Management for Professionals

The Springer series "Management for Professionals" comprises high-level business and management books for executives, MBA students, and practice-oriented business researchers. The topics cover all themes relevant to businesses and the business ecosystem. The authors are experienced business professionals and renowned professors who combine scientific backgrounds, best practices, and entrepreneurial vision to provide powerful insights into achieving business excellence.

The Series is SCOPUS-indexed.

Tobias Just • Harun Tanrıvermiş
Yeşim Tanrıvermiş
Editors

Understanding Türkiye's Real Estate Markets

Legal, Economic and Institutional Framework

Springer

Editors
Tobias Just
International Real Estate Business School (IREBS)
Regensburg University
Regensburg, Germany

Yeşim Tanrıvermiş
Department of Real Estate Development and Management, Faculty of Applied Sciences
Ankara University
Ankara, Türkiye

Harun Tanrıvermiş
Department of Real Estate Development and Management, Faculty of Applied Sciences
Ankara University
Ankara, Türkiye

ISSN 2192-8096 ISSN 2192-810X (electronic)
Management for Professionals
ISBN 978-3-032-13296-3 ISBN 978-3-032-13297-0 (eBook)
https://doi.org/10.1007/978-3-032-13297-0

This Springer imprint is published by the registered company Springer Nature Switzerland AG
The registered company address is: Gewerbestrasse 11, 6330 Cham, Switzerland

The original version of the book has been revised. A correction to this book can be found at https://doi.org/10.1007/978-3-032-13297-0_36

Acknowledgement

Publishing an interdisciplinary book on the real estate industry is always a challenge, and this challenge becomes even greater when the work spans several years, involves multiple universities, and requires coordination of many dozens of authors in several countries. This requires a shared goal, discipline, and mutual trust among the editors—above all, it requires a motivated team that is significantly larger than the small circle of editors.

We are delighted and grateful that we were able to work together with such a team. We would like to take this opportunity to thank these individuals.

This publication was made possible, among other things, by the tireless support of highly esteemed individuals, in particular Professor Dr Necdet Ünüvar, Rector of Ankara University, Türkiye. Thanks to his encouragement, moral support, and motivational endorsement, the project could be finalised timely. Without the invaluable support of the Rector of Ankara University, this book could not have been completed to this standard or within the given deadline.

We would also like to thank the *Regensburger Universitätsstiftung für Immobilienwirtschaft Hans Vielberth* for the financial support of this project. Of course, science thrives first and foremost on ideas and on the exchange among researchers, but this exchange requires freedom, and that freedom requires a solid financial foundation.

We would like to extend our special thanks to the faculty members involved from both Ankara University and Regensburg University: Assistant Professor Dr Monsurat Ayojimi Salami played an essential role in the realisation of this project. Frau Vanessa Dietl, Frau Claudia Skabrond, and Daniel Oeter contributed valuable content and put the chapters in an appropriate shape. And, of course, we would like to thank all the authors, without whose expertise, enthusiasm for the project, and patience—especially when the editors had questions—this book would never have been produced to the desired standard.

We would also like to thank the wonderful team at Springer Verlag GmbH, who not only ensured the project's swift completion in the final phase in an impressive manner, but also supported us throughout the entire process with advice, practical assistance, and, at times, the necessary reminders.

In closing, we hope that this book will spark many new ideas, that it will awaken or deepen interest in an intriguing and growing real estate market, and that it will serve as an interim report rather than the conclusion of the editors' journey of learning and researching on real estate markets in Türkiye.

March 2026
Regensburg and Ankara

Tobias Just
Harun Tanrıvermiş
Yeşim Tanrıvermiş

Contents

Contributors

Md Moynul Ahsan Department of Real Estate Development and Management, Faculty of Applied Sciences, Ankara University, Ankara, Türkiye

Toygun Atasoy Department of Real Estate Development and Management, Faculty of Applied Sciences, Ankara University, Ankara, Türkiye

Emine Baydan Department of Real Estate Development and Management, Faculty of Applied Sciences, Ankara University, Ankara, Türkiye

Sevilay Bostancı EGO General Directorate, Ankara Metropolitan Municipality, Ankara, Türkiye

Erol Demir Department of Real Estate Development and Management, Faculty of Applied Sciences, Ankara University, Ankara, Türkiye

Salih Demirkaya Department of Real Estate Development and Management, Faculty of Applied Sciences, Ankara University, Ankara, Türkiye

Vanessa Dietl International Real Estate Business School (IREBS), University of Regensburg, Regensburg, Germany

İskender Duman Van Metropolitan Municipality, Deputy Secretary General, Ankara, Türkiye

Ahmet Hilmi Erciyes Department of Real Estate Development and Management, Faculty of Applied Sciences, Ankara University, Ankara, Türkiye

A. Filiz Zorlu Kaman Department of Real Estate Development and Management, Faculty of Applied Sciences, Ankara University, Ankara, Türkiye

Ümit Gedik Department of Real Estate Development and Management, Faculty of Applied Sciences, Ankara University, Ankara, Türkiye

Gülnaz Şengül Güneş Department of Real Estate Development and Management, Faculty of Applied Sciences, Ankara University, Ankara, Türkiye

Parla Güneş Department of Real Estate Development and Management, Faculty of Applied Sciences, Ankara University, Ankara, Türkiye

Sinan Güneş Department of Real Estate Development and Management, Faculty of Applied Sciences, Ankara University, Ankara, Türkiye

Tuğba Güneş Department of Real Estate Development and Management, Faculty of Applied Sciences, Ankara University, Ankara, Türkiye

Üstün Hatipoğlu TALYA Real Estate Valuation and Consultancy Joint Stock Company, Zeytinburnu/Istanbul, Türkiye

Ali Hepşen Department of Finance, School of Business, İstanbul University, İstanbul, Türkiye

Tobias Just International Real Estate Business School (IREBS), Regensburg University, Regensburg, Germany

Ruşen Keleş Department of Political Science and Public Administration, Faculty of Political Sciences, Ankara University, Ankara, Türkiye

Esra Keskin Department of Real Estate Development and Management, Faculty of Applied Sciences, Ankara University, Ankara, Türkiye

Kh. Md Nahiduzzaman Citinnov for Integrated Territorial Planning and Smart Cities, Mohammed VI Polytechnic University (UM6P), Rabat, Morocco

Şebnem Akipek Öcal Department of Business Administration, Faculty of Economics and Administrative, TED University, Ankara, Türkiye

Department of Real Estate Development and Management, Faculty of Applied Sciences, Ankara University, Ankara, Türkiye

Ece Sert Özcan Office Leasing Manager, İstanbul Finance Centre, İstanbul, Türkiye

Arda Özkan Department of Basic Sciences, Faculty of Maritime, İstanbul Technical University, İstanbul, Türkiye

Akın Öztürk Department of Basic Sciences, Faculty of Maritime, İstanbul Technical University, İstanbul, Türkiye

Ali Parsa Westminster Business School, University of Westminster, London, UK

Monsurat Ayojimi Salami Department of Real Estate Development and Management, Faculty of Applied Sciences, Ankara University, Ankara, Türkiye

Sibel Canaz Sevgen Department of Real Estate Development and Management, Faculty of Applied Sciences, Ankara University, Ankara, Türkiye

F. Nihan Özdemir Sönmez Department of Real Estate Development and Management, Faculty of Applied Sciences, Ankara University, Ankara, Türkiye

Emir Sunguroğlu Department of Real Estate Development and Management, Faculty of Applied Sciences, Ankara University, Ankara, Türkiye

Harun Tanrıvermiş Department of Real Estate Development and Management, Faculty of Applied Sciences, Ankara University, Ankara, Türkiye

Yeşim Tanrıvermiş Department of Real Estate Development and Management, Faculty of Applied Sciences, Ankara University, Ankara, Türkiye

Sinan Terzioğlu Department of Real Estate Development and Management, Faculty of Applied Sciences, Ankara University, Ankara, Türkiye

Mustafa Tombul Department of Real Estate Development and Management, Faculty of Applied Sciences, Ankara University, Ankara, Türkiye

Emrullah Töremen Department of Real Estate Managemant and Development, Faculty of Applied Sciences, Ankara University, Ankara, Türkiye

Mustafa Tuna Department of Real Estate Development and Management, Faculty of Applied Sciences, Ankara University, Ankara, Türkiye

Abdurrahman Tursun Department of Real Estate Development and Management, Faculty of Applied Sciences, Ankara University, Ankara, Türkiye

Amani Micheal Uisso President Office Ethics Secretariat, Dodoma, Tanzania

Department of Real Estate Development and Management, Faculty of Applied Sciences, Ankara University, Ankara, Türkiye

Mehmet Ülger Department of Real Estate Development and Management, Faculty of Applied Sciences, Ankara University, Ankara, Türkiye

Gizem Ulusoy Department of Real Estate Development and Management, Faculty of Applied Sciences, Ankara University, Ankara, Türkiye

İlhan Yıldırım Department of Real Estate Development and Management, Faculty of Applied Sciences, Ankara University, Ankara, Türkiye

Muhammed Said Yılmaz Department of Real Estate Development and Management, Faculty of Applied Sciences, Ankara University, Ankara, Türkiye

Introduction to Türkiye's Real Estate Markets

Understanding Real Estate Markets in Türkiye: An Introduction

Tobias Just, Harun Tanrıvermiş, and Yeşim Tanrıvermiş

Abstract

This chapter summarises the key themes of the book. Türkiye is, in many ways, a bridge: between Europe and Asia, between thousands of years of history and modernity, and between powerful trends and equally powerful cycles. These characteristics shape the country's real estate markets. Understanding Türkiye's unique position is essential for identifying and seizing these opportunities. Nevertheless, these opportunities are inextricably linked to certain risks. This chapter also shows that only a multidisciplinary approach can really help understand the real estate market, and this requires not only practical experience but also analytical and academic excellence.

Keywords

Real estate · Cycles · Trends · Multidisciplinarity · Research and education

1 Türkiye: A Multidimensional Bridge

With regard to real estate, Türkiye is a remarkable country in many respects. Its history, economic and social development, cultural heritage, and the associated urban planning and real estate challenges and opportunities have resulted in a unique

T. Just (✉)
International Real Estate Business School (IREBS), Regensburg University, Regensburg, Germany
e-mail: tobias.just@irebs.academy

H. Tanrıvermiş · Y. Tanrıvermiş
Department of Real Estate Development and Management, Faculty of Applied Sciences, Ankara University, Ankara, Türkiye
e-mail: tanrivermis@ankara.edu.tr; aliefendioglu@ankara.edu.tr

T. Just et al. (eds.), *Understanding Türkiye's Real Estate Markets*, Management for Professionals, https://doi.org/10.1007/978-3-032-13297-0_1

character that has been shaped over thousands of years, connecting Europe and Asia. This has made the region both a source and a bridge for ideas, trade, and the production of numerous goods. These three functions have been the driving forces behind economic and cultural dynamism, fuelling urban development since the earliest civilisations. In this respect, it is no historical coincidence that the world's first city, Çatalhöyük, and the Göbekli Tepe complex were founded approximately 10,000 years ago in what is now Türkiye (Özdoğan et al., 2012; Diamond, 1999). The favourable geography brought early but also recurring strategic interest that repeatedly altered the course of the country's history because bridges can be used to transport goods and ideas just as easily as troops and weapons. This also shaped Türkiye until the twentieth century.

Today, Türkiye stands at the intersection of its long tradition and economic modernity between the West, with which it has close military ties through the NATO alliance, and the East, with which Türkiye shares an attempt to bind Asia's dynamism more closely to its own economy. It is as if Türkiye has to cross a new bridge into the future. In the real estate sector, significant changes are required, e.g. regulatory, legal, and economic reforms, which have long been discussed in the context of closer ties with the European Union. Technological progress is also essential, e.g. advancing digitalisation would improve data quality, increase market transparency, and enhance efficiency. Additionally, extensive investment in urban and rural infrastructure is necessary. At the same time, Türkiye will have to make substantial efforts to achieve its ambitious climate and energy goals.

This book reflects these upcoming decisions and their potential repercussions on the real estate markets in Türkiye. The authors address both quantitative and qualitative shortcomings and opportunities, not only in the residential asset class but also in numerous commercial real estate segments. Offering a thorough analysis of the present state, the book looks back to trace how the current situation evolved and, on this basis, outlines possible future scenarios for the Turkish real estate industry—including the political decisions needed to achieve them.

2 Structure, Cycles, and Trends

In "industrial economics," a sub-field of economics, there is a famous concept for analysing how markets function: the structure–conduct–performance (SCP) paradigm (Scherer & Ross, 1990; Ross, 2016). According to this model, the market structure—i.e. the institutional setting and the number of market players—shapes the behaviour of companies and consumers, which, in turn, determines the market's performance. Even though recent research indicates that the model is too simplistic for deterministic predictions—too many random factors and human influences lie beyond its scope—it remains useful for understanding the links between institutional frameworks and outcomes and for deriving policy recommendations. This can be adapted to the Turkish real estate markets. Thus, Chap. "The Institutional Structure of Real Estate in Türkiye" explains the institutional environment of the Turkish market players. It outlines important economic developments (income trends, population growth, etc.) and distinguishes the key market players, as well as the (partly) derived company sizes and governance structures. Companies remain comparatively small, traditionally organised, and active in only a few sub-markets, limiting their ability to benefit from economies of scale and scope. Chapter "An International Perspective on Real Estate Investments in Türkiye" builds on this by outlining the international perspective on Turkish real estate markets: Which determining factors are particularly important to international investors? Why is insufficient market transparency a challenge? An which structural market barriers need to be considered? The chapter also distinguishes the dynamics of major asset classes. Given that foreign capital has been an important driver of larger construction projects in recent years, it is crucial to understand the determinants of international capital flows. Changes in the flows of both capital and ideas are further clarified in Chaps. "Foreigners' Real Estate Acquisition and Citizenship Dynamics in Türkiye" and "Does Integrating PropTech into Turkish Sukuk Investment Provide an Effective Alternative for Delivering Affordable and Social Housing in Türkiye?".

Because international players, in particular, value verifiable, general information more than access to informal networks, it is essential to generate and provide more reliable data in Türkiye. Intensive efforts have been made in recent years to improve the quality and availability of real estate data. Chapter "Facts and Figures of Real Estate in Türkiye: Data Sources and Institutional Framework" provides insights into the main sources of real estate information and the conclusions that can be drawn from them.

Chapter "Socio-Economic Structure and Its Implications for Real Estate Markets" deepens the socio-economic analysis by examining how different qualification levels influence residential market parameters. The findings indicate that the educational level of a region is a strong predictor of both the levels and growth rates of housing prices.

Because taxation is one of the main ways in which the state can intervene in the market, it is essential to understand the tax legislation in Türkiye to grasp the structural framework, especially in real estate, where taxes affect markets in multiple ways: land, transactions, rental income, or services provided in the real estate business can all be taxed. Chapters "Real Estate Valuation System and Professionalisation in Türkiye" and "Evaluation of Tax Initiatives for the Improvement of Real Estate Markets within the Framework of Real Estate Taxation in Türkiye" show important regulatory tax provisions for the Turkish real estate markets.

All these conditions lead to predictable, systematic decisions by market players. Since these conditions differ across sub-markets (e.g. residential, retail, or office properties), it is crucial to assess these dynamics separately. Chapter "Real Estate Markets and Submarkets in Türkiye" deals with these differences and provides an asset-class-specific analysis of the most important sub-markets: residential, retail, office, logistics, and the tourist real estate segment, which is important for Türkiye. In terms of tourist destinations, the coastal region plays a key role in Türkiye. Chapter "The Effect of Coastal Areas Management on Real Estate", therefore, offers a *deep dive* into the legal and economic conditions of Türkiye's coastal areas and their implications for the real estate industry.

As possible speculative price exaggeration in the Turkish housing markets is currently intensely debated, Chap. "Dynamics of the Housing Market in Türkiye: Housing Prices and Bubble Risk" is devoted to this very topic and concludes that speculative exaggerations, i.e. irrational exuberances, are not the main reason for the sharp price increases in the Turkish housing markets. Instead, the primary cause is the general rise in inflation in Türkiye.

Most of these asset-class-specific chapters concern short-term, cyclical adjustments in the real estate markets. However, since real estate remains on the market for decades, it is equally important to monitor long-term trends. In addition to demographic developments (Chap. "Socio-Economic Structure and Its Implications for Real Estate Markets"), these are primarily digital and technological changes (Chap. "Digitalisation in the Real Estate Sector in Türkiye"), which can enable significant productivity gains and shifts in value creation structures, as well as energy efficiency measures driven by the challenges of global warming (Chap. "Policies and Practices for Reducing Emissions and Improving Energy Efficiency in Real Estate"). The overall trend towards sustainable real estate development and management is covered in Chap. "Sustainability in Real Estate Development Projects". These latter two trends (digitalisation and sustainability) make it clear that Türkiye still has considerable catching up to do compared to Western European countries. At the same time, it is also evident that major legal and technical efforts are underway to leverage this potential.

3 Interdisciplinary Approach

This book is not only a bridge between short- and long-term market dynamics within the SCP paradigm; it also illustrates that real estate economics goes beyond merely applying business administration to the real estate industry. A deep understanding of real estate market developments requires insights from multiple disciplines.

First and foremost, understanding the regulatory environment is essential. A dense network of regulations rightly restricts real estate markets, as real estate is a sensitive asset in many respects. There must be no serious technical defects, as these would pose a significant risk to life and limb. Moreover, real estate investments always involve large expenditures. For private households, real estate represents the single largest purchase in a lifetime.

This calls for prudent regulation that protects small private investors from severe financial risk. At the same time, the development and management of real estate can generate large profits. This sometimes leads to misconduct by market players, which must also be strictly limited through legal requirements. Chapters "Urban Policies and Urban Development in Türkiye" and "Urban Land and Spatial Management in Türkiye: Challenges and Perspectives" demonstrate that Türkiye's current regulatory framework is shaped by the country's unique historical trajectory while also highlighting aspects of urban space management.

Chapter "The Scope of Property Rights and Real Estate Ownership: A Comparative Analysis" provides a detailed overview of property law issues from a Turkish perspective. Chapter "Planning and Building Laws in Türkiye" examines the legal aspects of transactions and real estate developments with regard to the planning and public building law, thereby also providing a transition to two related aspects: on the one hand, the urban transformation process of the informal housing sector, discussed in Chap. "Urban Transformation and Informal Housing Areas Upgrading Practices and Policies in Türkiye" through various policy approaches and, on the other hand, the role of public infrastructure focused on in Chaps. "Urban Infrastructure Provision and Real Estate Markets" and "Public–Private Partnership Practices in Infrastructure and Real Estate Projects and Policy Implications". Infrastructure is a key value driver for real estate, as many manufacturing processes, service industries, and aspects of private well-being depend on a reliable network of utilities and high-quality social infrastructure. Recent experiences with operating models that lie between purely public and purely private solutions, i.e. public–private partnership (PPP) and their various forms, are especially important here. Market players and local authorities are increasingly gaining valuable expertise in this area.

However, even though the role of the public sector is important, the efficient interaction of many private sector players is crucial in real estate. In addition to the various types of developers already mentioned in Chap. "An International Perspective on Real Estate Investments in Türkiye", the size and complexity of construction projects require suitable financing structures. Chaps. "Assessments of Real Estate Finance System and Instruments in Türkiye", "Real Estate Investment Trusts in Türkiye", and "Real Estate Investments Options and Strategies in Türkiye" highlight multiple forms of investment and financing that play a particularly relevant role in Türkiye. These include real estate investment trusts (REITs), real estate investment funds (REIFs), and other instruments that are still in the early stages of development in the country. Chapter "Real Estate Investment Funds, Investment Options and the Requirements of Islamic Funds in Türkiye" also looks at Islamic funds, which are particularly important for a country that has been culturally shaped by Islam, and explains how their strategies differ from those of non-Islamic funds.

For all types of investments, it is essential to consider the specific risks associated with real estate investments and real estate financing. Private investors often wrongly consider real estate investments to be low-risk investments. However, it would be more accurate to view real estate investments as investments with specific risks and rewards. These risks can be systematically structured, their channels of influence understood, and investments managed accordingly.

This is the actual appeal of real estate investment, not its low risk (see Chap. "The Process of Risk Analysis and Decision Making in Real Estate Development Projects" in particular).

Ultimately, real estate development, investment, and financing are merely means to an end, enabling the actual purpose of real estate construction: the use of the property. Tailored real estate management is essential to ensure that this use is both efficient and effective for investors and users. Sometimes, such management requires the coordinated efforts of several distinct actors: the asset manager, the property manager, and the facility manager, who are responsible for the best possible operation of a property, strategically (asset manager), commercially (property manager), or technically (facility manager). In Türkiye, the professionalisation of these functions lags behind the developments in Western economies (Chap. "Facility, Property and Asset Management and the Practices"); yet there are signs of dynamic progress, with greater specialisation, larger-scale operations, and resulting productivity gains expected in the coming years. Chapter "Public Real Estate Management in Türkiye" illustrates that these experiences are not limited to the private real estate management sector but can also be transferred to public real estate management.

Finally, two distinctive features of the Turkish real estate market should be pointed out, which are of great importance for Türkiye and may be surprising, especially in comparison to US real estate market analyses: the first is the continued high importance of transactions involving, and the operation of, agricultural land well into the twenty-first century (Chaps. "Evaluation of Policies Regarding Productive Agricultural Land and Protected Natural Areas, Sustainability, and Their Impact on Real Estate Markets" and "Real Estate Education, Research Systems, and Professionalisation Trends in Türkiye").

The second is the significance of Türkiye's abundant cultural treasures, the result of a history spanning millennia. Chapter "Heritage Conservation Policies and Real Estate Markets Linkages" deals with the evaluation and preservation of this cultural heritage and its integration in construction processes in such a way that the interests of investors are safeguarded on the one hand and the overriding public interest in preserving cultural treasures is protected on the other.

4 Academic Excellence Meets Practical Know-How

This book builds a third important bridge for the real estate industry, namely the bridge between academic research and teaching excellence on the one side and the practical application of new findings on the other. In engineering, building physics, and the understanding of chemical processes, it is undisputed that sound academic knowledge is required to ensure that buildings are safe, stable, energy-efficient and not hazardous to health. Structural engineering without mathematics is inconceivable, and materials science based on gut feeling is dangerous. But these lessons also apply to the social science aspects of the real estate industry, business administration, economics, sociology, and planning law. People's lives in and around buildings could be improved everywhere if decisions were made according to a scientific approach, i.e. if decisions were based on verifiable and reliable data, analysed with sound methods, reproducible in their outcomes, and independent of irrational human influences.

However, it is equally true that many market players in the industry have long claimed that they can understand the markets solely through their professional experience. While such market experience is valuable, it can also be deceptive, as people are subject to a variety of biases (Kahneman, 2013). To avoid systematic errors, a scientific approach is essential, and the more market participants adopt this approach, the greater the pressure on each actor to conform to this standard.

This book strikes a balance between scientific contributions, using sophisticated methods, and more practice-oriented contributions. Science-based articles include Chap. "The Impacts of Recent Crises on REITs in Türkiye", which examines REIT price developments in the wake of two major shocks—the coronavirus pandemic and the 2022 earthquake—and Chap. "Real Estate Investment Funds, Investment Options and the Requirements of Islamic Funds in Türkiye", which provides an analysis of Islamic funds. These findings are based on extensive statistical and econometric analyses. If such insights can be translated into policy decisions, new institutions can be created, which, in turn, shape the behaviour of market players and, ultimately, deliver better market outcomes. In this respect, the recommendations in Chaps. "Public–Private Partnership Practices in Infrastructure and Real Estate Projects and Policy Implications" and "Evaluation of Policies Regarding Productive Agricultural Land and Protected Natural Areas, Sustainability, and Their Impact on Real Estate Markets", for example, illustrate how academic groundwork can become a far-reaching reality in the real estate industry. This works best when researchers and teachers engage intensively with market participants, policymakers, and the public.

The process is never complete: new insights emerge, geopolitical and macroeconomic conditions shift, the climate changes, and individual actors may play decisive roles. In this respect, it is important to regard all chapters in this book as an interim conclusion.

5 Concluding Remarks

This book is the third anthology in a series that aims to deepen the understanding of real estate markets through country-specific analyses. The first book, published in 2012, focused on the German market. A revised second edition of this book followed in 2017 (Just & Maennig, 2017). It describes the regulatory and economic frameworks of real estate markets in a Western industrialised nation. The degree of market development was reflected in the extent and quality of regulation, the sophistication of investment and financing instruments, and the availability of data. Although Germany is not regarded as one of the most transparent real estate markets in the Western world, it largely avoided the very severe corrections of the global financial and economic crisis. This resilience has made the German real estate market an attractive prospect for analysts from other countries.

The second book in this series, which examined the Chinese real estate market, has since appeared in its second edition (Wang & Just, 2021). It focuses on the real estate dynamics of an economy that has transformed from a developing country into a leading technologically advanced nation in just one generation. Given that the construction and real estate industries played a decisive role in the early stages of this transformation, China's experience offers valuable insights for countries seeking to emulate its path.

However, any such comparison should recognise that China's rise has been, and continues to be, accompanied by significant distortions.

In this respect, this third volume in the series logically extends the comparative perspective to Türkiye. This country can learn from both Germany and China as presented in the previous anthologies. This applies to areas such as the regulatory framework and crisis prevention. This anthology on Türkiye, therefore, attempts to strike a balance between the lessons learnt from its own history and those learnt from other jurisdictions. This is a favourable position, as it allows the country to avoid repeating the mistakes of others. Nevertheless, benchmarking has its limits, and Türkiye must follow its own path. Replicating the German or Chinese model is not recommended for Türkiye, not only because of its different history but also because of its distinct integration into the geopolitical and global economic constraints of a different era. The search for the right path for the future, therefore, requires, above all, the engagement of Turkish researchers and decision-makers, combined with the willingness to step back and reassess progress periodically. This is where the scientific approach proves its value: by experimenting, collecting data, and making better-informed decisions on that basis. We hope that this book will contribute to developing real estate strategies not only for companies but also for Türkiye as a whole.

References

Diamond, J. (1999). *Guns, germs and steel*. W. W. Norton & Company.

Just, T., & Maennig, W. (Eds.). (2017). *Understanding German real estate markets* (2nd ed.). Springer.

Kahneman, D. (2013). *Thinking, fast and slow*. Farrar, Straus and Giroux.

Özdoğan, M., Başgelen, N., & Kuniholm, P. (2012). *The Neolithic in Turkey, Western Turkey: New excavations and new research*. Archaeology and Art Publication.

Ross, D. R. (2016). Structure–conduct–performance. In M. Augier & D. Teece (Eds.), *The Palgrave encyclopedia of strategic management*. Palgrave Macmillan. https://doi.org/10.1057/978-1-349-94848-2_524-1

Scherer, F. M., & Ross, D. (1990). *Industrial market structure and economic performance*. University of Illinois at Urbana-Champaign's Academy for Entrepreneurial Leadership Historical Research Reference in Entrepreneurship. Available at SSRN https://ssrn.com/abstract=1496716

Wang, B., & Just, T. (Eds.). (2021). *Understanding China's real estate markets: Development, finance, and investment* (2nd ed.). Springer.

Tobias Just is Managing Director at the IRE|BS Immobilienakademie and professor for Real Estate at the Regensburg University. Tobias studied economics in Hamburg and Uppsala (Sweden). In 1997, he graduated and started to work at the University of the Federal Armed Forces Hamburg. His Ph.D. dissertation was awarded the university science prize in 2001. For more than ten years, Tobias worked at Deutsche Bank Research, the economics research unit of Deutsche Bank. He headed the units' sector and real estate research team and was a member of Deutsche Bank's group-wide Environmental Steering Committee. In summer 2006, Tobias was a Research Fellow at the American Institute of Contemporary German Studies at Johns Hopkins University in Washington, DC. Tobias published 17 books and more than 250 papers in professional and academic journals and books. Since November 2011, Tobias has been Managing Director at the IREIBS Immobilienakademie and holds a Chair for Real Estate at the University of Regensburg. He was President of the German Society of Property Researchers (GIF) from 2014-2021 and is editor of the ZIÖ—the German Journal of Real Estate Research. From 2016 to 2023, Tobias was a member of the Supervisory Board of Helaba Invest Kapitalanlagegesellschaft mbH. In 2017, Tobias became a Fellow of the RICS by nomination.

Harun Tanrıvermiş is a distinguished professor who occupies the esteemed position at the Ankara University top management level as founder and head of the Department of Real Estate Development and Management, and founder and current dean of the Faculty of Applied Sciences at Ankara University. Professor Tanrıvermiş also currently works as the vice rector at Ankara University. He attained his B.Sc., M.Sc., and Ph.D. degrees from the Department of Agricultural Economics at Ankara University, specialising in land and real estate economics, land and real estate valuation, as well as natural resources and environmental economics. Furthermore, he earned an M.Sc. in environmental management through the MED-CAMPUS Programme in 1996. Professor Tanrıvermiş has published approximately 400 papers, including 43 international and 55 national peer-reviewed articles, which have been published in various high-impact journals. Additionally, he has presented 48 international and 74 national proceedings, either in full or as abstracts, at numerous conferences. He is also credited with writing 39 books and 17 book chapters. Moreover, his works concentrate on the land and real estate valuation, land and real estate economics, real estate development and project appraisal, urban transformation and sustainability, sustainable real estate development, facility and real estate management, land management, administration and polices, measuring and reporting of real estate sustainability and ESG, digital transformation in real estate and real estate technologies.

Yeşim Tanrıvermiş holds the position of full professor in the Department of Real Estate Development and Management at the Faculty of Applied Sciences, Ankara University, Türkiye. She attained her Master of Science (M.Sc.) degree in 2011 from the Department of Agricultural Economics at Ankara University. She received her Ph.D. in 2011 as the first Ph.D. program graduate of the Department of Real Estate Development and Management at Ankara University. Her research interests encompass the management and conservation of land resources, land resource economics, as well as real estate analysis and economics, in addition to studies in real estate and asset valuation. She has been delivering lectures for several years and has published academic papers since 2006. Her publications consist of 50 international and 40 national peer-reviewed articles. Additionally, she has made contributions to 110 international and 25 national full or abstract proceedings at various conferences and congresses and has authored 35 books and 30 book chapters. Presently, she serves as the Deputy Head of her department at Ankara University. Moreover, she is an active participant in various academic and professional organisations. Her experience encompasses working as a researcher and consultant across diverse public and private sectors, with a focus on real estate asset analysis, real estate finance and valuation, land and building conservation practices, as well as real estate economics and management. Furthermore, she actively engages in enhancing cooperation with both domestic and international institutions, mobilising financial resources for research projects.

Macro Environment

The Institutional Structure of Real Estate in Türkiye

Harun Tanrıvermiş and Tobias Just

Abstract

This chapter investigates the institutional structure of the real estate market in Türkiye. Initially, it elucidates the institutional framework, concentrating on the activities and relationships among its participants. Furthermore, we delve into the Turkish real estate market by analysing Turkish Real Estate Investment Trusts (T-REITs) as a case study. We employed Atlas.ti for qualitative analysis. We examine the T-REITs' portfolios by looking at the components of the indices in which they invest, their staffing, the ages of board executives, and their portfolio beta in relation to market risk. The findings show that Turkish REITs invest in both real- and non-real-estate-related assets. The executive directors within the 50–59 age group represent the largest segment among executive directors in the Turkish real estate market. The real estate market is characterised by sensitivity and dynamism, necessitating experienced board directors for effective management. Most real estate firms in Türkiye employ fewer than 50 persons, while a minority of companies have more than 250 employees. This finding suggests that the Turkish real estate market remains at an early, unconcentrated stage. The real estate industry plays a pivotal role in stimulating economic growth and creating new jobs. So far, relatively few employees are engaged in Türkiye's institutional real estate sector.

H. Tanrıvermiş
Department of Real Estate Development and Management, Faculty of Applied Sciences, Ankara University, Ankara, Türkiye
e-mail: tanrivermis@ankara.edu.tr

T. Just (✉)
International Real Estate Business School (IREBS), Regensburg University, Regensburg, Germany
e-mail: tobias.just@irebs.academy

T. Just et al. (eds.), *Understanding Türkiye's Real Estate Markets*, Management for Professionals, https://doi.org/10.1007/978-3-032-13297-0_2

Keywords

Turkish REITs · Real estate assets · Financial institution · Technology · EPCIC · Facility management · Brokers · Government parastatals

1 Introduction

The real estate market is an institution composed of investors, developers, and regulators operating in an enabling environment. Previous research has often concentrated on market segments. Consequently, by focusing on specific real estate segments instead of delivering a comprehensive overview of the overall market, the institutional structure of the real estate market remains ambiguous. For instance, studies that concentrate on institutional investors (Cvijanović et al., 2022) and institutional real estate owners (Read et al., 2016) only show a fragment of the overall market's complexity. It has been contended that a lack of transparency and existing asymmetric information may lead to this focus (Cvijanović et al., 2022) rather than analysing the entire market. There is a lack of transparency for construction companies (Brady et al., 2018), as well as for the real estate market (Ionaşcu & Anghel, 2020). Thus, transparency issues may arise from multiple facets of the institutional framework of the real estate sector. As a result, better data availability has been recognised as a mechanism to provide potential investors and researchers with opportunities (Sadayuki et al., 2019) to evaluate the market. The capital market is an efficient provider of information. Therefore, it is argued that a deeper real estate capital market can help provide more and better information on the Turkish real estate market.

Although Real Estate Investment Trusts (REITs) were initially established in the United States as early as 1960 (Campbell & Sirmans, 2002), a comprehensive understanding of this economically significant institutional structure remains unclear. In several countries, institutional real estate markets remain inadequately researched, despite the fact that real estate market studies have continued since the 1990s (Wheaton, 1999). Acquiring insight into the structure of the real estate market is essential for thoroughly addressing transparency issues. Eastern Europe has initiated modifications to its institutional structure to align with EU regulations (Ionaşcu et al., 2021). A recent survey analysing the institutional framework of the real estate market in Switzerland focuses on the institutions, market participants, and regions that constitute the nation's real estate environment (Theurillat et al., 2015).

Furthermore, Han and Wang (2003) analysed the institutional structure of the inland property market in China, underscoring that there are only a few studies on the institutional structure of the real estate market. The institutional frameworks governing real estate markets across countries might reflect both commonalities and disparities, likely attributable to the fluid nature of the market, which is shaped by both formal and informal regulations (Abdullah, 2015; Han & Wang, 2003).

Consequently, this chapter offers a comprehensive illustration of the dimensions of the institutional structure of real estate in Türkiye, while considering the characteristics of Turkish Real Estate Investment Trusts (T-REITs).

The subsequent sections of this chapter are as follows: Section 2 elucidates the dimensions of Türkiye's real estate institutional structure. Section 3 outlines the coding methodology for the institutional market structure. Section 4 presents an overview of the key participants within the institutional framework of the Turkish real estate market. Section 5 delineates the structural and institutional trends within the real estate and construction sector. Section 6 provides a thorough analysis of Turkish Real Estate Investment Trusts (T-REITs) as a case study, and Sect. 7 concludes the chapter.

2 Institutional Real Estate Structure in Türkiye

Like most countries, Türkiye's institutional framework governing real estate consists of both horizontal and vertical structures, as depicted in Fig. 1. The horizontal real estate market structure includes residential properties, commercial factories, utilities, and various forms of infrastructural asset classes, whereas the vertical structure is classified into four categories of developers. These categories comprise primary, secondary, tertiary, and sophisticated developers, each exhibiting considerable variation in risk appetite and investment motivations. Primary developers are responsible for identifying new, undeveloped locations and enhancing their value to secure capital gains. In contrast, real estate developers engage in calculated risks by investing in specific parcels of land to realise future value benefits (Brill & Robin, 2020).

Mostly, primary developers acquire land in bulk at comparatively low prices. They divide the land into smaller units. The added value generated by primary (land) developers makes them key players in the real estate market. Primary developers do not focus on constructing buildings; rather, they prepare the land for secondary developers at a higher price. They may not hasten the sale of the land to safeguard profits from tax implications. In accordance with Turkish law, adherence to the required holding period is essential, as non-compliance will incur capital gains tax. Tax policy plays a vital role in mitigating land price inflation caused by speculators attempting to gain quick profits through their capability to anticipate market trends. When public organisations develop, they tend to pay less attention to transaction costs in comparison to private organisations (Wu et al., 2022). Typically, primary developers utilise surplus funds for the acquisition of land, given that there is no definitive timeline for the disposition of these

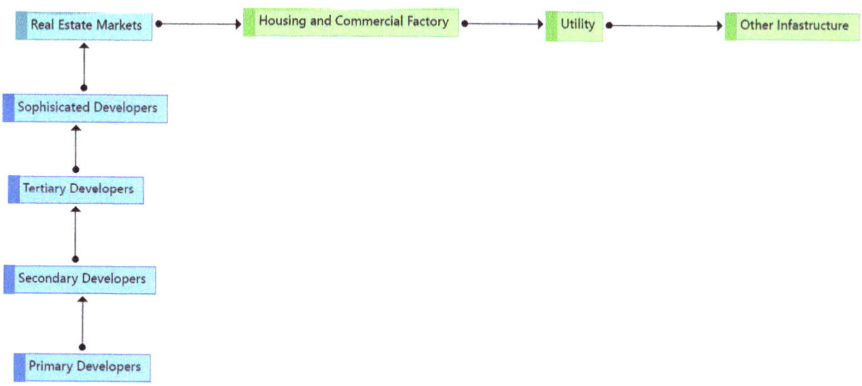

Fig. 1 Horizontal and vertical representations of the institutional real estate market in Türkiye. Source: own depiction

assets. Since the purchase of this land is typically not financed by bank loans, there is no imperative to expedite the sale, as interest charges are not applicable.

Secondary developers acquire land from primary developers. They construct buildings on the land or keep the land undeveloped for speculative purposes. Secondary developers take calculated risks, as the primary developer may have anticipated the potential for rapid development in that region. Should secondary developers choose to develop the land into residential or commercial properties, this could necessitate the installation of utilities and other necessary infrastructure. Alternatively, secondary developers may enhance the value of the land and subsequently sell it to tertiary developers. Similar to the situation in Singapore, the method of "en-bloc" redevelopment was implemented to enable private condominiums to collectively sell property at a significantly higher price to private developers (Oh & Shin, 2023).

The objective of tertiary developers is to transform land into structures for their utilisation or make the structures accessible to sophisticated developers interested in leasing properties for commercial purposes. Their investment objective is to utilise the facilities for either short-term or long-term endeavours, as they aspire to operate their businesses in multiple locations. Sophisticated developers in Türkiye are also known as asset management companies. Constructing buildings from the ground up may be regarded as excessively costly for sophisticated developers who plan to establish branches in various regions. In this context, leasing serves as their investment strategy within the real estate market, as it enables them to conserve time when initiating their businesses and facilitates convenient relocation should political challenges arise. At every stage, each developer endeavours to enhance the value of the land or allow it to appreciate before selling it to another developer to generate capital gains. Given the size of the residential asset class and the necessity of providing living space, residential development remains, by far, the focus of many market discussions.

3 Activities and Relationships in the Institutional Market Structure of Real Estate in Türkiye

Before examining the institutional structure, we collected both qualitative and quantitative data for 37 T-REITs from investing.com, Bloomberg, and TURKSTAT. The Atlas.ti software was used to create a word cloud analysis of the data collected, as illustrated in Fig. 2. Atlas.ti is a robust qualitative programme for uncovering latent information relevant to the objectives of this study (Demirsu & Cihangir-Tetik, 2019). This process revealed several essential terms. The significance of these codes is recognised within the context of the acquired document. The relationship between the codes and their relevance is fundamental for understanding the institutional framework of T-REITs. Coding additionally provides insights into the activities and relationships among participants in the Turkish real estate market. Data obtained from TURKSTAT supplies information regarding macroeconomic indicators.

Fig. 2 Word cloud of the Turkish institutional real estate markets. Source: Own depiction

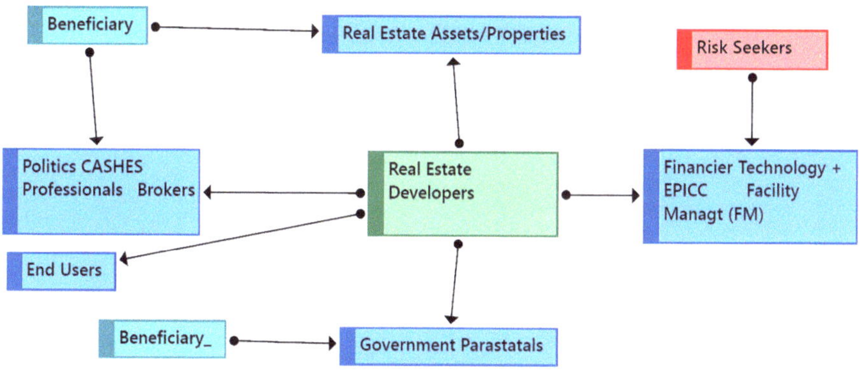

Fig. 3 Main players in the real estate market. Source: Own depiction

4 Players in the Turkish Real Estate Markets

Figure 3 illustrates the numerous stakeholders engaged in the Turkish real estate market, as well as their relationships. The blocks denoted in the figure depict the various activities, while the arrows show the relationships between these activities. The real estate market consists of key actors, including real estate developers, real estate brokers, government parastatals, and end users, who play pivotal roles in Türkiye's institutional real estate markets. Real estate developers add value for end users by acknowledging their needs and creating a use case through the development of space, ideas, and capital into buildings. Therefore, the developer is characterised as the core of the real estate market, while the needs of end users are crucial as they propel the real estate market forwards.

Developers recognise the value of the available land. They are committed to undertaking business risks by incorporating features that may enhance the perceived value of the land. The participants in the real estate market tolerate risk to varying degrees. Developers, financiers, technology providers, and Engineering, Procurement, Construction, Installation, and Commissioning (EPCIC) companies, along with operational management, commonly referred to as facility management, constitute the key stakeholders within the institutional framework of the real estate market. Conversely, political entities, Community, Affairs, Safety, Health, Environment, and Security (CASHES)[1] professionals, real estate brokers, and government parastatals benefit from the market while engaging in activities with a comparatively low risk exposure.

Figure 4 further elucidates the activities and connections within the T-REIT market. Developers collaborate with various stakeholders in the real estate sector to understand their needs and explore potential financial opportunities. In general terms, developers operate at significantly varying risk levels. Some beneficiaries, also known as investors, are either indirectly connected to real estate developers through real estate asset acquisitions or are connected through government parastatals. They may cooperate with financial institutions to secure mortgage loans. Furthermore, developers partner with professionals to augment their success in the timely delivery of housing. They provide services to developers in exchange for a blend of equity, monetary compensation, or a salary. This indicates that the risk

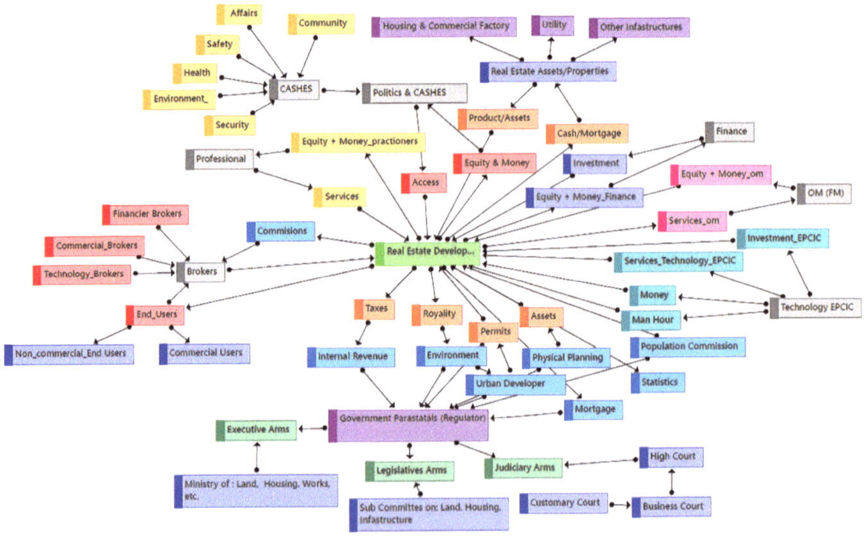

Fig. 4 Broad view of the institutional structure of the real estate market. Note that the directions of the arrows indicate the part of the entity with which they are grouped. In Fig. 4, most of the parameters are interconnected, indicating a high level of connectedness among the real estate institutions. The colour of each parameter indicates those parameters that share commonalities, but in some cases, they are interconnected with different parameters across various groups. Source: own depiction

[1] CASHES is an abbreviation of Community, Affairs, Safety, Health, Environment, and Security.

tolerance of different beneficiaries differs according to the amount of their financial commitment to partake in the project. Developers also establish connections with end users to achieve their business objectives. This suggests that developers play a pivotal role as institutional players in the real estate market.

Furthermore, developers extend cash or mortgage loans to the real estate sector in return for land or buildings. Financial institutions and investors offer capital (in the form of debt or equity) to developers in exchange for interest payments, a stake in the business, or a share of profits. Facility managers, who are also pivotal contributors, provide services to developers in return for a combination of equity or remuneration. The property developer evaluates costs and market prices to ascertain profitability from the real estate investment (Theurillat et al., 2015). Technology and EPCIC provide services, financial resources, and investment in return for remuneration and a defined percentage or an equity share. Many developers focus on specific segments of the real estate market, such as educational institutions, office buildings, hotels, and other property categories.

In many circumstances, developers collaborate with brokers to fulfil their real estate investment objectives. The internationalisation of real estate has heightened the importance of brokers within the market. The unbounded nature of investing, coupled with cross-border opportunities, encourages institutional arrangements between developers and other stakeholders to attain their investment goals. This internationalisation fortifies the relationship between real estate service providers and investors (D'Arcy, 2009). The brokers provide services that encompass facilitating connections between developers and financiers, real estate agents, and industry professionals, in addition to granting access to various technologies, all in exchange for commissions. They routinely negotiate reduced costs on behalf of developers and identify markets where building materials can be procured at a lower price. This represents the value that brokers provide to developers in exchange for their commissions. Their services can assist developers in efficiently and cost-effectively realising their business objectives. According to Read et al. (2016), property and asset managers should collaborate to enhance the cash flow and value of investment properties, thereby achieving their financial objectives.

Furthermore, developers collaborate with policymakers to understand the regulations and guidelines necessary for compliance and define the boundaries of their business interests. Due to inconsistencies in land allocation, pricing arrangements, and several other considerations, developers often maintain close relationships with governmental bodies (Han & Wang, 2003).

The regulatory authority establishes a set of regulations designed to mitigate irregularities within the real estate market. Numerous government parastatals play significant roles in these markets. Internal revenue is generated from developers in the form of taxes and royalties. Urban developers issue permits to builders, contingent upon the fulfilment of specific requirements. The Population Commission and the Department of Statistics provide essential data regarding the nation's population, along with other critical information, to assist developers in making informed decisions. Spatial planning can provide the government with real estate assets, including airports and ports; developers can manage that over extended periods of time. Moreover, the regulatory entities of the government overseeing the real estate markets encompass the executive, legislative, and judicial branches. The executive branch comprises ministries responsible for matters related to land, housing, and other relevant issues. The legislative branch includes various subcommittees dedicated to addressing concerns related to land, housing, and infrastructure. The judiciary addresses legal matters related to land and housing through customary courts, business courts, and high courts, as applicable.

5 Structure and Institutional Trends of Real Estate and Construction Sectors

In the early years of the Turkish Republic, the construction sector concentrated on developing infrastructure, encompassing the establishment of railway and significant water projects. This focus persisted until the 1950s. Investments in public infrastructure, along with contributions from the private sector, particularly in the industrial and housing domains, propelled the expansion of the construction sector during the 1950s and the 1960s. From the latter half of the 1980s onwards, the process of globalisation, marked by more liberal trade, capital exchange, and migration policies, began to impact the Turkish construction sector and related industries. The migration of individuals from rural areas to urban centres during the 1970s and the 1980s led to irregular and unplanned urbanisation, resulting in subsequent infrastructure challenges that highlighted the necessity for urban planning and multi-storey building construction as remedial measures. During this period, housing projects aimed at middle- and upper-income groups proliferated in various settlements, particularly within major cities. Following the 1960s, there was a notable rise in the development of residential and vacation properties on behalf of housing cooperatives. However, by the 2000s, their market share had significantly dropped due to less government support and the rising dominance and competitive advantage of the private sector. As urban expansion progressed, the heightened demand for housing prompted outward urban development. After the 1990s, the private sector emerged as the dominant force in housing production and commercial real estate investment.

Over the past 25–30 years, the construction and real estate sectors have experienced significant growth, largely driven by economic expansion and a favourable investment environment. The advancement of these sectors is frequently considered a pivotal element driving the economy. The effects of various determinants on economic growth have largely mitigated the adverse impacts of global crises and economic volatility. These determinants encompass the housing deficit induced by population growth and urbanisation, initiatives aimed at revitalising distressed urban environments and regions susceptible to disasters, extensive housing projects, and distinguished residential and mixed-use developments within urban centres, in addition to the establishment of new railways, highways, airports, ports, bridges, urban rail networks, and other infrastructural ventures. The expansion of the construction and real estate sectors has been bolstered by housing and project financing programmes, in conjunction with rises in household and per capita income, as well as governmental incentives for mass housing and urban redevelopment initiatives. Nevertheless, the growth of these sectors has also attracted scrutiny from various stakeholders (Tanrıvermiş, 2019).

Table 1 Changes in GDP, population, and per capita income in Türkiye

Years	GDP (at current prices, USD 1 million)	Growth rate (%)	Mid-year population (1000 people)	Per capita GDP (at current prices, USD)	Per capita real GDP based on PPP (at current prices, USD)
1980	67,457	−2.4	44,438	1518	2876
1990	149,195	9.3	56,203	2655	5832
2000	265,384	6.8	64,269	4129	9431
2005	481,497	8.4	68,435	7036	11,773
2010	731,608	9.2	73,142	10,003	17,281
2011	773,980	8.8	74,224	10,428	19,517
2012	786,283	2.1	75,176	10,459	20,549
2013	823,044	4.2	76,055	10,822	22,373
2014	799,370	3.0	76,903	10,395	24,105
2015	719,967	4.0	77,738	9261	25,856
2016	856,791	2.9	78,559	10,807	26,696
2017	851,491	7.4	80,313	10,602	28,193
2018	784,087	2.6	81,407	9632	28,299
2019	760,778	0.9	82,579	9127	28,461
2020	717,049	1.8	83,385	8599	28,680
2021	807,106	9.6	84,147	9539	31,638
2022	905,814	3.3	84,980	10,655	38,355
2023	1118,593	4.5	85,326	13,110	42,561

Source: TURKSTAT (2024)

In Türkiye, macroeconomic indicators have generally exhibited improvement since the 1980s, except for periods characterised by crises. Türkiye's gross domestic product (GDP), which was approximately USD 67.5 billion in 1980, increased to USD 265.4 billion in 2000, USD 731.6 billion in 2010, USD 717.1 billion in 2020, and USD 1118.6 billion in 2023. The gross national product (GNP) underwent significant declines during the years 1980, 1984, 1994, 1999, 2001, 2014, 2015, 2016, 2018, 2019, 2020, and 2021, primarily due to social and/or economic crises. The economic stability attained after 2001 began to deteriorate during the periods of 2014–2015 and 2018–2021. Per capita income rose from USD 1518 in 1980 to USD 4129 in 2000 and subsequently reached USD 13,110 in 2023. It is noteworthy that per capita income is considerably higher when calculated on a purchasing power parity (PPP) basis, as illustrated in Table 1. In addition to economic growth pertaining to production value, it is also essential to maintain a stable trajectory. Variations in the growth rate of the GDP, when expressed in constant prices, have been observed over time, and disparities exist between the growth rates of various sectors and the overall economic growth rate.

Furthermore, both public enterprises and private organisations participate in the construction of residential, social, and administrative buildings within urban areas. In 1984, Law No. 2983 was enacted to encourage savings and expedite public investments. Furthermore, the Mass Housing Law No. 2985 was introduced in 1984 to facilitate the necessary services mandated by this legislation. This initiative led to the establishment of the Housing Development Administration of the Republic of Türkiye (TOKİ). Law No. 2985 outlined the procedures and principles governing housing construction aimed at fulfilling housing needs, and the development of industrial construction techniques, tools, and equipment suited to national conditions and materials. It established a framework for State support. In addition to TOKİ, municipally owned companies have achieved notable success in land development and housing production. TOKİ represents 9.1% of housing construction, while its subsidiary, Emlak Konut Real Estate Investment Company (REIC), captures a 1.7% share, thereby bringing their combined share to 10.8%. Meanwhile, the 24 corporate construction and real estate development companies linked with the Association of Housing Developers and Investors (KONUTDER) hold a 1.6% share. In contrast, other corporate entities and traditional entrepreneurs account for 87.7% (Tanrıvermiş, 2019). Traditional enterprises dominate the Turkish housing sector, whereas large-scale private companies and foreign firms play a more important role in infrastructure projects, resulting in a dual-structured market.

The private sector comprises traditional enterprises, including partnerships, sole proprietorships (such as build-and-sell developers and contractors), cooperatives, and corporate construction and real estate firms. Key characteristics of traditional enterprises encompass informality, a deficiency in professional management, a lack of operational continuity, and limited capacity for innovation. Among these entities, build-and-sell developers and sole proprietorships represent the largest market share. However, comprehensive data regarding their total production volumes remains insufficient. In traditional business models, the total number of housing projects, small industrial sites, and collective workplace cooperatives has reached 57,858. In contrast, the number of cooperative unions is documented at 350. It is estimated that housing cooperatives have made significant contributions to the production of residential and vacation housing during the Republican era, amounting to approximately 1.5 million units (Tanrıvermiş, 2019). In addition to corporate construction and real estate development, the process of institutionalisation has been furthered by Real Estate Investment Trusts, real estate investment funds, and operating companies that manage investments in infrastructure and healthcare sectors—including highways, ports, and airports—alongside asset and facility management firms, asset leasing companies, and real estate valuation and consultancy firms. Out of a total of 57 Real Estate Investment Trusts (REITs), 48 have achieved the public status and are actively traded on Borsa İstanbul (BIST). Furthermore, the number of portfolio management companies authorised by the Capital Markets Board (SPK) to oversee investments has reached 34. In contrast, the total number of established real estate investment funds amounts to 230 (SPK, 2024). Project-based real estate investment funds may be established for ventures wherein more than half of the total gross area of independent units is allocated for residential purposes. This mechanism is anticipated to enhance the role of these funds in urban transformation and real estate development initiatives.

Since certain enterprises engaged in real estate development are classified in the "construction" sector and others in the "real estate" sector in accordance with the statistical classification system of economic sectors (Nomenclature statistique des activités économiques dans la Communauté européenne (NACE)), accurately determining the true magnitude of the sector presents an ongoing challenge. The number of companies in the construction sector rose from 139,976 in 2010 to 245,053 in 2020, ultimately reaching 261,576 at the end of 2023. However, this growth was not paralleled by a corresponding rise in the sector's added value. In 2010, entrepreneurs in the construction sector constituted 5.23% of the total number of companies, increasing to 7.42% in 2020 yet declining to 7.02% in 2023. In the real estate sector, the number of companies almost doubled from approximately 33,000 in 2010 to 64,000 in 2023. At the national level, the

Table 2 Structure of construction and real estate businesses in Türkiye

Years	NACE Rev. 2: sector name	Number of enterprises (k)	Total number of employees (k)	Number of compensated employees (k)	Value added at factor cost (bn, TL)	Production value by economic activities (bn, TL)	Share in total value added (%)
2010	Türkiye: Total	2679	10,929	8639	305.3	1230.5	24.8
	F: Construction	140	1001	913	20.5	127.0	16.1
	L: Real estate activities	33	71	41	2.6	11.3	22.9
2015	Türkiye: Total	2690	13,952	11,756	625.9	2664.7	23.5
	F: Construction	180	1646	1522	45,3	336.5	13.5
	L: Real estate activities	26	59	39	2.7	26.0	10.5
2020	Türkiye: Total	3304	15,954	13,228	1651.2	6030.5	27.4
	F: Construction	245	1434	1269	90.3	584.1	15.5
	L: Real estate activities	50	132	89	17.1	63.1	27.0
2021	Türkiye: Total	3579	17,494	14,540	2711.3	9845.0	27.5
	F: Construction	272	1694	1508	135.1	840.3	16.1
	L: Real estate activities	53	149	104	26.4	92.5	28.5
2022	Türkiye: Total	3785	18,648	15,542	5606.1	21,982.1	25.5
	F: Construction	281	1706	1516	271.0	1735.7	15.6
	L: Real estate activities	59	167	117	56.8	274.6	20.7
2023	Türkiye: Total	3724	19,099	16,097	9943.1	34,809.3	28.6
	F: Construction	262	1836	1671	544.9	3271.0	16.7
	L: Real estate activities	64	179	126	93.4	365.9	25.5

Note: Enterprise and employment numbers are rounded to the nearest thousand (k). Value added and production values are rounded to the nearest billion Turkish lira (TL). Percentages are rounded to one decimal place. Minor discrepancies may occur due to rounding
Source: TURKSTAT (2024)

percentage of companies in the real estate sector was recorded at 1.23% in 2010 and 1.72% in 2023. Table 2 illustrates that the combined share of companies in the construction and real estate sectors accounted for a total of 6.46% in 2010 and 8.75% in 2023.

Total employment in the construction and real estate sectors has reached nearly two million, accounting for 10.55% of total civilian employment. The share of compensated employees in the construction sector typically ranges between 89% and 92%. Conversely, the proportion of compensated employees in the real estate sector increased from 58.21% in 2010 to 70.26% in 2023. As the professionalisation of the real estate sector advances, the number of compensated employees is increasing, with businesses employing three or more employees becoming more prevalent, thus replacing one-person enterprises. The contribution of construction and real estate enterprises to the national added value has remained relatively stable, underscoring the necessity to leverage technology and undergo digital transformation to enhance productivity and efficiency in both sectors.

6 Turkish REITs as a Real Estate Market Institution

Based on the word cloud coding, Fig. 5 illustrates the institutional structure of T-REITs from a broader perspective.

Internal and external institutional structures categorise the institutional framework of the T-REIT market. The internal framework of the T-REIT market comprises all elements within the management's purview. Conversely, the external structure of the real estate market includes factors that lie beyond the control of T-REIT management yet possess the capacity to exert direct or indirect influence on the internal structure of the market.

The internal structure emphasises features pertinent to real estate investment and associated risk levels, which are evaluated through beta and employee involvement. The workforce includes both executives and non-executives. T-REIT executives oversee a portfolio comprising real estate investments, index investments, and tangible properties. It has been observed that T-REITs engage in investment activities that encompass a combination of tangible real estate and indices.

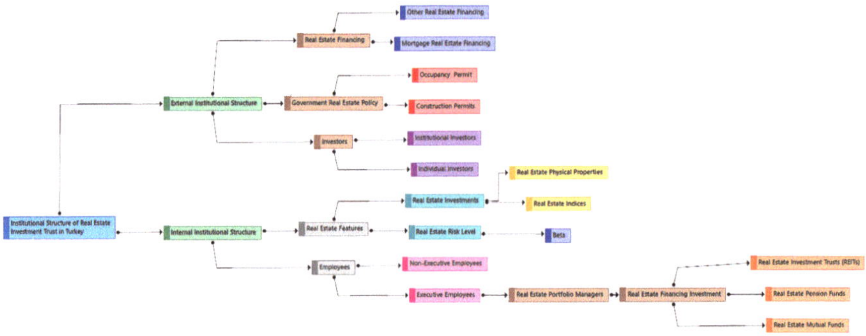

Fig. 5 Global view of the Turkish REITs' institutional structure. Source: Own depiction

The external structure of T-REITs is centred around investors, the government, and financial institutions. Investors in T-REITs encompass both institutional and non-institutional investors. Institutional investors comprise corporate organisations that allocate capital to real estate, as well as individuals who meet the criteria established by law. Conversely, non-institutional investors typically possess physical real estate for personal use or investment purposes. Furthermore, individual investors may also choose to invest in T-REITs. The government facilitates the process by issuing legal documents known as construction permits, which authorise developers to commence construction work. Additionally, it provides legal documents for occupancy, such as occupancy permits. Both documents are integral to establishing legal rights to physical real estate within the Turkish market. Finance constitutes another vital aspect of the institutional environment of T-REITs. Financing can be procured through mortgage loans or other sources, including familial and personal networks.

6.1 T-REITs' Executive Directors

Table 3 illustrates that there are not many REITs with young executive directors, aged 30–39 (Avrasya Real Estate Investment Trust Inc. and Reysas Real Estate). Executives aged 40–49 significantly contribute to Emlak Konut Real Estate, with most of their board members coming from Vakif Real Estate Investment Trust Inc.

It is important to note that Table 3 delineates the age range of board executives within the Turkish real estate market. Some real estate companies do not provide complete data on the ages of their board executives, as listed on the Bloomberg website. Ultimately, data regarding the age of approximately 128 board executives has been acquired and presented in the table above. The table does not include real estate companies that do not provide information concerning their board executives. Based on the available data, there are no board executive members below the age of 30, nor are there executive board members aged 90 years or older.

The demographic structure of executives within Türkiye's real estate companies predominantly features individuals aged between 50 and 59. Several factors may contribute to this, particularly the value of experience and the necessary network, coupled with the physical vitality required to fulfil the requisite duties. Given the dynamic nature of the real estate sector, it is imperative to emphasise core competencies. Notably, most of the board executive members of Akfen Industry, Mistral Real Estate Investment Trust Inc., and Torunlar Real Estate Investment Trust Inc. are within the age range of 60–69. Among the 27 T-REITs listed in Table 3 above, 12 entities are reported to have either one or two executive board members aged between 70 and 89 years old.

6.2 Employees in Turkish REITs

Additionally, Table 4 presents the number of employees working in the T-REIT sector. The findings indicate that most real estate companies in Türkiye employ fewer

Table 3 The age range of the board executives in the real estate market in Türkiye

T-REITs	30 < *Age* > 39	40 < *Age* > 49	50 < *Age* > 59	60 < *Age* >69	70 < *Age* > 89	Totals
Akfen Industry	2	1	2	3	2	10
Akis Real Estate Investment Trust Inc	2	0	2	1	0	5
Akmerkez Gayrimenkul Yatırım Ortaklığı A	2	0	5	1	1	9
Alarko Real Estate Investment Trust Inc	0	2	2	1	1	6
Ata Real Estate Investment Trust Inc	0	0	1	0	1	2
Avrasya Real Estate Investment Trust Inc	3	0	1	0	0	4
Baskent Real Estate Investment Trust Inc	0	0	1	0	0	1
Deniz Real Estate Investment Trust Inc	0	0	4	1	0	5
Dogus Real Estate Investment Trust Inc	0	0	2	2	0	4
Emlak Konut Real Estate Investment Trust Inc	1	4	1	0	0	6
Halk Real Estate Investment Trust Inc	0	2	3	1	0	6
Is Real Estate Investment Trust Inc	0	1	1	0	1	3
Kiler Real Estate Investment Trust Inc	0	0	3	0	0	3
Körfez Real Estate Investment Trust Inc	0	0	1	1	2	4

(Continued)

(Continued)

Martı Real Estate Investment Trust Inc	0	0	0	0	1	1
Mistral Real Estate Investment Trust Inc	0	0	2	5	1	8
Pera Real Estate Investment Trust Inc	0	0	3	0	0	3
Reysas Real Estate Investment Trust Inc	3	0	2	2	0	7
Servet Real Estate Investment Trust Inc	0	1	2	1	2	6
Sinpas Real Estate Investment Trust Inc	0	0	2	2	2	6
Torunlar Real Estate Investment Trust Inc	0	1	1	3	1	6
TSKB Real Estate Investment Trust Inc	1	1	1	0	0	3
Vakif Real Estate Investment Trust Inc	1	4	2	0	0	7
Yapi Kredi Koray Real Estate Investment Trust Inc	0	0	3	0	1	4
Yeni Gimat Gayrımenkul Yatırım Ortaklığı A	0	0	0	2	0	2
Yeşil Gayrimenkul Yatırım Ortaklığı A	0	2	4	1	0	7
Özak Real Estate Investment Trust Inc	0	2	3	0	0	5
Totals	15	19	50	28	16	128

Source: Own depiction

Table 4 Employees in the real estate market in Türkiye

Real Estate Market in Türkiye	1< E >50	51 < E > 100	101 < E >150	151 < E > 200	201 < E > 250	E >250
Akfen Industry	1	0	0	0	0	0
Akis Real Estate Investment Trust Inc	0	0	0	0	1	0
Akmerkez Gayrimenkul Yatırım Ortaklığı A	1	0	0	0	0	0
Alarko Real Estate Investment Trust Inc	1	0	0	0	0	0
Atakule Real Estate Investment Trust Inc	1	0	0	0	0	0
Avrasya Real Estate Investment Trust Inc	1	0	0	0	0	0
Baskent Real Estate Investment Trust Inc	0	0	0	0	0	1
Deniz Real Estate Investment Trust Inc	1	0	0	0	0	0
Dogus Real Estate Investment Trust Inc	1	0	0	0	0	0
Emlak Konut Real Estate Investment Trust Inc	0	0	0	0	0	1
Halk Real Estate Investment Trust Inc	1	0	0	0	0	0
Idealist Real Estate Investment Trust Inc	1	0	0	0	0	0
Is Real Estate Investment Trust Inc	0	1	0	0	0	0
Kiler Real Estate Investment Trust Inc	0	1	0	0	0	0
Kizilbuk Real Estate Investment Trust Inc	0	0	0	1	0	0
Körfez Real Estate Investment Trust Inc	1	0	0	0	0	0
Martı Real Estate Investment Trust Inc	1	0	0	0	0	0

(Continued)

(Continued)

Mistral Real Estate Investment Trust Inc	1	0	0	0	0	0
Nurol Real Estate Investment Trust Inc	1	0	0	0	0	0
Panora Real Estate Investment Trust Inc	1	0	0	0	0	0
Peker Real Estate Investment Trust Inc	1	0	0	0	0	0
Pera Real Estate Investment Trust Inc	1	0	0	0	0	0
Reysas Real Estate Investment Trust Inc	1	0	0	0	0	0
Servet Real Estate Investment Trust Inc	1	0	0	0	0	0
Sinpas Real Estate Investment Trust Inc	0	0	0	1	0	0
Torunlar Real Estate Investment Trust Inc	0	0	1	0	0	0
Trend Real Estate Investment Trust Inc	1	0	0	0	0	0
TSKB Real Estate Investment Trust Inc	1	0	0	0	0	0
Vakif Real Estate Investment Trust Inc	1	0	0	0	0	0
Yapi Kredi Koray Real Estate Investment Trust Inc	0	0	0	0	1	0
Yeni Gimat Gayrımenkul Yatırım Ortaklığı A	0	0	1	0	0	0
Yeşil Gayrimenkul Yatırım Ortaklığı A	1	0	0	0	0	0
Özak Real Estate Investment Trust Inc	0	0	0	0	0	1
Özderici Real Estate Investment Trust Inc	1	0	0	0	0	0
Totals	**23**	**2**	**2**	**2**	**2**	**3**

Note that E represents the number of employees in the Turkish real estate market
Source: Own depiction

than 50 persons, whereas three real estate companies in Türkiye employ more than 250 persons. This suggests that the Turkish real estate market remains underdeveloped from an institutional perspective, as no significant economies of scale have driven up company sizes. Moreover, the total number of employees within the industry remains low. This can be attributed to several factors: Türkiye encountered several financial crises in the early 2000s, followed by the global financial crisis in 2008, the COVID-19 pandemic in 2020, and the detrimental impact of the Russia–Ukraine conflict since 2022 (Salami et al., 2024). Out of the 37 analysed real estate companies, 25 T-REITs employed fewer than 50 employees. Concurrently, Is Real Estate Investment Trust Inc. and Kiler Real Estate Investment Trust Inc. maintained a workforce ranging from 50 to 100 employees. Furthermore, Torunlar Real Estate Investment Trust Inc. and Yeni Gimat Gayrımenkul Yatırım Ortaklığı employed between 100 and 150 persons. The workforce at Kizilbuk Real Estate Investment Trust Inc. and Servet Real Estate Investment Trust Inc. stayed below 200 employees. Akis Real Estate Investment Trust Inc. and Yapı Kredi Koray Real Estate Investment Trust Inc. employed between 200 and 250 individuals within Türkiye. Additionally, Baskent Real Estate Investment Trust Inc., Emlak Konut Real Estate Investment Trust Inc., and Özak Real Estate Investment Trust Inc. each employed more than 250 staff members. Among the T-REITs boasting over 250 employees, the government-linked real estate utility, which holds a monopolistic position in the gas-rendering sector, employs the largest staff, totalling 663.

6.3 Index Components of Turkish REITs

Table 5 presents a comprehensive overview of the indices in which Turkish Real Estate Investment Trusts (T-REITs) are represented. The top row denotes the codes corresponding to the index in which T-REITs have engaged in investment activities, as indicated in Table 6. In contrast, the first column lists the codes corresponding to the names of the reviewed T-REITs, following the coding scheme outlined in Table 6. Table 5 then shows that REIT A is represented in six different index components, namely BIST National All, BIST National 100, Index BIST 100, Financial, Other Real Estate Investment, and Index XYLDZ.

In total, T-REITs have been represented across 20 indices. Notably, nine T-REITs allocate resources to no fewer than four indices, which include the BIST National All, BIST National All 100, Financial, and Real Estate Investment indices. In comparison, three T-REITs are represented in a maximum of 11 indices. The scope of T-REIT investments may elucidate the degree of diversification observed within the real estate markets.

Table 6 explicitly delineates the individual T-REITs that are invested in indices, with the final column signifying the total index for each T-REIT. This table provides information on the diversification and performance expectations of each T-REIT, taking into account additional business-related engagements.

Table 5 Index components of Turkish REITs

Code	I	II	III	IV	V	VI	VII	VIII	IX	X	XI	XII	XIII	XIV	XV	XVI	XVII	XVIII	XIX	XX
A`	0	0	0	0	0	1	1	0	0	0	0	1	1	1	0	0	0	0	1	6
B`	0	1	0	0	0	1	0	0	0	0	0	0	1	1	0	0	0	1	1	6
C`	0	1	1	0	0	1	1	0	0	0	0	0	1	1	0	0	0	0	0	6
D`	1	0	1	0	0	1	0	0	0	0	0	1	1	1	0	1	0	0	1	8
E`	0	0	0	0	0	1	1	0	0	0	0	0	1	1	0	0	0	0	0	4
F`	0	0	0	0	0	1	1	0	0	0	1	0	1	1	0	0	0	0	0	5
G`	0	0	0	0	0	1	1	0	0	0	0	0	1	1	0	0	0	0	0	4
H`	0	0	0	0	1	1	1	1	1	1	1	1	1	1	0	0	0	0	1	11
I`	0	0	0	0	0	1	1	0	0	0	1	0	1	1	0	0	0	0	0	5
J`	0	1	0	0	0	1	1	0	0	0	0	0	1	1	0	0	0	0	0	5
K`	0	0	1	0	0	1	0	1	0	1	0	1	1	1	1	1	1	0	1	11
L`	1	1	1	0	0	1	0	0	0	0	0	0	1	1	0	1	0	0	1	8
M`	0	0	0	0	0	1	1	0	0	0	0	0	1	1	0	0	0	0	0	4
N`	1	0	0	0	0	1	0	0	0	1	0	1	1	1	0	1	0	0	1	8
O`	0	0	0	0	0	1	1	0	0	0	0	0	1	1	0	0	0	0	0	4
P`	0	0	0	0	1	1	1	1	0	0	1	0	1	1	0	0	0	0	0	7
Q`	0	0	0	0	0	1	1	0	0	0	1	0	1	1	0	0	0	0	0	5
R`	0	0	0	0	0	1	1	0	0	0	0	0	1	1	0	0	0	0	0	4
S`	0	0	0	0	0	1	1	0	0	0	1	0	1	1	0	0	0	0	0	5
T`	0	0	0	0	0	1	1	0	0	0	0	0	1	1	0	0	0	0	0	4
U`	0	0	0	0	1	1	1	1	1	1	1	1	1	1	0	0	0	0	1	11
V`	0	0	1	0	0	1	1	0	0	0	1	0	1	1	0	0	0	0	0	6
W`	0	0	0	0	1	1	1	1	0	0	1	0	1	1	0	0	0	0	0	7
X`	0	0	0	0	0	1	1	0	0	0	0	0	1	1	0	0	0	0	0	4
Y`	0	0	0	0	0	1	1	0	0	0	1	0	1	1	0	0	0	0	1	6
Z`	0	0	0	0	1	1	1	0	0	0	0	0	1	1	0	0	0	0	0	5
AA`	0	0	0	0	0	1	1	1	0	0	1	0	1	1	0	0	0	0	0	6
AB`	0	0	0	0	0	1	1	1	0	1	1	0	1	1	0	1	0	0	0	8
AC`	0	0	0	0	0	1	0	1	1	1	1	1	1	1	0	1	0	0	1	10
AD`	0	0	0	0	1	1	1	0	0	0	1	0	1	1	0	0	0	0	0	6
AE`	0	0	0	0	0	1	1	0	0	0	0	0	1	1	0	0	0	0	1	5
AF`	1	1	0	0	0	1	1	0	0	0	0	0	1	1	0	0	0	0	0	6
AG`	0	0	0	0	0	1	1	0	0	0	0	0	1	1	0	0	0	0	0	4
AH`	0	0	1	1	0	1	1	0	0	0	0	0	1	1	0	0	0	0	1	7
AI`	0	0	0	0	0	1	1	0	0	0	0	0	1	1	0	0	0	0	0	4
AJ`	0	0	0	0	0	1	0	1	0	1	1	0	1	1	0	0	0	0	1	7
AK`	0	0	0	0	0	1	1	0	0	0	1	0	1	1	0	0	0	0	0	5
	4	5	7	2	6	37	30	9	3	7	16	7	37	37	1	6	1	1	14	227

Source: Own depiction

Table 6 Interpretation of the code used in Table 5

Code′	REITs	Total	Index components	Code
1 = A′	Akfen Industry	6	Index: BIST 100–30	**I**
2 = B′	Akis Real Estate Investment Trust Inc	6	Index: BIST corporate management	**II**
3 = C′	Akmerkez Gayrimenkul Yatırım Ortaklığı A	6	Index: BIST dividend	**III**
4 = D′	Alarko Real Estate Investment Trust Inc	8	Index: BIST dividend 25	**IV**
5 = E′	Ata Real Estate Investment Trust Inc	4	Index: BIST IPO	**V**
6 = F′	Atakule Real Estate Investment Trust Inc	5	Index: BIST National all	**VI**
7 = G′	Avrasya Real Estate Investment Trust Inc	4	Index: BIST National all 100	**VII**
8 = H′	Baskent Real Estate Investment Trust Inc	11	Index: BIST participation 100	**VIII**
9 = I′	Deniz Real Estate Investment Trust Inc	5	Index: BIST participation 30	**IX**
10 = J′	Dogus Real Estate Investment Trust Inc	5	Index: BIST participation 50	**X**
11 = K′	Emlak Konut Real Estate Investment Trust Inc	11	Index: BIST participation all shares	**XI**
12 = L′	Halk Real Estate Investment Trust Inc	8	Index: BIST100	**XII**
13 = M′	Idealist Real Estate Investment Trust Inc	4	Index: Financials	**XIII**
14 = N′	Is Real Estate Investment Trust Inc	8	Index: Real estate investments	**XIV**
15 = O′	Kiler Real Estate Investment Trust Inc	4	Index: X030S	**XV**
16 = P′	Kizilbuk Real Estate Investment Trust Inc	7	Index: X100S	**XVI**
17 = Q′	Körfez Real Estate Investment Trust Inc	5	Index: X10XB	**XVII**
18 = R′	Martı Real Estate Investment Trust Inc	4	Index: XUSRD	**XVIII**
19 = S′	Mistral Real Estate Investment Trust Inc	5	Index: XYLDZ	**XIX**
20 = T′	Nurol Real Estate Investment Trust Inc	4	**Total**	**XX**
21 = U′	Pacific Real Estate Investment Trust Inc	11		
22 = V′	Panora Real Estate Investment Trust Inc	6		

(continued)

Table 6 (continued)

Code′	REITs	Total	Index components	Code
23 = W′	Peker Real Estate Investment Trust Inc	7		
24 = X′	Pera Real Estate Investment Trust Inc	4		
25 = Y′	Reysas Real Estate Investment Trust Inc	6		
26 = Z′	Seker Real Estate Investment Trust Inc	5		
27 = AA′	Servet Real Estate Investment Trust Inc	6		
28 = AB′	Sinpas Real Estate Investment Trust Inc	8		
29 = AC′	Torunlar Real Estate Investment Trust Inc	10		
30 = AD′	Trend Real Estate Investment Trust Inc	6		
31 = AE′	TSKB Real Estate Investment Trust Inc	5		
32 = AF′	Vakif Real Estate Investment Trust Inc	6		
33 = AG′	Yapi Kredi Koray Real Estate Investment Trust Inc	4		
34 = AH′	Yeni Gimat Gayrımenkul Yatırım Ortaklığı A	7		
35 = AI′	Yeşil Gayrimenkul Yatırım Ortaklığı A	4		
36 = AJ′	Özak Real Estate Investment Trust Inc	7		
37 = AK′	Özderici Real Estate Investment Trust Inc	5		
	Total	**227**		

Note that A′ to AK′ represents a list of Turkish REITs' names, while I to XIX represents a list of indices in which Turkish REITs are represented
Source: Own depiction

6.4 Turkish REITs' Portfolio Risk Relative to Market Risk

Table 7 illustrates the risk associated with the T-REIT portfolio in comparison to market risk. A value of 1 would indicate that the volatility of a specific REIT is the same as the overall market's volatility. The findings suggest that the volatility of 19 T-REITs is at or below 1, whereas 13 exceed this threshold. Given that the repercussions of the COVID-19 pandemic on real estate prices vary across different property types within the European commercial real estate market, it is important to differentiate (Hoesli & Malle, 2021): office buildings were significantly impacted

Table 7 Risk level of Turkish REITs' portfolio relative to market risk

	$\beta < 0$	$0 < \beta > 0.5$	$0.51 < \beta > 1$	$1.01 < \beta > 1.5$	$1.51 < \beta > 2$
Akfen Industry	0	0	1	0	0
Akis Real Estate Investment Trust Inc	0	0	1	0	0
Akmerkez Gayrimenkul Yatırım Ortaklığı A	0	0	1	0	0
Alarko Real Estate Investment Trust Inc	0	0	1	0	0
Ata Real Estate Investment Trust Inc	0	1	0	0	0
Atakule Real Estate Investment Trust Inc	0	0	0	1	0
Baskent Real Estate Investment Trust Inc	1	0	0	0	0
Deniz Real Estate Investment Trust Inc	0	0	0	0	1
Dogus Real Estate Investment Trust Inc	0	1	0	0	0
Emlak Konut Real Estate Investment Trust Inc	0	0	1	0	0
Halk Real Estate Investment Trust Inc	0	0	0	1	0
Idealist Real Estate Investment Trust Inc	0	0	1	0	0
Is Real Estate Investment Trust Inc	0	0	1	0	0
Kiler Real Estate Investment Trust Inc	0	0	0	1	0
Körfez Real Estate Investment Trust Inc	0	0	0	0	1
Martı Real Estate Investment Trust Inc	0	0	0	1	0
Mistral Real Estate Investment Trust Inc	0	0	1	0	0
Nurol Real Estate Investment Trust Inc	0	0	0	0	1
Panora Real Estate Investment Trust Inc	0	1	0	0	0
Peker Real Estate Investment Trust Inc	0	1	0	0	0
Pera Real Estate Investment Trust Inc	0	0	1	0	0
Reysas Real Estate Investment Trust Inc	0	0	1	0	0
Servet Real Estate Investment Trust Inc	0	0	0	0	1
Sinpas Real Estate Investment Trust Inc	0	0	0	0	1
Torunlar Real Estate Investment Trust Inc	0	0	0	1	0
	$\beta < 0$	$0 < \beta > 0.5$	$0.51 < \beta > 1$	$1.01 < \beta > 1.5$	$1.51 < \beta > 2$
Trend Real Estate Investment Trust Inc	0	0	0	1	0
TSKB Real Estate Investment Trust Inc	0	0	0	0	1
Vakif Real Estate Investment Trust Inc	0	0	1	0	0
Yapi Kredi Koray Real Estate Investment Trust Inc	0	1	0	0	0
Yeni Gimat Gayrımenkul Yatırım Ortaklığı A	1	0	0	0	0
Yeşil Gayrimenkul Yatırım Ortaklığı A	0	0	0	1	0
Özak Real Estate Investment Trust Inc	0	0	1	0	0
Totals	2	5	12	7	6

Note that β (beta) represents the level of risk of each T-REIT relative to the overall stock market risk at the time of this study
Source: Own depiction

during the COVID-19 pandemic, and a continuous transition towards hybrid working arrangements is being observed in the post-COVID-19 era (Naor et al., 2022).

The beta coefficients of Baskent Real Estate Investment Trust Inc. and Yeni Gimat Gayrımenkul Yatırım Ortaklığı A are recorded as being below zero, indicating that their portfolios exhibit a negative beta. As of the last quarter of 2022 (2022 Q4), Baskent Real Estate Investment Trust Inc. was noted to have a beta value of −0.77. The company operates as a government-owned entity, providing crucial natural gas services, including the transmission and delivery of natural gas through pipelines. The company specialises in the utility sector, with a distinct focus on investments in natural gas, and is represented across 11 indices. Given its workforce of 663 employees and its extensive diversification potential, the company is considered to carry a reduced level of risk.

As of the fourth quarter of 2022, Yeni Gimat Gayrımenkul Yatırım Ortaklığı's beta was recorded at −0.286. This indicates that the company has commenced performing positively in the aftermath of the COVID-19 pandemic. The organisation has made investments in the real estate sector and has engaged in trading activities across seven indices. The company currently employs a workforce of 113 persons, and its real estate investments are conducted through strategic partnerships with supermarket chains and hotel establishments.

7 Conclusion

In the real estate and construction sectors, the Housing Development Administration (TOKİ) and municipally owned companies have attained a considerable stake in land development and housing production. The private sector encompasses traditional enterprises, including general partnerships, sole proprietorships (such as build-and-sell developers and contractors), cooperatives, and corporate construction and real estate firms. Within the construction and real estate sectors, there are 325,671 active enterprises, the majority of which are sole proprietorships, including build-and-sell developers, as well as public and local government entities. Additionally, over the past 25–30 years, many Real Estate Investment Trusts (REITs) have been established, and these firms have specialised in valuation, financing, asset leasing, facility management, real estate management, and asset management, each evolving into distinct business sectors. Furthermore, businesses dedicated to real estate development—including the conversion of raw land into zoned parcels, architectural design, construction, financing, project management, marketing, and operations—have been established; however, the NACE classification system does not presently categorise such enterprises. To maximise the added value of positive developments in the national economy's construction and real estate sectors, regulatory reforms are essential in zoning, taxation, administration, and finance, alongside the implementation of policies aimed at promoting institutionalisation.

Despite their growing significance within the economy, the structural characteristics and informality of the construction and real estate sectors result in substantial tax and duty revenue losses, as well as challenges in accurately measuring the true scale of wealth and assessing the sector's potential. As the construction and real estate sectors continue to expand, the associated risks also escalate, leading to increased complexity in business operations over time. Economic risks and forecasts must not be disregarded during site selection, construction, or planning of investment projects. Nonetheless, the dynamics exhibited within the construction and real estate sectors significantly contribute to the economy, directly employing approximately two million persons, generating additional demand for goods produced across the economy, and consequently facilitating the emergence of new business fields and professions. Rapid population growth, advances in services and manufacturing, and the success of urban transformation projects lead to increased urban expansion, which, in turn, amplifies infrastructure expenditure for local administrations.

This chapter investigated the institutional structure of the real estate market in Türkiye. It used both qualitative and quantitative data pertaining to real estate in Türkiye. The real estate market in Türkiye comprises several key participants, including developers, who represent the ultimate risk-takers and engage with other market stakeholders. Other contributors within the risk-taking categories include financiers, facility management, technology providers, and Engineering, Procurement, Construction, Installation, and Commissioning (EPCIC) firms. In contrast, government regulators and professionals, as well as the categorisation of political and financial risks, assume a neutral role.

The real estate market structure is defined by the activities within the market and the relationships among its players. Essentially, a market is a venue where the exchange of goods and services occurs for a monetary value. Several activities transpire in the real estate market, including the exchange of land and cash between landowners and developers; the exchange of services and salaries between professionals and developers; the exchange of taxes, royalties, and permits between the regulator and developers; the exchange of investments and profits between financiers and developers; and the exchange of housing and money between developers and end users.

Regarding T-REITs, our findings indicate that their sensitivity to the market is assessed through their beta value. The external structure of T-REITs comprises government entities, financiers, and investors. These external market structures exist to facilitate the effective internal market structure of T-REITs.

The findings further indicated that T-REITs are represented across various indices. Specifically, T-REITs are engaged in investments that are described in at least four indices, in addition to a portfolio of physical real estate. The results also showed that some T-REITs employing more than 250 personnel are represented in a maximum of 11 indices. The findings suggested that T-REITs with a larger workforce exhibit greater diversification and reduced risk compared to the market. Furthermore, most T-REITs employ fewer than 50 individuals, with their risk levels relative to the market ranging between 0.5 and 1.5. These T-REITs are comparatively riskier than those that invest more broadly. Notably, executive directors aged between 50 and 59 years represent a significant demographic within T-REIT executive leadership.

A limitation of this study is its reflection of the institutional structure of the real estate sector in Türkiye during the post-COVID-19 era. This suggests that certain information may remain consistent before and after the COVID-19 pandemic. Future research on the institutional structure of the T-REIT market may focus on the sensitivity of T-REITs' risk profiles to seasonal variations to anticipate the resilience of the institutional framework.

References

Abdullah, M. R. B. (2015). Real estate market structure: Industrial organization perspectives. *International Journal of Management Studies, 22*(1), 57–72. https://doi.org/10.32890/ijms.22.1.2015.10420

Brady, D. A., Tzortzopoulos, P., Rooke, J., Formoso, C. T., & Tezel, A. (2018). Improving transparency in construction management: A visual planning and control model. *Engineering, Construction and Architectural Management, 25*(10), 1277–1297. https://doi.org/10.1108/ECAM-07-2017-0122

Brill, F. N., & Robin, E. (2020). The risky business of real estate developers: Network building and risk mitigation in London and Johannesburg. *Urban Geography, 41*(1), 36–54. https://doi.org/10.1080/02723638.2019.1637211

Campbell, R., & Sirmans, C. (2002). Policy implications of structural options in the development of real estate investment trusts in Europ: Lessons from the American experience. *Journal of Property Investment and Finance, 20*(4), 388–405.

Capital Markets Board of Türkiye (SPK). (2024). Retrieved November 08, 2024, from https://spk.gov.tr/portfoy-degerleri-GYO

Cvijanović, D., Milcheva, S., & van de Minne, A. (2022). Preferences of institutional investors in commercial real estate. *Journal of Real Estate Finance and Economics, 65*(2), 321–359. https://doi.org/10.1007/s11146-020-09816-y

D'Arcy, É. (2009). The evolution of institutional arrangements to support the internationalisation of real estate involvements: Some evidence from Europe. *Journal of European Real Estate Research, 2*(3), 280–293. https://doi.org/10.1108/17539260911000006

Demirsu, I., & Cihangir-Tetik, D. (2019). Constructing the partnership with Turkey on the refugee crisis: EU perceptions and expectations. *Journal of Balkan and Near Eastern Studies, 21*(6), 625–642. https://doi.org/10.1080/19448953.2018.1506291

Han, S. S., & Wang, Y. (2003). The institutional structure of a property market in inland China: Chongqing. *Urban Studies, 40*(1), 91–112. https://doi.org/10.1080/00420980220080181

Hoesli, M., & Malle, R. (2021). Commercial real estate prices and COVID-19. *Journal of European Real Estate Research, 15*(2), 295–306. https://doi.org/10.1108/JERER-04-2021-0024

Ionaşcu, E., & Anghel, I. (2020). Improvement of the real estate transparency through digitalisation. *Proceedings of the International Conference on Business Excellence, 14*(1), 371–384. https://doi.org/10.2478/picbe-2020-0036

Ionaşcu, E., Taltavull de La Paz, P., & Mironiuc, M. (2021). The relationship between housing prices and market transparency. Evidence from the metropolitan European markets. *Housing, Theory and Society, 38*(1), 42–71. https://doi.org/10.1080/14036096.2019.1672577

Naor, M., Pinto, G. D., Hakakian, A. I., & Jacobs, A. (2022). The impact of COVID-19 on office space utilisation and real estate: A Case study on teleworking in Israel as the new normal. *Journal of Facilities Management, 20*(1), 32–58. https://doi.org/10.1108/JFM-12-2020-0096

Oh, D. Y., & Shin, H. B. (2023). University as real estate developer: Comparative perspectives from the Global East. *Geoforum, 144*(March), 103764. https://doi.org/10.1016/j.geoforum.2023.103764

Read, D. C., Hopkins, E., & Goss, R. C. (2016). Working effectively with asset managers and institutional groups. *Property Management, 34*(4), 280–296. https://doi.org/10.1108/PM-07-2015-0031

Sadayuki, T., Harano, K., & Yamazaki, F. (2019). Market transparency and international real estate investment. *Journal of Property Investment and Finance, 37*(5), 503–518. https://doi.org/10.1108/JPIF-04-2019-0043

Salami, M. A., Tanrıvermiş, H., & Tanrıvermiş, Y. (2024). Influence of Ukraine invasion by Russia on Turkish markets. *The Journal of Economic Asymmetries, 29*, 1–17. https://doi.org/10.1016/j.jeca.2023.e00348

Tanrıvermiş, H. (2019). Türkiye Ekonomisinde İnşaat ve Gayrimenkul Sektörlerinin Rolleri ve Gelişme Eğilimlerinin Değerlendirilmesi (Assessment of the roles of construction and real estate sectors and their development trends in Turkey). In *Proceedings of Kent, İnşaat ve Ekonomi Kongresi, TMMOB Mimarlar Odası Gaziantep Şubesi, 2–4 Mayıs 2019, Gaziantep*, pp. 37–58.

Theurillat, T., Rérat, P., & Crevoisier, O. (2015). The real estate markets: Players, institutions, and territories. *Urban Studies, 52*(8), 1414–1433. https://doi.org/10.1177/0042098014536238

Turkish Statistical Institute (TURKSTAT). (2024). Retrieved November 8, 2024, from http://www.tuik.gov.tr

Wheaton, W. (1999). Real estate cycles: Some fundamentals. *Real Estate Economics, 27*(2), 209–230.

Wu, H., Qian, Q. K., Straub, A., & Visscher, H. J. (2022). Factors influencing transaction costs of prefabricated housing projects in China: A developer's perspective. *Engineering, Construction and Architectural Management, 29*(1), 476–501. https://doi.org/10.1108/ECAM-07-2020-0506

Harun Tanrıvermiş is a distinguished professor who occupies the esteemed position at the Ankara University top management level as founder and head of the Department of Real Estate Development and Management, and founder and current dean of the Faculty of Applied Sciences at Ankara University. Professor Tanrıvermiş also currently works as the vice rector at Ankara University. He attained his B.Sc., M.Sc., and Ph.D. degrees from the Department of Agricultural Economics at Ankara University, specialising in land and real estate economics, land and real estate valuation, as well as natural resources and environmental economics. Furthermore, he earned an M.Sc. in environmental management through the MED-CAMPUS Programme in 1996. Professor Tanrıvermiş has published approximately 400 papers, including 43 international and 55 national peer-reviewed articles, which have been published in various high-impact journals. Additionally, he has presented 48 international and 74 national proceedings, either in full or as abstracts, at numerous conferences. He is also credited with writing 39 books and 17 book chapters. Moreover, his works concentrate on the land and real estate valuation, land and real estate economics, real estate development and project appraisal, urban transformation and sustainability, sustainable real estate development, facility and real estate management, land management, administration and polices, measuring and reporting of real estate sustainability and ESG, digital transformation in real estate and real estate technologies.

Tobias Just is Managing Director at the IRE|BS Immobilienakademie and professor for Real Estate at the Regensburg University. Tobias studied economics in Hamburg and Uppsala (Sweden). In 1997, he graduated and started to work at the University of the Federal Armed Forces Hamburg. His Ph.D. dissertation was awarded the university science prize in 2001. For more than ten years, Tobias worked at Deutsche Bank Research, the economics research unit of Deutsche Bank. He headed the units' sector and real estate research team and was a member of Deutsche Bank's group-wide Environmental Steering Committee. In summer 2006, Tobias was a Research Fellow at the American Institute of Contemporary German Studies at Johns Hopkins University in Washington, DC. Tobias published 17 books and more than 250 papers in professional and academic journals and books. Since November 2011, Tobias has been Managing Director at the IRE|BS Immobilienakademie and holds a Chair for Real Estate at the University of Regensburg. He was President of the German Society of Property Researchers (GIF) from 2014-2021 and is editor of the ZIÖ—the German Journal of Real Estate Research. From 2016 to 2023, Tobias was a member of the Supervisory Board of Helaba Invest Kapitalanlagegesellschaft mbH. In 2017, Tobias became a Fellow of the RICS by nomination.

An International Perspective on Real Estate Investments in Türkiye

Tobias Just and Vanessa Dietl

Abstract

International real estate investors often view Türkiye with a mix of cautious pessimism and hopeful optimism. Positive demographic trends, substantial potential across key real estate sectors, and Türkiye's strategic geopolitical position support a long-term bullish outlook. Applying the beta convergence hypothesis, sustained growth is conceivable if institutional reforms align with Western standards, enabling convergence in per capita output. Despite an average annual GDP growth of 5% between 2010 and 2022—outpacing the EU27's 2%—Türkiye has lagged behind countries like Poland or Romania in real convergence. This shortfall is largely attributable to weak institutional frameworks, insufficient transparency, and regulatory shortcomings, which foster macroeconomic volatility and deter risk-averse investors.

Keywords

Economic development · Transparency · Real estate investment

T. Just (✉)
International Real Estate Business School (IREBS), Regensburg University, Regensburg, Germany
e-mail: tobias.just@irebs.academy

V. Dietl
International Real Estate Business School (IREBS), University of Regensburg, Regensburg, Germany
e-mail: Vanessa1.Dietl@wiwi.uni-regensburg.de

T. Just et al. (eds.), *Understanding Türkiye's Real Estate Markets*, Management for Professionals, https://doi.org/10.1007/978-3-032-13297-0_3

1 Introduction

All real estate is local. At least, that is what investor wisdom would have us believe. This refers to the lack of transparency in many real estate markets, which ultimately means that local market players determine what happens in real estate markets. However, the increasing internationalisation of goods and factor markets has contributed to both real estate users and real estate investors following this simple dictum of locality. Although a home bias for real estate capital markets can still be demonstrated (Imazeki & Gallimore, 2009; Gaar et al., 2022), which is primarily linked to the size of the potential investment markets and market transparency, this suggests that the professionalisation of real estate markets goes hand in hand with the internationalisation of markets and thus a reduction in home bias. Just and Uttich (2024) argue, with regard to German cross-border capital flows, that the much greater volatility of international real estate investment flows compared to national flows suggests that international investors react more strongly to deteriorating market data and that this contributes to a home bias.

Lieser and Groh (2014) show that the volume of international real estate investments depends on economic growth expectations, urbanisation, demographic developments, and varying degrees of transparency. Sociocultural aspects also play a role. In their analysis, Fuerst et al. (2015) conclude that market liquidity, measured by the share of market transactions in total real estate stock, is the most important indicator for explaining international capital flows. However, their data also suggests that transparency plays a major role.

In this chapter, we identify the key determinants of international real estate capital flows for Türkiye, i.e., economic growth, transparency, and demographic trends, before going on to examine individual market dynamics in detail. We illustrate that the volume of international transactions in Türkiye will only increase once the country has succeeded in stabilising its economic momentum and raising transparency, not only in the real estate markets, to Western European levels. Although much has improved in Türkiye in recent years, there is still work to be done, particularly with regard to financial institutions.

2 Macroeconomic Drivers of International Real Estate Investors

If we look solely at economic performance, measured by nominal gross domestic product, and economic development, measured by the change in price-adjusted gross domestic product, there is much to suggest that investor interest in real estate transactions in Türkiye is high: the average growth rate of Turkish GDP has been significantly higher than the Organisation for Economic Co-operation and Development (OECD) countries average since 2015, and comparatively high economic growth is also expected in the near future (see Fig. 1).

At the same time, the 85 million people in Türkiye generate an economic output that is slightly higher than that of Poland. Since Poland has a significantly smaller

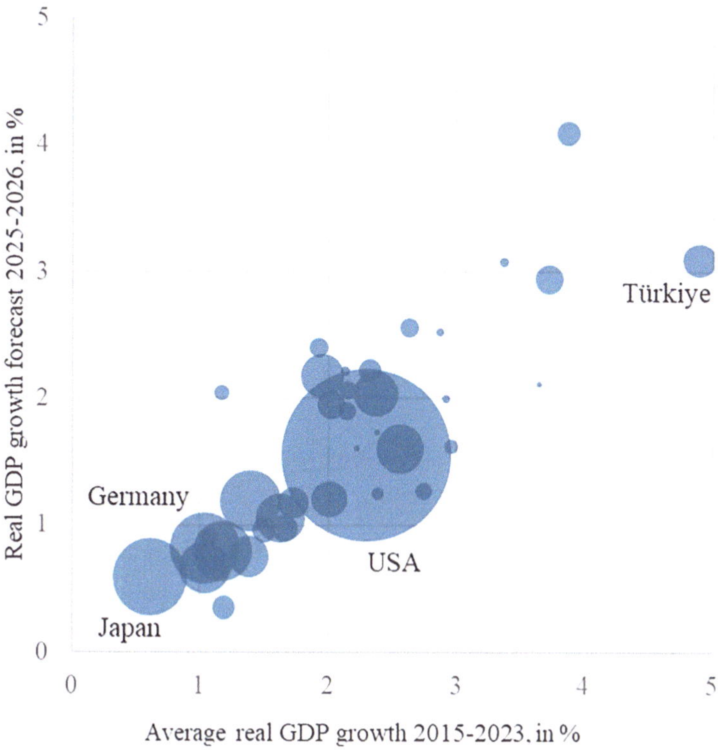

Fig. 1 Economic development of OECD countries. Note: The bubble sizes measure the total GDP in USD in 2024. Source: OECD (2025), own calculations

population than Türkiye, international investors can draw both positive and negative conclusions from this: on the one hand, Türkiye is clearly not achieving the productivity levels of Poland (or Western European countries), but on the other hand, this could be an advantage if Türkiye succeeds in catching up with European productivity levels in line with the convergence hypothesis.

Ultimately, capital strong and risk-aware institutional real estate investors (pension funds, insurance companies, and sovereign wealth funds) would be cautious if they had doubts about Türkiye's growth story and if monetary capital flows were not secure. Both are likely. On the one hand, economic development in Türkiye has not been stable in recent years, with the standard deviation of the economic growth rate around 50% higher than the average standard deviation of all OECD countries.

Even more serious, however, is the fact that the price stability of the Turkish currency could not be guaranteed in recent years. Turkish consumer prices have risen by double digits every year since 2017, which is not only significantly higher than in European countries but also higher than in many emerging markets (Fig. 2 also shows the inflation rates for India and China).

This lack of price stability poses several risks for international investors: the biggest risk is the associated devaluation of the Turkish lira. Since June 2020, the Turkish lira has fallen by 83% against the euro and by 82% against the US dollar.

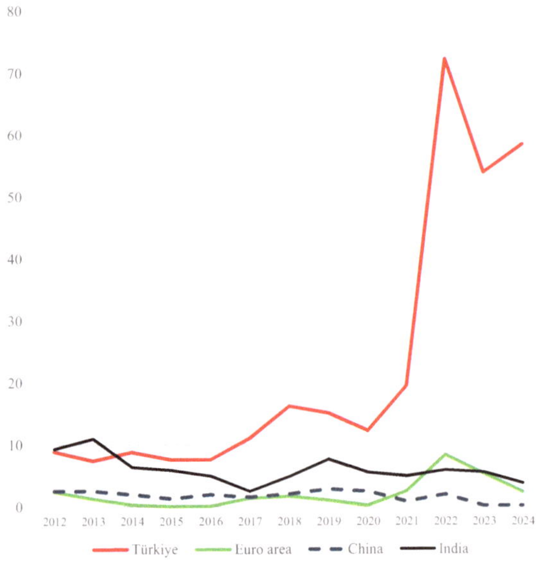

Fig. 2 Consumer price inflation in selected economies in % year-on-year. Source: OECD (2025)

Even if investors insist that rental agreements be concluded in foreign currencies, this only shifts the risk one step further to the customers or the users, who predominantly pay in lira. When analysing the risk, it is therefore important to ensure that the users of the properties conduct a large proportion of their business internationally. The second risk associated with this is the interest rate risk. High inflation rates are forcing central banks to raise interest rates. As a result, financing is becoming more difficult and economic momentum is slowing down. Here, too, foreign currency debt does not offer complete protection because the loss of economic momentum will weigh on every asset class. Currently (June 2025), the central bank interest rate stands at 46%, close to its highest level in decades. Above all, a look at the course of recent years shows that the central bank had lowered interest rates several times too early and too vigorously: the interest rate was lowered from 24% in 2019 to 8.25% in March 2020 (the coronavirus pandemic also played a role here, of course), only to have to raise it again to 18% just one year later. Similarly, the interest rate fell again to 8.5% by 2023, only to be raised shortly afterwards to the current dizzying levels. At least inflation rates have been falling month after month for a year. Inflation expectations are also falling but only very slowly. Most recently, inflation expectations for the next 12 months have also been well into double digits. Risk-averse European investors in particular are likely to remain cautious, given this outlook (Türkiye Cumhuriyet Merkez Bankasi, 2025).

3 International Investors Demand Transparency

In addition to overall economic demand dynamics and price trends, the stability of economic, financial, and legal institutions is considered an important determinant of international real estate investment. Table 1 compares the index values reported by

Table 1 Index of economic freedom by factors

Factor	Türkiye	Germany	China	India
Property rights	40.6	95.4	46.7	51.1
Government integrity	34.3	86.0	40.4	37.6
Judicial effectiveness	23.8	93.5	37.4	53.2
Tax burden	72.2	60.5	71.6	71.3
Government spending	71.9	26.9	67.1	74.2
Fiscal health	82.3	81.1	11.1	6.2
Business freedom	58.5	83.7	67.7	72.3
Labour freedom	48.4	53.3	57.9	59.0
Monetary freedom	37.9	69.0	74.6	69.9
Trade freedom	72.8	79.6	74.0	61.0
Investment freedom	70.0	60.0	20.0	40.0
Financial freedom	60.0	70.0	20.0	40.0
Overall score	56.1	71.6	49.0	53.0

Source: The Heritage Foundation (2025)

the Heritage Foundation (2025) for four countries. Türkiye ranks better than China or India on average across all these indicators. Still, the index values for Türkiye are significantly below those of Western European countries, as illustrated here by the values of Germany. The indices are calibrated so that the maximum value is 100 points and the minimum is zero points. Türkiye performs best in the categories of tax burden, fiscal health, government spending, and trade freedom. The Foundation's analysts see the greatest potential for improvement in the more politically driven categories and in the security of property rights. In these categories, Türkiye actually performs worse than China or India.

Property rights play a particularly important role in transactions, as does institutional transparency. JLL (2024) highlights this for real estate markets in its JLL Transparency Index (Fig. 3). This index is designed so that low values (a minimum of 1) represent higher transparency (more favourable). An index value of 5 points indicates the lowest transparency. The individual categories of the overall index paint a similar picture to the Heritage Foundation's figures. There is room for improvement in the regulatory/legal area, in the transaction process, and in sustainability issues. However, according to JLL's analysis, Türkiye does not perform significantly worse than China's major tier 1 cities in four of the six categories. Here, too, there is a lag behind Western European reference markets, as illustrated again in Fig. 3 with Germany. The country's potential, which was already evident in its economic growth, is reflected here in the fact that the market data is quite positive.

A key challenge in the coming years will therefore be to modernise central institutions and market regulations, as international investors need planning security and reliable data. At a time when the investment committees of large institutional investors are paying attention to all three pillars of the ESG (E = environmental, S = social, and G = governance) framework, Türkiye must become more transparent and focus more strongly on internal governance rules. It is no coincidence that Transparency International's Corruption Perception Index (2025) correlates highly with the JLL index. Investors associate the lack of institutions and data (often rightly so) with side agreements outside of contracts.

Fig. 3 Real estate market transparency by segments. Source: JLL (2024)

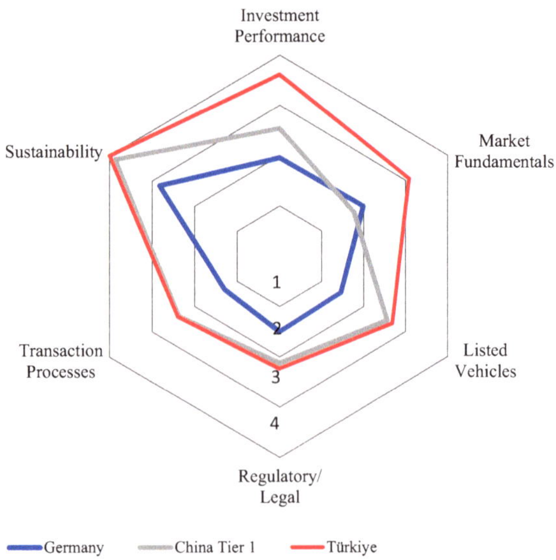

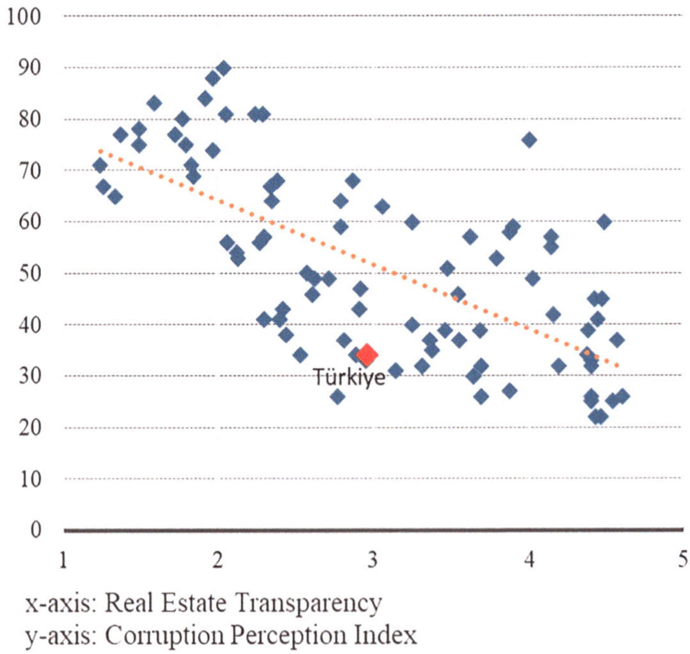

Fig. 4 Real Estate Transparency and Corruption Perception Index. Source: Transparency International (2025), JLL (2024)

It should be noted that the Corruption Perception Index in Fig. 4 is constructed in such a way that a low value represents a high level of perceived corruption and a high value represents low corruption. As a result, the indices from JLL and Transparency International are negatively correlated for around 90 countries.

4 Demographic Trends: Not Only about Population Growth

For international real estate investors, one of Türkiye's most important advantages is that its population will continue to grow significantly for several decades and that, compared to other European countries, the population is relatively young, with the birth rate in Türkiye falling from a significantly higher level. This means that the labour force potential will begin to decline much later than in Western and Eastern European reference countries (see Fig. 5). Between 2020 and 2024, the population in Türkiye grew by an average of 0.65% per year. At the same time, the average household size fell from 3.6 persons in 2014 to 3.1 in 2024, with a forecast of 2.7 by 2032. The increase in small households—for example, singles, single parents, or senior citizens—is particularly driving up demand for residential units.

Figure 5 shows the number of inhabitants from 1990 to 2050 according to the latest United Nations (UN) population projections from 2024 (x-axis) and the proportion of inhabitants between the ages of 15 and 64 (y-axis). A movement of the curve to the upper right (Türkiye until around 2035) thus indicates a country with a strong population growth and a growing proportion of working-age residents. For

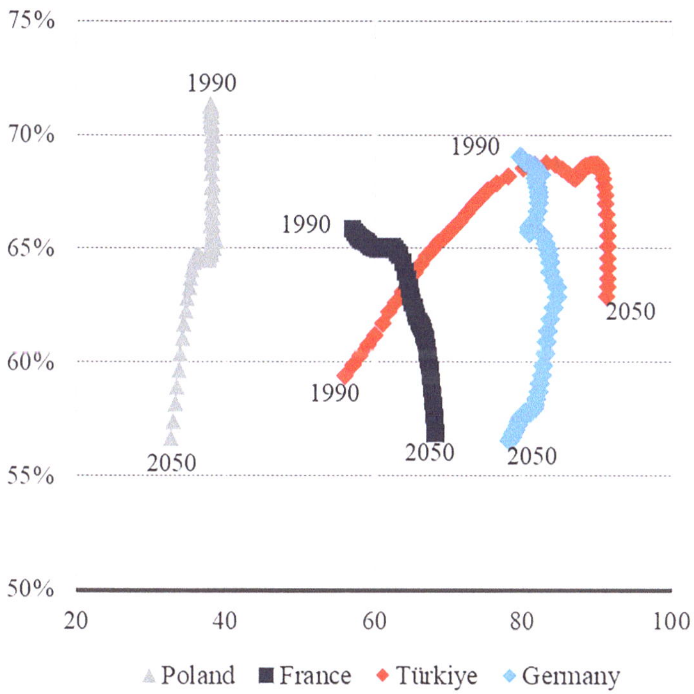

Fig. 5 Number of inhabitants and share of labour force. The x-axis shows the number of inhabitants in millions, and the y-axis shows the share of the labour force (age cohort: 15–64 years) for the time period 1990–2050. Source: UN Population Division (2024, median variant), own calculations

Poland, for example, the curve points downwards to the left, indicating that a decline in population is to be expected, accompanied by a decline in the proportion of the working-age population. The former limits growth in housing demand (in line with the trend), while the latter limits growth in commercial real estate demand (also in line with the trend).

Even more important for international real estate investors is that, according to the estimates by the UN Population Division (2018), the proportion of people living in cities is currently estimated to be 78%. By the middle of the century, this figure is expected to rise to 86%. The urban population in Türkiye is unevenly distributed across cities. The last census identified over 60 cities with more than 100,000 inhabitants, and ten cities have over a million inhabitants. Approximately half of Türkiye's urban population lives in these ten metropolitan areas. This means that the urban population is much more concentrated in a few metropolitan areas than in Germany or France. This concentration is both an advantage and a disadvantage: on the one hand, it facilitates market entry, as international investors can reach a market of 25 million people in Istanbul, Ankara, Izmir, and Bursa. On the other hand, however, concentration is also a problem, as market transparency is particularly lacking in smaller cities—and this includes even the smaller cities with over a million inhabitants. However, because urbanisation growth could be higher in smaller cities than in metropolitan areas over the next ten years, according to the United Nations projections, opportunities are at risk of being lost due to this transparency-driven ignorance of smaller cities.

5 Asset Classes

Residential Real Estate Markets

Strong population and income growth are the main drivers of higher housing prices. However, despite significant nominal price increases in the real estate sector, inflation-adjusted figures paint a different picture: in January 2025, nationwide house prices rose by 31.95% compared to the previous year, but adjusted for price changes, they fell by 7.16% (see Fig. 6).

Regional differences were pronounced, presenting international investors with risks rather than opportunities, as they need detailed information on individual markets in order to exploit potential opportunities, but this is difficult for them given the lack of market transparency: in Istanbul, price-adjusted residential property prices fell by 8.8%, in Ankara by 3.9%, and in Izmir by 8.8% (Global Property Guide, 2025). Consequently, the number of foreign residential property transactions declined by 32.1% in 2024, contrary to the actual market trend of higher sales figures. Overall, foreign investors currently account for only 1.6% of all transactions (Global Property Guide, 2025). This development reflects high inflation rates and, consequently, high interest rates. While 18.9% of residential property sales were still financed through mortgages in 2022, this share dropped to just 10.7% by 2024. The high financing costs had a noticeable negative impact on affordability (VS Partners & JLL, 2024).

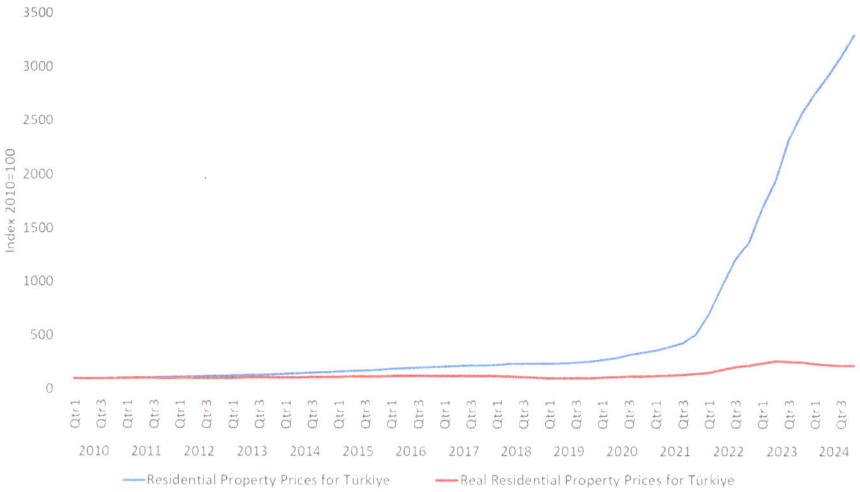

Fig. 6 Residential property prices in Türkiye (nominal and real; Q1 2010–Q1 2024). Source: Own illustration based on data from the BIS Residential Property Price Database (2025a, 2025b)

The increasing demand for energy-efficient and technologically integrated residential properties is likely to be important for international investors, as this has become a key component of institutional investors' investment strategies (Properstar, 2025). This also includes, in a broader sense, revitalisation, conversion of existing buildings, built-to-suit projects, sale-and-leaseback models, and ESG-compliant properties.

Office Properties and Logistics Real Estate

Two arguments are important for investments in commercial real estate: the sustained high economic momentum and the need to catch up, resulting from Türkiye's still comparatively low productivity levels. For example, in 2024, the megacity of Istanbul had no more than 6.66 million square metres of high-quality Grade A office space. This is significantly less than the space available in Paris (55.47 million square metres), London (23.46 million m^2), or Berlin (22.67 million m^2). Because the number of office workers in Istanbul grew by an average of 3.3% per year between 2015 and 2019, Istanbul regularly reaches its own space limits and has to upgrade or replace its existing stock (VS Partners & JLL, 2024). A key driver of this development is the sharp rise in the number of internationally active companies, which increased from 47,267 in 2015 to 86,418 in 2024 (VS Partners & JLL, 2024).

This gap is expected to be gradually closed over the next few years in line with economic growth; large development projects, such as the Istanbul International Financial Centre (IFC) with a planned total area of 3.4 million square metres, support this development (VS Partners & JLL, 2024).

The logistics real estate market is also benefiting from economic growth. Türkiye has significantly improved its position in the World Bank's Logistics Performance Index: in 2023, the country ranked 38th out of a total of 138 economies assessed—nine places higher than in 2018. This development underscores the country's growing importance as a strategic logistics hub, not least due to its favourable geographical location (Invest Türkiye, 2024).

Retail Properties

The gross leasable retail area (gross leasable area (GLA)) in Türkiye has expanded significantly since 2005.

While approximately 2 million m^2 of GLA were spread across 76 modern shopping centres in 2005, by 2024, the total had reached 14.3 million m^2 across 461 shopping centres (VS Partners & JLL, 2024). The geographical distribution has also broadened substantially: in 2005, only 21 cities had at least one modern shopping centre, whereas in 2024, that number has increased to 67 cities.

The highest GLA density is found in the metropolitan areas of Istanbul and Ankara, with 336 m^2 and 299 m^2 per 1000 inhabitants, respectively. In contrast, 14 cities still lack modern shopping centres, and in 13 additional cities, the available retail space remains below 20,000 m^2 (VS Partners & JLL, 2024).

Demand-side developments also reflect a dynamic trend: the Retail Sales Volume Index recorded an average annual growth rate of around 16% between 2021 and 2024. Non-food categories showed slightly above-average growth. For 2024, the index reported a year-on-year increase of 17.3% (VS Partners & JLL, 2024).

Tourism and Hotel Real Estate

The hospitality industry is particularly attractive to international investors, as this is easy to deduce from international travel statistics: in 2024, around 62.2 million international visitors came to Türkiye—an increase of 9% compared to 2023 and 20% compared to the pre-pandemic level of 2019. The resulting tourism revenues amounted to USD 56 billion, representing an increase of 8.3% compared to 2023 and as much as 55.4% compared to 2019. Per capita revenues have also risen significantly since 2019 (Properstar, 2025).

In February 2025, Türkiye's accommodation industry comprised a total of 22,091 registered establishments, with a total capacity of 952,982 rooms and 1,982,919 beds. The largest concentration of hotel rooms is in the tourist stronghold of Antalya, with a share of 32%, followed by Istanbul with 14% and the coastal province of Muğla in the south-west of the country with 12% (Properstar, 2025).

6 Capital Flows

Overall, population and economic growth are attractive factors for international investors; however, the lack of currency stability, uncertainty surrounding domestic institutions, and the absence of price stability are dampening the interest. In 2025, net foreign direct investment (FDI) in Türkiye, i.e., investment in real assets, amounted to USD 11.3 billion, approximately 8% more than in the previous year.

Above all, Türkiye was able to buck the Europe-wide trend of declining cross-border investment flows in 2024 (UNCTAD, 2024). The most important countries of origin were the Netherlands (23.6%), Germany (11.5%), and the United States (10.3%), followed by Ireland, Azerbaijan, Switzerland, the United Kingdom, the United Arab Emirates, France, and Norway. This broad diversification of capital sources illustrates both the economic and geopolitical peculiarities of Türkiye. Figure 7 demonstrates that this peculiarity has also led to highly volatile capital flows.

The manufacturing sector is particularly noteworthy, representing a very important target for international direct investment, with a share of 34.5% and a volume of USD 2.3 billion. In addition, 25.3% went to wholesale and retail trade and 7.2% to the transport and logistics sector (Invest Türkiye, 2024). Total FDI inflows into Turkish real estate remained at USD 2.8 billion after a decline of 20.6% in 2024. Investment activity on the Turkish real estate market developed unevenly in 2024. The retail property segment was particularly dynamic, although one-off effects and the low base in the previous year are likely to have played a role here: the foreign transaction volume in retail properties rose by 919% to around 1.07 billion euros. This gave Türkiye a market share of 3.2% of the total retail investment volume in the Europe and Middle East Asia (EMEA) region (VS Partners & JLL, 2024). In contrast to the relatively positive developments in the commercial segment, the residential property market declined for foreign buyers: the number of transactions by non-domestic buyers fell significantly from 67,490 in 2022 to around 23,781 in 2024. This decline is primarily attributable to a tighter legal framework, increased economic uncertainty, and the high volatility of the Turkish lira.

Prime yields showed a moderate decline but remained attractive by historical standards. Logistics properties proved stable at 8.5%, while yields for shopping centres fell slightly to 8.0% (a 25-basis-point decrease). High street retail recorded a yield of 6.5% (–50 basis points), and office space stood at 7.5%. However, this attractiveness is rapidly being eroded for foreign investors by financing and exchange rate risks (VS Partners & JLL, 2024). Portfolio investments, i.e. financial investments, have been even more volatile than FDI for years, mainly due to their high dependence on interest rate and exchange rate risks (see Fig. 7). This uncertainty is also reflected in the relatively high prices for credit default swaps (CDSs), which are an important indicator of perceived country risk: CDSs for five-year government bonds stood at 304 basis points in June 2025, corresponding to a default probability of over 5%. This means that swaps for Türkiye are very high compared with other European countries: CDSs for five-year bonds from Germany are at 9.43 basis points, those for Italy at 49.8 basis points, and CDSs for five-year bonds from China at 53.90 (World Government Bonds, 2025). Overall, the Turkish capital market is attracting growing but selective interest from international investors. High volatility, exchange rate risk, and political uncertainties are dampening broader engagement. At the same time, high bond yields, low valuations, and an improved rating environment point to attractive entry points.

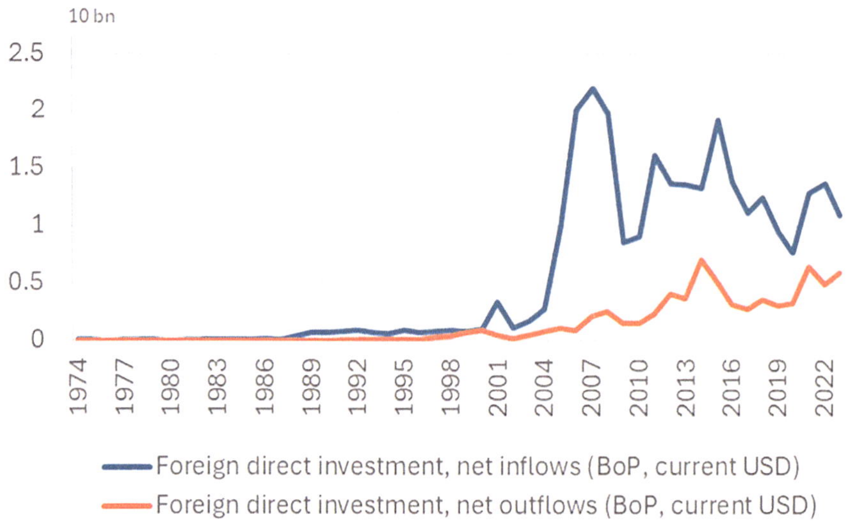

Fig. 7 Foreign direct investment (FDI) inflows and outflows (1974–2022, Balance of Payments (BoP), current US$). Source: Own illustration based on data from the World Bank (2024a, 2024b)

7 Concluding Remarks

When it comes to Türkiye, international real estate investors may find themselves torn between two conflicting emotions: joyful optimism and cautious pessimism. The optimistic outlook is supported by favourable demographic trends; significant catch-up potential in the most important real estate asset classes, both in terms of quality and quantity; and the associated economic momentum. Türkiye's unique geographical and political position underpins this long-term optimism.

Applying the convergence hypothesis in the context of the so-called beta convergence, the catch-up potential could then lead to long-term growth if institutions can be brought up to Western standards so that per capita economic output can converge with that of the West. So far, there has been an absolute improvement in Türkiye's economic indicators, but it is catching up slowly with the more prosperous EU member states. Between 2010 and 2022, the Turkish economy grew by an average of around 5% per year, while the average GDP growth in the EU27 area was only around 2%. Nevertheless, despite this growth differential, Türkiye has not been able to catch up with countries such as Poland or Romania to the same extent.

This is mainly due to the fact that, in the short term, the wait-and-see, pessimistic outlook of international investors remains justified by insufficient transparency and inadequate financial, capital, and regulatory institutions. This is reflected in high volatility, high inflation, and, as a result, high interest rates and high capital market volatility. This cocktail represents high market entry barriers for risk-conscious investors.

Overall, the picture of Türkiye remains similar to that outlined by Kudatgobilik et al. (2008) seventeen years ago: there are significant long-term opportunities, but institutional barriers continue to hinder progress in the short term and likely also the medium term.

References

Bank for International Settlements. (2025a). *Real residential property prices for Turkey [QTRR628BIS]*. FRED, Federal Reserve Bank of St. Louis. https://fred.stlouisfed.org/series/QTRR628BIS

Bank for International Settlements. (2025b). *Residential property prices for Turkey [QTRN628BIS]*. FRED, Federal Reserve Bank of St. Louis. https://fred.stlouisfed.org/series/QTRN628BIS

Fuerst, F., Milcheva, S., & Baum, A. (2015). Cross-border capital flows into real estate. *Real Estate Finance, 31*(3), 1–20.

Gaar, E., Scherer, D., & Schiereck, D. (2022). The home bias and the local bias: A survey. *Management Review Quarterly, 72*, 21–57. https://doi.org/10.1007/s11301-020-00203-8

Global Property Guide. (2025). *Turkey property price history*. https://www.globalpropertyguide.com/middle-east/turkey/price-history

Imazeki, T., & Gallimore, P. (2009). Domestic and foreign bias in real estate mutual funds. *Journal of Property Research, 26*(4), 367–389. https://doi.org/10.1080/09599916.2009.485419

Invest Turkey. (2024, April 17). *Türkiye's logistics sector aims for a top 25th global rank by 2028*. Retrieved June 23, 2025, from https://www.invest.gov.tr/en/news/news-from-turkey/pages/turkiyes-logistics-sector-aims-for-top-25th-global-rank-by-2028.aspx

Invest Türkiye. (2024, May 28). *Türkiye's FDI inflows reach USD 11.3 billion in 2024, defying global downturn*. https://www.invest.gov.tr/en/news/news-from-turkey/pages/turkiyes-fdi-inflows-reach-usd-11.3-billion-in-2024-defying-global-downturn.aspx

JLL, & LaSalle. (2024). *Global real estate transparency index 2024: Transparency in a time of transition*. Jones Lang LaSalle Incorporated.

Just, T., & Uttich, S. (2024, June 18). *Es sind nicht nur Gebäude: Was Anleger über Immobilienmärkte wissen müssen* (3rd updated ed.). Frankfurter Allgemeine Buch. https://www.beck-shop.de/just-uttich-gebaeude/product/36865489

Kudatgobilik, Z., Ruppert, E., Topintzi, E., & Just, T. (2008, August 26). *Real estate investment in Turkey: Look beyond Istanbul*. Deutsche Bank Current Issues.

Lieser, K., & Groh, A. P. (2014). The determinants of international commercial real estate investment. *Journal of Real Estate Finance and Economics, 48*, 611–659. https://doi.org/10.1007/s11146-012-9401-0

Organisation for Economic Co-operation and Development. (2025). *Currency conversions: US dollar exchange rate: Average of daily rates: National currency: USD for Turkey [CCUSMA02TRM618N]*. FRED, Federal Reserve Bank of St. Louis. https://fred.stlouisfed.org/series/CCUSMA02TRM618N

Properstar. (2025, June 7). *House prices in Turkey*. https://www.properstar.de/turkey/house-price

The Heritage Foundation. (2025). *Index of economic freedom*. https://www.heritage.org/index/pages/all-country-scores

Transparency International. (2025). *Corruption Perception Index 2024*. https://www.transparency.org/en/publications/corruption-perceptions-index-2024

Türkiye Cumhuriyet Merkez Bankasi. (2025, June). *Sectoral inflation expectations*. https://www.tcmb.gov.tr/wps/wcm/connect/EN/TCMB+EN/Main+Menu/Statistics/Tendency+Surveys/Sectoral+Inflation+Expectations/

UN Population Division. (2018). *World Urbanisation Project 2018*. https://population.un.org/wup/

UN Population Division. (2024). *World population prospects 2024*. https://population.un.org/wpp/

UNCTAD. (2024, January 17). *Global investment trends monitor (no. 48)*. United Nations Conference on Trade and Development. https://unctad.org/publication/global-investment-trends-monitor-no-48

VS Partners, & JLL. (2024). *Türkiye real estate market overview*. https://valuesolutionspartners.com/en/portfolio-item/vs-partners-jll-turkiye-real-estate-market-overview/

World Bank. (2024a). *Foreign direct investment, net inflows (BoP, current US$)—Turkey (BX.KLT.DINV.CD.WD)*. Retrieved June 23, 2025, from https://data.worldbank.org/indicator/BX.KLT.DINV.CD.WD?locations=TR

World Bank. (2024b). *Foreign direct investment, net outflows (BoP, current US$)—Turkey (BM.KLT.DINV.CD.WD)*. Retrieved June 23, 2025, from https://data.worldbank.org/indicator/BM.KLT.DINV.CD.WD?locations=TR

World Government Bonds. (2025). *Turkey 5 5-year CDS historical data*. Retrieved June 23, 2025, from https://www.worldgovernmentbonds.com/cds-historical-data/turkey/5-years/

Tobias Just is Managing Director at the IRE|BS Immobilienakademie and professor for Real Estate at the Regensburg University. Tobias studied economics in Hamburg and Uppsala (Sweden). In 1997, he graduated and started to work at the University of the Federal Armed Forces Hamburg. His Ph.D. dissertation was awarded the university science prize in 2001. For more than ten years, Tobias worked at Deutsche Bank Research, the economics research unit of Deutsche Bank. He headed the units' sector and real estate research team and was a member of Deutsche Bank's group-wide Environmental Steering Committee. In summer 2006, Tobias was a Research Fellow at the American Institute of Contemporary German Studies at Johns Hopkins University in Washington, DC. Tobias published 17 books and more than 250 papers in professional and academic journals and books. Since November 2011, Tobias has been Managing Director at the IRE|BS Immobilienakademie and holds a Chair for Real Estate at the University of Regensburg. He was President of the German Society of Property Researchers (GIF) from 2014-2021 and is editor of the ZIÖ—the German Journal of Real Estate Research. From 2016 to 2023, Tobias was a member of the Supervisory Board of Helaba Invest Kapitalanlagegesellschaft mbH. In 2017, Tobias became a Fellow of the RICS by nomination.

Vanessa Dietl is a research associate at the Chair of Real Estate at the University of Regensburg and the International Real Estate Business School (IREBS). She holds a B.Sc. in Business Administration and Economics from the University of Passau and an M.Sc. in Economics from the University of Regensburg. She is currently pursuing her PhD, with her research focusing on spatial economics, housing markets, and the impact of visibility networks on the commercial real estate market.

Urban Policies and Urban Development in Türkiye

Ruşen Keleş, Ahmet Hilmi Erciyes, and Muhammed Said Yılmaz

Abstract

Understanding the local and historical characteristics of the urbanisation process in Türkiye is essential for comprehending urbanisation. Global population growth and migration have led to a rapid transformation of cities, particularly since the 1950s, with urbanisation policies playing a significant role in this process. Türkiye embarked on its urbanisation journey with a limited urban heritage from the Ottoman Empire, and Turkish cities developed based on the principles established by the Republic. Ankara was designated as the capital upon the establishment of the Republic. Istanbul, a prominent port city, has retained its economic and cultural significance and has experienced a rapid and predominantly uncontrolled urbanisation process, accompanied by intense population growth. In Türkiye, which previously featured a predominantly rural population and an agriculture-based economy, the urban population has dramatically increased over the past few years, leading to a rise in the manufacturing and service sectors. Urban development can be categorised into five distinct periods: Türkiye's urbanisation experience commenced in the late Ottoman or pre-Republican era, with advancements in Istanbul. This was followed by the period between 1923 and 1950, during which rural development and the formation of Republican cities occurred. Subsequently, the period of uncontrolled migration and urban challenges followed between 1950 and 1980, succeeded by the globalisation period

R. Keleş (✉)
Department of Political Science and Public Administration, Faculty of Political Sciences, Ankara University, Ankara, Türkiye
e-mail: Rusen.Keles@politics.ankara.edu.tr

A. H. Erciyes · M. S. Yılmaz
Department of Real Estate Development and Management, Faculty of Applied Sciences, Ankara University, Ankara, Türkiye
e-mail: aherciyes@ankara.edu.tr; mhsyilmaz@ankara.edu.tr

T. Just et al. (eds.), *Understanding Türkiye's Real Estate Markets*, Management for Professionals, https://doi.org/10.1007/978-3-032-13297-0_4

from 1980 to 2000, marked by a significant increase in the movement of capital and goods. Finally, the period from 2000 to the present can be described as a phase of moderate growth.

Keywords

Urban policy · Urban development · Constitution of Türkiye · Development planning

1 Introduction

With a total population of approximately 85 million inhabitants, Türkiye constitutes more than 1% of the global population. At present, the majority of individuals worldwide reside in urban areas, and this is also evident in Türkiye, where over 77% of the population lives in urban agglomerations. Therefore, the management of cities is imperative for comprehensive economic development. Formulating effective urban policies has become a primary objective for both national and local governments. The practice of city management began during the latter phase of the Ottoman Empire, and Türkiye has continued to progress in alignment with this legacy. Data from the UN Population Division indicates that 65 million persons live in urban areas in Türkiye; seventy years ago, the percentage of the urban population did not exceed 25% (UN Population Division, 2018). This situation highlights the significant demographic, economic, and managerial transformations that have occurred over the past few decades. According to data from the Turkish Statistical Institute, more than 90% of the total population in Türkiye resides in urban areas today (TURSTAT, 2025).

Consequently, urbanisation ought to be scrutinised within its historical framework to comprehend the challenges faced by cities and the corresponding urban policies in Türkiye. This chapter delineates the historical evolution of Turkish cities and their urbanisation process.

2 Politics in the Urbanisation Process of Turkish Cities

2.1 Pre-Republican Period

The Ottoman Empire comprised two principal regions: Anatolia and Rumelia. Assessing the population of the Ottoman Empire during its final period poses considerable challenges for scholars: these problems arise from both methodological complexities and the reliability of the available sources. This difficulty is further aggravated by the empire's internal strife, wars, and intricate demographic structure (Shaw, 1978; Zamir, 1981; Karpat, 1985; Mutlu, 2003). The total population of the empire was recorded in the last census conducted in 1914, which included approximately 16 million individuals (Kayacan, 2022). The population of the capital,

Istanbul, recognised as the most significant urban centre of the Rumelia region, expanded from 400,000 to 700,000 during the sixteenth century, and accommodated nearly 40% of the total urban population of the country at that time. The primary reason for the low urbanisation rate was that individuals were encouraged to remain in rural areas, with agricultural policies taking precedence within the Ottoman Empire. By the nineteenth century, the urban population ratio in Anatolia, which was approximately 8.5% previously, increased to 25% due to the migration of the Muslim population from territories lost by the Ottoman Empire. However, concurrently, the population became more mobile owing to advancements in new transportation technologies. People migrated particularly to port cities, which were the economically pivotal centres of that era. As the population in these centres increased, the social, cultural, and technological infrastructure was enhanced: in Istanbul, new residential areas were constructed for the affluent, and suburbs developed (Tekeli, 1982). Population growth persisted until the 1870s (Ersoy & Şengül, 2003).

In the late nineteenth century, the population of Istanbul increased to one million inhabitants, resulting in the establishment of new residential and commercial areas, including banks and office buildings. The spatial transformations during this era rendered numerous administrative units, deeply rooted in the tradition of the Ottoman Empire, dysfunctional and inadequate in delivering urban services, thus necessitating independent management at the city level. Additionally, the city's swift adaptation can be attributed to the burgeoning economic relations with Europe (Ortaylı, 1990). Nevertheless, the new financial and commercial structure within the city, the ongoing transformation process, the lifestyle influenced by society's orientation towards European culture, and the bureaucratic framework introduced by the Tanzimat—a period characterised by extensive reforms in the nineteenth century—must be examined separately in the context of the management system's evolving requirements (Ökmen, 2002).

The initial action undertaken in urban management within the Ottoman Empire was the creation of the "Istanbul *Şehremaneti*" (Municipality of Istanbul). In light of the pronounced centralist tendencies of this era, this institution was not designed to engage with the local populace; instead, it functioned as a civil entity appointed by the central authority.

In 1857, The Sixth Department of the Municipality was established to serve the Beyoğlu and Galata regions, which were predominantly inhabited by the non-Muslim population. This structure may be regarded as a municipality (Lewis & Turna, 2008). Possessing privileged financial resources, it demonstrated greater success than *Şehremaneti* in delivering public services.

The inaugural municipal organisation of the Ottoman Empire, outside of Istanbul, was established in 1864 in accordance with the Provincial Regulations. The proposal featured the formation of assemblies comprising elected members for Sancak (Liva)[1] and town centres. Almost simultaneously, in 1868, the Sixth Department of the Municipality was restructured into 14 departments, which were then extended throughout Istanbul. However, these structures proved to be inadequate in terms of

[1] Sancak (Liva) are synonyms in Ottoman Turkish which describe a small district or shire.

technical, personnel, and financial resources (Ortaylı, 1990). In 1877, the *Dersaadet* Municipality Law and the Provincial Municipality Law were enacted to distinguish Istanbul from the provinces and enhance municipal administrations across the country. Subsequent to the enactment of this legislation, the newly established municipalities were entrusted with several responsibilities, including infrastructure management, provision of public services, sanitation, trade and health inspection, determination of fees for urban services, maintenance of immovable records, building inspection, expropriation, social assistance, and employment (Aytaç, 1990).

The initial significant milestone in urban planning occurred in 1848 with the enactment of the *Ebniye* Regulation, which established standards for roadways and edifices. The principal provision of this regulation, designed to address the challenges posed by the rapid growth of Istanbul, was the "free abandonment" principle, which stipulated equitable deductions from properties adjacent to roads that were to be widened within the city. Subsequently, the *Turuk* and *Ebniye* regulations of 1864 introduced guidelines concerning roadway width, building height, restrictions on construction activity, land parcelling, and cartographic procedures, in addition to regulations intended to mitigate fire hazards (Tüdeş, 2018). Furthermore, the *Ebniye* Law was implemented in 1882, prohibiting dead-end streets, mandating urban planning in areas devastated by fire, obligating property owners to erect necessary infrastructure, and allowing for objections to proposed plans (Ersoy & Şengül, 2003).

2.2 Early Republican Period of 1923–1950

The establishment of the Republic of Türkiye resulted in the emergence of new challenges at both the local and national levels that needed to be addressed concurrently. The severe repercussions of the war necessitated rectification, and a fundamental public administration system/body had to be instituted. Health-related issues began to proliferate across the nation, and, in conjunction with war-related demographic challenges, these became the predominant concerns of the era (Alada, 1990). The designation of Ankara as the new capital of the Republic garnered considerable attention in the initial years. During this formative period, in addition to the internal factors influencing national and local policies, the economic ramifications of the global economic crisis in 1929 and the prelude to the Second World War played pivotal roles. With the implementation of protectionist and statist policies, the first and second industrialisation plans were formulated (Keskinok, 2010). Central to these industrialisation policies was the establishment of state-owned factories and the development of new industrial cities. This restructuring and industrialisation also called for the construction of new infrastructure systems across the nation (Boratav, 2013) and facilitated the redistribution of the population to more remote regions (Keleş, 2015). According to Sencer (1979), strategies were adopted in Türkiye to augment the population by reducing mortality rates and increasing fertility rates (Yılmaz & Çiftçi, 2011).

During the Republican period, the foundations of municipal management policies were established through a series of legislative texts, commencing with the

Ankara *Şehremaneti* Law in 1924. This was subsequently followed by the Municipal and Hygiene Law in 1930 and the Building and Roads Law in 1933. Furthermore, this period witnessed the institutionalisation of urban management and interventions through the enactment of the Law on the Establishment of the Municipal Bank, the Law on Municipal Expropriation in 1933 and 1935, and the Law on the Establishment of the Municipal Reconstruction Administrative Committee No. 2763. Not only did new legislation emerge, but the implementation of regulations in Ankara also played a significant role in defining urban management and planning of the Republic, thus facilitating the professionalisation of urban management (Tekeli, 1998). Although the Municipality Law conferred upon municipalities the authority to prepare zoning plans, the financial constraints faced by these institutions prompted the *Nafia Nezareti* (Ministry of Public Works) to undertake zoning initiatives on behalf of the central government. In total, the Urban Development Administration Board, a subsidiary of the Ministry, approved 18 maps and 17 zoning plans up until June 1935 (Ersoy & Şengül, 2003).

According to the 1927 census, the total population in Türkiye was recorded at 13,648,270 in that year. However, 75.78% of the total population resided in rural areas, while 24.22% inhabited urban centres, and these proportions remained relatively stable until 1950. Despite the robust demographic growth in Türkiye, this reflected a 6% increase in the population of Ankara, attributed to migration (Işik, 2005) and considerable population expansion in Istanbul and Izmir (Sağlam, 2016). With regard to Ankara, civil servants prioritised addressing housing challenges (Keleş, 2015); for instance, civil servants were permitted to establish housing cooperatives. To secure accommodation, they were granted half of their salaries in advance and received housing compensation, and funds for civil servants' housing were allocated in the state budget. Nevertheless, due to significant population growth, an inadequate housing supply contributed to the emergence of slums, particularly in Ankara. Legal frameworks acknowledged the existence of slum structures, and their persistence could not be curtailed due to zoning amnesties, which were further exacerbated by the freezing of rents between 1939 and 1963.

2.3 The Period between 1950 and 1980

Following the end of World War II, particularly as a result of the extensive destruction of European cities, displacements, and economic development, movements towards urban areas intensified. This phenomenon was also observed in Türkiye, which, despite not participating in the war and thus not experiencing direct destruction, witnessed an increase in population movements from rural to urban areas, alongside the emergence of new costs and benefits associated with urbanisation (Yurt, 2020). Furthermore, liberal policies began to gain prominence in Türkiye, marking a departure from the statist policies that had previously prevailed (Yılmaz & Çiftçi, 2011). The proportion of the urban population saw a substantial increase, rising from 25.0% in 1950 to 34.4% in 1965 and further to 43.9% in 1980 (Işik, 2005). The mechanisation of agriculture, on the one hand, coupled with improved job opportunities in urban areas, on the other hand, acted as a catalyst for migration from rural areas to urban centres. However, this process was not sustained for a long period (Özaslan, 2006).

This migration pattern was exacerbated by the construction of new highways, which facilitated a transition from rail transport to road transport (Tekeli, 1998) and led to the implementation of new epidemic prevention policies (Işik, 2005). The influx of migrants to urban areas resulted in new issues, including unregulated construction activities, the rise of informal and marginal sectors, and inadequate infrastructure (Sağlam, 2006).

The rapid growth of urban populations and the inadequacy of housing supply led to an increase in slums within urban areas, thereby altering their overall quality. A new market for slums emerged, transforming the construction of slum areas into a lucrative investment that extended beyond mere housing needs. Consequently, certain groups of the population acquired an illegitimate level of income from these developments. The situation regarding slums escalated to an alarming degree, becoming one of the biggest challenges, particularly in cities such as Ankara and Istanbul. Despite the provisions outlined in the Municipal Law of 1930, which designated certain responsibilities for addressing the housing crisis at the local level as optional, municipalities consistently demonstrated a lack of resources to address housing production adequately; in fact, they were unable to fulfil even some of their compulsory obligations. This inadequacy prompted the establishment of municipal councils in 1950, aimed at rendering these responsibilities mandatory. Nevertheless, the reluctance of municipalities to engage with these duties persisted, with the central government remaining satisfied with formulating housing policies tailored specifically to Ankara (Keleş, 2015).

The number of housing cooperatives, which were first implemented in Ankara in 1934, experienced a sharp increase in the years following 1950. Various financing models were subsequently developed to assist workers in addressing housing challenges through social insurance (Bilgin & Taniyici, 2008). The establishment of the State Planning Organisation in 1960 marked the beginning of a new era of state-planned economic development, which notably influenced urban development. Although the housing dilemma was approached comprehensively in the development plans (Keleş, 2015), the allocation of resources towards industrial investments in these plans proved inadequate in meeting particular urban requirements, including housing and infrastructure provisions (Arslan, 2014). Moreover, despite the objective of the General Directorate of Land Office, established in 1969, to curb land speculation and facilitate the provision of additional building plots, these aims remained unfulfilled (Keleş, 2015).

As of 1960, notable changes were implemented in urbanisation policies in Türkiye that transcended merely addressing population growth. A significant transformation is evident in the 1961 Constitution, which addressed the housing needs of low-income individuals. The Flat Ownership Law of 1965 introduced vertical architecture and established independent property rights for units within buildings (Tekeli, 1998). Furthermore, the Municipal Law was amended in 1951, which expanded the responsibilities of municipalities and mandated their involvement in housing construction (Keleş, 2015). Although the state formulated policies to support cooperatives (Demirci Aksoy et al., 2024) aimed at meeting housing needs since the late 1960s, there was a persistent lack of success over the years, attributed to economic and political turbulence.

While the population in major cities grew strongly, certain settlements in other regions of Türkiye attained municipal status (Yılmaz & Çiftçi, 2011). Concurrently, the expansion of the formal urban areas was hindered by limited planning studies and the presence of slums in the city's periphery. With the increase of private automobile ownership in the 1970s, high-income households migrated from the city centre outwards, resulting in the development of suburbs (Tekeli, 1998). Zoning Law No. 6785, enacted in 1956, sought to establish and regulate the systematic development of urban areas. This legislation delineates the Master Zoning Plan and an associated Implementation Plan. The amendments to the Zoning Law in 1972 provided clarification regarding the concept and structure of metropolitan planning. Nevertheless, spatial and urban development studies remained inadequate (Ersoy & Şengül, 2003). During the 1950s, Istanbul was incorporated into urbanisation and zoning studies alongside Ankara. The expansion of Istanbul's road network and the establishment of wide boulevards were perceived as prestigious endeavours, and these efforts continued despite economic constraints. In these studies, the cultural and historical heritage of Istanbul was largely disregarded. A significant aspect of the zoning initiatives in Istanbul during this period was that policies related to the city were deemed matters of national interest and were consequently implemented under the auspices of the central government (Boysan, 1990).

A new legislation was enacted to address the issue of slums. Slums constructed prior to 1953 were legalised, while the establishment of new slums was prohibited until 1966. Nevertheless, this initiative could not avert the rise of new slums, although the challenge of homelessness was effectively managed. Throughout the planning period that began in 1960, strategies to confront the slum issue were formulated. These strategies included a provision allowing for the demolition of slums without the necessity of providing alternative housing for the affected residents, as well as the provision of essential public services.

Throughout the process, slums were integrated within urban planning frameworks. Urban services were rendered, and long-term residency rights were conferred to the proprietors of slums situated on public lands. The number of slum dwellings rose from 240,000 in 1960 to one million two decades later (Keleş, 2015). Concurrently, while unauthorised infrastructure and irregular structures proliferated within the built environment in Türkiye, particularly after 1960, new challenges such as congestion, air pollution, and various environmental and noise issues surfaced in urban areas (Yurt, 2020; Yılmaz & Çiftçi, 2011). Through zoning initiatives, the objective was to facilitate capital accumulation within the city, and urban renewal projects commenced in earnest (Şahin, 2006; Yurt, 2020; Yılmaz & Çiftçi, 2011).

2.4 The Period between 1980 and 2000

Following 1980, the Turkish economy was influenced by liberal, market-oriented policies, which resulted in an expansion of international trade and an increase in capital movements, thereby initiating a new wave of urbanisation. While several state-owned enterprises were privatised, the government retained a significant role in the economy. Public investments in manufacturing shrank, the private sector was actively encouraged, and the service sector expanded (Özaslan, 2006). The economic depression that occurred in the early 1990s, propelled by the crises of that period, alongside liberalisation and speculative capital movements, rendered concepts such as external debt and budget deficits as critical issues (Sönmez, 2004). During the 1990s, Istanbul's economic influence grew; simultaneously, cities in Anatolia, including Denizli and Gaziantep, emerged as new industrial centres. The increase in industrial production within these cities necessitated investment in new transportation and infrastructure.

The enactment of the Mass Housing Law led to the establishment of the Mass Housing Administration (TOKİ), under which the government initiated support for a housing construction system. Significant modifications were implemented in the legislation pertaining to slums, resulting in increased density. A new Zoning Law, instituted in 1985, terminated the limited oversight of the central government over zoning plans. This legislation introduced a comprehensive planning framework, endowing administrations with planning authority with enhanced rights concerning immovable properties. Farmlands located on the outskirts of the city were transformed into developable plots. The responsibility for formulating zoning plans was shifted from municipalities that lacked the necessary technical capabilities to İller Bank. Concurrently, local governments were granted the authority to approve these plans. Nevertheless, the obligation to develop and endorse various categories of zoning plans in designated areas, such as conservation zones and special development areas, was allocated to central institutions. This delegation resulted in persistent problems related to authority irregularity and fragmentation within the planning system (Işik, 1996).

Following the 1980 coup, numerous policy reforms were implemented across various sectors, particularly in relation to the Constitution. The Constitution, enacted in 1982, recognised the right to housing as a distinct title and articulated support for mass housing initiatives. The evaluation of the Mass Housing Law was to occur within this framework. Initially, only cooperatives reaped the benefits of the Mass Housing Fund established under this law; however, the scope was subsequently broadened to encompass all individuals, organisations, enterprises, and developers. From 1984 to 1995, the Housing Development Administration (TOKİ) extended loans for the construction of 949,079 residences through the fund, of which 816,091 were completed. Furthermore, housing units were erected on land owned by TOKİ and offered for sale under favourable payment arrangements (Türel, 1996). The build-and-sell model thrived, resulting in heightened property values in underprivileged neighbourhoods (Işik, 1996). The housing sector was regarded as a pivotal element contributing to the overall economy and was the focus of national policies.

An assessment of housing needs was conducted, leading to the anticipation that investments in housing should be directed towards identified priority regions (Keleş, 2015). Following the enactment of amnesty laws after 1983, slum areas underwent significant transformation. This transformation, facilitated by the Improvement Development Plans[2], included the construction of multi-storey apartment buildings (Şenyapılı, 2012).

In addition to recognising housing as a right under the 1982 Constitution, an important regulation concerning urban management was defined in Article 127: this article facilitated a specialised form of administration in major urban centres. The establishment of metropolitan municipalities arose from the inadequacy of Municipal Law No. 1580, which failed to manage large settlements more effectively and provide efficient services to the substantial populations residing in these cities (Bulut & Dönmez, 2019). Metropolitan municipalities, which are municipal governments, were first established by decree-law in 1984 through Law No. 3030, characterised by their scale (Keleş & Mengi, 2017)—the initial metropolitan municipalities were located in Ankara, Istanbul, and Izmir. Over time, numerous legal adjustments were made that altered their responsibilities and jurisdictions and increased the number of metropolitan municipalities. As the metropolitan system developed, the existing district municipalities were retained, with the duties and powers of the metropolitan municipalities incorporating those of the district municipalities. The metropolitan municipalities were assigned the task of delivering large-scale services within the urban area while ensuring coordination in the provision of selected services (Alici, 2013).

2.5 The Post-2000 Period

The Turkish population grew continuously after 1985; however, the growth rate was more gradual compared to the previous years. The most pronounced population growth was observed in the economically developed regions, including Ankara, Istanbul, Izmır, Adana, Bursa, and Kocaeli (Işik, 2005). Entering the 2000s, urbanisation entered a period of intensified transformation, during which cities underwent significant physical and legislative changes. In 2005, the legislation governing municipalities, the most effective local government entities in Türkiye, was amended. Responsibilities such as organising infrastructure, zoning and planning, establishing geographical information systems, and safeguarding citizens' rights were conferred upon municipalities, in addition to their pre-existing obligations. With the enactment of the revised Municipal Law, municipalities were empowered to deliver numerous services directly or through market-driven policies via private companies. Overall, the impact of private investment in urban areas was amplified through new construction projects, advancements in development, and the implementation of new technologies.

---

[2] Improvement development plans are special plans implemented ın Türkiye. A portion of them is used to rectify slum areas that have illegally and densely built up.

In the context of city management in Türkiye, significant reforms were instituted following the enactment of Law No. 6360 at the end of 2012. This legislation led to an increase in the number of metropolitan cities, which initiated a substantial transformation in urban policies. The legal entities of special provincial administrations and villages that had provided services to rural areas within the administrative borders of the metropolitan cities were dissolved, town municipalities within these metropolitan boundaries were disbanded, new districts were established, and the responsibilities and authorities of the abolished local administration units were transferred to the metropolitan municipalities (Güler, 2012). The new law introduced noteworthy modifications concerning municipal financial resources, representation and participation, and planning and development. Furthermore, based on a new definition enacted under this law, there was a sudden and considerable decline in the recorded percentage of the rural population (İzci & Turan, 2013). A significant consequence of this change pertains to the authority over development plans relevant to metropolitan municipalities and metropolitan district municipalities. Although both types of municipalities function within large cities and previously did not possess any legal hierarchical superiority over one another, metropolitan municipalities were endowed with extensive powers regarding development plans, thereby elevating their status in comparison to district municipalities in this specific regard. This has resulted in metropolitan municipalities having an influential role in planning activities at all levels within urban areas, consequently leading to more activities at the local level.

Privatisation has gained momentum in Türkiye since the 2000s, and the private sector has begun to offer urban services. In addition, the private sector has started to play an active role in urban planning activities that must be conducted in the public interest and are largely within the jurisdiction of municipalities. As a consequence, the struggle for a share of land rent began in urban areas, with planning activities emphasising benefits for individuals (Vural, 2015). Overall, Türkiye's cities underwent rapid transformation at a pace unprecedented in Turkish history, providing a large number of residential units across all cities, aided by TOKİ and private capital (Yurt, 2020). Additionally, slums have been transformed.

Private real estate markets have developed, and a rapidly increasing supply of housing has addressed the housing issue that originated in the 1950s. Simultaneously, housing has transformed into a means of capital accumulation, specifically as an asset class geared towards private investments. This transition stands in contrast to the nationalisation policies enacted during the early years of the Republic (Atasoy & Apaydin, 2023). Consequently, it has facilitated an increase in real estate investments, both domestically and internationally.

In a significant proportion of the projects undertaken, rent zones were established through zoning plans to minimise the utilisation of public resources and attract private capital investment. The residences underwent revitalisation via urban transformation initiatives, particularly within the central metropolitan areas. In regions where land values are elevated, new social challenges have arisen. Within the multi-actor framework of urban transformation, beneficiaries anticipate economic advantages rather than merely seeking shelter in a healthy environment.

Simultaneously, investors have emerged as the new proprietors of these areas, expecting rental returns. Gentrification has gained traction, and the rental income generated by higher living costs is retained by a minority rather than being distributed across the entire public sector (Köseoğlu & Sönmez, 2019). The issue of rising rents has become increasingly pertinent in Türkiye. Two important factors emerge in the discourse surrounding escalating rents: the commercialisation of public land through the provision of privileged zoning rights, facilitating its integration into the economy, and the establishment of rent on privately owned properties via amendments to zoning plans (Turan, 2008). To mitigate the problem of rising rents resulting from zoning modifications, a regulatory measure was enacted in 2020 with the objective of redistributing the resultant rental income to the public.

3 Administrative, Social, and Economic Structure of Turkish Cities

Türkiye has experienced rapid population growth and urbanisation, initially within the capital, Ankara, subsequently in Istanbul, and eventually across the entire nation. Urbanisation is a multidimensional process resulting in economic, social, cultural, and even political repercussions (Keleş, 2015). Similar to other developing countries, Türkiye has undergone a relatively unplanned urbanisation process, which has led to social, economic, and, particularly, environmental challenges within urban regions (Ulusoy & Vural, 2001). Sencer (1979) posits that urbanisation in Türkiye has occurred in an imbalanced manner concerning various distributional aspects (Yılmaz & Çiftçi, 2011). Urbanisation extends beyond mere economic advancement; it has also given rise to poverty and produced urban rents, slums, and inadequate housing conditions in Turkish metropolitan areas (Çetin, 2012). Certain issues persist unresolved, while new urban challenges have emerged.

Local governments, serving as extensions of the central government, have attained a degree of autonomy by augmenting their authority and responsibilities. Nevertheless, insufficient financial resources, limited local participation in decision-making processes, and the central government's substantial oversight continue to present challenges for local governments. Türkiye's reservations regarding the principles of proportionality, the unrestricted use of financial resources, and consultations with local authorities, as outlined in the European Charter of Local Self-Government, reflect its stance on adopting the provisions of the Charter (Keleş, 2020). In this context, while addressing various phenomena associated with urbanisation, it is imperative to enhance the skills and competencies of local governments in alignment with the UN Sustainable Development Goals (SDGs) and ensure autonomy in the realm of supervision, financing, and, particularly, local policy development.

When urbanisation in Türkiye is evaluated in terms of socio-economic development, discrepancies between regions in the process can be identified: since the 1990s, efforts have been made to diminish inter-regional disparities by providing national and supranational (European Union) funding (Çetin & Sevüktekin, 2016).

According to the General Directorate of Development Agencies of Türkiye, in 2017, the most developed provinces in Türkiye were Istanbul, Ankara, and Izmir, respectively. Within the framework of this research, cities were classified into six development categories based on 52 variables encompassing demography, employment, education, health, competitiveness and innovation, finance, accessibility, and quality of life. In simpler terms, the more advanced regions are located in the west, while the less developed regions are situated in the east of Türkiye (Fig. 1) (MOIT, 2025). The provinces that attract internal migration are also the most developed. However, this elevated level of development appears to be positively correlated with population density and negatively correlated with environmental efficiency in urban areas (Tunca, 2011).

At the foundation of the Republic, 76% of the population resided in rural areas, and the economy of the nation was predominantly agrarian. Following the initial census conducted in 1927, there was a rapid increase in the urban population, resulting in a shift in the ratio of rural to urban inhabitants, favouring urban centres. At the end of 2012, with the implementation of Law No. 6360, the number of metropolitan cities rose, and the designation of certain rural areas transitioned to urban. Consequently, a substantial increase in the urban population was recorded in 2013. Nevertheless, from a socio-economic perspective, it can be asserted that these regions, which have officially forfeited their rural designation, continue to exhibit characteristics commonly associated with rural areas. This observation accounts for the variances in urbanisation rates referenced at the outset of this article. A review of the 2024 population data from TURKSTAT reveals that 93.3% of the total population of Türkiye, amounting to 85,664,944 individuals, resides in urban regions, whereas 6.6% lives in rural locales (Fig. 2). According to the Ministry of Environment, Urbanisation and Climate Change of the Republic of Türkiye, the urban population rate recorded in 2020 stood at 76%, which aligns with the figure reported by the UN Population Division.

Fig. 1 Development level map by province. Source: MOIT (2025)

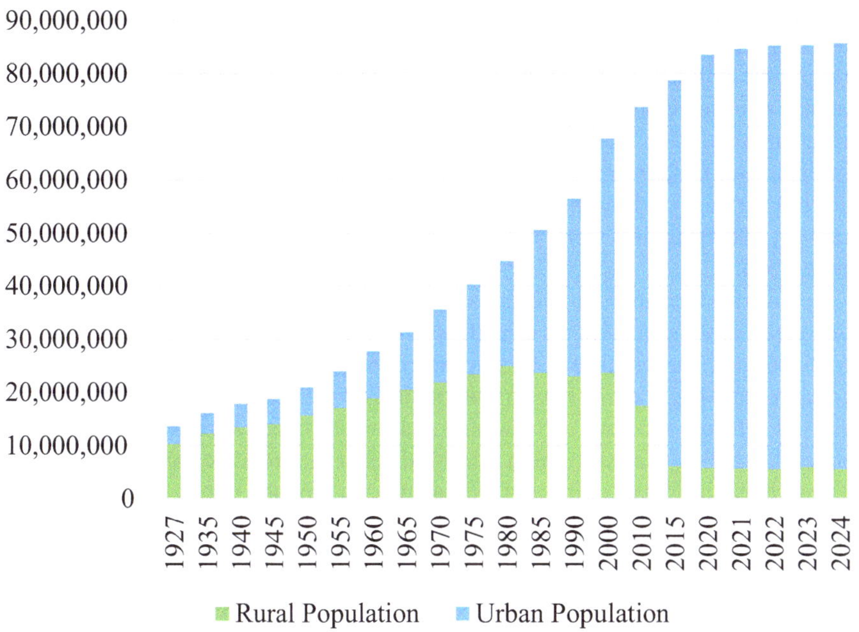

Fig. 2 The urban and rural population of Türkiye by year. Source: TURKSTAT (2025)

Zoning legislation constitutes one of Türkiye's most critical components of urban development. The legislation was shaped throughout the development process, resulting in a predominance of a gradual planning approach in contemporary practices. The strategies and policies established at the upper scale are subject to comprehensive regulation at the lower scale. Within the context of the Zoning Law, plans are categorised into three principal levels: spatial strategy plans, environmental plans, and zoning plans. The zoning plans are further divided into two distinct types: master zoning plans and implementation zoning plans. While the spatial strategy plans fall under the jurisdiction of the central government, both the central government and the local governments may formulate environmental plans. Zoning plans are developed within the framework of local governments. In the preparation of upper-scale plans, the principle of ensuring coordination among administrations operating across various thematic areas prevails. However, multiple laws have authorised several ministries concerned with tourism, conservation, and industrial zones. Moreover, institutions such as TOKİ and the Privatisation Administration have been granted the authority to create plans for the zoning frameworks included in the main structure. Thematic plans and the authorisation for the same plan to be prepared by different institutions introduce complexity into the planning process. This scenario impedes the integration of physical decisions, particularly in detailed spatial plans (Duyguluer, 2012).

Housing and accessible housing are ongoing issues in Turkish cities. Rapid urbanisation and population growth have not been effectively addressed due to global and national policy priorities, as well as a lack of financial resources. Generally, the emergence of slum areas on public lands has not been prevented, and public authorities, through zoning amnesties, have even recognised them. Attempts to solve the slum problem were made through improvement plans; however, a holistic solution in terms of urban planning was not presented. Nevertheless, in addressing the housing problem, non-refundable aid (subsidies) for civil servants and the middle-income population, support for housing cooperatives, and financing were provided by organisations such as social security institutions.

Urban transformation applications, which originated with the rehabilitation of slum areas, have been recognised as the predominant strategy employed under Law No. 6306 and in accordance with government policies.

At present, 93.2% of the housing supply in Türkiye is accomplished by construction in exchange for land and revenue sharing, in other words, a build-and-sell model. According to a 2021 report, prepared under the coordination of the Ministry of Environment, Urbanisation and Climate Change, public sector housing production accounts for 5.5% of the total, while housing cooperatives contribute 1.3%. Of the residences produced by TOKİ, 86% are deemed accessible (Kayapınar et al., 2021). These measures are significant due to the impact of the housing and construction sector on the economy and employment, as articulated in development plans, rather than the intention to achieve direct urban development. Furthermore, rent control policies, implemented through legislative measures or decisions by the Supreme Court of Appeals (YARGITAY), designed to enhance housing access, have arguably failed to exhibit the expected effectiveness in curbing market price escalations. As a result, substantial increases in property values and rental prices in recent years have aggravated the housing crisis. In response, the central government has established a nationwide objective for the period between 2023 and 2028 to develop 500,000 new housing units, 250,000 plots designated for residential construction, and 50,000 commercial units/workplaces (Ministry of Environment, Urbanisation and Climate Change, 2022).

4 Overall Assessment and Conclusion

Due to the extensive scale and scope of the urbanisation process in Türkiye, particularly in the years following World War II, significant challenges have arisen in transforming Turkish cities into contemporary living environments. These challenges stem from the abrupt increase in the urbanisation rate to 93%, alongside regulations that have elevated the number of metropolitan municipalities to 30, while simultaneously dissolving the legal entities of special provincial administrations, town municipalities, and villages within the metropolitan municipalities. Nevertheless, critical issues resulting from the elimination of special provincial administrations have not been thoroughly addressed, more than a decade after their identification, despite efforts to rectify concepts such as "rural neighbourhood" and "rural settlement" through regulations enacted in 2021.

Notwithstanding the efforts of the State Planning Organisation, established in the early 1960s, as well as the principles outlined in the Five-Year Development Plans, disparities in development and urbanisation persist across geographical regions to this day. The inequalities in the developmental progress of the provinces in the Western regions, evaluated against the development criteria of more than ten provinces encompassed within the South-Eastern Anatolia Project (GAP), remain unresolved. The dissolution and cessation of the State Planning Organisation within the Ministry of Development cannot be regarded favourably concerning urban development policies within the nation.

The inadequacy of addressing the housing needs of low- and middle-income individuals by state and municipal authorities has resulted in the nation confronting the issue of slums. It has been noted that the "improvement", "liquidation", and "prevention" mechanisms outlined in the Slum Law, effective since 1966, are inadequate to eradicate slums. The anticipated outcomes have not been realised through the practices dictated by the regulations established since the 2000s, which aimed at tackling the challenges posed by uneven and unbalanced urbanisation through urban transformation initiatives. Particularly during this time, the desired results were not achieved by the decisions aimed at enhancing living conditions in urban areas through investments in immovable property and housing.

As TOKİ, which was designated as a state institution in this domain, transcended its role of addressing the issues faced by low-income and economically disadvantaged citizens, it began to prioritise housing for families belonging to middle- and high-income groups and facilitate construction activities. Consequently, the "opportunity cost" of investments escalated, leaving the initial problems unaddressed. It stands as one of the most significant oversights that "housing cooperatives" were overlooked during this period..

More importantly, the sale and disposal of public lands by the treasury, along with all related public institutions, have significantly hindered the implementation of a robust urbanisation and housing policy. However, the rational utilisation of land—a non-renewable natural resource—by public institutions, emphasising the avoidance of its disposal, is critically important for promoting a healthy urbanisation policy.

The convention known as the European Charter of Local Self-Government, accepted by the Council of Europe, of which Türkiye is a member, and submitted for approval by the member states, mandates that local public services are to be executed by the administrative levels closest to the populace, specifically local administrations (municipalities). As a nation that has ratified this convention, Türkiye should assume a progressive role in the implementation of urbanisation policies, particularly in relation to urbanisation, urban public services, and housing matters, either independently from the central government or in collaboration with the state.

It can be inferred that Türkiye was not successful in determining and implementing a national urbanisation policy, including the efforts of the State Planning Organisation, since the transition to a multiparty democratic order following World War II. The political instabilities and the frequent necessity of forming coalition governments in the preceding years arguably contributed to this outcome. However, even in the past two decades—a period characterised by consistent political stability—it remains difficult to assert that Türkiye has effectively defined and executed urbanisation and housing policies that ensure that its citizens can reside in urban environments consistent with human dignity.

References

Alada, A. (1990). Türk Belediyeciliğine Kronolojik Yaklaşım. In İ. A. Ş. Metropol & Uila-Emme (Eds.), *Türk Belediyeciliği 60 Yıl Uluslararası Sempozyumu, 23–24 Kasım 1990* (pp. 119–143). Maya Matbacılık Yayıncılık.

Alici, O. V. (2013). Büyükşehir Belediyeleri ile İlçe Belediyeleri Arasında Yaşanan Sorunların Hukuki Temelleri. *Legal Hukuk Dergisi, 131*, 13–36.

Arslan, H. (2014). *Türkiye'nin Kentleşme Sürecinde Konut Politikalarının Evrimi*. Akademik Bakış Uluslararası Hakemli Sosyal Bilimler Dergisi.

Atasoy, T., & Apaydin, A. (2023). Türkiye'de Yabancı Gerçek Kişilerin Gayrimenkul Edinimlerinin Sınırlandırılması. In A. Çatalcalı Ceylan, S. Batal, A. Toptaş, & H. C. Öztürker Demir (Eds.), *Sosyal ve Beşerî Bilimlerde Uluslararası Çalışmalar*. Serüven Yayınevi.

Aytaç, F. (1990). Belediye Kanunu'nun Oluşumu, Uygulanması ve Değişiklikler. In A. Ş. Metropol İmar & Uila-Emme (Eds.), *Türk Belediyeciliği 60 Yıl Uluslararası Sempozyumu, 23–24 Kasım 1990* (pp. 86–106). Maya Matbacılık Yayıncılık.

Bilgin, N., & Taniyici, Ş. (2008). Türkiye'de Kooperatif ve Devlet ilişkilerinin Tarihi Gelişimi. *Karamanoğlu Mehmetbey Üniversitesi Sosyal ve Ekonomik Araştırmalar Dergisi, 2008*, 136–159.

Boratav, K. (2013). *Türkiye iktisat tarihi 1908–2009*. İmge Kitabevi.

Boysan, A. (1990). Adnan Menderes Belediyeciliği İmar Hareketi Uygulama ve Sonuçları. In Metropol İmar A.Ş. & Uila-Emme (Ed.), *Türk Belediyeciliğinde 60 Yıl Uluslararası Sempozyum* (pp. 225–233). Maya Matbacılık.

Bulut, Y., & Dönmez, D. (2019). 6360 Sayılı Düzenlemeyle Oluşan Büyükşehir Modelinde Büyükşehir Belediyesi ile İlçe Belediyeleri Arasında Yaşanan Sorunlar ve Çözüm Önerileri: Hatay İli Örneği. *Uluslararası Yönetim Akademisi Dergisi, 2*, 29–40.

Çetin, S. (2012). Kalkınmada Kentleşme ve Konut Politikalarının Önemi. *Hukuk ve İktisat Araştırmaları Dergisi, 4*, 293–304.

Çetin, I., & Sevüktekin, M. (2016). Türkiye'de Gelişmişlik Düzeyi Farklılıklarının Analizi. *Uluslararası Ekonomik Araştırmalar Dergisi, 2*, 39–61.

Çevre Şehircilik ve İklim Değişikliği Bakanlığı. (2022). *Cumhuriyet Tarihinin En Büyük Sosyal Konut Projesi "İlk Evim" "İlk İş Yerim"* [Online]. Retrieved September 20, 2022, from https://csb.gov.tr/cumhuriyet-tarihinin-en-buyuk-sosyal-konut-projesi-ilk-evim-ilk-is-yerim-bakanlik-faaliyetleri-36220

Demirci Aksoy, A., Tursun, A., & Atasoy, T. (2024). Konut Sorununun Çözümünde Yapı Kooperatiflerinin Değişen Rolü ve Önemi. *Vergi Sorunları Dergisi*, 87–99.

Duyguluer, F. (2012). *Turkish spatial planning practice in the neoliberal era: Over-fragmentation* (Master's thesis). Middle East Technical University.

Ersoy, M., & Şengül, H. T. (2003). *Yerel Yönetimlerin Yeniden Yapılandırılması Türkiye Deneyimi*.

Güler, B. A. (2012). *Hükümetin 8 Ekim 2012 Günlü Bütünşehir Yasa Tasarısı Üzerine*. Yerel Yönetim Araştırma Yardım ve Eğitim Derneği.

Işik, O. (1996). 1980 Sonrası Türkiye'de Kent ve Kentleşme. In F. Aral et al. (Eds.), *Cumhuriyet Dönemi Türk Ansiklopedisi Yüzyıl Biterken*. İletişim Yayınları.

Işik, Ş. (2005). Türkiye'de Kentleşme ve Kentleşme Modelleri. *Ege Coğrafya Dergisi, 14*, 57–71.

İzci, F., & Turan, M. (2013). Türkiye'de Büyükşehir Belediyesi Sistemi ve 6360 Sayılı Yasa ile Büyükşehir Belediyesi Sisteminde Meydana Gelen Değişimler: Van Örneği. *Süleyman Demirel University Journal of Faculty of Economics & Administrative Sciences, 18*.

Karpat, K. H. (1985). *Ottoman population, 1830–1914: Demographic and social characteristics*. The University of Wisconsin Press.

Kayacan, E. (2022). Türkiye'nin Nüfus Politikalarındaki Değişimin Kalkınma Planları Üzerinden Değerlendirilmesi. *Sosyal Politika Çalışmaları Dergisi, 22*(54), 107–139.

Kayapınar, Y. E., Yılmaz, A. N., Ağaçdiken, Ş., Çağlayan, A., Söylemez, E., Zoral, P., Eser, B., Ölmez, E., Karadoğan, T., Sezer, S., Yücel, A. G., & Yazar Yıldıztekin, M. (2021). *Türkiye Cumhuriyeti Yeni Kentsel Gündemin Uygulanmasına ilişkin Ulusal Rapor*. T.C. Çevre, Şehircilik ve İklim Değişikliği Bakanlığı Mekansal Planlama Genel Müdürlüğü.

Keleş, R. (2015). *Kentleşme politikası* (14th ed.). İmge Kitabevi.

Keleş, R. (2020). Yerel demokrasiyi merkezcilik virüsünden arındırmak. *Kent ve Çevre Araştırmaları Dergisi, 2*(1), 45–58.

Keleş, R., & Mengi, A. (2017). *Kent hukuku*. İmge Kitabevi.

Keskinok, Ç. (2010). Urban planning experience of Turkey in the 1930s. *METU Journal of the Faculty of Architecture, 27*, 173–188.

Köseoğlu, F. G., & Sönmez, F. N. Ö. (2019). Rant balonu ve soylulaştırmayı mümkün kılan bir araç olarak afet yasası. In *Göç, Mekan, Siyaset: Toplumsal - Mekansal Hareketlilik ve Planlama*. Berk Matbaacılık.

Lewis, B., & Turna, B. B. (2008). *Modern Türkiye'nin doğuşu*. Arkadaş Yayınevi.

MOIT. Republic of Türkiye Ministry of Industry and Technology. (2025). Socio-economic development ranking of provinces (SEGE-2025) [İllerin sosyo-ekonomik gelişmişlik sıralaması araştırması (İL-SEGE 2025)]. "https://www.sanayi.gov.tr/assets/pdf/birimler/2025-il-sege.pdf" https://www.sanayi.gov.tr/

Mutlu, S. (2003). Late Ottoman population and its ethnic distribution. *Turkish Journal of Population Studies, 25*(1), 3–38.

Ökmen, M. (2002). Osmanlı'dan Cumhuriyet'e Türkiye'de kent ve kentleşme. In H. C. Güzel, K. Çiçek, & S. Koca (Eds.), *Türkler Ansiklopedisi*. Yeni Türkiye Stratejik Araştırma ve Yayın Merkezi.

Ortaylı, İ. (1990). Yerel yönetim: Devraldığımız miras. In Metropol İmar A.Ş. & Uila-Emme (Ed.), *Türk Belediyeciliği 60 Yıl Uluslararası Sempozyumu, 23–24 Kasım 1990* (pp. 63–74). Maya Matbaacılık Yayıncılık.

Özaslan, M. (2006). Türkiye'de dışa açılma süreci ve sanayinin mekansal dağılımında değişimler. In *IV. Ulusal Coğrafya Sempozyumu Avrupa Birliği Sürecindeki Türkiye'de Bölgesel Farklılıklar Bildiri Metinleri, 25–26 Mayıs 2006* (pp. 265–288). Ankara Üniversitesi Basımevi.

Sağlam, S. (2006). Türkiye'de iç göç olgusu ve kentleşme. *Hacettepe Üniversitesi Türkiyat Araştırmaları (HÜTAD)*, 33–44.

Sağlam, S. (2016). 1923–1950 yılları arasında Türkiye'de kent ve kentleşme olgusu. *Journal of Sociological Studies/Sosyoloji Konferansları*.

Şahin, S. Z. (2006). Kentsel dönüşümün kentsel planlamadan bağımsızlaştırılması/ayrılması sürecinde Ankara. *Planlama Dergisi, 36*, 111–120.

Sencer, Y. (1979). *Türkiye'de kentleşme: Bir toplumsal ve kültürel değişme süreci*. Kültür Bakanlığı Yayınları.

Şenyapılı, T. (2012). Gecekondu ve evrimi. In M. Ersoy (Ed.), *Kentsel Planlama Ansiklopedik Sözlük*. Ninova Yayıncılık.

Shaw, S. J. (1978). The Ottoman census system and population, 1831–1914. *International Journal of Middle East Studies, 9*(3), 325–338.

Sönmez, M. (2004). *Türkiye ekonomisinin 80 yılı*. İstanbul Ticaret Odası Yayınları.

Tekeli, İ. (1982). *Türkiye'de kentleşme yazıları*. Turhan Kitabevi.

Tekeli, İ. (1998). Türkiye'de Cumhuriyet döneminde kentsel gelişme ve kent planlaması. In Y. Sey (Ed.), *75 Yılda Değişen Kent ve Mimarlık*. Tarih Vakfı Yayınları.

Tüdeş, T. (2018). *İmar planı uygulamaları: Kentsel alan düzenlemesi*. Ankara Üniversitesi Basımevi.

TURKSTAT. (2025). *Population of provincial/district centers vs. towns/villages* [Online]. Retrieved April 12, 2025, from https://data.tuik.gov.tr/Bulten/Index?p=Adrese-Dayali-Nufus-Kayit-Sistemi-Sonuclari-2024-53783

Tunca, H. (2011). Türkiye'deki illerin çevresel etkinliğinin ölçülmesi. *Uluslararası Ekonomi ve Siyaset Bilimleri Akademik Araştırmalar Dergisi, 5*, 47–57.
Turan, M. (2008). Kent yönetimine katılımda yeni bir sorun alanı: Kentsel rantların yönetimi. *Yerel Yönetimlere Katılım Bülteni, 64*, 39–49.
Türel, A. (1996). Toplu Konut İdaresi. In F. Aral, A. S. Aslandaş, T. Bora, A. Buğra, Y. Danzikyan, T. Eryılmaz, et al. (Eds.), *Cumhuriyet Dönemi Türk Ansiklopedisi Yüzyıl Biterken*. İletişim Yayınları.
Ulusoy, A., & Vural, T. (2001). Kentleşmenin sosyo ekonomik etkileri. *Belediye Dergisi, 7*, 8–14.
UN Population Division. (2018). *World urbanisation prospects* [Online]. Retrieved December 30, 2024, from https://population.un.org/wup/
Vural, T. (2015). Özelleştirme kavramının yerel yönetimler açısından değerlendirilmesi. *Maliye Araştırmaları Dergisi, 1*, 17–28.
Yılmaz, E., & Çiftçi, S. (2011). Kentlerin ortaya çıkışı ve sosyo-politik açıdan Türkiye'de kentleşme dönemleri. *Elektronik Sosyal Bilimler Dergisi, 10*, 252–267.
Yurt, R. G. (2020). Kentleşmenin tarihsel gelişimi/Historical development of urbanisation. *Disiplinlerarası Sosyal Bilimler Dergisi*, 19–44.
Zamir, M. (1981). Population statistics of the Ottoman Empire in 1914 and 1919. *Middle Eastern Studies, 17*(1), 85–106.1

Ruşen Keleş is a distinguished professor in the fields of urbanisation, local governments, and environmental policies in Türkiye. He was born in Trabzon in 1932. He completed his undergraduate (1954) and doctorate (1957) degrees at Ankara University's Faculty of Political Sciences (Mülkiye), where he subsequently became an associate professor in 1961 and a full professor in 1966. Spending a significant portion of his academic career at Mülkiye, Keleş held important administrative positions, including Head of the Department of Urbanisation and Environmental Problems, Dean (1971-1975), and Vice-Rector of Ankara University (1975-1979). He also engaged in international academic activities as a visiting professor in countries such as the Netherlands, Japan, and the USA, pioneering the development of academic disciplines in Türkiye related to urbanisation policies, municipal governance, housing, environmental law, and policy. An author of numerous books and articles considered seminal reference works in the field, such as "Kentleşme Politikası" (Urbanisation Policy), "Yerinden Yönetim ve Siyaset" (Decentralisation and Politics), and "Çevre Politikası" (Environmental Policy), Prof. Dr. Keleş continued his academic work and lecturing at various universities after his retirement, leaving a profound impact on the social sciences in Türkiye through the students he mentored and his significant contributions.

Ahmet Hilmi Erciyes is a research assistant in the Department of Real Estate Development and Management at Ankara University. He graduated from the Department of Public Administration at Süleyman Demirel University in 2013. He completed his master's degree in real estate development and management at Ankara University in 2019 and is currently pursuing his doctoral studies in the same field. As a certified real estate appraiser, his academic work primarily focuses on local governments, urban land management, zoning plans, and urban economics.

Muhammed Said Yılmaz is a lecturer at the Department of Real Estate Development and Management, Faculty of Applied Sciences, Ankara University, Türkiye. He graduated from the Department of City and Regional Planning at Middle East Technical University (METU) in 2014. He completed his master's degree in the Department of Real Estate Development and Management in 2020. He is currently pursuing his Ph.D. and working as a lecturer in the Department of Real Estate Development and Management at the Faculty of Applied Sciences, Ankara University. There, he conducts research in the fields of urban transformation, project development, and project financing.

Socio-Economic Structure and Its Implications for Real Estate Markets

Harun Tanrıvermiş, Monsurat Ayojimi Salami, and Abdurrahman Tursun

Abstract

This chapter examines the socio-economic structure of Türkiye and its implications for real estate markets. This chapter employed both qualitative and quantitative data. Qualitative investigations indicate that economic and social development significantly influences the trajectory of the real estate market, particularly in light of current global trends. Additionally, annual data from 11 provinces, spanning from 2013 to 2023, was used for quantitative analysis using the fully modified ordinary least squares (FMOLS) model. Dummy variables were introduced to capture the effects of the COVID-19 pandemic and the February 2023 earthquake. The findings from the study reveal that demographic changes have positive and significant impacts on the Turkish House Price Index (HPI). The results indicate a significant variance across different educational stages. Education exceeding that of a primary school certificate establishes a significant long-term relationship between housing sales (HS) and the Turkish HPI. Furthermore, we find a significant relationship between household size (HLDS) and the Turkish HPI for individuals holding master's and doctoral degrees but not for those possessing other degrees. Additionally, the findings illustrate a positive long-term relationship between population groups with varying educational levels (EDL) and the Turkish HPI, with the exception of those with only a primary school education. This indicates that a higher level of education correlates with an elevated Turkish HPI. The COVID-19 pandemic and the February 2023 earthquake exerted a significant positive influence on the Turkish HPI.

H. Tanrıvermiş (✉) · M. A. Salami · A. Tursun
Department of Real Estate Development and Management, Faculty of Applied Sciences, Ankara University, Ankara, Türkiye
e-mail: tanrivermis@ankara.edu.tr; masalami@ankara.edu.tr; atursun@ankara.edu.tr

T. Just et al. (eds.), *Understanding Türkiye's Real Estate Markets*, Management for Professionals, https://doi.org/10.1007/978-3-032-13297-0_5

Keywords

Socio-economic structure · Education · COVID-19 · Earthquake · Housing prices

1 Introduction

The level of economic and social development, along with the quality of life of individuals in a society, is referred to as the social structure. The social structure encompasses both the cultural and physical attributes of a society (Bayraktar, 2003). The cultural structure of a society includes characteristics such as lifestyle, beliefs, traditions, language, and family dynamics. Conversely, the physical structure of a society addresses aspects such as the economy, housing, education, and demographic characteristics. Given that the socio-economic structure provides insights into the quality of life and living standards of individuals and societies, it is of significant importance in the social sciences, especially in research that analyses socio-economic differentiation (Uçkan, 2019). Socio-economic status or structure encompasses various factors, including economic power, access to education and healthcare, employment opportunities, availability of resources, transportation, and communication infrastructure (Mutlu & Varol, 2017).

Furthermore, the socio-economic structure of a nation or society may be analysed from different perspectives, encompassing economic growth and economic development. Economic growth is defined as an increase in a nation's gross domestic product (GDP), which measures the monetary value of all goods and services produced within a designated time frame. Conversely, economic development describes the transformation of a nation's production structure to yield high-value-added goods while ensuring an equitable distribution of products across income groups, thereby enhancing living standards. Consequently, economic growth necessitates an augmentation of production capacity, whereas economic development requires structural modifications within both the economic and social dimensions. Therefore, rather than attempting to define socio-economic structure based exclusively on economically quantifiable variables in a narrow sense, such as per capita annual income, it should be evaluated more thoroughly by integrating factors such as population composition, employment, language, ethnicity, religion, traditions, education levels, access to services, and technological advancement (Case et al., 2005; Dinler, 2008; Kaynak, 2009). The determination and analysis of socio-economic conditions are particularly vital for urbanisation planning, real estate market regulation, and policy development, particularly in developing countries. To effectively investigate the fundamental structure of a nation or region, it is imperative to conduct a thorough analysis of its social and economic dynamics (Uçkan, 2019). This approach enables a more rational strategy for settlement planning, housing strategies, and real estate policies. In summary, there exists a correlation between demographic factors, such as population size, population structure, geographic distribution of the population, temporal changes (birth rates, mortality, marriage, divorce, and social mobility), and settlement patterns, as well as real estate markets.

The real estate market and property prices are closely interconnected with economic dynamics and cycles (Quigley, 1999; Wang, 2003). As human activities evolve, the real estate market also experiences analogous transformations. A significant portion of the real estate sector consists of residential properties, which play a crucial role in household expenditures, whether for personal use or as an investment. Mankiw and Weil (1989) demonstrated how demographic characteristics impact the housing market in the United States while also emphasising that taxation, economic factors, and social aspects must not be overlooked. Consequently, when evaluating the real estate sector, particularly housing investments, it is essential to consider sociological, psychological, political, cultural, artistic, and religious aspects within a holistic analytical framework. Housing investments are multifaceted and complex, as they can serve both as investment vehicles and personal residences while also possessing economic, social, and political significance.

Nonetheless, the real estate market is influenced by both physical and legal factors, as well as institutional and socio-economic characteristics. Furthermore, the direction of the real estate market is affected by societal characteristics, which are determined by variables such as GDP, unemployment rates, demographic factors, household income, interest rates, industrial production, household consumption, and other macroeconomic factors (Hon-Chung, 2009; Ludwig & Slok, 2004; Case et al., 2005; Bardhan et al., 2007; Goodhart & Hofmann, 2007; Zhang & Wu, 2008). These variables associated with the real estate market are also used to evaluate the socio-economic development of a region or society. Ovsiannikova et al. (2021) reveal in their study that the housing market and economic cycles exhibit simultaneous and similar cyclical patterns concerning the effects of socio-economic development on housing investments. Therefore, it can be contended that analogous variables influence both the socio-economic structure and real estate markets, wherein they interact with each other. Hon-Chung (2009) emphasises that the results from individual studies regarding the effects of these factors cannot be generalised across all countries and regions with differing contexts. Indeed, several studies examining the relationship between real estate markets and economic indicators have established a significant correlation between property prices and macroeconomic variables, including unemployment rates, stock market performance, current account balances, industrial production, and GDP (Case & Shiller, 2003; Malpezzi, 1999). Comparative studies on European countries reveal that these variables correlate to varying degrees, depending on the cultural and economic contexts. For instance, Égert and Mihaljek (2007) discovered that in Central and Eastern European countries, housing prices are highly sensitive to economic growth and fluctuations in financial markets. Similarly, Adams and Füss (2010) assert that in developed countries, housing prices maintain a long-term cointegration relationship with macroeconomic variables.

It is essential to recognise that the demand for real estate, particularly housing, is indicative of the socio-economic capacity of households. In essence, the ability of households to acquire and use (or consume) housing is inherently dependent upon their socio-economic characteristics. Socio-economic conditions are generally evaluated using indicators such as per capita gross national product (GNP) and the

United Nations Human Development Index (HDI). The HDI is a summary measure of income levels, life expectancy, and education levels. Still, the HDI is subject to considerable debate due to its limitations. It is often deemed an insufficient measure of human development, as it does not incorporate crucial indicators, such as unemployment, poverty, and environmental factors. Consequently, the socio-economic development index (SEDI) is regarded as an alternative to the HDI, as it seeks to address the deficiencies identified in the HDI. Conversely, a study examining the correlation between this index and real estate markets has yet to be conducted for Türkiye. Considering Grum and Govekar's (2016) assertion that socio-economic contexts must be taken into account, this chapter examines the impact of Türkiye's socio-economic context on the real estate markets using national data, underscoring its significance in spatial planning, real estate development, and investment decisions.

Furthermore, a concise review of prior studies concerning socio-economic development in Türkiye is provided. The methodology employed and the variables considered in defining socio-economic development in Türkiye were also scrutinised. To provide an overview of Türkiye's socio-economic circumstances, this chapter examines key indicators, including population, fertility rate, number of households, household types, average household size (HLDS), average household income, educational levels (EDL), employment rates, unemployment rates, and household earnings. In addition, the research assessed healthcare accessibility by analysing the number of hospitals, hospital beds, physicians, dentists, midwives, nurses, and pharmacists per 100,000 persons. To estimate the influence of socio-economic conditions on the real estate market, this chapter compared real estate sales statistics with the results of the Socio-Economic Development Ranking (SEGE, 2017), conducted by the Turkish Ministry of Industry and Technology, which ranks provinces based on their developmental levels. Within this context, housing sales (HS) at the provincial level were analysed, including mortgaged versus non-mortgaged transactions and first-hand versus second-hand property sales, in correlation with development ranking data. Moreover, the relationship between housing prices and socio-economic variables was investigated. The findings are delineated in the conclusion section, accompanied by policy recommendations for future research.

2 The Concept and Measurement of Socio-Economic Development

The concepts of socio-economic progress, socio-economic development, and socio-economic growth are frequently used interchangeably due to their inherent similarities (Turhan, 2020; Türkseven, 2020). In this context, growth is predominantly perceived as a one-dimensional concept, primarily employed to describe economic advancement. Conversely, the concept of progress, viewed from a broader perspective, encompasses meanings such as the institutional strengthening of the country, enhancement of its qualifications, and advances in cultural, social, and economic domains (Dincer et al., 2003). Particularly after the 1940s, it became apparent that while economic progress holds significance in the development process, it is also necessary to consider the environmental, social, and cultural dimensions of a country, alongside its economy, in the development trajectory. Over time, approaches centring on the human dimensions of progress have gained prominence. Consequently, the notions of economic progress and development have evolved to encompass not only economic growth but also environmental sustainability, cultural and social opportunities, equitable income distribution, employment, and the alleviation of poverty (Sakarya & İbişoğlu, 2015).

The concept of socio-economic progress has emerged as a consequence of examining both quantitative and qualitative growth within the broader frameworks of economic advancement and development. Socio-economic progress encompasses not only shifts in per capita income, employment levels, and production capacities but also social and cultural transformations (Özdemir & Altıparmak, 2005). The rate of socio-economic progress varies across nations, and even within the same country, it diverges across regions and provinces. Geographic and cultural disparities between regions or provinces result in variations in the levels of progress (Dinler, 2008), giving rise to classifications such as developed and underdeveloped regions (Sakarya & İbişoğlu, 2015).

2.1 Determination of Socio-Economic Progress Levels

To ensure nationwide socio-economic advancement and attain sustainable progress, it is imperative to identify disparities across regions. Consequently, research on the level of economic progress across different regions is essential. However, there is no universally accepted method or indicator to measure the levels of economic progress or evaluate the differences between regions, and discussions surrounding this matter persist (Akşahin, 2008). For a long time, gross domestic product (GDP) and gross national product (GNP) have been considered the best indicators of socio-economic development. Nevertheless, disparities in income distribution have prompted discussions regarding the adequacy of GDP or GNP as the only indicator. This discourse has ushered in a transition towards a multidimensional approach, whereby social development and welfare are assessed through a combination of various variables (Sakarya & İbişoğlu, 2015). Consequently, rather than concentrating on quantitative growth and transformation, there has been a shift towards qualitative development. This perspective includes factors such as economy, education, communication, accessibility, commercial capacity, culture, and healthcare, which are perceived to provide a more comprehensive representation of the socio-economic framework. As a result, SEDI has been introduced and employed in policymaking processes.

For instance, in India, Das (1999) established a development index using principal component analysis to assess socio-economic development disparities across states. This analysis incorporated four principal components: economy, healthcare, communication, and basic needs, which were broadly recognised at the national level (Sakarya & İbişoğlu, 2015). Similarly, for China, Wang (2007) employed the same methodology to formulate a socio-economic development index across provinces. This investigation used 70 distinct variables encompassing justice, education, human development, environment, economy, social security, industrial development, and public services. The findings reveal a substantial correlation between development levels and geographical regions (Yıldız et al., 2012). Moreover, the organisation for economic co-operation and development - OECD's indexing studies have also used principal component analysis across various fields and variables. In Türkiye, analogous socio-economic development evaluations have been executed at the provincial, district, and regional levels by the Turkish Ministry of Industry and Technology by employing the same methodology.

2.2 Studies on Determining Socio-Economic Development in Türkiye

Since 1963, five-year development plans have been formulated and executed in Türkiye, with the objective to foster progress across sectors, including education, transportation, health, economy, and justice, while simultaneously delineating the policies to be adopted in line with this aspiration. These plans establish policy frameworks intended to fulfil developmental aims, placing particular emphasis on the mitigation of regional disparities (Özaslan et al., 2006). In recent years, the incorporation of a sustainable development paradigm has further underscored the significance of evaluating disparities in socio-economic development levels across regions. The identification and comparative analysis of regional discrepancies through systematic evaluations have become imperative for SEDI studies, as well as for discerning the economic and sociocultural variables that underpin such assessments (Özaslan et al., 2006).

In accordance with the fundamental objectives of development plans, the pertinent ministry has undertaken socio-economic development ranking studies at the regional, provincial, and district levels. The SEDI studies, conducted by the Turkish Ministry of Industry and Technology, function as a monitoring and evaluation instrument for regional development policies. These studies yield critical insights by analysing and comparing socio-economic development levels and trends across regions, provinces, and districts. To date, seven SEDI studies at the district level (the most recent in 2022) and nine at the provincial level (the latest in 2017) have been completed (Turkish Ministry of Industry and Technology, 2022).

The most recent provincial-level study, SEDI-2017, integrated variables derived from endogenous growth theories, like the number of trademark and patent applications, Internet usage, mobile phone penetration, the number of students in higher education, and the number of individuals pursuing master's and doctoral degrees, all of which signify internal development potential. In this analysis, four demographic variables were used: population density, urbanisation rate, migration rate, and fertility rate. Several employment variables were included: daily earnings, labour force participation, the percentage of employees covered by the Social Security Institution (SGK), and the unemployment rate. A total of five education-related variables were analysed: the literacy rate among women, the university entrance exam (YGS) success rate, and the number of university or faculty graduates. Additionally, five healthcare variables were considered: the number of hospitals, physicians, dentists, and pharmacies per capita. Furthermore, 13 variables related to competitiveness and innovation capacity, six variables concerning financial status, five variables pertaining to accessibility, and seven variables regarding quality of life were included. In total, 52 variables were considered in the index development study, offering a comprehensive framework for policymaking (Turkish Ministry of Industry and Technology, 2017).

3 Assessment of Socio-Economic Conditions in Türkiye

Demographic variables are important indicators for the socio-economic state of societies. Likewise, demographic data, including population, birth rate, and the number of households, is essential in assessing the real estate market, particularly for the housing sector, and facilitating future projections (Mankiw & Weil, 1989; Just, 2013). Variables such as population growth rate, fertility rate, number and size of households, household income, employment opportunities, and the labour force ratio in both agricultural and non-agricultural sectors can be scrutinised in this context. As of 2023, Türkiye's total population was 85,372,377 persons, comprising 42,734,071 males and 42,638,306 females. These persons live in a total of 26,309,332 households; i.e. the average household size is 3.25 persons. The number of single-person households is 5,192,825, i.e. a share of 19.74% of all households. The number of two-person households is 5,919,212, accounting for 22.50% of the total households. Households consisting of three persons account for 19.99% of the total, while the share of households with four or more members shrinks with ever bigger households. Reviewing the distribution of the population by age groups, 52.01% fall within the 15–50-year range (Fig. 1), the 15–65-year group comprises 68.33%, and the dependent population includes 21.47% in the 0–14 age group and 10.22% in the group of persons above 66 years.

The fertility rate measures the average number of children a woman is anticipated to have during her reproductive years, typically defined within the 15–49 age range. The fertility rate, which was recorded at 2.38 in 2001, declined substantially to 1.51 in 2023 (TURKSTAT, 2024a). Income and consumption surveys offer valuable insights into the income distribution. The Gini coefficient, which measures income inequality, has remained near 0.40 between 2000 and 2024, signalling a relatively unequal income distribution, similar to levels reported for the United States. Türkiye is positioned between countries characterised by more equitable income distribution (where the Gini coefficient ranges from 0.25 to 0.35, e.g. Sweden or Norway) and those exhibiting the highest income inequality (where the Gini coefficient exceeds 0.60, such as Brazil or South Africa). Furthermore, the stability of the Gini coefficient could only be achieved by fiscal policies (Table 1).

A pivotal variable in evaluating socio-economic development is the educational status. There are 1,862,532 illiterate individuals in Türkiye, representing

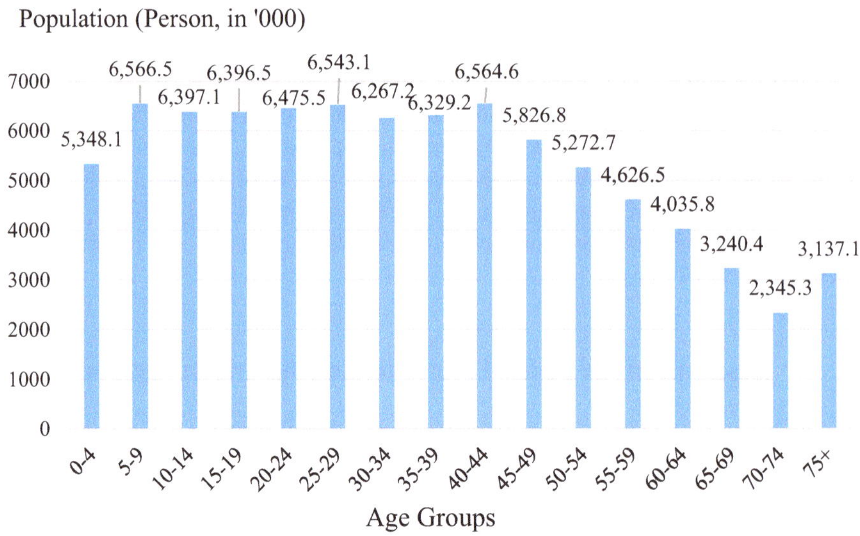

Fig. 1 Population distribution of Türkiye by age groups. Source: TURKSTAT (2024a)

approximately 2.5% of the total population aged 6 and older. At the same time, 11,637,287 persons have attained an associate degree (a two-year higher education programme) or a bachelor's degree (a four-year programme), and 1,628,574 persons have reached a postgraduate degree (either a master's or a doctoral degree). The total of individuals who have completed university education amounts to 13,265,861, corresponding to approximately 17.51% of the population aged 6 and older (TURKSTAT, 2024a). The educational status of other demographic groups is depicted in Fig. 2. The average duration of education among the population is 8.5 years, which is below the average duration observed in OECD countries (Aydın & Tuğrul, 2022).

Türkiye has a relatively young population, reflecting a strong labour supply. A part of the increase in labour supply was offset in the 1970s by people finding employment opportunities abroad, and this contributed to a reduction in unemployment during that period. However, in the 1980s, unemployment surged again. In Türkiye, alongside open unemployment, underemployment has also escalated to substantial levels (Uçkan, 2019). According to the Turkish Statistical Institute (TURKSTAT) (2024a), as of 2023, the total labour force aged 15 and more amounts to 65,637,000, of which 35,049,000 are actively participating in the labour market. Thus, the labour force participation rate is reported at 53.34%. When examining only the male population, the labour force participation rate is 71.1%, while the female participation rate is a mere 36.0%. A total of 80% of employment is concentrated in non-agricultural sectors, while 16% of the employees work in the agricultural sector. Furthermore, the share of agricultural labour is steadily declining. The agricultural employment rate, which was 21.1% in 2014, has declined gradually to

Table 1 Selected socio-economic status indicators in Türkiye

Selected indicators	Years								
	2000	2005	2010	2015	2020	2021	2022	2023	2024
Population (M)	64.7	68.9	73.7	78.7	83.6	84.7	85.3	85.4	85.7
Average household size (persons)	4.5	4.2	3.8	3.5	3.3	3.2	3.2	3.1	3.1
Labour force (1000 people)	23,078	21,321	24,516	29,550	30,725	32,743	34,317	34,881	35,705
Employment	21,581	19,357	21,810	26,501	26,685	28,827	30,725	31,607	32,590
Unemployment rate (%)	6.5	9.2	11.1	10.3	13.2	12.0	10.5	9.4	8.7
People per physician	759	663	597	557	488	461	438	418	417
Secondary school enrollment rate (%)	61.0	85.2	70.6	79.5	85.1	87.9	89.7	95.1	88.0
Gini coefficient	0.400	0.428	0.402	0.397	0.410	0.401	0.415	0.420	0.413

Note: Population rounded to one decimal and shown in millions (M)
Source: TURKSTAT (2025)

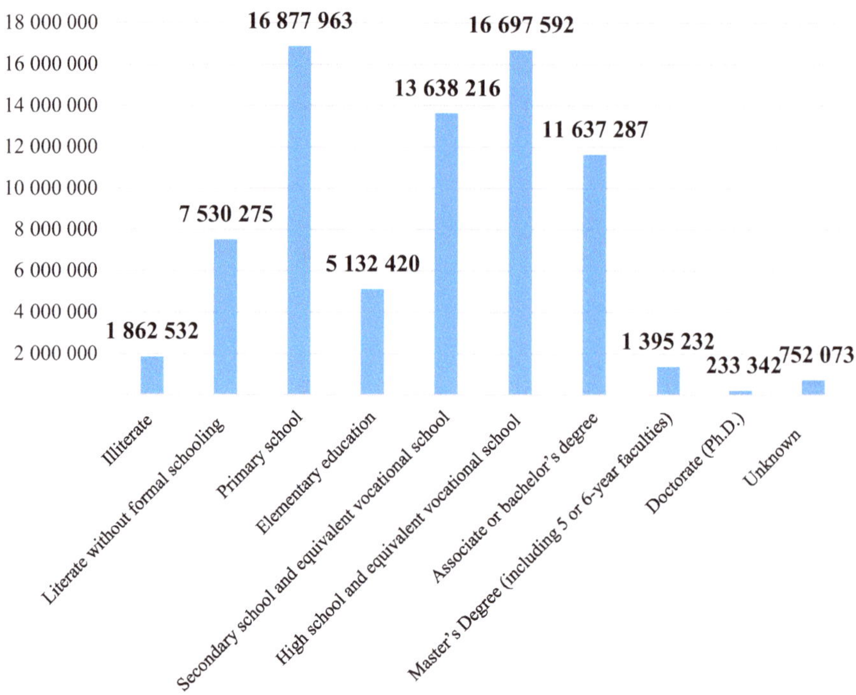

Fig. 2 Number of inhabitants in Türkiye by educational status. Source: TURKSTAT (2024a)

Table 2 Distribution of civilian employment by sectors

Years	Agriculture (%)	Industry (%)	Construction (%)	Services (%)
2005	25.5	21.4	5.6	47.4
2010	23.2	21.2	6.5	49.1
2015	20.2	20.2	4.7	52.4
2020	17.7	20.6	23.0	56.6
2021	17.2	21.4	6.1	55.3
2022	15.7	21.7	6.0	56.6
2023	14.6	21.3	6.3	57.8
2024	14.6	20.8	6.6	58.1

Source: TURKSTAT (2025)

16.8% in 2022. As emphasised by Tanrıvermiş and Bülbül (2007), the decreasing relative importance of agriculture in the economy and structural transformation are anticipated to yield a substantial increase in non-agricultural employment (Table 2).

The average labour income of household members increased consistently between 2006 and 2023. Throughout these 18 years, the average labour income rose by a factor of 13.3. However, this increase has primarily been due to inflation. When measuring income development in real terms, i.e., adjusted for increases in the

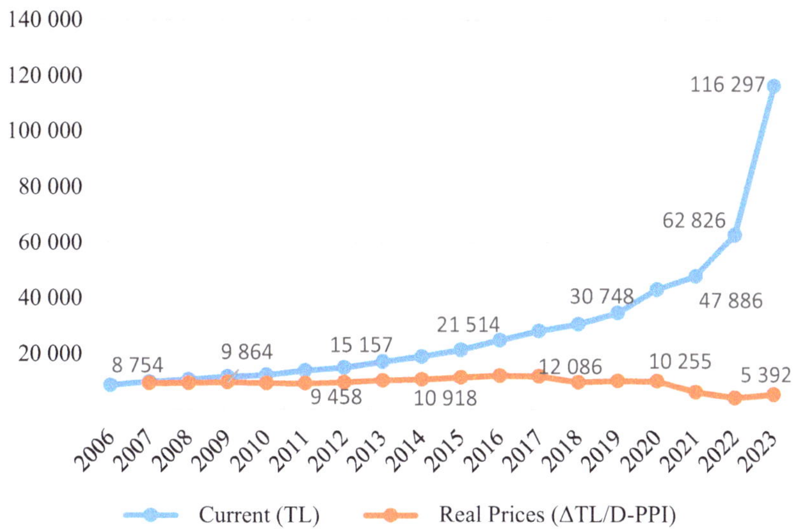

Fig. 3 Annual average labour income of household members. Source: TURKSTAT (2024b)

Domestic Producer Price Index (D-PPI), the annual average labour income of household members remained stable for a long time and began to decline in the past few years (Fig. 3).

The relationship between all socio-economic variables and healthcare is frequently regarded as the most intricate (Fuchs, 2004). However, the healthcare opportunities accessible to society act as a crucial indicator in evaluating socio-economic development (Dincer et al., 2003; Fuchs, 2004; Özaslan et al., 2006). Although the figures differ by region, the aggregate number of physicians per 100,000 inhabitants in Türkiye was 205 in 2020, and the total number of dentists per 100,000 inhabitants was 42. Similarly, the number of pharmacists per 100,000 inhabitants was recorded at 42. The number of nurses and midwives per 100,000 persons increased by 11.8%, from 306 in 2019 to 342 in 2020. In 2020, healthcare services were rendered in a total of 1534 hospitals, with an aggregate of 251,182 hospital beds (TURKSTAT, 2022a, c). According to the 2020 data, the number of hospital beds per 100,000 inhabitants was approximately 300. The quality of healthcare and educational services provided across cities in the country significantly influences the settlement choices of individuals, particularly migrant households (Tanrıvermiş & Gündoğan, 2021). Furthermore, the availability of elderly care facilities in cities such as Antalya, Muğla, Mersin, Aydın, and İzmir has facilitated the migration of elderly foreigners, who tend to prefer acquiring real estate and residing in coastal provinces like Antalya, Muğla, and Aydın (Tanrıvermiş, 2021).

4 Possible Effects of the Socio-Economic Development Level on Real Estate Markets

4.1 The Relationship between Development Indicators and Real Estate Markets

In the initial studies conducted to ascertain the socio-economic development levels of provinces and regions, methods such as indexing and using a taxonomy were employed. For these methods, the researchers assigned weights to variables deemed as development criteria. This may prompt discussions regarding the objectivity and reliability of these studies. Still, in recent years, multi-criteria decision theory has been extensively applied in ranking and classification studies. Decision theory facilitates the use of qualitative data; however, akin to the methods above, it remains vulnerable to the arbitrary choices of researchers in determining appropriate variable weights. Within this context, the SEDI-2017 study utilised 52 distinct variables across various categories, including demographics, healthcare, education, employment, competitiveness and innovation capacity, finance, accessibility, and quality of life, to determine the relative rankings and tiers of provinces (Turkish Ministry of Industry and Technology, 2017). Based on the computed development scores, the ranking of provinces (Fig. 4) was analysed in relation to real estate investments and market activity at the provincial level.

According to the 2017 SEDI study, Istanbul is the most developed province in terms of social development. Subsequently, the provinces are ranked as follows: Ankara, İzmir, Kocaeli, and Antalya. The five provinces identified as the least developed are Van, Hakkari, Muş, Ağrı, and Şırnak.

Demographic change affects the education system, labour market, housing market, and social security system (Mankiw & Weil, 1989), indicating a robust interrelationship between the housing market and socio-economic development. To analyse the effects of socio-economic development on the real estate market, the development scores of provinces calculated in 2017 were compared to the number of housing units sold in the same year. The housing market was chosen due to its importance as a fundamental component of the construction and real estate sectors, as well as the availability of data pertinent to the housing market. Thus, valuable insights can be obtained regarding the relationship between socio-economic development and real estate demand, particularly housing demand. Consequently, it is anticipated that the number of housing units sold in 2017 across various provinces should be proportional to their respective populations (Fig. 5). Indeed, for 2017, a correlation coefficient of $r = 0.96$ between the number of housing units sold and the population variables was found.

Comparing provincial development scores directly with the number of housing sales may yield misleading results when assessing the impact of socio-economic development on the real estate market. This is attributable to the fact that the number of houses sold correlates directly with the city's population. In contrast, the socio-economic development index encompasses 52 different variables in conjunction with demographic data, thereby making a direct comparison potentially

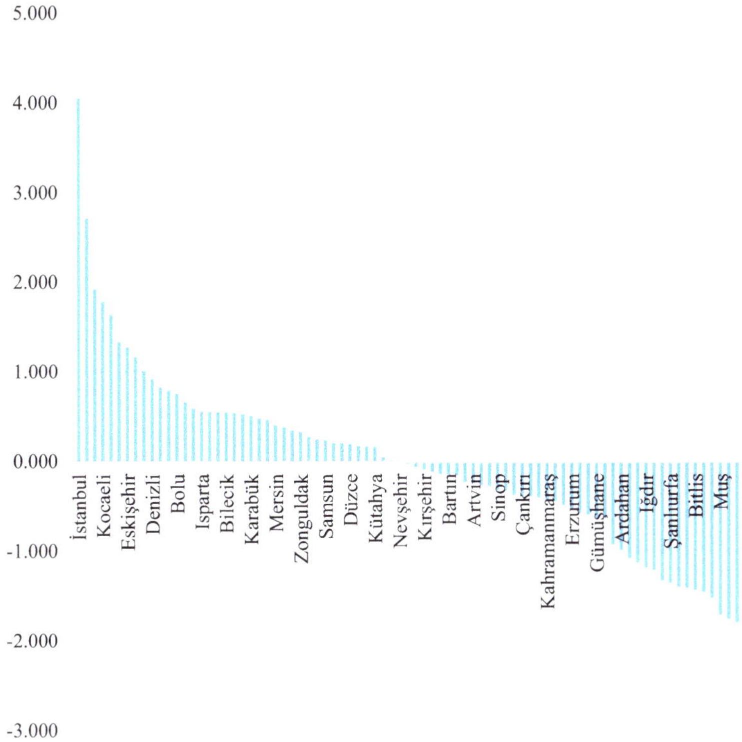

Fig. 4 Socio-economic development ranking of provinces (The vertical axis in this figure shows the economic development rate of Turkish provinces. A lower position on this axis indicates that the province makes a smaller socio-economic contribution to Türkiye's overall economic growth). Source: Turkish Ministry of Industry and Technology (2017)

misleading. Then, comparing the number of houses sold in each province relative to the population, specifically the percentage of per capita housing sales, against the socio-economic development score, would constitute a better approach. The results of this analysis yield a strong positive relationship (r = 0.63) between the socio-economic development score and the per capita mortgaged housing sales rate (Fig. 6). Similarly, a strong positive correlation (r = 0.55) is identified for the socio-economic development score and the per capita housing sales rate. Additionally, to examine the relationship between socio-economic development and newly constructed housing units, the number of first-hand housing sales in 2017 was analysed. A positive yet weaker correlation (r = 0.43) was found for the socio-economic development score and the per capita rate of first-hand housing sales.

It is widely recognised that regions and provinces characterised by elevated levels of socio-economic development exhibit a more active housing market. Furthermore, socio-economic development exerts an influence on real estate financing. In provinces marked by advanced socio-economic development, the

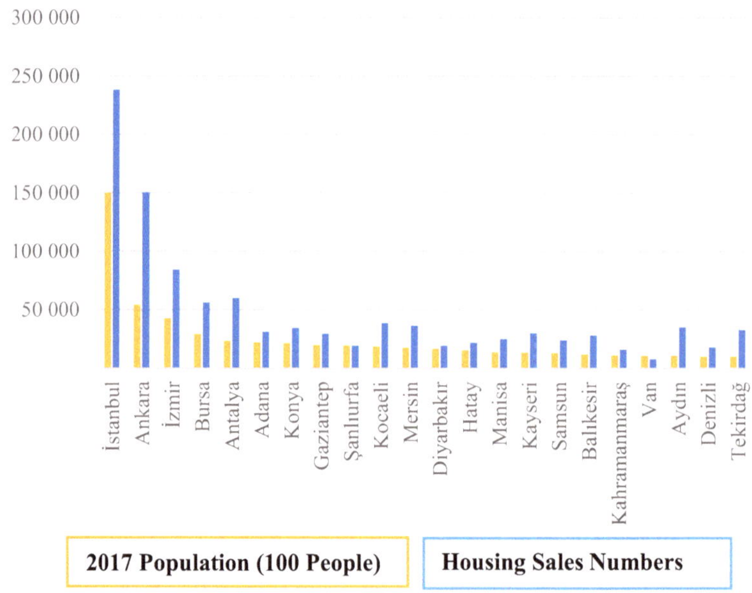

Fig. 5 Number of inhabitants and number of housing sales by provinces in 2017. Sources: TURKSTAT (2022a, 2022b, 2022c)

Fig. 6 Development scores of provinces and mortgaged housing sales. Sources: Turkish Ministry of Industry and Technology (2017), TURKSTAT (2022b)

procurement of financing for real estate acquisition is more prevalent, frequently facilitated through loans from financial institutions and the mortgage of the property. Although no official data delineates the socio-economic and demographic profile of individuals applying for mortgage housing loans, it is plausible that applicants typically reside in urban areas and possess a stable income at or exceeding the middle-income threshold, enabling them to afford the requisite down payment for such loans. Conversely, other individuals are either necessitated to resort to traditional methods of housing acquisition, such as inheritance, participation in housing cooperatives, borrowing from contractors and developers, or reliance on familial support, or they may choose to pursue rental housing options. This situation is particularly relevant for lower-to-middle-income households, where housing affordability remains a critical concern (Tanrıvermiş, 2019). In conclusion, each socio-economic group has unique housing requirements related to its specific socio-economic circumstances (Keskin, 2008).

4.2 The Impacts of Demographic Indicators on Real Estate Demand

4.2.1 Data and Methods

The annual data used in this chapter, spanning from 2013 to 2023, was procured from the Turkish Statistical Institute. A dummy variable was used to ascertain the impact of the COVID-19 pandemic. The data selection was contingent upon its availability. The analysis in this chapter is based on panel data, which encompasses both time series and cross-sectional information. Data for 11 provinces was included, representing fifty per cent of Türkiye's housing market. The provinces under examination are Ankara, Antalya, Bursa, Eskişehir, Istanbul, İzmir, Kocaeli, Muğla, Tekirdağ, Denizli, and Sakarya. The variables analysed consist of the Turkish House Price Index (HPI), housing sales, household size, population number (Pop), and educational attainment. The levels of education incorporated in this study range from primary education to doctoral degrees. This facilitates the investigation into the long-term effect of educational attainment on the Turkish House Price Index. Thus, the significance of demographic changes, such as educational attainment, on the Turkish House Price Index is scrutinised. Numerous studies have underscored that demographic changes are critical factors significantly influencing housing markets (Bampinas et al., 2017; Bramley & Watkins, 2016). Furthermore, the data used in this chapter was transformed into natural logarithms. The natural logarithm values allow for the estimated coefficient of the study to be interpreted as elasticities (Ruan & Yan, 2022).

$$y_{it} = Iny_{it} \quad (1)$$

$$x_{it} = Inx_{it} \quad (2)$$

where y_{it} denotes the Turkish House Price Index (HPI), serving as the dependent variable, and x_{it} symbolises the explanatory variables, inclusive of housing sales (HS), household size (HLDS), population number (Pop), and educational levels (EDL). Consequently, HPI is expressed as a function of the above-stated explanatory variables, and the generalised model is as follows:

$$HPI_{it} = f\left(HS_{it}, HLDS_{it}, Pop_{it}, EDL_{it}\right) \tag{3}$$

The panel version of the above model is expressed in a linear form, and the specific model is described in Eqs. (5)–(10) as follows:

$$LnHPI_{it} = \alpha_0 + \beta_1 LnHS_{it} + \beta_2 LnHLDS_{it} + \beta_3 Pop_{it} + \beta_4 LnEDL_{it} + \varepsilon_{it} \tag{4}$$

$$LnHPI_{it} = \alpha_{10} + \beta_{11} LnHS_{it} + \beta_{12} LnHLDS_{it} + \beta_{13} Pop_{it} + \beta_{14} LnPry_{it} + \varepsilon_{1it} \tag{5}$$

$$LnHPI_{it} = \alpha_{20} + \beta_{21} LnHS_{it} + \beta_{22} LnHLDS_{it} + \beta_{23} Pop_{it} + \beta_{24} LnLwr.Scnd_{it} + \varepsilon_{2it} \tag{6}$$

$$LnHPI_{it} = \alpha_{30} + \beta_{31} LnHS_{it} + \beta_{32} LnHLDS_{it} + \beta_{33} Pop_{it} + \beta_{34} LnUpp.Scnd_{it} + \varepsilon_{3it} \tag{7}$$

$$LnHPI_{it} = \alpha_{40} + \beta_{41} LnHS_{it} + \beta_{42} LnHLDS_{it} + \beta_{43} Pop_{it} + \beta_{44} LnBach_{it} + \varepsilon_{4it} \tag{8}$$

$$LnHPI_{it} = \alpha_{50} + \beta_{51} LnHS_{it} + \beta_{52} LnHLDS_{it} + \beta_{53} Pop_{it} + \beta_{54} LnMst_{it} + \varepsilon_{5it} \tag{9}$$

$$LnHPI_{it} = \alpha_{60} + \beta_{61} LnHS_{it} + \beta_{62} LnHLDS_{it} + \beta_{63} Pop_{it} + \beta_{64} LnPhD_{it} + \varepsilon_{6it} \tag{10}$$

where i represents provinces; t represents the study period; a_{10}, a_{20}, a_{30}, a_{40}, a_{50}, and a_{60} represent the fixed effect in the models that express different effects of educational levels; and ε is the white noise error term. *ln* is the natural logarithm of all variables. The parameters βs are the elasticities of the corresponding variables.

This study investigates the long-term relationship between the Turkish House Price Index (HPI) and demographic change. The fully modified ordinary least squares (FMOLS) methodology is widely regarded as robust and suitable for examining this long-run relationship. This modelling approach offers several advantages, including the ability to address heterogeneity (Ruan & Yan, 2022), resolve endogeneity issues (Lu et al., 2022), and produce robust cointegration results, even with limited sample sizes (Ruan & Yan, 2022). Cointegration is understood as a sequential combination of stationary variables. The FMOLS model is represented as outlined in the research conducted by Lu et al. (2022) and Gueye (2021), which is as follows:.

$$\hat{\theta}_{FMOLS} = \begin{pmatrix} \hat{\beta} \\ \hat{\gamma} \end{pmatrix} = \left(\sum_{T}^{t=2} Z_t Z_t^{'} \right)^{-1} \left(\sum_{T}^{t=2} Z_t y_t^{+} - T\left(\hat{\lambda}_{12} + 0\right) \right) \tag{11}$$

4.2.2 Empirical Findings and Discussions

The descriptive summary of the analysis pertains to the data used in the panel analysis. The conclusions concerning cointegration emphasise the long-term relationship between the Turkish House Price Index (HPI) and demographic changes, as elucidated in Tables 3 and 4.

Table 3 presents the descriptive statistics regarding demographic changes in Türkiye and the Turkish House Price Index (HPI) from 2013 to 2023 across the major provinces of Türkiye. The raw data for the mean value of the HPI is 21.8146, with a standard deviation of 27.3718. The mean of the Turkish HPI indicates a catastrophic occurrence, as denoted by a Kurtosis value of 3.3517. This suggests that the Turkish HPI has witnessed substantial fluctuations, thereby providing empirical evidence of instability within the index. Apart from the household size and population parameters with a Kurtosis value less than 3, all additional explanatory variables demonstrate signs of catastrophe. In addition, within the educational categories, individuals holding upper secondary education report the highest means, while those possessing a PhD exhibit the lowest means. Metin Özcan et al. (2021) also demonstrated, in their research concerning Turkish demographic changes, that those individuals with lower educational attainments have a higher mean age relative to those with graduate certificates. Another noteworthy finding pertains to the mean household size, which indicates a tendency for Turkish households to maintain smaller sizes. With the observed variation in the mean levels of education, there is

Table 3 Descriptive statistics of HPI and demographic change in Türkiye

Variables	Mean	Min.	Max.	Std. dev.	Skewness	Kurtosis	Jarque–Bera	Obs.
HPI	21.81	4.35	100.00	27.37	2.14	6.28	146.94[a] (0.0000)	121
House sales	65,156.7	12,591	276,223	65,923.4	1.78	5.21	88.39[a] (0.0000)	121
Household size	3.13	2.62	3.73	0.26	0.12	2.39	2.12 (0.3456)	121
Population (k)	1287	566	2618	650	0.61	1.97	12.81[b] (0.0017)	121
Primary education (k)	307	46	2370	401	3.01	12.57	644.61[a] (0.0000)	121
Lower secondary (k)	408	32	2530	526	2.65	9.79	373.96[a] (0.0000)	121
Upper secondary (k)	682	143	3434	789	2.16	6.83	167.93[a] (0.0000)	121
Bachelor's (k)	492	70	2784	620	2.19	7.16	184.08[a] (0.0000)	121
Master's (k)	57	4.5	410	86.6	2.39	8.27	255.13[a] (0.0000)	121
PhD (k)	11.5	1.2	63	15.9	1.79	4.95	83.90[a] (0.0000)	121

Note that superscripts [a] and [b] indicate 1% and 5% significance levels. Population- and education-related variables are shown in thousands (k). All values are rounded for clarity

Table 4 Long-run relationship between HPI and demographic change in Türkiye

Variables	Primary β	Lower secondary β	Upper secondary β	Bachelor's β	Master's β	PhD β
House sales	1.1526[b] (0.0004)	0.6301[b] (0.0001)	0.3978[b] (0.0147)	0.3532[c] (0.0752)	0.3724[b] (0.0361)	0.2905[c] (0.0689)
Household size	0.0715 (0.1435)	0.2677 (0.5620)	0.2323 (0.1025)	0.5341 (0.2471)	0.6159[b] (0.0352)	−0.2545 (−0.1420)
Population	−0.8480[a] (0.0000)	0.6920[a] (0.0000)	2.3799[a] (0.0000)	1.7613[a] (0.0000)	0.9448[a] (0.0000)	1.6576[a] (0.0000)
Primary education	0.3102[b] (0.0017)	–	–	–	–	–
Lower secondary	–	0.4542[b] (0.0008)	–	–	–	–
Upper secondary	–	–	0.3932[b] (0.0004)	–	–	–
Bachelor's	–	–	–	0.3772[b] (0.0002)	–	–
Master's	–	–	–	–	0.3580[a] (0.0000)	–
PhD	–	–	–	–	–	0.3722[a] (0.0000)
COVID-19	0.9504[b] (0.0004)	0.8612[b] (0.0005)	0.7334[a] (0.0000)	0.7377[b] (0.0001)	0.7320[b] (0.0007)	0.7027[a] (0.0000)
Earthquake 2023	1.5172[b] (0.0007)	1.7395[a] (0.0000)	1.4967[a] (0.0000)	1.5248[a] (0.0000)	1.5010[a] (0.0000)	1.4957[a] (0.0000)
Adjusted R^2	0.9739	0.9762	0.9830	0.9830	0.9875	0.9848
Wald Test	360.7280[b] (0.0012)	189.4467[b] (0.0005)	168.8513[a] (0.0000)	183.4628[b] (0.0027)	278.3205[a] (0.0000)	242.8603[b] (0.0042)
HQ^2 (3)	−0.075 (0.777)	−0.149 (0.038)	−0.055 (0.425)	−0.120 (0.101)	−0.124 (0.024)	−0.157 (0.005)
HQ^2 (6)	−0.025 (0.836)	−0.104 (0.055)	−0.078 (0.518)	−0.037 (0.199)	−0.144 (0.034)	−0.153 (0.005)

Superscripts [a] and [b] indicate 1% and 5% significance levels. The provinces studied are Ankara, Antalya, Bursa, Eskişehir, Istanbul, İzmir, Kocaeli, Muğla, Tekirdağ, Denizli, and Sakarya

substantial evidence to suggest that the mean differences in educational attainment across the population are significantly distinct, as evidenced by the gross ANOVA F-test ($F = 340.4595$, $p < 0.0001$) and the Welch F-test ($F = 304.5250$, $p < 0.0001$).

We further compared the significant differences in the mean education levels across the two groups, namely, primary and lower secondary education. The finding reveals a weak yet significant difference between those who acquired only primary education and those who acquired lower secondary school education, as indicated by the t-test result of −1.8407 with a p-value of 0.0621. In contrast, a significant difference exists between those with lower secondary education and those with upper secondary school certificates, as indicated by a t-test value of −4.9203 with a p-value of 0.0000. There is also a significant difference between those who acquired upper secondary certificates and those with bachelor's degrees, as predicted by a t-test with a p-value of 0.0005. Furthermore, a significant difference exists between those with bachelor's and master's degrees, as predicted by a t-test value of 17.0937 with a p-value =0.0000. Finally, a significant difference exists between master's and PhD degrees, as predicted by a t-test value of 10.2854 with a p-value = 0.0000. In contrast, the mean difference between primary and lower secondary education shows a weak yet significant difference. This further emphasises that at least a secondary school certificate is required to predict an increase in Turkish HPI.

Table 4 illustrates the correlation between demographic changes and the Turkish House Price Index (HPI). The results indicate that most demographic alterations established positive and statistically significant associations with the Turkish HPI. The relationship between the HPI and residential property sales is significant across all demographic variables. This suggests that an educational attainment exceeding a primary school certificate is necessary to establish a meaningful long-term relationship between residential sales and the Turkish HPI. Consequently, it is inferred that higher education plays a pivotal role in propelling the Turkish HPI upwards. This suggests that individuals with higher levels of education are more likely to prefer renting properties that align with their preferences, and the incorporation of value-added features may contribute to an increase in housing prices.

It is noteworthy that the household size unit establishes a significant relationship with the Turkish House Price Index (HPI) for individuals possessing master's and PhD degrees but not for those with other degrees. This suggests that individuals with master's and PhD degrees are perceived as owning their residences, as they may have chosen to live independently of their parents. This is regarded as the return on their educational investment. Numerous studies from both developed nations (e.g. Australia and the United States) and developing nations (e.g. Türkiye and Malaysia) have shown that education level constitutes a pivotal demographic change that warrants attention, as it significantly contributes to the rise in HPI through its positive associations (Bampinas et al., 2017; Reed, 2016; Tan, 2021). This finding is corroborated by Reed's (2016) assertion that household profiles have a significant influence on their housing decisions. Furthermore, population size exhibits a substantial positive long-term relationship with the Turkish HPI, except for populations possessing only primary school education. This suggests that as the population increases, the Turkish HPI is likely to rise, implying a higher demand for housing in the long run, as many individuals may prefer to either own or rent their homes. The COVID-19 pandemic and the February 2023 earthquake have exerted a notable positive influence on the Turkish HPI, indicating that the pandemic has contributed to the upward trend in the Turkish HPI (Aliefendioğlu et al., 2021; Salami et al., 2022, 2023).

5 General Evaluation and Conclusion

Population growth, the number of households, household income, employment, production, and access to economic resources—all considered in socio-economic development calculations—are critical indicators for analysing the real estate market. Consequently, the interaction between a region's socio-economic conditions and its real estate market is crucial. Given that official data on the housing market is accessible, housing market data has been used in comparisons with socio-economic development indicators. The housing market constitutes a fundamental component of the construction and real estate sectors, and the findings are generally deemed applicable to other forms of real estate as well. In examining Türkiye's socio-economic development status, it becomes apparent that significant disparities exist among provinces, which are likewise reflected in real estate markets.

The influence of socio-economic development on the real estate market in Türkiye has been examined by comparing the development scores of provinces calculated in 2017 with per capita housing sales and sales methods in the same year. A strong positive correlation was identified between the socio-economic development score and the per capita housing sales ratio. In contrast, a more pronounced positive correlation was found between socio-economic development and the ratio of mortgage housing sales. Furthermore, the quantity of first-hand housing sales was analysed to assess the relationship between newly constructed housing stock and socio-economic development. A positive, albeit weak, correlation was identified between the socio-economic development score and the per capita ratio of first-hand housing sales.

Alterations in housing demand and the real estate market in Türkiye have been noted due to shifting demographic and economic factors. Between the early 2000s and the 2010s, extensive housing projects were undertaken in Türkiye, during which initial housing sales accounted for a predominant share of total transactions. However, since 2018, due to escalating financial challenges, the proportion of initial housing sales within total housing transactions has begun to decline. Elevated interest rates and declining consumer confidence have made access to credit and the acquisition of new homes increasingly challenging. Considering the current elevated interest rates and deteriorating economic conditions, the persistent decline in initial housing sales, which has been observable since 2018, is expected to continue for several additional years. Indeed, the study conducted by Öztürk et al. (2018) emphasised that interest rates on housing loans and income levels exert a significant influence on housing demand. Nonetheless, variables such as population, household numbers, and average household size exhibit variation across cities within the nation, as do the quality and quantity of building stock, the occurrence of informal housing areas and structurally unsafe buildings, the status of urban transformation initiatives, and, consequently, per capita income, expenditure, and levels of housing accessibility. Therefore, it is reasonable to expect that the results derived from econometric analysis at the national level will differ at the provincial and regional levels.

In Türkiye, the data pertaining to the monitoring and evaluation of supply and demand parameters, vacant and rental property stock, and actual rental and sales values is inadequate for both the national and regional levels. In this regard, investment decisions at the micro-level are frequently made without the execution of comprehensive market research and feasibility studies prior to the development and implementation of projects. Consequently, an effective connection between the demands and preferences of potential customers and the characteristics of the project is not established. This results in overall weak interactions between supply and demand. Market research is an indispensable step in comprehending the preferences and behaviours of potential customers and in designing projects that respond to these needs. Nevertheless, in emerging markets such as Türkiye, such research is either not conducted at all or is performed superficially. Furthermore, issues on both the supply and demand sides of the housing market are influenced by several factors, including construction costs, access to credit, inflation, household incomes, rents, leasing conditions, and housing prices.

According to the results of the econometric analysis, a cointegration analysis was conducted at the national level between the House Price Index and demographic data. The research findings indicate that most demographic changes are positively and significantly correlated with the Turkish House Price Index (HPI). The results of the analysis reveal that demographic factors, particularly education and population growth, exert a long-term positive impact on housing prices in Türkiye. The level of education has emerged as a key factor in the housing market, and it is understood that individuals with a higher level of education both demand higher quality housing and contribute to price increases over the long term. Furthermore, external events such as pandemics and natural disasters increase volatility and demand in the housing market, thereby affecting the market's dynamics.

Real estate markets exhibit greater activity in regions and provinces characterised by higher socio-economic development in Türkiye. In other words, a larger number of real estate market transactions are conducted in proportion to the population. Furthermore, socio-economic development gives rise to specific disparities within real estate markets concerning real estate financing. Provinces ranked higher in terms of development experience elevated rates of mortgaged housing sales, whereas those ranked lower exhibit a comparatively smaller number of mortgaged transactions. This suggests that financial institutions are more frequently preferred for real estate financing in areas demonstrating higher levels of socio-economic development in Türkiye. Conversely, in provinces with lower socio-economic development, the preference for financial institutions in the context of real estate acquisition is smaller. There is a pressing need to enhance housing accessibility for middle- and lower-income households through the adoption of alternative financial models for shelter and housing acquisition.

References

Adams, Z., & Füss, R. (2010). Macroeconomic determinants of international housing markets. *Journal of Housing Economics, 19*(1), 38–50.

Akşahin, S. (2008). *Avrupa Birliği'nin Bölgesel Politikası, Yapısal Araçların Koordinasyonu ve Türkiye'nin Uyumu*. AB Uzmanlık Tezi.

Aliefendioğlu, Y., Tanrıvermiş, H., & Salami, M. A. (2021). House Price index (HPI) and Covid-19 pandemic shocks: Evidence from Turkey and Kazakhstan. *International Journal of Housing Markets and Analysis, 15*(1), 108–125. https://doi.org/10.1108/IJHMA-10-2020-0126

Aydın, İ., & Tuğrul, B. (2022). Türkiye Eğitim Verisinin OECD Ülkeleri ile Karşılaştırılması. In *SETSCI Conference Proceedings*, Vol. 14, pp. 1–7.
Bampinas, G., Konstantinou, P., & Panagiotidis, T. (2017). Inequality, demographics and the housing wealth effect: Panel quantile regression evidence for the US. *Finance Research Letters, 23*, 19–22. https://doi.org/10.1016/j.frl.2017.01.001
Bardhan, A., Edelstein, R., & Tsang, D. (2007). Global financial integration and real estate security returns. *Real Estate Economics, 36*(2), 285–311.
Bayraktar, C. (2003). Sosyal Yapı Özelliklerinin Spora Etkisi. *Uludağ Üniversitesi Eğitim Fakültesi Dergisi, 16*(1), 19–36.
Bramley, G., & Watkins, D. (2016). Housebuilding, demographic change and affordability as outcomes of local planning decisions: Exploring interactions using a sub-regional model of housing Markets in England. *Progress in Planning, 104*, 1–35. https://doi.org/10.1016/j.progress.2014.10.002
Case, K. E., & Shiller, R. J. (2003). Is there a bubble in the housing market? *Brookings Papers on Economic Activity, 2003*(2), 299–362.
Case, E. K., Quigley, J. M., & Shiller, R. (2005). Department of Economics. *The Berkeley Electronic Press, 5*(1), 1–29.
Das, A. (1999). Socio-economic development in India: A regional analysis. *Development and Society, 28*(2), 313–345.
Dincer, B., Özaslan, M., & Kavasoğlu, T. (2003). *İllerin ve Bölgelerin Sosyo-Ekonomik Gelişmişlik Sıralaması Araştırması*. DPT-BGYUGM.
Dinler, Z. (2008). *Bölgesel İktisat*. Ekin Kitabevi Yayınları.
Égert, B., & Mihaljek, D. (2007). Determinants of house prices in central and Eastern Europe. *Comparative Economic Studies, 49*, 367–388.
Fuchs, V. R. (2004). Sağlığın sosyo-ekonomik bağıntıları üzerine düşünceler. *Sağlık ekonomisi dergisi, 23*(4), 653–661.
Goodhart, C., & Hofmann, B. (2007). *House prices and the macroeconomy: Implications for banking and price stability*. Oxford University Press.
Grum, B., & Govekar, D. K. (2016). Influence of macroeconomic factors on prices of real estate in various cultural environments: case of Slovenia, Greece, France, Poland and Norway. *Procedia Economics and Finance, 39*, 597–604.
Gueye, G. N. (2021). Pitfalls in the cointegration analysis of housing prices with the macroeconomy: Evidence from OECD countries. *Journal of Housing Economics, 51*(4), 1–14. https://doi.org/10.1016/j.jhe.2021.101748
Hon-Chung, H. (2009). The impact of property market developments on Malaysia's real economy. *International Research Journal of Finance and Economics, 30*, 66–86.
Just, T. (2013). *Demografie und Immobilien* (2nd ed.). Odenbourg Verlag.
Kaynak, M. (2009). *Kalkınma İktisadı, Gözden Geçirilmiş ve Genişletilmiş 3. Baskı*. Gazi Kitabevi.
Keskin, B. (2008). Hedonic analysis of prices in the Istanbul housing market. *International Journal of Strategic Property Management, 12*, 125–138.
Lu, Q., Farooq, M. U., Ma, X., & Iram, R. (2022). Assessing the combined role of public-private investment in achieving green finance and renewable energy for carbon neutrality targets. *Renewable Energy, 196*, 1357–1365. https://doi.org/10.1016/j.renene.2022.06.072
Ludwig, A., & Slok, T. (2004). The relationship between stock prices, house prices and consumption in OECD countries. *Sonderforschungsbereireich, 504*, 1–26.
Malpezzi, S. (1999). A simple error correction model of house prices. *Journal of Housing Economics, 8*(1), 27–62.
Mankiw, N. G., & Weil, D. N. (1989). The baby boom, the baby bust, and the housing market. *Regional Science and Urban Economics, 19*(2), 235–258.
Metin Özcan, K., Üçdoğruk Birecikli, Ş., Ünlü, M., & Öktem Özgür, A. (2021). Economic and demographic determinants of overtime in the Turkish private sector. *International Journal of Working Conditions, 22*, 1–19. https://doi.org/10.25762/813y-vk56
Mutlu, E., & Varol, Ç. (2017). Sosyo-Ekonomik Farklılaşma ve Mekânsal Ayrışma: Bursa Metropoliten Alanı Analizi. *MEGARON, 12*(1), 87–105.

Ovsiannikova, T. Y., Rabtsevich, O. V., & Yugova, I. V. (2021). Analysis of housing investment market dynamics impact on social and economic development. *IOP Conference Series: Earth and Environmental Science, 666*, 062088. https://doi.org/10.1088/1755-1315/666/6/062088

Özaslan, M., Dincer, B., & Özgür, H. (2006). *Regional disparities and territorial indicators in Turkey: Socio-economic development index (SEDI), European regional science association (ERSA) conference paper, Volos, Greece.*

Özdemir, A. İ., & Altıparmak, A. (2005). Sosyo-ekonomik göstergeler açısından illerin gelişmişlik düzeylerinin karşılaştırmalı analizi. *Erciyes Üniversitesi İktisadi ve İdari Bilimler Fakültesi Dergisi, 24*, 97–110.

Öztürk, A., Kapusuz, Y. E., & Tanrıvermiş, H. (2018). The dynamics of housing affordability and housing demand analysis in Ankara. *International Journal of Housing Markets and Analysis, 11*(5), 828–851.

Quigley, M. J. (1999). Real estate prices and economic cycles. *International Real Estate Review, 2*(1), 1–20.

Reed, R. (2016). The relationship between house prices and demographic variables an Australian case study. *International Journal of Housing Markets and Analysis, 9*(4), 520–537. https://doi.org/10.1108/IJHMA-02-2016-0013

Ruan, F.-L., & Yan, L. (2022). Interactions among electricity consumption, disposable income, wastewater discharge, and economic growth: Evidence from megacities in China from 1995 to 2018. *Energy, 260*(1), 1–9. https://doi.org/10.1016/j.energy.2022.124910

Sakarya, A., & İbişoğlu, Ç. (2015). Türkiye'de İllerin Sosyo-Ekonomik Gelişmişlik Endeksinin Coğrafi Ağırlıklı Regresyon Modeli ile Analizi. *Marmara Coğrafya Dergisi, 32*, 211–238.

Salami, M. A., Tanrıvermiş, H., & Tanrıvermiş, Y. (2022). Performance evaluation and volatility of Turkey REITs during the COVID-19 pandemic. *Journal of Property Investment and Finance, 1*(1), 1–33. https://doi.org/10.1108/JPIF-02-2022-0017

Salami, M. A., Tanrıvermiş, H., & Aliefendioğlu, Y. (2023). Interdependence between foreigner housing acquisitions and housing price increase in Turkey during the COVID-19 pandemic era. *International Journal of Housing Markets and Analysis, 16*(3), 575–597. https://doi.org/10.1108/IJHMA-08-2022-0109

T.C. Sanayi ve Teknoloji Bakanlığı. (2017). *İllerin ve Bölgelerin Sosyo-Ekonomik Gelişmişlik Sıralaması Araştırması SEGE-2017*. Website. Retrieved September 30, 2022, from https://www.bebka.org.tr/admin/datas/sayfas/89/sege-2017_1581687211.pdf

T.C. Sanayi ve Teknoloji Bakanlığı. (2022). Web Sitesi. Retrieved September 30, 2022, from https://www.sanayi.gov.tr/merkez-birimi/b94224510b7b/sege

Tan, C. (2021). A study of boundedly rational behaviour in housing choice: Evidence from Malaysia. *International Journal of Housing Markets and Analysis, 1*, 1–16. https://doi.org/10.1108/IJHMA-08-2021-0094

Tanrıvermiş, H. (2019). Türkiye Ekonomisinde İnşaat ve Gayrimenkul Sektörlerinin Rolleri ve Gelişme Eğilimlerinin Değerlendirilmesi (Assessment of the roles of construction and real estate sectors and their development trends in Turkey). In *Proceedings of Kent, İnşaat ve Ekonomi Kongresi, 2–4 Mayıs 2019, TMMOB Mimarlar Odası Gaziantep Şubesi, Gaziantep*, pp. 36–57.

Tanrıvermiş, Y. (2021). Türkiye'de Yaşlı Yabancı Göçü ve Gayrimenkul Edinimi. In A. Özkan & G. Taşçı (Eds.), *Göç: Disiplinlerarası Bakış Açısıyla* (pp. 355–390). Nobel Yayıncılık.

Tanrıvermiş, H., & Bülbül, M. (2007). The role of agriculture in Turkish economy at the beginning of the European Union accession negotiations. *Journal of Applied Sciences, 7*(4), 612–625.

Tanrıvermiş, H., & Gündoğan, S. (2021). Göç ve Ekonomi. In A. Özkan & G. Taşçı (Eds.), *Göç: Disiplinlerarası Bakış Açısıyla* (pp. 47–86). Nobel Yayıncılık.

Turhan, Y. (2020). Kalkınma Kavramının Tarihsel Süreci ve Etimolojik Analizi. *Uluslararası İktisadi ve İdari İncelemeler Dergisi, 29*, 149–164.

Turkish Statistical Institute (TURKSTAT). (2022a). *Türkiye İstatistik Kurumu*. Web Sitesi. Retrieved October 01, 2022, from https://data.tuik.gov.tr/Search/Search?text=konut%20sat%C4%B1%C5%9F%20say%C4%B1lar%C4%B1

Turkish Statistical Institute (TURKSTAT). (2022b). *Türkiye İstatistik Kurumu*. Web Sitesi. Retrieved October 01, 2022, from https://biruni.tuik.gov.tr/medas/?kn=95&locale=tr
Turkish Statistical Institute (TURKSTAT). (2022c). *Sağlık İstatistikleri Yıllığı 2020 Haber Bülteni*. Web Sitesi. Retrieved October 09, 2022, from https://sbsgm.saglik.gov.tr/Eklenti/41611/0/haber-bulteni-2020pdf.pdf
Turkish Statistical Institute (TURKSTAT). (2024a). *Türkiye İstatistik Kurumu*. Web Sitesi. Retrieved September 09, 2024, from https://data.tuik.gov.tr/Search/Search?text=ya%C5%9F%20gru
Turkish Statistical Institute (TURKSTAT). (2024b). *Türkiye İstatistik Kurumu*. Web Sitesi. Retrieved September 09, 2024, from https://data.tuik.gov.tr/Search/Search?text=i%C5%9F%20gelirleri
Turkish Statistical Institute (TURKSTAT). (2025). *Türkiye İstatistik Kurumu*. Web Sitesi. Retrieved March 03, 2025, from https://data.tuik.gov.tr/
Türkseven, D. N. (2020). *Sosyal Sermaye ile Kalkınma İlişkisi: Ulusal ve Bölgesel Düzeyde Mukayeseli Analiz*. (Doktora Tezi). Sakarya Üniversitesi Sosyal Bilimler Enstitüsü.
Uçkan, M. (2019). *Gaziantep ilinin sosyo-ekonomik yapısının analizi. Hasan Kalyoncu Üniversitesi Sosyal Bilimler Enstitüsü İktisat Anabilim Dalı*, Master's thesis.
Wang, P. (2003). A frequency domain analysis of common cycles in property and related sectors. *The Journal of Real Estate Research, 25*(3), 325–346.
Wang, X. (2007). *Who's in first? A regional development index for the People's Republic of China's provinces*. ADB Institute Discussion Paper, No. 66, Metro Manila.
Yıldız, E., Sivri, U., & Berber, M. (2012). Türkiye'de illerin sosyoekonomik gelişmişlik sıralaması (2010). *Erciyes Üniversitesi İktisadi ve İdari Bilimler Fakültesi Dergisi, 39*, 147–167.
Zhang, Y. L., & Wu, J. (2008). Study on the periodic correlation between the real estate market and the stock market in China. *Chinese Real Estate*, 29–31.

Harun Tanrıvermiş is a distinguished professor who occupies the esteemed position at the Ankara University top management level as founder and head of the Department of Real Estate Development and Management, and founder and current dean of the Faculty of Applied Sciences at Ankara University. Professor Tanrıvermiş also currently works as the vice rector at Ankara University. He attained his B.Sc., M.Sc., and Ph.D. degrees from the Department of Agricultural Economics at Ankara University, specialising in land and real estate economics, land and real estate valuation, as well as natural resources and environmental economics. Furthermore, he earned an M.Sc. in environmental management through the MED-CAMPUS Programme in 1996. Professor Tanrıvermiş has published approximately 400 papers, including 43 international and 55 national peer-reviewed articles, which have been published in various high-impact journals. Additionally, he has presented 48 international and 74 national proceedings, either in full or as abstracts, at numerous conferences. He is also credited with writing 39 books and 17 book chapters. Moreover, his works concentrate on the land and real estate valuation, land and real estate economics, real estate development and project appraisal, urban transformation and sustainability, sustainable real estate development, facility and real estate management, land management, administration and polices, measuring and reporting of real estate sustainability and ESG, digital transformation in real estate and real estate technologies.

Monsurat Ayojimi Salami is an assistant professor in the Department of Real Estate Development and Management, Faculty of Applied Sciences, Ankara University, Türkiye. She graduated from the International Islamic University Malaysia (IIUM) and served as a Postdoc fellow between 2018 and 2019 at the IIUM Institute of Islamic Banking and Finance (II*i*BF). She specialises in the fields of financial economics, Islamic finance, real estate finance and investment, digitalisation in real estate, tokenisation, smart contracts and proptech. She holds multiple international certifications, including the Certified Quantitative Risk Management (CQRM). She has made significant contributions to over 50 academic publications indexed in prestigious databases such as the Social Sciences Citation Index (SSCI), Scopus, and the Emerging Sources Citation Index (ESCI). Her research predominantly focuses on financial inclusion, sustainable finance, risk management, and the application of Islamic financial instruments. Additionally, she has co-authored several chapters in academic books published by renowned international publishers, including Edward Elgar, Springer and Routledge. She has participated as a member of the scientific committee at various global conferences concerning Islamic finance and real estate.

Abdurrahman Tursun currently serves as a research assistant at the Department of Real Estate Development and Management, Faculty of Applied Sciences, Ankara University. He completed M.Sc. and Ph.D. programs in the field of Real Estate Development and Management at Ankara University. He obtained his bachelor's degree in mathematics from Sakarya University. His research interests encompass housing markets, system dynamics, real estate valuation, and alternative financing models. Dr. Tursun has authored a substantial number of academic publications, which include peer-reviewed journal articles, book chapters, and conference proceedings. Furthermore, he has participated as a member of the organising committee for various international conferences.

Facts and Figures of Real Estate in Türkiye: Data Sources and Institutional Framework

Tuğba Güneş, Sibel Canaz Sevgen, and Mehmet Ülger

Abstract

Public and private sector organisations in Türkiye have achieved notable advancements in enhancing data quality and transparency within the real estate sector, propelled by technological innovations. This chapter delineates the scope and quality of critical data sources in Türkiye. It elaborates on the public institutions tasked with collecting, producing, and disseminating statistics pertaining to real estate. Furthermore, the chapter analyses macroeconomic and social indicators pertinent to the real estate sector, including housing stock, construction activities, land registry, transaction data, as well as information concerning mortgage loans and real estate-backed financial instruments. Additionally, it encapsulates data on real estate and rental prices furnished by both public and private institutions.

Keywords

Official statistics · Data sources · Real estate price index · Real estate data

1 Introduction

Real estate prices, value appreciation, a country's socio-economic conditions, the legal framework, and environmental factors significantly influence investment decisions. Access to comprehensive, reliable, and transparent data of high quality and currency has become essential for investors. Türkiye boasts an active property market, averaging two million transactions annually, and attracts both domestic and

T. Güneş (✉) · S. C. Sevgen · M. Ülger
Department of Real Estate Development and Management, Faculty of Applied Sciences, Ankara University, Ankara, Türkiye
e-mail: gunest@ankara.edu.tr; ssevgen@ankara.edu.tr; mehmet.ulger@ankara.edu.tr

T. Just et al. (eds.), *Understanding Türkiye's Real Estate Markets*, Management for Professionals, https://doi.org/10.1007/978-3-032-13297-0_6

foreign investors. While public institutions serve as the primary data sources for the real estate sector and related industries, the private sector also gathers and supplies information about property and rental prices, as well as statistics regarding construction and real estate activities nationwide. This chapter reviews the public institutions in Türkiye that disseminate data and statistics pertinent to the real estate sector. Subsequently, it summarises the key data sources related to real estate prices, including contributions from both the public and private sectors.

2 Authorities Responsible for Official Statistics on Real Estate

Official statistics in Türkiye are collected, analysed, produced, and disseminated by the Turkish Statistical Institute (TURKSTAT) (*Türkiye İstatistik Kurumu* (TÜİK)) (TURKSTAT) within the framework of the Official Statistics Programme (OSP). The OSP has been developed over five years to establish fundamental principles and standards for official statistics and is published at both the national and international levels. The stakeholder institutions delineated in the OSP (TURKSTAT, 2021) are mandated to collaborate in the production of statistics. In collaboration with TURKSTAT, ministries, affiliated agencies, municipalities, and other public institutions also engage in the creation and dissemination of a diverse array of statistics, both within and beyond the scope of the OSP. A summary of the primary institutions responsible for producing statistics on real estate markets is provided below.

1. The General Directorate of Civil Registration and Citizenship Affairs, a division of the Ministry of Interior (İçişleri Bakanlığı), has instituted an information system entitled the "Address Registration System" to manage the addresses of Turkish citizens as well as foreign individuals residing in Türkiye. In 2011, the National Address Database (*Ulusal Adres Veri Tabanı* (UAVT)) was superseded by the Spatial Address Registry System (*Mekânsal Adres Kayıt Sistemi* (MAKS)). Subsequently, it has been refined by correlating addresses with their geocoordinates (Spatial Address Registry System (Mekânsal Adres Kayıt Sistemi)). The MAKS also promotes the concurrent development and/or enhancement of various other pertinent information systems and databases.
2. The General Directorate for Land Registry and Cadastre (GLDRC) (*Tapu ve Kadastro Genel Müdürlüğü* (TKGM)) (General Directorate for Land Registry and Cadastre (Tapu ve Kadastro Genel Müdürlüğü)), functioning under the authority and supervision of the Ministry of Environment, Urbanisation and Climate Change is formally entrusted with the responsibilities of maintaining property registry data, facilitating real estate transactions, and producing housing sales statistics.
3. Municipalities systematically maintain statistics related to building construction and occupancy permits, architectural projects, zoning development plans, and supplementary information. This data is stored in digital format within munici-

palities that are equipped with "Urban Information System" tools. Land tax values are established by ad hoc property valuation commissions operating within these municipalities, while real estate tax values are documented in the pertinent municipality's records (Güneş & Yıldız, 2016; Töremen, 2020).

4. The Turkish Statistical Institute (TURKSTAT) is tasked with disseminating construction statistics and executing the Population and Housing Census within the country (TURKSTAT, 2021).
5. The Central Bank of the Republic of Türkiye (*Türkiye Cumhuriyet Merkez Bankası* (TCMB)) constructs the Residential and Commercial Property Price Indices (CBRT, 2024b, 2024c).
6. The Central Securities Depository and Trade Repository of Türkiye (*Merkezi Kayıt Kuruluşu* (MKK)) functions as the principal registry and securities depository in Türkiye. This financial institution is tasked with the collection and management of data pertaining to capital markets within a singular centralised system (Central Securities Depository and Trade Repository of Türkiye (Merkezi Kayıt Kuruluşu - MKK)). Information concerning real estate-backed financial assets, including real estate certificates, lease certificates, covered bonds, mortgage-backed securities, and real estate investment funds and trusts, is conveyed to the MKK.

3 Real Estate Market Data in Official Statistics

3.1 Macroeconomic and Social Indicators

Fundamental macroeconomic indicators, such as economic growth, inflation, foreign trade volumes, foreign direct investment, production volumes, and other industry-related data, as well as socio-economic indicators, including demographic development, education levels, health-related data, and data on housing, are published by the Turkish Statistical Institute (TURKSTAT) and the Central Bank of the Republic of Türkiye (CBRT). The Banking Regulation and Supervision Agency (BRSA, or *Bankacılık Düzenleme ve Denetleme Kurumu* (BDDK)) and the Capital Markets Board (CMB, or *Sermaye Piyasası Kurulu* (SPK)) are tasked with the regulation of banking and capital markets while disseminating pertinent data. Furthermore, various public institutions collect data relevant to their domains of activity and share it with appropriate entities and stakeholders. The enhancement of accessibility and transparency has been achieved through the implementation of sophisticated information systems and extensive databases.

Information concerning the residences of Turkish citizens and foreigners residing in Türkiye is reconciled with the population registers by utilising identification numbers and address codes through TURKSTAT's Address-Based Population Registration System (*Adrese Dayalı Nüfus Kayıt Sistemi* (ADNKS)). Demographic data, encompassing total population, gender, age, marital status, household size, respective growth rates, internal and external migration patterns, and population projections, is publicly accessible on the TURKSTAT website. The integration of the ADNKS and MAKS systems with TURKSTAT's other ongoing projects and collaborations with stakeholder institutions will facilitate access to real estate data and relevant information, thereby enabling accurate estimates and housing demand projections at the local level. The development of the Population Attributes Database by TURKSTAT is currently underway and will provide additional socio-economic information. Data related to residence permits and international or temporary protection statuses for foreigners is maintained in the Migration Registration System (GöçNet) within the framework of the Presidency of Migration Management. Initiatives to ensure the regular transfer of GöçNet data to TURKSTAT are in progress (TURKSTAT, 2021).

Labour statistics are generated in accordance with the classifications of economic activities, occupations, and sectors established by the Turkish Statistical Institute (TURKSTAT). Labour statistics offer pertinent information concerning workforce capacity and variations in employment trends pertaining to the real estate and construction sectors, derived from TURKSTAT's economic classifications. This data serves as a vital source of indicators for real estate prices and their trends.

The CBRT disseminates data regarding interest rates, the weighted average mortgage rates offered by banks, exchange rates, foreign trade, and foreign direct investments, as well as property price indices and public finance (CBRT, 2024a).

3.2 Housing Stock and Construction Sector Data

The construction sector represents one of the foremost industries in Türkiye. Over the past decade, it has, on average, contributed approximately 6.5% to Türkiye's gross domestic product (GDP). Data pertaining to the construction sector, as part of the Official Statistics Programme, is presented in Table 1 (TURKSTAT, 2021).

The MAKS has initiated the process of gathering data on the characteristics of all buildings (e.g. size, number of rooms, and geo-coordinates) throughout the nation. Following the establishment of the MAKS, a "Building and Housing Registration System" will be developed based on this framework. Furthermore, the European Union advises that nations undertake a "population and housing census" in years that conclude with the digit "0" to account for the entire population and housing inventory of a country. Due to the limited availability of data sources, TURKSTAT surveyed in 2021 to collect information on "Building and Dwelling Characteristics" and published the findings in December 2022 (TURKSTAT, 2022).

Figure 1 illustrates the number of construction permits for dwellings and the number of occupancy permits over the past decade. Additional housing supply significantly declined between 2018 and 2020, with construction permits falling below the number of occupancy permits for the first time during this period. While the number of dwellings that were granted occupancy permits was nearly 1.4 million in 2017, it decreased to 670,000 in 2018 and further to 320,000 in 2019. Despite the gradual increase observed since 2020, it is apparent that the housing supply in the past four years is unlikely to meet the housing demand in the forthcoming years, considering that the annual average of newly constructed dwellings between 2012

Table 1 Construction data and sources

	Frequency of dissemination	Institution
Building permit statistics (occupancy and construction permits)	Quarterly	TURKSTAT (TURKSTAT Central Data Delivery System (TÜİK Merkezi Dağıtım Sistemi))
Construction sector labour input indices	Quarterly	TURKSTAT (TURKSTAT Central Data Delivery System (TÜİK Merkezi Dağıtım Sistemi))
Construction turnover index	Monthly	TURKSTAT (TURKSTAT Central Data Delivery System (TÜİK Merkezi Dağıtım Sistemi))
Construction cost index	Monthly	TURKSTAT (TURKSTAT Central Data Delivery System (TÜİK Merkezi Dağıtım Sistemi))
House sales statistics	Monthly	TURKSTAT (TURKSTAT Central Data Delivery System (TÜİK Merkezi Dağıtım Sistemi))
Residential property Price index	Monthly	Central Bank (CBRT, 2024a)
Commercial property Price index	Quarterly	Central Bank (CBRT, 2024a)

Source: Own depiction

and 2017 was approximately one million, while demand continues to rise. This trend is also evident in the statistics regarding house sales: the share of new housing transactions relative to total house sales was 47% in 2018 but decreased to 31% by the close of 2023 (TURKSTAT Central Data Delivery System (TÜİK Merkezi Dağıtım Sistemi)) (Fig. 2).

One of the primary factors contributing to the decline in housing supply is the substantial increase in construction costs that has transpired since the latter half of 2020. While the annual growth rate of construction costs at the end of 2020 was 25% per year, it escalated to 67.8% by the end of 2021 and reached a peak annualised rate of 119.8% by the end of the fourth quarter of 2022 (TURKSTAT Central Data Delivery System (TÜİK Merkezi Dağıtım Sistemi)). This escalation was accompanied by deteriorating exchange rates (see Fig. 3), which impacted material and labour costs.

In conjunction with the COVID-19 pandemic and the escalation of energy costs impacting nearly all nations, unfavourable conditions within the national economy in recent years—including the substantial depreciation of the Turkish lira (TL), the unavoidable contraction in purchasing power attributable to rising inflation, and rapid increases in raw material and labour costs—have instigated a negative chain reaction within the Turkish economy. Notably, the surging construction costs have resulted in substantial increases in real estate prices (Fig. 8).

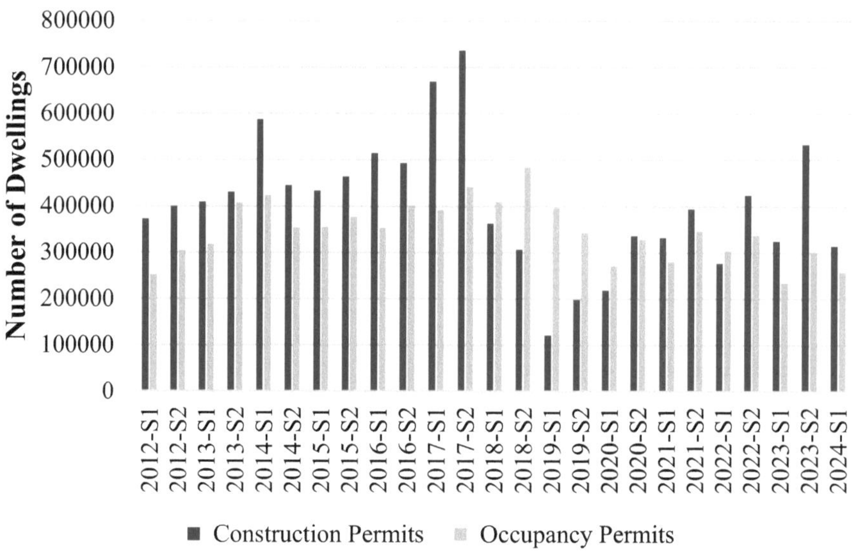

Fig. 1 Dwelling construction statistics. Source: Building permit statistics, Turkstat (TURKSTAT Central Data Delivery System (TÜİK Merkezi Dağıtım Sistemi))

3.3 Land Registry and Property Transaction Data

The TKGM serves as the public institution responsible for the execution and documentation of all property transactions.[1] Land registration and cadastral operations for properties nationwide are conducted, alongside the maintenance of relevant registers. The General Directorate of Land Registry and Cadastre (TKGM), which traces its origins to the Ottoman Empire, manages and operates through 81 cadastre offices and 973 land registry directorates, all functioning under the supervision of 23 regional directorates across the country. Cadastral data pertaining to all properties is digitally stored within the TKGM's Spatial Property System (*Mekânsal Gayrimenkul Sistemi* (MEGSIS)). Since 2012, descriptive information regarding properties and all property transactions—from sales to inheritance—has been maintained and processed by the Land Registry and Cadastre Information System (*Tapu ve Kadastro Bilgi Sistemi* (TAKBIS)). According to the current legislation, all land registry records for properties are retained in hard copy documents, including notebooks and land registry books (GDLRC, 2024a). The integration of TKGM's two information systems, TAKBIS and MEGSIS, is presently 99% complete (GDLRC, 2024b). TAKBIS and MEGSIS provide property owners with electronic access to information concerning their properties.

The descriptive information contained within the TAKBIS records encompasses various elements, including location data (such as province, district,

[1] Effective by the beginning of 2023, the law enabling real estate transactions to be conducted through notaries was enacted in June 2022.

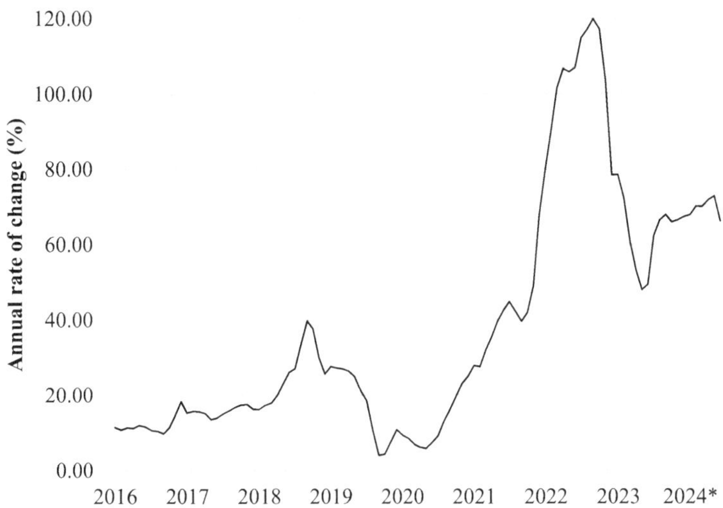

Fig. 2 Construction cost index (annual rate of change %) (**by the first half of 2024*). Source: Construction cost index, Turkstat (TURKSTAT Central Data Delivery System (TÜİK Merkezi Dağıtım Sistemi))

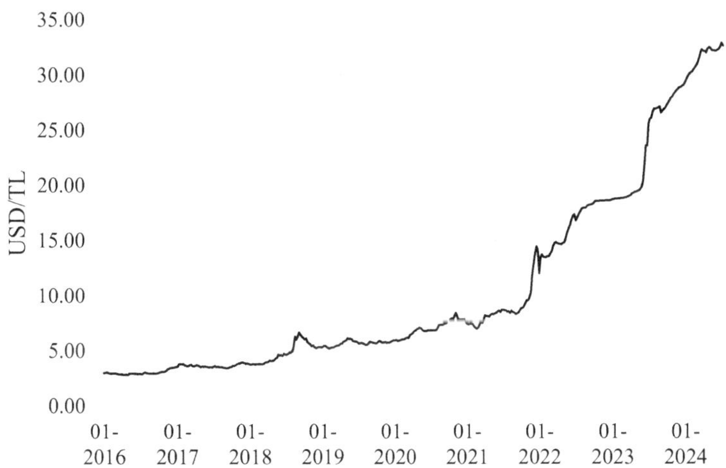

Fig. 3 US dollar/TL exchange rate (2016–2024). Source: CBRT (2024a)

neighbourhood, block, and parcel number, as well as individual unit number), lot size, purpose of acquisition, transaction date, and details pertaining to both current and previous property owners. Additionally, it includes rights and obligations (for instance, mortgages, easements, and seizures), alongside reported prices from sellers and property owners.

Significant deficiencies in data quality and standardisation persist. One of the primary challenges is that numerous data entries are conducted manually. For instance, property types lack standardisation due to typographical errors, the use of synonyms, or the inclusion of additional information regarding the property. Consequently, any statistics categorised by property type are generated by executing queries based on various assumptions. Another critical issue involves the inconsistencies between the current usage purpose and the property type listed in the official records. For example, a residential property documented in official records may be utilised as an office. The third major concern is that illegal constructions are inadequately documented. Notably, although unlawful buildings and individual units are not officially registered in the land registry, they receive all municipal services. This underscores the importance of integrating data from TKGM with data from municipalities and highlights the necessity for collaboration to address and rectify these issues (Güneş & Yıldız, 2016). Another significant limitation is the absence of data on the indoor characteristics of buildings (e.g. number of rooms, balcony, and elevator) and individual units within the official TKGM records. These features are documented for buildings constructed in the past two decades, as detailed in the hard copy architectural projects preserved in the archives of the land registry directorates. Copies of most architectural projects are also available in the municipalities. However, the archives do not house complete architectural projects, and most of the existing records are inaccessible through an electronic information system. Furthermore, the projects may not correspond with the properties' current usage due to renovations and/or alterations.

According to the TKGM records, Türkiye possesses 58 million parcels and boasts a highly active property market, with an annual average of approximately 2 million property transactions. The Residential Property Price Index, as reported by the Central Bank, reveals a substantial increase in house prices since 2020. Conversely, as illustrated in Fig. 4, an average of 1.4 million residential units have been sold annually over the past few years.

Simultaneously, home ownership rates have not increased; in fact, they have declined significantly according to the data from TURKSTAT. The home ownership rate in Türkiye has decreased from slightly above 61% in 2014 to 56.2% in 2023 (Fig. 5, TURKSTAT, 2024b). This suggests that current property acquisitions are primarily motivated by investment purposes rather than residential use while also indicating that affordability has emerged as a significant challenge for many private households in Türkiye.

TKGM provides comprehensive land registry information, including location, boundaries, and land size for all properties, through its ParselSorgu (ParcelQuery) application. Transacted properties are also represented on the map within ParselSorgu; access to this information incurs a fee. ParselSorgu is extensively used by real estate agents and the general public (Parcel Query App (Parsel Sorgu)).

In recent years, there has been a significant increase in property acquisitions by international homebuyers in Türkiye (Fig. 6, TURKSTAT, 2024c). Previously, property acquisitions in Türkiye were conducted on a reciprocal basis until 2022, whereby only citizens of countries that permitted Turkish nationals to purchase property within their own country were allowed to acquire property in Türkiye. This reciprocity requirement was abolished on May 12, 2012, thereby opening the

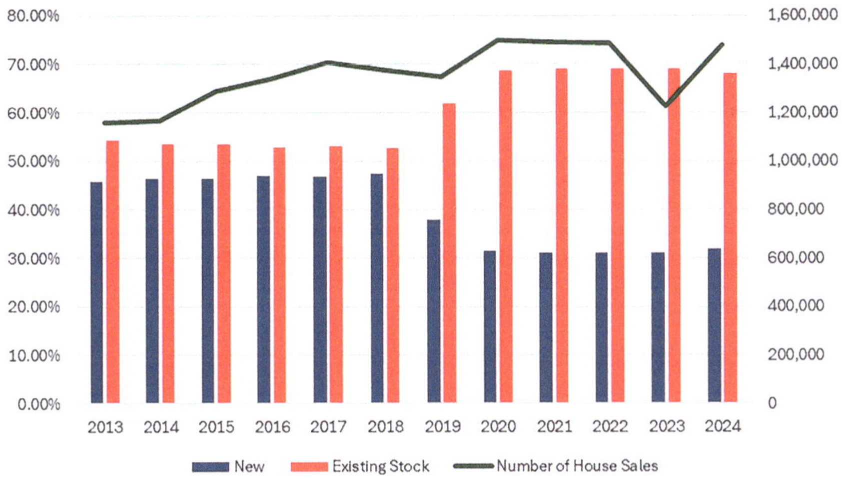

Fig. 4 House sales statistics (*by the first half of 2024). Source: House Sales Statistics, Turkstat (TURKSTAT Central Data Delivery System (TÜİK Merkezi Dağıtım Sistemi))

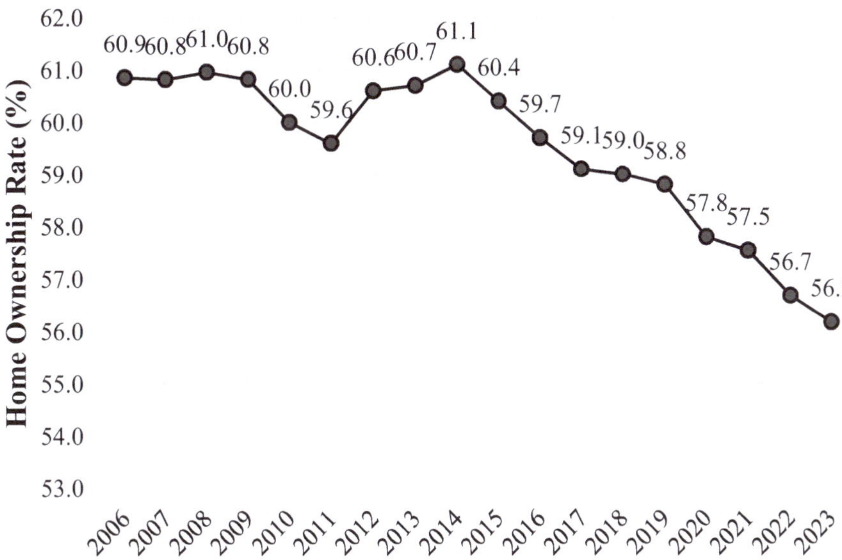

Fig. 5 Home ownership rate. Source: TURKSTAT (2024b)

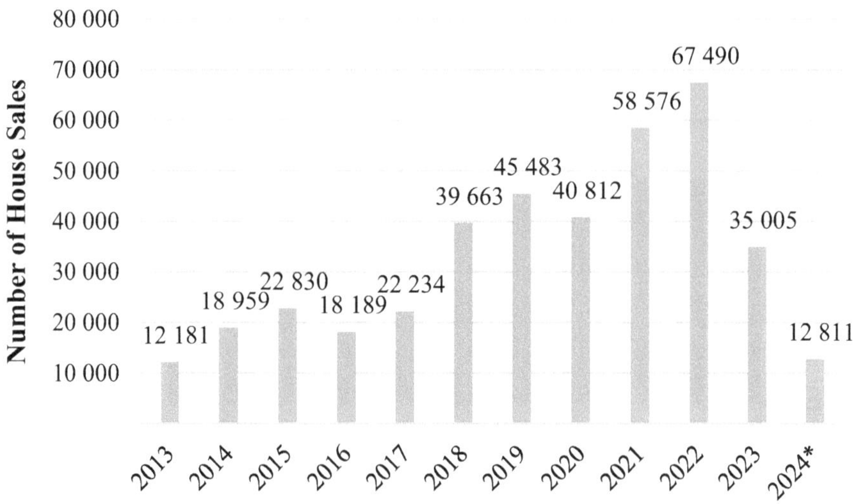

Fig. 6 Number of house sales by foreign buyers (*by the first half of 2024). Source: TURKSTAT (2024c)

Turkish property market to a broader foreign audience. As of January 12, 2017, Turkish citizenship was conferred upon foreigners who made a property investment valued at a minimum of USD 1 million and maintained it for three years. This investment threshold was subsequently reduced to USD 250,000 on September 19, 2018, and later increased to USD 400,000 on June 13, 2022. Citizenship through real estate investment programmes has facilitated the acquisition of properties by numerous foreigners in Türkiye. A significant demand has emerged from international investors in the southern and eastern regions of Türkiye seeking to purchase real estate. For these foreign homebuyers, Istanbul and Antalya are the most favoured provinces for property acquisition in Türkiye.

3.4 Mortgage Loans and Real Estate-Backed Financial Assets

The mortgage system in Türkiye remains relatively underdeveloped when compared to those in the United States and Western European countries. The initial step in establishing a contemporary mortgage framework in Türkiye was accomplished with the enactment of Law No. 5582 in 2007. Subsequently, the new Capital Market Law No. 6362, enacted in 2012, has provided the foundation for the current mortgage system and the legislative regulations governing financial instruments secured by real properties. Additionally, financial assets such as mortgage-backed securities, asset-backed securities, covered bonds, leases, and real estate certificates have been integrated into the legal framework.

Monthly statistics on house sales, encompassing both mortgaged and non-mortgaged transactions, are published by TURKSTAT and the Central Bank. The

Banking Regulation and Supervision Agency provides detailed information on consumer loan amounts, which includes mortgage loans, the total number of borrowers, and the ratio of non-performing loans. Additionally, the Central Securities Depository of the Turkish capital markets compiles and disseminates prospectuses for financial instruments, along with relevant data. Both the prospectuses and the monthly and annual summary statistics can be accessed on the Capital Market Board's website (Capital Market Board). Furthermore, data pertaining to assets and stock companies is also available through the Borsa Istanbul's (BIST) website.

Figure 7 illustrates a negative correlation between mortgage rates and the number of sales financed by mortgages, in line with expectations. Figure 7 presents the total number of housing sales, the proportion of mortgage-financed sales, and the average mortgage rates in Türkiye over the past decade. While the annual average of house sales constituted 30% of mortgage sales between 2013 and 2017, this proportion decreased to 20% in 2018.

The central government sought to lower mortgage rates by introducing two housing support schemes in June 2020 and May 2022. These initiatives facilitated an increase in household sales, encompassing both cash- and mortgage-financed transactions. Nonetheless, the expected rise in mortgage-financed sales has not materialised, attributed to significant inflationary pressures, escalating housing prices, and prevailing unfavourable economic conditions. Following the implementation of the housing support scheme in 2020, the proportion of mortgage-financed sales nearly doubled, reaching 38%. However, mortgage-financed sales experienced a precipitous decline, plummeting to 14.5% by 2023 (TURKSTAT Central Data Delivery System (TÜİK Merkezi Dağıtım Sistemi)).

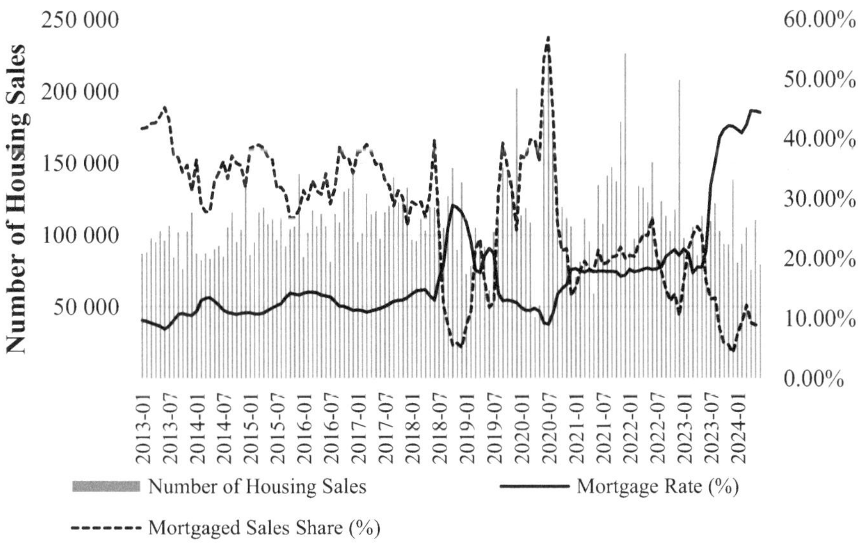

Fig. 7 House sales and average mortgage rates. Source: CBRT (2024a) and TURKSTAT Central Data Delivery System (TÜİK Merkezi Dağıtım Sistemi)

It is noteworthy that the volume of financial instruments backed by real estate has remained limited within Turkish capital markets. According to data from the Capital Markets Board, there are 53 Real Estate Investment Trusts (REITs), with a total volume of TL 396 billion, approximately equivalent to EUR 10 billion, and 150 real estate investment funds, possessing a total value of TL 82.5 billion, or approximately EUR 2 billion, as of the first quarter of 2024 (CMB, 2024b).

Additionally, lease certificates valued at TL 133 billion, approximately EUR 3.5 billion, were issued in 2023 (CMB, 2024a). The proportion of real estate certificates, mortgage-backed securities, and covered bonds within the capital market continues to be negligible. The presidential decree issued at the end of 2019, which involved the treasury's transfer of initial capital and participation in the establishment of a mortgage finance institution, constitutes a significant step towards fostering a broader securitisation of mortgage loans.

4 Real Estate Price Indices

4.1 Real Estate Prices in Official Records

According to the current legislation, specifically the Law on Fees, property transaction fees are predicated upon the reported transaction prices submitted by sellers and buyers; these prices are not permitted to be lower than the property's officially stated value. As delineated by the Property Tax Law, the central government is responsible for establishing the valuation methodology for estimating property tax values and revaluation rates. This valuation process is conducted by ad hoc valuation commissions within the municipalities. A regulation enacted by the Revenue Administration in 2009 specifies that professional valuation experts and private sector resources may be utilised when deemed necessary. Nevertheless, the composition of the commission's members frequently includes individuals with limited to no experience in property valuation. As a result, property tax values are often determined without adherence to a scientific methodology and are substantially lower than prevailing market prices. Consequently, property buyers and sellers typically report the transaction price as equivalent to the property tax value for non-mortgaged sales and approximately equal to the loan amount for mortgage-financed sales, thereby enabling them to evade substantial transaction fees. Furthermore, using property values as a basis for calculating various other taxes imposed on real estate also facilitates tax evasion. The transaction prices documented in the TKGM's official records are often deemed unreliable (Güneş & Yıldız, 2016). Pilot studies on mass valuation conducted in the provinces of Istanbul and Ankara between 2013 and 2015, as part of the TKGM's Land Registry and Cadastre Modernisation Project, supported by the World Bank, have demonstrated that the market prices of properties are considerably higher than the assessed values according to property tax values (GDLRC, 2022).

Due to the inadequacy of official transaction price records, property price indices in Türkiye are formulated based on real estate valuation reports created for mortgage purposes. The CBRT produces property price indices applicable to both residential and commercial properties.

4.2 Real Estate Sales and Rental Price Data from the Private Sector

The primary data source of the private sector is the real estate valuation reports prepared for mortgage loans. Pursuant to the Capital Market Law, these valuation reports are required to be submitted to the Appraisers Union of Türkiye (Türkiye *Değerleme Uzmanları Birliği* (TDUB)) (Appraisers Union of Türkiye (Türkiye Değerleme Uzmanları Birliği - TDUB)). To enhance the quality of valuations and facilitate the activities of its members, the responsibility for the establishment of a real estate information centre, which enables the dissemination of real estate value data, has been assigned to the TDUB within its legal framework. The TDUB Real Estate Information Centre Corporation was founded in 2016 and subsequently transferred to the Central Securities Depository and Trade Repository of Türkiye (MKK) in 2021. Since that time, it has continued its operations under the designation of "MKK Real Estate Information Centre Corporation" (MKK Real Estate Information Centre Corporation). The Corporation periodically publishes summary statistics concerning valuation expertise and valuation reports. However, information regarding the context of valuation reports (e.g. property values or attributes) is not available in these reports.

In Türkiye, various real estate listing websites (e.g. Real estate listing website) and data vendors furnish data and statistics, including real estate price indices (e.g. Real estate data vendor website). A range of summary statistics and concise information is accessible at no cost on these platforms. However, more comprehensive datasets typically incur charges. Since real estate agents or sellers publish these advertisements on the listing websites, they often contain inaccurate information or errors pertaining to property attributes and speculative pricing. Location information frequently fails to accurately represent the properties' actual locations due to concerns about potential business losses on the part of real estate agents or security issues for homeowners. There is a notable lack of standardisation in many of these advertisements. The extent of data coverage on property characteristics depends on individual preferences when entering information on websites. Additional data provided in the supplemental inputs section may encompass important insights, warranting data processing and statistical analyses to extract more information regarding the real estate market. The primary advantage of these websites lies in their capacity to furnish clearer insights into the prevailing market conditions. Nonetheless, they may feature manipulated prices and/or negotiating margins. The Ministry of Treasury and Finance (Revenue Administration) published the General Communiqué on Tax Procedure Law (No. 538) in the Official Gazette in 2022. According to the communiqué, online listing websites are required to submit advertisements for all movable and immovable properties and services to the Revenue Administration on a monthly basis. The primary objective of this regulation is to monitor speculation in property markets. Despite delays in data submissions, the collected data may serve as a significant resource for market monitoring. The integration of this dataset with TKGM's official land registry records would yield more reasonable and valuable information.

4.3 Production Methods and Comparison of Real Estate Price Indices

Property price indices are typically calculated exclusively for residential properties. The computation of price indices for other real estate categories is constrained by two factors: (1) the insufficiency of transaction data, as the volume of transactions involving other types of real estate is low, and (2) the greater heterogeneity in property characteristics and types contrasting with residential properties. Residential property indices generated by the CBRT and private sector firms differ in their data sources, coverage, definitions, methodologies, base years, and release dates.

Considering that the proportion of mortgage-financed transactions constitutes less than 20% of total transactions and is virtually absent in numerous provinces, it becomes difficult to evaluate the reliability of the CBRT property price indices, which are derived from valuation reports associated with mortgage loans. The methodologies employed by the CBRT in the computation of property price indices are summarised below:

1. The Residential Property Price Index for New Dwellings (NRPPI) is estimated for properties constructed within the past two years. In contrast, the Residential Property Price Index for Existing Dwellings (ERPPI) pertains to properties constructed more than two years prior. In contrast, the comprehensive Residential Property Price Index (RPPI) includes all properties.
2. The RPPI is developed at the national and Nomenclature of Territorial Units for Statistics 2 (NUTS2) levels, whereas the NRPPI and the ERPPI are generated only at the national level. The Commercial Property Price Index is established for both the national and provincial levels, specifically encompassing the provinces of Istanbul, Ankara, and İzmir. It primarily focuses on office and retail properties.
3. The property indices are formulated utilising the hedonic regression methodology, where prices are computed by controlling for quality alterations linked to observed housing characteristics.
4. The average value and quantity of households are employed in the valuation of each stratum's residential property price indices. Conversely, the commercial property price indices are weighted according to the average value of office and retail properties, in addition to the regional GDP.
5. The Tukey's Hinges method and Cook's Distance are utilised to analyse extreme values for Residential and Commercial Property Price Indices, respectively.
6. The indices of residential property prices have been made available on a monthly basis since 2010, whereas the index of commercial property prices has been reported on a quarterly basis since 2015.

Due to the relative ease of data accessibility through real estate agents and online listing services in the private sector, REIDIN has developed the Residential Property Price Index. Additionally, an alternative index has been established through a collaboration between the Association of Real Estate Investment Companies

(GYODER) and a private entity known as Endeksa since 2023. Several other online listing services and vendors also provide insights into real estate markets and pricing trends. REIDIN formulates the house price index using the Stratified Real Estate Price Index method, alongside the Laspeyres formula. This index encompasses all provinces within the country. For the provinces of Adana, Ankara, Antalya, Bursa, Istanbul, İzmir, and Kocaeli, the base year is set at June 2007, while January 2012 or January 2015 is used as the base for all remaining regions. The data is obtained from various providers, including local online listing websites, asset management firms, correspondents, real estate development companies, and consultancy firms (REIDIN, 2024b).

As the property price indices produced by the CBRT utilise the hedonic regression methodology, they are deemed superior to those generated by the private sector. However, it should be noted that these indices do not comprehensively represent the entire property market, as they are limited to properties eligible for mortgage collateral and do not reflect transaction prices. Moreover, price fluctuations are portrayed as the same average value across more localised areas due to the lack of granularity in the geographic coverage of the indices. Additionally, it is important to highlight that the data is published with a delay of 15–60 days (Hülagü et al., 2016; CBRT, 2024b, 2024c).

Given their diverse characteristics, it is challenging to compare the property indices published by the Central Bank of the Republic of Türkiye (CBRT) and those from the private sector. Figure 8 illustrates the Residential Property Price Indices of the CBRT and REIDIN (REIDIN, 2024a). Figure 9 presents the Rental Price Indices of the Turkish Statistical Institute (TURKSTAT) and REIDIN for residential properties. The rental price index provided by TURKSTAT is based on "actual rentals for housing", which is derived from the "Consumer Price Index (2003=100)" dataset and is categorised into main and sub-main groups (TURKSTAT, 2024a). As demonstrated in Figs. 8 and 9, the residential property price indices for housing sales from the CBRT and REIDIN follow reasonably similar trends. In contrast, a growing disparity is evident between the rental price indices of TURKSTAT and REIDIN for residential properties, a trend that has been particularly pronounced since 2020.

5 Conclusion

This chapter underscores that, despite certain deficiencies, an extensive and expanding compendium of data pertaining to the Turkish real estate market exists. Moreover, technological advancements and information systems are proficiently utilised in the compilation and dissemination of data. Most of this data is generated and distributed by public institutions. The private sector additionally publishes reports and datasets pertaining to the construction of property price indices, property valuations, and market implementations. All properties throughout the nation are systematically documented, encompassing their descriptive characteristics and fundamental information, and this data is accessible to real estate proprietors. Nonetheless, discrepancies between the legal and actual status of property

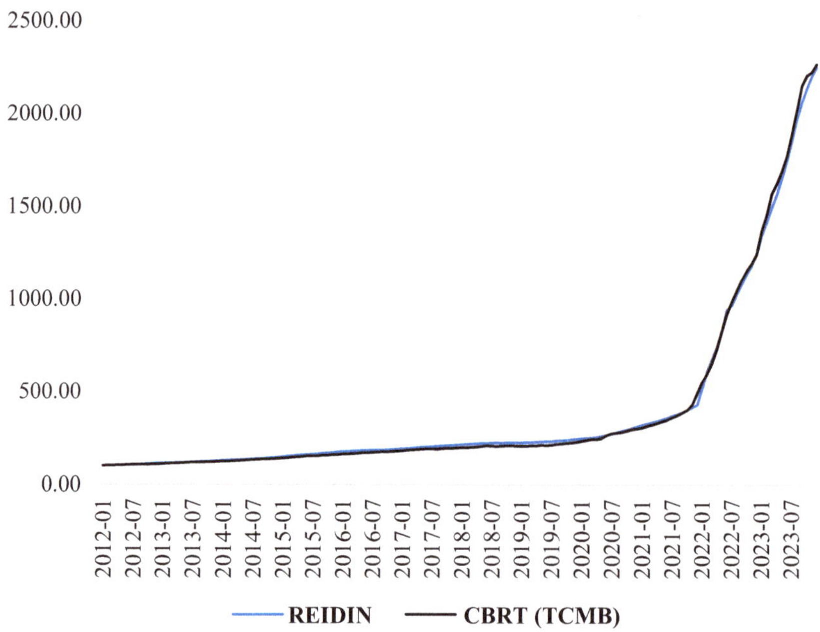

Fig. 8 Residential property price index comparison (January 2012 = 100). Source: REIDIN (2024b) and CBRT (2024a)

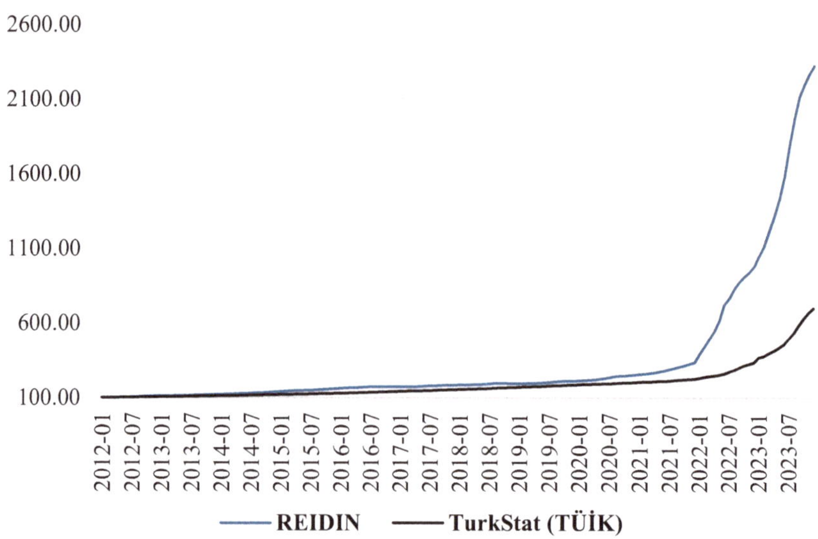

Fig. 9 Residential properties' rental price index comparison (January 2012 = 100). Source: REIDIN (2024b) and TURKSTAT (TURKSTAT Central Data Delivery System (TÜİK Merkezi Dağıtım Sistemi))

attributes, unreliable transaction prices, the lack of detailed information regarding building and individual unit features within the official land registers, and inadequate data quality represent significant drawbacks in the official records. These limitations result in complications in property taxation and necessitate the formulation of property price indices based on property valuation reports rather than transaction prices. Given the minimal proportion of mortgage sales within total transactions, property price indices are not developed for all provinces and property types. The absence of standardisation and coverage deficiencies in the official datasets yield misleading statistics and hinder access to information regarding housing stock and vacancy rates. Collaborative efforts among public institutions and the integration of data would significantly improve data quality and coverage. The private sector engages in more limited statistical analyses and data collection in comparison to its counterparts in developed nations.

References

CBRT. (2024a). *Electronic data delivery system by the Central Bank of the Republic of Türkiye* [Online]. Retrieved August 4, 2025, from https://evds2.tcmb.gov.tr/

CBRT. (2024b). *Metadata for residential property price index* [Online]. Retrieved August 4, 2025, from https://www.tcmb.gov.tr/wps/wcm/connect/EN/TCMB+EN/Main+Menu/Statistics/Real+Sector+Statistics/Residential+Property+Price+Index/

CBRT. (2024c). *Metadata for commercial property price index* [Online]. Retrieved August 4, 2025, from https://www.tcmb.gov.tr/wps/wcm/connect/EN/TCMB+EN/Main+Menu/Statistics/Real+Sector+Statistics/Commercial+Property+Price+Index/

CMB. (2024a). *Capital market board's activity report, 2023* [Online]. Retrieved August 4, 2025, from https://spk.gov.tr/data/61e48f651b41c60d1404d687/2023%20Y%C4%B11%C4%B1%20SPK%20%C4%B0dare%20Faaliyet%20Raporu.pdf

CMB. (2024b). *Monthly Statistical Bulletin of the Capital Markets Board of Turkey, May 2024* [Online]. Retrieved August 4, 2025, from https://spk.gov.tr/istatistikler/aylik-istatistik-bultenleri/2024-yili-istatistik-bultenleri

GDLRC. (2022). *Various reports on the property valuation component of the Land Registry and Cadastre Modernisation Project* [Online]. Retrieved August 4, 2025, from https://www.tkgm.gov.tr/tasinmazd-db/raporlar

GDLRC. (2024a). *About and projects by the General Directorate of Land Registry and Cadastre* [Online]. Retrieved August 4, 2025, from https://www.tkgm.gov.tr/en

GDLRC. (2024b). *Land Registry and Cadastre Data Integration Statistics* [Online]. Retrieved August 4, 2025, from https://cbs.tkgm.gov.tr/istatistik/MegsisGenel.aspx

Güneş, T., & Yıldız, Ü. (2016). Property valuation and taxation for enhancing local governance in Turkey. *Land Tenure Journal, 15*, 141–160.

Hülagü, T., Kızılkaya, E., Gencay, A., & Tunar, P. (2016). A hedonic house price index for Turkey. In *Chapters from NBP conference publications* (pp. 179–202). Narodowy Bank Polski, Economic Research Department.

REIDIN. (2024a). *Blog: Everything you need to know about real estate* [Online]. Retrieved August 4, 2025, from https://reidin.com/tr/blog/

REIDIN. (2024b). *REIDIN Emlak Endeks 2024 Şubat Ayı Sonuçları* [Online]. Retrieved August 4, 2025, from https://reidin.com/wp-content/uploads/2024/03/REIDIN-EMLAK-ENDEKS-202402.pdf

Töremen, E. (2020). Emlak vergisine esas arsa birim değerlerinin belirlenmesindeki sorunlar ve çözüm önerileri. *Niğde Ömer Halisdemir Üniversitesi Sosyal Bilimler Enstitüsü Dergisi, 2*, 21–42.
TURKSTAT. (2021). *Official statistics program (2022–2026)* [Online]. Retrieved August 4, 2025, from https://www.resmiistatistik.gov.tr/
TURKSTAT. (2022). *Survey on building and dwelling characteristics, 2021* [Online]. Retrieved August 4, 2025, from https://data.tuik.gov.tr/Bulten/Index?p=Survey-on-Building-and-Dwelling-Characteristics-2021-45870&dil=2
TURKSTAT. (2024a). *Consumer Price Index (2003=100) by main and sub-main groups* [Online]. Retrieved August 4, 2025, from https://data.tuik.gov.tr/Kategori/GetKategori?p=Enflasyon-ve-Fiyat-106
TURKSTAT. (2024b). *Distribution of non-institutional population by equivalised household disposable median income groups and problems with the dwelling and environment, 2006–2023* [Online]. Retrieved August 4, 2025, from https://data.tuik.gov.tr/Bulten/Index?p=Yoksulluk-ve-Yasam-Kosullari-Istatistikleri-2023-53713
TURKSTAT. (2024c). *House sales to foreigners, 2013–2024* [Online]. Retrieved August 4, 2025, from https://data.tuik.gov.tr/Bulten/Index?p=Konut-Satis-Istatistikleri-Haziran-2024-53760

Online References

Appraisers Union of Türkiye (Türkiye Değerleme Uzmanları Birliği - TDUB). https://tdub.org.tr/
Capital Market Board. www.spk.gov.tr
Central Securities Depository and Trade Repository of Türkiye (Merkezi Kayıt Kuruluşu - MKK). https://www.mkk.com.tr/en
General Directorate for Land Registry and Cadastre (Tapu ve Kadastro Genel Müdürlüğü). https://www.tkgm.gov.tr/en
MKK Real Estate Information Centre Corporation. https://mkkgabim.com.tr/
Parcel Query App (Parsel Sorgu). https://parselsorgu.tkgm.gov.tr/
Real estate data vendor website. https://reidin.com/tr/
Real estate data vendor website. https://www.endeksa.com/tr/
Real estate listing website. www.sahibinden.com
Real estate listing website. www.hepsiemlak.com
Spatial Address Registry System (Mekânsal Adres Kayıt Sistemi). https://maks.nvi.gov.tr/
TURKSTAT. www.tuik.gov.tr
TURKSTAT Central Data Delivery System (TÜİK Merkezi Dağıtım Sistemi). https://biruni.tuik.gov.tr/medas/

Tuğba Güneş holds a Bachelor of Science and a Master of Science degree in statistics. She completed her doctorate in the Department of Real Estate Development and Management at Ankara University, concentrating on studies related to real estate finance and automated valuation models. She dedicated one year of her doctoral program as a visiting scholar in the Land Economy Department at the University of Cambridge. Dr. Güneş is a licensed property appraiser and has been employed as a statistician with senior expertise in mass valuation at the General Directorate of Land Registry and Cadastre in Türkiye. Furthermore, she actively contributes to property valuation and taxation projects endorsed by the World Bank. Her research interests include property valuation, real estate economics and finance, urban economics, and the applications of machine learning.

Sibel Canaz Sevgen is an assistant professor in the Department of Real Estate Development and Management, Faculty of Applied Sciences, Ankara University. She is a researcher and specialises in the applications of machine learning within the field of real estate science. She is recognised as an expert in Geographic Information Systems (GIS) as well as remote sensing technologies. She has made significant contributions to various studies that integrate advanced data-driven models with land cover monitoring and real estate mass appraisal studies. Her areas of expertise include deep learning, statistical modelling, and geospatial analysis. She has collaborated on interdisciplinary projects that merge artificial intelligence with the discipline of real estate science. Furthermore, she has published several articles in high-impact academic journals and is actively involved in scientific conferences.

Mehmet Ülger earned his B.Sc. with a Civil Engineering degree from Erciyes University and holds an M.Sc. in Coastal Engineering from Gazi University. He completed his PhD in Real Estate Development and Management at Ankara University, specialising in modelling shoreline changes and their effect on real estate values. He has published numerous papers in top journals, including Q1 publications, addressing topics such as coastal erosion, real estate valuation, and coastal area planning. He is responsible for teaching graduate and doctoral courses in coastal area management and planning, building information modelling (BIM) in the real estate sector, and real estate and asset analysis at the department. His professional expertise encompasses numerical modelling of coastal sediment transport, assessing the impacts of climate change on coastal properties, and investigating Building Information Modelling (BIM) applications in infrastructure projects. Dr. Ülger's research focuses on the nexus of coastal engineering, real estate economics, and advanced modelling techniques for sustainable coastal and property development.

The Impacts of Recent Crises on REITs in Türkiye

Harun Tanrıvermiş, Monsurat Ayojimi Salami, and Tobias Just

Abstract

This chapter analyses the effects of recent crises, including the COVID-19 pandemic, Russia's invasion of Ukraine, and the earthquake of February 6, 2023, on the Turkish real estate market. The research used weekly data covering the period from March 2020 to March 2023. The data was segmented based on the periods of crises to facilitate a descriptive statistical analysis. Conversely, the primary analysis employed the Multivariate Generalised Autoregressive Conditional Heteroscedasticity (MGARCH)–Baba-Engle-Kraft-Kroner (BEKK) methodology, which captured the effects of the crises by using dummy variables. The results indicate that real estate prices experienced significant fluctuations during the COVID-19 pandemic and Russia's invasion of Ukraine. Notably, during these two periods, reversible means were not considered. Given that perceptions of the crises may differ among investors and customers, the intensity of the reaction to a crisis may also suggest an asymmetric response. The findings indicate that Turkish Real Estate Investment Trusts (REITs) should adopt more diversified investment strategies to better prepare for times of crisis.

Keywords

Turkish real estate market · COVID-19 pandemic · Russia's invasion of Ukraine · Earthquake · MGARCH-BEKK · Turkish REITs

H. Tanrıvermiş · M. A. Salami (✉)
Department of Real Estate Development and Management, Faculty of Applied Sciences, Ankara University, Ankara, Türkiye
e-mail: tanrivermis@ankara.edu.tr; masalami@ankara.edu.tr

T. Just
International Real Estate Business School (IREBS), Regensburg University, Regensburg, Germany
e-mail: tobias.just@irebs.academy

T. Just et al. (eds.), *Understanding Türkiye's Real Estate Markets*, Management for Professionals, https://doi.org/10.1007/978-3-032-13297-0_7

1 Introduction

The COVID-19 pandemic and Russia's invasion of Ukraine attracted significant attention from various stakeholders, leading to increased uncertainty in the global economy. This effect also extended to real estate-related sectors. For instance, an escalation in mortgage defaults emerged as a consequence of the COVID-19 pandemic's impact on the banking system (Pfeifer & Steurer, 2022). The COVID-19 pandemic profoundly impacted access to essential amenities, thereby complicating rent and mortgage payment obligations. The market's response to this crisis was revealing: survival took precedence over all other priorities during the initial wave, including the acquisition of luxury properties and real estate. Nevertheless, investment patterns evolved in response to changes in survival rates, precautionary measures, and vaccine availability (Eisfeld & Just, 2024). This adaptation permitted real estate investments to surpass the performance of stocks and bonds (Eisfeld & Just, 2021). This transformation in market behaviour underscores the astuteness of market participants, which, in turn, affects market trends and real estate investments.

Numerous individuals perceived urban centres as susceptible to particular risks,[1] which enabled the implementation of remote working Work from Home (WFH) practices and ultimately led to a significant reduction in the utilisation of downtown office spaces, where actual occupancy was recorded to have reached a historic low in 2020, and this persisted into 2021 (Gupta et al., 2022). The induced uncertainty resulting from the COVID-19 pandemic has precipitated a significant global downturn in the real estate sector, with (abnormal) returns ranging from −0.7% to −42.69% (Baker et al., 2020). The pandemic has served as a reminder to investors that external shocks, in addition to national economic policies, fundamental market factors, and the expectations of market participants, can have profound impacts on real estate markets (Pilinkiene et al., 2021). The adverse effects of the COVID-19 pandemic on real estate returns have been thoroughly documented, and the pandemic has particularly impacted firms with higher leverage (Chu et al., 2021). Numerous studies report that the real estate sector is of high economic importance, and its volatility has the potential to induce financial instability, potentially undermining the entire economic system (Pilinkiene et al., 2021). In light of this, this chapter examines the impact of recent crises on the Turkish real estate market, with a specific focus on the returns of Turkish Real Estate Investment Trusts (REITs). The results of this analysis will provide valuable insights for stakeholders for their future decision-making, particularly in preparing for periods characterised by multiple crises (Aliefendioğlu et al., 2021; Pilinkiene et al., 2021; Yarovaya & Mirza, 2022).

The Turkish real estate industry is recognised as one of the largest contributing sectors to the economy (Çamlıbel et al., 2021). The significance of the Turkish real estate market in the economic development of Türkiye can be traced back to the period following 2001 (Çamlıbel et al., 2021). The COVID-19 pandemic has

[1] See Eisfeld and Just (2024) for an analysis of the density-related risks associated with the COVID-19 pandemic.

impacted a sector characterised by both resilience and susceptibility. Nonetheless, it can be asserted that the pandemic has led to a decline in the demand for office space (Naor et al., 2022) and other real estate asset classes across varying intensities (e.g. Just & Plößl, 2022).

Real Estate Investment Trusts (REITs) in these sectors experienced the strongest adverse impacts (Allaberganov et al., 2021; Ling et al., 2020). Other sectors, including residential real estate, experienced a lesser degree of impact (Eisfeld & Just, 2021).

Although the pandemic has been officially declared over, its residual effects on specific asset classes within the real estate markets will continue for an extended period (see contributions in Just & Plößl, 2022).

The pandemic had not yet ended when Russia commenced its invasion of Ukraine on February 24, 2022, leading to a substantial increase in several input prices across the globe. The invasion by Russia prompted a considerable outflow of migrants from both nations seeking refuge in neighbouring countries, including Türkiye. While the international community continues to endeavour to bring an end to the conflict, Türkiye encountered a third crisis: the catastrophic earthquake on February 6, 2023. This calamitous event inflicted further shocks upon the Turkish economy and, as a result, the Turkish real estate market. The sequence of these three disastrous occurrences, each differing in intensity, underscored the importance of the objectives of this study, which serves as its underlying motivation.

This chapter elucidates the volatility of the Turkish real estate market and its clustering throughout the study period. This volatility is concentrated both temporally and across various asset classes. Furthermore, the article illustrates the impact of leverage on volatility within the Turkish real estate market. It may be inferred that the real estate market is fragile, and any forthcoming crisis could similarly exert a detrimental effect on the nation's economy.

The remainder of this paper is organised as follows: Section 2 discusses the literature review, while Sect. 3 presents the data and describes the methodology. Sections 4 and 5 outline the empirical findings and provide a conclusion for the study.

2 Literature Review

2.1 COVID-19 Pandemic Studies

Chu et al. (2021) discovered that the COVID-19 pandemic has adversely impacted real estate returns asymmetrically, indicating that larger firms necessitate a more diversified strategy to mitigate the effects of the pandemic (or similar events). Similarly, Tanrıvermiş (2020) showed that the COVID-19 pandemic has exerted a detrimental impact on Turkish real estate from the outset, influencing multiple facets, including transaction trading volume and the number of new project completions, which has ultimately led to a significant reduction in the real estate sector's contribution to the national economy.

For Vietnam's real estate markets, Ha (2021) demonstrated that the COVID-19 pandemic had a detrimental impact on real estate prices by using data derived from land use rights, house ownership, other assets associated with the land, and registration fee records spanning from April 2020 to April 2021. Del Giudice et al. (2020) used the modelled average housing price as a function of average household income, unemployment, per capita income, an index for overall transaction volume, a temporal variable, and a judicial execution index to assess foreclosures as an indication of the adverse impact of the COVID-19 pandemic on real estate prices.

Pfeifer and Steurer (2022) studied various real estate indicators, including price and rent indices, price–rent ratios, market volume, time on market, market turnover, and sentiment indicators, during the COVID-19 crisis in London and Vienna. The analysis was based on the data collected from November 2018 to December 2020. It was observed that the sentiment indicator remained stable concerning the real estate sales volume, although it was slightly negative in the rental market in London throughout 2020.

Hromada (2021) analysed the conditions of the Czech real estate market during the COVID-19 pandemic. The variables considered included the rental and selling prices of the apartments, as well as their technical conditions and energy performance. Similarly, Pilinkiene et al. (2021) examined the impact of the COVID-19 pandemic on the Lithuanian real estate market utilising an Autoregressive Distributed Lag (ARDL) model. The findings indicated that the economic stimulus contributed to the stabilisation of the market.

Tomal (2021) evaluated the volatility of real estate returns during the COVID-19 pandemic in developed economies, including the United States and Australia; emerging economies, such as Türkiye and Poland; and frontier economies, like Morocco and Jordan, employing the Generalized Autoregressive Conditional Heteroscedasticity (GARCH) model on the data spanning from March 2020 to April 2021. The analysis concluded that the initial wave of the COVID-19 pandemic negatively impacted the returns on US real estate stocks. In contrast, the real estate stock returns of Poland and Jordan experienced adverse effects only during the second and third waves of the pandemic. Furthermore, an increase in the volatility of real estate returns was observed in the Polish real estate stock market.

Aliefendioğlu et al. (2021) reported on the impact of the COVID-19 pandemic and the house price index (HPI) on data spanning from January 2010 to May 2020 while controlling for the Consumer Price Index (CPI). The authors employed the Non-linear Autoregressive Distributed Lag (NARDL) model. They concluded that the COVID-19 pandemic had both short- and long-term asymmetric effects on Türkiye's real estate price index. Furthermore, the authors identified that the COVID-19 pandemic had symmetric implications for the house price index of Kazakhstan. Similarly, Salami et al. (2022) used a Multivariate Generalised Autoregressive Conditional Heteroscedasticity (MGARCH)–BEKK to demonstrate that Turkish REITs consistently underperformed during the COVID-19 pandemic, using data from April 1, 2020, to May 16, 2022.

Kaklauskas et al. (2021) conducted a systematic review of construction investment and real estate development (CIRED) pre-, during, and post-COVID-19 pandemic and real estate, revealing that the COVID-19 pandemic had a significant impact on the property market.

Therefore, this paper's hypothesis 1 (H_1) is as follows:

H1: The COVID-19 pandemic increased volatility in the Turkish real estate market.

2.2 Russia–Ukraine Invasion Studies

The subsequent shock analysed pertains to Russia's invasion of Ukraine in February 2022, which had a detrimental effect on multiple economies and was expected to similarly impede the returns of Turkish Real Estate Investment Trusts (REITs).

This analysis was conducted using an event study that encompassed 531 firms. In a cross-sectional examination of companies within the G7 nations, Abbassi et al. (2022) revealed that Russia's invasion of Ukraine significantly contributed to the majority of firms' abnormal negative returns. The authors found that smaller firms outperformed their larger counterparts, and that firms located in France and the United States experienced only small impacts. The study indicates an asymmetric influence of the shocks across the G7 stock markets.

Aslam et al. (2022) analysed how the Russia's invasion of Ukraine influenced commodities, including oil and natural gas, using intra-day data with 30-minute intervals over seven months. The findings indicate a decline in the efficiency of major oil markets. In contrast, the natural gas market was noted to exhibit greater efficiency compared to the period prior to Russia's invasion of Ukraine. Overall, their findings suggest that Russia's invasion of Ukraine ultimately destabilised the primary energy-related sectors and appeared to affect global welfare adversely.

Mattera and Soto (2022) assessed the impact of more volatile fossil fuels by comparing the performance of companies within the Spanish IBEX-35 index that adopted renewable energy sources with those that did not. This analysis was conducted following the examination of energy firms listed in the Spanish IBEX-35 index during the period of the Russian invasion of Ukraine. The findings indicate that companies with a greater reliance on renewable energy exhibited better performance and encountered reduced levels of uncertainty (volatility). Furthermore, adherence to the Sustainable Development Goals (SDGs) pertaining to climate issues contributed positively to the firms' overall performance.

Yarovaya and Mirza (2022) reported findings pertaining to 1281 mutual funds across 40 countries. The results indicate that the repercussions of the war most severely impacted mutual funds in Russia, Ukraine, and NATO. Conversely, mutual funds from nations that opted not to endorse war petitions demonstrated superior performance, experiencing positive abnormal returns.

Salami et al. (2024) used daily real estate market data from February 24 to June 14, 2022. This data indicated that the Russian invasion had a significant positive impact on housing prices in Türkiye. The study further noted that the sensitivity of the Turkish real estate market to its surrounding conditions contributed to the upward shift in housing prices, which subsequently resulted in elevated living expenses.

Hypothesis 2 (H_2) is as follows:

H2: The Russian invasion of Ukraine induced shocks and increased volatility in the Turkish real estate market.

2.3 Earthquake Studies

The territory of Türkiye encompasses multiple tectonic plates, including the Aegean, Arabian, and Anatolian plates. This frequently leads to geological tensions and seismic activity within Türkiye, exemplified by the Marmara earthquake that occurred on August 17, 1999 (Gürer & Bayrak, 2007; Şahin Güçhan, 2007); the 2011 Van earthquake (Altiner et al., 2013); and the earthquakes of 1942 and 1943, which were among the most catastrophic seismic events documented in Türkiye (Akin et al., 2011). Only a limited number of analyses were conducted to comprehend the impact of earthquakes on real estate values in Türkiye. Consequently, research gaps remain, and hypothesis 3 (H_3) is articulated as follows:

H3: The earthquake on February 6, 2023, heightened the volatility of the Turkish real estate market.

This chapter addresses the existing research gap by modelling the effects of three distinct shocks: the COVID-19 pandemic, the Russia's invasion of Ukraine, and the earthquake that occurred on February 6, 2023, on the real estate stock markets in Türkiye.

3 Methodology

3.1 Data

Weekly Turkish Real Estate Investment Trust (REIT) prices were sourced from the data platform www.investing.com, covering the period from December 5, 2010, to March 3, 2023. REITs have undergone a global upward trend since the early 1990s (Bonato et al., 2021). Researchers analyse REIT data to assess the effects of crises on real estate markets, as this data is more frequently and reliably available compared to the data for direct real estate investments. A total of 640 observations were obtained, encompassing all three unrelated crises: the COVID-19 pandemic, Russia's invasion of Ukraine, and the earthquake. This provides a unique opportunity to examine the influence of the COVID-19 pandemic and Russia's invasion of Ukraine on Turkish REIT returns. The data was transformed into the natural logarithm of returns, as expressed below:

$$R_{Y_t} = \frac{\ln Y_{t-1} - \ln Y_t}{\ln Y_t} \tag{1}$$

where R_{Y_t} represents the log returns of Turkish REITs, and Y_{t-1} and Y_t represent the lagged and unlagged REIT prices, respectively.

3.2 Method

3.2.1 MGARCH Modelling

We used Multivariate Generalised Autoregressive Conditional Heteroscedasticity (MGARCH) models to assess the impact of the COVID-19 pandemic and Russia's invasion of Ukraine on the Turkish Real Estate Investment Trust (REIT) market. The MGARCH-BEKK model, introduced by Engle and Kroner in 1995, is a variant of the model proposed by Engle and Baba, as well as Engle, Kraft, and Kroner. This model was employed in the study to analyse the volatility of REITs. The parsimonious characteristics and the capability to estimate multiple markets simultaneously render the MGARCH framework a suitable model. Although GARCH (1,1) may exhibit greater parsimony, its restrictive assumptions result in numerous limitations (Wang et al., 2016). Employing the dynamic MGARCH model to examine the volatility of the Turkish real estate markets is anticipated to yield a comprehensive reaction.

According to Bekkerman (2011), the MGARCH framework is applied in order to model multiple market components simultaneously. Mensi et al. (2014) used the MGARCH model to simultaneously capture the returns and volatility of eight energy and cereal commodity markets. The BEKK model also accounts for volatility spillovers (Hung, 2020; Li, 2015). Moreover, it is important to recognise that BEKK models capture, firstly, the effects of their innovations on the current conditional volatility; secondly, the lagged volatility and cross-market shocks; and thirdly, the volatility transmission from other markets (Mensi et al., 2014). We adopted the diagonal BEKK model for two reasons: firstly, the BEKK model is suitable for modelling persistent volatility and the spillover of its innovations across other markets (Mensi et al., 2014), and secondly, the BEKK model is parsimonious.

Due to their consistent findings, Zhou (2016) ranked BEKK as one of the most effective analytical tools for examining REITs. It is a common approach among researchers exploring volatility transmission from one market to another (Abbas et al., 2013). Therefore, the present study examines volatility spillover, volatility persistence, and volatility clustering, thereby deriving perceived asymmetric reactions among all Turkish REITs analysed in this research.

We adopted the bivariate BEKK model, as specified by Mensi et al. (2014) and Salami et al. (2022). To meet our model specification for the multivariate BEKK model, the conditional variance–covariance matrix (H_t) of the residuals (Türkiye REITs) is specified as follows:

$$\varepsilon_t \mid \Omega_{t-1} \sim N\left(0, H_t\right), H_t \equiv \begin{bmatrix} Turkey\ REITs_t^{1,1} & \cdots & Turkey\ REIT_t^{1,n} \\ \vdots & \ddots & \vdots \\ Turkey\ REITs_t^{n,1} & \cdots & Turkey\ REITs_t^{n,n} \end{bmatrix} \quad (2)$$

where ε_t is the $(n \times 1)$ vector of residuals of the mean equation and Ω_{t-1} is the set of all available reactions up to $(t - 1)$. A simplified equation of H_t for this model is given by the specification that is shown below:

$$H_t = CC' + A\varepsilon_{t-1}\varepsilon_{t-1}^{'}A + BH_{t-1}B' \tag{3}$$

where C is an $(n \times n)$ upper triangular matrix of constants with elements $C_{i,j}$. A is a $(n \times n)$ matrix of coefficients $A\varepsilon_{ij}$ that capture the effects of own shocks and cross-REIT markets' interactions shocks, and B is a $(n \times n)$ matrix of coefficients b_{ij} that capture the own volatility persistence. The volatility interactions between Turkish REITs i and j. MGARCH-BEKK model estimation is carried out in the quasi-maximum likelihood (QML) method, where the conditional distribution of ε_t is assumed to have followed a joint Gaussian log-likelihood function for a sample of T observations and $k = n$ in a multivariate model as follows:

$$logL = -\frac{1}{n}\sum_{T}^{t=1}\left[klog\left(n\pi\right) + \ln\left|H_t\right| + \varepsilon_t^{'}H_t^{-1}\varepsilon_t\right] \tag{4}$$

4 Empirical Findings

Figure 1 shows the price development of 20 Turkish REITs (Investing.com, 2025) for the analysed period. The chart illustrates a significant shift in price movement, particularly from late 2019. It is also noted that Turkish REITs responded to the COVID-19 pandemic announcement in 2020. The subsequent news, including Russia's invasion of Ukraine and the earthquake on February 6, resulted in a series of volatility shocks in the Turkish REIT markets. For further clarification, Figs. 2 and 3 illustrate the volatility of Turkish REITs during the COVID-19 pandemic, Russia's invasion of Ukraine, and following the earthquake on February 6, 2023.

Table 1 presents descriptive statistics for each REIT across these three events. The mean during the COVID-19 pandemic is lower in comparison to the other two events. This indicates that Turkish REITs encountered greater challenges during the COVID-19 pandemic than during Russia's invasion of Ukraine and the devastating, albeit regionally confined, earthquake. Although the price movements of Turkish REITs during the pandemic demonstrated both upward and downward trends throughout the entire period, the impact of the Russian invasion was predominantly positive, particularly for residential REITs, likely due to the invasion inciting a surge in migration. The influx of migrants necessitated shelter, daily necessities, and services, thereby further stimulating demand for real estate services. This positive influence is evidenced by the increase in the mean value of Turkish REITs during the study period. While the earthquake constituted a natural disaster, its effects were limited to one region, resulting in shifts in demand to other areas and prompting supplementary construction activities. As a result, the impact was constrained in both temporal and spatial dimensions, even though it was initially more pronounced than in the early phase of the pandemic. Those settlements have considered relocating to other provinces, which could have a detrimental effect on house prices.

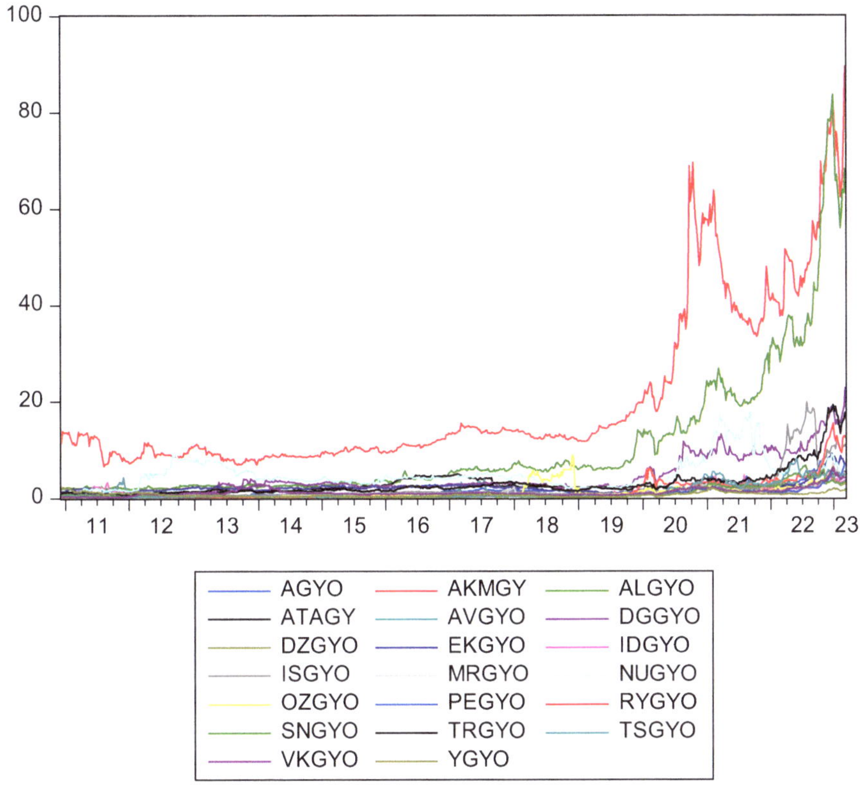

Fig. 1 Price movement of Turkish REITs between 2011 and 2023. Source: Investing.com (2025)

Furthermore, the analyses revealed that many Turkish REITs experienced considerable volatility during Russia's invasion of Ukraine, with 18 out of 20 Turkish REITs exhibiting significant fluctuations during this period, as anticipated by the standard deviation. This suggests that the earthquake on February 6 in Türkiye represented an even greater initial shock to Turkish REIT investors than the pandemic. Nevertheless, the pandemic has had a substantially deeper and more enduring impact than the earthquake, as indicated by the respective Kurtosis data for both events.

We estimated MGARCH-BEKK (1,1,1) using a maximum likelihood estimator. The findings meet the two underlying assumptions: the coefficient of Autoregressive Conditional Heteroscedasticity (ARCH) (α), which captures its volatility, and GARCH (β), which captures the cross-volatility, must be significantly different from zero, and the sum of α *and* β should be smaller than one if the mean reversion is ascertained; otherwise, Turkish REITs have experienced strong excess volatility during the study period. Table 2 presents the findings on the coefficient of the REITs model during the COVID-19 pandemic, Russia's invasion of Ukraine, and the Turkish earthquake on February 6, 2023. The sum of ARCH and GARCH

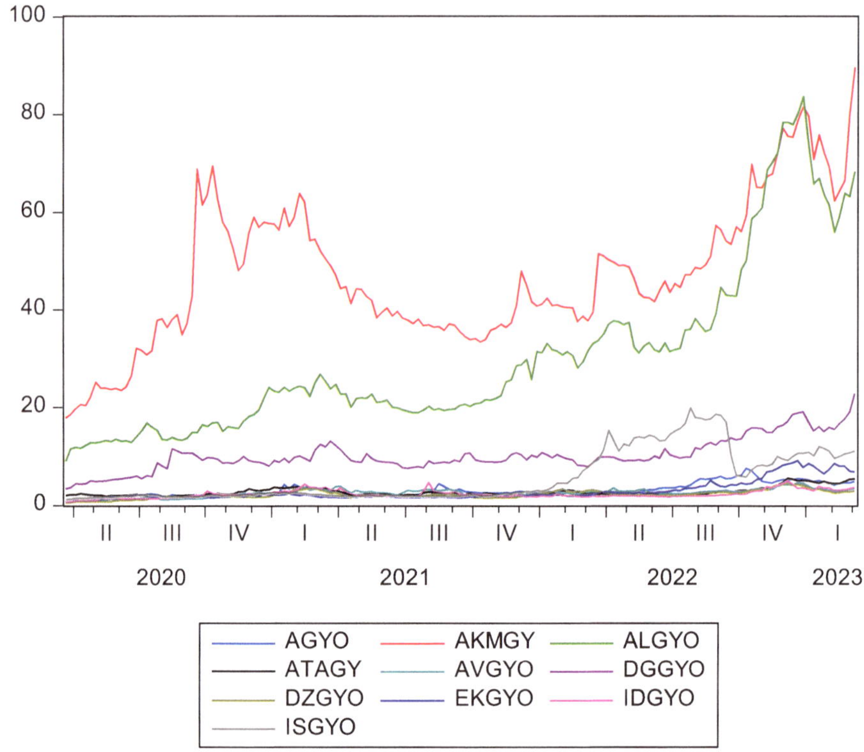

Fig. 2 Volatility of the Turkish REITs No. 1–10 examined during the COVID-19 pandemic, Russia's invasion of Ukraine, and the Turkish earthquake of February 6, 2023. Source: Investing.com (2025)

coefficients is highly significant and is greater than unity (>1) for the majority of REITs examined. This implies that most Turkish REITs have shown strong and persistent volatility; the shocks' effect on volatility did not fade quickly, and volatility remained elevated.

4.1 Volatility Spillover

Furthermore, the Autoregressive Conditional Heteroscedasticity (ARCH) model revealed significant reactions regarding the volatility of each Turkish Real Estate Investment Trust (REIT), with most exhibiting notable volatility, except for DGGYO, OZGYO, RYGYO, and TSGYO during the COVID-19 pandemic crisis, ATAGY and IDGYO during Russia's invasion of Ukraine, and PEGYO during the Turkish earthquake event. AGYO exhibited the highest volatility across the three events. Additionally, the cross-volatility among all Turkish REITs remains persistently significant. The volatility of Turkish REITs continues to be elevated. The findings further indicate that the cross-volatility is significantly greater than zero for

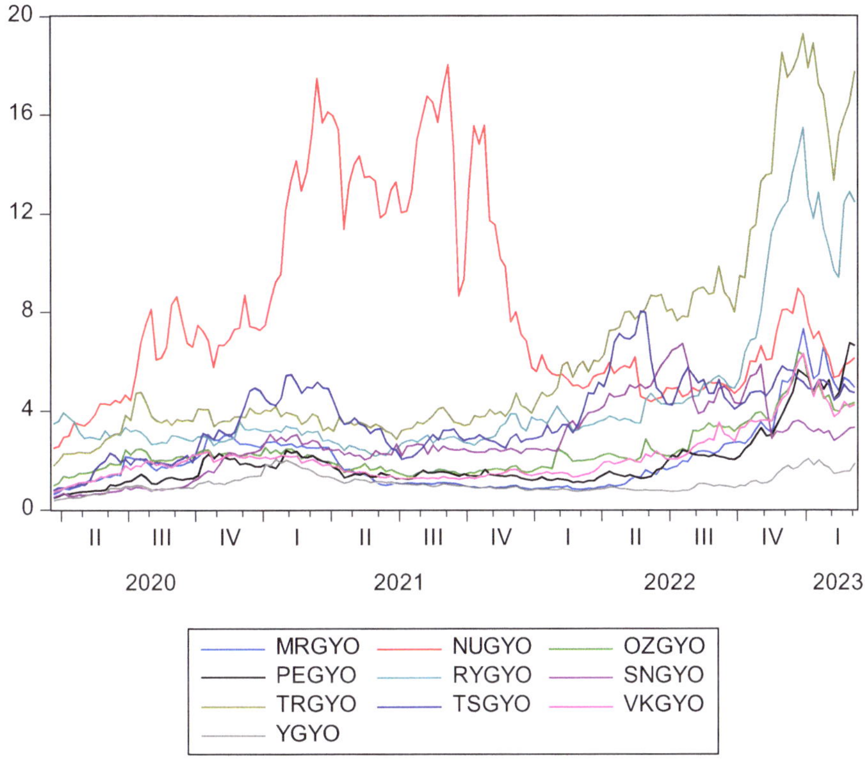

Fig. 3 Volatility of the Turkish REITs No. 11–20 examined during the COVID-19 pandemic, Russia's invasion of Ukraine, and the Turkish earthquake of February 6, 2023. Source: Investing.com (2025)

all Turkish REITs during these events. Volatility spillover represents a widespread phenomenon among Turkish REITs. Similarly, Bonato et al. (2021) and Chang and Chen (2014) conclude that global crises tend to amplify the volatility of REITs, and the operational and valuation methods within the Turkish REIT markets have undergone marked changes due to the cascade of the three crises. However, it is noteworthy that market volatility did not escalate further following the Turkish earthquake on February 6, nor were increases in cross-volatility observed. This phenomenon is likely attributable to the temporary and regional constraints posed by this natural disaster. Additionally, the close international ties that Türkiye maintains contributed to a swift recovery after the earthquake, facilitated by substantial national and international support from both governmental and non-governmental organisations; this may have mitigated the surge in volatility. These findings underpin the conclusions drawn by Çamlıbel et al. (2021) that Turkish REITs are highly volatile across their study period. The authors emphasise that policy flexibility provisions with corporate tax exceptions do not prevent markets from being volatile.

Table 1 Descriptive statistics for all analysed Turkish REITs

	REITs	Mean	Max.	Min.	Std. Dev.	Skewness	Kurtosis	Obs.
Covid	AGYO	2.5046	4.52	1.04	0.7003	0.6283	**3.6729**	97
R_UJ	AGYO	**4.4602**	7.63	2.55	**1.309**	0.1384	2.1857	50
EarthQ	AGYO	**4.1775**	4.96	4.55	0.1731	0.7002	2.1051	4
Covid	AKMGY	41.6442	69.62	17.99	12.1846	0.2385	2.5152	97
R_U_I	AKMGY	56.4354	81.7	37.9	**12.6969**	0.4985	1.9368	50
EarthQ	EarthQ	**75.35**	89.8	64.5	11.9668	0.271	1.3875	4
Covid	ALGYO	19.8018	33.26	9.15	5.3346	0.3866	2.691	97
R_UJ	ALGYO	47.6422	83.8	29.49	**16.9491**	0.7671	2.0889	50
EarthQ	ALGYO	63.7625	68.45	59.3	3.7486	0.1026	1.9793	4
Covid	ATAGY	2.4637	3.789	1.842	0.5051	1.2573	**3.4594**	97
R_U_I	ATAGY	3.0828	5.49	2.106	**1.0759**	0.9448	2.3976	50
EarthQ	ATAGY	5.02	5.4	4.47	0.4297	**−0.4207**	1.5748	4
Covid	AVGYO	2.2816	4.03	0.665	**0.8038**	0.0166	1.9981	97
R_U_l	AVGYO	3.1654	4.66	2.44	0.5629	1.0307	**3.4396**	58
EarthQ	AVGYO	3.23	3.55	2.92	0.2768	0.04553	1.5311	4
Covid	DGGYO	8.8	13.29	3.5	2.055	−0.6777	**3.1069**	97
R_U_l	DGGYO	**12.6968**	19.15	8.04	**3.19**	0.3264	1.8329	50
EarthQ	DGGYO	**19.1125**	22.92	16.7	2.7221	0.735	2.0005	4
Covid	DZGYO	1.9154	3.663	0.644	0.6344	0.4755	3.5342	97
R_UJ	DZGYO	2.8754	4.68	2.1	**0.6874**	0.977	3.0075	50
EarthQ	DZGYO	**2.82**	2.98	2.62	0.2523	−0.4023	1.8732	4
Covid	EKGYO	1.8924	2.421	1.144	0.3077	−0.4119	3.2342	97
R_UJ	EKGYO	4.6658	9.22	2.161	**2.2297**	0.7224	2.0438	50
EarthQ	EKGYO	7.54	8.09	6.9	0.6393	−0.0394	1.0523	4
Covid	IDGYO	2.221	4.81	0.806	0.7486	0.9413	**4.2654**	97
R_UJ	IDGYO	2.5964	5.05	1.88	**0.8647**	1.1368	3.063	50
EarthQ	IDGYO	3.46	3.8	3.21	0.2583	**0.4702**	1.7625	4
Covid	ISGYO	2.0738	4.55	1.21	**0.4744**	2.1262	10.511	97
R_UJ	ISGYO	12.1076	19.89	5.78	3.7357	2614	**2.1179**	50
EarthQ	ISGYO	10.61	11.11	10.01	0.4616	−0.341	1.8872	4
Covid	MRGYO	1.6443	3.074	0.641	0.725	0.5064	**1.7613**	97
R_U_l	MRGYO	**2.807**	7.35	0.85	**1.8225**	0.9105	2.6712	50
EarthQ	MRGYO	**5.0725**	5.34	4.81	0.241	0.022	1.3751	4
Covid	NUGYO	9.5364	18.08	2.51	4.3178	0.237	1.8009	97
R_U_l	NUGYO	5.758	8.98	4.38	**1.1776**	1.1315	3.3915	50
EarthQ	NUGYO	**5.86**	6.17	5.42	0.3184	−0.6397	2.0283	4
Covid	OZGYO	1.8584	2.54	0.99	0.3654	0.1579	1.995	97
R_U_l	OZGYO	3.286	6.4	1.99	**1.1789**	0.808	2.8977	50
EarthQ	OZGYO	4.1975	4.35	3.98	0.1565	−0.6624	2.0645	4
Covid	PEGYO	1.4371	2.4	0.494	0.4319	0.1931	**2.794**	97
R_U_l	PEGYO	2.5964	5.66	1.1	**1.3758**	0.9323	2.5844	50
EarthQ	PEGYO	5.97	6.75	4.73	0.9379	**−0.5321**	1.6874	4
Covid	RYGYO	3.0201	3.95	2.195	**0.3868**	0.3053	2.8642	97

(continued)

Table 1 (continued)

	REITs	Mean	Max.	Min.	Std. Dev.	Skewness	Kurtosis	Obs.
R_U_I	RYGYO	6.7036	15.5	3.25	3.6694	0.9721	**2.4364**	50
EarthQ	RYGYO	11.81	12.9	9.4	1.6194	−1.0991	2.2957	4
Covid	SNGYO	1.9328	3.068	0.512	0.7965	−0.6327	**1.7937**	97
R_U_I	SNGYO	**4.4425**	6.75	2.81	**1.0299**	0.3898	2.3665	50
EarthQ	SNGYO	**3.175**	3.34	2.94	0.1836	−0.4168	1.5827	4
Covid	TRGYO	3.5866	4.77	1.79	0.6046	−0.7085	3.7844	97
R_U_I	TRGYO	10.65	19.3	5.59	**4.2131**	0.8602	2.2836	50
EarthQ	TRGYO	**16.355**	17.8	15.22	1.0961	0.4279	1.8667	4
Covid	TSGYO	2.9425	5.506	0.808	1.1353	0.3629	2.6721	97
R_U_I	TSGYO	5.255	8.06	3.46	**0.9885**	1.1546	4.094	50
EarthQ	TSGYO	4.8	5.07	4.6	0.1982	0.561	2	4
Covid	VKGYO	1.6318	2.373	0.742	0.3856	0.0744	**2.1073**	97
R_U_I	VKGYO	3.0517	6.35	1.354	**1.2752**	0.8197	2.8001	50
EarthQ	VKGYO	4.1775	4.39	3.91	0.2019	**−0.4289**	1.9228	4
Covid	YGYO	1.0415	2.03	0.37	**0.3439**	0.9305	4.1156	97
R_U_I	YGYO	1.092	2.04	0.73	0.3965	1.1315	**2.8374**	50
EarthQ	YGYO	1.615	1.88	1.49	0.1786	1.0782	2.2821	4

4.2 Volatility Clustering

The phenomenon of volatility clustering, defined as significant deviations of volatility from long-term averages, is evidenced in the analysis of REITs during the COVID-19 pandemic and the Russian invasion of Ukraine. However, no additional instances of heightened volatility were detected concerning the Turkish earthquake that occurred on February 6, as the impact was promptly contained. The volatility clustering elucidated the price movement patterns during both favourable and unfavourable events, which have the potential to forecast abnormal negative and positive returns. The volatility clustering observed during the COVID-19 pandemic and Russia's invasion of Ukraine indicates that periods characterised by lower persistence in excess returns are succeeded by periods of strong persistence in excess returns. In addition, Lin et al. (2021) argue that price increases in real estate markets typically occur in a clustered manner. This emphasises that once the signal of volatility clustering occurs, the policymakers may prompt their intervention decision before the worst is felt.

4.3 Asymmetric Reaction

Furthermore, there exists evidence of asymmetric reactions among Turkish Real Estate Investment Trusts (REITs), as the impact of volatility differs across these entities, and adverse news seems to exert a more prolonged effect than favourable news. This observation is consistent with the behavioural finance literature (Weng & Gong, 2017). This suggests that Turkish REIT managers should consider this asymmetry and that investors may benefit from it.

Table 2 Volatility of REITs during the COVID-19 pandemic, the Russian invasion, and Earthquake, December 2010–March 2023

	COVID-19 pandemic			Russian invasion			Earthquake		
REITs	α	β	γ	α	β	γ	α	β	γ
Constant	$3.46E^{-05a}$	$3.46E^{-05a}$	$3.46E^{-05a}$	$1.81E^{-05a}$	$1.81E^{-05a}$	$1.81E^{-05a}$	$3.69E^{-05a}$	$3.69E^{-05a}$	$3.69E^{-05a}$
R_AGYO	0.30^{a}	0.97^{a}	$5.80E^{--07}$	0.16^{a}	**0.99^{a}**	0.08^{b}	**0.90^{a}**	0.00	0.83^{a}
R_AKMGY	0.21^{a}	0.98^{a}	−0.00	0.04^{c}	**1.00^{a}**	-0.07^{b}	0.20^{a}	0.01	0.98^{a}
R_ALGYO	0.10^{a}	**0.99^{a}**	0.13^{b}	0.20^{a}	0.99^{a}	−0.02	0.07^{b}	0.00	1.00^{a}
R_ATAGY	0.22^{a}	0.97^{a}	0.29^{b}	0.04	**1.00^{a}**	0.02	0.22^{a}	0.00	0.99^{a}
R_AVGYO	0.26^{a}	**0.97^{a}**	−0.01	0.30^{a}	0.97^{a}	0.00	0.35^{a}	0.00	0.97^{a}
R_DGGYO	0.01	0.98^{a}	-0.26^{a}	0.05^{c}	**1.00^{a}**	0.08^{b}	0.13^{b}	0.30^{a}	0.97^{a}
R_DZGYO	0.11^{b}	**0.98^{a}**	0.32^{a}	0.25^{a}	0.98^{a}	0.18^{b}	0.52^{a}	0.00	-0.94^{a}
R_EKGYO	0.16^{b}	0.97^{a}	0.39^{a}	0.14^{a}	**1.00^{a}**	0.03	0.19^{a}	0.00	1.00^{a}
R_IDGYO	0.58^{b}	0.90^{a}	−0.02	0.07	**0.99^{a}**	-0.23^{a}	0.17^{a}	0.00	0.99^{a}
R_ISGYO	0.10^{b}	0.98^{a}	0.47^{a}	0.33^{a}	**0.98^{a}**	0.02	0.09^{a}	0.00	1.01^{a}
R_MRGYO	0.13^{b}	0.99^{a}	-0.24^{a}	0.16^{a}	**0.99^{a}**	0.15^{b}	0.26^{a}	0.01	0.99^{a}
R_NUGYO	0.15^{b}	0.97^{a}	-0.40^{a}	0.06^{c}	**0.98^{a}**	-0.36^{a}	0.20^{a}	0.01	0.99^{a}
R_OZGYO	0.01	**1.00^{a}**	0.08	0.25^{a}	0.98^{a}	0.01	0.16^{a}	0.12^{b}	0.99^{a}
R_PEGYO	0.21^{b}	0.99^{a}	−0.00	0.09^{b}	0.99^{a}	-0.27^{a}	0.03	0.25^{a}	0.99^{a}
R_RYGYO	0.05	**0.99^{a}**	0.17^{b}	0.11^{b}	0.99^{a}	-0.23^{a}	0.04^{b}	0.00	1.00^{a}
R_SNGYO	0.25^{b}	0.98^{a}	−0.00	0.26^{a}	**0.98^{a}**	0.00	0.26^{a}	0.00	0.98^{a}
R_TRGYO	0.10^{b}	0.99^{a}	0.25^{a}	0.15^{a}	**0.99^{a}**	-0.15^{a}	0.25^{a}	0.00	0.99^{a}
R_TSGYO	0.03	**1.00^{a}**	−0.02	0.78^{a}	0.88^{a}	−0.04	0.17^{b}	0.29^{a}	0.99^{a}
R_VKGYO	0.09^{a}	0.99^{a}	0.17^{a}	0.14^{a}	**1.00^{a}**	−0.04	0.11^{a}	0.05	1.00^{a}
R_YGYO	0.06^{c}	**1.00^{a}**	0.02	0.06^{b}	0.99^{a}	0.04	0.12^{a}	0.00	1.00^{a}
Wald test	72.7797^{a}			30.6533^{c}			116.9926^{a}		
$HQ^2(6)$	2513.382^{c}			2637.428^{a}			2582.866^{b}		
$HQ^2(12)$	4947.782^{c}			5080.266^{b}			4914.651		
$HQ^2(18)$	7107.817			7242.291			7064.787		

All values are rounded to two decimal places. Superscripts a, b, and c represent significance levels of 1%, 5%, and 10%, respectively. The ARCH coefficient (α) explains own volatility, the GARCH coefficient (β) explains cross-volatility, and the asymmetry reaction coefficient (γ) indicates whether news shocks are positive or negative

During the Russia–Ukraine conflict, the findings indicated that 10 out of 20 Turkish Real Estate Investment Trusts (REITs) analysed demonstrated significant asymmetric reactions. In contrast, all 20 Turkish REITs assessed exhibited considerable asymmetric responses during the earthquake in Türkiye on February 6, 2023. This phenomenon may elucidate the degree of flexibility in dividend payments associated with Turkish REIT investments. Although dividend distributions are discretionary within the Turkish real estate sector, nearly all REITs reflected the long-term ramifications of the COVID-19 pandemic in their dividend allocations. However, the impact of the COVID-19 pandemic varies across different Turkish REITs. The nature and extent of portfolio diversification among various Turkish REITs could provide further insight into this discrepancy.

This finding may reflect the stance of the Turkish authorities during the invasion, as it aimed to resolve the issue prior to the escalation of the conflict. Türkiye is also a nation that has advocated for ceasefires during the Russian and Ukrainian invasions. Consequently, the resolution of the invasion may be favoured in Türkiye due to the degree of intervention. Nevertheless, the responses of various countries to the level of intervention may differ significantly. Ultimately, Turkish intervention may elicit an asymmetric reaction, even among Turkish citizens. Lastly, Table 3 presents the results of diagnostic tests that substantiate the validity of the findings, thereby ruling out spuriousness.

5 Conclusion

This study analysed the influence of the recent series of crises on Türkiye's real estate markets, particularly the REIT markets. The research is centred around the most recent sequence of crises. The epidemic crisis commenced in the last quarter of 2019, which was declared a pandemic in March 2020 and significantly disrupted the global economy until the first quarter of 2022. In this quarter, Russia initiated its invasion of Ukraine, redirecting global attention from the pandemic to this new crisis. Similarly, the earthquake that struck approximately 11 provinces in Türkiye in 2023 diverted public and professional attention within the country.

This study employed weekly Turkish REIT returns as a proxy for the development of the Turkish real estate market. The data for this research spanned from March 2020 to March 2023, encompassing the three significant events. The findings revealed that the COVID-19 pandemic and Russia's invasion of Ukraine exacerbated the volatility of the Turkish REIT market. A strong indication of volatility spillover was detected for these shocks, accompanied by volatility clustering and asymmetric reactions for the initial two shocks, namely, the pandemic and the invasion. This suggests that the Turkish REIT market is intricately linked to macroeconomic and political factors; thus, government intervention may be effective and even essential should another disruption impact the Turkish real estate markets.

Additionally, the asymmetric effect of the crisis indicates that Turkish REITs respond differently to positive and negative signals, reflecting the phenomenon whereby adverse news takes longer to normalise in Türkiye's REIT markets.

Table 3 Model diagnostic tests

	COVID−19 pandemic			Russian invasion			Earthquake		
REITs	Skewness	Kurtosis	Jarque–Bera	Skewness	Kurtosis	Jarque–Bera	Skewness	Kurtosis	Jarque–Bera
Constant									
R_AGYO	−1.61[a]	10.36	41.89[a]	−0.85[a]	6.09[a]	78.97[a]	−0.73[a]	4.15[b]	21.98[a]
R_AKMGY	−1.88[a]	10.82	50.84[a]	−2.09[a]	12.26[a]	658.51[a]	−1.40[a]	5.87[a]	102.79[a]
R_ALGYO	−0.56[b]	5.89[a]	28.71[a]	−0.22	2.20[b]	5.31[c]	−0.11	2.61	1.29
R_ATAGY	−0.05	3.77[b]	5.52[b]	−0.20	2.80	1.30	−0.08	1.70[b]	10.29[b]
R_AVGYO	0.19	6.78[a]	54.91[a]	0.35[c]	4.29[b]	13.61[b]	0.19	2.47	2.67
R_DGGYO	−2.64[a]	17.34[a]	87.78[a]	−0.53[b]	3.57	9.24[b]	−0.82[a]	4.47[a]	30.73[a]
R_DZGYO	−1.56[a]	10.62[b]	44.07[a]	−0.37[c]	2.87	3.68	−0.77[a]	3.56	16.98[b]
R_EKGYO	−0.07	2.03[b]	8.61[b]	−0.15	2.62	1.49	−0.01	2.23[c]	3.82
R_IDGYO	−1.77[a]	8.28[a]	65.88[a]	−0.35[c]	6.11[a]	64.95[a]	0.31	10.71[a]	381.26[a]
R_ISGYO	3.36[a]	21.30[a]	232.00[a]	1.28[a]	10.00[a]	354.19[a]	0.31	6.58[a]	84.00[a]
R_MRGYO	−0.80[a]	3.97	16.10[a]	−0.40[b]	4.45[a]	17.52[a]	−0.96[a]	6.62[a]	106.83[a]
R_NUGYO	2.04[a]	13.04	53.81[a]	0.97[a]	6.00[a]	81.28[a]	1.76[a]	15.87[a]	1134.74[a]
R_OZGYO	−0.79[a]	10.07[a]	92.45[a]	−0.97[a]	8.38[a]	208.77[a]	−0.81[a]	5.67[a]	62.24[a]
R_PEGYO	−1.67[a]	11.86[b]	49.52[a]	−0.97[a]	9.25[a]	273.10[a]	−2.58[a]	15.87[a]	1226.06[a]
R_RYGYO	−0.13	3.10	0.79	−0.02	3.00	0.01	−0.47[b]	2.51	7.12[b]
R_SNGYO	1.44[a]	7.95	34.77[a]	−0.76[a]	9.45[a]	279.94[a]	0.05	12.11[a]	529.28[a]
R_TRGYO	−1.99[a]	12.61	52.15[a]	−3.28[a]	22.98[a]	2819.24[a]	−4.20[a]	31.68[a]	5693.50[a]
R_TSGYO	−0.05	3.70[b]	4.84[c]	−54755.51[a]	11.12[a]	$7.88E^{+14}$	−45948.85[a]	880.23[a]	$4.94E^{+14}$[a]
R_VKGYO	−0.97[a]	6.24[b]	23.37[a]	−0.37[c]	25.73[a]	3298.03[a]	−10.15[a]	161.21[a]	162196.2[a]
R_YGYO	−0.93[a]	4.96	18.14[a]	0.90[a]	10.50[a]	378.97[a]	19.51[a]	299.35[a]	569587.9[a]
Joint	589.92[a]	376.23[a]	966.16	$7.65E^{+10}$[a]	$7.88E^{+14}$[a]	$7.88E^{+14}$[a]	$5.38E^{+10}$[a]	$4.94E^{+14}$[a]	$4.94E^{+14}$[a]

All values are rounded to two decimal places. Superscripts a, b, and c represent significance levels of 1%, 5%, and 10%, respectively

Moreover, the results suggest that certain Turkish REITs are significantly more affected than others. Given the nature of the shocks, this is logically justifiable, as the pandemic impacted the commercial real estate markets, particularly affecting residential real estate markets to a lesser degree. Consequently, Turkish REIT portfolio managers are advised to scrutinise their real estate diversification components closely.

In addition, characteristics indicative of significant volatility, such as volatility spillover, persistence in volatility, volatility clustering, and asymmetric reactions, have been established. However, the impact of the earthquake on Türkiye differed: the shock was more temporally and spatially confined, resulting in no additional increase in long-term volatility.

In summary, the Turkish REIT market exhibited sensitivity to global crises and transient responses to natural disasters. Future research on Turkish real estate markets may explore the enduring effects of earthquake shocks on these markets. This study's findings regarding the Turkish earthquake are constrained by their generalisation, lacking a detailed assessment of the earthquake's impact across the 11 provinces affected. Specifically related to the earthquake, a more comprehensive and focused analysis of direct real estate investments would serve as an appropriate follow-up research topic.

References

Abbas, Q., Khan, S., & Shah, S. Z. A. (2013). Volatility transmission in regional Asian stock markets. *Emerging Markets Review, 16*, 66–77. https://doi.org/10.1016/j.ememar.2013.04.004

Abbassi, W., Kumari, V., & Pandey, D. K. (2022). What makes firms vulnerable to the Russia–Ukraine crisis? *Journal of Risk Finance, 23*(6), 1–16. https://doi.org/10.1108/JRF-05-2022-0108

Akin, M. K., Kramer, S. L., & Topal, T. (2011). Empirical correlations of shear wave velocity (Vs) and penetration resistance (SPT-N) for various soils in an earthquake-prone area (Erbaa, Turkey). *Engineering Geology, 119*(1–2), 1–17. https://doi.org/10.1016/j.enggeo.2011.01.007

Aliefendioğlu, Y., Tanrıvermiş, H., & Salami, M. A. (2021). House Price Index (HPI) and the COVID-19 pandemic shock: Evidence from Turkey and Kazakhstan. *International Journal of Housing Markets and Analysis, 15*(1), 108–125. https://doi.org/10.1108/IJHMA-10-2020-0126

Allaberganov, A., Preko, A., & Mohammed, I. (2021). Government commitment to the tourism and hospitality sector during the COVID-19 pandemic. *Tourism Critiques: Practice and Theory*, 1–17. https://doi.org/10.1108/trc-02-2021-0004

Altiner, Y., Söhne, W., Güney, C., Perlt, J., Wang, R., & Muzli, M. (2013). A geodetic study of the 23 October 2011 Van, Turkey earthquake. *Tectonophysics, 588*, 118–134. https://doi.org/10.1016/j.tecto.2012.12.005

Aslam, F., Slim, S., Osman, M., & Tabche, I. (2022). The footprints of Russia–Ukraine war on the intraday (in)efficiency of energy markets: A multifractal analysis. *Journal of Risk Finance, 23*(6), 1–16. https://doi.org/10.1108/JRF-06-2022-0152

Baker, S. R., Bloom, N., Davis, S. J., Kost, K. J., Sammon, M. C., & Viratyosin, T. (2020). *The unprecedented stock market impact of COVID-19*. National Bureau of Economic Research. https://www.nber.org/papers/w26945

Bekkerman, A. (2011). Time-varying hedge ratios in linked agricultural markets. *Agricultural Finance Review, 71*(2), 179–200. https://doi.org/10.1108/00021461111152564

Bonato, M., Çepni, O., Gupta, R., & Pierdzioch, C. (2021). Do oil price shocks predict the realised variance of U.S. REITs? *Energy Economics, 104*, 105689. https://doi.org/10.1016/j.eneco.2021.105689

Çamlıbel, M. E., Sümer, L., & Hepşen, A. (2021). Risk-return performances of real estate investment funds in Turkey, including the COVID-19 period. *International Journal of Strategic Property Management, 25*(4), 267–277. https://doi.org/10.3846/ijspm.2021.14957

Chang, G. D., & Chen, C. S. (2014). Evidence of contagion in global REITs investment. *International Review of Economics and Finance, 31*, 148–158. https://doi.org/10.1016/j.iref.2013.12.005

Chu, X., Lu, C., & Tsang, D. (2021). Geographic scope and real estate firm performance during the COVID-19 pandemic. *Journal of Risk and Financial Management, 14*(7), 309–315. https://doi.org/10.3390/jrfm14070309

Del Giudice, V., De Paola, P., & Del Giudice, F. P. (2020). COVID-19 impacts real estate markets: Short- and mid-term effects on housing prices in the Campania region (Italy). *Social Sciences, 9*(9), 114. https://doi.org/10.3390/socsci9070114

Eisfeld, R. K., & Just, T. (2021). *Die Auswirkungen der COVID-19-Pandemie auf die deutschen Wohnungsmärkte: Eine Studie im Auftrag der Hans-Böckler-Stiftung*. IREBS International Real Estate Business School Universität Regensburg.

Eisfeld, R. K., & Just, T. (2024). Urban density versus regional dispersion: On the risks in high-density conurbations in Germany during COVID-19. *Sustainable Cities and Society, 108*, 105503. https://doi.org/10.1016/j.scs.2020.105503

Gupta, A., Mittal, V., Peeters, J., & Van Nieuwerburgh, S. (2022). Flattening the curve: Pandemic-induced revaluation of urban real estate. *Journal of Financial Economics, 146*(2), 594–636. https://doi.org/10.1016/j.jfineco.2021.10.008

Gürer, A., & Bayrak, M. (2007). Relation between electrical resistivity and earthquake generation in the crust of West Anatolia, Turkey. *Tectonophysics, 445*(1–2), 49–65. https://doi.org/10.1016/j.tecto.2007.06.009

Ha, N. H. P. (2021). Factors affecting real estate prices during the COVID-19 pandemic: An empirical study in Vietnam. *Journal of Asian Finance, Economics and Business, 8*(10), 159–164. https://doi.org/10.13106/jafeb.2021.vol8.no10.0159

Hromada, E. (2021). Development of the real estate market in the Czech Republic in connection with the COVID-19 pandemic. In *15th Economics and Finance Virtual Conference, Prague*, pp. 169–176. https://doi.org/10.20472/efc.2021.015.014

Hung, N. T. (2020). An analysis of CEE equity market integration and their volatility spillover effects. *European Journal of Management and Business Economics, 29*(1), 23–40. https://doi.org/10.1108/EJMBE-01-2019-0007

Investing.com. (2025). *GYO company search*. Retrieved May 25, 2025, from https://www.investing.com/search/?q=gyo

Just, T., & Plößl, F. (2022). *European cities after COVID-19: Strategies for resilient cities and real estate*. Springer Fachmedien.

Kaklauskas, A., Zavadskas, E. K., Lepkova, N., Raslanas, S., Dauksys, K., Vetloviene, I., & Ubarte, I. (2021). Sustainable construction investment, real estate development, and COVID-19: A literature review. *Sustainability (Switzerland), 13*(13), 7420. https://doi.org/10.3390/su13137420

Li, S. (2015). Volatility spillovers in the CSI300 futures and spot markets in China: Empirical study based on discrete wavelet transform and VAR-BEKK-bivariate GARCH model. *Procedia Computer Science, 55*, 380–387. https://doi.org/10.1016/j.procs.2015.07.085

Lin, Y. C., Lee, C. L., & Newell, G. (2021). Varying interest rate sensitivity of different property sectors: Cross-country evidence from REITs. *Journal of Property Investment and Finance, 40*(1), 68–98. https://doi.org/10.1108/JPIF-09-2020-0099

Ling, D. C., Wang, C., & Zhou, T. (2020). A first look at the impact of COVID-19 on commercial real estate prices: Asset-level evidence. *Review of Asset Pricing Studies, 10*(4), 669–704. https://doi.org/10.1093/rapstu/raaa014

Mattera, M., & Soto, F. (2022). Dodging the bullet: Overcoming the financial impact of the Ukraine armed conflict with sustainable business strategies and environmental approaches. *Journal of Risk Finance*, 1–21. https://doi.org/10.1108/JRF-04-2022-0092

Mensi, W., Hammoudeh, S., Nguyen, D. K., & Yoon, S. M. (2014). Dynamic spillovers among major energy and cereal commodity prices. *Energy Economics, 43*, 225–243. https://doi.org/10.1016/j.eneco.2014.03.004

Naor, M., Pinto, G. D., Hakakian, A. I., & Jacobs, A. (2022). The impact of COVID-19 on office space utilisation and real-estate: A case study about teleworking in Israel as new normal. *Journal of Facilities Management, 20*(1), 32–58. https://doi.org/10.1108/JFM-12-2020-0096

Pfeifer, N., & Steurer, M. (2022). Early real estate indicators during the COVID-19 crisis. *Journal of Official Statistics, 38*(1), 319–351. https://doi.org/10.2478/jos-2022-0017

Pilinkiene, V., Stundziene, A., Stankevicius, E., & Grybauskas, A. (2021). Impact of the economic stimulus measures on the Lithuanian real estate market under the COVID-19 pandemic's conditions. *Engineering Economics, 32*(5), 459–468. https://doi.org/10.5755/J01.EE.32.5.28057

Şahin Güçhan, N. (2007). Observations on earthquake resistance of traditional timber-framed houses in Turkey. *Building and Environment, 42*(2), 840–851. https://doi.org/10.1016/j.buildenv.2005.09.027

Salami, M. A., Tanrıvermiş, H., & Tanrıvermiş, Y. (2022). Performance evaluation and volatility of Turkey REITs during the COVID-19 pandemic. *Journal of Property Investment and Finance, 40*(2), 1–33. https://doi.org/10.1108/JPIF-02-2022-0017

Salami, M. A., Tanrıvermiş, H., & Tanrıvermiş, Y. (2024). Influence of Ukraine invasion by Russia on Turkish markets. *The Journal of Economic Asymmetries, 29*, e00348. https://doi.org/10.1016/j.jeca.2023.e00348

Tanrıvermiş, H. (2020). Possible impacts of the COVID-19 outbreak on the real estate sector and possible changes to adopt: A situation analysis and general assessment from the Turkish perspective. *Journal of Urban Management, 9*(3), 263–269. https://doi.org/10.1016/j.jum.2020.08.005

Tomal, M. (2021). Modelling the impact of different COVID-19 pandemic waves on real estate stock returns and their volatility using a GJR-GARCHX approach: An international perspective. *Journal of Risk and Financial Management, 14*(8), 374. https://doi.org/10.3390/jrfm14080374

Wang, Y., Wu, C., & Yang, L. (2016). Forecasting crude oil market volatility: A Markov switching multifractal volatility approach. *International Journal of Forecasting, 32*(1), 1–9. https://doi.org/10.1016/j.ijforecast.2015.02.006

Weng, Y., & Gong, P. (2017). On price co-movement and volatility spillover effects in China's housing markets. *International Journal of Strategic Property Management, 21*(3), 240–255. https://doi.org/10.3846/1648715X.2016.1271369

Yarovaya, L., & Mirza, N. (2022). The price reaction and investment exposure of equity funds: Evidence from the Russia–Ukraine military conflict. *Journal of Risk Finance, 23*(5), 669–676. https://doi.org/10.1108/JRF-07-2022-0174

Zhou, J. (2016). Hedging performance of REIT index futures: A comparison of alternative hedge ratio estimation methods. *Economic Modelling, 52*, 690–698. https://doi.org/10.1016/j.econmod.2015.10.009

Harun Tanrıvermiş is a distinguished professor who occupies the esteemed position at the Ankara University top management level as founder and head of the Department of Real Estate Development and Management, and founder and current dean of the Faculty of Applied Sciences at Ankara University. Professor Tanrıvermiş also currently works as the vice rector at Ankara University. He attained his B.Sc., M.Sc., and Ph.D. degrees from the Department of Agricultural Economics at Ankara University, specialising in land and real estate economics, land and real estate valuation, as well as natural resources and environmental economics. Furthermore, he earned an M.Sc. in environmental management through the MED-CAMPUS Programme in 1996. Professor Tanrıvermiş has published approximately 400 papers, including 43 international and 55 national peer-reviewed articles, which have been published in various high-impact journals. Additionally, he has presented 48 international and 74 national proceedings, either in full or as abstracts, at numerous conferences. He is also credited with writing 39 books and 17 book chapters. Moreover, his works concentrate on the land and real estate valuation, land and real estate economics, real estate development and project appraisal, urban transformation and sustainability, sustainable real estate development, facility and real estate management, land management, administration and polices, measuring and reporting of real estate sustainability and ESG, digital transformation in real estate and real estate technologies.

Monsurat Ayojimi Salami is an assistant professor in the Department of Real Estate Development and Management, Faculty of Applied Sciences, Ankara University, Türkiye. She graduated from the International Islamic University Malaysia (IIUM) and served as a Postdoc fellow between 2018 and 2019 at the IIUM Institute of Islamic Banking and Finance (II*i*BF). She specialises in the fields of financial economics, Islamic finance, real estate finance and investment, digitalisation in real estate, tokenisation, smart contracts and proptech. She holds multiple international certifications, including the Certified Quantitative Risk Management (CQRM). She has made significant contributions to over 50 academic publications indexed in prestigious databases such as the Social Sciences Citation Index (SSCI), Scopus, and the Emerging Sources Citation Index (ESCI). Her research predominantly focuses on financial inclusion, sustainable finance, risk management, and the application of Islamic financial instruments. Additionally, she has co-authored several chapters in academic books published by renowned international publishers, including Edward Elgar, Springer and Routledge. She has participated as a member of the scientific committee at various global conferences concerning Islamic finance and real estate.

Tobias Just is Managing Director at the IRE|BS Immobilienakademie and professor for Real Estate at the Regensburg University. Tobias studied economics in Hamburg and Uppsala (Sweden). In 1997, he graduated and started to work at the University of the Federal Armed Forces Hamburg. His Ph.D. dissertation was awarded the university science prize in 2001. For more than ten years, Tobias worked at Deutsche Bank Research, the economics research unit of Deutsche Bank. He headed the units' sector and real estate research team and was a member of Deutsche Bank's group-wide Environmental Steering Committee. In summer 2006, Tobias was a Research Fellow at the American Institute of Contemporary German Studies at Johns Hopkins University in Washington, DC. Tobias published 17 books and more than 250 papers in professional and academic journals and books. Since November 2011, Tobias has been Managing Director at the IRE|BS Immobilienakademie and holds a Chair for Real Estate at the University of Regensburg. He was President of the German Society of Property Researchers (GIF) from 2014-2021 and is editor of the ZIÖ—the German Journal of Real Estate Research. From 2016 to 2023, Tobias was a member of the Supervisory Board of Helaba Invest Kapitalanlagegesellschaft mbH. In 2017, Tobias became a Fellow of the RICS by nomination.

Institutional and Legal Framework

The Scope of Property Rights and Real Estate Ownership: A Comparative Analysis

Şebnem Akipek Öcal and Esra Keskin

Abstract

In this chapter, real estate rights, which reflect the economic and social structures of societies and are subject to ongoing discussions, are assessed distinctly within each legal system. The State is responsible for organising the legal and administrative framework to safeguard the inviolable rights associated with real estate and ensure compliance with these rights. Furthermore, real estate rights are also protected by international regulations. In the 1961 and 1982 Constitutions of the Republic of Türkiye, property rights are enshrined as fundamental rights, stipulating that they may only be restricted in the public interest or for the benefit of society. However, the 1982 Constitution mandates that any limitation on real estate rights must be proportionate. Protocol 1 of the European Convention on Human Rights (ECHR) governs real estate rights. Numerous rulings of the Constitutional Court closely correspond with those of the European Court of Human Rights. In Türkiye, real estate rights confer extensive powers upon owners while simultaneously imposing specific duties and responsibilities. This chapter examines the regulations governing real estate rights in Türkiye, provides a general overview, and discusses their scope and application.

Ş. A. Öcal
Department of Business Administration, Faculty of Economics and Administrative, TED University, Ankara, Türkiye
e-mail: sebnem.akipekocal@tedu.edu.tr

E. Keskin (✉)
Department of Real Estate Development and Management, Faculty of Applied Sciences, Ankara University, Ankara, Türkiye
e-mail: esrkeskin@ankara.edu.tr

T. Just et al. (eds.), *Understanding Türkiye's Real Estate Markets*, Management for Professionals, https://doi.org/10.1007/978-3-032-13297-0_8

Keywords
Right to ownership · Real estate ownership · Scope of the real estate right · Ownership restrictions

1 Introduction

Real estate rights are essential and recognised as inviolable by international law. While the owner exercises this right, it bestows upon the owner a comprehensive array of rights and powers; however, it simultaneously obligates the owner to honour the interests of society. Although the legislator holds the authority to define the precise content of real estate rights and the scope of associated obligations, such authority is not without limitations. This right ensures the safeguarding of all other fundamental rights and freedoms. It has been codified in numerous national and international regulations, including human rights declarations, constitutions, and other foundational legal frameworks.

The assertion that the Constitution and other legislative frameworks provide adequate guarantees for real estate rights is not universally perceived as sufficient for the protection of these rights (Başpınar, 2016: 637). It is imperative to also consider the sanctions that may be imposed in the event of an infringement of such regulations. While the legal restrictions do not curtail the extensive authority associated with real estate rights, it remains a reality that the freedoms of the property owner are significantly constrained (Oğuzman et al., 2018: 274). This chapter delineates the substance of property rights in Türkiye, alongside the relevant regulations in both national and international legislative contexts. Moreover, it elucidates the responsibilities of property owners, the scope and limitations of property rights, and the various factors that may result in the forfeiture of real estate.

2 Right to Real Estate

The rights associated with real estate delineate the relationship between the owner and the property (Fendoğlu, 1994: 143). In other words, ownership constitutes an absolute and tangible entitlement that bestows upon the individual the authority to utilise (*usus*), generate income (*fructus*), and dispose of (*abusus*) the real estate.

The concept of a right is typically defined as the powers and interests that are acknowledged and safeguarded by the positive legal order (Guriz, 2009: 49). The right to own real estate confers direct control over properties and can be enforced against all individuals, thereby establishing it as one of the absolute rights (Ertaş, 2011: 3). Real estate rights not only bestow powers but also impose obligations on the right holder; in this context, there exist varying perspectives on ownership. One perspective characterises private real estate as absolute and inviolable, while another perspective endorses collective ownership. A third perspective, while recognising private real estate, constrains the utilisation of the right in the interest of public welfare (Bulut, 2006: 15). In Türkiye, the Constitution guarantees real estate rights.

Although regarded as an absolute right, it is acknowledged that these rights may be legally limited in the interest of public welfare.

2.1 Legal Regulations on the Real Estate Right

In Turkish jurisprudence, rights associated with real estate were originally protected by the "*Kanun-i Esasi*" (Constitutional Law) promulgated in 1876. Article 21 of the *Kanun-i Esasi* asserts: "Everyone is duly assured of their real estate and possessions; real estate in the possession of any individual cannot be taken unless the necessity for the benefit is determined, and the value is paid in advance in accordance with the law".

Although the 1921 Constitution does not explicitly guarantee the right to own real estate, the decisions of *Tekalif-i Milliye* are recognised as a significant advancement during this period (Başpınar, 2016: 648; Etgü, 2009: 149). These decisions clarified that the State is obligated to provide compensation for properties confiscated during and after the war. This provision indicates that real estate rights were, at the very least, somewhat protected under wartime conditions. In the 1961 Constitution, real estate rights are addressed in Article 36, which is included within the section on social and economic rights and duties. The 1961 Constitution delineated the parameters of real estate rights in relation to public and community benefits.

In contrast, the 1982 Constitution delineates the right to real estate within the section addressing personal rights in Article 35: "Everyone has the right to own, bequeath, and inherit real property". These rights may only be curtailed by law in the public interest. The exercise of the right to real estate should not contradict public interest. Consequently, real estate rights in Türkiye conform to the third approach referenced above (Tuğrul, 2004: 133; Bulut, 2006: 25).

The third paragraph of Article 35 of the Constitution stipulates that the exercise of the right in question must not infringe upon the public interest, thereby imposing a positive duty upon the owners of real estate rights (Guriz, 2003: 161). This concept is further elucidated in subsequent articles of the Constitution: for instance, Article 43 reaffirms that the coastal areas are subject to the jurisdiction and control of the State, Article 44 specifies restrictions on land ownership, Article 46 addresses the process of expropriation, Article 47 explains nationalisation, and Article 169 delineates the non-transferability of ownership concerning State forests. Additionally, provisions relating to limitations and exceptions are also presented (Tanör & Yüzbaşıoğlu, 2024: 167).

Subsequent regulations offer extensive protection for real estate rights on a global level. For example, the European Convention on Human Rights (ECHR) regulates property rights through its First Additional Protocol. The Constitutional Court in Türkiye consistently complies with the ECHR's rulings in numerous cases (Akça, 2015: 543).

2.2 Subject and Scope of Real Estate Rights

In accordance with the principles of late Roman law, real estate rights confer three fundamental powers upon their owner: the right to use (*usus*), the right to exploit (*fructus*), and the right to dispose of (*abusus*) the property. Within this context, real estate rights embody the right *in rem*, which grants the holder the most comprehensive powers. These powers are articulated as the positive content of the real estate right (Oğuzman et al., 2018: 274).

Article 683 of the Turkish Civil Code articulates, "A person who owns something has the authority to use, benefit from, and dispose of it as they wish, within the limits of the legal order". The authority to safeguard real estate is referred to as the negative aspect of property rights (Oğuzman et al., 2018: 276). In this context, property rights empower owners to initiate legal proceedings for compensation and inhibit any unlawful seizure. The owner endeavours to affirm their property rights and reclaim the property through a compensation lawsuit. In instances of seizure prevention, the owner, whose property is subjected to encroachment, seeks to terminate the ongoing infringement.

In accordance with the principle of certainty, only specified properties that possess independent existence may be subjected to the right to real estate (Oğuzman et al., 2018: 286). In relation to real estate, a dual distinction is made between movable real estate and immovable property, such as land.

3 Ownership of Immovable Property and Its Scope

According to Article 704 of the Turkish Civil Code, real estate is defined as "land, independent and permanent rights recorded on a separate page in the land registry, and independent sections registered in the condominium registry". Based on this legal provision, Turkish law recognises three distinct types of property.

Article 718 of the Turkish Civil Code delineates the parameters of real estate ownership: "As beneficial as it is to utilise ownership of the land, it includes the airspace above and the subsurface layers below. This real estate encompasses buildings, vegetation, and resources, subject to legal restrictions".

In real estate law, real estate encompasses not only the boundaries of the land but also the airspace above it and the subsurface layers beneath it (Sirmen, 2021: 370).

3.1 Acquisition of Real Estate

The fundamental distinction in acquiring real estate rights resides in the difference between actual and sublet acquisition. When the right to ownership is transferred from one individual to another, it is attained through a transfer. Contracts pertaining to the transfer of real estate ownership must be formally drafted in accordance with Article 706 of the Turkish Civil Code. Specifically, the sales price of a property must be meticulously documented. The purpose of the official form requirement is acknowledged as protecting the parties from impulsive actions and ensuring the reliability of the legal transaction that underpins the registration (Oğuzman et al., 2018: 359; Kocayusufpaşaoğlu, 2010: 271). In cases where an individual has not previously owned real estate, this situation is referred to as actual acquisition.

Another distinction made in the acquisition of real estate pertains to the registration within the land registry. The fundamental principle concerning the acquisition of real estate rights is the principle of registration, which establishes these rights. Unregistered acquisition is permissible solely in specific instances prescribed by law, possessing exceptional characteristics (Albaş, 2007: 1). The circumstances in which real estate may be acquired without registration are delineated in Article 705 of the Turkish Civil Code as "inheritance, court decision, forced execution, occupation, expropriation, and other situations prescribed by law". However, even in those scenarios where the property is obtained prior to registration, the lawful owner who secures the real estate may exercise their rights of disposition over the property, contingent upon the registration of the real estate rights in the land registry. Furthermore, some perspectives argue that the statute of limitations for extraordinary acquisitions represents one of the categories of unregistered acquisition of real estate (Albaş, 2007: 3).

Article 713 of the Turkish Civil Code governs the acquisition of real estate through extraordinary acquisitive prescription. The relevant provision states, "A person who has held real estate uninterruptedly for twenty years, which is not registered in the land registry and without a lawsuit, may request the registration of ownership rights for the entirety, a part, or a share of that real estate in the land registry". Under the same conditions, an individual who possesses the entirety or a portion of real estate registered in the name of an unidentifiable owner or for whom an absenteeism ruling was granted twenty years prior may also seek the registration of ownership rights over the entirety, a part, or a share of that real estate in the land registry. Although possession is not explicitly referred to in the Turkish Civil Code, Article 973 defines a person with de facto control over real estate as a possessor. A person who does not recognise another's possession of the real estate is considered to hold possession with the title of ownership (Akkanat, 2011: 321). It is crucial for an individual seeking to acquire ownership of real estate through extraordinary acquisitive prescription to first initiate a lawsuit to claim the registration of the property in their name. Upon the submission of the lawsuit, the court publicly announces the subject matter of the case via newspapers and public notifications. Should no objections be presented within three months, the court shall render a decision on registration; however, this decision is explanatory and not definitive (Oğuzman et al., 2018: 361).

To acquire ownership rights, registration must be associated with a legitimate and valid legal foundation (Akkanat, 2011: 318). In the absence of a legally valid foundation, the registration will be considered invalid. In accordance with Article 712 of the Turkish Civil Code, it is stipulated that, "If the person who is registered as the owner of the land registry without a valid legal reason continues his possession of the real estate uninterruptedly for ten years without a lawsuit and in good faith, the right to ownership that he/she has acquired in this way cannot be challenged". Thus, real estate may be obtained through the standard means of acquisitive prescription. Provided that the criteria outlined in the Turkish Civil Code are met, the invalid registration is automatically corrected, and the right to the real estate is granted (Akkanat, 2011: 331). However, public properties are exempt from this regulation. For real estate to be acquired through the ordinary statute of acquisitive prescription, it must be duly recorded in the land registry. Moreover, the registration itself must be invalid.

3.2 Restrictions on Real Estate Ownership

International treaties and the Turkish Constitution impose restrictions on real estate rights due to various factors, including public and general interests (Şahin, 2009: 90). A distinction is established between common interest and public interest. Public interest pertains to the safeguarding of the established order. When the established order is predicated upon private property, public interest signifies the protection of such private property. Conversely, public interest also encompasses the collective interests of all citizens residing in the nation (Dik, 2005: 4).

While the right to real estate was delineated in the 1876 Constitution with a strong emphasis on its protection, it is characterised as a limited right in the Constitutions of 1924, 1961, and 1982. However, the 1924 Constitution failed to specify any criteria for such limitations. In the 1961 and 1982 Constitutions, it was explicitly stated that the right to real estate must not contradict the public interest (Şahin, 2009: 95). Following the amendment enacted by Law No. 4709 on October 3, 2001, criteria such as the principle of proportionality and conformity to the letter and spirit of the Constitution, along with the requirements of the democratic social order and the secular republic, were established. Furthermore, Article 15 of the Constitution asserts that rights and freedoms may be subject to restrictions; it declares: "In cases of war, mobilisation or emergency, the exercise of fundamental rights and freedoms may be partially or entirely suspended, or measures may be taken against the guarantees envisaged in the Constitution, to the extent required by the situation, provided that duties arising from international law are not violated".[1]

The right to real estate is considered one of the fundamental rights and freedoms that may be subject to restrictions under exceptional circumstances; however, given that real estate is perceived as the most significant guarantee of rights and freedoms, the principles of liberty and the rule of law are generally not compromised when this right is relinquished (Başpınar, 2016: 24).

Limitations on real estate rights are delineated within the frameworks of both private and public law. Expropriation serves as a significant constraint under administrative law, which is a component of public law. This process pertains to the acquisition of real estate by the State and public legal entities for the public good, compensated by a monetary value alongside a unilateral declaration of intent (Sirmen, 2021: 377–378). Article 754 of the Turkish Civil Code articulates

[1] Constitutional Court, January 10, 1991, 1990/25, D. 1991/1

restrictions founded upon specific legal provisions. Special legislation, including the Development and Settlement Law, the Law on the Protection of Cultural and Natural Assets, and the Coastal, Environment, Forestry, and Land Law, presides over these restrictions. Within the context of criminal law, the notions of seizure and confiscation warrant examination from this perspective. Confiscation denotes the State's appropriation of properties utilised in the commission of a crime, along with the proceeds derived from the crime, in the interest of public safety, general morality, and public order (Güngör & Toroslu, 2016: 1970).

The rights of purchase, re-purchase, and pre-emption represent significant limitations arising from the legal transactions executed by the owner (Oğuzman et al., 2018: 530). Consequently, through a unilateral declaration of intent, a sales relationship is established between the parties upon the exercise of the right to purchase, which obligates the owner to transfer ownership of the real estate to the holder of this right. If duly annotated, this right is fortified and can be enforced against third parties. By conferring the right to purchase upon an individual, the owner implicitly restricts their ownership rights. Furthermore, through the issuance of annotations, ownership rights are limited for subsequent owners, thereby establishing a situation of indebtedness concerning the properties (Oğuzman et al., 2018: 533). The right to re-purchase enables the individual who has transferred property to another party to reclaim the real estate via a unilateral declaration of intent. Its annotation is similar to that of the right to purchase. Regarding the right to pre-emption, should the real estate owner convey the property to another individual, the holder of the pre-emption right is entitled to acquire the property.

3.3 The Loss of Real Estate Ownership

A distinction may be established between the loss of real estate prior to and subsequent to its abandonment (Oğuzman et al., 2018: 460). In situations wherein the ownership of real estate is transferred between parties, particularly when it is acquired through such a transfer, there exists a relative loss of ownership for the individual ceding the right to ownership. Article 717 of the Turkish Civil Code specifies that the right to ownership will cease upon the abandonment or destruction of the property. In cases of destruction, abandonment, or expropriation of the property, an absolute loss of ownership is deemed to have occurred.

3.4 Responsibility of the Real Estate Owner

The real estate right constitutes a right *in rem* that grants its owner the most extensive powers. In this context, while the owner retains the authority to utilise, derive benefits from, and dispose of the property, he or she is also empowered to safeguard these rights by instituting a lawsuit for compensation and preventing unlawful seizure. Furthermore, the owner has certain obligations to fulfil, including the duty to refrain from acts of extortion and tolerate the expropriation of property for societal benefit (Tuğrul, 2004: 67).

The responsibilities and obligations that arise between neighbours concerning real estate rights are encapsulated within the term "neighbour rights" as articulated in the Turkish Civil Code. The responsibility in question is attributed to the cause (Badur, 2001: 878), and it is recognised that this responsibility arises even in the absence of fault, as delineated in the case law established by the Supreme Court. It is deemed sufficient to establish a causal relationship between the harm or potential harm and the act. Given that the owner's responsibility is characterised by strict liability, it is acknowledged that the owner cannot evade responsibility by asserting a lack of fault in the occurrence of the damage or by presenting evidence of equivalent validity relief.[2]

In Article 730 of the Turkish Civil Code, titled "Responsibility of the Real Estate Owner", a dual distinction is delineated: Article 730/f. 1 articulates "a liability arising from the use of real estate in violation of legal restrictions", as stated in 730/f.2. Additionally, there exists a "responsibility for excesses that occur as a result of using real estate in accordance with the law" (Yılmaz, 2018: 1146). In the first distinction, reinstatement is necessitated by the elimination of danger and damage resulting from an unlawful act. In the second distinction, compensation for damages and equitable equalisation are stipulated. The term exuberance pertains to actions that surpass the normal tolerance limits of the neighbourhood and result in damage to the real estate.[3] It is within the judge's purview to ascertain whether the real estate owner's actions exceed the tolerable limits that can reasonably be expected by their neighbours and may, therefore, be classified as excessive (Yılmaz, 2018: 1154).[4]

According to Article 730 of the Turkish Civil Code, "anyone who is harmed or faces the danger of harm as a result of a real estate owner's exercise of their property rights in violation of the legal restrictions governing these rights may sue for restitution of the situation, elimination of the danger, and compensation for the damage suffered. The judge may decide to award damages arising from unavoidable outbursts following local custom at an appropriate price. While Article 2 of the Turkish Civil Code prohibits the abuse of rights, it also delineates the limits of real estate rights (Yılmaz, 2018: 1155)".

In accordance with Article 683 of the Turkish Civil Code, "the owner may file a lawsuit against the person who is unjustly possessing his real estate, or he/she may sue to prevent all forms of unlawful seizure". Conversely, an individual who has experienced harm or is at potential risk of damage due to the owner's use of the real estate is entitled to initiate legal proceedings for the restoration of the situation and the abatement of both the danger and the damages incurred.

Numerous perspectives exist regarding the legal basis for a real estate owner's liability. One viewpoint asserts that individuals who benefit from real estate should also be held accountable for any damage inflicted upon their surroundings (Saymen & Elbir, 1963: 379). In contrast, an alternative viewpoint contends that liabilities

[2] Law department No. 14 of The Supreme Court, September 26, 2018, 2252/5989

[3] Law department No. 14 of The Supreme Court, June 6, 2013, 7927/9417

[4] Law department No. 14 of The Supreme Court, October 3, 2018, 2775/6298

arise exclusively from the mere existence of real estate (Eren, 2021: 218). Furthermore, some authors regard responsibility as stemming from potential hazards (Ayan, 2020: 434).

4 Real Estate Rights in Constitutional Court Decisions

Although the concepts of community interest and public interest are governed by the same article pertaining to the limitation of real estate rights in both the 1961 and 1982 Constitutions, neither Constitution provides a legal definition for these concepts. In the rulings of the Constitutional Court, the terms "community interest" and "public interest" are often used interchangeably, signifying a collective benefit that surpasses individual interests (Akça, 2015: 518).

In a ruling issued by the Constitutional Court on May 24, 2001, the Court underscored that limitations on the right to real estate may solely be imposed through legislative means, and it is impermissible to restrict the right to property through a Decree decision[5]; in the case of annulment filed on the grounds of the unconstitutionality of specific articles of the Free Zones Law, the Court emphasised the provision in the Constitution that states that "no person or organisation shall deviate from the liberal democracy outlined in this Constitution and the legal order adopted in accordance with its requirements". Furthermore, in a more recent line of argument, the Court clarified that democracy, in this context, aligns with the Western (classical) understanding of democracy.

The rulings of the Constitutional Court further elucidated that real estate rights, acknowledged as fundamental rights and freedoms, must not be subjected to any restrictions that foster inequality among religions or impede the freedom of belief and worship (Akça, 2015: 577).

5 Right to Real Estate in International Regulations

The Swiss Civil Code, authored by Eugen Huber, was formally adopted by the Republic of Türkiye in 1926, with no significant modifications (Kolly, 2012: 247). The right to individuals to acquire and dispose of real estate freely is pivotal from economic, social, and legal perspectives. Therefore, the rights associated with real estate are protected by the relevant provisions enshrined in the constitutions and laws of various nations. Article 1 of the First Protocol of the European Convention on Human Rights (ECHR) asserts that the real estate rights of foreign nationals may be subject to certain restrictions. In the context of real estate rights outlined in the Treaty establishing a Constitution for Europe, it is posited that individuals may be deprived of their rights to real estate for the purpose of public benefit, provided that just compensation is awarded, and that legislation may be enacted to regulate real estate rights to the extent deemed necessary for the public interest (Ankara Bar Association, 2004; Mutlu, 2005: 267).

[5] Constitutional Court, 06.10.1986, 1985/21, D. 1986/23

Real estate law is governed by specific regulations in Belgium, Germany, Denmark, Greece, Finland, Italy, Luxembourg, Latvia, Lithuania, Malta, Portugal, Poland, Sweden, Slovenia, Slovakia, Spain, the Czech Republic, and Hungary (Başpınar, 2009: 157). The constitutions of the EU member states recognise real estate as a fundamental right, reflecting the principle that "everyone has the right to own real estate", which is analogous to Turkish law. In the constitutions of Denmark, Estonia, and Ireland, the right to real estate is deemed inviolable, paralleling the provisions of the French Declaration of the Rights of Man and of the Citizen (Başpınar, 2016: 645).

In the Czech and Slovak Constitutions, a substantial margin of appreciation has been conferred upon the legislature regarding the exceptions applicable to the State concerning real estate rights. Under Article 11 of the Charter of Fundamental Rights in the Constitution of the Czech Republic, real estate rights may be restricted to address societal needs, economic development, and public welfare (Constitute Project, 2022). A similar provision is present in Article 4 of the Constitution of the Slovak Republic. Furthermore, it is stipulated that the right to real estate cannot be exercised to the detriment of others or in contravention of the general interests protected by law (Gönenç, 2005: 94). According to Article 64 of the Polish Constitution, the right to real estate may only be limited by law without encroaching upon its essence. The Constitution of the Republic of Bologna, adopted in 1796, is predicated on the principle that every nation aims to secure freedom, security, property, and equality. This Constitution delineates the right to real estate as the right to benefit from and dispose of its fruits (Başpınar, 2016: 639). Article 23 of the American Declaration of Human Rights and Duties, promulgated in 1948, asserts a "right to property", stating that "every person has a right to own such private property as meets the essential needs of decent living and helps to maintain the dignity of the individual and the home" (Ghdirmic, 2018; Aktan, 2000: 144).

In the US law, it is impermissible to interfere with an individual's real estate rights without their explicit consent (Başpınar, 2016: 640). Article 10 of the Massachusetts Bill of Rights underscores that legal regulations are in place to protect real estate rights and mandates that just compensation must be provided should the State encroach upon such rights. Furthermore, the amendments to the US Constitution assert that no individual may be unlawfully deprived of their property rights. Through the fifth and 14th Amendments, the right to real estate is confirmed as a fundamental right (Başpınar, 2016: 640). While the US law acknowledges that private real estate may be subject to restrictions for the public interest, similar to Türkiye, such restrictions are not permitted, even for the sake of public benefit (Başpınar, 2016: 641).

6 Conclusion

Real estate rights constitute fundamental entitlements that can be asserted against any individual, thereby bestowing upon the owner the authority to utilise, exploit, and dispose of their properties. The parameters governing this right, along with the powers and responsibilities of the legislator, are delineated in Turkish law, as articulated in Articles 2, 13, and 35 of the Constitution. The boundaries of this right are shaped by considerations of public interest, personal rights and freedoms, and the democratic social order. It is impermissible for the owner of the real estate to exercise this right in a manner that contradicts the public interest (Eren, 2016: 21). Nevertheless, the legislator is prohibited from encroaching upon the essence of the right to real estate while exercising the authorities granted by the Constitution.

The duties assigned to the owner of real estate rights and the privileges it entails are frequently examined. In this context, Article 35 of the Constitution characterises real estate as a right rather than a duty (Eren, 2016: 23). In a manner akin to fundamental rights and freedoms, authorities perceive rules and responsibilities as exceptions (Eren, 2016: 24). Furthermore, Article 13 of the Constitution specifies that real estate rights shall not be limited in a manner that contravenes the democratic social order. In a ruling from 1976 rendered by the Constitutional Court, the expropriation procedures that do not provide full compensation were deemed inconsistent with the essence of the right.

Comprehending the State as a social institution is implausible within a framework that does not uphold private land ownership. Consequently, real estate rights, which safeguard fundamental rights and freedoms, are upheld by public law, international law, and private law.

References

Akça, K. (2015). Anayasa Mahkemesi kararlarında mülkiyet hakkı. *İnönü University Journal of Faculty of Law Special Issue, 1*(2015), 543–596.

Akkanat, H. (2011). Taşınmaz mülkiyetinin olağan zamanaşımı yoluyla kazanılması. *Istanbul University Journal of Faculty of Law, 62*(1–2), 317–332.

Aktan, C. C. (2000). *Hak ve özgürlükler antolojisi*. Confederation of Right Trade Unions.

Albaş, H. (2007). Tapu siciline kayıtlı taşınmazlar bakımından olağanüstü zamanaşımı ile taşınmaz mülkiyetinin kazanımında mirasçılar arasında zamanaşımının işlememesi sorunu. *Journal of Dokuz Eylul University Faculty of Law, 9*(2), 1–28.

Ankara Bar Association. (2004). *Avrupa için bir anayasa oluşturan antlaşma*. İnteks Print and Publication.

Ayan, M. (2020). *Eşya hukuku II: Mülkiyet*. Filiz Publications.

Badur, E. (2001). Gayrimenkul malikinin sorumluluğu. *Journal of the Union of Turkish Bar Associations*, 2001(3), 835–880.

Başpınar, V. (2009). *Mülkiyet hakkını ihlâl eden müdâhaleler*. Yetkin Publications.

Başpınar, V. (2016). Mukayeseli hukukta ve Türk Hukuku'nda mülkiyet hakkı teminatı. *Journal of Ankara University Faculty of Law, 65*(3), 633–658.

Bulut, N. (2006). Mülkiyet konusundaki temel yaklaşımlar ve Türk Anayasasında mülkiyet hakkı. *Erzincan University Journal of Faculty of Law, 10*(3–4), 15–26.

Constitute Project. (2022). *Czech Republic's Constitution of 1993 with Amendments through 2013*. Retrieved October 16, 2022, from https://www.constituteproject.org/constitution/Czech_Republic_2013.pdf?lang=en

Dik, E. (2005). Kamu yararı anlayışında değişim baskısı. *Mustafa Kemal University Journal of Institute of Social Sciences, 2*(4), 15–26.

Eren, F. (2016). *Mülkiyet hukuku*. Yetkin Publications.

Eren, F. (2021). *Borçlar hukuku genel hükümler*. Yetkin Publications.

Ertaş, Ş. (2011). Eşya Hukuku. Barış Publications.
Etgü, M. A. (2009). *Kamu hukukunda mülkiyet hakkı ve Avrupa İnsan Hakları Mahkemesi'nin mülkiyet hakkına bakışı*. On İki Levha Publications.
Fendoğlu, H. T. (1994). *Hukuk tarihimizde temel haklar*. Mimoza Publications.
Ghdirmic, B. (2018). The American declaration of the rights and duties of man: An underrated gem of international human rights law. *Journal of Law and Public Administration, 10*(4), 50–61.
Gönenç, L. (2005). Özelleştirme ve Anayasalar: Orta Avrupa deneyimi. *Ankara University Journal of Faculty of Law*, 91–98.
Güngör, D., & Toroslu, H. (2016). Müsadere ve hükmün açıklanmasının geri bırakılması ilişkisi üzerine kısa birdeğerlendirme. *JAnkara University Journal of Faculty of Law, 65*(4), 1967–1980.
Guriz, A. (2003). Hukuk Felsefesi. Siyasal Publications.
Guriz, A. (2009). Hukuk Başlangıcı. Siyasal Publications.
Kocayusufpaşaoğlu, N. (2010). *Borçlar hukuku genel hükümler*. Filiz Publications.
Kolly, G. (2012). Türk Anayasa Mahkemesi, İsviçre Federal Mahkemesi ve Ortak Medeni Kanun. *Constitutional Judiciary, 29*, 247–254.
Mutlu, L. (2005). Yabancı kişilerin taşınmaz mal edinimi yönünden Avrupa Birliği ve Türkiye. *Journal of the Union of Turkish Bar Associations, 59*, 264–309.
Oğuzman, K., Seliçi, Ö., & Oktay Özdemir, S. (2018). *Eşya hukuku*. Filiz Publications.
Şahin, A. (2009). Ulusalüstü insan hakları hukukunda ve Türk Anayasa Hukukunda mülkiyet hakkının sınırlandırılması sorunu. *Journal of Liberal Thought, 54*, 85–103.
Saymen, F. H., & Elbir, H. K. (1963). *Türk eşya hukuku dersleri*. Filiz Publications.
Sirmen, L. (2021). *Eşya hukuku*. Yetkin Publications.
Tanör, B., & Yüzbaşıoğlu, N. (2024). *1982 Anayasasına göre Türk Anayasa Hukuku*. Beta Publications.
Tuğrul, S. (2004). *Kamu hukuku açısından mülkiyet hakkı ve sınırlandırılması*. Kazancı Publications.
Yılmaz, Y. (2018). Taşınmaz malikinin sorumluluğu. *Marmara University Faculty of Law Journal of Legal Studies, 24*(2), 1146–1173.

Şebnem Akipek Öcal serves as a professor at TED University in Ankara. She commenced her academic journey at the Faculty of Law at Ankara University, where she distinguished herself by ranking at the top of her class and achieving first place overall during her graduation. She obtained her master's degree from the London School of Economics and earned her PhD in Civil Law from Ankara University, where she wrote a dissertation focusing on consumer credit. Her career at the Faculty of Law encompassed roles such as assistant professor, associate professor, and full professor. Throughout the years, she assumed various administrative positions, including Director of the Ankara University Vocational School of Justice, Legal Advisor at Middle East Technical University, and Dean of the Faculty of Law at Kadir Has University. She concluded her tenure in November 2018 but remains actively engaged in academia as a faculty member at TED University, where she previously served as Vice Rector.

Esra Keskin is an assistant professor in the Department of Real Estate Development and Management at the Faculty of Applied Sciences of Ankara University. Following her graduation from the Faculty of Law at Gazi University, she practised as a lawyer registered with the Ankara Bar Association for nearly a decade. She earned her master's and PhD degrees from the Department of Real Estate Development and Management at Ankara University, where she also served as a research assistant during her doctoral studies. In 2023, she was appointed as a visiting scholar at the Georgia Institute of Technology through a fellowship from TÜBİTAK (The Scientific and Technological Research Council of Türkiye). In 2024, she was appointed as an assistant professor. Her research primarily concentrates on urban transformation, real estate law, contract law, contract management, and facility and property management.

Urban Land and Spatial Management in Türkiye: Challenges and Perspectives

Yeşim Tanrıvermiş, Ümit Gedik, Parla Güneş,
and Amani Micheal Uisso

Abstract

Historically, cities have been examined from many different perspectives, particularly regarding the social and economic development of nations. Throughout each era, cities have been on the agenda due to political shifts, financial impacts, planning strategies, and administrative structures. When a town achieves city status, urban areas encounter a multitude of challenges that necessitate resolution and are continually subject to legal and administrative interventions. In addition to zoning processes, the shape of cities is influenced by political, economic, and social dynamics, which must not be considered in isolation while analysing the urban space. Within the literature on planning, sustainable urban development is frequently discussed in conjunction with the concept of urban form. This relationship arises from the necessity for an ideal physical development framework that comprehensively defines and manages the future development of a city. Furthermore, urban planning requires robust institutional mechanisms capable of transforming urban spaces at both macro- and micro-levels. The individuals who constitute the most critical element of space also play a pivotal role in its formation. Likewise, the selection of settlement locations has been influenced by transportation accessibility, proximity to services, and the availability of essential resources. Consequently, spatial analysis should align with these fundamental criteria. Factors such as the relocation of people, density patterns, economic structures, spatial organisation, and real estate dynamics can only be compre-

Y. Tanrıvermiş (✉) · Ü. Gedik · P. Güneş
Department of Real Estate Development and Management, Faculty of Applied Sciences, Ankara University, Ankara, Türkiye
e-mail: aliefendioglu@ankara.edu.tr; umitgedik@ankara.edu.tr; parlagunes@ankara.edu.tr

A. M. Uisso
President Office Ethics Secretariat, Dodoma, Tanzania
e-mail: amani.uisso@maadili.go.tz

T. Just et al. (eds.), *Understanding Türkiye's Real Estate Markets*, Management for Professionals, https://doi.org/10.1007/978-3-032-13297-0_9

hended through a proper understanding of space. Urbanisation, driven by dynamic socio-spatial and economic variables, is inherently connected to the spatial distributional challenges resulting from rapidly growing urban populations, an issue of global significance. As the share of the urban population increases, the demand for spatial development grows, exerting pressure on scarce natural resources and environmental values. Urbanisation operates as a key indicator of national development levels. In this context, cities are systematically planned through a process that spans broader regional scales to detailed local frameworks within a planning cycle that shapes urban morphology.

Keywords

Urban land · Land and land readjustment · Spatial management

1 Introduction

In urban environments, the increasing population, coupled with advancements in infrastructural development, underscores the imperative for authorised multidimensional plans. Furthermore, their spatial implications must effectively contribute to the city while ensuring orderly progression in urban planning. In accordance with the Zoning Law, Land and Parcel Arrangement (LPA) practices are designed to support comprehensive planning methodologies within urban areas. These practices seek to allocate the requisite urban spaces for development, identify appropriate zones for construction, and establish public spaces intended for communal use.

The land required for implementation may be obtained either through purchase or expropriation; however, such implementations can also take place in optional, fragmented areas, without the need for land acquisition. Numerous challenges arise from the initiation of the implementation of Article 18 up to the final stage. Practical solutions to these arising issues expedite the process and offer multiple benefits.

In Türkiye, administrative units and local governments have been granted legal authorisation through the Zoning Law to regulate and organise urban spaces. These administrative units undertake a variety of tasks and operations to develop and manage housing, commercial, social, and public spaces necessary within urban environments. According to Karaağaç (2019), during the implementation process, these units encounter challenges that are not only related to technical personnel, budgets, and technological infrastructure but also involve organisational deficiencies, political concerns, and a lack of comprehensive planning.

Two principal factors predominantly drive the implementation of zoning regulations: the initiation of new development areas and the revitalisation of declining zones. These factors necessitate the formulation of new plans for the designated areas. However, it is imperative to acknowledge that the primary concern extends beyond the mere development of plans; rather, it encompasses their practical application in real-world contexts. A zoning plan applied to the land can be regarded as the initial step in spatial development. It is underscored that land use arrangements conducted within and around the urban centre, in conjunction with consolidation practices in both urban and rural regions, generate local spatial disparities and establish a foundation for social and economic advancement.

2 Theories and Practices Related to Land Readjustment

The theory of land distribution principally constitutes regulatory actions designed to address social, economic, and demographic needs while simultaneously fostering regional development. As stated by the International Federation of Surveyors (FIG), the demand for land is essentially propelled by social and economic forces and their corresponding needs (Wallace, 2010). This demand centres on the efficacy of land development or redevelopment in fulfilling public or private interests. Consequently, the theory of land distribution underscores the potential for land to be rendered usable to satisfy a range of social and economic requirements (Wallace, 2010; Msangi, 2011; Lupala & Chiwanga, 2014).

According to the FIG, the fundamental tools of land distribution theory, applicable to both public and private purposes, are classified into two primary models: market-based acquisition systems and human rights-based acquisition models (Wallace, 2010). The market-based approach functions through the principles of supply and demand to ascertain compensation (or value) for land acquisition and delivery. In contrast, the human rights-based model addresses the challenges encountered in nations where market-based solutions for establishing compensation predominantly govern informal land markets. This model considers the rights of both legal and informal landholders, with the aim of safeguarding these rights throughout the land distribution process.

In Türkiye, land readjustment (LR) practices are crucial for the establishment of new development areas within urban environments, the formulation of planning decisions, the development of strategic initiatives, the enhancement of efforts, and the assurance of appropriate land utilisation. These practices are employed to optimise the economic utilisation of cadastral parcels. Furthermore, they offer practical insights into averting protracted implementation timelines and achieving efficiency in expansive areas (Doebele, 2007).

Through the implementation of these measures, cadastral parcels situated within the boundaries of zoning plans are converted into zoning parcels. This conversion significantly impacts the value of real estate properties. To balance the resultant increase in land value and allocate land for public-use areas, a deduction referred to as the Land Readjustment Contribution Share is required and is governed by relevant laws and regulations.

In Türkiye, zoning practices may be classified as either compulsory, which involves mandatory participation of citizens, or voluntary, contingent upon the preferences of landowners (Koçoğlu, 2019). In implementations for compulsory zoning, all properties within the designated adjustment area become integral to the project. Land acquisition for zoning practices may occur through the process of expropriation. Given that one of the principal prerequisites for expropriation in Türkiye is public interest, property owners within the designated public project area possess limited agency. They are obliged to relinquish their land for a predetermined compensation.

Municipalities and governorates possess the authority to expropriate land for zoning purposes; however, their contributions through such implementations are comparatively limited in practice. Within the context of expropriation by the authorities, individual parcels are not directly redistributed to individuals. Nevertheless, in privately developed facilities, there may be authorisations aimed at circumventing the deduction of the full 45% Land Readjustment Contribution Share or because the parcels do not have legally established development (land use) rights. This specific authority is exercised in accordance with Article 10 of the Zoning Law.

3 Implementation of Article 18 beyond Necessity and the Role of Land Readjustment

Article 18, when applied beyond its intended necessity, is fundamentally executed through land subdivision, in accordance with its original purpose. Nevertheless, when delays arise due to the functioning of Article 17, landowners frequently demand expedited access to their land. In response to these demands, it becomes feasible for independent parcels to attain "land" status under Articles 15 and 16 (Aksay, 2005). Conversely, when a property intersects with public-use areas such as parks, green spaces, or roads, it becomes impracticable to establish an independent parcel, and the owner is unable to secure a zoning parcel; rather, the property transitions into the subdivision process under Article 18 (Karaağaç, 2019).

Academics and researchers engaged in urban land development and transformation regard land readjustment as an essential instrument. Nevertheless, this methodology is not universally applicable to every land development or planning circumstance, and land development in isolation is inadequate to resolve all challenges. The success of land readjustment is significantly contingent upon the participation of the affected landowners (Sorensen, 2000), and the degree of acceptance of this method is a determinant of its overall effectiveness (Home, 2007).

One of the most significant challenges in implementing land readjustment is the accurate assessment of land value, both before and after redistribution. Although numerous factors influence property values, and mathematical models may be employed, estimating values in a manner that guarantees equitable distribution remains a formidable task (Çete, 2010; Tüdeş, 2019). Optimal outcomes from this method are generally achieved within urban contexts characterised by robust market conditions and escalating land values. Conversely, under circumstances of weak market conditions, land readjustment procedures may prove impractical or ineffective. These procedures can be intricate and protracted, akin to other land development methodologies such as expropriation or land acquisition.

The land readjustment approach is typically more feasible when implemented in new development zones situated on the urban fringe (greenfield) or within smaller areas, as opposed to urban redevelopment regions such as brownfields (abandoned industrial sites/developed areas). This is attributable to property owners' propensity to oppose the expenses associated with demolition and relocation (Home, 2007).

Another limitation of land readjustment is its failure to adequately address the needs and concerns of tenants who do not own land. These processes typically involve landowners while neglecting the perspectives of tenants and renters during the negotiation phases. This often results in inequitable outcomes, where the interests of tenants may be disregarded, particularly when landowners and tenants are not considered equal stakeholders (Thomas Lie, 2010).

Urban spaces are assessed according to various criteria that embody differentiation within urban areas. Concepts such as urban growth, sprawl, and fringe development represent key dynamics that influence the macroform of cities and shape spatial organisation. The advancement of each space, based on these criteria, signifies both the trajectory and magnitude of urban development. The erosion of a clear distinction between urban and rural spatial organisation is not merely a consequence of inappropriate planning decisions; rather, the effective management of the process also impacts changes in spatial value (Güneş, 2021).

A key concept observed in the development cycles of urban spaces is the establishment of a compact and dense urban fabric. This concept inherently pertains to the transformation of the central urban fabric. The notion of a singular city centre has significantly influenced decisions regarding urban density, and the distribution of various land use types has adapted accordingly. As cities undergo decentralisation, they often become more compact, resulting in an expansion of spaces. When spatial organisation is concentrated in a single area, it impacts the characteristic form of space and directs value distribution likewise. Conversely, when cities attain a balanced spatial distribution devoid of a dominant centre, the distribution of value evolves more equitably. As the understanding of spatial density progresses within this context, mobility is likely to increase, and the criteria for site selection will consequently be influenced (Güneş, 2021) (Table 1).

4 Challenges Encountered In Land Readjustment

Although land readjustment procedures and practices in Türkiye are conducted entirely under public supervision and within the framework of legal regulations, challenges arise at every stage for a variety of reasons. When categorising these challenges broadly, they can be classified into issues prior to implementation, issues encountered during implementation, and issues that arise after implementation. The sub-categories include technical and procedural errors, problems stemming from the misapplication of legislation, issues related to land readjustment contributions, and errors in parcelling.

It should be emphasised that a city's planned development relies more on the feasibility of implementing the generated plans than on the construction of superstructures. The data used in zoning implementations are derived from the land registry cadastre and zoning plans. The implementations under Article 18 are based on these plans and cadastral data. Challenges may arise at all stages of the process,

Table 1 Comparison of spatial concepts

Evaluation criteria	Urban growth	Urban sprawl	Urban scattering/ urban fringes	Compact/dense city
Physical texture of space	•	•	•	•
Urban form		•	•	•
Population	•	•	•	•
Impact of mobility		•		
Impact of generated land value		•	•	
Changes in property preferences	•	•	•	
Economic impact	•	•	•	•
Political cycle	•	•		
Perception of the city Centre		•		•
Transportation routes	•	•	•	
Land use types	•	•	•	
Rural/urban texture transformation	•	•	•	
Density	•	•	•	•
Spatial organisation	•	•	•	•
Rural land use rates		•	•	
Changes in mixed uses	•			•
Formation of sub-regions	•	•	•	
Infrastructure development	•	•	•	•
Social impact		•	•	

Source: Güneş (2021)

both for the administration that commissions the implementation and for the contractors involved.

The preparation of zoning plans necessitates the use of both current base maps and cadastral maps. Given that plans and maps must be used in conjunction, any inconsistencies that arise during their production may result in errors. A primary technical challenge is the use of disparate coordinate systems for plans and maps; it is essential to recognise that inaccuracies resulting from coordinate transformations can have significant repercussions on the entire system. The methodologies employed in production and the precision of the cadastral base and maps used are critical factors that warrant meticulous consideration. Such resultant errors may yield inaccurate area measurements of enclosed spaces depicted on plans and maps. If efforts to rectify these errors prove successful, subsequent work should be predicated on accurate area measurements. If these enclosed spaces pertain to property, the adjustment of the area can be executed with the property owner's consent. If this is not feasible, rectification may be attained through the application of Article 41 of the Cadastre Law No. 3402. Considering the preparatory, approval, public announcement, and registration processes of Article 18 implementations, it is imperative to avert these setbacks or address them as efficiently and practically as possible.

Although procedural errors are relatively straightforward to rectify and do not represent significant impediments, they frequently lead to judicial determinations for annulment. An illustration of such a procedural error arises when a subordinate authority renders a decision that is requisite during the zoning implementation process.

The legislation pertaining to zoning implementations within Turkish law is notably comprehensive and explicit. However, any inconsistencies in the application of legal provisions at any stage can result in significant issues. Even if an error in one of the procedural steps stipulated by the legislation impacts only a single parcel, it may become necessary to revise the entire zoning plan to rectify this situation. In such instances, the zoning implementation should be annulled, and any alterations made on-site during the duration required for this annulment can considerably complicate the process, potentially resulting in irreversible consequences.

Estimating the deduction designated as the Deduction for Public Facilities (DOP) represents a critical phase within the zoning plan. The applicable laws and regulations delineate precise methodologies for calculating this ratio, along with stipulations regarding the utilisation of land acquired through the deduction. Given that inaccuracies at this juncture may adversely impact the comprehensive plan and its execution, the calculations and planning processes must be performed with utmost diligence and meticulous consideration.

Parcelling represents the final technical phase in the implementation of zoning. It necessitates careful attention and diligence, both in administrative procedures and in design considerations. When evaluating the objections raised by property owners directly involved in the implementation process, this phase tends to receive the majority of objections. Given that the resolution of objections pertaining to parcelling cannot typically be conducted in isolation for the objected property, it may become necessary to redo the entire parcelling process for the whole of the zoning block or potentially for the entire implementation area.

5 Legal Aspects of Land and Plot Readjustment and Implementation

The foundation of zoning plans in Türkiye is grounded in the Constitution. As early as 1848, with the introduction of the *Ebniye Nizamnamesi* (Building Regulations), regulations were instituted that encompassed decisions regarding the layout of streets and avenues, as well as provisions pertaining to expropriation (Yıldız, 1999). These early regulations signified the commencement of formal spatial planning in Türkiye. Throughout the nineteenth century, comprehensive legal regulations concerning land and plot readjustment were implemented, culminating in the enactment of Law No. 6785 in 1956. This law legally established the land readjustment distribution ratio at 25%, which possesses significant legal importance within the country's zoning and land management framework.

Regulations pertaining to planning processes hold a significant position within Türkiye's legal system, with particular emphasis on the prioritisation of legal applications within these processes. According to Article 2 of the Zoning Law No. 3194, it is stipulated that "Plans to be made and all public and private structures to be constructed within and outside municipal and adjacent area boundaries shall be subject to the provisions of this Law." By virtue of this provision, the principles and rules that govern spatial planning and form in the country are regulated under the Zoning Law (Erkün, 1999). Examples of legislation pertinent to zoning include the following:

- Law No. 4708 on Building Inspection
- Law No. 5216 on Metropolitan Municipalities
- Law No. 1580 on Municipalities
- Law No. 3458 on Engineering and Architecture
- Law No. 634 on Condominium Ownership
- Law No. 775 on Squatter Settlements (*Gecekondu*)
- Law No. 2464 on Municipal Revenues
- Law No. 2863 on the Conservation of Cultural and Natural Assets
- Law No. 2942 on Expropriation
- Law No. 2985 on Mass Housing

In accordance with Article 45 of Zoning Law No. 3194, the Ministry of Environment, Urbanisation and Climate Change is vested with the authority to designate development zones and permit municipalities to amend local zoning regulations. This delegation of authority imposes limitations on municipalities' powers. Although the powers of municipalities are not explicitly delineated within this regulation, decisions made by municipal councils may be encompassed within the regulation, contingent upon the distinctive attributes of each region.

The technical specifications of the zoning regulations under Law No. 3194 are dictated by the accompanying regulations, with Article 44 delineating the legal foundation for these regulations. In addition to Article 44, numerous regulations pertain to settlements and the readjustment of land or plots. Examples of these regulations include the following:

- The Regulation on the Principles Regarding Land and Plot Readjustment Under Article 18 of the Zoning Law
- The regulation regarding the procurement of base maps and the ground-level implementation of land and plot readjustment works
- The Model Zoning Regulation for Municipalities Outside the Scope of Law No. 3030
- The regulation of the High Council for the Protection of Cultural and Natural Assets and the Conservation Boards
- The Village Settlement Area Implementation Regulation
- The Bosphorus regulation
- The Zoning Regulation, which is applicable in areas lacking approved plans, both within and outside the boundaries of municipal and adjacent areas (Ünal, 2010)

6 Spatial Development and Management Forms

Numerous factors significantly influence the development and progression of cities globally. As urban areas evolve, their systems of transformation also grow, and technological innovations have a substantial impact on the composition of urban environments. Decisions regarding urban land use have facilitated urban expansion and contributed to widespread urban sprawl (Kahn & Glaeser, 2004). The economic and social dynamics within cities have evolved over the years, which is particularly relevant for developing countries. With population growth altering spatial use, the continuity of spaces, perceptions of accessibility, and the capability to access services collectively influence the urban landscape.

Urban growth exerts a direct influence on the urban life cycle and facilitates a balance between urban and rural land use. Although spatial resources are limited, it is imperative to create spaces for efficient use to cultivate healthy environments within urban areas (Turner & Duranton, 2012).

As presented in Fig. 1, based on the specific conditions of the country, land consolidation tools can be categorised into three primary categories: (i) voluntary sale

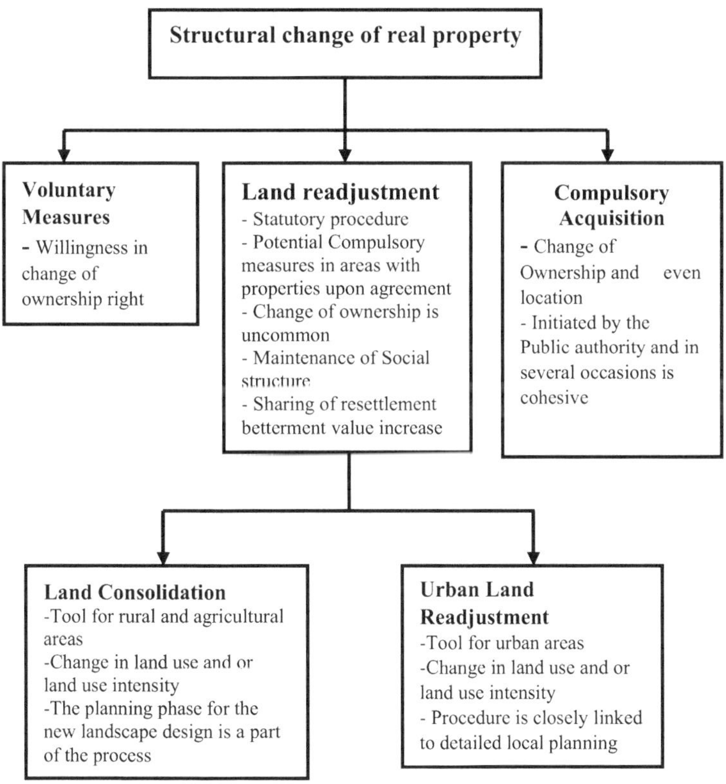

Fig. 1 Structural change in land development and property rights. Source: Lozano-Gracia et al. (2013)

agreements (land acquisition by mutual consent), (ii) compulsory land acquisition (expropriation or through governmental authority's influence), and (iii) land readjustment (Alterman, 2007; Wallace, 2010; Abd-Elkawy, 2018). The degree of implementation of a land development model predominantly relies on a country's legal and institutional framework (O'Brien et al., 2020). Notably, both compulsory acquisition and voluntary sale agreements are contingent upon market-determined values to facilitate the exchange. While compulsory acquisition encompasses an element of coercion, the latter is predicated on mutual consent (Uisso, 2023; Uisso & Tanrıvermiş, 2025).

During the land readjustment process, it is customary for implementers, including the state or municipalities, landowners, and individuals affected by the project, to collaborate seamlessly throughout the entire process (Yau & Cheng, 2010). Landowners may actively participate in the process, contributing their perspectives, thereby ensuring that an effective monitoring mechanism is established for the land readjustment project. Furthermore, land readjustment plays a pivotal role in promoting a fair distribution of redevelopment gains and project costs, alongside the collective sharing of consolidation and redevelopment values and associated risks among various stakeholders (Doebele, 2007; Yau & Cheng, 2010; Tan & Heerink, 2017).

The state possesses the capacity to acquire land through expropriation or market transactions; however, it may also gain from the enhanced value shared among stakeholders due to land readjustment (Tan & Heerink, 2017). This approach, which entails the exchange of undeveloped land for land that is suitable for development, is particularly appropriate for nations where governmental financing of public infrastructure investments proves challenging (Shoup, 1983a). Consequently, this mechanism serves as a self-financing alternative. Within this framework, it becomes a viable solution that assists municipalities in addressing the obstacles encountered during land development (Lozano-Gracia et al., 2013). Given financial considerations, the expropriation of substantial tracts of land to satisfy the demand for infrastructure development in urban settings is perceived to be considerably difficult in many countries (De Souza et al., 2018). Amid stringent budgetary limitations, an exclusive reliance on compulsory purchase methods for acquiring land intended for public use may impede local governments' capacity to execute new land use plans (Fig. 2) (Doebele, 2007).

Land readjustment can be regarded as an alternative method of urban development that diminishes the transaction costs associated with both market-based and government-led expropriation processes, thereby ultimately ensuring an equitable distribution of value gains (Türk, 2004; Ndjovu, 2016; Adam, 2019). In contrast to expropriation and compulsory purchase strategies, which necessitate substantial resources from municipalities or central governments to finance the projects, land readjustment has been recognised as a participatory and cost-efficient approach (De Souza et al., 2018). Within this framework, the method facilitates effective urban renewal and expansion by promoting seamless collaborations with affected individuals through their participation (Sorensen, 2000; Yoshino et al., 2018).

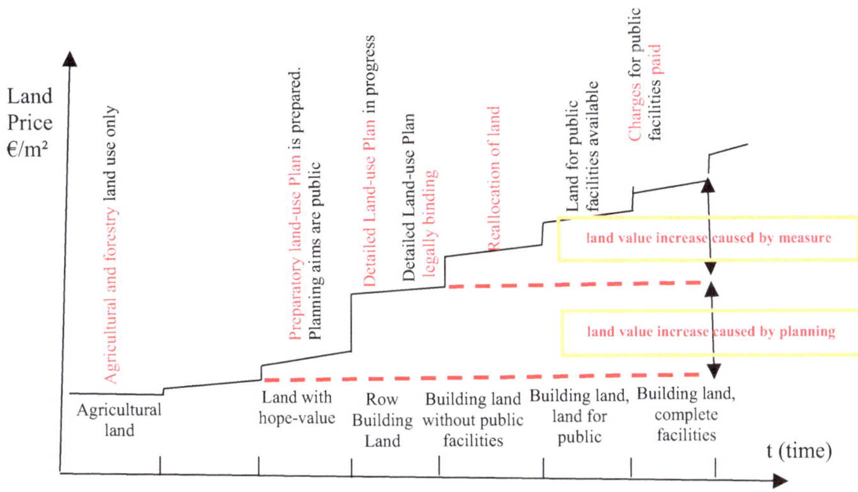

Fig. 2 Urban land development levels related to value. Source: Own illustration based on De Vries and Voss (2018)

Although this method is actively employed in Türkiye, it should be emphasised that deductions are made under the title of Deduction for Public Facilities (DOP) on the principal properties owned by participants. These lands, acquired without compensation, are used to establish the requisite public-use areas. In situations where land value appreciates due to readjustment within public or non-registrable spaces and a reduction exceeding 45% is mandated based on the size of the properties, implementation may occur in accordance with Article 7181 of the Law No. 7181 (Official Gazette, 10 July, 2019).

Furthermore, it is essential to note that in Türkiye, the allocation of new zoning parcels is based on area rather than value, which does not fully ensure equity (Bayraktar, 2019). The land readjustment mechanism is garnering interest in numerous developing countries due to its ability to enhance local infrastructure, safeguard the environment, and offer land for green spaces and other public amenities (Shoup, 1983b; Uzun & Şimşek, 2018). Given the limited financial resources available for land acquisition, developing nations possess an alternative prospect for land development (Shultz & Schnidman, 1990; Larsson, 1997; Sorensen, 2000; Thomas Lie, 2010).

Considering that Türkiye holds a prominent position among developing nations, it has initiated a development process, following numerous years of economic adversity and post-war rehabilitation. Furthermore, land readjustment practices have assumed a crucial role in this endeavour. The advantages of zoning and consolidation practices are apparent for both citizens and public sector institutions (Yılmaz & Demir, 2015; Uisso & Tanrıvermiş, 2024).

From the perspective of landowners, the advantages encompass enhanced property values, the regularisation of irregularly shaped plots, access to building entitlements, the amalgamation of fragmented small parcels, and the capacity to

Table 2 Benefits of spatial readjustments for landowners and public institutions (Bayraktar, 2019)

Benefits for landowners	Benefits for government
• after the project, land values rose significantly, making it more valuable for landowners.	• compensation expenses for public-use land are significantly reduced, allowing for the provision of public areas to be captured more economically.
• A cadastral parcel is reshaped and transformed into a site lot that can be utilised more economically.	• A zoning plan is implemented quickly, and urban land development projects are completed rapidly.
• small, fragmented parcels are consolidated into a new building parcel, maximising land use.	• tax revenue is increasing within the project area, providing an additional source of funds for the government.
• since the effects of the LR project are uniform for all landowners, disputes regarding land planning injustices are minimised.	• the land development programmes in urban fringe areas are executed systematically.
• at the end of the project, basic public services will be provided to new lots. Therefore, the latest social services will be introduced into the project area.	• the existing cadastral records are updated and reorganised, and cadastral administration is improved.

Source: Own depiction

collectively obtain public services without incurring supplementary costs. Conversely, from the standpoint of public institutions, this method offers benefits regarding land acquisition, significantly reduces compensation payments, facilitates the prompt execution of urban projects, augments tax revenues, updates the cadastral database, and establishes a systematic foundation for regional development (Table 2).

7 Conclusion and Evaluation

In line with spatial usage determinations, efforts for renewal and effective space utilisation hold significant importance. In cities that expand and evolve without strategic planning, the relevance of zoning plans and decisions emerges as a pivotal concern in spatial organisation, particularly when considering future projections. Within the context of spatial organisation, the equitable distribution of value, the cultivation of a sense of belonging, and the just incorporation of increased value into the spatial form are prioritised. In this regard, consistent practices in Türkiye play a vital role at both the local and national levels. Each zoning decision influences the equilibrium of urban growth and development. Ensuring that the distribution of value does not disrupt this equilibrium over time facilitates the appropriate direction of public investments and urban development through judicious location choices.

Following decisions regarding spatial usage, the distribution implemented at the parcel level facilitates spatial management through the strategic positioning of infrastructure and social facilities. Decisions made at the parcel scale impact not only local administrations but also overarching economic strategies at the city level.

Patterns of settlement in urban centres and their peripheries advance based on a comparative analysis of land use decisions across various regions. The equilibrium of rural–urban settlement structures can solely be attained through effective spatial organisation, while practices of land and plot readjustment at the parcel scale seek to foster the healthy development of these regions.

In consideration of the principle of value equality, urban land readjustment practices frequently employ area-based distribution models rather than evaluating each parcel based on its unit value, as evidenced in land consolidation projects. This methodology diminishes the probability of attaining fair outcomes. A plethora of academic studies has indicated that the application of a value-based distribution model for zoning and, ultimately, for parcelling in urban areas fosters a more equitable system. Furthermore, it is advised that real estate professionals collaborate with technical personnel engaged in these implementations to guarantee sound decision-making.

In circumstances where the Dedication for Public Facilities (DOP) mechanism, as acknowledged by legislation as the land acquisition model for common-use areas, proves inadequate, the expropriation method is frequently used. However, the public often perceives this method unfavourably. In such scenarios, land consolidation or the modification of zoning boundaries to ensure that the DOP rate remains below 45% can be advantageous for zoning implementations.

Zoning practices, which are considerably relevant within the Turkish legal framework and are subject to laws, regulations, and judicial precedents, are regarded as a fundamental mechanism for urban and spatial management. Although land and plot readjustment is a widely used and effective strategy, both in Türkiye and globally, for promoting the planned development of urban peripheries and the amalgamation of rural and urban areas, it is crucial to acknowledge the substantial challenges encountered during the implementation process. The number and nature of lawsuits filed in courts indicate that disputes related to property are quite common. Consequently, any initiatives aimed at reviewing and improving the methods employed in these processes will be of paramount importance for both the Turkish state and its citizens.

References

Abd-Elkawy, A. A. M. (2018). Requirements of implementation of the limited land readjustment tool in developing informal deteriorated areas (Case study: Daier el Nahea area - Dokki District – Giza governorate). *International Journal of Development and Sustainability, 7*(1), 381–408.

Adam, A. G. (2019). Land readjustment as a tool for urban development: A comparative analysis. *Land Use Policy, 83, 289–297.*

Aksay, B. (2005). *Hukuki Açıdan Arazi ve Arsa Düzenlemesi*. Makro Yayınları.

Alterman, R. (2007). Much more than land assembly: Land readjustment for the supply of urban public services. *Lincoln Institute for Land Policy*, 57–86.

Bayraktar, S. (2019). *Türkiye'de Uygulanan Arsa Düzenleme Yönteminin Swot Analizi ile Değerlendirilmesi (Yüksek lisans tezi)*. Karadeniz Teknik Üniversitesi Fen Bilimleri Enstitüsü.

Çete, M. (2010). Turkish land readjustment: Good practice in urban development. *Journal of Urban Planning and Development, 136*(4), 373–380. https://doi.org/10.1061/(ASCE)UP.1943-5444.0000031. Retrieved December 10, 2019.

De Souza, F. F., Ochi, T., & Hosono, A. (2018). *Land readjustment: Solving urban problems through an innovative approach*. JICA Research Institute.

De Vries, W. T., & Voss, W. (2018). Value capture and land readjustment: An international comparison. *Land Use Policy, 77, 362–372.*

Doebele, W. A. (2007). Foreword. In Y.-H. Hong & B. Needham (Eds.), *Assembling land for urban development* (pp. vii–xv). Lincoln Institute of Land Policy.

Erkün, M. (1999). *Zoning law. Ankara: Yetkin Publications.*

Güneş, P. (2021). *Kentsel büyüme, yayılma ve kentsel saçaklanma ile gayrimenkul piyasası ilişkilerinin değerlendirilmesi: Ankara ili Alacaatlı, Bağlıca ve Dodurga mahalle örnekleri (Yüksek lisans tezi)*. Ankara Üniversitesi Fen Bilimleri Enstitüsü, Gayrimenkul Geliştirme ve Yönetimi Anabilim Dalı.

Home, R. (2007). Land readjustment as a method of development: Land assembly: A comparative overview. *Town Planning Review*. https://doi.org/10.3828/tpr.78.4.4. Retrieved December 10, 2019.

Kahn, M. E., & Glaeser, E. L. (2004). Sprawl and urban growth. In *J. V. Henderson & J. F. Thisse (Eds.), Handbook of regional and urban economics. Elsevier.*

Karaağaç, M. F. (2019). *3194 Sayılı İmar Kanununun 18. Maddesinin Uygulanmasında Karşılaşılan Sorunlar ve Çözüm Önerileri (Yüksek lisans tezi)*. Erciyes Üniversitesi Fen Bilimleri Enstitüsü.

Koçoğlu, M. (2019). *Değer Esaslı Arsa Düzenlemesi Modeli ve Ülkemizde Uygulanabilirliği (Yüksek lisans tezi)*. Konya Teknik Üniversitesi Lisansüstü Eğitim Enstitüsü.

Larsson, G. (1997). Land readjustment: A tool for urban development. *Habitat International, 21*(2), 141–152. https://doi.org/10.1016/S0197-3975(96)00059-8. Retrieved December 10, 2019.

Lozano-Gracia, N., Young, C., Lall, S. V., & Vishwanath, T. (2013). *Leveraging land to enable urban transformation: Lessons from global experience* (Policy Research Working Paper No. 6312). The World Bank.

Lupala, J., & Chiwanga, P. (2014). Urban expansion and compulsory land acquisition in Dodoma National Capital, Tanzania. *Journal of Land Administration in Eastern Africa (JLAEA), 2*(2).

Msangi, D. (2011). *Land acquisition for urban expansion: Process and impacts on the livelihoods of peri-urban households* (Licentiate thesis). Swedish University of Agricultural Sciences, Faculty of Natural Resources and Agricultural Sciences

Ndjovu, C. E. (2016). Understanding the causes of dissatisfaction among compensated landowners in expropriation programs in Tanzania. *International Journal of Scientific and Technology Research, 5*(1).

O'Brien, P., Lord, A., & Dembski, S. (2020). How do planners manage risk in alternative land development models? An institutional analysis of land development in the Netherlands. *Land Use Policy, 91*, 104409.

Shoup, D. C. (1983a). *The economics of urban land development. Urban Institute Press.*

Shoup, D. C. (1983b). Intervention through Property Taxation and Public Ownership. Urban Land Policy: Issues and Opportunities, A World Bank Publication, Oxford University Press, 132–152.

Shultz, M. M., & Schnidman, F. (1990). The potential application of land readjustment in the United States. *The Urban Lawyer, 22*(2), 197–243.

Sorensen, A. (2000). Conflict, consensus or consent: Implications of Japanese land readjustment practice for developing countries. *Habitat International, 24*(1), 51–73. https://doi.org/10.1016/S0197-3975(99)00029-6. Retrieved December 10, 2019.

Tan, R., & Heerink, N. (2017). Public and self-organised land readjustment in rural China – A comparison. *Journal of Rural Studies, 53*, 45–57. https://doi.org/10.1016/j.jrurstud.2017.04.006. Retrieved December 10, 2019.

Thomas Lie. (2010). *Bir başkentin oluşumu: Avusturyalı, Alman ve İsviçreli mimarların izleri.* Goethe-Institut Ankara.

Tüdeş, T. (2019). *İmar planı uygulamaları: Kentsel alan düzenlemesi.* Ankara Üniversitesi Gayrimenkul Geliştirme ve Yönetimi Anabilim Dalı Yayını.
Türk, Ş. Ş. (2004). The applicability of urban land acquisition methods for the provision of serviced residential land in the Turkish case. *International Development Planning Review, 26*(2), 141–167.
Turner, M. A., & Duranton, G. (2012). Urban growth and transportation. *The Review of Economic Studies, 79(4), 1407–1440.*
Uisso, A. M. (2023). *Gelişmekte olan ülkelerde kentsel gelişme ve dönüşüm için arazi düzenleme modelleri: Tanzanya'da arazi düzenlemede alternatif modellerin uygulanabilirliğinin değerlendirilmesi (Doktora tezi).* Ankara Üniversitesi Fen Bilimleri Enstitüsü, Gayrimenkul Geliştirme ve Yönetimi Anabilim Dalı.
Uisso, A. M., & Tanrıvermiş, H. (2024). Impediments to urban land development and transformation in Tanzania: Evaluating conventional approaches and proposing innovative solutions. *Survey Review, 56*(1), 1–12. https://doi.org/10.1080/00396265.2024.2370599
Uisso, A. M., & Tanrıvermiş, H. (2025). Gelişmekte olan ülkelerde kentsel gelişme ve dönüşüm için arazi düzenleme modelleri: Tanzanya'da alternatif modellerin uygulanabilirliği. *İDEALKENT, 17*(47), 342–373. https://doi.org/10.31198/idealkent.1529698
Ünal, Z. (2010). *İmar mevzuatı kapsamında yapılaşmaya ilişkin süreçler, uygulamada yaşanan sorunlar ve çözüm önerileri (Yüksek lisans tezi).* Gazi Üniversitesi Fen Bilimleri Enstitüsü.
Uzun, B., & Şimşek, N. C. (2018). Land readjustment for minimising public expenditures on school lands: A case study of Turkey. *Arabian Journal of Geosciences, 11*(10), 1–12.
Wallace, J. (2010, April). *Land acquisition in developing economies.* Article of the Month – February 2010, International Federation of Surveyors (FIG), presented at FIG Congress in Sydney.
Yau, Y., & Cheng, C. Y. (2010). Applicability of land readjustment in urban regeneration in Hong Kong. *Journal of Urban Regeneration & Renewal, 4*(1), 19–32.
Yıldız, F. (1999). *İmar bilgisi, Nobel Yayınclık Ltd.Şti.*
Yılmaz, A., & Demir, H. (2015). Evaluation of Turkish land readjustment. In *FIG Working Week 2015: From the wisdom of the ages to the challenges of the modern world, Sofia, Bulgaria, May 17–21, 2015.*
Yoshino, N., Paul, S., Sarma, V., & Lakhia, S. (2018). *Land acquisition and infrastructure development through land trust laws: A policy framework for Asia (No. 854).* ADBI Working Paper.

Yeşim Tanrıvermiş is a full professor in the Department of Real Estate Development and Management at the Faculty of Applied Sciences, Ankara University, Türkiye. She attained her Master of Science (M.Sc.) degree in 2011 from the Department of Agricultural Economics at Ankara University. She earned her PhD in 2011, becoming the first PhD graduate of the Department of Real Estate Development and Management at Ankara University. Her research interests encompass the management and conservation of land resources, land resource economics, real estate analysis and economics, and real estate and asset valuation. She has been delivering lectures for several years and has published academic papers since 2006. Her publications consist of 50 international and 40 national peer-reviewed articles. Additionally, she has contributed to 110 international and 25 national full or abstract proceedings at various conferences and congresses, and has authored 35 books and 30 book chapters. Presently, she serves as the Deputy Head of her department at Ankara University. Moreover, she is an active participant in various academic and professional organisations. Her experience includes work as a researcher and consultant across diverse public and private sectors, with a focus on real estate asset analysis, real estate finance and valuation, land and building conservation practices, and real estate economics and management. Furthermore, she actively enhances cooperation with domestic and international institutions and mobilises financial resources for research projects.

Ümit Gedik is lecturing in the Department of Real Estate Development and Management at Ankara University. He earned his bachelor's degree in Geomatics Engineering from Yıldız Technical University and completed his master's in real estate development and management at Ankara University. His research focuses on land administration and related fields, and he is pursuing a PhD on a model that integrates blockchain technology with land administration systems.

Parla Güneş is a research assistant at the Department of Real Estate Development and Management, Faculty of Applied Sciences, Ankara University, Türkiye. She is currently pursuing her doctoral studies in the Department of Real Estate Development at Ankara University's Graduate School of Natural and Applied Sciences. She completed her master's degree in the Department of Real Estate Development and Management at Ankara University, with her thesis investigating the relationships between urban growth, sprawl, and the real estate market in the Alacaatlı, Bağlıca, and Dodurga neighbourhoods of Ankara. Ms Güneş's academic work primarily focuses on urban spatial perception, urban identity, spatial analysis, urban transformation processes, sustainability, and the preservation of urban values. Her research emphasises the importance of understanding the social and economic dynamics of urban spaces, evaluating public participation processes, and refining spatial planning strategies. She primarily focuses her research on urban transformation, socio-spatial dynamics, land-use planning, and real estate development, employing an interdisciplinary framework that combines sociology, city and regional planning, and real estate economics. These topics are vital not only for expanding academic knowledge but also for guiding policymaking and professional practices in real estate and urban planning

Amani Michael Uisso is an expert in real estate development, urban transformation, and land management, with an extensive academic and professional career spanning Tanzania and Türkiye. He holds a Doctorate and a master's degree in real estate development and management from Ankara University, Türkiye, as well as a bachelor's degree in Land Management and Valuation from Ardhi University, Tanzania. Dr Uisso's research centres on urban development, land management, and administration, and has provided valuable insights to the discipline through numerous publications. His work effectively bridges academic rigour with practical applications, addressing significant challenges in urban transformation and sustainable land use. Currently, Dr Uisso serves in the President's Office, where he applies his expertise to inform policy and strategic initiatives. In addition to his public service, he is a certified real estate appraiser and a highly sought-after consultant in real estate development, offering specialised guidance on projects that shape urban environments. With a steadfast commitment to advancing knowledge and practice in real estate and urban development, Dr Uisso consistently and significantly contributes to both academia and industry.

Real Estate Valuation System and Professionalisation in Türkiye

Harun Tanrıvermiş and Yeşim Tanrıvermiş

Abstract

The institutionalisation of valuation studies and the establishment of real estate departments at universities commenced in the 1900s. A substantial body of knowledge concerning professional standards and institutionalisation has since been accumulated across many countries. Currently, the formulation of uniform standards on a global scale, including those pertinent to real estate measurement, is widely accepted. However, in Türkiye, real estate and asset valuation studies diverge significantly from international standards, necessitating enhancements in quality. Until the early 2000s, valuation was predominantly pursued as a "secondary activity" by various professional disciplines, with a neglect of professionalisation and institutionalisation. To address valuation issues encountered within the money and capital markets, the Capital Markets Board (CMB) of Türkiye issued a Communiqué on August 12, 2001, which delineated licensed valuers and valuation companies and instituted licensing regulations. During the 2000s, the expansion of housing and real estate finance, infrastructure projects, urban transformation, real estate investment trusts (REITs), asset management, and real estate-based capital market instruments—propelled by macroeconomic stability—necessitated rational valuation of real estate, projects, related rights, and movable properties. The Housing Finance System Law No. 5582 of 2007 led to the establishment of the Turkish Association of Appraisers (TDUB), a professional organisation endowed with the character of a public institution, thereby ensuring the membership of valuation experts and companies within the Association and the supervision of their work. Currently, there are 154 valuation companies licensed by the CMB and approximately 18,000 licensed valuers.

H. Tanrıvermiş (✉) · Y. Tanrıvermiş
Department of Real Estate Development and Management, Faculty of Applied Sciences, Ankara University, Ankara, Türkiye
e-mail: tanrivermis@ankara.edu.tr; aliefendioglu@ankara.edu.tr

T. Just et al. (eds.), *Understanding Türkiye's Real Estate Markets*, Management for Professionals, https://doi.org/10.1007/978-3-032-13297-0_10

Excluding periods of economic crisis, between 1.2 and 1.5 million valuation reports are generated annually. Roughly 37% of the total 2 million lawsuits filed in civil courts are related to real estate, with an average of two reports obtained per case. Most expert witness reports presented in courts do not adhere to valuation science or international standards. Despite the enactment of Law No. 6754 on Expert Witnessing, there has been no significant improvement in the quality of reporting, thus highlighting the necessity to develop new methods and approaches within this discipline. Furthermore, objectives include organising the real estate valuation system within the public sector, grounding values for taxes and fees on valuation reports, and thereby reducing tax loss and evasion. It appears essential to unify valuation practices stipulated in legal regulations under a single authority, to reinforce the public valuation organisation, and to establish a public authority responsible for monitoring and evaluating the activities of private individuals and institutions.

Keywords
Real estate and asset valuation · Valuation profession · International valuation and financial reporting standards · Institutionalisation · Valuation quality · Supervision

1 Introduction

The acquisition and use of real estate have transformed over time, making property systems a key part of public order. Besides acquisitions for practical and social purposes, real estate development projects and capital market instruments based on these projects are popular investment options for both individual and institutional investors due to their expected potential for future growth. In many countries, real estate accounts for over 40% of household wealth and the total assets of businesses (Bender et al., 1997; Akçay, 1999). According to data from the World Bank, this proportion can reach as high as 70% (International Valuation Standards (IVS), 2017). With declining inflation rates in both developed and developing countries and considering the risk-return profiles of alternative investment options, interest in real estate has increased, highlighting the need to assess the utility and value of real estate and other assets.

Valuation is a comprehensive set of systematically completed analyses, interpretations, and classification activities conducted to reliably determine the value of real estate, movable properties, real estate projects, limited real rights, and intangible and personal properties. At the core of valuation activities lie the wants and needs of individuals, which introduces a certain degree of subjectivity into the work. Although nearly every good and service has a market price in market economies, individual or mass valuation is necessary for various reasons: Due to the heterogeneous nature of real estate and the absence of an efficient market in many residential areas, the valuation of such assets has become a distinct area of expertise in almost every country. With increasing levels of development, subspecialities such as real estate securitisation, financial reporting, company and asset valuation, and the valuation of personal property, environmental assets, antiques, and art have also emerged as independent professions. Furthermore, legal regulations and institutional requirements are significant factors that necessitate valuation activities (Tanrıvermiş, 2017).

After the first economic crisis of 1929–1931, significant progress was made in institutionalising the valuation profession, developing standards, and organising these services in both the public and private sectors. In many countries, the science of valuation has been widely applied in assessing property taxes, title deed fees, and capital gains for wealth taxation. Valuation studies are critically important in many areas, especially for determining tax values for plots, land, buildings, and facilities; collateral valuation for residential and commercial loans; expropriation; managing public real estate; urban transformation; privatisation; asset assessment; calculating income from real property and capital gains; foreign acquisition of real estate by natural and legal persons; and matters related to inheritance and partition of indivisible property. Furthermore, company mergers, capital contributions in kind, proceedings pertaining to execution and bankruptcy, combating financial crimes, financial reporting, and valuation of movable or intangible assets are also within this scope. Determination of compensation for illegal or wrongful users, identification of the ideal operational period and easement fees in project finance models, and insurance valuations are also key areas of application (Demirci et al., 2007; Tanrıvermiş, 2019). Beyond public projects, valuation is also essential in many private sector activities, including project development, money and capital market transactions, insurance, investment decisions, sale and purchase transactions, partnerships, marriage and divorce proceedings, and corporate management (Çağatay & Tecim, 2013; Hışır, 2009; Tanrıvermiş, 2017).

In Türkiye, valuation activities remained insufficiently professionalised for many years, largely confined to expert witness reports submitted to courts until the early 2000s. Over the past 20 years, valuation has been mandated by legal regulations in areas such as money and capital markets, expropriation, urban transformation, enforcement, bankruptcy, and accounting. However, significant issues persist regarding quality, professionalisation, training, and adherence to international standards. This chapter explores the development of the valuation profession, its main fields of activity, specialisation and standardisation processes, and current challenges by analysing relevant institutional records and valuation reports prepared by experts and companies. The historical development and legal framework of real estate, accounting, and asset valuation activities have been examined. Practical issues have been identified through an analysis of reports prepared by independent experts, and potential solutions have been proposed. Specifically, selected valuation reports and judicial decisions have been analysed and compared with International Valuation Standards (IVS) to evaluate compliance. The valuation infrastructure planned for establishment within the public sector, as outlined in recently announced macroeconomic programmes and policy documents, has been compared to examples from selected countries, and conditions for success have been identified. Furthermore, an analysis of the changing role of valuation experts, the need for professional development and specialisation, and licensing and educational programmes has been conducted, highlighting that existing programmes must remain aligned with international standards. In conclusion, restructuring the national valuation system for the public and private sectors and establishing an effective valuation framework are vital for the sustainability of the economic system.

2 Historical Development and Analysis of the Current State of Real Estate and Asset Valuation

2.1 The Scope of Valuation Studies and the Development of the Valuation Profession

Real estate and asset valuation involve studies that determine the values, benefits, or useful lives of goods for various purposes. Valuation methods differ depending on the good and the purpose of the valuation, resulting in varying content and approaches in each study (Mülayim, 2008). Private and institutional investors require that the value of goods be assessed at their fair value under competitive market conditions for reasons such as sales, collateral, investment, or financial reporting; this necessitates the preparation of valuation reports, which may be mandatory or optional. Valuation encompasses analysing the characteristics of real and movable properties and their related rights; assessing their value or benefits based on local market conditions; determining the duration of limited real rights; calculating rent and easement fees; and establishing the economic life, salvage, or scrap value of long-lived assets (Tanrıvermiş, 2017).

In the early legal regulations of the Republican era, the notion of the "expert witness" (bilirkişi), previously referred to as ehlivukuf, was employed; however, the absence of licensing and the inability to evaluate, supervise, or monitor their activities professionally or administratively adversely impacted the process of institutionalisation and the quality of services. The valuation profession was initially defined in the "Communiqué on the Principles Regarding Companies That Will Provide Real Estate Valuation Services within the Framework of Capital Market Legislation and Their Inclusion on the Board's List", published in the Official Gazette No. 24491 on August 12, 2001, which designated the expert as an individual licensed under this Communiqué. To offer valuation services within the domains of money and capital markets, the establishment of a valuation company is obligatory. According to Article 76 of the Capital Market Law No. 6362 of 2012, licensed valuation experts and valuation companies are mandated to be members of the Turkish Association of Appraisers (TDUB). The term "market value" was adopted as the primary benchmark for valuation in transactions related to money and capital markets, a methodology later referred to as "fair value" in the "Regulation on Banks' Procurement of Valuation Services and the Authorisation and Activities of Institutions Providing Valuation Services to Banks, which became effective in 2017. Pursuant to Turkish Accounting Standards (TMS-40), this metric pertains to the potential revenue derived from a sale or the amount payable in debt settlement (TMS 40, Art. 5).

A valuation expert is a licensed individual under the regulations of the Capital Markets Board (CMB) of Türkiye, authorised to perform valuations of real estate, projects, and the rights and benefits associated with these assets. Such experts may operate independently or provide services on a full-time or contractual basis with valuation companies. Engaging with a valuation company is obligatory for providing services to banking institutions. Given the significant role of the real estate sector in Türkiye, valuation expertise must evolve into a profession requiring interdisciplinary knowledge. Obtaining a licence alone is insufficient for competent practice. The valuation process necessitates expertise in fields such as construction, architecture, urban planning, business administration, agriculture, and law. Additionally, proficiency in market analysis, legal competencies for transactions with official institutions, interpersonal effectiveness, and multifaceted thinking are essential qualities for a valuation expert (Töre, 2004). Consequently, departments of real estate development and management have been established in numerous countries, undergraduate and postgraduate education programmes have been initiated, and international accreditations have been promoted. For sound investment decisions, elements such as legal status, location, physical characteristics, market rent, and property value must be evaluated through expert assessment. The legal status encompasses ownership, zoning, building permits, annotations in the land registry, easements, liens, and tax liabilities. Simultaneously, locational and physical factors include transportation, environment, building quality, age, orientation, view, and parking. These factors are categorised as internal and external. Internal factors comprise physical condition, scarcity, utility, and transferability, whereas external factors relate to the economic, social, and legal environment (Alp & Yılmaz, 2007).

External factors encompass elements such as demographic composition, environmental characteristics, natural disaster risks, security conditions, and access to social amenities and public services. For instance, a prospective decline in the population of a designated area for residential development could disrupt the supply–demand equilibrium, resulting in substantial declines in property values, thereby threatening the expected return on investment. Environmental factors are also important. The development trajectory of the area, infrastructural investments, occupancy rates, and ongoing construction activities can directly influence both the current and prospective value of real estate assets. In this regard, for investment decisions related to real estate or real estate projects to be well-founded, it is imperative to consider not only the current utility or yields but also potential future cash flows. Concerning natural disaster risks such as earthquakes, floods, landslides, avalanches, and rockfalls, it is essential to evaluate not only the structural resilience of the buildings but also the capacity for post-disaster response, the security level of the environment, and the proximity to social or commercial centres (Atik et al., 2015).

The scope and service areas of valuation activities have expanded significantly over time, with research on securities valuation and, notably, intangible assets gaining prominence in recent years. Applications include: agricultural lands (such as fields, vineyards, orchards, greenhouses, and meadows), zoned plots; residential and commercial properties (apartments, detached houses, mansions, waterside mansions, villas, shops, and offices); commercial buildings (business centres, plazas, shopping malls); industrial facilities (factories, production plants, workshops, warehouses); livestock facilities (cattle and small ruminant farms, poultry farms, aquaculture facilities, integrated meat and dairy processing plants); energy and fuel structures (gas stations, refineries, power plants); service-oriented properties (hospitals, daycare centres, schools, dormitories, parking lots, sports facilities); tourism facilities (hotels, guesthouses, holiday villages), marinas, shipyards, and ports; mass housing projects; logistics structures; entertainment venues (theatres, cinemas, concert halls); and highway rest areas, as well as special-purpose properties such as mining sites and stone, sand, lime, and marble quarries.

The valuation process concludes with the preparation of a valuation report based on the data. To initiate this process, a contractual agreement must be signed with the valuation expert, accompanied by a letter of authorisation. During fieldwork, the expert is required to obtain records and documents from various public institutions, depending on the nature of the property, such as the Land Registry Directorate, Cadastre Directorate, municipality, provincial special administration, National Real Estate Directorate, forestry and agriculture directorates, conservation boards, law enforcement agencies, and courts. In the preliminary phase, cadastral maps and zoning plans are examined, and the property's location is identified with the assistance of GPS technology. For properties with existing structures, an analysis of architectural plans is performed, and an on-site inspection is conducted to compare the current condition of the property with the project documentation. The purpose of this inspection is to identify the property's strengths and weaknesses by evaluating its internal and external features. The valuation is carried out considering the physical and environmental characteristics of the property, along with the economic and social context of its location. In this regard, the property's value is determined through market, income, cost, or hybrid valuation methods. Additionally, in the utility analysis of the property and project, factors such as local development trends and proximity to centres of interest are carefully scrutinised. With the aid of Geographic Information Systems (GIS), the property's distance to various zones, transportation options, and accessibility to social and cultural amenities are assessed and compared with similar properties.

The principal methods employed in individual valuation practices encompass the market (comparison) approach, the income approach, the cost approach, and hybrid valuation techniques. Due to their simplicity of application and widespread familiarity, the market and cost methods are predominantly preferred in numerous valuation studies. In addition to these traditional methods, advanced techniques such as hedonic valuation, multiple regression analysis, artificial neural networks, fuzzy logic, spatial data analysis, and nominal valuation have been increasingly used in recent years. These methods are favoured in mass appraisal studies. Automated valuation models (AVMs), specifically developed for this purpose, facilitate the rapid and systematic computation of a property's value by algorithms (Barańska, 2013; Mora-Esperanza, 2004; Glumac & Des Rosiers, 2020). These systems operate on extensive datasets to automatically estimate market value. Although automated valuation methods offer advantages in terms of speed and transaction costs, their capacity to fully incorporate local conditions and exceptional circumstances—particularly in developing markets such as Türkiye—may limit their accuracy. Nevertheless, when properly configured, these systems hold the potential to provide effective solutions, especially when time is constrained.

In determining the valuation methods to employ, the property's location, characteristics, rental and income expectations, risks, and the relationship between return and investment are considered. For zoned parcels, whether developed or not, comparison methods will produce optimal results if there is enough reliable comparable sales data and information on zoning and usage characteristics to benchmark this value. It is appropriate to value real estate and intangible assets by applying suitable income approaches based on anticipated future income or cash flows they can generate (such as rental housing, offices, shopping malls, residences, workplaces, land, industrial facilities, and operating and usage rights). For incomplete buildings and facilities that do not directly generate income, as well as owner-occupied residences, the market value is determined based on the cost approach. In valuation practice, care is typically taken to use two or more valuation methods together to derive the most suitable result.

The lack of standards, data infrastructure, and value maps that enhance the effectiveness of valuation studies in Türkiye means that valuation activities are often not carried out within a standardised framework. In particular, the absence of fundamental data, such as the physical characteristics of properties and comparable sales, in central databases forces experts to collect data from the field and relevant institutions for each study. This reliance on manual data collection from institutions like land registries, cadastre offices, and municipalities creates administrative difficulties, which in turn slow down the process and negatively impact valuation quality. The underdeveloped technical infrastructure in the country leads to the use of different parameters and methods across institutions and fields of application, resulting in the calculation of different values for the same property. Existing regulations permit such practices to produce ad hoc solutions, but the legal framework remains insufficient, especially in cases requiring mass appraisal (Erdem, 2017, 2018). To restructure the tax system and reduce the informal economy, greater use of mass appraisal methods is necessary. The first regulation in this direction in Türkiye was established in 2018. Consequently, these mass- and regional-scale studies are conducted using techniques such as hedonic valuation, e.g. by means of multiple regression analysis, artificial neural networks, fuzzy logic, spatial data analysis, and nominal valuation. To overcome difficulties in accessing the physical and financial data essential for valuation, especially in metropolitan areas, the use of advanced mathematical and software-based approaches like artificial intelligence, artificial neural networks, and fuzzy logic is recommended. While these methods may not be practical for individual (single) valuations, they can offer significant advantages in applications requiring large-scale and rapid results.

2.2 Development Trends of Valuation Studies in the Republican Era

In Türkiye, valuation studies were underdeveloped at a professional level for a long time and, until the early 2000s, were predominantly limited to expert witness services provided to judicial authorities. Initially, valuation activities were carried out through expert witness reports submitted to judicial bodies in accordance with the Civil Procedure Code, Law No. 1086 of June 18, 1927 (subsequently repealed by the Civil Procedure Law, Law No. 6100 of February 4, 2011), and the specific regulations within its framework. However, with the progress of financial markets, valuation services began to institutionalise and transform into a professional discipline from the 2000s onwards. In response to challenges faced by publicly traded and multi-partner companies during economic crises and driven by the need to develop capital markets and safeguard investors, substantial legal regulations were introduced under the Capital Market Law No. 6362 (December 6, 2012) and the previous Law No. 2499, which it repealed. Within this context, the foundation of the valuation profession was established by two communiqués issued by the Capital Markets Board (CMB): the "Communiqué on the Principles Regarding Companies That Will Provide Real Estate Valuation Services within the Framework of Capital Market Legislation and Their Inclusion on the Board's List" (Serial: VIII, No: 35, August 12, 2001) and the "Communiqué on the Principles of Licensing and Record-Keeping for Those Operating in the Capital Market" (Serial: VIII, No: 34, August 11, 2001). Moreover, the Housing Finance Law No. 5582 of March 6, 2007, further underscored the significance of the valuation profession, effectively completing its institutionalisation. For lending institutions, it is obligatory that valuation reports prepared during the securitisation of mortgaged properties in secondary markets adhere to international standards and remain valid and that an insurance system is established. Simultaneously, it became a requirement for companies exceeding specified thresholds in total assets, net sales revenue, and number of employees to obtain asset valuation services as part of their independent audits. Valuation services have increasingly been subject to legislative regulations across various fields, notably in capital markets, enforcement and insolvency processes, taxation, urban transformation, and expropriation (Yalçın, 2006).

The valuation profession in Türkiye has acquired an institutional identity and has advanced towards specialisation through the regulations implemented by the Capital Markets Board (CMB). The enforcement of a minimum service fee schedule under Law No. 6362, along with the mandatory membership of licensed valuation experts and valuation firms in the Turkish Association of Appraisers (TDUB), established by Law No. 5582, has played a significant role in standardising the sector and fostering the robust development of real estate markets. The primary objective of the Board in this domain is to ensure that investors are accurately informed and protected in transactions such as real estate purchases and sales, project development, leasing, and capital contributions in kind by publicly traded companies and real estate investment trusts (REITs). Consequently, the licensing of professionals authorised to conduct real estate valuations and the inclusion of companies founded by these professionals on the Board's approved list fall under the jurisdiction of the CMB. Over time, the licences conferred by the Board have gained acceptance as authoritative references among other public and private sector organisations. Presently, many banks, private companies, and public institutions prefer to use valuation services provided by licensed experts and valuation firms listed by the CMB.

The rapid economic growth and urbanisation process in Türkiye since the 2000s has, on the one hand, led to uncontrolled increases in urban land and property values and, on the other, caused an intensification of development activities and the emergence of increased economic rent through the rapid development of new residential, industrial, and commercial areas. However, it is observed that unregulated construction, urban transformation, and development zones within cities have also resulted in significant property and valuation challenges. As economic growth accelerated, inflation and interest rates declined to single-digit levels, achieving macroeconomic stability; consequently, real estate and real estate-based investments gained importance. The integration of these investments into financial and capital markets has, in turn, heightened the necessity for valuation studies. The primary issues encountered in real estate valuation studies conducted for various purposes in urban and rural areas include the failure to generate the normative data required for valuation methods based on legal and scientific principles; difficulties in accessing existing data, information, and architectural plans; insufficient application of international valuation standards; inadequate knowledge of real estate and project valuation methods; the inability to accurately identify the positive and/or negative factors influencing valuation; and the failure to develop adjustment parameters for these factors. Furthermore, the inability to create value maps at the settlement level, shortcomings in the institutionalisation of valuation services, and the inadequacy of project development and valuation services adversely impact the potential for the efficient and productive use of private and public real estate, resulting in property values significantly diverging from expected levels. These cumulative deficiencies lead to increased risks across various sectors, notably finance and construction, and within the broader economy (Aliefendioğlu & Tanrıvermiş, 2015; Tanrıvermiş & Aliefendioğlu, 2017).

For the guidance of urban development and the regulation of land markets, the effective provision of valuation services and the production of value maps have become essential. However, according to the Condominium Law No. 634 of 1965, when establishing full condominium ownership or preliminary condominium ownership, the land shares allocated within the project for each of the independent units of the main property must be clearly indicated based on principles of common ownership, in proportion to the values calculated according to their location and size (Art. 3). Despite this, since 1965, in practice, the land shares of independent units are not distributed proportionally to the total value of the main property and the value of each independent unit; instead, project developers arbitrarily determine land shares and execute the relevant title deed transactions. Such erroneous land share distributions significantly and adversely impact urban development and transformation processes. Furthermore, a notable deficiency lies in the fact that land readjustment and plot production activities conducted under the Zoning Law No.

3194, as well as land consolidation efforts within the framework of the Law on Agricultural Reform Regarding Land Consolidation in Irrigation Areas No. 3083, continue to be solely based on surface area. Determining the pre- and post-regulation land values in urban and rural land markets is crucial for preventing the loss of rights and unfair practices that result from subjecting parcels within the application area to uniform percentage deductions based solely on surface area. In this context, transitioning to a value-based regulation system serves the public good and societal benefit. Moreover, under the Regulation on the Assessment of Tax Values to be Used as the Basis for Property Tax, tax authorities may prepare tax maps by collecting essential data for property valuation from various institutions such as Directorates of Public Works, Agriculture, Zoning and Housing, Forestry, Land Registry and Cadastre, as well as municipalities and special provincial administrations. In this framework, when preparing value maps for buildings and plots, residential areas should be divided into zones based on building and plot values. These zones should then be further subdivided into smaller areas, such as squares, coastlines, main avenues, streets, and other thoroughfares. However, no comprehensive or systematic study has thus far been undertaken in this regard.

In conjunction with the progression of commerce and finance, valuation has also become an obligatory aspect within the field of execution and bankruptcy proceedings. Initially, an amendment to the Execution and Bankruptcy Law No. 2004 mandated the procurement of a valuation report for secured loans. Subsequently, it became a requirement to obtain such a report during the phases of bankruptcy and the postponement thereof. The Law on Pledge of Movables in Commercial Transactions No. 6750, enacted on January 1, 2017, facilitated the pledging of all plausible movable assets as collateral, thereby enhancing access to finance and boosting the competitive capacity of small and medium-sized enterprises—a vital component of economic and social advancement—ultimately augmenting their contribution to national economic growth. To expand financing opportunities for enterprises investing in industrially less developed or developing regions, where access to funding is frequently impeded by the limited value of land assets and the consequent inadequacy of real estate and other collateral, the Ministry of Commerce's Movable Pledge Registry (TARES) Regulation was implemented. Under this framework, transactions within TARES are executed by the Ministry within the jurisdiction of the Union of Notaries of Türkiye, enabling merchants, artisans, farmers, producer organisations, and self-employed professionals to use the system for obtaining credit through the pledging of assets to cover their requisite collateral. This development is significant for commercial banks and financial institutions. An analysis of sectoral practices indicates that commercial banks tend to exercise considerable caution in accepting movable assets as collateral, and the volume of collateral-based transactions, especially by private banks, remains at low levels. The main factors contributing to this include:

- Uncertainties concerning the preservability of the value of movable assets, the fact that the values of these assets can fluctuate due to numerous variables, and the monitoring and control challenges that may emerge if they are physically relocated all represent high-risk elements for banks.

- The limited number of valuation firms capable of appraising movable and other tangible or intangible assets highlights a capacity shortage within the sector.
- The need for valuation firms to go beyond simply determining values and to develop models and processes that enable the definition, monitoring, and reporting of collateralised asset values in a manner that assesses credit risk is one of the most critical requirements in practice.

Furthermore, it is essential to evaluate whether movable assets can be valued in conjunction with the real estate and commercial enterprises to which they are attached. The value stated in valuation reports for pledged movables needs to reflect market conditions accurately. Additionally, this value must be preserved during the collateral's liquidation process, and an assessment should be made to determine whether dismantling the assets is economically viable.

Following the global financial crisis of 2007, many countries granted permanent residence and citizenship rights in exchange for economic activities such as buying real estate, establishing a business, and creating employment to attract qualified foreign investors. In this context, an amendment to the Regulation on the Turkish Citizenship Law, published in the Official Gazette No. 29946 on January 12, 2017, states that foreign individuals who purchase real estate valued at least USD 1 million, with an annotation in the title deed records stating it cannot be sold for three years and confirmed by the Ministry of Environment and Urbanisation, are eligible to acquire Turkish citizenship through exceptional means. Presidential Decree No. 418, published in the Official Gazette No. 30618 on December 7, 2018, expanded this provision by allowing citizenship if a notarised promise-to-sell agreement for a property with established condominium ownership or preliminary condominium ownership, purchased for at least USD 250,000 or equivalent in foreign currency or Turkish lira in cash, includes a note in the land registry stating it cannot be transferred or relinquished for three years. Furthermore, a regulation effective as of January 6, 2022, revised the minimum real estate purchase amount for citizenship applications to USD 400,000 or its equivalent in a foreign currency. Since this change, there has been a marked preference among individual foreign investors to acquire citizenship by purchasing property in Türkiye, and consequently, housing sales to foreigners rose. The growing interest of foreigners in buying real estate in Türkiye has led real estate developers, property consultants, and legal firms operating in the sector to enhance their understanding of the legal and administrative procedures involved in these purchases. These developments signify that acquiring real estate for citizenship has evolved into a highly active area, marked by complex legal and economic considerations along with practical challenges.

A circular issued by the Republic of Türkiye Ministry of Environment, Urbanisation, and Climate Change, General Directorate of Land Registry and Cadastre, Department of Foreign Affairs, mandates the procurement of a real estate valuation report for sale and purchase transactions in Türkiye involving foreign natural persons. Such valuation reports must be prepared in accordance with established valuation standards and obtained from valuation and consultancy firms authorised by the Capital Markets Board (CMB) and the Banking Regulation and

Supervision Agency (BRSA). A real estate valuation report is obligatory for all sales transactions where foreign persons participate, whether as buyers or sellers. The submitted reports to the Land Registry Directorate remain valid until the transaction is completed, provided that the application is made within 3 months from the date of issuance.

After the global financial crisis, the risks stemming from flawed valuation studies and errors during the securitisation phase, along with their effects, are now better understood. As a result, strict regulations and standards are being implemented in many countries within this field (Aliefendioğlu & Tanrıvermiş, 2015). The presence of quality issues in collateral valuation and real estate-based capital market valuation studies not only creates a risk to the financial system but also negatively impacts real estate investments and the issuance of real estate-based capital market instruments. In valuation for tax purposes and sales, the fact that transaction values are much lower than market conditions causes central and local authorities to suffer significant revenue losses and results in an inequitable distribution of income and wealth. Conversely, in urban transformation, renewal, conservation areas, and infrastructure projects, the long duration of land acquisition and valuation studies increases land acquisition and expropriation costs, sometimes rendering many projects unfeasible. This chapter examines the overall structure of countries that could serve as models for valuation organisations. The chapter also outlines, based on macro policy objectives, a model for establishing a public valuation system in Türkiye. The regulation of valuation studies by a single public authority, conducting valuations for tax purposes, and designing a framework to produce macro-indicators for real estate markets, market observation, and analysis—thus strengthening the existing valuation system for money and capital markets and benefiting from accumulated expertise—would represent significant advances. For this purpose, a brief overview of how valuation studies are organised in the public sector of selected countries will be provided, along with proposals for an organisational model of valuation studies—particularly for taxation—in the public sector of Türkiye.

2.3 Analysis of the Legislation for Valuation Studies and the Methods to Be Used

The value of an asset varies depending on its economic characteristics and the purpose of its appraisal. Consequently, the initial step in the valuation process involves defining the purpose of the appraisal and adhering to a methodological framework suitable for that purpose. In real estate valuation processes, analysing the supply–demand equilibrium, price levels, and prevailing market conditions is essential. Valuation approaches are generally categorised as (i) traditional valuation methods, (ii) statistical or mathematical valuation techniques, and (iii) modern or advanced valuation strategies. In practice across many nations, traditional methods are preferred, particularly for individual valuation tasks, owing to their simplicity and high comprehensibility. These include the market value approach, the cost approach, the income approach, and hybrid methodologies. Conversely, statistical and modern techniques are predominantly employed within the context of mass appraisal exercises and scientific research (Tanrıvermiş, 2017).

Within the Turkish legal system, provisions governing real estate valuation are explicitly delineated in various legislative instruments and are categorised according to their respective applications. Although fiscal legislation prescribes distinct valuation methodologies for property classifications such as land, plots, and buildings, a definitive differentiation between the concepts of "urban plot" and land has not been established. In practice, there have been instances where definitions such as "land to be considered as a plot" are employed. Additionally, valuation techniques are comprehensively detailed for domains such as expropriation, confiscation without expropriation, and zoning procedures. Moreover, regulations pertaining to money and capital markets, including the Housing Finance Law No. 5582, CMB Communiqués, and BRSA regulations, do not explicitly specify the valuation methods to be used.

Although Turkish legislation has established criteria for valuing movable and immovable assets for various purposes within specific legal frameworks, the valuation methods employed in sectors such as real estate, financial markets, environmental compensation, and legal damages assessment remain undefined. This regulatory ambiguity grants valuation experts broad discretion in choosing methods, leading to significant discrepancies in value reports for the same subject. The absence of explicit valuation standards creates a substantial gap, particularly in cases such as determining land shares for individual units under Condominium Law No. 634, assessing betterment fees in residential complexes or cooperatives, and calculating value differences between renovated and non-renovated buildings in urban renewal and transformation zones. These uncertainties result in diverse valuation approaches in practice and produce varying outcomes for properties of a similar nature. Additionally, judicial decisions markedly influence real estate valuation practices. However, many of these rulings do not align with scientific principles or international valuation standards and often contain contradictory judgements. This disconnect between legal rulings and established valuation principles underscores the necessity of aligning the discipline more closely with legal practices.

2.4 Assessment of Approaches Used in Valuation Studies and Their Compliance with International Standards

Since the 2000s, international valuation and financial reporting standards have served as a fundamental basis for valuation research conducted for various purposes. Indeed, numerous countries, including Türkiye, have adopted international standards as essential documents to be considered alongside domestic legal regulations in valuation practices. Within this context, valuation reports in Türkiye, prepared for purposes such as participation in money and capital markets or financial reporting, are independently drafted by licensed experts affiliated with authorised firms, in accordance with the International Valuation Standards (IVS), International Financial Reporting Standards (IFRS), and Turkish Financial Reporting Standards

(TFRS). Here, 1500 valuation reports from the period 2020 to 2024, obtained from publicly accessible sources, were analysed to discuss the valuation data and methodologies employed in previously prepared reports, the differences among the results yielded by various valuation methods, the procedures for establishing the final value, and the reliability of these values.

An analysis of the reports revealed that the IVS used market value, cost, and income methods, with the market approach or comparison method being the most widely applied. The second most common method identified was the income approach, which was preferred for valuing commercial real estate and land. The cost method was less often applied, mainly for workplaces and structures. It was considered essential for properties without a market price or income, as well as for expropriation transactions. The analysis also revealed the difficulties in obtaining actual transaction data, with listing or asking prices often acting as substitutes. The use of official unit costs in setting cost prices is common, and this method is generally viewed as a secondary valuation approach next to the market value.

While the sales prices and rents advertised in the market for comparable properties are generally used in valuation reports, the sales information recorded at the land registry tends to be significantly lower than the market value (Tanrıvermiş, 2017; Taş et al., 2017). Experts try to simplify their work. Conversely, obtaining actual transaction prices from official sources such as the land registry or tax records involves challenges. Directly using such data in valuation is impractical because the property values declared at the land registry and tax records do not reflect the true market conditions. Limited time available for report preparation often leads experts to avoid collecting data through methods such as surveys and interviews with local real estate sales, project development and consultancy firms, municipalities, land registry offices, tax offices, or other reliable sources, and testing their validity. The review's findings suggest that the comparable property data used in valuation reports are not based on actual market transaction prices (or transaction costs), which adversely affects their consistency with the IVS.

The income methods, which require a detailed analysis of income and expenses and the determination of a discount rate, are generally used for commercial real estate and are applied only when necessary. Reports indicated that property rents, operating expenses, and other data, categorised by property type, were processed based on the business manager's declarations rather than financial records. Business managers' expectations inevitably influence valuations through inaccurate income and expense declarations. For this reason, the income value in many reports does not always align with the market value.

In income capitalisation, the average annual net income is transformed into a valuation by dividing it by a discount or capitalisation rate or by multiplying it by a multiplier. In the valuation reports, gross rent multipliers range from 10 to 15 times annual rent for workplaces, 20 to 25 times for structures, and 10 times for plots and land. The discount or capitalisation rates were determined in the reports either through a crude build-up method or were adopted from previously used rates; these rates also varied according to the property type and usage. The methodologies employed for selecting discount rates were inconsistent, and the applied methods were inadequately documented. In discounted cash flow analysis, the value of the real estate is obtained by discounting the net operating income of the property (after deducting expenses) to its present value using an acceptable discount rate. Instead of applying a standard rate or conducting calculations based on established techniques, it was observed that various rates were used arbitrarily, without any explanation provided for these choices.

In the valuation reports, the final value was frequently ascertained by the application of two valuation methodologies, and occasionally by a single method. Outside of project development contexts, the employment of three valuation methods remains uncommon. Typically, at least two valuation approaches are used for high-value projects, whereas one or two methods are customary for properties of relatively lower value. During the reconciliation of differing valuation outcomes, preference is accorded to the conclusions derived from market and income approaches. When a decision must be made between results obtained from different methodologies, the market value is generally regarded as the basis. Conversely, the "weighting method", which is emphasised in the International Valuation Standards effective from January 2025 (IVS, 2024), has not been found in valuation reports. Techniques such as discounted cash flow analysis, development appraisal, residual value analysis, and replacement cost valuation are seldom used.

Reports usually bear the signatures of two experts, with the supervising valuation expert conducting quality control. They are prepared based on fieldwork results by the valuation expert and are typically signed by the supervising expert after a desk review. In reports signed by three experts, the third expert reviews and controls the report before signing. The preference for two or three experts to prepare and sign reports in accordance with company policy, rather than the type of real estate. As highlighted by Tanrıvermiş (2008, 2019), the maximum time allocated for a valuation report on specialised properties such as shopping malls, mixed-use real estate, industrial complexes, and large-scale multifamily condominiums is 10 to 15 days. There is a relationship between the time allocated for fieldwork and reporting, its scope, and the cost and quality of the work.

What is more, the format of valuation reports varies depending on the client and company. Therefore, there is a need to standardise the report format based on the purpose of the valuation. Companies or clients should not dictate these formats; instead, they should be arranged according to the valuation's objective, with standardisation ensured. The reports include comprehensive details about the location of the property and business, macro- and microeconomic data, as well as the technical features of the property. The reports also contain site and architectural plans of the plot and structures, photographs, satellite images, and detailed analyses of factors influencing the location, competition, and value. For assessing the property's location and physical features, useful analyses are carried out using satellite imagery and secondary data, with an emphasis on visualisation. However, valuation reports often lack a thorough combined analysis of factors affecting the asset's value and situational analyses—such as PEST (political, economic, societal, and technological), PESTEL (political, economic, societal, technological, ecological, and legal), and SWOT (strengths, weaknesses, opportunities, and threats), especially in linking these factors to market and income values and assessing the impact of market risks and uncertainties.

2.5 Assessment of the Development Trends of Valuation Studies

The decline in inflation rates to single-digit levels and the acceleration of economic growth in the Turkish economy have boosted interest in real estate investments. Developments in the real estate and construction sectors have gained momentum due to rising domestic and foreign demand, leading to a substantial increase in the number of construction companies, real estate investment trusts (REITs), asset management firms, and real estate investment funds operating within these sectors. These developments have necessitated that real estate, associated rights, movable properties, and real estate projects be valued based on rational and scientific criteria. With the Law on the Housing Finance System No. 5582, the valuation profession gained institutional recognition; consequently, the Turkish Association of Appraisers (TDUB), a professional organisation functioning as a public institution, was established, and membership became mandatory for licensed valuation experts and valuation companies. Simultaneously, the aim was to supervise valuation activities and uphold professional standards through this body.

Following the initiatives of the Capital Markets Board (CMB) of Türkiye, the valuation profession has garnered increased prominence since the early 2000s. It has become a requirement for individuals aspiring to operate within this domain to graduate from relevant undergraduate university programmes, succeed in the "Real Estate Valuation Expertise Licence Exam", and meet a specific experience criterion. Although there has been a consistent rise in examination applications over the years, the sector's demand for qualified experts has not yet been fully satisfied. At the end of 2024, there were 17,938 licensed experts in Türkiye, including 16,245 with a real estate valuation expert licence and 1693 with a residential valuation expert licence. Nonetheless, due to limited sector activity, deficiencies in working conditions, and job satisfaction concerns, only 62.2% (approximately 11,157 individuals) actively practice in the field. The remaining licensed experts have designated their licences as inactive, primarily working in public institutions or other sectors.

The consideration of real estate as a financial instrument has necessitated the valuation of these assets in accordance with international standards. In this context, during the mid-1990s, Türkiye's inaugural valuation entity, Gayrimenkul Değerleme ve Danışmanlık A.Ş. (GEDAŞ), was established in 1994 pursuant to a decision by the Council of Ministers as a subsidiary of Emlak ve Kredi Bankası. Subsequently, in 1995, Vakıfbank founded Vakıf Gayrimenkul Değerleme A.Ş., and a significant number of new valuation firms have become operational, particularly since the early 2000s. Today, 154 companies have received licensure from the Capital Markets Board (CMB) and the Banking Regulation and Supervision Agency (BRSA). These companies employ approximately 6500 licensed valuation professionals (see Table 1). The remaining licensed experts are engaged within real estate investment trusts, investment funds, portfolio management companies, construction and real estate development companies and public institutions. An analysis of the undergraduate backgrounds of these professionals shows that 54.4% bear degrees in engineering and architecture, 38.4% in economics and administrative sciences, with smaller proportions originating from fields such as arts and sciences (1.9%), agriculture (1.6%), law (1.3%), and education (1.0%). Additionally, around 15% of these professionals possess postgraduate qualifications in real estate development or related disciplines. This data underscores the ongoing need for a qualified workforce within the sector. Consequently, supporting postgraduate educational opportunities, especially for professionals from diverse academic backgrounds, is of strategic importance for both careers and the improvement of professional standards.

Experts working for valuation firms, either full-time or on a contract basis, make up roughly one-fourth of all licensed professionals; these actively practising experts collectively produce between 1.2 and 1.5 million valuation reports annually for the money and capital markets (fewer in the crisis years 2018 and 2024). The main reasons for the rapid rise in the number of valuation experts over the past 4 years include the expansion of powers granted to the profession through new legal regulations, rising unemployment in other fields, and the mandatory TDUB membership required to conduct official expert witnessing and valuation in the money and capital markets. The number of reports fell by 4.12% in 2017 and by another 25.18% in 2018; in October 2018, the decline was even 50% yoy, but stronger data for May offset this. (Table 2). In 2016, 1,209,438 reports were prepared, followed by 1,159,568 reports in 2017. There is a noteworthy linear relationship between the annual number of valuation reports and the volume of housing loans, as well as total real estate and construction loans. Particularly in the post-COVID-19 period, rising inflation and increasing loan interest rates have restricted home purchases through credit, causing this share to fall below 15% of total sales. Consequently, the number of valuation reports prepared for collateral purposes has also fallen.

The topics of valuation reports and their distribution at the city level are also interesting: Over the years, there were shifts in the number of valuation reports, their share within the country, and occasionally in provincial rankings. However, the provinces of Istanbul, Ankara, Izmir, and Antalya consistently rank as the top four, with their national shares ranging from 17% to 20% for Istanbul, 8% to 10% for Ankara, 6% for Izmir, and between 4% and 6% for Antalya. Recently, the lowest number of valuation reports across the country was recorded in Tunceli, Hakkari, and Bayburt (Table 3). A clear relationship exists between the number of reports produced in each province, the growth of the construction and real estate sectors, and the provinces' development index. This structure has resulted in 82% of existing valuation company headquarters being situated in the three major provinces, which makes it necessary for large companies to focus on regional organisational structures and collaborate with contract-based experts rather than salaried staff.

Current analyses for the valuation sector show that the sector's profit margins are low, the level of organisational capacity at the provincial level is inadequate, and the number of licensed specialists falls significantly short of the demand in many regions. An analysis of the reports generated by these firms indicates that, although specialised areas such as monetary and capital markets, project valuation, and urban transformation are significant, the volume of reports produced in these domains varies considerably, and business diversification remains limited. An analysis of the sectoral distribution of valuation reports from 2018 to 2024 reveals that the banking

Table 1 Development of TDUB membership structure

	Years								
Indicators	2016	2017	2018	2019	2020	2021	2022	2023	2024
Licensed real estate valuers	4402	5262	6885	5815	6008	5855	6496	6427	6340
Licensed real estate valuation firms	132	133	134	137	139	148	154	159	154
Total	4534	5395	7019	5952	6147	6003	6650	6586	6494
Rate of change (%)	–	18.99	30.10	−15.2	3.28	−2.34	10.78	−0.96	−1.40

Source: Turkish Association of Appraisers (2025)

Table 2 Monthly distribution of valuation reports prepared by TDUB members (in thousands)

	Years								
Months	2016	2017	2018	2019	2020	2021	2022	2023	2024
January	79	99	84	56	116	65	90	109	72
February	98	100	81	61	117	75	95	93	73
March	111	124	97	92	115	98	131	114	74
April	99	97	84	75	43	75	125	91	44
May	101	99	101	68	52	52	126	103	69
June	103	84	90	44	204	99	151	68	47
July	68	90	72	63	191	68	80	73	65
August	102	87	46	90	122	88	102	83	65
September	94	88	52	125	95	106	99	71	73
October	118	103	51	122	86	98	96	69	82
November	122	99	53	115	81	125	108	64	80
December	115	88	56	126	66	135	117	66	88
Total	**1209**	**1160**	**868**	**1036**	**1290**	**1084**	**1321**	**1005**	**831**

Note: All values are rounded to the nearest thousand
Source: Turkish Association of Appraisers (2025)

sector comprises 95.36% of the total reports, while reports for specific purposes constitute 4.12%, and reports related to the capital markets account for merely 0.52%. These data suggest that the sector is predominantly engaged in traditional, collateral-based valuation activities. In contrast, the volume of work in project-based, innovative, or investment-oriented valuation types is limited.

According to legislation, real estate valuation companies must be organised as joint-stock companies and recognised as capital market institutions. These entities are authorised to appraise not only plots, land, residential and commercial real estate, industrial and specialised properties and projects, but also movable assets such as infrastructure facilities, machinery, equipment, ships, aircraft, and land vehicles. However, the predominant share among the valued properties pertains to housing, with a share between 59% and 73% in the last few years, reaching 61% in 2024. In the distribution of property types over time, housing, shops, plots, and offices are identified as the most frequently valued asset categories, although the rankings of certain categories, such as shops and fields, fluctuate periodically. In 2024, the number of valuation reports for developed properties increased, primarily attributable to economic developments (see Table 4). Nonetheless, it is deemed that valuation practices have matured in an application-oriented manner. Yet, the institutionalisation of valuation theory and its internalisation as a corporate necessity among all public and private sector stakeholders has not been fully realised, and this process will require time.

The fact that reports prepared by valuation companies and experts are solicited for various purposes by different institutions and organisations, each subject to distinct legal regulations, can give rise to complexities and irregularities. To mitigate these, it is essential to ensure legislative cohesion, update valuation standards in accordance with national conditions, standardise report formats, and implement

Table 3 Distribution of reports prepared by TDUB members by province and year (values in thousands)

Provinces	2018		2020		2022		2023		2024	
	Number of reports	Share (%)	Number of reports	Share (%)	Number of reports	Share (%)	Number of reports	Share (%)	Number of reports	Share (%)
Istanbul	160	18.39	259	20.13	246	18.95	170	16.88	147	17.65
Ankara	79	9.12	126	9.80	108	8.30	87	8.64	74	8.88
İzmir	52	6.05	81	6.30	73	5.63	59	5.89	52	6.24
Antalya	37	4.26	61	4.71	75	5.78	54	5.35	39	4.74
Bursa	32	3.63	47	3.63	44	3.37	33	3.33	29	3.52
Mersin	25	2.82	39	3.00	35	2.72	28	2.80	22	2.63
Kocaeli	24	2.81	36	2.78	33	2.55	25	2.45	21	2.52
Adana	22	2.58	32	2.48	30	2.30	21	2.06	20	2.47
Tekirdağ	20	2.35	28	2.21	28	2.18	21	2.11	17	2.08
Konya	20	2.33	28	2.19	35	2.67	31	3.06	22	2.70
Gaziantep	18	2.06	26	2.03	24	1.83	16	1.63	17	2.03
Manisa	17	2.02	24	1.83	25	1.95	22	2.18	17	2.05
Aydin	18	2.12	27	2.08	28	2.18	24	2.40	18	2.14
Balıkesir	17	1.92	24	1.88	28	2.13	24	2.36	18	2.21
Muğla	16	1.83	25	1.92	27	2.07	21	2.06	17	2.05
Kayseri	14	1.65	22	1.68	22	1.71	18	1.76	15	1.80
Hatay	14	1.61	19	1.46	17	1.33	7	0.75	9	1.03
Diyarbakır	13	1.55	18	1.42	21	1.60	16	1.57	15	1.87
Samsun	13	1.49	19	1.47	19	1.43	15	1.53	12	1.47
Şanlıurfa	13	1.45	16	1.25	20	1.51	14	1.42	13	1.62
Sakarya	13	1.45	18	1.40	19	1.43	14	1.36	10	1.23
Eskişehir	11	1.28	16	1.24	18	1.42	13	1.33	10	1.23
Denizli	12	1.39	18	1.36	20	1.53	17	1.69	13	1.59
Kahramanmaraş	9	1.03	11	0.88	14	1.11	8	0.82	8	0.93

Note: The number of reports is rounded to the nearest thousand
Source: Turkish Association of Appraisers (2025)

Table 4 Distribution of valued properties by type

	Valuation year and rate				
Property type	2018 (%)	2020 (%)	2022 (%)	2023 (%)	2024 (%)
Residential	67	73	62	59	61
Field	7	6	12	14	9
Shop	9	7	9	9	8
Plot	6	5	7	7	7
Office	5	4	2	2	2
Others	6	5	8	9	13

Source: Turkish Association of Appraisers (2025)

regular monitoring and evaluation of all valuation activities conducted. In particular, a comprehensive assessment and alignment of the provisions within the Turkish Commercial Code No. 6102, the Capital Market Law No. 6362, the Banking Law No. 5411, the Execution and Bankruptcy Law No. 2004, the Law on Expert Witnessing No. 6754, the Law on Pledge of Movables in Commercial Transactions No. 6750, and other relevant legislation—within the framework of the IVS, IFRS, and TFRS—is of paramount importance for both enhancing the operational conditions of valuation firms and improving the quality of reporting. For valuation firms to operate in accordance with established standards, these organisations must undergo regular and effective audits. The heightened competition within the sector has, at times, led to unethical practices, particularly due to the direct relationship between real estate valuation activities and financial interests. Consequently, the development of more specific and robust regulatory and supervisory mechanisms by the CMB is imperative. Conversely, the authorities granted to the TDUB by law contribute positively to the institutionalisation and growth of the profession, as well as playing a vital role in fostering standardisation within the sector.

The "Communiqué on International Valuation Standards in the Capital Market" (Serial: VIII, No: 45) established the principles for valuation procedures to be carried out by partnerships, institutions, and issuers subject to capital market legislation. This Communiqué entered into force following its publication in the Official Gazette (No: 26100) on March 6, 2006. The international valuation standards included in the annexe of the Communiqué were translation-based adaptations of texts published by valuation organisations in the 1990s. They were thus incorporated into the national regulatory framework. However, given the dynamic nature of valuation activities, a need for continuous updates to legislation and standards has arisen. Particularly after the global financial crisis in 2007/2008, the standards outlined in the annexe of the Communiqué were abolished and replaced by more current and comprehensive valuation standards, which were made accessible to all valuation firms. In this context, the "Communiqué on Valuation Standards in the Capital Market" (III-62.1), enacted by the Capital Markets Board (CMB) on February 1, 2017, repealed the earlier Communiqué dated March 6, 2006, along with its annexes. The new Communiqué mandated adherence to the International Valuation Standards (IVS) as published by the Valuation Standards Issuing Body (TDUB) and the Turkish Capital Markets Association (TCMA). Furthermore, it was stipulated that, in cases of discrepancy between the regulations of the Board and the standards published by the TDUB or TCMA, the regulations of the CMB would take precedence. In conclusion, although standards are predominantly followed in valuation reports, their application remains limited in specialised areas such as project development, the valuation of historic buildings, machinery and equipment, and intangible assets. Despite the mandatory requirement for the valuation of business assets within the scope of financial reporting to be carried out in accordance with IFRS/TFRS, public and private sector entities are not sufficiently interested in obtaining valuation reports for accounting purposes to prepare their financial statements. In summary, for areas outside the scope of money and capital markets, the specific conditions regarding when, by whom, and under what circumstances valuations should be performed must be explicitly defined within legislation and implementation principles to ensure consistency in practice (Tanrıvermiş, 2017).

The strength of valuation activities depends on their reliance on sound market data. Consequently, the validity of the data influences the accuracy of the valuation. In practice, however, the under-declaration of property values in title deed transactions to pay lower taxes and fees impedes the International Valuation Standards (IVS) from accurately reflecting market prices. In this context, market prices are predominantly acquired through hearsay from individuals active within the sector, and the listed prices of properties for sale are employed as comparable values in valuation reports. Such practices significantly compromise the reliability of valuation reports and highlight the necessity for more detailed and enforceable legal regulations.

A comprehensive data network that would facilitate the systematic processing and sharing of extensive data used in the preparation of valuation reports has been largely overlooked. An accurate and objective valuation process necessitates multifaceted studies, including project reviews at municipal levels, tax value inquiries, analysis of zoning plans and associated notes, access to land registry data, review of decisions made by conservation boards, data collection from relevant ministries, local market research, and on-site property inspections. Conversely, the practice whereby numerous municipalities impose fees for project review procedures increases the cost of valuation reports and, in some instances, results in the omission of these reviews. This practice diminishes the effectiveness of valuation reports; therefore, making these services free of charge or exclusively accessible online to licensed valuation experts could enhance data sharing efficiency. Moreover, in certain land registry offices, file reviews are conducted only on specific days of the week, thereby causing procedural delays. Such practices ought to be standardised through legislative regulation. The unit values assigned to plots and land, which serve as the basis for property taxation, are determined by appraisal commissions during each declaration period. However, these values often remain significantly below current market rates, with notable price disparities identified even on streets and avenues situated between neighbouring districts, particularly in metropolitan areas. This discrepancy arises because these values are based on subjective opinions and desk-based evaluations rather than market conditions and the valuation criteria stipulated in legislation, thereby adversely impacting the tax revenues of both local and central administrations (Aliefendioğlu & Tanrıvermiş, 2017).

2.6 Analysis of Development Trends in the Field of Expert Witnessing

The institution of expert witnessing is governed by laws pertaining to procedural rules, which constitute the comprehensive set of regulations that delineate the procedures and principles necessary to ensure that a lawsuit or claim presented before a court is adjudicated in a lawful, systematic, and rational manner. An expert witness is an individual who helps the judicial process and facilitates the court's decision-making through a report on specialised and technical matters requiring expertise. Expert witnesses, chosen by a judge, are appointed based on their specific knowledge and technical competence, and such appointments may involve a single individual or multiple individuals (Yıldırım et al., 2011). In cases where the resolution is significant and clarification or determination requires specialised or technical knowledge, the third party or parties whose opinions and views are sought by the court are designated as expert witnesses. The expert witness may be regarded as a judicial assistant and an instrument of evidence, much like a fact witness, particularly in establishing the material facts of a case. The work performed by an expert witness can be considered, in a sense, as a consultancy service. The institution of expert witnessing holds considerable significance for the effective functioning of the judicial system and for ensuring a fair trial (Meriç et al., 2016).

In real estate markets, many lawsuits are filed for purposes such as protecting ownership and usage rights, determining a property's rent and value, setting the price and duration of usufruct rights, claiming damages to property, and calculating and paying fees for unlawful occupation, eviction, and compensation for expropriation and de facto seizure (Table 5). Over the past 25 years, civil court cases have most frequently concerned inheritance, compensation, expropriation, protection of minors' assets, title deed cancellation, and dissolution of co-ownership, and the topics of these lawsuits have diversified over time. Currently, 37.44% of the filed cases in civil courts relate to real estate. When cases filed in administrative courts—such as those for the cancellation of zoning plans, projects, decisions of public interest, and Environmental Impact Assessments (EIA), as well as lawsuits for compensation arising from de facto expropriation—are included, the proportion of real estate-related cases within the total number of lawsuits is at least 50%. The process of handling inheritance procedures in rural areas is noted to be connected to eligibility for state support, and the number of cases concerning inheritance issues, co-ownership dissolution to facilitate construction on a parcel, and especially the establishment and termination of superficies (building rights) linked to project finance applications have increased.

A significant portion of the problems faced in the field of expert witnessing is directly linked to the competence and impartiality of the witnesses themselves. Key issues include appointing individuals as expert witnesses outside their area of expertise, experts losing impartiality due to social relationships or repeated appointments of the same individuals, the failure to enforce the oath, which should emphasise conscientious responsibility properly, and the improper administration of that oath. Moreover, some expert witnesses cause a miscarriage of justice by preparing reports

Table 5 The share of real estate-related cases within lawsuits in Turkish civil courts (numbers in thousands)

Case types	Number of cases filed								
	2000	2005	2010	2015	2020	2021	2022	2023	2024
Inheritance (writ of)	1	2	430	303	363	182	559	622	571
Compensation / damages	86	91	108	132	132	170	139	141	198
Expropriation	39	30	47	61	36	39	74	98	94
Title deed cancellation and registration	37	37	47	41	44	60	55	54	69
Eviction of leased property	41	36	41	38	28	37	32	62	70
Protection of minors' assets	–	–	31	38	25	28	27	31	29
Dissolution of co-ownership (İzale-i Şuyuu)	20	23	27	29	38	54	42	17	41
Inheritance	2	2	7	16	34	46	28	30	32
Prevention of de facto expropriation (inverse condemnation)	0	3	19	14	17	22	15	14	17
Condominium ownership	1	2	3	7	9	12	–	10	13
Cadastre	21	32	44	12	10	15	10	10	8
Annulment of disposition	0	1	3	5	11	14	17	14	21
Correction in land registry record	–	–	23	7	5	10	–	–	–
Rent / lease	12	7	4	4	3	5	21	44	67
Right of way / easement of access	3	3	3	2	4	6	–	–	–

Family residence annotation - annulment - Establishment of usufruct	–	–	1	1	1	1	–	–	–
Objection to enforcement proceedings	0	0	45	42	9	48	–	15	16
(Matrimonial) Property regime	–	–	2	5	16	22	26	28	34
Establishment of superficies (building rights)	3	3	0	0	0	0	–	–	–
Total number of real estate-related cases	**265**	**270**	**883**	**757**	**770**	**772**	**907**	**1048**	**1082**
Grand total of cases	**851**	**1021**	**1887**	**2168**	**1984**	**2565**	**1550**	**2888**	**3195**
Share of real estate-related cases filed (%)	**31.19**	**26.48**	**46.77**	**34.92**	**38.84**	**30.10**	**58.52**	**36.29**	**33.85**

Note: The number of cases filed is rounded to the nearest thousand
Source: Republic of Türkiye Ministry of Justice, General Directorate of Criminal Records and Statistics (2025)

that distort or conceal the truth, neglecting to report conflicts to appropriate authorities when outside their expertise, and having reports prepared by sub-experts in unrelated fields. When files are not thoroughly examined, or when information about the dispute is unclear or documents are incomplete, experts may overstep their duties and make errors in assessment. Some expert witnesses establish direct contact with parties in a lawsuit, which is not legally appropriate, often to complete missing documents or seek clarification. Additionally, unethical practices such as soliciting fees beyond those approved by the court have been observed. The failure to provide sufficient justification in reports, the inclusion of only vague assessments, and the preparation of reports not based on adequate research and investigation are also factors that reduce the quality of these reports.

Practices such as appointing experts as a panel of three to five individuals who fail to work in a coordinated manner, with only one expert preparing the report while others merely sign it, undermine report reliability. The failure to submit reports on time—an issue not taken seriously enough by judicial bodies or the experts themselves—and the absence of disciplinary or penal sanctions against experts who do not deliver reports promptly also diminish the process's effectiveness. When courts refer cases to expert witnesses using vague phrases like "for the referral of the file to the expert witness", or "for the submission of the file and its annexes to the expert witness", or "for obtaining the expert witness" opinion in light of the parties' claims and defenses", they fail to clearly define the scope of work or specify the questions to be answered. This results in reports that lack adequate content. Lastly, the tendency of courts to frequently resort to expert witnesses, even in minor matters or general legal issues, creates multiple problems. Because the fees for expert witnesses are kept disproportionately low relative to the dispute amount, the role is often not preferred by capable individuals, performed reluctantly or without seriousness, and may even lead to beneficiaries soliciting benefits from the parties (Meriç et al., 2016).

As a result of extensive discussions and efforts aimed at mitigating issues within the field of expert witnessing, a significant milestone was achieved with the enactment of Law No. 6754 on Expert Witnessing. This legislation has enabled individuals possessing at least 5 years of professional experience in a specific domain and holding a basic training certificate to be appointed as expert witnesses. The content of the foundational training programmes is determined by the Ministry of Justice, with a primary focus on the scope and limitations of an expert witness's duties and the National Judiciary Informatics System (UYAP). The primary and sub-speciality areas permissible for expert testimony have been delineated by committees established within the Ministry, and applications to these fields are contingent upon possession of specific diplomas, proficiency certificates, or other qualifications. Additionally, an amendment to Law No. 2942 (Expropriation Law) mandates that expert panels for real estate valuation include at least one member holding a master's or doctoral degree in real estate development and/or being licensed under Law No. 6362 (Capital Market Law). Circulars issued by the Ministry of Justice, Department of Expert Witnessing, emphasise that accepting postgraduate education as a criterion for expert witness selection signifies an important advancement in defining expertise. However, it is observed that the areas of expertise, initially established through comprehensive scientific and technical research, have been restructured due to political influence, deviating from scientific standards—particularly with regard to expanding the role of lawyers as expert witnesses. In this context, criticisms have been raised that Law No. 6754, enacted to address judiciary challenges related to expert witnessing, has effectively created a more centralised system susceptible to executive influence. Such developments undermine the reformist objectives initially envisioned by the legislation.

2.7 The Need for Organisation of Valuation Studies and Development Trends

In nearly all countries, valuation activities that are conducted as part of official transactions—such as tax assessments, title deed procedures, expropriations, and the management of public real estate—are distinguished from valuations performed for financial markets, accounting practices, investment planning, and other specialised purposes. Valuation procedures for such official transactions are frequently executed within the framework of specific legal regulations, where the effectiveness and institutional capacity of public structures are prioritised. In countries such as the United States, the United Kingdom, and the Netherlands, particular emphasis is placed on ensuring the independence, transparency, and reliability of valuation processes; consequently, valuation activities are regarded as highly institutionalised, both structurally and through supervisory mechanisms. These countries have adopted different institutional structures and organisational models tailored to different valuation purposes, with valuation standards developed and implemented based on international standards (e.g. IVS and Royal Institution of Chartered Surveyors (RICS)). Additionally, the development of valuation guides, training of valuation experts, and the qualification criteria for professionals are often managed collaboratively by public authorities and professional organisations. As a result, disciplines including real estate development, management, investment, and finance have evolved into autonomous professional fields, with specialists in these areas playing a crucial role in the institutionalisation of valuation services (Aliefendioğlu & Tanrıvermiş, 2019).

The licensing of individuals who conduct valuation services and the process of institutionalisation differ between the public and private sectors. The legislation and practices for organising valuation studies in the public sector and authorising private valuation offices and companies vary according to national conditions. In some countries (like the United Kingdom, the Netherlands, Germany, Slovenia, Denmark, Sweden, Finland, Russia, the USA, or Canada), valuation for official transactions is either carried out or commissioned by various public institutions. However, in almost every country, valuation studies for purposes such as money and capital markets, real estate sales and purchases, collateral, project development, capital contributions in kind to legal entities, the issuance of real estate-based capital market instruments, securitisation, insurance, and accounting are provided entirely by private firms or licensed valuation experts. In the public sector of many countries, valuation procedures for wealth taxation, zoning applications, land consolidation, expropriation, and the management of public real estate are conducted, in part or in full, by public institutions (Demirci et al., 2007; Tanrıvermiş, 2019).

The inability to produce comprehensive value maps and calibrate individual valuation studies has hindered the control of property values and the analysis of value fluctuations at the neighbourhood, village, district, and provincial levels. The establishment of the Real Estate Information Centre Inc. (GABIM), a subsidiary of the Central Registry Agency of Türkiye (Central Securities Depository and Trade Repository of the Turkish Capital Markets, MKK), which is affiliated with Borsa İstanbul, is regarded as a structure that will benefit not only professional experts and public institutions but all stakeholders. This company's inception was driven by necessity, enabling the creation of a database and the conduct of report audits relevant to society, accessible to all real estate owners. It is envisaged that a real estate value index should be developed at the neighbourhood and street levels, subject to auditing not only by entities authorised under narrower laws, such as the Capital Markets Board (CMB), but also by nationally authorised organisations regulated by other legislation (Taş et al., 2017). Furthermore, it is believed that valuable information, such as real estate value and rent indices, holds public interest; this information should be freely accessible rather than fee-based, open to the public and academic circles, with appropriate legal regulations enacted accordingly. The "Regulation on the Establishment and Management of the Real Estate Value Information Centre", drafted by the General Directorate of Land Registry and Cadastre (TKGM) and presented for stakeholder feedback to establish a national Real Estate Value Information Centre by aggregating data from all public and private institutions, courts, and enforcement offices, is substantially complete. This initiative aims to provide more accurate information and comparative opportunities regarding the validity of the final appraised value to both public and private institutions, as well as individual property owners.

A significant portion of real estate acquisitions, construction, and project development activities is supported by financial institutions. These institutions, which provide funding, seek to secure the credit they extend. In case of non-repayment for any reason, the quickest way for the financial institution to recover its credit is through the real estate itself. Therefore, accurately assessing the property's value is crucial for securing the loan (Wu et al., 2015). Real estate valuation services are supplied by licensed valuation companies employing expert personnel. These valuation companies are joint-stock companies and must be authorised by the CMB and the BRSA. The number of CMB-licensed real estate valuation companies listed by the BRSA is 136, and this list is updated periodically. Valuation companies primarily serve financial institutions rather than individuals. They provide this service based on the real estate valuation fees announced annually by the TDUB, under the condition of adhering to yearly contracts with the general and regional bank directorates. Unlike the commissions and expert witnesses of the past, real estate valuation companies operate as independent firms, not affiliated with any institution, and conduct the task of preparing valuation reports that are valid for a set period. These reports are used as a basis in judicial and financial organisations. Professional valuation services are delivered by licensed real estate valuation specialists, licensed residential valuation specialists, and their assistants.

Practically, there is a frequent requirement for the valuation of movable assets for various purposes such as accounting, sales and acquisitions, collateral security, insurance, and loss assessment. Significantly, the Law on Pledge of Movables in Commercial Transactions No. 6750, enacted on October 20, 2016, seeks to facilitate access to financing by broadening the application of the non-possessory pledge right as a security interest, expanding the range of movable assets subject to this pledge, ensuring transparency through public disclosure of movable promises, and providing alternative liquidation methods. Consequently, it became possible for the involved parties to determine the value of the movable asset subject to the pledge according to the procedure specified in the second paragraph before establishing the pledge right. Nevertheless, although considerable advancements have been achieved in valuation research concerning money and capital markets and in response to investor needs, there remains a deficiency in valuation studies concerning real estate, income, corporate, inheritance, and transfer taxes and fees. Additionally, research in areas such as expropriation, project development, creation of limited real rights, zoning, and land share distribution in the formation of condominium ownership continues to be inadequate. Furthermore, valuation procedures employed in expert witness reports submitted to judicial authorities are frequently observed to fall short of acceptable standards within the domains of valuation science, international norms, and legislative requirements.

An amendment published in the Official Gazette on July 15, 2018 (No. 30479) restructured Section 34 of Presidential Decree No. 4, which governs the duties and powers of the General Directorate of Land Registry and Cadastre. This decree allocated new responsibilities to the General Directorate, explicitly clarifying its role in conducting mass appraisals of real estate, performing individual valuations to generate requisite data, establishing and managing the Real Estate Value Information Centre, and producing and maintaining current value maps. The effective execution of these tasks necessitates the formation of a **Department of Real Estate Valuation**. However, considering current practices, it is proposed that organising this unit as a higher-level authority, such as a General Directorate of Real Estate Valuation or a Real Estate Valuation Board, would more effectively support the institutionalisation of the valuation field. Meanwhile, the valuation values used as the basis for sales, purchases, and other disposition transactions at land registry offices continue to rely on a declaration system or a minimum value application. Nonetheless, initiatives to replace this practice with a system grounded on formal valuation reports are reportedly advancing swiftly, encompassing legislative activities, software infrastructure development, and system installation efforts.

With Presidential Decree No. 30, published in the Official Gazette on February 5, 2019, the phrase "to regulate and conduct mass appraisal activities" was added to the objectives of the General Directorate of Land Registry and Cadastre. The same Decree also explicitly defined the following aspects as duties and powers of the General Directorate: the determination of the value of real estate through mass appraisal methods, the establishment and management of the Value Information Centre, and ensuring the production and updating of value maps. Furthermore, the Decree established a new unit within the General Directorate of Land Registry and Cadastre, named the "Department of Real Estate Valuation", tasked with real estate valuation employing mass appraisal methods, harmonising standards with national conditions, developing value maps, and conducting relevant research and reporting. Through this regulation, the General Directorate of Land Registry and Cadastre endeavours to create a systematic framework for valuing real estate nationwide, developing value maps, and executing title deed transactions based on individual valuations.

In the realm of wealth taxation, the most equitable approach is grounded in declaration. Accurately reporting one's earnings, income, and sale-purchase values is not merely a civic duty but, more importantly, a conscientious obligation. It is conceivable that this conscientious decision might not always be executed correctly for various reasons, such as economic conditions, perceived tax injustice, or high tax rates. It is the responsibility of the state to check and verify the accuracy of these declarations on behalf of all citizens. Real estate transactions involving sale and purchase are subject to a title deed fee of 2% for the buyer and 2% for the seller, computed based on the actual sale and purchase price, which cannot be less than the property's tax value. The basis for the title deed fee is the declaration furnished by the buyer and seller. Should the declared sale and purchase value be lower than the property's tax value, the higher tax value shall be employed in the calculation of the title deed fee. Within the declaration-based tax assessment system, regarded as the most consistent framework, establishing minimum declaration values or tax base determination procedures within statutory law represents a means to ensure tax security. For the title deed fee, this threshold has been established as the property tax value. Nevertheless, it is also acknowledged that, for various reasons, property tax values often do not accurately reflect the true market situation and tend to become outdated—that is, they fall below the actual value—rendering this lower value the primary basis for calculation in real estate transactions.

Türkiye's Twelfth Development Plan (2024–2028) emphasises that "a mechanism for monitoring the real value of real estate will be established to contribute to the efficient functioning of the real estate market". Furthermore, the Plan states that "a technical infrastructure will be developed for monitoring real estate value changes and creating real estate value maps", and "legislative infrastructure studies will be carried out for the correct determination of real estate value" (Presidency of the Republic of Türkiye, Strategy and Budget Office, 2023). The plan envisages the establishment of a comprehensive database that records the current values of real estate in coordination with relevant institutions, as well as the implementation of computer-assisted mass appraisal methods, primarily for taxation purposes. However, it does not include a policy framework regarding the individual valuation reports prepared for the money and capital markets or judicial proceedings.

Although it is anticipated that the tax base for the title deed fee will be declared and calculated based on market values as determined by valuation reports, such a regulation would necessitate an amendment to Law No. 492 on Fees. Presently, the profession of real estate valuation is governed under the Capital Market Law, with comprehensive valuation procedures conducted by licensed experts authorised by the Board. The residual question remains: what would be the impact if an alternative public institution engaged in value determination, and such a value was subsequently used for tax transactions? Currently, property tax values are established quadrennially by appraisal commissions at the provincial and district levels for each street and avenue. It is unlikely that members of these administrative commissions possess the requisite technical expertise in valuation. In numerous provinces and districts, the tax value of plots ranges between 20% and 30% of the market value. Furthermore, since residential and commercial structures on these plots are appraised based on cost, the overall tax value remains markedly below prevailing market transaction values. Consequently, in many instances where tax value serves as the basis, both central and local administrations encounter significant revenue losses, thereby impairing the quality of public services. However, when a dynamic, current, and transaction-based valuation that accurately reflects market conditions cannot be provided—an issue subject to debate from a public policy perspective owing to the extensive and costly nature of such procedures—then a system predicated on valuations performed by licensed experts as needed, supported by up-to-date value maps derived from these valuations, would be more meaningful and dependable than a fixed valuation by public authorities, even if the latter represents an improvement compared to the existing system. To establish a functional and transparent financial system, it is imperative to reduce the title deed fees applied to real estate transactions. Subsequently, adopting a system that bases transactions on valuation reports reflecting actual market values—prepared by licensed experts at the time of each transaction—would be appropriate. Such a system would obviate the need for periodic revaluations, and through effective control mechanisms during both the valuation and transaction stages, it would be possible to reduce tax losses and evasion.

It is essential to recognise that the genuine strength of the valuation industry relies on accurate market data, which remains valid solely when it is dependable. The undervaluation recorded in the land registry, intended to keep taxes and fees low, does not accurately reflect the true market prices, as per the IVS. Under these circumstances, it is understood that market prices are obtained from stakeholders within the real estate sector, often based on hearsay, and that the advertised sale prices of properties are used as comparable data in valuation reports. This practice compromises the reliability of valuation reports and underscores the necessity for appropriate legal and institutional regulations. Additionally, valuations are frequently conducted within limited time frames. Valuation reports typically specify a period of 3 to 5 days for assessment, which may be inadequate for comprehensive on-site inspections, data collection, analysis, and reporting. Furthermore, the availability of essential data—encompassing technical, financial, economic, environmental, and social information—is often restricted in many cities. This situation is worsened by the costs associated with activities such as examining completed sales at land registry offices, obtaining copies of land registry records, and analysing zoning plans and architectural projects in municipal offices. The requirement to visit these institutions at designated times further increases costs and reduces the efficacy of valuation reports. It would be advantageous if all information required for valuation could be made accessible to experts via online platforms without charge. Moreover, consolidating data such as zoning plans, three-dimensional architectural designs, and other relevant information into a comprehensive database and making it available for valuation purposes—justified by the public benefit derived from the work of valuation professionals—would markedly improve the overall process.

3 Conclusion and Recommendations

Real estate assets hold strategic significance from both economic and social viewpoints. The housing and construction sector is considered one of the core industries with the potential to stimulate economic growth during periods of stability and crisis alike. Like other core sectors, the construction industry currently encounters structural challenges. Nonetheless, it is conceivable to mobilise approximately 100 related sectors, primarily within the real estate domain, through the revitalisation of the construction industry. Although the classification of the real estate sector within the national accounts system presents complexities, the sector's value is predominantly derived from the stock of plots, land, and buildings. The foundation of land management is established by real estate economics, development, administration, and policy, alongside cadastre, zoning planning, value-based zoning applications, and land consolidation activities. Central to these areas must be an institutionalised and effective real estate and asset valuation system. While real estate economics and management constitute a multidimensional discipline, the establishment of a transparent and scientifically grounded valuation infrastructure is essential for the functionality of this system.

In Türkiye, considerable progress has been achieved in valuation studies concerning the money and capital markets, responding effectively to investor needs. Conversely, however, valuation activities conducted in realms such as property, income, corporate, and inheritance and transfer taxes and fees, as well as in expropriation, project development, the establishment of limited real rights, zoning applications, and the distribution of land shares in the formation of condominium ownership, are deemed insufficient. Moreover, the valuation procedures documented in expert witness reports submitted to the courts frequently do not meet academically accepted standards, international valuation standards, or applicable legislation. Thus, the aim "to develop the real estate valuation system, mass appraisal, and value map production", as articulated in the macro policy documents published by the Presidency of the Republic of Türkiye, is of paramount importance for enhancing the quality of valuation studies for public services and for addressing current issues. Nonetheless, efforts since the 2000s to structurally institutionalise valuation activities within the public sector have yet to reach fruition. Consequently, the Department of Real Estate Valuation, established within the General Directorate of Land Registry and Cadastre, possesses a limited capacity to realise the objectives outlined in the macro policy documents comprehensively.

Although Türkiye has an existing real estate valuation system, it faces structural issues. Therefore, instead of creating an entirely new system, a more sensible approach would be to overhaul the current one, strengthen the valuation authority within public institutions, formalise the valuation profession, and align it with international standards. Additionally, how the proposed real estate valuation system will be incorporated with existing practices will be a key factor in its success. In this context, it is considered feasible to establish institutions such as a value information system and a real estate exchange under a public authority, preferably within Borsa Istanbul. This approach is crucial for securing property information, protecting investors, and facilitating the public use of the data generated.

Enhancing the effectiveness of the national real estate valuation system can largely be achieved by integrating international standards into local contexts. In this regard, adherence to standards established by organisations such as the International Valuation Standards (IVS), the Royal Institution of Chartered Surveyors (RICS), and the International Property Measurement Standards (IPMS) will help to create a more reliable and transparent valuation process for both local and global investors (IVS, 2024; RICS, 2024). However, realising this requires promoting widespread professionalisation of valuation processes, strengthening professional education, and improving reporting standards. These steps will boost Türkiye's institutional capacity in real estate valuation and reinforce its competitive position in the international market. Applying valuation methods grounded in scientific principles and executed correctly will ensure that economic decisions in both public and private sectors are based on sound reasoning, thereby supporting sustainable economic growth. Alongside individual valuation reports for financial institutions and judicial bodies, reports are also prepared for central and local administrations for purposes such as expropriation, real estate transactions, urban transformation, rent assessment, and project development. Nonetheless, the content and presentation standards of these reports, prepared within both the public and private sectors, still have room for improvement. Therefore, promoting professionalisation remains essential.

As in many countries, Türkiye needs to strengthen its institutional capacity so that mass appraisal methods can be effectively used within public policies such as taxation, zoning plannıng, and land consolidation. Developing the public valuation infrastructure in this direction is crucial for reducing losses in tax and fee revenues, enabling public institutions and the private sector to assess the value of their real estate assets more accurately, and for establishing the valuation profession as a recognised discipline. In this context, the education-research-application cooperation protocols that have been in place since 2010 among the General Directorate of Land Registry and Cadastre, the General Directorate of National Real Estate, İller Bank Inc., the Ministry of Environment, Urbanisation and Climate Change, the Union of Municipalities of Türkiye, and the Ankara University Department of Real Estate Development and Management serve as a valuable model for training experts in the field. Notably, employing RICS-accredited graduates as "experts" is a vital step towards both improving the quality of valuation services in Türkiye and enhancing the confidence of foreign investors. In this framework, it is important to emphasise that professional disciplines related to real estate development, management, valuation, and finance are central to both the national system and international integration.

In many developed countries, the valuation profession is recognised as a field requiring specific academic and professional qualifications. For instance, in the USA, the United Kingdom, the Netherlands, or Poland, graduating with an undergraduate or postgraduate degree accredited by RICS or an equivalent professional certification is indispensable for becoming a valuation expert. An undergraduate degree explicitly in the real estate sector is deemed a fundamental prerequisite for valuation activities in these countries. In contrast, graduates from law and engineering faculties are expected to pursue master's or certificate programmes in real estate. In the USA, many states empower individuals with undergraduate or postgraduate education in real estate and finance to conduct valuation work within both the public and private sectors. Conversely, in Türkiye, valuation activities historically conducted by value appraisal commissions, price determination commissions, and tender commissions within public institutions, as well as expert witness panels in the judiciary, were predominantly performed by individuals lacking formal education in real estate and valuation. This situation resulted in considerable issues regarding service quality. However, over the past 20 years, driven by growth in real estate investments, project development, and capital market-based real estate instruments, "real estate development expertise" has evolved into a distinct professional discipline in Türkiye. Particularly in the United States, Canada, the United Kingdom, the Netherlands, or Germany, the provision of valuation services in accordance with professional ethical standards and international norms is exclusively ensured through competent, internationally accredited specialists. In Türkiye, although the initial employment of graduates from diverse disciplines in real estate valuation, management, or finance was driven by necessity, current efforts are actively developing undergraduate and postgraduate programmes tailored to these areas. Concurrently, a legal framework has been established to delineate the roles and authorities of "real estate development and management expertise".

In a valuation system designed to be integrated with the existing GIS and Land Registry and Cadastre Information System (TAKBİS) infrastructure, it would be more effective for these services to be provided by experts who have graduated from relevant departments of internationally accredited universities, as emphasised in the Law on Expert Witnessing No. 6754 and the circulars of the Ministry of Justice, rather than having the public sector directly produce valuation services. Through these experts, both the execution of valuation activities and the development of data foundations for mass appraisal should be ensured. Additionally, comprehensive value maps should be prepared for submission to all stakeholders, especially municipalities and development agencies. In this context, the Central Bank and the banking sector could use these value maps to conduct risk analyses of mortgage pools and to ensure proper execution of risk measurement and credit rating activities in securitisation processes. Similarly, effective planning of urban transformation and renewal policies, as well as the comparative auditing of valuation reports obtained by judicial bodies and other stakeholders over time, would become feasible. Indeed, as stated by Aliefendioğlu and Tanrıvermiş (2017) and Tanrıvermiş (2019), if the tax values of properties were aligned more closely with their market values according to their types, a two- to threefold increase in total tax revenues could be achieved, even if current tax and fee rates were reduced to one-third of their present levels. To realise this potential, the real estate valuation system must be structured rationally. In this regard, all regulations pertaining to tax, zoning, land registry, cadastre, urban transformation, as well as the money and capital markets, in addition to tax laws and related regulations, must be reviewed with a holistic approach. Otherwise, the integrity of the system cannot be guaranteed, and the targeted structural transformation will remain unachievable.

References

Akçay, B. (1999). Gayrimenkul yatırım ortaklıkları. Bilkamat.

Aliefendioğlu, Y., & Tanrıvermiş, H. (2015). Kentsel dönüşüm sürecinde taşınmaz ve proje değerleme işlemleri ve sorunlarının analizi: Kayseri Büyükşehir Belediyesi Sahabiye ve Fatih mahalleleri dönüşüm projesi örneği çerçevesinde değerlendirme. *Uluslararası Sosyal Araştırmalar Dergisi, 8*(39), 736–769.

Aliefendioğlu, Y., & Tanrıvermiş, H. (2017). Türkiye'de belediye gelirlerinin araştırılması açısından taşınmaz değerleme sisteminin geliştirilmesi ve olası etkileri. In Uluslararası Kentsel Politikalar Konferansı (International Conference on Urban Politics) (pp. 230–256). Gazimağusa, KKTC.

Aliefendioğlu, Y., & Tanrıvermiş, H. (2019). Türkiye'de gayrimenkul ve varlık değerleme çalışmalarının gelişimi ve kurumsallaşma eğilimlerinin değerlendirilmesi (Analysis of real estate and assets valuation studies and institutionalization tendencies in Türkiye). In Kent, İnşaat ve Ekonomi Kongresi, Bildiriler Kitabı (pp. 86–107). Gaziantep, Türkiye.

Alp, A., & Yılmaz, M. U. (2007). *Gayrimenkul finansmanı ve değerlemesi* (3. Baskı). İMKB Yayını.

Atik, M., Köse, Y., Yılmaz, B., & Erbaş, M. (2015). Şehirlerin ilerleme yönlerinin gayrimenkul değerleri üzerindeki etkisinin ölçülmesi. *Çankırı Karatekin Üniversitesi İktisadi ve İdari Bilimler Fakültesi Dergisi, 5*(2), 443–458.

Barańska, A. (2013). Real estate mass appraisal in selected countries–functioning systems and proposed solutions. *Real Estate Management and Valuation, 21*(3), 35–42.

Bender, A., Din, A., Favarger, P., Hoesli, M., & Laakso, J. (1997). An analysis of perceptions concerning the environmental quality of housing in Geneva. *Urban Studies, 34*(3), 503–513.

Çağatay, U., & Tecim, V. (2013). Avrupa Birliği sürecinde taşınmaz değerleme bilgi sistemi. *Dokuz Eylül Üniversitesi Sosyal Bilimler Enstitüsü Dergisi, 15*(3), 375–393.

Demirci, R., Tanrıvermiş, H., & Aliefendioğlu, Y. (2007). Türkiye'de arazi yönetimi ve piyasası: Temel özellikleri, yasal ve kurumsal düzenlemeler, sorunlar ve değerleme çalışmaları üzerine etkileri. *Üçüncü Sektör Sosyal Ekonomi Dergisi (eski adıyla Türk Kooperatifçilik Kurumu), 42*(4), 38–63.

Erdem, N. (2017). Türkiye için bir taşınmaz değerleme sistemi yaklaşımında temel veri yönetimi. *Geomatik Dergisi, 2*(2), 66–85.

Erdem, N. (2018). Türkiye taşınmaz değerleme sisteminin yeniden yapılandırılmasına yönelik bilimsel çalışma ve öneriler üzerine bir değerlendirme. *Ömer Halisdemir Üniversitesi Mühendislik Bilimleri Dergisi, 7*(1), 159–170.

Glumac, B., & Des Rosiers, F. (2020). Practice briefing—automated valuation models (AVMs): Their role, their advantages and their limitations. *Journal of Property Investment and Finance, 39*(5), 481–491.

Hışır, M. (2009). Türkiye'de taşınmaz değerleme ve harita mühendisliği. In *12. Türkiye Harita Bilimsel ve Teknik Kurultayı.* TMMOB Harita ve Kadastro Mühendisleri Odası.

International Valuation Standards Council [IVS]. (2017). Building trust in valuations through international partnerships: Annual report 2016–17. London, UK.
International Valuation Standards Council [IVS]. (2024). *International valuation standards (IVS)*. Effective January 2025. Publication date: 25 September 2024. London, UK.
Meriç, A., Erkuş, H., & Kaygusuzoğlu, M. (2016). Bilirkişilik müessesesinde yaşanan sorunlarla ilgili muhasebe meslek mensupları ve hakimlerin algısı üzerine bir araştırma. Muhasebe ve Finansman Dergisi, Temmuz. (pp. 23–48).
Mora-Esperanza, J. G. (2004). Artificial intelligence applied to real estate valuation: An example for the appraisal of Madrid. CATASTRO. (pp. 255–265).
Mülayim, Z. G. (2008). *Tarımsal değer biçme ve bilirkişilik* (Genişletilmiş 3. Baskı). Yetkin Yayınları.
T.C. Adalet Bakanlığı Adli Sicil ve İstatistik Genel Müdürlüğü (Republic of Türkiye Ministry of Justice, General Directorate of Criminal Records and Statistics), 2025. www.adlisicil.adalet.gov.tr/hukukpdf.html, Accessed: 3/5/2025.
T.C. Cumhurbaşkanlığı Strateji ve Bütçe Başkanlığı (Presidency of the Republic of Türkiye, Strategy and Budget Office), 2023. On İkinci Kalkınma Planı (2024-2028), Ankara, Türkiye.
Tanrıvermiş, H. (2008). Taşınmaz değerlemede gelir çarpanları yaklaşımı ve Türkiye'de kentsel ve kırsal taşınmaz değerleme uygulamalarında kullanım olanakları. *Vergi Sorunları Dergisi, 241*, 106–148.
Tanrıvermiş, H. (2017). Gayrimenkul değerleme esasları. SPL Sermaye Piyasası Lisanslama Sicil ve Eğitim Kuruluşu.
Tanrıvermiş, H. (2019). Dünyada kamu sektöründe değerleme çalışmaları ve Türkiye için uygun model arayışları. *Tapu ve Kadastro Mülkiyet (E-Dergi), 1*(Ocak), 31–44.
Tanrıvermiş, H., & Aliefendioğlu, Y. (2017). Yusufeli Barajı ve hidroelektrik santrali projesi kamulaştırma alanı içindeki mahallelerde kamulaştırılacak arsa vasfındaki taşınmazların parsel düzeyinde değerleme çalışmaları (Yayın No: 32). Ankara Üniversitesi Uygulamalı Bilimler Fakültesi Gayrimenkul Geliştirme ve Yönetimi Bölümü.
Taş, O., Mert, H., & Aydın, R. (2017). A study on real estate appraisal and assessment reports conducted in Türkiye. *Journal of Economics, Finance and Accounting (JEFA), 4*(3), 316–330.
The Royal Institution of Chartered Surveyors [RICS]. (2024). RICS valuation—global standards. Effective from 31 January 2025. London, UK.
Töre, E. (2004). *Gayrimenkul değerlemesi (The appraisal of real estate, çeviri)* (12. Baskı). İstanbul Üniversitesi Sosyal Bilimler MYO.
Türkiye Değerleme Uzmanları Birliği. (2025). 2016–2024 yılları arası değerleme sektörü analizi raporları. İstanbul.
Wu, J., Gyourko, J., & Deng, Y. (2015). Real estate collateral value and investment: The case of China. *Journal of Urban Economics, 86*(2), 43–53.
Yalçın, S. (2006). *Gayrimenkul değerlemesinde değerleme uzmanlığı üzerine bir inceleme (Yüksek lisans tezi)*. İstanbul Üniversitesi Fen Bilimleri Enstitüsü.
Yıldırım, R., Odyakmaz, Z., Çoban Atik, A., Çalışkan, Z., Ersöz, A. K., & Dengiz, Y. (2011). İdare mahkemeleri örneğinde bilirkişilik uygulamaları. Selçuk Üniversitesi Hukuk Fakültesi Dergisi, 9–38.

Harun Tanrıvermiş is a distinguished professor who occupies the esteemed position at the Ankara University top management level as founder and head of the Department of Real Estate Development and Management, and founder and current dean of the Faculty of Applied Sciences at Ankara University. Professor Tanrıvermiş also currently works as the vice rector at Ankara University. He attained his B.Sc., M.Sc., and Ph.D. degrees from the Department of Agricultural Economics at Ankara University, specialising in land and real estate economics, land and real estate valuation, as well as natural resources and environmental economics. Furthermore, he earned an M.Sc. in environmental management through the MED-CAMPUS Programme in 1996. Professor Tanrıvermiş has published approximately 400 papers, including 43 international and 55 national peer-reviewed articles, which have been published in various high-impact journals.

Additionally, he has presented 48 international and 74 national proceedings, either in full or as abstracts, at numerous conferences. He is also credited with writing 39 books and 17 book chapters. Moreover, his works concentrate on the land and real estate valuation, land and real estate economics, real estate development and project appraisal, urban transformation and sustainability, sustainable real estate development, facility and real estate management, land management, administration and polices, measuring and reporting of real estate sustainability and ESG, digital transformation in real estate and real estate technologies.

Yeşim Tanrıvermiş holds the position of full professor in the Department of Real Estate Development and Management at the Faculty of Applied Sciences, Ankara University, Türkiye. She attained her Master of Science (M.Sc.) degree in 2011 from the Department of Agricultural Economics at Ankara University. She received her Ph.D. in 2011 as the first Ph.D. program graduate of the Department of Real Estate Development and Management at Ankara University. Her research interests encompass the management and conservation of land resources, land resource economics, as well as real estate analysis and economics, in addition to studies in real estate and asset valuation. She has been delivering lectures for several years and has published academic papers since 2006. Her publications consist of 50 international and 40 national peer-reviewed articles. Additionally, she has made contributions to 110 international and 25 national full or abstract proceedings at various conferences and congresses and has authored 35 books and 30 book chapters. Presently, she serves as the Deputy Head of her department at Ankara University. Moreover, she is an active participant in various academic and professional organisations. Her experience encompasses working as a researcher and consultant across diverse public and private sectors, with a focus on real estate asset analysis, real estate finance and valuation, land and building conservation practices, as well as real estate economics and management. Furthermore, she actively engages in enhancing cooperation with both domestic and international institutions, mobilising financial resources for research projects.

Evaluation of Tax Initiatives for the Improvement of Real Estate Markets Within the Framework of Real Estate Taxation in Türkiye

Emrullah Töremen and Erol Demir

Abstract

The real estate sector enables transactions and economic activities related to real estate production, and both create numerous jobs. All economic activities in the country are subject to taxation unless specified by special legislation. A wide range of stakeholders engage in the real estate production process, which typically lasts about a year, and this process carries various tax obligations. Taxes are levied on earned income, expenses, and transactions, which means that duplicate taxes could occur during real estate production. The study thoroughly examined the tax responsibilities related to real estate production within a specific classification framework. This framework outlines potential tax liabilities that may arise before, during, and after the production process. Additionally, specific exceptions, exemptions, and deductions linked to tax liabilities in the real estate market are recognised as tax incentives. The study aims to thoroughly delineate the tax obligations within Türkiye's real estate production process and provide valuable insights to the industry and relevant stakeholders through a comprehensive account of the associated tax initiatives.

Keywords

Real estate · Taxation · Property market

E. Töremen(✉) · E. Demir
Department of Real Estate Development and Management, Faculty of Applied Sciences, Ankara University, Ankara, Türkiye
e-mail: toremene@ankara.edu.tr; eroldemir@ankara.edu.tr

T. Just et al. (eds.), *Understanding Türkiye's Real Estate Markets*, Management for Professionals, https://doi.org/10.1007/978-3-032-13297-0_11

1 Introduction

The real estate sector plays a crucial role in the Turkish economy. Due to its substantial economic value and diverse functions, this sector is subject to various forms of taxation. From a tax perspective, the sector is regulated differently, facing numerous liabilities related to income, transaction, and ownership taxes. In addition to the classification of real estate (immovable property) within the construction and real estate sector for purposes of sale, investment, or residential use, the derivation and sale of real estate securities based on real estate have recently established this sector as a significant participant in both money markets and capital markets.

People have always aimed to live in a healthy and safe environment. Whether in developed or developing countries, individuals often strive to attain this goal as efficiently and economically as possible. However, they face numerous obstacles in their quest for suitable housing, including its accessibility (Yalçıner, 2018).

Housing represents the most vital component within the real estate sector. The housing market encompasses all enterprises and transactions pertaining to the production, marketing, and utilisation of residential properties. Individuals obtain shelter and generate income through strategic investments. The output of real estate extends over several years and influences multiple sectors, thereby providing substantial economic value to the nation. The government receives a portion of this economic value, referred to as "tax". Taxes are levied to fund public expenditures (Mutluer et al., 2019); such taxes are unrequited and grounded in legal frameworks. They are assessed on properties and remitted by either individuals or legal entities (K'Akumu & Olima, 2005).

Taxation broadly includes economic values, legal transactions, and tangible assets, alongside the associated processes and events (Buchanan, 1979). It is commonly recognised that the financial burden of taxes rests on those who can afford it (Harold, 2001). Thus, individuals interacting with taxation-related components may incur applicable taxes, regardless of their geographic location within the country (Marcio, 2012). As a result, taxes can be classified as public revenue generated from individuals' spending, income, and assets.

Universally, taxes must align with individuals' financial solvency. In other words, tax liabilities should factor in a reasonable framework pertaining to the capacity to bear the tax burden (Utz, 2023). In this context, with respect to optimal tax compliance, it is expected that individuals will endorse a tax policy that minimises the tax burden (Neumark & McLure, 2023). In this regard, coherent taxation signifies that individuals are equally responsible for their wealth and earnings and derive analogous satisfaction in their lives (Flew, 1980).

In this context, the tax liabilities associated with the real estate production process are examined across three distinct stages: prior to the initiation of real estate production, throughout real estate production, and subsequent to the completion of real estate production. Furthermore, the tax liabilities at each stage are delineated with respect to income taxes, transaction taxes, and ownership-based taxes.

2 Tax Liabilities in the Real Estate Production Process

The construction of real estate entails a multitude of activities and processes. Various taxes, fees, participation shares, and costs are associated with these activities and processes. This situation has been analysed in three distinct stages. The first stage takes place prior to the initiation of the real estate production process. The second stage pertains to real estate as a commercial enterprise, wherein transactions occur during the production phase. The final stage encompasses the utilisation or transfer of real estate subsequent to its production (Table 1).

2.1 Before Starting the Real Estate Production Phase

Prior to commencing real estate development, it is essential to evaluate the condition of the land (soil) where the structure will be built. If there are no zoning regulations in the intended construction area, the proper administrative authority must start or support a parcel operation in this locale. The relevant administrative body acts in accordance with Law No. 3194, Article 5. If the municipality is outside the designated zones, jurisdiction will shift to the municipality, the affected areas, and the governorships (special administration).

The initial parcellation process, designated as "first parcelling", incurs fees in accordance with pertinent legal regulations. Furthermore, in certain cases, merging or separating parcels within areas designated for construction may be a requisite; accordingly, these operations are executed. The differentiation of parcels is referred to as "subdivision", while the amalgamation of several contiguous parcels into a single unit is termed "unification". These transactions are subject to a "subdivision and unification fee". For the endorsement of the plan by the pertinent administration, the process of plan and project approval incurs a "plan and approval fee". During this procedure, a "registration and copy fee" is imposed. Should a copy of any plans, projects, or sketches pertaining to the structure be required, a registration and copying fee is applicable. The establishment of the foundation within the construction site and the subsequent relocation of soil from this foundation to the specified location, as delineated by the relevant administration, will incur a "ground opening and land excavation" fee (Law No. 2464, article 80).

A fee is levied for the "zoning status certificate" by the respective municipalities or their affiliated administrations (Law No. 2464, article 97). This certificate serves to verify the construction status of the land and the types of structures permitted within the zoning plan. Furthermore, the transfer and relinquishment of real estate by the land registry administration are subject to a land registry regulations fee (Law No. 492, article 63 and schedule IV attached article 20/a). Moreover, a revolving fund fee is applicable during transactions at the land registry office (Law No. 6083, article 8/6).

A building permit is essential for construction activities on the designated land (Law No. 3194, article 21). Upon the issuance of the building permit, a construction fee is mandated, with variations depending on whether the building is residential or

Table 1 Tax liabilities during the real estate production process

Stage before starting real estate production	During real estate production	Sale or transfer stage of real estate produced
• Zoning fees (parcelling, subdivision and unification and plan and project approval fee) • Registration or copy fee • Ground opening and land excavation fee • Zoning status certificate fee • Land registry and cadastre fee • Land Registry and Cadastre circulating capital fee • Building permit fee • Road, sewerage and water facility expenses participation fee • Technical infrastructure fee • Stamp duty (contract) • Notary fee (notary, contract) • Occupation fee (construction waste, etc.) • Value-added tax (VAT) (land delivery in return for a flat) • Announcement and advertisement tax	**1. Taxes levied due to transfers and transactions** • Land registry and cadastre in case of transfer • Inheritance and transfer tax in case of a gratuity/inheritance • VAT 1 (taxpayer) • VAT 2 (as responsible) • Stamp duty (declaration) • Stamp duty (withholding tax) • Mortgage loans BITT/Resource Utilisation Support Fund (RUSF) • Converting from land to building fee • Building use permit fee **2. In earning** • Personel income or corporate tax • Withholding tax (personal income tax) • Personel income tax withholding (in contracting business) • Provisional tax **3. Taxes based on ownership** • Land (property) tax • Immovable cultural assets share • Announcement and advertisement tax • Environmental cleaning tax	• Land registry and cadastre fee • Land Registry and Cadastre circulating capital fee • Inheritance and transfer tax (gratuitous inheritance) • VAT • Real estate capital income (rental income tax) • Value increase gain (income tax) • Building (property) tax • Valuable housing tax • Immovable cultural assets share

Source: Töremen and Demir (2020)

commercial (Law No. 2464, additional article 1). Furthermore, specific costs incurred by municipalities or municipal institutions are allocated as "shares for participation" among property owners (Law No. 2464, articles 86–88).

When a structure is erected in exchange for land, stamp duty is levied on the agreements between the contractor and the landowner (Law No. 488, article 1). Should a floor easement be established, both a title deed fee and a revolving fund fee will be required for its creation. An occupation fee is incurred for temporarily obstructing roads or pavements to facilitate the removal of construction debris or to install construction prevention barriers during the building process (Law No. 2464, article 52). Consequently, the daily occupation fee must reflect the amount stipulated in the applicable tariff.

When an individual seeks to develop property on another person's land, a contract is established for the provision of apartments, shops, or workspaces to be constructed. This contract encompasses two parties: the landowner and the contractor. Within this agreement, one party designates its plot in exchange for the completed independent sections of the other party. This provision is subject to value-added tax in accordance with relevant tax regulations. The event that triggers the tax liability occurs upon the delivery of the pertinent independent sections. Nevertheless, if the land is registered for business purposes or if the work is conducted on a continuous basis, the tax will be applicable. Otherwise, no tax will be assessed, as it does not generate commercial returns (Kolotoğlu, 2019).

2.2 In the Production Phase of Real Estate

Taxes on Transfers and Transactions Upon the initiation of construction, the transactions associated with the project, encompassing floor-to-altitude and prepaid transactions, as well as any unforeseen transfers, become significant in economic considerations. Should the property be sold during the construction phase, a title deed fee shall be applicable. Additionally, a revolving capital fee will be necessary for transactions facilitated through the title deed administration. At this juncture, if the transaction pertains to a transfer through donation or inheritance, it shall be subject to duty and transfer tax as stipulated by the relevant legislation. This tax is determined based on the direct real estate tax base, which is calculated in accordance with the provisions set forth in Law No. 7338, Article 1, Section 10.

Contractors engaged in the delivery and execution processes of real estate development are subject to value-added tax. In accordance with the applicable regulations, the institutions and organisations concerned do not remit the full value-added tax on the delivery or service fees they receive; rather, they remit a portion of the calculated tax by deducting the amount owed and subsequently declaring it to the relevant tax authority. This deduction process is commonly referred to as "withholding or stoppage". As of March 1, 2021, the withholding rate is established at TL 5 million (VAT included) and 4/10 for the production work executed (Demir et al., 2022).

The signatures on documents outlined in the relevant law incur an applicable stamp duty (Law No. 488, Article 1). The signatory of these documents is the taxpayer. In this regard, a tax rate of 9.48 per thousand is applied to contracts, commitments, appeals, concessions, and advances. Moreover, all tender decisions subject to tender law are liable for a stamp duty of 5.59 per thousand (Demir, 2015).

Taxes on Earnings Earnings taxes are imposed on the profits gained from real estate development. Tax obligations may apply to either individual taxpayers or corporate entities, depending upon the classification of the individual or organisational entity. While the income of individuals is subject to income tax, corporate tax is primarily levied on the revenue generated by corporations possessing legal personality. To clarify further, the revenue gained from real estate is principally categorised as commercial income. In accordance with applicable legislation, commercial gains are designated as withholding and temporary taxes on a case-by-case basis throughout the taxation period. Moreover, capital gains and income derived from real estate are also included within the taxes collected on income.

Commercial Earnings Profits gained from real estate sales by individuals who frequently transact through a commercial organisation are taxed as commercial profits according to the relevant legal procedures. Legal entities engaged in such activities must pay corporate tax.

The production process in the real estate sector typically extends beyond 1 year. As stipulated by the pertinent tax legislation, the taxation period for income generated from construction activities that exceed 1 year is established upon the project's completion. Conversely, income tax withholding is required under the taxation of commercial profits at the time the construction work is executed. According to the relevant legislation (Law No. 193, Article 42), the income tax withholding associated with construction concerns "years of common construction and repair works". The law further delineates that the profit or loss derived from construction activities is recognised in the year the construction is completed and is reported in that same year. Moreover, income is accounted for in the year it is reported.

In the context of taxation, tax deductions are applied based on the income obtained from construction projects, due to the deferral of tax payments until the work is completed. Therefore, those responsible for settling claims on behalf of individuals involved in construction activities are mandated to remit taxes to the tax administration by withholding a portion of the claims as tax liability in accordance with the relevant legal provisions. The applicable rate is set at 5%. Furthermore, the withheld amount is deducted from either the income tax or corporate tax liabilities of the recipients of the payment (Law No. 193, article 94).

The provisional tax is an advance tax remitted by withholding income taxes over three-month intervals, with the exception of the fourth period,[1] without delaying

[1] With the Law dated 14.10.2021 and numbered 7338, the application of provisional tax was terminated with the accounting period of 2022.

until the annual tax period (Law No. 193, duplicate article 120). According to the relevant law, there is no temporary tax on construction contracting works.

Ownership-Based Taxes Taxes derived from ownership are commonly designated as wealth taxes. A representative example of this category of taxation is the property tax. Moreover, an environmental clean-up tax is imposed on real estate proprietors to offset the cleaning services provided by municipalities. In addition, if construction firms or other enterprises necessitate announcements or advertising services for the introduction of a business or product, they are required to remit taxes to the relevant municipalities, categorised under announcement and advertising tax.

In the context of real estate development, a land tax is imposed on parcels designated for construction. The Land Appreciation Commission conducts a review and establishes the base unit value for this tax computation every 4 years. Throughout the intervening years, the values from the initial year remain constant, while subsequent years reflect increases correlated to half of the tax reappraisal rate. Presently, the land tax rate is set at 3 per thousand, whereas for metropolitan municipalities, it is set at 6 per thousand. As specified in construction contracts, the landowner is accountable for the land and, therefore, is obliged to remit the land tax (Töremen, 2020).

Conversely, a tax-related obligation associated with property taxes pertains to the contribution share. This share is intended for the preservation of immovable cultural assets that require protection. Its foundation is the property tax value, which is set at 10% (Law No. 2863, article 12). Municipalities collect this share through property taxes and subsequently transfer it to the relevant administrations.

2.3 Taxes After Real Estate Production

Upon completion, the real estate may be used or sold by the individuals or entities responsible for its construction. At this juncture, the builders are required to remit income tax on the profits accrued from the sale of the real estate. Should the constructed property be utilised or remain in situ during a tax period, property taxes and transaction taxes will be applicable in the event of a transfer of the real estate.

Taxes on Earnings When assessing taxes on earnings after the creation of the structure, several important factors emerge. To begin with, taxes apply to earnings from the contractor's structure sales, resales within a designated period, or from renting the developed property. In this regard, individual income taxpayers are taxed on their earnings during a fiscal period at rates varying from 15% to 40%, based on the tax base defined in the applicable law (Law No. 193, article 103). Regarding corporate tax, a fixed rate is set, with taxpayers obligated to pay a corporate tax of 20% on the earnings reported for the taxation period (Law No. 5520, article 32). In contrast, a rate of 22% was imposed on corporate earnings for the years 2018, 2019, and 2020 (Law No. 5520, temporary article 10). For 2021, a rate of 25% was established, while a rate of 23% has generally been accepted for 2022. Additionally, some financial institutions, insurance companies, and pension firms are subject to a corporate tax rate of 25% (Law No. 5520, temporary article 13).

Conversely, the new regulations propose a corporate tax rate of 30% for projects carried out under the build-operate-transfer model and for profits generated by institutions involved in the public special cooperation model. This regulation is applicable to institutions directly engaged in contracts for the designated projects, becoming effective in 2025 and for future taxation periods (Law No. 7524, articles 35, 60).

Real estate capital earnings comprise revenues obtained from the leasing of goods and rights as delineated in the pertinent legislation (Law No. 193, article 70). Real estate capital gains are subject to taxation as they constitute the capital income of proprietors, tenants, possessors, holders of easements and usufruct, or occupants of these assets and rights (Özkök Çubukçu et al., 2009). With certain exceptions, the tax exemption for residential properties in 2024 is established at TL 33,000 (Income Tax General Communiqué No. 324, article 3).

Capital Gain Ownership of real estate is subject to periodic transitions. In this context, an increase in value may result in a gain subject to income tax. According to applicable legislation, a gain on appreciation is recognised when the relevant assets or rights are transferred within a five-year timeframe, with the exception of gratuitous acquisitions (Law No. 193, duplicate article 80/6). The difference between the original acquisition price of the real estate and the disposal price is taxable at the rates specified in the income tax brackets (Law No. 193, Article 70). For the year 2024, the amount exempt from taxation is established at TL 87,000 (Income Tax General Communiqué No. 324, article 3).

Temporary Tax A tax is levied in advance on the earnings of relevant taxpayers, with the exception of the last quarter, which is due within three months. This tax, which is collected in advance in compliance with applicable laws, is subsequently deducted from the annual tax on earnings at the conclusion of the term. However, a temporary tax does not apply if there is no other activity resulting from years of construction work (Law No. 193, duplicate article 120).

Ownership-Based Taxes Property tax comprises two primary components: building tax and land tax (Morton, 1955). A real estate tax is imposed on the building upon the completion of the real estate development project. In accordance with the real estate tax law, all structures and facilities established as fixed constructions are classified as buildings (Law No. 1319, article 2). The tax obligation for newly constructed buildings commences in the year following the completion date of the structure (Law No. 1319, Article 9). The applicable tax rate is established at 1 per thousand for residential buildings and 2 per thousand for all other classifications of buildings. In metropolitan areas, this rate is subject to a 100% increase (Law No. 1319, article 8). The fundamental components of the building tax, or tax value, consist of two significant elements: the value of the plot upon which the building is located and the construction value associated with the building.

Land appreciation commissions assess the value of the base unit in relation to the assessed tax value of the land. Each year, the two pertinent ministries establish the unit value for the construction component of the building (Töremen, 2020). Consequently, the tax value represents the value of the building as outlined in the list determined by the relevant administrations (Appraisal Institute, 1980). In addition, a fee of 10% is imposed on the tax accrued to safeguard immovable cultural assets, as previously indicated (Law No. 2863, article 12).

Another type of tax associated with property, specifically the building tax, is the valuable housing tax, which constitutes a property tax levied on high-value residences. The provisions pertaining to the valuable housing tax have been incorporated into the property tax legislation (Dogrusöz, 2020). For this tax, reference is made to the relevant provisions of law (Law No. 1319, articles 42–46). The estate tax matrix must exceed a specified amount for the applicable year[2] and be inhabited.

The tax base is determined by the property's 2024 real estate tax value, which is over TL 12,880,000.[3] For instance, if the taxable value of the housing amounts to TL 15,700,000, the computed tax liability (15,700,000–12,880,000) will equate to TL 2,820,000. Furthermore, only residential properties that exceed the designated threshold are eligible for exemption from the valuable housing tax. For example, a taxpayer with a taxable value of TL 13 million will qualify for exemption from the valuable housing tax. If a taxpayer owns three residential properties with taxable values of TL 12.5 million, TL 15 million, and TL 18.5 million, the tax will not be imposed on the property with the lowest taxable value (TL 12.5 million); however, the valuable housing tax will be applicable to the properties with taxable values of TL 15 million and TL 18.5 million (as per the amount for the year 2024). The tariff for the valuable housing tax is outlined in the pricing procedure, resembling an ascending rate tariff (Table 2).

Taxes and Fees Due to Transfers and Transactions Upon completion of the land structure, a conversion fee will be imposed for the transition from land to building (Law No. 492, Schedule IV, Article 13/a) due to the transformation of the land into a structure. In accordance with the pertinent zoning law, a certificate of permission for the utilisation of the structure is issued, which allows its use without impediment (Law No. 2463, article 80/f). This document entails a fee for the permission to utilise the structure (Law No. 492, article 55). Furthermore, according to the relevant legislation, if a floor alliance has been established on the parcel, a title deed fee is assessed to create condominiums from the floor elevation after the completion of construction (Law No. 2464, article 97). Should a service be solicited from the appropriate municipalities during the construction phase, a fee shall be charged in exchange, referred to as the municipal fee. Municipalities collect fees upon the issu-

[2] This amount is increased by half of the revaluation rate each year.

[3] This amount is increased by half of the revaluation rate each year.

Table 2 Valuable housing tax tariff (for 2024)

Tax base	Rate (per thousand)
This applies to amounts exceeding TL 12,880,000 TL and up to TL 19,321,000, including the latter amount	3
For amounts not exceeding TL 25,763,000 (inclusive of this figure), a fee of TL 19,323 is applicable for amounts ranging from TL 19,321,000 to the next greater amount, and a fee of TL 19,323 is likewise applicable for amounts exceeding this threshold	6
Individuals possessing assets exceeding TL 25,763,000 must submit an application reflecting an amount of TL 57,975 for the specified threshold of TL 25,763,000	10

Source: Real Estate Tax Law General Communiqué, No: 84

ance of elevator, fire, and parking certificates in return for the services they provide in this context.

In the event of the sale of structures produced after the completion of construction or upon a change of ownership, such as through a gift (heritage or donation), a title deed or inheritance tax shall be applicable. Upon the completion of construction, it will be subject to the land registry fee as specified in the sale agreement. Moreover, a revolving capital fee will be levied during transactions administered through the title deed administration. Should the real estate from this phase be transferred via donations or alternative means, it will be subject to an inheritance tax (Due, 1967).

In this context, the sale of real estate generated within the framework of commercial earnings will be subject to VAT. The applicable rates for VAT are 1%, 10%, or 20% as delineated in Law No. 3065, article 28, and Presidential Decision No. 7346. Additionally, a stamp duty is proposed on the declarations to be issued for the specified taxes and on insurance premium declarations.

Consequently, for the year 2024, the stamp duty is required to be remitted as follows: TL 624.10 for corporate tax returns, TL 467.20 for income tax returns, TL 308.30 for other tax returns (excluding stamp duty), and TL 228.80 for declarations pertaining to insurance premiums (The General Communique on Stamp Tax Law, Serial No: 68). In this context, stamp tax is levied on the amounts above via declarations and insurance premium statements submitted by enterprises operating within the construction industry throughout the year.

3 Tax Initiatives

Tax incentives for construction and real estate were examined within the context of tax initiatives. Consequently, taxation scenarios, income, corporate taxpayers, value-added tax, procedural law, and additional tax regulations concerning delivery and services are assessed.

Income taxes are typically progressive. Consequently, individuals with higher incomes are subjected to higher tax rates. This phenomenon leads to more income taxes from wealthier individuals, thereby aiding in the alleviation of income inequality within society through the mechanism of taxation (Schiller, 2007).

3.1 Taxation of Earnings in Income and Corporate Tax

The taxpayer of income tax is an individual. Consequently, consideration is given to the personal and family circumstances of the individual. In other words, certain deductions are provided based on the individual's payment capacity. Therefore, incentives may exist to alleviate the tax burden in accordance with the personal and family situation of the individual (Buchanan, 1960). The construction and real estate sector generally involves processes that extend beyond 1 year. As the real estate production process has exceeded the standard taxation period, special taxation provisions pertaining to construction activities regarding income taxes have been instituted.

Taxation of Earnings in Construction Works The execution of construction projects necessitates a confluence of specific conditions pertinent to materials, craftsmanship, climate, and economic factors. In light of designated work failing to yield results within a taxation period, certain activities demand diverse expertise to complete the structure, which encompasses tasks ranging from land acquisition to project execution for the benefit of another party or for investment or utilisation purposes. Various taxation regulations have been instituted within construction undertakings for the reasons above. As a result, construction activities are subject to taxation based on two fundamental principles pertaining to the commitment to specialised construction endeavours (Karakoyun, 2019).

Private construction works refer to projects that are not bound by a formal commitment and are undertaken by the building owner on their own behalf. These projects encompass various independent sectors, including residential constructions, workplaces, and apartment complexes. The building owner engages in these constructions primarily for investment purposes, akin to practices for personal usage. Moreover, the marketing of independent units is typically managed by the builders themselves. This industry exemplifies a productive activity, as the constructions intended for investment are subsequently sold. This distinction delineates private construction from contractual work. Although spanning several years, private construction works do not fall within the classification of construction projects that exceed a taxation period as stipulated under tax regulations. As a result, no specific arrangements have been established for special constructions. The revenue generated from special construction works is categorised as commercial earnings according to the relevant clause. No particular taxation provisions were anticipated for the taxation of private construction work. The general provisions for determining commercial gain will similarly apply to the specified construction works. Furthermore, private construction enterprises will encounter temporary tax liability (Demir, 2015).

Construction Contracting Works Although construction contracting activities do not typically conclude within a single taxation period, certain projects may be both initiated and completed within such a timeframe. In construction contracts, the dates at which work is scheduled to commence or conclude are distinctly specified. The duration of construction commitment activities shall be evaluated in accordance with Article 42 of the pertinent legislation. Accordingly, in the taxation of the aforementioned construction works, the tax is declared upon the completion of the project, and the profit or loss is recognised as income or loss for the fiscal year in which it is claimed. For an undertaking to qualify as a construction contracting business, it must involve work that extends beyond 1 year, be related to construction, and be conducted on a commitment basis. In construction contracting, should additional work be performed outside the confines of the primary construction tasks, depreciation on machinery and equipment pertaining to these associated expenses is allocated in proportion to the days of work utilised (Şentürk, 2013).

In the realm of construction contracting, a 5% deduction is instituted on payments rendered to contractors by the building owners (Law No. 193, article 94/3 and Law No. 5520, article 15). These deducted amounts are subject to income and corporate tax considerations. Nevertheless, it is noteworthy that no temporary tax applies to construction contracting work. Conversely, should the work extend beyond the determined taxation period, a tax deduction will be enacted at the specified rate (Demir, 2015).

Discounted Corporate Tax on Incentivised Investments This analysis focuses on calculating the contribution amount to the investment, which is derived from investment expenses, and the taxation of the declared corporate income at a reduced rate until the entire contribution amount is fully invested (Law No. 5520, Article 32/A). It is essential to note that business partnerships with financial and insurance institutions are not eligible for the discounted rate. Furthermore, income generated from contracting work (Law No. 4283 and Law No. 3996) is excluded from consideration regarding certain investments (Ernst & Young, 2021).

Exception for Real Estate Sales Earnings A portion of profits from real estate sales, registered as an active business within 2 years, will be exempt from corporate tax for corporate taxpayers (Law No. 5520, Article 5/1-e). The institution must actively manage the real estate for at least two full years. Delays in registering the real estate under the institution's name may occur, but if two full years remain in the operation, the exemption can still apply. To accurately account for the entire two-year duration, the economic history of the real estate needs thorough documentation. Regarding the real estate circuit (Law No. 5520, articles 19, 20), both the acquisition date and the date of transfer or division of the institution should be considered (Koşar et al., 2021).

The profits made by companies involved in real estate trading and leasing do not fall under the stated exception. However, this exception does extend to the profits derived from real estate that these companies utilise in their operations. An entity that is not part of these specified activities may still qualify for the exception if it rents out real estate that it does not use. It is not unusual for transactions involving transfers, assignments, or exchanges of real estate to occur without cash being involved. Therefore, land deliveries for construction purposes, in exchange for the land itself, will not be considered an exception. Additionally, the sale price of real estate must be received within 2 years of the sale date. If the payment is not received within this timeframe, it indicates that any tax not collected during this period is forfeited due to the exception. The amount of the specified exception is held in a passive fund for 5 years, and this immunity applies during the sales period. Furthermore, it is not used to calculate earnings for any other exceptions related to the values sold in this scenario. Lastly, the foreign currency exchange rate differences in sales are assessed in this context (Akarca & Safak, 2021).

Conversely, the term "immovable property" as outlined in the pertinent legislation has been eliminated by Law No. 7456. Nevertheless, a provisional arrangement has been established. Consequently, a corporate tax exemption of 25% may be applicable to the sale of real estate categorised within the enterprise's assets prior to July 15, 2023, contingent upon compliance with the previously stipulated conditions (Law No: 5520, temporary article 16). Therefore, no discount shall be applied to the sale of immovable properties activated after the specified date.

3.2 Value Added Tax Application

Value-added refers to the value a producer contributes to the raw material or the purchase cost of a product or service prior to its sale (Alan, 1988). The value-added tax (VAT) system is characterised by a value-added tax structure that is implemented at every stage, encompassing the production of goods and services up to the point of consumption, with value-added created in each phase. This calculation is executed by applying value-added tax to those responsible for delivering goods and providing services at each phase of production. Additionally, the delivery of these services and goods also entails the remittance of this tax. This system is administratively resolved by deducting the tax collected at each stage of production from the value-added tax remitted, in accordance with the expenses received or incurred, for the added value generated throughout the process (Oktar, 2007).

VAT Rate in Housing Delivery In accordance with the pertinent regulatory process (Presidential Decision 5359, Law No. 3065, temporary article 43), a new application has been mandated since April 1, 2022 (Bilir & Oktar, 2022). Furthermore, the VAT rates of 8% and 18% have been revised to 10% and 20%, respectively, effective July 10, 2023 (Presidential Decision 7346). Consequently, the location of the housing unit within a metropolitan municipality, the property tax value of the area, and the construction class are inconsequential. The tax rate applicable to housing up to 150 m^2 on sale is set at 10%. Moreover, the VAT rate on land and land deliveries, which serves as a critical input in housing construction, shall be applied at a rate of 10%. For the delivery of any real estate other than the specified housing, land, and associated properties, the value-added tax rate will be 20%. Additionally, as stipulated in Law Number 6306, the value-added tax rate for housing constructed in areas assessed within the risk or reserve concept defined under the scope of disaster risk, and whose net area surpasses 150 m^2, is established at 1%. The value-added tax rate applied to real estate deliveries is 20% (GİB, 2022).

Pursuant to Article 17/4-r of the pertinent legislation, the sale of real estate that has been part of institutional assets for 2 years is exempt from value-added tax. Nonetheless, this practice has been nullified with the enactment of the new regulation. However, the provisions for exceptions prior to the modification shall apply to immovable properties held by institutions as of 15 July 2023 (Law No. 3065, temporary article 43).

Sale of Housing to Foreigners As of April 1, 2017, this regulation applies to the initial delivery of buildings constructed for use as residences or workplaces. The pricing is denominated in foreign currency and brought to Türkiye. With the exception of those specified in the relevant regulation, Turkish citizens residing abroad for a duration exceeding 6 months with a work or residence permit, foreign natural persons lacking residency status in Türkiye, as well as the delivery of residential or workplace facilities to institutions that do not possess their legal or business centre in Türkiye and do not derive income in Türkiye through a workplace or permanent representative, are exempt from value-added tax (Law No: 3065, article 13/i).

Regulation on VAT Refund Recently, new regulations have been enacted in the VAT Law, in conjunction with the pertinent legislation concerning VAT refunds (Law No. 7524, articles 19, 20, 22). Consequently, this legal regulation has been applied retroactively, and the period for discounts on VAT charged prior to January 01, 2030, has been restricted to five calendar years. As it is feasible to obtain a refund for "non-deductible VAT" in transactions that are fully exempt as stipulated in the VAT Law, temporary exemptions with full exemption status and transactions subject to a reduced rate permit any VAT that cannot be deducted due to other transactions to be carried forward to subsequent periods indefinitely. This amount may be deducted from the VAT calculated for a given period by including it in the "VAT Carried Forward from Previous Period" line of the VAT return in subsequent periods without being subject to any indexation. Consequently, taxpayers who were previously permitted to deduct their "VAT Carried Forward" without limitation are now confined to a deduction period of 5 years under the new regulation. In this context, a statute of limitations issue may arise concerning both the transfer of VAT and the VAT incurred.

For taxpayers in the construction and real estate sectors, particularly those operating over several years, the "Refund of Transferred VAT" issue has sparked considerable public dialogue. This requirement to wait a minimum of 2 to 3 years during the construction phase for cash refunds leads to a waiting period of up to 3 years for refunds of previously charged VAT. VAT represents a significant "financing cost" for these sectors, which urgently need to mitigate it. However, the anticipated legal regulation enabling "the refund of charged VAT to taxpayers if it cannot be set off through a discount within 12 months" has yet to be enacted. Instead, a new regulation is set to be introduced in 2030, allowing for "Carried Over VAT" amounts—held in a special account for five calendar years or more—to be considered an expense for income or corporate tax purposes, based on an audit requested by the taxpayer.

3.3 Stamp Duty and Resource Utilisation Support Fund Dedication

The relevant secondary regulation introduces a zero tax rate for specific construction works subject to stamp duty. This includes officially recognised real estate sales contracts, prepaid housing sales contracts, legitimate land equity or revenue-sharing construction contracts, as well as construction agreements between original contractors and subcontractors related to formal land exchanges or revenue-sharing projects. Additionally, consultancy service contracts linked to land exchanges or revenue-sharing construction projects have also been assigned a zero tax rate for construction supervision service contracts since March 15, 2017 (Resolution of the Council of Ministers, No: 2017/9973).

The Resource Utilisation Support Fund (RUSF) represents a significant consideration in the context of tax and comparable financial obligations relating to loan interest. In this context, the funds specified at a rate of 15% are designated as interest on the loans extended by the credit provider. This fund is derived from all consumer credit transactions. However, housing loans are exempt from this fund. Furthermore, commercial loans are excluded from the RUSF (GİB, 2023).

In this context, the party obligated to repay, particularly to syndicated banks as a consequence of project financing, is designated as a Special Purpose Vehicle (SPV). Furthermore, it is feasible to secure low-cost loans from SPVs. Consequently, it is imperative to facilitate the provision of loans from SPVs. This mechanism allows for the disbursement of loans at reduced costs, thereby providing loans without the deduction of RUSF, akin to those offered by banks and financial institutions.

3.4 Property Tax and Valuable Housing Tax

Property taxes constitute a fiscal instrument that markedly influences land use patterns, particularly in urban environments. Consequently, the structure of land taxes substantially dictates land use preferences (Bird & Slack, 2004). The supply of land is of paramount importance in the construction sector. In this context, the Housing Administration, which plays an essential role in housing production, is exempt from land tax (Law No. 1319, article 15/i).

Property tax shall not be imposed on real estate owned by the Treasury for 5 years, commencing from the beginning of the year subsequent to the date of sale. The classification of this real estate as either a building or land is inconsequential (Law No: 4706, article 7/4). Thus, when a real estate tax resident that the Treasury owns is acquired by an individual who is a real estate taxpayer, property tax shall be exempt for 5 years from the date of sale for this real estate (İVDB, 2015). As a critical cost factor in the land acquisition for residential development, a purchased parcel of real estate bypasses a considerable tax liability.

With regard to the real estate tax applicable to buildings, newly completed residential housing is granted an exemption from the building tax for a predetermined period (Law No. 1319, article 5/a). Therefore, in instances where the completed structure is used as a residential building and the assessed value exceeds TL 2500, 25% of the property tax will be exempted for 5 years following the completion of its construction. In situations involving extensions to existing structures, exemptions continue to apply for a specified period and under particular conditions, which are exclusively confined to the portion that has been expanded.

Valuable Housing Tax In the context of construction activities, an exemption from the valuable housing tax is anticipated in specific circumstances to alleviate the financial burden on this sector (Law No. 1319, article 46). Consequently, businesses primarily engaged in construction are exempt from this tax if the properties they have yet to sell, subsequent to their production, fall within the purview of the valuable housing tax. Furthermore, with respect to construction works, the exemption also extends to independent units retained by the contractor after the housing construction on the land has been completed.

The residence tax exemption applies primarily to a single home. Additionally, for individuals owning multiple qualifying properties, the home with the lowest value will be exempt from this tax. Therefore, the valuable housing tax establishes the single-residence exemption in two ways. First, if a taxpayer owns only one residence within Türkiye, they qualify for the exemption. Second, among multiple properties that meet the criteria for the valuable housing tax, the property with the lowest value is exempt. Conversely, taxes must be paid for all other residences.

3.5 Tax Procedure Law

Real Estate Valuation Within the Scope of the Tax Procedure Law The provisions related to the taxation of real estate or economic assets subject to valuation, such as real estate, are regulated in the Tax Procedure Law numbered 213. In this context, articles 269–273 of the Law include provisions regarding the valuation of real estate and economic assets subject to valuation, such as real estate (Demir, 2019).

According to Article 262 of the Law, the cost price is defined as the total of payments made for the acquisition of an economic asset or for enhancing its value, in addition to all associated expenses. The expenses to be incorporated into the cost price are also enumerated.

Re-evaluation Re-evaluation pertains to the reassessment of values documented in an enterprise's balance sheet, which arises from price increases within the economy. Consequently, the enactment of the Tax Procedure Law has guaranteed that fixed assets are recorded at their fair value, along with appropriate depreciation, as outlined in Article 298 (Özyer, 2001).

Renewal Fund The profit derived from the sale of depreciated economic assets or the compensation received from insurance in the event of damage can be used as a renewal fund, contingent upon specific conditions. In this context, Article 328 of the Tax Procedure Law stipulates the renewal of economic values by using the sales profits generated from the disposal of certain depreciated economic assets. This is commonly referred to as the "renewal fund" (Dogrusöz, 2021). Enterprises are required to establish a separate and dedicated renewal fund to replenish the value of sold goods, utilising the sales profit as a source of economic value. This necessity must be elucidated prior to the conclusion of the term. For the profit from the sale to be incorporated into the renewal fund, the asset sold must be an economic asset subject to depreciation. The profit from the sale must be allocated towards the acquisition of economic capital of equivalent value.

The renewal fund is maintained in a temporary account designated for the passive coverage of renewal costs. This fund is required to be used within 3 years. In instances of acquiring new economic capital, the depreciation associated with the newly received assets is offset by deducting the corresponding amount from the renewal fund. Furthermore, in instances of abandonment, transfer, or liquidation of the business prior to the conclusion of the third calendar year following the year in which the sale occurred, the profit retained within the account is incorporated into that year's profit and loss statement. Moreover, this fund is specifically established for taxpayers who maintain their financial records in accordance with the balance sheet method. The business account is inherently linked to the renewal fund (Arslan, 2016). Through this application, businesses can effectively renew their existing economic value.

Cost Increase in Real Estate As previously indicated, real estate valuation is conducted based on the acquisition cost. Various expenses associated with real estate may augment the overall cost of ownership. In this context, expenses related to real estate need to be incorporated into the total economic capital, contingent upon the fulfilment of specific criteria. The relevant legal provision stipulates that the date of expenditures does not apply to repair and cleaning expenses (Arslan, 2016; Demir, 2019). Consequently, this practice leads to an inflated valuation of real estate, resulting in a price that exceeds its actual worth.

Tax Status of Real Estate Investment Trusts (REITs) Real estate constitutes a significant component of both institutional investment portfolios and portfolios held by individual investors. Investors in real estate are increasingly gravitating towards alternative forms of real estate investments, whereby real estate investment funds or trusts hold paramount importance (Mazurczak, 2011). In accordance with the implementation of the Corporate Tax Act, funds that are subject to regulation and supervision by the Capital Market Board, as well as foreign funds resembling these, are classified as capital companies. It is imperative to differentiate between mutual funds and investment partnerships. While investment partnerships attain the status of joint-stock companies, mutual funds are acknowledged as capital companies (Demir, 2019). REITs may be established to manage a portfolio of infrastructure investments and services, or a portfolio of other assets and rights, and to invest in specific projects or infrastructure investments and services. Moreover, they may also be established to operate within a defined field (Yalçıner, 2018).

Real Estate Investment Trusts (REITs) are to be structured as joint-stock companies, and are liable to corporate taxation as capital enterprises. In this regard, they must adhere to the general regulations that govern corporate taxpayers. As per the relevant legislative provisions, the earnings generated by REITs and Real Estate Investment Funds (REIFs) are exempt from corporate taxation. Nevertheless, as delineated in Law No. 5520, Article 5/1-d, the earnings of these entities, with the exception of those established for the management of a portfolio consisting of real estate, real estate projects, and real estate-based rights pertinent to their primary area of activity, are not eligible for this exemption. Moreover, to qualify for the specified exemption as stipulated in the most recent regulations, a minimum of 50% of the earnings derived from real estate must be disbursed as dividends. Conversely, it is essential to recognise that these funds are subject to this regulation, especially given that a 10% domestic minimum corporate tax will be instituted commencing from the 2025 tax period, as articulated in Law No. 5520, Article 32/C. According to Article 17/4-g of the Value Added Tax (VAT) Law, various transactions involving foreign exchange, currency, stamp duty, securities, stocks, bonds, and metal deliveries are exempt from value-added tax. In this context, the procurement and disposal of securities, including stocks, by REITs are exempt from VAT. Additionally, purchase and sale agreements exclusively pertaining to real estate portfolios by REITS are exempt from stamp duty (Özkök Çubukçu et al., 2009).

4 Conclusion

The principles of taxation concerning construction and real estate activities encompass several specialised issues within the unique framework of the sector. However, it has been observed that certain challenges stem from the distinctive characteristics of the construction sector and the current tax legislation. The construction and real estate sector is regarded as a crucial economic activity, particularly in Türkiye, where there is a significant demand for housing. The manufacturing process within the construction and repair sector stimulates the related sectors by supplying inputs from several industries and invigorates economic activities such as production and employment by providing the outputs generated at the conclusion of the processes as inputs to other sectors. Upon examining real estate production within the construction and real estate sector, it becomes apparent that numerous tax liabilities are associated with the real estate production process, both prior to its commencement and subsequent to its completion. These taxes can be categorised into three groups: taxes arising from earnings, taxes pertaining to transactions, and taxes based on ownership. Consequently, taxation related to the sector should not be addressed solely through this classification but rather in regard to the overall tax burden or instances of duplicate taxation.

Upon evaluating the construction and real estate sector with respect to tax obligations and initiatives, the framework is both intricate and fragmented. Tax obligations and initiatives are governed by provisional or daily regulations alongside various tax categories that lack a unified approach. In light of the identified dispersion and complexity, it is advantageous to implement a taxation system for the sector that adopts a comprehensive perspective on taxation while ensuring equitable treatment for all stakeholders.

One of the significant challenges encountered within the construction and real estate sector pertains to the inconsistent determination of the actual value of real estate, which varies across diverse contexts, including expropriation, sales, mortgage valuation, and tax assessments. Consequently, to accurately assess the value of real estate in accordance with its scale, valuation criteria that comply with international real estate standards must be implemented, and this undertaking should be carried out by professionals possessing expertise in this domain. In this manner, an anticipated increase in public revenues can be expected.

The construction and real estate sector represents a multifaceted domain that makes a significant contribution to the nation's economy. The intricacies of the pertinent legislation, the rigour of tax and legal obligations, the absence of a systematic accounting framework and document organisation, as well as the insufficient oversight, among other factors, hinder the desired efficiency within the sector. It is a well-established fact that the construction and real estate sector plays a pivotal role in transitioning from economic stagnation to growth. Recognising its importance, it is advantageous to extend support from public authorities for the expedited implementation of regulations aimed at addressing its financial challenges.

Furthermore, a multitude of initiatives and facilities are present within the framework of tax initiatives related to the construction and real estate sectors. Certain initiatives are characterised as tax exemptions, while others are enacted as tax reductions. When the specified tax initiatives are systematically and deliberately designed to impact the sector, they are evaluated as exerting a favourable influence on the advancement of the construction and real estate industries.

In this context, it is essential to minimise tax practices in the construction and real estate sectors to a manageable level. This includes simplifying the tax structure, considering stakeholders' opinions when drafting new regulations, and identifying areas that lead to double taxation while aiming to reduce redundancy. This approach will help decrease informality in the economy, boost the share of direct taxes in overall tax revenues, and ultimately reduce income inequality.

References

Akarca, A., & Safak, M. (2021). Tasinmaz satis kazanci istisnasi uygulamasinda kapsam ve süre. https://www.ekonomim.com/kose-yazisi/kurumlarda-tasinmaz-satis-kazanci-istisnasi-uygulamasinda-kapsam-ve-sure/618665. Accessed September 7, 2022.

Alan, A. T. (1988). *Value added Tax: International practice and problem*. International Monetary Fund.

Appraisal Institute. (1980). The appraisal of real estate. (11th ed.). Chicago.

Arslan, M. (2016). Vergi Hukuku. (9th ed.). Dora Yayinlari.

Bilir, Ö., & Oktar, K. (2022). KDV oranlarinda degisiklik, issue/2022-11. (p. 2). https://www.pwc.com.tr/tr/hizmetlerimiz/vergi/dolayli-vergi/bultenler/kdv-otv-bultenleri/2022/kdv-oranlarinda-degisiklik.html. Accessed September 15, 2022.

Bird, R. M., & Slack, E. (2004). *International handbook on land and property taxation*. Edward Elgar. https://doi.org/10.4337/9781845421434

Buchanan, J. M. (1960). *The public finances*. Richard D. Irvin, Inc.

Buchanan, J. M. (1979). Constitutional constraints on governmental taxing power. ORDO, 30.

Demir, E. (2015). *Insaat ve Gayrimenkul Muhasebesi*. Gazi Kitabevi.

Demir, E., Tanrıvermiş, Y., & Töremen, E. (2022). Türkiye'de gayrimenkul ve insaat islerinin vergilendirilmesinin incelenmesi ve özellik gösteren durumlarin degerlendirilmesi. *Avrasya Isletme ve Iktisat Dergisi, 28*, 79–100.

Demir, S. (2019). *Gayrimenkuller ve Menkul Kiymetlerin Vergilendirilmesi ve Degerlemesi*. Seçkin Yayinlari.

Dogrusöz, B. (2020). Dkv ve verginin yasalligi ilkesi. https://www.bumindogrusoz.com/article/dkv-ve-vergnn-yasalligi-lkes. Accessed September 24, 2023.

Dogrusöz, B. (2021). Son degisikliklerle yenileme fonu. https://www.ekonomim.com/kose-yazisi/son-degisikliklerle-yenileme-fonu/642702. Accessed: September 5, 2022.

Due, J. F. (1967). Maliye: Bir Iktisadi Analizi (Çev. S. Görgün, I. Önder). Fakülteler Matbaasi.

Ernst & Young. (2021). Indirimli kurumlar vergisi rehberi. (p. 21). https://www.vergidegundem.com/files/ebooks/2021/sep/IKV/files/downloads/EY_indirimli%20kurumlar%20vergisi_2021.pdf. Accessed September 7, 2022.

Fees Law (Law No. 492), Official Gazette No. 11756, July 17, 1964.

Flew, A. (1980). Who are the equals? *Philosophia, 9*, 133. https://doi.org/10.1007/BF02379114

GİB. (2022). KDV oranları listesi. https://www.gib.gov.tr/yardim-ve-kaynaklar/yararli-bilgiler/kdv-oranlari-listesi. Accessed April 7, 2022.

GİB. (2023). KKDF Mevzuat. https://www.gib.gov.tr/kkdf-mevzuat. Accessed April 8, 2023.

Harold, D. S. Jr. (2001). The taxation of life insurance policies in OECD countries: Implications for Tax policy and planning. Insurance and Private Pensions Compendium for Emerging Economies. (Vol. 1, Part 1, Section 7-b). https://www.oecd.org/finance/insurance/1815326.pdf. Accessed January 3, 2023.

Inheritance and Gift Tax (Law No. 7338), Official Gazette No. 10231, June 15, 1959.

İVDB. (2015). *Hazineden alınan taşınmazın emlak vergisinden muaf olup olmadığı*, İstanbul Vergi Dairesinin 8/10/2015 tarihli Özelgesi. https://www.gib.gov.tr/node/105837/pdf. Accessed May 4, 2023.

K'akumu, O. A., & Olima, W. H. A. (2005). *Theoretical basis of land value taxation*. https://www.researchgate.net/publication/253454074. Accessed December 10, 2022.

Karakoyun, F. (2019). Vergi tekniği bakımından yıllara yaygın inşaat ve taahhüt işlerinin vergilemesi ve damga vergisi sorunsalı. *Vergi Sorunları Dergisi, 368*, 86–107.

Kolotoğlu, O. (2019). Gerçek kişilere ait arsanın kat karşılığı teslimi. *Vergi Sorunları Dergisi, 374*, 24–36.

Koşar, S., Aykar, Ö., & Şahin, O. (2021). Tüm yönleriyle gayrimenkul vergi rehberi. Adalet Yayınevi.

Marcio, A. (2012). Sovereignty and the international tax law. *Revista da Faculdade de Direito da UERJ, 2*(22), 2.

Mazurczak, A. (2011). Development of real estate investment trust (REIT) regimes in Europe. *Journal of International Studies, 4*(1), 115–123.
Morton, W. A. (1955). *Housing tax*. The University of Wisconsin Press.
Mutluer, M. K., Kuzeyli, D., & Nilay, N. (2019). *Vergi hukuku: Genel ve özel hükümler* (620th ed.). Yetkin Yayınları.
Neumark, F., & McLure, C. E. (2023). *Principles of taxation*. https://www.britannica.com/money/topic/taxation/Principles-of-taxation. Accessed January 23, 2023.
Oktar, K. (2007). *KDV istisnalar ve iadeler* (7 Baskı ed.). Maliye ve Hukuk Yayınları.
Özkök Çubukçu, D., Pınar, A., & Öz, N. S. (2009). Gayrimenkulde vergilendirme: Gayrimenkul yatırım ortaklıkları ve konut finansman sistemi (Mortgage). Ankara Üniversitesi Fen Bilimleri Enstitüsü, Gayrimenkul Geliştirim Anabilim Dalı Yayın No: 3, Ankara.
Özyer, M. A. (2001). *Vergi usul kanunu uygulaması*. Maliye Hesap Uzmanları Derneği Yayını.
Schiller, B. R. (2007). *Essentials of economics* (6th ed.). McGraw-Hill International Edition.
Şentürk, M. (2013). Birden fazla takvim yılına sirayet eden inşaat ve onarma işlerinde ortak genel giderlerin dağıtımı. *Vergi Sorunları Dergisi, 292*, 49–54.
Töremen, E. (2020). Emlak vergisine esas arsa birim değerlerinin belirlenmesindeki sorunlar ve çözüm önerileri. *Niğde Ömer Halisdemir Üniversitesi Sosyal Bilimler Enstitüsü Dergisi, 2*(1), 21–42.
Töremen, E., & Demir, E. (2020). İnşaat ve gayrimenkul sektörü açısından vergi ve yasal yükümlülükler ile son düzenlemeler kapsamında değerli konut vergisi. ICREDM2020, II. Uluslararası Gayrimenkul Geliştirme ve Yönetimi Konferansı, Ankara.
Utz, S. (2023). Ability to pay 2002. Faculty Articles and Papers, (133). https://opencommons.uconn.edu/law_papers/133. Accessed January 11, 2023.
Value Added Tax (Law No. 3065), Official Gazette No. 18563, November 2, 1984.
Yalçıner, K. (2018). *Gayrimenkul finansmanı*. Detay Yayıncılık.

Emrullah Töremen earned his bachelor's degree in public administration from Hacettepe University and completed his Master's and Doctoral degrees at Ankara University. The title of his doctoral study is "Tax Awareness and Perception in Businesses Operating in Construction and Real Estate Sector: An Evaluation from the Perspective of Housing Producers and Sellers in Ankara Province". His areas of expertise include tax law, fiscal law, real estate tax legislation, fiscal sociology, urban policy, local administrations, and local administration taxes. Dr. Töremen held various positions at the Ministry of Treasury and Finance between 1998 and 2019. He currently serves as Deputy Director-General at the General Directorate of Local Administrations under the Ministry of Environment, Urbanisation, and Climate Change.

Erol Demir is a full professor at the Department of Real Estate Development and Management, Faculty of Applied Sciences, Ankara University, Türkiye. He holds a Ph.D. in Agricultural Economics from Ankara University and an M.Sc. in Business Administration from Gazi University. His research focuses on real estate taxation, accounting practices in the construction and property sectors, cooperative finance, and public sector economics. He has published extensively in peer-reviewed journals and authored several books. Prof. Demir has also served as Deputy Dean and contributed to multiple academic committees within Ankara University. He is currently an editorial board member of cited journals.

Real Estate Financing and Investment

Assessments of Real Estate Finance System and Instruments in Türkiye

Gülnaz Şengül Güneş, İlhan Yıldırım, and Erol Demir

Abstract

The scarcity of resources necessitates the effective and efficient use of existing resources to enhance the activities of the real estate sector, thereby facilitating economic development. Furthermore, advances in information and communication technology, coupled with increasing demands arising from globalisation, have imposed more active and novel roles on the real estate sector—not only serving as a means to address housing needs but also functioning as a target of production activity aimed at ensuring economic development and sustainability. Given the growing significance of the real estate development process, the introduction of alternative financing methods beyond traditional capital market financing becomes essential. This development, however, is contingent upon a robust capital market and the enhanced role of real estate derivatives as intermediaries within this market. Additionally, the level of development across countries varies, influenced by the strength of their money and capital markets, as well as the diversity of instruments used. In this context, it is highly important to aim at improving the integration of Türkiye's real estate markets with international markets, in conjunction with money and capital markets, to initiate new real estate and financial instruments based on derivatives, and to enhance existing instruments.

Keywords

Real estate financing · Project finance · Derivative financial instruments related to real estate · Financial institutions

G. Ş. Güneş (✉) · İ. Yıldırım · E. Demir
Department of Real Estate Development and Management, Faculty of Applied Sciences, Ankara University, Ankara, Türkiye
e-mail: gsengul@ankara.edu.tr; ilhan.yildirim@msb.gov.tr; eroldemir@ankara.edu.tr

T. Just et al. (eds.), *Understanding Türkiye's Real Estate Markets*, Management for Professionals, https://doi.org/10.1007/978-3-032-13297-0_12

1 Introduction

Depending on the level of capital market development in Türkiye, the interaction between the construction and real estate sectors and the financial markets is evolving. Consequently, the range of products used in real estate financing is transforming, with an increase in both the number of users of these products and transaction volumes. Given that both sectors are pivotal to the nation's economy and social transformation, the demand for financing to ensure their continuity and diversity is becoming critical.

The reality that demand remains strong while resources are finite presents a challenge for individuals seeking to finance their real estate for either housing or investment purposes. Real estate investments necessitate a considerable allocation of resources, which can result in an inability to satisfy all financing requirements, subsequently creating a demand for supplementary financial instruments. Thus, the acquisition of real estate through funds procured via borrowing becomes imperative. Borrowing may be accessed either directly or indirectly through intermediaries representing funding providers, contingent on the developmental stage of the respective countries (Hepşen, 2014). Furthermore, the sale of real estate to suppliers is crucial for the sustainability of the project. Construction companies engaged in substantial projects require long-term loans accompanied by a designated grace period to finalise their endeavours, as continuous cash flow to the project cannot be guaranteed.

The real estate sector plays a crucial role in the economic development of Türkiye and is engaged in a continuous and dynamic interaction with the financial markets. Given that real estate markets entail long-term investments and necessitate substantial capital, they are primarily influenced by monetary and capital markets, while concurrently affecting these markets through instruments derived from real estate assets.

Real estate investments entail substantial expenses for both producers and purchasers. Consequently, the paramount consideration in actualising real estate investments is the establishment of sufficient financing (İçellioğlu, 2013). Furthermore, housing finance, a subset of real estate finance, holds considerable significance for countries. The imperative of housing to fulfil individuals' need for shelter necessitates the examination of housing not only as an investment but also as a social phenomenon (Ayan, 2011).

The primary objective of real estate financing is to facilitate the development of real estate projects or to acquire real estate for residential or investment purposes. An effective real estate financing system involves the collection of necessary funds from entities with surplus resources and their subsequent transfer to institutions or individuals in need of financing (Hepşen, 2014). Consequently, the capacity of the financial system to provide adequate credit, the accessibility of such credit to users, and the structure of long-term loan repayment are critical indicators of the system's effectiveness (Tanrıvermiş, 2017a, 2017b). This chapter will examine Türkiye's real estate financing system and its instruments, discuss the sources and methods of financing real estate, and offer a brief overview of real estate investment funds, lease certificates (Islamic financial certificate-*Sukuk*), real estate certificates, and real estate investment trusts, which serve as instruments of real estate-based financing.

2 Sources of Financing for the Real Estate Market

The process of collecting funds from individuals or institutions possessing surplus resources and subsequently transferring these funds to both public and private entities in need of financing for real estate acquisition, along with the repayment of these funds via long-term loans, is crucial for the establishment of an effective real estate finance system (Hepşen, 2011; Tapan, 2020). Nevertheless, the requirement for funding should extend beyond individuals or institutions seeking real estate; it should also encompass those who are providing it. While individual or household income is recognised as the primary source of financing in real estate transactions, it remains feasible to categorise the funding sources of real estate markets into four distinct categories: (i) non-corporate, (ii) corporate, (iii) public, and (iv) foreign resources (Demir & Kurt Palabıyık, 2005; Yalçıner, 2018).

(i) ***Non-corporate Finance:*** This constitutes a system in which formal rules do not dictate activities, but rather these are based on traditions and practices. Informality prevails, and legal regulations do not predominantly govern operations (Alp, 2000; Tapan, 2020). This approach is frequently used in construction and real estate endeavours within underdeveloped or developing nations, where specialised financial institutions are not readily available. This method primarily attracts middle-upper and upper-income households. Non-corporate or institutional financing sources encompass "household savings, funds from relatives, friends and close family circle, funds from employers or colleagues at work, savings in precious metals, funds from moneylenders and similar structures, loans from non-institutional sources such as savings and loan associations, loans from contractors and housing cooperatives" (Demir & Kurt Palabıyık, 2005; Hepşen, 2014; Yalçıner, 2018). Previous research conducted in Türkiye indicates that the acquisition of real estate through non-corporate financing sources is exceedingly prevalent. Personal savings and financial support from relatives and close acquaintances play a significant role in facilitating appropriate financing.

(ii) ***Corporate Finance Sources:*** The institutions include all institutions, organisations, principles, and structures that have been laid down and authorised in line with regulations grounded in legal frameworks, as well as the resources allocated within this context. Accordingly, mortgage banks, real estate companies, specialised housing finance institutions, banks, pension funds, insurance companies, and social security institutions represent significant sources of corporate finance. The operations of these institutions are subject to public scrutiny and must be transparently disclosed to the public (Demir & Kurt Palabıyık, 2005; Tanrıvermiş, 2017b; Yalçıner, 2018). The primary objective of financial institutions specialising in real estate finance is to extend loans to individuals seeking funding in exchange for mortgages. Consequently, the core activities of these institutions differ from those in the financial sector. Generally, the funding sources for these institutions include capital raised through the issuance of securities. Thus, these institutions, particularly prominent in developed countries, alongside organisations that accrue capital through market mechanisms, such as commercial banks, which provide real estate financing, encounter significant challenges in maintaining competitiveness within the real estate financing sector (Tapan, 2020).

(iii) ***Public Finance:*** These entail fund transfers by the public, including housing projects constructed by the public, as well as indirect fund transfers, such as subsidies and incentives (tax reductions) provided by the public. The financial support extended by the central government to these real estate markets serves as a significant social policy instrument for lower- and lower-middle-income groups (Demir & Kurt Palabıyık, 2005, Tanrıvermiş 2017b). In Türkiye, the Housing Development Administration (TOKİ) was established in 1984 and plays a critical role in providing affordable housing, particularly in the realm of social housing construction. Moreover, TOKİ offers interest-free housing loans to families of casualties and individuals with disabilities affected by terrorism. As of 2024, the total volume of loans disbursed amounts to Turkish Lira (TL) 315,571,500 (Table 1).

The Social Security Institution (SSI) and the Army Assistance Institution (OYAK) exemplify the financial support extended by public institutions. These entities facilitate housing construction and offer low-interest housing loans to their members. Notably, OYAK continues to provide mortgage housing loans. Furthermore, the public leverages various models to finance real estate projects that require substantial investments, encompassing sectors such as energy, health, transportation, and infrastructure. To implement these projects, which require substantial financial resources, models such as build-operate-transfer, build-operate, and

Table 1 Housing loans extended by TOKİ

Years	Number of people	Loans extended (TL)
2014	1709	140,637,493
2015	1347	110,241,61
2016	1316	118,337,000
2017	2043	205,815,526
2018	1758	193,954,333
2019	1641	215,040,727
2020	997	147,523,500
2021	875	148,846,500
2022	489	112,415,500
2023	362	137,750,100
2024	495	315,571,500

Source: TOKİ (2025)

public-private partnerships have been employed since the 1990s, alongside the establishment of suitable legal frameworks.

(iv) ***International Resources:*** The support provided by the World Bank and the international financial institutions via technical assistance is significant but constrained (Demir & Kurt Palabıyık, 2005; Yalçıner, 2018).

3 Approaches Used in Real Estate Financing

The methods employed to secure the financial resources necessary for the production or acquisition of real estate differ based on the characteristics of real estate projects or their financing. In the selection of the appropriate method, various factors are considered, including the size of the property, the amount and maturity of the loan, the rights conferred to ownership alongside construction and usage rights, the cost of financing, project planning, the duration of construction, and the anticipated cash flow and profit levels from the project (Hepşen, 2017; Yalçıner, 2018). Depending on the economic and social structures of the respective countries, the following methods are frequently used in real estate financing: "(i) direct financing", "(ii) accumulation against contract", "(iii) deposit financing", and "(iv) mortgage banking".

The mechanism commences with households and prospective real estate purchasers allocating funds to general and savings banks, insurance companies, and pension funds. However, in the absence of this transfer, real estate may be acquired through direct engagement with real estate sellers (direct financing method). Alternatively, buyers may also finance their real estate acquisitions through general and savings banks by using their deposits (deposit financing). Funds may additionally be transferred by executing contracts between real estate buyers and financial intermediaries (contract method). Lastly, mortgage banks can furnish funds for real estate purchases after securing the intended property with a mortgage (mortgage banking) (Fig. 1).

(i) ***Direct Financing:*** In circumstances where savings are insufficient and additional financing is necessary, the systems available arise directly from individuals or institutions with surplus funds, established through interpersonal relationships between the involved parties. These systems include family members, friends, professional organisations, credit unions, contractors, and cooperatives. The direct financing approach is preferred in countries with underdeveloped corporate real estate markets (Hepşen, 2010). The effectiveness of this approach depends on the amount of available funds. However, the limited capacity of the resources generated by this approach makes it impossible to cover the entire financing requirement in proportion to needs. (Yalçıner, 2006).

In Türkiye, contractors, commonly referred to as builders and sellers, participate in the development of housing projects on land in exchange for securing residential

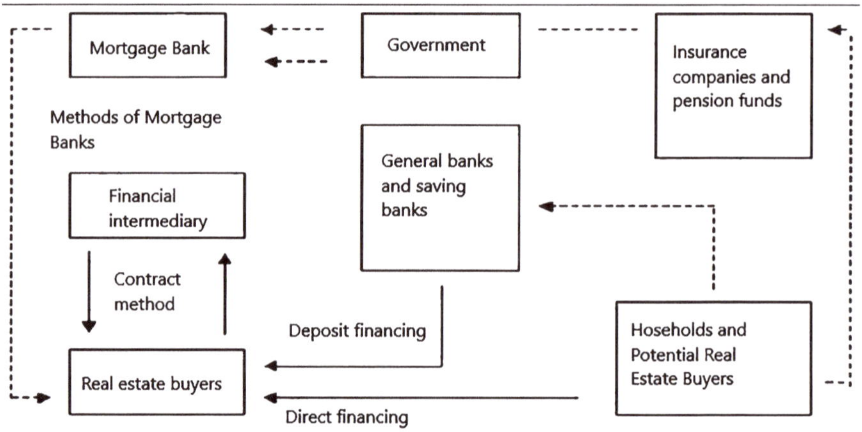

Fig. 1 Operation of real estate financing methods. Source: Hepşen (2014)

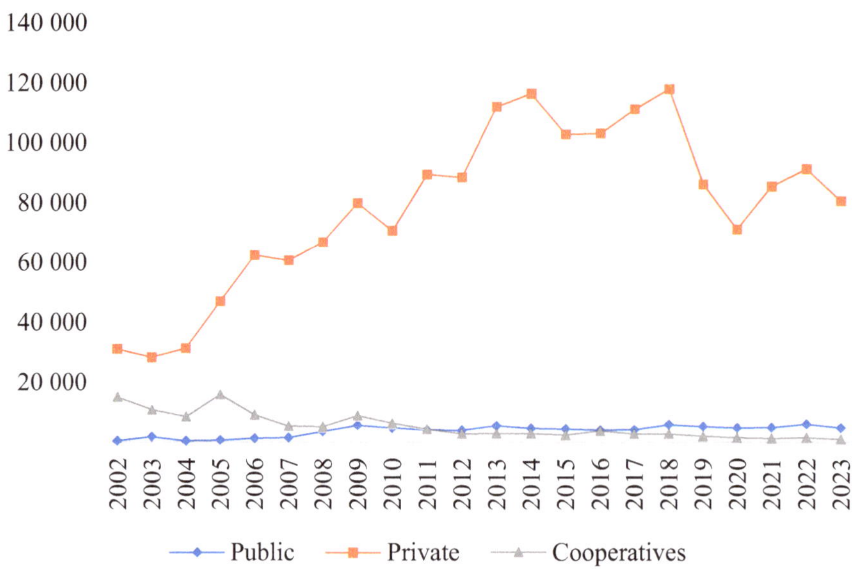

Fig. 2 Distribution of building use permit documents by year. Source: TURKSTAT (2024)

flats. Furthermore, building cooperatives represent an alternative approach to housing production, facilitating homeownership for their members through the contributions received from them. However, the effectiveness of building cooperatives has significantly declined in recent years. Their share in building use permits has steadily declined over the last few years, while the share of private sector enterprises has risen sharply (Fig. 2).

(ii) ***Contractual Savings:*** Economic entities endeavouring to acquire real estate save at a rate that is lower than the existing market interest rates at predetermined intervals through institutionalised and specialised real estate financial institutions, thereby obtaining the right to secure loans proportional to their savings. Upon repayment of the loan, interest is calculated at a rate that is below the market interest rate (Hepşen, 2010). To maintain the continuity of this cycle, new participants must join the system to provide financing for those who entered earlier. Given that this approach does not cover the entire expense of the real estate to be acquired (a maximum of 40%), additional funds need to be added (Yalçıner, 2006, Tanrıvermiş, 2017b). This system originated in the UK (Building Societies) and exists in Germany (Bausparkassen), France (savings institutions) and several developed European nations, Brazil, Mexico, and the Philippines. Although Türkiye does not have equivalent savings institutions, the "Regulation on Housing Account and State Contribution", which was enacted following Council of Ministers Decree No. 2016/8559, seeks to establish a comparable savings framework (Tanrıvermiş, 2017b).

(iii) ***Deposit Financing:*** The system operates on the premise that financial institutions, which accept deposits—including but not limited to commercial banks, investment banks, savings associations, and building societies—provide all or a portion of the deposits they accumulate as mortgage loans to individuals seeking to acquire real estate. Within this framework, funds are sourced either through the collection of market interest rates or via securities issued against mortgage-backed housing loans characterised by extended maturities (Yalçıner, 2006; Hepşen, 2010). In Türkiye, the issuance of housing loans has experienced a notable increase following the enactment of the "Law on Housing Finance No. 5582 dated 21.02.2007". The practice of commercial banks of lending deposits they have received as housing loans raises the question of "maturity mismatch". The brevity of the deposit durations in Türkiye, juxtaposed with the protracted term of housing loans, presents a significant risk for commercial banks. For both housing and consumer loans extended by banking institutions, the period of 3–12 months is favoured as of March 2024, succeeded by loans with maturities ranging from 19 to 24 months (The Banks Association of Türkiye, 2024). The proportion of mortgaged sales within the overall housing market has fluctuated over the years, and its share in total sales stood at 10.7% as of 2024 (Table 2).

As of December 2023, the total amount of housing loans disbursed reached TL 438,232 million, with the predominant share provided by deposit banks. Specifically, among deposit banks, state-owned banks accounted for a 59.81% share of the sector. The proportion of banks participating in the utilisation of housing loans stood at 9.68% (Table 3).

Table 2 Number of housing sales by year

Year	Total	Mortgage sales		Other sales	
		Number	Share (%)	Number	Share (%)
2013	**1,157,190**	460,112	39.8	697,078	**1,157,190**
2014	**1,165,381**	389,689	33.4	775,692	**1,165,381**
2015	**1,289,320**	434,388	33.7	854,932	**1,289,320**
2016	**1,341,453**	449,508	33.5	891,945	**1,341,453**
2017	**1,409,314**	473,099	33.6	936,215	**1,409,314**
2018	**1,375,398**	276,820	20.1	1,098,578	**1,375,398**
2019	**1,348,729**	332,508	24.7	1,016,221	**1,348,729**
2020	**1,499,316**	573,337	38.2	925,979	**1,499,316**
2021	**1,491,856**	294,530	19.7	1,197,326	**1,491,856**
2022	**1,157,190**	460,112	39.8	697,078	**1,157,190**
2023	**1,165,381**	389,689	33.4	775,692	**1,165,381**
2024	**1,289,320**	434,388	33.7	854,932	**1,289,320**

Source: TurkStat (2025)

Table 3 Mortgage loan distribution by banks in 2024

	Number of banks	Sector share (%)	Mortgage loan volume distribution (TL million)
Total deposit bank	32	90	448,178
Public deposit banks	3	48	239,766
Domestic private deposit banks	8	29	142,277
Foreign deposit banks	21	13	66,135
Development and investment banks	13	0	496
Participation banks	6	10	47,945
Total	**51**	**100**	**496,129**

Source: The Association of Real Estate Investors (2025a)

(iv) ***Mortgage Banking:*** A mortgage[1] serves as collateral to secure a debt, which can result from a mortgage loan that has either already occurred or is anticipated to occur in the future. Conversely, the mortgage market is a complex system that encompasses the production, marketing, and sale of real estate, as well as the assessment of savings in both money and capital markets, including securitisation.

The mortgage banking system is predicated upon the "housing finance system". It is imperative to allocate funds through the issuance of mortgage loan receivables as securities within secondary markets. Consequently, this approach diverges from

[1] A mortgage is a real estate pledge listed in Article 850 of the "Turkish Civil Code No. 4721", and it is not affected by the owner's change for real estate on which it is established. It must be established in official written form as a condition of validity.

traditional housing loans (Eroğlu, 2010). In addition, this application, which is based on long-term real estate mortgages, is widely used not only in the real estate sector but also for investments in agriculture, industry, and commerce. (Öztop & Şekeroğlu, 2016; Tanrıvermiş, 2017a; Yalçıner, 2018).

In Türkiye, the issuance of asset-backed securities based on loans granted for mortgage banking was realised in 1992 with the amendment made to Capital Markets Law No. 2499. Subsequently, Law No. 5582 established regulations for covered bonds (CB), asset-guaranteed securities (AGS), mortgage-backed securities (MBS), and asset-backed securities (ABS) as new capital market instruments to facilitate the implementation of the mortgage banking system. Law No. 5582 encompasses capital market institutions for institutional structuring. Furthermore, Asset Financing Funds (AIFs) and Housing Finance Funds (HFFs), designated to function as Special Purpose Vehicles (SPVs) and manage asset transfers during the securities issuance process, are also regulated. Additionally, Mortgage Finance Institutions (MFIs) are classified as organised secondary market institutions (Capital Markets Board, 2024b). These regulations have been maintained in the revised "Capital Markets Law No. 6362" of 2012. The infrastructure for housing finance and asset finance funds in Türkiye was initially established through the articles (38/a—Housing finance, 38/b—Housing finance fund, 38/c—Asset finance fund) integrated into Article 38 of Law No. 2499 of 1981. The scope of these provisions was expanded by Law No. 6362 in 2012, incorporating regulations aimed at enhancing the development of the secondary market. The housing finance system is delineated under the section titled "Housing and Asset Finance and Mortgage Finance Institutions" of Law No. 6362 (Heper Baran, 2020). Housing finance is defined in Article 57 of the Law as follows: "Providing loans to consumers for the acquisition of housing, leasing housing through financial leasing, providing loans to consumers under the collateral of the housing they own, and providing loans for refinancing of these loans". Additionally, Sub-Regulations were established through the "Communiqué on Securities Based on Assets and Mortgages (III – 58,1)", "Communiqué on Secured Securities (III – 59,1)", "Communiqué on Principles Regarding Mortgage Finance Institutions (III– 60,1)", and "Communiqué on Lease Certificates (III – 61,1)".

4 Financial Institutions and Financing Instruments in the Real Estate Market

Financial institutions, which are indispensable for the establishment of an institutional framework within the real estate financing system, are categorised into two distinct groups: legal entities and non-legal entities. Funds, which are designated as unincorporated financial institutions, do not possess an institutional structure akin to commodity groups and are created for a predetermined duration. Financial institutions that hold legal personality are divided into five categories: (i) Housing Finance Institutions, (ii) Mortgage Finance Institutions, (iii) Real Estate Investment Trusts (REITs), (iv) Real Estate Appraisal Companies, and (v) Asset Leasing

Companies (ALCs). Conversely, financial institutions without legal personality comprise (i) Real Estate Investment Funds (REIF), (ii) Housing Finance Funds, and (iii) Asset Finance Funds.

Housing finance institutions encompass conventional banks, participation banks, financial leasing companies, and financing companies. These entities were initially incorporated into the legal framework by the Financial Leasing Law No. 3226 of 1985. They were subsequently broadened under the Financial Leasing, Factoring, Financing, and Savings Finance Companies Law No. 6361 of 2012. Among the financial leasing and financing companies recognised by the Banking Regulation and Supervision Agency, those classified as suitable for housing financing are designated as housing finance institutions. Participation banks are also included in this category based on the loans they extend to consumers or the financial leasing they conduct for similar purposes.

The Capital Markets Board permits the establishment of mortgage finance institutions as joint stock companies. These entities shall acquire, transfer, and manage assets of the type and nature specified for housing and asset financing and use the assets as collateral.

Housing and asset finance funds are assets that do not possess legal personality. These funds are established in accordance with the internal regulations derived from the principles of fiduciary asset management. The funds provided by the Housing Finance Funds (HFFs) in exchange for the Mortgage-Backed Securities (MBS) are transferred to the accounts of the MBS holders. Conversely, Asset Finance Funds (AFFs) operate on behalf of the Asset-Backed Securities (ABS) holders, using the funds provided in exchange for the ABS.

4.1 Real Estate Investment Funds (REIFs)

Real estate investment funds (REIFs) are "assets without legal personality, which are established for a period or indefinitely to operate the portfolio formed on behalf of the shareholders with the savings collected from qualified investors in return for their participation shares". In Türkiye, REIFs were introduced as a financial instrument with the issuance of the "Communiqué on Principles Regarding Real Estate Investment Funds (III–52.3)" dated January 3, 2014. REIFs, which facilitate the transformation of real estate into more liquid assets through securitisation, are primarily aimed at institutional investors in Türkiye (Yalçıner, 2018).

The distribution of the total value of the fund in REIFs is regulated by legislation. Consequently, a minimum of 80% must be comprised of real estate investments. Furthermore, these funds may be traded on the stock exchange within the market for qualified investors. REIFs can be managed by real estate portfolios, portfolio management firms, or venture capital companies. The fund portfolio comprises real estate, independent sections in specific real estate projects, or rights related to real estate, as well as funds collected from qualified investors in exchange for

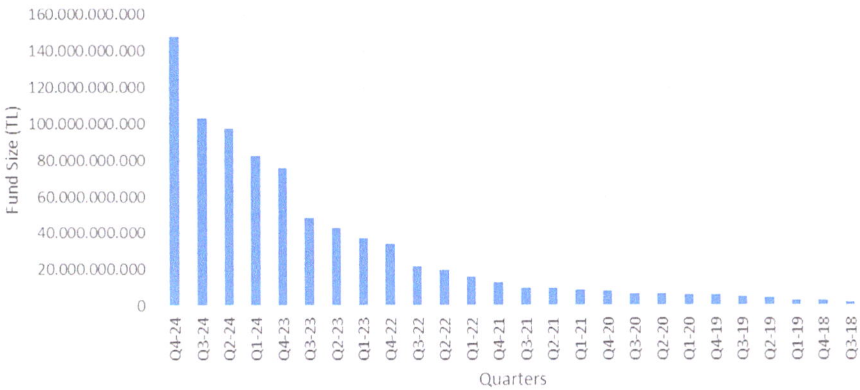

Fig. 3 The total market size of REIFs. Source: The Association of Real Estate Investors (2025b)

participation shares. The legal status of REIFs, which do not possess legal personality, is confined to registration with the title deed registry and the processes for cancellation and rectification. Specific obligations are imposed on the funds; for example, the portfolio value of the fund must reach at least TL 10,000,000 within 1 year following the issuance of the fund units. Valuation institutions approved by the Capital Markets Board (CMB) evaluate the value of real estate investments.

The legislation pertaining to tax liabilities for REIFs includes specific privileges. In accordance with legal requirements, the assets of the founder, portfolio custodian, and portfolio manager are separated from the assets of the fund, thereby safeguarding the portfolio custodian's and manager's assets. Furthermore, with respect to debts, liabilities, and receivables, no settlements are conducted in the relationships between the founder and/or portfolio manager and third parties. The market size of REIFs in Türkiye has consistently expanded over the years, with the projected market size for 2024 estimated to be approximately TL 148 billion (Fig. 3).

4.2 Sukuk (Lease Certificate)

Sukuk are defined as "financial instruments representing shares of equal value in the assets of a good, benefit, service, a specific project and/or investment" (Durmuş, 2010). The interest-free financial system in Türkiye was initially introduced in 1983 by the Special Finance Institution. In 2005, the designation and status of the Special Finance Institutions were altered, leading to their transformation into "Participation Banks", which provide banking services related to Islamic finance (Aslan, 2012). On April 1, 2010, the "Communiqué on the Principles Regarding Lease Certificates and Asset Leasing Companies No: Series III, No: 43" established a legal basis for lease certificates in Türkiye. Subsequently, on June 7, 2013, the application principles were delineated in the "Communiqué on Lease Certificates No. III–61.1".

Lease certificates, akin to REIFs, are regarded as a relatively novel financing instrument and are issued in two distinct ways in Türkiye, contingent upon real estate factors. These methods include (i) public offerings and (ii) private placements. Lease certificates issued through public offerings are mandated to be listed on a stock exchange. Conversely, sales conducted without a public offering may be executed in one of two ways: "allocated sale" or "sale to a qualified investor". For lease certificates that are based on ownership, partnerships, and work contracts, the issuance limit is established at 90% of the assessed value. Article 7/A of the "Law No. 4749 on the Regulation of Public Finance and Debt Management", dated March 28, 2002, instituted the Treasury Asset Leasing Company Inc., which is affiliated with the Treasury, pursuant to the authority conferred to the Ministry of Treasury and Finance. Thus, the transfer of public real estate to the Treasury Asset Leasing Company Inc. is conducted through sales (Ministry of Treasury and Finance, 2024). The Ministry of Treasury and Finance issues lease certificates featuring "fixed lease payments", "Indexed to CPI", or "based on gold" (Capital Markets Board, 2024a). The issuance process for leasing certificates conducted by Treasury Asset Leasing Company Inc. involves a seven-step operational mechanism in which the Department of the Treasury, Treasury Asset Leasing Company Inc., and investors participate jointly. The action that initiates this process is the transfer of public real estate to the Treasury Asset Leasing Company Inc. via the Ministry of Treasury and Finance (Fig. 4).

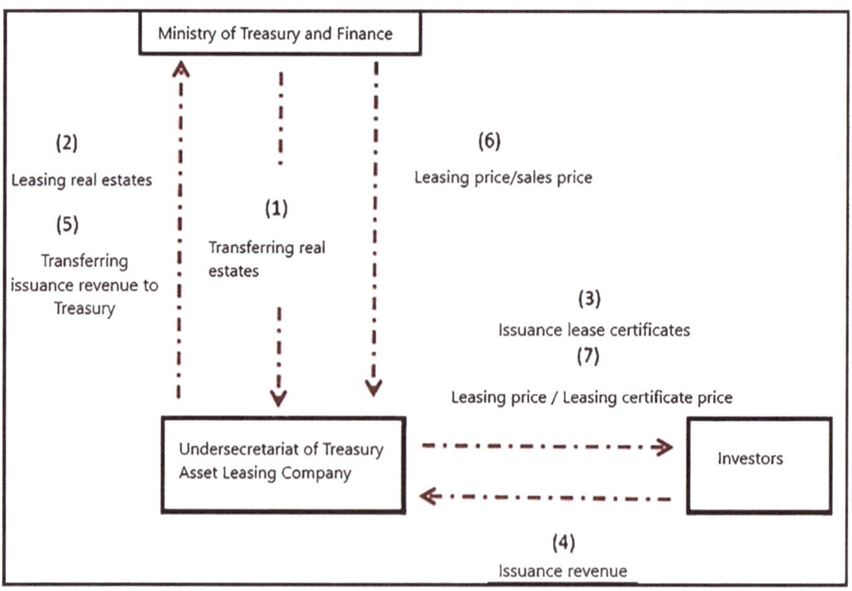

Fig. 4 Lease certificate issuance procedure. Source: Ministry of Treasury and Finance (2024)

Interest in Islamic finance products has increased in Türkiye over the last few years. Sukuk issuances, a specific type of Islamic finance product, have experienced a notable rise. Particularly, in 2013, sukuk issuances began to grow as public banks began to issue sukuk. As of 2024, the largest issuance to date was executed by Ziraat Participation Bank. The distribution of issuances by banks is presented in Table 4.

Table 5 presents the values of Sukuk issuances, both domestically and internationally, as reported by the Ministry of Treasury and Finance, denominated in Turkish Lira (TL), other currencies, and gold. The TL-denominated value of domestic Sukuk issuances has trended upward for many years; however, it began to decline in 2021. However, the domestic Sukuk issuances denominated in gold have been exhibiting consistent growth over the years.

4.3 Real Estate Certificates

A real estate certificate is defined as "a capital market instrument issued by joint stock companies and public institutions and organisations authorised to issue capital market instruments to represent certain independent sections or a certain unit on an area basis of a real estate project to be built or under construction". The primary objective of these certificates is to facilitate financing for real estate projects, enabling owners of savings to obtain a share in the project (Köroğlu, 2016; Sırma, 2018; Heper Baran, 2020). Certificates that enable the securitisation of real estate are transacted on the stock exchange. Consequently, the value of these certificates is determined by the principles of supply and demand within the stock market and is susceptible to price fluctuations (Turan, 2017; Heper Baran, 2020).

Certificates of real estate, issued by authorised entities, are rendered null upon the completion of either primary or secondary acquisition processes. Moreover, construction progress reports are acquired from building inspection firms by designated institutions, contingent upon the disbursement of the issuance income tranche and the successful completion of the project, as illustrated in Fig. 5.

Real estate certificates in Türkiye commenced trading on the "Borsa İstanbul Inc. Collective Investment Products and Structured Products Market" as of April 7, 2017, with TOKİ issuing the inaugural certificates. The real estate certificate was issued for the Park Mavera III Project, constructed in the Başakşehir district of Istanbul, pursuant to the "Revenue Sharing Business in Return for Land Sales" agreement entered into between TOKİ and "Makro Construction Company" on April 6, 2016. Initially offered to the public, the certificates were traded at a base price of TL 42.50, with 10.47% acquired by one participation bank and 13.65% by two pension investment funds. According to data from investors, real estate certificates were requested from 79 provinces, with most demand originating from Istanbul and Ankara. A significant proportion of the demand for certificates arises from individuals aged 30 to 40 (Heper Baran, 2020).

Table 4 Sukuk issuance volumes of participation banks (2013–2024)

Years		Albaraka Türk	Emlak participation	Kuveyt Türk	Türkiye finance	Vakıf participation	Ziraat participation
2013		–	–	150,000	–	–	–
2014		–	–	287,000	299,000	–	–
2015		–	–	1,524,091	1,050,000	–	–
2016		350,000	–	1,723,614	985,000	–	300,000
2017		900,000	–	2,330,000	1,258,000	1,620,000	1,100,000
2018		3,338,470	–	5,100,000	4,278,100	4,367,304	3,454,000
2019		8,990,000	–	5,891,000	8,440,000	9,012,696	8,150,000
2020		13,092,000	4,804,198	6,311,370	7,550,000	9,934,830	12,450,000
2021		22,213,000	12,917,764	19,085,000	15,150,000	16,172,000	11,400,000
2022		8,190,000	15,350,000	12,660,000	16,460,000	15,350,000	15,900,000
2023		3,220,000	25,250,000	11,590,000	8,200,000	17,400,000	16,500,000
2024		24,001,000	28,664,350	26,262,300	8,500,000	15,553,000	32,700,000

Source: Association of Participation Banks of Türkiye (2025)

Table 5 Ministry of treasury and finance domestic and international Sukuk issuance volumes (2012–2022 August)

Years	Overseas (USD)	Domestic (1000TL)	USD	EUR	GOLD (Gram)
2012	1,500,000	1,624,483	–	–	–
2013	1,250,000	3,332,627	–	–	–
2014	1,000,000	3,172,784	–	–	–
2015	–	3,390,299	–	–	–
2016	1,000,000	6,262,257	–	–	–
2017	1,250,000	4,259,965	–	–	1,318,542
2018	–	7,253,675	–	565,565	2,485,747
2019	2,000,000	7,601,170	–	1,836,950	65,473,071
2020	–	37,155,160	2,427,292	488,464	51,105,190
2021	2,500,000	11,477,850	232,929	697,360	77,550,300
2022/August	3,000,000	46,619,860	–	–	34,833,955
Total	**13,500,000**	**132,150,129**	**2,660,221**	**3,588,339**	**232,766,805**

Source: Association of Participation Banks of Türkiye (2024)

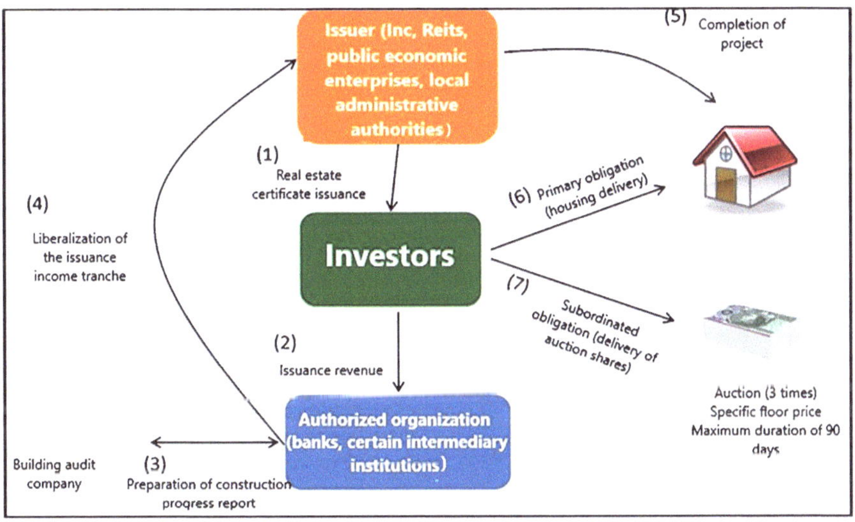

Fig. 5 The issuance process of real estate certificates. Source: Capital Markets Board (2024b)

4.4 Real Estate Investment Trusts (REITs)

The initial regulation governing real estate investment trusts in Türkiye was established through the "Communiqué on Principles Regarding Real Estate Investment Trusts No: VI No: 7" dated July 22, 1995. This was succeeded by the issuance of "Communiqué No. 11" in 1998, which incorporated subsequent amendments. Ultimately, the "Communiqué on Principles Regarding Real Estate Investment Trusts (III–48.1)" delineated the legal framework for REITs. The inaugural REIT

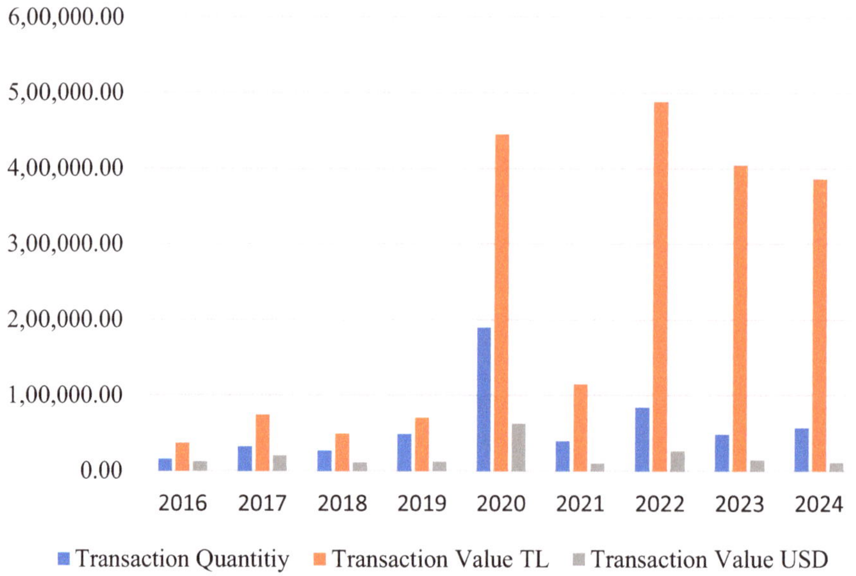

Fig. 6 Transaction quantities and values of REITs. Source: The Association of Real Estate Investors (2025c)

was established in Türkiye in 1995, with its public offering taking place in 1997 (Kaçıra, 2009). The number of REITs in Türkiye has increased to 49 REITs as of the first quarter of 2025. REITs are mandated to allocate a minimum of 51% of their total assets to real estate investments and are permitted to manage exclusively one real estate portfolio. Over the years, transaction volumes of REITs in Türkiye have escalated. After years of rising transaction values, a significant decline was observed in 2021. As of 2024, the transaction value of REITs reached approximately TL 385,933 million (Fig. 6).

5 Conclusion

The real estate markets are defined not only by the assets but also by the securities that represent the rights conferred by real estate, along with the frameworks within which monetary or comparable assets are exchanged. From a macroeconomic perspective, public investments of diverse qualities and scales are undertaken by the public sector to facilitate and sustain economic development. To bolster the real sector and, thereby, foster economic advances, a robust capital market is essential, necessitating an enhancement of the role of real estate as an instrument within this market. The establishment of a real estate financing system is anticipated to stimulate demand for real estate and to meet financial requirements under terms and conditions that guarantee the persistence of this demand. However, the achievement of this objective relies heavily on cultivating a healthy relationship among market participants, including governmental entities, financial institutions, producers, developers, and households. In accordance with classifications established by international valuation and accounting standards, it is imperative to devise new financial instruments that provide the requisite financing to fulfil the demand for the use, sale, or investment in real estate, which is categorised as tangible fixed assets on the balance sheets of enterprises by both domestic and international banks and financial institutions. Real estate-based capital market instruments and institutions were established to address the need for access to such financing. The aim is therefore to support both investors and private individuals who wish to purchase residential property, while at the same time offering alternative financing options for real estate development projects. Furthermore, small investors get the opportunity to capitalise on price fluctuations within the real estate market.

In Türkiye, the number of financial instruments related to real estate that are traded in capital markets is increasing. Consequently, the variety of products employed in real estate financing is evolving, and there is a significant rise in the number of buyers of these products. Nevertheless, it is observed that a considerable portion of the funds allocated for housing access continues to originate from commercial banks. The instruments used by commercial banks when distributing housing loans are the deposit accounts presented by investors as funding sources. Therefore, the utilisation of deposits accumulated in commercial banks to finance real estate projects raises the issue of maturity mismatch, as real estate is inherently a long-term asset. This problem of maturity mismatch presents a risk to both banks and the country's overall economy. Hence, the imperative to adapt new products within the system and ensure a diverse array of offerings to sustain financing needs becomes increasingly critical.

The financial system must furnish adequate funding, facilitate accessible loan opportunities for eligible users, and establish a structured framework for long-term loan repayment to cultivate a robust real estate financing infrastructure. This issue is directly associated with the establishment of long-term repayment mechanisms and, more notably, the sufficient development of secondary markets. Consequently, the expansion of mortgage banking is deemed imperative, with its foundations laid in Türkiye through Law No. 5582, "Law on Amendments to Various Laws Regarding the Housing Finance System". Furthermore, it is essential to regulate secondary markets, encourage the introduction of real estate derivative instruments traded within these markets, and undertake research aimed at enhancing investor engagement in these sectors.

References

Alp, A. (2000). Modern konut finansmanı (No. 216). SPK Yayınları.

Association of Participation Banks of Türkiye. (2024). *Sukuk*. https://tkbb.org.tr/Documents/Sukuk_Ozet_Sunum_2022_Agustos.pdf. Accessed October 15, 2024.

Association of Participation Banks of Türkiye. (2025). *Sukuk ihraç hacimleri*. https://tkbb.org.tr/veripetegi-detay/8. Accessed April 25, 2025.

Aslan, H. (2012). Alternatif bir yatırım ve finansman aracı olarak sukuk: Yapısı, işleyişi ve Türkiye piyasası için öneriler (Master's thesis, Marmara University, Department of Financial Markets and Investment Management), 147 p., İstanbul.
Ayan, E. (2011). Konut finansmanı sistemi ve Türkiye'de TOKİ uygulamalarının analizi. *Journal of Accounting and Finance, 49*, 139–156.
Capital Markets Board. (2024a). *Sermaye piyasası araçları: 1.* https://spl.com.tr/wp-content/uploads/2024/07/1003_MKT_30062024_202407170758.pdf. 161 p. Accessed August 20, 2024.
Capital Markets Board. (2024b). *Sermaye piyasası araçları: 2.* https://spl.com.tr/wp-content/uploads/2024/07/1004_MKT_30062024_202407171732.pdf (196 p.) Accessed August 20, 2024.
Demir, H., & Kurt Palabıyık, V. (2005). Konut ediniminde uzun vadeli ipotek kredisi sistemi. *Journal of Geodesy, Geoinformation and Land Management, 93*, 3–11.
Durmuş, A. (2010). Modern bir finansal araç olarak sukuk ve fıkhi açıdan tahlili. *Journal of Islamic Law Research, 16*, 1–22.
Eroğlu, E. (2010). Mortgage sisteminde ikincil piyasa ürünleri ve dünya uygulamaları. *Journal of Business Research, 2*(4), 19–38.
Heper Baran, L. (2020). Türkiye'de gayrimenkul finansmanı yönünden gayrimenkul sertifikaları (Master's thesis, Ankara University, Natural and Applied Sciences), 194 p., Ankara.
Hepşen, A. (2010). Gayrimenkul piyasaları ve finansmanı. Literatür Yayıncılık, 222 p.
Hepşen, A. (2011). Finansal krizlerde gayrimenkul finansman piyasalarının rolü ve gayrimenkul fiyat endekslerinin önemi. Literatür Yayıncılık.
Hepşen, A. (2014). Gayrimenkul değerleme esasları. SPL Yayınları, 231 p.
Hepşen, A. (2017). Gayrimenkul değerleme esasları ve finans boyutu. Literatür Yayıncılık.
İçellioğlu, C. Ş. (2013). Gayrimenkul ekonomisi. Derin Yayınları, 160 p.
Kaçıra, F. B. (2009). Gayrimenkul yatırım ortaklıkları. Beta Yayınları, 410 p.
Köroğlu, A. (2016). Gayrimenkul sertifikası modeli ve Türkiye'de uygulanabilirliği. *Gazi Journal of Economics and Business Administration, 2*(1), 25–42.
Ministry of Treasury and Finance. (2024). *Kira sertifikası.* https://www.hmb.gov.tr/yatirimci-klavuzu-kira-sertifikasi. Accessed August 20, 2024.
Öztop, H., & Şekeroğlu, M. B. (2016). Konut sorunu. Detay Yayıncılık, 228 p., Ankara.
Sırma, İ. (2018). Gayrimenkul sertifikalarının ihracında yatırımcıların korunması. *Journal of Financial Research and Studies, 10*(18), 125–136.
Tanrıvermiş, H. (2017a). Gayrimenkul (taşınmaz) değerleme ilkeleri ve uygulamaları (Vol. 1). Course Notes, Ankara.
Tanrıvermiş, H. (2017b). Gayrimenkul değerleme esasları. SPL Yayınları, 512 p., Ankara.
Tapan, F. M. (2020). *Gayrimenkul finansmanı ve gayrimenkul projelerinin derecelendirme teknikleri* (Master's thesis, İstanbul Gelişim University, Finance Institute, Capital Markets Department), 214 p.
The Association of Real Estate Investors. (2025a). *Konut kredileri.* https://gyodergosterge.com/detay/konut%20kredileri. Accessed April 25, 2025.
The Association of Real Estate Investors. (2025b). *GYF'ler.* https://gyodergosterge.com/detay/gyf%C2%B4ler. Accessed April 25, 2025.
The Association of Real Estate Investors. (2025c). *GYO'lar.* https://gyodergosterge.com/detay/gyo%C2%B4lar. Accessed April 25, 2025.
The Banks Association of Türkiye. (2024). *Tüketici kredileri ve konut kredileri—Mart 2024.* https://www.tbb.org.tr/Content/Upload/istatistikiraporlar/ekler/4390/Tuketici_Kredileri-Mart_2024.pdf. Accessed August 20, 2024.
TOKİ. (2025). *Faizsiz konut kredileri.* https://www.toki.gov.tr/faizsiz-konut-kredileri. Accessed August 20, 2024.
Turan, N. (2017). Gayrimenkul (emlak) sektörünün gelişmesinde ve konut sorununun çözümünde gayrimenkul işletme kooperatifleri ve gayrimenkul sertifikaları modellerinin alternatif olarak değerlendirilmesi. *Third Sector Journal of Social Economy, 52*, 24–40.

TURKSTAT. (2024). *Yapı ruhsatına göre kullanma amacı ve yapı sahipliği, Ocak-Mart 2024.* https://data.tuik.gov.tr/Bulten/Index?p=Yapl-Izin-Istatistikleri-I.-Ceyrek:-Ocak-Mart,-2024-53750. Accessed August 20, 2024.

TURKSTAT. (2025). *Konut satış istatistikleri, Aralık 2023.* https://data.tuik.gov.tr/Bulten/Index?p=Konut-Satis-Istatistikleri-Aralik-2023-49516. Accessed August 20, 2024.

Yalçıner, K. (2006). İpotek karşılığı menkulleştirilmiş krediler (İKMEK–Mortgage). Gazi Yayınları, 166 p., Ankara.

Yalçıner, K. (2018). Gayrimenkul finansmanı. Detay Yayıncılık, 296 p., Ankara.

Gülnaz Şengül Güneş serves as a research assistant within the Department of Real Estate Development and Management at Ankara University. She holds a Ph.D. in Real Estate Development and Management, with an academic focus that encompasses sustainable real estate markets, real estate finance, real estate economics, and ESG-based investment instruments. Dr. Güneş has authored numerous articles and book chapters and has presented her work at international conferences. Her doctoral research concentrates on the development of a sustainability index for Türkiye's real estate markets. Furthermore, she has also held the position of visiting researcher at the University of Regensburg, facilitated by a TÜBİTAK 2214 fellowship programme.

İlhan Yıldırım is a doctor and completed his master's and doctorate degrees at the Department of Real Estate Development and Management at Ankara University in 2024. He is currently employed as an expert at the Ministry of National Defence. Dr. Yildirim's areas of expertise encompass real estate finance, real estate law, real estate valuation, real estate projects, project valuation, and the management of public real estate.

Erol Demir is a full professor at the Department of Real Estate Development and Management, Faculty of Applied Sciences, Ankara University, Türkiye. He holds a Ph.D. in Agricultural Economics from Ankara University and an M.Sc. in Business Administration from Gazi University. His research focuses on real estate taxation, accounting practices in the construction and property sectors, cooperative finance, and public sector economics. He has published extensively in peer-reviewed journals and authored several books. Prof. Demir has also served as Deputy Dean and contributed to multiple academic committees within Ankara University. He is currently an editorial board member of cited journals.

Real Estate Investment Trusts in Türkiye

Ali Hepşen, Gizem Ulusoy, and Abdurrahman Tursun

Abstract

This chapter examines the development of real estate investment trusts (REITs) in Türkiye, along with the relevant legal regulations and market conditions. Furthermore, it delineates the advantages and disadvantages associated with these real estate-based securities within secondary markets, underscoring their significance to the Turkish economy. The chapter offers comprehensive insights into the establishment, operations, and activities of REITs. It evaluates their economic contributions, encompassing the total number of REITs, their market values, and asset sizes. The objective of this study is to furnish a snapshot of the current situation for readers who aspire to gain a deeper understanding of the real estate markets in Türkiye. A compilation of relevant legislation and literature was executed, succeeded by the utilisation of secondary data published by both public and private institutions in the study.

Keywords

Real estate sector · Real estate investments · Securities fund · Real estate investment trusts

A. Hepşen
Department of Finance, School of Business, İstanbul University, İstanbul, Türkiye
e-mail: ali.hepsen@istanbul.edu.tr

G. Ulusoy (✉) · A. Tursun
Department of Real Estate Development and Management, Faculty of Applied Sciences, Ankara University, Ankara, Türkiye
e-mail: gulusoy@ankara.edu.tr; atursun@ankara.edu.tr

T. Just et al. (eds.), *Understanding Türkiye's Real Estate Markets*, Management for Professionals, https://doi.org/10.1007/978-3-032-13297-0_13

1 Introduction

Real Estate Investment Trusts (REITs) are professionally managed entities that facilitate investors' access to extensive income-generating real estate investments without the necessity of direct ownership or operation (Baker et al., 2019; Smith & Green, 2009). By aggregating capital from a multitude of investors, REITs acquire or finance real estate assets and distribute a portion of the earnings, along with specific tax advantages, to shareholders (Akkaya et al., 2005). They benefit from a favourable tax treatment when disbursing at least 90% of their taxable income as dividends each fiscal year (Baker et al., 2019). Additionally, REITs are esteemed for their ability to mitigate inflation effects and increasingly contribute to diversified investment portfolios (Akkaya et al., 2005; Chan et al., 2002). The growth in their market capitalisation and the rising levels of institutional ownership highlight their increasing attractiveness globally (Chan et al., 2002).

The United States House of Representatives initially proposed the concept of REITs as a real estate-backed security fund in 1960, with the intention of enabling small investors to benefit from real estate opportunities. Danso (2022) examines this strategy by analysing data for 40 countries. Globalisation and a rise in free market economies in the 1980s coincided with an increased interest in REITs. The introduction of REITs into the Turkish real estate market transpired in the late 1980s, marked by the offering of a housing certificate in 1989 and a land certificate in 1990. However, REITs became officially operational only in 1995, following the establishment of the first legal guidelines[1] in 1992. In 1997, REIT trading commenced on the Istanbul Stock Exchange (Erdoğan & Özaslan, 2021; Coskun et al., 2021). According to Turkish regulation, REITs engage in investments pertaining to real estate, development projects, and real estate-based rights, utilising the capital acquired from investors in return for shares. As significant institutions within the capital market, REITs are instrumental in channelling dormant resources into the economy by mitigating unregistered real estate investments. Consequently, investors in REITs are afforded the opportunity to benefit from asset valuation and to achieve liquidity by exchanging their shares for cash on the stock market (Hepşen, 2017; Hepşen et al., 2017).

REITs can undertake specific real estate projects or acquire particular properties, using their income to engage in other lawful activities. They are stock market institutions that enjoy tax exemptions. Real estate investment trusts are entities that facilitate group investments and manage their portfolios within a corporate framework. The "Communiqué on Principles Regarding Real Estate Investment Companies," dated July 22, 1995, Serial: VI No: 7, served as the foundation for their operations in our country. The most recent significant regulation is the "Communiqué on Principles Regarding Real Estate Investment Companies," dated May 28, 2013, Serial: III No: 48-1.

[1] With amendments to the Capital Market Law and Tax Laws, it is stated that "Investment Trusts are joint stock companies established to operate capital market instruments, real estate, gold, and other precious metal portfolios."

Real estate investment partnerships have historically been perceived as appealing instruments for real estate financing, owing to the tax advantages instituted in response to Türkiye's housing and real estate crisis. Until August 2024, REITs and Real Estate Investment Funds (REIFs) enjoyed a complete exemption from corporate taxation on their earnings. However, a significant legislative amendment—Law No. 7524, published in the Official Gazette on August 2, 2024 and entitled "Law on Amendments to Tax Laws and Certain Laws and Decree Law No. 375"—has considerably altered this framework. Under the newly established regulation, the corporate tax exemption is now contingent upon the distribution of at least 50% of the income generated from real estate assets as dividends. This distribution must be finalised by the conclusion of the second month following the corporate tax return deadline to qualify for the exemption.

The institutions that operate under the REIT shall allocate a minimum of 75% of their total assets to investments in real estate, real estate projects, and rights based on real estate. By engaging in real estate and associated ventures that yield a high rate of return, REITs primarily strive to generate income through rental yields and trading activities. REITs distribute profits to their shareholders annually in the form of dividends. Consequently, owners of REITs may benefit from the robust returns generated by the properties within their portfolio. In addition to the dividends distributed, shareholders may also experience potential appreciation in the value of REIT shares on the stock market.

Investors who utilise the strategy of real estate investment partnerships can circumvent the issue of low liquidity by acquiring shares in companies that have already engaged in real estate investments, rather than investing directly in low-liquidity real estate assets. In addition to real estate investments, REITs are prohibited from providing contracting services in Türkiye; however, they may finance corporations' real estate projects. The primary focus of REITs in this context involves the management of the portfolios they possess and develop in relation to real estate. Conversely, REITs are not permitted to include machinery and equipment among their assets. The nature of the activities undertaken by a given organisation indicates that REITs may be classified as such if they are consistent with their operational domains. Various factors, including the project's scale, profitability potential, ownership rights, and financing costs, significantly influence the financing strategies chosen by REITs for relevant real estate projects.

1.1 Establishment of Real Estate Investment Trusts

In accordance with the Communiqué on Principles Regarding Real Estate Investment Trusts, partnerships may be established directly as REITs. Additionally, existing joint-stock companies have the opportunity to convert into REITs by modifying their articles of association to ensure compliance with the provisions of Capital Markets Law (Law) No. 6362 and the stipulations detailed in this Communiqué. The Capital Markets Board (CMB) is responsible for approving applications pertaining to the establishment or transformation of companies, adhering to specific restrictions. Alternatively, the conditions stipulated in the Communiqué for real estate investment trusts are as follows:

(a) Establishing a joint-stock company with registered capital or applying to the Board to transition to the registered capital system, which resembles that of a joint-stock company.
(b) The initial capital necessary for establishment and transformation, along with the existing paid-in or issued capital, should be at least TL 30,000,000.
(c) If the capital amount specified in subparagraph (b) of the relevant article is less than TL 60,000,000, a minimum of 10% of the shares must represent capital of TL 60,000,000 or higher, totalling TL 6,000,000 in capital. The current assets category encompasses cash, cash equivalents, and financial investments, as delineated in the independently audited unconsolidated or individual financial statements for the most recent accounting period. Where the aggregate amount of these items reaches or exceeds the ratio or monetary threshold specified in this paragraph, such requirement shall be deemed to have been fulfilled.
(d) Incorporating the phrase "Real Estate Investment Trust" within its trade name or petitioning the Board to amend its title to encompass this phrase.
(e) The founding partners and current partners are required to fulfil the conditions detailed in this Communiqué.
(f) The articles of association adhere to the provisions outlined in the Law and this Communiqué, or they endeavour to amend the existing articles of association in accordance with the stipulations established by the Law and this Communiqué.
(g) The general manager, along with the members of the Board of Directors, is required to fulfil the conditions outlined in this Communiqué; the general manager's appointment should take place on or before the specified registration date.
(h) The qualifications of the assets included or to be received in the portfolio, along with their respective weights in the total assets of the partnership, adhere to the qualifications and limitations delineated in this Communiqué.
(i) The amount of the start-up capital has been delineated in accordance with Article 9 of this Communiqué.
(j) It has been formally communicated to the Board that the initial capital, representing 25% of its issued capital, will be offered to the public within the specified time and in accordance with the principles outlined in this Communiqué.
(k) The capital has not experienced an increase over the past 2 years from the funds generated by adjusting the assets to their fair value.

1.2 REITs and Valuation

Real estate investment trusts are required to select the valuation firms from which they will procure services, as outlined in the Communiqué, within 1 month following the end of each fiscal year. The REITs should actively pursue valuation services for their assets, and alterations to the appointed valuation firm or firms are permissible with the endorsement of the Board of Directors, contingent upon communication of the rationale for such changes. Moreover, support may be sought from designated valuation firms for a duration of up to three consecutive years. Following a minimum engagement period of 2 years with a valuation firm that has been retained for three successive years, it becomes possible to request a revaluation service.

The Communiqué delineates the information that REITs are required to collect. The chosen valuation firm must maintain independence from firms listed by the CMB that provide real estate appraisal services. The Communiqué specifies the following:

(a) Acquiring or disposing of real estate, along with rights associated with real estate and projects connected to the property within the portfolio.
(b) Lease of real estate from the portfolio.
(c) Lease Agreement for Real Estate.
(d) The renewal or extension of lease agreements for the properties contained within the portfolio.
(e) Acceptance of a real estate mortgage.
(f) Before construction on real estate projects can commence, it is imperative that the legal procedures are observed and that all required documents are accurately prepared.
(g) The inclusion and exclusion of additional assets deemed appropriate for valuation within the portfolio by the Capital Markets Board.
(h) Assessing the year-end values of the assets within the partnership's portfolio for which the fair value has not been established for any reason during the previous 3 months of the accounting period.
(i) Altering the category or classification of real estate, including the associated rights and related projects within the portfolio.
(j) Contributing capital in kind to the partnership.

Personnel should engage in activities within 3 months following a company's establishment or the amendment of its articles of association registered with the trade registry. This action is essential for the company to qualify as a real estate investment trust, either from its inception or by revising its articles of association in accordance with the applicable Law and Communiqué. This process entails providing the necessary tools and facilities, establishing the required framework, appointing a general manager in partnerships formed as real estate investment trusts, and fulfilling obligations concerning the assets intended for inclusion in the portfolio. Moreover, the public offering application form must be completed, with the principles to be determined by the Board, and all documents specified in this form should be finalised (Hepşen, 2017; Hepşen et al., 2017).

In order to divest their shares by offering them to the public, facilitating the requisite equipment and venues, establishing the necessary organisational structure, appointing a general manager in partnerships established as real estate investment trusts, and adhering to their obligations concerning the assets intended for inclusion in the portfolio, it is essential to complete the public offering application form, the particulars of which shall be determined by the Board. All documents delineated in this form must be submitted to the Board for the approval of the prospectus relating to the public offering of the shares representing 25% (Hepşen, 2017; Hepşen et al., 2017).

1.3 REITs and Fields of Activity

The authorised fields of operation for REITs are delineated in the pertinent Communiqué and encompass the following:

(a) To attain trading profits or rental income, individuals may engage in the buying, selling, renting, leasing, or committing to purchase or sell various forms of real estate. This includes, but is not limited to, land, residential properties, office spaces, shopping centres, hotels, logistics centres, warehouses, parks, hospitals, and other related assets.
(b) In addition to the property they possess, they may undertake the development of real estate projects or invest in such initiatives by securing a construction right on land owned by other parties with whom they have entered into revenue sharing or land sale agreements in exchange for a predetermined fee.
(c) They can guarantee that real estate necessitating specific minimum equipment for operation, such as hotels, hospitals, or comparable establishments, is sufficiently equipped prior to leasing.
(d) They may establish a construction right, usufruct, and time-share easement in their favour on real estate owned by others and may transfer these rights to third parties.
(e) They may establish construction rights, usufruct, and time-share easements on the real estate they own in favour of other parties, thus permitting the transfer of these rights to third parties.
(f) Without prejudice to special regulations, entities may undertake projects developed through the build-operate-transfer model by granting the right of construction either in their favour or in favour of others, provided that the conditions outlined in the regulations are met.
(g) Entities may engage in the buying and selling of capital market instruments, execute Takasbank money market and reverse repo transactions, and open deposit or participation accounts in Turkish Lira or a foreign currency. Furthermore, they are permitted to lend capital market instruments, contingent upon their non-involvement in intermediary activities. In accordance with a contract that adheres to the pertinent regulations established by the Board, entities may lend up to 50% of the market value of the capital market instruments within their portfolio at any given time, provided that the requisite collateral is supplied.
(h) For operating companies, other real estate investment trusts, enterprises established under build-operate-transfer projects, and those formed internationally that engage solely in real estate—restricted to the incorporation of specific properties or rights pertaining to real estate, in addition to infrastructure ser-

vices associated with real estate, real estate-based rights, or real estate projects enumerated in and/or designated for inclusion in their portfolios for entities based in Türkiye—which constitute a minimum of 75% of the total assets reported in the financial statements of the participating company; such entities may only engage with these organisations if mandated by the legal obligations delineated in the pertinent legislation governing companies established or to be established to provide these services.

(i) If specific contractual provisions are accessible, entities may procure real estate from third parties and subsequently lease it again to generate rental income.
(j) In order to mitigate potential risks, organisations may participate in swap and forward transactions, formulate options, and acquire futures contracts, with the exception of those linked to tangible goods.
(k) In projects that are executed in exchange for a fixed fee and revenue sharing, landowners ought to establish a construction right in favour of the partnership, either at no cost or for a nominal fee. Should the land be transferred, mortgages or other limited real rights will be established on the properties within the partnership's portfolio to guarantee the project in favour of the landowner. Moreover, when acquiring real estate, real estate projects, and property-based rights, they may establish mortgages, pledges, and other limited real rights on the assets within the portfolio solely for the purpose of financing these transactions or to secure loans for investments.
(l) Entities may borrow an amount equivalent to five times their unconsolidated equity, as reflected in the financial statements prepared and presented to the public at the conclusion of the accounting period, in order to address their short-term funding requirements or to offset the expenses associated with their portfolios.
(m) They are able to issue debt instruments in accordance with the provisions set forth in capital market legislation.
(n) In accordance with the regulations established by the Board, they have the authority to issue securities that are secured by assets backed by real estate certificates, receivables derived from property sales within the portfolio, sales contracts or contracts promising sale, as well as the associated rental income.
(o) They may establish a formal partnership with one or more partners solely to complete a project. Similarly, the activities that real estate investment trusts are restricted from performing are delineated in the Communiqué above.

Additionally, they are restricted in the following ways:

(a) In accordance with the Banking Law, entities are prohibited from collecting deposits and from engaging in any business or transaction that may result in the accumulation of deposits.
(b) They shall not engage in commercial, industrial, or agricultural activities beyond those transactions that are permitted.

(c) They are unable to provide project development, project control, financial feasibility assessments, oversight of legal permits, and similar services to other individuals and organisations through their personnel, except for projects that are, or will be, included in the portfolio.
(d) As articulated in the Board's financial reporting regulations, offering loans or establishing debt–credit relationships with related parties is strictly prohibited unless such arrangements are founded upon transactions involving the purchase and sale of goods or services.
(e) No undocumented expense or commission payment that deviates from the prevailing market value may be made.
(f) They are unable to engage in ongoing short-term real estate transactions.

The constraints imposed on investments by real estate investment trusts are delineated as follows:

(a) They are prohibited from engaging in short selling of capital market instruments, trading on credit securities, or borrowing capital market instruments.
(b) They are prohibited from engaging in transactions that surpass the designated level of protection through the utilisation of derivative instruments.
(c) They are prohibited from incurring commission fees and similar expenses that exceed 3% of the asset value when purchasing and selling assets from the portfolio. This provision excludes taxes, fees, and other associated costs for which they hold legal responsibility.
(d) They are prohibited from investing in assets or rights that are encumbered by transferability limitations.

Hepşen (2017) analyses the subsequent activities that real estate investment trusts may engage in as follows:

(a) Ability to Provide Collateral: In projects conducted by real estate investment trusts in exchange for a fixed fee, if the proprietors of the land upon which the project is to be developed confer the construction right in favour of the partnership at no expense or for a nominal fee, it becomes feasible to establish a mortgage or limited real rights in favour of the landowner as security for the project. Moreover, during the acquisition of real estate, real estate projects, and rights pertaining to real estate, in addition to pledges and other limited real rights, can be established on the portfolio assets exclusively for the purpose of financing these transactions or securing loans for investments.
(b) When preparing and disclosing their financial accounts to the public following an accounting period, real estate investment trusts can borrow up to five times their unconsolidated equity to mitigate short-term cash shortages or expenses associated with their portfolios.
(c) Real estate certificates and asset-backed securities may be issued by real estate investment trusts, pursuant to Board regulations, under the Board's assurance of their receivables arising from the sale of real estate certificates and portfolio

properties, as well as sales contracts or promises of sale, within the overarching framework of those regulations.

(d) Affiliates: Exclusively affiliates, operating companies, other real estate investment trusts, companies formed within the framework of build-operate-transfer projects, and companies established abroad, whose activities are confined solely to real estate linked to a specific portfolio of properties or real estate-based rights, appraisals of real estate or real estate rights at the date of acquisition. Infrastructure services related to real estate, real estate rights, or real estate projects that are included in and/or are intended to be included in their portfolios for companies registered in Türkiye, where the value of the company's balance sheet assets constitutes at least 75%. If mandated, companies established or to be established to provide these services solely under the relevant legislative obligations may participate in these companies. However, the participation of the partnerships in the operating companies cannot exceed 10% of the total assets reflected in the financial statements of the partnerships that are prepared and publicly announced after the accounting period.

1.4 Functioning Structure of REITs

There exist units with diverse job descriptions at various stages, encompassing contractors, consultancy firms, operational companies, and real estate appraisal companies, all of which are among the parties involved in the operation of REITs currently under investigation. The responsibilities of each unit are managed by distinct firms organised within that unit and selected by the CMB. These firms operate within the confines of their contractual agreements with the relevant REITs (Özcan, 2011). A "Contractor" refers to a natural or legal person who undertakes construction activities for the real estate projects in their portfolio. The respective REIT's "Operating Company" is responsible for managing the properties in its portfolio for profit. The pertinent REIT's "Consultant Company" provides services for portfolio development and the exploration of alternative investment opportunities. The "Real Estate Appraisal Company" offers valuation services for rights associated with real estate within the REIT's property portfolio.

2 REITs in Figures

The inaugural REIT was established in Türkiye in 1995. As of the first quarter of 2025, 49 REITs exist, which are elucidated within the context of the prevailing laws in Türkiye (Table 1). As previously indicated, REITs are financial entities that invest in real estate, real estate-related assets, and financial securities. By offering these to the public, REITs aggregate the funds collected from numerous investors and utilise them to conduct profitable and substantial real estate transactions. Consequently, while individual investors can indirectly participate in real estate investments that they are unable to undertake independently or solely with their savings, the

Table 1 Structure of real estate investment trusts in Türkiye

Year	Number of REITs	Market value		Net assets	
		Million TL	**Million $**	**Million TL**	**Million $**
2011/12	23	11,708	6224	20,770	11,041
2012/12	25	15,782	8857	24,087	13,518
2013/12	30	18,632	8730	37,573	17,604
2014/12	31	21,981	9462	41,791	18,022
2015/12	31	21,465	7356	50,907	17,508
2016/12	31	25,447	7231	59,329	16,799
2017/12	31	26,924	7138	68,896	18,081
2018/12	33	18,384	3481	81,817	15,552
2019/12	33	27,777	4676	88,519	14,902
2020/12	33	54,163	7379	98,801	13,316
2021/12	36	94,951.87	7317	151,577	11,372
2022/12	39	245,216.51	13,116	313,853	16,785
2023/12	48	343,242	11,676	760,318	25,828
2024/12	49	532,839	15,127	–	–

Sources: CMB Monthly Bulletin, 2024 and GYODER4 Indicator Turkish Real Estate Sector 2024 4th Quarter Report—Issue 38

investment risk may be mitigated through a diversified portfolio approach and professional asset management (Hepşen, 2017; Hepşen et al., 2017). To establish a genuine market for illiquid real estate through the sale of their shares on the Stock Exchange, REITs may engage in real estate projects that conform to corporate values and a professional methodology (Table 1).

Concerning the investors and the advantageous influence on the nation's economy, the stability and value generation of the real estate sector are of great importance. While REITs are regarded as highly efficient and favoured financial instruments, the primary factors contributing to their declining trading volumes include an absence of transparency regarding net asset value, insufficient investor relations, and limited public offerings. Moreover, unreliable and inconsistent sectoral data, the existing dividend policy, the diversity and magnitude of REIT portfolios, and regulatory uncertainty further reduce confidence in this instrument. Consequently, the overall asset and market valuations of REITs vary, as each of these factors affects the value of REIT shares in distinct ways.

3 Contribution of Real Estate Investment Trusts to the Economy

Large-scale real estate projects, including shopping malls, business complexes, hospitals, and supermarkets, are frequently financed through REITs. Companies are required to manage the financial obligations necessary to complete such extensive undertakings. Businesses that depend on loans for capital due to inadequate equity generally incur interest payments. However, smaller investors can easily obtain financing for these significant projects in return for shares in real estate investment partnerships (Hepşen et al., 2017). As a result, the financial burden on the firm is notably alleviated. This circumstance typically yields advantages for the economy by fostering national economic growth and reinforcing essential industries.

According to Özcan and Gürol (2020), REITs should possess a substantial equity structure if they aspire to achieve high performance. REITs, characterised by robust equity structures during the planning stage of a project, are able to secure the necessary financing through their equity. This structural integrity allows them to enhance performance through better profitability, attributable to minimal levels of financing charges arising from foreign capital costs throughout project construction and disposal. While REITs may possess sufficient equity to execute the project, the opportunity cost of that capital could be perceived as a significant cost (Şarkaya, 2007).

3.1 Advantages of Real Estate Investment Trusts

Real estate investment partnerships are increasingly considered attractive for real estate financing owing to the tax advantages introduced in response to the state's housing and real estate crisis, which is broadly acknowledged as a public issue. From the investors' perspective, factors such as risk mitigation through portfolio diversification, funding investment projects, and depreciation are perceived as potential benefits. Conversely, real estate investments tend to foster a sense of trust and stability. Investors possess the ability to sell their shares in real estate investment trusts on the stock market, thereby reaping the potential rewards associated with price increases of these shares. Additionally, superior outcomes can be attained compared to individual investments, as professionals in the real estate sector manage the company's portfolio. International corporations frequently invest in REITs. These institutions favour shares of real estate investment trusts, which are traded in secondary markets, over direct real estate investments to generate returns from real estate in emerging markets, given that REIT investors enjoy higher liquidity compared to direct investors. Furthermore, REITs offer protection against inflation, as they typically do not necessitate substantial capital commitments, often required for real estate acquisitions (Akkaya et al., 2005).

By submitting an enquiry to one of the investment firms authorised to engage in trading on the stock market, investors who wish to participate in shares of real estate investment trusts can acquire the REIT shares they seek. However, when a real estate investment trust is offered to the public, individuals can also invest in it through the primary market. It is advisable to monitor the circular releases and submit applications for such investments at designated sales locations. A distinctive advantage that sets REITs apart from other business entities is their capacity to convert real estate into securities, thereby enabling smaller investors to engage in large-scale investments (Yaslıdağ & Layout, 2021). REITs, which are fundamentally involved in real estate operations, were integrated into the system following the 1990s, introducing a new array of financing methods to the industry and facilitating the transfer of resources via the capital market. This approach contrasts with traditional financing observed in the real estate sector, which depends on funding from savings or external sources, such as bank loans. Public offerings distribute capital to the foundational level and promote urbanisation by enabling the execution of large-scale projects (Şarkaya, 2007).

By directing corporate capital towards the real estate sector, which is characterised by a scarcity of financing sources, and in the development of substantial, high-quality projects, REITs serve as fundamental investment instruments that address liquidity concerns. The establishment of a funding source for the real estate industry, which encounters significant difficulties in this respect, is regarded as a big advantage of REITs in Türkiye (Önder et al., 2014). Conversely, REITs mitigate the risk of unchecked urbanisation by facilitating small investments that generate capital for substantial real estate developments, thus contributing to more sustainable urban growth (Hepşen, 2017; Hepşen et al., 2017).

3.2 Possible Disadvantages

(1) REITs, similar to most high-yield investment instruments, offer investors an easy way to acquire shares in income-generating real estate and thus achieve significant returns. Still, they are accompanied by elevated risks in comparison to lower-yield alternatives, such as Treasury bills. While investments in real estate are characterised by a long-term advantage concerning returns, their prices are prone to significant fluctuations in reaction to external events and market dynamics. This volatility, in conjunction with the potential for distorted pricing, may be regarded as a risk factor in unstable markets (Coşkun et al., 2021; Hung & Glascock, 2010).

(2) If a REIT fails to establish public accessibility within a timeframe of 3 to 6 months, its licence is revoked. In the event that the licence is revoked, various risks, including retroactive tax penalties and damage to reputation, may ensue, notwithstanding the financial advantages previously attained.

(3) Following their initial public offering, REIT shares frequently experience a decline in value ranging from 30% to 40%. This scenario presents a significant risk when acquiring real estate owned by third parties at discounts of 30% to 40%.

(4) The institutionalisation and procedural requirements associated with CMB applications impose considerable pressure on corporate management.

(5) The Central Bank of the Republic of Türkiye (*Türkiye Cumhuriyet Merkez Bankası* (TCMB)) constructs the Residential and Commercial Property Price Indices (CBRT, 2024b, 2024c).

(6) The licence must be strictly observed in relation to modifications in real estate and construction. In the absence of alterations to the zoning plan, the developmental costs associated with anticipated projects within the portfolio cannot be augmented. Annually, institutions licensed by CMB undertake valuation activities. However, should the valuation fail to comply with the licensing standards, the properties may be excluded from the portfolio.

It is argued that REITs can benefit passive equity investors by mitigating relevant investment risks. Time-varying risk aversion can be accomplished through the prospective implementation of a hedge-on/hedge-off strategy (Demirer, 2021).

4 Conclusion and Evaluation

Since their inception in the Turkish capital markets, REITs—also referred to as corporate structures—have emerged as a highly regarded investment strategy among savers, primarily due to the psychological trust evoked by real estate. These investment trusts are classified as either indirect or direct investments and offer opportunities through securities funds, thereby enhancing the competitive landscape and increasing mobility within secondary markets. Conversely, the growing number of shopping malls and office buildings in Türkiye provides financing for substantial real estate investments, presenting a significantly more attractive funding option.

REITs aggregate the capital of many investors, enabling individual investors to reap the benefits of real estate investments without the necessity of financing, acquiring, or managing properties. While REITs typically offer a more stable income stream, they generally yield lower returns than direct real estate investments. Publicly traded REITs are prevalent and exhibit significantly greater liquidity compared to direct real estate investments. However, Türkiye does not possess a sufficiently developed market for REITs. A primary factor contributing to this challenge is the restriction placed on the managers appointed within the REIT, encompassing their borrowing capacity, the eligibility of properties for inclusion in the portfolio, areas of expertise, and subsidiaries, as delineated by existing regulations. Furthermore, the competitive landscape, in which the concept of contracting as a developer predominates, further exacerbates the circumstances.

Nonetheless, corporate taxpayers in possession of shares in real estate investment funds, which are a related investment vehicle, are exempt from the obligation of paying this tax. In contrast, no such exemption exists for investors who generate income through REITs. By improving the legal competitiveness of REITs and fostering opportunities for growth, these entities are positioned to substantially contribute to the expansion of the Turkish real estate market and to assist in the realisation of larger projects.

References

Akkaya, G. C., Kutay, N., & Tükenmez, M. (2005). Real estate investment trusts and the fundamentals of real estate investments: A case study of Türkiye. *Management and Economics: Journal of Celal Bayar University, Faculty of Economics and Administrative Sciences, 12*(1), 39–46.

Baker, H. K., Filbeck, G., & Kiymaz, H. (2019). Real estate investment trusts: The savvy investor's guide to pooled investments.

Chan, S. H., Erickson, J., & Wang, K. (2002). *Real estate investment trusts: Structure, performance, and investment opportunities*. OUP Catalogue.

Capital Markets Board (CMB). (2024). *CMB monthly bulletin*—https://www.spk.gov.tr/SiteApps/Yayin/Aylik%20Statistics%20bulletins. Accessed April 11, 2025.
Coskun, Y., Erol, I., & Morri, G. (2021). Why do Turkish REITs trade at a discount to net asset value? *Empirical Economics, 60*, 2227–2259.
Danso, E. I. (2022). Examining the relationship between real estate prices and REITs. Real Estate Finance.
Demirer, R. (2021). On the hedge benefits of REITs: The role of risk aversion and market states. [Working paper No. 739898418].
Erdoğan, O., & Özaslan, A. (2021). The development of real estate investment trust (REIT): Emlak Konut as a REIT in Türkiye. *Black Sea Journal of Social Sciences, 13*(25), 679–700.
GYODER. (2024). *Indicator: Turkish real estate sector 2024 4th quarter report—Issue: 38*. https://www.gyoder.org.tr/yayinlar/gyoder-gosterge. Accessed April 11, 2025.
Hepşen, A. (2017). *Real estate valuation principles and financial dimensions*. Literature Publications.
Hepşen, A., Berberoglu, M. G., & Aydın, O. (2017). Real estate investment trusts in Turkey: Structure, analysis, and strategy. *Journal of Business Economics and Finance, 6*(2), 191–199.
Hung, S. Y. K., & Glascock, J. L. (2010). Volatilities and momentum returns in real estate investment trusts. *Journal of Real Estate Finance and Economics, 41*, 126–149. https://doi.org/10.1007/s11146-008-9165-8
Önder, E., Taş, N., & Hepşen, A. (2014). REITs in Turkey: Fundamentals vs. market. *The International Journal of Latest Trends in Finance and Economic Sciences, 4*(1), 662–676.
Özcan, N., & Gürol, B. (2020). Examining the performance of real estate investment trusts: A study on real estate investment trusts in Türkiye. *Celal Bayar University Journal of Social Sciences, 18*, 1–16.
Özcan, O. (2011). Real estate investment partnerships are an application and financial tool in the formation process of urban space.
Şarkaya, C. (2007). A study on real estate investment companies and sector analysis in Türkiye. *Journal of Social Sciences, 1*, 175–190.
Smith, C. R., & Green, H. (2009). Real-estate investment trusts. Darden Case: Business Communications (Technical note).
Yaslıdağ, B. H., & Layout, M. (2021). Stock exchange performance analysis of real estate investment companies listed on Borsa Istanbul between 2010 and 2020. *Journal of Business Studies, 13*(2), 1592–1609.

Ali Hepşen completed his high school education at Bornova Anatolian High School in İzmir province and then pursued his studies at Istanbul University's Faculty of Business Administration (English programme), graduating in 2002. Upon graduation, he commenced the Finance Master's Programme at the Istanbul University Social Sciences Institute, graduating in 2004 and earning the designation of Finance Specialist. He pursued his doctoral studies at the same institute, culminating in 2010 with the attainment of the title of Doctor of Philosophy. In recognition of his academic contributions, he was conferred the title of associate professor in 2012 and subsequently full professor in 2018. Since 2002, he has been employed at the Istanbul University Faculty of Business Administration, Department of Finance, where he has published three books and numerous articles in the realm of real estate finance, his area of expertise.

Gizem Ulusoy is a research assistant at the Department of Real Estate Development and Management, Faculty of Applied Sciences, Ankara University, Türkiye. She completed her high school education at Ankara Atatürk Anatolian High School and obtained a bachelor's degree in international relations from the Faculty of Political Sciences at Ankara University. Subsequently, she engaged in professional endeavours across various institutions within both the private and public sectors, before she was appointed a research assistant at Ankara University. She completed her master's degree, presenting a thesis titled "The Role and Importance of International Real Estate Investment in Emerging Economies" at the Ankara University Department of Real Estate

Development and Management. Currently, Gizem Ulusoy is pursuing her doctoral studies in the same department and has authored publications on international real estate investments.

Abdurrahman Tursun currently serves as a research assistant at the Department of Real Estate Development and Management, Faculty of Applied Sciences, Ankara University. He completed M.Sc. and Ph.D. programs in the field of Real Estate Development and Management at Ankara University. He obtained his bachelor's degree in mathematics from Sakarya University. His research interests encompass housing markets, system dynamics, real estate valuation, and alternative financing models. Dr. Tursun has authored a substantial number of academic publications, which include peer-reviewed journal articles, book chapters, and conference proceedings. Furthermore, he has participated as a member of the organising committee for various international conferences.

Foreigners' Real Estate Acquisition and Citizenship Dynamics in Türkiye

Harun Tanrıvermiş, Yeşim Tanrıvermiş, and Toygun Atasoy

Abstract

The right to property constitutes a fundamental human entitlement, and in many jurisdictions, the acquisition of real estate is regarded as a prerogative accessible to all. However, in many countries, the purchase of property by foreigners is subject to monitoring and restrictions through direct or indirect measures, often limiting the location, type, size, or physical attributes of the asset. In Türkiye, the initial statutory principles regulating foreign ownership were established through the Village Law (Law No. 442 of 1924) and the Land Registry Law (Law No. 2644 of 1934). From the 1920s to the 1980s, this matter rarely appeared on the national agenda, and foreign demand remained limited. Following the Economic Stabilisation Programme of January 24, 1980, an outward-oriented growth strategy prompted successive legislative amendments (1983–2012) aimed at attracting foreign investors, many of which were subsequently annulled by the Constitutional Court. Currently, the acquisition of real estate by foreign individuals has been significantly facilitated under Law No. 2644, as amended by Law No. 6302, dated May 18, 2012. The pursuit of security amid conflicts and political instability in neighbouring nations, the Lira's exchange-rate advantage, and the citizenship-by-investment programme have all contributed to a marked increase in foreign demand for Turkish property. Although foreign acquisitions are occasionally viewed with sensitivity, analysing this phenomenon solely through the lens of foreign direct investment is inadequate. A multidimensional assessment—encompassing economic, social, spatial, and environmental implications—is essential for a comprehensive understanding of its impacts.

H. Tanrıvermiş · Y. Tanrıvermiş (✉) · T. Atasoy
Department of Real Estate Development and Management, Faculty of Applied Sciences, Ankara University, Ankara, Türkiye
e-mail: tanrivermis@ankara.edu.tr; aliefendioglu@ankara.edu.tr; atasoy@ankara.edu.tr

T. Just et al. (eds.), *Understanding Türkiye's Real Estate Markets*, Management for Professionals, https://doi.org/10.1007/978-3-032-13297-0_14

Keywords
Property rights · Real estate ownership · Foreign people · Foreign legal entity · Citizenship · Investment economics

1 Introduction

Property ownership is recognised as a universal right under the Universal Declaration of Human Rights and applies equally to citizens and non-citizens (DeVerteuil, 2021; Gorback & Keys, 2020; Levi, 2006). Nonetheless, many nations—either explicitly or implicitly—impose restrictions on this right through various criteria (Tanrıvermiş et al., 2013). Definitions and limitations concerning foreign ownership vary considerably across jurisdictions, ranging from outright prohibitions to restrictions based on location, property type, quantity, or specific attributes (Aslan, 2023; Atasoy, 2015). Some states address this issue within the broader context of foreign direct investment, while others consider it in terms of property rights and the legal status of non-nationals. Within the European Union, regulations adhere to the principle of the free movement of capital, as articulated in the Treaty on the Functioning of the European Union (TFEU). Collectively, these diverse approaches highlight the lack of a uniform practice among nations regarding the foreign acquisition of real estate (Salami et al., 2023; Tanrıvermiş et al., 2013).

In Türkiye, regulations concerning foreign ownership of real estate distinguish between private individuals and legal entities. The rights of foreigners to acquire property are delineated in Articles 35 and 36 of the Land Registry Law (Law No. 2644, 1934), which also impose quantitative and procedural restrictions. Article 35 states that, "*Subject to statutory restrictions, foreign people who are nationals of countries designated by the President—where international bilateral relations or the interests of the State necessitate—may acquire immovable property and limited real rights in Türkiye*", and that "*Commercial companies possessing legal personality and incorporated under the laws of foreign states may acquire immovable property and limited real rights solely within the framework of specific laws*". The same regulation imposes quantitative limits on foreign holdings: "*The total surface area of immovable properties and limited real rights of an independent and permanent nature acquired by each foreign person shall not exceed thirty (30) hectares nationwide, nor surpass ten per cent of the privately-owned land area within any particular district*". Regarding acquisition procedures, "*Foreign people and legal entities incorporated under foreign laws must, within two years, submit their development project to the competent ministry for approval for any undeveloped immovable property they purchase, and are required to execute this project, utilise the land, and operationalise it*". In 2012, an amendment expanded the scope of permissible acquisitions, permitting foreign investors to purchase vacant rural and urban immovable properties, in addition to offices, commercial premises, and residences, with the objective of attracting increased foreign capital. Nevertheless, an effective mechanism to monitor and evaluate whether the required development projects are actively implemented on these vacant properties following acquisition has yet to be established.

Despite that, there are two limitations for foreigners to acquire real estate in Türkiye according to the legislation. As of the end of 2024, a total of 383,163 foreigners had acquired real estate, including 42,039 individuals who obtained primary residences and 344,124 individuals who acquired independent units. Among parcel owners, 21.81% are German citizens; among unit owners, 12.53% are Russian. Additionally, Türkiye hosted 83,542 foreign-capital companies, of which 6150 had acquired real estate—comprising 13,409 parent parcels and 21,177 units—totalling 34,586 properties with a combined surface area of 900,799,454 m^2. Foreign legal entities are also known to rely extensively on easements and long-term leases rather than freehold titles. Following the 2018 revision of citizenship regulations, foreigners who purchase real estate exceeding a specified threshold and register a three-year no-sale restriction are eligible for exceptional naturalisation. Under Law No. 5901, a total of 34,139 individuals have received certificates of eligibility for Turkish citizenship; 21% are Iranian, 12% Afghan, and 10% Iraqi.

This chapter examines the impact of legal regulations aimed at promoting foreign investment in Türkiye, particularly during its period of outward-oriented economic growth and liberalisation. These effects are discussed in the context of the progress report on Chapter 4 titled "Free Movement of Capital", which is part of the European Union's 35-chapter acquis pertaining to Türkiye's accession. This chapter analyses the legal regulations and practices related to real estate acquisition by foreigners and the promotion of direct foreign investment following the enactment of the January 24, 1980, Economic Stabilisation Measures. Furthermore, it explores this subject within the context of citizenship rights conferred upon foreigners who acquire real estate in the post-2018 period. For the evaluation of real estate acquisitions by foreigners, this chapter synthesises data from the Department of Foreign Affairs of the General Directorate of Land Registry and Cadastre, the Turkish Statistical Institute (TurkStat), relevant judicial decisions, as well as findings from previous field studies. The economic and social impacts of foreign property acquisition are assessed within a broad framework, and a comprehensive analysis is conducted in accordance with European Union law and the acquis. Additionally, policy recommendations are formulated to address key issues. The chapter identifies challenges faced by foreigners acquiring property for investment purposes and presents targeted solutions to resolve these issues.

2 Evolution of Foreign Direct Investments in Türkiye

Foreign direct investment (FDI) inflows represent capital that foreign investors commit directly to productive activities within the host country. In Türkiye, annual FDI fluctuated between USD 9.51 billion in 2020, the lowest level of the 2015–2024 period, and USD 19.26 billion in 2015, the peak year (Table 1). In 2024, FDI reached USD 11.25 billion, representing a 5.62% increase from the previous year. The upward trend observed in 2021 and 2022 transitioned into a downward movement

Table 1 Foreign direct investment inflows to Türkiye

Indicators (USD $)	2015	2016	2017	2018	2019	2020	2021	2022	2023	2024
Foreign direct investment (FDI) inflows to Türkiye (bn)	19,3	13,8	11.2	15.5	9.5	7.5	12.7	13.8	10.7	11.3
FDI equity capital (bn)	12.2	7.6	7.4	6.7	5.9	5.8	7.1	7.0	5.9	6.7
Real estate investment (bn)	4.2	3.9	4.6	5.9	5.0	4.0	5.6	6.3	3.6	2.9
Other (bn)	2.9	2.4	−0.9	−0.2	−0.1	−0.2	−0.1	0.5	1.2	1.7
Ratio of real-estate investment to fdi inflows (%)	21.6	28.1	41.5	47.5	52.4	52.6	44.5	45.5	33.4	25.1
Ratio of real-estate investment to fdi equity capital (%)	34.1	51.3	62.7	88.3	84.7	68.3	78.9	90.1	60.8	42.2

Note that all monetary values are shown in billion USD (bn) and rounded to one decimal place. Percentages rounded to one decimal place. Negative values represent outflows.
Source: Central Bank of the Republic of Türkiye (2025)

in 2023. By country of origin, the Netherlands contributed the largest cumulative share of inflows, followed by the United States, Germany, Ireland, and the United Kingdom. Throughout the 2015–2024 period, Türkiye received an approximate total of USD 122.13 billion in direct investment inflows. Notably, during this period, real estate investments comprised USD 45.83 billion of the total, representing 37.53% of all direct investments.

Foreign investment in Turkish real estate reached its lowest point at USD 2.8 billion in 2024 and achieved a recent peak of USD 6.27 billion in 2022. Overall, foreign direct investment remains predominantly focused on the manufacturing sector, with subsequent investments in finance and insurance activities, as well as the mining and real estate sectors. Repeated legal amendments concerning foreigners' property rights and citizenship-by-investment schemes[1] have maintained real estate inflows on an upward path. Although transaction volumes remained substantial immediately following the pandemic, the nominal value of purchases dropped in

[1] Law No. 6302 (in force since 18 May 2012) amended Article 35 of the Land Registry Law (Law No. 2644) and abolished the reciprocity requirement, which had conditioned foreigners' property rights on equivalent rights for Turkish citizens in the buyer's home country. The same regulation allowed nationals of bordering states—except in the border provinces themselves—to purchase property in Türkiye. In 2017, foreigners and Turkish citizens residing abroad under a work permit became eligible for a value-added-tax exemption on residential purchases, provided the sale price is transferred to Türkiye in foreign currency. Another important regulation that makes the housing market attractive to foreigners was implemented in 2018 with an amendment to the Turkish Citizenship Law No. 5901. With this amendment, the minimum real estate value required for foreigners who purchase real estate in Türkiye to obtain Turkish citizenship was reduced from $1 million to $250,000. However, due to the rapid depreciation of the Turkish lira in 2022, this amount was increased to 400,000 dollars.

2023 and 2024; nonetheless, the proportion of real estate within net FDI inflows remained elevated. After increasing to USD 5.6–6.3 billion in 2021 and 2022, foreign real estate investments declined to USD 3.6 billion in 2023 and USD 2.8 billion in 2024. These investments, driven by domestic macroeconomic conditions and the political-social climate in neighbouring countries, continue to constitute a significant share of Türkiye's FDI stock and flows. Given the ongoing appeal of the real estate sector, further growth appears feasible, contingent upon enhancements in market transparency, adequate protection of investor rights and assets, and continued improvement of local living standards.

Foreign purchasers of real estate in Türkiye are predominantly middle- or lower-income individuals above the age of 50. Evidence suggests that the buyers primarily consider these properties as assets to occupy or rent out for income generation (Tanrıvermiş et al., 2013; Uyar et al., 2022). In recent years, this trend has sparked debate about whether home acquisitions by older foreigners hinder Turkish citizens' access to housing (Salami et al., 2023). However, with foreign investment in Turkish real estate having declined significantly, this controversy over the adverse effects has diminished. This decline in inflows reflects both global economic uncertainty and the perceived economic and political risks within Türkiye. High inflation and exchange-rate volatility have reduced the country's appeal to international investors, while rising domestic housing prices have similarly constrained foreign demand (Badurlar, 2008; Yıldırım et al., 2021).

3 Evolution of the Legal Framework Governing Foreign Ownership of Real Estate

Following the declaration of the Republic in 1923, Türkiye granted specific rights to foreigners in line with principles of international law. Article 70 of the Turkish Constitution of 1924 (Teşkilât-ı Esasiye) initially recognised property and inheritance rights for Turkish citizens. As Levi (2006) observes, the ability of foreigners to acquire real estate was later regulated through a series of international agreements to which Türkiye was a party. Although the dominant approach did not promote foreign ownership within Turkish territory, Article 71 of the same Constitution protected any proprietary rights that foreign nationals had previously established.

In accordance with the Village Law (Law No. 442 of March 18, 1924), foreign nationals were restricted from residing within village boundaries unless they acquired a specific permit from the Ministry of the Interior. Moreover, the law forbade their purchase of real estate within villages. This Law No. 442 was repealed by the Act of March 7, 2003 (Law No. 4916, "Amending Various Laws and the Decree Law on the Organisation and Duties of the Ministry of Finance"). Subsequently, a statutory amendment enacted in 2012 ultimately authorised foreigners to acquire property in rural villages.

The initial noteworthy regulation explicitly concerning acquisitions by foreign people was the Land Registry Law (Law No. 2644 of December 22, 1934). While this legislation established various restrictions, it permitted foreigners with no administrative or social ties to a specific village to acquire certain types of property, such as standalone farms and agricultural land. Consistent with the principle of reciprocity, only nationals from countries that authorised Turkish citizens to acquire real estate were entitled to the same rights within Türkiye. During the period spanning from the 1920s to the 1980s, however, foreign acquisitions of Turkish real estate remained infrequent and elicited minimal public discourse.

The Economic Stabilisation Programme, announced on January 24, 1980, adopted an outward-oriented growth approach, including measures to liberalise protections for the domestic market and encourage export-focused production (Tanrıvermiş & Bülbül, 2007). Following a significant policy change in 1983, the government sought to address Türkiye's capital shortage by attracting foreign investment, resulting in the relaxation of regulations pertaining to real estate acquisitions by non-nationals. Law No. 3029, enacted on June 21, 1984, amended Article 35 of the Land Registry Law (Law No. 2644) by adding a clause that authorised the Council of Ministers to waive the reciprocity requirement for select countries (Yılmaz, 2013). However, the Constitutional Court annulled this clause on June 13, 1985 (Aykul, 2011).

An important modification was enacted in the Land Registry Law (article 35) through the "*Law on Amendments to Articles 19, 30, and Temporary 2 of Law No. 4916 on Amendments to Various Laws and the Decree Law on the Organisation and Duties of the Ministry of Finance*", published in the Official Gazette on July 3, 2003. Among the provisions in question, Article 19 of Law No. 4916 stipulates that "*provided that it is reciprocal and legal restrictions are observed, foreign nationals may acquire real estate within the borders of the Republic of Türkiye. In the application of the principle of reciprocity, the rights granted by a foreign state to its citizens in real estate acquisition must also be granted to citizens of the Republic of Türkiye*". The amendment also mandated that nationals of non-reciprocal states liquidate any properties they had previously inherited in Türkiye—and any assets located in areas subject to statutory restrictions—with compensation to be paid at assessed market value. This clause addressed several practical issues. In cases of testamentary transfers (mortis-causa dispositions other than statutory succession) to foreign people, any registration exceeding 30 hectares was required to be liquidated, and the price paid, unless the Council of Ministers issued specific approval. The reciprocity condition was declared inapplicable to the establishment of limited real rights on property in favour of foreign people. Finally, the Council of Ministers retained the authority to designate areas where the article would not apply on grounds of "public interest and national security".

On March 14, 2005, the Constitutional Court annulled Article 19 of Law No. 4916 (File No. 2003/70, Decision No. 2005/14). To address the legal gap created, Parliament enacted the Law Amending the Land Registry Law (Law No. 5444, January 7, 2006), which replaced Article 35 of Law No. 2644 (issued on December 22, 1934) and introduced Provisional Article 2. This legislation stipulates that foreign nationals may acquire immovable property within designated or registered areas for use as a residence or workplace in Türkiye, if reciprocity and legal restrictions are observed, and that similar conditions apply for establishing limited real rights. It limits such acquisitions to a total of 2.5 hectares by foreign individuals, with the Council of Ministers authorised to increase this limit up to 30 hectares under the same conditions. The law also clarifies that these restrictions do not apply to real estate inherited legally by citizens of countries with reciprocity agreements with Türkiye. In inheritance cases, existing records and restrictions remain applicable. Conversely, properties inherited by citizens of non-reciprocity countries must be transferred out through liquidation procedures. The principle of reciprocity prescribes that factual and legal conditions will be used to establish relevant criteria, and that this principle does not confer ownership rights to individuals; instead, it ensures that the rights granted to foreign citizens by their respective countries for real estate acquisition are similarly given to Turkish citizens. In Decision No. 2007/48 dated April 2007, the Constitutional Court partially annulled the new provisions introduced by Article 1 of Law No. 5444, specifically the fourth sentence in Article 35 of Law No. 2644, which authorised the Council of Ministers to increase the surface area limit up to 30 hectares, and the part of paragraph 7 that limited foreign people' property acquisitions at the provincial level to no more than five per thousand of the surface area of the province and its districts.

Article 1 of Law No. 5444, which pertains to the Amendment of the Land Registry Law—an act that operates within and derives its authority from the Land Registry Law—introduced a series of restrictive amendments applicable to foreign people. These amendments, enacted in response to issues highlighted by the Constitutional Court's 2003 annulment decision, establish limitations on the purposes for which foreigners may acquire immovable property, the permissible surface area of such property, the extent of real rights that may be based thereon, and the authorities delegated to the Council of Ministers in these matters. Furthermore, within this framework, regulations concerning inheritance and other mortis-causa dispositions were incorporated into Law No. 5444—mutatis mutandis—in accordance with the prior provisions of Law No. 4916.

Law No. 5444 also introduces amendments concerning the purpose, location, and size of the property to be purchased. It clarifies that registration is only possible for immovable property intended as a workplace or residence. Consequently, foreigners can only acquire parcels that are designated and registered for these uses within an implementation zoning plan or a partial development plan. The law further states that the area a foreign person may acquire is limited to 2.5 ha. However, the Council of Ministers has the authority to raise this limit to up to 30 hectares per individual. Moreover, the Council can establish, at the provincial level, a maximum land acquisition proportion—up to five ten-thousandths (0.05%) of a province's total surface area—ensuring that the total land acquired within a province does not exceed this threshold.

By Decision No. 2007/48 of April 11, 2007 (Case E. 2006/35), the Constitutional Court held that the clause granting the Council of Ministers the power to increase the per-person acquisition ceiling from 2.5 hectares to 30 hectares—representing a 12-fold increase—was deemed "disproportionate". It thus constituted an unlawful transfer of legislative authority to the executive branch, making the provision unconstitutional. In the same judgment, the Court also invalidated the clause allowing the

Council of Ministers to set, on a provincial basis, the maximum proportion of immovable property that foreign people may acquire, provided it did not exceed five per ten thousand (0.05%) of the surface area of the province, ruling that this delegation was also unconstitutional.

Following the partial annulment by the Constitutional Court, Parliament enacted Law No. 5782 on July 3, 2008, which again amended Article 35 of the Land Registry Law. The amendment authorised foreign people to acquire immovable property and establish limited real rights within the scope of implementation and partial development zoning plans, up to 10% of the total surface area in each metropolitan centre (central district) and district municipality. The provision allowing the Council of Ministers to increase this individual ceiling to 30 ha remained unchanged; consequently, the acquisition limit per person remained at 2.5 ha. Subsequently, Law No. 6302—entitled "Amending the Land Registry Law and the Cadastre Law"—came into effect on May 18, 2012, undertaking a comprehensive revision of Article 35 and updating the conditions under which foreign people may acquire real estate. The revised text stipulates that, "subject to statutory restrictions, foreign people who are nationals of countries designated by the Council of Ministers—considering bilateral relations and the national interest—may acquire immovable property and limited real rights in Türkiye". Additionally, the reciprocity principle was abolished, and paragraph 3 now empowers the Council of Ministers, "whenever required in the national interest, to determine, restrict, partially or wholly suspend, or prohibit the acquisition of immovable property by foreign people—by country, individual, geographical region, duration, number, ratio, type, nature, surface area, or amount". The European Commission's 2012 Progress Report on Türkiye noted that the abolition of reciprocity would facilitate real estate purchases by foreigners and could potentially enhance capital inflows, while also observing that the Government retains discretion to decide which countries' nationals are eligible to purchase property in Türkiye.

The Land Registry Law No. 2644 stipulates that "*the total surface area of immovable properties and limited real rights of a permanent and independent nature acquired by foreign people shall not exceed ten per cent of the privately-owned land area within any given district, nor thirty hectares nationwide per individual*". Nonetheless, in practice, both the Treasury and other public entities—including local authorities—possess substantial real estate portfolios. However, the definition of "public land" remains expressly undefined. Consequently, only the land owned by the Treasury is typically excluded from the denominator, which effectively preserves the land acquisition cap for foreigners at a relatively elevated threshold.

The latest revision of Article 35 stipulates that any foreign individual acquiring undeveloped land—regardless of zoning—must prepare a development plan and submit it for approval within 2 years. Upon approval, the ministry shall record the project's commencement and completion dates in the 'annotations' column of the land register and shall continue to monitor its progress. According to the law, if the project is not finalised within this timeframe and the owner fails to liquidate the property, along with any limited real rights, within a grace period of up to one year—granted by the Ministry of Finance—the property shall be automatically liquidated and converted into cash. The proceeds shall be paid to the rights-holder.

Article 17 of the Universal Declaration of Human Rights affirms that "*everyone has the right to own property alone as well as in association with others. No one shall be arbitrarily deprived of his property*", thus explicitly securing the right to property worldwide (Council of Europe, 1948). Similarly, Protocol No. 1 to the European Convention on Human Rights states that "Every natural or legal person is entitled to the peaceful enjoyment of his possessions. No one shall be deprived of their possessions except in the public interest and in accordance with the law and international principles. However, these provisions do not restrict the right of the state to enforce laws necessary to regulate property use in the public interest or to collect taxes, contributions, or penalties" (Council of Europe, 1952). Both the 1948 and 1952 texts do not differentiate between citizens and foreigners regarding property rights, allowing countries to impose certain restrictions if they meet international law standards and serve a public interest purpose (Tanrıvermiş et al., 2013).

In Türkiye, the provisional regulations enacted following the 1960 military intervention maintained the existing regime under the 1924 Constitution regarding foreign ownership of real estate. The 1961 Constitution, under the section titled "Social and Economic Rights and Duties", incorporated the right to property and inheritance: Article 36 articulated that "*everyone has the right to property and inheritance. These rights may only be restricted by law and for the public interest. The exercise of the right to property shall not conflict with the interests of society*", thereby reaffirming the principle of equality between citizens and foreigners. In the second part concerning Fundamental Rights and Duties, Article 13, titled "Status of Foreigners", stipulates that "*the rights and freedoms set forth in this Part may, with respect to foreigners, be restricted by law in conformity with international law*" (see Table 2).

Within the framework of the Turkish constitutional system, the right to property—enshrined in Article 35—is founded on principles of equality and is comprehensively acknowledged within domestic legislation. While it is lawful for national legal frameworks to impose certain restrictions, Article 16 of the Constitution explicitly states that "*fundamental rights and freedoms may be restricted by law, with respect to foreigners, in conformity with international law*". Consistent with these provisions, the rights granted to all individuals stipulate that foreigners are also subject to the same rights. Furthermore, under the section titled "Status of foreigners", it is understood that, in accordance with the provision that "*fundamental rights and freedoms may be restricted by law for foreigners in accordance with international law*", foreigners are entitled to the same rights as Turkish citizens. Both the Constitution and the corresponding legislation are notably progressive, facilitating not only the acquisition of real estate by foreigners for investment purposes but also, and perhaps more importantly, their eventual attainment of citizenship (see Table 2).

Law No. 6302 implemented a comprehensive reform of Türkiye's regulations regarding foreign property ownership. It abolished the reciprocity requirement—currently maintained in certain European countries—and, for the first time,

Table 2 Legislative instruments governing foreign ownership of real estate in Türkiye and their quantitative limits

Legal instrument (article-based)	Entry into force	Characteristics and quantitative limits of foreign nationals' real-estate acquisitions				
		Main parcel	Independent units[a]	Limited real rights	Undeveloped land	Ceiling per person /other quantitative limit
Land Registry Law No. 2644, Arts. 35–36	Dec 22, 1934—Official Gazette 2891	+	–	–	–	30 ha
Law No. 3029 (Article 35 of Land Registry Law, Article 87 of Village Law)	Jun 21, 1984	+	+	–	–	30 ha
Law No. 3278 (Article 35 of Land Registry Law; Article 87 of Village Law)	Apr 22, 1986	+	+	–	–	30 ha
Law No. 4916 (Article 35 of Land Registry Law)	Jul 3, 2003	+	+	+	–	30 ha
Law No. 5444 (Article 35 of Land Registry Law)	Dec 29, 2005	+	+	+	–	2.5 ha — Cabinet may be raised to 30 ha
Law No. 5782 (Articles 35 and 36 of Land Registry Law)	Jul 3, 2008	+	+	+	–	2.5 ha
Law No. 6302 (Articles 35 and 36 of Land Law)	May 18, 2012—Official Gazette 28,296	+	+	+	+	30 ha — President may raise to 60 ha

[a] "Independent unit" refers to condominiums/apartments registered as separate property under the Building Ownership Law. Legend: "+" = permitted; "–" = not permitted under the relevant law and period
Source: own compilation

permitted foreigners to purchase vacant plots and other undeveloped land. The amendment notably simplified the conditions for foreign nationals seeking to acquire property in Türkiye, although some restrictions remain applicable to citizens of neighbouring countries. Prior to 2012, only citizens of 53 countries — primarily European and North American countries — had the right to acquire property in Türkiye; however, the amendment extended eligibility to citizens of 183 countries, including numerous nations in Africa and Asia. The key legislative milestones governing foreign real estate ownership in Turkish law are summarised in Table 2.

Despite the implementation of such a radical reform aimed at strengthening EU–Türkiye relations and fostering increased foreign investment, the European Commission considered it inadequate. The 2018 Türkiye Report (Progress Report) indicated, under Chapter 4 concerning the free movement of capital, that by 2019, Türkiye should "*prepare and adopt an action plan to eliminate restrictions and enhance transparency regarding the acquisition of real estate by foreigners*" (European Commission, 2018). The Report highlighted that "*the current Turkish regulations on foreign ownership of real estate are complex and are not applied uniformly to all EU citizens in a non-discriminatory manner.* Türkiye *must develop and execute an action plan to further liberalise real estate purchases by foreigners, aligning with the EU acquis. Currently,* Türkiye *grants citizenship to foreign investors under specific conditions, such as making a fixed-capital investment, purchasing real estate exceeding a certain value, and committing not to sell within three years. Additionally, foreign ownership remains restricted in sectors including radio and television broadcasting, transportation, education, and the electricity market*".

The European Commission's 2023 Türkiye report notes, in accordance with Articles 35 and 36 of the Land Registry Law, only nationals from countries designated by the President are allowed to acquire property in Türkiye; as of October 2022, a total of 185 countries were included on this list, which is not publicly available due to its absence from the website of the General Directorate of Land Registry and Cadastre. The Commission warns that this lack of transparency creates risks, including money laundering, tax evasion, terrorist financing, corruption, and infiltration by organised crime. Furthermore, the Commission's 2024 Türkiye Report emphasises that the legislation governing foreign ownership of real estate is not applied in a non-discriminatory manner towards all EU citizens and that nationals of neighbouring states remain prohibited, on national security grounds, from purchasing property in border regions.

4 Assessment of Foreign Real Estate Acquisitions

4.1 Acquisition by Foreign People

The acquisition of immovable property by foreigners is governed by Articles 35 and 36 of the Land Registry Law (Law No. 2644), which limit holdings to 30 hectares per individual nationwide and prohibit foreign ownership from exceeding 10% of the privately owned land area within any given district. As of the end of 2024, 373,089 individual foreigners owned properties in Türkiye (the details are shown in Table 3). The significant increase in the number of main parcels in recent years can be attributed to the amendment introduced by Law No. 6302, which, for the first time, permitted foreigners to purchase "vacant" or "undeveloped urban and rural land".

Table 3 Real-estate holdings of foreign people in Türkiye

Land category	Number of people	Number of properties
Main parcel	42,039	40,232
Independent units	344,064	332,857
Total	383,163	373,089

Source: General Directorate of Land Registry and Cadastre, TKGM (2025)

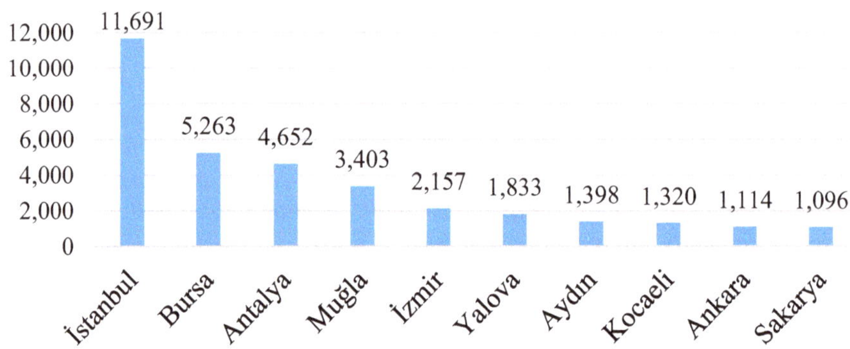

Fig. 1 Provinces with the highest number of main properties acquired by foreigners. *Source*: TKGM (2025)

The highest number of principal parcels registered to foreigners is in Istanbul Province, followed by Bursa, Antalya, and Muğla. Foreign acquisitions in Istanbul constitute 29.06% of all parcels purchased by foreigners, totalling 11,691 parcels. The second-highest figure, in Bursa, is 13.08% (5263 units), while Antalya and Muğla account for 11.56% (4652 units) and 8.46% (3403 units) respectively (Fig. 1). The provinces and districts where foreigners predominantly acquire property are primarily relatively developed regions characterised by a high quality of life.

Istanbul consistently also has the highest number of unit acquisitions by foreigners. The city accounts for 38.59% of all registrations, totalling 128,466 units, followed by Antalya, which represents 26.91% or 89,575 units of the total unit registrations (Fig. 2).

Among the various categories of real estate acquired by foreign investors, residential properties constitute the majority, suggesting that foreign buyers primarily acquire properties for short-term residences (such as holidays), pre- or post-retirement living, and rental income. Of all properties acquired by foreigners, 81.64% are residential units, 13.16% are main parcels, and 5.19% are commercial properties (Fig. 3).

The majority of foreigners acquiring primary parcels are German nationals. German citizens constitute 21.81% (8775 individuals) of all foreign acquisitions of primary parcels, followed by Greek citizens at 17.71% (7125 individuals), and citizens of the United Kingdom at 9.75% (3921 individuals) (Fig. 4).

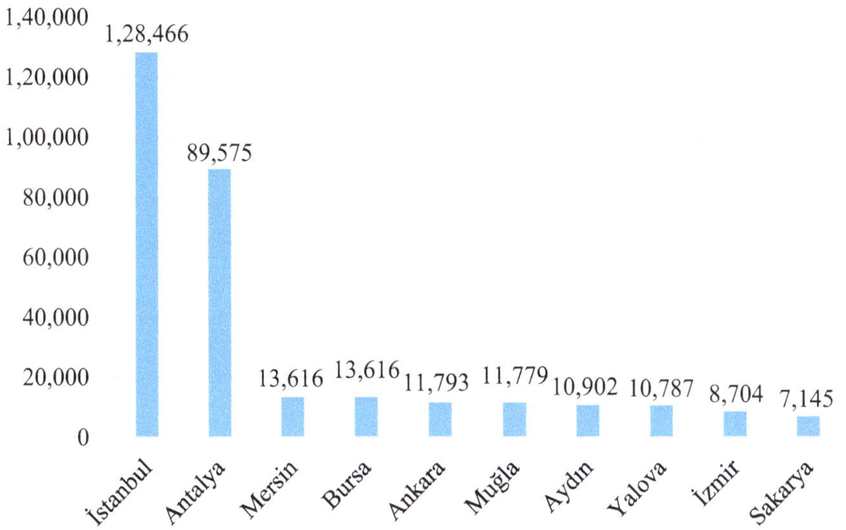

Fig. 2 Provinces with the highest number of independent units acquired by foreigners. *Source*: TKGM (2025)

Fig. 3 Types of real estate acquired by foreigners. *Source*: TKGM (2025)

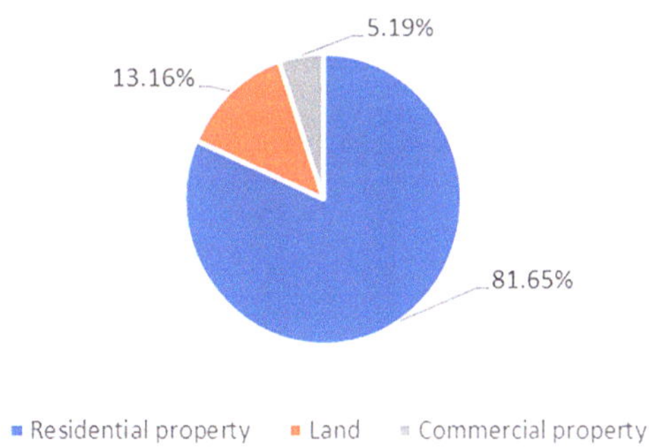

Russian nationals made up the majority of acquisitions of independent units. Russian citizens account for approximately 16.70% (55,601 people) of all unit owners. They are followed by Iranian citizens, at 12.53% (41,694 people), and Iraqi citizens, at 11.17% (37,194 people) (Fig. 5).

Data from 2010 to 2024 show the surface areas and owner counts of properties acquired by foreigners at both the main parcel and unit levels. Records indicate that foreigners purchased 292 main parcels in 2010, reaching a peak of 5781 main parcels in 2022. During the same period, the highest annual total of unit acquisitions was 64,563 units in 2022. Notable year-on-year increases are observed in 2013, 2014, 2021, and 2022 (Table 4).

When evaluating overall housing transactions in Türkiye without differentiating between international and domestic purchasers, the proportion of foreign acquisitions in total registrations ranges from 1.05% to 4.50% over the period from 2013 to

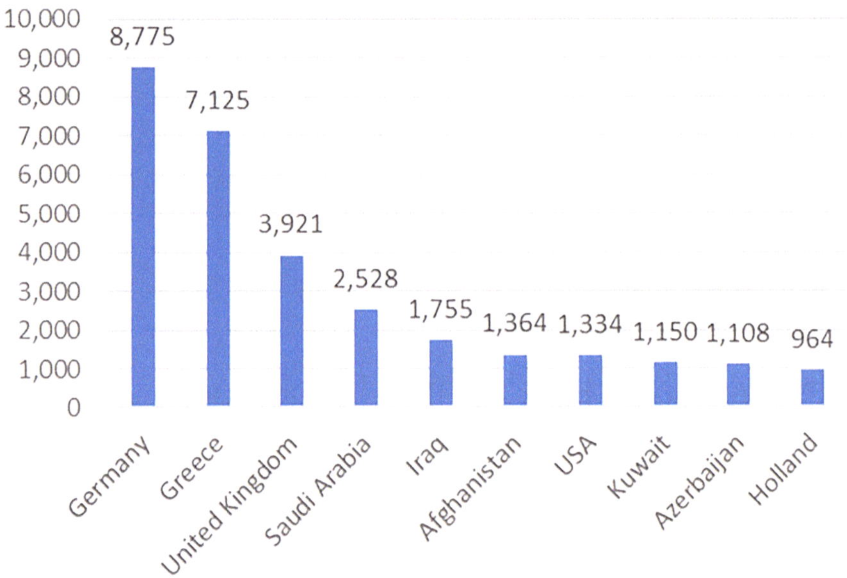

Fig. 4 Nationalities of foreigners who acquired main parcels. *Source*: TKGM (2025)

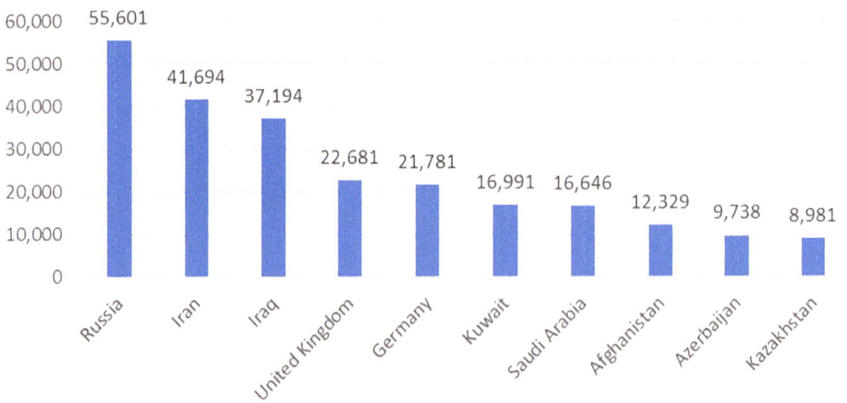

Fig. 5 Nationalities of foreigners who acquired units. *Source*: TKGM (2025)

2024. Despite the amendments enacted in 2022, aimed at simplifying the process of obtaining Turkish citizenship through real estate investments, the foreign share of total registrations for that year remained just below 5% (Table 5). There has been an increased demand for residency rights and property in Türkiye and certain European countries, primarily in response to social unrest and conflict that have compromised living standards in parts of the Middle East, Africa, and Asia.

Based on a survey of 3163 foreign nationals—selected from at least two distinct districts in each of the 28 provinces in Türkiye that foreigners most prefer for real estate acquisition—the main criteria they consider when purchasing property are:

Table 4 Number of main parcels and units acquired by foreigners

Years	Main parcel	Independent units	Total properties	Main-parcel share (%)	Unit share (%)
2010	292	2034	2326	12.55	87.45
2011	364	2336	2700	13.48	86.52
2012	521	2816	3337	15.61	84.39
2013	845	5245	6090	13.88	86.12
2014	1108	8830	9938	11.15	88.85
2015	1669	11,788	13,457	12.40	87.60
2016	1386	10,168	11,554	12.00	88.00
2017	1318	11,625	12,943	10.18	89.82
2018	2235	24,684	26,919	8.30	91.70
2019	3134	31,791	34,925	8.97	91.03
2020	2114	26,937	29,051	7.28	92.72
2021	4115	45,305	49,420	8.33	91.67
2022	5781	64,563	70,344	8.22	91.78
2023	5283	43,966	49,249	10.73	89.27
2024	4950	30,755	35,705	13.86	86.14

Source: TKGM (2025)

Table 5 Share and change in dwellings sold to foreigners

Years	Total dwellings sold in Türkiye (including sales to foreigners)	Dwellings sold to foreigners in Türkiye	Share of dwellings sold to foreigners in Türkiye (%)
2013	1,157,190	12,181	1.05
2014	1,165,381	18,959	1.63
2015	1,289,320	22,830	1.77
2016	1,341,453	18,189	1.36
2017	1,409,314	22,234	1.58
2018	1,375,398	39,663	2.88
2019	1,348,729	45,483	3.37
2020	1,499,316	40,812	2.72
2021	1,491,856	58,576	3.93
2022	1,485,622	67,490	4.50
2023	1,225,926	35,005	2.90
2024	1,478,025	23,781	1.60

Source: TURKSTAT (2025)

employment opportunities in Türkiye, 21.1%; suitability of travel, holiday facilities, natural beauty, and climate, 15.1%; forced migration from, or risk of deportation out of, the home country, 14.3%; and obtaining information and making the purchase decision via the internet, 13.3%. The detailed factors influencing foreign nationals' real estate transactions were identified as: guidance from relatives, family members, and acquaintances residing in Türkiye, 6.3%; favourable economic and trading conditions, 4.5%; Türkiye's appeal and attractiveness, 3.8%; marriage to a Turkish citizen, 3.5%; ease of acquiring property, 3.2%; overall ease of living, 3.1%; the deepening of nationalist sentiment, 2.5%; relocation for educational purposes,

2.2%; prior residence in the country, 3.2%; the intention to settle in Türkiye after retirement, 1.6%; and other motives—including escape from conflict and war, health concerns, religious tensions, and miscellaneous reasons—9.6% (Tanrıvermiş et al., 2013).

Economic growth and social unrest emerge as the two most influential drivers of foreign acquisitions. Empirical data suggest that capital inflows and property acquisition demands have escalated from Europe, Asia, the Gulf, the Middle East, and Africa, in response to social upheavals, uprisings, and attempted revolutions across the Balkans, Eastern Europe, the Baltic states, Central Asia, and various African countries, coupled with increasing mistrust towards Western nations. Unlike European investors, who predominantly focus on the same provinces and districts that drive domestic demand, investors from Arab countries exhibit a clear preference for the cooler northern provinces and thermal spa centres. Overall, both the selection of provinces or districts and the type of real estate acquired differ according to the investment motives and the nationality of the investors (Tanrıvermiş et al., 2013).

4.2 Acquisition of Real Estate by Foreign Legal Entities in Türkiye

Foreign investment activity in Türkiye was initially formalised by the enactment of the Foreign Capital Law No. 6224 in 1954. This legislation remained in effect until 2003 and contained liberal provisions concerning both domestic and foreign sources of capital. According to the 2024 report by the Ministry of Industry and Technology, there are currently 83,542 foreign-capital companies operating in Türkiye. Among these, 21,487 are engaged in wholesale trade and trade brokerage (excluding motor vehicles and motorcycles); 12,157 in construction and real estate activities; and 10,304 in retail trade, excluding motor vehicles and motorcycles, as well as in the repair of personal and household goods (Table 6).

According to Article 35 of Law No. 2644 (Land Registry Law), specific rules govern the acquisition of real estate by foreign legal entities in Türkiye. Commercial companies registered in foreign countries can buy property in Türkiye only under certain conditions. For example, foreign-established companies may purchase property for their Turkish operations if allowed by specific laws, such as Law No. 6491 (Turkish Petroleum Law), Law No. 2634 (Tourism Promotion Law), and Law No. 4737 (Industrial Zones Law). Additionally, foreign-owned companies established in Türkiye are entitled to the same real estate rights as Turkish companies under Law No. 5782 (Foreign Direct Investment Law). Along with Article 36 of Law No. 2644 and Article 28 of the Turkish Citizenship Law, Law No. 5782 states that any legal entity in which foreign individuals, foreign companies, or international organisations hold at least 50% of the shares—or control—can acquire ownership or limited real rights over immovable property to develop and operate activities outlined in its articles of association. By the end of 2024, active registry records show that 6151 foreign-capital companies had purchased real estate in Türkiye, owning a total of

Table 6 Sectoral distribution of foreign-capital companies operating in Türkiye

Sector	Number of companies
Wholesale trade and trade brokerage, except motor vehicles and motorcycles	21,487
Construction and Real Estate Activities	12,157
Retail trade except motor vehicles and motorcycles; repair of personal and household goods	10,304
Other Business Activities	5138
Supporting and Auxiliary Transportation Activities; Activities of Travel Agencies	4734
Hotels and Restaurants	3375
Computer and Related Activities	2543
Production and Distribution of Electricity, Gas, Steam and Hot Water	1709
Land transport and transport via pipelines	1534
Other Service Activities	1494
Manufacture of furniture; manufacture of other products n.e.c.	1458
Sale, maintenance and repair of motor vehicles and motorcycles; retail sale of motor fuel	1401
Manufacture of textile products	1276
Healthcare and social work	1045
Agriculture, hunting and related service activities	1001
Manufacture of chemicals and chemical products	967
Entertainment, recreational, cultural and sporting activities	946
Other	10,973
TOTAL	*83,542*

Source: Ministry of Industry and Technology (2025)

Table 7 Real-estate holdings of foreign-capital companies operating in Türkiye

Property type	Units	Surface Area (m^2)
Main parcel	13,409	201,812,682.30
Independent units	21,177	698,966,771.70
Total	34,586	900,779,454.00

Source: TKGM (2025)

34,586 properties. These cover a combined area of approximately 900,779,454 m^2, comprising 13,409 main parcels and 21,177 units (Table 7).

Foreign-capital companies' real estate holdings have also been examined at the provincial level. By the end of 2024, the highest concentration was in Istanbul, where firms owned 10,785 properties. Istanbul was followed by Muğla, with 2571 properties, and Antalya, with 2126. Across the country, there is a strong positive correlation (correlation coefficient: +0.76) between the number of properties held by foreign companies and each province's socio-economic development index. This indicates that corporate acquisitions tend to increase in more developed provinces (Table 8).

Table 8 Property acquisitions by foreign-capital companies and the socio-economic development-index values of the provinces where the properties are located

Provinces	Main parcel acquisitions	Independent section acquisitions	Total properties acquired	Provincial socio-economic development-index value
Istanbul	1018	9767	10,785	4.051
Muğla	736	1835	2571	1.642
Antalya	1113	1013	2126	0.278
Mersin	396	1115	1511	1.336
Uşak	1423	32	1455	2.718
Bursa	575	831	1406	0.923
Ankara	459	935	1394	0.413
İzmir	796	393	1189	1.926
Kocaeli	404	304	708	1.175
Gaziantep	130	353	483	0.250

Sources: TKGM (2025); Ministry of Industry and Technology (2025)

For firms operating within the sectors of hotels, restaurants, energy, mining, and quarrying, real estate requirements are typically satisfied not through outright purchase but via the establishment of limited real rights over state-owned land. In accordance with the Electricity Market Law (Law No. 6446), the Mining Law (Law No. 3213), the Tourism Promotion Law (Law No. 2634), the Turkish Petroleum Law (Law No. 6491), and analogous statutes, foreign-capital companies are permitted to acquire easement rights over Treasury land necessary for their projects. When private land falls within the scope of a project, it is subject to expropriation. The licence or permit holder receives compensation, the land is subsequently re-registered in the name of the Treasury or relevant public entity, and the company is authorised to utilise it for the duration of the licence. Consequently, the surface area figures presented for foreign-capital companies' freehold properties are minimal, and parcels subject to easement rights are excluded from the table. It is essential to note that these companies may only acquire ownership or limited rights for activities specified in their articles of association. Nevertheless, the relevant public authorities have not established an effective system for monitoring and evaluating compliance.

5 Acquisition of Turkish Citizenship Through Real-Estate Purchase

According to the Turkish Citizenship Law (Law No. 5901, 2009), a "Turkish citizen" is defined as an individual who is bound to the Republic of Türkiye through the bond of citizenship, while "multiple citizenship" refers to a situation whereby a Turkish citizen concurrently possesses more than one nationality. A "foreigner" is characterised as any individual who does not have that bond to Turkish citizenship. Citizenship can be acquired either by birth or through naturalisation after birth.

Birth-based citizenship is conferred automatically either by descent (ius sanguinis) or by place of birth (ius soli). Consequently, a child born in or outside Türkiye to two married Turkish parents is regarded as Turkish by birth. Additionally, a child born out of wedlock to a Turkish mother and a foreign father is also considered Turkish. Conversely, a child born out of wedlock to a Turkish father and a foreign mother attains Turkish citizenship once paternal filiation is legally established. A child born in Türkiye who does not acquire foreign nationality from parents is deemed Turkish from birth, and a foundling discovered within Türkiye is presumed—absent contrary evidence—to have been born in Türkiye. Postnatal acquisition of citizenship, also referred to as subsequent naturalisation, occurs through a decision by the competent authority, adoption, or the exercise of the right of option; these pathways collectively constitute exceptional naturalisation. Notably, individuals who make substantial capital investments (movable or immovable) exceeding defined thresholds, or who have achieved distinguished accomplishments in science, art, or sport, may be granted Turkish citizenship by presidential decree.

Article 20, titled "*Exceptional acquisition of Turkish citizenship, required documents for application, and procedures*", of the Regulation on the Implementation of the Turkish Citizenship Law—issued on the basis of Article 46 of Law No 5901—states that a foreigner may acquire Turkish citizenship under Article 12 of the Law if any of the following conditions are satisfied.

a) *Investing at least USD 500,000 (or the equivalent in another foreign currency) in fixed capital, as certified by the Ministry of Industry and Technology.*
b) *The purchase of real estate valued at a minimum of USD 400,000 (or its equivalent in another foreign currency) is permissible provided that a three-year no-sale annotation is registered in the land register. Alternatively, if the property is subject to condominium or construction servitude, a notarised promise-to-sell agreement must be executed, with a minimum of USD 400,000 paid in advance and a three-year non-transfer undertaking recorded in the land register, as certified by the Ministry of Environment, Urbanisation and Climate Change.*
c) *Creating jobs for at least 50 people, as certified by the Ministry of Labour and Social Security.*
d) *Depositing a minimum of USD 500,000 (or its equivalent in another foreign currency) into a bank operating within Türkiye and undertaking to retain the funds for 3 years, as certified by the Banking Regulation and Supervision Agency.*
e) *Purchasing government debt instruments valued at no less than USD 500,000 (or equivalent in another foreign currency) and maintaining possession thereof for 3 years, as certified by the Ministry of Treasury and Finance.*
f) *Acquiring shares of a real estate investment fund or venture capital investment fund valued at no less than USD 500,000 (or the equivalent in another foreign currency) and retaining them for a minimum duration of 3 years, as verified by the Capital Markets Board.*
g) "*Contributing a minimum of USD 500,000 (or the equivalent in another foreign currency) to the private pension system, maintaining the contribution in funds designated by the Insurance and Private Pension Regulation and Supervision*

Agency, and sustaining membership in the system for three years, as certified by said Agency".

By the end of 2024, a total of 34,139 individuals had obtained a certificate of eligibility for Turkish citizenship through the acquisition of property, 6670 women and 27,469 men. Of these, 28,939 people—approximately 85% of all recipients—purchased property in Istanbul (see Fig. 6). Advantageous conditions for business development generally characterise the provinces and districts where foreigners acquire property for citizenship purposes. These regions are particularly favoured by elderly individuals seeking retirement in Türkiye, as well as entrepreneurs interested in establishing businesses.

When eligibility certificates are analysed by nationality, Iran ranks first with 7169 recipients, followed by Afghanistan with 3937 and Iraq with 3414. Yemen, China, and Russia occupy the subsequent positions (Fig. 7). The prominence of buyers from countries experiencing economic or political turmoil has stimulated domestic debate; critics frequently contend that demand from neighbouring states, motivated by citizenship considerations, substantially enhances Türkiye's property market and contributes to upward price pressures.

The transition from foreigner to citizen signifies a fundamental change in an individual's status, shifting from that of a temporary resident or guest to one of permanent membership. This change grants access to the rights and responsibilities associated with integration into the host society. Several critical factors influence this process: the migration policies and experiences of the receiving state, its cultural composition, economic and political environment, and notably, the willingness of the host community to accept foreigners and incorporate them into democratic life (Yıldız, 2017). While citizenship is primarily acquired by birth, the proliferation of "citizenship-by-investment" programmes—designed to prioritise economic contributions—has expanded globally in recent years. Initially, schemes that confer

Fig. 6 Number of foreigners granted a certificate of eligibility for Turkish citizenship, by province. *Source*: TKGM (2025)

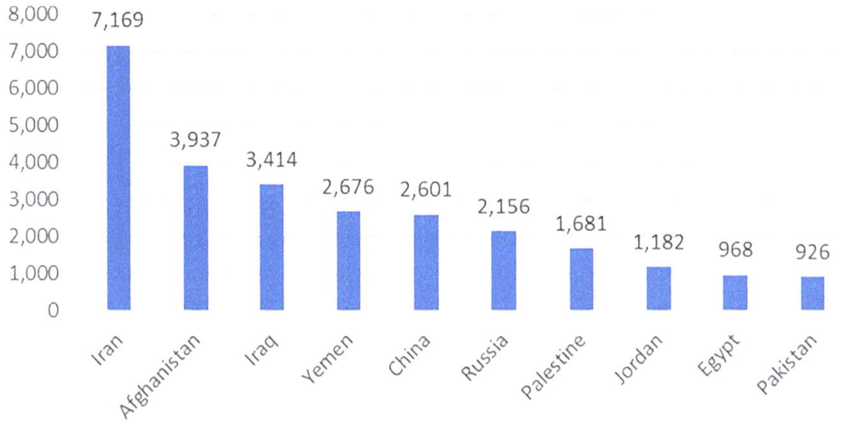

Fig. 7 Number of foreigners granted a certificate of eligibility for Turkish citizenship, by nationality. *Source*: TKGM (2025)

citizenship without a residence requirement emerged in the Caribbean; within the European Union, the Republic of Cyprus pioneered this practice, followed by Malta and Bulgaria (Kaya, 2021). However, the sale of access to EU citizenship has faced substantial criticism from EU institutions and other member states (Bauböck, 2018). Countries such as the United States, the United Kingdom, Canada, Belgium, Australia, Portugal, Greece, Italy, and Hungary operate programmes that impose residence requirements (Kaya, 2021).

Türkiye, which introduced a citizenship-by-investment scheme in 2017, now attracts both capital and human inflows through this programme. As a candidate for European Union membership, the EU oversees the operation of this scheme. Member states offering such programmes are expected to establish oversight mechanisms to address security concerns. The inclusion of investment-based naturalisation in the EU accession process remains a subject of ongoing debate (Deniz & Çetinkaya, 2023; European Commission, 2019; Yıldız, 2017). Regarding real estate investments, once applicants fulfil the financial criteria, the Ministry of Environment, Urbanisation and Climate Change issues an investment verification and eligibility certificate. Given the involvement of property transactions, the Foreign Affairs Department of the General Directorate of Land Registry and Cadastre (TKGM) provides guidance circulars outlining procedures and requirements for obtaining citizenship through real estate investment. Applications are evaluated on two criteria: (i) compliance with regulations and (ii) security screening results (Toksoy, 2023). Although foreign real estate transactions have increased since the programme's inception, only 13.5% of individuals who purchased independent units after 2017 received an eligibility certificate (TURKSTAT, 2024). Consequently, while the potential for citizenship has fostered substantial foreign demand for housing in Türkiye (Güler & Gökçe, 2020), not all purchases are made with this objective, and not every transaction results in the issuance of a certificate.

6 Impacts of Foreign Real Estate Acquisitions

At the regional level, foreign purchases have multifaceted economic effects on housing markets, influencing price dynamics and affordability. Often, inflows of foreign-capital drive prices higher, risking that local households will struggle to meet their housing needs. Many studies have examined the impact of increasing foreign investment on prices, revealing that foreign buyers are typically willing to pay more than local purchasers, which creates barriers for domestic households and distorts market competition (Cvijanovic et al., 2020). While foreign demand can stabilise housing markets during downturns, it may also reduce local demand when trading volumes are high (Liao et al., 2015). A significant presence of foreign investors can boost national income, encourage economic growth, and increase construction activity (Tanrıvermiş et al., 2024). However, rising prices can also worsen affordability for residents (Masron & Md Nor, 2016). These tensions can cause friction between foreigners and locals, raising broader concerns about access and fairness (DeVerteuil, 2021; Jen, 2022). Governments might address these issues by imposing taxes on foreign buyers and using the revenue to support low- and middle-income households, thereby improving social welfare (Chao & Yu, 2015).

Research for several countries illustrates the impact of international demand on regional housing markets. In the United States, for instance, a surge in purchases by Chinese investors has driven up prices and constrained supply; a 1% rise in foreign-capital inflows correlates with an approximate 0.27% increase in local property prices (Gorback & Keys, 2020). In Cape Town, South Africa, Davids et al. (2020) observe that non-resident foreigners pay 10.42% more than domestic purchasers, thereby contributing to a 3.39% elevation in prices. Regarding England and Wales, Sa (2016) indicates that foreign acquisitions within the UK contribute to rising prices—particularly in regions with inelastic supply—although the total housing inventory remains unaffected.

In Türkiye, the acquisition of real estate by foreign nationals entails substantial economic, social, spatial, and legal implications at both regional and national levels. Such transactions directly impact urban development and policymaking; an increase in foreign populations can exert additional pressure on municipal finances, leading to overstretched public services (Tanrıvermiş et al., 2013). From a social standpoint, foreigners generally report minimal difficulties in cohabiting with Turkish residents and adapting to the local culture (Oğuz, 2018). Conversely, local residents express satisfaction in sharing neighbourhoods with foreign homeowners but oppose further relaxation of purchase conditions for foreigners (Baltacı, 2011). Furthermore, high concentrations of foreign buyers in specific areas may result in the out-migration of local residents and pose a risk of ghettoisation.

Access to housing and the rise of housing prices have recently become key topics of debate in Türkiye. In urban areas, increased foreign demand has driven up both sale and rental prices, especially impacting low-income households in provinces and districts with high foreign ownership (Tanrıvermiş et al., 2013). Salami et al. (2023) find that foreign investment in real estate has negative economic effects on the Turkish housing market, suggesting the need for government intervention. They highlight that when housing costs surpass 30% of household income, the likelihood of low- and middle-income families owning homes drops significantly.

Exchange-rate fluctuations represent the most decisive factor: the depreciation of the Turkish lira increases foreign demand for real estate (Yanar & Demir, 2022; Süleymanlı, 2019). The consequent surge in purchases has, consequently, led to a price escalation (Karadağ & Alıcı, 2024). The 2018 decision to establish the citizenship-by-investment threshold at USD 250,000 further augmented Türkiye's attractiveness, resulting in a significant increase in transactions by foreigners seeking both property and Turkish citizenship (Aslan, 2023).

7 Overseas Real-Estate Investments by Turkish Investors

In recent years, Turkish investors have increasingly shifted their focus towards international real estate markets, driven by a range of structural factors. Elevated mortgage rates and limited access to housing credit have impeded homeownership opportunities for the middle class. Conversely, yield-oriented investors, confronted with a sluggish domestic housing market—partly attributable to a decline in foreign demand—have reallocated their capital towards interest-bearing financial instruments. Simultaneously, domestic investors seeking more promising opportunities have begun to explore overseas markets. Affluent investors, in particular, are attracted to foreign real estate markets that offer more stable and dependable returns. Economic uncertainties and exchange-rate volatility further motivate investors to secure assets abroad (Süleymanlı, 2019). The depreciation of the Turkish lira accentuates the preference for assets denominated in foreign currencies. Diversification also serves as a key motive: by engaging in international property markets, investors aim to hedge against economic risks within Türkiye and to attain geographical diversification of their portfolios. These investors are drawn to foreign property markets that promise consistent income streams, higher rental yields, or access to "golden visa" residence schemes (Üret, 2021). Notably, these investments predominantly occur in developed markets—where property values tend to appreciate and rental incomes remain steady—most prominently in the United States, the United Kingdom, and Germany, as well as in countries offering golden visa programmes, such as Greece and Portugal.

An increasing volume of foreign currency outflows reduces the pool of capital available for domestic investment. A decline in overall investment and expenditure within Türkiye's real estate sector may further exacerbate the ongoing stagnation in the construction sector. Concurrently, capital expatriated in foreign currency could impede Türkiye's capacity to finance its current account deficit. Consequently, a weakening of domestic demand may adversely affect the construction and real estate industries (Çiftci, 2014; Hatipoğlu & Tanrıvermiş, 2017). The migration of investors towards foreign markets might jeopardise investment and employment within the domestic sector. As the construction industry constitutes a vital driver of the Turkish economy, a contraction in this sector could exert downward pressure on overall economic growth (Yamak et al., 2018). Real estate investments made abroad, unlike those undertaken within Türkiye, do not directly contribute to the Turkish tax income; this omission could result in decreased government tax revenues and lower proceeds from real estate transactions such as VAT and deed fees. Moreover, when investors transfer their foreign currency assets abroad, Türkiye's foreign exchange reserves diminish, which may heighten economic uncertainty and place additional pressure on the exchange rate, potentially leading to further depreciation of the Turkish lira.

Housing acquisitions primarily drive the overseas real estate activities of Turkish investors; nevertheless, sectors such as mining, quarrying, construction, and various manufacturing subsectors also attract capital, with the financial industry receiving a substantial influx as well. This diversity suggests that Turkish investors are approaching foreign opportunities with a comprehensive perspective. Over the past decade, the total dollar value of real estate purchased abroad by Turkish citizens has increased significantly. Annual data reveal a marked surge following 2022: the value of acquisitions escalated from approximately USD 791 million in 2022 to USD 2.08 billion in 2023, and further to USD 2.51 billion in 2024. From 2015 to 2024, outward real estate investment by residents grew approximately 2.64 times in 2023 compared to the previous year, followed by a 20.6% increase in 2024. Conversely, year-on-year declines were recorded in 2016, 2018, 2019, and 2020 (Table 9).

An analysis of Turkish residents' overseas investments highlights sectoral patterns: In 2015, mining and quarrying accounted for the largest portion at 35.65%, followed by manufacturing at 16.22% and financial and insurance activities at 15.28%. Real estate ranked fifth with 7.44%. By 2023, real estate had emerged as the top destination, accounting for 36.78% of outward investments, and it continued to lead in 2024 with 38.18%. The total value of these investments was USD 5.24 billion in 2015, decreased to below USD 4 billion from 2016 to 2020, then increased to USD 5.62 billion in 2023 and USD 6.59 billion in 2024 (see Table 10). Recent years show real estate as the largest share of outbound capital, followed by mining and financial and insurance activities. Notably, Turkish investments in European countries, such as Greece, Italy, and Luxembourg, have expanded significantly.

To address the capital outflows driven by overseas property investments and to bolster the Turkish economy, various incentives and regulatory measures could be implemented. The main focus would be on improving the domestic investment environment, stabilising the exchange rate, and increasing investor confidence—all of which would promote capital retention within Türkiye. These initiatives would create a more sustainable and appealing investment climate. Additionally, reducing exchange-rate volatility and controlling inflation would boost confidence among local investors; as economic uncertainty decreases, investors are more inclined to keep their assets domestically rather than moving them abroad. Lastly, re-establishing balance in the domestic property market to moderate prices could present advantageous opportunities for middle-income investors.

Table 9 Overseas real-estate acquisitions by residents of Türkiye (million USD)

Year/ Month	January	February	March	April	May	June	July	August	September	October	November	December	Total	Increase over the previous year (%)
2015	21	12	25	27	13	20	27	25	8	31	100	81	390	–
2016	17	18	39	8	24	52	31	40	23	40	34	33	359	−7.95
2017	120	30	90	94	20	28	22	44	25	32	21	41	567	57.94
2018	30	29	36	29	72	59	20	52	32	23	35	16	433	−23.63
2019	19	15	40	13	114	35	18	15	18	20	22	43	372	−14.09
2020	19	49	31	8	18	18	25	20	17	15	15	47	282	−24.19
2021	34	49	43	29	42	30	37	58	36	28	59	81	526	86.52
2022	45	21	31	24	34	47	102	48	93	152	104	90	791	50.38
2023	94	125	149	127	209	138	185	231	186	275	199	167	2085	163.59
2024	133	166	298	177	288	177	231	209	155	240	202	239	2515	20.62

Source: Central Bank of the Republic of Türkiye (2025)

Table 10 Overseas real-estate acquisitions by residents of Türkiye (million USD)

Sectors	2015	2016	2017	2018	2019	2020	2021	2022	2023	2024
Mining and Quarrying	1869	1094	1007	831	734	692	1004	932	963	996
Manufacturing	850	515	390	533	635	437	921	860	480	505
Electricity, gas, steam and air-conditioning supply	117	50	18	387	33	383	88	81	187	214
Construction	322	40	150	66	477	93	166	125	159	404
Wholesale and Retail Trade	70	86	120	45	104	108	154	157	188	472
Accommodation and food-service activities	44	56	121	161	30	12	67	81	60	120
Information and communication	656	72	107	66	40	358	65	116	86	145
Financial and insurance activities	801	551	453	1189	462	625	934	1242	996	742
Real-estate activities	390	359	567	433	372	282	526	791	2085	2515
Others	**123**	**291**	**243**	**214**	**545**	**160**	**691**	**494**	**464**	**473**
Total	*5242*	*3114*	*3176*	*3925*	*3432*	*3150*	*4616*	*4879*	*5668*	*6586*

Source: Central Bank of the Republic of Türkiye (2025)

8 Overall Assessment and Conclusions

A review of Türkiye's legislation regarding foreign real estate ownership indicates that significant modifications transpired between 1984 and 2012, a period characterised by the nation's promotion of an outward-oriented growth strategy. During this interval, the legislation established quantitative limits both per individual and per district; however, Law No. 6302 of 2012 abolished the reciprocity principle along with numerous restrictions concerning property types. Regulations pertaining to foreign people are delineated in Article 35 of the Land Registry Law (No. 2644). Two constraints are imposed: an individual is restricted from acquiring more than 30 hectares nationwide, and foreign holdings are limited to no more than 10% of privately owned land within any district. When developing an undeveloped parcel, the purchaser is required to initiate a development project and submit it for approval within 2 years of registration. Upon approval, the project is entered into the land register, and the Ministry supervises its prompt execution. Should the project remain incomplete within the designated timeframe, the law stipulates that the owner must liquidate the property or constrain the real right within a period determined by the Ministry of Treasury and Finance, which may extend up to 1 year. Failure to comply results in authorities liquidating the asset ex officio, with the proceeds subsequently distributed to the owner.

Despite Türkiye's relatively liberal reforms, the levels of foreign direct investment and real estate acquisitions for commercial purposes have not yet attained the anticipated scale. To date, 42,039 foreign nationals have acquired primary parcels, and 344,064 have obtained individual units, totalling 386,103 foreign owners. Collectively, foreign nationals currently own 373,089 properties, comprising 40,232 main parcels and 332,857 independent units. Acquisition of primary parcels is predominantly concentrated in select provinces: 29.06% in Istanbul, 13.08% in Bursa, 11.56% in Antalya, and 8.46% in Muğla. Registrations of units illustrate an even more pronounced concentration: 38.59% of all units purchased by foreigners are situated in Istanbul, with 26.91% in Antalya. Regarding nationality, 21.81% of foreign primary-parcel owners are German citizens, 17.71% are Greek, and 9.75% are British. It has been determined that 16.70% of foreign people who acquired independent units are Russian citizens, 12.53% are Iranian citizens, and 11.17% are Iraqi citizens.

From 2010 to 2024, the highest number of registrations for both parent parcels and independent units acquired by foreign people occurred in 2021 and 2022. This increase appears to be attributable to the enhancements introduced in recent years to facilitate the acquisition of Turkish citizenship. Türkiye hosts 83,542 foreign-capital companies, of which 6151 have engaged in real estate acquisition. These companies hold a total of 34,586 properties, comprising 13,409 parent parcels and 21,177 units. Among the provinces, Istanbul (10,785 properties), Muğla (2571), and Antalya (2126) represent the largest corporate holdings. A positive correlation between provincial socio-economic development-index scores and the volume of corporate acquisitions confirms that property purchases tend to increase as a province's level of development advances.

A total of 34,139 foreign nationals have obtained certificates of eligibility for Turkish citizenship through real estate acquisitions, comprising 6670 women and 27,469 men. Of these recipients, 85% purchased property in Istanbul. By nationality, 21% are Iranian, 12% Afghan, and 10% Iraqi. Although acquiring Turkish citizenship through property investment is not exceedingly prevalent, the practice has attracted significant public criticism; numerous observers contend that, rather than granting citizenship, foreign buyers should be issued fixed-term or indefinite residence permits. Increasing demand from foreigners seeking refuge from conflicts and political instability in neighbouring nations, or to leverage exchange-rate advantages, has exerted additional pressure on the market, leading to a rise in rental and sale prices (Tanrıvermiş et al., 2024). Considering that current policies regarding foreign property investment are expected to persist, it remains crucial to implement targeted measures that enhance Turkish citizens' access to housing.

A comprehensive approach is imperative to evaluate the economic, spatial, environmental, social, cultural, and political implications of foreign real estate acquisitions. To date, policy initiatives have predominantly focused on the economic aspect, often neglecting the broader interdisciplinary effects. Furthermore, although foreign property ownership should be a concern for multiple public agencies, the internal policies and information systems within the agencies responsible for settlement and living conditions remain inadequate. In regions such as provinces, districts, villages, and neighbourhoods where foreign property acquisition is prevalent, a distinct requirement exists for both integration initiatives and pragmatic measures to support foreign investors in their daily activities.

References

Aslan, A. S. (2023). Türkiye'de yabancıların mülk edinimi: Yalova konut sektörü örneği. *Kent Akademisi, 16*(Türkiye Cumhuriyetinin 100. Yılı Özel Sayısı), 616–633.

Atasoy, T. (2015). *Türkiye'de yabancı gerçek kişilerin taşınmaz ediniminin sınırlandırılması: Antalya ili Alanya ilçesi örneği* [Master's thesis, Ankara Üniversitesi].

Avrupa Komisyonu. (2012). *Türkiye 2012 yılı ilerleme raporu: Komisyon tarafından Avrupa Parlamentosu'na ve Konsey'e sunulan bildirim*. Brüksel.

Avrupa Komisyonu. (2018). *Türkiye raporu, 2018: Avrupa Parlamentosu, Konseye, Ekonomik ve Sosyal Komiteye ve Bölgeler Komitesine sunulan bilgilendirme*. Strazburg.

Avrupa Komisyonu. (2019). *Avrupa Birliği'nde yatırım yoluyla vatandaşlık ve ikamet planları*. Brüksel.

Avrupa Komisyonu. (2023). *Türkiye raporu: Avrupa Parlamentosu, Konseye, Avrupa Ekonomik ve Sosyal Komitesine ve Bölgeler Komitesine sunulan komisyon bilgilendirmesi*. Brüksel.

Avrupa Komisyonu. (2024). *Türkiye raporu: Avrupa Parlamentosu, Konseye, Avrupa Ekonomik ve Sosyal Komitesine ve Bölgeler Komitesine sunulan komisyon bildirimi*. Brüksel.

Avrupa Konseyi. (1948). *İnsan Hakları Beyannamesi*. https://www.coe.int

Avrupa Konseyi. (1952). *İnsan Hakları ve Temel Özgürlüklerin Korunmasına İlişkin Sözleşme'ye Ek Protokol*. https://www.coe.int [Retrieved May 5, 2025].

Aykul, Ö. (2011). *Yabancılara arazi satışı konusunda Anayasa Mahkemesi'nin 2644 sayılı Tapu Kanunu değişikliği ile ilgili 5872 sayılı kanun hakkında son kararının değerlendirilmesi*. http://barobirlik.org.tr [Retrieved April 12, 2025].

Badurlar, İ. Ö. (2008). Türkiye'de konut fiyatları ile makro ekonomik değişkenler arasındaki ilişkinin araştırılması. *Anadolu University Journal of Social Sciences, 8*(1), 223–238.

Baltacı, F. (2011). *İkinci konut turizmi kapsamında Alanya'da konut edinen yabancıların kentin sosyal, kültürel ve ekonomik yapısına etkileri* [Master's thesis, Akdeniz Üniversitesi].

Bauböck, R. (2018). What is wrong with selling citizenship? It corrupts democracy! In R. Bauböck (Ed.), *Debating transformations of national citizenship* (pp. 37–41). Springer Nature AG.

Chao, C.-C., & Yu, E. S. H. (2015). Housing markets with foreign buyers. *Journal of Real Estate Finance and Economics, 50*(2), 207–218. https://doi.org/10.1007/S11146-014-9454-3

Çiftci, N. (2014). Türkiye'de cari açık, reel döviz kuru ve ekonomik büüyüme arasındaki ilişkiler: Eş bütünleşme analizi. *Anadolu Üniversitesi Sosyal Bilimler Dergisi, 14*(1), 129–142.

Cvijanovic, D., Cvijanovic, D., & Spaenjers, C. (2020). "We'll always have Paris": Out-of-country buyers in the housing market. *Social Science Research Network*. https://doi.org/10.2139/SSRN.3248902

Davids, A., Georg, C.-P., & Georg, C.-P. (2020). The Cape of Good Hope: Exchange rate depreciations, foreign demand and house prices. *Social Science Research Network*. https://doi.org/10.2139/SSRN.3349815

Deniz, A., & Çetinkaya, S. C. (2023). Citizenship by investment in Türkiye: Who buys citizenship and why? *Southeast European and Black Sea Studies*, 1–22.

DeVerteuil, G. (2021). *Overseas investment and the real estate market: Global and local frictions and the great acceleration* (pp. 19–29). Springer. https://doi.org/10.1007/978-3-030-77466-0_2

General Directorate of Land Registry and Cadastre. (TUKSTAT) (2024). Data on Real Estate Acquisition by Foreigners 2024.

General Directorate of Land Registry and Cadastre. (TKGM). (2025). Data on Real Estate Acquisition by Foreigners 2025.

Gorback, C. S., & Keys, B. J. (2020). Global capital and local assets: House prices, quantities, and elasticities. *National Bureau of Economic Research*. https://ideas.repec.org/p/nbr/nberwo/27370.html

Güler, İ., & Gökçe, A. (2020). Analyzing the relationship between housing sales to foreigners and the housing bubble with GSADF tests: The case of Istanbul, Antalya Provinces and throughout Turkey. *Third Sector Social Economic Review, 55*(2), 989–1007. https://doi.org/10.15659/3.sektor-sosyal-ekonomi.20.05.1353

Hatipoğlu, Ü. & Tanrıvermiş, H. (2017). Assesment of supply and demand factors that affect housing investment decisions In Turkey. *Bankacılar Dergisi, 28*(100), 49–75.

Karadağ, H., & Alıcı, V. A. (2024). Türkiye ekonomisinde konut fiyat endeksi ile yabancılara yapılan konut satışı arasındaki ilişki. In A. Kamacı & H. Güneş (Eds.), *Uluslararası ticarette güncel sorunlar* (pp. 141–153). Eğitim Yayınevi.

Kaya, T. (2021). Dünyadaki örnekler ışığında yatırım yoluyla vatandaşlık uygulamasına eleştirel bir bakış. *İnönü Üniversitesi Hukuk Fakültesi Dergisi, 12*(1), 115–132.

Levi, S. (2006). *Yabancıların taşınmaz mal edinmeleri*. Legal Yayıncılık.

Liao, W.-C., Zhao, D., Lim, L. P., & Wong, G. K. M. (2015). Foreign liquidity to real estate market: Ripple effect and housing price dynamics. *Urban Studies, 52*(1), 138–158. https://doi.org/10.1177/0042098014523687

Masron, T. A., & Md Nor, A. H. (2016). Foreign investment in real estate and housing affordability. *Jurnal Ekonomi Malaysia, 50*(1), 15–28. https://doi.org/10.17576/JEM-2016-5001-02

Oğuz, Ş. (2018). *Türkiye'de yabancıların taşınmaz ediniminin sosyoekonomik açıdan değerlendirilmesi: Aydın ili Didim ilçesi örneği* [Unpublished master's project]. Ankara Üniversitesi, Fen Bilimleri Enstitüsü.

Sa, F. (2016). The effect of foreign investors on local housing markets: Evidence from the UK. *Social Science Research Network*. https://papers.ssrn.com/sol3/papers.cfm?abstract_id=2877263

Salami, M. A., Tanrıvermiş, H., & Tanrıvermiş, Y. (2023). Interdependence between foreign housing acquisitions and housing price increase in Turkey during the COVID-19 pandemic era. *International Journal of Housing Markets and Analysis, 16*(3), 575–597.

Süleymanlı, C. (2019). Türkiye'de yabancıların konut edinimi ile döviz kuru arasındaki ilişki: Eşbütünleşme analizi (2013–2019). *Bingöl Üniversitesi İktisadi ve İdari Bilimler Fakültesi Dergisi, 3*(2), 117–136. https://doi.org/10.33399/BIIBFAD.595840

Ministry of Industry and Technology (2025). Web Site: https://www.sanayi.gov.tr/istatistikler/yatirim-istatistikleri

Tanrıvermiş, H., & Bülbül, M. (2007). The role of agriculture in Turkish economy at the beginning of the European Union accession negotiations. *Journal of Applied Sciences, 7*(4), 612–625.

Tanrıvermiş, H., Doğan, V., Akipek Öcal, Ş., Kurt, Y., Akyılmaz, S. G., Tanrıbilir, F. B., Dardağan Kibar, E., Başpınar, V., Aliefendioğlu, Y., Apaydın, A., Çabuk Kaya, N., Şit, B., & Baskıcı, M. (2013). *Türkiye'de yabancıların taşınmaz edinimi ve etkilerinin değerlendirilmesi projesi*, İçinde: *Türkiye'de tarihsel gelişim süreci içinde yabancıların taşınmaz edinimlerinin analizi* (Vol. 3). TÜBİTAK Proje No: 110G020.

Tanrıvermiş, Y., Salami, M. A., & Tanrıvermiş, H. (2024). Impact of foreign investors on the Turkish construction industry. *E3S Web of Conferences, 535*, 02003. https://doi.org/10.1051/e3sconf/202453502003.

TC Merkez Bankası. (2025). *Ödemeler dengesi istatistikleri*. https://evds2.tcmb.gov.tr/index.php?. Accessed 07.04.25.

Toksoy, G. E. (2023). *Yatırım yoluyla vatandaşlık kazanılması: Problemler ve çözüm önerileri* [Unpublished master's thesis]. İhsan Doğramacı Bilkent Üniversitesi, Sosyal Bilimler Enstitüsü.

Üret, G. (2021). Between lifestyle migration and comfortable exit strategies: Turkish Golden Visa investors in Greece. *Diaspora: A Journal of Transnational Studies, 21*(2), 166–187. https://doi.org/10.3138/DIASPORA.21.2.2021.05.21

Uyar, R.U., Aliefendioğlu, Y. & Tanrıvermiş H. (2022). Determination of the parameters that constitute the price of residential properties: The case of çankaya district, ankara province. *Erciyes University Journal of Faculty of Economics and Administrative Sciences*, (62), 205–224. https://doi.org/10.18070/erciyesiibd.1081522

Yamak, N., Koçak, S., & Samut, S. (2018). Türkiye'de inşaat sektörünün kısa ve uzun dönem dinamikleri. *Ekonomi ve Yönetim Araştırmaları Dergisi, 7*(1), 96–113.
Yıldırım, S., Kırmızı, B. K., & Zeren, F. (2021). Türkiye'de konut fiyatlarını belirleyen makroekonomik göstergelerin analizi (Analysis of macroeconomic indicators determining housing prices in Turkey). *Uluslararası Ekonomi İşletme ve Politika Dergisi, 5*(1), 1–15.
Yıldız, A. (2017). Göç ve entegrasyon politikalarında vatandaşlık. *Göç Araştırmaları Dergisi, 3*(1), 36–67.
Yılmaz, A. Ç. (2013). 6302 sayılı Kanun hükümleri uyarınca yabancı gerçek kişilerin Türkiye'de taşınmaz edinimi. *Gazi Üniversitesi Hukuk Fakültesi Dergisi, 17*(1–2), 1095–1126.

Harun Tanrıvermiş is a distinguished professor who occupies the esteemed position at the Ankara University top management level as founder and head of the Department of Real Estate Development and Management, and founder and current dean of the Faculty of Applied Sciences at Ankara University. Professor Tanrıvermiş also currently works as the vice rector at Ankara University. He attained his B.Sc., M.Sc. and Ph.D. degrees from the Department of Agricultural Economics at Ankara University, specialising in land and real estate economics, land and real estate valuation, as well as natural resources and environmental economics. Furthermore, he earned an MSc in environmental management through the MED-CAMPUS Programme in 1996. Professor Tanrıvermiş has published approximately 400 papers, including 43 international and 55 national peer-reviewed articles, which have been published in various high-impact journals. Additionally, he has presented 48 international and 74 national proceedings, either in full or as abstracts, at numerous conferences. He is also credited with writing 39 books and 17 book chapters. Moreover, his works concentrate on the land and real estate valuation, land and real estate economics, real estate development and project appraisal, urban transformation and sustainability, sustainable real estate development, facility and real estate management, land management, administration and polices, measuring and reporting of real estate sustainability and ESG, digital transformation in real estate and real estate technologies.

Yeşim Tanrıvermiş holds the position of full professor in the Department of Real Estate Development and Management at the Faculty of Applied Sciences, Ankara University, Türkiye. She attained her Master of Science (M.Sc.) degree in 2011 from the Department of Agricultural Economics at Ankara University. She received her Ph.D. in 2011 as the first Ph.D. program graduate of the Department of Real Estate Development and Management at Ankara University. Her research interests encompass the management and conservation of land resources, land resource economics, as well as real estate analysis and economics, in addition to studies in real estate and asset valuation. She has been delivering lectures for several years and has published academic papers since 2006. Her publications consist of 50 international and 40 national peer-reviewed articles. Additionally, she has made contributions to 110 international and 25 national full or abstract proceedings at various conferences and congresses and has authored 35 books and 30 book chapters. Presently, she serves as the Deputy Head of her department at Ankara University. Moreover, she is an active participant in various academic and professional organisations. Her experience encompasses working as a researcher and consultant across diverse public and private sectors, with a focus on real estate asset analysis, real estate finance and valuation, land and building conservation practices, as well as real estate economics and management. Furthermore, she actively engages in enhancing cooperation with both domestic and international institutions, mobilising financial resources for research projects.

Toygun Atasoy is a mathematician currently employed as a research assistant at the Department of Real Estate Development and Management, Ankara University, where he also earned his Ph.D. Dr. Atasoy has worked as a researcher on real estate analysis and valuation, urban transformation, and development projects undertaken by the department. Dr. Atasoy's academic work centres on mathematical and econometric models, real estate analysis, real estate project development, and real estate investment analysis. His research covers real estate markets, with a particular emphasis on housing prices, macroeconomic indicators, foreign real estate acquisition, and real estate derivative models.

Real Estate Investments, Options, and Strategies in Türkiye

Gizem Ulusoy, Üstün Hatipoğlu, Amani Micheal Uisso, and Tuğba Güneş

Abstract

This chapter analyses direct and indirect real estate investment alternatives in Türkiye. Real estate investments in Türkiye are analysed with regard to macroeconomic indicators. Concerning investment strategies, it is possible to identify the potential of real estate investments in Türkiye, whether they take the form of direct investment—the purchase of physical real estate or ownership of real estate-based rights—or indirect investment—investments in real estate-based assets traded on capital markets. This also requires taking a closer look at Türkiye's socio-economic indicators. The real estate and construction sector significantly contributes to GDP and attracts foreign investment, but faces challenges like economic instability, housing price rises, and limited investment options. Opportunities include granting citizenship, improving housing finance systems, and expanding financial instruments. Options for direct and indirect real estate investment are sketched, and these options and strategies are summarised in this chapter.

G. Ulusoy (✉) · T. Güneş
Department of Real Estate Development and Management, Faculty of Applied Sciences, Ankara University, Ankara, Türkiye
e-mail: gulusoy@ankara.edu.tr; gunest@ankara.edu.tr

Ü. Hatipoğlu
TALYA Real Estate Valuation and Consultancy Joint Stock Company, Zeytinburnu/Istanbul, Türkiye
e-mail: uhatipoglu@talyagd.com

A. M. Uisso
President Office Ethics Secretariat, Dodoma, Tanzania
e-mail: amani.uisso@maadili.go.tz

T. Just et al. (eds.), *Understanding Türkiye's Real Estate Markets*, Management for Professionals, https://doi.org/10.1007/978-3-032-13297-0_15

Keywords
Real estate sector · Foreign direct real estate investments · Direct investments · Indirect investments

1 Introduction

For governments, private companies, and private households, "investment" refers to managing savings and available resources to generate a return while taking various risks to enable higher future expenditures. Investments can produce both short- and long-term gains and can help to increase purchasing power. Investments are the result of the decision between liquidity, risk, and expected returns on the investment. In that sense, real estate investments are comparatively illiquid and offer specific risks and returns.

Residential real estate provides utility, such as giving shelter, security, privacy, and social prestige, while commercial real estate facilitates value creation in other sectors. Both can be valuable for private or commercial investors. The purchase of a parcel of land, a building, a boat, or a right can be treated as a real estate investment, and this also holds for rights to one or more properties or financial instruments based on real estate (Erdoğdu & Büyükduman, 2018; Esra & Seven, 2019; Gümüş, 2018; Ulusoy, 2018). Due to their continuous rental income potential and their specific risk compared to other investment options, real estate is considered an asset class of its own for individuals and legal entities. Because a special feature of (direct) property investment is that properties are difficult to divide, large individual expenses are often associated with property investments. With a long planning horizon, this can result in the "Black Day Coin Dilemma" (also known as The Nest Egg Dilemma): You save too much and have too few funds for the present, or you save too little and have too few savings later (Mcgreevy & Eldred, 2006). While real estate investments in Türkiye have been a domestic issue for a long time, this has changed in the last few decades, given the European Union's Free Movement of Capital policy, which has helped Türkiye to become a global investment destination.

1.1 Real Estate in Türkiye

Real estate is fundamentally categorised as "tangible assets that are fixed and cannot be moved from one place to another". The term "immovable" or "immovable property" is also used to describe it (Tanrivermiş & Tanrivermiş, 2022). Real estate is defined as "land, autonomous and permanent rights documented on a separate page in the land registry, independent parts registered in the condominium registry" under Article 704 of the Turkish Civil Code No. 4721.[1] Real estate is divided into

[1] Official Gazette, Date: 12/8/2001, Nr: 24607.

two categories under the Real Estate Tax Law No. 1319[2]: buildings and land. Article 2 of the Law defines "building" as "any fixed construction, whether on land or water, regardless of the material it is built of". It is specified individually as "land and plot" in the law's section on land taxes. While land is defined in the 12th article of the law as land parcelled by the municipality inside the municipality's boundaries, it is up to the President to determine whether land that is not parcelled out within or beyond the municipal boundaries is still regarded as land.

Residential, commercial, industrial, agricultural, and special-purpose real estate are categories of real estate. These investments require specific expenses to allow rental returns and capital gains. For financial assets, the net present value is defined as the sum of the predicted future net cash flows of the real estate, i.e. all future excess returns discounted by an appropriate interest rate. Long-term cash-yielding real estate is traded on capital markets and compared to other income-producing and cash-yielding financial assets (stocks and bonds). These investments in real estate-based assets include both direct and indirect real estate investments. In contrast, direct investments include purchasing and owning real estate (Tanrivermiş & Tanrivermiş, 2022).

1.2 Key Economic Indicators Within the Real Estate Sector

The real estate market is typically a long-term investment option, with the status of the economy and expectations greatly influencing investor choices. The real estate market and the building industry are usually among the most significant sectors of the economy. While the share of these two sectors in the Gross deomestic product (GDP) was above 15% on average between 2000 and 2017, this share dropped to 11% in the 6 years thereafter and even to 9.6% in 2023 (Fig. 1). The drop in this share was driven by weakening economic conditions, including, but not limited to, the depreciation of the Turkish lira, rising energy prices, rising consumer and construction prices, and the COVID-19 pandemic.

While the average annual inflation rate from the early 2000s to the end of 2017 was 8.5%, it rapidly rose in the second half of 2018. While the annual change was 14.6% by the end of 2020, it reached 36.8% in 2021 and 64.7% at the end of 2023 (Turkstat, 2024a). At the same time, and mirroring the rising inflation rates, the Turkish lira has significantly depreciated against the USD and the Euro (EUR) since the second half of 2018. The exchange rate rose from 5.26 USD/TL in 2018 to 12.98 USD/TL in 2021 and 32.6 USD/TL by July 2024 (CBRT, 2024a).

Real estate is a long-term asset that can protect against inflation and inflation uncertainty in the long run (Tanrivermiş & Tanrivermiş, 2022). According to Yanar and Demir (2022), when the country's currency depreciates against the USD, an inflationary economic climate can make real estate markets more appealing, especially for foreign investors. Despite the increase in residential property sales until 2023, the homeownership rate in Türkiye has recently fallen from 60% to 56.2%.

[2] Official Gazette, Date: 8/11/1970, Nr: 13576.

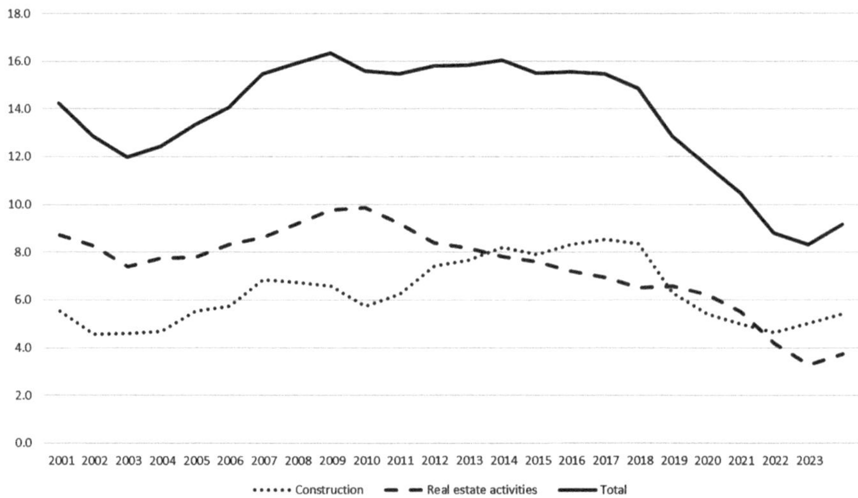

Fig. 1 Share of real estate activities and construction sector in GDP in %. *Source*: TurkStat (2024d)

This indicates that private housing purchases are also an important investment and not only a consumption good (TurkStat, 2024b). Foreign direct investment (FDI) inflows have increased significantly since the early 2000s, and according to the international direct investment inflows, there was a net direct investment inflow of USD 10,607 million in 2023, of which 33.5% was real estate investments with USD 3560 million (STB, 2024). In 2021, real estate FDI stood at USD 5.8 billion, accounting for 41% of all foreign direct investments. The Turkish real estate market drew more foreign investors' attention until 2022; however, this momentum sharply ended in 2023. The citizenship-by-investment programme is another significant driver of demand from overseas investors. According to the TKGM, foreign investors acquired, on average, 50,000 properties annually in the last ten years. The peak was reached in 2022, and the value dropped to 35,000 in 2023 (Fig. 2).

Given that real estate requires substantial investment volumes, pure equity investments are rare; therefore, modern real estate markets are built on deep real estate capital markets. The first step in establishing a modern mortgage system in Türkiye was taken with the enactment of Law No. 5582 in 2007. The new Capital Market Law No. 6362, enacted in 2012, has served as the basis for the current mortgage system. Mortgage-financed sales accounted for 31% of all residential property transactions between 2013 and 2019. Following the central government's housing support schemes in June 2020, aimed at reducing mortgage rates in the country, the share of mortgage-financed sales increased to 38% in 2020. However, this share dramatically decreased in the following years and declined to 14.5% in 2023 (Turkstat, 2024c). Mortgages in Türkiye usually have a maturity of 10 years, and the weighted average of mortgage rates was over 42% by the end of 2023 (CBRT, 2024b). The adverse impact of high mortgage rates on mortgage-financed sales levels was demonstrated by Güneş and Apaydin (2021) and Atasoy and Tanrivermiş (2021).

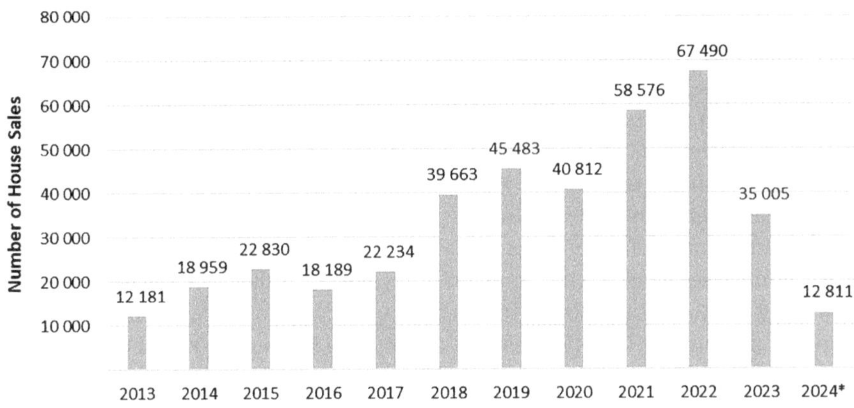

Fig. 2 Real estate acquisitions by foreigners in figures *(* by the first half of 2024). Source*: TurkStat (2024d)

2 Direct Investment Options and Strategies

Real estate investments can be made in many different real estate segments, including housing, office, or retail properties, both in existing stock and new developments (Tanrivermiş, 2019). As developing real estate requires a significant amount of time, long-term investment strategies, strategic planning, and economically founded predictions of key supply and demand drivers are crucial for estimating the expected risks and returns (Pagliari Jr, 2020). The main real estate investment strategies include buying a real estate property at market price and renting it for the long term (buy-and-hold), or buying and renovating the property, allowing the market price to rise, and putting it up for sale (flippers), and seizing the opportunities brought by time and/or region and sell with capital gains (Haight & Singer, 2005; Pagliari Jr, 2020). In Türkiye, real estate sales and rental prices have been on a rapid upward trend in recent years, making real estate a good investment option that incorporates all three strategies.

Since the 1980s, Türkiye has actively sought foreign direct investment (FDI) to accelerate its economic development and has implemented liberal FDI policies and regulations to attract foreign capital (Çetin, 2024). FDI contributes to Türkiye's development by providing capital, creating employment, transferring technology and improving management skills (Kalyoncu et al., 2015). Türkiye has historically received relatively low volumes of FDI compared to similar economies (Balasubramanyam, 1996).

2.1 Land Development and Real Estate Investments

Land, as an important factor of production, is of great importance for real estate investments. In Türkiye, land development and land supply have been pioneered by the local government through municipalities by ensuring the availability of the infrastructure land services and public services such as roads, streetlights, way-leaves, parks, and buildable urban land plots, especially for the areas experiencing fast urbanisation (Tuhral & Psilander, 2005). Land readjustment is employed for land development and zoning in urban areas, while in the adjacent rural regions, land consolidation is deployed specifically to prevent land fragmentation and to improve agricultural land productivity (Ertunç, 2020; Turk, 2007). Public institutions which govern the land cadastre, planning, valuation, and land ownership are important to facilitate the process. These institutions and the Urban Land Development Law No. 3194, the decentralisation in planning, led to a significant trickle-down effect on the availability of serviced land, housing production, and the flourishing of the real estate sector (Tuhral & Psilander, 2005; Türel & Koç, 2015).

2.2 Housing Development and Supply Policies

The development of housing in Türkiye can be illustrated by examining different periods in history, starting from the 1950s, when the supply of affordable housing was immense, leading to the emergence of informal settlements, also known as "gecekondu", unregistered properties, and an ambiguous land tenure and ownership system (Çelik, 2021). Until the 1980s, affordable houses were still limited to cover the demand of low-income groups, financed by social security funds, government bodies, commercial banks, and other institutions and cooperatives (Erol & Patel, 2004). The second phase of extensive activities into affordable housing started with the financial banking crisis in January 2000 in Türkiye, when the Turkish government enhanced the housing sector by creating a base for housing finance, and by providing further institutional and legal regulatory changes to make a significant achievement in the settlement and housing sector (Çelik, 2021). This momentum experienced growing headwinds during the following cascade of crises, like the global financial and economic crisis of 2007/2008, followed by the global COVID-19 pandemic (Çelik, 2021; Özdemir Sari, 2019; Tanrivermiş, 2020).

The Housing Development Administration designed policies in housing development, and commercial banks played a new role in real estate financing, particularly for the demand-oriented policies. At the same time, supply-oriented policies encouraged investments in housing by providing tax incentives, such as reducing VAT (Türel & Koç, 2015).

2.3 Real Estate Investment Strategies

In line with the changing economic, environmental, and social conditions, investors' preferences regarding the real estate segment are also changing. Some investors favour maximum profits; others prefer a rapid payback. Government decisions can strongly impact the exact preference: In the residential property market in Türkiye, rental prices increased by 0.85% per month on average in 2020 and 2021. However, this rate sharply increased to 4.8% in 2022 and 2023 (Turkstat, 2024a). Rental price increases are often linked to the country's average consumer price index (CPI). Thus, the change in the CPI reaching 80% created a huge payment shock for the tenants. In June 2022, the government imposed a cap of 25% on rental price increases for contract renewals. However, this limitation rule was terminated in July 2024.

The rise in rents accelerated in metropolitan areas after the earthquake in and around Kahramanmaraş in February 2023 (BBC, 2023). Despite this rise in rental prices, it is noteworthy that the return period of housing investments increased from an average of 16.6 years (200 months) in 2012 to 22.1 years (265 months) in June 2022, meaning that prices climbed faster than rents (GYODER, 2022a). Although the prolonged payback period is seen as a burden for domestic and foreign real estate investors, this situation did not last long. As of Q1 2024, the payback period for housing investment decreased to 17.1 years again. However, in addition to investor demand and the level of real estate supply, payback periods vary on a regional basis depending on factors such as tourism, population mobility, security, and seasonality. For example, according to GYODER (2022a), Russian and Ukrainian investors' interest in Antalya province and the Aegean region has increased rental prices, resulting in a seasonally shorter return on investment periods.

Factors like the granting of citizenship rights in return for real estate investments, lower real estate prices compared to developed European countries, the geographical and strategic location, as well as historical, cultural, touristic, and natural appeal, fast and effective banking and title deed procedures, make the Turkish real estate market an important option for foreign investors. In addition, due to the unfavourable political conditions in their home countries, acquiring Turkish citizenship by investing in real estate offers an advantage for citizens of countries like Iraq, Iran, or Afghanistan. According to TurkStat data, Turkish real estate is particularly bought by investors from the Russian Federation, Iran, Ukraine, Germany, Iraq, Kazakhstan, Azerbaijan, Saudi Arabia, the USA, and Afghanistan (TurkStat, 2024d).

It is observed that the share allocated to real estate within the foreign direct capital flows entering Türkiye has risen in the last 10 years, but has been very volatile. In this sense, it is thought that the pandemic negatively affected the demand of foreigners for real estate investments due to reasons such as closed borders and restrictions imposed at certain levels. The popularity of Airbnb and similar websites and investing in real estate for renting out has created a new framework encompassing long-term rental contracts and short-term rentals in both holiday destinations and urban centres with historical and cultural sites. In other words, developing technology and individual preferences have provided the opportunity to create a new real estate investment strategy. For example, in September 2019, there were 32,000 rental housing advertisements in Istanbul and 5000 rental housing advertisements in Izmir, while as of September 2024, these numbers have increased to 50,000 for Istanbul and 13,000 for Izmir (Airdna, 2024).

The COVID-19 outbreak has significantly affected the real estate sector. In addition to the burden it created, it also enabled opportunities for investors: According to GYODER (2022b), Türkiye's retail and office sectors were more fragile in the 2 years following the pandemic, while the housing and logistics markets were more resilient. People's preferences for housing type and accommodation for tourism have also changed. According to the data from the real estate data provider company Endeksa (2020), during the 6 weeks from March 11, 2020, when the first COVID-19+ case was registered in Türkiye, to April 28, 2020, housing sales prices increased on average by 11%, and rental prices increased by 6%, while calls to "Stay at Home" increased the demand for detached houses offering living spaces with gardens instead of apartments. The sales prices of detached houses increased by an average of 25%, and rents by 18%.

During the COVID-19 pandemic, housing preferences have shifted to detached houses, and there has been an increase in the rate of second home acquisition. In addition to the houses acquired for renting, existing residences have also become an investment opportunity. These secondary residences, which are generally not used except at specific times of the year, have become an element of the tourism sector with the COVID-19 pandemic and have become an opportunity to provide a return on investment. Offering an isolated vacation opportunity instead of hotels where groups are in close contact, these (detached) residences have attracted great interest (Zoğal & Emekli, 2020). This is also reflected in the statistics: According to TurkStat (2024b), Türkiye's homeownership rate decreased from over 60% in 2019 to 56.2% in 2023. The increase in housing and rental prices has made housing an important investment option. At the same time, it is observed that there was an increase in demand for land in rural areas during the pandemic.

In addition to factors affecting the real estate sector worldwide, such as technological developments and the COVID-19 pandemic, incidents specific to Türkiye can also offer real estate investment opportunities. For example, millions of asylum seekers who have come to Türkiye since 2011 have caused housing sales and rental prices to rise in some parts of the country (Balkan et al., 2018). Therefore, it has become an investment option to purchase housing in areas where refugees are concentrated to respond to increasing rental demand. Similar opportunistic or strategic behaviour is also exhibited in response to the potential increase in profits that public investments will provide in real estate (such as taking advantage of the benefits of urban transformation by purchasing old houses that have the potential to be declared risky areas).

3 Indirect Investment Options

With the Law No. 5582 on the Amendment of Various Laws Regarding the Housing Finance System, enacted in 2007, and the new Capital Markets Law No. 6362, from 2012, and the communiqués issued by the Capital Markets Board (CMB), Türkiye established a modern real estate finance system, initiating mortgaged bonds and mortgage-backed securities. Similarly, other real estate-based financial instruments, such as real estate and lease certificates, investment trusts, and funds, were regulated. Thus, the options for making indirect investments in the real estate sector were included in several steps (Table 1).

3.1 Real Estate Investment Trusts

Fund management involves investing the capital pool in various asset classes, including real estate. Shares based on real estate investments can be a suitable way to reduce the liquidity limitations of real estate investments, diversify risk and/or yield higher returns (Baum, 2015). Real estate investment trusts (REITs), which were introduced in Türkiye in 1995, are *"capital market instruments that can invest in real estate, real estate projects, real estate-based rights, and capital market instruments, that can be established to realise certain projects or invest in a specific real estate, and that can engage in other permitted activities, and whose income is exempted from corporate tax"*. By the first quarter of 2024, there were 53 REITs in Türkiye with a market capitalisation of TL 396 billion (CMB, 2024) (see also section 12). Real estate investment trusts provide resources for large-scale real estate projects, especially those with high financing needs, relieving companies of the burden of credit and supporting Türkiye's economic development. For investors,

Table 1 CMB regulations on financial instruments backed by real properties

Series - No	Name of communiqué	Official gazette
III - 58.1	Communiqué on asset- or mortgage-based securities	January 9, 2014 – 28877
III - 59.1	Collateralised securities communiqué	January 21, 2014 – 28889
III - 60.1	Communiqué on principles regarding mortgage financing institutions	July 17, 2014 – 29063
III - 48.1	Communiqué on principles regarding real estate investment trusts	May 28, 2013 – 28660
III - 61.1	Communiqué on lease certificates	June 6, 2013 – 28670
VII - 128.2	Communiqué on real estate certificates	July 5, 2013 – 28698
III - 52.3	Communiqué on principles regarding real estate investment funds	January 3, 2014 - 28871

Source: Authors' own depiction

shares securitised through real estate create an environment of trust in portfolio diversification and expert fund management, making this type of indirect investment attractive.

3.2 Real Estate Investment Funds

Real estate investment funds (REIFs) sell "participation shares" to savers within the scope of their portfolios, which consist of various real estate properties and real estate-based rights. Conversely, savers can benefit from real estate, such as rental income or appreciation gains. The important point is that while providing a competitive environment for the real estate sector, these participation shares will also contribute positively to developing capital markets, as they will be sold in secondary markets. The primary difference between REIFs and REITs is that REIFs are not publicly traded (CMB, 2016; Hepşen et al., 2017). There were 150 Real Estate Investment Funds in Türkiye by the first quarter of 2024, and the total size of REIFs has reached TL 82.5 billion (CMB, 2024).

3.3 Real Estate and Lease Certificates

The first application of real estate certificates in Türkiye was established with the issuance made by the Mass Housing and Public Partnership Administration under the name of housing certificate (Istanbul Halkalı Mass Housing). The implementation did not continue due to the high initial issuance price, the demand for goodwill, the 5 years required to acquire a house, and the fact that the yield remained below the inflation rate (Yalçiner, 2006). Real estate certificates, which were reissued with the CMB communiqué published in 2013, have been criticised due to the previous negative experience, and according to the CMB's May 2024 report, real estate certificates have not yet found a place in Türkiye (CMB, 2024).

Lease certificates (Sukuk) in Türkiye had a total volume of TL 277 billion by the end of 2023. While the Treasury issued 95% of the certificates, the private sector issued the rest. The Treasury's share of domestic issuances was 71%. Figure 3 shows a rapid increase, particularly in the Treasury's domestic issues, in recent years. Two green lease certificates were issued in Türkiye. According to the report of the Presidential Finance Office (2022), the total value of green Sukuk issuances made by Türkiye Emlak Katılım Bankası in November 2021 and by Türkiye Varlık Fund in December of the same year was TL 651.8 million. The *"Green Debt Instrument, Sustainable Debt Instrument, Green Lease Certificate, Sustainable Lease Certificate Guide"*, which was prepared based on the Green Bond Principles of the International Capital Markets Association (ICMA) and the first draft of which was made available to the public in November 2021, was officially published by the

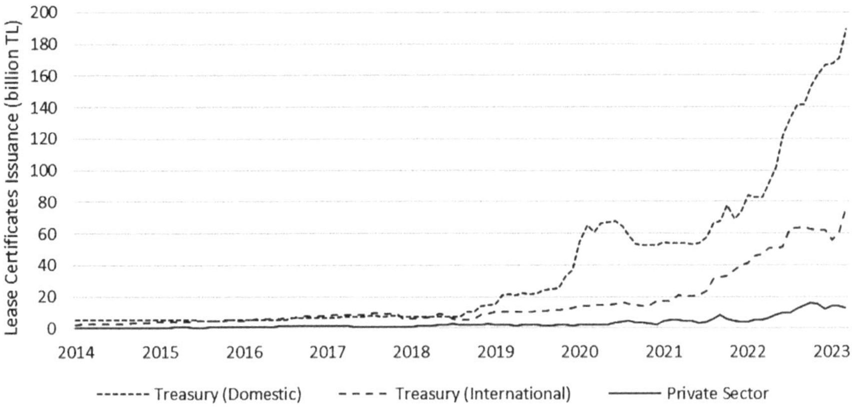

Fig. 3 Lease certificate issuance. *Source*: BRSA (2024)

CMB in February 2022. To encourage environmentally beneficial investments, it was decided to offer a 50% discount on the fees made to the CMB in the issuances within the scope of the Guide (CMB, 2022).

3.4 Mortgaged Bonds (Mortgage-Covered Bonds)

As in most European countries, there are legally covered bonds in Türkiye as well (ECBC, 2023; Larsson, 2013). Article 59 of the Capital Markets Law, amended in 2012, titled "Mortgage and asset-backed securities", sets out the principles and procedures for covered bonds. The principles and procedures regarding covered bonds are regulated by the "Communiqué on Covered Bonds (III - 59.1)" (as amended several times over the years) published by the Capital Markets Board on January 21, 2014. Accordingly, mortgaged bonds can be issued by housing finance institutions (KFK) or mortgage finance institutions (IFK). IFKs are joint stock companies established by Article 60 of the Capital Markets Law. KFKs, on the other hand, are banks that can provide loans or financial leasing to consumers for housing financing, or financing companies that the Banking Regulation and Supervision Agency (BRSA) has approved to engage in housing finance activities.

According to the "European Covered Bonds Market-2023" report of the European Covered Bond Council (ECBC), the total outstanding volume of Turkish mortgage-covered bonds by the end of 2022 was EUR 280 million, corresponding to only 0.01% of the total mortgage-covered bond volume in Europe. While the total outstanding volume of covered bonds in Türkiye was EUR 2.6 billion in 2019, a rapid deterioration in the market was observed in the following few years. The new covered bond issuances amounted to EUR 227 million in 2019, EUR 16 million in 2021, with no new covered bonds being issued in 2020 and 2022 (ECBC, 2023).

3.5 Mortgage-Backed Securities

Various laws[3] were amended with the Law mentioned above (Nr. 5582), also known as the "Mortgage Law", in the public. This law aimed to create a secondary mortgage market in Türkiye. It enabled issuing mortgage-backed securities and mortgage-covered bonds backed by collateral pools created from mortgage loans. The Law provided definitions of the capital market instruments backed by mortgages, determined the definition and scope of the housing finance system and institutions, and drew a distinction between mortgage-backed and asset-backed securities. The communiqués published by the CMB between 2007 and 2009 identified the principles of mortgage or asset-backed securities and covered bonds. Final regulations on the mortgage system were issued with the assistance of the new Capital Market Law, which was enacted in 2012, and the CMB communiqués issued for asset- or mortgage-backed and covered bonds in subsequent years. According to the regulations, only a housing finance fund or a mortgage finance institution (IFK) can issue mortgage-backed securities.

Securitisation is widely regarded as one of the most significant financial innovations of the last century, and a cornerstone of the secondary mortgage market. Mortgage-backed securities produced by securitisation have remained relatively limited in Türkiye. The Presidential decree issued at the end of 2019, which involved the Treasury's transfer of initial capital to and participation in a mortgage finance institution establishment, represents a significant step towards the securitisation of mortgage loans.

In the Eleventh Development Plan covering the period of 2019 to 2023, it is mentioned that *"The main objective is to form a financial sector with a strong institutional structure that can sufficiently satisfy financing needs of the real sector at a lower cost; offer various financial instruments to investors in a wide spectrum through reliable institutions…"*. The Plan also has brought measures by stating that *"The issuance limit of the Mortgage Finance Institution (MFC) will be made independent of its capital"* and *"To decrease issuance costs of MFC, transaction costs such as CMB board fee and Central Securities Depository of Türkiye (CSD) custody fee will be reduced"*. The CMB has reflected these measures in the regulations by amending the Communiqués on Asset and Mortgage-Backed Securities and Debt Instruments in June 2020 to encourage the issuance of mortgage-backed securities.

[3] https://word-edit.officeapps.live.com/we/wordeditorframe.aspx?ui=tr-TR&rs=en-US&hid=MoGP4ugE0Uuk2M5/J9FAjQ.0&wopisrc=https://wopi.onedrive.com/wopi/files/59577DAF9D935F7C!1270&wdo=2&wde=docx&sc=host=&qt=Default&wdp=3&uih=OneDrive&jsapi=1&jsapiver=v2&corrid=17695b04-afce-4846-87dc-71c6fe57562a&usid=17695b04-afce-4846-87dc-71c6fe57562a&newsession=1&sftc=1&wdorigin=Other&instantedit=1&wopicomplete=1&wdredirectionreason=Unified_SingleFlush.

4 Conclusion

This chapter analysed the current situation regarding the real estate investments made by institutional and private investors in the Turkish real estate market. Like other countries, the main motivation for real estate investments in Türkiye is to provide a reasonable compromise between demand for liquidity, expected returns and exposed risks. Economic and global indicators, including the COVID-19 pandemic, have obviously impacted real estate investment choices in Türkiye over the last few years; some segments suffered (retail, office), others flourished (e.g. residential, logistics).

Decisions and strategies of real estate investors in Türkiye have been adversely affected by various factors, including rises in construction and labour costs, depreciation of the Turkish lira, and increasing energy costs. Rises in housing sales and rental prices have been major drivers of the investment choices of both domestic and international investors in deciding real estate segments and their potential. Housing and land development policies (e.g. urban transformation, housing acquisition support schemes implemented through reduced mortgage interest rates) and tax incentives can influence investment options and investor preferences. The construction and real estate industries are important for the Turkish economy because they boost GDP and draw in foreign direct investment, in accordance with the popularity of sukuks. But the industry has to contend with issues including unstable economies, soaring housing costs, and a dearth of varied indirect investment opportunities. Possibilities include extending real estate-backed financial instruments, enhancing housing finance systems, and awarding citizenship to overseas investors. However, there are still serious issues with risks like opaqueness and poor tracking of local supply–demand patterns.

Indirect investment options (financial assets backed by real estate) have fallen behind the direct investments in Türkiye and have been used at a more limited level compared to developed countries. Due to the insufficient economic and political stability in Türkiye, the underlying reason for investors' preference is the sense of safety created by making direct investments through physically acquiring real estate. Increasing the incentives for issuing financial instruments backed by real estate may offer more variety in the capital market and make these assets more attractive to investors. Economic stability, as in all sectors, is at the core of real estate investment strategies, and various incentives and policies can increase its contribution to the country's economy.

References

AIRDNA. (2024). *Airbnb Rental Data* [Online]. https://www.airdna.co/ [Accessed].

Atasoy, T., & Tanrivermiş, H. (2021). Türkiye'de Konut Kredisi Hacmi ile Seçilmiş Makroekonomik Faktörler Arasındaki İlişkinin Değerlendirilmesi. *Erciyes Üniversitesi İktisadi ve İdari Bilimler Fakültesi Dergisi*, 461–484.

Balasubramanyam, V. N. (1996). *Foreign direct investment in Turkey. The economy of Turkey since liberalisation*. Springer.

Balkan, B., Tok, E., Torun, H., & Tumen, S. (2018). *Immigration, housing rents, and residential segregation: Evidence from Syrian refugees in Turkey*.

Baum, A. (2015). *Real estate investment: A strategic approach*. Routledge.

BBC. (2023). https://www.bbc.com/turkce/articles/c3g0xylry03o. Accessed 21.08.24.

BRSA. (2024). Lease Certificates Issued by the Treasury and Private Sector [Online]. Available: https://www.bddk.org.tr/BultenAylik/en/Home/Gelismis [Accessed 02.09.2024].

CBRT. (2024a). *Exchange Rates(Daily), USD/TL* [Online]. https://evds2.tcmb.gov.tr/index.php?/evds/serieMarket. [Accessed].

CBRT. (2024b). *Weighted Average Interest Rates for Banks' Loans and Housing (TRY)* [Online]. https://evds2.tcmb.gov.tr/index.php?/evds/serieMarket [Accessed].

Çelik, Ö. (2021). The roles of the state in the financialisation of housing in Turkey. *Housing Studies*, 1–21.

Çetin, R. (2024). Analysis of foreıgn direct investment policies and of the performance of FDI flows into Türkiye. *Kahramanmaraş Sütçü İmam Üniversitesi Sosyal Bilimler Dergisi, 21*, 118–127.

CMB. (2016). *Gayrimenkul Yatırım Fonu Tanıtım Rehberi*. T.C. Başbakanlık Sermaye Piyasası Kurulu.

CMB. (2022). *Yeşil Borçlanma Aracı, Sürdürülebilir Borçlanma Aracı, Yeşil Kira Sertifikası, Sürdürülebilir Kira Sertifikası Rehberi Basın Duyurusu* [Online]. https://www.spk.gov.tr/Duyuru/Goster/20220224/0. [Accessed].

CMB. (2024). *Monthly Statistical Bulletin of the Capital Markets Board of Turkey, May 2024* [Online]. https://spk.gov.tr/istatistikler/aylik-istatistik-bultenleri/2024-yili-istatistik-bultenleri [Accessed].

ECBC. (2023). *18th edition of the ECBC European Covered Bond Fact Book*.

ENDEKSA. (2020). *Salgın sonrası talep edilen konut satış fiyatı %11, kira %6 arttı, Endeksa Raporu* [Online]. https://www.endeksa.com/tr/blog/yazi/salgin-sonrasi-talep-edilen-konut-satis-fiyati-11-kira-6-artti [Accessed].

Erdoğdu, C., & Büyükduman, A. (2018). *Sorularla gayrimenkul yatırımı*, CERES YAYINLARI.

Erol, I., & Patel, K. (2004). Housing policy and mortgage finance in Turkey during the late 1990s inflationary period. *International Real Estate Review, 7*, 98–120.

Ertunç, E. (2020). Analysis of the effect of land consolidation projects on land fragmentation and parcel shapes: The case of Konya, Turkey. *Arabian Journal of Geosciences, 13*, 1–13.

Esra, A., & Seven, Ü. (2019). Türkiye Konut Piyasasında Etkinlik Analizi. *Istanbul Business Research, 48*, 84–112.

Finance Office. (2022). *Yeşil Sukuk Çalışma Raporu: Mevcut Durum, Tespitler ve Öneriler*. T.C. Cumhurbaşkanlığı Finans Ofisi.

Gümüş, G. K. (2018). Yatırım Analizinin Kavramsal Temelleri. In A. Bayrakdaroğlu & A. Gündoğdu (Eds.), *Güncel Yaklaşımlarla Yatırım Projelerinin Değerlendirilmesinde Ekonomik Analizler. Kavram - Yapı - Uygulama* (2nd ed.). Seçkin.

Güneş, T., & Apaydin, A. (2021). Mortgage volume and macroeconomic factors: Evidence from Turkey. *Business & Management Studies: An International Journal, 9*, 1504–1520.

GYODER. (2022a). *Gyoder Gösterge: Türkiye Gayrimenkul Sektörü 2022*, 2.Çeyrek Raporu - Sayı:29.

GYODER. (2022b). REstate Turkey: A Close Look at Comparable Markets, Issue 6, GYODER and Colliers.

Haight, G. T., & Singer, D. D. (2005). *The real estate investment handbook*. John Wiley & Sons.

Hepşen, A., Berberoglu, M. G., & Aydin, O. (2017). Real estate investment trusts in Turkey: Structure, analysis, and strategy. *Journal of Business Economics and Finance, 6*, 191–199.

Kalyoncu, H., Tuluce, N., & Yaprak, Z. (2015). Determinants of foreign direct investment: An empirical analysis for Turkey. *Journal of Economic and Social Studies, 5*.

Larsson, C. F. (2013). What did Frederick the great know about financial engineering? A survey of recent covered bond market developments and research. *The North American Journal of Economics and Finance, 25*, 22–39.

Mcgreevy, P., & Eldred, G. W. (2006). *Investing in real estate*. John Wiley & Sons.

Özdemir Sari, Ö. B. (2019). Redefining the housing challenges in Turkey: An urban planning perspective. In *Urban and regional planning in Turkey*. Springer.
Pagliari, J. L., Jr. (2020). Real estate returns by strategy: Have value-added and opportunistic funds pulled their weight? *Real Estate Economics, 48*, 89–134.
STB. (2024). *Uluslararası Doğrudan Yatırım Girişleri (Net Yükümlülük Oluşumu), Sanayi ve Teknoloji Bakanlığı (STB) - The Ministry of Industry and Technology* [Online]. https://sanayi.gov.tr/istatistikler/yatirim-istatistikleri/mi0803011615 [Accessed].
Tanrivermiş, H. (2019). *Gayrimenkul Projelerinin Stratejik Planlaması*. Lisansüstü Eğitim Ders Notları.
Tanrivermiş, H. (2020). Possible impacts of COVID-19 outbreak on real estate sector and possible changes to adopt: A situation analysis and general assessment on Turkish perspective. *Journal of Urban Management, 9*, 263–269.
Tanrivermiş, H., & Tanrivermiş, Y. (2022). *Gayrimenkul EKonomisi ve Yönetimi Dersnotu*. Ankara Üniversitesi Fen Bilimleri Enstittüsü Gayrimenkul Geliştirme ve Yönetimi Anabilim Dalı.
Tuhral, M., & Psilander, K. (2005). *Real estate development process in Turkey*. Royal Institute of Technology.
Türel, A., & Koç, H. (2015). Housing production under less-regulated market conditions in Turkey. *Journal of Housing and the Built Environment, 30*, 53–68.
Turk, S. S. (2007). An analysis on the efficient applicability of the land readjustment (LR) method in Turkey. *Habitat International, 31*, 53–64.
TURKSTAT. (2024a). *Consumer price index (2003=100) according to main and sub-main groups, 2005–2024* [Online]. https://data.tuik.gov.tr/Kategori/GetKategori?p=Enflasyon-ve-Fiyat-106 [Accessed].
TURKSTAT. (2024b). *Distribution of non-institutional population by equivalised household disposable median income groups and problems with the dwelling and environment, 2006–2023* [Online]. https://data.tuik.gov.tr/Bulten/Index?p=Yoksulluk-ve-Yasam-Kosullari-Istatistikleri-2023-53713 [Accessed].
TURKSTAT. (2024c). *House sales by type and state, 2013–2024* [Online]. https://data.tuik.gov.tr/Bulten/Index?p=Konut-Satis-Istatistikleri-Mart-2024-53767 [Accessed].
TURKSTAT. (2024d). *House sales to foreigners, 2013–2024* [Online]. https://data.tuik.gov.tr/Bulten/Index?p=Konut-Satis-Istatistikleri-Haziran-2024-53760 [Accessed].
Ulusoy, T. (2018). Yatırım Projelerinin Ulusal Ekonomi Açısından Değerlendirilmesi: Ekonomik Analiz (Toplumsal Karlılık Analizi). In A. Gündoğdu & A. Bayrakdaroğlu (Eds.), *Güncel Yaklaşımlarla Yatırım Projelerinin Değerlendirilmesinde Ekonomik Analizler. Kavram - Yapı - Uygulama* (2nd ed.). Seçkin.
Yalçiner, K. (2006). *İpotek Karşılığı Menkulleştirilmiş Krediler Mortgage (İKMEK-MORTGAGE)*. Gazi Kitabevi.
Yanar, R., & Demir, C. Ş. (2022). Döviz Kurundaki Değişimlerin Yabanci Konut Talebine Etkileri: Türkiye Örneği. *İşletme Ekonomi ve Yönetim Araştırmaları Dergisi, 5*, 56–71.
Zoğal, V., & Emekli, G. (2020). Türkiye'de Covid-19 Salgini SürecInde İkIncI Konutlarin DeğIşen Anlamlari. *International Journal of Geography and Geography Education*, 168–181.

Gizem Ulusoy is a research assistant at the Department of Real Estate Development and Management, Faculty of Applied Sciences, Ankara University, Türkiye. She completed her high school education at Ankara Atatürk Anatolian High School and obtained a bachelor's degree in international relations from the Faculty of Political Sciences at Ankara University. Subsequently, she engaged in professional endeavours across various institutions within both the private and public sectors, before she was appointed a research assistant at Ankara University. She completed her master's degree, presenting a thesis titled "The Role and Importance of International Real Estate Investment in Emerging Economies" at the Ankara University Department of Real Estate Development and Management. Currently, Gizem Ulusoy is pursuing her doctoral studies in the same department and has authored publications on international real estate investments.

Üstün Hatipoğlu earned his Bachelor of Science degree from the Middle East Technical University Civil Engineering Department, his master's degree from the same department, and his Ph.D. degree from the Real Estate Development and Management Department at Ankara University. From 1989 to 1998, he served as an engineer, construction manager, and project manager for various private enterprises. In 1998, he began his tenure at one of Türkiye's largest private banks, where he concluded his service in the Construction and Real Estate Department in 2018. He held the position of Director of the Education Academy from 2020 to 2021 under the Turkish Appraisers Association (TDUB). Between 2019 and 2021, he was engaged as a Guest Lecturer at Kadir Has University. Since 2021, Dr. Hatipoğlu has served as General Coordinator at a real estate appraisal firm.

Amani Micheal Uisso is an expert in the fields of real estate development, urban transformation, and land management, boasting an extensive academic and professional career that spans both Tanzania and Türkiye. He holds a Doctorate and a master's degree in real estate development and management from Ankara University, Türkiye, along with a bachelor's degree in Land Management and Valuation from Ardhi University, Tanzania. Dr. Uisso's research centres on urban development, land management, and administration, providing valuable insights to the discipline through numerous publications. His work effectively bridges academic rigour with practical applications, addressing significant challenges in urban transformation and sustainable land use. Currently, Dr. Uisso holds a position within the President's Office, where he applies his expertise to inform policy and strategic initiatives. In addition to his contributions to public service, he is a certified real estate appraiser and a highly sought-after consultant in real estate development, offering specialised guidance to projects that shape urban environments. With a steadfast commitment to advancing knowledge and practice in the fields of real estate and urban development, Dr. Uisso consistently and significantly contributes to both academia and industry.

Tuğba Güneş holds a Bachelor of Science and a Master of Science degree in statistics. She completed her Doctorate in the Department of Real Estate Development and Management at Ankara University, concentrating on studies related to real estate finance and automated valuation models. She dedicated one year of her doctoral program as a visiting scholar in the Land Economy Department at the University of Cambridge. Dr. Güneş is a licensed property appraiser and has been employed as a statistician with senior expertise in mass valuation at the General Directorate of Land Registry and Cadastre in Türkiye. Furthermore, she actively contributes to property valuation and taxation projects endorsed by the World Bank. Her research interests include property valuation, real estate economics and finance, urban economics, and the applications of machine learning.

Real Estate Investment Funds, Investment Options, and the Requirements of Islamic Funds in Türkiye

Gülnaz Şengül Güneş, Monsurat Ayojimi Salami, and Erol Demir

Abstract

This chapter examines real estate investment funds (REIFs) as the investment options available for Islamic funds in Türkiye. Quarterly and long-term net asset value (NAV) data were obtained to analyse the correlation and long-term relationships between several variables. A generalised method of moments (GMM) model is employed to estimate a dynamic panel regression. Furthermore, the information gathered on Türkiye REIFs (T-REIFs) has enabled the categorisation of T-REIF companies into three broad investment options: conventional REIFs, full-fledged Islamic REIFs, and hybrid T-REIF windows, in which investors in T-REIFs can invest. The findings indicate that not all T-REIFs have made substantial investments in the real estate sectors. Additionally, the portfolio diversification of these T-REIFs is markedly different from that of other T-REIFs. Some T-REIFs have experienced a sudden price increase, while others have appreciated only gradually. The findings also show that lagged T-REIF prices, time deposits, public debt instruments, and investments in various sectors have a significant impact on current price movements in T-REIFs (Islamic T-REIFs). However, real estate investment (REI) did not significantly predict price movements in T-IREIFs. In contrast, REI and time deposits exert a significant impact on price movements in conventional T-REIFs (T-CREIFs). Future event studies, along with improved data, are recommended.

G. Ş. Güneş · M. A. Salami (✉) · E. Demir
Department of Real Estate Development and Management, Faculty of Applied Sciences, Ankara University, Ankara, Türkiye
e-mail: gsengul@ankara.edu.tr; masalami@ankara.edu.tr; eroldemir@ankara.edu.tr

T. Just et al. (eds.), *Understanding Türkiye's Real Estate Markets*, Management for Professionals, https://doi.org/10.1007/978-3-032-13297-0_16

Keywords
Turkish Real Estate Investment Funds (T-REIFs) · Turkish Conventional REIFs (T-CREIFs) · Turkish full-fledged Islamic REIFs (full-fledged T-IREIFs) · Hybrid T-REIFs Windows (T-CREIFs and T-IREIFs)

1 Introduction

Real estate has rapidly developed in this century, and it has become a distinctive asset which is growing steadily in several countries, including Türkiye (Aliefendioglu et al., 2021; Çamlibel et al., 2021; Tanrivermiş, 2020), China (Hong, 2014), and many other countries. As real estate is relatively illiquid, real estate investment funds (REIFs) address the sector's illiquidity challenges. A REIF is an investment vehicle that appeals to high-net-worth investors across all markets. A REIF provides opportunities for qualified investors to invest in real estate assets through REIFs with low risk. Besides risk mitigation, investors could use their limited investment capital to benefit from the performance of several properties in which REIFs are invested. Investors can include real estate in their portfolios (Pivo, 2009) either directly owning physical real estate or investing in shares of listed real estate companies (Wang et al., 2009). In addition, Fachrudin and Fachrudin (2015) listed a set of properties, including flats, land, shopping centres, dry ports, shops, apartments, office towers, residential houses, hospitality services, and infrastructure, that could be invested in.

However, the policy guiding investments in real estate varies across countries. For instance, Morri and Lee (2009) reported that managing companies in some European markets, such as Germany and Italy, made some of their real estate products available only to private investors or institutional investors. In Türkiye, qualified investors, as defined according to the Communiqué on Principles regarding Mutual Funds and the Communiqué on the Principles of Sales and Distribution and Delivery of Capital Market Instruments, are *"domestic and foreign investment funds, pension funds, investment partnerships, intermediary institutions, banks, insurance companies, portfolio management companies, mortgage finance institutions, retirement and aid funds, foundations, public benefits associations, funds established under the temporary Article 20 of the Social Security Law No. 506, and other investors to be defined by the board according to the similarity of these institutions in terms of their qualification."* Similarly, qualified investors are natural and legal persons who own at least TL one million and/or foreign currency and capital market instruments on the date of a public offering of their fund participation shares. As a result, only investors who meet the required criteria are considered. Still, the number of shares sold to the investors in REIFs may vary, and qualified investors obtain participation certificates to indicate their investment shares. Investors in REIFs typically manage direct investments in real estate, companies within the real estate sector, or both.

REIFs invest directly in an investment vehicle (Mattarocci & Siligardos, 2012), which could be generally defined as assets where savings are collected in a pool and investments are made in real estate by professionals. Savings can be in the form of money, real estate, independent sections within the scope of real estate projects as specified in the third paragraph of Article 18, or rights based on real estate. These are the assets regulated and audited by the Capital Markets Board in Türkiye, which appeal to domestic and foreign savers. Here, all shareholders benefit in proportion to their shares. In other words, REIFs are a corporate structure that allows individual savings to be bundled and evaluated collectively by real estate investment professionals. At the same time, sufficient attention should be given to best practices and professionalism in the real estate sector. Jadevicius (2020) identified non-listed real estate investment best practices and professionalism as features that attract investors, elevating them to major real estate investment conduits.

Despite this, the funds do not have a legal personality; they can only have a limited legal personality applicable to title deed registration procedures. Similarly, earnings from investments are distributed over the fund. REIFs can be established for a term or an indefinite period and are categorised into different types based on specific features, including the number of shares. Therefore, REIFs are funds that manage inter alia income-producing commercial real estate, such as shopping centres, hospitals, plantations, industrial properties, hotels, and office blocks (Abd-Sukor et al., 2020). However, REIFs can also be invested in non-real estate assets. With a broad range of investment opportunities, REIFs can diversify and thus generate better returns for investors, even though dividend payments are not mandatory for Turkish REIFs (T-REIFs). According to Erol and Tirtiroglu (2011), T-REIFs are unique because dividend payments are not mandatory, and investors can still enjoy tax exemptions.

This chapter focuses on Türkiye's REIFs for several reasons. Firstly, although real estate investment in Türkiye is growing fast, the introduction of REIFs is relatively recent compared to some developed countries. Secondly, there are only a few studies on T-REITs compared to REITs. Thirdly, none of these studies on T-REIFs examines the correlation or investigates the price determination of REIFs based on their investment allocation. Therefore, T-REIFs are classified into broader forms of investment options. The perspective of available investment options, along with empirical findings based on the available information, may help to reduce ambiguity about where investors can invest.

The remainder of this chapter is structured as follows: Sect. 2 discusses T-REIFs, and Sect. 3 explains the investment options for T-REIFs. Section 4 presents a literature review of international REIF studies; Sect. 5 presents the data and methodology; Sect. 6 reveals our analyses of T-REIF requirements and the empirical results; Sect. 7 discusses these results and concludes.

2 Real Estate Investment Funds (REIFs) in Türkiye

REIFs have been available in developed and developing countries for several decades (Schacht & Wimschulte, 2008). In 2014, the concept of REIFs was brought to Türkiye with the 'Communiqué on Principles Regarding Real Estate Investment Funds', which summarises the features that should be included in the REIFs:

(i) Funds can have a certain period or can be established indefinitely.
(ii) The authority to establish funds is given to portfolio management or real estate portfolio management companies.
(iii) The portfolio manager or founder manages the fund in accordance with the principles of fiduciary ownership.
(iv) Savers who provide cash flow to the fund must consist of qualified investors.
(v) Savers are given participation shares in return for the funds they have collected.
(vi) The fund lacks a legal personality.
(vii) The fund's acquisition of legal personality is limited to transactions involving title deeds.

Although some of these features of T-REIFs are universal and found also in other countries, there are country-specific features of REIFs.

3 Investment Options in Real Estate Investment Funds (REIFs)

Regarding country-specific differences, investment options in REIFs may be similar to those in other countries or distinct from them. REIF investment options are the REIFs in which qualified real estate fund investors can invest. As presented in Table 1, there are several direct real estate segments in which T-REIFs could invest, with capital gains or rental income being the primary objectives of investing. Similarly, in the Western world, where REIFs originated (Schacht & Wimschulte, 2008), Islamic finance is recently gaining new attention. Therefore, previous real estate investment options did not account for the Islamic classification of the funds as a separate option. Earlier investment options in REIFs were viewed from several perspectives, such as open-end REIFs, closed-end REIFs, leasing REIFs, and opportunity REIFs (Schacht & Wimschulte, 2008). Open-end REIFs and closed-end REIFs are the most common among these investment options. Most of the newly introduced REIFs made available to investors are due to the level of development of a country. In general, open-end REIFs are more liquid than closed-end REIFs (Schacht & Wimschulte, 2008), whereas closed-end REIFs used to constitute a larger proportion of REIFs than open-end REIFs for many years. These classifications suggest that investment options in REIFs are not rigid but rather flexible, allowing them to be more readily tailored to suit each country's unique characteristics. In China, a proposition for the pilot REIFs has been made, and it has been concluded that they can only be operated under special regulations (Wang et al., 2009).

In Türkiye, the classifications of REIF investment options in Table 1 are very broad, as the goal is either to gain appreciation or rental income, which does not account for investors' beliefs or preferences and fails to meet the necessary conditions of this research purpose. If investors' value expectations are considered, the classification of investment options in T-REIFs can be viewed differently from the Western world's approach. The effort to nurture investment options in T-REIFs from

Table 1 Türkiye real estate investment options based on years of establishment of T-REIFs

REIFs	Year of establishment	Real estate properties	Goal
T-REIF-1	2017	Strategic lands and landed properties	Gain appreciation
T-REIF-2	2018	Strategic lands and landed properties	Gain appreciation
T-REIF-3	2018	Shopping centres	Rental income
T-REIF-4	2019	Commercial real estate, mainly office space	Rental income
T-REIF-5	2020	Invested in various properties, especially housing, which is undervalued	Gain appreciation
T-REIF-6	2020	Investment in commercial real estate, land, residences, offices, shopping centres, hotels, logistics centres, warehouses, parking lots, dormitories, and hospitals	Rental income

Note that Table 1 broadly categorises investment options of REIFs in a general form without tailoring them to the preferences of investors' beliefs, which prevents this classification from meeting the expectations of this analysis. Deficiencies in this classification led to the development of more specific investment options in T-REITs, as presented in Table 2
Source: Authors' extraction from Çamlibel et al. (2021)

the perspective of *Shariah* (Islamic law) provides the authors with the opportunity to further classify T-REIF investment options into three categories, namely, Turkish conventional REIFs (T-CREIFs), Turkish full-fledged Islamic REIFs (full-fledged T-IREIFs) and hybrid T-REIF windows (T-IREIFs and T-CREIFs). The primary distinction between conventional and Islamic REIFs lies in their adherence to Shariah principles (Sukor et al., 2020).

T-CREIFs are REIFs that do not consider Shariah as a guiding principle for direct investment in real estate and other sectors. In other words, T-CREIFs may hold direct investments in Shariah- and non-Shariah-compliant real estate projects, as well as other non-Shariah-compliant investments. Non-Shariah compliant real estate projects are those assets that are used for gambling, alcohol and intoxicant-related businesses, and any other companies considered unlawful investments from the perspective of Shariah. From an Islamic perspective, those businesses are forbidden, and any income generated from them is considered impure and cannot be used for further investment or growth. On the other hand, full-fledged T-IREIFs are those T-REIFs that directly invest in only Shariah-compliant real estate properties and consider Shariah rulings before investing in other sectors. At the same time, hybrid T-REIFs are REIF companies that invest in both conventional and Islamic REIFs. Practising hybrid T-REIF windows may have several reasons, ranging from the fund's willingness to meet the needs of different qualified investors to preventing the loss of some investors who prefer one REIF to another.

This classification, which utilises investors' perspectives, is justifiable because qualified investors are the pillar for the success of REIFs. This classification of investment options in REIFs may also help to address the issue of investor

Table 2 T-REIFs investment options based on investors' preferences

Investment options		Companies	REIFs	Code
Conventional REIFs (T-CREIFs)		Akfen real estate PMC	Birinci	ABI
		Neo PMC	Birinci	VVF
		Omurga real estate and venture capital company	İkinci	OG1
			Ufuk karma	OG2
Full-fledged T-IREIFs		24 real estate PMC	Altın Başak	YD1
			Al Zamil Kira Getirili	YD2
			Primo	YD3
			Portakal Çiçeği	YD4
			A1	YD5
			İkinci Al Zamil Kira Getirili	YD7
		Albaraka real estate PMC	One tower	AG6
			Batışehir	AG8
			Dükkan	AG5
			Metropol	AG7
		Arz real estate and venture capital company	Birinci	AZ1
			İkinci	AZ2
			Üçüncü	AZ3
			Dördüncü	AZ6
			Beşinci	AZ7
		Aura PMC	Konut alfa	UKA
		Fiba PMC	Re-pie	FRG
		Ak PMC	İkinci	IKG
		Mükafat PMC	Ataşehir Metropol	MPG
		Oyak PMC	Birinci	OGM
		Qinvest PMC	Re-pie	ERP
Hybrid T-REIF windows	T-IREIFs windows	Is PMC	Quasar İstanbul Konut Katılım	IIK
		Re-pie PMC	Anadolu Stratejik	RP2
			Milenyum	RP5
			Novada Urfa	RP1
			Avrupa Stratejik	RP3
			Avrasya Stratejik	RP4
			Asya Stratejik	RAS

Note that hybrid T-REIF windows offer REIFs that are designed to cater to various categories of qualified investors. At the same time, T-CREIFs and T-IREIFs focus on specific categories of investors who prefer the direct real estate investment strategies offered by their form. Table 2 presents three companies that provide T-CREIFs, nine companies that offer full-fledged T-IREIFs, and several companies that provide hybrid T-REIFs, enabling the adoption of both T-IREIFs and T-CREIFs within REIF companies. It was later discovered that five hybrid T-CREIF windows, including KL2 (2017Q3-2019Q2), YD6 (2018Q3-2019Q4), GTG (2018Q3-2019Q1), KL1 (2018Q3-2019Q2), and MBG (2018Q4-2020Q1), had stopped functioning
Source: Own compilation

confidence in the emerging real estate market. Today, a lack of investor confidence is highly detrimental to emerging real estate markets (Onofrei & Anghel, 2012). In addition, Wang et al. (2009) proposed the need to attract institutional and retail investors for the survival of the first REIFs in China. Similarly, Hoesli and Lekander (2006) noted that the long-term benefits and risk-adjusted returns of investing in property are among the key features that attract institutional investors to real estate investments. Furthermore, the essentiality of qualified investors in REIFs is also traced to the lack of institutional investors such as 'insurance companies, pension funds, unit trusts, and investment trusts' in the Romanian real estate development market before 2005, which was argued to have prevented the functionality of the market during the period (Onofrei & Anghel, 2012). As a result, the classification of investment options in REIFs based on investors' value perception would allow qualified investors to invest their capital based on their beliefs and have some expectations that such REIFs should meet.

Table 2 provides details of T-REIFs based on qualified investors, categorised by value-based beliefs. With several REIFs catering to various categories of investors, newly identified T-REIF investment options in this study may become more appealing to these investors. This could eventually serve as a strong strategy to drive growth despite the relatively recent emergence of T-REIFs. This classification also allows the authors to identify five T-REIFs throughout this analysis.

4 Related Studies on REITs

Real estate investments have been widely studied, and the majority of the studies focus on REITs (see, e.g., Yat-Hung et al., 2008; Ong et al., 2012; Yuksel, 2016; Almudhaf & Hansz, 2018; Sukor et al., 2020; Capellán et al., 2021). Even though studies on REIFs are rare (see, e.g., Jadevicius, 2020; Çamlibel et al., 2021) researchers used the findings from the REIT studies to support their conclusions in the REIF studies. The findings could also be attributed to the fact that REITs and REIFs have more similarities than differences. This also holds for studies on T-REIFs, where some studies have measured the behaviours of REIF managers and the performance of REIFs (Şengül Güneş, 2020; Şengül Güneş & Tanrıvermiş, 2020).

Furthermore, available studies either investigate the relationship between real estate investment and other financial assets (Tsai & Chiang, 2013; Yuksel, 2016), evaluate the volatility of real estate investment (Brown & Klingenberg, 2015; Jain et al., 2017), or compare cross-border REIT prices and performance (Quek & Ong, 2008).

Yuksel (2016) employed a co-integration approach to examine the relationship between real estate and stock prices, using daily data on REITs, interest rates, and stock prices during the 2008 global financial crisis. The analysis concluded that the long-run equilibrium was no longer maintained after the outbreak of the global financial crisis. Furthermore, the correlation between real estate and stock prices has been extensively studied using data from developed nations, such as the United

States and the United Kingdom (Eichholtz & Hartzell, 1996; Ibbotson & Siegel, 1984).

Yat-Hung et al. (2008) investigate the correlation between real estate investment trusts (REITs), real assets, and financial assets, such as stocks and bonds, in developed markets. Although their findings show that REITs can provide diversification benefits in a multi-asset portfolio, they caution against viewing them as a perfect substitute for direct property investment.

Almudhaf and Hansz (2018) studied the behaviour of REIT subsectors using 21 years of data from 1994 to 2015. They employed a variance ratio test to conclude that different REIT subsectors behave differently, as aggressive investments characterise some, while others are more recession-resistant. Furthermore, they supported the application of technical trading rules rather than the 'buy and hold' approach in subsectors.

Ong et al. (2012) examined the performance of conventional and Islamic REITs in Malaysia, from 2005 to 2010, using the Treynor and Sharpe models. The study concluded that REITs were negatively affected during the Global Financial Crisis (GFC) but outperformed during the post-GFC period. Recently, Salami et al. (2023) examined T-REITs using data from the COVID-19 pandemic, applying Treynor and Sharpe models to establish that the REITs underperformed during the pandemic, characterised by persistently high volatility, volatility clustering, and an asymmetric impact of shocks.

Sukor et al. (2020) obtained quarterly data from 13 conventional and Islamic REITs, conducting multiple regression analyses that revealed Islamic REITs exhibit better diversification than conventional REITs. In addition, Jadevicius (2020) also demonstrated that developed markets, such as Europe, the USA, and the Asia-Pacific, maintain a globally diversified core real estate fund portfolio.

The portfolio diversification benefits of T-IREIFs have not been systematically investigated. Alcock et al. (2013) also noted that, despite numerous studies on real estate, a research study on the drivers of the return-generating process is still lacking in private equity real estate. In support of quantifying the investment allocation of T-REIFs in relation to price determination, emphasis has been placed on reliably, consistently, and transparently pricing real estate, a major concern for several stakeholders, including national governments, the valuation profession, and the public (Roulac et al., 2006). To extend previous findings on REIFs, this chapter aims to fill gaps by examining the extent of portfolio diversification of T-REIFs through their series of investment allocations and quantifying the determinants of T-REIF pricing. Therefore, the following hypotheses have been developed:

H_1: There is uncertainty about the investment allocation of T-IREIFs.

H_2: The price of T-IREIFs is correlated with direct real estate investment (REI) and investment in other sectors.

H_3: There is a long-run relationship between T-IREIF's price and Time Deposit (TD) and Public Debt Instruments (PDI).

To the best of the authors' knowledge, and as can be inferred from the preceding discussion, the magnitude of the correlation between the investment allocation and the price of REIFs or the investment allocation responsible for driving the prices of REIFs has been examined before. This is supported by the argument presented in the study by Roulac et al. (2006) regarding the research gap in the contribution of real estate investment to predicting realised returns.

5 Data and Methodology

We obtained quarterly data on T-REIF's net asset value (NAV) in Turkish currency (TL) as well as the percentage of their investment allocations from the website www.tcmb.gov.tr, covering the period from Q3 2016 to Q4 2020. The data obtained was unbalanced due to the different times T-REIFs were introduced. Fourteen REIF companies were examined and further classified into 3 T-CREIFs, 9 full-fledged T-IREIFs, and 2 hybrid T-IREIFs, which had issued a total of 32 individual T-REIFs. The amount invested in each fund for each quarter was estimated based on the percentage of each investment allocation. T-REIFs allocated their investment capital to real investment (REI), time deposit (TD), public debt instruments (PDI), and other sectors (Other_Sectors) during the study period.

Before the analysis, the quarterly invested amount in each sector was converted into a logarithmic value. At the same time, the unit price of REIFs was expressed in currency terms to reflect the price changes over the study period in TL.

$$\text{lnAsset allocated value in TL}_{\text{it}} = \log\left(\text{Asset allocated value}\right) \tag{1}$$

For the main analysis, we used the Generalised Method of Moments (GMM) estimator developed by Blundell and Bond (1998) to investigate the dynamic relationship between T-REIFs prices and selected explanatory variables. The GMM estimator was chosen over other estimators for two reasons. Firstly, the OLS estimator ignores the panel data structure; second, by incorporating a lag variable, this model mitigates the high persistence effects of explanatory variables and controls for endogeneity bias (Aslam & Haron, 2020). The model is suitable as it alleviates the problem of weak instrumental variables associated with a single GMM estimator (Nguyen et al., 2014). Therefore, the influence of regressors on the dependent variable is expressed in the regression model below:

$$\begin{aligned} T-REIFs_{it} &= \alpha_0 + \beta_1 T-REIFs_{it-1} + \beta_2 REI_{it} + \beta_3 TD_{it} + \beta_4 PDI_{it} + \beta_5 Other\_Sectors_{it} \\ &+ \sum_{k=1}^{p} REI_{it} + \sum_{k=1}^{q} TD_{it} + \sum_{k=1}^{r} PDI_{it} + \sum_{k=1}^{s} Other\_Sectors_{it} + \varepsilon_{it} \end{aligned} \tag{2}$$

where the dependent variable $T - REIFs_{it}$ is the price of REIF i in the quarter t in TL. The parameters to be estimated are β_1, β_2, β_3, β_4, and β_5 to quantify the relationship between the lag of T-REIFs, investment directly in real estate (REI), time deposits (TD), public debt instruments (PDI), investment in other sectors

(Other_Sectors), and the price of T-REIFs. There is no standard a priori expectation for the magnitude and sign of parameters to be estimated other than that the findings for both T-IREIFs and T-CREIFs are not expected to converge. This is because IREIFs have additional guiding principles that differ from those guiding CREIFs.

After performing diagnostic tests on the instrument's validity, heteroskedasticity, and serial correlation, a dynamic one-step system GMM estimator was chosen as the best model. Similarly, the GMM estimator supports a small sample size, and it is supported by Ledhem (2020).

To better understand the data, we presented descriptive statistics and a correlation matrix and ran a dynamic panel regression of the studied variables. The standard deviation of each asset allocated was used to explain the level of uncertainty in T-REIFs' prices and investment in REI, TD, PDI, and CB, as well as Other_Sectors. Brown and Klingenberg (2015) considered uncertainty an inherent problem related to future investment income, capital, or both. Similarly, the correlation coefficient between the price of T-REIFs and the explanatory variables is used to predict the degree of diversification of T-REIFs' portfolios.

6 Requirements of Islamic Real Estate Investment Funds in Türkiye

There is no legislation specifically for Islamic REIFs in Türkiye. However, when the foundation charter of the fund states that investments will be made in accordance with Islamic principles, the fund is managed in accordance with Islamic law (Shariah). With the money or real estate collected from qualified investors, a fund could be established on behalf of the shareholders to operate a portfolio of real estate rights, comprising real estate, cash, and capital market instruments, in accordance with the principles outlined in the certificate of authorisation, incorporating Islamic finance principles. The primary difference here is that real estate and other investments must conform to the approved portfolio, as indicated by a certificate approved by the advisory board.

The strategy can differ by fund. Generally, the main strategy of the fund is to invest in various types of real estate assets, including land, commercial real estate, residences, fields, dwellings, offices, shopping centres, hotels, logistics centres, warehouses, parks, parking lots, dormitories, hospitals, and other approved assets, as determined by the Board. This would increase the value of the fund portfolio, leading to a capital gain or rental income. For this purpose, the fund may purchase, sell, rent, and lease real estate or execute preliminary sales or purchase contracts accordingly. Stock shares and real estate certificates of joint-stock companies and other real estate investment funds can also be purchased.

Shariah-compliant real estate refers to property dedicated to and utilised by Shariah-compliant businesses, which can generate income or appreciate in value. In some countries, dividend payments are mandatory, in which case a substantial portion of the realised profits should be distributed to investors. In Türkiye, most IREIFs have huge direct investments in real estate and few investments in other assets. However, the dividend payment is not mandatory for T-REITs (Salami et al., 2023).

Observations from T-IREIT's investment allocations suggest a lack of statistical evidence that IREIFs invested in the money market and reverse repo, potentially indicating non-compliance with Shariah principles. Similarly, different IREIFs invested in combining various assets while adhering to Shariah compliance. This has necessitated an investigation into whether the funds can effectively manage their investment allocation by examining the diversification benefits through the correlation matrix of each T-IREIF. Due to space constraints, a statistical summary report is available upon request; the main correlations of the T-IREIFs are presented in Table 3.

6.1 Correlation Result

Table 3 presents the correlations between the investment allocation and explanatory variables for both full-fledged T-IREIFs and hybrid T-IREIF windows and prices. Some variables exhibit a high correlation coefficient with IREIFs' prices and, as such, may have a significant impact on the price movement. This suggests that any highly correlated sector may experience significant fluctuations in the price of T-IREIFs. A correlation coefficient greater than 0.75 is considered highly correlated. Nearly all the T-IREIFs have a direct investment in REI except Altın Başak (YD1). The majority of T-IREIF prices are positively correlated with REI. This indicates significant fluctuations in the REI investment, which may be translated into a pattern of direction in which T-IREIF prices are likely to move. Similarly, the correlation between T-IREIFs prices and explanatory variables ranges from low to moderate, except for Altın Başak (YD1) and Milenyum (RP5), which exhibit a very high correlation coefficient between T-IREIFs prices and investment in other sectors, at $r = 0.963$ and $r = 0.976$, respectively. This implies that if a significant shock affects investment in various sectors, the prices of T-IREIFs may be substantially impacted.

Similarly, the number of sectors in which T-IREIFs are invested is also crucial in mitigating risk, as it can serve as a means to diversify the portfolio. A T-REIFs portfolio with a low to medium correlation in the opposite direction is generally considered a diversified portfolio. For instance, all AGs, Ataşehir Metropol (MPG), Birinci (OGM), and Avrupa Stratejik (RP3) IREIFs may be regarded as well-diversified T-IREIFs because their investments are allocated across several sectors with varying magnitudes and directions of correlation. In other words, T-IREIFs with direct investment allocated across several sectors, each with different magnitudes and correlation directions, are regarded as diversified IREIFs. However, the degree of its efficiency may vary depending on several factors: More or less, all T-IREIFs are diversified, but the degree of diversification may differ substantially. This is supported by the fact that REIT companies tend to vary in risk levels (Almudhaf & Hansz, 2018). Lodging REITs are regarded as aggressive investments, while

Table 3 Nonlinear correlations (Spearman Rank) T-IREIFs

	Correlation of investment allocation in T-IREIFs with T-REIFs prices							
T-IREIFs	Code	P	REI	TD	PDI	CB	Other_Sectors	Investors
Altın Başak	YD1	1			−0.274		0.963	1
Al Zamil Kira Getirili	YD2	1	0.802		0.077		0.171	1
Primo	YD3	1	0.979		0.306		0.087	14
Portakal Çiçeği	YD4	1	0.289		−0.058		0.009	12
A1	YD5	1	0.939		0.290		−0.261	3
İkinci Al Zamil Kira Getirili	YD7	1	0.411		−0.274		0.489	1
One tower	AG6	1	0.758	−0.436	0.149	0.124	0.139	28
Batışehir	AG8	1	−0.150	0.036	0.364	0.283	0.004	81
Dükkan	AG5	1	0.448	−0.589	−0.427	0.024	0.176	16
Metropol	AG7	1	0.890	−0.099	0.055		0.226	5
Birinci	AZ1	1	0.868	−0.507		0.507	0.429	20
İkinci	AZ2	1	0.909	−0.225		0.506	0.492	16
Dördüncü	AZ6	1	−0.600			0.894	0.100	5
Üçüncü	AZ3	1	0.764				−0.473	9
Konut alfa Katılım	UKA	1	0.177				0.100	13
Re-pie	FRG	1	0.900				−0.300	15
Ataşehir Metropol	MPG	1	0.350	−0.228	−0.555	0.678	0.733	9
İkinci	IKG	1	0.941	−0.511	−0.367	−0.430	0.448	16
Birinci	OGM	1	0.593		−0.314	0.334	−0.401	27
Re-pie	ERP	1	0.967	−0.320			−0.083	14
Avrupa Stratejik	RP3	1	0.166	0.174	−0.640		0.133	13

Quasar İstanbul Konut Katılım	IIK	1	0.536	0.464			−0.107	19
Anadolu Stratejik	RP2	1	0.732				0.446	46
Milenyum	RP5	1	0.533				0.976	5
Novada Urfa	RP1	1	0.548				0.383	2
Avrasya Stratejik	RP4	1	0.406				0.154	16
Asya Stratejik	RAS	1	0.590				−0.488	4

Note: The correlation coefficient for AZ7 was not estimated due to the limited number of available data points. AZ7 has only 3 quarters of data. Therefore, the correlation coefficient of AZ7 REIF is missing in Table 3. In addition, *P* Price, *REI* Real Estate Investment, *TD* Time Deposit, *PDI* Public Debt Instruments, *CB* Corporate Bonds, *I* Investors 2022) healthcare, self-storage, and similar properties are considered recession-resistant (Block, 2012).

Furthermore, more qualified investors invested in full-fledged T-IREIFs relative to investors in hybrid T-IREIFs. This may suggest that qualified investors prefer REIFs with clear policies over hybrid T-REIF policies. Due to uncertainty in their investment returns, which may not be purely Islamic, qualified investors who prefer halal investment may not find hybrid T-REIFs companies appealing.

6.2 Regression Results

Next, we conducted dynamic regressions for both T-IREIFs and T-CREIFs using the GMM model. We conducted the Sagan diagnostic test and ran robust models. The Sagan test is performed to determine the validity of instrumental variables (Nguyen et al., 2014). Since the number of observations is relatively small, we could not proceed with a two-step model. Despite this, we conducted a robust model to prove that the findings are not spurious. We could not reject the null hypothesis:

- H_0: The Sagan Test is valid. The instrumental variable is valid; the instruments are uncorrelated, and the error terms are uncorrelated with the regressor and the explanatory variables.

The inability to reject the null hypothesis indicates that the model is correctly specified (Nguyen et al., 2014).

Table 4 presents the dynamic relationship between T-REIFs' prices and their investment-allocated sectors. The findings established that the price of T-IREIFs is predicted by the lag of the T-IREIFs' price, time deposits, public debt instruments, and investment in other sectors, but not by real estate investments. The finding shows that the lag of the T-IREIFs price predicts the price for the next quarter. As noticed, the prices of T-IREIFs either increase steadily, as in the case of YDs, AZs, AG7, UKA, IKG, OGM, IIK, RAS, and RP1-RP3, or prices jump, as in the case of AG5, AG6, AG8, FRG, MPG, ERP, and RP4, while only RP5 shows a pattern of price decrease for the period under consideration. This implies that T-IREIFs offer a diverse range of REIFs capable of meeting the needs of various categories of qualified investors. This feature may make T-REIF widely patronised by different qualified investors.

Interestingly, there is no significant relationship between the T-IREIFs price and the investment allocated to the REI parameter. This finding suggests that T-IREIFs focus on value gain and appreciation of real estate properties, which can be time-consuming. This finding further supports the idea that T-IREIFs are guided by *Shariah*. Therefore, their investment in real estate should be societal value-added rather than immediate or short-term profit. All of this may contribute to the insignificance of REI in predicting the current price of T-IREIFs. Furthermore, Almudhaf and Hansz (2018) argued that information efficiency differs within subsectors of

Table 4 Dynamic regression of T-IREIFs price and its investment allocated sectors

	T-IREIFs			T-CREIFs		
Variables	Coefficient	Z	*p*-value	Coefficient	Z	*p*-value
Constant	−300.2119	−0.92	0.356	0.2467	0.67	0.506
$Price_{(-1)}$	1.3037	4.05	0.0000	0.1781	0.66	0.512
REI	$1.11e^{-08}$	0.11	0.909	$1.80e^{-09}$	4.38	0.000
TD	$-2.75e^{-06}$	−3.45	0.001	$3.93e^{-08}$	1.73	0.084
PDI	$6.58\ e^{-07}$	2.97	0.003			
Other_Sectors	$2.47\ e^{-07}$	2.03	0.042			
Diagnostic						
χ^2	1.6061		0.6580	4.3584		0.3597
Wald test	40.57		0.0000	3.04		0.2192

Note that parameters such as Price, REI, TD, PDI, and Other_Sectors represent the unit price of REIFs, Real Estate Investment, Time Deposit, Public Debt Instrument, and REIFs in other sectors, respectively. T-IREIFs and T-CREIFs represent Turkish Islamic Real Estate Investment Funds and Turkish Conventional Real Estate Investment Funds, respectively

REIFs. This may support the reason behind some investment allocations of REIFs significantly predicting REIFs' price, while others do not.

Additionally, the finding revealed a negative correlation between the current price of T-IREIFs and investment in a time deposit. This implies that T-IREIFs reduce their investment in TD as the price of T-IREIFs increases. This may also support the idea that T-IREIFs constantly observe their investments in various sectors and minimise non-*Shariah* investment activities. The finding further reveals an increase in the relationship between T-IREIFs' current price, public debt investment, and investment in other sectors. This indicates that increasing investment in public debt instruments and other sectors contributes to an increase in the current price of T-IREIFs. In addition, the significance of the lagged price indicates that T-IREIFs pricing displays a certain degree of predictability. A positive and significant relationship between T-IREIFs prices and PDI supports the raising of funds through public investments to finance real estate investment (Kıyılar & Hepşen, 2010).

Regarding T-CREIFs, REI and TD predict the current price of T-CREIFs at 1% and 10% significance levels, respectively; however, the price lag did not apply to T-CREIFs. Since T-CREIFs do not have additional restrictive guiding principles besides conventional rules on REIFs, this may not prevent them from investing in any real estate property and may easily contribute to an increase in T-CREIF prices.

The findings clearly show that the pricing determinant components of both T-IREIFs and T-CREIFs differ. The greater predictability of T-IREIF prices is likely the result of improved transparency in T-IREIF pricing, which is lacking in T-CREIF pricing, underscoring the need for greater transparency in achieving returns within the private equity real estate investment industry (Alcock et al., 2013). In addition, the significance of REI in T-CREIFs' pricing reveals the opportunity to invest in real estate as long as it fulfils profit maximisation rather than societal or community benefit. Furthermore, the inverse relationship between time deposits with T-IREIFs and T-CREIFs consistently supports *Shariah* principles guiding the type and nature of authorised investments permissible from an Islamic standpoint. Despite this, T-IREIFs may have a similar opportunity to invest in any sector under the law governing REIFs; however, T-IREIFs are restricted by Islamic law.

Table 5 presents a robust model for the pricing of T-IREIFs and T-CREIFs. All signs of estimated variables, as well as their level of statistical significance, remain stable. We ran one robust model for T-IREIFs and two robust models for T-CREIFs because the REI was not a significant predictor of T-IREIF prices; therefore, it was omitted. The models remained statistically significant and well-fitted. While both coefficients of the independent variables indicating the importance of T-CREIFs' price are significant, the model also fits when one variable is dropped. This implies that long-run findings demonstrating the relationship between T-REIFs and their investment allocation are not misleading.

7 Discussion and Conclusion

This chapter examined REIFs, investment options, and Islamic real estate investment fund requirements in Türkiye. We explored various classifications of investment options in REIFs and found that there are numerous classifications based on the extent of REIFs' development in a particular market or country. Since the success of T-REIFs heavily depends on qualified individual or institutional investors, we viewed investment options in T-REIFs from the perspective of investors. Thus, investment options in T-REIFs are broadly classified into T-CREIFs, full-fledged T-REIFs and hybrid T-REIF windows. The T-CREIFs are any REIFs that do not impose religious-related conditions as their guiding principles for investing in REIFs; rather, they are guided by Western rules and regulations. The full-fledged T-IREIFs are REIFs that only invest in real estate properties and are related based on the permissibility of Islamic law. The hybrid T-REIFs windows enable both T-REIFs and T-CREIFs to operate simultaneously within the same REIFs company.

We obtained quarterly net asset value (NAV) data for each T-REIF and used asset allocation percentages to estimate the investment allocated to each sector in which T-REIFs invested. We conducted a descriptive analysis to examine the behaviour of each investment allocated to different sectors. We further quantified the degree of correlation among the variables under study and then conducted a dynamic panel regression using the GMM method. The findings confirmed that the price determinants of T-IREIFs and T-CREIFs are not converging. The findings suggest that T-IREIFs are guided not only by Western rules and regulations but also by Islamic law, which restricts the types of investments into which T-IREIFs are permitted to venture. Clustering REIFs according to investors' perspectives provides an interesting finding which would not have been otherwise.

These findings filled the gaps in the REIFs literature, especially in the context of T-REIFs, and provided essential information to portfolio managers and policymakers. The main limitation of this study is the data constraint due to REIFs' relatively new status in Türkiye. Similarly, Yat-Hung et al. (2008) reported a data constraint, which they attributed to different market maturity levels across the countries they studied. Therefore, a future event study on T-REIFs is suggested.

Table 5 T-IREIFs price and T-CREIFs price: Robust models

	T-IREIFs			T-CREIFs					
Variables	Coeff.	Z	*p*-value	Coeff.	Z	*p*-value	Coeff.	Z	*p*-value
Constant	−53.3603	−0.30	0.764	0.9001	7.06	0.0000	1.0174	2.16	0.031
$Price_{(-1)}$	1.3105	5.05	0.0000	−0.0235	−0.25	0.800	0.1060	0.25	0.806
REI				$1.33e^{-09}$	4.57	0.0000			
TD	$-2.77e^{-06}$	−4.27	0.000				$-4.55e^{-08}$	−2.47	0.014
PDI	$6.50e^{-07}$	3.76	0.000						
Other sectors	$2.37e^{-07}$	3.48	0.000						
Diagnostic									
χ^2	2.4067		0.6614	19.2580		0.1553	6.5241		0.4800
Wald test	60.29		0.0000	0.06		0.8000	13.91		0.0010

Note that the definitions of the parameters are identical to those in Table 4

References

Abd-Sukor, M. E., Sujak, Z. A., & Noordin, K. (2020). Conventional REITs, Islamic REITs and macroeconomic variables in Malaysia : A review. *ISRA International Journal of Islamic Finance, 12*(1), 131–143.

Alcock, J., et al. (2013). The role of financial leverage in the performance of private equity real estate funds. *The Journal of Portfolio Management*, 99–110.

Aliefendioglu, Y., Tanrıvermiş, H., & Salami, M. A. (2021). House Price index (HPI) and COVID-19 pandemic shocks: Evidence from Turkey and Kazakhstan. *International Journal of Housing Markets and Analysis, 1*, 1–18.

Almudhaf, F., & Hansz, A. J. (2018). Random walks and market efficiency : Evidence from real estate investment trusts (REIT) subsectors. *International Journal of Strategic Property Management, 22*, 81–92.

Aslam, E., & Haron, R. (2020). The influence of corporate governance on intellectual capital efficiency : Evidence from Islamic banks of OIC countries. *Asian Journal of Accounting Research, 5*(2), 195–208.

Block, R. (2012). *Investing in REITs* (4th ed.). Wiley. https://doi.org/10.1002/9781119202325

Blundell, R., & Bond, S. (1998). Initial conditions and moment restrictions in dynamic panel data models. *Journal of Econometrics, 87*(1), 115–143.

Brown, R., & Klingenberg, B. (2015). Real estate risk: Heavy tail modelling using excel. *Journal of Property Investment and Finance, 33*(4), 393–407.

Çamlibel, M. E., Sümer, L., & Hepşen, A. (2021). Risk-return performance of real estate investment funds in Turkey, including the COVID-19 period. *International Journal of Strategic Property Management, 25*(4), 267–277.

Capellán, R. U., Ollero, J. L. S., & Pozo, A. G. (2021). The influence of the real estate investment trust in the real estate sector on the Costa del Sol. *European Research on Management and Business Economics, 27*(1), 1–13.

Eichholtz, P., & Hartzell, D. (1996). Property shares, appraisals and the stock market: An international perspective. *The Journal of Real Estate Finance and Economics, 12*, 163–178.

Erol, I., & Tirtiroglu, D. (2011). Concentrated ownership, no dividend payout requirement and capital structure of REITs : Evidence from Turkey. *Journal of Real Estate Finance Economics, 43*, 174–204.

Fachrudin, K. A., & Fachrudin, H. T. (2015). The study of investment portfolio management and sustainability of property and real estate companies in Indonesia stock exchange. In *2nd global conference on business and social Science-2015, GCBSS-2015, 17–18 September 2015, Bali, Indonesia* (Vol. 1, pp. 177–183).

Hoesli, M., & Lekander, J. (2006). Real estate portfolio strategy and product innovation in Europe. *Journal of Property Investment & Finance, 26*(2), 162–176.

Hong, L. (2014). The dynamic relationship between real estate investment and economic growth : Evidence from Prefecture City panel data in China. *IERI Procedia, 7*, 2–7.

Ibbotson, R., & Siegel, L. (1984). Real estate returns: A comparison with other investments. *AREUEA Journal, 12*, 219–241.

Jadevicius, A. (2020). Real estate portfolios—The case for globally diversified core property funds. *Journal of Property Investment & Finance, 38*(1), 82–86.

Jain, P., et al. (2017). Hospitality REITs and financial crisis: A comprehensive assessment of market quality. *Journal of Property Investment and Finance, 35*(3), 277–289.

Kıyılar, M., & Hepşen, A. (2010). Performance appraisal of real estate investment trusts (REITs): A practice in Istanbul stock exchange. *Yonetim, 21*(65), 11–23.

Ledhem, M. A. (2020). Does Sukuk financing boost economic growth? Empirical evidence from Southeast Asia. *PSU Research Review, 1*, 1–17.

Mattarocci, G., & Siligardos, G. (2012). Investor attention for retail and institutional investors : A test on the real estate market. *Journal of Property Investment and Finance, 31*(4), 314–328.

Morri, G., & Lee, S. L. (2009). The performance of Italian real estate mutual funds. *Journal of European Real Estate Research, 2*(2), 170–185.
Nguyen, D., Diaz-Rainey, I., & Gregoriou, A. (2014). Determinants of the capital structure of listed Vietnamese companies. *Journal of Southeast Asian Economies, 31*(3), 412–431.
Ong, T. S., et al. (2012). Malaysian real estate investment trusts : A performance and comparative. *International Journal of Economics and Finance, 4*(5), 73–84.
Onofrei, M., & Anghel, I. (2012). Risks and rewards of leverage in Romanian real estate investment. *Procedia - Economics and Finance, 3*(12), 481–488.
Pivo, G. (2009). Social and environmental metrics for US real estate portfolios sources of data and aggregation methods. *Journal of Property Investment and Finance, 27*(5), 481–510.
Quek, M. C. H., & Ong, S. E. (2008). Securitising China real estate : A tale of two China-centric REITs. *Journal of Property Investment and Finance, 26*(3), 247–274.
Roulac, S., et al. (2006). Real estate value: Creation and destruction. *Journal of Property Investment and Finance, 24*(6), 474–489.
Salami, M. A., Tanrıvermiş, H., & Tanrıvermiş, Y. (2023). Performance evaluation and volatility of Turkey REITs during COVID-19 pandemic. *Journal of Property Investment and Finance, 41*(5), 473–505. https://doi.org/10.1108/JPIF-02-2022-0017
Schacht, U., & Wimschulte, J. (2008). German property investment vehicles and the introduction of G-REITs : An analysis. *Journal of Property Investment and Finance, 26*(1), 232–246.
Şengül Güneş, G. (2020). Türkiye'de Borsada İşlem Gören Gayrimenkul Yatırım Fonlarının Performans Analizi. *Business & Management Studies: An International Journal, 8*(5), 4438–4462.
Şengül Güneş, G., & Tanrıvermiş, H. (2020). A research on real estate investment fund managers in Turkey. *Business and Economics Research Journal, 11*(2), 431–444.
Sukor, M. E. A., Sujak, Z. A., & Noordin, K. (2020). Conventional REITs, Islamic REITs and macroeconomic variables in Malaysia: A review. *ISRA International Journal of Islamic Finance, 12*(1), 131–143.
Tanrivermiş, H. (2020). Possible impacts of COVID-19 outbreak on real estate sector and possible changes to adopt: A situation analysis and general assessment on Turkish perspective. *Journal of Urban Management*, 1–7.
Tsai, M. S., & Chiang, S. L. (2013). The asymmetric price adjustment between REIT and stock markets in Asia-Pacific markets. *Economic Modelling, 32*(1), 91–99.
Wang, H., Sun, Y., & Chen, Y. (2009). Special considerations for designing pilot REITs in China. *Journal of Property Investment and Finance, 27*(2), 140–161.
Yat-Hung, C., Joinkey, S. C., & Bo-sin, T. (2008). Time-varying performance of four Asia-Pacific REITs. *Journal of Property Investment and Finance, 26*(3), 210–231.
Yuksel, A. (2016). Central Bank review the relationship between stock and real estate prices in Turkey : Evidence around the global financial crisis. *Central Bank Review, 16*(1), 33–40.

Gülnaz Şengül Güneş serves as a research assistant within the Department of Real Estate Development and Management at Ankara University. She holds a Ph.D. in Real Estate Development and Management, with an academic focus that encompasses sustainable real estate markets, real estate finance, real estate economics, and ESG-based investment instruments. Dr. Güneş has authored numerous articles and book chapters and has presented her work at international conferences. Her doctoral research concentrates on the development of a sustainability index for Türkiye's real estate markets. Furthermore, she has also held the position of visiting researcher at the University of Regensburg, facilitated by a TÜBİTAK 2214 fellowship programme.

Monsurat Ayojimi Salami is an assistant professor in the Department of Real Estate Development and Management, Faculty of Applied Sciences, Ankara University, Türkiye. She graduated from the International Islamic University Malaysia (IIUM) and served as a Postdoc fellow between 2018 and 2019 at the IIUM Institute of Islamic Banking and Finance (II*i*BF). She specialises in the fields of financial economics, Islamic finance, real estate finance and investment, digitalisation in real estate, tokenisation, smart contracts and proptech. She holds multiple international certifications, including the Certified Quantitative Risk Management (CQRM). She has made significant contributions to over 50 academic publications indexed in prestigious databases such as the Social Sciences Citation Index (SSCI), Scopus, and the Emerging Sources Citation Index (ESCI). Her research predominantly focuses on financial inclusion, sustainable finance, risk management, and the application of Islamic financial instruments. Additionally, she has co-authored several chapters in academic books published by renowned international publishers, including Edward Elgar, Springer and Routledge. She has participated as a member of the scientific committee at various global conferences concerning Islamic finance and real estate.

Erol Demir is a full professor at the Department of Real Estate Development and Management, Faculty of Applied Sciences, Ankara University, Türkiye. He holds a Ph.D. in Agricultural Economics from Ankara University and an M.Sc. in Business Administration from Gazi University. His research focuses on real estate taxation, accounting practices in the construction and property sectors, cooperative finance, and public sector economics. He has published extensively in peer-reviewed journals and authored several books. Prof. Demir has also served as Deputy Dean and contributed to multiple academic committees within Ankara University. He is currently an editorial board member of cited journals.

Does Integrating PropTech into Turkish Sukuk Investment Provide an Effective Alternative for Delivering Affordable and Social Housing in Türkiye?

Monsurat Ayojimi Salami, Harun Tanrıvermiş, and Yeşim Tanrıvermiş

Abstract

This chapter proposes the integration of property technology (ProptTech) in *Sukuk* contracts to promote affordable and social housing investment in Türkiye. This chapter also assesses the need for employing innovative approaches in utilising *Sukuk* investments to address social and affordable housing needs. Technology adoption has led to a shift in the nature and type of housing required in the nineteenth century compared to those needed in the twenty-first century. Therefore, it is crucial to make modifications to the existing housing structure and adopt a more technological approach in the newly constructed housing. Since the provision of housing should be a collective effort beyond public institutions, the use of *Sukuk* investment is suggested as an alternative source of funds that could be diverted to address national issues on real estate at an affordable price and with an ethical profit for investors. For this analysis, quarterly data from 2014Q1 to 2024Q3 is collected, and a Panel ARDL analysis is applied on 20 provinces in Türkiye. *Sukuk* investment is a dependent variable, while first house, second house, mortgage, real estate CPI, HPI, other finance, and turnover are independent variables. House sales and the COVID-19 pandemic are control variables. The findings reveal that *Sukuk* and houses establish long-term relationships with different speeds of adjustment to short-term shocks in provinces.

Keywords

Sukuk · Housing · Mortgage · HPI · Affordable Housing · Social Housing · PropTech · Türkiye

---

M. A. Salami · H. Tanrıvermiş (✉) · Y. Tanrıvermiş
Department of Real Estate Development and Management, Faculty of Applied Sciences, Ankara University, Ankara, Türkiye
e-mail: masalami@ankara.edu.tr; tanrivermis@ankara.edu.tr; aliefendioglu@ankara.edu.tr

T. Just et al. (eds.), *Understanding Türkiye's Real Estate Markets*, Management for Professionals, https://doi.org/10.1007/978-3-032-13297-0_17

1 Introduction

The origin of *Sukuk* has been traced to 700 A.D., while the persistent endorsement of utilising *Sukuk* for financing projects has significantly contributed to the substantial growth of *Sukuk*'s market value. The Islamic International Financial Market (IIFM) reported that *Sukuk* first emerged in 1990, with a niche market value of USD 30 million, and had grown to USD 150 billion by 2012 (IIFM, 2013). Since 1990, *Sukuk* has begun to grow and flourish (Borhan & Ahmad, 2018). As of 2023, Islamic finance was predicted to have a worth of USD 3.8 trillion, and as a result, its expansion made it one of the significant agents of economic growth (Ledhem, 2020). Modern-day *Sukuk* has gained recognition in recent years, and the birth of AAIOFI (Accounting and Auditing Organisation for Islamic Financial Institutions) has made a magnificent contribution towards this achievement (Katterbauer et al., 2022). The persistent endorsement of using *Sukuk* for financing projects has attracted investors, perceiving that the growth of *Sukuk* will continue.

Sukuk is an Islamic financial instrument used to raise capital in accordance with Islamic law. *Sukuk* shares features with traditional bonds: they enable investors to lend money to a government or corporation in exchange for periodic payments. However, unlike conventional bonds, *Sukuk* is structured to avoid interest, which is prohibited under Islamic law. Thus, *Sukuk* have experienced significant growth in Muslim countries; still, non-Muslim investors also find *Sukuk* to be an attractive investment option (The Star, 2016). This increase in *Sukuk*'s market value suggests that its benefits extend beyond the Islamic economy. Given this, *Sukuk* can be adopted to address the global issue of providing social and affordable housing fairly.

Therefore, this chapter examines the role of *Sukuk* in providing affordable and social housing in Türkiye, while suggesting the adoption of PropTech (Property Technology) to attract investors. PropTech serves as a solution provider for challenges facing real estate markets (Tagliaro et al., 2024). The results could be called value added in real estate-related Sukuk investment. Most studies on *Sukuk* are conducted at the national level, whereas projects financed by *Sukuk* funds are implemented across states or provinces. Therefore, this analysis examined the use of *Sukuk* holdings to provide financing, especially for securing first housing or to act as a value-enhancement to existing housing projects. Traditionally, the house could be acquired through a mortgage or other financing. In Türkiye, data indicate that many people prefer alternative financing options over mortgages. This preference may be due to factors surrounding mortgage approval or the impact of interest rates.

The findings from this analysis suggest that Sukuk investment applications could serve as a more effective source for providing affordable and social housing. The findings reveal that the speed of adjustment to short-term shocks varies by rates and provinces. This offers opportunities for policymakers to tailor *Sukuk* in different provinces, as evidenced by the lags in Sukuk adoption in several provinces. Particular attention should be paid to how each province responds to the pattern of adjustment speed for first and second houses.

The remainder of the chapter is structured as follows: Sect. 2 discusses the application of *Sukuk* in real estate, followed by a proposed PropTech—*Sukuk* Model for addressing affordable and social housing in Sect. 3. Section 4 presents the data and methodology. Section 5 shows the results, and Sect. 6 discusses them. Section 7 concludes.

2 *Sukuk* Application in Real Estate

Sukuk is a *Shariah*-compliant bond-like instrument, ranked among the Islamic economy's most successful and fast-growing financing instruments (Khan et al., 2022), and an Islamic capital market instrument suitable for corporate and government use (Oseni & Hassan, 2014) in capital-intensive financing projects. *Sukuk* is employed to acquire housing debt (Katterbauer et al., 2022). *Sukuk* is a "*certificate of equal value put into use as common shares and rights in tangible assets, usufructs, and services or as equity in a project or investment activity*" (AAOIFI; Rafay et al., 2017). Guermazi (2020) stress that *Sukuk* do not always represent ownership of the underlying assets. *Sukuk* is considered a relatively low-risk financial instrument compared to stock investments and complies with Islamic beliefs, but investors are exposed to potential loss to benefit from monetary gain (Guermazi, 2020). *Sukuk* is a security-backed real estate, defined as "*Islamic investment trust certificates*" (Hasan et al., 2019). The fact that *Sukuk* is structured to avoid interest is a key aspect of its design. *Sukuk* is categorised under the risk-sharing paradigm without interest (Guermazi, 2020). Therefore, *Sukuk* investment could be used to finance housing or capital-intensive projects, and investors who purchase the Sukuk would receive periodic payments based on the performance of these projects.

Sukuk can be used to facilitate affordable and social housing initiatives by establishing a real estate investment trust (REIT) dedicated to real estate assets, including apartments, office buildings, or shopping malls. Community land trusts may be employed to develop and manage such housing projects, with *Sukuk* serving as an additional funding mechanism. Furthermore, *Sukuk* could be deployed to finance microfinance institutions that offer small loans and other financial services to low-income individuals and households.

3 Proposed PropTech: *Sukuk* Investment Model for Addressing Affordable and Social Housing in Türkiye

Affordable and social housing have become a global issue (Leung et al., 2022). Although the effect may vary across nations, the demand for affordable housing remains high in every country. The lack of housing affordability is broader than just access to shelter, as it affects the family ties, access to education and other wealth-related opportunities within the community (Öztürk et al., 2018). This makes housing affordability a global concern, as it has the potential to lower the productivity and well-being of the population. If the magnitude is so big, it may create unrest and indirectly obstruct the unaffected population. With PropTech blended into the real estate *Sukuk* investment, it has the potential to reach interested investors.

PropTech has increased by over 300% in the last few years (Kim & Kim, 2021). Also, social housing has to meet decent home standards (Kempton, 2008) according to the UK housing corporation. However, the short supply of social housing is likely to leave the occupiers with no option but to accept available houses (Kempton, 2014) without considering the decency standard. The fact that everyone deserves a decent home, and that *Sukuk* could be an alternative investment option for raising investment funds, calls for consideration. The proximity of social housing to other residential properties may be another factor contributing to its limited supply. Negative spill-overs of social housing are reported, for example, by Sequeira and Filippova (2020).

Although records reveal an upward trend in *Sukuk* investment in Türkiye, the ratio of *Sukuk* investment relative to other Islamic financial products remains low. *Sukuk*, considering technological progress, is crucial for efficient and effective outcomes. Figure 1 shows that the ratio ranges from 8.34% of total Shariah-compliant financing in Q1 2014 to 32.15% in Q3 2023 (ifsb.org, 2025). There is still a significant amount of unused *Sukuk* in the Turkish market that could be utilised to achieve housing affordability.

This also indicates that *Sukuk* investment in Türkiye has not been substantially attractive. Otherwise, it could have been used to address aspects of national concerns, such as affordable and social housing, by involving investors across different sectors. A national call for *Sukuk* investment could be made available for various investors to select their preferred option voluntarily, and transparency could be

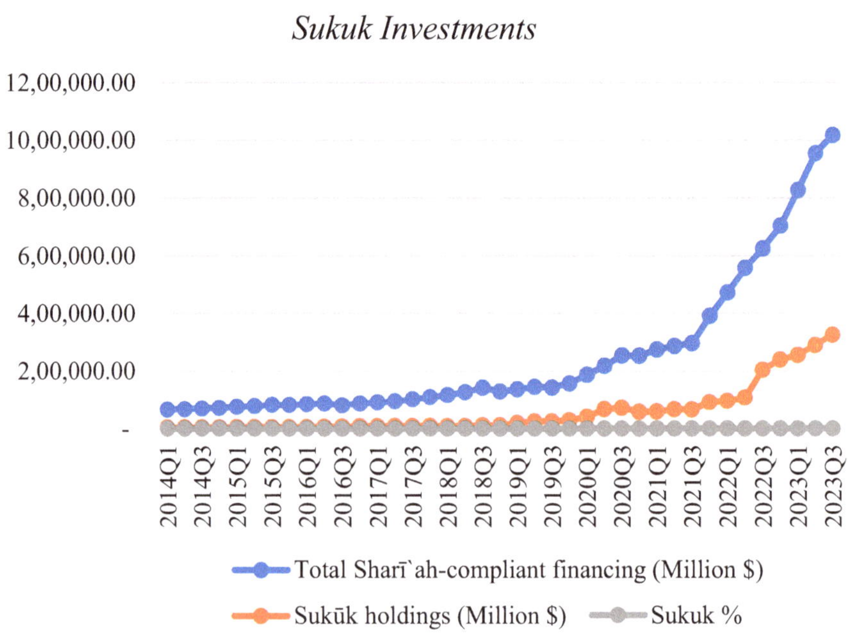

Fig. 1 Turkish Sukuk investment. *Source*: ifsb.org (2025)

ensured through a PropTech application. Integration of PropTech has an advantage for both investors and house buyers. Figure 2 presents an interesting model for various stakeholders who aim to facilitate affordable housing or social housing initiatives.

Sukuk can be used as a means of providing affordable housing and social housing in several ways. A government, corporation, or non-profit organisation responsible for financing social housing could issue Sukuk to raise funds for constructing new housing units. Social housing refers to housing provided by the government or a non-profit organisation and is intended for low-income households unable to afford market-rate housing. *Sukuk* funds could be used to finance housing construction, and the investors who purchase the *Sukuk* would receive periodic payments based on the performance of the housing units.

Furthermore, *Sukuk* could be used to provide affordable housing and finance social housing by establishing a real estate investment trust (REIT) for assets, such as apartments, office buildings, or shopping malls. A *Sukuk*-based REIT could be created to invest in affordable housing and finance social housing, allowing investors to participate in ownership and support the construction and management of new housing units while still complying with Islamic law.

Besides those, *Sukuk* could finance the rehabilitation and modernisation of existing affordable housing units, allowing landlords to make necessary improvements

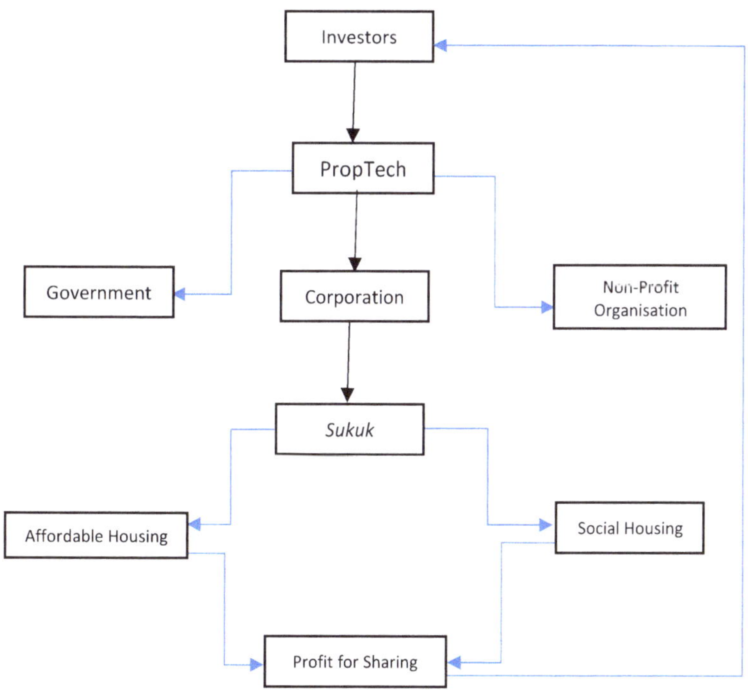

Fig. 2 *Sukuk* as the source of providing affordable and social housing. *Source: own depiction*

and upgrades while complying with Islamic law. *Sukuk* could also finance community land trusts and non-profit organisations that acquire land for community benefits. Community land trusts can be utilised to develop and manage affordable and social housing, and the use of *Sukuk* to finance these projects could provide an additional funding source.

Additionally, *Sukuk* can be used to finance microfinance institutions, which are financial institutions that provide small loans and other financial services to low-income individuals and households. These institutions could utilise the funds raised through the sale of Sukuk to offer loans for the construction or purchase of affordable housing, thereby increasing access to housing for low-income individuals and families.

In summary, *Sukuk* offers several potential benefits as a means of providing affordable housing and financing social housing, thereby raising capital in compliance with Islamic law by attracting a wide range of investors who can assist in achieving housing initiatives.

Figure 2 shows that investors could invest in housing projects of any kind through either the government, the corporation or a non-profit organisation into a *Sukuk* investment portfolio. During the investment application process, all relevant information about the type of real estate will be clearly stated, allowing the investor to make an informed and uninterrupted investment decision. The investor decides unilaterally the channel through which the investment is channelled, such as affordable or social housing. *Sukuk* financing has the potential to grow strongly in Türkiye. The profit from the investment is not expected to be substantial, as the primary motive is not primarily financial.

Real estate investors may find *Sukuk* investment a valuable tool for achieving more affordable and socially responsible housing, provided they are integrated into the ecosystem in a way that makes them active participants. PropTech can provide this feature. Individual investors will have the liberty to see a virtual image of the real estate that they invest in.

4 Data and Methodology

4.1 Data

Quarterly data for the variables used include Turkish Sukuk holdings, new house data, second house ownership, mortgage, other financial means, turnover, CPI (Consumer Price Index), HPI (House Price Index), and house sales. *Sukuk* holdings were employed as a financing proxy for economic growth in South Asia (Ledhem, 2020). The HPI serves as an indicator of the overall performance of the real estate market, encompassing sub-indices that assess price movements, rental yields, affordability, and other related metrics (Eulerpool). The duration of the data ranges from Q1 2014 to Q3 2024, resulting in 860 data points. The period was chosen based on the availability of data. The data was obtained from IFSB and TurkStat. The analysis employed a panel ARDL model for 20 provinces. For better information, the province was selected based on the Income and Wealth Index Priority and House Index Priority. Affordable houses could be provided in provinces with a priority in the income and wealth index. In contrast, social housing could be provided in provinces with a priority in the housing index. This selection is assumed to be better as it could justify the form in which *Sukuk* could be better applied in different provinces.

Most studies on *Sukuk* use national data, though states or provinces within a country are not homogeneous. Hence, those projects being financed by *Sukuk* funds should be evaluated separately. Therefore, this analysis examined the use of *Sukuk* funds to provide financing for securing affordable first-home projects or as a value-added on existing real estate projects. Traditionally, the house could be acquired through mortgage loans or other financing means. In Türkiye, data indicate that the majority of households prefer alternative financing options to mortgage loans. Less consideration for a mortgage loan may be due to factors such as the interest rate.

4.2 Methodology

The Panel ARDL model is employed to examine the provision of affordable and social housing in Türkiye through *Sukuk* investment and enhanced outreach using PropTech. The general long-term equation is expressed as follows:

$$\begin{aligned} Sukuk_{i,t} = \int 1st\_House_{i,t}, 2nd\_House_{i,t}, Mortgage_{i,t}, Other\_financing_{i,t}, \\ Turnover_{i,t}, CPI_{i,t}, HPI_{i,t}, House\_Sales_{i,t} \end{aligned} \quad (1)$$

To make the model dynamic, lagged *Sukuk* is incorporated into the model, along with the lags of explanatory variables, as proposed by Pesaran et al. (1999) in the ARDL (p, q) framework. Dynamic panel ARDL enable the capture of heterogeneous features embedded in the data used for the analysis (Assi et al., 2021). The model is rewritten as follows:

$$lnSukuk_{i,t} = \alpha_i + \sum_{p}^{j=1} \delta_{i,j} lnSukuk + \sum_{q}^{j=0} \gamma_{i,j} Z_{i,t-j} + \varepsilon_{i,t}. \quad (2)$$

where $Z_{i,t-j}$ represents the set of explanatory variables for the analysis across the provinces examined. The explanatory variables are first and second houses, mortgage, CPI, HPI, other finance, and turnover. The study controls for house sales and the COVID-19 pandemic for unbiased findings.

5 Findings

5.1 Preliminary Analysis

Preliminary tests, including the panel unit root, descriptive statistics, and correlation matrix, help to determine the most appropriate model. The unit root test revealed that the data series is integrated of I~(0) and I~(1) This makes the model more appropriate for ARDL. The fact that 20 provinces were examined simultaneously necessitated the use of panel ARDL in this study.

5.2 Descriptive Summary

Table 1 presents a descriptive summary of the data employed. *Sukuk* holdings in Türkiye are in millions of Turkish liras (TL). All the variables are found to be positively skewed and exhibit kurtosis, except the first houses variable, where the kurtosis coefficient is below 3. The kurtosis coefficient indicates that used houses have experienced catastrophes over the study period. The average *Sukuk* holdings throughout the analysis are TL 86,487.28 million; the minimum Turkish *Sukuk* holdings are TL 5687.08 million. Maximum Turkish *Sukuk* holdings are TL 365,915.4 million. The spread between the maximum and minimum *Sukuk* shows a significant difference, indicating that Turkish investment in *Sukuk* is increasing over time. Furthermore, *Sukuk* holdings could present an investment opportunity for Türkiye to address the challenges of social and affordable housing in the country. Similarly, the minimum and maximum first houses acquired for the study are 80,370 units and 196,936 units, respectively. On the other hand, the minimum second houses acquired is 137,641 units, and the maximum acquired is 375,073. It can be deduced that most real estate acquirers in Türkiye perceived their investment in the sector as a good decision, which in turn attracts repeated housing acquisitions. It can be observed that more of the second houses are acquired. On average, there are more purchases of second houses than of first houses.

The minimum number of houses acquired with a mortgage is 16,864 units, and the maximum number of houses acquired by mortgage is 242,316 units, while those houses acquired through other means of financing range from 146,656 units as the minimum to 430,043 units as the maximum. This implies that housing acquirers prefer to seek financing through alternative means rather than approaching banks. This might have been due to indirect means of reducing costs, such as seeking financing that is not interest charge-related or avoiding continuous currency fluctuations and subsequent inflation effects. This can also be translated into the opportunity to use non-interest-related financing, such as *Sukuk*, to motivate more investors in the Turkish housing acquisition, which may increase housing suppliers. This may speed up the authority to attain equilibrium in making houses available for different levels of demand and eventually reduce the continuous increase in rents and housing prices.

The minimum housing turnover during the period of the study was 32.0767, and the maximum housing turnover was 808.7995, which is 25.2145 times the minimum. CPI and HPI have responded to these turnover rates. The HPI coefficient ranges from 4.6967 to 157.2367, and the CPI ranges from 8.9600 to 41.8333. This implies that the adverse effects of substantial changes in real estate are reflected in the HPI and CPI, and the general population may be feeling the negative consequences. Therefore, increase the population towards an unaffordable range.

Table 1 Descriptive summary

	Mean	Maximum	Minimum	Std. Dev.	Skewness	Kurtosis	Jarque–Bera	Obs
Sukuk(m)	86487.28	365915.4	5687.077	115015.7	1.3732	3.3077	273.6593	860
First House	131781.9	196936.0	80370.00	32488.34	0.1239	1.9052	45.15213	860
Second House	207277.4	375073.0	137641.0	53893.56	1.4898	4.9350	452.2821	860
MORTGAGE	87773.42	242316.0	16864.00	42875.20	0.8045	4.9270	225.8189	860
OTHER_FIN_	251285.9	430043.0	146656.0	58959.07	0.9457	3.6231	142.0954	860
TURNOVER	156.6709	808.7995	32.0767	198.5341	2.1296	6.4361	1073.139	860
CPI	14.5060	41.8333	8.9600	5.7949	2.8438	12.7652	4576.207	860
HPI	31.7289	157.2367	4.6967	40.45700	1.7592	4.6889	545.7945	860
HOUSE_SALES	12293.88	96773.00	1922.000	13264.97	3.0369	13.0757	4959.721	860

Note that Other Fin represents the financing raised from family and friends. It is considered another source of financing real estate without approaching the banks

Source: own calculation

As presented in Table 1

Table 2 illustrates the degree of correlation between the variables. The correlation coefficient reveals that the first house acquisition, mortgage financing, and house sales had a negative correlation with Sukuk financing. In contrast, the second house acquisition, other types of financing, housing turnover, CPI and HPI showed a positive correlation with *Sukuk* financing. This implies that providing *Sukuk* for housing availability will make it more attractive to acquire housing without being affected by interest rate fluctuations. This suggests that using *Sukuk* financing could serve as a useful indicator for policy makers aiming to provide social and affordable housing. The second house, mortgage, other financing, and house sales displayed a positive correlation with the first house acquisition. Conversely, turnover, real estate CPI, and HPI exhibited a negative correlation with the first house acquisition. The low correlation between the first and second house acquisitions indicates that fewer people who purchase the first house are able to acquire a second. This may be influenced by several macroeconomic factors, which are beyond the scope of this chapter. Higher coefficient of turnover and HPI revealed that acquiring more than the first house may be triggered by business motives rather than by pure necessity. Therefore, policy makers may consider imposing higher taxes that could prevent unnecessary housing speculation in the Turkish housing market.

Table 3 presents the results of the long-term relationship between Turkish *Sukuk* holdings and housing sales, mortgage financing, other financings, turnover, HPI, and CPI. Housing acquisitions, HPI, and CPI established a positive and significant relationship with Turkish *Sukuk* holdings. Increasing *Sukuk* holdings contributes significantly to housing acquisitions, potentially leading to an increase in housing availability. It may increase the bargaining power of tenants and eventually lower housing affordability. Increasing *Sukuk* holdings increases the HPI, which could indicate an increase in economic performance in the real estate sector, as *Sukuk* holdings are diverted to address Turkish housing issues. There is also a positive long-term relationship between *Sukuk* holdings and CPI. This might indicate better economic performance as a result of using *Sukuk* holdings to address economically challenging issues. This implies that the appropriate use of *Sukuk* holdings matters in the extent at which it contributes towards economic enhancement.

With regards to mortgage and other financing, turnover and the COVID-19 pandemic, there is a significant negative relationship with *Sukuk* holdings. This revealed that the more the *Sukuk* holdings are made available for housing-related projects, the less the need for mortgage and other financing for housing acquisition for the purchasers in the long term. This suggests that *Sukuk* holdings have the potential to alleviate future housing challenges in Türkiye, and the success of such initiatives could be emulated by countries facing similar issues. The negative relationship between turnover and *Sukuk* holdings might suggest that speculative motives in the Turkish housing market tend to decrease as *Sukuk* use for real estate increases drastically.

Table 2 Correlation matrix of the variables relationship

	Sukuk	First house	Second house	Mortgage	Other_Fin	Turnover	CPI	HPI	House_Sales
Sukuk	1								
First House	−0.5251	1							
Second House	0.2858	0.1501	1						
Mortgage	−0.5398	0.5040	0.3123	1					
Other_Fin	0.3644	0.3217	0.7696	−0.1640	1				
Turnover	0.9289	−0.4358	0.1841	−0.5465	0.3256	1			
CPI	0.1606	−0.2724	0.3707	−0.0750	0.2433	0.0880	1		
HPI	0.9728	−0.4765	0.2033	−0.5602	0.3306	0.9841	0.1319	1	
House_Sales	−0.0187	0.1114	0.1519	0.1024	0.1258	−0.0237	0.0279	−0.0264	1

Table 3 Long-term regression analysis of *Sukuk* holdings and independent variables

Variables	β
$ln1st\_House_{it}$	16.1883**
$ln2nd\_House_{it}$	12.8848**
$lnMortgage_{it}$	−8.0717**
$lnOther\_Finance_{it}$	−21.6607**
$lnTurnover_{it}$	−6.5494**
$lnHPI_{it}$	1.8775**
$lnCPI\_Business_{it}$	0.1921
$COVID\_19_{it}$	−1.3375**

Note that superscript ** indicates 5% significance level

5.3 Short-Term Speed of Adjustment Findings

Table 4 illustrates how the short-term deviation adjusts to short-term shocks in the long-term relationship between Sukuk and the independent variables. The short-term deviation caused by the shock typically adjusts at a rate of 22.69%. Sukuk, first house sales, and second house sales adjust at different rates, while mortgage, other finance, turnover, HPI, CPI, and COVID-19 struggled to revert from short-term deviations. The difficulty in adjusting these variables to short-term shocks may have slowed the transition towards the long-term relationship. The findings indicate a positive trend, suggesting a potential for future repetition of long-term relationships among the study's variables.

5.4 Short-Term Speed of Adjustment Findings: Provinces Findings

Table 5 shows the speed of adjustment to short-term shocks on the long-term relationship between *Sukuk* and the independent variables as presented in column 3. The short-term shock in Gaziantep Province was the slowest at 9.69%, followed by Tekirdağ (11.91%) and Hatay (13.99%), all of which have adjustment rates below 15%. The adjustment to short-term shocks in seven provinces—Muğla (17.51%), Kocaeli (18.8%), Adana (18.9%), Konya (19.18%), Mersin (19.05%), Sakarya (19.06%), and İzmir (19.41%)—remains under 20%. The adjustment to short-term shocks in provinces such as Kayseri (20.68%), İstanbul (22.38%), Aydın (22.55%), and Ankara (23.18%) stays below 25%. Adjustment in provinces like Antalya (27.29%) and Manisa (26.88%) remains under 30%. In provinces including Samsun (30.76%) and Bursa (31.42%), the adjustment rate stays under 35%. Eskisehir (35.44%) and Balıkesir (45.65%) show higher adjustment rates compared to other provinces. This suggests that the *Sukuk* application could serve as an effective alternative strategy for addressing real estate issues, including housing affordability and social housing, across various provinces. Table 6 summarises the data presented in Table 5.

Table 4 Short-term deviation adjustment

Variables	β
α	8.7090***
CointeQ01	−0.2269***
$\Delta lnSukuk_{(-1)}$	−0.7072***
$\Delta lnSukuk_{(-2)}$	−1.3945***
$\Delta\ ln\ 2ndHand$	1.8042***
$\Delta\ ln\ 2ndHand_{(-1)}$	−0.1580
$\Delta\ ln\ 2ndHand_{(-2)}$	−0.4444***
$\Delta\ ln\ 1stHand$	−3.0919***
$\Delta\ ln\ 1stHand_{(-1)}$	−1.6548***
$\Delta\ ln\ 1stHand_{(-2)}$	−0.1446
$\Delta lnMortgage$	1.6681***
$\Delta lnMortgage_{(-1)}$	0.6617***
$\Delta lnMortgage_{(-2)}$	0.3913***
$\Delta lnOtherFinance$	3.8449***
$\Delta lnOtherFinance_{(-1)}$	1.5501***
$\Delta lnOtherFinance_{(-2)}$	0.3469**
$\Delta lnTurnover$	0.8303***
$\Delta lnTurnover_{(-1)}$	0.9839***
$\Delta lnTurnover_{(-2)}$	0.5691***
$\Delta lnHPI$	0.7707**
$\Delta lnHPI_{(-1)}$	3.3133***
$\Delta lnHPI_{(-2)}$	3.2932***
$\Delta lnCPIBusiness$	0.0287
$\Delta lnCPIBusiness_{(-1)}$	0.0244
$\Delta lnCPIBusiness_{(-2)}$	−0.2504***
$\Delta COVID-19$	0.7804***
$\Delta COVID-19_{(-1)}$	0.5197***
$\Delta COVID-19_{(-2)}$	0.2821***
$\Delta lnHouse\ Sales$	−0.0443
@Trend	0.0835***
Wald Test	31.6358***

Note that superscripts ** and *** indicate 5% and 1% significance levels, respectively

According to Table 7 the speed of adjustment to a short-term shock is relatively higher in the first lag compared to the second lag in all provinces except Gaziantep. This indicates that *Sukuk* takes time to respond to shocks, which is likely due to its stable structure, resulting in less volatility of the asset class. Across all provinces, the shock to the first house acquisition in the *Sukuk* investment relationship adjusts instantly to short-term shocks. This demonstrates in the *Sukuk* and first house acquisition relationship, suggesting that financing the first house acquisition may be a preferable option. Conversely, in some provinces, shocks related to the second house acquisition and *Sukuk* struggle to adjust either immediately, as in Istanbul, or

Table 5 Speed of adjustment due to short-term shocks across provinces

Provinces	α	Cointegration β	*Sukuk* β	First House β	Second House β	Mortgage β	Turnover β	HPI β	CPI β	Other Fin. β	COVID- 19 β	House Sales β	Trend β
Adana	6.8367 (0.2258)	−0.1890 (0.0001)	−0.4074 (−1) (0.0004)	−2.2020(0) (0.0001)	−1.3987 (0) (0.0023)	1.3405 (0) (0.0000)	0.5427(0) (0.0019)	−0.7705(0) (0.0085)	0.0289(0) (0.0007)	2.7911(0) (0.0003)	0.5761(0) (0.0000)	0.0061 (0.5167)	0.0759 (0.0000)
			−1.1496 (−2) (0.0000)	−0.7868 (−1) (0.0018)	−0.1158 (−1) (0.2692)	0.4889 (−1) (0.0000)	0.9377(−1) (0.0008)	2.0414(−1) (0.0010)	0.1944(−1) (0.0000)	0.6811(−1) (0.0048)	0.41170(−1) (0.0001)		
Antalya	9.0164 (0.3575)	−0.2729 (0.0002)	−0.5030 (−1) (0.0002)	−2.5930(0) (0.0001)	−2.9711 (0) (0.0006)	1.9192 (0) (0.0000)	1.5149(0) (0.0001)	−0.7623(0) (0.0067)	0.1419(0) (0.0000)	3.8894(0) (0.0002)	0.5758(0) (0.0000)	0.1131 (0.0430)	0.1079 (0.0000)
			−1.5894 (−2) (0.0000)	−0.6312 (−1) (0.0020)	−0.8493 (−1) (0.0033)	0.8666 (−1) (0.0000)	1.4863(−1) (0.0003)	1.2953(−1) (0.0003)	0.2374(−1) (0.0000)	0.8348(−1) (0.0000)	0.4904(−1) (0.0000)		
Ankara	5.6098 (0.3908)	−0.2318 (0.0001)	−0.6941 (−1) (0.0000)	−2.8703(0) (0.0001)	−2.2272 (0) (0.0008)	1.6608 (0) (0.0000)	1.0684(0) (0.0004)	0.1237(0) (0.3366)	0.0999(0) (0.0000)	3.7669(0) (0.0002)	0.7639(0) (0.0000)	0.2778 (0.0002)	0.0868 (0.0000)
			−1.2616 (−2) (0.0000)	−1.9094 (−1) (0.0001)	−0.3322 (−1) (0.0237)	0.8046 (−1) (0.0000)	1.1870(−1) (0.0003)	2.9140(−1) (0.0003)	0.0058(−1) (0.1843)	1.8259(−1) (0.0005)	0.5724(−1) (0.0000)		
Aydin	8.9070 (0.4049)	−0.2255 (0.0002)	−0.5649 (−1) (0.0005)	−2.9564(0) (0.0004)	−1.4390(0) (0.0155)	1.5077(0) (0.0002)	1.0930(0) (0.0055)	0.0304(0) (0.8330)	0.0423(0) (0.0007)	3.2349(0) (0.0023)	0.5933(0) (0.0000)	−0.0690 (0.0205)	0.0850 (0.0000)
			−1.4142 (−2) (0.0001)	−1.0528(−1) (0.0028)	−0.0407(−1) (0.8008)	0.6085(−1) (0.0005)	1.3256(−1) (0.0025)	2.8047(−1) (0.0010)	0.0523(−1) (0.0012)	0.5750(−1) (0.0377)	0.4214(−1) (0.0005)		
Balikesir	28.6385 (0.2637)	−0.4565 (0.0011)	−2.0628(−1) (0.0000)	−5.9228(0) (0.0000)	−4.4551(0) (0.0004)	3.4491(0) (0.0000)	2.1422(0) (0.0000)	3.1585(0) (0.0004)	0.1208(0) (0.0000)	8.1737(0) (0.0003)	1.3745(0) (0.0000)	−1.3580 (0.0000)	0.1734 (0.0000)
			−3.1623(−2) (0.0000)	−3.5833(0) (0.0001)	−0.6657(0) (0.0091)	1.4647(−1) (0.0000)	0.9599(−1) (0.0002)	7.1609(−1) (0.0004)	−0.2361(−1) (0.0000)	3.6673(−1) (0.0005)	1.6051(−1) (0.0000)		
Bursa	18.0423 (0.2447)	−0.3142 (0.0003)	−1.0228(−1) (0.0001)	−4.1123(0) (0.0002)	−3.1029(0) (0.0020)	2.5430(0) (0.0001)	1.3918(0) (0.0009)	1.1306(0) (0.0065)	0.1270(0) (0.0000)	5.8295(0) (0.0008)	1.0884(0) (0.0000)	−0.6950 (0.0001)	0.1119 (0.0000)
			−2.0826(−2) (0.0000)	−3.0568(−1) (0.0002)	−0.3009(−1) (0.0484)	1.0524(−1) (0.0001)	1.0755(−1) (0.0006)	4.8651(−1) (0.0004)	0.0356(−1) (0.0018)	3.2660(−1) (0.0009)	1.1073(−1) (0.0001)		

Kayseri	2.7230 (0.8404)	−0.2068 (0.0002)	−0.6945(−1) (0.0002)	−3.2182(0) (0.0022)	−1.6385(0) (0.0318)	1.4594(0) (0.0011)	0.8313(0) (0.0272)	1.2724(0) (0.0469)	−0.0297(0) (0.0103)	3.6539(0) (0.0092)	0.8429(0) (0.0001)	0.5424 (0.0074)	0.0724 (0.0000)
			−0.8327(−2) (0.0008)	−2.0531(−1) (0.0071)	−0.2210(−1) (0.6156)	0.6877(−1) (0.0026)	1.2228(1) (0.0112)	3.0886(−1) (0.0519)	−0.0166(−1) (0.1749)	1.8370(−1) (0.0261)	0.4486(−1) (0.0022)		
Eskisehir	18.7243 (0.3537)	−0.3544 (0.0001)	−1.0690(−1) (0.0001)	−4.2716(0) (0.0002)	−4.2035(0) (0.0048)	2.9819(0) (0.0002)	1.5674(0) (0.0013)	0.3279(0) (0.1513)	0.2588(−1) (0.0000)	6.6126(0) (0.0018)	1.1580(0) (0.0000)	−0.6697 (0.0002)	0.1264 (0.0000)
			−2.3350(−2) (0.0001)	−3.0051(−1) (0.0002)	−0.9579(−1) (0.0106)	1.3322(−1) (0.0001)	1.3278(−1) (0.0007)	5.1700(−1) (0.0005)	0.2071(−1) (0.0000)	3.5582(−1) (0.0014)	1.2448(−1) (0.0001)		
Kocaeli	5.0230 (0.3453)	−0.1880 (0.0002)	−0.7961(−1) (0.0000)	−2.8587(0) (0.0002)	−1.2116(0) (0.0082)	1.3724(0) (0.0001)	0.3331(0) (0.0153)	0.4978(0) (0.0517)	0.0697(0) (0.0001)	3.2575(0) (0.0008)	0.8121(0) (0.0000)	0.2038 (0.0007)	0.0719 (0.0000)
			−1.2938(−2) (0.0000)	−1.7006(−1) (0.0006)	−0.1015(−1) (0.4071)	0.5786(−1) (0.0001)	0.3752(−1) (0.0144)	3.6078(−1) (0.0022)	0.0468(−1) (0.0010)	1.6249(−1) (0.0008)	0.4640(−1) (0.0001)		
Gaziantep	2.2214 (0.8179)	−0.0969 (0.0001)	−0.4013(−1) (0.0046)	−2.2649(0) (0.0029)	0.0628(0) (0.9080)	0.6539(0) (0.0054)	0.2990(0) (0.2359)	1.0398(0) (0.1317)	−0.1238(0) (0.0012)	1.9572(0) (0.0225)	0.6361(0) (0.0001)	0.1597 (0.0786)	0.0295 (0.0000)
			−0.3665(−2) (0.0123)	−0.8225(−1) (0.0421)	0.6963(−1) (0.0283)	0.0446(−1) (0.3804)	1.0011(−1) (0.0333)	1.6629(−1) (0.0420)	0.0063(−1) (0.7137)	0.1346(−1) (0.6185)	−0.0948(−1) (0.1363)		
Konya	3.3944 (0.6234)	−0.1918 (0.0001)	−0.7548(−1) (0.0001)	−3.5510(0) (0.0007)	−1.3376(0) (0.0242)	1.5277(0) (0.0004)	0.5095(0) (0.0212)	1.1230(0) (0.0240)	−0.1055(0) (0.0001)	3.7646(0) (0.0044)	0.8319(0) (0.0000)	0.4122 (0.0003)	0.0623 (0.0000)
			−1.1667(−2) (0.0002)	−2.3457(−1) (0.0014)	0.3528(−1) (0.0590)	0.5081(−1) (0.0008)	0.9879(−1) (0.0023)	3.7134(−1) (0.0023)	−0.1169(−1) (0.0003)	1.7935(−1) (0.0077)	0.4839(−1) (0.0004)		
Istanbul	7.1004 (0.7987)	−0.2238 (0.0001)	−0.5038(−1) (0.0004)	−2.5969(0) (0.0003)	1.5956(0) (0.0064)	1.4943(0) (0.0001)	1.1387(0) (0.0010)	−1.3167(0) (0.0054)	0.1725(0) (0.0000)	3.2455(0) (0.0008)	0.7879(0) (0.0000)	0.0791 (0.0919)	0.09552 (0.0000)
			−1.1482(−2) (0.0001)	−1.2924(−1) (0.0013)	−0.3198(−1) (0.0718)	0.7602(−1) (0.0001)	1.5948(−1) (0.0009)	2.3725(— 1) (0.0021)	0.2527(−1) (0.0000)	1.3192(−1) (0.0040)	0.5574(−1) (0.0002)		
Tekirdag	4.4358 (0.5496)	−0.1191 (0.0000)	−0.3580(−1) (0.0024)	−2.4886(0) (0.0005)	−0.4852(0) (0.0991)	1.0564(0) (0.0002)	−0.0430(0) (0.6424)	1.1179(0) (0.0595)	−0.0565(0) (0.0002)	2.6755(0) (0.0021)	0.6874(0) (0.0000)	−0.0071 (0.8649)	0.0428 (0.0000)
			−1.1172(−2) (0.0002)	−1.4737(−1) (0.0022)	0.4259(−1) (0.0323)	0.2277(−1) (0.0010)	0.1924(−1) (0.1705)	2.4707(−1) (0.0103)	0.0622(−1) (0.0053)	1.1711(−1) (0.0087)	0.1779(−1) (0.0041)		
Izmir	11.8877 (0.4991)	−0.1941 (0.0001)	−0.5906(−1) (0.0009)	−2.2033(0) (0.0008)	−1.0717(0) (0.0293)	1.3856(0) (0.0003)	0.3384(0) (0.0485)	1.9105(0) (0.0294)	−0.0770(0) (0.0002)	2.8849(0) (0.0025)	0.6128(0) (0.0000)	−0.4861 (0.0040)	0.0709 (0.0000)
			−1.2157(−2) (0.0002)	−0.9979(−1) (0.0053)	0.3555(−1) (0.0887)	0.4247(−1) (0.0008)	0.6795(−1) (0.0008)	1.8352(−1) (0.0347)	−0.0038(−1) (0.6817)	0.7899(−1) (0.0025)	0.4835(−1) (0.0010)		

(continued)

Table 5 (continued)

Provinces	α	Cointegration β	*Sukuk* β	First House β	Second House β	Mortgage β	Turnover β	HPI β	CPI β	Other Fin. β	COVID- 19 β	House Sales β	Trend β
Mersin	4.5415 (0.4737)	−0.1905 (0.0001)	−0.2909(−1) (0.0011)	−2.2557(0) (0.0000)	−1.4638(0) (0.0016)	1.3651(0) (0.0000)	0.5846(0) (0.0010)	−1.1855(0) (0.0084)	0.0574(0) (0.0001)	2.7763(0) (0.0002)	0.5514(0) (0.0000)	0.2647 (0.0045)	0.0747 (0.0000)
			−1.1011(−2) (0.0000)	−0.8779(−1) (0.0010)	−0.2551(−1) (0.0623)	0.5515(−1) (0.0000)	1.1146(−1) (0.0008)	2.0108(−1) (0.0009)	0.2511(−1) (0.0000)	0.8145(−1) (0.0140)	0.3775(−1) (0.0001)		
Samsun	13.5818 (0.2073)	−0.3076 (0.0003)	−1.1070(−1) (0.0000)	−3.8528(0) (0.0001)	−2.4087(0) (0.0009)	2.1313(0) (0.0000)	1.0538(0) (0.0003)	3.0405(0) (0.0014)	−0.0183(0) (0.0029)	5.1479(0) (0.0002)	0.8968(0) (0.0000)	−0.2575 (0.0002)	0.1071 (0.0000)
			−1.9710(−2) (0.0000)	−2.0979(−1) (0.0001)	−0.6666(−1) (0.0047)	0.8700(−1) (0.0000)	0.9157(−1) (0.0004)	5.7632(−1) (0.0003)	−0.3183(−1) (0.0000)	2.4615(−1) (0.0004)	0.5864(−1) (0.0000)		
Sakarya	6.1300 (0.3872)	−0.1906 (0.0001)	−0.8040(−1) (0.0001)	−2.8419(0) (0.0002)	−1.3297(0) (0.0077)	1.4022(0) (0.0001)	0.3875(0) (0.0230)	0.7196(0) (0.0185)	0.0595(0) (0.0002)	3.3709(0) (0.0014)	0.8229(0) (0.0000)	0.0983 (0.0226)	0.0730 (0.0000)
			−1.2855(−2) (0.0001)	−1.5622(−1) (0.0007)	−0.1484(−1) (0.3230)	0.5740(−1) (0.0001)	0.3283(−1) (0.0474)	3.6240(−1) (0.0037)	0.0388(−1) (0.0002)	1.5470(−1) (0.0023)	0.4547(−1) (0.0002)		
Mugla	2.7819 (0.7522)	−0.1751 (0.0001)	−0.3002(−1) (0.0036)	−2.8167(0) (0.0002)	−0.7723(0) (0.0453)	1.2031(0) (0.0001)	0.7753(0) (0.0027)	−0.5841(0) (0.0441)	0.0435(0) (0.0003)	2.4970(0) (0.0020)	0.6126(0) (0.0000)	0.4393 (0.0018)	0.0627 (0.0000)
			−1.2064(−2) (0.0001)	−0.9979(−1) (0.0022)	0.3322(−1) (0.0453)	0.3565(−1) (0.0005)	1.4043(−1) (0.0010)	2.2854(−1) (0.0010)	0.1798(−1) (0.0001)	0.2721(−1) (0.1110)	0.2186(−1) (0.0022)		
Manisa	9.4356 (0.3090)	−0.2688 (0.0002)	−0.8678(−1) (0.0001)	−3.7245(0) (0.0002)	−1.9766(0) (0.0043)	1.9237(0) (0.0001)	0.7494(0) (0.0034)	2.4979(0) (0.0027)	−0.0399(0) (0.0007)	4.6087(0) (0.0010)	0.8715(0) (0.0000)	0.0551 (0.0076)	0.0893 (0.0000)
			−1.6678(−2) (0.0001)	−2.5430(−1) (0.0004)	−0.3134(−1) (0.0669)	0.7804(−1) (0.0001)	0.8871(−1) (0.0016)	5.4920(−1) (0.0020)	−0.2340(−1) (0.0000)	2.6131(−1) (0.0015)	0.5483(−1) (0.0001)		
Hatay	5.1483 (0.4344)	−0.1399 (0.0001)	−0.3519(−1) (0.0027)	−2.2359(0) (0.0051)	−1.0589(0) (0.1472)	0.9842(0) (0.0029)	0.9842(0) (0.1734)	2.0422(0) (0.0121)	−0.1975(0) (0.0000)	2.7594(0) (0.0282)	0.5108(0) (0.0000)	0.0038 (0.5560)	0.0512 (0.0000)

Note that the reported parameters are based on the instant response ($_0$) of the market and the first lag response ($_{-1}$) of the market. P-value is presented in parentheses

Table 6 Extent of the speed of adjustment

	Speed of adjustment to short-term shocks						
Provinces	Extremely low	Very low	Quite low	Moderately low	Low	Moderately fast	Fast
Gaziantep	√						
Tekirdağ		√					
Hatay		√					
Adana			√				
Kocael			√				
Konya			√				
İzmir			√				
Mersin			√				
Sakaraya			√				
Muğla			√				
Ankara				√			
İstanbul				√			
Aydın				√			
Kayseri				√			
Antalya					√		
Manisa					√		
Bursa						√	
Samsun						√	
Eskisehir							√
Balıkesir							√

The sign "√" indicates the category to which the speed of adjustment of the province belongs at a glance

do not adjust instantly, as seen in Gaziantep. Additionally, delays in adjustment during the first lag are observed in the relationship between second house acquisition and *Sukuk* in Gaziantep, Konya, Tekirdağ, İzmir, and Muğla. The first lag in the relationship between second house acquisition and *Sukuk* remains unadjusted in Adana province.

According to the findings in Table 7, *Sukuk* could be used to address housing issues in the provinces shown above. Using *Sukuk* investment to provide a first house may lead to more economic development than using *Sukuk* investment to provide a second house, especially in provinces such as Gaziantep, Tekirdağ, Konya, İzmir, Muğla, and İstanbul. The finding could be translated to a reduction in real estate concentration on a few individuals, which may assist effective policy implementation in provinces such as Ankara and İstanbul.

Further findings in Table 5 revealed that short-term shocks to the relationship between mortgage and other forms of finance with *Sukuk* struggle to adjust across all provinces. This suggests that numerous house buyers in Türkiye show a preference for *Sukuk* over other real estate financing options. Furthermore, short-term shocks to the relationship between housing turnover and *Sukuk* also experienced difficulty in adjustment, with the exception of Tekirdağ province, where the

Table 7 Appropriation of Sukuk investment to proposed housing type

Provinces	*Sukuk* holdings housing financing	
	First house	Second house
Gaziantep	√	Nill
Tekirdağ	√	Nill
Hatay	√	√
Adana	√	√
Kocael	√	√
Konya	√	Nill
İzmir	√	Nill
Mersin	√	√
Sakaraya	√	√
Muğla	√	Nill
Ankara	√	√
İstanbul	√	Nill
Aydın	√	√
Kayseri	√	√
Antalya	√	√
Manisa	√	√
Bursa	√	√
Samsun	√	√
Eskisehir	√	√
Balıkesir	√	√

This sign "√" indicates that *Sukuk* can be applied to the type of housing for the specified province. Those provinces that do not adjust or hardly adjust to short-term shocks in the second housing column are represented by NILL. In this case, policy intervention may be required by assigning a low tax to the first house acquirer and imposing a higher tax on those who exercise continuous housing acquisition, as it should be viewed as every other subsequent housing acquisition for business purposes

turnover adjusted at a notably low rate. Overall, this may represent a strategic approach to normalise recent volatility within housing markets and could potentially facilitate progress towards housing affordability and the sustainability of social housing provision over time.

Furthermore, the HPI and *Sukuk* relationship instantly adjusts to short-term shocks in provinces such as Adana, Antalya, Istanbul, Mersin, and Muğla. The relationship between the CPI and *Sukuk* shows an immediate adjustment to short-term shocks in provinces such as Balıkesir, Kayseri, Gaziantep, Konya, Tekirdağ, İzmir, Samsun, Manisa, and Hatay. The findings indicate evidence of lag adjustment to the short-term shock in the relationship between the COVID-19 pandemic and *Sukuk* within the Gaziantep and Hatay provinces. Conversely, the relationship shows more difficult adjustments in the remaining provinces. Additionally, the trend variable is positive and statistically significant across all provinces examined.

In provinces such as Antalya, İzmir, Kocaeli, and Tekirdağ, affordable houses could be considered for *Sukuk* real estate investment to address challenges that could come along with residing in an income and wealth index priority zone. In contrast, social housing could be considered in the provinces that fall within the range of house index priority, such as Sakarya and Eskisehir provinces. In some cases, provinces such as Ankara are grouped under both the Income and Wealth Index priority and the House Index Priority; therefore, both affordable and social housing may be provided in the proportion that policy allows. İstanbul province could be considered a saturated province.

6 Discussion

This suggests that *sukuk* could be used to finance new real estate projects or to increase the value of existing real estate projects.. In addition, the findings show that *Sukuk* financing works differently in each province. For instance, *Sukuk* could add value to existing projects in big cities such as Istanbul, Ankara, and Antalya. Attention should be paid to due diligence to mitigate negative long-term effects. There is a need to pay attention to the speed of adjustment. The greater the speed of adjustment, the more swiftly the shock will be rectified, and the trajectory will be redirected and rescheduled. *Sukuk's* investment to finance new buildings in the above three provinces may not provide a significant long-term impact. Given the required attention to other provinces that have the potential to develop, so that they could contribute more to the national economy. In several provinces, *Sukuk* investment could be used in providing both first and second housing, while considering factors of over-congestion in some provinces that are earthquake-prone. Findings also revealed that *Sukuk* could be used to finance new real estate projects.

7 Conclusion

Sukuk investment can be applied with different durations. This makes Sukuk investment appropriate for a long-term project. For the efficient use of real estate *Sukuk* investment, integrating PropTech applications could play a substantial role. This could allow foreign investors to invest in Turkish real estate via Sukuk investment. At the same time, the authority should maintain some control over speculation and continuous fluctuations in the Turkish housing market. This indicates that, despite the world's transition from traditional to digital approaches, investment strategies have also undergone a shift with caution. Still, the application of PropTech in raising capital for affordable housing and social housing vis Sukuk should be given more attention. Therefore, PropTechs in *Sukuk* investment can help enhancing liquidity and promoting transparency.

This chapter showed that *Sukuk* and the Turkish housing market established a long-term relationship. The chapter found that macroeconomic factors, such as CPI, play a significant role in this relationship. In the findings, a positive trend in the relationship indicates that the Turkish housing market has potential for growth. Heterogeneity in the speed of adjustment to short-term shocks was found, which could be insightful for policymakers in deciding the kind of housing investment to construct in different provinces. HPI is expected to respond upward when the affordability and social housing are continuously addressed. Also, investors could make uninterrupted decisions on where to invest and what type of project to invest in. As PropTech Sukuk investment provides clearer information investors can make better informed decisions. Since *Sukuk* is an Islamic finance vehicle, ethical investment and contribution to society should be important to the *Sukuk* investors over profit maximisation.

The analysis' constraint was its limited scope to 20 provinces, focusing on the integration of PropTech in real estate-related Sukuk investment as an effective approach to raise investment funds for affordable and social housing through different stakeholders. Future research may consider the environmental aspect of investment and focus on raising green funds for providing affordable and social housing in Türkiye.

Acknowledgement This chapter was prepared using data titled "Levels of Utilisation of Technology in Real Estate Businesses in Türkiye, Establishment of Real Estate Technologies Centre (Proptech Centre/Hub) and Development Opportunities" (Türkiye'de Gayrimenkul İşletmelerinde Teknolojiden Yararlanma Düzeyleri, Gayrimenkul Teknolojileri Merkezi (Proptech Centre/Hub) Kurulması ve Geliştirilebilme Olanakları), Project Code: SBG-2025-3879, financed by the Ankara University Scientific Research Projects Coordination (BAP) Office. The authors thank the reviewers for their valuable recommendations on the chapter and thank Ankara University Rectorate for providing financial and technical assistance for the project.

References

Assi, A. F., Zhakanova Isiksal, A., & Tursoy, T. (2021). Renewable energy consumption, financial development, environmental pollution, and innovations in the ASEAN + 3 group: Evidence from (P-ARDL) model. *Renewable Energy, 165*, 689–700. https://doi.org/10.1016/j.renene.2020.11.052

Borhan, N. A., & Ahmad, N. (2018). Identifying the determinants of Malaysian corporate Sukuk rating. *International Journal of Islamic and Middle Eastern Finance and Management, 11*(3), 432–448. https://doi.org/10.1108/IMEFM-02-2017-0045

Guermazi, I. (2020). The determinants of Sukūk issuance in GCC countries. *Islamic Economic Studies, 28*(1), 25–45. https://doi.org/10.1108/IES-08-2019-0026

Hasan, R., Ahmad, A. U. F., & Parveen, T. (2019). Sukuk risks – a structured review of theoretical research. In Journal of Islamic Accounting and Business Research (Vol. 10, Issue 1, pp. 35–49). Emerald Group Publishing Ltd. https://doi.org/10.1108/JIABR-06-2015-0026

ifsb.org. (2025). Sukuk Data Source: https://data.ifsb.org/data/datasets obtained February, 2025

Katterbauer, K., Syed, H., Cleenewerck, L., & Genc, S. Y. (2022). Robo-Sukuk pricing for Chinese equities. *Borsa Istanbul Review, 22*(5), 854–860. https://doi.org/10.1016/j.bir.2022.06.002

Kempton, J. (2008). Mixed tenure estates: Implications for asset management in the registered social landlord sector. *Structural Survey, 26*(1), 7–16. https://doi.org/10.1108/02630800810857408

Kempton, J. (2014). Asset Management of low-zero carbon technology in social housing. *Structural Survey, 32*(1), 14–31. https://doi.org/10.1108/SS-09-2012-0027

Khan, N., Kchouri, B., Yatoo, N. A., Kräussl, Z., Patel, A., & State, R. (2022). Tokenization of sukuk: Ethereum case study. *Global Finance Journal, 51*, 1–16. https://doi.org/10.1016/j.gfj.2020.100539

Kim, J., & Kim, J. (2021). An integrated analysis of value-based adoption model and information systems success model for proptech service platform. *Sustainability (Switzerland), 13*(23), 1–17. https://doi.org/10.3390/su132312974

Ledhem, M. A. (2020). Does Sukuk financing boost economic growth? Empirical evidence from Southeast Asia. *PSU Research Review*, 1–17. https://doi.org/10.1108/prr-09-2020-0028

Leung, K. M., Yiu, C. Y., & Lai, K. K. (2022). Responsiveness of subdivided unit tenants' housing consumption to income: a study of Hong Kong informal housing. *Housing Studies, 37*(1), 50–72. https://doi.org/10.1080/02673037.2020.1803799

Oseni, U. A., & Hassan, M. K. (2014). The regulation and supervision of sukuk in global capital markets. In Handbook on Islam and Economic Life (pp. 394–416). https://doi.org/10.4337/9781783479825.00029

Öztürk, A., Kapusuz, Y. E., & Tanrıvermiş, H. (2018). The dynamics of housing affordability and housing demand analysis in Ankara. *International Journal of Housing Markets and Analysis, 11*(5), 828–851. https://doi.org/10.1108/IJHMA-08-2017-0079

Pesaran, M. H., Shin, Y., & Smith, R. P. (1999). Pooled Mean Group Estimation of Dynamic Heterogeneous Panels. *Journal of the American Statistical Association, 94*(446), 621–634. https://doi.org/10.1080/01621459.1999.10474156

Rafay, A., Sadiq, R., & Ajmal, M. (2017). Uniform framework for Sukuk al-Ijarah – a proposed model for all madhahib. *Journal of Islamic Accounting and Business Research, 8*(4), 420–454. https://doi.org/10.1108/JIABR-09-2015-0042

Sequeira, V., & Filippova, O. (2020). Does concentration of social housing influence house prices? Evidence from New Zealand. *International Journal of Housing Markets and Analysis, 14*(4), 720–744. https://doi.org/10.1108/IJHMA-04-2020-0032

Tagliaro, C., Pomè, A. P., Migliore, A., & Danivska, V. (2024). Technology "like a fork". How PropTech shapes real estate innovation. *Journal of European Real Estate Research, 18*(1), 4–26. https://doi.org/10.1108/JERER-05-2024-0035

Further Readings

Aliefendioğlu, Y., Tanrivermiş, H., & Salami, M. A. (2022). House Price Index (HPI) and Covid-19 Pandemic Shocks: Evidence from Turkey and Kazakhstan. *International Journal of Housing Markets and Analysis, 15*(1), 108–125. https://doi.org/10.1108/IJHMA-10-2020-0126

IIFM. (2013). *Sukuk Report: A Comprehensive Study of the Global Sukuk Market*. International Islamic Financial Market.

Salami, M. A., Tanrıvermiş, H., Aliefendioğlu, Y., & Tanrıvermiş, Y. (2023). Interdependence between Foreigner Housing Acquisitions and Housing Price Increase in Turkey during the COVID-19 Pandemic Era. *International Journal of Housing Markets and Analysis, 16*(3), 575–597.

Salami, M. A., Tanrıvermiş, H., & Erciyes, A. H. (2022). The Growth, Opportunities and Challenges Facing Islamic Finance in Nigeria: Evidence from Waqf and Sukuk (Chapter 10). In M. K. Hassan, A. Muneeza, & K. N. M. Sonko (Eds.), *Islamic Finance in Africa, The Prospects for Sustainable Development* (pp. 193–207). Edward Elgar Publishing.

Sarea, A., Echahabi, A., Salami, M. A., & Mahmood A. (2025). *Artificial Intelligence for Sustainable Innovation Management and Risk Management: A Systems (and Network) Perspective*. (SSDC, Volume 227), https://link.springer.com/book/9783031953095

Tanrıvermiş, H. (2020). Possible impacts of COVID-19 outbreak on the real estate sector and possible changes to adopt: a situation analysis and general assessment from a Turkish perspective. *Journal of Urban Management, 9*(3), 263–269.

The Star. (2016). *Malaysia says US$1.5 1.5bil Sukuk oversubscribed*, available at: www.thestar.com.my/business/business-news/2016/04/21/malaysia-says-sukuk-oversubscribed/. Accessed 17.08.25.

Monsurat Ayojimi Salami is an assistant professor in the Department of Real Estate Development and Management, Faculty of Applied Sciences, Ankara University, Türkiye. She graduated from the International Islamic University Malaysia (IIUM) and served as a Postdoc fellow between 2018 and 2019 at the IIUM Institute of Islamic Banking and Finance (II*i*BF). She specialises in the fields of financial economics, Islamic finance, real estate finance and investment, digitalisation in real estate, tokenisation, smart contracts and proptech. She holds multiple international certifications, including the Certified Quantitative Risk Management (CQRM). She has made significant contributions to over 50 academic publications indexed in prestigious databases such as the Social Sciences Citation Index (SSCI), Scopus, and the Emerging Sources Citation Index (ESCI). Her research predominantly focuses on financial inclusion, sustainable finance, risk management, and the application of Islamic financial instruments. Additionally, she has co-authored several chapters in academic books published by renowned international publishers, including Edward Elgar, Springer and Routledge. She has participated as a member of the scientific committee at various global conferences concerning Islamic finance and real estate.

Harun Tanrıvermiş is a distinguished professor who occupies the esteemed position at the Ankara University top management level as founder and head of the Department of Real Estate Development and Management, and founder and current dean of the Faculty of Applied Sciences at Ankara University. Professor Tanrıvermiş also currently works as the vice rector at Ankara University. He attained his B.Sc., M.Sc. and Ph.D. degrees from the Department of Agricultural Economics at Ankara University, specialising in land and real estate economics, land and real estate valuation, as well as natural resources and environmental economics. Furthermore, he earned an MSc in environmental management through the MED-CAMPUS Programme in 1996. Professor Tanrıvermiş has published approximately 400 papers, including 43 international and 55 national peer-reviewed articles, which have been published in various high-impact journals. Additionally, he has presented 48 international and 74 national proceedings, either in full or as abstracts, at numerous conferences. He is also credited with writing 39 books and 17 book chapters. Moreover, his works concentrate on the land and real estate valuation, land and real estate economics, real estate development and project appraisal, urban transformation and sustainability, sustainable real estate development, facility and real estate management, land management, administration and polices, measuring and reporting of real estate sustainability and ESG, digital transformation in real estate and real estate technologies.

Yeşim Tanrıvermiş holds the position of full professor in the Department of Real Estate Development and Management at the Faculty of Applied Sciences, Ankara University, Türkiye. She attained her Master of Science (M.Sc.) degree in 2011 from the Department of Agricultural Economics at Ankara University. She received her Ph.D. in 2011 as the first Ph.D. program graduate of the Department of Real Estate Development and Management at Ankara University. Her research interests encompass the management and conservation of land resources, land resource economics, as well as real estate analysis and economics, in addition to studies in real estate and asset valuation. She has been delivering lectures for several years and has published academic papers since 2006. Her publications consist of 50 international and 40 national peer-reviewed articles. Additionally, she has made contributions to 110 international and 25 national full or abstract proceedings at various conferences and congresses and has authored 35 books and 30 book chapters. Presently, she serves as the Deputy Head of her department at Ankara University. Moreover, she is an active participant in various academic and professional organisations. Her experience encompasses working as a researcher and consultant across diverse public and private sectors, with a focus on real estate asset analysis, real estate finance and valuation, land and building conservation practices, as well as real estate economics and management. Furthermore, she actively engages in enhancing cooperation with both domestic and international institutions, mobilising financial resources for research projects.

Sustainability in Real Estate Development Projects

Harun Tanrıvermiş, Yeşim Tanrıvermiş, and Sinan Güneş

Abstract

The real estate sector makes a significant contribution to addressing climate change, as buildings are responsible for approximately 40% of annual carbon emissions. This chapter examines how principles of sustainability can be integrated into each phase of the real estate development process, from land acquisition to sale, employing the "Quadruple Net Value Analysis" methodology, which established assessment models inspire. This approach evaluates real estate development initiatives across economic, environmental, social, and sensory dimensions, illustrating that sustainability extends beyond technical solutions to encompass institutional learning and multi-stakeholder governance processes. Case studies demonstrate that sustainable projects can result in savings of up to 30% in operating costs, enhance asset values by 15–20%, and yield rental returns that are 10–15% higher. The integration of innovative methodologies such as smart building technologies, building information modelling (BIM), and circular construction practices into project development facilitates developers in optimising both environmental performance and financial returns. The significance of environmental, social, and governance (ESG) criteria in investment decisions, coupled with the proliferation of green finance instruments, is expanding access to funding for sustainable real estate development projects. Nonetheless, the transition in real estate development presents several challenges. These include delays in the supply of sustainable materials, a fragmented regulatory environment, and a deficiency of green building expertise among construction teams. Future projects grounded in regenerative design principles and circular economy approaches are anticipated to revolutionise the sector from a "do less harm" phi-

H. Tanrıvermiş · Y. Tanrıvermiş (✉) · S. Güneş
Department of Real Estate Development and Management, Faculty of Applied Sciences, Ankara University, Ankara, Türkiye
e-mail: aliefendioglu@ankara.edu.tr; tanrivermis@ankara.edu.tr; sngunes@ankara.edu.tr

T. Just et al. (eds.), *Understanding Türkiye's Real Estate Markets*, Management for Professionals, https://doi.org/10.1007/978-3-032-13297-0_18

losophy to a strategy of "active environmental contribution". Sustainable real estate development introduces a new paradigm for urban growth by harmonising environmental responsibility, economic efficiency, and social justice.

Keywords
Sustainable real estate · Green buildings · Energy efficiency · Environmental performance · Smart building technologies

1 Introduction

During the process of urban growth, the natural environment is gradually replaced by the built environment, a transformation that has significant environmental impacts. The real estate sector, which, together with infrastructure investments, makes up nearly the entire built environment, plays a strategic role in the fight against climate change, accounting for approximately 40% of the world's annual carbon emissions and 36% of total energy use (Tanrıvermiş & Tanrıvermiş, 2021). In this context, sustainable real estate development signifies a multidimensional transformation that diverges from traditional approaches, aiming to reduce environmental impacts, promote social equity, and ensure economic sustainability. This chapter explores the concept of sustainability via the Quadruple Net Value Analysis approach, examining projects across four key dimensions (Booth et al., 2013). These dimensions are (i) economic benefit, (ii) environmental impact, (iii) social and cultural value, and (iv) sensory/perceptual quality. These four aspects require not only the development of environmentally friendly structures but also the creation of livable, healthy, accessible, and culturally harmonious urban spaces.

This chapter examines comprehensively the conceptual foundations, institutional structures, technological tools, and market dynamics of sustainable real estate developments. The approaches discussed aim to assess the impacts of real estate development on the physical environment, on social fabrics, on cultural perceptions, and on economic systems. Several limitations should be considered when interpreting the chapter's findings: Since the research focuses on Türkiye and a few developed countries, the relevance of the suggested strategies in different climatic, economic, and institutional settings is limited. Additionally, the chapter's qualitative, analysis-driven methodology highlights the need to empirically test the effectiveness of the "Quadruple Net Value Analysis" approach. In a rapidly evolving field where sustainable technologies and green finance instruments are continually advancing, the relevance of the findings, based on data up to 2025, must also be recognised. Furthermore, as the chapter focuses on large-scale commercial projects, the sustainability aspects relevant to the residential sector and smaller development projects are addressed only to a limited extent. While these limitations define the scope of the chapter, they also emphasise the necessity for future research involving broader geographical areas, quantitative methods, and projects of various sizes.

In practical terms, this chapter examines the cost-benefit trade-offs of sustainable projects, their impact on user behaviour, and their market performance through international and local case studies. It further investigates the legal, technical, and institutional barriers that impede the widespread adoption of sustainable practices and proposes solutions within multi-stakeholder governance models, technological innovations, and policy measures. In this context, the chapter, aligned with the Sustainable Development Goals (SDGs), establishes a foundational basis for policies and strategies that facilitate the transformation of the real estate sector, while also offering a reference framework for researchers, investors, and policymakers.

2 Integration of Real Estate Development and Sustainability Concepts

2.1 Sustainability and Change in Development

The real estate development process is a multi-stage and multi-stakeholder activity primarily aimed at value creation (Squires et al., 2017). According to Peiser (2015), developers not only construct new structures but also possess the capacity to enhance the economic, social, and spatial value of real estate through the transformation or repurposing of existing building stock. This process encompasses several interconnected stages, including land acquisition, design development, financing, securing legal approvals, construction, leasing, management, and eventual sale, as presented in Fig. 1.

Sustainable real estate development redefines the traditional process not solely from the perspective of economic return but also in accordance with the principles of environmental protection, social inclusion, and long-term resilience. The essential transformation lies in the acknowledgement that a development extends beyond the construction of physical structures to encompass social responsibility, which holistically influences the quality of urban life.

The key element that distinguishes a good real estate development project from an unsustainable one is its ability to enhance social welfare (Peiser, 1990). While creating new residential or commercial spaces can increase physical access, ignoring the impacts of these structures, such as the use of natural resources, carbon emissions, or ecosystem damage, may reduce overall social welfare. Therefore, sustainable development surpasses traditional cost-benefit analyses by adopting a multidimensional impact assessment. In this context, Perera and Mensah (2019) highlight two main approaches that underpin the theory of sustainability. The first is the *normative approach*, which views sustainability, as defined in the Brundtland

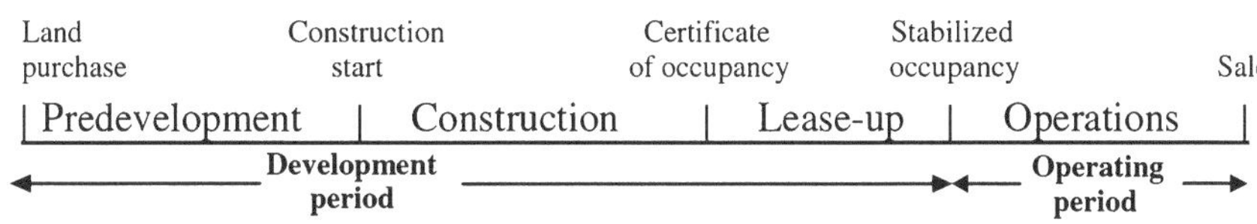

Fig. 1 Real estate development process. *Source*: Peiser and Hamilton (2012)

Report from 1987, as a development model that satisfies current needs without hindering future generations from meeting their own needs. This approach, which seeks to balance economic, environmental, and social factors, has been criticised for defining sustainability within a predominantly measurable, technical, and static framework, and for failing to incorporate social and contextual dynamics fully. The second is the *institutional approach*, which considers sustainability as a socially constructed, context-dependent, and dynamic process. This perspective suggests that a development is influenced not only by technical decisions but also by social values, power relations, and shifting stakeholder priorities. In this framework, a sustainable real estate development involves participatory planning, social learning, and adaptable governance mechanisms; thus, sustainability is seen as an issue that encompasses not only environmental and economic aspects but also institutional and societal factors.

Key components of the institutional approach include principles such as institutional capacity and organisational learning, multi-level governance structures, inter-actor trust and effective communication, as well as context sensitivity and flexibility. This framework plays a critical role, particularly in enhancing public participation in real estate projects, adopting user-centric approaches, and developing long-term adaptation capabilities. Conversely, the real estate development process has experienced a dynamic evolution over time. Healey (2007) delineates this process within the framework of three principal periods: the physical period, the financial period, and the governance period. The *physical period* denotes an era in which development was focused on the production and sale of structures, predominantly characterised by architectural and tectonic approaches. The *financial period* represents the stage during which projects were assessed mainly based on their investment values, with financial sustainability becoming the paramount criterion. *The governance period* signifies an era in which concepts such as participatory planning, multi-stakeholder process management, and spatial justice emerged, and sustainability became associated with institutional frameworks. This evolutionary perspective demonstrates that sustainable real estate development is not merely a technical process but also an outcome of societal values and institutional capacity. Consequently, the effective integration of sustainability principles is facilitated not only through legal regulations but also via institutional learning, stakeholder balance, and sensitivity to the local context.

The multifaceted nature of the sustainability concept and the role of the real estate sector within this spectrum can be better understood through the connections between different ecological paradigms. This spectrum, stretching from weak sustainability to strong sustainability, highlights the interplay of diverse environmental philosophies. Ranging from technology-centred approaches, such as Cornucopian environmentalism, to holistic views like deep ecology and transpersonal ecology, this range illustrates the variety of sustainability ideas related to the built environment and real estate developers. Figure 2 illustrates this theoretical diversity on a horizontal axis, showing the positions of various institutions, actors, and strategies along this spectrum. It therefore offers a comprehensive theoretical framework for sectoral actors to position their sustainability strategies.

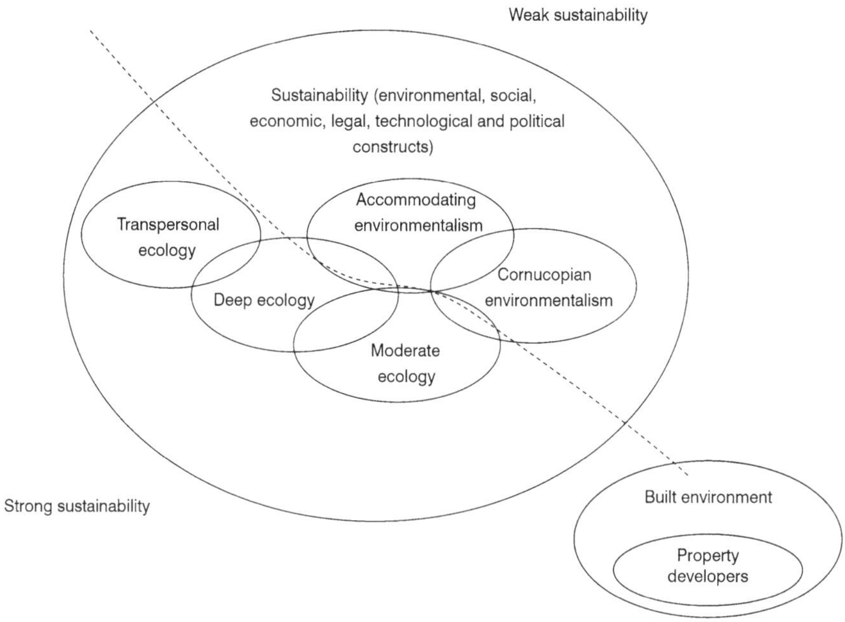

Fig. 2 The position of the built environment and real estate organisations within the spectrum of sustainability concepts. *Source*: Wilkinson et al. (2015)

2.2 The Fundamental Principles of Sustainable Real Estate Development

To evaluate the multidimensional impacts of sustainable real estate projects, this chapter proposes an original and multifaceted framework inspired by existing assessment models. The proposed model facilitates the evaluation of real estate projects not solely based on economic efficiency but also considering environmental integrity, social benefits, and sensory/perceptual experiences. The four fundamental criteria delineated within this framework are elaborated below (Booth et al., 2013):

Economic net value encompasses the project's financial sustainability, return on investment (ROI), cash flow, enhancement in market value, and long-term income-generating potential. Furthermore, considerations such as the appreciation of real estate value, maintenance and operational expenses, as well as the amortisation period, are included within this scope.

Environmental net value includes elements such as the project's carbon footprint, energy and water efficiency, green infrastructure implementations, waste management, and ecological impacts. Life cycle analysis (LCA) and environmental impact assessment (EIA) serve as the principal analytical instruments for this domain.

Social net value evaluates the project's contribution to social inclusion, spatial justice, accessibility, safety, local employment, and social integration. It also emphasises how well projects support the aim of equal opportunity across different social groups.

Sensory net value emphasises individuals' perceptual and experiential interactions with the environment. It considers parameters such as visual aesthetics, acoustic quality, thermal comfort balance, indoor environmental quality, and user satisfaction. Although this aspect is frequently neglected in sustainability discussions, it holds crucial significance for the quality of life.

The assessment of these four dimensions provides a comprehensive and comparable analysis of sustainable real estate development projects. The proposed framework aims not only to evaluate existing impacts but also to steer decision-making by considering how projects evolve, ensuring traceability during implementation phases, and enabling a comparative analysis of outputs from a sustainability perspective. This approach enables the comparison of alternative scenarios in real estate development processes, establishes monitoring and feedback mechanisms during implementation, and assesses performance after project completion. To ensure the practical application of the Quadruple Net Value Analysis approach, the specific evaluation factors within each dimension have been defined (Table 1). The *economic dimension* encompasses direct financial impacts, such as return on investment, job creation, and increased tax revenue, as well as indirect economic benefits, including energy savings, reduced insurance costs, and lower maintenance expenses. The *environmental dimension* covers direct ecological impacts, including waste reduction, carbon emission control, and water resource protection, as well as criteria related to life-support systems such as biodiversity conservation and indoor air quality. The *social dimension* evaluates criteria based on collective welfare indicators, including safety, recreational opportunities, social inclusion, and cultural diversity. The *sensory dimension* examines environmental factors that directly impact user perception, encompassing visual aesthetics, acoustic comfort, tactile experience, and thermal comfort. This comprehensive matrix of factors enables the analysis of the impacts of sustainable real estate projects across multiple dimensions in a measurable, comparable, and traceable manner.

As highlighted by Perera and Mensah (2019), the process of sustainable real estate development inherently entails tensions among the conflicting economic, environmental, and social interests and values of stakeholders, as well as the associated power relations. From this perspective, sustainable real estate development signifies a specific developmental outcome that aligns with the broadest shared meaning derived from the collective values of all stakeholders.

The institutional real estate development model encompasses three tiers of analysis. Firstly, the *empirical observation level* involves identifying specific events, significant institutions, and the power dynamics among them. Secondly, the *strategic and interest level* entails examining actor strategies and interests relating to resources, regulations, and the conceptual frameworks guiding the development process. Thirdly, the *social relations level* facilitates the assessment of connections with the production model, regulatory mode, and societal ideology within which development takes place. This theoretical framework can be integrated with the subsequent seven fundamental principles of sustainable real estate development:

Table 1 Factors used in the Quadruple Net Value Analysis

Economic factors	
Return on investment	Profitability, occupancy rates, and investor return
Increased tax revenue	Increased property value, sales tax contribution
Increased employment	Construction period and long-term employment opportunities
Economic and infrastructure development	Local development, transportation infrastructure, and improvement of public services
Cost avoidance	Reduction in energy, maintenance and transportation costs
Insurance and legal costs	Fire, flood, health, and litigation expenses
Environmental factors	
Waste reduction	Construction waste, landfill use and sewage load
Carbon reduction	Energy efficiency, embodied energy, and landscape applications
Water conservation	Rainwater harvesting, flood management
Biodiversity	Ecological conservation, native species, wildlife
Indoor air quality and health effects	Clean air, walkability, access to nature, greenways
Food production	Gardens, urban agriculture, and preservation of agricultural lands
Shelter	Structural safety, climatic comfort
Social factors	
Safety and security	Crime prevention, accident prevention
Recreation and community interaction	Parks, open spaces, and public gathering areas
Private space	Quietness, spiritual places, and personal experiences
Diversity	Ethnic, socio-economic, and cultural diversity
Convenience	Access to shopping, transportation, education, and employment
Sensory factors	
Sight	Architectural quality, natural scenery
Sound	Quietness, natural sounds, noise control
Taste	Social relationships and experiential tastes
Touch	Textural diversity, material quality
Smell	Vegetation, environmental diversity, and sources of odours
Temperature and heat	Thermal comfort, humidity, sun-shade balance, and wind direction

Source: Booth et al. (2013)

1. *Life cycle assessment:* Conducting a comprehensive analysis of environmental impacts from raw material extraction through to the building's demolition; identifying areas for improvement utilising tools such as embodied carbon calculators.
2. *Circular material flows:* Abandoning linear "take-make-dispose" production models and embracing closed-loop systems.
3. *Resilience planning:* Designing structures that are resilient to climate stressors such as floods and heatwaves and can sustain their functionality during crises.

4. *Stakeholder collaboration:* Involving architects, engineers, local communities, and policymakers early in the design process to align ecological objectives with local needs.
5. *Energy systems reform:* Prioritising strategies for energy efficiency is essential, given that buildings are responsible for approximately 30% of global energy consumption.
6. *Water management networks:* Developing comprehensive and integrated water management systems in accordance with projections indicating that urban water demand will exceed supply by 40% by the year 2030.
7. *Human-centric environments:* Prioritising user health, comfort, and well-being through the application of biophilic design principles.

From an institutional perspective, sustainable real estate development is characterised as a non-linear process involving feedback loops. In this context, stakeholder knowledge is transient, limited, and frequently tacit. Consequently, participation and consensus-building are not only decision-making tools but also serve as mechanisms for disseminating knowledge, fostering social learning, transforming values, and creating collective meaning over time. The primary characteristics of the social learning process are outlined as follows:

- It operates as an incremental process.
- It provides continuous improvement through feedback loops.
- It accepts the evolution of stakeholder values over time.
- It supports the creation of shared meaning through consensus building.

2.3 Sector Structure and Actors

The real estate industry involves a diverse range of actors across various subdisciplines and specialised areas. Although it accounts for around 20% of the gross domestic product in the United States (Urban Land Institute, 1997), its economic impact is relatively smaller in developing countries, such as Türkiye (Tanrıvermiş, 2019). The sector can generally be divided into three main categories: investors and property owners, financiers, and professionals offering specialised services.

The development process necessitates the coordination of numerous experts throughout the entire lifecycle, from pre-project stages to sales and operations. This process encompasses a broad range of specialisations, including brokers, planners, engineers, marketers, construction contractors, and legal professionals. Various stakeholders participate in each phase, undertaking vital roles in land selection, design, construction, sales, and property management. The efficient operation of this comprehensive process depends not only on technical expertise but also on effective communication, regulatory compliance, and financial coordination (Peiser & Hamilton, 2012; Table 2).

Each category of real estate essentially functions as a separate sector, addressing distinct purposes, target markets, and user profiles. This diversity signifies that each

Table 2 Actors within the real estate sector

Process stage	Relevant actors
1. Land selection	Real estate brokers, title deed companies, market consultants, contract attorneys
2. Feasibility study	Market consultants, economic consultants, cost estimators, surveyors, mortgage brokers and bankers, land-use attorneys, and engineers
3. Design	Architects; urban planners/landscape architects; general contractors/construction managers
4. Marketing	Real estate brokers, public relations firms, advertising agencies, graphic designers, and internet service providers
5. Financing	Mortgage brokers and bankers, construction lenders, permanent lenders and syndicators, title deed companies, appraisers
6. Construction	Architects; general contractors; engineers; landscape architects; surety companies; authorised auditors
7. Operation	Property managers, specialised maintenance and facility service teams
8. Sale	Real estate brokers, appraisers
Process-wide	Attorneys (title deed, contract, land use, litigation, etc.)

Source: Peiser and Hamilton (2012)

segment possesses unique development strategies, operational dynamics, and investment evaluation criteria. Generally, real estate investments may be categorised as follows:

- *Residential:* Single-family houses, apartment buildings, and gated residential communities.
- *Office:* Central Business District (CBD) office buildings and suburban office parks.
- *Commercial:* Shopping malls, high-street retail, and retail chains.
- *Industrial:* Warehouses, manufacturing facilities, and logistics centres.
- *Hospitality:* Hotels, holiday villages, and resort complexes.
- *Land:* Undeveloped or redevelopment-ready parcels.

Although there are notable differences in development requirements between industrial warehouses and apartment blocks, they share a common institutional framework in many respects, such as land acquisition, access to financing, legal procedures, and construction processes. This suggests that there are structural similarities to some degree among different types of real estate, and therefore, sectoral expertise can be applicable across multiple segments.

2.4 Integrated System Approaches in Sustainable Building Design

The physical expression of sustainable real estate development is reflected in how buildings are designed, constructed, and operated. Nowadays, green building design has shifted from focusing on single-system solutions to adopting multi-system approaches that work together in an integrated and synergistic way. Through this integration, buildings cease to be mere structures providing shelter and become "living organisms" that simultaneously enhance environmental performance, economic efficiency, and user well-being.

The spatial experience upon entering a sustainable building differs significantly from that of conventional structures. In this context, an exemplary illustration is the Bullitt Center (Seattle, USA), which effectively exemplifies the integrated system approach characteristic of sustainable design. Digital panels located in the building's entrance hall provide real-time data on current energy production, water usage, and indoor air quality to visitors. This transparency extends beyond a mere technical information display; it fosters an awareness-oriented experience that fundamentally alters the users' relationship with the building. The integrated systems employed within the Bullitt Centre are meticulously designed to ensure that all processes related to energy, water, waste, and material management operate synergistically. While photovoltaic panels aim to generate surplus energy throughout the year, rainwater harvesting and on-site water treatment systems serve to decrease the building's reliance on external resources. Additionally, composting toilets constitute part of a circular system that transforms wastewater into fertiliser. The heating and cooling demands are met by 26 geothermal wells installed underground, and automatic window systems facilitate natural ventilation. The materials selected for construction, comprising recycled concrete and low-toxicity, sustainable wood, further emphasise the commitment to sustainability. Through this integrated approach, the building is characterised not merely as an environmentally conscious structure but as a systemic entity that interacts with its users, thereby embedding sustainability awareness into daily life (Shehadi, 2020).

At the core of the transformation in sustainable building design are the extensive modelling, analysis, and simulation capabilities offered by Building Information Modelling (BIM) technology. BIM-based parametric design tools allow architects and engineers to evaluate, in real-time, the impacts of a decision—such as selecting a facade material—on energy performance, maintenance requirements, visual aesthetics, and user comfort. As a result, the design process shifts away from purely intuition-driven decisions towards a more scientifically precise approach, utilising multidimensional data.

In sustainable building design, energy efficiency remains one of the most visible and measurable components of sustainable design. However, current practices are evolving towards more holistic approaches that go beyond merely reducing energy consumption. An example of this is the Vauban settlement in Freiburg, Germany. Families living in residences built to Passivhaus standards here consume only 15 kWh/m^2 of energy annually, yet this low consumption is achieved without sacrificing comfort. These buildings, which combine super-insulation, airtight facade systems, and ventilation solutions with heat recovery, reduce their energy demand by approximately 90% compared to traditional structures. They also enhance user comfort through consistent indoor temperatures, quietness, and high air quality (Fraker, 2013).

A significant intersection between sustainable building design and digitalisation concerns intelligent building systems that emphasise user interaction. In this context, the Edge building in Amsterdam exemplifies such integration by achieving an energy efficiency rate of 98.4% through automated adjustments of lighting and temperature settings based on occupancy, facilitated by its Internet of Things (IoT) infrastructure. Nevertheless, what truly distinguishes this building is its capability to enable employees to control lighting and temperature at their desks, and the status of coffee machines, via their smartphones (Jalia et al., 2019). These customisation options demonstrate that sustainability can be realised through an approach that enhances the user experience rather than diminishes it, by combining energy efficiency with individual comfort.

Another example from Türkiye is the Garanti BBVA Technology Campus in Pendik, Istanbul. This LEED Gold-certified building features daylight-integrated lighting systems, as well as heating and cooling solutions designed in accordance with sustainability principles. Dynamic sun-shading systems on the building's facade respond to climatic conditions, enhancing energy efficiency (Arkiv, 2025). Flexibility in workspace design and optimal utilisation of natural light were key criteria. Additionally, Garanti BBVA's data centre in Pendik saves approximately TL 1.8 million annually by using innovative technologies aimed at reducing its carbon footprint.

2.5 Holistic Solutions in Water Management

Water management is a crucial aspect of sustainable building design where environmental responsibility and practical needs meet. In this context, smart water systems are not just an ideal solution but are increasingly becoming a vital infrastructure element. For example, Singapore's Punggol Eco-Town project exemplifies comprehensive water management solutions. The closed-loop hydrology systems used in the project enable 100% of wastewater to be treated with membrane bioreactors for reuse. The treated water is then used for irrigation and toilet flushing, supporting the water needs of 42,000 households with minimal reliance on the city grid (Material Economics, 2020). This system not only conserves water but also embodies the integration of ecological cycles into the built environment.

Similarly, the Bullitt Centre in Seattle garners attention due to its innovative water management solutions enacted at the architectural level. The building's 250,000-gallon rainwater harvesting system reduces dependency on municipal water supplies by 34% annually. Furthermore, the transparent water storage and filtration systems incorporated within the structure allow occupants to observe the processes of rainwater collection, treatment, and reuse. This visual transparency transforms water conservation from an abstract environmental policy into a comprehensible, traceable, and embedded aspect of daily life.

2.6 Circular Approaches in Material Innovation

The construction sector's dependence on energy-intensive materials such as concrete and steel accounts for approximately 23% of global carbon emissions. This situation necessitates a fundamental transformation in material selection that emphasises not only aesthetics and structural integrity but also environmental sustainability. In this context, innovative materials such as cross-laminated timber (CLT) are at the forefront of sustainable construction practices. The Vergé building in Switzerland can sequester roughly 1200 tons of CO_2 equivalent through biogenic carbon storage, owing to the utilisation of CLT. Nevertheless, the advantages offered by CLT extend beyond environmental performance; the natural texture and warmth of the wood contribute to enhancing users' emotional connection with the space, thereby reducing stress levels and fostering psychological well-being.

Furthermore, in material innovation, it is not only low-emission production that matters, but also re-evaluating the material throughout its entire life cycle. An advanced example of this approach is the *Circle Tower* project in Amsterdam. In this project, 12,000 building elements were digitally tracked, and material passports were created for each one, outlining future reuse possibilities. The fact that approximately 85% of these components will be reused in other projects at the end of their lifespan, rather than becoming waste, demonstrates the construction industry's shift from a linear "take-make-dispose" model to a circular economy. Another benefit of using circular materials is that it encourages sustainability awareness among users. Each recycled building element is not just a material but also a story, adding semantic depth to the space. This layered experience makes sustainability more than a technical aim; it becomes an integral part of everyday life.

2.7 Human-Centred Design and Biophilic Approaches

One of the most significant developments in sustainable building design in recent years has been the emphasis on human health and well-being, alongside technological performance. Biophilic design principles incorporate people's fundamental connection with nature into the spatial experience, offering both environmental and psychological benefits. Spaces that include natural light, greenery, and non-toxic materials significantly improve workplace environmental conditions, with studies showing satisfaction improvements of up to 110% in air quality and thermal comfort. Research demonstrates measurable productivity gains, with employees reporting a 16% improvement in work performance efficiency and working 16% more than expected by their employers (Gray & Curtis, 2017).

The WELL Building Standard facilitates the systematic implementation of this comprehensive approach. This standard, which requires air quality monitoring, ergonomic arrangements, and the spatial integration of natural elements, demonstrates that health benefits can lead to economic gains by reducing absenteeism by 19% in certified offices. Additionally, all workplace well-being metrics show statistically significant improvements, including employee satisfaction with how the workplace supports their health and analytical work (Gray & Curtis, 2017). Nonetheless, the true significance of the WELL standard resides in its ability to create environments where employees feel valued and are aware that their health is a top priority.

In environments where natural lighting is optimised, employees not only conserve energy but also synchronise with their natural biorhythms by experiencing variations in light throughout the day. This experience mitigates stress levels while enhancing productivity and focus. In areas where acoustic comfort is assured, users enjoy the tranquillity provided by protection from noise pollution. At the same time, the privacy afforded by sound insulation enables them to engage in higher-quality social interactions.

2.8 Technological Integration and Smart Systems

The strength of contemporary sustainable architecture stems not only from individual systems but also from their synergistic integration. The Internet of Things (IoT) technology enables buildings to become intelligent entities that can perceive their environment and respond accordingly. Elements such as occupancy sensors, air quality and temperature monitors, and system performance trackers allow for real-time optimisation of building operations.

An illustrative example of this methodology is Spine Tower, situated in Maslak, Istanbul. Over 2500 sensors are integrated into the structure, continuously monitoring and optimising energy consumption, indoor air quality, lighting levels, and security parameters. With a comprehensive data collection and analysis infrastructure, the building attains approximately 35% in energy savings and a 28% reduction in operational costs. Simultaneously, personalised comfort experiences, sensitive to individual needs, are also provided. Furthermore, artificial intelligence (AI) algorithms are capable of learning the behavioural patterns of building occupants and automatically optimising environmental conditions, thereby establishing comfort parameters based on individual preferences. Predictive maintenance applications can intervene by identifying potential failures in system components in advance through machine learning algorithms, resulting in a 25–30% reduction in maintenance costs while ensuring the user experience remains uninterrupted and sustainable.

3 Regulatory Frameworks and Certification Systems

Regulatory frameworks and certification systems play a crucial role in the growth of sustainable real estate development. These systems not only ensure quality assurance but also serve as guiding signals to the market.

3.1 Global Standards Shaping Real Estate Development Practices

In the real estate sector, there is a high probability of developing large office buildings, regional shopping centres, and hotels, especially in city centres and suburban transit zones, often situated at the intersections of major highways and public transportation hubs. Such projects are not only beneficial for urban density and accessibility but also adhere to sustainability criteria aimed at reducing environmental impacts. In this context, global green building certification systems play an important role in guiding industry transformation through benchmarking in sustainable real estate development.

Initiatives operating within the sustainable real estate ecosystem exhibit diversity in terms of their target audiences, measurement frameworks, and sustainability focus areas (Table 3). These initiatives can be categorised into four principal groups: certification systems, performance assessment tools, reporting frameworks, and management standards. Certification systems, such as LEED and BREEAM, ensure quality assurance in building design and construction processes, while performance assessment tools, including GRESB and Energy Star, evaluate the operational performance of existing structures. Reporting frameworks, such as GRI-CRESS and CDP, facilitate corporate transparency, whereas management standards, like ISO 14001, provide a methodology for systematic environmental management. This multi-layered and complementary structure allows for the comprehensive monitoring, evaluation, and management of sustainability objectives within the real estate sector, thereby supporting transformation at a global level.

3.2 Turkish Applications: YeS-TR and ÇEDBİK

The development of domestic certification systems in Türkiye constitutes a strategically significant endeavour in incorporating the nation's climatic and cultural attributes into certification standards. In this regard, two prominent systems, established through both official and private initiatives, are particularly noteworthy.

i. *The YeS-TR (Green Certificate) System:* YeS-TR represents the national green building certification framework established by the Turkish Ministry of Environment, Urbanisation, and Climate Change (ERKE Design, 2024). The "Certification System Manual" was formulated in 2018, the software infrastructure was developed in 2019, and the system achieved full operational status in the first quarter of 2021 (Ministry of Environment, Urbanisation and Climate Change, 2020; 2022a, b).

The system comprises five principal modules that take into account Türkiye's geographical and climatic features. These modules include Integrated Building Design, Construction, and Management (BBT); Building Material and Life Cycle Assessment (YDD); Indoor Environmental Quality (İOK); Energy Use and

Table 3 Key initiatives in the sustainable real estate sector

System	Full name	Target audience	Key sustainability issues	Rationale for the system
ULI—Green print	Urban land institute—Green print	Building owners, operators, and users	Climate change, energy, water, waste	Data collection, analysis, comparison, and reporting
GRI—CRESS	Global reporting initiative—Construction and real estate sector supplement	Companies that invest in, develop, construct, or manage buildings or infrastructure	Economy, environment, labour practices, human rights, society, product responsibility	Sustainability reporting
UN PRI	United Nations—Principles for responsible investment	Institutional investors	Environment, social, governance	Signed principles + reporting framework
GRESB	Global real estate sustainability benchmark	Institutional investors	Energy, greenhouse gas emissions, water, waste	Sustainability performance benchmarking
Energy star—Portfolio manager	Energy star—Portfolio manager	Building owners, operators, and users	Energy, water, greenhouse gas emissions	Monitoring and benchmarking
CDP	Carbon disclosure project	Investors and companies (primarily)	Climate change, water, and forests	Measurement and reporting
USGBC—LEED	US green building council - leadership in energy and environmental design	Developers and building owners, operators, and users	Green buildings	Green building certification
BREEAM	Building research establishment environmental assessment methodology	Developers and building owners, operators, and users	Green buildings	Green building certification
WBCSD—EEB	World business Council for Sustainable Development—Energy efficiency in buildings	Owners and managers of large building portfolios	Energy	Decision making/ overcoming barriers to energy efficiency
ISO 14001—Environmental Management	International Organization of Standardization 14,001—Environmental management	Companies	(Variable)	Framework for developing environmental management systems

Source: own compilation

Efficiency (EKV); and Water and Waste Management (SAY) (Sustainable Future, 2023). Based on the evaluation, four distinct certification levels are conferred: "Pass", "Good", "Very Good", and "National Excellence" (Aşan, 2022).

Following the update of regulations in 2022, the Turkish Environment Agency was officially designated as the assessing authority (Ministry of Environment, Urbanisation and Climate Change, 2022a, b). The system is managed exclusively via a digital platform. YeS-TR is applicable to both newly constructed and existing buildings, encompassing a broad spectrum of building types, including residential, office, educational, healthcare, and industrial structures (AECO, 2024).

ii. *ÇEDBİK (Çevre Dostu Yeşil Binalar Derneği - Eco-Friendly Green Buildings Association) and the B.E.S.T System:* ÇEDBİK is a non-governmental organisation established in October 2007, comprising a team of 23 individuals and companies, with the aim of advancing Türkiye's construction industry in accordance with sustainable principles (Çevre Dostu Yeşil Binalar Derneği, 2024; Cevreciyiz, 2024). The organisation functions as a member of the World Green Building Council (WGBC) (Yeşil Aşkı, 2020).

ÇEDBİK's most significant contribution is the development of the B.E.S.T certification system. The initial version of the system was launched in 2015 and was updated to version 2.0 in August 2019 (ÇEDBİK, 2024). The B.E.S.T system offers assessments across two categories: residential and commercial buildings, and creates criteria tailored to local conditions.

Both systems offer green building assessments customised for Türkiye's local conditions. While YeS-TR, as an official certification system, has a legal foundation, B.E.S.T. acts as a sectoral pioneer as a civil initiative. Although YeS-TR is recognised less due to its novelty (AECO, 2024), it holds strong potential for widespread adoption due to its official backing. Both systems align with international standards but have the advantage of better reflecting local characteristics.

3.3 Policy Instruments Driving Market Transformation

Government policies and regulations catalyse the growth of sustainable real estate development. The policy tools suggested in this context help speed up sectoral change through mandatory standards, financial incentives, and market-based mechanisms.

i. *Building Energy Codes and Regulations:* Many countries are progressively strengthening their regulations concerning building energy efficiency. In this context, the European Union's Energy Performance of Buildings Directive (EPBD) was amended on 12 April 2024, establishing a noteworthy threshold. According to the amended directive, all new constructions are required to be zero-emission buildings by 2030. Additionally, from 2028 onwards, new buildings owned by public institutions must also attain zero-emission status (European Commission, 2024; Narter & Partners, 2024a).

In Türkiye, the "Regulation Amending the Regulation on Energy Performance in Buildings", prepared by the Ministry of Environment, Urbanisation and Climate Change, was published in the Official Gazette on February 19, 2022 and became effective on January 1, 2023 (Ministry of Environment, Urbanization and Climate Change, 2023). According to this regulation, as of January 1, 2023, it is mandatory for all buildings exceeding 5000 m^2 to be constructed with an energy performance rating of at least "B" and to derive at least 5% of their energy consumption from renewable energy sources. Starting 1 January 2025, this requirement will be extended to all buildings larger than 2000 m^2, provided that at least 10% of the energy used originates from renewable sources. These regulations aim to promote energy-efficient construction practices and to enhance the utilisation of renewable energy.

ii. *Carbon Pricing Mechanisms*: Carbon pricing is increasingly recognised as a vital policy instrument in the pursuit of sustainability objectives. Such systems internalise environmental externalities by imposing a per-ton CO_2 charge on traditional construction techniques, thereby augmenting the economic attractiveness of sustainable alternatives.

Türkiye has taken its initial step in this domain by initiating a pilot application of its Emissions Trading System (ETS) on October 15, 2024 (Sustainable Future, 2024). Following a two-year transition period, the first phase of implementation is scheduled to commence on 15 October 2026 (Narter & Partners, 2024b). The pilot phase of the ETS will encompass facilities classified under Category C of the Turkish National Monitoring, Reporting, and Verification (MRV) System, which includes approximately 130 facilities that emit more than 500 kt CO2e. This system possesses the potential to convert the low carbon footprint of sustainable building projects into a competitive economic advantage. Consequently, investments in green buildings will not only benefit the environment but also enhance financial performance.

4 Technological Innovations Reshaping Real Estate Development

Technological innovations play a central role in sustainable real estate development, driving and enriching the transformation processes within the sector. These innovations not only enhance the environmental and economic performance of buildings but also comprehensively improve the user experience.

Technological solutions applicable throughout the sustainable real estate value chain provide a comprehensive range, from the design phase to end-of-life management. Within this framework, during the design phase, Building Information Modelling (BIM) and 3D mapping technologies support multi-stakeholder planning, enabling the development of solutions that are sensitive to energy performance. Throughout the construction process, material efficiency, modular construction techniques, and prefabricated components reduce resource consumption and minimise waste production. In the operational phase, smart asset optimisation, HVAC (heating, ventilation, and air conditioning) analytics, and building automation systems make energy consumption traceable and manageable, thereby decreasing the carbon footprint. During the retrofit period, adaptation solutions and life-cycle extension strategies ensure the integration of existing buildings with sustainability objectives in mind. At the end-of-life stage, zero-waste management and material recovery systems transform into practical applications that facilitate the transition to a circular economy (World Economic Forum, 2016).

Throughout these procedures, digital transformation tools—such as data management platforms, predictive maintenance systems, and digital tagging solutions—enhance the quality of decision-making processes and improve operational efficiency. Moreover, green lease agreements and "soft landing" strategies promote the establishment of more effective and transparent collaborations among property owners, tenants, and service providers.

4.1 Smart Building Technologies

The integration of information and communication technologies with building systems is transforming structures from reactive to proactive and predictive entities. This smart transformation introduces innovative and radical solutions for improving building performance. In this field, two technologies are especially important: the integration of the Internet of Things (IoT) and artificial intelligence/machine learning.

IoT technology transforms buildings into intelligent systems that perceive their environment and respond accordingly. Sensor networks monitoring occupancy, environmental conditions, and system performance enable real-time optimisation of building operations. The Bullitt Centre in Seattle is a pioneering example in this field. Equipped with a comprehensive IoT ecosystem of 1400 sensors, the building achieves net-zero energy and water consumption while reducing maintenance costs by 40% (Jax, 2025). This success demonstrates the power of an integrated systems approach.

Artificial intelligence algorithms, however, improve the learning and adaptation ability of building systems to optimise performance. These technologies evaluate historical data to forecast future needs and proactively modify system settings. Predictive maintenance applications utilise machine learning algorithms to identify potential failures in building systems before they occur. This method reduces maintenance costs by 25–30% while enhancing system reliability.

4.2 Renewable Energy Integration

The integration of renewable energy technologies into real estate development projects has become a fundamental element of environmental performance and economic value enhancement today. According to data from IRENA (2025), global renewable energy capacity expanded by 15.1% in 2024, reaching 4448 GW, highlighting the rapid pace of transformation. These developments demonstrate that in the real estate sector's pursuit of energy independence, renewable technologies are now a necessity rather than an option.

Building-integrated photovoltaic (BIPV) systems represent the most visible aspect of this transformation. According to BCC Research (2025), the global BIPV market reached USD 17.1 billion in 2024; this figure is projected to increase to USD 42 billion by 2029. These systems substitute traditional building materials, maintaining aesthetic appeal while generating energy. According to an analysis by Paradise Energy Solutions (2024), commercial solar energy systems yield an average return on investment of 13.52%, with payback periods ranging from 9 to 16 years. These figures establish highly appealing economic parameters, particularly for long-term real estate investments.

Türkiye's substantial geothermal potential presents considerable prospects for alternative energy technologies. As noted by the U.S. Department of Energy (2024), geothermal heat pump systems achieve a coefficient of performance ranging from 3.5 to 4.0, offering a return on investment within five to 10 years. Moreover, hybrid systems and sophisticated energy storage innovations enhance energy security and strengthen independence (Pacific Northwest National Laboratory, 2024).

From an economic perspective, the case for integrating renewable energy grows stronger every day. According to a report by IRENA (2024), the Levelised Cost of Energy (LCOE) for solar power is 56% lower than that of fossil fuels. While this gap helps reduce operating expenses, incentives such as the 30% Investment Tax Credit in the U.S. make investing in renewable energy even more appealing (U.S. Environmental Protection Agency, 2024).

The regulatory framework also promotes integration. The EU's RED III (2023) directive aims for 42.5% renewable energy use by 2030. The EPBD, updated in 2024, requires that all new buildings be zero-emission from 2030 onwards (European Parliament and Council, 2023 and 2024).

Looking towards the future, technological advancements are enhancing the potential for integration. The efficiency of perovskite solar cells has increased from 3% in 2009 to 26% in 2024, with commercial application anticipated to commence in 2025/2026 (U.S. Department of Energy, 2024). Artificial intelligence and Internet of Things (IoT) systems, in turn, provide predictability and efficiency in energy management. Nonetheless, as articulated by the International Energy Agency (2024), high capital costs in developing nations remain one of the principal obstacles to this transformation.

4.3 Circular Construction Techniques

Applying circular economy principles to the construction sector fosters innovative methods that enhance waste reduction and resource efficiency in property development projects. This shift signifies a move from the traditional "cradle-to-grave" model to a "cradle-to-cradle" approach, ensuring that building materials are revalued as resources at the end of their lifespan. The ambition of pioneering cities like Amsterdam to fully adopt a circular economy by 2050 illustrates that this approach has become not just an environmental aspiration but also an economic imperative.

Digital material passports constitute the technological backbone of this transformation. These systems facilitate the digital tracking of building components throughout their life cycle, thereby optimising recovery and reuse processes. A study conducted in the Amsterdam Metropolitan Area revealed that the 2.6 million tons of building materials resulting from annual renovation and demolition activities are valued at EUR 688 million (Metabolic, 2024). These figures illustrate the potential of material passports to generate both environmental and economic value. Initiatives supported by the European Union, such as the Buildings as Material Banks (BAMB) project, have implemented practical applications of material passports, demonstrating that buildings can be conceived as future dismantlable repositories of materials.

Modular and prefabricated construction technologies represent some of the most tangible applications of circular construction techniques. Off-site manufacturing processes, enabled by precision production conducted within controlled factory environments, substantially diminish construction waste and enhance quality control. According to a report by the Waste and Resources Action Programme (WRAP), modular construction approaches can achieve waste reductions of up to 90% for materials such as wood, cardboard, plastic, and concrete compared to conventional methodologies (Modular Building Institute, 2024). This high level of performance is achieved through precise cutting operations executed within factory settings and the recycling of waste materials within the same facility.

From an economic perspective, modular construction techniques provide significant benefits for real estate developers. An analysis conducted by McKinsey and Company (2022; 2024) indicates a potential for up to 20% savings in overall project costs when employing modular construction methods (World Economic Forum, 2025). Additionally, a sector report authored by Allied Modular Building Systems (2025) notes that these savings are achieved through shorter project durations, reduced material waste, and decreased labour expenses (Selo Group, 2021; Allied Modular Building Systems, 2025). Particularly in projects characterised by labour-intensive activities, cost advantages may range from 15 to 25% by utilising standardisation and economies of scale.

In terms of environmental impact, circular construction techniques have the potential to reduce the carbon footprint of the real estate sector significantly. A study conducted by Elements Europe on the Camp Hill project in Birmingham found that the steel modular construction method yields an approximate 35% reduction in embodied carbon throughout the entire project life cycle (World Economic Forum, 2025). Furthermore, a report by the Modular Building Institute indicates that modular buildings consume 67% less energy during the construction phase compared to traditional structures, underscoring the sustainability benefits of this technology.

In Türkiye, circular construction techniques are still in the developmental stage but hold significant potential. The country's young population, developing technology infrastructure, and increasing environmental awareness create a suitable environment for the widespread adoption of these technologies. Especially in regions with high earthquake risk, the quick installation and safety advantages of modular structures offer considerable advantages over traditional construction methods (Center for American Progress, 2024). Furthermore, in line with Türkiye's 2053 Net Zero Emission target, circular construction techniques are emerging as a crucial tool for reducing carbon emissions in the construction sector.

From a future perspective, circular construction techniques not only provide solutions to current environmental issues but also have the potential to develop new business models in the real estate sector. Reassessing building materials at the end-of-life stage creates additional revenue streams for developers while also significantly contributing to sustainability goals. For example, Amsterdam's aim of reducing primary raw material use by 50% by 2030 is pioneering the development of regulatory frameworks that promote the adoption of circular construction methods.

5 Financial Impacts and Market Dynamics

The financial aspect of sustainable real estate development is a key factor in the sustainability of sectoral transformation. Analysing this aspect shows impacts across a wide range, from investment choices to market trends.

5.1 Cost-Benefit Analysis of Sustainable Real Estate Development

The financial performance of sustainable buildings demands a thorough assessment of both upfront investment costs and long-term benefits. The performance analyses demonstrate the economic validity of sustainability.

i. *Capital Cost Analysis:* Each type of real estate essentially functions as a separate industry, catering to different purposes, markets, and clients. Although industrial warehouses have completely different development needs compared to apartment buildings, they share a common institutional framework regarding land, financing, legal matters, and even construction.

Understanding the financial structure of real estate development projects requires a comprehensive analysis of cost components and income streams. Development costs mainly include land acquisition and construction expenses, while the financing structure relies on a balanced mix of equity and debt financing. The ratio of land cost to total investment varies based on the project's location and type, but generally falls between 15 and 25% (Peiser, 2015). Construction costs, by contrast, vary depending on technical specifications, quality levels, and technologies employed.

Within the financing structure, an increase in the equity ratio reduces the debt service burden; however, it simultaneously increases the cost of equity. In assessing operating income, Net Operating Income (NOI) is derived by deducting vacancy rates and operating expenses from gross rental income. The residual cash flow available to the investor is then calculated by subtracting debt service payments from the total cash flow. Such financial modelling serves as an essential instrument for evaluating how the incremental costs associated with sustainable projects can be balanced against long-term economic benefits (Peiser, 2015).

Green buildings incur initial costs that are 2–7% higher than those of traditional constructions, primarily due to the use of advanced systems, premium materials, and bespoke design processes (Biswas et al., 2024). Nonetheless, this cost differential is progressively diminishing as sustainable technologies mature and economies of scale are realised. To accurately assess the true value of this initial expense disparity, a thorough analysis of the operational performance of green buildings, supported by empirical data, is essential (Tanrıvermiş & Tanrıvermiş, 2021). A comprehensive field investigation conducted in Haryana, India, provides substantial evidence on this matter (Kanika et al., 2016). The comparative evaluation of Indoor Environmental Quality (IEQ) performance between four Green Rated Integrated Habitat Assessment (GRIHA) certified green buildings and four proximate traditional buildings demonstrates the viability of sustainable investments across five pivotal parameters. In this chapter, each building's floors were divided into five distinct zones (east, west, north, south, and central), with detailed measurements taken during both winter and summer seasons. This methodological approach facilitated a comprehensive assessment of the impacts of local climate variations and seasonal changes on building performance (Table 4).

The comparative analysis results demonstrate that green buildings exhibit a statistically significant superiority across four of the five fundamental performance parameters. The most notable disparity is observed in air quality management, with green buildings maintaining substantially lower pollutant levels than conventional structures during both winter (82%) and summer (74%) seasons. This superiority is attributable to the implementation of advanced ventilation systems, utilisation of low-emission materials, and enhanced building envelope design.

The results from natural lighting performance clearly show the energy efficiency potential of green buildings. The improvement in lighting ranges from 215% to 309%, reducing the need for artificial lighting and leading to significant energy savings, while also enhancing visual comfort and productivity for users. This performance is achieved through the combined effect of smart glass technologies, optimised window design, and interior space arrangements.

The findings on thermal comfort demonstrate the success of energy management strategies in green buildings. Indoor temperatures that are 7 °C higher in winter and 19 °C lower in summer offer a potential for 25–30% savings in HVAC energy use. The improvement in noise control of more than 25 dB provides clear benefits for employee focus and overall well-being.

Table 4 IEQ performance comparison of green and traditional buildings

Performance parameter	Green building	Traditional building	Performance difference
Air pollutants (ppm)			
Winter average	0.99	5.43	82% cleaner
Summer average	1.39	5.43	74% cleaner
Temperature control °C			
Winter comfort level	20.4	13.04	+7.36 °C more comfortable
Summer comfort level	26.8	45.77[a]	−18.97 °C more comfortable
Natural lighting (lux)			
Winter lighting level	873	277	215% brighter
Summer lighting level	1135	277	309% brighter
Noise control (dB)			
Winter noise level	45.5	71.12	−25.62 dB quieter
Summer noise level	45.8	71.12	−25.32 dB quieter
Humidity rate (%)			
Winter humidity level	51.8	56.46	Close to the optimal level
Summer humidity level	62.7	56.46	+6.24% difference

[a] The average summer temperature was calculated from the 39 to 49 °C range
Source: own compilation

The mixed results concerning humidity control highlight an area for optimisation to consider in the design and operation of green buildings. Although some green buildings exhibited higher humidity levels, this is generally attributed to the buildings' increased air exchange rates and natural ventilation strategies.

Empirical evidence suggests that the initial 2–7% increase in costs associated with green buildings is more than offset by the value gained from enhanced operational performance, energy efficiency, and improvements in occupant health and comfort. Particularly in markets with high-energy prices, this superior performance makes green buildings a financially compelling investment alternative. In addition to the benefits in indoor environmental quality, the savings realised during the operational phase substantially contribute to recovering the initial investment costs. These savings encompass a wide range, from direct expense reductions to indirect productivity gains (Table 5).

ii. *Operational Cost Savings:* Life-cycle analyses show that well-designed, properly commissioned, and effectively managed certified green buildings deliver operating expense savings of between 15 and 35% through energy and water conservation, reduced maintenance needs, and enhanced system efficiency. Data from the U.S. Green Building Council (2024) indicate that LEED-certified buildings use 25% less energy and 11% less water, along with a 20% decrease in maintenance costs. In industrial green buildings, reported savings include 23% in operational costs and 15% in maintenance costs (Zuo & Zhao, 2021). Although research by the World Green Building Council (2022) suggests that green buildings can attain savings of up to 37% in operating costs, a more realistic expectation for the average user is a reduction of 15–25%. These savings generate

Table 5 Operational savings and financial impact potential of green buildings

Saving area	Potential impact
Energy savings	25–30% HVAC savings with advanced thermal control
Lighting cost	15–20% electricity savings with 300% better natural lighting
Employee health	Reduced risk of sick building syndrome with 80% cleaner air
Productivity increase	8–15% efficiency increase with optimal comfort conditions
Maintenance costs	20–25% maintenance savings with quality systems

Source: own depiction

Table 6 Comparative analysis of sustainable and traditional real estate

Criterion	Sustainable real estate	Traditional real estate
Initial cost	Higher due to green materials and technology	Lower upfront costs, but higher operating costs
Operational cost	Lower due to energy efficiency and reduced maintenance	Higher due to inefficient energy use and material degradation
Real estate value	Higher due to market demand for eco-friendly buildings	Moderate appreciation depending on market trends
Tenant attraction	Higher due to demand for sustainable living and lower utility costs	Lower due to a lack of environmental benefits
Regulatory compliance	Meets or exceeds green building regulations	May require future retrofitting to meet new standards
Long-term ROI	Higher due to cost savings, tax benefits, and market preference	Moderate, but sensitive to fluctuations in energy prices

Source: Borromeo et al. (2025)

significant financial value through compound effects over the building's lifecycle and tend to provide long-term economic benefits, with payback periods typically ranging from 2 to 4 years (Turner et al., 2008).

A comparative analysis of sustainable versus traditional real estate development can be conducted based on six fundamental criteria. The disadvantage concerning initial investment costs is mitigated by savings in operational expenses, appreciation in market value, and benefits related to regulatory compliance. Sustainable projects demonstrate a clear advantage in tenant attraction and long-term investment yields, while also exhibiting increased resilience to fluctuations in energy prices (Table 6).

iii. *Market Performance and Value Appreciation:* Green buildings provide advantages in market performance; among these, higher rents, increased occupancy rates, and greater tenant satisfaction stand out. However, global market data indicates that rent premiums often fall below commonly cited claims. In mature markets, these premiums usually range from 3% to 9%. According to a detailed analysis by CBRE, which covers 20,600 U.S. office buildings, LEED-certified buildings offer a 4% rent premium when location, building age, and renovation levels are controlled for (CBRE, 2022). Geographical differences significantly influence these premiums; while rent premiums of 3 to 5% are observed in North American markets, the average rate in Asia-Pacific markets is 9.9% (World Economic Forum, 2024).

Although precise percentage data on faster lease-up rates are limited, CoStar data reveals that LEED-certified buildings have 3.8% higher occupancy rates. According to JLL's (2024) prediction, 65% of the demand for low-carbon workspace will be unmet by 2030. Regarding tenant retention performance, there is a limited amount of quantitative data available in the academic literature. Existing studies indicate increased user satisfaction in green buildings; however, definitive comparisons in terms of retention rates have not yet been established in the literature (GSA, 2018). These performance indicators reveal that sustainability investments are valued by the market, while also emphasising that the returns provided vary significantly depending on market maturity, geographical location, and certification level.

Empirical studies within the international academic literature demonstrate that green-certified buildings consistently outperform in market performance (Table 7). These studies, which cover diverse geographical regions, sectors, and certification frameworks, reveal rent premiums ranging from 1 to 11% and sales price premiums from 2 to 19%. Additionally, occupancy rates increase by 1 to 18%. Notably, buildings with low energy performance face market discounts, while the premiums for

Table 7 Examples of green premium/incentive studies

Location/sector	Green certificate	Observed impact
Australia/ residential	Energy efficiency rating	2–6% sales premium with energy rating, increasing with higher rating
USA/class A offices	LEED/ Energy star	No sales premium, 2–4% higher occupancy rate, 30% lower occupancy cost
USA/offices	LEED/ Energy star	3% rent premium; 19% sales premium
USA/offices	LEED/ Energy star	3–5% rent premium, ~15% price premium, 1–3% higher occupancy rate
The Netherlands/ residential	EPC	3–10% price premium for ABC, 1-5% discount for EFG
Singapore/ residential	Green mark	3–6% price premium, up to 14% for platinum
Australia/offices	Green star	1% rent premium, 2% price premium for the highest rating, discount for lower rating
USA/class A offices	LEED/ energy star	10–18% higher occupancy rates for certified buildings
Ireland/ residential	Energy efficiency rating	6–11% sales premium for A/B; 2–4% rent premium for A/B. Discount for lower rating
Other Western Europe/ residential	Energy rating	Austria: 4% rent premium, 8% price premium per grade; Belgium: 3–5% price premium per 100 points; France: 4% price premium per grade; Ireland: 3% price premium per grade
UK/residential	EPC	6–14% premium compared to the lowest grade, regional differences

Sources: McAllister (2012) and World Economic Forum (2016)

high-performance buildings are gradually rising. These findings confirm that sustainability investments are justified not only by environmental reasons but also by strong financial rationales.

5.2 Innovative Financing Mechanisms

In the financing of sustainable real estate initiatives, innovative financial instruments are increasingly gaining prominence alongside conventional methods. Such instruments serve to lower the financing expenses of projects while incentivising sustainability performance. Development finance primarily comprises two components: equity financing and debt financing. Equity financing represents the most challenging and expensive source of capital for developers, as equity investors receive cash flows subsequent to mortgage payments during operation and following the repayment of debt upon the sale of the property.

In the domain of sustainable real estate finance, Environmental, Social, and Governance (ESG) criteria have become the primary determinants influencing investment decisions. Environmental criteria encompass ecological performance metrics, including energy consumption, carbon footprint, water management, and waste reduction. Social criteria encompass social impact assessments, including public accessibility, employee health, community relations, and human rights. Governance criteria are predicated on corporate quality indicators, including transparency, accountability, ethical practices, and risk management. This tripartite framework enables investors to systematically assess sustainability performance and orient their financing choices accordingly (Dimmelmeier, 2024) (Table 8).

Innovative financial instruments are increasingly becoming significant in financing sustainable real estate initiatives (ESMA, 2024). In this context, the two main mechanisms are green loans and green bonds (Canikli, 2022): Green loans are credit tools designed to finance projects that support environmental aims, such as energy efficiency and reducing carbon emissions. In these loans, interest rates are determined based on how well companies meet their sustainability targets, and projects with strong environmental performance can secure more favourable financing options (Canikli, 2022). In this context, the USD 212.5 million green loan provided by the World Bank to Vietnam's VPBank is one of the early examples of this mechanism.

Green bonds are debt instruments whose proceeds are directed exclusively to the financing of environmental projects. The green bond market, which stood at USD 1 billion in 2007, reached USD 1 trillion by 2020. According to 2019 data, geographically, Europe ranked first with USD 307.4 billion, while North America, with USD 190.4 billion, and the Asia-Pacific region, with USD 183.6 billion, held considerable shares. A substantial portion of green bond proceeds is allocated to renewable energy and energy efficiency initiatives, resulting in an approximate reduction of 37 million tons of CO_2 emissions. Furthermore, these investments have yielded renewable energy equivalent to the electricity requirements of 1.5 million households (Canikli, 2022).

Table 8 ESG criteria matrix

Environmental	Social	Governance
Air quality output	Access and affordability of product/service	Accounting and audit process
Biodiversity impacts	Consumer rights	Board structure
Carbon footprint	Corporate philanthropy	Business ethics
Climate change resilience	Customer relations	Compliance
Energy consumption	Data security and customer privacy	Executive compensation
Environmental policy	Diversity issues	Lobbying and political contributions
Freshwater use	Employee engagement	Ownership structure
Groundwater depletion	Fair disclosure and labelling	Reporting and public disclosure
Impacts on the cryosphere	Health and safety of communities	Shareholder rights
Impacts on food supply	Human capital management	Succession planning
Land use	Human rights	Transparency
Natural resource management	Product quality and safety	Voting procedures
Ocean productivity and acidification	Responsible R&D	Advisory board powers and structure
Regulatory and legal risks	Stakeholder and community relations	Client compliance and fee structure
Supply chain management	Supply chain management	Fund governance
Vulnerability to extreme weather		
Waste and hazardous materials management		

Source: Walter (2020) and Coakley (2024)

Türkiye made a significant advancement in sustainable finance by successfully issuing its inaugural sovereign green bond amounting to USD 2.5 billion on April 5, 2023. This seven-year instrument garnered substantial demand from international investors; 64% of the allocation was assigned to investors located in Europe and the United States. As of September 2024, all funds have been allocated to 86 distinct projects, with the largest portion (56%) allocated to clean transportation, followed by climate change adaptation (20%) and sustainable water management (13%) (Ministry of Treasury and Finance, 2024).

The Sustainable Finance Framework, published in 2021, underpins this successful issuance process. Developed in accordance with the principles of the International Capital Market Association (ICMA), it has also received approval from Sustainalytics. Moreover, Türkiye's ratification of the Paris Climate Agreement in 2021, establishing a net-zero emission target for 2053, and its elevation of the Nationally Determined Contribution (NDC) target to 41% have further reinforced this process at the institutional level.

Pioneering steps have also been taken on the private sector side. The Turkish Industrial Development Bank (TSKB) became the first implementer with its USD

300 million green bond issuance in 2016. Following this, organisations such as YDA Construction, Rönesans, Garanti Bank, and Zorlu Enerji have also created resources for sustainable projects using similar green financing instruments. To support these developments, the Sermaye Piyasası Kurulu (2021) published the "Green Debt Instrument, Sustainable Debt Instrument, Green Lease Certificate, Sustainable Lease Certificate Guide", aiming to ensure standardisation and reliability in the market.

6 Successful Sustainable Real Estate Projects in Türkiye

Türkiye's sustainable real estate sector has developed through pioneering projects in the past decade. These initiatives have successfully gained international green building certifications across various use types, setting industry standards. This section examines three notable projects in the education, office, and commercial sectors:

6.1 Pioneering Application in the Education Sector: Özyeğin University Çekmeköy Campus

An example within Türkiye's sustainable educational infrastructure is the Özyeğin University Çekmeköy Campus. Designed by the internationally acclaimed architectural firm RMJM, known for their work on the Cambridge and Princeton campuses, this campus was finalised between 2011 and 2013 and has achieved the distinction of being Türkiye's first university campus to receive LEED Gold certification (Enerji Günlüğü, 2013; Özyeğin University, 2025).

The sustainability strategies implemented across the campus, which encompasses an area of 127,000 to 143,000 m^2, demonstrate a comprehensive approach spanning numerous aspects, including energy efficiency, water management, and green space planning (Table 9). Particularly, in terms of energy performance, the campus outperforms standard buildings by 35%. This considerable achievement has been realised through the deployment of integrated solutions such as centralised energy distribution, high-efficiency mechanical systems, and smart building automation.

The campus has implemented innovative water management solutions, such as rainwater harvesting and greywater treatment systems. According to the project

Table 9 Özyeğin University campus sustainability indicators

Category	Performance indicator	Achieved result
Energy efficiency	Savings compared to standard buildings	35%
Green space ratio	Green portion of the campus area	>50%
Certification status	LEED gold certified	Received in 2013
Fresh air ratio	As per the ASHRAE 62.1 standard	Over 30%
Area usage	Total campus area	127,000–143,000 m^2

Source: Altensis (2019)

report by Altensis (2019), significant water savings have been achieved through the treatment and reuse of greywater collected from taps in toilet facilities. Furthermore, more than 50% of the campus area is designated as green space, and water consumption, alongside chemical fertiliser use, has been reduced by selecting native and adapted plant species.

In addition to its environmental performance, Özyeğin University, which has also obtained the ISO 14001 Environmental Management System and ISO 45001 Occupational Health and Safety Management System certifications, holds the distinction of being the first university in Türkiye to acquire all three of these certifications concurrently (Özyeğin University, 2025).

6.2 Innovative Approach in Commercial Real Estate: Kağıthane OfisPark

Kağıthane OfisPark, a notable example of sustainability within the office sector, was completed in 2012 by Tekfen Real Estate Development. The project gained recognition by earning a LEED Gold (Core & Shell) certificate and became one of the most distinguished office developments of its era (Tekfen Real Estate, 2025).

Contrary to the traditional single-block concept, the project comprises four blocks connected by social courtyards, increasing natural ventilation and daylight usage (Emre Arolat Architecture, 2024). It is also notable for its energy efficiency, achieving 24% energy savings according to the ASHRAE 90.1 American Building Energy Efficiency Standard (Emlak Web TV, 2012). This performance offers significant benefits for users in terms of operating costs. Additionally, the project's 4.30-metre floor height provides more spacious working environments compared to standard office buildings (Table 10).

The project's success has also been validated through recognition from international awards. The "Highly Commended" accolade at the MIPIM Architectural Review Future Project Awards in 2009, the European Commercial Property Awards in 2010, and the 2012 National Architecture Awards in the building category serve as evidence that the project's excellence in both design and sustainability has achieved international acknowledgement (Arkitera, 2019).

Table 10 Kağıthane OfisPark project features

Feature	Detail
Total area	53,000 m^2 gross area
Number of blocks	4 blocks (connected by bridges)
Floor height	4.30 meters
Energy savings	24% (according to ASHRAE 90.1)
Certificate	LEED gold (Core & Shell)
Completion	2012

Source: Emre Arolat Architecture (2024)

6.3 Sustainability in the Retail Sector: Magnesia Shopping Mall

Magnesia Shopping Mall, recognised for its sustainable initiatives within the retail sector, received certification at the "Good" level in 2013, in accordance with the BREEAM Europe Commercial 2009 criteria (TurkEco, 2020). As the inaugural shopping centre in the city of Manisa in Western Anatolia, it has also significantly contributed to regional development (Table 11).

The design features two entrance levels that utilise the natural elevation difference, enhancing aesthetics and minimising environmental impact through reduced excavation (Arkitera, 2013). This approach improves functionality while minimising environmental impact. The main entrance on Mimar Sinan Boulevard, along with nearby cafes and restaurants overlooking the surrounding buildings and mountains, creates a social square. The lower-level entrance offers direct access to a green parking area for visitors arriving by car.

The sustainability strategies implemented under the BREEAM certification encompass high-efficiency mechanical systems, fixtures with low water consumption, and waterless urinals. To enhance indoor air quality, natural and low-VOC materials were prioritised, and specialised insulation materials were employed to ensure that heat loss and gain performance surpasses local standards (TurkEco, 2020).

The three projects from Türkiye highlight how sustainability can be successfully integrated into real estate sectors. Each project was a pioneer, setting a benchmark for future initiatives. The tangible outcomes, particularly in energy efficiency, water management, material selection, and user comfort, demonstrate that sustainable real estate offers both environmental and economic benefits.

7 Systemic Challenges to Sustainable Real Estate Development

The proliferation of sustainable real estate development confronts interconnected systemic challenges primarily along three axes: technological transition and supply chain issues; a lack of institutional coordination; and inadequate human resources. Research conducted internationally with circular economy experts by Oluleye et al. (2023) indicates that these challenges are not solely technical but also fundamentally linked to social learning processes and the enhancement of institutional capacity.

Table 11 Comparison of successful sustainable real estate projects in Türkiye

Project	Use type	Certificate	Completion	Noteworthy feature
Özyeğin university campus	Education	LEED gold	2013	35% energy efficiency
Kağıthane OfisPark	Office	LEED gold	2012	Courtyard concept and 24% energy savings
Magnesia shopping mall	Commerce	BREEAM good	2013	Use of natural elevation and regional leadership

Source: TurkEco (2020)

7.1 Supply Chain Fragility and Technological Transition Issues

The bottlenecks in the global supply chain for sustainable building materials are a major obstacle to sectoral transformation. The production capacity for innovative solutions, such as cross-laminated timber (CLT), recycled steel composites, and bio-based insulation materials, is insufficient to meet the increasing worldwide demand, resulting in project delivery times of 18–24 months. According to an analysis by McKinsey and Company (2025), the scarcity of materials not only raises costs but also erodes the confidence of developer firms in sustainable technologies, leading to a trend of reverting to traditional materials.

The situation is more delicate in Türkiye's specific case. The fact that around 70% of sustainable building materials rely on imports leaves the country exposed to global supply chain disruptions. Domestic projects, such as the 50,000 m^3 annual capacity CLT production plant commissioned by Kastamonu Entegre in 2023, are encouraging but can only satisfy 15% of the national demand, leaving the sector dependent on imports. The core issue behind this is the erosion of trust resulting from the gap between the claimed performance of new technologies and their actual real-world results. According to a report by the Building Performance Institute Europe (2024), the failure of 30% of green buildings to meet their expected energy performance fosters technological scepticism among decision-makers, negatively influencing investment decisions.

7.2 Institutional Coordination Gaps and the Fragmented Nature of Regulations

The second significant challenge encountered in sustainable real estate development originates from the lack of coordination within multi-level governance frameworks. The proliferation of over 140 distinct green building certification systems globally increases compliance costs by 12 to 15%, particularly affecting international projects and consequently reducing sectoral efficiency. Berglund-Brown et al. (2024) establish that this fragmented configuration results not only in increased costs but also in a diminution of trust and the emergence of conflicts among stakeholders.

In Türkiye, discrepancies between the central government and local authorities in executing projects hinder effective timing and budget management. Significant tension exists between municipalities' long-term environmental objectives and developers' short-term profit expectations. Implementing new, multi-stakeholder governance structures is crucial for addressing and balancing these competing priorities.

Transforming the sector requires not only that the workforce stay proficient in modern technologies but also that architects, engineers, and project managers remain up-to-date with the latest advancements. Unfortunately, current professional training programmes fail to keep pace with these changes. McKinsey and Company (2024) reports that 40% of architecture and engineering curricula rely on technologies that are over 5 years outdated. This gap hampers the adoption of new technologies and slows the dissemination of innovative solutions within the industry.

8 The Future of Sustainable Real Estate Development: A Transformative Evolution

The future of sustainable real estate development indicates a multidimensional evolutionary process moulded by the dynamic interaction of technological convergence, financial innovation, and societal transformation (World Economic Forum, 2021). This progression encompasses not only the technical transformation of the construction sector but also the redefinition of urban living, environmental sustainability, and economic growth.

The transition from the conventional 'do less harm' philosophy to an active benefit strategy exemplifies a fundamental paradigm shift in sustainable real estate development. The regenerative design methodology reconceptualises buildings as living systems that restore and enhance their environments; notably, the Bosco Verticale project in Milan, capable of capturing 1.2 kg CO_2/m^2 daily, stands as a pioneering example of this transformation.

The technological infrastructure underpinning this paradigm shift consists of bio-based materials. Innovative materials, such as mycelium insulation, algae-derived concrete, and agricultural waste composites, have the potential to reduce embodied carbon by 50 to 70% compared to conventional construction products. With the advancement of AI-supported generative design algorithms, it has been demonstrated that building layouts can be optimised for energy efficiency 40% more rapidly than by human designers. Through digital twin technologies, structures are transformed into intelligent learning systems throughout their entire life cycle.

Alongside this transformation, material passports and blockchain-based tracking systems are significantly revolutionising circular economy practices within the construction sector. For instance, in the Circle Tower project in Amsterdam, between 85% and 95% of building components are digitally monitored with the aim of reuse, shifting from a "cradle-to-grave" to a "cradle-to-cradle" paradigm. The updated circular economy criteria of the EU Taxonomy, revised in 2023, establish robust regulatory frameworks that expedite this transition, particularly in the construction and real estate industries.

The transformation taking place in the financial system is reshaping both the scale and accessibility of sustainable real estate investments. According to data from ING Think (2024), global sustainable debt issuance reached USD 800 billion in the first half of 2024, with the strong performance of green bonds having broadened the financing options for projects in this field. Research by Morri et al. (2024) reveals a positive correlation between ESG factors and financial performance, underscoring the significant role of the environmental dimension, particularly in influencing investment value.

ESG criteria now serve as the foundation for investment decisions; according to a report by Deloitte Global (2024), real estate developers are adapting their strategies in response to stakeholder demands for sustainable development. In this context, the increasing adoption of green lease agreements emerges as a crucial instrument that enhances ESG performance by aligning tenant behaviours with sustainability objectives.

Over 130 countries' net-zero emission commitments exert substantial regulatory pressure on the real estate sector. Meanwhile, the European Union's updated Energy Performance of Buildings Directive (EPBD), effective from 2024, requires all new buildings to be zero-emission by 2030. Türkiye's 2053 Net Zero Emission goal further demands a 3–5% annual enhancement in building energy performance, creating both major opportunities and considerable responsibilities for the industry.

The global adoption of carbon pricing systems and the expansion of the EU ETS to include the buildings sector are increasing the financial appeal of sustainable real estate projects. All these developments necessitate the reorganisation of long-term investment strategies in the sector around the theme of sustainability, demonstrating that sustainability is becoming a competitive advantage that boosts market competitiveness through innovative technologies, performance-driven design models, and policy-supported mechanisms.

9 Strategic Transformation Roadmap

In assessing the strategic roadmap for sustainability, macro-policy documents were reviewed, and the results are summarised below:

Short-Term Intervention Areas (2024–2027) The initial steps to promote sustainable real estate development should focus on aligning regulations and enhancing financial incentives to support sustainable development. Harmonising the ÇEDBİK system with international standards and establishing mutual recognition agreements with global certifications, such as LEED and BREEAM, will help gain worldwide acceptance of the national certification system. Additionally, implementing extensive training programmes and providing technical support to bolster local government capacities are essential for improving sector coordination. To diversify financial incentives, applying a 25–50% property tax discount for buildings with an Energy Performance Certificate and expanding the low interest "Sustainable Real Estate Loan" for SMEs will help steer the market towards sustainability.

Medium-Term Transformation Goals (2027–2030) To improve technological infrastructure, establishing 'Sustainable Building Technologies Research Centres' in universities and strengthening their links with industry should be a priority. Creating a "Türkiye Building Performance Database" will accelerate sectoral learning and support evidence-based decisions. Regarding human resources, introducing certification programmes for sustainable building expertise through professional chambers and making these certifications mandatory for project approval will ensure the systematic progress of sectoral skills.

Long-Term Transformative Vision (2030–2053) Starting from 2035, the design of all new public buildings will adhere to regenerative design principles, while promoting the private sector's participation in this transition. The formulation of a comprehensive legal framework, coupled with economic incentives, aims to achieve a 90% material recycling rate within the construction sector by 2040, thereby facilitating the complete integration of circular economy principles.

10 Evaluation and Conclusion

Sustainable real estate development is central to the fight against climate change, one of the most urgent societal issues of the twenty-first century, signifying not only a sectoral transformation but also a societal paradigm shift. The comprehensive analysis in this chapter demonstrates that sustainable practices have transitioned from a niche to mainstream, allowing for the simultaneous creation of value across economic, environmental, social, and technological dimensions.

Research indicates that sustainable real estate projects, evaluated within the "Quadruple Net Value Analysis" framework, generate integrated value across economic, environmental, social, and sensory dimensions. They can achieve up to 30% savings in operating expenses, increase asset value by 15 to 20%, and improve user health by up to 28%, supporting the "triple bottom line" approach. Additionally, green buildings offer 82% cleaner indoor air, 215 to 309% higher natural lighting levels, and noise levels that are 25 dB lower than those of traditional buildings. This suggests that sustainability is a multifaceted approach that encompasses both environmental and holistic strategies, ultimately enhancing human well-being.

The integration of technologies such as artificial intelligence, the Internet of Things, digital twins, and bio-based materials is driving a significant shift in the real estate paradigm. These innovations are transforming buildings from simple reactive systems into proactive, learning, and adaptable structures. They also promote regenerative design and enhance the sector's ability to lower its environmental impact. Türkiye's potential to lead this change depends on its young population, robust construction infrastructure, and expanding technological skills.

ESG criteria have now become a key part of investment decisions. Research by Morri et al. (2024) confirms a positive relationship between environmental performance and financial returns. This indicates that sustainable investments are consistent with economic logic. The global sustainable finance market has grown to a transaction volume of USD 800 billion, and the robust performance of green bonds is broadening financing options for these projects and supporting sectoral change.

Situated at the crossroads of Türkiye's 2053 Net Zero Emission goals and the EU's Green Deal, the country could emerge as a regional leader in sustainable real estate development. Its solar energy capacity, advantageous geography, and a growing green finance sector underpin this potential. The successful issuance of a USD 2.5 billion sovereign green bond in 2023 serves as a key indicator of this capability, complemented by the expansion of domestic technology production, which enhances Türkiye's global competitiveness.

Three success factors are essential for this transformation: First, promoting technological innovations such as regenerative design, AI integration, and the circular economy. Second, enhancing governance across multiple stakeholders, encouraging social learning, and utilising participatory design approaches. Third, creating a new financial innovation framework that includes green finance tools, performance-based incentives, and risk-sharing mechanisms.

In conclusion, sustainable real estate development serves as a critical instrument for transformation, bridging environmental, economic, and social priorities. This shift significantly impacts not only the real estate industry but also the urban quality of life, societal well-being, and global climate goals. Unlocking this potential is crucial for fostering sustainable communities and promoting social justice and economic competitiveness.

References

AECO. (2024). *YeS-TR Ulusal Yeşil Bina Sertifikası*. https://www.yes-tr.com/

Allied Modular Building Systems. (2025). *How modular construction reduces costs & speeds up your building project*. https://alliedmodular.com/modular-construction-cost-savings/

Altensis. (2019, 13 Nisan). *Özyeğin Üniversitesi Kampüsü*. https://www.altensis.com/proje/ozyegin-universitesi-kampusu/

Arkitera. (2013, 25 Mart). *Magnesia Alışveriş Merkezi*. https://www.arkitera.com/proje/magnesia-alisveris-merkezi/

Arkitera. (2019, 24 Temmuz). *Emre Arolat Architects Tarafından Tasarlanan Tekfen Kağıthane OfisPark, 2012'ye Hazır*. https://www.arkitera.com/haber/emre-arolat-architects-tarafindan-tasarlanan-tekfen-kagithane-ofispark-2012ye-hazir/

Arkiv. (2025). *Garanti BBVA Teknoloji Kampüsü*. https://www.arkiv.com.tr/proje/garanti-teknoloji-kampusu/4432

Aşan, D. (2022, 16 Mart). *Türkiye Yeşil Bina Sertifikaları*. https://www.dilekasan.com/turkiye-yesil-bina-sertifikalari/

BCC Research. (2025). *Building-Integrated Photovoltaics (BIPV): Technologies and Global Markets*. Globe Newswire.

Berglund-Brown, J., Pandey, A., Duarte, F., et al. (2024). Stakeholders' perceptions of and willingness to pay for the circular economy in the construction sector. *npj Urban Sustainability, 4*, 46. https://doi.org/10.1038/s42949-024-00182-9

Biswas, N., Saha, P., Mitra, S., & Majumdar, G. (2024). Green building material (GBM) vs conventional building material (CBM) to reduce environmental impact. *Science and Technology for Energy Transition, 79*(3). https://doi.org/10.2516/stet/2024040

Booth, G., Clayton, M. J., & Kim, J. B. (2013). A framework for designing sustainable real estate developments using Quadruple Net Value Analysis and Building Information Modelling. In *Proceedings of the 19th International CIB World Building Congress*.

Borromeo, M. R. E., Cabug-os, R. S., Maranan, T. M. C., & Yambao, F. M. P. (2025). *Exploring the Role of Sustainable Real Estate Development as Long-Term Business Strategy: Challenges and Opportunities*.

Building Performance Institute Europe (BPIE). (2024). *Renovation Wave Progress Assessment*.

Canikli, S. (2022). Sürdürülebilir finans mekanizmaları, araçları ve sürdürülebilir kalkınma ilişkisi. *Akdeniz İİBF Dergisi, 22*(1), 26–39.

CBRE. (2022). *Green is good: The enduring rent premium of LEED-certified U.S. office buildings*. https://www.cbre.com/insights/viewpoints/green-is-good-the-endurance-of-the-rent-premium-in-leed-certified-us-office-buildings

Center for American Progress. (2024). *Increasing affordable housing stock through modular building*. https://www.americanprogress.org/article/increasing-affordable-housing-stock-through-modular-building/

Çevre Dostu Yeşil Binalar Derneği - ÇEDBİK- (2024). *Yeşil Bina*. https://www.cedbik.org/yesilbina

Cevreciyiz. (2024). *ÇEDBİK - Çevre Dostu Yeşil Binalar Derneği*. http://www.cevreciyiz.com/sergi-detay/71/cedbik-cevre-dostu-yesil-binalar-dernegi

Coakley, D. (2024). ESG investment in commercial real estate: A structured literature review. *SSRN*. https://doi.org/10.2139/ssrn.4948030.

Deloitte Global. (2024). *2024 ESG in Real Estate Insights*. https://www.deloitte.com/global/en/Industries/real-estate/research/esg-real-estate-insights.html

Dimmelmeier, A. (2024). Expanding the politics of measurement in sustainable finance: Reconceptualizing environmental, social and governance information as infrastructure. *Journal of Cultural Economy, 17*(1), 89–108. https://doi.org/10.1177/23996544231209149

Emlak Web TV. (2012, November 6). *Kâğıthane OfisPark'ta hayat başladı*. https://www.emlak-webtv.com/k-githane-ofispark-ta-hayat-basladi/1616

Emre Arolat Architecture. (2024, January 12). *Kağıthane OfisPark*. https://emrearolat.com/project/kagithane-ofispark/

Enerji Günlüğü. (2013, March 12). *Özyeğin Üniversitesi'ne LEED Gold Sertifikası*. https://www.enerjigunlugu.net/ozyegin-universitesine-leed-gold-sertifikasi-2684h.htm

ERKE Tasarım. (2024). *Yeşil Sertifika YeS TR Belgesi Nedir?* https://erketasarim.com/yestr-yesil-sertifika

European Commission. (2024). *Energy Performance of Buildings Directive*. https://energy.ec.europa.eu/topics/energy-efficiency/energy-efficient-buildings/energy-performance-buildings-directive_en

European Parliament and Council. (2023; 2024). *EU Directives on Renewable Energy and Building Energy Performance*.

European Securities and Markets Authority (ESMA). (2024). *Sustainable Finance Roadmap 2022–2024*. https://www.esma.europa.eu/sites/default/files/library/esma30-379-1051_sustainable_finance_roadmap.pdf

Fraker, H. (2013). *The hidden potential of sustainable neighborhoods: Lessons from low-carbon communities* (pp. 97–119). Island Press.

Gray, W. A., & Curtis, T. (2017). *WELL post-certification survey analysis report: ASID*. Delos Insights—Applied Research Program, Delos Living, LLC.

GSA. (2018). *The impact of high-performance buildings*. U.S. General Services Administration. https://www.gsa.gov/governmentwide-initiatives/federal-highperformance-green-buildings/resource-library/integrative-strategies/the-impact-of-highperformance-buildings

Healey, P. (2007). *Urban complexity and spatial strategies: Towards a relational planning for our times*. Routledge.

ING Think. (2024). *The global sustainable finance market is changing for the better*. https://think.ing.com/articles/global-sustainable-finance-market-changing-for-the-better/

International Energy Agency. (2024). *Renewables 2024: Analysis and forecast to 2030*.

IRENA. (2024; 2025). Renewable power generation costs and renewable capacity statistics. International Renewable Energy Agency.

Jalia, A., Bakker, R., & Ramage, M. (2019). *The edge, Amsterdam: Showcasing an exemplary IoT building*. Technical report, Centre for Digital Built Britain, University of Cambridge, UK.

Jax, A. (2025). *Circular principles for real estate development: Adjustments for project selection and their application in practice*.

JLL. (2024). *The green tipping point: We're approaching the point when carbon commitments change lease markets at scale*. https://www.us.jll.com/en/trends-and-insights/research/the-green-tipping-point

Kanika, S. K., Rana, K., & Dahiya, M. (2016). A comparative study on green and conventional buildings. *International Journal of Home Science, 2*(2), 338–343.

Material Economics. (2020). *Understanding the economic case for decarbonising cities: Why economic case analysis for city decarbonization is crucial.*

McAllister, P. (2012). *Studies of price effects of eco-labels in real estate markets.* University of Reading. http://www.henley.reading.ac.uk/web/FILES/REP/Eco_labels.pdf

McKinsey & Company. (2022). *Modular construction: From projects to products.* McKinsey Global Institute.

McKinsey & Company. (2024). *From trials to triumphs in building materials circularity: Takeaways from Davos.* https://www.mckinsey.com/industries/engineering-construction-and-building-materials/our-insights/from-trials-to-triumphs-in-building-materials-circularity-takeaways-from-davos

McKinsey & Company. (2025). *How circular economy can make the built environment more sustainable.* https://www.mckinsey.com/industries/real-estate/our-insights/how-circularity-can-make-the-built-environment-more-sustainable

Metabolic. (2024). *Materials passport for a circular economy.* https://www.metabolic.nl/news/circular-economy-materials-passports/

Ministry of Environment, Urbanisation and Climate Change. (2020). *Number of "Green Buildings" to increase with domestic green certificate system YeS-TR.* https://csb.gov.tr/yerli-yesil-sertifika-sistemi-yes-tr-ile-yesil-bina-sayisi-artacak-bakanlik-faaliyetleri-29700

Ministry of Environment, Urbanisation and Climate Change. (2022a). *Green Certificate Regulation for Buildings and Settlements.* https://meslekihizmetler.csb.gov.tr/binalar-ile-yerlesmeler-icin-yesil-sertifika-yonetmeligi-haber-272022

Ministry of Environment, Urbanisation and Climate Change. (2022b). *Regulation on energy performance in buildings. Official Gazette, 31755.*

Ministry of Environment, Urbanization and Climate Change. (2023). *Renewable energy obligation in buildings starts on 1 January.* https://www.csb.gov.tr/binalarda-yenilenebilir-enerji-zorunlulugu-1-ocakta-basliyor-bakanlik-faaliyetleri-37361

Ministry of Treasury and Finance. (2024). *Republic of Türkiye.* https://ms.hmb.gov.tr/uploads/2024/09/MoTF-Green-Bond-Allocation-Report-2024.pdf

Modular Building Institute. (2024). *How modular construction leads to zero waste and eco-efficiency.* https://www.modular.org/2023/12/26/how-modular-construction-leads-to-zero-waste-and-eco-fficiency/

Morri, G., Yang, F., & Colantoni, F. (2024). Green investments, green returns: Exploring the link between ESG factors and financial performance in real estate. *Journal of Property Investment & Finance, 42*(5), 435–452. https://doi.org/10.1108/JPIF-09-2023-0084

Narter & Partners. (2024a, April 15). *Avrupa Birliği Binalarda Enerji Performansı Direktifi Revizyonu.* https://www.narterlaw.com/avrupa-birligi-binalarda-enerji-performansi-direktifi-revizyonu/

Narter & Partners. (2024b, April 29). *Türkiye Emisyon Ticaret Sistemi.* https://www.narterlaw.com/turkiye-emisyon-ticaret-sistemi/

Oluleye, B. I., Chan, D. W., Antwi-Afari, P., & Olawumi, T. O. (2023). Modeling the principal success factors for attaining systemic circularity in the building construction industry: An international survey of circular economy experts. *Sustainable Production and Consumption, 37*, 268–283.

Özyeğin University. (2025). *Sertifikalar.* https://www.ozyegin.edu.tr/tr/hse/sertifikalar

Pacific Northwest National Laboratory. (2024). *Energy storage cost and performance database.* U.S. Department of Energy.

Paradise Energy Solutions. (2024). *Commercial solar panel ROI analysis.*

Peiser, R. B. (1990). Who plans America: Planners or developers. *Journal of the American Planning Association, 56*, 496–503.

Peiser, R. B. (2015). Real estate development. In *International encyclopedia of the Social & Behavioral Sciences* (Vol. 20, 2nd ed.).

Peiser, R., & Hamilton, D. (2012). *Professional real estate development: The ULI guide to the business.*

Perera, U., & Mensah, C. A. (2019). Conceptualizing sustainability in the real estate development process. *SUSTINERE: Journal of Environment & Sustainability, 3*(1), 1–13.
Selo Group. (2021). *How modular construction saves money*. https://selogroup.co/how-modular-construction-saves-money/. Accessed June 28, 2025.
Sermaye Piyasası Kurulu. (2021). *Yeşil Borçlanma Aracı ve Yeşil Kira Sertifikası Rehberi*. https://www.spk.gov.tr/Sayfa/Dosya/1350. Accessed June 26, 2025.
Shehadi, M. (2020). Net-zero energy buildings: Principles and applications. In *Zero-Energy Buildings—New Approaches and Technologies*.
Squires, G., Heurkens, E., & Peiser, R. (2017). Real estate development: An overview. In *Routledge companion to real estate development* (pp. 1–10).
Sustainable Future. (2023, June 1). *Yeşil Sertifika (YeS-TR)*. https://sustainablefuture.com.tr/yesil-sertifika-yestr/. Accessed 13.06.25.
Sustainable Future. (2024, February 22). *Türkiye Emisyon Ticaret Sistemi'nin bir ön analizi*. https://sustainablefuture.com.tr/turkiye-emisyon-ticaret-sisteminin-bir-on-analizi/. Accessed 23.06.25.
Tanrıvermiş, H. (2019). Türkiye ekonomisinde inşaat ve gayrimenkul sektörlerinin rolleri ve gelişme eğilimlerinin değerlendirilmesi (Assessment of the roles of construction and real estate sectors and their development trends in Turkey). In *Kent, İnşaat ve Ekonomi Kongresi* (pp. 36–58), 2–4 May 2019, Gaziantep.
Tanrıvermiş, H., & Tanrıvermiş, Y. (2021). Linkages between urbanisation, real estate investments and sustainability in Turkey. In R. T. Abdulai & K. G. Baffour Awuah (Eds.), *Sustainable real estate in the developing world* (pp. 13–37). Emerald Publishing Limited. https://doi.org/10.1108/978-1-83867-837-120211011
Tekfen Real Estate. (2025). *Kağıthane OfisPark*. https://tekfengayrimenkul.com/kagithane.aspx. Accessed 24.06.25.
TurkEco. (2020, December 30). *Manisa Magnesia Mall | BREEAM Certification, Energy Modeling*. https://turkeco.com/manisa-magnesia-mall-breeam-certification-energy-modeling/. Accessed 25.06.25.
Turner, C., Frankel, M., & U.S. Green Building Council. (2008). Energy performance of LEED for new construction buildings. *New Buildings Institute, 4*(4), 1–42.
U.S. Department of Energy. (2024). *Perovskite solar cells & geothermal systems*.
U.S. Environmental Protection Agency. (2024). *Inflation Reduction Act provisions*.
U.S. Green Building Council. (2024). *Benefits of green building*. https://www.usgbc.org/press/benefits-of-green-building. Accessed 22.06.25.
Urban Land Institute. (1997). *America's real estate: Natural resource, national legacy*. The Urban Land Institute.
Walter, I. (2020). Sense and nonsense in ESG ratings. *Journal of Law, Finance and Accounting, 1–40*. https://doi.org/10.2139/ssrn.3568104
Wilkinson, S. J., Sayce, S., & Christensen, P. H. (2015). *Developing property sustainably* (Vol. 296). Routledge.
World Economic Forum. (2016). *Environmental sustainability principles for the real estate industry*. https://www.weforum.org/publications/environmental-sustainability-principles-for-the-real-estate-industry/. Accessed 27.06.25.
World Economic Forum. (2021). *A framework for the future of real estate: Insight report*. https://www.weforum.org/publications/a-framework-for-the-future-of-real-estate/. Accessed 28.06.25.
World Economic Forum. (2024). *JLL forecasts 70% shortage of low-carbon buildings by 2030*. https://www.weforum.org/stories/2024/04/jll-low-carbon-office-shortage/. Accessed 10.06.25.
World Economic Forum. (2025). *How modular construction drives productivity and circularity*. https://www.weforum.org/stories/2025/01/modular-construction-productivity-circularity/. Accessed 10.06.25.
World Green Building Council. (2022). *The business case for green building: A review of the costs and benefits for developers, investors and occupants*. https://worldgbc.org/article/the-

business-case-for-green-building-a-review-of-the-costs-and-benefits-for-developers-investors-and-occupants/. Accessed 10.06.25.
Yeşil Aşkı. (2020, May 10). *Yeşil bina değerlendirme sistemleri*. https://www.yesilaski.com/yesil-bina-degerlendirme-sistemleri.html. Accessed 19.06.25.
Zuo, J., & Zhao, Z. Y. (2021). Comparative life-cycle cost (LCC) study of green and traditional industrial buildings in Sri Lanka. *Energy and Buildings, 231*, 110598. https://doi.org/10.1016/j.enbuild.2021.110598

Harun Tanrıvermiş is a distinguished professor who occupies the esteemed position at the Ankara University top management level as founder and head of the Department of Real Estate Development and Management, and founder and current dean of the Faculty of Applied Sciences at Ankara University. Professor Tanrıvermiş also currently works as the vice rector at Ankara University. He attained his B.Sc., M.Sc. and Ph.D. degrees from the Department of Agricultural Economics at Ankara University, specialising in land and real estate economics, land and real estate valuation, as well as natural resources and environmental economics. Furthermore, he earned an MSc in environmental management through the MED-CAMPUS Programme in 1996. Professor Tanrıvermiş has published approximately 400 papers, including 43 international and 55 national peer-reviewed articles, which have been published in various high-impact journals. Additionally, he has presented 48 international and 74 national proceedings, either in full or as abstracts, at numerous conferences. He is also credited with writing 39 books and 17 book chapters. Moreover, his works concentrate on the land and real estate valuation, land and real estate economics, real estate development and project appraisal, urban transformation and sustainability, sustainable real estate development, facility and real estate management, land management, administration and polices, measuring and reporting of real estate sustainability and ESG, digital transformation in real estate and real estate technologies.

Yeşim Tanrıvermiş holds the position of full professor in the Department of Real Estate Development and Management at the Faculty of Applied Sciences, Ankara University, Türkiye. She attained her Master of Science (M.Sc.) degree in 2011 from the Department of Agricultural Economics at Ankara University. She received her Ph.D. in 2011 as the first Ph.D. program graduate of the Department of Real Estate Development and Management at Ankara University. Her research interests encompass the management and conservation of land resources, land resource economics, as well as real estate analysis and economics, in addition to studies in real estate and asset valuation. She has been delivering lectures for several years and has published academic papers since 2006. Her publications consist of 50 international and 40 national peer-reviewed articles. Additionally, she has made contributions to 110 international and 25 national full or abstract proceedings at various conferences and congresses and has authored 35 books and 30 book chapters. Presently, she serves as the Deputy Head of her department at Ankara University. Moreover, she is an active participant in various academic and professional organisations. Her experience encompasses working as a researcher and consultant across diverse public and private sectors, with a focus on real estate asset analysis, real estate finance and valuation, land and building conservation practices, as well as real estate economics and management. Furthermore, she actively engages in enhancing cooperation with both domestic and international institutions, mobilising financial resources for research projects.

Sinan Güneş is lecturing in the Department of Real Estate Development and Management at Ankara University. He obtained his bachelor's degree in civil engineering from Erciyes University in 2013 and subsequently completed a master's degree in real estate development and management at Ankara University in 2019. His master's thesis focused on the decision-making processes pertaining to the repair or demolition of earthquake-affected reinforced concrete buildings. Mr. Güneş completed in doctoral studies at the same department at Ankara University in 2025. His research interests encompass financial economics, engineering management, numerical methods, and construction management, with a particular focus on energy efficiency and sustainability in the built environment. He has authored numerous academic publications addressing sustainable building practices, energy consumption forecasting, and near-zero energy building strategies. Through his teaching and research, he makes significant contributions to the advancement of knowledge in sustainable real estate development and energy-efficient building strategies.

Real Estate Market Characteristics

Real Estate Markets and Submarkets in Türkiye

Ali Parsa, Ece Sert Özcan, and Salih Demirkaya

Abstract

Türkiye's real estate market is emerging and continues to attract significant investment. The country is a major hub for tourism, logistics, and office services. In recent years, substantial retail and residential developments have been made. Türkiye is also considered an important transit point for human migration from the Middle East and Eastern countries, and it is an appealing centre for Europe and the Gulf Region due to its natural and historical attributes. Simultaneously, it is becoming a land of opportunity for economic investments. The COVID-19 pandemic has had a profound impact on the world, with its subsequent economic effects continuing to linger. It is essential to note that restrictions on energy use and production have adverse consequences. Similarly, the construction sector and the real estate sector in Türkiye have been affected, mirroring global trends. The economic repercussions within these sectors' subsectors have led to a shift in balance. This chapter assesses the factors influencing the real estate market in Türkiye, considering recent economic developments supported by economic data.

A. Parsa (✉)
Westminster Business School, University of Westminster, London, UK
e-mail: a.parsa@westminster.ac.uk

E. S. Özcan
Office Leasing Manager, İstanbul Finance Centre, İstanbul, Türkiye
e-mail: Ece.sertozcan@ifm.gov.tr

S. Demirkaya
Department of Real Estate Development and Management, Faculty of Applied Sciences, Ankara University, Ankara, Türkiye
e-mail: sdemirkaya@ankara.edu.tr

T. Just et al. (eds.), *Understanding Türkiye's Real Estate Markets*, Management for Professionals, https://doi.org/10.1007/978-3-032-13297-0_19

Keywords

Real estate · Logistics · Retail · Office · Residential · Tourism

1 Introduction

Since the 2000s, there has been a growing interest from foreign investors in the Turkish real estate market, especially since 2005. Notably, foreign companies like Redevco (acquired by Blackstone in July 2012), Multi Development (acquired by Blackstone in July 2013), and Corio (acquired by Klepierre in 2014) have made substantial investments in the Turkish retail sector. However, after 2017, this trend started to slow down, as indicated by the sale of several properties. Between 2017 and 2018, Carrefour sold three major assets. While there were more local transactions in 2019, significant deals in 2020 and 2021 including the sale of the company owning İstinye Shopping Centre to QIA, the transfer of Palladium Shopping Centre to Ak Portföy, the sale of Mersin Palm City to Yenişehir AVM LTD by Bainbridge Holding, and CarrefourSA's sale of Adana Carrefour to a local investor. In 2022, it was observed that foreign investors like Klepierre and Multi began transferring their properties to domestic investors. Moreover, as of 2021, the Turkish retail investment market exhibited a large transaction volume relative to many European countries, appealing to opportunity-driven investors.

An analysis of office market transactions indicated that local investors primarily purchased buildings for their own use. Companies in sectors such as energy, insurance, banking, and technology have notably increased their investments in office properties. Although foreign developers encounter restrictions in the housing market, Turkish investors and developers are importing technology and labour from abroad, thus capturing a significant share of the Turkish market. Conversely, foreign investment in the housing sector largely occurs through sales to international buyers. Furthermore, the logistics sector might experience limited foreign investment due to the constraints above.

The Investment Markets Transparency Index, evaluated by JLL based on 256 parameters across 151 cities in 89 countries, ranks Türkiye 46th in 2024, marking an 8-position decline since 2022. Furthermore, Türkiye stands at 23rd among 27 European economies. It is placed in the semi-transparent category, which is ranked third out of 5 categories. This category mainly includes developing economies that have not yet fully matured in their corporate governance practices and market regulatory frameworks (McAuley et al., 2024).

An analysis of the Turkish real estate market reveals that its institutional structure and regulatory framework align closely with those of developed markets. Various stages of the real estate life cycle—development, management, and acquisition—are governed by institutional structures and regulatory bodies. These mechanisms effectively manage several key areas, including buying and selling activities, zoning regulations, construction, and oversight processes. Consequently, the real estate development cycle can take comparatively long. This suggests that one primary reason for the supply lagging behind demand is the interdisciplinary nature of real estate markets, resulting in numerous institutions having an interest in the sector.

Currently, the organisations authorised to create zoning plans include İller Bankası Inc., the Privatisation Administration, the Ministry of Environment and Urbanisation, the Housing Development Administration (TOKİ), Municipalities, Governorships, the Ministry of Agriculture and Forestry, the Ministry of Industry and Technology, and the General Directorate of State Railways. This multitude of institutions engaged in spatial planning introduces jurisdictional ambiguity, complicating the development of a unified planning strategy. While various institutions and organisations provide feedback during real estate development processes, it is crucial to shift these processes towards achieving virtual consensus whenever possible, establish a centralised information system, and implement robust legal frameworks that govern real estate development and management. To keep pace with technological advancements, public initiatives have been initiated to digitise processes and improve transparency. The Real Estate Valuation System and the Department of Real Estate Valuation, founded in 2019, exemplify these efforts. In addition to the integration of technology into the real estate sector, the introduction of the Webtapu system is expected, which will include features such as 3D land registry extracts and digital remote access rights to land registry extracts.

In June 2012, Türkiye removed the reciprocity rule, enabling citizens from 42 countries to purchase real estate, mainly for investment purposes, including land for housing. This change has notably increased acquisitions by several countries, particularly for residential purposes, resulting in heightened demand within the construction sector. However, this development is perceived as foreign exchange income. Conversely, the inability of local citizens to satisfy the demands of the real estate market has led to housing issues in cities like Antalya, Mersin, Gaziantep, Istanbul, and Trabzon, especially in tourist areas favoured by foreigners. However, successful project implementations are rare due to the lengthy and complex development processes, along with investors' limited understanding of local regulations, which hinder timely project completions. Consequently, foreigners acquiring real estate often struggle to develop projects on schedule, resulting in earnings primarily through buying and selling rather than project development. Investing in foreign properties solely for rental income is not ideal. Similar to global trends, the Turkish real estate sector was impacted by the COVID-19 pandemic. By 2022, as restrictions eased, the real estate and investment market began to revive. The decreasing profit margins caused by shifts in the income-expense dynamics of commercial real estate have resulted in stagnation in investments, leading investors to consider disposing of inefficient assets. In contrast, the housing market remains robust against inflation and exchange rate fluctuations. The investment outlook for zoned land containing housing components appears promising for development purposes.

2 Turkish Retail Real Estate Market

2.1 General Overview

The impressive expansion of the Turkish retail market is mainly fuelled by a vast consumer base, a large young population, growing purchasing power, and as a consequence strong retail demand, all driven by evolving consumer habits. With about

85.7 million people, Türkiye ranks as the second-largest country in Europe, following Russia (TURKSTAT, 2024a). According to TUIK, the population is projected to reach 91.5 million by 2040 (TURKSTAT, 2024b). For 2024, Türkiye's median age is 34.4 years, with individuals under 15 accounting for 20.9% of the overall population. In the medium to long term, household incomes and purchasing power are expected to increase (TURKSTAT, 2024a).

Investment in shopping centres in Türkiye skyrocketed until 2008, especially in cities that lacked these facilities, resulting in lasting projects. However, after 2009, the growth of shopping mall investments slowed due to economic stagnation, leading to a complete halt of some projects. This stagnation continued until 2010, but as economic conditions improved, investment activity quickly regained momentum.

2.2 Supply and Demand

By the end of 2024, Türkiye had 14.1 million m^2 of leased space in 446 active shopping centres. Once the 10 shopping malls under construction are completed, the gross leasable area (GLA) is expected to rise to 14.5 million m^2. Istanbul, Türkiye's most populous and economically vibrant city, dominates the retail market with 38.5% of the total supply. Following Istanbul is Ankara, which has a leasable area of 5.4 million m^2 across 128 shopping centres and a GLA of 1.6 million m^2 in 43 shopping malls (GYODER, 2024).

In 2024, nine shopping malls opened in Türkiye, increasing the total leasable area by 246,000 m^2 (Kurban, 2025). Nevertheless, the number of shopping malls under construction and the leasable area capacity have declined compared to previous years (Table 1).

The total Gross Leasable Area (GLA) serves as an essential measure for evaluating retail supply in the market, while retail space per capita indicates saturation levels. In Türkiye, Istanbul stands out with the highest total retail supply density, followed by Ankara, Karabük, Kayseri, and Bolu, which show retail densities of 342, 277, 271, 264, and 242 m^2 per 1000 residents, respectively (GYODER, 2024).

The Consumer Confidence Index, a key demand indicator, recently exceeded the 85 mark for the first time since 2019, reaching 86.7 in March 2021. Throughout the first half of 2021, the index varied between 77 and 87, but it dropped to 68.9 in

Table 1 Current and pipeline-organised retail supply, (*) by the end of 2025

		Operational	Under construction*	Total
İstanbul	Unit	128	5	133
	GLA (m^2)	5,441,525	220,000	5,661,525
Ankara	Unit	43	1	44
	GLA (m^2)	1,604,458	27,000	1,631,458
Other cities	Unit	275	4	279
	GLA (m^2)	7,083,378	122,274	7,205,652
Türkiye	Unit	446	10	456
	GLA (m^2)	14,129,361	369,274	14,498,635

Source: GYODER (2024)

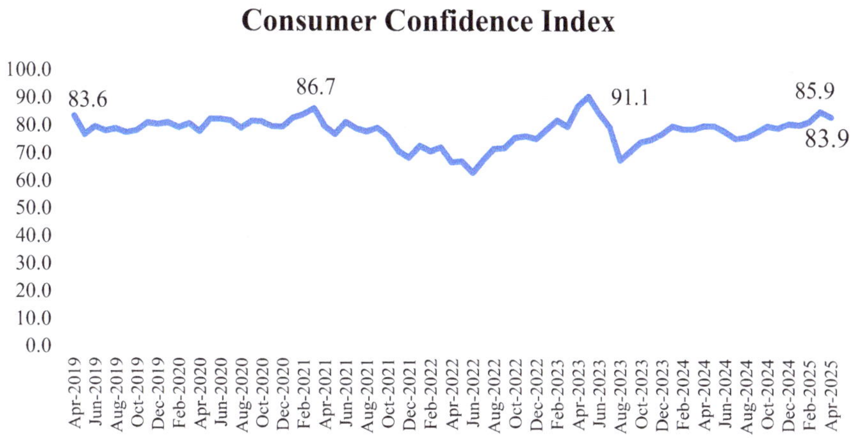

Fig. 1 Consumer confidence index. *Source*: TURKSTAT (2025a)

December 2021, indicating a 3.1% decline from the previous month and a 14.0% drop compared to December 2020. In December 2022, the index recorded a value of 75.6, representing a 9.8% improvement from the same month a year earlier. This upward trend persisted into year-end 2023, with a 2.4% rise. By the end of 2024, the consumer confidence index had further improved to 81.3, reflecting a 5% increase. In March 2025, it was measured at 85,9, illustrating a recovery as the economy normalises following COVID-19, despite ongoing high inflation (Fig. 1).

The retail sales volume index trended steadily upward until 2015, but starting in 2016, political and economic market conditions began to affect it negatively. Although the industry faced fluctuations in 2020 due to the COVID-19 pandemic, it rebounded strongly and achieved record numbers as of February 2025, reaching an index level of 174.6 (Fig. 2).

2.3 Performance Indicators

The effects of the COVID-19 pandemic on retail spaces have been felt severely in Türkiye and globally. Curfews, time and category restrictions on shopping centre activities, inadequate clean air ventilation in many centres, economic recession, and the prevailing uncertainty affecting consumer confidence have all impacted the organised retail market, resulting in reduced visitor numbers and lower sales in shopping centres. Investors with robust financial resources supported their tenants by offering rent-free periods and rent reductions to ensure a diverse tenant mix. As vaccination efforts ramped up and COVID-19 restrictions gradually eased, shopping malls were beginning to recover. Additionally, the tourism sector's significantly rebounded, following the lifting of travel restrictions, and this positively impacted retail market performance.

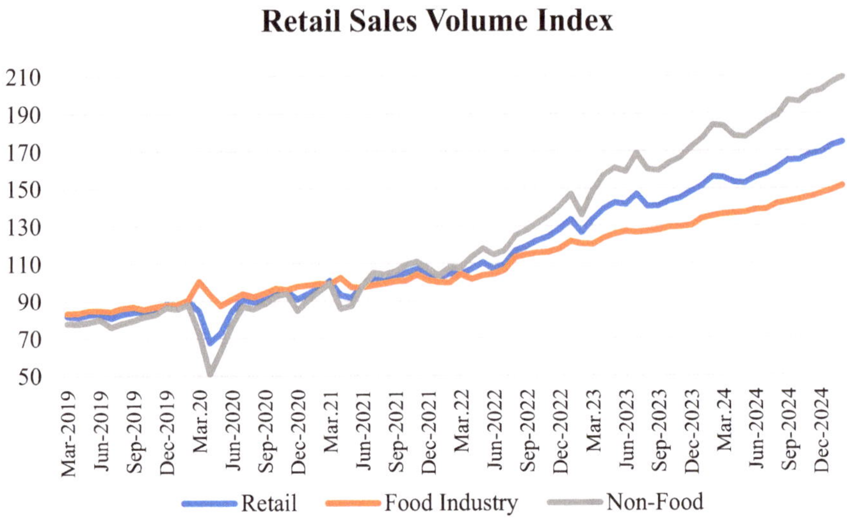

Fig. 2 Retail sales volume index. *Source*: TURKSTAT (2025b)

A crucial metric for assessing retail market performance is turnover per square meter. In this regard, the Shopping Mall Retail Turnover Index, developed collaboratively by the Council of Shopping Centres (AYD) and Akademetre, is published monthly. This index compares data from the same month as the previous year without adjusting for inflation. As of Q4 2024, the turnover index surged by 49.75% compared to the previous year. (Fig. 3) The year-end statistics also showed a significant rise of 43.8% in December 2024, elevating the index to 4095 points (Alışveriş Merkezleri ve Yatırımcıları Derneği, 2024). However, this growth did not exceed the reported annual inflation rate of 44.38% (TURKSTAT, 2025c). The turnover per m^2 in December 2024 was noted at TL 19,183 in Istanbul and TL 13,228 in Anatolian cities, with the average turnover across Türkiye standing at TL 15,610 (Alışveriş Merkezleri ve Yatırımcıları Derneği, 2024). By March 2025, the turnover per m^2 dropped to TL 16,400 in Istanbul, while it increased to TL 13,394 in Anatolian cities, and the Turkish average decreased to TL 14,597. This overall decline was also evident in the index, which fell to 3.697 as of March 2025 (Alışveriş Merkezleri ve Yatırımcıları Derneği, 2025).

In March 2025, the retail turnover categories showed that apparel sales experienced the largest increase at 53.8%, followed by hypermarkets at 39.8%, food and beverage at 37%, footwear at 23.6%, other categories at 23.5%, and electronics at 22.3% compared to the same month of the previous year (Alışveriş Merkezleri ve Yatırımcıları Derneği, 2025).

Another important metric, the shopping centre visitor index (Fig. 4), saw a notable improvement of 86% in Q3 2021, rising from 43 to 80, marking the post-pandemic recovery. The index stabilised at these levels for three quarters, then increased by 18%, reaching 91 in Q2 2022. In Q3 2023, there was another increase of 16%, elevating the index to 106. Performance in 2023 and 2024 remained robust,

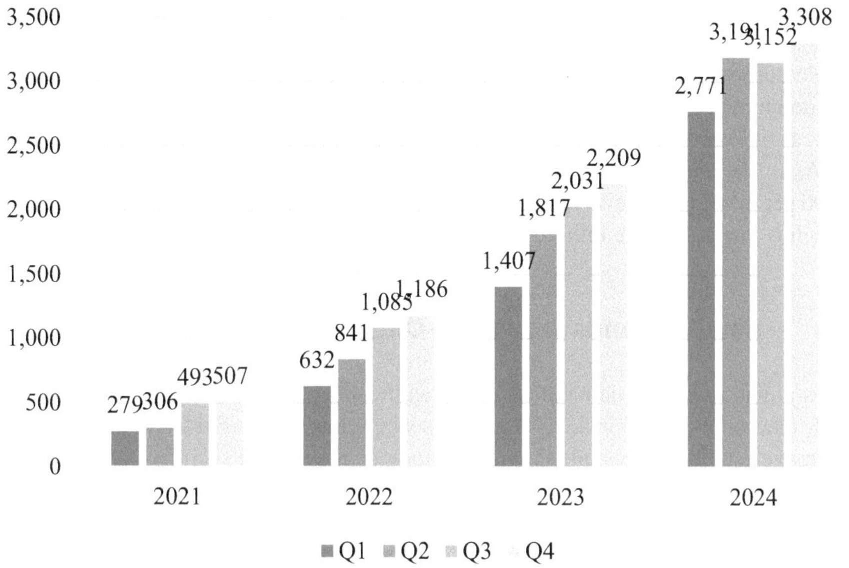

Fig. 3 Square meter productivity index based on Q4 figures. *Source*: Alışveriş Merkezleri ve Yatırımcıları Derneği (2025)

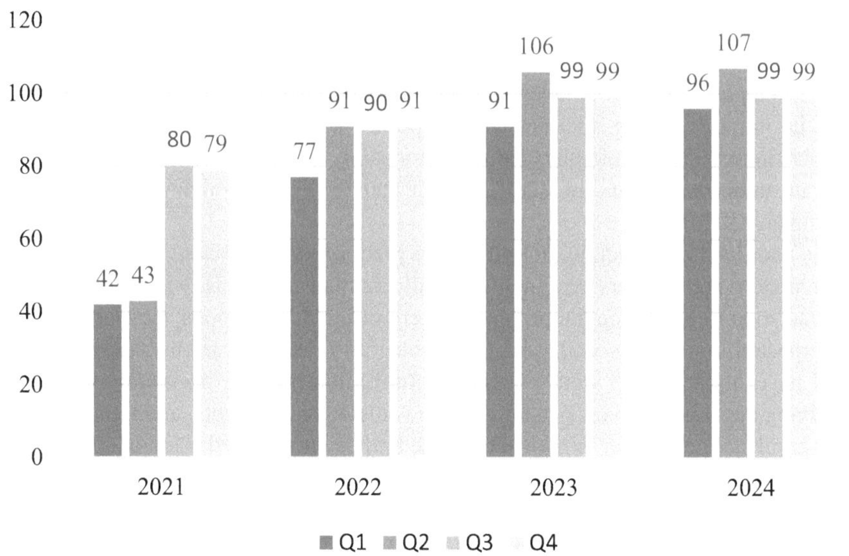

Fig. 4 Shopping centre visitor index based on Q4 figures. *Source*: Alışveriş Merkezleri ve Yatırımcıları Derneği (2024)

with Q2 peaking at 106 and 107, respectively. However, by Q4 2024, the visitor index held steady compared to the same quarter the previous year. This suggests that while turnover per square meter in shopping malls shows a remarkable post-pandemic recovery, this positive trend has not been mirrored in visitor footfall. In fact, as of February 2025, the index dropped to 78, reflecting a 21% decline.

As of the end of 2024, the prime rent, a key indicator of demand, stood at TL 4500 per m^2 and EUR 125 EUR per m^2. This marks a year-on-year growth of 35.4%, which is lower than the inflation rate (Kurban, 2025).

2.4 Retailer Trends and Future Outlook

On a global scale, the demand for open retail concepts, which foster a more hospitable environment by considering human scale, is increasing. Furthermore, food and beverage establishments, along with restaurants, necessitate such indoor spaces. In Türkiye, shopping malls are anticipated to incorporate more open spaces and integrate more green areas.

In retail environments, where space efficiency and profitability are lacking for multiple reasons, current trends indicate a shift towards cautious growth strategies and resizing existing sales areas. Furthermore, portfolio management and optimisation have become increasingly important for both retailers and investors. This includes expected re-evaluations of leasable spaces in shopping centres, with empty areas being transformed into alternative real estate uses, such as urban distribution centres, co-working facilities, educational institutions, and various entertainment venues.

The pandemic has brought lasting shifts in retail behaviour, particularly a marked rise in online shopping and contactless options like delivery and pickup. As consumers increasingly avoid physical stores for safety and convenience reasons, retailers are under enormous pressure to adapt their business models (McKinsey and Company, 2020).

In addition to enhancing numerous sales platforms (omnichannel), it is projected that in-store pick-up services, including fully automated outlets, will become widespread soon to guarantee the prompt delivery of purchased goods. Consequently, it is expected that brands with significant integration across various sales channels will have implemented store portfolio optimisation models, accurately assessing evolving customer demands and providing value-added products, and retail formats that emphasise customer experience. These brands have gained traction in the post-COVID-19 era.

Businesses must act swiftly to thrive in the fast-evolving retail environment. Embracing the "new normal" will require a complete transformation of their strategies and operations. Retailers need to assess their strengths and weaknesses in five essential areas: pricing and revenue enhancement, operational flexibility, digital advancement, strategic investments, and opportunities for growth through partnerships or acquisitions (McKinsey and Company, 2020).

In the near future, the retail investment sector will encounter new challenges: Increased construction costs for new developments, significantly affected by currency fluctuations, include expenses related to interior design. Furthermore, incentives like rent-free periods for retailers establishing new outlets, rising management and shared area expenses due to ongoing high inflation, changes to the Shopping Centre Management Bylaws—particularly recent amendments on common area expense calculations—and sustainability concerns will become crucial elements influencing decision-making and profitability for both existing and upcoming investments.

3 Turkish Office Real Estate Market

3.1 General Overview

Türkiye's economic transformation accelerated significantly following the 2001 crisis. The rise in foreign direct investment and the local market's adaptation to this capital inflow have made Istanbul a focal point for numerous domestic and international companies, positioning it as the core of Türkiye's economy and business operations.

In 2021, Türkiye's economy expanded by 11% during the post-COVID-19 era. Economic growth for 2022 was 5.5%, while the economy grew by 5.1% in 2023 (TURKSTAT, 2025d). In 2024, the growth rate was recorded at 3.2%. In comparison, global growth rates for 2021, 2022, and 2023 were 6%, 3.2%, and 2.7%, respectively (International Monetary Fund, 2024). The medium-term program for 2025 to 2027 (MTP) outlines Türkiye's growth forecasts at 3.1%, 2.8%, and 2.5% for 2025, 2026, and 2027, respectively (Republic of Türkiye Presidency of Strategy and Budget, 2024).

3.2 Supply and Demand

Istanbul, Türkiye's largest city in terms of population and economic advancement, serves as the cornerstone of its economy and business sector, thanks to its strategic location. It is the country's most developed office market, accounting for around 80% of the national supply of modern, high-quality offices. The Grade A office space in Istanbul primarily resides within the Central Business District (CBD), particularly in the Levent-Etiler, Gayrettepe-Şişli, and Zincirlikuyu-Maslak areas along Büyükdere Street on the European Side. Levent stands out as the most prestigious office sub-market due to its exceptional transportation links, infrastructure, and premium office offerings. On the Anatolian Side, key office sub-markets include Kozyatağı, Ataşehir, Altunizade, Kavacık, and Maltepe-Kartal. In fact, Kozyatağı and Ataşehir rival the CBD in rental rates, aided by the recent influx of high-quality office space.

The Istanbul Finance Centre (IFC) project, situated near Ataşehir, features public institutions and organisations including Vakıflar Bank, Ziraat Bank, and Halk Bank, and will also host the Capital Markets Board, the Banking Regulation and Supervision Agency, the Central Bank, and the Istanbul Stock Exchange. Ataşehir has gained popularity due to the relocation of entities like İlbank, Emlak Konut GYO, and Halkbank, which seek to be neighbours to these institutions in the area.

By the end of 2024, Istanbul's active Grade A office supply will be 7.1 million m^2, with pipeline projects amounting to 500,000 m^2 (Cushman and Wakefield, 2024). Analysing the distribution of office supply across sub-markets at the end of 2024, newly emerging office areas like Ataşehir, Kartal, Maltepe, Kağıthane, and Bomonti account for 36% of new office space. The CBD follows with a share of 27%. Non-CBD Europe represents 21%, while the lowest share belongs to non-CBD Asia at 17% (PROPIN Property Investment Consultancy, 2024). This shift reflects the expansion of office spaces into alternative locations.

By the end of 2023, the prime rent in Istanbul's office market was USD 38 per m^2, which increased to USD 42 per m^2 in Q2 2024 and USD 45 per m^2 in Q3 2024 (Cushman and Wakefield, 2024). For companies using TL, this represents a 50% year-over-year increase, reaching TL 1500 TL per m^2 (Kurban, 2024). The rise in prime rents was primarily due to the absence of new completions, especially for Grade-A office space (Fig. 5).

An analysis of vacancy rates in the Istanbul Class A office market reveals that the CBD has the highest rate at 12.4%. Within sub-markets, Taksim and Nişantaşı, the historical CBD, exhibits the highest vacancy rate at 19.1%. This is followed by

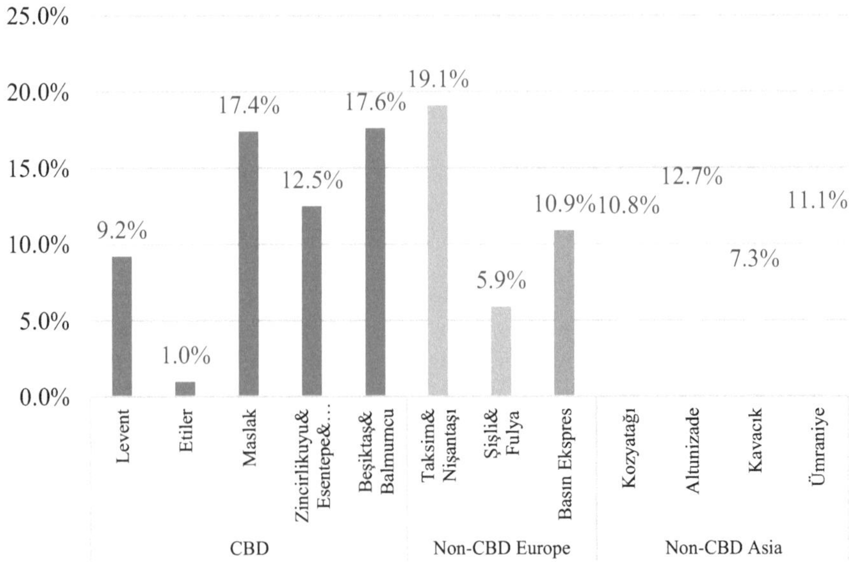

Fig. 5 Vacancy rates based on office submarkets. *Source*: PROPIN Property Investment Consultancy (2024)

Beşiktaş and Balmumcu, which have a comparatively low supply of modern offices. Maslak ranks third with a vacancy rate of 17.4%, attributed to recent project completions. In contrast, the Etiler submarket boasts the lowest vacancy rate at 1%, also accounting for the smallest portion of the office supply.

Propin estimates that the demand for office leasing and sales is approximately 282,000 m^2, indicating a slight rise of 1% (PROPIN Property Investment Consultancy, 2024). Additionally, economic stagnation, businesses increased their focus on maximising existing office space utilisation, and a lack of new, modern office supply due to low completions have considerably curtailed demand for new office transactions.

3.3 Occupier Trends and Future Outlook

Office occupiers in Türkiye prioritise their employees as the focus in developing workspace strategies that are consistent with global trends. Locations are frequently selected in the proximity of public transportation hubs and consider the prestige of the building and its surrounding area.

In workplace interior design, employee productivity and space efficiency are essential. While private workspaces are getting smaller, there is a rise in user-friendly, high-tech meeting rooms and cafeterias, along with areas specifically created to enhance communication and collaboration and for employees needing a quiet space to concentrate on their tasks.

The COVID-19 pandemic has instigated significant changes in the dynamics of business operations, leading to more companies adopting hybrid working models. Currently, the office environment has transitioned into a space primarily designated for learning, social interaction, and connectivity, with employees no longer expected to maintain a constant physical presence in the workplace. Consequently, there is a noticeable shift away from personalised, desk-based work, and it is anticipated that co-working spaces will gain in popularity (JLL, 2021). These novel working models were already established as the prevailing standard, prompting companies to downsize their physical office spaces accordingly.

Another trend that emerged in the aftermath of COVID-19 is the rise in healthy building certifications. During the period described as the "New Normal," alongside widely recognised certificates such as LEED, ASHRAE, BREAM, and Energy Star, which are pivotal in the realm of environmental sustainability, certification programs that assess the "wellness" attributes of buildings and workspaces have gained substantial traction. These certifications encompass WELL, Fitwel, and RESET. They offer structured frameworks for evaluating air quality, lighting, acoustics, biophilic design, levels of physical activity, and social engagement. Regardless of their focus on physical or social quality, these certifications present effective strategies to maximise the value of investments. Concurrently, offices that resist seismic activity, feature operable windows, and ensure the provision of 100% clean air are expected to remain desirable. Workspaces that foster well-being and promote healthy environments are anticipated to influence the design of future office spaces significantly.

4 Turkish Real Estate Logistics Market

4.1 General Overview

Due to its geographic positioning and its geopolitical relevance, transportation infrastructure, and significant demand, Türkiye is one of the emerging logistics markets within the EMEA (Europe, Middle East, and Africa) region. Given its strategic location at the confluence of the European and Asian continents, alongside its notable geographical features such as the Bosphorus, it can be considered the most critical hub in Türkiye concerning trade, maritime, and logistics operations. Moreover, considering the industrial production capabilities and the industrial activities of the neighbouring cities in the Marmara Region, Istanbul contributes most to the nation's economy and production endeavours.

By the end of 2023, Istanbul accounted for about 30% of Türkiye's total GDP, 55% of tax revenues, and 30% of foreign trade. According to the Ministry of Industry and Technology, 171 of Türkiye's top 500 companies are tied to the Istanbul Chamber of Industry. At the same time, 48 are connected to the Ankara Chamber, and 35 to the Kocaeli Chamber. Due to their extensive business operations, production, import-export functions, and logistics, Istanbul and Kocaeli surpass other Turkish cities (ISO 500, 2023). Hence, robust land, sea, and air transport networks are vital for the logistics efficacy of both cities.

The Ministry of Transport, Maritime and Communications of the Republic of Türkiye released the 2053 Transport and Logistics Master Plan in April 2022 as part of the 11th Development Plan (2019 to 2023). This plan aims to boost mobility, balance different transportation modes, and improve service quality as well as operational efficiency within the logistics sector. It is important to highlight that prioritising safety, sustainability, workforce quality and efficiency, technology, and levels of digitalisation is essential for achieving these objectives.

The plan aims to position Türkiye within the top 10 of the World Bank's Logistics Performance Index (LPI) by means of a sustainable development strategy. Additionally, it aims to double the number of Logistics Centres from 13 to 26. Notably, the report highlights the importance of energy efficiency and social sustainability.

4.2 Supply and Demand

Türkiye's premier logistics market, distinguished for its high-quality facilities, predominantly comprises the Marmara Region, which encompasses the provinces of Istanbul and Kocaeli. On the European side of Istanbul are Hadımköy and Esenyurt, whereas Tuzla is situated on the Anatolian side. The principal submarkets within the Marmara Region include Kocaeli, Gebze, Çayırova, and Dilovası. Enhanced accessibility in these regions promotes the influx of new logistics supplies into the market.

In the development and rental market, built-to-suit projects tailored to meet the technical specifications required by tenants are now favoured. Conversely, developers with available land tend to prioritise securing tenants who provide rental guarantees before proceeding to invest in warehouses.

According to the GYODER, 2024 report, the total logistics supply in the Istanbul and Kocaeli region was approximately 11.3 million m^2. Excluding owner-occupied storage areas, this figure is still about 7.9 million m^2 (GYODER, 2024). As stated in the VSP 2024 Macroeconomic and Real Estate Market Figures of Türkiye report, the total supply is expected to reach 10.3 million m^2 by the end of 2025, with 500,000 m^2 under construction and a projected pipeline supply of 11.8 million m^2. Vacancy rates for logistics supply are relatively low compared to the office market, measured at 5% for the year-end of 2024, slightly above the 2023 year-end figure of 4.9%. Within this 5%, the European part of Istanbul accounts for 2%-points, Kocaeli for 1.8%-points, and Istanbul Anatolian Side for 1.2%-points (Kurban, 2025).

In the year 2024, the volume of logistics rental transactions reached 211,600 m^2, signifying a substantial increase of 56% compared to the previous year, thus recovering from the downturn experienced in 2022 and 2023. Nonetheless, this figure remains below the 2021 data, which recorded 232,000 m^2 (Kurban, 2025; Fig. 6) Despite the heightened demand for premium logistics and storage facilities, particularly due to the rise in e-commerce activities following the COVID-19 pandemic, the market encounters difficulties in fulfilling the demand for advanced storage solutions. This is primarily attributed to a lack of quality supply and a shortage of suitable land for the development of logistics warehouses. Persistently high construction costs, along with a scarcity of developable land, are obstructing the introduction of new logistics supply. Consequently, this situation creates a disparity between the increasing demand for larger spaces, especially in prime locations, and the market's capability to meet such demand, thereby motivating international corporations to explore growth opportunities in secondary markets.

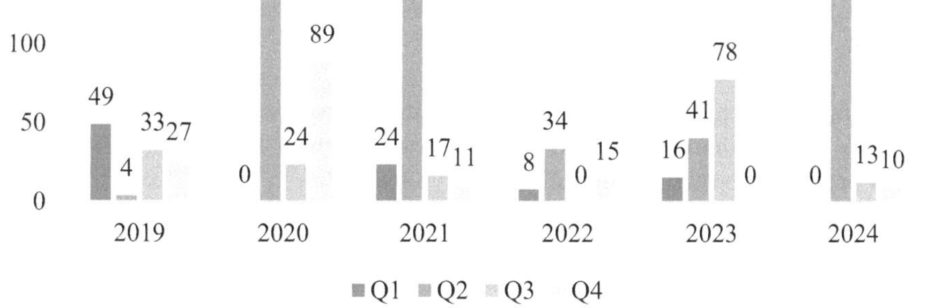

Fig. 6 In Türkiye, primary logistics market leasing transactions 1000 m^2. *Source*: GYODER (2024)

Analysing the distribution of industrial and logistics investment transactions by sector reveals that, in 2024, most transactions are attributed to third-party logistics (3PLs), e-commerce, retail, and electronics firms. A significant factor driving the growth of 3PL companies is the surge in e-commerce, triggered by restrictions on retail operations. During the peak of the pandemic, traditional retail was heavily disrupted, leading to a seismic shift towards e-commerce that has now become an essential aspect of everyday life. Even though these restrictions have been fully lifted, consumer behaviours have irreversibly transformed. Notably, Kocaeli accounted for the largest share of leasing transactions in the logistics and industrial sectors (Kurban, 2024).

At the end of 2024, prime rents for logistics markets hit USD 10 per m^2 and TL 350 per m^2. This marks a 14.3% increase in USD and a 34.6% rise in TL compared to the same period last year (Kurban, 2025).

4.3 Occupier Trends and Future Outlook

Current trends among users in the logistics sector show a growing availability of storage space within facilities (in-house logistics), a surge in e-commerce, and a consolidation of logistics supply fuelled by institutionalisation.

Türkiye has emerged as a significant force in digital commerce, currently ranking as the 18th largest e-commerce market worldwide. Since 2019, the sector has shown remarkable growth, with its share of retail sales climbing to 6.5% by 2023. Additionally, its contribution to GDP has more than doubled, increasing from 2.7–6.8% during the same period. A tech-savvy youth demographic drives this expansion, as does the prevalent use of digital payments and a competitive marketplace environment (Uzunoglu, 2024).

The expected swift expansion of the retail sector is likely to positively impact the logistics market in the near to medium term. Nonetheless, prohibitively high land prices and scarcity remain significant obstacles hindering the establishment and leasing of new facilities. The elevated land costs related to logistics in Türkiye, when compared to Europe, pose a major challenge to development efforts and deter international investments. Furthermore, the persistent rise in construction expenses and high inflation resulting from fluctuating exchange rates indicate that stagnation in the development of key logistics warehouses is expected to continue for the foreseeable future.

The COVID-19 pandemic has profoundly affected the creativity, resilience, and adaptability of leading companies in the logistics sector. As the economy begins to recover post-pandemic, the need for a new supply chain framework has become apparent. Transformations in global supply chains due to regional conflicts have made Türkiye an attractive option for international investors looking for nearby alternatives. Recent investments from companies such as Germany's BLG Logistics, Felix Schoeller, and Brazil's WEG S.A. underscore Türkiye's rising allure (Cushman & Wakefield, 2025).

Due to disruptions in the supply chain, Türkiye has emerged as a strategic manufacturing hub, serving essential markets in Europe, the Middle East, and the Eastern Seaboard of the United States. The country possesses notable strengths in exports, which include automotive products, apparel, power grid equipment, and home appliances. The top seven export categories account for 40.2% of total global exports and 52.6% of shipments to the European Union (Birch et al., 2024).

Technological advances will drive the transformation of supply chains. Throughout this evolution, proficient risk management and system regulations will enable smooth business operations, paving the way for a transition from traditional supply management to digital supply networks (Kilpatrick & Barter, 2020).

Consumer preferences have increasingly shifted towards online shopping, which is valued for its convenience, cost-effectiveness, and efficiency. Despite occasional fluctuations, the overall trend suggests that e-commerce is becoming an essential part of Türkiye's economy. The sector's resilience to economic changes indicates significant growth potential as digital platforms continue to merge with Turkish consumption patterns. This is expected to generate new demand for logistics transactions and development initiatives.

Alongside this, urban logistics facilities, often referred to as last-mile distribution centres, are relatively rare but provide significant benefits in terms of delivery speed and efficiency for online orders. With advances in technology, including the growing use of electric vehicles and the expanding installation of electric vehicle charging stations, the presence of distribution robots is anticipated to rise. Consequently, city liveability is expected to improve, and carbon emissions will decline due to reduced transportation travel—at least in the medium term (JLL, 2022).

Lastly, with respect to sustainability, it is anticipated that the demand for storage facilities equipped with advanced technological infrastructure, capable of minimising energy consumption, particularly in air conditioning, and meeting various sustainability standards, will remain substantial.

5 Turkish Tourism Market

5.1 Supply and Demand

In recent years, Türkiye has become a prominent tourism hub, attributable to the remarkable allure of its natural landscapes, historical heritage, and advantageous climatic conditions. This progression signifies that Türkiye functions as a destination where both cultural and business tourism activities have experienced substantial growth. It is recognised as the most desirable locale for Mediterranean holidays, featuring 567 Blue Flag beaches, which ranks as the third highest globally (FEE, 2025). Furthermore, the nation is home to 21 UNESCO World Heritage Sites, comprising 19 cultural and 2 mixed classifications, along with an additional 81 sites listed on the Tentative List of UNESCO World Heritage Sites (UNESCO World Heritage Centre, 2025).

Considering health and education opportunities, Türkiye has gained substantial international recognition. Recent years have seen a significant rise in tourism activities, including health and education tourism, leading to over a 50% increase in visitors over the past decade. Notably, even during 2020, which is regarded as a peak year for the pandemic, Türkiye welcomed almost 13 million tourists. The following year, 2021, marked a strong rebound with a 94% increase in foreign visitors. A similar pattern emerged in 2022 with an 80% rise. By 2023, the number of foreign visitors hit an unprecedented 49 million, and by the end of the year, this figure soared to 52.6 million (Table 2).

The pandemic revealed a significant decline in tourism revenues. Notably, tourism earnings plummeted from USD 42.9 million in 2019 to nearly 65% less in 2020. However, a substantial recovery occurred in 2021, with tourism income almost doubling. A similar pattern was seen in tourism revenues, peaking at USD 55.9 million and exceeding this to reach USD 60.5 million in 2024, equivalent to about UL 1.97 trillion.

In 2024, Türkiye's travel and tourism sector contributed TL 5 trillion to the national economy, making up about 12% of the country's GDP. This industry also employed 3.2 million people, which is 10% of the national workforce. It has continuously provided stable job opportunities in various fields such as hospitality, transportation, gastronomy, and cultural tourism. For 2025, projections indicate that Türkiye's travel and tourism market will contribute TL 5.2 trillion to the economy, sustaining its share of around 12% of the total GDP. This anticipated growth will likely come from both domestic and international visitors, with foreign tourists alone estimated to spend TL 2.6 trillion, highlighting Türkiye's increasing appeal as a global travel destination (WTTC, 2025).

Taking into account factors such as international travel and accommodation restrictions, the fact that Türkiye hosts approximately 53 million foreign tourists underscore Türkiye's potential standing in the tourism industry. The number of facilities reached 12,844 facilities in 2019 and increased to a total of 13,454 facilities in 2020. As this trend persists, Türkiye is anticipated to provide 1.83 million beds in 15,046 facilities by the year 2024 (Table 3).

Despite the evident decline in hotel occupancy levels during the year 2020, it is important to emphasise that the temporary reduction in employment and the downturn in local economies within tourist regions are not at a point of irreparable damage. The recovery observed post-2021 indicates that the tourism sector continued to advance positively in the subsequent years (Fig. 7). Regarding the overall occupancy rates of hotel rooms, both in Türkiye and İstanbul, the year 2022 represented the apex, reflecting the fulfilment of deferred tourism demand immediately following the pandemic. A significant trend to note is that Istanbul has consistently demonstrated superior occupancy rates relative to the overall performance of Türkiye throughout the years.

In Türkiye, when assessing hotel bed occupancy rates across its metropolitan cities, Antalya and Muğla experienced higher occupancy levels in both the pre-pandemic era and in 2023 and 2024. This can be largely attributed to their significant role in summer tourism, featuring numerous beaches and five-star facilities.

Table 2 Foreign tourism mobility and direct tourism revenues in Türkiye

Year	Income (USD) (Thousands)	Number of foreign visitors
2010	24,930,997	28,632,204
2011	28,115,692	31,456,076
2012	35,717,337	31,782,832
2013	40,186,327	34,910,098
2014	41,316,834	36,837,900
2015	37,700,923	36,244,632
2016	26,539,007	25,352,213
2017	31,253,835	32,410,034
2018	35,920,910	39,488,401
2019	42,851,778	45,058,286
2020	15,169,371	12,734,213
2021	30,309,722	24,712,266
2022	49,857,030	44,564,395
2023	55,874,176	49,209,180
2024	60,497,018	52,629,283

Source: TURKSTAT (2025e)

Table 3 An analysis of facility and bed capacity (2024)

Number of municipal certified facilities	Number of municipal certified rooms	Number of municipal certified beds
9603	280,307	627,572
Number of facilities certified by the ministry	Number of rooms certified by the ministry	Number of beds certified by the ministry
5443	573,368	1,206,543
Total number of facilities	Total number of rooms	Total number of beds
13,454	853,675	1,834,115

Source: T.C. Kültür ve Turizm Bakanlığı, Yatırım ve İşletmeler Genel Müdürlüğü (2024)

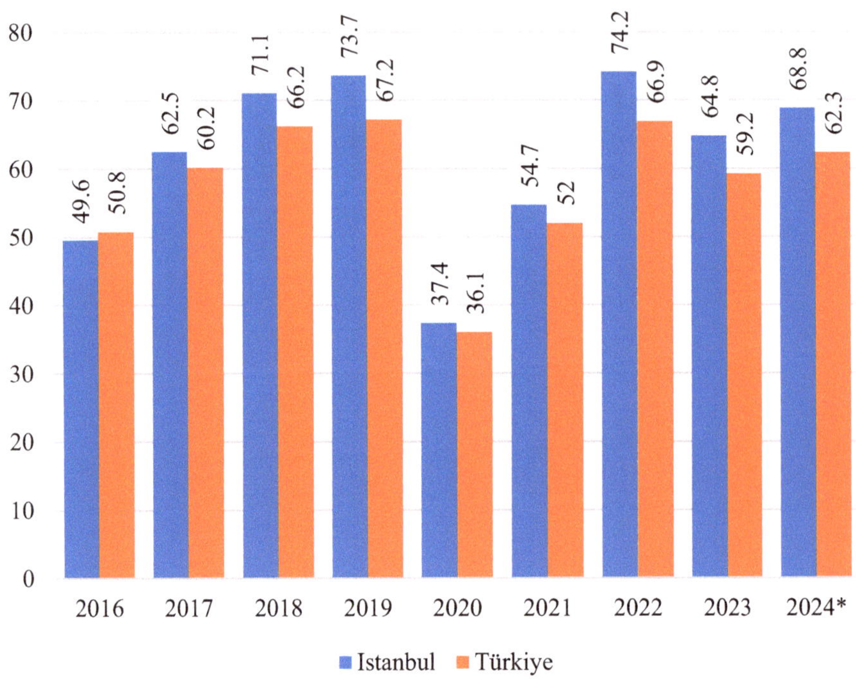

Fig. 7 Comparison of hotel occupancy rates for Türkiye and Istanbul in %. *Source*: GYODER (2024)

Istanbul was the third-ranked city for occupancy, while İzmir and Ankara fell below the Turkish average during this time, catering to a diverse clientele (Fig. 8).

5.2 Future Predictions

Evaluating the current trends, Türkiye's travel and tourism sector is set for strong and sustained growth in the coming years. According to WTTC forecasts, the industry is expected to contribute TL 7 trillion to the economy by 2035, representing

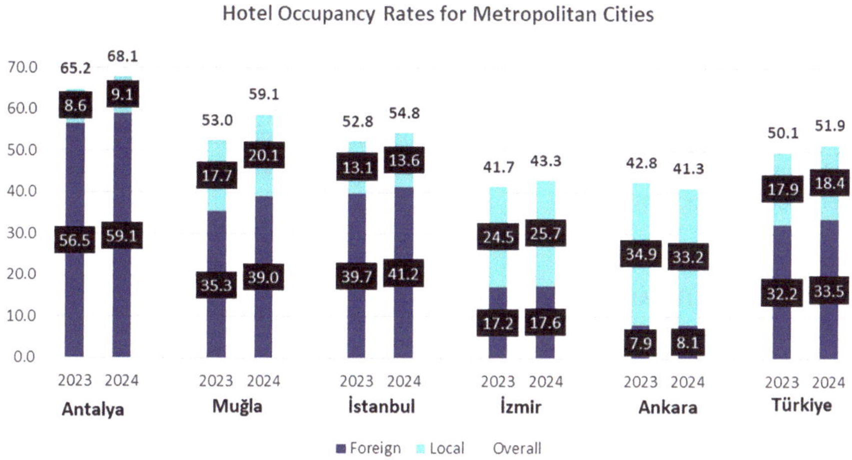

Fig. 8 Comparison of hotel occupancy rates for Türkiye and Istanbul in %. *Source*: Republic of Türkiye Ministry of Culture and Tourism (2025)

nearly 13% of GDP and maintaining 3.8 million jobs. This means over half a million new jobs will be created in the next decade. The projected growth will come from both international visitors, with foreign spending estimated at TL 3.4 trillion, and TL 1.7 trillion from domestic tourism activities. These statistics highlight the essential role of tourism in Türkiye's economy, ensuring stable employment and drawing in investments. With rising global demand and a vibrant domestic travel market, the sector is primed for long-term growth (WTTC, 2025).

The post-pandemic period shows a growing preference for boarding house-style lodgings and boutique hotels rather than large hotels, largely due to a wish to avoid crowded settings. Moreover, the rising popularity of summer homes and caravan accommodations has impacted hotel occupancy rates. Nevertheless, as recovery continues, hotels are expected to regain their favoured status, with an ongoing growth in tourism facilities. In addition to cultural tourism, the availability of extensive health facilities, especially those offering geothermal services, plays a significant role in the growth of health tourism. In this context, geothermal hotels are becoming increasingly popular. Furthermore, as Türkiye is further established as a centre for education, trade, and marketing, its tourism sector is projected to grow rapidly in the next few years.

6 Turkish Residential Real Estate Market

6.1 General Information

The notion of housing, classified among personal rights, signifies one of the fundamental needs essential for human wellbeing, as articulated in Maslow's Hierarchy of Needs. The fulfilment of housing requirements throughout historical periods and geographical contexts has been a substantial challenge. Addressing this necessity has played a pivotal role in the establishment of settlements and the development of urban environments (Asasoğlu, 2013; Özturan, 2005). The housing need, recognised as a critical issue, has been addressed in classical city models and post-modern urbanisation theories, ranging from the formation of villages and towns to the emergence of megacities, and continues to be a crucial consideration in real estate investment decisions across all eras.

6.2 Demand and Supply

In addition to the increasing resident population in Türkiye, the shrinking household size also contributes to a rise in the number of households. Conversely, when considering issues such as the desire to renew the existing housing stock and seismicity, it should be noted that housing production in Türkiye is experiencing a significant upward trend in both construction and real estate markets. Although the country's economic conditions fluctuated during this period, this situation also heightened demand for housing projects, which are viewed as a safe investment (Table 4).

The increasing demand for housing, driven by a growing number of households, necessitates that the housing supply has to catch up. Failure to do so can result in challenges related to meeting housing needs, thereby leading to affordability issues such as rising housing prices and rental prices. In addition to the economic contraction observed, particularly since 2018, the deceleration in the construction sector in Türkiye during the COVID-19 pandemic has impeded housing production since 2019. Throughout this period, the issuance of building permits for housing exhibited an upwardtrend, notably in 2017, before commencing a decline in subsequent years. The years 2017 and 2018 are particularly significant as they marked the peak in the acquisition of building occupancy permits, after the completion of the construction phase. Between the years 2018 and 2023, an increase and revitalisation in the acquisition of building permits was observed (Table 5).

The fluctuations in population and household size significantly influenced the housing supply. Moreover, emerging trends in housing developments, including smart homes, sustainable housing, and green buildings, are gaining popularity in

Table 4 The relationship between housing numbers and households

Year	Number ofhouses	Number of houses produced	Population	Number of households	Household size
2017	23,467,467	824,627	80,810,525	23,032,955	3.51
2018	24,292,094	873,034	82,003,882	23,599,727	3.47
2019	25,027,128	735,034	83,154,997	24,822,387	3.35
2020	25,625,196	598,068	83,614,362	25,337,685	3.30
2021	26,249,112	623,916	84,680,273	26,216,803	3.23
2022	27,049,037	648,941	85,279,553	26,902,067	3.17
2023	27,583,591	534,554	85,372,377	27,188,655	3.14

Source: TURKSTAT (2024c)

Table 5 Housing production according to the number of building licenses in Türkiye

Years	2010	2015	2016	2017	2018	2019	2020	2021	2022	2023
Building permit										
Number of buildings	139,616	125,741	134,099	161,921	104,509	55,717	96,204	138,449	123,467	139,600
Number of houses	907,451	897,230	1,006,650	1,405,447	669,165	319,720	555,012	722,576	646,628	855,265
Building use permit certificates										
Number of buildings	82,131	110,204	111,383	118,802	127,117	93,880	77,849	92,173	100,090	86,790
Number of houses	429,755	732,948	754,174	833,517	894,240	738,816	600,003	626,904	648,941	534,554

Source: TURKSTAT (2024c)

Türkiye and are regarded as markers of prestige. This trend particularly encourages the creation of branded housing projects. Conversely, the housing production facilitated by public institutions, such as TOKİ and municipalities, is viewed as a mechanism that serves both to implement social housing projects and to act as a stabilising component in the market. Notably, during periods of economic contraction, the provision of housing by public entities plays a vital role in market regulation and in fulfilling housing needs. It is anticipated that the housing supply will be appropriately balanced, satisfying demand while addressing housing requirements. Consequently, it is imperative to monitor the level of housing sales closely. Specifically, the sales figures of newly constructed housing projects are instrumental in informing decisions related to the ongoing production of housing.

This chapter indicates that the volume of title deed transfers and real estate sales in Türkiye fluctuates yearly. From 2017 to 2023, there was an annual average of 2.8 million sales. Istanbul accounted for the largest portion of these sales at 10.72%, with Ankara and Izmir following at 6.95% and 4.86%, respectively (Table 6).

First-hand and second-hand sales analysis shows that first-hand sales, seen as a key demand indicator, prompt manufacturers to create new housing projects. In Türkiye, the number of house sales ranged from 1.35 million to 1.5 million from 2017 to 2023, averaging 1.4 million (Fig. 9).

During this period, the volume of first-hand house sales declined significantly. In 2017, first-hand sales accounted for 46.81% of total sales, resulting in 659,698 units, but this quantity fell dramatically to 30.96% by 2023. The emergence of branded and prestigious housing projects directly impacts house sales. While economic factors mainly influence changes in first-hand house sales, modifications in housing policies also play a vital role, particularly concerning the launch of new housing projects (Table 7).

Balancing equity and credit usage is crucial for purchasing a home. Acquiring a property through loans, especially when there is stable and sufficient income, effectively supports both housing finance systems and secondary housing markets. However, fluctuations in mortgage housing sales over the years revealed a significant drop in 2021, with sales falling by approximately 50% compared to the previous year. Forecasts indicate that the mortgage sales rate may decline to 14.50% by 2023. This downturn is mainly due to rising housing loan interest rates and the instability of many households' incomes, exacerbated by a growing unemployment rate from economic contraction. Additionally, a slowdown in housing production and soaring housing prices are creating challenges for acquiring homes. Notable factors contributing to the rise in housing sales include transactions of previously acquired but unregistered dwellings between 2021 and 2023, current homeowners leveraging loans to fund essential economic activities through family transfers, and homeowners opting for higher-quality construction by selling their earlier purchases along with their savings (Table 8).

The rise in second-hand house sales during the same period indicates that tenants are increasingly leaning towards homeownership. Specifically, the proportion of housing costs relative to household income significantly influences this shift. Housing and rent costs remain the most substantial component of household

Table 6 Total title deed transactions and sales volumes (2017–2023)

Transaction type	2017	2018	2019	2020	2021	2022	2023
Total transactions	7,824,067	8,323,839	9,907,090	10,934,112	14,623,843	16,761,236	18,285,900
Sales in quantity	2,653,817	2,593,602	2,411,553	2,754,550	3,020,225	3,234,200	2,949,437
Share of sales transaction (%)	33.9	31.1	24.3	25.1	20.6	19.3	16.1
İstanbul transactions	953,174	998,981	1,158,686	1,246,943	1,579,440	1,720,462	1,632,205
Ankara transactions	593,045	609,879	715,002	818,884	1,017,686	1,085,612	1,180,754
İzmir transactions	442,366	460,287	526,020	450,965	696,257	824,213	812,121

Source: TURKSTAT (2024c)

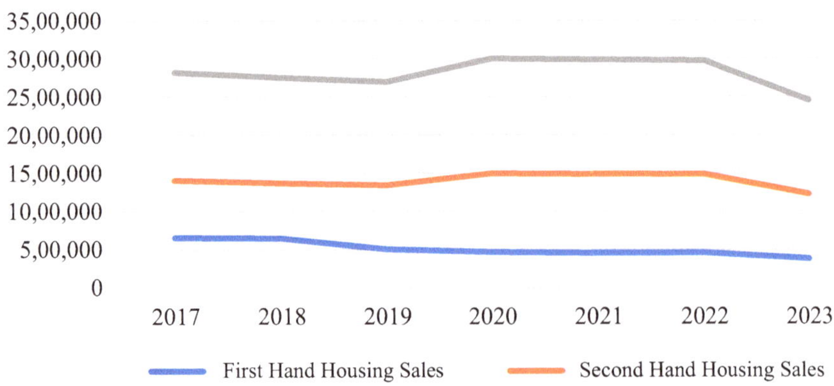

Fig. 9 Change of housing sales by year (first-hand and second-hand sales). *Source*: TURKSTAT (2024c)

Table 7 Analysis of Housing Sales and Forms by Years

Years	Firsthand housing sales	Share in total (%)	Second-hand housing sales	Share in total (%)	Total housing sales
2017	659,698	46.81	749,616	53.19	1,409,314
2018	651,572	47.37	723,826	52.63	1,375,398
2019	511,682	37.94	837,047	62.06	1,348,729
2020	469,740	31.33	1,029,576	68.67	1,499,316
2021	461,523	30.94	1,030,333	69.06	1,491,856
2022	460,079	30.97	1,025,543	69.03	1,485,622
2023	379,542	30.96	846,384	69.04	1,225,926

Source: TURKSTAT (2024c)

Table 8 Analysis of housing sales and types by years—mortgage sales

Year	Total housing sales	Mortgage sales	Other sales	Share of mortgaged housing (%)
2017	1,409,314	473,099	936,215	33.57
2018	1,375,398	276,820	1,098,578	20.13
2019	1,348,729	332,508	1,016,221	24.65
2020	1,499,316	573,337	925,979	38.24
2021	1,491,856	294,530	1,197,326	19.74
2022	1,485,622	280,320	1,205,302	18.87
2023	1,225,926	177,748	1,048,178	14.50

Source: TURKSTAT (2024c)

expenditures. This is primarily because most households are still renting, and the repayment of loans taken out for housing takes up a considerable portion of their income (Table 9).

This chapter shows a significant increase in the number of homeowners. Over the years, the percentage of owner-occupiers rose by 12%. In contrast, the segment of non-owners not paying rent has grown considerably by 16%. Interestingly, many

Table 9 Share of housing and rent in household consumption expenditure

Types of expenses	Distribution of household consumption expenditure									
Years	2002	2005	2010	2015	2016	2017	2018	2019	2022	2023
Housing and rent (%)	27	26	27	26	25	25	24	24	22	26

Source: TURKSTAT (2024c)

Table 10 Analysis of ownership status in residential use

Years	Homeowner	Tenant	Lodging	Not a landlord but does not pay rent	Total
2017	13,219,372	6,057,146	343,011	3,413,426	23,032,955
2018	13,217,732	6,767,371	371,762	3,242,863	23,599,728
2019	14,715,951	6,406,945	325,353	3,578,879	25,027,128
2020	14,811,363	6,724,051	317,752	3,772,029	25,625,196
2021	14,909,496	7,055,761	309,740	3,974,116	26,249,112

Source: TURKSTAT (2024c)

occupants in these rent-free homes tend to be close relatives, such as parents or siblings. Furthermore, the number of individuals using rental housing has also increased by approximately 16%. Profiles of tenants show that households unable to buy a home due to financial constraints often rent properties, sometimes while owning another house, as they invest in non-residential real estate or financial securities. Finally, the proportion of individuals using housing as tenants remains relatively low at about 26% (Table 10).

Türkiye has recently attracted attention from foreigners, particularly from Gulf countries like Saudi-Arabia, Syria, but also from Afghanistan. It also draws immigrants from Europe such as Russia, Ukraine, Germany, and the United Kingdom. This rise in migration is driven by advances in global transport and shifting economic and political landscapes. This trend has significantly boosted the sale of properties to foreigners in Türkiye. With domestic demand already exceeding supply, this influx adds strain to house prices, particularly in coastal and tourist regions. Analysing trends in housing sales reveals a dip in 2020, coinciding with the peak of the pandemic. However, 58,576 housing transactions in 2021 and 67,490 in 2022 were completed by foreign buyers. Projections suggest a decline in 2023 and subsequent years due to the prevailing economic conditions (Fig. 10).

When the supply fails to meet the demand, the second-hand housing market is mobilised, which affects housing prices. Upon examining the underlying reasons, the rise in the costs of necessary inputs for housing production and the inability to secure workers, e.g. due to work limitations imposed by the COVID-19 Pandemic (Ministry of Interior, Türkiye, 2024) exert pressure on the development of new projects. Labour restrictions have become problematic in the procurement of raw materials, the production of intermediate materials, and the final stages of production. The decline in housing production is the consequence. Therefore, the labour force in the construction sector is regarded as a vital input that must be acknowledged as a critical factor of production.

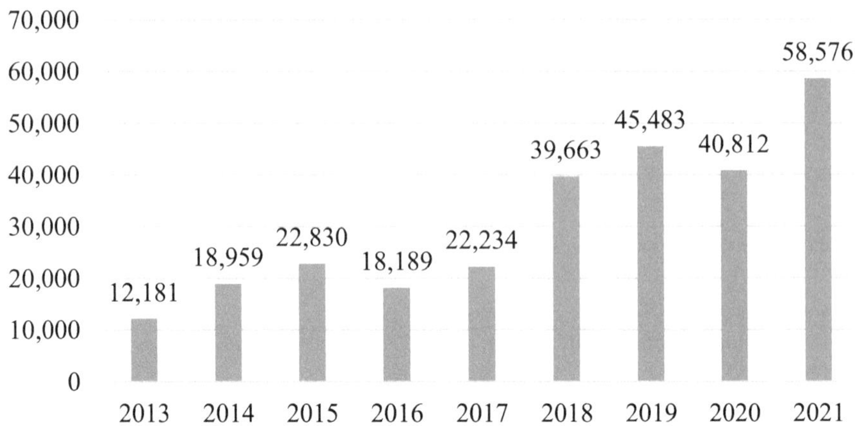

Fig. 10 Housing sales to foreigners by year. *Source*: TURKSTAT (2024c)

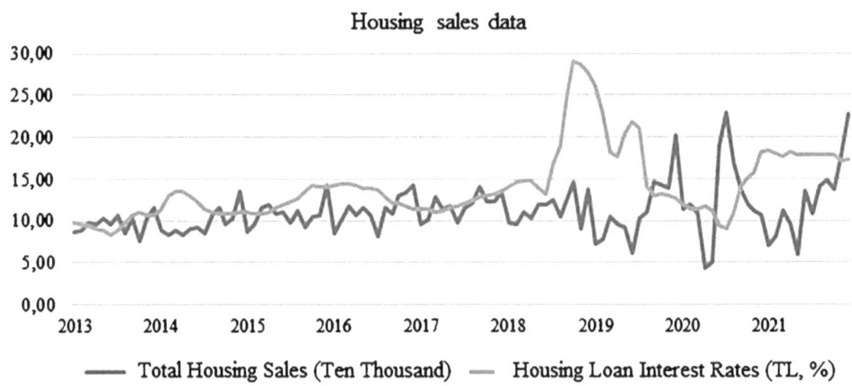

Fig. 11 Loan interest rates and sales data comparison. *Sources*: TURKSTAT (2024c) and Bankacılık Düzenleme ve Denetleme Kurumu [BDDK] (2024)

It is noteworthy that fluctuations in interest rates, in conjunction with economic developments significantly influence housing acquisition. An inverse relationship is evident between interest rates and the demand for housing loans. However, this also precipitates a fall in housing prices as a reflection of the supply-demand equilibrium. Given the inherent characteristics of the real estate cycle, housing loan rates play a crucial role in price variations. Concurrently, during phases of economic contraction, the anticipation of future value appreciation in housing investments generates heightened interest from investors. Particularly, the insufficiency of housing stock may result in issues related to housing utilisation, prompting ongoing discussions regarding the escalation of rent and housing values (Fig. 11).

The credit-to-value ratio is an important factor in obtaining housing, playing a crucial role in the effective use of housing loans. Although a higher loan-to-value ratio might seem negative in terms of repayment periods and increased monthly payments, it is recommended that investors adopt this strategy, especially during

Table 11 Change in the loan-to-value ratio over the years

Effective starting date	Loan/Value ratio (%)
01.01.2011	75
27.09.2016	80
18.03.2020	90

Source: Bankacılık Düzenleme ve Denetleme Kurumu [BDDK] (2024)

Table 12 Loan-to-value ratios valid as of 23.06.2022

	Energy class		
House value	A	B	DİĞER
Maximum credit amount that can be used for the purchase of first-hand housing sales			
Value <= 2 billion TL	90	85	80
2 billions TL < value <= 5 billions TL	70	65	60
5 billions TL < value <= 10 billions TL	Max. 3.5 billion TL	Max. 3.25 billion TL	Max. 3 billion TL
10 billion TL < value	x	x	x
Maximum credit amount that can be used for the purchase of second-hand housing sales			
Value <= 500 bin TL	90	90	90
500 thousands TL < value <= 2 billions TL	70	65	60
2 billions TL < value <= 5 billions TL	50	45	40
5 billions TL < value <= 10 billions TL	Max. 2.5 billion TL	Max. 2.25 billion TL	Max. 2 billion TL
10 billion TL < value	x	x	x

Source: Bankacılık Düzenleme ve Denetleme Kurumu [BDDK] (2024)

periods of high inflation. Importantly, the low down payment rates create favourable conditions for both regular income earners and investors. The latest change to the loan-to-value ratio took effect on March 18, 2020, allowing loans to be secured at a loan-to-value ratio of up to 90% (Table 11).

The 2022 regulation concerning loan-to-value ratios requires setting a clear level to differentiate between loan rates and the quality and value of real estate. Consequently, it is essential to ascertain the credit value ratio, which depends on factors such as energy class, whether the sale is first-hand, and the property's value (Table 12).

6.3 Future Predictions

The housing sector in Türkiye plays a crucial role in real estate activities. Factors such as population growth and migration, trends in foreign housing acquisitions, the emergence of advanced housing projects, and the renewal of housing stock, it is expected that the housing sector will grow rapidly in the coming years. Rising inflation, including high rental and housing prices, has encouraged both investors and consumers to seek housing. Although the COVID-19 pandemic caused a downturn in the construction sector, putting pressure on housing production, it is essential to continue construction to meet real estate demands. Even though high input costs currently restrict existing housing producers and developers from launching new projects, the sustainability of housing production is upheld and occasionally bolstered by other real estate developers like TOKI. Providing suitable credit options can act as a beneficial subsidy for developers, facilitating housing production or acquisition. As a result, construction activities can be revitalised. Despite the domestic market's unmet demand for housing, increasing interest from foreign investors in buying homes in Türkiye has significantly driven up housing prices, motivating producers to expand their housing production. Thus, steady demand, a housing stock that is not growing sufficiently fast, and rising prices are expected to spur increased housing production in the upcoming years.

7 General Evaluation and Conclusion

Türkiye has emerged as a centre for the real estate industry in the last few years. This can be attributed not only to internal demand factors, such as a large consumer base, a young and densely living population, rapidly increasing purchasing power, and evolving user preferences, but also to external influences, including substantial migration, both temporary and permanent. Moreover, political and economic events have significantly accelerated these migration trends. Additionally, Türkiye's natural beauty, rich historical context, advancing urban infrastructure, and improved socioeconomic conditions have drawn interest from both domestic and international investors, resulting in the swift growth of the real estate sector. The global impact of the COVID-19 pandemic has brought changes in technology and affected real estate markets, including retail, transportation, communication, and work habits, as well as the design and attributes of residences. Furthermore, shifts in energy usage, production technologies, and regulatory constraints have influenced real estate markets.

It is important to recognise that across Türkiye, the real estate sector and its associated fields are anticipated to grow considerably in the next few years. In addition to advances in real estate development, management, and facility oversight, a stable real estate market is likely to emerge through professionalisation initiatives and the recruitment of skilled experts in the industry. Despite the temporary slowdown caused by the COVID-19 pandemic, which has resulted in issues like raw material shortages and labour constraints, the increasing pressures from population growth, urban renewal needs, and seismic risks underscore the necessity for a renewed approach to building stock management. Consequently, the temporary stagnation is expected to be resolved.

The 2023 general elections in Türkiye impacted markets and caused stagnation in the real estate sector. However, the growing demand for real estate developments is expected to drive construction activities, aiding economic stability.

Energy is a significant global challenge. In particular, the diversification of effective electricity generation and utilisation is a fundamental challenge, with considerable emphasis placed on renewable energy sources. Anticipating that energy efficiency and sustainability will play pivotal roles in the development of real estate projects, initiatives such as green building practices, smart building technologies, and the establishment of smart cities are prominently featured, all of which are poised to impact real estate markets substantially in the future. Within this framework, the promotion of designs and applications for automation systems across various real estate sub-sectors emerges as a vital area for development and advancement.

As Türkiye emerges as a hub in the real estate markets of the developing world, it offers significant benefits for investors. However, this can also result in rising operational costs and systemic challenges for users and administrators. In contexts where legal systems play a crucial role in shaping real estate activities in developing countries, establishing legal frameworks that meet the needs of both users and providers is essential. Moreover, it's necessary to clarify technical specifications through regulations to promote healthy urbanisation and ensure the sustainability of real estate activities and the sector overall. Thus, there is a critical need for legal reforms to tackle the current challenges. Notably, these reforms are essential not only for domestic and international investors and users in Türkiye, which has become an appealing centre due to its real estate sector in a global context, but also for the overall impact on the domestic economy. It is expected that adaptation studies will occur in response to emerging technologies and changing usage patterns, especially in areas like real estate development, marketing, facility management, land asset planning, and management practices.

References

Alışveriş Merkezleri ve Yatırımcıları Derneği. (2024, December). *Shopping mall turnover index December 2024* [AVM ciro endeksi Aralık 2024]. Retrieved April 25, 2025, from https://ayd.org.tr/avm-ciro-endeksi-aralik-2024

Alışveriş Merkezleri ve Yatırımcıları Derneği. (2025, March). *March 2025 turnover index* [Mart 2025 ciro endeksi]. Retrieved April 25, 2025, from https://ayd.org.tr/mart-2025-ciro-endeksi

Asasoğlu, A. (2013). Konut ve konut alanları örneğinde mimarlık serüveni [Architecture adventure in the example of housing and residential areas]. *ICONARP: International Journal of Architecture and Planning, 1*, 58–66.

Bankacılık Düzenleme ve Denetleme Kurumu [BDDK]. (2024). *Banking Regulation and Supervision Agency Board Decision* (Decision No: 2022/10249). Retrieved April 19, 2025, from https://www.bddk.org.tr/Mevzuat/DokumanGetir/1126

Birch, A., Rogers, C., Oak, E., & Leyland, J. (2024). *Turkey as a supply chain reshoring centre: Opportunities and challenges*. S&P Global Market Intelligence. Retrieved April 19, 2025, from https://www.spglobal.com/market-intelligence/en/news-insights/research/turkey-supply-chain-reshoring-center-opportunities-challenges

Cushman and Wakefield. (2024). *Türkiye country snapshots: Third quarter 2024*. Retrieved April 19, 2025, from https://cw-tr.com/en/research-detail/1824/turkiye-marketbeat-q3-2024

Cushman and Wakefield. (2025). *Türkiye real estate market overview, year-end 2024*. Retrieved April 19, 2025, from https://cw-tr.com/en/research-detail/1894/turkiye-real-estate-market-overview-year-end-2024

Foundation for Environmental Education (FEE). (2025). *All Blue Flag sites*. Blue Flag. Retrieved May 3, 2025, from https://www.blueflag.global/all-bf-sites

GYODER. (2024). *GYODER indicator: From data to information in real estate* [GYODER gösterge: Veriden bilgiye gayrimenkul]. Retrieved April 22, 2025, from https://www.gyoder.org.tr/yayinlar/gyoder-gosterge

International Monetary Fund. (2024). *World Economic Outlook*. Retrieved April 15, 2025, from https://www.imf.org/en/publications/weo

ISO 500. (2023). *500 big industrial institutions of Turkey*. Retrieved April 23, 2025, from https://www.iso500.org.tr/500-big-industrial-institutions-of-turkey

JLL. (2021). *Creating places people want to be*. Retrieved October 3, 2023, from https://www.jll.co.uk/en/trends-and-insights/research/creating-places-people-want-to-be

JLL. (2022). *Global real estate perspective: August 2022*. Retrieved October 1, 2023, from https://www.jll.co.uk/content/dam/jll-com/documents/pdf/research/global/jll-global-real-estate-perspective-august-2022-summary.pdf

Kilpatrick, J., & Barter, L. (2020). *COVID-19: Managing supply chain risk and disruption*. Deloitte. Retrieved October 3, 2023, from https://www2.deloitte.com/content/dam/Deloitte/global/Documents/risk/gx-covid-19-managing-supply-chain-risk-and-disruption.pdf

Kurban, R. (2024). *Q3 2024 Türkiye real estate market figures*. Value Solution Partners. Retrieved April 23, 2025, from https://valuesolutionpartners.com/en/portfolio-item/q3-2024-turkiye-real-estate-market-figures/

Kurban, R. (2025). *2024 year-end macroeconomic and real estate market figures of Türkiye: MIPIM edition*. Value Solution Partners. Retrieved April 23, 2025, from https://valuesolutionpartners.com/portfolio-item/gyodervsp-macroeconomic-and-real-estate-market-figures-of-turkiye-mipim-edition/

McAuley, M., Kelly, J., & Gorab, E. (2024). *Global real estate transparency index*. JLL. Retrieved April 10, 2025, from https://www.jll.com/en-us/insights/global-real-estate-transparency-index

McKinsey and Company. (2020). *Perspectives on retail and consumer goods*. Retrieved April 23, 2025, from https://www.mckinsey.com/~/media/McKinsey/Industries/Retail/Our%20Insights/Perspectives%20on%20retail%20and%20consumer%20goods%20Number%208/Perspectives-on-Retail-and-Consumer-Goods_Issue-8.pdf

Ministry of Interior, Turkey. (2024). *New restrictions and measures circulars in the context of combating coronavirus* [Koronavirüs ile mücadele kapsamında—Yeni kısıtlama ve tedbirler genelgeleri]. Retrieved August 10, 2024, from https://www.icisleri.gov.tr/koronavirus-ile--mucadele-kapsaminda-sokaga-cikma-kisitlamalari%2D%2D-yeni-kisitlama-ve-tedbirler--genelgeleri

Özturan, Ö. (2005). Çağdaş kentlerde konut oluşumları [housing formations in contemporary cities]. In A. M. Bozdayı (Ed.), *Çağdaş kent yaşamında konut sorunları* (p. 33). Hacettepe University Publications.

PROPIN Property Investment Consultancy. (2024). *2024 4th quarter–Istanbul office market* [2024 4. çeyrek–İstanbul ofis pazarı]. Retrieved April 20, 2025, from https://propin.com.tr/raporlar/periyodik/2024-4-ceyrek

Republic of Turkey Ministry of Culture and Tourism. (2025). *Tourism statistics* [Turizm istatistikleri]. Retrieved May 1, 2025, from https://yigm.ktb.gov.tr/TR-9851/turizm-istatistikleri.html

Republic of Türkiye Presidency of Strategy and Budget. (2024). *Medium-term program (2025–2027)* [Orta Vadeli Program (2025–2027)]. Retrieved April 23, 2025, from https://www.sbb.gov.tr/wp-content/uploads/2024/09/Orta-Vadeli-Program_2025-2027.pdf

T.C. Kültür ve Turizm Bakanlığı, Yatırım ve İşletmeler Genel Müdürlüğü. (2024). *Tourism statistics* [Turizm istatistikleri]. Retrieved August 15, 2024, from https://yigm.ktb.gov.tr/TR-9851/turizm-istatistikleri.html

TURKSTAT. (2024a). *Address-based population registration system results, 2024* [Adrese dayalı nüfus kayıt sistemi sonuçları, 2024] (Publication No. 53783). Retrieved April 27, 2025, from https://data.tuik.gov.tr/Bulten/Index?p=Adrese-Dayali-Nufus-Kayit-Sistemi-Sonuclari-2024-53783

TURKSTAT. (2024b). *Seasonal gross domestic product, Q4: October–December 2024* [Dönemsel gayrisafi yurt içi hasıla, IV. çeyrek: Ekim–Aralık, 2024] (Publication No. 53699). Retrieved April 27, 2025, from https://data.tuik.gov.tr/Bulten/Index?p=Donemsel-Gayrisafi-Yurt-Ici-Hasila-IV.-Ceyrek:-Ekim-Aralik,-2024-54163.

TURKSTAT. (2024c). *TURKSTAT statistics* [TURKSTAT İstatistikler]. Retrieved August 15, 2024, from https://data.tuik.gov.tr/Search/Search?text=konut

TURKSTAT. (2025a). *Consumer confidence index, April 2025* [Tüketici güven endeksi, Nisan 2025] (Bulletin No. 53881). Retrieved April 27, 2025, from https://data.tuik.gov.tr/Bulten/Index?p=Tuketici-Guven-Endeksi-Nisan-2025-53881

TURKSTAT. (2025b). *Trade sales volume index (2021=100), February 2025* [Ticaret satış hacim endeksi (2021=100), Şubat 2025] (Bulletin No. 54111). Retrieved April 27, 2025, from https://data.tuik.gov.tr/Bulten/Index?p=Ticaret-Satis-Hacim-Endeksi-Subat-2025-54111

TURKSTAT. (2025c). *Consumer price index, December 2024* [Tüketici fiyat endeksi, Aralık 2024] (Bulletin No. 53621). Retrieved April 27, 2025, from https://data.tuik.gov.tr/Bulten/Index?p=Tüketici-Fiyat-Endeksi-Aralık-2024-53621&dil=1

TURKSTAT. (2025d). *Population projections, 2023–2100* [Nüfus projeksiyonları, 2023–2100] (Publication No. 54163). Retrieved April 27, 2025, from https://data.tuik.gov.tr/Bulten/Index?p=Donemsel-Gayrisafi-Yurt-Ici-Hasila-IV.-Ceyrek:-Ekim-Aralik,-2024-54163

TURKSTAT. (2025e). *Tourism statistics Q4: October–December and annual, 2024* [Turizm istatistikleri IV. Çeyrek: Ekim–Aralık ve yıllık, 2024]. Retrieved May 1, 2025, from https://data.tuik.gov.tr/Bulten/Index?p=Turizm-Istatistikleri-IV.-Ceyrek:-Ekim-Aralik-ve-Yillik,-2024-53660

UNESCO World Heritage Centre. (2025). *World Heritage List*. Retrieved May 3, 2025, from https://whc.unesco.org/en/list/

Uzunoglu, C. (2024, June 20). Turkish e-commerce market: Trust in online marketplaces on the rise. *ECDB*. Retrieved April 27, 2025, from https://ecdb.com/blog/turkish-ecommerce-market-trust-in-online-marketplaces-on-the-rise/4571

World Travel and Tourism Council (WTTC). (2025, April 29). *Türkiye's travel & tourism to reach a record ₺5.2TN this year* [Press release]. Retrieved May 2, 2025, from https://wttc.org/news/turkiyes-travel-tourism-to-reach-a-record-5-point-2tn-this-year

Ali Parsa is a professor and senior academic with over 30 years of experience in teaching and research, currently based at the University of Westminster. He holds a PhD in International Planning and Construction from Newcastle University. He is a Fellow of both the Royal Institution of Chartered Surveyors (RICS) and the Royal Society for the Arts, Manufactures and Commerce (RSA). His academic career spans seven UK universities, and he currently holds a visiting professorship at UTHM University (Malaysia). He was the Aubrey-Orchard Lyle Senior Research Fellow (1991-1996) and Director of Property Research at London South Bank University between 1991 and 2007, Rotary International Professor of Urban Planning and Business Development at the University of Ulster (2007-2010), and appointed as Professor of Real Estate at the University of Salford (2010-2012). He was Dean of Real Estate and Land Management at the Royal Agricultural University (2012- 2019). Professor Parsa has been a visiting faculty member with the University of Salford, the University of Manchester and Northumbria University since 2019. He is actively engaged in international academic collaboration, having served as an external examiner for several institutions, including the National University of Singapore, the University of Hong Kong, the University of Malaya, the City University Business School, Birmingham City University, De Montfort University and Wolverhampton University. His research focuses on global cities, sustainable urban regeneration, housing market analysis, land policy, and Sharia-compliant real estate investment and development. He works closely with universities, government agencies, and private firms across Asia, the Middle East, and Europe. In 2025, he was appointed as a mentor to the Kofi Annan Changemakers Initiative.

Ece Sert Özcan is an expert in real estate, with over 15 years of experience in property strategy and urban development. Currently, she serves as the Office Leasing Manager at the Istanbul Financial Centre, where she is responsible for developing leasing plans and negotiating contractual agreements. As a certified professional recognised by the Royal Institution of Chartered Surveyors (RICS), she has provided advisory services to prominent clients regarding property valuations and investment opportunities. Similarly, her expertise centres on developing real estate projects that are both profitable and sustainable. Özcan holds a bachelor's degree in urban and Regional Planning from Istanbul Technical University, along with a master's degree in Community Planning with a specialisation in Economic Development from the University of Cincinnati, where she graduated with the highest honours. Residing in Istanbul, she actively advocates for the advancement of women within the real estate sector.

Salih Demirkaya graduated from the Department of Architecture at Gazi University in 2010. He completed his master's degree at the Department of Real Estate Development and Management in 2017 and finalised his PhD at the same department in 2025. His master's thesis explored the relationship between building materials and construction costs. During his doctoral studies, Demirkaya examined office buildings in England and continued his research at Bradford University (UK) for one year, while also conducting studies on office buildings in Ankara. He focused on the relationship between user satisfaction and office spaces, concluding his doctoral research by analysing facility management in offices, real estate markets, user interactions with spaces, and the pandemic's impact. Between 2010 and 2013, he worked as a project manager, project developer, and construction manager at Kırşehir Municipality, while also serving as a project preparation and construction controller on large-scale projects. Since 2013, he has continued his academic and technical research at Ankara University, Department of Real Estate Development and Management. Dr Demirkaya remains actively engaged in areas such as real estate development, facility management, project development, effective and efficient use of built environment and space, user satisfaction, construction costs, and cost management in real estate development projects.

Dynamics of the Housing Market in Türkiye: Housing Prices and Bubble Risk

Md Moynul Ahsan, Abdurrahman Tursun, and Kh. Md Nahiduzzaman

Abstract

Housing constitutes a fundamental human need and a basic human right. In contemporary society, efforts are made to address the demand for housing, which serves not only as a prerequisite for basic living but also fulfils various roles, including fostering a sense of ownership, facilitating social interaction, and providing personal security. Despite its significant importance, housing remains a major challenge, particularly in terms of financing. Considering this, this chapter focuses on the financial challenges associated with housing, including housing prices and real estate bubbles, as well as the inherent risks and the social and economic dimensions of housing. This chapter endeavours to critically examine the concept of a housing bubble in Türkiye, as well as its formation and assessment. In recent years, housing prices have escalated significantly, and a sudden decline in housing prices appears highly improbable. Therefore, by analysing several indicators related to housing market dynamics, this chapter argues that the increasing housing prices are not merely a consequence of a housing bubble.

Keywords

Housing market dynamics · Housing price · Housing bubble · Bubble risk

M. M. Ahsan (✉) · A. Tursun
Department of Real Estate Development and Management, Faculty of Applied Sciences, Ankara University, Ankara, Türkiye
e-mail: mahsan@ankara.edu.tr; atursun@ankara.edu.tr

K. M. Nahiduzzaman
Citinnov for Integrated Territorial Planning and Smart Cities, Mohammed VI Polytechnic University (UM6P), Rabat, Morocco
e-mail: KhMd.Nahiduzzaman@um6p.ma

T. Just et al. (eds.), *Understanding Türkiye's Real Estate Markets*, Management for Professionals, https://doi.org/10.1007/978-3-032-13297-0_20

1 Introduction

Housing fulfils multiple functions that can be transacted in the marketplace, and it may be utilised as collateral to leverage the appreciation of property value. Consequently, it is feasible to generate rental income concurrently while the capital appreciates. Housing is also acknowledged as a reflection of social, cultural, and economic living standards; therefore, the housing market constitutes a pivotal segment of the economy. In addition to the public housing sector, the private sector typically demonstrates greater operational efficiency, particularly with regard to the supply of housing (Bolat & Şenol, 2020).

Changes in housing prices and their valuation accuracy are critical indicators, not just for the housing sector but also for various other industries and the overall economy. Housing prices are influenced by market conditions, which are based on the balance of supply and demand. The demand for housing is primarily driven by population changes (notably, the number of households), income growth, consumption preferences, and fluctuations in interest rates (Taşdemir et al., 2015). The supply side reflects the number of new housing units, which can be impacted by several factors, including construction costs, taxes, emerging technologies, and regulations imposed by public agencies (both central and local), third-sector organisations (such as housing associations and foundations), and housing cooperatives or private investors supported by state grants (Bortel & Gruis, 2019). Assuming all other conditions stay constant, a rise in housing demand generally leads to increased prices, while a boost in housing supply tends to decrease prices (Taşdemir et al., 2015).

A house is a relatively immobile asset, yet its location-specific features enhance its diversity, making it essential to analyse market characteristics on a local scale. While market mechanisms influence prices in the housing market, their unique aspects, compared to other goods and services, are often more pronounced (Yalçıner, 2018).

The real estate sector, particularly the housing segment in Türkiye, has emerged as one of the most significant contributors to the Turkish economy (Demir, 2015). Over the past 2 years, housing prices in Türkiye have more than doubled, sparking considerable discourse regarding the possibility of a housing bubble and raising a crucial inquiry: does this trend indicate a robust and expanding real estate market, or is it a reflection of a speculative bubble (Erol, 2015)? To effectively address this matter, it is essential to characterise the bubble first. A speculative bubble, or exuberance, denotes a prolonged deviation of prices from their fundamentally justified levels—those are typically influenced by factors such as demographic changes, variations in income, fluctuations in interest rates, or escalating input costs. If these fundamental drivers are insufficient to account for the rise in real estate prices, it implies the possibility of speculative behaviour.

2 State of the Housing Market in Türkiye

Following the 1950s, the phenomenon of rural-urban migration in Türkiye has led to rapid population growth and the emergence of slums and unplanned settlements within urban areas, characterised by inadequate infrastructure, basic services, and facilities. As a result, these unplanned developments have elicited various challenges across spatial, environmental, social, economic, and financial domains (Ishak et al., 2017; Nahiduzzaman, 2012). The challenges associated with addressing the housing issue in Türkiye primarily arise from a disparity between housing supply and demand. Indeed, the housing supply has consistently failed to meet existing demand for housing. The migration from rural to urban areas, particularly by young people, represents a robust and enduring trend (Ahsan & Duman, 2022), thereby contributing to urban problems, notably unemployment and an uneven income distribution. This predicament has been further exacerbated by a dysfunctional and non-institutionalised housing finance system, which has intensified unplanned urbanisation (Berberoğlu & Teker, 2005). This section of the chapter investigates the social, economic, and legal dimensions of housing, the dynamics of the housing market and its evolution, as well as the key determinants influencing the housing market in Türkiye.

2.1 Social, Economic, and Constitutional Facets of Housing

The number of households present within the community can estimate the overall necessity for housing. Should the number of households increase at a rate that exceeds the introduction of new housing units (whether 'open' or 'hidden'), pressure within the housing market will likely intensify. While a (mathematical) ratio encompassing households and housing units signifies the demand for 'visible' or 'open' housing, a comparable methodology ought to be employed to assess the 'hidden' housing requirements. This category includes instances of overcrowded accommodations, provisions for multiple families, as well as unstable, substandard, unsafe, and low-quality living environments. Consequently, a sustainable resolution to the housing issue must be informed by comprehensive and long-term investigations into population dynamics and migration patterns, emphasising the identification of hidden housing requirements through an exhaustive synthesis (İnşaat Mühendisleri Odası- İMO, 2008).

Housing is not only a means of meeting the need for shelter but also fulfils many essential functions, such as social integration, peace and confidence, socialisation, individual protection, and the provision of fundamental services for the elderly. Today, societies regard housing as an indicative outcome of social, cultural, and economic living standards (Mutlu Çamoğlu & Çakır, 2020; Nahiduzzaman, 2017). Historically, housing reflected the lifestyle, behaviours, and preferences of the society to which households belong. Housing fulfils basic human needs (Ören & Yüksel, 2013) and is widely recognised as a basic social right.

In addition to serving as a social and cultural asset, housing plays an important economic role, considering its construction value as well as the value added through other real estate services and financial sectors. A house is also regarded as a financial investment, capable of being traded and utilised as collateral. Consequently, this has transformed housing into a crucial component of the economy by establishing a new derivatives market and introducing novel financing opportunities (Önver, 2016). Nonetheless, the perception of housing as an economic commodity should not overlook its social and cultural dimensions.

In Türkiye's legal framework, the right to housing is governed by multiple constitutional and legal provisions. The 1961 Constitution recognised housing as a social right, defining it as a responsibility of the state. Specifically, Article 49 mandates that the state must ensure individuals can maintain their physical and mental well-being and receive medical care: "[...] the State shall take measures to provide poor and low-income families with dwellings that meet sanitary requirements". Since access to shelter is essential for health, the state should create opportunities that address the housing needs of all citizens. Furthermore, the 1982 Constitution required the state to take necessary actions to meet housing demands. Article 56 asserts that "[...] everyone has the right to live in a healthy and balanced environment", while Article 57 mandates that "[...]. The State shall take measures to meet the need for housing within the framework of a plan that takes into account the characteristics of cities and environmental conditions and also supports community housing projects" (Constitution of the Republic of Türkiye, 1982).

2.2 Development of the Housing Market

The significant proportion of young people in Türkiye can be linked to a sustained demand for new housing. The increase in industrialisation since the 1950s has catalysed urbanisation throughout the nation, leading to rapid social and demographic changes. Urbanisation has necessitated the construction of high-rise buildings to accommodate the expanding population in urban areas. Furthermore, the migration to cities has also contributed to the formation of numerous unplanned neighbourhoods, which have established a social structure and urban fabric in which informal settlements have become an integral part of urban life. Essentially, housing policy has transitioned to function as a "hoarding policy" instead (Çetin, 2012).

Over the past decade, it is estimated that Türkiye has sold an average of 1,342,000 houses annually. Between 2017 and 2021, sales of new homes declined, while the inventory of existing homes expanded. Generally, transactions involving new homes occur with less frequency compared to those for second-hand properties. Concurrently, during this period, sales of second-hand homes increased, while sales of new homes decreased (Ahsan & Sadak, 2021). This transition can be attributed to escalating construction costs, rising domestic consumer prices, and various economic challenges, notwithstanding a modest overall increase in transaction volumes during these years.

2.3 Factors Affecting the Housing Market

Housing encompasses a range of legal, social, economic, technological, and cultural dimensions, fulfilling various functions. The demand for housing arises when households possess sufficient financial resources to acquire a residence or pay for housing services, such as rent. Similar to numerous other countries, variations in the housing market represent a crucial macroeconomic factor in Türkiye, exerting significant influence on the national economy (Uysal & Yiğit, 2016).

Housing constitutes a heterogeneous asset, primarily attributable to its location-specific characteristics. Nevertheless, the housing market is significantly influenced by both regional and national economic indicators. Factors impacting the housing market encompass demographics, such as population growth and the number and structure of households, consumer and producer price inflation (Uysal & Yiğit, 2016), household income (Çamoğlu & Çakır, 2020), input prices, including labour and material costs (Kolcu & Yamak, 2018), interest rates, and financing conditions (Ahsan & Sadak, 2021; Atasoy & Tanrıvermiş, 2021; Bochkarova, 2024). These factors exert an influence on housing prices and result in modifications to building (construction) permits or building occupancy permits (Öztürk et al., 2018). Figure 1 illustrates the timeline of the Consumer Price Index (CPI), the Domestic Producer Price Index (PPI), the Cost of Construction Index (CCI), and the Housing Price Index (HPI) in Türkiye, thereby demonstrating a close relationship between these indicators for the period from 2018 to 2024.

The observation that the Housing Price Index (HPI), which reflects developments in residential property prices in Türkiye, closely correlates with the consumer price index (CPI) and, to a slightly lesser extent, with the producer price index (PPI)

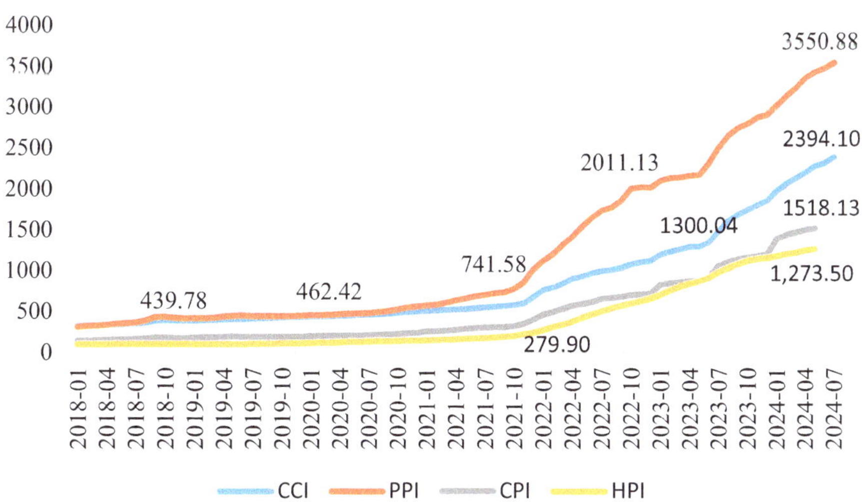

Fig. 1 Changes in HPI, CPI, PPI, and CCI for the period 2018–2024 in Türkiye. *Sources*: TurkStat (2024a, b, c) and CBRT (2024)

and the construction cost index (CCI) is noteworthy. Figure 1 illustrates the dynamics of these linkages. It is pertinent to emphasise that the HPI has escalated by a factor of 8.7 since the beginning of 2021, while the CPI has increased by a factor of more than 10; additional factors are also displaying significant price variations. In October 2018, the purchasing power parity (PPP) was recorded at 439.78, which surged to 3550.88 by July 2024, signifying an approximate quintupling over this duration. Rapid changes transpired during the COVID-19 pandemic and have persisted subsequently across all indices, reflecting an estimated fivefold increase from July 2020 to July 2024. Indeed, the Turkish housing market is intricately interconnected with other macroeconomic factors, demonstrating a strong and bidirectional relationship (Atasoy & Tursun, 2022).

3 Housing Prices and Bubble Risk

A bubble is identified as a major discrepancy between market prices and their fundamentally justified values. Thus, it is essential to analyse market dynamics closely to understand bubble risk. With this perspective, this chapter assesses the dynamics of the Turkish housing market from 2015 to 2024. Various methodologies, including price-to-income and price-to-rent ratios, were utilised to evaluate bubble risks. The results indicate that these ratios do not substantiate the presence of a bubble in the Turkish housing market (Coskun & Pitros, 2022). Recent empirical research on global housing bubbles also supports this conclusion. For example, Said and Hicham (2025) developed a Dynamic Stochastic General Equilibrium model for Morocco, illustrating how housing prices respond to monetary policy. Similarly, Chen et al. (2025) conducted a counterfactual treatment analysis to differentiate between structural dynamics and speculative activities. This study emphasises the condition of housing prices, the concept of housing bubbles, indicators of housing bubbles, and bubble risks in Türkiye.

3.1 Housing Price in Türkiye

The balance between supply and demand is influenced by factors such as population demographics and growth rates, rising household incomes, costs, and other economic factors. This balance also affects housing prices (Çadırcı & Güner, 2022).

Individuals acquire residential properties either to meet their housing needs or as an investment. When considering purchasing versus leasing, investment choices are typically guided by analyses of risk and return ratios. Within this framework, the utility value of a residence serves as a critical element when viewed as a consumer product, whereas factors such as profitability and risk gain prominence when a residential unit is regarded as an investment, particularly in relation to alternative investment opportunities. Consequently, the acquisition of a property for investment purposes ought to be predicated upon a comprehensive assessment of its profitability and the associated risks (Öztürk & Fitöz, 2009).

To monitor fluctuations in housing prices, the Turkish government utilises the Housing Price Index and considers the valuation reports prepared by the Central Bank for properties currently available for sale. This index has been calculated since 2015, with a reference point set in 2017 at a value of 100. This Key Performance Indicator (KPI) was recorded at 104.10 in the first quarter of 2018, escalating to 1273.50 by the fourth quarter of 2024. Consequently, it experienced an approximate 12.23-fold increase during the period from the first quarter of 2018 to the fourth quarter of 2024 (Fig. 2).

More specifically, a significant spike was observed during the period from October 2021 to May 2024, demonstrating a more than sixfold increase in housing prices, which reflects the aforementioned pronounced rise in overall input prices and consumer prices. Inflation-adjusted (real) property prices ought to be considered in conjunction with current prices to assess this rise in housing prices in relation to broader economic performance. Consequently, the variations in real house prices from January 2015 to May 2024 are scrutinised and illustrated in Fig. 3. Real house prices in Türkiye experienced a decline of one-third between 2016 and 2021, followed by an increase of nearly two-thirds. The inflation-hedging characteristics do not necessarily apply to each year; rather, they are evident over the long term, as illustrated in Fig. 3. Ultimately, the pronounced increase in nominal prices appears to be driven more by overall inflation than by real appreciation, that is, productivity gains or income growth associated with the property.

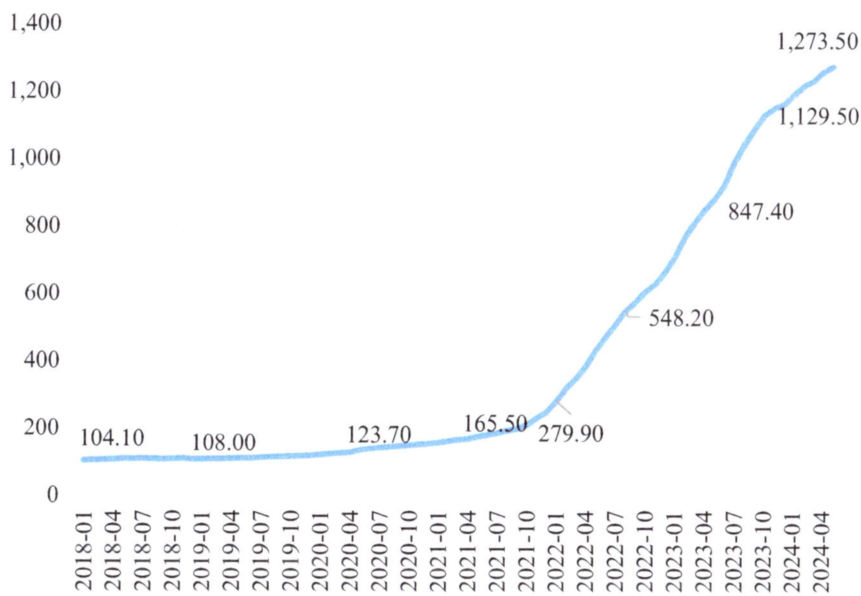

Fig. 2 Housing prices for the period 2018/1–2024/5. *Source*: CBRT (2024)

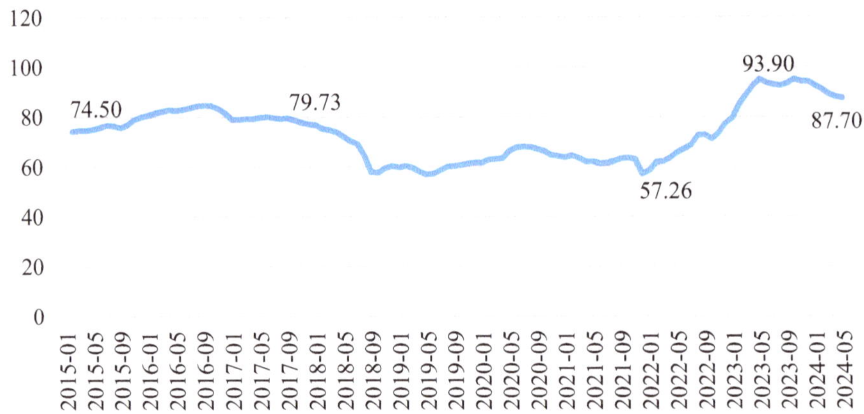

Fig. 3 Housing prices for 2015/1–2024/5 (Real). *Sources*: CBRT (2024); TurkStat (2024b)

3.2 The Concept of the Housing Bubble

The concept of a bubble is commonly exemplified by a marked increase in prices, followed by a sudden decline, or by a collapse occurring subsequent to a prolonged period of price appreciation (Oran, 2011). Thus, a bubble, by definition, can be identified only after it has burst. Consequently, a more precise definition often utilised in both academic and professional market analyses delineates a bubble as a situation wherein prices surpass fundamental values or when a product is acquired at a cost that exceeds its intrinsic value, with the anticipation of selling it at a significantly higher price in the future. Housing is considered an investment good, and to accurately identify a housing bubble, it is imperative to evaluate the true value of housing based on the internal dynamics of the housing market (Smith & Smith, 2006). This definition implies the existence of an underlying fundamental value, thereby necessitating a clear delineation of this intrinsic value (Oran, 2011).

Numerous factors have been proposed in countries facing a housing bubble risk. These factors encompass insufficient regulation and oversight of market mechanisms, excessively high demand fuelled by speculation, and a lack of market control. The emergence of a housing bubble signifies a sudden escalation in housing prices, followed by a rapid decline when expectations are undermined by new information (Lind, 2009). Subsequently, when investors in the sector incur financial losses, this may have an adverse impact on the national economy and occasionally result in regionally detrimental economic conditions.

The price of any product can be determined not solely by its intrinsic value, but rather by the expectations towards the main price drivers. This is particularly true for housing, given its long-term investment good nature. Given that these assets provide services over an extended period, the intrinsic value is shaped by expectations, which irrational biases may influence in the market (Kladakis et al., 2025). Once these biases dissipate, expectations are adjusted, resulting in a decline in prices. A comparable psychological pattern has been noted in speculative digital markets. Huang and Goetzmann (2023) illustrated how exaggerated expectations regarding Non-Fungible Tokens led to unsustainable pricing trends, which offer parallels for asset markets such as housing. Suppose the rationale behind the elevated housing prices observed today is the belief among investors that prices will continue to rise in the future. In that case, this suggests the existence of a housing bubble (Stiglitz, 1990). Certain prices, including those of stocks and housing, may occasionally correspond to these irrational beliefs and expectations (Erdem, 2019). When housing bubbles emerge from speculative activities, investors can realise short-term profits from these assets due to accelerated price movements.

3.3 Indicators of Housing Bubble

The emergence of a housing bubble results in substantial increases in housing prices, driven by factors unrelated to fundamental market dynamics. During this phenomenon, prospective buyers, anticipating the potential for selling the property at a markedly elevated price in the future, opt to pay amounts that exceed the property's true value.

There exists no universally accepted criterion for determining the excessive escalation of housing prices. Evaluations may be conducted by comparing housing prices to household income or by observing that real housing prices have increased by more than 100% within five years (Gong et al., 2024). The elevation in the price-to-income ratio is regarded as an indication of a housing bubble, which cannot be solely attributed to rising incomes. Another significant indicator is the rent multiplier, which illustrates the relationship between housing prices and rental rates. An increase in the rent multiplier and price-to-income indicators, in isolation, is insufficient; rather, these indicators should ideally be compared to the long-term averages and trends over the last 20 to 30 years (Bulat & Şenol, 2020). Furthermore, it is feasible to estimate housing prices utilising scoring or regression models. At the same time, the comparison of household formation with the development of housing stock also serves as a potential indicator of underlying demand (Barut & Bilgin, 2023).

3.4 Bubble Risk in Türkiye

Housing prices are contingent upon the dynamics of the housing market, and these prices are ascertained within the framework of such dynamics. Since 2010, the Housing Price Index and the New Housing Price Index have been computed by the Central Bank of the Republic of Türkiye (based on 2017 = 100) to monitor housing prices. Additionally, fluctuations in housing prices are tracked in accordance with the relevant index rates. A multitude of factors, including individual preferences and tastes, construction expenses, the overall state of the nation's economy, financing options, interest rates, and the inherent diversity of properties (wherein each house differs from another), profoundly influence the determination of house prices.

The concept of a housing bubble in Türkiye has been a topic of considerable discussion for several years, primarily attributable to escalating prices within the housing market. The rise in prices has been mainly driven by elevated construction costs and a resultant shortage of adequate supply, given the increasing demand (Hatipoğlu & Tanrıvermiş, 2017). In general, housing prices have surged predominantly due to intensified housing demand, rising interest rates on housing loans, and increasing expenses associated with house construction. In addition to these core factors, the scope for further discourse regarding a bubble remains limited. Tenreyro and Thwaites (2016) demonstrated how loan-to-value (LTV) policy instruments can effectively contain excessive leverage and speculation, thereby diminishing the risk of a bubble.

In other words, the escalation of prices over the past 2 years should not be characterised as a housing bubble. Furthermore, a sudden and drastic decline in housing prices is not anticipated in Türkiye, as speculative activities or non-intrinsic values have not driven the realised price increase. This assertion can be readily demonstrated by adjusting the housing price index for inflation (Fig. 3). The fact that the increase in housing prices arises from the dynamics of the housing market, rather than speculation, significantly reduces the probability of a sudden downturn in housing prices. In the first quarter of 2025, the housing market has exhibited signs of stabilisation. However, investors are advised to proceed with full awareness and undertake comprehensive research before making investment decisions.

4 Concluding Remarks

The construction and real estate sectors assume a pivotal role in the Republic of Türkiye. Given that the housing construction sector is a big component of the overall construction industry, it has a significant impact on the Turkish economy. It is estimated that an average of 1,342,000 residences have been sold annually in the Turkish housing market over the past decade. From 2017 to 2021, sales of new residences declined, while the number of second-hand properties increased. It has been observed that the volume of housing production contracted after 2018, leading to a decrease in the share of new sales within total housing sales, a trend that persisted into the first half of 2024.

From January 2018 to May 2024, the Housing Price Index, which represents the country's house prices, generally moved in conjunction with the consumer price index (CPI), the domestic producer price index (PPI), and the consumer confidence index (CCI). Moreover, the Turkish housing market displays a strong correlation with various macroeconomic variables. This chapter shows that house prices have nearly doubled over the past 2 years. However, upon analysing the consumer-price-adjusted house prices, it appears that the risk of a housing bubble is limited. Therefore, it is concluded that the increase in current prices is not primarily attributable to speculation or productivity gains, but is rather significantly influenced by monetary impulses, i.e. by consumer price inflation.

The emergence of a housing bubble signifies that housing prices are escalating beyond their intrinsic and fundamentally justified values. In light of the dynamics of the housing market, substantial declines are not currently observable; therefore, the occurrence of a housing bubble is unlikely. The price escalations predominantly stem from fundamental factors within the Turkish housing market.

References

Ahsan, M. M., & Duman, D. (2022). Kırsal Yerleşimlerde Gençlerin Göç Etme Eğilimleri ve Etkileri: Bitlis İli Adilcevaz İlçesi Örneği (in English: Migration tendencies and effects of young people in rural settlements: A study of Adilcevaz District in Bitlis Province). *Journal of Academic Value Studies, 8*(3), 231–243. https://doi.org/10.29228/JAVS.63782

Ahsan, M. M., & Sadak, C. (2021). Exploring housing market and urban densification during COVID-19 in Türkiye. *Journal of Urban Management, 10*(3), 218–229. https://doi.org/10.1016/j.jum.2021.06.002

Atasoy, T., & Tanrıvermiş, H. (2021). Türkiye'de konut kredisi hacmi ile seçilmiş makroekonomik faktörler arasındaki ilişkinin değerlendirilmesi. *Erciyes Üniversitesi İktisadi ve İdari Bilimler Fakültesi Dergisi, 59*, 461–484.

Atasoy, T., & Tursun, A. (2022). Türkiye'de Konut Piyasası ve Birinci El Konut Satışlarının Analizi. *Eurasian Academy of Sciences Eurasian Business & Economics Journal, 29*, 23–40.

Barut, Z., & Bilgin, T. T. (2023). Konut Fiyatlarının Tahmini için Polinomsal Regresyon ve Yapay Sinir Ağları Yöntemlerinin Uygulamalı Karşılaştırılması. *Süleyman Demirel Üniversitesi Fen Bilimleri Enstitüsü Dergisi, 27*(1), 152–159.

Berberoğlu, M. G., & Teker, S. (2005). Konut Finansmanı ve Türkiye'ye Uygun Bir Model Önerisi. *İTÜ-B Dergisi, 2*(1), 58–68.

Bochkarova, M. (2024). Stimulating the development of residential development through mortgage lending. *Economics & Education, 9*(2), 14–19. https://doi.org/10.30525/2500-946X/2024-2-2

Bolat, M., & Şenol, L. (2020). Konut pİyasasinda fiyatlandirma ve konut balonu. In Ö. Gökkaya, İ. Kılıçaslan, B. Demir, & K. Kahraman (Eds.), *International Marmara social sciences congress (İmascon 2020–autumn) proceedings book* (pp. 216–221).

Bortel, G. V., & Gruis, V. (2019). Innovative arrangements between public and private actors in affordable housing provision: Examples from Austria, England and Italy. *Urban Science, 3*(2), 52. https://doi.org/10.3390/urbansci3020052

Çadırcı, B. D., & Güner, B. (2022). TRA1 Bölgesi Konut Piyasasında Fiyat Oluşumu Balon Mu? *Elektronik Sosyal Bilimler Dergisi, 21*(81), 291–307.

Çamoğlu, S., & Çakır, E. (2020). Piyasa değeri ve mülkiyete göre hanehalkı konut talebi: Ordu örneği. *Süleyman Demirel Üniversitesi İktisadi ve İdari Bilimler Fakültesi Dergisi, 25*(1), 111–123.

CBRT. (2024). *T.C. Merkez Bankası*. https://evds2.tcmb.gov.tr/index.PHP?/evds/serieMarket/collapse_26/5949/DataGroup/turkish/bie_hkfe/. Accessed: 20.08.2024.

Çetin, S. (2012). Kalkınmada Kentleşme ve Konut Politikalarının Önemi. *Hukuk ve İktisat Araştırmaları Dergisi, 4*(1), 293–304.

Chen, Y., Phillips, C.B. P., & Shi, S. (2025). *Bubble Mitigation Policies: Counterfactual Analysis and Treatment Effect Inference*. Cowles Foundation Discussion Papers. 2844. https://elischolar.library.yale.edu/cowles-discussion-paper-series/2844

Constitution of the Republic of Türkiye. (1982). *Official Gazette of the Republic of Türkiye*, November 9, 1982, No. 17863. https://www.mevzuat.gov.tr/mevzuat?MevzuatNo=2709&MevzuatTur=1&MevzuatTertip=5

Coskun, Y., & Pitros, C. (2022). Is there a bubbly euphoria in the Turkish housing market? *Journal of Housing and the Built Environment, 37*(4), 2013–2032. https://doi.org/10.1007/s10901-022-09931-7

Demir, E. (2015). *İnşaat ve Gayrimenkul Muhasebesi*. Gazi Kitabevi.
Erdem, A. (2019). *Konut balonu kavramı ve Türkiye'de konut balonuna ilişkin bir uygulama. Yayınlanmamış Yüksek Lisans Tezi*. Marmara Üniversitesi.
Erol, I. (2015). 'Türkiye'de konut balonu var mı? konut sektörü kapitalizasyon oranları analizi' Taymaz, E and Özçelik, E. (eds.). Türkiye Ekonomisinin Dünü, Bugünü Yarını: Yakup Kepenek'e ve Oktar Türel'e Armağan.: İmge Kitapevi, 323–344.
Gong, B., Yang, S., & Zhu, M. (2024). *The detection and inspection of bubbles in the NASDAQ*. The Leading Edge Academic Publications. The Centre on Contemporary China and the World, the University of Hong Kong.
Hatipoğlu, Ü., & Tanrıvermiş, H. (2017). Türkiye'de arz ve talep açısından konut yatırım tercihlerini etkileyen faktörlerin değerlendirilmesi. *Türkiye Bankalar Birliği: Bankalar, 100*, 49–75.
Huang, D., & Goetzmann, W. N. (2023). Selection-neglect in the NFT bubble (No. w31498). National Bureau of Economic Research.
İnşaat Mühendisleri Odası (İMO). (2008). Türkiye'de konut sorunu ve konut ihtiyacı raporu. *Teknik Güç, 188*, 7–10.
Ishak, M., Nahiduzzaman, K. M., & Aldosary, A. S. (2017). Pro-poor urban housing provision in Ghana: A review of implementation challenges and prospects. *Open House International, 42*(4).
Kladakis, G., Lux, N., & Skouralis, A. (2025). Exploring the non-linear dynamics between commercial real estate and systemic risk. *Journal of Empirical Finance, 82*. https://doi.org/10.1016/j.jempfin.2025.101607
Kolcu, F., & Yamak, N. (2018). Gelir ve faiz oranlarının konut fiyatları üzerindeki kısa ve uzun dönem etkileri. *Uluslararası İktisadi ve İdari İncelemeler Dergisi, (Dr. Harun Terzi Özel Sayısı)*, 141–152.
Lind, H. (2009). Price bubbles in housing markets: Concept, theory, and indicators. *International Journal of Housing Markets Analysis, 2*(1), 78–90.
Mutlu Çamoğlu, S., & Çakır, E. (2020). Piyasa değeri ve mülkiyete göre hanehalkı konut talebi: Ordu örneği. *Suleyman Demirel University Journal of Faculty of Economics & Administrative Sciences, 25*(1), 111–123.
Nahiduzzaman, K. M. (2012). *Housing the Urban Poor: An Integrated Governance Perspective*. The Case of Dhaka, Bangladesh. Dissertation, the Royal Institute of Technology (KTH), Sweden.
Nahiduzzaman, K. M. (2017). *Finding an Affordable Housing Option: Social Business as the 'New' Policy Tool?* Policy Brief, Johnson Shoyama Graduate School of Public Policy, University of Regina & Saskatchewan, Canada. https://www.schoolofpublicpolicy.sk.ca/documents/research/policy-briefs/JSGS-policybriefs-Affordable%20Housing_web.pdf. Accessed: 25.02.25.
Önver, M. Ş. (2016). *Konut ve Konut Politikasi*. Ijopec Publication.
Oran, A. (2011). Balonları daha iyi tanımaya çalışmak: balon tanımları, modelleri ve lale çılgınlığı örneği. *Dokuz Eylül Üniversitesi İktisadi İdari Bilimler Fakültesi Dergisi, 26*(1), 151–161.
Ören, K., & Yüksel, H. (2013). Türkiye'de konut sorunu ve temel dinamikleri. *Süleyman Demirel Üniversitesi Sosyal Bilimler Enstitüsü Dergisi, 18*, 47–84.
Öztürk, N., & Fitöz, E. (2009). Türkiye'de konut piyasasının belirleyicileri: ampirik bir uygulama. *ZKÜ Sosyal Bilimler Dergisi, 5*(10), 21–46.
Öztürk, A., Kapusuz, Y. E., & Tanrıvermiş, H. (2018). The dynamics of housing affordability and housing demand analysis in Ankara. *International Journal of Housing Markets and Analysis, 11*(5), 828–851.
Said, R., & Hicham, O. (2025). House Prices and the Effectiveness of Monetary Policy in an Estimated DSGE Model of Morocco. *Economies, 13*(4), 87.
Smith, M. H., & Smith, G. (2006). Bubble, bubble, where's the housing bubble? *Brookings Papers on Economic Activity, 1*, 1–67.
Stiglitz, J. E. (1990). Symposium on bubbles. *The Journal of Economic Perspectives, 4*(2), 13–18.
Taşdemir, M., et al. (2015). *Gayrimenkul ekonomisi*, Anadolu Üniversitesi Yayın No:2766: 104.
Tenreyro, S., & Thwaites, G. (2016). Pushing on a string: US monetary policy is less powerful in recessions. *American Economic Journal: Macroeconomics, 8*(4), 43–74.
TURKSTAT. (2024a). *Turkish Statistical Institute*. https://data.tuik.gov.tr/Kategori/GetKategori?p=insaat-ve-konut-116&dil=1. (Accessed: 20.08.24).

TURKSTAT. (2024b). *Turkish Statistical Institute*. https://data.tuik.gov.tr/Kategori/GetKategori?p=Enflasyon-ve-Fiyat-106. (Accessed: 20.08.24).
TURKSTAT. (2024c). *Turkish Statistical Institute*. https://data.tuik.gov.tr/Kategori/GetKategori?p=Insaat-ve-Konut-116. (Accessed: 20.08.24).
Uysal, D., & Yiğit, M. (2016). Türkiye'de konut talebinin belirleyicileri (1970-2015): ampirik bir çalışma. *Selçuk Üniversitesi Sosyal Bilimler Meslek Yüksek Okulu Dergisi, 19*(1), 185–209.
Yalçıner, K. (2018). *Gayrimenkul Finansmanı*. Detay Yayıncılık.

Md Moynul Ahsan is an associate professor who previously held a faculty position in the Department of Real Estate Development and Management at Ankara University, Ankara, Türkiye, and later joined as a researcher in the Department of Economic and Social Research at SESRIC (a subsidiary organ of the OIC). He obtained his Ph.D in Urban and Environmental Sciences from Ankara University, Türkiye. He possesses over 11 years of professional experience in teaching and research within the domains of urban planning and development, housing, climate change, disaster management, and water across various universities in Bangladesh, Brunei, and Türkiye. Additionally, he has served as a Town Planner in Land and Real Estate firms in Bangladesh. His current research interests include urban planning and development, water resources, housing, strategic planning, sustainable cities and real estate, public policy, climate change, and migration. He has published 22 peer-reviewed articles, 8 book chapters, and more than 35 conference proceedings/abstracts, and has participated in over 45 national and international conferences.

Abdurrahman Tursun currently serves as a research assistant at the Department of Real Estate Development and Management, Faculty of Applied Sciences, Ankara University. He completed M.Sc. and Ph.D. programs in the field of Real Estate Development and Management at Ankara University. He obtained his bachelor's degree in mathematics from Sakarya University. His research interests encompass housing markets, system dynamics, real estate valuation, and alternative financing models. Dr. Tursun has authored a substantial number of academic publications, which include peer-reviewed journal articles, book chapters, and conference proceedings. Furthermore, he has participated as a member of the organising committee for various international conferences.

Kh Md Nahiduzzaman is an associate professor at Citinnov for Integrated Territorial Planning and Smart Cities at Mohammed VI Polytechnic University (UM6P) in Morocco. Additionally, he has held academic positions at the University of British Columbia (UBC) Okanagan in Canada, King Fahd University of Petroleum and Minerals (KFUPM) in Saudi Arabia, and the Royal Institute of Technology (KTH) in Sweden. His areas of expertise include urban and territorial planning, resilience, human-centric smart cities, and climate risk assessment. He has secured in excess of $5 million in research funding and has published more than 100 scholarly works across journals, book chapters, conference proceedings, and workshops. As a recognised authority in these disciplines, he collaborates on research initiatives with governmental entities, industry partners, and communities globally, including those in Canada, Italy, Spain, Romania, Germany, the USA, and Saudi Arabia. His contributions to non-structural flood resilience, floodplain mapping, and land-use planning strategies in British Columbia, Canada, have had a significant impact on provincial policies.

Facility, Property, and Asset Management and the Practices

Harun Tanrıvermiş, Esra Keskin, and Salih Demirkaya

Abstract

The lifecycle of real estate begins with land acquisition and includes phases of planning, project development, construction, facility development, resource allocation, property management, asset management, and concludes with demolition. Each phase requires collaboration between various disciplines, including project management and human resources management. On the back of a notable contribution of the real estate sector to Türkiye's economic growth, the sectors of facility and property management are experiencing growth at an even faster rate than asset management. Furthermore, compared to European and American countries, Türkiye has yet to achieve progress in establishing standards for facility, property, and asset management, as well as in professional development, licensing, institutionalisation, and accreditation. Nonetheless, the expanding and diversifying market for facility and property management services, along with increasing business activities and employment opportunities, positions Türkiye as an emerging market with large potential for further growth. The demand for academic institutions and professional organisations specialising in facilities, property, and asset management, as well as for licensing education and training in this field, continues to grow, too. This chapter examines the current state of built environment management, including its status and developmental trends, and suggests solutions to promote standardisation, enhance collaboration, and foster human resource development.

H. Tanrıvermiş (✉) · E. Keskin · S. Demirkaya
Department of Real Estate Development and Management, Faculty of Applied Sciences, Ankara University, Ankara, Türkiye
e-mail: tanrivermis@ankara.edu.tr; esrkeskin@ankara.edu.tr; sdemirkaya@ankara.edu.tr

T. Just et al. (eds.), *Understanding Türkiye's Real Estate Markets*, Management for Professionals, https://doi.org/10.1007/978-3-032-13297-0_21

Keywords
Facility management · Property management · Built environment management · Asset management and professionalisation

1 Introduction

Facility and property management were established in the early 1900s in the United States, when large high-rise buildings called for more professional management services. The demand for various services, including cleaning, security, maintenance, and repair, necessary for these high-rise buildings, prompted the development of facility and property management (Bell, 1992). Over time, such services have become increasingly diverse, and the scope of both fields has expanded rapidly. Activities that directly influence the quality of life and contribute to building sustainability—such as security, cleaning, catering, air conditioning, maintenance of mechanical systems, car parking, landscaping, pest control, and rental services for large-scale buildings—are now encompassed within facility management (FM) (Terzioğlu & Tanrıvermiş, 2020). Alongside the growth in commercial real estate, mass housing, mixed-use developments, public buildings, stations, harbours, parks, and recreational areas worldwide, including Türkiye, facility and property management have become ever more vital and specialised.

Facility Management (FM) services primarily encompass the execution of technical services related to real estate. The activities conducted daily within the real estate sector, including appropriate rental procedures and maintenance tasks, are referred to as property management. In addition to these responsibilities, asset management involves overseeing the owner's real estate assets as an investment. Asset managers may engage only superficially with the ongoing operations at the facilities' locations, placing greater emphasis on investment strategies (Edwards & Ellison, 2009). These three concepts are interrelated, and their distinctions cannot be clearly and precisely delineated. Moreover, the disciplines of property and asset management have undergone significant evolution over the past 10–20 years, emerging as independent business domains (Keskin, et al., 2023a, b; Read, 2017; Tanrıvermiş, 2019). Increasing competitive pressures in the market have necessitated a broadening of services among professionals in these three fields, and this also applies to market participants holding substantial real estate portfolios. This has led to closer cooperation in achieving investment objectives. Many market participants have described this broadening of activity fields as a "blurring of the lines" between facilities, property, and asset management functions (Read, 2017). Consequently, a structure has been established that complicates the ability to distinguish between these three areas in practice. Still, property and asset managers pursue common goals, centred on value creation.

As a result of competition and rising incomes, housing companies in many countries are shifting their focus from meeting basic housing needs to providing high-quality, more comfortable living environments for households. To fulfil these obligations, investment companies must deliver a wide range of management services efficiently and to a high standard (Chotipanich, 2004). This serves as the foundation for FM services. FM can integrate these services under one umbrella by utilising resources for both investors and clients (Atkin & Bildsten, 2017). Given these critical responsibilities, FM forms strategic partnerships with all stakeholders (Nutt, 2000). The primary goal of delivering housing services efficiently and ensuring their sustainability can only be achieved through integrating these services within the framework of FM (Noor & Pitt, 2009). In other words, a FM company is a management or service enterprise that provides human-oriented services in the real estate sector, particularly in large buildings, aimed at achieving high levels of customer satisfaction by adopting a customer-centric approach and complying with international standards and national legal regulations. Furthermore, while national legal regulations, which often exceed international standards, are introduced in property management, both global standards and national laws significantly influence asset management (Tanrıvermiş, 2019).

FM aims to improve the satisfaction of all stakeholders receiving services from the facility by using existing resources efficiently and effectively across both public and private sectors, as well as within the broader built environment. The level of satisfaction with the service can positively influence investment value, depending on the sector. This factor makes FM a multidisciplinary and multifunctional service (Barrett & Baldry, 2003). Due to FM's unified service structure, the number of subsectors within service areas tends to grow and become more complex as the scope of services expands. Conversely, property and asset management operate on a larger scale, focusing on preserving and increasing investment value. FM addresses technical and operational issues, while property and asset management deal with higher-level or strategic challenges.

2 Built Environment Production and Management Needs in Türkiye

Facility and property management can only be efficient and effective if they are integrated into a network of other management functions and aligned with corporate governance policies. In organisations, the mission, vision, roles, and goals of strategic management, along with subsequent management policies, are established by the board of directors. One responsibility of senior management is to develop an asset management policy consistent with other management policies. The resulting property and asset management policies encompass various elements, including, but not limited to, the asset portfolio composition, strategic asset management plans, asset management systems, and the selection of individual assets. In accordance with the property and asset management policies, it is essential to develop and implement an FM policy that also addresses technical considerations.

As a core element of asset management, property management includes management of land, land parcels, buildings, facilities, infrastructure, and the rights related to real estate, along with the administration of these rights and other relevant issues. FM typically covers building operations, maintenance and repairs, customer service requirements, and personnel management. In this context, within the organisational framework, facilities, property, and asset management exhibit a hierarchical structure, akin to a pyramid (Fig. 1). While operational involvement is prominent in FM, strategic participation increases as one ascends the pyramid (Tanrıvermiş, 2021).

Facilities, property, asset and investment management, corporate real estate management, and social responsibility are commonly used terms in both public and private institutions. Asset management involves the strategic handling of all activities that influence risk, return, and performance throughout the asset life cycle. Corporate real estate management covers a broad range of strategic and operational tasks, including the procurement of land as raw material, transforming it into developed land according to established plans, developing and designing suitable projects based on demand analyses, obtaining construction permits, overseeing construction, delivering projects to end users, and conducting maintenance, repairs, and similar FM activities post-delivery (Tanrıvermiş, 2021). Corporate property management aims to improve organisational performance by ensuring that the real estate portfolio aligns with the overall business strategy. The concept of corporate property management has begun to gain recognition within the private sector. However, progress in the public sector indicates that the methods and tools of corporate real estate management can be effectively applied in both industries (Haynes et al., 2017; RICS, 2016). When used in the public sector, the term 'public real estate management' is often used.

During the rapid urbanisation process in Türkiye following 1950, there was a significant increase in the building stock. The total number of buildings in urban areas has reached 9.50 million units, with an estimated 74.92–77.13% (76.08% on average) being residential buildings constructed between 2000 and 2023. The total number of residential buildings has reached 7.3 million, while the number of housing units has reached 30 million. Commercial buildings – including shops, stores,

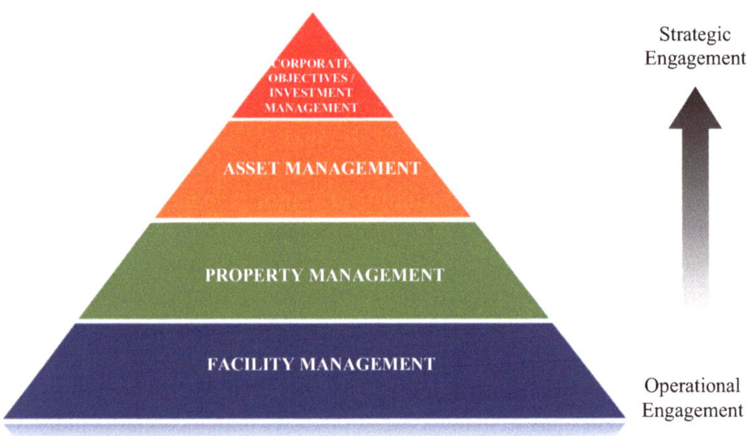

Fig. 1 Facility, real estate, asset, and investment management relationship. Source: Tanrıvermiş (2021)

arcades, business inns, bazaars, offices, cinemas, theatres, opera houses, cinema studios, hotels, motels, pensions, holiday villages, apart-hotels, bus station buildings, airport buildings, petrol and service stations, ferry pier buildings, railway stations, warehouses, garages, hangars, kiosks, bars, nightclubs, wedding halls, weighbridge buildings, public houses, restaurants, casinos, coffee houses, billiard and game halls, pharmacies, banks, and insurance buildings—constitute between 6.00% and 6.24% of the total number of buildings. Although the number of buildings designated for other purposes increased from 1,254,707 to 1,307,468 between 2000 and 2023, their proportion in the overall number of buildings declined from 16.01% to 13.42% (averaging 14.52%), despite rapid development in commercial real estate investments and markets. The share of industrial buildings in the total number of buildings experienced a slight increase from 1.83% to 2.11% (with an average of 2.02%) during the period from 2000 to 2023 (TURKSTAT, 2024) (Table 1).

The total number of buildings was recorded as 7.8 million in 2000 by the survey. The production and use of both residential and non-residential buildings, which are crucial for urban development, were analysed using macro data from 2000 to 2023. Data on building production was studied at both the building level and the unit level, considering features such as function, ownership, heating system, fuel type, and the number of storeys. Over this period, there was a general rise in the number of buildings and units. In 2000, there were 90,849 buildings, with 245,155 units. By 2023, these figures decreased to 86,818 buildings, but the number of units increased to 535,115. Clearly, the average size of a building had grown, meaning more units per

Table 1 Development of building assets by type in Türkiye

Years	Total number of buildings	Residential	Commercial	Industrial	Buildings of public recreational, educational, hospital or care	Others
2000	7,838,675	5,872,808	470,524	143,209	97,427	1,254,707
2005	8,108,366	6,096,499	493,822	157,121	99,342	1,261,582
2010	8,181,749	6,158,509	500,290	159,167	99,834	1,263,949
2011	8,249,805	6,215,248	505,346	161,923	100,505	1,266,783
2012	8,325,874	6,279,342	512,043	164,283	101,215	1,268,991
2013	8,420,646	6,360,107	519,972	167,216	102,066	1,271,285
2014	8,502,777	6,430,874	524,833	170,058	103,034	1,273,978
2015	8,601,116	6,516,710	530,854	172,974	103,916	1,276,662
2016	8,696,879	6,599,534	537,348	175,476	104,772	1,279,749
2017	8,817,812	6,702,236	547,953	178,655	106,020	1,282,948
2018	8,942,322	6,807,296	558,315	182,262	107,474	1,286,975
2019	9,052,526	6,902,192	565,428	184,405	108,686	1,291,815
2020	9,163,909	6,997,964	571,616	187,774	110,077	1,296,478
2021	9,282,711	7,102,406	577,702	190,557	111,456	1,300,590
2022	9,409,828	7,212,801	584,400	194,483	113,084	1,305,060
2023	9,503,708	7,293,964	590,205	197,298	114,773	1,307,468

Source: TURKSTAT (2024)

building (Fig. 2). Notably, from 2000 to 2023, while the number of buildings increased by 40%, the number of units grew by 260%. The development plan for 2019–2023 aims for horizontal growth to be the foundation of urbanisation. Measures that will improve urban life, foster community, promote neighbourhood culture, and enhance urban awareness will be expanded. Furthermore, successful model settlements reflecting human-centred architecture will be identified, and an evaluation report will be prepared (Presidency of Strategy and Budget, 2023).

Buildings and units encompass residential, commercial, industrial, cultural, religious, sanitary, social, and administrative categories. Between 2002 and 2023, there was a notable increase in the construction of residential buildings, which accounted for 76.93% of the total building output. Subsequently, commercial and office structures also contributed significantly, with the private sector's development occupying a considerable share (Table 1). Following the acceleration of slum area transformation and the remediation of disaster-prone structures in numerous cities after 2012, new buildings and residential districts have emerged, leading to an increase in the completion of high-rise structures. The ongoing process of urban transformation—including demolition and reconstruction—is anticipated to persist in cities for the next 15–20 years, driven by sustained demand for quality housing, office space, and residences fuelled by rising incomes.

Most units completed between 2000 and 2021 were completed in three-storey buildings. In 2000, these multi-unit buildings accounted for 85.84%, and by 2021, this share had increased to 93.50%. A detailed analysis of the building structure shows a rise in the number of units within buildings that have 4, 5, 6, 7, and 10 or

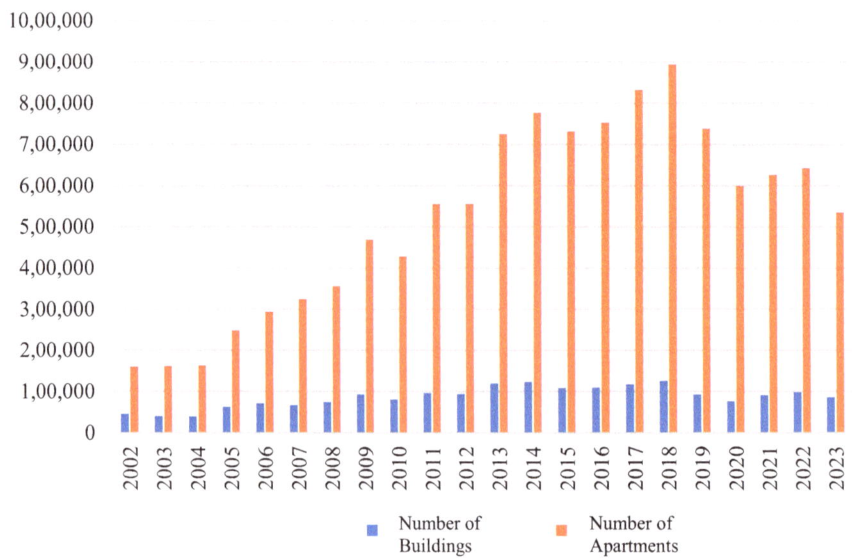

Fig. 2 Buildings and independent sections for which occupancy permits were obtained by years. Source: Presidency of Strategy and Budget (2023)

more storeys (TURKSTAT, 2024). This change can be linked to the need to reduce escalating land and acquisition costs on overall construction expenses, driven by rapid urbanisation and progress in construction technology. The increasing number of multi-storey residential buildings, offices, homes, and hotels that have emerged in recent years further emphasises this trend (Table 2).

This trend towards taller buildings is reinforced by financing initiatives that improve zoning density within transformative projects.

High-rise structures are mainly used for offices, plazas, luxury residences, and hotels. They face challenges related to services such as maintenance and repair operations, heating and cooling systems, elevators, security, cleaning, and fire suppression. The management costs associated with these buildings are considerably higher compared to structures with five or fewer storeys, leading to substantial difficulties during their operation. The issues caused by high-rise buildings negatively affect quality of life, and their financial risks must be evaluated alongside environmental hazards.

3 Status and Development of Facility Management in Türkiye

3.1 Scope and Development of Facility Management

FM originated from the need to provide adequate shelter and construct physical structures in response to these requirements. In Türkiye, the concept of FM remains in its early stages, as demonstrated by global cases and the current state of the sector (Erentürk, 2016). This situation is seen as a recent improvement in the quality of life for stakeholders receiving services within buildings and facilities in our country.

Over time, significant progress has been achieved in defining and delineating the concept of FM. The British Institute of Facilities Management (BIFM) has adopted the definition of FM articulated by the European Committee for Standardisation (CEN) and endorsed by the British Standards Institution: "Facilities help to ensure the functionality, comfort, safety, and efficiency of buildings and grounds, infrastructure, and real estate. Within the context of the built environment, it is performed strategically and systematically. It meets operational objectives for day-to-day delivery, ensuring the environment remains safe and efficient." The British Institute of Facilities Management has refined this concept, stating, "Facilities Management encompasses the management of multidisciplinary activities in the built environment and their impact on people and workplaces". This supplementary definition recognises that managers are engaged in various disciplines. It also establishes the connection between the workplace and its stakeholders. The International Facility Management Association (IFMA) defines FM as follows: "FM is an organisational function that integrates people, place, and process within the built environment with the purpose of improving the quality of life for people and the productivity of the core business". FM encompasses not only multidisciplinary activities and the effectiveness of core operations and the workplace's

Table 2 Classification of buildings according to number of units in Türkiye

Years	Units	Number of Stories										
		Total	1 storey	2 storey	3 storey	4 storey	5 storey	6 storey	7 storey	8 storey	9 storey	10 or more storeys
2000	Number of buildings	90,849	7908	25,696	15,476	13,764	11,165	8697	2772	1487	1112	2772
	Number of units	245,155	6437	28,265	23,682	32,631	45,372	45,239	16,112	9937	8256	29,224
2005	Number of buildings	64,126	9002	23,241	13,376	6069	5409	3810	1361	584	413	861
	Number of units	249,816	4382	28,632	26,772	27,523	48,023	45,294	21,679	10,537	9633	27,341
2010	Number of buildings	82,131	10,764	20,252	16,570	8839	10,748	7029	2786	1379	854	2910
	Number of units	429,755	5885	27,774	37,123	43,565	86,617	73,535	37,229	22,859	17,567	77,601
2011	Number of buildings	98,339	11,950	23,795	17,876	11,452	14,193	9728	3784	1544	1153	2864
	Number of units	556,769	6308	33,923	43,704	60,452	115,413	101,095	50,464	24,515	23,518	97,377
2012	Number of buildings	95,763	11,456	22,946	17,447	11,602	13,958	9575	3467	1380	1132	2800
	Number of units	556,331	5736	33,166	48,061	66,190	116,911	101,997	48,068	22,244	21,083	92,875
2013	Number of buildings	120,933	13,518	25,483	22,209	15,666	18,578	13,056	5071	2046	1545	3761
	Number of units	726,339	7730	32,075	64,251	86,968	154,524	131,698	67,438	31,328	29,366	120,961
2014	Number of buildings	124,510	14,061	26,345	21,780	16,207	18,186	13,703	5663	2028	1682	4855
	Number of units	777,596	7074	38,663	64,199	91,939	141,276	139,671	74,123	33,260	32,660	154,731
2015	Number of buildings	110,204	11,126	20,638	18,209	15,461	18,151	13,564	5501	1833	1692	4029
	Number of units	732,948	4829	31,770	59,068	89,090	145,546	141,005	72,394	28,583	31,792	128,871
2016	Number of buildings	111,383	11,228	21,074	19,485	15,165	17,844	13,339	5579	1756	1475	4438
	Number of units	754,174	4741	31,994	63,333	88,923	142,656	138,226	74,026	30,462	28,816	150,997

2017	Number of buildings	117,441	10,232	21,849	20,818	17,096	19,286	14,027	5979	1990	1685	4479
	Number of units	824,627	4676	33,877	72,577	102,837	157,940	152,954	81,193	33,058	33,946	151,569
2018	Number of buildings	124,116	12,528	23,015	22,142	18,238	19,575	13,603	6213	2289	1733	4780
	Number of units	873,034	5537	36,647	76,990	110,458	165,558	153,154	88,701	40,111	36,871	159,007
2019	Number of buildings	93,279	9110	17,175	15,649	12,379	15,284	10,035	4948	1976	1694	5029
	Number of units	734,373	4212	25,729	51,975	77,228	130,290	117,478	74,224	35,799	37,715	179,723
2020	Number of buildings	77,865	9865	15,969	12,317	9480	11,055	7834	4116	1500	1489	4240
	Number of units	600,096	5696	24,392	41,624	60,124	96,954	93,697	62,167	28,731	34,406	152,305
2021	Number of buildings	92,182	13,976	22,630	14,701	10,126	11,424	8667	4161	1519	1202	3776
	Number of units	627,082	8273	32,507	48,291	64,897	103,354	105,423	64,638	28,224	26,553	144,922

Source: TURKSTAT (2024)

impact on individuals' productivity, but it also aims to achieve organisational effectiveness by ensuring that the working environment and support services are aligned and integrated with business processes and the organisation's strategic objectives (Haynes et al., 2017).

FM remains a priority for executive management within organisations, especially concerning cost control. However, FM serves not only as a functional and physical aspect of companies but also provides social benefits to both organisations and stakeholders. It plays a vital role in building a strong brand image, ensuring employee and customer satisfaction, promoting health and safety, and enhancing perceptions of corporate social responsibility (RICS, 2016). Therefore, it is clear that modern companies no longer see FM simply as a cost; they are equally dedicated to maintaining a strong brand identity and addressing corporate social responsibility. Issues such as adopting Leadership in Energy and Environmental Design (LEED) standards across sectors, reducing carbon emissions, and providing a healthy, safe, high-quality, and sustainable working environment have become increasingly important (IAM, 2015).

FM involves multiple functional groups within an organisation. The decisions made by one group can significantly impact another; therefore, effective FM requires a comprehensive, end-to-end management process. To ensure that all groups work together harmoniously and efficiently, FM policies should be formulated and developed in alignment with the company's asset and property management policies. For these reasons, property management goes beyond merely locating and utilising space; it represents a systematic and interconnected life cycle focused on optimising the investment in and use of real estate (Tanrıvermiş, 2019).

In Türkiye, FM was first introduced in smart buildings, shopping centres, and large hotels during the 1990s. Subsequently, a series of mixed real estate projects and public investments emerged. Corresponding with advances in technology, smart buildings were constructed more frequently, with automation playing a crucial role in building management. The need to monitor and manage service expenses more efficiently has led to the adoption of more professional methods within FM (Tanrıvermiş, 2019). In recent years, investment firms have notably demonstrated FM practices within their organisations to attract greater customer interest and control operational costs. The development of mixed-use projects, including residential, office, and retail spaces, has positioned FM as a strategic partner for all stakeholders, especially investor companies responsible for construction and clients benefiting from these initiatives (Evcioğlu, 2013). Furthermore, the development of FM within the public sector has recently gained momentum through the provision of management services by the rights holder via operation and maintenance (O + M) contracts established during the tender phase for specialised infrastructure projects, such as city hospitals, airports, toll roads, and bridges, implemented as public-private partnerships. Consequently, the number of entities operating within the FM sector continues to grow.

In conjunction with the ongoing progress of FM in Türkiye, prominent corporations established within the FM sector in the United States and Europe are engaging in the Turkish market through local partnerships with Turkish firms. This collaborative approach facilitates the growth of the FM industry in Türkiye by disseminating the expertise of new international companies specialising in their respective fields. In conclusion, FM alleviates a substantial burden on investor companies, enabling them to focus on their core business activities, and promotes a more comfortable living space by ensuring clients receive superior service.

Professional Facility Management (FM) in Türkiye continues to exhibit significant deficiencies. Despite global progress and emerging trends in FM, the oversight of this sector within Türkiye faces challenges due to legal regulations established in the 1960s, which do not meet contemporary needs and modern standards. Consequently, there is a pressing need to enact comprehensive and guiding legislation to foster the sustainable development of FM in Türkiye (Tanrıvermiş, 2019). Numerous companies of various scales are engaged in facility services, with the market size estimated at approximately USD 15 billion (Temeljotov-Salaj et al., 2021). The primary driver of growth in the FM market can be attributed to the rise of mixed-use housing, commercial real estate, urban hospitals, and ports, particularly in major urban centres such as Istanbul. Therefore, FM is expected to continue to evolve. It is anticipated that, with the adoption of international standards, the sector may even surpass its recent growth trajectory.

Facility and property management activities contribute approximately 5–10% to the Gross Domestic Product (GDP) of developed countries. The total value of FM activities, including support services, makes up about 8.2% of the UK's GDP. According to a survey by Berger (2001), 70% of American companies and 50% of European companies see their real estate as a strategic resource (Ebinger & Madritsch, 2012). Effective FM requires that the portfolio of facilities and infrastructure aligns well with the company's vision and mission, that facilities have the right asset mix, that assets are acquired efficiently, that components of facilities and infrastructure are adequately protected, and that facilities comply with legal standards. Companies are increasingly recognising FM not just as a back-office function managing daily operations, but as a strategic and integrated role that greatly benefits the organisation overall. Today, businesses tend to hire professional facility and property management companies to lower operating costs, reduce energy consumption, support sustainability goals, improve efficiency, and streamline facilities processes. Unlike institutions in developed countries, many public and private institutions in Türkiye do not view real estate assets as a strategic resource. Extensive research is needed to create an effective facility and real estate management system, as the FM market's share of GDP remains below 1%. This ratio is lower than in advanced countries and the EU (Markets and Data, 2024).

3.2 Facility Management Models and General Structure of the Market

Currently, facilities operate across a diverse range of environmental conditions to fulfil various functions or purposes. Consequently, management practices in Facility Management (FM) vary according to these distinctions. A study conducted by Barrett and Baldry (2003) categorises FM models into six categories: the office or office manager's model, the single-campus model, the local campus model, the multiple-campus model, the international model, and the public sector model. In Türkiye, several additional FM models have been identified, including the service companies model, the construction companies model, the condominium owners' management model, the building owners' (investors') management model, and the professional management model, see below (Keskin, et al., 2023a, b; Tanrıvermiş, 2021):

1. *The Service Company's Model:* The main services provided by providers involved in FM include security, cleaning, gardening, and landscaping. Service companies appeared in the 1990s, during the early stage of the service sector, initially specialising in cleaning and security services for buildings, business centres, and factories. Over the following years, these companies expanded their expertise by offering additional services like garden maintenance, pest control, and catering. Today, service provider firms provide cost-effective and efficient services in sectors where quality expectations are moderate and do not require advanced technological solutions.
2. *The Construction Company's Model:* Currently, numerous construction firms have chosen to implement Facility Management (FM) services for their development projects. The primary reason for this trend is the economic infeasibility for many construction companies to bear the operational and maintenance costs associated with their projects when engaging a professional FM provider. As a result, a considerable number of construction firms, predominantly driven by economic factors, attempt to undertake FM activities despite lacking prior experience, familiarity with service standards, regulations, and quality expectations, and facing difficulties in identifying professional solutions. Consequently, it is observed that the overall satisfaction levels of facility users in such models tend to be low.
3. *The Condominium Owner's Model:* The performance of site or residential real estate management is conducted by the management staff elected by the condominium owners or by an external manager. In this management model, the oversight of the budget, expenditures, and requirements is executed by the management appointed by the condominium owners during the general assembly of the site. This management model often lacks professionalism and a focus on cost and is marked by internal disputes. Furthermore, this model exhibits low flexibility and efficiency.
4. *The Building Owner's Model:* The Building Owner's Model involves managing a building by individuals who own more than 50% of its total gross area and represent the majority of the owners. This approach is common in mixed-use developments where retail centres, office spaces, and residential units coexist. Management is carried out either by the building owners or by a team they appoint from outside. This team is formed by contracts with independent companies, providing services such as security, cleaning, heating and cooling, maintenance and repair, and rental management. Consequently, the management cannot operate as a cohesive unit. This fragmentation leads to suboptimal man-

agement of workplace conditions, the work environment, and overall quality of life, causing widespread dissatisfaction.

5. *The Professional Management Model:* Here, facility services are executed by professional companies with specialised expertise in their respective fields. These companies employ managers, project managers, technical staff, accounting personnel, and legal experts who are essential to the overall management services within their organisation. They may also hire additional personnel beyond these core roles or hire external subcontractors. Professional FM companies emphasise the competence and expertise of their personnel during the staffing process (Erentürk, 2016; Gümüştekin & Mutlu, 2013; Kaya & Emiroğulları, 2013).

The FM market in Türkiye is currently growing significantly. However, this growth is impeded primarily by inadequate professionalisation and a tendency to prioritise cost reduction over service quality. In both residential and commercial real estate developments, facility and property management services are provided by various models within the framework of management projects that are implemented concurrently with the delivery of housing and workplace environments. In public housing initiatives, all management activities—such as maintenance, repair, and commissioning of machinery and equipment in shared areas, as well as the collection and monitoring of dues, procurement of different goods and services, recruitment, management, and administration of personnel necessary for service provision—are conducted under the authority and responsibility of the management company.

The operating projects related to management services and/or activities are included in the estimated expense items for the initial year. The increases in common expense shares or management fees established at the end of the period are carried out in accordance with the provisions of Condominium Law No. 634, considering factors such as historic expense realisations, benefits gained by vendors and/or institutions, and minimum wage adjustments. Common expenses incurred within the framework of the operating projects of each estate are consolidated into bank accounts registered under the name of the estate management, which are used to cover the expenses incurred. All requests arising from common expenses are systematically reviewed by site management to ensure smooth continuation of transactions related to management services and activities. The same legal provisions apply to commercial real estate, including condominiums, offices, and residences subject to condominium ownership. For shopping centres and street stores, transactions are governed by Law No. 6585 regarding the Regulation of Retail Trade and the Regulation on Shopping Centres. Beyond these, there are no specific regulations applicable to the management of industrial facilities, public buildings, educational institutions, healthcare facilities, and infrastructure facilities. Various legal regulations have been established concerning energy, security, and waste management within facilities; however, no specific regulation addresses FM. Additionally, the responsibilities and areas of authority for FM expertise and companies remain ambiguous.

To establish collective building management at a site, the site must be based on one or more zoning parcels as delineated in an approved settlement plan. Sufficient infrastructure facilities and common-use areas must also be available, and should be interconnected in their management. When buildings are located on more than one parcel, a single management plan must be prepared, despite any previously developed separate management plans. The manager is required to consult the condominium owners' board regarding essential works and repairs. However, in situations necessitating immediate attention, e.g., to prevent damage, the individual may incur necessary expenses without prior approval from the condominium owners' board. Under Article 28 of the Condominium Law No. 634, a management plan can only be amended with the affirmative votes of four-fifths of all condominium owners. Additionally, Article 33 of the law reserves the right to appeal to the court. Except in circumstances where the law stipulates unanimous consent, a four-fifths majority of all condominium owners' votes is required to amend the management plan. Challenges often arise with timeshare properties, seasonal homes, and locations with a high proportion of foreign owners at certain times of the year.

Law No. 634 regulates the rules for collective building management, which includes blocks or groups of blocks located on a single parcel or multiple parcels. The main aim of the legislator's regulation for collective buildings under Law No. 634 is to define the rights of rightful owners and those responsible for determining the participation share in the communal areas and facilities of the collective building, along with the related costs. Additionally, the legal qualifications required for the administrator have been specified. Article 69 of the Law sets out the framework for management and the methods applied to the communal areas and facilities within the collective structure; the boards are authorised to handle issues related to the communal premises and facilities and to make decisions, while the procedure for the election and formation of these boards is detailed. The legislator has chosen not to mandate specific provisions for the management of collective buildings, allowing for various management models, provided these models comply with the management plan's stipulations. The provisions concerning the management of collective buildings hold a supplementary legal character. These rules are implemented in the absence of an agreement among parties regarding the collective building. In managing collective buildings, activities are primarily carried out according to the management plan. Nonetheless, even with customised management plans, they must conform to the framework established by Law No. 634.

3.3 Professionalisation in Facility Management and Management Services

A stylised image of a FM company shows a company that handles the main functions of an organisation while managing smaller, routine tasks. However, this image is insufficient when it comes to professional FM in Türkiye, especially in light of current and future FM trends. Currently, the main organisation concentrates on its core competencies and areas of expertise, while the rest of the workload involves FM. In other words, within many organisations, FM is responsible for providing services such as legal counsel, accounting, organising facility spaces, maintenance and repair operations, property management, and leasing services, which are seen as secondary and outside the organisation's primary business activities. The rapid progress in technology, along with increasing competition and the urgent need for swift professionalisation, is raising expectations of FM. As a result, FM professionals and companies will face considerable challenges.

Given the high level of competition across nearly all sectors, both cost and quality have become increasingly important for various types of services and products. The professionalisation of services is essential for achieving cost efficiency and quality in service delivery and production (Deighton, 2016). Professional FM must establish skilled human resources within the scope of the authority delegated by the organisation they represent and address issues that require expertise, including contract management, service management, energy management, risk management, and service level management, all while complying with applicable legal regulations and management contracts.

Professional FM companies usually perform specialised management tasks with their experienced staff (Adewunmi & Ajayi, 2016). While they oversee services such as cleaning and security, which demand less expertise, they assign the implementation of personnel to their in-house specialists. This creates highly complex and integrated business processes. Many contacts exist between professional management and the employer organisation in administering service processes. Experts must identify these contact points to ensure effective and efficient service delivery. Additionally, coordinating subcontractors at the service site is equally important. Setting the minimum expected service level, anticipated quality, work schedules, shift hours, occupational safety, and operational management are essential factors that influence the success of the service in the field.

Particularly after March 2020, the heightened hygiene requirements, initial mandates for social distancing (although there are currently no specific social distancing requirements), and demands for proper indoor air quality management imposed by companies, combined with a significant rise in material costs since the start of the pandemic, increasing energy prices, and difficulties in meeting the demand for certain commodities due to challenges in supply and distribution by producers, have led to higher prices and increased management service costs (Tanrıvermiş, 2020). In this context, the sharp rise in input costs for facilities management services suggests that further cost increases are expected after 2022 (CBRE, 2022). This trend indicates that, in many major cities, particularly in the management of residential and commercial real estate, costs are nearing rental expenses. However, the proportion of administrative costs to rents varies between 10% and 35%, based on the comparison of declared rents and administrative costs in major cities. Since there is still insufficient data on administrative costs and rents, these estimates should be interpreted with caution.

4 Property Management and Businesses in Türkiye

4.1 Scope and Objectives of Property Management

Property management encompasses leasing operations, collection of rent and operating expenses, the annual delivery of service fees, and liaison with tenants. It also involves fulfilling legal obligations, ensuring appropriate environmental conditions, complying with contractual terms, maintaining the sustainable operation of real estate, collecting taxes and service fees, supervising and enforcing all tenant obligations under lease agreements, resolving issues, and initiating litigation when necessary. Furthermore, it includes more operational and routine activities, such as regular communication with tenants, assessing their requests, maintaining and updating tenant-related records, monitoring and implementing rent increases as stipulated in contracts, renewing and extending agreements, vacating and recovering properties, obtaining insurance, securing guarantees, performing requisite maintenance and repairs, and ensuring compliance with legal regulations to maintain a healthy and safe environment (RICS, 2016). Additionally, property management significantly overlaps with the operational functions of organisations. It necessitates the execution of professional and technical tasks, as well as providing relevant services upon request, to sustain the desired condition of the real estate. This also encompasses activities such as the disposal, construction, or acquisition of new properties, valuation of real estate, management of relationships between property owners and tenants, and business and real estate valuation (Haynes et al., 2017).

Many entities operate in property management, with numerous institutions responsible for overseeing public real estate. The Treasury, several ministries, and metropolitan, provincial, and district municipalities, along with other organisations, are either tasked with or authorised to manage the buildings, facilities, and properties belonging to central and local public bodies. Conflicts often occur in managing public areas and green spaces, especially within metropolitan boundaries. These spaces face pressure from development and construction activities, motivated by the prospect of higher rental yields. Large housing projects within urban areas characterise new settlements and make these zones more attractive. However, rapid development in these areas leads to new construction activities, accelerating urbanisation and resulting in uncontrolled growth and sprawl.

Turkish land prices experience significant fluctuations due to the inherent characteristics of real estate and the country's broader economic conditions. These fluctuations stem from factors such as cadastral renewal, zoning applications, changes to administrative boundaries, expropriation, and infrastructure investments. It is crucial to compile an inventory of real estate owned by various public and private institutions, as well as individual stakeholders, to identify properties with notable volatility in values and to develop appropriate strategies for these assets. To achieve this, establishing real estate inventories based on their acquisition purposes and preparing comprehensive current status and valuation reports at an independent unit level are essential. To keep pace with rapid market changes, comparing past and present conditions and making relevant forecasts will be beneficial. Additionally, preparing periodic valuation reports tailored to specific needs and automating processes through property management software, especially for corporate real estate, is recommended. Gathering spatial, environmental, economic, and technical data regarding the real estate holdings of institutions or individuals is necessary. An information repository should be set up to enable customers to access the required data and documents online.

4.2 Property Management Services and Institutionalisation

- *Property management*: This relates to the daily operations of properties acquired for investment, maintaining the relationship between tenant and owner, and ensuring the real estate is managed professionally to maximise its profitability for the owner. Property management companies differ from FM companies, as they concentrate on the management aspects of the property, while FM focuses on the technical aspects. The responsibilities of property management companies are detailed in their contracts. Typically, these contracts cover the following elements:
- *Determining rents:* Management companies exhibit substantial expertise in evaluating the rental value of real estate and establishing pricing strategies that attract prospective tenants. Institutional owners generally favour engaging valuation experts to determine rent levels and analyse shared expenses. Furthermore, these companies possess comprehensive knowledge of the market in which the properties are located. They are capable of promptly analysing the reasonable value and rental rates of properties, owing to their routine comparisons with neighbouring properties.
- *Rent collection:* Management companies guarantee a consistent cash flow by setting specific date ranges for rent collection and implementing a strict follow-up system to minimise potential delays. They also encourage tenants to pay on time through measures such as late payment interest.
- *Regulation of the rental price:* Management companies may adjust the rent annually, taking into account fluctuations in the producer or consumer price index, market trends, the rental history of comparable properties, and the specific terms of the contract.
- *Communication between tenant and real estate owner*: One of the key responsibilities of management companies is to establish effective communication with tenants. This process begins with a comprehensive analysis of tenants and the dependable placement of tenants within the real estate sector, encompassing all transactions related to tenant complaints and evictions.
- *Tenant placement*: Management companies are responsible for marketing, which includes leasing, purchasing, and selling real estate. Real estate firms work with agencies that exceed established standards in each rental area. These agencies know the best channels for sharing information about properties and the key content that advertisements should include. They are familiar with both online and offline media sources, including websites, and understand the criteria pro-

spective tenants prioritise when searching for residential, commercial, and other types of properties. As a result, they help speed up the real estate rental process.
- *Analysing prospective tenants and finalising contracts*: Management companies are responsible for evaluating applications and selecting tenants. This involves an ongoing assessment process, which includes retrospective research. These surveys help identify reliable tenants. Property managers interact with a diverse range of tenants, often developing more practical strategies for tenant selection. They stay aware of tenants' punctual rent payments, the length of lease agreements, and the avoidance of critical issues.
- *Dealing with emergencies and complaints*: Management companies are responsible for overseeing maintenance and repair requests, waste management, and the regulation of air and noise pollution. Furthermore, specialised teams are available to offer support and assistance during emergencies, including search and rescue operations, fire suppression efforts, and medical interventions, depending on the size of the facility and its affiliated real estate.
- *Dealing with evictions*: When a tenant vacates a residential or commercial property, the property manager is responsible for receiving and inspecting the premises, managing the security deposit, assessing any damage caused, and determining the appropriate amount of the security deposit to refund to the tenant. After the tenant's eviction, the manager is tasked with maintaining and repairing the property and preparing it for new tenants.
- *Dealing with the eviction case process*: If the tenant fails to submit monthly rent on time or behaves in a way that breaches the terms of the contract, the property manager is obliged to initiate the eviction process and determine the most appropriate method to carry out the eviction.
- *Maintenance and repair responsibility*: Management companies are responsible for the physical management of facilities and estate, including both general and emergency maintenance as well as repairs. They must continually identify and address maintenance and repair needs to maintain the property's physical integrity. With support from their regular collaborators, they identify issues such as leaks, wall cracks, and landscaping concerns that may develop over time. This process enhances tenant satisfaction and makes it easier to find new tenants. If a problem arises regarding the physical condition of the property, the management company dispatches a team for urgent maintenance and repairs. Typically, management companies oversee a network of electricians, plumbers, carpenters, and contractors.

Management companies should possess comprehensive knowledge of the legal regulations governing real estate ownership, management, and leasing operations, particularly within the residential and commercial sectors. Professional property management firms bear the important responsibility of accurately informing property owners and users. Within this framework, they develop a systematic plan of action, ensuring compliance with relevant laws during the execution of management transactions. Tasks include negotiating rent rates and management expenses, designing lease contracts, managing deposits, assessing prospective tenants, overseeing the duration and termination of leases, conducting tenant evictions, managing archives and account summaries, collecting rent, forwarding the collected rent to property owners, and managing the funds in the account. Furthermore, the management company provides a monthly account statement to the property owner, which covers all expenses related to the property as well as any associated maintenance and repair costs. The company is responsible for archiving all contracts, maintaining insurance and tax documentation, recording maintenance and repair requests, processing offers and complaints, and keeping records of rent collection. Additionally, the management company is obliged to inform property owners about the taxation of real estate to facilitate tax transactions and to monitor tax obligations as specified in the contract. These procedures help to preserve the value of the property and ensure the effective management of individual assets.

Real estate decisions are now recognised as vital components in determining the success or failure of businesses, with flexible, customer-oriented approaches becoming a common topic of discussion. Active management of real estate portfolios is essential, offering benefits such as improved asset and FM performance, along with the potential for capital raising through various outsourcing options. More often, these portfolios are managed holistically at a strategic level of corporate integration (Tanrıvermiş, 2019). Traditionally, real estate and estate-based rights were not seen in the same light as other corporate assets; however, today, companies are adopting a more strategic approach to property management. Corporate real estate management has become a key concept that combines the management of financial, physical, and operational assets owned by companies, alongside all related professional services. Corporate real estate and asset managers are required to hold both undergraduate and postgraduate degrees in this field to gain the necessary knowledge and skills in areas such as business planning, real estate strategies, data analysis for business and real estate, accounting, performance measurement, understanding the links between corporate strategy and real estate strategy, and developing integrated solutions to problems using appropriate analytical tools, as well as space planning, design, building and location assessment, and environmental and sustainability considerations.

Corporate real estate management involves the integration, administration, and support of an organisation's business processes, objectives, positioning, values, strategic assets, and core assets, including personnel and premises. The effective strategic implementation of corporate real estate management creates opportunities for positive impact on the organisation's performance (Haynes & Nunnington, 2010). Outsourcing plays a vital role in effective business strategies within corporate real estate management, significantly influencing the reduction of real estate-related costs while enhancing overall business performance. Corporate real estate management aligns with the business environment, organisational context, position, and culture. Additionally, it entails selecting properties in appropriate locations that support the organisation's strategic and financial objectives. This interdisciplinary field aims for harmony and coordination among people management, productivity, performance measurement, the working environment, human environment interaction, and health. The strategic alignment model for corporate real estate management enhances corporate strategy, improves performance, and ensures that all stakeholders collaborate toward achieving shared goals (Haynes et al., 2017). Furthermore, corporate real estate management contributes to organisational performance by providing a portfolio aligned with the business strategy. Although the application of corporate real estate management initially began in the private sector, recent progress and developments in the public sector demonstrate that it is also pertinent within the public domain (Haynes et al., 2017).

5 Asset Management and Companies in Türkiye

5.1 Scope and Objectives of Asset and Investment Management

Asset management was extensively adopted in both the private and public sectors following the 1980s, primarily for the administration of physical assets (IAM, 2015). Over time, significant progress has been made in the comprehension and implementation of asset management principles through the development of a series of approaches, standards, and models on a global scale. As a result, asset management has developed into a more prominent sector. Numerous organisations and institutions have adopted asset management, recognising its considerable potential to create and oversee assets comprehensively, thereby attaining increased value addition. Asset management encompasses all coordinated activities and business processes through which an organisation derives value from its assets. The organisation needs to reach an optimal balance between cost, performance, and risk to generate value. The asset management policy formulates a strategic asset management plan, and the organisation defines a portfolio. Moreover, asset management ensures the presence of the appropriate assets in the correct locations at the right times, thereby facilitating the efficient and effective collaboration of assets (IAM, 2015).

Asset management involves the study of the creation, operation, maintenance, repair, and replacement of assets. Asset management systems are inherently intricate, interdependent, dynamic, and capable of rapid change. By formulating an asset management policy, organisations can delineate the scope and applicability limits of the asset management system. The phases of asset management are assessed from a lifecycle perspective. Although the terminology and number of phases may vary across industries, they typically include four fundamental stages: planning, acquisition, operation, maintenance, and disposal (ISO, 2014). In response to developments in the field, the Institute of Asset Management (IAM) was established in 1994. Particularly after 2002, initiatives commenced to foster the discipline of asset management and to establish a unified perspective in collaboration with numerous organisations worldwide. In 2014, the International Standards Organisation (ISO) promulgated the ISO 55000 standard to facilitate the dissemination, standardisation, and professional development of asset management best practices (IAM, 2015).

Asset management requires the integration of activities throughout the entire lifecycle, rather than focusing on individual stages. This involves several disciplines working together across the phases of the asset lifecycle and at all tiers of the asset portfolio, thereby encouraging different specialities from various functions and disciplines to develop a shared understanding and perspective. Modern asset management demands a results-driven approach and an interdisciplinary practice. Asset management is a professional field that deals with issues such as establishing, operating, evaluating, and developing management systems (IAM, 2015).

Asset management involves structuring an organisation in accordance with its optimal corporate interests. Efforts are focused on ensuring asset coordination aligns with the organisation's corporate goals. Professionals with the requisite knowledge and experience in this field are regarded as the organisation's most critical assets for the effective and holistic management of assets (Haynes et al., 2017). Given that asset management represents a fundamental aspect of the organisation, a thorough understanding of its context is essential. Influencing factors include both external and internal elements: external factors encompass social, cultural, political, legal, technological, and economic developments, while internal factors comprise the organisation's structure, capacity, competencies, responsibilities, tasks, authorities, resources, procedures, and personnel (IAM, 2015).

To achieve effective asset management, it is important to recognise and regularly review the needs and expectations of all relevant stakeholders. Internal stakeholders include employees, shareholders, and management teams. External stakeholders comprise customers, tenants, suppliers, service providers, contractors, non-governmental organisations, consumer organisations, government agencies, regulatory authorities, politicians, investors, local communities, financial institutions, rating agencies, insurers, employee representatives, and the wider public. Since stakeholders' views can significantly influence the organisation's asset-related decisions, it is crucial to identify, document, and consider their perspectives. Therefore, the needs and expectations of all stakeholders should be identified, analysed, and integrated into the strategic asset management plan (ISO, 2014).

Understanding the methodologies by which decisions related to assets are formulated constitutes a fundamental aspect of asset management. The criteria guiding these decisions are shaped by the requirements of both internal and external stakeholders, the asset management policy, and the organisation's risk tolerance. The initiatives undertaken by internal and external stakeholders to define these decision-making criteria are pivotal in establishing priorities and resolving conflicting demands. Such criteria should mirror the relevance and complexity of the decisions to be made. They should serve as a basis for evaluating alternative options to achieve asset management objectives, as well as for developing comprehensive asset management plans. The requirements may be articulated in different formats to facilitate quantitative, semi-quantitative, or qualitative decision-making processes. The methods employed to delineate the decision-making criteria that underpin asset management practices should be transparent and thoroughly documented. It is essential that stakeholders are informed about decisions that may impact them, and that they are reasonably involved in decisions that could affect them, and that they engage in necessary communications with relevant stakeholders (ISO, 2014).

The scope and framework of the company's asset management system should be established through an analysis of the organisation's content, demand assessments, as well as the needs and expectations of stakeholders. The framework and feasibility of the asset management system ought to be incorporated into the strategic asset management plan, and relevant information should be communicated to all pertinent internal and external stakeholders within the organisation. In defining the scope of asset management, considerations such as asset portfolios, boundaries, interdependencies, requirements, outsourcing, organisational structure, functions, responsibilities, liabilities, obligations, and authorities of all business units—including their interactions with other units—must be properly considered (Tanrıvermiş, 2021). For an asset management system to be effective, management processes, activities, data flows, and other organisational functions must be integrated. Moreover, interactions with ongoing business processes should be effectively communicated to all relevant personnel. Given the finite nature of resources, it is essential to determine the priorities and development sequence accordingly.

The asset management policy serves as a formal document outlining the principles the organisation intends to follow to achieve its corporate objectives. It is crucial that senior management enforces the asset management policy, and that all relevant stakeholders work together in line with this policy. The organisation should then develop and approve a strategic asset management plan. Asset management strategically connects business needs, asset diversification, and future investments (Tanrıvermiş, 2021).

5.2 Asset Management Practices and Their Place in the Financial System

The first regulation governing the establishment of asset management companies was laid down in the Regulation on the Establishment and Operating Principles of Asset Management Companies, dated October 1, 2002, which came into effect subsequent to the Law on Restructuring of Debts to the Financial Sector and Amendment of Certain Laws, dated January 1, 2002, and numbered 4743. This regulation was subsequently repealed by the Regulation on the Establishment and Operating Principles of Asset Management Companies, dated November 1, 2006, which remains in effect. Article 143 of Law No. 5411 on Banking delineates the objectives of establishment and the scope of activities for asset management companies. Their independent audits, conducted within their accounting and reporting systems, are performed in accordance with the framework established by Law No. 6102, the Turkish Commercial Code. Furthermore, the Regulation on the Sale of Receivables of Public Capital Banks and Financial Institutions that are subsidiaries of these banks to asset management companies, published by the Banking Regulation and Supervision Agency on August 11, 2017, specifies the procedures and principles related to the transfer of receivables from public banks to asset management companies. Türkiye Halk Bank Inc. has conducted the initial implementation.

The increase in non-performing loans presents a significant threat to banks, the financial sector, and the national economy (Kingu et al., 2018). Failure to recover the principal and interest on loans provided by banks promptly and fully is a significant credit risk (Ertürk, 2010). A decline in the asset quality of banks' loan portfolios is seen as one of the key indicators of financial crises (Kaya & Uzay, 2020; Messai & Jouini, 2013; Temur & Döğer, 2017). Non-performing loans act as a gauge of the economic environment and indicate the debt repayment ability of households and the corporate sector. During periods of economic downturn, when households face unemployment and reduced well-being, there is a noticeable increase in non-performing loans. The sizeable amount of such loans makes banks susceptible to external influences like inflation, budget deficits, foreign exchange risk, and current account deficits (Kartal & Demir, 2017).

Asset management companies can acquire non-performing loans from financial institutions at reduced prices through receivables assignment and seek to recover these loans using their expertise. In this context, asset management companies work as entities that take over the non-performing loan portfolios of banks and financial institutions. Asset managers thus are duly authorised to collect these receivables (Kaya & Uzay, 2020). The institutions they serve include savings deposit insurance funds, banks, financial leasing firms, factoring companies, financing entities, and insurance companies providing credit insurance services. Currently, twenty-three asset management companies operate in Türkiye (BRSA, 2025). These companies play a crucial role in improving the operational efficiency of the financial system by acting as intermediaries between financial institutions and borrowers. They are exempt from stamp duty, fee payments, banking and insurance transaction taxes (BITT), resource utilisation support fund (KKDF), and obligations to the Competition Authority for the year of their establishment and the next 5 years. Furthermore, they benefit from VAT exemption as stipulated in the Value Added Tax Law No. 3065, without any time limit.

The classification of loans in banking institutions is carried out in accordance with the Regulation on the Procedures and Principles for the Classification of Loans and the Provisions to be set aside for them. Under this Regulation, loans are divided into five distinct categories:

1. First Group—Standard Quality Loans (Disbursed punctually and not exceeding 30 days of delinquency).
2. Second Group—Loans Under Close Monitoring (loans where collection is delayed for more than 30 days but does not exceed 90 days).
3. Third Group—Loans with Limited Collectability (Loans that are more than 90 days overdue, but do not exceed 180 days).
4. Fourth Group—Doubtful Collectability (Loans overdue for more than 180 days but not exceeding 1 year).
5. Fifth Group—Non-Performing Loans (Loans overdue for more than a year).

Banks categorise loans with a collection period exceeding 90 days as non-performing loans. Delays in collection occur when the repayment terms established between the bank and the borrower are breached. The probability of incurring a loss becomes significant, thereby classifying these loans as non-performing (Aktaş, 2000). Non-performing loans refer to cases in which the borrower is unable to fulfil the obligations arising from the debt that must be repaid promptly (Ağaoğlu, 2011; Kartal & Demir, 2017; Mesutoğlu, 2001). Some scholars characterise a non-performing loan as a debt payment that is either partially or wholly overdue by 90 days (Yüksel, 2016). According to Article 15 of the Regulation, non-performing loans constitute the fifth category. Banks are required to allocate provisions of 20%, 50%, and 100% for these three categories of non-performing loans, respectively.

Driven by overall inflationary pressure, the total loan volume of banks in Türkiye increased sharply by a factor of 304 between 2002 and 2024, while non-performing loans rose by a factor of 26 at current prices. In line with the surge in total loans, a noticeable upward trend in non-performing loans has been observed; however, the growth rate of non-performing loans has been relatively restrained. The main reason for this is the sale of non-performing loans by banks to asset management companies. Additionally, this scenario has effectively maintained the share of non-performing loans at a stable average level of 4.97%. Excluding crisis years (notably 2002 and 2003), the proportion of non-performing loans in total loans fluctuates between 2% and 7%, averaging approximately 3.5% (see Table 3).

Changes in loans within the banking system from 2008 to 2024 include housing and consumer loans. The non-performing loan rate is lower for housing loans compared to consumer loans. The average non-performing loans ratio is 3.29% for total consumer loans, and only 0.66% for housing loans (Table 4). The non-performing loan rate for consumer loans matches the overall non-performing loan ratio across all loans. Non-performing loans negatively impact banks by tying up their limited resources, leaving them idle. In response, banks pursue legal and administrative procedures for non-performing loans. If these loans remain uncollectible despite follow-up efforts, banks may sell collateral assets—such as negotiable instruments, lease agreements, housing, or vehicles—to recover the loan. When asset sales are not feasible, banks might acquire them and record them as part of their assets against the debt. Properties bought by banks are classified under "Assets Held for Sale" in their financial statements. By 2022, 63 deposit, development investment, and participation banks held investment real estate worth of TL 5.33 billion, increasing to TL 12.89 billion in 2023 (TBB, 2024). The share of net fixed assets in total bank assets ranges from 0.82% to 1.0%, while the proportion of real estate within fixed assets varies from 5.0% to 7.0%.

5.3 Challenges of Asset Management and Changing Asset Management Structure

Financial institutions provide loans that need to be repaid according to set payment schedules and to cover deposit interest. When borrowers fail to meet repayment deadlines, it causes complications and imposes costs on banks (Kartal & Demir,

Table 3 Loan and non-performing loan sizes of deposit banks

Years	Total Loans (Billion TL)	Change (% yoy)	Non-performing Loans (Billion TL)	Change (% yoy)	Non-performing Loans/Total Loans (%)
2002	44.74	–	10.25	–	*22.91*
2003	61.28	36.97	8.45	−17.56	*13.79*
2004	94.03	53.44	6.18	−26.86	*6.57*
2005	143.98	53.12	7.34	18.77	*5.10*
2006	207.43	44.07	8	8.99	*3.86*
2007	267.90	29.15	9.66	20.75	*3.61*
2008	349.48	30.45	13.01	34.68	*3.72*
2009	361.41	3.41	20.34	56.34	*5.63*
2010	487.07	34.77	18.54	−8.85	*3.81*
2011	633.32	30.03	17.37	−6.31	*2.74*
2012	728.17	14.98	21.59	24.29	*2.96*
2013	957.29	31.47	26.93	24.73	*2.81*
2014	1138.06	18.88	32.75	21.61	*2.88*
2015	1338.50	17.61	42.7	30.38	*3.19*
2016	1556.48	16.29	54.1	26.70	*3.48*
2017	1867.03	19.95	59.43	9.85	*3.18*
2018	2085.78	11.72	86.83	46.10	*4.16*
2019	2304.25	10.47	138.81	59.86	*6.02*
2020	3089.47	34.08	139.48	0.48	*4.51*
2021	4.149,63	34.32	144.47	3.58	*3.48*
2022	6506.85	56.81	148.12	2.53	*2.28*
2023	9915.11	52.38	175.61	18.56	*1.77*
2024	13,591.87	37.08	265.05	50.93	*1.95*
Average	–	*30.52*	–	*18.16*	*4.97*

Source: Banking Regulation and Supervision Agency (2025)

2017). As non-performing loans increase, banks lose equity, which leads them to reduce the amount of new loans they are willing to give. A major consequence of these bad loans is the decline in asset quality shown in the bank's balance sheet. A high level of non-performing loans harms the bank's performance, damages its reputation, and restricts growth. This situation negatively impacts competitiveness and growth. Funds that could be invested elsewhere for higher returns are tied up, causing banks to face income losses (Kartal & Demir, 2017).

Banks are required to monitor non-performing loans closely. Alongside these monitoring mechanisms, early warning systems are also developed, which help ensure the quick implementation of necessary measures. Loan restructuring could be suggested as an additional solution. Many of these challenges can be addressed by transferring loans to asset management companies. Through such transfers, the volume of non-performing loans on banks' balance sheets can decline, the amount of necessary capital can be lowered, and the return on assets will improve. However, concerns remain that such transfers could lead to a more reckless approach by banks in their lending practices (Kartal & Demir, 2017). The operations of asset

Table 4 Development of the share of non-performing loans in total loan volume

Years	Loans (Billion TL)	Consumer loans and credit cards (Billion TL)	Mortgage loans (Billion TL)	NPL Ratio		
				Overall (%)	Mortgage loan (%)	Consumer loan (%)
2008	367	117	39	3.68	1.30	3.66
2009	393	130	45	5.27	2.10	6.00
2010	526	173	61	3.66	1.40	4.13
2011	683	224	75	2.70	0.90	2.88
2012	795	266	86	2.86	0.80	2.95
2013	1047	332	111	2.75	0.60	2.87
2014	1241	356	126	2.85	0.49	3.38
2015	1484	385	144	3.20	0.47	4.48
2016	1733	420	164	3.34	0.52	4.45
2017	2096	487	192	3,04	0.41	3.58
2018	2393	502	189	3.91	0.51	3.56
2019	2652	580	199	5.60	0.64	3.46
2020	3575	821	278	4.22	0.33	2.06
2021	4900	987	299	3.26	0.29	2.47
2022	7568	1530	360	2,14	0.16	1.94
2023	11,630	2669	438	1,65	0.11	1.68
2024	15,901	3807	511	1,81	0.14	2.91
Average	–	–	–	*3.29*	*0.66*	*3.32*

Source: Banking Regulation and Supervision Agency (2025)

management companies are subject to regular audits by the Banking Regulation and Supervision Agency (BRSA), and implementing measures is considered vital for the system's effective functioning (Kaya & Uzay, 2020). To collect receivables transferred to these companies, an initial analysis of all debtor assets is performed; this requires specialised personnel. Most asset management companies lack experts in real estate development and management, resulting in difficulties in monitoring debtor real estate assets, investigating fraudulent real estate activities, and pursuing legal action for relief, shifting the focus toward debt collection.

In Türkiye, asset management as well as the structure and operation of real estate asset management companies differs from international examples. Currently, asset management companies are established and authorised by authorities to recover non-performing loans that banks have extended to their retail and corporate clients. These authorised asset management companies play a vital role in collecting non-performing receivables, which are crucial for the ongoing operations of banks and the proper functioning of the financial system. This process also helps to resolve issues reflected in banks' financial statements. Additionally, there has been a significant rise in demand for asset management services in sectors such as retail trade, electronic commerce, hospitality, and especially for short-term housing rentals. This has led to the establishment of new companies dedicated to these sectors.

Various public and private organisations have acknowledged that asset management provides opportunities for developing and overseeing assets, thus adding value through a comprehensive approach to effective property management. This involves managing assets more effectively by identifying key performance indicators (KPI), actively measuring success, and aligning all efforts with organisational objectives (Kavrakov, 2016). The fields of asset management, property management, and facilities management are interconnected; consequently, they require the integration of asset management adequately (Then, 2002). Asset management must be grounded in fundamental principles within a real estate portfolio management system. The core principles are (1) goals and leadership, (2) performance orientation, (3) compliance with organisational objectives, (4) complete transparency, (5) competitiveness, (6) sustainability, and (7) the development and implementation of management systems (Tezbaşar, 2019).

There is a big need to align property management and FM decisions with the corporate strategy, actively oversee these elements, and incorporate physical asset needs into a unified business resource management model. Professional property management involves a dynamic and integrated process that optimises technological, financial, and other knowledge-based resources, especially the skills of qualified personnel, to achieve corporate goals and objectives. To effectively carry out these operations and meet business needs, a thorough understanding of the tasks involved is essential, along with promoting awareness within the organisation and adopting a management approach supported by senior leadership. To reach corporate objectives, it is crucial to recruit and develop qualified personnel according to international standards and who have matching competencies and skills in asset management, property management, and FM (Tanrıvermiş, 2021).

6 General Outlook of the Sector and Necessity of Development

In Türkiye, large corporations and financial institutions began investing in smart buildings for administrative operations during the 1990s, leading to a gradual increase in the number of companies offering services in plazas and towers after the mid-1990s. Throughout the 2000s, the indoor areas of modern, large-scale complexes and structures have nearly doubled. This rapid market growth attracted global companies within the FM sector to focus on Türkiye and pursue business development efforts. The number of companies operating directly in this field within the private sector continues to rise, with those engaged in FM, management and services, building and collective structure management, as well as real estate and project management, actively participating in this sector, with their organisational structures showing considerable diversity.

The organisational structures of companies engaged in facility and property management exhibit considerable variation in legal frameworks, including sole proprietorships, family-owned enterprises, limited liability entities, and joint-stock corporations. Entrepreneurs operating within this domain are categorised within the real estate sector as well as administrative and support services within the broader macroeconomic framework. The total number of registered companies under the broader category of asset and property-related services increased from 21,760 in

2010 to 31,735 in 2023. However, it is estimated that only approximately 1% of these companies are exclusively dedicated to core facility and property management activities. The majority conduct operations in adjacent sectors or incorporate FM/PM as secondary services within a diversified portfolio of business activities. Among these entities, service offerings may include solely FM, substantial components of FM, or a combination of facility and property management services. The total workforce of these companies exceeds 650,000 persons, representing nearly 4% of the civilian employment. Considering that numerous FM firms outsource services such as security, cleaning, catering, landscaping, maintenance, and repairs, there is potential for the workforce to double. While many companies employ fewer than 100 persons and are not operating professionally, some organisations employ more than a thousand persons. In these latter companies, institutionalisation is significantly higher, resulting in a dualistic structure within the sector.

According to the NACE classification, FM companies are categorised under "real estate activities" with the code "management of real estate on a fee or contract basis." Among the companies involved in real estate, 1000 companies participate in facility and property management along with related activities. Notably, some FM companies are classified under "accommodation activities", while others are under "administrative and support services" because they manage timeshare facilities. It would be advisable to consolidate companies engaged in FM, building and structure management, property management, and timeshare management under a new code, and to limit FM companies to their core activities (see Table 5).

Based on the results of comprehensive interviews conducted with sector experts, the current condition of the facility management market in Türkiye, as well as the identified areas requiring improvement, include: (1) the necessity to advance the facilities management market within both the public and private sectors; (2) insufficient coverage of facilities management and service contracts; (3) heightened expectations from owners and users regarding facilities management, compounded by structural challenges and the substandard service quality provided by facilities management firms; (4) the increasing demand for facilities management services in the retail trade and service sectors during the post-COVID-19 era; (5) the imperative for FM in urban settings and the heightened need for urban FM following urban transformation; (6) the lack of qualified human resources; and (7) the inadequacy and disorganisation of FM legislation, along the absence of clear definitions concerning the public institution responsible for and authorized in this domain (Keskin, et al., 2023a, b; Temeljotov-Salaj et al., 2021). It is pertinent to emphasise that similar situations and challenges are evident within the fields of property and asset management. In fact, even in property and asset management, the levels of institutional development, the establishment of standards, the formation of professional companies, the availability of licensed experts, and the provision of effective service delivery are deficient. Efforts to improve this situation are essential across all three business areas. Facility Management companies have established seven national-level associations; sector employees have formed one association; and these associations have created two federations. Conversely, asset management companies have formed a single association. Currently, there are no civil organisations within

Table 5 Facility and property management companies (entrepreneurs) in Türkiye and their fields of activity

Sectors	Section and group	NACE Rev. 2- Description	2010	2015	2020	2021	2022	2023
–	–	*Türkiye*	*2,678,787*	*2,941,233*	*3,304,088*	*3,578,931*	*3784,464*	*3,723,944*
L-real estate activities	68	Real estate activities	33,007	39,169	49,810	52,701	59,624	64,147
	682	Renting out or operating the real estate owned or leased	8049	1626	1003	1206	1285	1408
	683	Real estate activities based on a fee or contractual basis	24,578	36,769	47,827	50,471	57,292	61,659
N-administrative and support services	81	Building-related services and landscaping activities	5012	11,549	11,844	12,488	12,999	12,920
	811	Combined on-site support services	78	305	459	487	517	526
	812	Cleaning activities	4186	9581	9055	9391	9654	9435
	813	Landscaping and maintenance activities	748	1663	2330	2610	2828	2959
	82	Office management, office support and business support activities	8699	11,828	14,497	15,001	16,286	17,407
	821	Office management and support activities	949	1024	1071	1105	1193	1175
	822	Activities of call centres	222	694	968	1093	1229	1465
Total Facility and property management	–	–	21,760	25,003	27,344	28,695	30,570	31,735

Source: TÜRKSTAT (2024)

the realm of property management. The contributions made by these organisations towards sectoral development, professionalisation, and professional growth remain limited.

7 Conclusion

Türkiye's current facility, property, and asset management market remains in its developmental stage. Nonetheless, the facility and property management sectors have shown rapid growth in recent years. However, when compared to Western Europe, there remains a lack of progress in critical areas such as the institutionalisation of the FM market, the establishment of standards, the accreditation of service providers, the institutionalisation of companies, the development of FM legislation, the design of employment and service contracts, and the formulation and implementation of best practice guidelines, as well as workforce qualification. Although certain studies are conducted by the Turkish Vocational Qualifications Authority and TSE, FM is gradually gaining recognition as an independent and professional discipline within the domestic market. The necessity of professionalising FM, particularly within commercial facilities, high-rise residential buildings, office and residential complexes, mixed-use real estate, hospitals, airports, and other infrastructure investments, is widely acknowledged. It would be beneficial for FM companies to attain institutionalisation, with their service delivery capacities structured to meet the expectations of investors and users within the domestic market. The service areas of established companies should be limited to FM, with management companies restricted from engaging in auxiliary fields, particularly in construction and real estate marketing (brokerage and consultancy). Nonetheless, there are many cases where facility and property management have been merged and consolidated within a single entity. Progress in asset management, real estate portfolio management, corporate real estate, and investment management is essential for effectively overseeing asset and investment portfolios, especially for large public and private entities, as well as for individual and institutional investors.

By regulating both the supply and demand side of the property management services market and improving the use of outsourcing within public institutions, the market for this sector is set to expand. This expansion will support the efficient and timely implementation of more effective regulatory activities. Classifying management companies that offer single services and integrate space, personnel, and processes within the sector—along developing performance measurements and standards—will be key to enhancing service quality. Furthermore, restructuring entities that provide single services and supporting facilities management companies, including security, catering, cleaning, software, technology sectors, and professional groups, will further advance this effort.

Establishing a legal and institutional framework for service provision, contracting, standard development, identifying the responsible or authorised public institution, and accurately regulating its duties in FM is critical. Experts and companies engaged in FM are enthusiastic about forming associations; however, these associations are fragmented and often lack organisation. Consequently, it is essential to implement a structured framework, such as an FM council or federation, and to develop national FM policies. Cooperation between academic institutions and FM associations with organisations such as Eurofm, Global FM, and IFMA is anticipated, especially alongside educational institutions conducting academic studies with European and US universities. This collaboration is expected to enhance the sector's capacity in training specialised personnel and in facility and property management research and education significantly. The demand for academic institutions and professional companies capable of providing teaching, research, and consultancy services in basic FM, as well as advanced facility, property, and asset management, is high. It is vital to ensure collaboration between FM consultancy institutions and construction and real estate development companies, and to mandate the inclusion of FM consultancy within the project development teams for projects above a certain scale. To promote a professional approach to facility and property management across both public and private sectors, thereby enabling the industry to operate more efficiently and effectively while creating employment opportunities. The first step has to be granting licences to the entities intending to operate within the sector through a central regulatory institution, and to certify individuals wishing to work in a more authorised industry.

Despite these challenges, stakeholders have recognised that built environment management should be regarded as a professional sector during the COVID-19 pandemic, and significant progress has been achieved in this domain. In the construction and real estate sectors, individuals and organisations providing facility and property management services are expected to play a key role and act as "strategic partners" or "consultants" in projects and facilities. The demand for national facilities and property management markets is increasing, and sharing experiences in this field with other countries is feasible. Knowledge and skills can be improved through developing occupational standards in collaboration with international organisations, training qualified personnel, and employing them within the sector. The market is forecast to grow by the expansion of national facilities and property management companies into other countries, as well as through enhanced networking and cooperation opportunities. In Türkiye, there is still no exclusive regulation governing facility and property management, nor has there been the necessary administrative structuring within the public sector. Management services need to be standardised using a professional property and asset management approach in order to enable future growth and thus facilitating employment.

References

Adewunmi, Y. A., & Ajayi, O. D. (2016). Attitudes of Nigerian facilities management professionals to the benefits of benchmarking. *Facilities, 34*(7/8), 468–492. https://doi.org/10.1108/F-06-2014-0057

Ağaoğlu, A. (2011). *Krizi sonrasında sorunlu aktiflerin çözümlenmesinde kamunun ve varlık yönetim şirketlerinin önemi*. Master's thesis, İstanbul Kültür University, Institute of Social Sciences, Department of Economics.

Aktaş, R. (2000). *Sorunlu Krediler*. Banks Association of Türkiye Training and Promotion Group Seminar Notes.

Atkin, B., & Bildsten, L. (2017). A future for facility management. *Construction Innovation, 17*(2), 116–124. https://doi.org/10.1108/CI-11-2016-0059

Banking Regulation and Supervision Agency. (2025). *Varlık yönetim şirketleri*. Retrieved February 18, 2025, from https://www.bddk.org.tr/Kurulus/Liste/82.

Banking Regulation and Suppervission Agency (BRSA). (2025). Asset Management Companies. https://www.bddk.org.tr/Kurulus/Liste/82

Barrett, P., & Baldry, D. (2003). *Total facilities management towards best practice*. John Wiley & Sons.

Bell, J. (1992). Facilities management and changing professional boundaries. *Facilities, 10*(10), 21–22. https://doi.org/10.1108/EUM0000000002211

Berger, R. (2001). *Trend Studie für Facility Management*. Roland Berger Strategy Consultants und GEFMA.

CBRE. (2022). *Facility management cost trends 2022*. Retrieved May 12, 2024, from https://www.cbre.com/insights/reports/2022-fm-cost-trends-report

Chotipanich, S. (2004). Positioning facility management. *Facilities, 22*(13/14), 364–372. https://doi.org/10.1108/02632770410563086

Deighton, M. (2016). *Facility integrity management: Effective principles and practices for the oil, gas and petrochemical ındustries*. Gulf Professional Publishing.

Ebinger, M., & Madritsch, T. (2012). A classification framework for facilities and real estate management: The Built Environment Management Model (BEM2). *Facilities, 30*(5/6), 185–198.

Edwards, V., & Ellison, L. (2009). *Corporate real estate management: Aligning real estate with business strategy*. John Wiley & Sons.

Erentürk, M. K. (2016). Dış Kaynak Kullanımı ile tesis yönetiminin konutlardaki yaşam kalitesine katkıları ve bir inşaat firması üzerinde çalışma. *TURAN-SAM: TURAN Center for Strategic Studies, 10*(39), 105–113.

Ertürk, H. (2010). Bankacılık sektörünün karşılaştığı riskler ve risk yönetimi. *Denetişim, 4*(62), 70.

Evcioğlu, K. (2013). *Ülkemiz için modern tesis yönetimi projesi* (Modern Facility Management for Türkiye). Retrieved September 14, 2024, from http://egeteknikmudurler.com

Gümüştekin, E., & Mutlu, L. (2013). *Bina ve site yöneticiliği*. Publication of Anatolian University, No: 1946.

Haynes, B. P., & Nunnington, N. (2010). *Corporate real estate asset management*. Elsevier.

Haynes, B. P., Nunnington, N., & Eccles, T. (2017). *Corporate real estate management: Strategy and implementation*. Routledge.

IAM. (2015). *Asset management and anatomy*. The Institute of Asset Management.

ISO. (2014). *ISO 55000: Asset management—overview, principles and terminology* (1st ed.), 2014-01-15.

Kartal, M. T., & Demir, C. H. (2017). Türkiye'de katılım bankacılığında sorunlu kredilerin varlık yönetim şirketlerine satışı üzerine bir inceleme ve yöntem önerileri. *Journal of Islamic Economics and Finance, 2017*(1), 89–115.

Kavrakov, D. (2016). Asset vs. facility management - spot the difference, 1. *Central Eastern Europe Real Estate Congress*, 26-27 October 2016, Warsaw, Poland.

Kaya, A., & Emiroğulları, H. (2013). Bina yönetim sistemi. VI. *Proceedings of control automation and building electronic systems symposium*, 21–24 November 2013, İzmir.

Kaya, H. P., & Uzay, Ş. (2020). Varlık yönetim şirketlerinin finansal sistem içindeki yeri ve önemi. *Muhasebe ve Denetime Bakış, 2020*(59), 53–74.

Keskin, E., Temeljotov-Salaj, A., & Tanrıvermiş, H. (2023a). Development trends and current status of facility management and professionalization of facility services in Turkey. *Facilities, 41*(7/8), 510–525. https://doi.org/10.1108/F-03-2022-0050

Keskin, E., Yang, E., Tanrıvermiş, H., & Erdoğmuş, E. (2023b). Facility management perspective in urban transformation projects: The opportunities and challenges in Turkey. *Facilities, 41*(3/4), 248–264.

Kingu, P. S., Macha, S., & Gwahula, R. (2018). Impact of non-performing loans on banks' profitability: Empirical evidence from commercial banks in Tanzania. *International Journal of Scientific Research and Management, 6*(1), 71–79.
Markets and Data. (2024). Global facility management market assessment, by type [hard services, soft services], by service model [insourced, outsourced], by industry type [organised, unorganised], by end-user [industrial, commercial, government], by region, opportunities and forecast, 2017-2031F. Retrieved August 2, 2025, from https://www.marketsandata.com/industry-reports/facility-management-market
Messai, A. S., & Jouini, F. (2013). Micro and macro determinants of non-performing loans. *International Journal of Economics and Financial Issues, 3*(4), 852–860.
Mesutoğlu, B. (2001). *Sorunlu aktiflerin varlık yönetimi şirketlerince tasfiyesi-ülke örnekleri* (pp. 1–50). BDDK MSPD Work Reports.
Noor, M. N. M., & Pitt, M. (2009). A critical review of innovation in facilities management service delivery. *Facilities, 27*(5/6), 211–228. https://doi.org/10.1108/02632770910944943
Nutt, B. (2000). Four competing futures for facility management. *Facilities, 18*(3/4), 124–132. https://doi.org/10.1108/02632770010315670
Presidency of Strategy and Budget (2023). Twelfth Development Plan. https://www.sbb.gov.tr/wp-content/uploads/2025/08/Konut-Politikalari-OIK-Raporu_0108225.pdf
Read, D. (2017). *Real estate asset management: A process and a profession*. IREM, Institute of Real Estate Management.
RICS. (2016). *RICS professional guidance. Real estate fund, asset and real estate management: Investment services*. RICS Information Paper.
Tanrıvermiş, H. (2019). Türkiye ekonomisinde inşaat ve gayrimenkul sektörlerinin rolleri ve gelişme eğilimlerinin değerlendirilmesi (assesment of the roles of construction and real estate sectors and their development trends in Türkiye). In *TMMOB Chamber of Architects Gaziantep Branch, Urban, Construction and Economy Congress*, May 2-3-4 2019, Gaziantep.
Tanrıvermiş, H. (2020). Possible impacts of COVID-19 outbreak on real estate sector and possible changes to adopt: A situation analysis and general assessment on Turkish perspective. *Journal of Urban Management, 9*(3), 263–269.
Tanrıvermiş, H. (2021). *Tesis ve kaynak yönetimine giriş*. Lecture Notes, Ankara University Faculty of Applied Sciences, Department of Real Estate Development and Management.
Temeljotov-Salaj, A., Ural Keskin, E., Tanrıvermiş, H., & Alatlı, L. (2021). Facility management development trends in South-Eastern Europe: The case of Türkiye. In *14th IFM Congress, 11th and 12th of November 2021 at TU Wien, Austria*.
Temur, F., & Döğer, H. (2017). Varlık Yönetim Şirketlerine Hukuki Bakış. *GSI Articletter, 2*(11), 161–176.
Terzioğlu, S., & Tanrıvermiş, Y. (2020). In S. T. Yönetimi & Y. D. Uslu (Eds.), *Dünyada Hastane Yönetiminin Tesis Yönetimi İlkeleri Açısından İncelenmesi*. Nobel Publications.
Tezbaşar, A. (2019). *Gayrimenkul portföy yönetimi sistemi ve Türkiye'de seçilmiş işletmelerdeki uygulamalarının kullanıcılar yönünden değerlendirilmesi*. Master's thesis, Ankara University, Graduate School of Natural and Applied Sciences, Department of Real Estate Development and Management.
Then, D.S.S. (2002). Integration of facilities provision and facilities support services provision: A management process model. *International Council for Building W070 Symposium on Facilities Management and Asset Maintenance*, 18–20 September 2002, Glasgow, Scotland.
Türkiye Bankalar Birliği (TBB). (2024). *Bankalarımız 2023*. TBB Publications.
TURKSTAT (Turkish Statistical Institute). (2024). *Turkish real estate data*. Retrieved February 15, 2024, from https://data.tuik.gov.tr/Kategori/GetKategori?p=nufus-ve-demografi-109&dil=1
Yüksel, S. (2016). Bankaların takipteki krediler oranını belirleyen faktörler: Türkiye için bir model önerisi. *Journal of Bankers, 98*, 41–56.

Yeşim Tanrıvermiş holds the position of full professor in the Department of Real Estate Development and Management at the Faculty of Applied Sciences, Ankara University, Türkiye. She attained her Master of Science (M.Sc.) degree in 2011 from the Department of Agricultural Economics at Ankara University. She received her Ph.D. in 2011 as the first Ph.D. program graduate of the Department of Real Estate Development and Management at Ankara University. Her research interests encompass the management and conservation of land resources, land resource economics, as well as real estate analysis and economics, in addition to studies in real estate and asset valuation. She has been delivering lectures for several years and has published academic papers since 2006. Her publications consist of 50 international and 40 national peer-reviewed articles. Additionally, she has made contributions to 110 international and 25 national full or abstract proceedings at various conferences and congresses and has authored 35 books and 30 book chapters. Presently, she serves as the Deputy Head of her department at Ankara University. Moreover, she is an active participant in various academic and professional organisations. Her experience encompasses working as a researcher and consultant across diverse public and private sectors, with a focus on real estate asset analysis, real estate finance and valuation, land and building conservation practices, as well as real estate economics and management. Furthermore, she actively engages in enhancing cooperation with both domestic and international institutions, mobilising financial resources for research projects.

Esra Keskin is an assistant professor in the Department of Real Estate Development and Management at the Faculty of Applied Sciences of Ankara University. Following her graduation from the Faculty of Law at Gazi University, she practised as a lawyer registered with the Ankara Bar Association for nearly a decade. She earned her master's and PhD degrees from the Department of Real Estate Development and Management at Ankara University, where she also held the position of research assistant during her doctoral studies. In 2023, she was appointed as a visiting scholar at the Georgia Institute of Technology through a fellowship from TÜBİTAK (The Scientific and Technological Research Council of Türkiye). In 2024, she was appointed as an assistant professor. Her research primarily concentrates on urban transformation, real estate law, contract law, contract management, and facility and property management.

Salih Demirkaya graduated from the Department of Architecture at Gazi University in 2010. He completed his master's degree at the Department of Real Estate Development and Management in 2017 and finalised his Ph.D. at the same department in 2025. His master's thesis explored the relationship between building materials and construction costs. During his doctoral studies, Demirkaya examined office buildings in England and continued his research at Bradford University (UK) for one year, while also conducting studies on office buildings in Ankara. He focused on the relationship between user satisfaction and office spaces, concluding his doctoral research by analysing facility management in offices, real estate markets, user interactions with spaces, and the impact of the pandemic. Between 2010 and 2013, he worked as a project manager, project developer, and construction manager at Kırşehir Municipality, while also serving as a project preparation and construction controller on large-scale projects. Since 2013, he has continued his academic and technical research at Ankara University, Department of Real Estate Development and Management. Dr. Demirkaya remains actively engaged in areas such as real estate development, facility management, project development, effective and efficient use of built environment and space, user satisfaction, construction costs, and cost management in real estate development projects.

Digitalisation in the Real Estate Sector in Türkiye

Emir Sunguroğlu, Sibel Canaz Sevgen, and Mehmet Ülger

Abstract

Digitalisation, and the strategically broader concept of digital transformation, have been increasingly prevalent across various fields in recent years. One notable area where digitalisation has gained relevance is the real estate sector. In general terms, digitalisation pertains to the conversion and processing of data originally stored in analogue formats to a digital environment. Numerous datasets within the real estate domain have been converted to digital formats, and a variety of applications have emerged to facilitate the transfer of this data to digital platforms. This chapter examines the applications, policies, data, and technologies associated with digitalisation in the real estate sector in Türkiye.

Keywords
Digitalisation · PropTech · Real estate technologies · Big data

1 Introduction

The Third Industrial Revolution is commonly described as a revolution in manufacturing based on Information and Communication Technology and Clean Energy. Digitalisation of processes is thus an important part of this Digital Revolution. With the invention of the Internet, email communication has become prevalent in and between companies since the 1980s. At the same time, personal computers, server-based IT applications, and desktop computing became standard processing machines. As computers became increasingly integrated into daily life, information

E. Sunguroğlu (✉) · S. C. Sevgen · M. Ülger
Department of Real Estate Development and Management, Faculty of Applied Sciences, Ankara University, Ankara, Türkiye
e-mail: esunguroglu@ankara.edu.tr; ssevgen@ankara.edu.tr; mehmet.ulger@ankara.edu.tr

T. Just et al. (eds.), *Understanding Türkiye's Real Estate Markets*, Management for Professionals, https://doi.org/10.1007/978-3-032-13297-0_22

technologies were employed to automate production processes, and the concept of digitalisation, which pertains to the conversion and processing of analogue information into digital form, became widespread. The act of using digitalised information is termed digitisation, which leverages existing data to generate new insights and integrates this information across various business sectors. The processing of digital information to automate existing processes is called digitalisation, and the complete integration of a new digital business model is known as digital transformation. Among the types of data significantly impacted by digitisation is spatial data, which was previously stored in analogue formats. For instance, maps of varying scales and characteristics were traditionally drawn on paper, while attribute data was documented as land registry entries in physical registers. Physical copies were necessary for sharing this information with others. Over time, paper-based information was digitised into electronic files using computers. The advent of Computer-Aided Design (CAD) software facilitated the digitisation and transformation of paper-based data into electronic files. This enabled the creation of 2D and 3D drawings, designs, and analyses, as well as the storage, retrieval, sharing, distribution, and processing of digital geographic information, which became significantly more streamlined due to the Internet and social media platforms that facilitate the widespread sharing of information and ideas. Since the beginning of the new millennium in particular, progress and innovation in the field of digital technologies have continued to accelerate.. The evolution of sensor technologies, coupled with the swift transition from mobile phones to smartphones shortly following their market introduction, as well as the internet connectivity and communication capabilities of these and other mobile devices, has precipitated the onset of the Fourth Industrial Revolution. The Fourth Industrial Revolution has seen the emergence of technologies such as artificial intelligence, big data analysis, virtual and augmented reality, cloud computing, and 3D printing, which have transformed the collection and analysis of spatial data. These improvements enable real-time access to spatial data, facilitate the querying of valuable information within extensive datasets, and contribute to the processing of existing data to generate new insights.

According to Sui et al. (2013), an average of 1–5 exabytes (1 EB = 10^6 TB) of data was produced globally every day as of 2013, with 90% of the world's digital data being generated within the preceding 2 years. This volume of data is projected to double every 2 years. In 2010, the data volume first reached 1 zettabyte (one ZB = 10^3 EB), and in 2011, it had increased to 1.8 ZB. By 2020, the global data volume was anticipated to be 50 times bigger than the volume recorded in 2011, and the global data production in 2025 could be as high as 150 ZB. It is asserted that 80% of the big data generated worldwide comprises spatial information or data related to spatial information (Gantz & Reinsel, 2011; Huang & Wang, 2020; Saralioglu & Gungor, 2020).

It is recognised that spatial data and technology have a significant impact on both built and natural environments. Here, it is essential to consider the life cycle of real estate, which is relevant to these environments. In this context, PropTech, an abbreviation for property technology, refers to the application of spatial data and technologies within the real estate sector. According to Andrew Knight, the Global Data and Technology Leader at the RICS (Royal Institution of Chartered Surveyors), the narrow definition of PropTech—specifically, the application of technology to any phase of the real estate life cycle—is deemed insufficient to fully capture the essence of the term. He favours a broader definition of PropTech, describing it as 'the impact of technology on any aspect of the real estate life cycle'. Knight asserts that, akin to the real estate sector itself, there is a multitude of concepts associated with real estate and related technologies, including ConTech (Construction Technologies), PlanTech (Planning Technologies), CRETech (Corporate Real Estate Technologies), InfraTech (Infrastructure Technologies), and FinTech (Finance Technologies). Although these concepts intersect and overlap in their applications, they can all be classified under the umbrella of PropTech. In other words, PropTech solutions are noted to encompass the concepts above. For instance, a technology associated with the payment of maintenance fees can be classified as both FinTech and PropTech.

In addition to the prevailing definition of PropTech, the expectations regarding its scope are also noteworthy: The real estate life cycle process adapts when integrated with data and technology, a phenomenon referred to as digitalisation in real estate.

The objective of digitalisation, akin to that of disruptive technologies, should be either to render feasible what was previously impossible or to enhance existing processes. In the context of real estate digitalisation, notable achievements include the elimination of the need to physically view properties and the elimination of long waiting times for real estate transactions. For instance, the utilisation of virtual reality glasses allows for viewing numerous properties at one's convenience without the need for physical presence at the location. Additionally, the Web Tapu system, as implemented by the General Directorate of Land Registry and Cadastre (TKGM), exemplifies this progress. 'Web Tapu is a system where citizens can manage their real estate properties online without going to the land registry offices, view the land registry records and location information of their properties' (TKGM, 2022a).

Every 5 years, the European Commission formulates the European Union's strategy and converts it into policies and initiatives based on the priorities established by the Commission. The current priorities comprise six categories selected between 2019 and 2024 (EC, 2019). These priorities, determined by the European Commission, are significant for both local and central administrations, as they concern their roles in providing financing and closely monitoring global developments. Among these priorities, 'A Europe fit for the digital age', which is directly associated with digitalisation and digital transformation, in addition to the 'European Green Deal' and 'An economy that works for people', which are connected to real estate, are of paramount importance to all stakeholders, encompassing both real estate technologies and digitalisation.

This chapter presents an overview of the applications of digitalisation and real estate technologies within the real estate sector in Türkiye. It investigates the digital transformation in the real estate industry and the legal regulations and public policies pertaining to digitalisation in this domain, both conceptually and practically.

2 Türkiye's Digitalisation Policy

In 2018, the Presidential Decree established the Digital Transformation Office to steer Türkiye's digital transformation efforts, enhance inter-institutional cooperation, and ensure coordination across all domains pertinent to digital transformation, including the real estate sector. The primary responsibility of the Digital Transformation Office is to create a robust digital transformation ecosystem by fostering collaboration among all sectors, non-governmental organisations, and academic institutions, as well as promoting engagement in digital transformation initiatives. It offers recommendations to the Presidency of Strategy and Budget on these issues and oversees the development of projects related to digital transformation. Furthermore, it formulates strategies for utilising big data and its analysis within the public sector, supports existing applications, and ensures the requisite coordination.

In Türkiye, the Presidency of Strategy and Budget formulates a development plan every 4 years. The existing Twelfth Development Plan, encompassing policies from 2024 to 2028, was enacted by the Grand National Assembly of Türkiye on October 31, 2023. The Twelfth Development Plan has introduced substantial digitalisation policies pertaining to real estate. Certain objectives and policies outlined in the development plan coincide with the priorities set forth by the European Commission for the pertinent period.

The Eleventh Development Plan (2019–2023) addressed the concepts of a sustainable environment and livable cities, delineating crucial policies aimed at the development and digitalisation of real estate technologies as part of a comprehensive approach to urban digitalisation. Some of these policies are still in the planning phase, while others have been formulated, and implementation initiatives have already commenced. The plan encompassed policies related to real estate, including mapping, property, valuation, and housing (Table 1).

In the Twelfth Development Plan (2024–2028), the objectives pertaining to real estate are categorised under the titles of 'Qualified People, Strong Family, Healthy Society' and 'Disaster-Resistant Living Spaces, Sustainable Environment', within the areas of focus titled 'Income Distribution', 'Urban Transformation', and 'Urbanisation'. These objectives can be categorised into three themes: real estate valuation, urban transformation, and project financing. Upon exploring the keywords 'Digitalisation' and 'Digital Transformation', objectives emerge under five distinct headings. This suggests the anticipation that the development and emergence of disruptive technologies will progress significantly across nearly all dimensions of the real estate sector (including construction, management, housing, investment, urbanisation, finance, etc.), resulting in transformation of existing business practices.

In 2019, the Ministry of Environment, Urbanisation, and Climate Change (ÇŞİDB) in Türkiye developed the National Smart Cities Strategy and Action Plan (UAŞSEP), which encompassed the period from 2020 to 2023. This action plan introduced the concept of smart buildings, defined as systems designed to enhance the quality of life by addressing the fundamental needs of all buildings within a city,

Table 1 Policies created for real estate in the eleventh development plan

Subject	Policy	Status
Mapping	The completion of cadastral and mapping processes will be conducted in a multidimensional format.	Ongoing
Property	Transactions related to property will be incorporated into the electronic environment in compliance with legal regulations.	Completed
	A unified coordinate system will be established, and the efforts pertaining to cadastral modernisation will be completed.	Completed
	All documents pertaining to title deed transactions will be digitised, thereby facilitating the execution of transactions through electronic means.	Ongoing
Value	An information centre dedicated to real estate valuation will be integrated into the Land Registry and Cadastre Information System. This centre will document declared prices in title deed transactions, monitor fluctuations in value, identify increases attributable to public investments and regulations, provide data for location selection analyses, and generate real estate value maps.	Ongoing
Housing	An integrated system will be established to provide access to housing sector data from a single source.	Ongoing

Source: UAŞSEP (2019)

including housing quality, living standards, climate control, energy systems, and safety measures, through a technological and intelligent approach. The action plan was disseminated to relevant institutions and organisations across all provinces via a circular letter from the President, published in 2019, which instructed necessary actions to be undertaken in accordance with the strategies outlined in the action plan. Progress regarding this action plan can be monitored at www.akillisehirler.gov.tr. Efforts have commenced to renew the action plan. The draft for the 2024–2030 National Smart Cities Strategy and Action Plan has been prepared; however, it has not yet received official endorsement.

The UAŞSEP emphasised the importance of a green certificate for smart buildings, highlighting the need to promote adequate public awareness about energy efficiency and green building practices. In this context, the Ministry promulgated the Green Certificate Regulation for Buildings and Settlements in 2022, and the implementation of the Green Certificate Evaluation Guide for Buildings followed. This guide aimed to mitigate reliance on conventional energy sources (e.g. oil, coal) by promoting the appropriate use of renewable energy technologies (e.g. wind, geothermal, solar, hydro, bioenergy) that are both environmentally sustainable and economically viable, while also encouraging the adoption of advanced energy-efficient technologies. Furthermore, the Ministry initiated the development of the National Green Certificate System (YeS-TR).

With respect to the governance of smart buildings within UAŞSEP, the objectives encompass ensuring resource and organisational management, completing and implementing planning stages, as well as monitoring, evaluation, sustainability, interoperability, coordination among stakeholders, and service management. It is noteworthy that, with the shift from apartment complexes to larger residential developments, it has become imperative to consider building governance capabilities in conjunction with facility management.

In the pursuit of transforming buildings into smart ones, it is imperative to use Building Information Modelling (BIM) to create and manage digital representations that encapsulate spaces' functional and physical characteristics. This modelling facilitates collaborative efforts among all project disciplines, encompassing architectural, structural, electrical, mechanical, and other areas of expertise. Furthermore, it is essential to establish a data-driven system for the building prior to issuing a construction permit.

The Local Government Survey, which was prepared and implemented as an integral component of the UAŞSEP project, revealed that the implementation of smart buildings in urban areas is notably insufficient, as evidenced by certain inquiries regarding smart buildings (Table 2).

The UAŞSEP emphasised the necessity of establishing a Building Disaster Emergency Management framework, as well as an Integrated Building Security System specifically designed for smart buildings. In this regard, the implementation of the following proposals was recommended:

- Early Warning Systems
- Emergency Systems
- Building Security Systems
- Instant Notification Systems for Emergency Services
- Remote Security Control Systems
- Information Systems Designed for the Implementation of Security Measures in Shelters and Disaster Living Areas

These initiatives are designed to integrate smart buildings into a centralised system and to mitigate the loss of life and property during disaster situations.

The establishment of disaster emergency management systems and robust building security frameworks is imperative for nations such as Türkiye, which are situated in seismic zones. Consequently, the enhancement of buildings to be earthquake-resistant was embraced as a principal policy initiative. A key objective is the development of intelligent buildings that provide adequate protection against earthquakes and other calamities during the construction phase, the classification of existing structures based on their seismic risk assessments, and the implementation of requisite upgrades.

Table 2 Applications of smart buildings in local governments and their implementation rates

Applications	Implemented cities (%)
Smart water meters	8%
Building integrated waste management	7%

Source: UAŞSEP (2019)

Furthermore, measures such as permeable concrete, green roofs, and flood barrels are planned for incorporation into buildings to mitigate the effects of flooding and waterlogging.

The Local Government Survey on integrated security systems in smart buildings, prepared and implemented as a component of the UAŞSEP project, indicates that these implementations remain in the initial stages (Table 3).

In 2021, the General Directorate of Geographical Information Systems of the Ministry of Environment, Urbanisation, and Climate Change published the Smart City Reference Architecture Guide. The systems encompassed within Smart Buildings include: Instant Notification to Emergency Services, Adaptive Ventilation Systems (HVAC), Disaster Living Rooms and Shelters, Smart Building Disaster Living Rooms and Shelters, Smart Building Lighting Systems, Enhancement of Smart Building Energy Efficiency (e.g., Glass Buildings), Smart Building Integrated Emergency Systems, Smart Building Integrated Security Systems, Smart Building Insulation System, Smart Building Renewable Energy Systems, Smart Water Meters, Building Information Modeling, Integrated Emergency Systems, Integrated Heating and Cooling Systems, Early Warning Systems, User Information Systems for Security Measures, Utilisation of Natural Resources for Healthy Climate Control, Remote Security Control Systems, Building Data Management, Accessibility of Buildings, and Green Certified Buildings.

One of the initiatives undertaken in the realm of smart buildings is the MatchUp Project, which is a component of Türkiye's smart cities initiative. The MatchUp Project constitutes a smart city initiative that has garnered funding through the European Union's Horizon 2020 program. Its objective is to devise and enhance integrated solutions across the domains of Environment, Energy, Information and Communication Technologies, and Transportation Technologies.

Within the parameters of the project, Türkiye's largest urban transformation initiative, the Kepez Santral Neighbourhood Urban Transformation Project, has been selected as a pilot implementation. This initiative aims to incorporate essential technological applications for smart buildings, encompassing components for smart

Table 3 Applications for smart buildings in local governments and their implementation rates

Applications	Implemented cities (%)
Early warning systems	10%
Emergency systems	13%
Smart building integrated security systems	8%
Instant notification to emergency services	12%
Remote security control systems	15%
Smart building disaster living rooms and shelters	11%
Information systems aimed at implementing security measures	13%

Source: UAŞSEP (2019)

Fig. 1 Kepez Santral neighbourhood urban transformation project. Source: Marmara Şehircilik (2024)

homes and building control in both residential and public structures, as well as renewable energy and storage solutions, smart lighting, and smart meters. It will serve as a reference for smart housing applications and policies in Türkiye (Fig. 1).

3 Development of the PropTech Field in Türkiye

The development of PropTech in Türkiye experienced significant growth during the 2000s, like the trends observed in other countries with socio-economic structures comparable to Türkiye's. Nonetheless, the definition of activities encompassed by the term 'PropTech' remains in a state of evolution. Upon reviewing private sector investments and initiatives, the initial study aimed at identifying PropTech stakeholders in Türkiye was conducted in 2019 by the EurAsia PropTech Initiative, a non-profit organisation headquartered in Istanbul. This study ascertained the market size and analysed the market structure, culminating in the establishment of the Türkiye PropTech Map in January 2019 (EPTI, 2019a).

According to this research study, Türkiye experiences more than 1.5 million real estate transactions annually. The nation is distinguished by its substantial population of more than 80 million inhabitants, the magnitude and progress of its construction sector, its dynamic characteristics concerning both internal and external migrations, and its ongoing and active process of urbanisation. Furthermore, considering the risk associated with natural disasters, seven million structures in Türkiye need structural renewal. The study also highlights the presence of over 35 million active mobile banking users and a mortgage market worth USD 50 billion, which presents considerable potential for growth compared to other countries. The

Table 4 Overview of real estate technologies in Türkiye according to EurAsia PropTech initiative studies

Publication date	Number of institutions	Innovations	Published Map
January 2019	81	–	EPTI (2019a)
September 2019	97	Categories for construction technologies (ConTech) and owner applications have been added.	EPTI (2019b)
September 2020	132	Cloud market/kitchen category added.	EPTI (2020)
January 2021	145	–	EPTI (2021)

Sources: EPTI (2019a, 2019b), EPTI (2020), EPTI (2021)

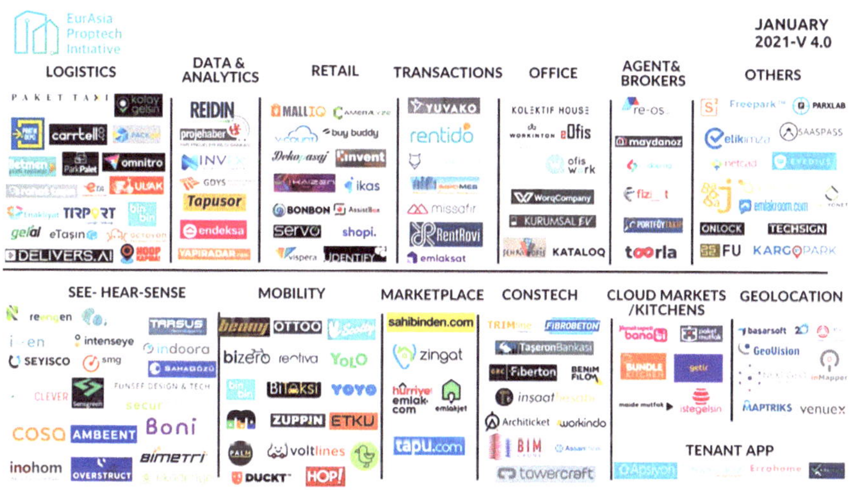

Fig. 2 January 2021 Türkiye PropTech Map. Source: EPTI (2021)

Türkiye PropTech Map of 2019 identified 81 organisations, classified according to their respective areas of activity into categories such as Marketplace, Data & Analytics, Transaction, Office, Retail, Logistics, Location Services, Mobility, Sensing-Seeing-Hearing, Hospitality, Intermediary Services, and Others.

The EurAsia PropTech Initiative conducted the study again in September 2019, September 2020, and January 2021, as demonstrated in the table below (Table 4). Consequently, following the most recent study, the Türkiye PropTech Map was revised in January 2021 (Fig. 2).

In recent years, influenced by the global ramifications of the pandemic, startups within the logistics sector, akin to the sector, have experienced considerable growth. The latest study underscores significant advances in online real estate management, the demand for flexible office spaces, applications that integrate electronic and biometric signatures, applications that unify access and identity verification, applications that amalgamate data production, usage, and communication, as well as developments in mobility, construction technologies, cloud marketplaces, and cloud kitchens.

To enhance the digitalisation of the real estate sector in Türkiye, the financial returns on investments in this domain must be effectively communicated to both the public and private sectors. Additionally, PropTech should place a high priority on scientific research and foster an ecosystem through collaborative models between universities and industry.

Türkiye is anticipated to exhibit competitiveness in the PropTech market when compared to nations with similar characteristics or within a regional context. Future endeavours aimed at evaluating the level of PropTech development or conducting comparative analyses among countries will augment the findings of this study.

4 Digital Transformation in the Real Estate Sector in Türkiye

The process of digitalisation within the real estate sector in Türkiye is progressing at a considerable pace. Significant subjects pertaining to digitalisation in real estate encompass big data, virtual reality, and online real estate platforms, among others. This section delineates digitalisation initiatives in Türkiye's real estate sector that have either been executed or are currently in the planning phases.

4.1 Big Data and Machine Learning in Real Estate

In recent years, advances in technology and an increase in data storage capacity have resulted in the emergence of the concept of big data. As the volume of data has expanded, new research domains concerning big data have developed, addressing challenges such as speed and performance degradation that were observed with traditional methods, particularly through the application of artificial intelligence and its subfield, machine learning algorithms. Machine learning involves creating a model by instructing a computer using data and relevant variables, thereby enabling the automatic prediction of outcomes from the data. The applications of machine learning algorithms are vast, spanning across fields such as medicine, engineering, finance, and social sciences.

In recent years, machine learning algorithms have been increasingly used within the real estate industry, particularly for bulk property valuation (Kontrimas & Verikas, 2007). The machine learning methodology typically manages big datasets and can perform property valuations either individually or collectively. When several properties are appraised concurrently, this is referred to as Bulk Valuation. Bulk valuation is thus undertaken simultaneously for multiple properties rather than on an individual basis within a specific time frame. In many developed nations, property values are determined or updated through the application of these methods.

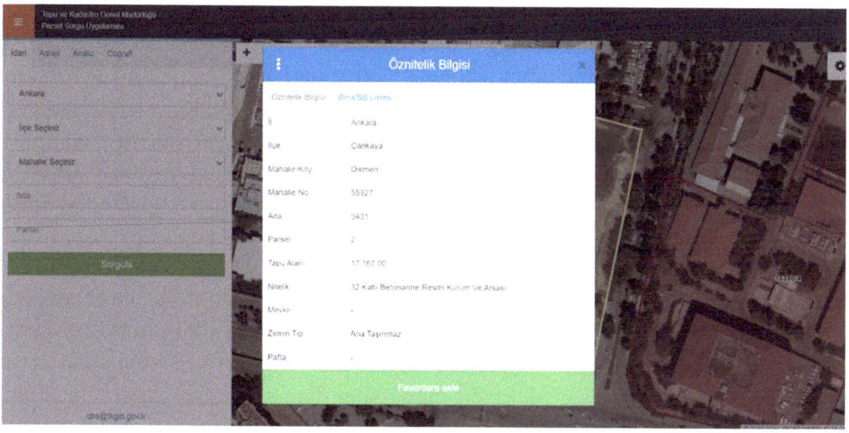

Fig. 3 A view of the parcel query screen. Source: TKGM (2022b)

In Türkiye, bulk valuation studies using machine learning algorithms have commenced within the academic community over the past decade. According to the Eleventh Development Plan of the Presidency, 'A real estate value information centre will be established, integrated with the Land Registry and Cadastre Information System, to create property value maps and keep data related to property values along with ownership information'. This indicates that a bulk valuation system is anticipated to be implemented shortly in the country, and it is acknowledged that TKGM (General Directorate of Land Registry and Cadastre) and ÇŞB (Ministry of Environment, Urbanisation and Climate Change) have completed pilot studies for real estate bulk valuation.

In addition to bulk valuation, TKGM has conducted various digitalisation and big data initiatives in the real estate sector. One initiative is the Land Registry and Cadastre Information System (TAKBIS), which has facilitated the transfer of property data into an electronic format since 2012 (TKGM, 2012). Another noteworthy application of digital transformation by TKGM is the Parcel Query Application, which enables users to access fundamental information regarding land registry and cadastre data electronically, as well as the geometrical details of adjacent parcels. It is available for public use (Fig. 3).

4.2 Internet of Things and Real Estate

The Internet of Things (IoT) refers to a network of physical objects that are equipped with sensors, software, and various technologies designed to connect and exchange data with other devices and systems via the Internet. IoT serves as a bridge between the physical and digital realms, enabling individuals and devices to connect at any time and from any location, thereby facilitating interactions with everything and everyone (Georgios et al., 2019). A notable subcategory of IoT technologies is the 'smart home system'. Advanced control systems are available for managing engineering systems within buildings and facilities (Pupentsova et al., 2019). Infrastructure elements, including cameras and sound systems, permit the online collection of data in the realm of real estate, particularly within residential properties. With recent technological advancs, mobile devices now provide the capability for remote access to smart buildings within a network, enabling functionalities such as activating heating systems and initiating electronic appliances. In Türkiye, particularly in Istanbul, the concept of smart homes and offices is prevalent. IoT also significantly contributes to the development of energy-efficient buildings.

A prevalent illustration of Internet of Things (IoT) applications is the concept of smart living. While variations exist depending on real estate utilisation, a discernible trend towards enhancing tools and equipment within residential spaces via information technology is evident, encompassing data collection, communication, and control functionalities. This development culminates in innovative and, importantly, comprehensive applications across various domains including heating, cooling, lighting, energy consumption, safety and security, access control, and the optimisation of routine tasks such as waste collection, cleaning, and dishwashing, as well as the procurement of consumables (Altamira, 2022; DSBRR, 2016).

Another illustration pertains to the implementation of intelligent maintenance within the realm of facility management (Altamira, 2022). The integration of sensors and various information technologies facilitates the continuous monitoring of facility infrastructure for anomalies such as leaks, moisture levels, temperature fluctuations, and the overall performance of existing materials and infrastructure, thereby promoting preventive maintenance.

4.3 Augmented Reality, Digital Twin, and 3D Modelling

Augmented reality technologies facilitate the conversion of real-world environments into digital formats, enabling individuals to perceive the reality of their surroundings through instruments such as computers and 3D glasses. Contemporary concepts encompass augmented reality, mixed reality, and virtual reality, collectively referred to as extended reality (Fig. 4).

Virtual reality enables the 3D representation of previously collected information about an environment, thereby enhancing its application in the real estate sector, particularly in the acquisition and rental of residential properties. For instance, virtual tours of listed properties—especially residential ones—are essential, as they offer insights and mitigate time expenditure. Globally, there are numerous virtual tour and sales platforms for properties that allow for 3D virtual tours before purchase. In Türkiye, several real estate websites are providing and developing 3D virtual home tours. For instance, sahibinden.com, one of Türkiye's largest real estate platforms, features 3D property listings that can be interacted with virtual reality devices.

Another area of technology that's emerging with the convergence of digitalisation and real estate is the concept of the 'digital twin'. A digital twin is a digital

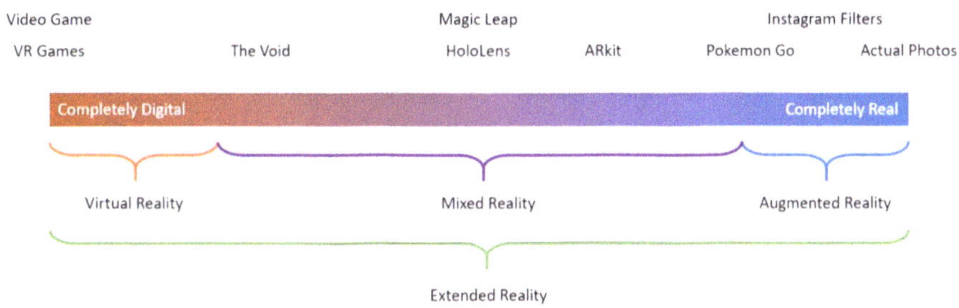

Fig. 4 Augmented reality scale and concepts from real to virtual. Source: Liu (2018)

replication of a physical object. When this object pertains to real estate, it is designated as a digital twin in real estate. The development of digital twins within the real estate sector presents several advantages, including enhanced building maintenance and the facilitation of sustainable construction practices. Additional benefits include (Agente Studio, 2020):

- Lowers maintenance expenses, enhances the sustainability of the building, and improves the quality of life for tenants.
- Facilitates timely decision-making. Digital twins enable owners and operators of buildings to access the virtual twin at any time and use statistical data and predictive analytics.
- Diminishes labour costs related to facility management.
- Enhances user satisfaction by ensuring prompt resolution of issues and providing superior tenant customer service.
- The efficiency of the development process is significantly enhanced. Digital twins enable continuous comparisons between the design and the ongoing work.
- Facilitates sustainability through the management of CO_2 emissions, the reduction of noise pollution, and the implementation of distinct waste collection practices.

It is acknowledged that creating digital twins for properties constitutes one of the primary objectives of the Ministry of Environment, Urbanisation, and Climate Change in Türkiye. A broader scope of digital twins and virtual reality entails the development of 3D models of cities and, consequently, of real estate and buildings, collectively referred to as the built environment. Therefore, 3D city models offer opportunities across sectors, ranging from smart cities to real estate planning. Furthermore, 3D city models update the building stock, conduct spatial analyses of buildings, and extend their functions beyond these primary uses. In Türkiye, stemming from initiatives established by the Ministry of Environment, Urbanisation, and Climate Change in 2016, the General Directorate of Land Registry and Cadastre has generated 3D city models for Amasya and Kütahya. The project, overseen by the General Directorate of Spatial Information Systems, has successfully concluded digital twin studies for 21 provinces. The 3D tours of these cities are accessible

Fig. 5 3D city model visual created by TKGM for Amasya city. Source: TKGM (2022c)

Fig. 6 3D city model visual created for Amasya by the general directorate of spatial information systems. Source: GDSIS (2022)

through web interfaces. Figure 5 illustrates an example of the 3D model of Amasya completed by TKGM, and Fig. 6 exhibits the updated model presented by the General Directorate of Spatial Information Systems in 2022.

The Ministry of Environment, Urbanisation, and Climate Change characterises the models depicted in Figs. 5 and 6 as digital twins. However, given the ongoing evolution of digital twins, the question of whether these models meet the criteria of digital twins or have the potential to evolve into digital twins may warrant further research.

5 Conclusion

In recent years, the real estate sector in Türkiye has embraced digitalisation, driven by global trends, technological innovations, and national development strategies. This chapter examined the integration of technologies, including PropTech, big data analytics, IoT, virtual reality, and digital twins, into the sector and their role in driving transformation. A foundational framework for digital transformation has been established through national policies, including the Eleventh and Twelfth Development Plans, in addition to the National Smart Cities Strategy and Action Plan (UAŞSEP). Government-led initiatives, including the Web Tapu system, the TAKBIS, and pilot projects involving 3D city models and smart buildings, have been implemented to facilitate the transition towards a more digital and data-driven real estate ecosystem.

Türkiye's PropTech ecosystem is evolving, propelled by a dynamic construction sector, rapid urbanisation, an increasing volume of real estate transactions, and a young, digitally literate population. Proptech solutions have progressively contributed to enhancing efficiency, transparency, and user experience through innovations such as online platforms, virtual tours, and intelligent facility management systems. In line with these developments, the establishment of a dedicated PropTech Centre at Ankara University has been officially announced for 2025. This centre aims to foster innovation, interdisciplinary research, and collaboration among academia, industry, and public institutions, thereby enhancing the national capacity for digital real estate transformation. Still, several challenges have arisen, including the integration of data systems, aligning legal frameworks, workforce preparedness, and the scalability of pilot projects. It has been emphasised that enhanced collaboration among the public and private sectors, academic institutions, and civil society is essential to realise the benefits of digitalisation fully.

In summary, Türkiye is anticipated to maintain a competitive stance within the regional PropTech and digital real estate sector. This potential may be leveraged through ongoing strategic investments, the formulation of supportive policies, and a commitment to inclusive and sustainable digital transformation. Digitalisation is projected to revolutionise the processes involved in developing, managing, and transacting real estate, thereby contributing to the creation of more resilient, efficient, and future-ready urban environments.

References

Agente Studio. (2020). Why digital twins are important for commercial real estate. *Agente Studio*, 9 Ocak 2020.

Altamira. (2022). Altamira software internet of things applications in real estate page. Retrieved October 10, 2022, from https://www.altamira.ai/blog/iot-applications-for-real-estate/

DSBRR. (2016). Deloitte smart buildings research report. Retrieved October 10, 2022, from https://www2.deloitte.com/content/dam/Deloitte/nl/Documents/real-estate/deloitte-nl-fsi-real-estate-smart-buildings-how-iot-technology-aims-to-add-value-for-real-estate-companies.pdf

EC. (2019). The European Commission's priorities. Retrieved September 1, 2024, from https://commission.europa.eu/strategy-and-policy/priorities-2019-2024_en
EPTI. (2019a). EurAsia Proptech Initiative Turkey Real Estate Technology January 2019 Overview. Retrieved September 30, 2022, from https://www.proptecheurasia.com//news/-
EPTI. (2019b). EurAsia Proptech Initiative Turkey Real Estate Technology September 2019 Overview. Retrieved September 30, 2022, from https://www.proptecheurasia.com//news/turkey-proptech-map%2D%2Dversion-2
EPTI. (2020). EurAsia Proptech Initiative Turkey Real Estate Technology September 2020 Overview. Retrieved September 30, 2022, from https://www.proptecheurasia.com/news/istanbul-proptech-scene%2D%2Dsept-2020
EPTI. (2021). EurAsia Proptech Initiative Turkey Real Estate Technology January 2021 Overview. Retrieved September 30, 2022, from https://www.proptecheurasia.com/news/istanbul-proptech-scene-january-2021
Gantz, J., & Reinsel, D. (2011). Extracting value from chaos, Aug. 2011, [online] Available: https://web.archive.org/web/20180308060055/https://www.emc.com/collateral/analyst-reports/idc-extracting-value-from-chaos-ar.pdf
GDSIS. (2022). General Directorate of Spatial Information Systems. Retrieved September 30, 2022, from https://3dsehir.csb.gov.tr/
Georgios, L., Kerstin, S., & Theofylaktos, A. (2019). Internet of Things in the Context of Industry 4.0: An overview.
Huang, B., & Wang, J. (2020). Big spatial data for urban and environmental sustainability. *Geo-spatial Information Science, 23*(2), 125–140. https://doi.org/10.1080/10095020.2020.1754138
Kontrimas, V., & Verikas, A. (2007). Neural networks-based screening of real estate transactions. *Neural Network World, 17*(1), 17.
Liu, J. (2018). *The difference between AR, VR, MR, XR and how to tell them apart*. HackerNoon.
Marmara Şehircilik. (2024). Antalya Büyükşehir Kepez Santral Mahallesi Kentsel Dönüşüm Projesi. https://marmarasehircilik.com.tr/
Pupentsova, S., Leventsov, V., Livintsova, M., Alexeeva, N., & Vodianova, S. (2019). Assessment of the Internet of Things projects on the real estate market. In *IOP conference series: Materials science and engineering* (Vol. 618, No. 1, p. 012041). IOP Publishing.
Saralioglu, E., & Gungor, O. (2020). Crowdsourcing in remote sensing: A review of applications and future directions. *IEEE Geoscience and Remote Sensing Magazine, 8*(4), 89–110.
Sui, D., Goodchild, M., & Elwood, S. (2013). Volunteered geographic information, the exa-flood, and the growing digital divide. In *Crowdsourcing geographic knowledge* (pp. 1–12). Springer-Verlag.
TKGM. (2012). General Directorate of Land Registry and Cadastre. TAKBIS Information Page. Retrieved September 30, 2022, from https://www.tkgm.gov.tr/projeler/tapu-ve-kadastro-bilgi-sistemi-takbis
TKGM. (2022a). TKGM Web Title Service Page. Retrieved October 10, 2022, from https://webtapu.tkgm.gov.tr/
TKGM. (2022b). TKGM Parcel Inquiry Page. Retrieved September 30, 2022, from https://parselsorgu.tkgm.gov.tr/
TKGM. (2022c). TKGM. Retrieved September 13, 2022, from https://amasya3b.tkgm.gov.tr/#/
UAŞSEP. (2019). Türkiye developed the National Smart Cities Strategy and Action Plan. Retrieved September 30, 2022, from https://akillisehirler.gov.tr/wp-content/uploads/EylemPlani.pdf

Emir Sunguroğlu is a lecturer at the Department of Real Estate Development and Management, Faculty of Applied Sciences, Ankara University, Türkiye. He acquired a Bachelor of Science degree in Computer Engineering and a Master of Science degree in Real Estate Development and Management. He is interested in investigating emerging technologies, such as artificial intelligence, in relation to their applicability within the real estate and construction sectors. Furthermore, he possesses a strong interest in the Proptech industry and digitalisation, particularly in Türkiye. Currently, Mr Sunguroğlu is engaged in doctoral research on the topic of "Assessment of Digital

Transformation in Facility Management with Capability Maturity Model." He holds a position as a full-time lecturer in the Department of Real Estate Development and Management at Ankara University, where he contributes to courses on information technology, computer-aided design, and construction project analysis.

Sibel Canaz Sevgen is an assistant professor in the Department of Real Estate Development and Management, Faculty of Applied Sciences, Ankara University. She is a researcher and specialises in the applications of machine learning within the field of real estate science. She is recognised as an expert in Geographic Information Systems (GIS) as well as remote sensing technologies. She has made significant contributions to various studies that integrate advanced data-driven models with land cover monitoring and real estate mass appraisal studies. Her areas of expertise include deep learning, statistical modelling, and geospatial analysis. She has collaborated on interdisciplinary projects that merge artificial intelligence with the discipline of real estate science. Furthermore, she has published several articles in high-impact academic journals and is actively involved in scientific conferences.

Mehmet Ülger earned his B.Sc. with a Civil Engineering degree from Erciyes University and holds an M.Sc. in Coastal Engineering from Gazi University. He completed his PhD in Real Estate Development and Management at Ankara University, specialising in modelling shoreline changes and their effect on real estate values. He has published numerous papers in top journals, including Q1 publications, addressing topics such as coastal erosion, real estate valuation, and coastal area planning. He is responsible for teaching graduate and doctoral courses in coastal area management and planning, building information modelling (BIM) in the real estate sector, and real estate and asset analysis at the department. His professional expertise encompasses numerical modelling of coastal sediment transport, assessing the impacts of climate change on coastal properties, and investigating Building Information Modelling (BIM) applications in infrastructure projects. Dr. Ülger's research focuses on the nexus of coastal engineering, real estate economics, and advanced modelling techniques for sustainable coastal and property development.

The Process of Risk Analysis and Decision-Making in Real Estate Development Projects

Akın Öztürk and Harun Tanrıvermiş

Abstract

This chapter examines the integration of risk analysis and decision-making into real estate development projects, highlighting the growing importance of data-driven and systematic methods amid increasing complexity and uncertainty. Based on a comprehensive review of existing literature and field research with leading construction firms, this chapter demonstrates how Decision Support Systems (DSS) enhance developers' ability to identify, assess, and manage project risks. Key risk factors are categorised at both company and project levels, including political instability, financing challenges, site selection, and development delays. Different risk assessment and decision-making techniques are examined, such as scenario analysis, Monte Carlo simulations, the Analytic Hierarchy Process (AHP), and fuzzy logic. Results indicate a prevalent lack of systematic risk management in the real estate industry, despite widespread recognition of its importance. The chapter concludes by underscoring the need to combine risk analysis with DSS to enable informed, strategic, and sustainable decision-making, and advocates for institutional backing, data transparency, and the cultivation of specialised human resources.

Keywords

Risk analysis · Decision-making · Real estate development · DSS · Uncertainty · Scenario analysis

A. Öztürk · H. Tanrıvermiş (✉)
Department of Real Estate Development and Management, Faculty of Applied Sciences, Ankara University, Ankara, Türkiye
e-mail: akin.ozturk@ankara.edu.tr; tanrivermis@ankara.edu.tr

T. Just et al. (eds.), *Understanding Türkiye's Real Estate Markets*, Management for Professionals, https://doi.org/10.1007/978-3-032-13297-0_23

1 Introduction

Decision Support Systems (DSS) enhance risk management in real estate projects by facilitating more informed, objective, and data-driven decision-making. These systems integrate various risk management models and analytical tools to assess factors such as investment risks, development costs, and market conditions, even in complex and uncertain environments (Lin et al., 1996; Mosallaeipour et al., 2019; Valverde, 2011a). For example, sophisticated DSS frameworks that utilise spatial analysis, big data, and intelligent algorithms enable detailed regional risk prediction. This helps stakeholders identify and visualise risk, supporting strategic decisions related to location, investment, and project development (Anelli & Tajani, 2023; Sun, 2023; Xie et al., 2023). By combining qualitative and quantitative data, DSS enables dynamic monitoring, scenario analysis, and actionable reporting, ultimately promoting sustainable and profitable real estate development by reducing uncertainties (Anelli & Tajani, 2023; Lin et al., 1996; Mosallaeipour et al., 2019; Sun, 2023; Valverde, 2011b).

Risk management has been a subject of discussion for over a century (Knight, 1921) and remains highly relevant today (Prat & Uctum, 2019). The success of a real estate development project depends not only on its specific features but also on external factors such as the overall economic climate, construction policies, and cost fluctuations. In decision support systems, making accurate decisions requires systematic and logical reasoning. Evaluating risk, costs, and benefits during the process of identifying viable options demands rigorous, methodical thinking. While prompt and informed decisions can bring advantages such as increased influence, reputation, prestige, and financial rewards, delays or errors can lead to significant tangible and intangible losses. Therefore, decision-makers need to develop action plans based on quick, accurate, and adaptable decisions that respond effectively to changing circumstances (Öztürk, 2020). This study examines the sources of risk in real estate development and investment projects, the tools employed for risk management, the need for decision support systems, and their potential effects, drawing on both a literature review and survey findings.

2 Decision-Making and Risks in Real Estate Projects

Risk includes the possibility of positive or negative developments, resulting in either a gain or a loss premium. The complex and long-term nature of development projects raises the question of how risks can be comprehensively managed within a project (Tanrıvermiş, 2017). Due to the variety of risks involved, it is necessary to consider each risk type separately. To manage risks effectively, an appropriate decision-making system must be established. Risks should be examined in greater detail and incorporated into the overall project analysis and valuation to ensure they are considered during the decision-making process.

In the decision-making process, accurately identifying alternatives and using suitable analytical techniques are essential for real estate developers. The alternatives are developed based on past experiences and current data on potential future developments. The developer must make project development decisions by considering the expectations, needs, interests, and possible trends within the customer portfolio. At the same time, the developer takes on a guiding role for investors and other stakeholders. In the development of residential, mixed-use, or commercial real estate, creating and delivering spaces that are not currently available in the market but are needed will add significant value to the project.

In real estate investment projects, risk premiums differ from one project to another. The types of risks each project faces and their impact levels are analysed on a case-by-case basis and included in the project plan. Developers require decision support systems to monitor project risks throughout the project lifecycle. These systems identify and evaluate risks, allowing the calculation of risk premiums by linking them to relevant sector weightings. The risk premium varies between projects. Projects are influenced not only by their internal risks but also by external risks. For example, the value depreciation of luxury real estate projects may be greater than that of other types. When making investment decisions for development projects, locations along the development axes of cities are generally preferred. In this context, higher-level spatial plans, zoning policies, and investor trends guide the selection of suitable locations and land for the projects.

2.1 Risk Analysis

Risk management involves identifying and analysing the effects of uncertainties and then mitigating these effects or transforming them into opportunities (ISO 31000, 2018). This process is crucial for the success of strategic decisions in businesses, public institutions, and projects. Risk refers to the difference between expected and realised outcomes (Aven, 2015). This difference can lead to adverse situations (a loss), but it can also create positive impacts. Therefore, the modern concept of risk management includes not only threats but also potential opportunities. According to the ISO 31000 standard, the risk management process comprises the following steps:

1. *Establishing the context:* The organisation's internal and external environments, stakeholders, and risk tolerance levels are established.
2. *Risk identification:* Risks are recognised and their potential manifestation is identified.
3. *Risk analysis:* The probability and impact of the risk are evaluated.
4. *Risk evaluation:* The level of risk acceptability is determined.
5. *Risk treatment:* Strategies are designed to mitigate, accept, transfer (such as via insurance), or eliminate the risk.
6. *Monitoring and review:* The process is regularly monitored and maintained with updates.
7. *Communication and consultation:* The success of risk management is enhanced through the establishment of effective communication with stakeholders.

Risk management constitutes a fundamental component essential for achieving success in disciplines characterised by substantial uncertainty, such as project management and finance. For example, the Project Management Institute (PMI) notes that a considerable proportion of project failures are attributable to the lack of implementation of suitable risk management procedures (PMI, 2017). Conversely, Beck's (1992) "risk society" theory posits that contemporary societies are progressively cultivating increased risk, thereby rendering risk management critical not only at the individual level but also within societal and organisational frameworks.

Risk analysis typically occurs in two main forms: qualitative and quantitative. Some sources also note that these methods can be combined into a mixed-methods approach (Bentahar & Cameron, 2015; Yorulmaz & Sezen, 2023). In qualitative risk analysis, the likelihood and impacts of risks are evaluated, along with the overall risk value or interactions between risks. Quantitative analysis, on the other hand, involves expressing risks and their relationships through numerical data. Usually, instead of analysing every identified risk separately, the focus is on specific risk types, such as fluctuations in housing interest rates. First, the specific characteristics of the risk are identified. For interest rate risks, forecasts are made for possible changes at the start and during the project, and project plans are adjusted accordingly. Since project value can vary over time, planning should not rely solely on current interest rates. From an investment perspective, estimating future interest rates involves calculating the weighted average cost of capital (WACC) and discount rates (Tanrıvermiş, 2017). Since project values are based on these forecasts, the actual values realised during the project carry inherent risk. For example, a downward trend in interest rates could lead to higher sales and lower investment costs. Therefore, when analysing interest rate risk, changes in treasury bond rates are considered, and the likelihood and impact of these changes are evaluated (Öztürk, 2020).

The methods for analysing risk types and assessing their impact have both pros and cons. Hanafizadeh and Latif (2011) discussed the advantages and disadvantages of sensitivity analysis, scenario analysis, Monte Carlo simulation, and the real options approach (Table 1).

2.2 Decision-Making

Alan Turing's, 1950 article "*Computing Machinery and Intelligence" is regarded as a cornerstone of the field of artificial intelligence, as it explores* the possibility of machines developing human-like thinking abilities. In this context, Turing's vision for artificial intelligence has served as a major source of inspiration for the development of modern decision support systems. These systems aim to optimise users' decision-making processes by establishing meaningful connections within complex datasets and information. Turing's question, "Can machines think?", provides the fundamental motivation for modern decision support systems to deliver real-time, intelligent, and effective recommendations through algorithmic intelligence and learning capabilities. Therefore, by enhancing human-machine collaboration,

Table 1 Comparison of risk analysis methods

Approach	Advantage(s)	Disadvantage(s)
Sensitivity analysis	– Requires minimal information. Suitable for uncertain conditions where there is a lack of statistical data about variables. – Highlights variables related to managerial behaviours during implementation.	– Assessing concurrent variations in uncertain parameters is highly complex. – Unsuitable when variables are statistically dependent.
Scenario analysis	– Suitable for conditions of uncertainty where there is a lack of statistical information about variables.	– Not suitable for the use of historical data. – It is not easy to identify all scenarios; the best- and worst-case scenarios may not be found.
Monte Carlo simulation	– Utilises historical data. – Allows monitoring of simultaneous changes in uncertain variables.	– Provides the distribution of the present value, but does not determine a single value. – Does not account for the variances of uncertainty variables.
Real options approach	– Decision-making is flexible. – Uses the probabilities of scenarios in the present value calculation. – Applies information learned from past outcomes to future decisions.	– Does not account for project exit or delays. – Does not account for the variances of uncertainty variables.

Source: Hanafizadeh and Latif (2011)

decision support systems translate the principles of artificial intelligence advanced by Turing into practical applications. Making the right decision is critically important at every stage of every project (Harrison, 1999). Decision theory is a field of study that investigates how individual judgements can be modelled and how these models influence them. This modelling can take different forms, such as probability-based models, loss functions, or statistical representations of judgements. Many decision theories focus on how decisions are actually made, relying on the observation of past decisions (Elizabeth et al., 2008). Overall, the decision-making process can be summarised as follows (Fig. 1) (Öztürk, 2020) (Table 1).

In decision-making, two main models stand out: rational and normative. Rational models rely on cognitive judgements and help in choosing logical options. These models include techniques such as decision matrix analysis, the Pugh matrix, SWOT analysis, Pareto analysis, and decision trees with a selection matrix. In rational models, the problem is defined, success criteria for the outcome and process are set, all possible solutions are considered, the consequences of these solutions are evaluated, and the best choice is made by comparing the probabilities of meeting the criteria. The normative decision-making model, however, is used when constraints may affect the decision process, such as time limits, complexity, uncertainty, and resource scarcity. In normative models, individuals often work with limited information and make decisions using heuristic shortcuts or by finding "good enough" (satisficing) solutions (Atherton et al., 2008).

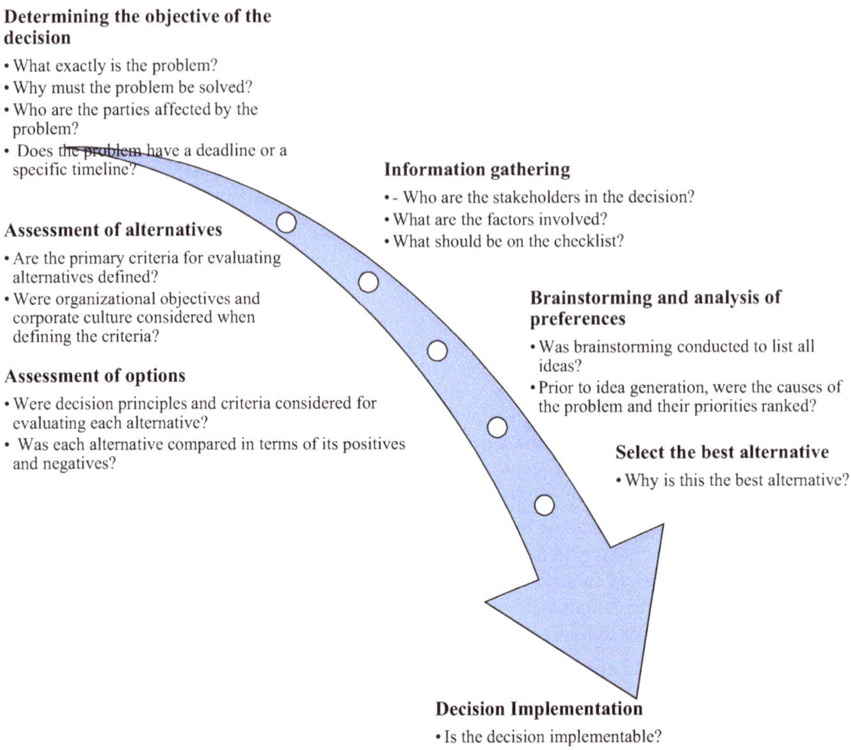

Fig. 1 Steps of a generally accepted decision-making process. *Source*: own depiction

Decision models in academic research are usually categorised into the following three types:

- *Descriptive Analysis:* Models that explain how decisions are made.
- *Normative (Predictive) Analysis:* Models that suggest how decisions *should* be made.
- *Predictive (Prescriptive) Analysis:* Models that assist decision-makers by employing normative frameworks with cognitive variables.

2.3 Decision-Making Methods

Decision-making is the process by which individuals or organisations choose the most appropriate option from several alternatives. This process involves many factors, including uncertainty, risk, values, and objectives. It is studied across various fields, including psychology, economics, business, engineering, and political science, with different models (Simon, 1979). Different disciplines and applications use different decision-making methods, often categorised as Simple Additive

Weighting, Ordered Weighted Averaging, the Analytic Hierarchy Process, fuzzy logic, artificial neural networks, and Bayes' Theorem (Erpul, 2019). Each method has its strengths and weaknesses. The suitability of a process depends on specific conditions, and there is no single "best" approach. Instead, evaluating the three most appropriate methods for the current context can help decision-makers identify potential changes in project value and develop aligned action plans. A comprehensive review of all these methods is beyond the scope of this chapter.

2.3.1 Rational Decision-Making Method

Here, the decision-maker rationally analyses all alternatives and their potential outcomes to select the option that will yield the highest utility. Nobel laureate Herbert A. Simon made this approach more realistic with the concept of "bounded rationality". According to Simon, decision-makers act with limited information, time, and cognitive capacity (Simon, 1979). For example, when a company plans to invest in three different real estate projects, it chooses the one that will provide the highest return by evaluating the growth potential and risk level of each.

2.3.2 Intuitive Decision-Making

In this approach, individuals make decisions based on their previous experiences and instincts rather than on conscious and systematic analysis. This approach is often preferred, especially in environments with high time pressure (Gigerenzer, 2007). For example, a project employee working in a purchasing unit may choose a suitable supplier by reviewing the supplier's past delivery performance. Such a decision is grounded in experience gained from similar past situations.

2.3.3 Multi-Criteria Decision-Making

The multi-criteria decision-making method is employed in situations where multiple criteria are considered. In this approach, decisions rely on several variables rather than just one. It is widely favoured, especially in fields such as engineering, supply chain management, and public administration.

2.3.4 Analytical Hierarchy Process (AHP)

This method, developed by Saaty, organises decision criteria into a hierarchy and assigns importance weights through pairwise comparisons (Saaty, 1980). For instance, when selecting a new campus location, a university can use the Analytic Hierarchy Process (AHP) to evaluate options based on criteria such as transportation access, cost, student attraction, and infrastructure, thereby identifying the most suitable choice.

2.3.5 Technique for Order Preference by Similarity to Ideal Solution (TOPSIS)

This approach enables the ranking of each alternative based on its proximity to an ideal solution. For instance, a municipality can determine the most appropriate alternative by evaluating various transportation projects according to criteria such as environmental impact, cost, and user satisfaction within the framework of the TOPSIS method (Technique for Order Preference by Similarity to Ideal Solution).

2.3.6 Probabilistic Methods and Decision Trees

A decision tree is a tool for visualising decision-making under uncertainty. It organises options and their possible outcomes into branches (Raiffa & Schlaifer, 1961). For instance, a pharmaceutical company might use a decision tree to evaluate potential results when deciding to invest in clinical trials for a new drug, incorporating the likelihoods of success and failure.

2.3.7 Game Theory

Game theory is an analytical framework that investigates decision-making strategies in scenarios involving multiple decision-makers (actors). It is extensively applied across disciplines such as economics, political science, and negotiation strategies (Von Neumann & Morgenstern, 1944). An illustrative example is the scenario where two competing companies plan to enter a market concurrently, which can be analysed through the concept of the Nash equilibrium. A Nash equilibrium describes a strategic situation in which no actor can unilaterally gain by changing his strategy if the other actor's strategy remains unchanged.

2.3.8 Decision-Making with Fuzzy Logic

Fuzzy logic, in contrast to classical logic, allows the incorporation of imprecise or uncertain information within the decision-making process (Zadeh, 1965). It emerges as an effective methodology, especially in domains where human judgement is essential. For example, a hotel enterprise can translate qualitative assertions, such as "cleanliness is good" or "location is very good," into numerical scores using a fuzzy logic approach to assess customer satisfaction.

2.4 Decision-Making in Real Estate Projects

A real estate developer creates a project and decision-tracking system that serves multiple purposes throughout the development process. To support multidimensional decision-making, the monitored variables are identified first. In this context, to develop a successful project that boosts brand value, yields expected profits, and ensures high customer satisfaction, the developer must carefully observe and assess these variables throughout the decision-making process. Since humans can make errors, this monitoring should be carried out and documented systematically (Fig. 2). For developers, a Decision Support System (DSS) primarily clarifies which data to collect within project management frameworks and which tools to use for processing this data. The initial step involves reviewing administrative records produced nationally, followed by the creation of a dataset of macroeconomic indicators. This dataset also incorporates market analysis results and data from similar sample projects whenever possible. However, past experiences of firms and individuals remain valuable. Because location is the most critical success factor in real

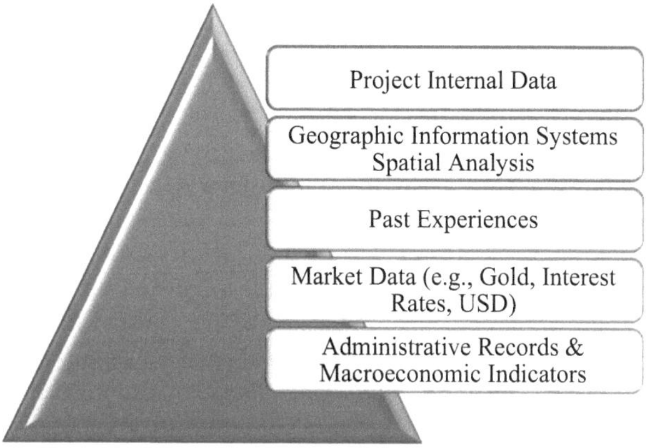

Fig. 2 General decision support system variables. Source: own depiction

Table 2 PMI project success factors

Is the final product good? 1. Zero-defect transition 2. Use with minimal defects 3. Optimal service and increased performance across the facility lifecycle	Did the project meet its delivery objectives? 1. Time 2. Budget 3. Production delay
Were stakeholders satisfied with the project? 1. Happy clients 2. Happy users 3. Happy subcontractors 4. Good community relations	Was the project management successful? 1. Solid, reliable records 2. Good contract management 3. Few changes 4. Few disputes 5. Smooth, clean, and orderly site 6. Predictability and control of cost, time, quality, and risk

Source: Williams (2016)

estate projects, Geographic Information Systems (GIS) and spatial analysis outputs are integrated into the process. The dataset is analysed using various risk management techniques to determine the impact values of identified risks. This analysis establishes the foundational structure for the DSS. When a DSS can generate at least three alternative options for each sub-discipline using appropriate data and methods, it qualifies as a knowledge-based decision support system.

Projects are carried out within a specific timeframe and budget, producing a targeted output. All projects have general performance indicators. Furthermore, the project success factors defined by PMI also hold a crucial role in the literature (Table 2). In project development, simply obtaining the product in any form is not regarded as sufficient. Besides the product, it is also essential that deviations from project objectives are minimal and that these objectives have been accurately defined and communicated.

The objectives and variables of each project differ. In the literature, the primary decision variables of projects are generally listed as cost, time, profit generation, and brand value protection. Decision support systems also facilitate the making of decisions that align with other project objectives. The impact of a one-unit change in the time variable on cost and quality can be measured with a well-structured system. Variables must be interrelated, the connections between them clearly defined, and expressed mathematically.

The PMI project success factors are used to identify essential variables for the decision support system (Williams, 2016). While a decision support system aims to maximise the value of the investment, it also considers other variables and endeavours to fulfil all relevant objectives. For a typical decision support system, the variables at each decision stage may include time, financial resources, quality, risk, and stakeholder satisfaction (Table 3). The variables within decision support systems are more numerous than those listed here. The target variables differ depending on each organisation and institution. The identified variables have been compiled from those generally regarded as important by various firms.

2.5 Analysis of Risks in Real Estate Projects

During the development phase of projects, additional studies are required to determine how identified risk variables will be considered and to measure their degrees of impact. Öztürk (2020) employed scenario analysis to assess the risks associated with a sample mixed-use project. When examining the specific outputs of the five scenarios generated as examples, a deviation of 36% was identified in the Net Present Value (NPV) calculation depending on the change in risk variables (Table 4).

Once risks are identified and analysed, four primary response strategies can be developed to address these risks. Avoidance is defined as the complete elimination

Table 3 General decision support system variables

Variables	Description
Time	This variable is the most crucial to watch in any project, as it directly influences success and costs. Both the sales price in the open market and a cost item can fluctuate over time. Therefore, it is essential to monitor what actions to take and when to implement them.
Money	This is one of the most important variables to monitor in projects. Both budgetary conditions and profit are monitored through this variable.
Quality	The products generated from the project should meet the expectations of all stakeholders. Merely accomplishing time and profit objectives is inadequate for ensuring financial sustainability.
Risk premium	This is the decision variable that supports risk management in the project. Whether the level of risk is tolerable must be monitored.
Stakeholder satisfaction	The satisfaction of all project stakeholders' expectations (e.g. timely payments, achieving the expected profit, maintaining brand value, and client satisfaction).

Source: own depiction

Table 4 The effects of base scenarios on NPV

Scenario	Description	Pessimistic NPV[a] (A)	Base NPV	Optimistic NPV (B)	Percentage Difference (%)
1	The most fundamental scenario model illustrates the change in project value resulting from changes in interest rates (±3%).	157	183.5	214	36
2	The most fundamental scenario model shows the change in project value when rental incomes vary by 5% from the expected rate over periods.	175	183.5	190	9
3	The most fundamental scenario model shows the change in project value when costs vary by 5% from the expected rate.	180	183.5	186	3
4	The most fundamental scenario model shows the change in project value when costs and rental incomes vary by 5% from the expected rate.	167	183.5	198	19
5	The most fundamental scenario model shows the change in project value based on the prediction that interest rates change (±1) while costs and rental incomes vary by 5% from the expected rate.	159	183.5	208	31

Source: own depiction
[a]The percentage difference between the pessimistic and optimistic values = (B/A*100–100)/100

of a risk's impacts. To mitigate risks, measures such as modifying the work, redefining the scope, or augmenting resources can be implemented to address these concerns. In transfer, another strategy aims to prevent a direct impact on the project plan by transferring the risk to another party. Transfer strategies include instruments such as insurance, guarantees, and collateral. The third strategy, mitigation, aims to minimise the potential impacts of a risk. Within this scope, action plans are prepared, and rapid response strategies are developed by creating "what-if" scenarios. The fourth and final strategy, acceptance, refers to the situation where all consequences that arise if the risk materialises are accepted, and no response strategy is developed. In risk response planning, an appropriate response strategy is selected for each risk (specifically those falling into red and yellow zones), and a project team member is assigned to monitor that risk. By choosing one of these approaches, a comprehensive risk response plan is created. For example, in their study, Fisher and Robson (2006) produced a sample table of risk responses while measuring the risk perceptions of office developers (Öztürk, 2020). Appropriate reactions to specific risks are also determined and implemented during the development stages (Table 5).

Table 5 Risk response examples

Risks	Avoidance	Mitigation	Transfer	Acceptance
Planning risk	Change of location choice Different land use	Site selection Design change	Insurance	Budgeting for risk
Procurement risk	Purchase of materials	Securing connections	Joint venture	
Sales risk	Establishing a cooperative	Running promotions	Agreements with banks	Acting according to the market
Interest rate risk	Using principal capital	Sourcing external debt	Joint venture	
Occupational accidents	Team building and strict monitoring for occupational safety	Creating a safe environment	Insurance and comprehensive coverage	
Legal risks	Full compliance with plans	Gathering information from relevant parties and providing information about the plan	Procuring insurance against legal risks	
Design risk	Plan modification	Market research	Flexible design Purchase guarantee	

Source: based on Fisher and Robson (2006)

2.6 Audit and Control

Monitoring fluctuating conditions and expectations in real estate projects influences the project's trajectory. A control mechanism is essential to remain adaptable throughout the project's progression. Control mechanisms act as an early warning system for decision-makers, offering a clear indication of potential risks and opportunities. The control parameters that need to be monitored at decision points during the project's ongoing phase are outlined under five headings: timeliness, cost variation, revenue variation, quality variation, and changes in risk (Table 6).

2.7 Decision-Making and Risk Studies in Real Estate Projects

The history of decision support systems and risk management research dates back a long time. Knight's (1921) survey is among the earliest studies to explore the concept of risk. Hertz (1964) concentrated on risk analysis related to capital investments, while Byrne and Cadman (1984) investigated risk, uncertainty, and decision support systems in real estate development. Wiegelmann (2012) classified feasibility studies in real estate development into six categories: market, location, project concept analysis, risk analysis, competitors, and profitability analysis (see Fig. 3; competition and profitability analysis are dropped in the chart). The risk component

Table 6 Monitoring methods for risk treatment variables

Variable	Description	Applicable method(s)
Timeliness	Conformance of tasks to the timeframes specified in the project plan	Instantaneous system entry of initiated, ongoing, and completed work.
Cost change	Monitoring changes in input costs	Monitoring and noting the status of contracts and suppliers
Revenue change	Monitoring changes in sales and other revenues	Monitoring price changes
Quality change	Monitoring of work performed and materials used	Conformity tests for incoming materials and verification of completed work
Changes in risks	The materialisation status of identified risks and the investigation of new risk situations	Monitoring changes in the probability and status of identified risks; examining the status of risks not included in the project.

Source: own depiction

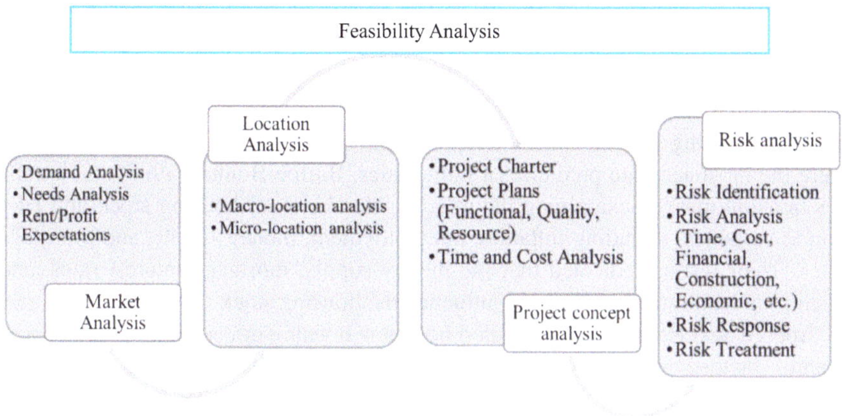

Fig. 3 Feasibility analysis in real estate development. *Source*: based on Wiegelmann (2012)

plays a crucial role in feasibility analysis, with particular emphasis on accurately identifying and analysing risks to produce a dependable feasibility report.

Naeem et al. (2023) thoroughly explored the digital transformation in real estate across four key themes: information and communication technologies (ICT), data collection technologies, data network tools, and digital decision support systems. ICT forms the backbone for data management and analysis, enhancing methods for planning and overseeing real estate projects. Data collection technologies facilitate decision-making by enabling the rapid and precise collection of large and diverse real estate data. Data network tools support the integration of information from multiple sources, making it possible to analyse complex datasets. Digital decision support systems derive valuable insights from this data, helping investors and developers make strategic choices related to risk assessment, valuation, and project execution. The study highlights that digitalisation drives a multi-faceted and comprehensive transformation in real estate development, opening up innovative opportunities within the sector.

Anelli and Tajani (2023) used a model applied to Rome, Italy, to show how spatial decision support systems can effectively assess risks in real estate redevelopment. By combining the Analytic Hierarchy Process (AHP) with Geographic Information Systems (GIS), they developed a "Basic Risk Index" (ISRR). The findings indicated that risky areas were mapped spatially, enabling decision-makers to make better-informed choices.

The objective of market research is to identify the optimal product at an appropriate price, establishing a balance between supply and demand. As is typical with economic challenges, a precise point cannot be determined. The market researcher collects data utilising numerous variables to identify the correct equilibrium. In supply and demand analyses, assuming linear functions, an attempt is made to ascertain the intersection point of these two functions. During the development phase, the quantities of supply and demand significantly influence the project's success at both microeconomic and macroeconomic levels. An increase in supply, while demand remains constant, results in a lower price (Novak, 1996).

Birgönül and Dikmen (1996) showed that Monte Carlo simulation can provide more precise estimates of project costs and durations in construction. Dua and Miller (1996) employed a Bayesian Vector Autoregression (B-VAR) approach to predict home sales across the US, analysing sales volume, prices, mortgage rates, income, building permits, and unemployment. They found that building permits were the most accurate predictor of home sales. Baffoe-Bonnie (1998) studied the US housing market, examining the relationships between housing stock and economic variables, including inflation, unemployment, money supply, and mortgage rates. Their results indicated that the money supply, mortgage interest rates, and unemployment rates significantly influence the housing stock.

Apergis and Rezitis (2003) studied how new housing prices relate to macroeconomic factors in Greece through an EC-VAR (Error Correction-Vector Autoregression) model. The findings indicate that housing prices respond to shifts in mortgage loan rates, inflation, and employment. Variance decomposition revealed that the mortgage (housing) loan rate is the most influential factor affecting housing price changes, with inflation and employment trailing behind. The influence of the money supply on housing prices, however, was deemed statistically insignificant.

Durkaya and Yamak (2004), in their study that examines the housing market from the demand perspective, developed housing demand equations using time series data from 1964 to 1997. They analysed the effects of variables such as income, overall price levels, real housing costs, population, and industrialisation on housing demand. The results indicate that factors like per capita income, real costs, population growth, migration, and urbanisation significantly influence housing demand. As income levels rise, the tendency for individuals to choose higher-quality housing increases. Therefore, including various economic, social, and cultural variables (e.g. income, income distribution, prices of own and substitute goods, population movements, age distribution, gender, marital status, education level, migration, and urbanisation) in analyses of housing demand enables more comprehensive and informed evaluations.

Leamer (2007) asserts that the housing sector assumes a pivotal role in most economic recessions within the United States. The research indicates that declines in housing investment frequently serve as precursors to economic downturns and typically precede recessions. The housing sector offers more robust signals in economic cycles compared to consumer expenditure and business investments. Stevenson (2007) concentrated on the short-term forecasting of housing supply in the Irish housing market. The study employed ARIMA (Auto-Regressive Integrated Moving Average), VAR, and OLS (Ordinary Least Squares) models, subsequently comparing their predictive performances. Variables such as housing prices, construction permits, interest rates, and economic growth were analysed as potential determinants influencing housing supply.

Demir and Bostancı (2010) used an integrated approach combining discounted cash flow (DCF), Monte Carlo Simulation (MCS), and sensitivity analysis to identify risk factors in housing development projects. They applied two scenario-based cash flow models to pinpoint key variables for risk management and decision support. In a case study of a real estate project in Istanbul, they found that cash flows were most sensitive to the sales price. The study also highlighted the importance of monitoring changes in construction costs, occupancy rates, and land costs, and suggested that investors should carefully track regional unit sales values. The analysis showed that sales prices influence the project's internal rate of return (IRR) and present value by 61–65% under normal conditions, and by 29–36% during economic crises.

In Wiegelmann's (2012) study, the project objectives were categorised under five headings: to attain objectives; to comprehend the risks undertaken to achieve objectives and the extent of associated risk; to identify opportunities and threats about risks in the pursuit of objectives; to establish the firm's risk terminology and perception; and to incorporate risk management as an integral component of the system.

Hepşen and Aşıcı (2013) explored the link between housing prices, the current account deficit, national income, and inflation in Türkiye, finding a positive correlation between the current account deficit and changes in housing prices. Özpolat's (2014) study focuses on macroeconomic factors influencing housing demand in Türkiye. Using quarterly data, the analysis examined the relationships between building use permits (housing supply), GDP, stock market index, inflation, interest rate, and money supply. Results indicated a significant positive relationship between real GDP and housing demand. Additionally, the money supply positively influenced demand, whereas higher interest rates had a negative effect. These findings illustrate how housing demand is driven by economic growth and monetary policies.

Aydoğan and Köksal (2014) examined the risks faced by firms developing international projects on a country-specific basis using a meta-analysis[1] method. According to the findings, political stability, the enforceability of laws, and exchange rate fluctuations stood out as the most decisive among the 18 analysed risk types. In a survey in the Netherlands, Gehner et al. (2006) asked participants to rank the most important risks and to explain why they prioritised these risks. Risk categories were created by breaking down high-level risks into sub-components. As a result of the study, planning errors, delays, marketing, and technical risks were identified as the most critical risk groups (Table 7).

[1] https://himmelfarb.gwu.edu/tutorials/studydesign101/metaanalyses.html

The study by D'Alpaos and Canesi (2014) presents a new valuation model for assessing uncertainties and risks in real estate investments during periods of global economic crisis. The study emphasises that the uncertainties faced by investors in their decision-making processes can lead to the postponement or cancellation of investments. In particular, the Caserma Garibaldi project in Milan was selected as a case study, and quantitative algorithms were developed to evaluate economic risks. These algorithms enable investors to tailor their decisions to various risk tolerances and preferences. The study emphasises the importance of uncertainty and risk analysis in real estate investments, as well as the influence of these analyses on investment decisions (Table 8).

The study concluded that the results are useful for decision-making processes. Evaluation criteria like market impact and value sharing for each investment can serve as specific risk indicators. Depending on risk variable values, investment plan adjustments might be needed. When a comprehensive framework for defining risk and uncertainty is introduced, analytical tools are used more effectively by investors and practitioners (D'Alpaos & Canesi, 2014). Political instability and weak laws are significant risk factors. This highlights that political stability and a strong legal system in a country lower its risk rating (Table 9).

The concept of Value at Risk (VaR) is integral to contemporary financial risk management practices. VaR methodologies are extensively employed by financial

Table 7 Important risk classifications and weights

Risk	Response	(%)	Risk	Response	(%)
Risks of the planning approach	15	100	Archaeological excavation	3	20
Delay in the development process	15	100	Land pollution	3	20
Marketing risks	15	100	Protected flora and fauna	2	13
Technical / construction risks	15	100	Liability risks	2	13
Legal/judicial risks	12	80	Financing risks	2	13
Abandonment risks	10	67	Financial risks	2	13
Objections to building plans	8	53	Monumental building risks	1	7
Tender—construction costs	5	33	Vacancy	1	7
Changes in politics	4	27	Longer time to lease/sell	1	7
Legislative changes	4	27	Financial risks	2	13
Design flaws	4	27	Monumental building risks	1	7
Acquisition-purchase risks	4	27	Vacancy	1	7
Interest rate risk	4	27	Longer time to lease/sell	1	7
Opposition from the administrative machinery	3	20	Lease/sale price risks	1	7
Delay in construction time	3	20	Bankruptcy of consultants/contractors	1	7
Building readiness risks	3	20	Construction defects	1	7

Source: Gehner et al. (2006)

Table 8 Economic risk classification

Market risks	Capital Market Risk (CMR)	MCR/ACR	
	Valuation Risk (VR)	NBD/AP	
	Market Growth Rate Risk (MGRr)	(UIRR-ACR)/MGR	This risk measure is used to compare the value of the asset. It examines the relationship between the general market growth rate and the asset's growth rate.
Real estate operational risks	Yield risk (Ya)	OOR/TOE	
	Developmental risk (DR)	(NOI-ACR)/CC2	
	Leasing risk (LR)	(LU1y/MA1y)/(BV/MV)	
	Lease / head rent risk (LHR)	GRI/MR	
	Leverage risk (LVR)	UIRR/KD	
	Tax risk (TR)		Tax risk is the possibility of facing a different tax liability than originally anticipated, due to a specific action or inaction.
	CC: Construction/renovation cost LU1y: Leased square meters representation BV: Vacancy rate OG: Market-specific vacancy GRI: Gross rental income MR: Market average rent KD: Cost of debt UIRR: Unlevered internal rate of return MCR: Mean market capitalisation rate	ACR: Asset's capitalisation rate NPV: Net present value AP: Acquisition/construction cost MGR: Market growth rate OOR: Sum of operating and other revenues TOE: Total operating expenses NOI: Net operating income MA1y: Market absorption by year	

Source: D'Alpaos and Canesi (2014)

institutions to ensure the maintenance of capital at prudent levels and to quantify the risk associated with assets. VaR is a metric that estimates the maximum potential loss that could occur under typical market conditions, at a designated confidence level, over a specified time horizon. In essence, assuming "normal" market conditions, it offers risk managers an informed projection of potential losses (Grotke, 2010).

Economic risks play a crucial role in real estate development, directly impacting project revenue. Khumpaisal (2015) surveyed 210 experts and assessed economic

Table 9 Country risk factors and their ratings

Risk factors	Rating
Political stability	17
Laws and regulations	17
Exchange rate risk	13
Cultural differences	13
Inflation	10
Expropriation	8
Tax discrimination	7
Language barrier	7
Bribery and corruption in the host country	7
Force majeure	6
Social conflicts	6
GDP	6
Restrictions on profit transfer	5
Entry restrictions	5
Socio-economic stability	5
Interest rate	5
Hostilities with neighbouring countries	3
Bureaucracy	2

Source: Aydoğan and Köksal (2014)

risks and their impact values using factor analysis (Exploratory Factor Analysis[2]—EFA) (Table 10). The study revealed that practitioners worry about economic risks, which they link to fluctuations in material prices, exchange rates, and the absence of economic and political stability.

3 Application of Risk Analysis in Real Estate Projects

3.1 Data Source and Survey Preparation

In this section, a field analysis is presented that evaluates how macroeconomic variables influence real estate projects. Members or affiliates of 121 companies of the Turkish Contractors Association (TCA) were surveyed electronically. Altogether, members of 34 large companies completed the survey. No sampling method was employed; instead, the aim was to reach the entire population, resulting in a response rate of 30%. The surveys were filled out by real estate specialists within the firms, using a Likert scale and open-ended questions. The main goal was to assess risk perceptions and gather data for calculating risk weightings.

[2] Used to reduce the number of variables. A statistical method that serves to find a smaller number of related variables from a larger set of variables.

Table 10 Economic risks and valuation methods

Economic risk	Valuation methods (outcome and probability)
Brand recognition	The developer's reputation during the development phase.
Supply and demand	The degree of competitiveness of similar property types in the study area
Supply and demand	The degree of misestimation of supply and demand for similar real estate
Market liquidity	The sales volume of the same type of real estate in the local market
Market liquidity	The sales prices of the same type of real estate in the local market
Customer purchasing power	The customer's ability to repay the mortgage
Marketing strategy	The impact of project sales volume and the resulting prices
Availability of resources and project funds	The amount of funds injected into the project and the availability of funds from project investors
Interest rate	Loan interest rates
Cash flow liquidity	The ability to pay the contract price to subcontractors
Return on investment	Internal rate of return (IRR) and capitalisation rate
Project depreciation	The depreciation rate of tangible fixed assets (straight-line method)
Construction material price changes	Consumer price index (for construction materials)

Source: Khumpaisal (2015)

3.2 Methods Used in Analysis of Results

Initially, participant responses were analysed and interpreted. For multiple-choice questions, the Weighted Average Rating (WAR) method, a widely used and reliable technique, was applied. Generally, the WAR is calculated as follows (Kumar & Thakur, 2018):

$$WAR \approx \frac{v}{v+m}^{*} R + \frac{m}{v+m}^{*} C \tag{1}$$

where R denotes the average score of the item, v is the total votes for the item, m is the minimum vote threshold, and C is the overall average score of all items in the system.

For example, if a question gets 30 votes with an average score of 4.5, and the overall average score for all questions (C) is 3.8, with a minimum vote count (m) set at 50, the WAR method calculates a value of 4.06. This shows that, despite the question's high, simple average, the WAR value offers a more balanced and fair assessment. The benefits of the WAR method include: (i) providing a fairer evaluation by rewarding popular items while preventing less-voted items from being overly ranked, (ii) being resistant to manipulation, and (iii) ensuring reliability in dynamic systems.

In the second stage of the study, the Chi-squared (χ^2) method was employed to assess whether a significant relationship exists between the responses. For this Chi-square analysis, hypotheses are initially formulated:

H_0: The two variables are independent of each other.
H_1: The two variables are dependent on each other.

A cross-tabulation (contingency table) is constructed for the questions whose relationship is to be tested. The test statistic is calculated by squaring the differences between each cell's observed value (O_{ij}) and the expected frequency (E_{ij}). If this calculated value exceeds the table's critical value, the null hypothesis (H_0) is rejected. The detailed formula for computing the test statistic is provided in Eq. (2).

$$\chi_0^2 = \sum_{j=1}^{c}\sum_{i=1}^{r}\frac{\left(O_{ij} - E_{ij}\right)^2}{E_{ij}} \tag{2}$$

$$\chi_0^2 \geq \chi_{tab}^2$$

In the third stage of the study, responses to general expectations and open-ended questions were analysed, and efforts were made to identify sector-specific needs in risk management. The expectations of firms, especially from the public sector, were categorised using a response grouping method.

3.3 Evaluation of Survey Results

The survey results indicate an average discrepancy of 8 years between the companies' years of establishment and their years of entry into the real estate sector. It was noted that companies whose primary business is not real estate have also ventured into the construction sector, motivated by the profits generated. Generally, the participating firms undertake either residential (3.58/5) or mixed-use (2.36/5) projects. The headquarters of these companies are predominantly situated in major cities of Türkiye, such as Istanbul, Izmir, and Ankara. An examination of their main fields of activity reveals a particular concentration in superstructure projects. In recent years, an increasing demand for luxury housing and shelter-oriented accommodations for refugees have been identified, encouraging firms to invest in these sectors.

Risks are categorised into two main groups: company-level and project-specific. Based on survey results, the four most critical risk factors at the company level are political instability, income reduction, financing risk, and currency (foreign exchange) risk (Table 11).

Based on the survey findings, project-level risks—such as delays in the development process, land selection, rental and sales uncertainties, and postponements in the construction schedule—constitute the most significant risk factors. Land represents a vital input for real estate development projects, as it encompasses additional

Table 11 Company-level risks and their impact degrees in real estate development processes

Company-level risks	Per cent (%)
Political instability	3.87
Revenue changes	3.65
Financing risks	3.57
Exchange rate risk	3.48
Construction cost changes	3.46
Sales management	3.44
Legislative changes	3.42
Advertising and promotions	3.41
Legal/judicial risk	3.36
Interest rate risk	3.33
Procurement risks	2.96
Vacancy rates	2.79
Change in expectations	2.79
Increase in substitute products	2.76
Other	2.57
Difficulties in labour and material supply	2.54
Changes in brand value	2.4
Unemployment	2.04

Source: own depiction

factors including frontage, proximity to the city centre, development rights, and environmental considerations (Table 12).

According to the survey results, more than half of the firms reported that they lack a direct risk management system, whereas 6% indicated that their efforts in this regard are ongoing. TürkiyeApproximately 40% of the participating firms have implemented risk management systems at various levels. Due to the nature of the real estate sector, risk management practices exhibit considerable variability among different firms. However, the existence of a risk management system does not necessarily imply its integration across all processes and sub-processes, nor its utilisation at a strategic level. In practical terms, risk management is often regarded as a secondary concern by some firms, owing to factors such as a demanding work pace, time constraints, and limited resources. It is frequently addressed solely as a mandatory requirement in specific circumstances, such as during tender submissions or management presentations (Table 13).

There are many ways to analyse risk. However, the most effective and simplest method is generally preferred. Risk analysis methods used by real estate companies include intuition/experience and scenario analysis. Checklists, sensitivity analysis, and external experts are also valuable tools for risk analysis (Table 14).

Risk levels faced by firms fluctuate over time. The risk level changes based on the status of non-systematic (not project-specific) and systematic (project-specific) risk variables. Half of the surveyed firms reported that their risk levels are increasing. This can be attributed to factors such as exchange rate volatility, geopolitical

Table 12 Project-level risks and their impact degrees in real estate development processes

Project-level risks	Per cent (%)
Location (land) selection	4.07
Developmental delay	3.88
Delay in construction time	3.63
Lease/sale risks	3.63
Planning-related risks	3.54
Objections to building plans	3.28
Design flaws	3.18
Technical/construction risks	3.14
Occupational accidents	3.04
Subcontractor risks	2.96
Construction defects	2.93
Archaeological excavation	2.81
Others	2.58
Vacancy risks	2.50
Formation of land pollution	2.38

Source: own depiction

Table 13 Reasons for risk management in companies

Reasons for risk management	(%)
Top management request	62.50
Controlling/preventing potential losses	50.00
Following sectoral trends	50.00
Audit requirements	50.00
Integrated decision making	50.00
Following customer needs/changes	37.50
Capital budgeting	31.25
Gaining a competitive advantage	25.00
Countermeasures against legal regulations	12.50
Others	6.25

Source: own depiction

risks, and political instability. Only 6% of the firms believe that their risk levels are decreasing (Table 15).

56% of the firms believe that the risk level is changing, and they cite economic unpredictability, market fluctuations, political turbulence, and currency fluctuations as the most significant reasons for this change. Firms are not comfortable with external factors affecting their projects when calculating their risks (Table 16).

Firms often need to modify their plans after a project has begun. These adjustments are sometimes driven by necessity and other times by profit motives. Approximately 75% of all companies must modify their plans once the project is

Table 14 Risk management methods in companies

Risk management implementation tools	(%)
Intuition/experience	67.74
Scenario analysis	48.39
Checklist	45.16
Sensitivity analysis	35.48
External expert	32.26
Total value at risk	22.58
Possible methods	22.58
Qualitative description	16.13
Risk premium	16.13
Decision tree	12.90
Group techniques (e.g. delphi)	0.00

Source: own depiction

Table 15 Risk level faced by companies

Company risk level status	(%)
Increasing	50.00
Decreasing	21.88
Not changing	21.88
Becoming uncertain	6.25

Source: own depiction

Table 16 Reasons for differentiation of companies' risk levels over time

Reasons for risk level differentiation	(%)
Economic unpredictability	72.41
Market changes	68.97
Political turbulence	58.62
Currency fluctuations	58.62
Interest rate changes	48.28
External influences	27.59
Lack of information	17.24
Lack of project management	13.79
Data pollution	10.34
Terrorism	10.34
Lack of risk management	6.90

Source: own depiction

underway. Changes are more frequently prompted by economic crises, financing issues, and sales pressures than by legal regulations, as shown in Table 17.

Companies are modifying their real estate strategies in response to plan changes, such as transforming properties into high-rise buildings, broadening credit options, and delaying projects. A major concern is deciding who will oversee risk management. The survey indicates that senior executives and the board of directors mostly assign this task to themselves (Table 18).

Table 17 Reasons for plan changes in the last 10 years

Reasons for risk plan changes	Per cent (%)
Economic crises	46.43
Economic reasons	46.43
Sales statistics	42.86
Legal regulations	35.71
Regional impacts	32.14
Environmental impacts	28.57
Political changes	25.00
Macroeconomic changes	17.86
Material-labor, etc. resources	10.71
Other	10.71

Source: own depiction

Table 18 Risk owners in businesses

Units responsible for risk management	(%)
Board of directors	65.63
Chief executive officer	62.50
Project manager	34.38
Finance manager	15.63
CFO	12.50
Board of auditors	6.25
Chief risk officer (CRO)	3.13
Inspection board	3.13
Risk management committee	0.00
Other (please specify)	0.00

Source: own depiction

68.77% of companies do not calculate a risk premium. They determine their project costs and expected profits, accepting potential losses from risks as lower profits (Table 19)

Companies recognise that risk is not merely a ratio but an essential aspect of project management. Identifying and ranking risks, followed by risk valuation and analysis, and being prepared for potential risks, are all crucial elements of risk management. The approaches companies take to risk management vary (Table 20).

In an economy, demand typically generates supply and supply can trigger demand. For a real estate developer, demand or estimated transaction volume is crucial when developing a project. When assessing project risk, understanding how macroeconomic indicators influence the project's net present value becomes clearer. Macro data are used to build risk and decision support systems (see Table 21). The outcomes align with academic expectations and are consistent overall.

A DSS is crucial for making informed decisions, as it helps to evaluate options and reduce human mistakes. The survey indicates that 73% of companies do not use a DSS and mostly depend on basic desktop programmes. Therefore, it is recommended that firms implement IT systems to enhance their integrated decision-making processes (Table 22).

Table 19 Risk management characteristics

Management preferences	Strongly disagree	Disagree	Agree	Strongly agree	WAR
Risk management should be prioritised for the company to achieve its goals	9.38	6.25	46.88	37.50	3.13
Risks must be taken to achieve goals	6.25	18.75	59.38	15.63	2.84
It should be known how much risk is taken to achieve goals	3.13	6.25	56.25	34.38	3.22
In relation to risk, opportunities and threats to achieve goals should be examined	0.00	12.50	62.50	25.00	3.13
A risk terminology and perception should be established in the company	0.00	6.25	65.63	28.13	3.22
Risk management should be conducted and addressed as an integrated part of a system	3.13	6.25	56.25	34.38	3.22

Source: own depiction

Table 20 Characteristics of risk studies

Characteristics	Strongly disagree (%)	Disagree (%)	Agree (%)	Strongly agree (%)	WAR
The identification, analysis, and securing of risks with a specific risk assessment approach in your company	6.25	3.13	65.63	25.00	3.09
A risk management plan should be prepared	3.13	9.38	65.63	21.88	3.06
Only the main risks should be identified in the company	9.38	40.63	40.63	9.38	2.5
The probabilities of risk occurrence should be calculated	3.13	9.38	65.63	21.88	3.06
The impact degrees of risks should be calculated	3.13	6.25	68.75	21.88	3.09

Source: own depiction

In the survey conducted among firms, the perspectives of experts in developer roles were solicited through open-ended questions (Table 23). These insights may serve as valuable inputs, particularly in the formulation of real estate policies (Öztürk et al., 2016). In the survey, sector evaluations were obtained via a total of nine open-ended questions. The target audience was identified not only by quantitative measures, but also by business development directors and real estate developers from large-scale enterprises. Participants were initially queried regarding the prospects of the construction sector. The responses that were received suggest that the construction and real estate industries function as the locomotive of the Turkish economy, that quality should be emphasised and that firms are experiencing sales pressures (Table 23).

Evaluations of Turkish entrepreneurs' activities abroad show that, although there is substantial effort in the sector contributing to the country's economy, support is

Table 21 Risk Decision Support System (DSS) macro datasets

	(%)
Demand (housing sales)	81.25
Interest rates	75.00
Construction costs	71.88
Inflation	62.50
Barter (exchange)	59.38
Economic confidence	59.38
Supply (building permits)	56.25
Construction sector confidence index	50.00
Market vacancy rate	46.88
Income	46.88
Rental rates	40.63
Sales to foreigners	40.63
Population (migration)	37.50
Birth rates	31.25
Number of marriages	28.13
Unemployment	15.63
Industrial production	15.63
Number of arriving tourists	12.50
Other (please specify)	9.38
Gold prices	6.25
Current account deficit	6.25
Automobile sales	3.13
Imports/exports	3.13
Foreign debt	0.00

Source: own depiction

Table 22 Risk management—IT support

	(%)
We use a system integrated with the general IT infrastructure.	10.00
We utilise a standalone system that can be seamlessly integrated with our general IT infrastructure.	10.00
We use standard desktop software (MS project, Visio, excel, etc.).	50.00
We do not use any applications.	30.00

Source: own depiction

also necessary for managing exchange rate fluctuations, government assistance, and access to loans. The key takeaway is that firms are primarily expanding abroad to mitigate risks (Table 24).

General evaluations of the prospects of the real estate sector indicate that Türkiye possesses considerable real estate potential for both domestic and international investors. This is attributed to factors such as its young population, the necessity for housing renewal owing to its location in an earthquake-prone zone, and its strategic geographical position. In conjunction with shifting global balances and domestic

Table 23 Thoughts on the future of the construction sector in Türkiye

Positive	Negative
• As it is a locomotive sector, it should always be given momentum and supported. • Current population increases and a dense young population drive its rapid growth. • Excessive growth slows over the long term and stabilises at a certain point, settling into a standard. There will be no significant decline. • Quality is improving. • It is a very important, strategic sector and should continue to grow. • It will continue to develop depending on government policies. • It is a very important, strategic sector and should continue to grow.	• There is an excessive housing supply; a mechanism should control this. • The outlook is negative owing to its reliance on the economy and the prevailing economic uncertainty. • More qualified labour and higher quality workmanship are required. • There is a lack of coordination. Competition is lowering profitability. Interest rates are high. Construction costs are rising continuously while purchasing power is declining. • The state still does not provide adequate support for overseas construction services. • There are planning deficiencies. • It must be ensured that it is carried out by competent individuals with effective supervision. • There are uncertainties in zoning and licensing matters. • The sector is very active, but firms that are not from the construction industry are entering the sector solely to offset VAT liabilities.

Source: own depiction

Table 24 Opinions of Turkish entrepreneurs on international contracting and project development activities

Positive	Negative
• Firms are very successful in their overseas projects. With its Turkish engineering strength and sectoral experience, the company is capable of developing projects worldwide. • They generate an important external resource. They contribute to the Turkish economy. • Türkiye ranks second on the ENR (engineering news-record) 225 list; this indicator shows that work abroad is progressing well. • They continue on their path in a competitive position. • Firms are diversifying their risks by expanding abroad. • Firms are professionalising and gaining prestige through their international work. • They are undertaking major projects, especially in Russia. • Public projects realised in recent years have encouraged firms to undertake international work and have increased their know-how levels.	• As domestic demand is insufficient, firms are turning to overseas projects. • Like other countries, Türkiye should also provide support to its firms. • Other countries, especially Western ones, provide data and intelligence support to their firms. • Double taxation, letter of guarantee costs, the inadequacy of Turkish banks' guarantees on international platforms, exchange rate fluctuations, and legislation of countries where business is conducted pose serious problems. • There is a need for engineering, labour, tax, and political support. • Firms should be directed towards larger, more profitable construction jobs.

Source: own depiction

political stability, the real estate sector continues to develop and maintain its presence. Its position at the heart of international transit routes, including the Silk Road and energy corridors, has historically rendered Türkiye an important centre for investment and attraction. Consequently, real estate projects that are unrestricted and sell regardless of their construction, as observed in the past, are no longer successful (Table 25).

There is a necessity for projects that are meticulously planned on an appropriate scale to effectively address specific deficiencies within a region, supported by comprehensive market analysis, alternative financing options, and investment funds. Recognising uncertainties and adapting to evolving conditions are regarded as essential for achieving success. In particular, in real estate endeavours in Istanbul, approximately 30% of sales and marketing strategies are tailored for a foreign clientele. Recent terrorist incidents have undermined the previously accelerating momentum in this sector. It is well understood that Türkiye possesses considerable potential; however, this potential can only be standard if stability and a climate of

Table 25 Thoughts on the future of the real estate sector in Türkiye

Positive	Negative
• Real estate is always and everywhere the most valuable investment; land is very valuable in Türkiye's geography. • The real estate sector is expected to remain dynamic in the future due to reasons such as the necessity of urban transformation, the continuation of population growth, and the increasing rate of standardization. • The diversification, proliferation, and increased application of real estate-backed securities, thereby strengthening the sector's relationship with the financial industry, and the development of sustainable alternative financing methods are also among the expectations. • It will continue to be important due to urban transformation, renewal, and other reasons. • Demand for new housing will increase in parallel with population growth, the decrease in the number of nuclear family members, and the rise of individualism. • We can achieve great gains by attracting the interest and investment of our entire near geography.	• As costs rise and revenues fall, the continuation of poor-quality construction will not cease. • While land values continue to rise, a decrease is expected in developer profit—One of the components that make up the total value—Due to increasing competition and supply/demand imbalance. • Attention must be paid to supply-demand ratios. • Uncertainties are rapidly increasing. • While population growth increases the need for infrastructure investments and housing, urban transformation practices also require new investments. However, the shortcomings in the tendering system are leading to a decline in the number of specialist "construction" companies and an increase in the number of non-specialist companies carrying out collective work. The sector will continue to develop, but its sensitivity to international economic fluctuations will remain. • The production of low-quality housing continues. • There are seven million poor-quality buildings that must be demolished and rebuilt. • A serious contraction has occurred in housing and office purchases due to the shrinking of industry and production. Prices are not at a level that salaried people can afford. • Political predictability should be increased, and the legal system should be brought to a good level.

Source: own depiction

trust, fundamental to foreign investment, are restored (Öztürk et al., 2016; Tanrıvermiş, 2019).

In evaluations concerning the final opinions of participants and stakeholders acting collaboratively, the reduction of uncertainties, along with the establishment of effective databases and systems, emerges as one of the primary expectations of the companies. Although there is a certain level of awareness regarding risk management within these firms, the absence of necessary legal infrastructure, data access, and appropriate toolsets presents a significant obstacle to the effective implementation of this process across all projects. The key recommendations provided by the participants for the progress of risk management and decision support systems within the construction and real estate sectors are summarised below:

1. The arbitrary practices of public institutions cause serious financial losses for firms.
2. It is essential to disseminate professional software, establish units dedicated to quality management and risk analysis, and standardise certification procedures.
3. Under the "risk" heading in every project, a systematic analysis must be conducted, risk lists created, and probability-based evaluations performed.
4. Companies ought to incorporate risk management into their internal procedures.
5. In Türkiye, the roles and responsibilities of contractors and stakeholders of construction and real estate are not only intertwined, but they are also not clearly defined. To resolve this issue, collaboration must be fostered among universities, the industry, governmental agencies, and the corporate sector.

Success is assured when projects are developed that can appeal to all segments of society, designed to consider the history, culture, and natural resources, alongside the needs and habits of the international customer profile. In assessments concerning the responsibilities of stakeholders in establishing risk management and decision support systems for the construction and real estate sectors, the development of a database for analysis and forecasting studies emerges as the most significant requirement. Non-governmental organisations (NGOs) and public entities have expectations regarding legal regulations, transparency, and clarity to enable more secure actions and informed future planning (Table 26).

When analysing survey results for statistical testing, both parametric and non-parametric methods are used. Parametric tests typically assume that the data are at the interval or ratio level, follow a normal distribution, and have equal group variances (Apaydın et al., 2005). Given the sample size and data distribution in this section, non-parametric tests were deemed appropriate for examining relationships between variables. Therefore, the dataset was tested using the Chi-Square test to assess whether significant differences existed between categorical variables. The survey's categorical questions were analysed with Chi-square tests to identify any significant relationships. Results indicated a significant association between the implementation of risk management and the presence of a decision support system in firms. The Pearson Chi-Square p-value was less than 0.05 (Table 27). This outcome aligns with academic expectations, implying that firms employing risk

Table 26 Tasks falling to stakeholders

Public	• Tax incentives should be provided to support the transition to implementation, along with public activities aimed at raising awareness. • Bureaucracy should be reduced and expedited. • Regions with ready infrastructure should be created to prevent unplanned urbanisation. Proper zoning plans should be made. • The legal system and bureaucracy must be made service-oriented. • Stability must be achieved with a clear, open, and finalised planning logic from the highest to the lowest scale plan, within a structure where bureaucratic procedures are fast, equal, and fair for everyone. • The public sector should create legislation and improve its implementation. • The markets must be kept in balance. • The public sector should conduct planning and provide direction to the private sector. • The institutionalisation of the sector should be encouraged, and by ensuring the preparation and public disclosure of sectoral data, regulations that promote and regulate the sector should be made. • There is a need for improvement in data generation, transparency, and clarity. • The regulatory clutter must be removed.
Contractors association	• It should protect the interests of companies more. • It should contribute by organising training sessions. • It should contribute to matters of state support and zoning. • Companies should be informed about the benefits of their processes during the bidding stages and of risk analysis. • It should bring solutions to the sector's problems and support its institutionalisation. • It should take the lead in system establishment. • It should gather all contractors under its umbrella. It should establish professional criteria. • Efficient systems should be established through the work it will conduct with its members. • Reasonable demands should be made of the public sector. • A database for analysis and forecasting studies should be created.
Real estate plantform	• It should make active contributions. • It should raise awareness among its members. • It should organise training and pave the way for its members to receive services on advantageous terms. • The formation of cartels should be prevented. • Studies indicating the importance of risk management should be conducted. • It should bring solutions to the sector's problems and support its institutionalisation. • Efficient systems should be established through the work it will conduct with its members. • A database for analysis and forecasting studies should be created.

(continued)

Table 26 (continued)

Developer association	• Awareness-raising activities should be carried out. • It should organise training and pave the way for its members to receive services on advantageous terms. • It should provide statistics. • Studies indicating the importance of risk management should be conducted. • It should bring solutions to the sector's problems and support its institutionalisation. • Standards, technical and ethical rules should be established. • It should contribute to the formation of efficient systems through its work with its members. • A database for analysis and forecasting studies should be created.
Other	• The most important issue is financing, and here, funds and different financing models should be created for investors. • All NGOs should work in coordination.

Source: own depiction

Table 27 Chi-Square (χ^2) test result (relationship between risk management and decision support systems)

		Presence of a decision support system for risk management in the company			
		Yes	No	In Progress	Total
Is there a risk management system used/adopted in your company?	***Yes***	6	6	1	13
	No	0	14	1	15
	In Progress	0	2	0	2
Total		**6**	**22**	**2**	**30**
Chi-Square test					
	Value		**Df**	**Likelihood ratio**	
Pearson Chi-Square	10,322		4	0.035	
Possibility	12,758		4	0.013	
Linear relationship	4421		1	0.035	
N of valid sases	30				

Source: own depiction

management methods tend to require a decision support system. In contrast, those who do not practice risk management are less likely to need one.

If firms calculate a risk premium, one can speak of a decision-making mechanism within the firm. According to the Chi-Square test results, a significant relationship was found between risk premium calculation and decision support systems. According to the survey results, if a risk premium is not calculated in a firm, it becomes meaningless to speak of a decision support system (Table 28).

Table 28 Chi-Square (χ^2) test result (relationship between risk premium and decision support systems)

		Presence of a decision support system for risk management in the company			Total
		Yes	No	In progress	
Is there a risk premium calculated in your company?	***Yes***	4	4	0	8
	No	2	18	2	22
Total		**6**	**22**	**2**	**30**
Chi-Square test					
		Value	**Df**	**Likelihood ratio**	
Pearson Chi-Square		6446	2	0.040	
Possibility		6295	2	0.043	
Linear relationship		5696	1	0.017	
N of valid cases		30			

Source: Own Depiction

4 General Evaluation and Conclusion

The processes of real estate investment and project development encompass numerous risks, and the origins of these risks are continually diversifying in response to evolving environmental conditions. Enterprises must formulate more rational projects by considering the increasing risks, deriving lessons from experience, and recognising the inherent existence of risk. To facilitate comprehensive analyses in real estate development decisions, an extensive database containing all sectoral data is essential. The fundamental questions in project development are "what should be done" and "when should it be done". Consequently, sales data must be thoroughly analysed, and the associated risk factors identified. From a risk management and decision support systems perspective, calculating risk perception and weightings is of paramount importance. In this context, the relationship between real estate risks and decision support systems was examined through a risk perception survey administered to firms. The results indicate that, although location selection is the most significant source of risk, the demand for decision support systems escalates as risk perception increases.

However important the project's endogenous risks may be, measuring and monitoring country-specific realities and systematic risks will be vital. The project's start time must be carefully determined through the use of real options, scenario analysis, and simulation methods during its development. The most critical aspect of risk management is not the risk's impact value but rather the awareness that the risk exists and having the appropriate methods ready for its analysis. Monitoring real estate values, performing mass appraisals using machine learning, and continuously tracking rental and sales prices help to reduce sales price risk. Real estate development activities are not solely aimed at generating profit or returns. When converting a finite resource, such as land, into real estate, social, environmental, and future-oriented risks must be considered alongside economic risks. The present value of a project isn't limited to the benefits during its economic life. In real estate development, economic, financial, environmental, and social sustainability are fundamental to a project's success. In this context, sustainability analysis is a crucial part of the project lifecycle and closely linked to risk management.

The study's findings underscore the necessity for qualified human capital to analyse risk factors, develop management techniques, and incorporate these into decision-making processes. It is evident that in dynamic countries where macroeconomic variables, property and development rights, as well as environmental and social conditions are rapidly evolving, the integration of risk analysis and management models into decision-making mechanisms is of paramount importance. Within this context, it becomes apparent that topics such as land acquisition, project development, design, contractual agreements, construction, and operational phases, along with the assessment and management of risks in real estate development projects, will occupy a significant position within real estate development research. Furthermore, national, regional, and local studies in this domain should be regarded as essential and prioritised. In conclusion, it is imperative for all public and private sector entities engaged in real estate project development and execution to perform risk analyses, develop Decision Support Systems (DSS), and recognise that these activities should constitute key components of their "business development departments." Making decisions regarding project execution without adequate analysis constitutes a substantial deficiency that may hinder success. Consequently, it is critically important that these activities are executed professionally, and that sector-specific expertise is prioritised within organisations. In this framework, employing more graduates university programmes specialising in real estate development and management will contribute to the professionalisation of real estate activities. This, in turn, will enhance the infrastructure necessary for making informed project development and investment decisions, thereby reducing the likelihood of flawed investments.

References

Anelli, D., & Tajani, F. (2023). Spatial decision support systems for effective ex-ante risk evaluation: An innovative model for improving the real estate redevelopment processes. Land Use Policy. https://doi.org/10.1016/j.landusepol.2023.106595

Apaydın, A., Kutsal, A., & Atakan, C. (2005). *Uygulamalı İstatistik* (p. 498 s). Kilavuz Kitabevi.

Apergis, N., & Rezitis, A. (2003). Real interest rate linkages between mortgage loans and housing prices: Evidence from Greece. *Applied Economics Letters, 10*(9), 561–565. https://doi.org/10.1080/1350485032000104887

Atherton, E., French, N., & Gabrielli, L. (2008). Decision theory and real estate development: A note on uncertainty. *Journal of European Real Estate Research, 1*(2), 162–182.

Aven, T. (2015). *Risk analysis*. Wiley.

Aydoğan, G., & Köksal, A. (2014). History related risk factors in international construction: Meta-analysis. *MEGARON, 9*(3), 190–200.

Baffoe-Bonnie, J. (1998). The dynamic impact of macroeconomic aggregates on housing prices and stock of houses: A national and regional analysis. *The Journal of Real Estate Finance and Economics, 17*(2), 179–197. https://doi.org/10.1023/A:1007753421236

Beck, U. (1992). *Risk society: Towards a new modernity*. Sage Publications.

Bentahar, O., & Cameron, R. (2015). Design and implementation of a mixed-methods research study in project management. *Electronic Journal of Business Research Methods, 13*(1), 3–15.

Birgönül, T. M., & Dikmen, İ. (1996). İnşaat Projelerinde Risk Yönetimi. *IMO Teknik Dergi, Yazı 97*, 1305–1326.

Byrne, P., & Cadman, D. (1984). *Risk, uncertainty and decision-making in property development*. E.&F.N. Spon.

D'Alpaos, C., & Canesi, R. (2014). Risk assessment in real estate investments during global crises. *WSEAS Transactions on Business and Economics, 11*, 369–379. https://doi.org/10.37394/23207.2020.11.37

Demir, H., & Bostancı, B. (2010). Decision-support analysis for risk management. *African Journal of Business Management, 4*(8), 1586–1604. 18 July, 2010. Available online at http://www.academicjournals.org/AJBM ISSN 1993-8233 ©2010 AcademicJournals, Accessed Apr 21, 2017

Dua, P., & Miller, S. M. (1996). Forecasting Connecticut home sales in a BVAR framework using coincident and leading indexes. *The Journal of Real Estate Finance and Economics, 13*(3), 219–235. https://doi.org/10.1007/BF00217392

Durkaya, M., & Yamak, R. (2004). Türkiye'de Konut Piyasasının Talep Yönlü Analizi. *İktisat İşletme ve Finans, 19*(217), 75–83. ISSN: 1300-610X.

Elizabeth, A., Nick, F., & Laura, G. (2008). Decision theory and real estate development: A note on uncertainty. *Journal of European Real Estate Research, 1*(2), 62–182.

Erpul, G. (2019). *Karar Destek Sistemleri*. Akara Üniversitesi Açık Ders Notları.

Fisher, P., & Robson, S. (2006). The perception and management of risk in UK Office Property Development. *Journal of Property Research, 23*(2), 135–161.

Gehner, E., Halman, J. I. M., & Jonge, H. (2006). Risk management in the Dutch real estate development sector: A survey. In *6th international postgraduate research conference*. Delft University of Technology.

Gigerenzer, G. (2007). *Gut feelings: The intelligence of the unconscious*. Penguin.

Grotke, J. (2010). *An introduction to the mathematics of value-at-risk. Rochester Un*. Mathematics Department Notes.

Hanafizadeh, P., & Latif, V. (2011). Robust net present value. *Mathematical and Computer Modelling., 54*, 233–242.

Harrison, E. F. (1999). *The managerial decision-making process*. Houghton Mifflin.

Hepşen, A., & Aşıcı, M. (2013). The association between current account deficit and house prices in Türkiye. *Journal of Applied Finance & Banking., 3*(3), 65–79.

Hertz, D. B. (1964). Risk analysis in capital investment. *Harvard Business Review, 64*.

International Organization for Standardization (ISO). (2018). ISO 31000:2018 Risk management—Guidelines.

Khumpaisal, S. (2015). An examination of economic risks' perception of thai real estate developers. *International Journal of Trade, Economics and Finance, 6*(1), 14–21.

Knight, F. H. (1921). *Risk, uncertainty, and profit, Boston and New York* (p. 388s). Houghton Mifflin Co., The Riverside Press.

Kumar, A., & Thakur, R. (2018). Analysis of different rating aggregation techniques for online reviews. In *Proceedings of the international conference on advances in computing and data sciences* (pp. 381–390). Springer. https://doi.org/10.1007/978-981-13-1819-1_36

Leamer, E. E. (2007). *Housing is the business cycle* (NBER working paper no. 13428). National Bureau of Economic Research. https://doi.org/10.3386/w13428

Lin, R., Wang, Q., Hu, J., Gao, L., & Lu, L. (1996). An intelligent decision support system for real estate investment. In *Proceedings of the IEEE international conference on industrial technology (ICIT'96)* (pp. 801–805). https://doi.org/10.1109/ICIT.1996.601708

Mosallaeipour, S., Shavarani, S., Steens, C., & Erős, A. (2019). A robust expert decision support system for making real estate location decisions: A case of investor-developer-user organisation in the Industry 4.0 era. *Journal of Corporate Real Estate, 22*, 21–47. https://doi.org/10.1108/jcre-03-2019-0019

Naeem, M., Ali, S., & Ahmed, S. (2023). Digital transformation in real estate: A comprehensive review of information and communication technologies, data collection, network tools, and digital decision support systems. *Journal of Real Estate Technology and Innovation, 5*(2), 123–145. https://doi.org/10.1007/s44268-023-00016-0

Novak, L. R. (1996). *Market and feasibility studies: A how-to guide*. Uoregon University. Website: https://pages.uoregon.edu/rgp/PPPM613/downloads/How%20to%20do%20a%20Market%20Analysis.pdf, Accessed Nov 28, 2010

Özpolat, A. (2014). *Türkiye'de kentleşme politikaları ve konut talebini etkileyen faktörler: Svec analizi*. Doktora Tezi, Gaziantep Üniversitesi, Sosyal Bilimler Enstitüsü, İktisat Anabilim Dalı.

Öztürk, A. (2020). *Taşınmaz Geliştirme Projelerinde Karar Destek Sistemleri ve Risk Yönetimi: Ankara İlinde Taşınmaz Geliştirme Projelerinde Bir Uygulama*. Doktora Tezi, Ankara Üniversitesi Fen Bilimleri Ens. Gayrimenkul Geliştirme ve Yönetimi Anabilim Dalı.

Öztürk, A., Kapusuz, Y. E., & Tanrıvermiş, H. (2016, June 8–11). Housing issues and policy requirements: Time series analysis of household and macroeconomic indicators in the case of Ankara Province. European Real Estate Society (ERES) 23rd Annual Conference, Regensburg, Germany.

Prat, G., & Uctum, R. (2019). Term structure of interest rates: Modelling the risk premium using a two-horizon framework. *Journal of Economic Behavior & Organization, 182*, 421.

Project Management Institute (PMI). (2017). *A guide to the project management body of knowledge* (PMBOK® Guide) (6th ed.).

Raiffa, H., & Schlaifer, R. (1961). *Applied statistical decision theory*. Harvard University Press.

Saaty, T. L. (1980). *The analytic hierarchy process*. McGraw-Hill.

Simon, H. A. (1979). Rational decision making in business organizations. *The American Economic Review, 69*(4), 493–513.

Stevenson, S. (2007). Forecasting housing supply: Empirical evidence from the Irish market. *European Journal of Housing Policy, 7*(1), 1–17. https://doi.org/10.1080/14616710601132518

Sun, Z. (2023). Research on product decision of real estate project based on big data analysis. *Frontiers in Business, Economics and Management*. https://doi.org/10.54097/fbem.v11i2.12593

Tanrıvermiş, H. (2017). *Gayrimenkul Değerleme Esasları, SPL Sermaye Piyasası Lisanslama Sicil ve Eğitim Kuruluşu*. Lisanslama Sınavları Çalışma Kitapları Ders Kodu: 1014 (Konut Değerleme Sınavı, Gayrimenkul Değerleme Sınavı).

Tanrıvermiş, H. (2019). *Türkiye Ekonomisinde İnşaat ve Gayrimenkul Sektörlerinin Rolleri ve Gelişme Eğilimlerinin Değerlendirilmesi* (Assesment of the roles of construction and real estate sectors and their development trends in Türkiye), Kent, İnşaat ve Ekonomi Kongresi. May 2–4, 2019, Gaziantep (pp. 37–58).

Turing, A. M. (1950). Computing machinery and intelligence. *Mind, 49*, 433–460.

Valverde, R. (2011a). A business intelligence system for risk management in the real estate industry. *International Journal of Computer Applications, 27*, 14–22. https://doi.org/10.5120/3276-4458

Valverde, R. (2011b). A risk management decision support system for the real estate industry.

Von Neumann, J., & Morgenstern, O. (1944). *Theory of games and economic behavior*. Princeton University Press.

Wiegelmann, W. T. (2012). *Risk management in the real estate development industry investigations into the application of risk management concepts in leading european real estate development organizations*. Doctor of Philosophy, Institute of Sustainable Development& Architecture, Bond University.

Williams, T. (2016). Identifying success factors in construction projects: A case study. *Project Management Journal, 47*(1), 97–112.

Xie, J., Liu, P., & Deng, X. (2023). Real estate risk analysis based on support vector machine. In *International conference on statistics, data science, and computational intelligence (CSDSCI 2022), Qingdao, China*. https://doi.org/10.1117/12.2656749

Yorulmaz, M., & Sezen, K. (2023). Denizcilik alanında kullanılan risk analizi yöntemleri ve fine kinney yöntemiyle bir uygulama. *Afet ve Risk Dergisi, 6*(3), 622–637.

Zadeh, L. A. (1965). Fuzzy sets. *Information and Control, 8*(3), 338–353.

Akın Öztürk graduated from the Department of Industrial Engineering at Ankara Çankaya University in 2004. He holds a master's degree from the Department of Computer Engineering at the Institute of Science and Technology at Ankara Baskent University in 2008. In 2021, he received his doctorate from the Department of Real Estate Development and Management, Graduate School of Natural and Applied Sciences at Ankara University. With 21 years of experience, Dr. Öztürk has worked as a data scientist and software developer, specialising in decision-making and risk management in real estate development. His areas of expertise encompass artificial intelligence, time series analysis, project management, business intelligence, metadata management, decision support systems, decision making, risk analysis and management.

Harun Tanrıvermiş is a distinguished professor who occupies the esteemed position at the Ankara University top management level as founder and head of the Department of Real Estate Development and Management, and founder and current dean of the Faculty of Applied Sciences at Ankara University. Professor Tanrıvermiş also currently works as the vice rector at Ankara University. He attained his B.Sc., M.Sc., and Ph.D. degrees from the Department of Agricultural Economics at Ankara University, specialising in land and real estate economics, land and real estate valuation, as well as natural resources and environmental economics. Furthermore, he earned an M.Sc. in environmental management through the MED-CAMPUS Programme in 1996. Professor Tanrıvermiş has published approximately 400 papers, including 43 international and 55 national peer-reviewed articles, which have been published in various high-impact journals. Additionally, he has presented 48 international and 74 national proceedings, either in full or as abstracts, at numerous conferences. He is also credited with writing 39 books and 17 book chapters. Moreover, his works concentrate on the land and real estate valuation, land and real estate economics, real estate development and project appraisal, urban transformation and sustainability, sustainable real estate development, facility and real estate management, land management, administration and polices, measuring and reporting of real estate sustainability and ESG, digital transformation in real estate and real estate technologies.

Urban Planning and Restructuring

Planning and Building Laws in Türkiye

Esra Keskin and Şebnem Akipek Öcal

Abstract

As a consequence of urbanisation and rapid population growth in Türkiye, the rate of construction and the demand for land and planning studies have increased significantly. One of the primary objectives of urban planning is to establish physical environmental conditions that fulfil the needs of individuals. Legal statutes, regulations, and judicial rulings guide the evolution of the urban environment. However, practical challenges inevitably arise. Deficiencies in legislation and occurrences of misapplication are apparent across numerous issues, including the development of areas that are unsuitable for construction, noncompliance with restrictions mandated by laws during and subsequent to the construction phase, inconsistencies between implementation and land use plans, as well as conflicts among institutions concerning authorisation. This chapter elucidates the planning process and various plan types in Türkiye and criticises the legislation addressing existing challenges.

Keywords

Planning · Zoning Law · Zoning plans · Urbanisation

E. Keskin (✉)
Department of Real Estate Development and Management, Faculty of Applied Sciences, Ankara University, Ankara, Türkiye
e-mail: esrkeskin@ankara.edu.tr

Ş. A. Öcal
Department of Business Administration, Faculty of Economics and Administrative, TED University, Ankara, Türkiye
e-mail: sebnem.akipekocal@tedu.edu.tr

T. Just et al. (eds.), *Understanding Türkiye's Real Estate Markets*, Management for Professionals, https://doi.org/10.1007/978-3-032-13297-0_24

1 Introduction

Due to rapid urbanisation supported by strong population growth in Türkiye, the demand for housing has surged, and the construction sector has become a pivotal component of the Turkish economy. This development has underscored the significance of zoning plans in facilitating organised urbanisation. Zoning plans should strive to take social, economic, and cultural aspects into account alongside physical dimensions (Brown et al., 2018; Domingo et al., 2021; Nolon & Bacher, 2008). Consequently, the public, local governments, and legislators have to collaborate as key stakeholders in the planning process (Amado et al., 2010; Damer & Hague, 1971; Fagence, 2014; Lane, 2005; Sanoff, 1999; Selman, 2004). The distribution of planning authority through various legal regulations, coupled with deficiencies in the laws, results in inconsistent practices. Given that it is not feasible to develop long-term plans without considering the emerging needs during and after the planning process, the enhancement of zoning rights through plan amendments and modifications in land use frequently culminates in disputes necessitating legal intervention. Although the pertinent legislation and jurisprudence guide in addressing these challenges, they remain inadequate in certain respects. This chapter assesses the evolution of planning legislation in Türkiye alongside its legal foundation. After elucidating the types of zoning plans and the hierarchy among these categories within the relevant legislation, the challenges encountered due to zoning plans are examined from various angles.

2 Historical Development of Legislation on Planning

The inaugural planning regulation in Türkiye was the Ebniye Regulation, which was promulgated in 1848 during the Ottoman Empire. This regulation established the architectural styles and certain zoning regulations pertaining to structures in the central area of Istanbul. In 1864, the Türuk (Roads) and Ebniye Regulations were enacted, encompassing the whole country, and the principle of generality was implemented in practice.

The inaugural legislation about zoning during the Ottoman period was the Ebniye Law of 1882. The Ministry of Development and Housing was established on October 13, 1923, followed by the enactment of Law No. 352 regarding the Duties and Authorities of the Ministry. Pursuant to the Law on Umuru Belediyeye Müteallik Ahkamı Criminal Penalty Law, dated April 16, 1924, and numbered 486, it was mandated that constructions in violation of the Ebniye Law are subject to demolition. In 1928, municipalities were first required to implement a zoning plan, as outlined in Law No. 1351 for the Capital, Ankara. Subsequently, this requirement was extended to all municipalities with the introduction of Municipal Law No. 1580, enacted in 1930 (Erkün, 1999, p. 12).

The initial regulations established during the Republican period introduced Zoning Law No. 6785, which came into effect in 1957. This law, enacted on July 9, 1956, represents the first comprehensive legislative framework addressing modern urban planning (Muzmul, 2004, p. 15). However, it only governed construction activities within municipal boundaries and was subsequently repealed in 1985 (Ural et al., 2019). Zoning Law No. 3194, which was enacted in 1985, aimed to ensure that settlements adhere to established plans, as well as scientific, health, and environmental standards. A noteworthy aspect of this law is the delegation of authority for the preparation, approval, and implementation of zoning plans to municipalities or governorships.

3 Legal Basis of Planning Legislation in Türkiye

Physical planning in Türkiye is implemented within the framework of zoning legislation. Additional legal foundations for zoning studies include the Constitution of the Republic of Türkiye, the Turkish Civil Code, Zoning Regulations, and various Circulars (Yıldız, 2020, p. 47). Zoning Law is defined as the regulations that govern the characteristics that buildings must adhere to when constructed on a property (Zevkliler, 1982, p. 165). From another perspective, zoning law encompasses the principles that establish the legal regime applicable to buildings erected on a property (Yılmaz, 2002, p. 21).

The primary regulatory focus of zoning law encompasses the settlements and structures located within designated areas. The Zoning Law, enacted to ensure that structures are established in accordance with formal plans, scientific principles, health regulations, and environmental considerations, has been in effect since 1985. The jurisdiction of this law is delineated by the stipulation that "all official and private structures to be built, with plans to be made, in places within and outside the borders of the municipality and the adjacent area". Given that Zoning Law No. 3194 cannot comprehensively regulate all aspects within the domain of zoning, various technical issues are governed by regulations such as the Regulation on the Principles of Plan Making, the Zoning Regulation for Unplanned Areas, the Development Amnesty Regulation, and the Parking Lot Regulation (Kalabalık, 2022, p. 39).

No explicit provision in the 1961 and 1982 Constitutions mandates the preparation of zoning plans. However, Article 166, entitled "Planning", refers to a general planning activity. It is widely recognised that Article 35 of the Constitution, which governs property rights, constitutes a component of the constitutional foundation for development plans (Orta, 2005, p. 5; Mengi & Keleş, 2003, p. 20).

The limitation imposed on the utilisation of property rights shall be duly considered in light of the public interest as delineated within the zoning plan. An additional cornerstone is Article 23 of the Constitution, which governs the circumstances under which the freedom of establishment may be curtailed. Furthermore, Article 56, about the right to a healthy environment, and Article 57, concerning the right of living in adequate housing, represent additional provisions that form the foundation of fundamental zoning law.

In instances where the stipulations of Law No. 775 are not applicable to the properties for which a title deed allocation document exists, the stipulations of Law No.

3194 shall be employed, contingent upon the title deed allocation document establishing ownership and possessing the characteristics of a title deed.

Article 14 of Coastal Law No. 3621 stipulates that the provisions of Zoning Law No. 3194 shall apply to buildings constructed in the areas governed by Coastal Law. Article 20 of the Environmental Law mandates that buildings that violate laws and regulations about the protection of potable and drinking water shall be demolished in accordance with the principles delineated in Zoning Law No. 3194. Article 16 of Law No. 2863 regarding the Protection of Cultural and Natural Assets asserts that buildings in violation of these rules shall be penalised in accordance with the Zoning Law. Furthermore, in the sixth paragraph of Article 57 of the same law, it is noted that all forms of construction and physical interventions must be conducted with the approval of the conservation regional board, with the exception of modifications and repairs that conform to Article 21 of Zoning Law No. 3194.

Other pertinent legislations associated with zoning encompass National Parks Law No. 2873, Forest Law No. 6831, Soil Conservation and Land Use Law No. 5403, Pasture Law No. 4342, Law No. 3573 regarding the Rehabilitation of Olive Cultivation and Vaccination of Wilds, Military Restricted Zones and Security Zones Law No. 2565, Law No. 4562 concerning Organised Industrial Zones, and Law No. 2981.

In the context of statutory ordinances (KHK), which are classified as administrative acts, statutory ordinance No. 595 about building supervision, issued in the year 2000, serves as an exception to the absence of a direct regulation within the Zoning Law (Şaşmaz, 2010, p. 26). The regulations encompass the Regulation on the Principles of Plan Making, the Regulation on Unplanned Areas, the Planned Areas Type Zoning Regulation, and the Regulation on the Principles of Land and Land Arrangement, which is to be enacted under Article 18 of the Zoning Law.

3.1 Zoning Plans

Urbanisation in Türkiye occurred primarily through strong internal migration from rural regions to urban areas, especially in the 1950s, leading to various challenges, such as squatting. Administrations require regulatory frameworks to facilitate healthy urbanisation and to develop solutions to prevailing issues. In order to achieve sustainable urbanisation, effective planning serves as an essential instrument for attaining specific objectives and aiding developing countries and regions in addressing social, economic, physical, and legal challenges (Akdemir, 2021, p. 133; Norton, 2008). In other words, planning can be defined as the decision-making process targeting future development (Üstündağ & Şengün, 2011, p. 2). The Regulation on the Principles of Plan Preparation stipulates that zoning plans are designed to fulfil the social and cultural requirements of the urban population, to establish a healthy and secure environment, and to enhance the quality of life, utilising comprehensive research and data pertaining to the economic, demographic, social, cultural, historical, and physical attributes of the city. This document comprises maps, reports, and annotations that delineate urban settlement and development trends, presenting alternative solutions that encompass land usage, protection measures, restrictions, organisational structures, and implementation principles. Zoning plans constitute administrative procedures and represent a regulatory act with significant legal implications (Özkaya Özlüer, 2015, p. 436).

In accordance with the ruling issued by the sixth Chamber of the Council of State, designated as E: 1986/1023, Dated November 25, 1986, the objectives of the zoning plans are established as follows: "To accurately ascertain the present circumstances, possibilities, and prospective development of the designated region, geographical data, urban utilisation, infrastructure, and financial information will be analysed based on the gathered data from research and survey studies, to identify optimal solutions for existing or proposed structures among diverse urban functions; to facilitate a healthy physical environment that positively influences personal and familial well-being within human, societal, and environmental relationships. Furthermore, an additional objective of the zoning plans is to guide the selection of locations and developmental trends for investments, to ascertain the most rational balance between environmental protection and land utilisation, to ensure favourable living conditions for the inhabitants of the city, and to develop various plans consistent with the city's distinctive lifestyle, character, demographics, spatial relations, environmental considerations, and regional context. This plan is formulated with consideration for the interconnections among individuals, their social and cultural needs, and matters related to safety and health.

Plans are classified based on their objectives and intended applications, including development plans, regional plans, environmental plans, provincial environmental plans, master zoning plans, and implementation zoning plans. In accordance with Article 6 of Zoning Law No. 3194, spatial plans encompass environmental plans and zoning plans. These plans are categorised as environmental plans and zoning plans and must be formulated in alignment with the spatial strategy plan. Furthermore, the spatial strategy plan should be congruent with the development plans.

Subsequently, zoning plans are prepared in the format of a master zoning plan and an implementation zoning plan. These plans must align with the plans above. The metropolitan zoning plan is excluded from this stratification. Article 9 of the Zoning Law empowers the Ministry to create, possess, amend, and approve metropolitan development plans ex officio. According to their configuration, zoning plans are classified into three categories: revision zoning, local zoning, and supplementary zoning plans (Ünal, 1991). Furthermore, building on this classification with the planning system also integrate various socieconomic, spatial and special-purpose plans organised under specific categories, as presented in Fig. 1 below.

Before the amendment of Article 6 of the Zoning Law, dated November 29, 2018, plans were systematically classified into regional and zoning plans, based on the areas they encompassed and the objectives they were intended to achieve. The zoning plans were further categorised into master zoning plans and implementation zoning plans. Following the 2018 amendment, spatial plans and Spatial Strategy Plans were introduced.

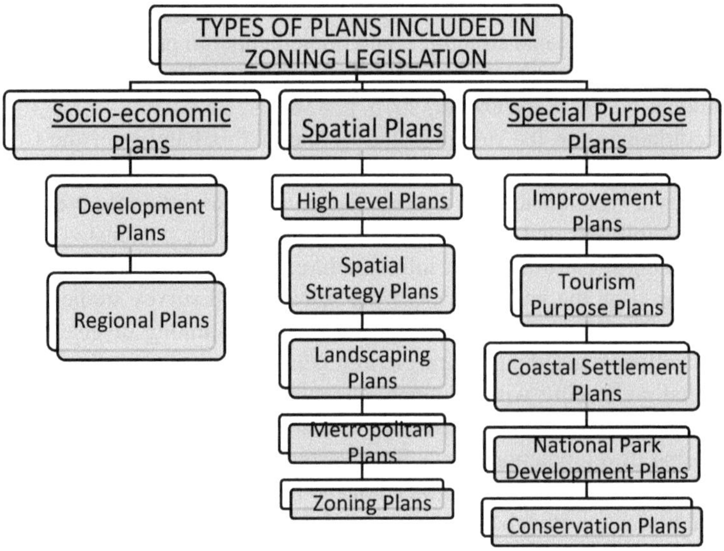

Fig. 1 Types of plans included in zoning legislation. *Source*: own depiction

3.2 Hierarchy of Plans

The primary objective of development and regional plans is to ascertain the allocation of investments that will facilitate growth and advancement within the designated areas subject to the plan (Üstündağ & Şengün, 2011, p. 5). Regional plans govern aspects such as the distribution of settlements and infrastructure within the area by establishing foundational principles derived from development plans. Both plans aim to foster social and economic development.

The plan hierarchy delineates the preparation of each plan by a superior plan (Fleischmann & Meyr, 2003). Through the appropriate application of this principle, plans that contradict the superior plan are effectively prevented. Nevertheless, the decisions made at the upper-plan level are elaborated upon with respect to lower-scale plans, which serve as a guiding framework (Akdemir, 2021, p. 136). The sixth Chamber of the Council of State, in its ruling dated June 5, 2003, in cases 2002/853E and 2003/3482 K, emphasises that: "The lower-scale zoning plans must follow the upper-scale zoning plans. A plan on the scale of 1/1,000 cannot contradict a plan on the scale of 1/5,000" This hierarchy among plans pertains not only to the variance in scale but also facilitates a progression from the abstract to the specific, incorporating distinct characteristics and details (Ersoy, 2000a, p. 225).

The environmental plan is articulated in Article 5 of the Zoning Law, which states that it is "a plan prepared for the region, basin, or province as a whole, which determines the land-use principles and criteria in accordance with the spatial strategy plan". Furthermore, it is stipulated in the fifth paragraph of Article 6 of the Spatial Plans Construction Regulation that environmental plans must adhere to the parameters set forth in the development and regional plans: "While preparing the spatial strategy plans and environmental plans, the targets set by the development plan, regional plans, regional development strategies, and other strategy documents are taken into account". Clause B of Article 8 of the Zoning Law articulates that "Zoning Plans consist of a master zoning plan and an implementation zoning plan". When appropriate, the master and implementation zoning plans for areas within the municipality's jurisdiction are developed by the pertinent municipalities, ensuring conformity with the stipulations of regional plans and environmental plan decisions. This implies that the master zoning plan, when available, should be synchronised with the regional and environmental plans.

An implementation zoning plan is defined as: "[...] a plan that has been drawn up according to the principles of the master zoning plan, with the cadastral status, if any, processed on the maps that have already been approved, and that illustrates the building blocks of various regions, their density and arrangement, the roads, the implementation stages, and other information that will serve as the basis for the zoning application programs required for implementation". Article 5 of the Zoning Law emphasises that the implementation of the zoning plan will be organised in accordance with the principles of the master zoning plan within the hierarchy of plans. Concerning special-purpose plans, it is considered that they will be executed in the event of a conflict with the primary plans (Yayla, 1975, p. 134; Akdemir, 2021, p. 162).

4 Zoning Planning Processes and Inspection

Municipalities have the authority to formulate plans. This is derived from Article 8 of Law No. 3194. Article 18 of the Zoning Law stipulates provisions about land and land regulation. Following the identification of the area subject to the plan, a comprehensive land analysis is conducted, accompanied by the collection of data through the acquisition of opinions from various ministries and directorates. The procurement of these opinions is vital for the successful implementation of the process. Throughout the data collection phase, the report must encompass details regarding the age of the buildings, their construction status, material quality, and floor utilisation. All data obtained from the research is analysed, and the lands and regions suitable for the zoning plan are specified. After the plan is prepared, it is submitted to Parliament. The plan sheets are approved if no one objects to the plan after the suspension process. Similarly, this sequence of actions constitutes the fundamental of the statutory planning workflow and guarantees that each phase is executed with administrative responsibility and technical precision. In practice, the planning process follows a systematic progression, advancing from data collection and analysis through public consultation to final approval. The primary stages of this workflow are depicted in Fig. 2 below.

Numerous statutes in Türkiye empower institutions and organisations to formulate and endorse zoning plans. The process for approving zoning plans, whether developed or commissioned by these institutions and organisations, differs according to the regulations prescribed by the respective laws that grant them authority. In addition to local governmental bodies, entities such as the Ministry of Environment, Urbanisation and Climate Change, the Ministry of Culture and Tourism, as well as

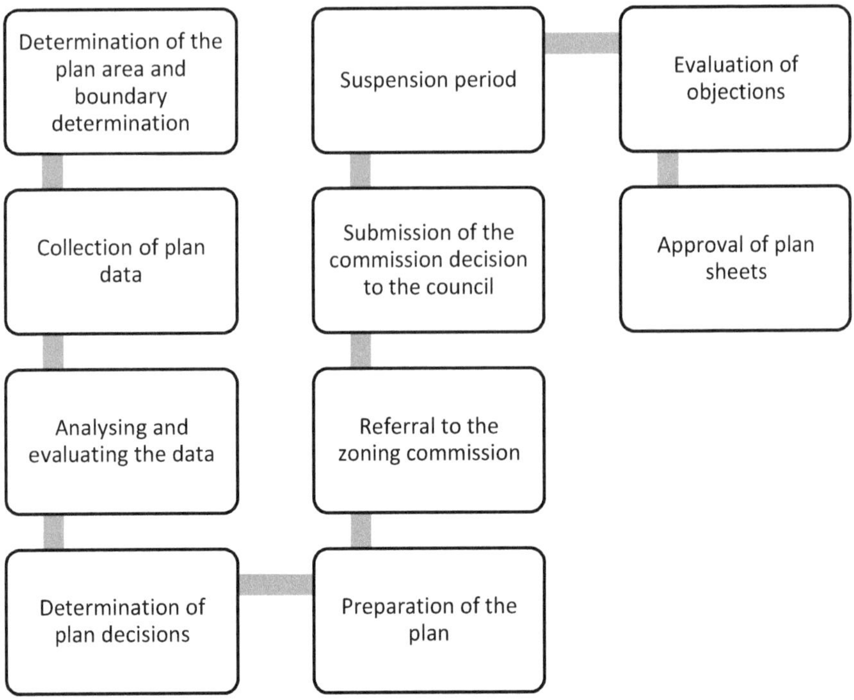

Fig. 2 Zoning planning process. *Source*: own depiction

the Housing Development Administration, may also be entrusted with the responsibility of preparing and approving zoning plans.

Given that municipal councils are integral to the process and serve as decision-makers in zoning plan procedures, it would be inappropriate for them to conduct the audit, as this would create a conflict of interest for the institutions and individuals responsible for establishing regulatory procedures to oversee the same processes. Various types of audits can be distinguished: the zoning external audit, such as guardianship audits conducted by the Ministry of Interior and other relevant ministries' audit bodies; a financial audit carried out by the Court of Accounts; and a judicial audit, which is limited to judicial and public audits concerning zoning plans. However, not all zoning plans are subject to judicial review. In this context, the audit mechanism does not operate with optimal effectiveness in the approval processes of zoning plans.

5 Problems Encountered in Planning

In Türkiye, there are discussions regarding zoning regulations and practices. Various legal frameworks empower different institutions, which leads to ambiguity. Plans are devised by exploiting the legislative gaps, resulting in modifications that lead to zoning distortions, rent-seeking behaviours, and unlawful construction activities.

5.1 Authorisation Problems

The legislation governing zoning in Türkiye authorises several institutions and organisations. While planning encompasses the stages of physical planning, implementation, and control, it is typically formulated with the assistance of architects and engineers. Throughout the planning process, numerous issues stemming from the legislation are encountered and subsequently become subjects of discussion. The challenges arising from authority are significant.

Article 8 of the Zoning Law delineates that the authority to formulate plans "consists of the Master Zoning Plan and the Implementation Zoning Plan". If available, the master and implementation zoning plans for the areas within the municipality are prepared or developed by the relevant municipal institutions, ensuring compliance with the regional plan and environmental plan decisions. According to the Decree on the Organisation and Duties of the Ministry of Environment and Urbanisation, the Ministry is the sole authority in all matters related to planning. The third paragraph of Article 7 of Decree-Law No. 644 states: "The Ministry develops and approves the national and regional physical plans". Metropolitan municipalities develop environmental plans within their borders, and the Ministry in non-metropolitan provinces creates, maintains, and approves them. Besides the Zoning Law, Municipal Law No. 5393, the Metropolitan Municipality Law No. 5216, and the Law on the Special Provincial Administration No. 5302 have conferred upon various institutions the authority to formulate zoning plans.

5.2 Problems Caused by Legislation

While the compatibility of master and implementation zoning plans, as well as their relationship with higher-level plans, is evaluated within the framework of the "plan hierarchy principle", the conflicts concerning special-purpose zoning plans disclose an additional challenge. As articulated in Article 4 of the Zoning Law, the legal provisions pertaining to zone planning for areas designated with special status are scrutinised. Nonetheless, due to the multi-authority arrangement present in the legislation, it is feasible to confront the issue of assessing special-purpose development plans under the ambit of more than one law concurrently (Orta, 2005, p. 103).

Article 6 of Law No. 3194 categorises plans into regional and zoning plans. Other plans are excluded from this Article. Given that the title of the item is 'Planning levels', the absence of a regulation encompassing all plans within the hierarchy results in inconsistencies with other provisions and contradictions in the application of the plan hierarchy. While this deficiency undermines the integrity of planning, it also engenders contradictions during the implementation phase of the plan hierarchy.

Institutions or organisations authorised by specific legislation have the authority to conduct activities in accordance with their stipulations within areas governed by specialised regulations. These activities, irrespective of the location and construction conditions specified in prevailing zoning plans or other pertinent legislation, may conflict with decisions made in upscale planning.

5.3 Practical Problems

The inability to establish fixed vertical and horizontal relationships between various plan types underscores the challenges associated with this practice. Given that it is unnecessary to formulate plans at higher scales in grading, inconsistencies may arise. Furthermore, instances exist where upper-scale plans were modified in response to changes made at the parcel level. As decisions concerning upper-scale plans will inform and constrain lower-scale plans, scenarios ought to be developed in accordance with scientific principles. Failing to do so may lead to a disconnection from evolving needs over time.

In Türkiye, urbanisation has led to the emergence of slums. The implementation of zoning amnesties has resulted in the acceptance of slum settlements and structures that contravene zoning regulations, consequently undermining trust in zoning plans and encouraging the utilisation of buildings that violate zoning standards (Keleş, 2000, p. 11).

While the preparation of zoning plans and amendments to these plans is extensively addressed in the regulations, the absence of regulation is often attributed to a deficiency of qualified experts. The technical aspect of this issue remains incompletely understood (Ersoy, 2000b, p. 69). The modifications proposed by the land use plan can be enacted through the development plan. The metropolitan municipalities carry out the changes that are the responsibility of the district municipalities. There is ongoing discourse regarding whether alterations to the social and technical infrastructure, as established during the land use planning process, will compromise the principal determinations of the plan (Ünal, 2020, p. 30). Although the Regulation on the Principles of Plan Making specifies that such amendments can only be enacted in instances of necessity, it remains unclear what constitutes such cases of necessity. It is widely acknowledged that adjustments to the location and size of social and technical infrastructure areas, as prescribed by the land use plan, can be made in implementation development plans, provided that they do not infringe upon the overall standards. Modifications to social and technical infrastructure, as well as density, may result in adverse consequences in practice and detrimentally affect the primary objectives of the plan. Consequently, the principle of refraining from making such modifications unless warranted is endorsed. The Council of State acknowledges that changes which do not fundamentally alter the land use plan may be implemented through the development of plans and subsequently integrated into the land use plan. In certain instances, the Council of State deems the later amendment of the land use plan, as delineated in the implementation zoning plan, to be inconsistent with urban planning principles, the public interest, and development plans. As a result, it orders the annulment of the amendment to the land use plan. A comprehensive approach should be adopted when assessing the upper-scale plan. The frequency of plan amendments should also be considered, as repeated requests for plan amendments are not desirable. If changes are necessary, they should be instituted to preserve the fundamental character, continuity, and integrity of the land use plan, with the justifications articulated clearly.

Given that zoning planning is a multidimensional endeavour, effective participation constitutes one of the crucial elements for success (Jorden & Hentrich, 2003; Steele, 1987). This framework aims to ensure the inclusion of non-governmental organisations, professional chambers, universities, and all stakeholders impacted by the plan, thereby allowing for the consideration of diverse perspectives (Orta, 2005, p. 187; Gülan, 2000, p. 141). The transparency of the process is of paramount importance, particularly in mitigating objections. With the implementation of Zoning Law No. 3194, the bureaucratic procedures were streamlined, and zoning planning was enhanced. It was essential to empower local governments with the authority to approve zoning plans (Ersoy, 2000b, p. 46).

5.4 Buildings Contrary to Zoning Law

In the twentieth paragraph of Article 4 of the Zoning Regulation applicable within the Areas Without a Plan, both within and outside the borders of the Municipality and Adjacent Areas, as well as in the fourth paragraph of Article 4 of the Regulation on the Implementation of Law No. 2981, it is stipulated that: "Public services such as roadways, green areas, parking lots in the adjacent parcel, and zoning plans that contravene the license and its annexes, scientific and health regulations, floor order, floor area, distances between neighbours, zoning roads, front lines, building depth, zoning principles, and structures that infringe upon areas designated for facilities and are constructed in locations where a construction ban is explicitly enforced, are deemed contrary to zoning".

According to Article 20 of the Zoning Law, obtaining a license is a prerequisite for the construction of buildings. Furthermore, Article 21 stipulates that acquiring licenses from municipalities or governorates for all buildings is mandatory. The concept of a license represents permissions for construction, serving as one of the fundamental tools of zoning law (Çal, 2012, p. 18). In this context, the license is an essential instrument for maintaining the zoning order (Özkaya Özlüer, 2018, p. 314). In instances where construction has commenced without a license or has been completed in violation of the license, such construction contravenes zoning regulations. Pursuant to Article 32 of the Zoning Law, "on the determination, technical responsibility and notification of the construction by the relevant administration, in which the construction was started without obtaining a license or in the buildings that can be built without a license, and its annexes or without a license, the municipality or governorships current construction status is determined. The building is sealed, and the construction is stopped immediately". Numerous disputes regarding violations or illegal constructions arise in practice (Yener, 2016, p. 2967).

6 Conclusion

Planning is intended to address future needs and promote the well-being of urban areas. Amendments to plans are often applied to economic investments and projects. As a result, zoning plans and modifications are susceptible to litigation, given that rents or capital values may escalate. Due to the incomplete establishment of participatory mechanisms in the planning process, numerous lawsuits are initiated for the infringement of interests. While efforts are undertaken to enforce oversight over zoning plans based on the principle of "public interest", this measure is not invariably adequate.

The deficiencies within the legislation serve as the fundamental cause of the challenges faced in practice. Article 70 of the Special Provincial Administration Law and Article 84 of the Municipal Law state: "In case of contradiction with the provisions of this Law in the Zoning Law No. 3194 limited to the duties and services for which the municipality is responsible and authorised by this Law, the provisions of this Law shall apply". The existence of this provision, along with similar provisions, can give rise to authorisation issues. Article 5 of Zoning Law No. 3194 stipulates that environmental plans have to be developed in conjunction with regional plans. Furthermore, implementation development plans must be prepared in alignment with the environmental plans, and these plans need to be further refined in accordance with the land use plan. Nevertheless, numerous instances exist where the hierarchical structure of the plans is not adhered to. In certain legislations, such as Law No. 4706 on the Evaluation of Property Owned by the Treasury and Amending the Value Added Tax Law, authorisation is granted irrespective of the restrictions delineated in zoning legislation. Additionally, the zoning amnesties initiated by the Law on Encouraging the Construction of Buildings and Unauthorised Buildings, numbered 6188 and enacted in 1953, are frequently debated within the context of Turkish Zoning Law.

One potential solution is to establish a framework in which the increased value resulting from urban development is equitably distributed among the property owner, the municipality, and the residents. Furthermore, it remains essential to clarify the regulations pertaining to illegal construction, implement deterrent measures, and refrain from seeking zoning amnesties, all of which are frequently emphasised in key solution proposals. A comprehensive urbanisation policy is imperative for the development of cities as livable environments that prioritise the public interest. It is posited that a majority of the challenges faced can be effectively addressed through the establishment of a legal foundation for municipal zoning practices, which should be aligned with specific standards and aimed at rectifying existing legislative shortcomings.

References

Akdemir, B. (2021). İmar planlarında hiyerarşi. *Journal of Konya Bar Association, 2021*(1), 133–173.

Amado, M. P., Santos, C. V., Moura, E. B., & Silva, V. G. (2010). Public participation in sustainable urban planning. *International Journal of Human and Social Sciences, 5*(2), 102–108.

Brown, G., Sanders, S., & Reed, P. (2018). Using public participatory mapping to inform general land use planning and zoning. *Landscape and Urban Planning, 177*, 64–74.
Çal, S. (2012). *Türk İdare Hukukunda ruhsat*. Seçkin Publications.
Damer, S., & Hague, C. (1971). Public participation in planning: A review. *Town Planning Review, 42*(3), 217.
Domingo, D., Palka, G., & Hersperger, A. M. (2021). Effect of zoning plans on urban land-use change: A multi-scenario simulation for supporting sustainable urban growth. *Sustainable Cities and Society, 69*, 102833.
Erkün, S. (1999). *Türk İmar Hukuku'nun ana çizgileri*. Yem Publications.
Ersoy, M. (2000a). *İmar mevzuatımızda planlama kademeleri ve üst ölçek planlama sorunu*. Middle East Technical University, Department of City and Regional Planning.
Ersoy, M. (2000b). *İmar planı değişiklikleri ve yargı denetimi*. Yargı Publications.
Fagence, M. (2014). *Citizen participation in planning*. Elsevier.
Fleischmann, B., & Meyr, H. (2003). Planning hierarchy, modelling and advanced planning systems. In *Handbooks in operations research and management science* (Vol. 11, pp. 455–523).
Gülan, A. (2000). Türk İmar Hukuku'nda 'hamur kuralı' uygulaması. 3194 Sayılı İmar Kanunu'nun 18. maddesi uygulamasına ilişkin teorik bir yaklaşım. Unpublished associate professorship thesis, İstanbul.
Jorden, D. A., & Hentrich, M. A. (2003). Public participation is on the rise: A review of the changes in the notice and hearing requirements for the adoption and amendment of general plans and rezonings nationwide and in recent Arizona land use legislation. *Natural Resources Journal*, 865–886.
Kalabalık, A. (2022). *Imar hukuk dersleri*. Seçkin Publications, Ankara.
Keleş, R. (2000). Kent ve çevre değerleri bağlamında kamu yararı kavramı, mekan planlama ve yargı denetimi. In M. Ersoy & H. Ç. Keskinok (Eds.), Yargı Publications.
Lane, M. B. (2005). Public participation in planning: An intellectual history. *Australian Geographer, 36*(3), 283–299.
Mengi, A., & Keleş, R. (2003). *İmar hukukuna giriş*. İmge Publications.
Muzmul, O. (2004). İmar alanında Türkiye'de mülkiyet hakkı ihlalleri. *Hukuk Dünyası, 2004*(1), 1–15.
Nolon, J. R., & Bacher, J. (2008). Zoning and land use planning. *Real Estate Law Journal, 37*(1), 90.
Norton, R. K. (2008). Using content analysis to evaluate local master plans and zoning codes. *Land Use Policy, 25*(3), 432–454.
Orta, E. (2005). *İmar hukukunda plan hiyerarşisi ve planların çatışması*. Master's thesis, İstanbul University, Institute of Social Sciences, Department of Public Law.
Özkaya Özlüer, I. (2015). Mekânsal Planlar Yapım Yönetmeliği ışığında imar planlarında yetki sorunu. *Journal of Ankara University Law Faculty, 64*(2), 435–457.
Özkaya Özlüer, I. (2018). İmar barışı düzenlemesine hukuki bir yaklaşım. *Journal of İnönü University Faculty of Law (İÜHFD), 9*(2), 313–340.
Sanoff, H. (1999). *Community participation methods in design and planning*. John Wiley & Sons.
Şaşmaz, C. (2010). *İmar mevzuatına aykırı yapı kavramı ve denetimi*. Master's thesis, Istanbul Kültür University, Institute of Social Sciences, Department of Public Law.
Selman, P. (2004). Community participation in the planning and management of cultural landscapes. *Journal of Environmental Planning and Management, 47*(3), 365–392.
Steele, E. H. (1987). Community participation and the function of rules: The case of urban zoning boards. *Law & Policy, 9*(3), 279–303.
Ünal, Y. (1991). *Kentleşme ve kentleşme politikaları*. TÜSES Turkish Social Economic Research Foundation.
Ünal, Y. (2020). *Türk şehir planlama hukuku*. Yetkin Publications.
Ural, E., Keleş, R., & Aliefendioğlu, Y. (2019). Planlamada karşılaşılan sorunlar açısından Türkiye ve İngiltere örneğinin karşılaştırılması. *Dumlupınar Üniversitesi Sosyal Bilimler Dergisi, 60*, 100–112.

Üstündağ, Ö., & Şengün, M. T. (2011). Türk imar mevzuatındaki plan türleri ve fiziki planlama - coğrafya ilişkisi üzerine genel bir değerlendirme. *Fırat University Journal of Social Sciences, 2*(21), 1–25.

Yayla, Y. (1975). *Şehir planlamasının başlıca hukuki meseleleri ve İstanbul örneği*. Publication of İstanbul University.

Yener, M. D. (2016). Yargıtay kararları kapsamında imara aykırı yapılarda tescil ve tazminat talepleri. *Marmara Üniversitesi Hukuk Fakültesi Hukuk Araştırmaları Dergisi, 22*(3), 2967–2976.

Yıldız, F. (2020). *İmar bilgisi*. Nobel Publications.

Yılmaz, M. (2002). *İmar yaptırımları ve yargısal korunma*. Seçkin Publications.

Zevkliler, A. (1982). *İmar kurallarına aykırı ve zarar verici inşaat*. Publication of Ankara University Faculty of Law.

Esra Keskin is an assistant professor in the Department of Real Estate Development and Management at the Faculty of Applied Sciences of Ankara University. Following her graduation from the Faculty of Law at Gazi University, she practised as a lawyer registered with the Ankara Bar Association for nearly a decade. She earned her master's and PhD degrees from the Department of Real Estate Development and Management at Ankara University, where she also served as a research assistant during her doctoral studies. In 2023, she was appointed as a visiting scholar at the Georgia Institute of Technology through a fellowship from TÜBİTAK (The Scientific and Technological Research Council of Türkiye). In 2024, she was appointed as an assistant professor. Her research primarily concentrates on urban transformation, real estate law, contract law, contract management, and facility and property management.

Şebnem Akipek Öcal serves as a professor at TED University in Ankara. She commenced her academic journey at the Faculty of Law at Ankara University, where she distinguished herself by ranking at the top of her class and achieving first place overall during her graduation. She obtained her master's degree from the London School of Economics and earned her PhD in Civil Law from Ankara University, where she wrote a dissertation focusing on consumer credit. Her career at the Faculty of Law encompassed roles such as assistant professor, associate professor, and full professor. Throughout the years, she assumed various administrative positions, including Director of the Ankara University Vocational School of Justice, Legal Advisor at Middle East Technical University, and Dean of the Faculty of Law at Kadir Has University. She concluded her tenure in November 2018 but remains actively engaged in academia as a faculty member at TED University, where she previously served as Vice Rector.

Urban Transformation and Informal Housing Areas Upgrading Practices and Policies in Türkiye

F. Nihan Özdemir Sönmez, Emine Baydan, and Parla Güneş

Abstract

In many developing nations, urbanisation is often linked to informal or unplanned settlements where urban poverty has flourished. In this regard, Türkiye is one of these countries. However, similar to the circumstances observed in other developing nations, Türkiye has, to some extent, succeeded in transforming such areas. This chapter examines the policies implemented to prevent the further proliferation of informal housing areas, particularly gecekondu settlements, from a historical perspective. Amnesty laws for informal housing areas, which originated in the 1950s, have been replaced by comprehensive urban transformation projects supported by a series of regulations. The urban transformation experiences presented reveal a significant absence of social impact assessments, irrespective of the legal frameworks on which they were founded. Moreover, the lack of social impact assessments in these transformed areas may lead to gentrification, displacing the poor to alternative informal housing contexts.

Keywords

Informal housing areas · Gecekondu · Urban transformation policies · Gentrification

F. N. Ö. Sönmez (✉) · E. Baydan · P. Güneş
Department of Real Estate Development and Management, Faculty of Applied Sciences, Ankara University, Ankara, Türkiye
e-mail: sonmezo@ankara.edu.tr; ebaydan@ankara.edu.tr; parlagunes@ankara.edu.tr

T. Just et al. (eds.), *Understanding Türkiye's Real Estate Markets*, Management for Professionals, https://doi.org/10.1007/978-3-032-13297-0_25

1 Introduction

The spatial implications of the economic and political changes encountered during the final quarter of the twentieth century have manifested as significant transformations within cities. 'Urban Transformation Projects', which commenced implementation in Western developed countries during the 1970s, emerged as instruments utilised by local governments to restructure deteriorated urban locales (Akkar, 2006; Atkinson, 1999; Uzun, 2006). In this context, the outdated residential zones for the working class that developed following the industrial revolution, along with industrial areas that have lost their functionality due to the adoption of new production methodologies, represent the initial instances of urban transformation executed in Western cities. Since the 1980s, when liberal economic policies were instituted, urban transformation projects have been undertaken in these areas through specialised projects formulated by public–private partnerships (Özdemir Sönmez, 2006).

Theories elucidating the transformation processes in Western nations predominantly concentrate on discussions related to gentrification (Smith, 1979, 1996). The concept of gentrification can be used to develop a framework for understanding the urban transformation experiences of cities in developing countries to some extent as well. Explanations of gentrification, particularly those relating to supply, as contained in Smith's Rent Gap Theory, are more readily applicable to comparable transformation processes in developing countries.

Nonetheless, the Rent Gap Theory neglects the engagement of various stakeholders in the gentrification process, which is applicable to both developed and developing nations. In particular, the influence of landowners as principal stakeholders in the redevelopment process, along with their relations with local governments, constitutes a significant factor that is insufficiently addressed within this theory. Therefore, a thorough evaluation of stakeholder roles is imperative when applying the Rent Gap Theory to the transformative experiences of developing countries.

Comprehensive urban transformation practices have been implemented in Türkiye. Through periodic squatter amnesty laws enacted since the 1950s, unplanned urban areas have been reclassified as officially designated development zones. However, particularly after the 1980s, the conversion of low-income residential neighbourhoods and deteriorating urban areas into prestigious projects aimed at attracting private sector investment is occasionally viewed as a strategy that transcends national boundaries. Regulations have further expedited the progression of such projects (Balaban, 2012; Uzun, 2020). It is noteworthy that within the urban transformation initiatives undertaken post-2000, the participation of the private sector has increased (Yetişkul et al., 2016).

This chapter initially examines the concept of urban transformation alongside its diverse implementation methods. Subsequently, considering the extensive timeline of informal housing development in Türkiye, the second section provides a succinct historical overview of gecekondu areas. The third segment analyses policies formulated for the rehabilitation of these areas within the framework of urban transformation projects. The concluding section is dedicated to a concise review and potential policy recommendations.

2 Conceptual Framework

2.1 What Is Urban Transformation?

While the notion of urban transformation typically pertains to the physical modification of declining urban locales, the alterations taking place in social and economic contexts are among the foremost subjects of discourse. Tekeli (2003) characterises urban transformation as an 'inclusive engagement that aims to bring an enduring solution to the complicated economic, physical, and social problems of an area and offers comprehensive solutions to these problems' and emphasises the environmental, economic, and social facets of urban transformation.

In this context, urban transformation can be regarded as a complex array of policies and procedures implemented to address the economic, social, physical, and environmental deficiencies of undervalued urban areas. This comprehensive approach necessitates consideration of both the enhancement of social conditions and the improvement of physical aspects. In its most general sense, 'urban transformation can be defined as the renewal, change, development and revitalisation of the urban fabric (which is either ageing, obsolete, worn out or where the potential land value exceeds the existing superstructure value) in accordance with the contemporary socio-economic and physical conditions' (Özden, 2002).

2.2 Different Methods of Urban Transformation

Urban transformation practices, which have been executed through historical processes, are designated differently depending on the results of these implementations. These diverse applications can be categorised as urban renewal, urban rehabilitation, urban regeneration, and urban conservation (Özdemir Sönmez, 2012).

2.2.1 Urban Renewal

Urban renewal entails the dismantling of the existing urban fabric, subsequently followed by the construction of a new settlement in its place. Such methodology encompasses radical interventions, characterised as transformation practices involving demolition and reconstruction (Tekeli, 2003), and is now increasingly being abandoned in contemporary urban transformation projects. Urban renewal practices face criticism for their adverse effects on the social groups residing in the intervention area, as well as for the resultant degradation of the urban fabric that warrants protection. Consequently, urban renewal is regarded as an acceptable approach solely in regions characterised by significantly deteriorated and unprotected structures (for instance, slum areas) or in zones identified as high-disaster-risk areas. The urban renewal strategy generally anticipates the resettlement of residents to an alternative location within the city, imposing substantial social and environmental costs. This method, which has largely fallen out of favour among the majority of developed nations, proves ineffective in preventing the reemergence of problematic areas that existed prior to the renewal in other locations within the city, as it fails to address underlying social issues.

2.2.2 Urban Rehabilitation

Urban rehabilitation is a strategy used to enhance areas that were developed in accordance with zoning plans but have subsequently undergone deterioration or exhaustion over time. These areas are characterised by high-density populations, inadequate infrastructure, and living conditions that do not align with contemporary standards. This approach prioritises the preservation and restoration of the existing building stock. Rehabilitation possesses the potential to rejuvenate such regions with minimal investment. By employing the urban rehabilitation methodology, it becomes feasible to maintain the integrity of urban characteristics through the preservation of the current urban fabric, as opposed to initiating new construction or completely demolishing older structures. Moreover, this method facilitates the retention of residents within the same area subsequent to spatial improvements.

2.2.3 Urban Regeneration

Urban regeneration constitutes a systematic approach aimed at revitalising urban areas by addressing and rectifying the factors contributing to urban decline, particularly in socio-cultural, economic, and physical dimensions. This process encompasses the restoration of historically significant buildings and urban infrastructures that have been neglected and were previously designated for functions such as storage and manufacturing, and that were heavily used by economically disadvantaged groups. Furthermore, this method seeks to redefine and diversify the economic activities within the area through comprehensive spatial improvement programmes, thereby enhancing the overall quality of urban life.

2.2.4 Urban Conservation

Urban conservation is defined as the preservation of the spatial structure of society, which reflects the social and economic conditions, as well as the cultural values of the past, from being compromised by contemporary social and economic circumstances. Its objective is to ensure the survival of preserved areas through their integration with modern society and current needs. Furthermore, urban conservation seeks the long-term preservation of historical, architectural, cultural, and visual values by employing scientific methods and techniques; assigning functions that align with the characteristics of the city's planned development areas; and ensuring the maintenance of contemporary living standards.

3 Historical Background of Gecekondu Areas in Türkiye

Following the Second World War, Türkiye experienced rapid urbanisation, leading to numerous socio-economic and socio-spatial challenges. One notable consequence was the emergence of informal housing areas, referred to as gecekondu areas. Initially, these areas developed on unclaimed public land; however, the practice of acquiring a plot, followed by constructing a house without the necessary building permits on illegally acquired land and in housing markets, has become prevalent.

This process has been furthered by government policies concerning informal settlements that either mitigate regulations or entirely exempt them. Since the 1940s, informal housing developments have proliferated throughout the nation. However, Ankara experienced rapid urbanisation in the early 1920s following its designation as the new capital of the country. It is feasible to analyse this process of informal housing development and the corresponding government policies across four distinct periods:

- The initial period—the early Republican era (spanning from 1923 to 1950).
- The second period, referred to as the stability period of gecekondus, transpires between 1950 and 1960.
- The third period, which extended from 1960 to 1980, encompassed the consolidation of gecekondu areas in both spatial and social dimensions.
- The fourth period pertains to the inception of neo-liberal policies within the urban context, which began in 1980 and persists to the present day.

3.1 The First Period (1923–1950)

In contrast to other cities in Türkiye, Ankara has emerged as a central hub for migration following its designation as the new capital of the Republic of Türkiye. 'During these early days, the city's planned development was the top priority of the new élites who wanted to create a new capital as a symbol of the creation of a new nation. Even during the early days, Ankara was attracting people from rural areas as a capital city' (Danielson & Keleş, 1985).

Nevertheless, the existing housing inventory is insufficient to satisfy the rising demand. The construction of personal sheds, especially on Altındağ Hill, represents the sole method by which newcomers may alleviate the housing crisis. These sheds served as the forerunners to the informal housing developments that would later be recognised as slums.

In the initial stages, the government displayed considerable hostility towards the development of residential housing. As early as 1924, only 1 year after the establishment of the Republic, the first regulation was passed. To address the prevailing antagonism towards these structures, this regulation proposed the elimination of the barracks. However, by the 1940s, these disparate sheds began to establish permanence and evolved into gecekondu areas, which ultimately resulted in the enactment of the first amnesty law in 1948.

3.2 The Second Period (1940–1960)

A multi-party political system characterised the decade spanning from 1950 to 1960, accompanied by significant rural-to-urban migration, predominantly driven by a transformation in agricultural production. This migration led to the proliferation of gecekondu areas within major urban centres. However, the absence of legal, economic, and political instruments within housing policy was conspicuously evident and constituted the primary cause underpinning the accelerated development of unauthorised housing. In response to the rising concerns regarding the necessity for legal restrictions on the ongoing development of gecekondus, Law No. 6188 was enacted in 1953. This legislation also retroactively legalised all gecekondu dwellings constructed prior to 1953 and recommended the demolition of houses erected after that date.

Notwithstanding, the proliferation of gecekondus persisted, accompanied by an enhancement in their quality. More resilient construction materials, including bricks, cinder blocks, and concrete, began to be utilised. By the end of the designated period, informal housing markets began to receive acknowledgement, facilitating the rental, sale, and acquisition of gecekondu residences within this informal marketplace. Simultaneously, urban services gradually became attainable, aligning with the augmented bargaining power of gecekondu residents.

3.3 The Third Period (1960–1980)

During the 1960s, the self-help aspect of the entire gecekondu production process emerged. By the end of the 1960s, the existing legislative framework was revealed to be inadequate, which led to a renewed focus on the development of comprehensive legislation within the governmental structure. In this context, Gecekondu Law No. 775 was enacted. However, this legislative measure proved to be inadequate in curtailing the proliferation of gecekondu areas.

The informal land and housing market in gecekondu areas has facilitated the emergence of a new modality of land acquisition: joint title ownership through division. While this method of ownership is sanctioned within the legal framework, the construction of gecekondus on these parcels remains classified as unlawful. This arrangement affords a degree of security to landowners relative to the unauthorised occupation of public land.

3.4 The Period from 1980 Onward

During this period, a series of new legislative measures concerning gecekondu areas were enacted, specifically Law No. 2805 and Law No. 2981 (Official Gazette, 08.02. 1984, No. 18335). These statutes were analogous to their predecessors in granting official pardons as a primary response to the challenges presented. In conjunction with this strategy, all gecekondus and other unauthorised constructions established on public land prior to 1984 were to be exempted through the relaxation of the relevant zoning laws. Furthermore, in addition to the amnesty conferred upon such structures, new development rights were assured through the implementation of specialised plans referred to as 'Improvement Plans'. The subsequent outcome was a vigorous and rapid transformation of the gecekondu areas resulting from the execution of these specialised plans.

While the transformation of gecekondu areas in accordance with improvement plans is ongoing, certain regions have been redeveloped through 'special transformation projects' in locales where urban land prices are comparatively elevated. These initiatives were executed through a collaboration between the public and private sectors. Furthermore, as will be elaborated upon in the subsequent section of the article, a series of regulations have been enacted for the transformation and prevention of gecekondu areas (i.e. laws 5393, 5104 and 6306).

4 Legal and Institutional Structure of Urban Transformation in Türkiye

As detailed in the preceding sections of this article, urban transformation may be defined as the physical, social, and economic modification of underprivileged urban areas into more viable environments through the execution of specialised initiatives, including renewal, rehabilitation, regeneration, and conservation, among others. Essentially, it can be regarded as a process designed to tackle the challenges encountered by neglected and economically distressed urban areas. The regions experiencing urban transformation in Türkiye are as follows:

- Regions that are characterised by natural hazards
- Informal residential areas
- Socially, physically, and economically deprived areas
- Historically and naturally designated preservation areas.

Many legislations concerning urban transformation in Türkiye exist. These legislations regulate the transformation processes of diverse categories of urban areas, including irregular housing settlements, conservation areas, and hazardous zones.

4.1 Gecekondu Amnesty Law (No. 2981/3290)

This legislation signifies the inaugural implementation of the most extensive transformation initiatives in gecekondu areas through improvement plans. In this legislation, these specific plans are defined as: 'Improvement Plans are the urban development plans which enable the unauthorised and unhealthy housing areas to be converted into regular and healthy ones through the provision of urban services by following the present land-use and ownership patterns of the settlement as much as possible' (Official Gazette, 08.02. 1984, No. 18335; Official Gazette, 23.07. 1986, No. 19173). Furthermore, the legislation specifies that eligible gecekondu owners are those who constructed their gecekondus prior to November 1984 and who do not possess other building parcels or residences within the same town.

Steps Towards the Transformation of Gecekondu Areas through Improvement Plans:

- Owners of eligible gecekondu properties may apply for a 'temporary title deed,' known as a title deed assignment certificate, by paying a designated application fee.
- Municipalities formulate and approve enhancement plans.
- Owners of gecekondu who have obtained a temporary title deed are awarded title deeds for the new building parcel or a share in the new building parcel, contingent upon the dimensions of the original parcel, enacted through land readjustment procedures.
- Redevelopment is executed in alignment with the determinations specified in the improvement plan, facilitated through contractual agreements between landowners and small-scale developers.

In practice, nearly all municipalities nationwide, including gecekondu areas, developed improvement plans. At that time, Ankara was among these cities, with over 50% of its population residing in gecekondu areas. Specifically, in 1980, 72.4% of the total population inhabited gecekondu areas (Keleş, 2021).

The Municipality of Ankara designated 22 gecekondu settlements as improvement planning zones at the end of 1984. Subsequently, in 1984, the district municipalities of Ankara—specifically Altındağ, Çankaya, Keçiören, Mamak, and Yenimahalle—assumed the responsibility of developing improvement plans for their respective districts. As illustrated in Table 1, by the end of 1992, more than 78.3% of the total gecekondu areas had been planned within 8 years (Özdemir, 1998).

Nevertheless, the implementation of these specialised improvement plans has revealed their substantial inadequacy in creating a healthy living environment for gecekondu areas, as they do not comply with the minimum infrastructure standards prescribed by a conventional zoning plan.

Table 1 Improvement planning works by district municipalities (1992)

	Altındağ	Çankaya	Keçiören	Mamak	Yenimahalle	Total
Total *gecekondu* area (ha.)	2427	2171	2487	3615	2206	12,906
The total area encompassed by the improvement plans	1990	1395	2119	3615	999	101,118
%	81.9	64.2	85.2	100.0	45.2	78.3
Unplanned *gecekondu* areas (ha.)	437	776	368	–	1207	2788
%	18.1	35.8	14.8	–	54.8	21.7

Source: Özdemir (1998)

4.2 Municipality Law (No. 5393-Article 73)

Article 73 delineates municipalities' responsibilities regarding the declaration of urban transformation areas and the preparation and execution of urban transformation projects within these designated regions. Conversely, in metropolitan areas, these responsibilities are allocated to the larger metropolitan municipalities, in accordance with the provisions of the Metropolitan Municipality Law (No. 5216, Article 7/c).

Steps Towards Urban Transformation via *Municipality Law—Article 73*

- Initially, the sector designated for urban transformation is identified, and the boundaries of this sector receive approval from the municipal council. The sector must encompass a minimum area of 5 hectares and a maximum of 500 hectares (1 hectare = 10,000 m^2).
- Consequently, all resolutions regarding existing plans, whether related to the development plan, implementation plan, or improvement plan, are hereby suspended within this jurisdiction.
- In the subsequent phase, entitled, landowners will be identified. Should the area encompass gecekondus, the Gecekondu Amnesty Law (No. 2981/3290) shall be applicable. If not, all legitimate flat and landowners will be incorporated into the urban transformation project as legal partners.
- Contracts are executed between the municipality and each eligible partner concerning the terms of payment.
- Each partner is assigned a residence within the recently developed housing blocks, considering the previous dimensions of their properties as well as their current market value.
- In the event that the market value of the real estate is determined to be insufficient for the purchase of the new apartment, the shareholders are obliged to make up the shortfall.
- In numerous instances, the prevailing market value of previously owned properties is insufficient to facilitate the acquisition of a new apartment, thereby necessitating individuals to allocate a considerable sum to secure a single dwelling.

This situation is particularly exacerbated in low-income gecekondu areas, where individuals are often compelled to forgo the project entirely and vacate the premises.

- In specific instances, eligible gecekondu proprietors may be relocated to housing areas that are specifically developed for their accommodation and distinct from their original locations through resettlement initiatives.
- The predominant strategy for the redevelopment of the transformation area entails establishing a contractual arrangement between the Housing Development Administration of Türkiye, known as TOKİ, and the municipal government. Additionally, it is feasible to agree with another real estate development company. In this context, TOKİ may also devise new development and implementation proposals for the urban transformation area.
- The Housing Development Administration (TOKİ) is responsible for the preparation and implementation of development plans for both transformation and resettlement areas, as deemed appropriate.

Since the enactment of the pertinent legislation, it has become the predominant approach for urban transformation, particularly within metropolitan regions. The Ankara Metropolitan Municipality has placed considerable emphasis on urban transformation projects carried out in accordance with Article 73 of the Law (Official Gazette, 03.07. 2005, No. 25874). Between the years 2005 and 2020, the Ankara Metropolitan Municipality designated a total of 45 urban transformation projects, encompassing an area of 6483.78 hectares. Nevertheless, approximately 30% of these 45 urban transformation projects have been subjected to legal proceedings, resulting in the annulment of plans or boundaries. As a consequence, a total of 31 urban transformation projects, covering an area of 3642.98 hectares, were successfully executed between 2005 and 2020 (Fig. 1).

The implementation of Article 73 has initiated a physical and market-oriented transformation process, utilising the size of the project area as a fundamental criterion for urban transformation projects. Following the amendment enacted in 2010, the scope of metropolitan municipalities' authority to declare urban transformation was significantly expanded. This amendment resulted in a substantial increase in the size of the transformation area after 2010 (Fig. 1). However, alongside these developments, the number of lawsuits has also increased. Such lawsuits are typically filed with requests for the annulment of plan changes, the declaration of the urban transformation project area, and the invalidation of the project area boundary change (Cihangir Çamur & Korkmaz, 2021).

4.3 Preservation and Perpetuation of Historical and Cultural Assets Law (Law no. 5366)

This statute was enacted to facilitate the execution of redevelopment and renewal projects within historical and cultural sites, with the aim of preserving and perpetuating these areas (Article 1). The statute bestows authority upon local governments

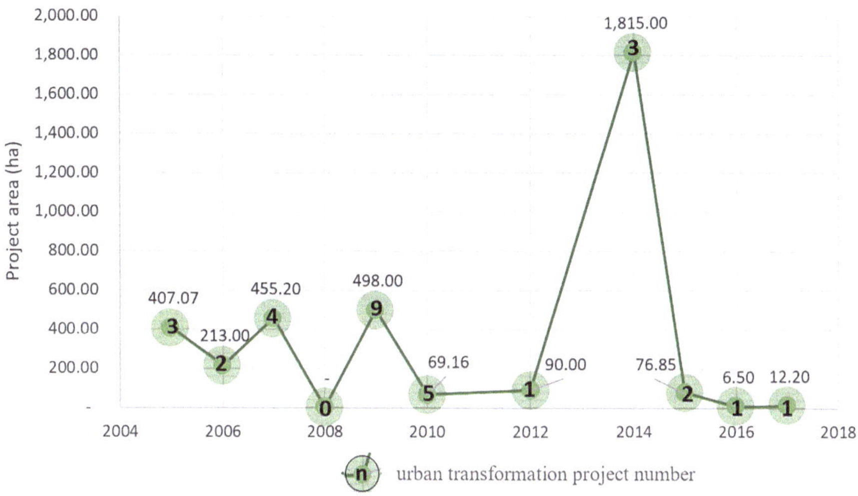

Fig. 1 Information about urban transformation projects implemented under Article 73 in Ankara. Source: Own depiction based on data from the Ankara Metropolitan Municipality archive (2024)

Fig. 2 Tarlabaşı before transformation. Source: Göker (2014)

to designate 'renovation areas' for the implementation of specialised renewal and redevelopment projects, which, in effect, also signifies the transformation of the area.

This legislation has been enacted through various redevelopment initiatives, particularly in İstanbul and Ankara. Notable examples include the Tarlabaşı Renovation Project in İstanbul and the Ulus Historical Centre Renovation Project in Ankara. While the Tarlabaşı Renovation Project is currently underway and has not yet been completed, the Ulus Historical Centre Renovation Project was deemed illegal and subsequently annulled by a court ruling (Figs. 2 and 3).

The municipality articulates the objective of the Tarlabaşı transformation project in the following manner: '*The renovation has significantly mitigated or entirely eradicated the existing physical and socio-economic challenges within the area*

Fig. 3 Visualisation of the Tarlabaşı transformation project proposal. Source: Göker (2014)

through various initiatives and training programmes. Furthermore, the factors that pose a risk to both the area and its adjacent surroundings are anticipated to diminish. The residents of this area, as well as those in the immediate vicinity, will benefit from the added value generated by the renovated area. Additionally, the project is expected to serve as a model for future renovation projects'. However, since the project's inception in 2006, it has remained uncompleted, and the residents, who were promised social improvement, have long been compelled to vacate the area.

4.4 Urban Transformation Law for Northern Ankara Entrance (No. 5104)

This legislation was specifically enacted to facilitate the implementation of a redevelopment project within a designated area in northern Ankara. Through the enactment of a special law, the restriction of 'eligible ownership', as defined by Law No. 2981/3290, which is essential for participation in transformation projects, was circumvented. The law permitted gecekondu owners who constructed their gecekondus subsequent to November 1984, the stipulated deadline for the Gecekondu Amnesty Law (No. 2981/3290), to be integrated into the project as entitled partners. Consequently, the number of eligible legal gecekondu owners has increased, thereby alleviating the social and political costs associated with the project. TOKİ has managed the project in collaboration with the Ankara Metropolitan Municipality.

The area connecting Ankara Esenboğa Airport and the city centre is designated as the 'Northern Ankara Entrance'. Despite the significance of this thoroughfare for the capital, unplanned and illegal constructions were notably prevalent in the region prior to the implementation of Law No. 5104. The project is underpinned by two principal components (Erman, 2016; Korkmaz & Balaban, 2020; Yüksel, 2007). The first component comprises relatively high-quality, low-density housing areas equipped with public services, referred to as 'luxury housing areas'. In contrast, the second consists of relatively low-quality, high-density housing areas that lack essential public services, identified as 'resettlement housing areas' for eligible gecekondu owners.

The financing of the project pertaining to the urban transformation of the Northern Ankara Entrance has been suitably regulated by legal statutes. This initiative encompasses resettlement housing areas designated for property owners, as well as luxury housing segments intended to generate funding for the project. These provisions also include workplaces, shopping centres, and areas designed for social enhancement, which may further be allocated to individual beneficiaries. The primary objective is to utilise the revenue derived from the sales of luxury residences and workplace properties administered by the Municipality and the Administration to finance the project (Yasin, 2005).

4.5 Urban Transformation Law of Hazardous Areas (No. 6306)

Through this legislation, the Ministry of Environment, Urbanisation, and Climate Change has been vested with the authority to oversee the comprehensive management of the transformation process in hazardous areas, thereby superseding local governments. The substantial power conferred upon the Ministry is deemed essential for accelerating the transformation process in these critical regions, where immediate action is imperative under such circumstances.

The law introduces three novel concepts pertinent to the execution of transformation projects: 'hazardous area', 'hazardous building', and 'reserve area'. A hazardous area is defined as the 'area that carries the risk of causing loss of life and property due to the ground structure or the construction on it'. Conversely, a hazardous building is characterised as a building that 'is located either within or outside the hazardous area, has completed its economic life, or is at risk of collapse or significant damage, which is determined based on scientific and technical data'. Lastly, the reserve area is defined as the areas 'designated by the Ministry, with the authorisation of the Ministry of Treasury and Finance, to be used as a new settlement area' in accordance with this Law (Official Gazette, 31.05. 2012, No. 28309).

In Hazardous Areas:

- Firstly, the Ministry designated the 'hazardous area'.
- If the construction of new and secure housing units in the same area is deemed technically feasible, a transformation project has been devised for that region.
- If that is not the case, the transformation project is executed within the 'reserve area', which is also designated by the Ministry.
- In both instances, the Ministry prepares and sanctions the development and implementation plans meticulously.
- In this context, either TOKİ or a private development company may undertake the transformation project as stipulated by the terms of the contract established with the Ministry.

By the year 2018, 4 years after the enactment of the law, 244 hazardous areas comprising a cumulative area of 12,697 hectares were officially designated across 53 provinces in Türkiye. Within these specified areas, the total number of

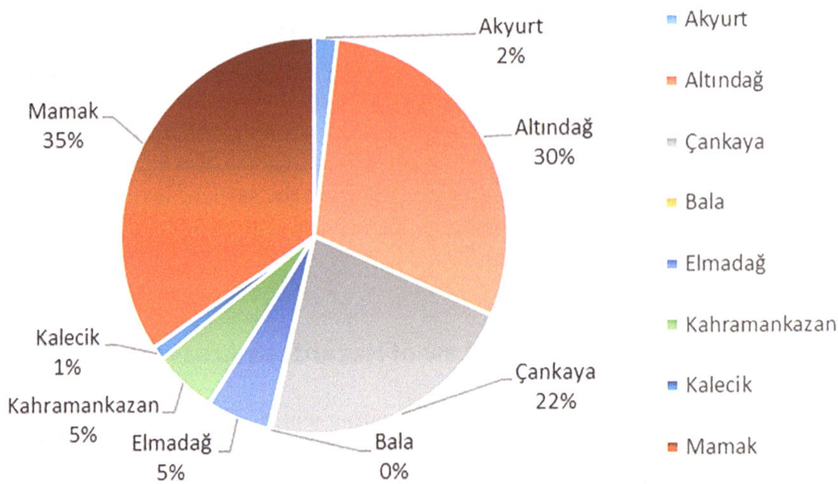

Fig. 4 The distribution of hazardous areas in Ankara according to Law No. 6360. Source: Own depiction based on data from the Ankara Metropolitan Municipality archive (2024)

independent units is approximately 662,000. The population residing in these regions is estimated to be around 1,832,000 individuals (Berk, 2019).

Meanwhile, 987.1 hectares across eight distinct zones in Ankara have been classified as 'hazardous areas' by the Ministry. An analysis of the spatial distribution of these hazardous areas reveals that 35% are situated in Mamak, 30% in Altındağ, and 22% in Çankaya (Fig. 4). The primary rationale for the designation of these hazardous areas in the Mamak, Altındağ, and Çankaya Districts is attributed to the soil structure and the substandard quality of construction on the ground.

In Buildings Considered Hazardous:

- The risk assessment report is obtained from authorised institutions.
- The demolition or reinforcement of the structure may commence following the completion of the assessment report.
- In either instance, a contract is executed between property owners and the real estate development company.
- This contract establishes the valuation of both existing and newly constructed flats, specifies the dimensions of the newly constructed flats, and outlines the total financial contribution for rent to be paid during the construction period.
- In the concluding phase, small-scale developers implement and finalise the transformation at the plot level.

Legislation has conferred certain advantages upon private developers to expedite the transformation of hazardous buildings.

Developers are exempt from:

- All payments related to transactions, contracts, transfers, registrations, and any other applications must be appropriately processed.

Table 2 Distribution of building transformations by districts (2015–2022)

	Altındağ	Çankaya	Keçiören	Mamak	Yenimahalle	Total
2015	1102	**6250**	1532	1124	2132	**12,140**
Total in 2022	2325	**12,652**	3258	7232	4563	**30H.030**

Source: Own depiction based on data from the Ministry of Environment, Urbanisation and Climate Change archive (2024)

- Notary fees, title deed fees, and all other fees imposed by municipal authorities.
- Inheritance and transfer taxes, along with other associated taxes.

Moreover, the loans acquired by the developers are exempt from the taxation that applies to bank and insurance transactions. The remediation of hazardous buildings has represented the primary method of transformation since the enactment of the pertinent legislation. In Ankara, for instance, since 2012, a total of 12.140 buildings have been redeveloped in compliance with Law No. 6360. Nonetheless, the exemptions conferred upon developers have led to the transformation of designated middle-income residential areas, where urban rent exceeds that of other regions. Table 2 illustrates the distribution of these single-building transformation figures across the major districts of Ankara. As indicated in the table, the Çankaya district stands out as the leading area, characterised by the highest urban land rent in the city.

5 Concluding

This chapter examined the proliferation of informal housing sectors in Türkiye and the policies designed to alleviate this trend through urban transformation initiatives. Following the 1980s, the conversion of low-income residential zones into upscale developments, along with the subsequent influx of private sector investments, has become common practice within urban transformation. The primary concern revolves around the underlying causes of the demand for transformation. Although the main stakeholders in the implementation of the Gecekondu Amnesty Laws (No. 2981), which facilitated the comprehensive redevelopment of such areas, were the gecekondu proprietors, it has now become apparent that these gecekondu owners have emerged as the most resistant group to the ongoing urban transformation projects.

Experiences indicate that the enhancement of social and economic conditions for individuals residing in such areas has become increasingly significant, alongside the physical transformation of these regions. Nonetheless, achieving physical, social, and economic transformation through a holistic approach via urban transformation projects necessitates a participatory model, despite the challenges associated with its implementation. In many instances, the eligibility criteria for these transformation projects may inadvertently exclude the urban poor from participation while simultaneously facilitating the transfer of urban rent to middle- and upper-income groups.

The measures that may be pursued for this purpose can be listed as follows:

- The origins and justification for the demand for transformation should be recognised, and compelled transformation projects should not be executed.
- By employing the social impact assessment method, it is essential to ascertain that the proposed transformation will augment the quality of life within the neighbourhood. Consequently, well-planned and inclusive processes should be employed.
- The project ought to be economically viable and accessible for individuals within the urban disadvantaged groups who engage in urban transformation initiatives.
- Applications and strategies relevant to the domains where urban transformation initiatives are executed should be formulated.
- The increment value resulting from the urban transformation projects ought to be distinctly defined, accompanied by the determination of its distribution.
- The delineation of boundaries for urban transformation areas should be established using scientific and technical methods.

References

Akkar, M. (2006). Kentsel dönüşüm üzerine batı'daki kavramlar, tanımlar, süreçler ve Türkiye. *Planlama, 2006*(2), 29–38.

Atkinson, R. (1999). Discourses of partnership and empowerment in Contemporary British Urban Regeneration. *Urban Studies, 36*, 59–72.

Balaban, O. (2012). The negative effects of construction boom on urban planning and environment in Türkiye: Unravelling the role of the public sector. *Habitat International, 36*(1), 26–35.

Berk, K. (2019). *6306 sayılı kanun kapsamında gerçekleştirilen riskli alan projelerinde merkezi idare ile yerel yönetimlerin rolü* (Yayımlanmış Tezsiz Yüksek Lisans Dönem Projesi). Ankara Üniversitesi, Fen Bilimleri Enstitüsü.

Cihangir Çamur, K., & Korkmaz, C. (2021). İnşaat odaklı ekonomide kentsel dönüşüm mevzuatının dönüşümü, pratiği ve planlama ilke-esasları çatışması: Mahkeme kararlarında Ankara örneği. *Planlama, 31*(1), 95–107.

Danielson, M. N., & Keleş, R. (1985). *The politics of rapid urbanisation: Government and growth in modern Türkiye*. Holmes & Meier.

Erman, T. (2016). *Mış gibi site*. İletişim Yayınları.

Göker, M. (2014). *Tarlabaşı bölgesinin kamusal mekan açısından değerlendirilmesi: Tarlabaşı yenileme projesi öncesi ve sonrası* (Yüksek Lisans Tezi). Mimar Sinan Güzel Sanatlar Üniversitesi.

Keleş, R. (2021). *Kentleşme politikası*. (18. Baskı). İmge Yayınevi.

Korkmaz, C., & Balaban, O. (2020). Sustainability of urban regeneration in Türkiye: Assessing the performance of the North Ankara Urban Regeneration Project. *Habitat International, 95*, 102081. https://doi.org/10.1016/j.habitatint.2019.102081

Official Gazette. (1984, March 8). *Law No. 2981*, No. 18335.

Official Gazette. (1986, July 23). *Implementation of the Code of Law No. 2981 and 3290*, No. 19173.

Official Gazette. (2004, March 4). *Law No. 5104*, No. 25400.

Official Gazette. (2005, July 3). *Law No. 5393*, No. 25874.

Official Gazette. (2012, May 16). *Law No. 6306*, No. 28309.

Özdemir, N. (1998). *Transformation of squatter settlements into authorised apartment blocks: A case study of Ankara*. Published PhD Thesis, University of Kent.
Özdemir Sönmez, N. (2006). Düzensiz konut alanlarında kentsel dönüşüm modelleri üzerine bir değerlendirme. *Planlama, 2*, 121–127.
Özdemir Sönmez, N. (2012). Kentsel dönüşüm. In F. Eke & A. Sat (Eds.), *Kent planlamasına giriş* (pp. 365–376). Ankara Üniversitesi Yayınları.
Özden, P. (2002). Türkiye'de kentsel dönüşümün uygulanabilirliği üzerine düşünceler. *İ.Ü. Siyasal Bilgiler Fakültesi Dergisi, 35*, 215–233.
Smith, N. (1979). Towards a theory of gentrification: A back-to-the-city movement by capital, not people. *Journal of the American Planning Association, 45*, 538–548.
Smith, N. (1996). *The new urban frontier: Gentrification and the revanchist city*. Routledge.
Tekeli, İ. (2003). Kentleri dönüşüm mekanı olarak düşünmek. In *TMMOB Kentsel Dönüşüm Sempozyumu* (2–7 Haziran), İstanbul.
Uzun, N. (2006). Yeni yasal düzenlemeler ve kentsel dönüşüme etkileri. *Planlama, 2006*(2), 49–52.
Uzun, N. (2020). Kentsel yenileme ve dönüşüm. In S. S. Özdemir, B. Ö. Sarı, & N. Uzun (Eds.), *Kent planlama* (pp. xx–xx). İmge Yayınları.
Yasin, M. (2005). Kentsel dönüşüm uygulamalarının hukuki boyutu. *TBB Dergisi, 60*, 105–138.
Yetişkul, E., Kayasü, S., & Özdemir, S. Y. (2016). Local responses to urban redevelopment projects: The case of Beyoğlu, Istanbul. *Habitat International, 51*, 159–167.
Yüksel, Ö. (2007). *Kentsel dönüşümün fiziksel ve sosyal mekana etkisi: Kuzey Ankara Kent Girişi Kentsel Dönüşüm Projesi* (Yüksek Lisans Tezi). Gazi Üniversitesi, Fen Bilimleri Enstitüsü.

F. Nihan Özdemir Sönmez is a professor at the Department of Real Estate Development and Management, Faculty of Applied Sciences, Ankara University, Türkiye. She graduated from Middle East Technical University in 1987 with a degree in City and Regional Planning. She subsequently obtained her master's degree in the same field from the University's City Planning Master's Programme in 1990. In 1998, she earned her Ph.D. in Urban Studies from the University of Kent, United Kingdom, with a dissertation entitled "The Transformation of Squatter Settlements into Authorised Apartment Blocks: A Case Study of Ankara, Türkiye". She commenced her academic career as a research assistant in the Department of City and Regional Planning at Gazi University in 1988. In 2005, she advanced to the position of assistant professor and was subsequently promoted to associate professor in 2012. Since March 2016, she has been a faculty member of Ankara University's Department of Real Estate Development and Management, achieving the rank of full professor in 2018. She specialises in research areas including urban planning, urban policies, and urban transformation.

Emine Baydan graduated from the Department of City and Regional Planning at Middle East Technical University in 2012. In 2021, she earned her master's degree from the Department of Real Estate Development and Management at the Graduate School of Natural and Applied Sciences at Ankara University. Her master's thesis examined planning and property relations in conservation areas, featuring a case study of the Cappadocia region in middle Anatolia. She is currently a Ph.D. candidate in the same department, concentrating on the interplay between transportation planning, land use, and real estate markets. Mrs. Baydan commenced her academic career in 2018 as a research assistant in the Department of Real Estate Development at Ankara University. Her research interests encompass urban planning, real estate development, transportation, spatial transformation, and the application of digital tools, including sentiment analysis and artificial intelligence, in analysing real estate and urban policies.

Parla Güneş is a research assistant at the Department of Real Estate Development and Management, Faculty of Applied Sciences, Ankara University, Türkiye. She is currently pursuing her doctoral studies in the Department of Real Estate Development at Ankara University's Graduate School of Natural and Applied Sciences. She completed her master's degree in the Department of Real Estate Development and Management at Ankara University, with her thesis investigating the relationships between urban growth, sprawl, and the real estate market in the Alacaatlı, Bağlıca, and Dodurga neighbourhoods of Ankara. Ms. Güneş's academic work primarily focuses on urban spatial perception, urban identity, spatial analysis, urban transformation processes, sustainability, and the preservation of urban values. Her research emphasises the importance of understanding the social and economic dynamics of urban spaces, evaluating public participation processes, and refining spatial planning strategies. She primarily focuses her research on urban transformation, socio-spatial dynamics, land-use planning, and real estate development, employing an interdisciplinary framework that combines sociology, city and regional planning, and real estate economics. These topics are vital not only for expanding academic knowledge but also for guiding policymaking and professional practices in real estate and urban planning.

Urban Infrastructure Provision and Real Estate Markets

Mustafa Tuna, Sinan Güneş, Mustafa Tombul, and Sevilay Bostancı

Abstract

Urban infrastructure encompasses a diverse array of services, which include communication, transportation, energy distribution, recycling and refining processes, solid waste collection, wastewater and sewage management, as well as the provision and distribution of safe drinking water. It entails the management and planning of these services, in addition to the construction, maintenance, renewal, and operation of associated networks and facilities. In Türkiye, the processes pertaining to the financing, planning, projection, management, and operation of urban infrastructure are executed by central administrations (ministries), local authorities, water and sewage administrations, and transportation authorities. This chapter explores the concept of urban infrastructure and its historical development in Türkiye from 1980 to 2021. Furthermore, it examines the allocation of public investments within the sector, encompassing infrastructure investments and their proportion of Gross Domestic Product (GDP), as well as infrastructure developments, financing methodologies, associated risks, and challenges. The influence of infrastructure on real estate markets is also evaluated.

Keywords

Urban infrastructure · Real estate financing · Public-private cooperation

M. Tuna · S. Güneş (✉) · M. Tombul
Department of Real Estate Development and Management, Faculty of Applied Sciences, Ankara University, Ankara, Türkiye
e-mail: mustafatuna@ankara.edu.tr; sngunes@ankara.edu.tr; mtombul@ankara.edu.tr

S. Bostancı
EGO General Directorate, Ankara Metropolitan Municipality, Ankara, Türkiye
e-mail: Sevilay.bostanci@ego.gov.tr

T. Just et al. (eds.), *Understanding Türkiye's Real Estate Markets*, Management for Professionals, https://doi.org/10.1007/978-3-032-13297-0_26

1 Introduction

Urban infrastructure transcends a collection of engineered facilities, utilities, and systems. It serves as a platform for multi-level governance, spanning from local administrations to national policy frameworks, and interweaving issues related to economic growth, climate change, and municipal waste (Ferrer et al., 2018). Contemporary research highlights that sustainable urban infrastructure requires extensive interventions and collaborative efforts from various stakeholders, encompassing not only public–private partnerships but also innovative methods for evaluating impact and the development of advanced financing instruments for green infrastructure initiatives (Ferrer et al., 2018; Meng et al., 2024).

The World Bank, recognised as the largest multilateral financier of urban development, allocates an average of USD 5 billion annually towards urban development, resilience, and land, thereby contributing to Sustainable Development Goal No. 11: Make cities inclusive, safe, resilient, and sustainable (World Bank, 2025). With over 50% of the global population currently residing in urban areas, projections indicate that nearly 7 out of 10 people will live in cities by 2050. The demand for urban infrastructure systems is thus rising steadily (World Bank, 2025).

Public-private partnerships (PPPs) have emerged as vital financing mechanisms for infrastructure development. Numerous nations are endeavouring to leverage this model to augment the economic value of infrastructure outputs (Liu et al., 2024; World Bank, 2022). The escalating complexity associated with financing infrastructure projects, along with the imperative for sustainable development, has compelled governments worldwide to explore innovative funding mechanisms that can bridge the widening infrastructure investment gap (Global Infrastructure Outlook, 2020).

Türkiye outlines policies and measures pertaining to urban technical infrastructure within its Eleventh Development Plan. The main objective of the Development Plan is articulated as follows: "Ensuring that the population has access to healthy and reliable potable and utility water, minimising the effects of wastewater on human and environmental health, achieving effective management of these resources; reducing waste to mitigate its impacts on human and environmental health, promoting recycling and recovery, and eliminating waste as well as creating safe and sustainable urban transportation systems that are efficient in both time and cost."

This chapter outlines the concept and characteristics of infrastructure, examining the evolution of urban infrastructure in Türkiye from 1980 to 2021. The analysis concludes in 2021 due to data availability constraints and to ensure methodological consistency with the most recent, complete, and official statistics available. It addresses the allocation of public investments alongside infrastructure investments and their proportion of GDP. Furthermore, it analyses developments in infrastructure, financing methods, associated risks, and pertinent issues. The influence of infrastructure on real estate markets is also analysed.

2 Historical Process of Urban Infrastructure in Türkiye

Between 1980 and 1990, the public sector in Türkiye refrained from implementing policies aimed at promoting investment in the mining and manufacturing sectors. During this time, the proportion of investments allocated to energy, communication, transportation, and social infrastructure increased in relation to total assets, while the percentage of public investments directed towards the mining and manufacturing sectors in Türkiye began to decline in the 1980s, decreasing from 31.7% to 8.6%, and ultimately reaching 3.4% by 1990. Despite the observed decline in the mining and manufacturing industries, a notable increase was observed in the proportion of infrastructure investments within the transportation and other public service sectors as part of the public assets. This upward trend signifies that public services and transportation industries were prioritised in public investment policies during this period (Kalem, 2015).

The distribution of public investments by sector from 2010 to 2021 reveals that the transportation sector is of great importance. Conversely, the inclusion of industries such as health and energy, which are categorised as infrastructure investments, among the sectors receiving the most substantial public asset investments underscores the significant portion of infrastructure services within these investments (Table 1).

Public investments were restricted to infrastructure due to regulations outlined in the 1980 investment policies, increasing the proportion of assets held by the private sector. Furthermore, guidelines were established to attract foreign investors to Türkiye (Kılıçbay, 1991). Figure 1 delineates the allocation of resources across the health, transportation, energy, and education sectors within public fixed capital investments from 1998 to 2021. Excluding the effects of the pandemic, infrastructure investments have exhibited consistent growth since 2004. However, the funding for infrastructure was concentrated on the transportation sector.

The correlation between infrastructure investments, GDP, and economic growth shows that the proportion of infrastructure investments has declined in recent years. The primary factor contributing to the decline in the share of infrastructure investments is the heightened competition for infrastructure services in Türkiye, accompanied by variations in exchange rates (Table 2).

The significant migration to urban centres following the declaration of the Republic emerged as a big challenge to Türkiye's urbanisation path during the 1920s. Over the subsequent decades, Türkiye gradually developed its urban infrastructure capabilities through successive development plans and policy reforms, ultimately transforming its municipalities through comprehensive policies implemented in urban infrastructure. This evolutionary process culminated in one of the most profound and transformative urbanisation experiences globally (World Bank, 2015). In recent years, a systematic method has been employed to achieve the objectives outlined in the Eleventh Development Plan—the most comprehensive policy devised for urban infrastructure. It has been noted that the initiatives concerning

Table 1 Distribution of public investments by sector (million USD)

	2010	2011	2012	2013	2014	2015	2016	2017	2018	2019	2020	2021
Agri-culture	5988	5665	6402	6879	5416	5243	4906	4985	4197	2227	1593	2055
Mining	1040	1279	1240	936	798	878	416	435	1068	1087	1708	1808
Manufacturing	426	341	406	475	325	289	200	174	128	121	309	144
Energy	3225	2581	2434	2145	2102	1453	1027	1037	937	2328	2841	2228
Trans-porta-tion	18,565	14,906	13,831	14,596	10,638	10,661	8458	8108	19,937	9595	12,031	10,624
Tou-rism	173	196	206	190	112	175	94	254	249	66	66	43
Hou-sing	454	456	293	291	192	13	450	535	347	424	277	419
Edu-cation	2655	2489	2742	2842	2456	7488	5536	4064	2578	3584	1870	3743
Health	916	852	816	774	3476	3332	1905	1536	2193	1057	366	2522
Other services	3402	2938	2608	17,086	14,239	14,450	9688	7256	14,023	8960	5376	7327

Source: PSB (2022)

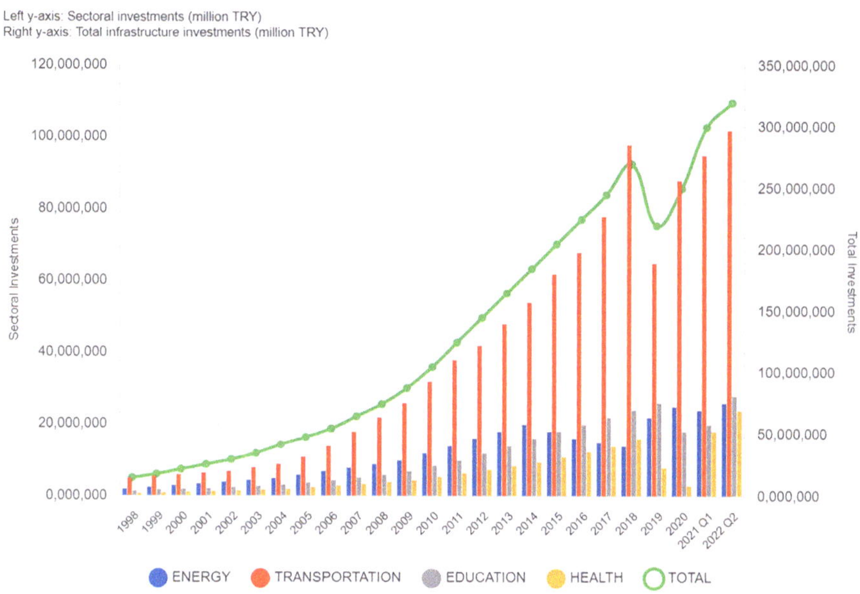

Fig. 1 The share of the infrastructure investments within the public fixed capital investments in Türkiye. Source: PSB (2022)

Table 2 Infrastructure investments in Türkiye and growth relations

Years	Infrastructure Investments (thousands of USD)	GDP (million USD)	Share in the GDP (%)	Annual Growth (%)
2010	62,122,121,20	772,365	8.04	8.4
2011	58,684,466,45	831,696	7.06	11.2
2012	61,130,972,64	871,125	7.02	4.8
2013	72,578,314,23	950,355	7.64	8.5
2014	62,404,422,65	934,857	6.68	4.9
2015	57,568,232,08	861,879	6.68	6.1
2016	55,914,146,88	862,746	6.48	3.3
2017	55,578,052,86	852,618	6.52	7.5
2018	49,104,463,46	789,043	6.22	5.0
2019	33,530,528,55	760,778	4.41	0.9
2020	29,657,690,54	717,049	4.14	1.8
2021	30,919,288,71	802,678	3.85	11.0

Note: The amounts were converted from TL to USD using the average exchange rate calculation for each year. Source: Own depiction based on data from TSI (2022) and the World Bank (2022)

potable water and sewerage have been substantially advanced. Nonetheless, it is important to emphasise that the advances achieved in wastewater management have not yet attained the requisite level, necessitating a focus on sewage in forthcoming endeavours (Table 3).

Table 3 Urban infrastructure indicators within the scope of the eleventh development plan

	2018	2020	% Change
Total number of municipalities	1399	1389	−0.71
Number of municipalities provided with potable and utility water supply networks.	1397	1387	−0.72
The number of municipalities served by the sewerage network.	1357	1362	0.37
The percentage of the municipality's population that is served by potable and utility water networks, in relation to the total population of the city (%)	98.60	98.70	0.10
The percentage of the municipality's population that is served by a sewerage network in relation to the total population of the city (%)	90.70	91.10	0.44
The total volume of water extracted from the potable and utility water network (in million m^3)	6193	6492	4.83
The total volume of water distributed through the potable and utility water network is measured in million cubic meters (m^3).	4045	4309	6.53
The cumulative volume of water processed in the water refining facilities (in million m^3)	3574	3900	9.12
The total volume of water discharged into the receiving environments (million m^3)	4795	4960	3.44
The total volume of wastewater processed in the wastewater treatment facilities (million m^3)	4236	4358	2.88
The percentage of wastewater refined (%)	88.30	87.90	−0.45
The percentage of untreated wastewater discharged (%)	11.70	12.10	3.42
The mean daily quantity of water consumed per capita (litres/person-day)	224	228	1.79
The average daily volume of wastewater discharged per capita (litres/person-day)	188	189	0.53
Total number of wastewater treatment facilities.	4196	4276	1.91
The quantity of potable water and utility water refining facilities located within municipalities.	629	714	13.51
The percentage of the municipality's population that is served by wastewater treatment facilities, in relation to the total population of the city (%)	78.70	77.70	−1.27
The percentage of recycled treated wastewater (%)	2.30	1.60	−30.43
The percentage of potable water seepage loss (%)	34.70	33.60	−3.17
The percentage of waste recovery associated with the zero-waste initiative (%)	13	19	46.15
The number of buildings participating in the zero-waste program (in thousands).	13	61	369.23
The proportion of the population in the municipalities that is regularly provided with storage service (%)	75	99	32.00
Cumulative length of the urban rail system (km)	747	782	4.69
Cumulative length of bicycle lanes (in km)	1048	1426	36.07

Source: TSI (2022)

3 Financing of the Infrastructure Investments

In Türkiye, the responsibility for most infrastructure investments has progressively been delegated to local administrations as part of more extensive decentralisation and localisation reforms. While infrastructure services, including energy supply, transportation systems, environmental sanitation, bridge and underpass construction, and urban water provision, were traditionally under the jurisdiction of the central government, these responsibilities have gradually been transitioned to local governments in accordance with the provisions of the Metropolitan Municipality Law No. 6360.

The financing of infrastructure investments, whether undertaken by local or central authorities, is facilitated through a combination of institutional support and financial mechanisms, a structure that has evolved significantly since the early 1990s (Public Administration Research, 1992). Key actors in this domain include İlbank (Provincial Bank) and various domestic and international banking institutions. The financial models employed to support these investments encompass a broad array of public-private partnership (PPP) modalities, such as long-term leasing, build-operate-transfer (BOT), transfer of operational rights, rehabilitate-operate-transfer (ROT), design-build-finance-operate (DBFO), build-lease-transfer (BLT), and pure build-operate schemes.

In addition to these models, financing through municipal affiliates encompasses instruments such as income-sharing certificates, privatisation-linked financial structures, and bond issuance. Local administrations in Türkiye also generate funds through revenues derived from real estate and asset management, operational and industrial income, and self-generated income streams. These models are frequently complemented by transfers from the central budget and various forms of earmarked taxes, fines, and borrowing instruments (Çelebi, 2003). Alternative and increasingly prominent financing instruments include direct borrowing, mezzanine financing, municipal bond issuance, Sukuk (Islamic leasing certificates), and a range of refinancing options specifically designed to meet long-term infrastructure needs.

Investing in and financing sustainable infrastructure is paramount, not only for addressing the needs stemming from urbanisation and service provision but also due to the integrated environmental, social, and economic benefits it provides (Meng et al., 2024). In addition to its direct utility, investments in infrastructure contribute to shaping urban form, facilitating higher population densities, and influencing private investment decisions, thereby serving a catalytic role in sustainable urban development (Collier & Venables, 2016).

3.1 Providing Financing from the Provincial Bank

İller Bank is a development and investment bank established in accordance with Law No. 6107, with a capital of TL 30 billion. The institution assists and advises in the construction of infrastructure and superstructure for urban projects, with shareholders comprising all provincial and municipal administrations. Its primary responsibility is to support the financing requirements of cities and their associated administrations, in addition to exceptional regional administrations and local government unions. The regional bank extends credit to local administrations for infrastructure investments, including urban transformation, underpasses and overpasses, potable water systems, sewerage systems, road construction, rail transportation systems, and intersection arrangements. Furthermore, the institution is tasked with facilitating the provision of treasury-guaranteed funds in foreign currency from international donor organisations, financial institutions, and investment banks.

3.2 Providing Financing from Domestic Banks Through Borrowing

Türkiye should pursue financing options from both domestic and foreign banking institutions through borrowing, as local administration revenues are insufficient for the execution of infrastructure investments. The regional administrations are permitted to borrow up to 10% of their respective budgets, a proposition that must be submitted to the town council for approval. This process is governed as follows: "Domestic borrowings exceeding this amount may be made with the decision of an absolute majority of the full number of council members and the approval of the Ministry of Environment, Urbanism, and Climate Change". Furthermore, the cumulative total of foreign and domestic borrowing cannot exceed the amount assessed according to the revaluation rate of the most recently finalised budget revenues, as stipulated by the local administrations in compliance with the Tax Procedure Law numbered 213.

3.3 Providing Financing from Foreign Banks through Borrowing

In accordance with Municipality Law 5393, municipalities in Türkiye are empowered to secure loans for services pertaining to their official responsibilities. Local administrations were granted the authority to procure funds from foreign sources as outlined in the "Regulation of Principles and Procedures for the Provision of Foreign Financing within the Scope of Law No. 4749", which was instituted in 2009. They can access foreign financing through two avenues: pursuing treasury-guaranteed funding sources and obtaining loans without a treasury guarantee.

Financing for infrastructure investments may be secured through national resources in Türkiye, or funding and donations could be provided by international institutions such as the World Bank. It is uncommon for metropolitan municipalities to approach the World Bank, given that the process of obtaining recognition or contributions from the institution is both lengthy and complex.

3.4 Public–Private Cooperation

Upon reviewing the progress of projects executed in Türkiye through public–private cooperation (PPC) from 1990 to 2021, 2011 witnessed the highest number of projects completed, while 2015 marked a significant year, with the largest investment amount, approximately USD 45 billion. The electricity sector was the biggest domain where the PPC model was applied, both in terms of the quantity of projects and the total investment, as per the industry classification of investments. This was subsequently followed by the development of airport and highway services (World Bank, 2022). Türkiye has undertaken numerous large-scale infrastructure projects employing the Build-Operate-Transfer (BOT) model and continues to initiate comparable initiatives (Table 4).

Türkiye's infrastructure investment requirements from 2022 to 2040 are projected to be USD 569 billion. By the end of 2021, Türkiye had established 28,284 km of dual carriageways and 1213 km of high-speed rail. Furthermore, it manages 344.9 million tons of maritime container transport and operates 56 airports nationwide (Fig. 2).

Table 4 Big infrastructure projects in Türkiye are performed with the BOT model

Project	Investment amount (US dollars)	Remark
İstanbul Airport	USD 6.5 billion	It has an annual capacity of 150 million passengers.
Eurasia Tunnel (Istanbul Strait Highway Tube Passage Project)	USD 1.2 billion	It establishes a connection between the European and Asian sides through a highway tunnel that spans 14.6 km beneath the sea.
Canal Istanbul		Six bridges span 45 kilometres, with a depth of 21 metres and a width of 275 metres.
Yavuz Sultan Selim Bridge (Third Strait Bridge)	USD 3.5 billion	The structure measures 59 metres in width and was commissioned in 2016.
Ankara-Istanbul High-Speed Railway	USD 544.7 million	
Gebze-Halkalı Railway		It includes 10 stations, 31 viaducts (8 km long), and 53 tunnels (120 km long), covering a total distance of 213 km. The passenger capacity is 13 million per year, while the load capacity is 12 million tons annually.
Gebze-Orhangazi-Izmir Expressway	Investment amount of USD 6.5 billion	The construction of a 427 km expressway comprises a 43 km connection and an additional 384 km segment.
1915 Çanakkale Bridge	USD 2.8 billion	The project was commissioned in 2022 and possesses a medium level of openness, measuring 2023 metres in length.

Source: Kocabıyık (2016)

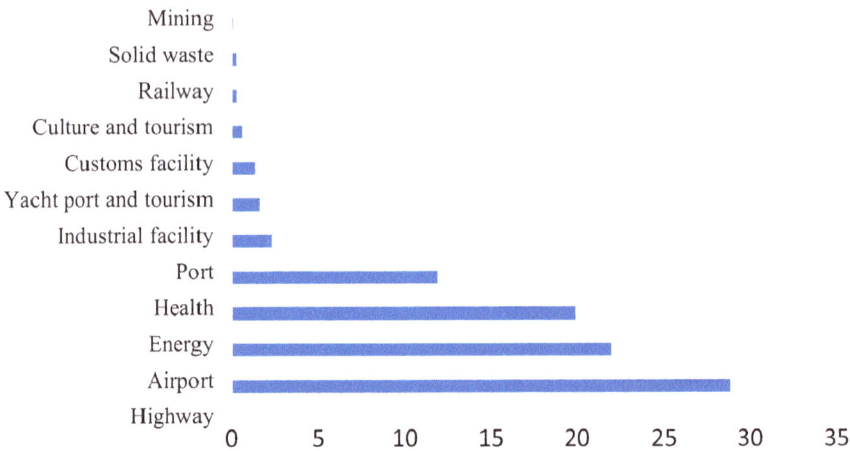

Fig. 2 Sectoral distribution of investment amounts for PPC projects, in percentage (%). Source: PSB (2022)

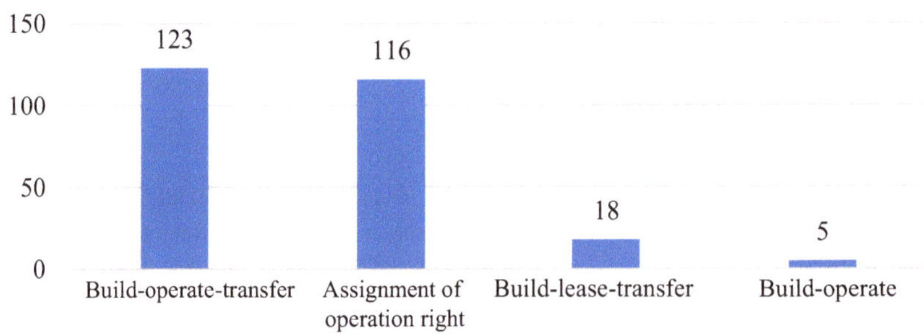

Fig. 3 PPC models are the most frequently used in PPC projects performed in Türkiye. Source: PSB (2022)

Türkiye's geopolitically strategic location, coupled with the increasing volume of international trade, necessitates the advancement of infrastructure investments within the country. An analysis of sector-based investment amounts for projects conducted using the Public–Private Collaboration (PPC) method indicates that investment in highways ranks first, followed by investment in airports, and then the energy sector, all assessed at 2022 prices. The hierarchy of the most frequently used models in projects executed via the PPC method in Türkiye is as follows: build-operate-transfer (123 tasks), assignment of operational rights (116 projects), build-lease-transfer (18 projects), and build-operate (5 projects) (Fig. 3).

Secondary legislation, encompassing laws, statutory decrees, and regulations, supports the legal framework for urban infrastructure in Türkiye. The primary structure for urban infrastructure has been constructed through the provisions of the "Law on Public Improvement" (numbered 3194), the "Law of Municipality" (numbered 5393), the "Law of Metropolitan Municipality" (numbered 5216), and the "Law of Provincial Special Administration" (numbered 5302). This framework is executed at the secondary legislation level through statutory decrees issued concerning the actions and transactions of the "Ministry of Transportation and Infrastructure, Ministry of Environment, Urbanism and Climate Change, and Ministry of Agriculture and Forestry", along with the "Regulation of Metropolitan Municipalities Coordination Centers, Regulation of Planned Areas Type Improvement, and Construction Regulation for Spatial Plans", in addition to regulations addressing issues such as water pollution, wastewater treatment, and environmental impact.

Given that the majority of Türkiye's urban population resides in metropolitan areas, coordinating local administrations in the urban infrastructure sector has become increasingly important. Consequently, metropolitan municipalities have instituted an Infrastructure Coordination Centre (ICC), which facilitates the coordination of urban infrastructure services within each municipality's organisational framework. The ICC is tasked with examining the compliance of proposed infrastructure investments with the city's development plan and annual programmes, thereby ensuring that the assets conform to the overarching strategic plans and programmes.

The configuration of the division of labour among institutions and entities engaged in urban infrastructure, along with the coordination of metropolitan municipalities and the responsibilities and authorisations of the relevant institutions and entities, is illustrated in Fig. 4. Cities play a crucial role in supplying rainwater, wastewater, drinking water, and utility water, in addition to providing electricity distribution and telecommunications services—collectively referred to as infrastructure services—particularly in urban areas.

The considerable number of institutions authorised and accountable for urban infrastructure signifies the necessity for strong inter-institutional coordination. Figure 5 depicts the institutions and entities associated with infrastructure in Türkiye. Additionally, the regions within the urban area have been categorised into natural disaster areas, village settlements, informal settlements, cultural tourism zones, industrial zones, development regions, forested areas, and national parks. The pertinent ministries and entities are likewise presented.

4 Infrastructure Problems and Risks

A notable challenge in developing large-scale infrastructure is the widespread dissemination of misinformation regarding the associated costs, expected benefits, and inherent risks. This misinformation frequently leads to cost overruns, insufficient benefits, and inefficiencies in resource allocation (Harper et al., 2010).

In Türkiye, numerous contemporary infrastructure challenges can be attributed to the urbanisation policies instituted in the 1920s. The failure to effectively manage rapid population growth, combined with constrained planning capacity and a shortage of financial and technical resources during the early Republican era, led to the widespread occurrence of unplanned, uncontrolled, and often illegal construction

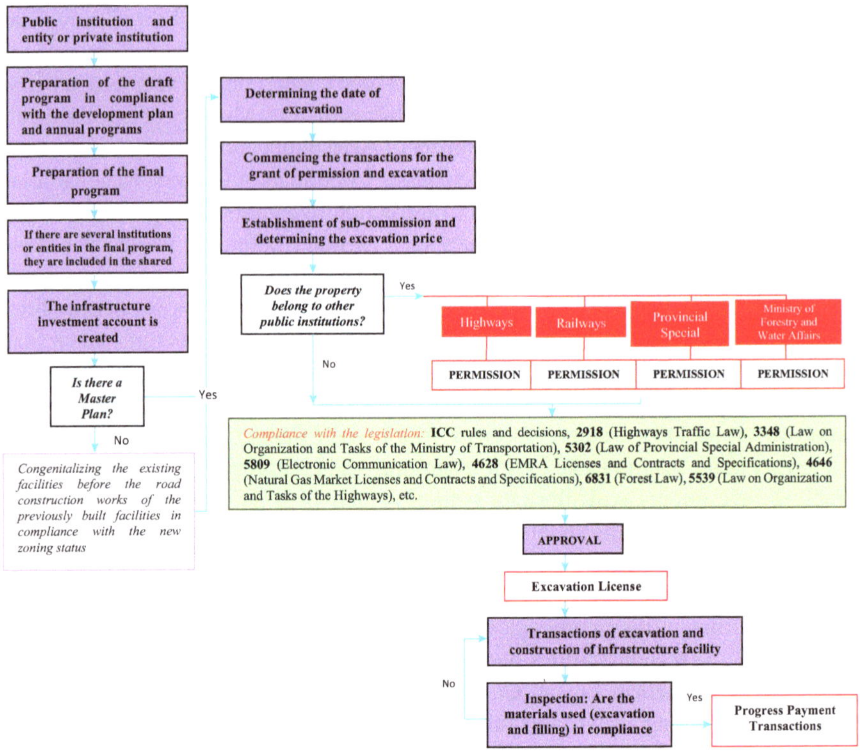

Fig. 4 Infrastructure coordination in metropolitan municipalities. Source: PEUAD (2017)

within urban areas. These dynamics have engendered enduring challenges in guaranteeing equitable, effective, and high-quality infrastructure service delivery—an issue that has continued into the twenty-first century.

In response, the 2000s witnessed a renewed emphasis on investing in urban infrastructure, particularly through collaboration with municipalities. Although these endeavours generated some enhancements, the ongoing presence of systemic and inherited issues, alongside Türkiye's macroeconomic constraints and sociopolitical dynamics, has resulted in infrastructure service provision remaining a significant concern.

Current risks associated with infrastructure are multifaceted, encompassing financial constraints, environmental and ecological concerns, institutional and technical limitations, and governance challenges. The high capital costs, restricted availability of public funds, and the requirement for substantial upfront investment frequently render it unfeasible for local and central governments to rely exclusively on equity financing. As a result, infrastructure projects are often associated with elevated financing costs (Tuna & Bostancı, 2021). Additionally, the lack of qualified personnel within institutions tasked with infrastructure planning and service delivery, along with inadequately developed information systems, hinders the precise identification and resolution of these intricate challenges.

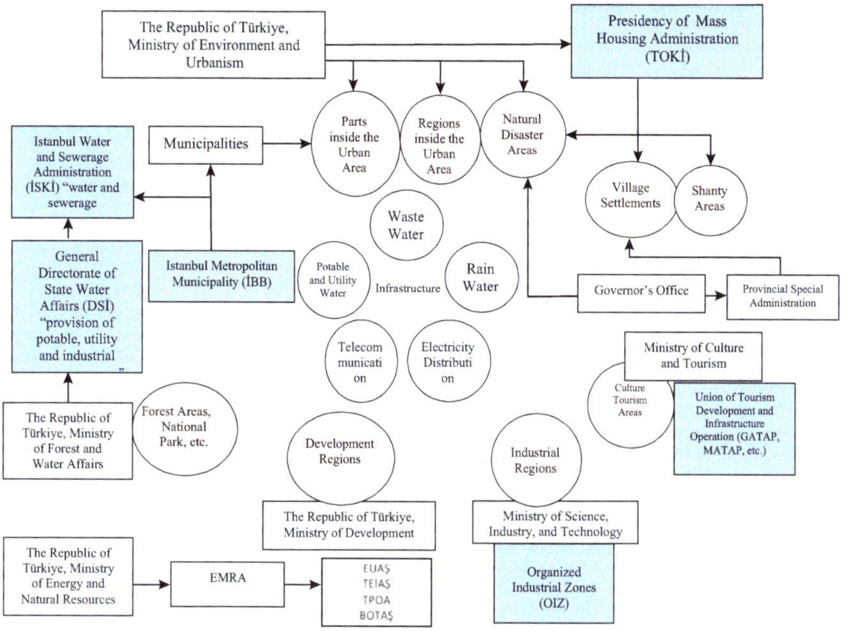

Fig. 5 Relations with the institutions and entities concerning infrastructure in Türkiye. Source: PEUAD (2017)

5 Urban Infrastructure and Real Estate Market in Türkiye

The zoning practices regulated by local or central administration on undeveloped land during the real estate development process contribute to the enhancement of the value of immovable property, a phenomenon referred to as development value. Subsequently, urban infrastructure services are provisioned in the real estate market after this phase. The value of the "increment fee" is determined upon the completion of urban infrastructure services, which encompass roads, sewerage, water supply, and other related services. Ultimately, urban infrastructure services are recognised as significant factors influencing the real estate market through the concept of "land value capture". This concept denotes the increase in value resulting from qualified infrastructure projects, such as urban transportation and urban transformation, on immovable property (MEUCC, 2017), after the value increases generated by zoning and construction activities (Fig. 6).

Urban infrastructure services are regarded as one of the fundamental factors affecting the value of urban real estate properties (Hong & Brubaker, 2010). Considering the significant role that urban infrastructure services play in the real estate markets in Türkiye, the costs associated with infrastructure investments and the use of emerging value have become urgent concerns (Yılmaz, 2020). Numerous methods exist to transfer the value increase that is generated by publicly managing and executing urban infrastructure services to the broader public. These methods

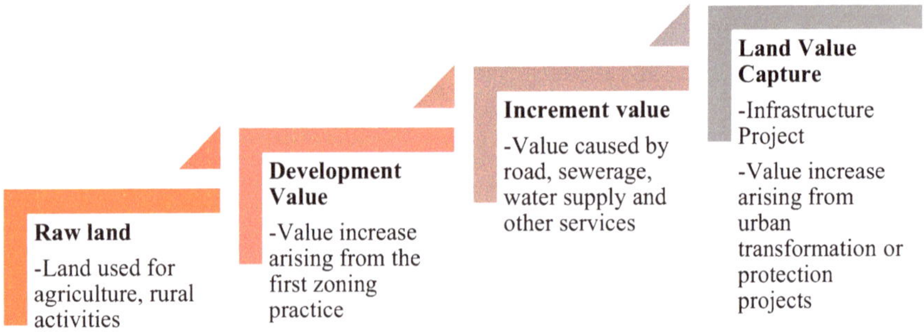

Fig. 6 Position of urban infrastructure in the real estate markets in Türkiye. Source: Tanrıvermiş (2022)

are generally categorised into two groups: the transfer of investment-focused value increases to the public through taxation, and the direct transfer of value increases to the public. Consequently, an indirect increase in the value of urban real estate properties within the affected area can be observed, as the decisions made by public authorities influence the investments above. The primary methods historically and currently employed in Türkiye for transferring the value increase derived from urban infrastructure services to the public encompass valuation duty (betterment), regulatory partnership share, contribution to expenses, urban income tax, and value increase share.

Betterment The municipalities have been authorised to receive a portion of the benefits derived from the services they render, in accordance with the prevailing legal regulations in Türkiye. The share allocated to the administration is determined based on the advantages received by beneficiaries, or by employing one of the methods that involves apportioning the costs of the provided services. Taxes levied on a supportive basis are referred to as betterment, whereas methods that emphasise the division of expenses are designated as participation shares (Bulutoğlu, 1976). This is defined as the payment acquired from immovable properties whose value appreciates due to infrastructure services in alignment with the increased value (Keleş et al., 1999).

Regulation Partnership Share Article 18 of the "Law of Zoning, numbered 3194", encompasses provisions that regulate land and lots. Municipalities are authorised to consolidate the lands and lots within their zoning boundaries with other properties in the area of authorisation, distributing them according to whether they are classified as condominiums or independent shares, as well as for re-parcelling (Aslan, 2014). Up to 45% of the surface area of the land or lot prior to administration may be considered as partnership shares, in relation to the value increases resulting from the application of these regulations. Parcels are designated for use in urban infrastructure services within the areas acquired by the local administration through this method.

Contribution to Expenses Contributions to costs may be derived from individuals or entities benefiting from pertinent services, including those provided by municipal water facilities, sewer systems, and roadways, which are frequently maintained by cities (Yılmaz, 2008). Given that these expenditures contribute to the enhancement of real estate value, such contributions are correlated with property ownership within the region.

Urban Income Tax The valuation of real estate may experience an upward trend due to the local administration's enforcement of zoning regulations, which facilitates the conversion of agricultural lands into residential lots, along with the provision of enhancements such as the completion of urban infrastructure services (Aslan, 2014). Once these projects are finalised, the economic capacity of real estate proprietors within the region, which has undergone substantial development, can be realised through the urban income tax generated by the increased property values, thereby benefiting the public from this growth.

Value Increase Share This method offers the public a significant enhancement in value, mirroring the increase in real estate property values resulting from revisions to the master plans. Additionally, it has been designated as a requisite for governing plan amendments, contingent upon a value increase, in a manner that enables the addressing of the region's social and technical infrastructure needs as well.

6 Conclusion

Notwithstanding the progress made in urban infrastructure services in Türkiye since the 2000s, notable gaps remain in both legislation and practical implementation, primarily stemming from challenges associated with historical urbanisation. It is imperative to establish a secure, accessible, and sustainable urban transportation system in Türkiye that is both efficient in terms of time and cost within the context of urban infrastructure. The actions, strategies, and plans pertaining to the sustainable utilisation, development, and preservation of water resources must exemplify a sense of coherence. Wastewater and potable water services should be delivered in compliance with established standards to ensure adequate and effective provision. The investment efficiency and operational performance of the accountable institutions and entities should also be augmented. Opportunities for improvement must be cultivated both financially and technically to enhance the effectiveness of solid waste management, encompassing the rehabilitation of illegal dumping sites as well as the processes of recovery, transportation, separate collection, source sorting, and waste reduction. Implementation models, such as PPC, should advocate for environmental responsibility and resource efficiency in solid waste management. Facilities tasked with managing domestic solid waste and conducting recovery and transfer operations by local administrations with constrained financial resources should receive the requisite financial support. Decisions, policies, and investments related to transportation and zoning within urban areas ought to be assessed in a coordinated manner. The principal transportation plan and master plans should be prepared harmoniously and updated regularly in Türkiye. To mitigate air pollution, accidents, and traffic congestion in urban areas, demand-driven policies should be formulated for urban transportation rather than those based on supply, thereby promoting the use of mass transportation systems over private vehicle use. Sustainable, environmentally friendly transportation modes should be established, and non-motorised transportation methods should be facilitated within the urban transport network. To foster more effective planning, accurately manage transportation demands, enhance traffic safety, and optimise the use of existing infrastructure, a national intelligent transportation systems (ITS) strategy should be developed, the ITS framework should be advanced, and ITS practices should be broadly implemented.

The urban infrastructure services that the administration has to provide or manage, including water and sewerage, energy, transportation, natural gas, potable water, health, education, and communication, constitute significant investments that pose challenges in securing financing. Within this framework, it is imperative to diversify methods aimed at enhancing value, primarily derived from public urban infrastructure investment services. Relevant regulations must be instituted to facilitate these practices. Furthermore, policies should be formulated to encourage the widespread adoption of Public-Private Partnership (PPP) models in infrastructure investments. The demand for infrastructure investment is increasing and diversifying in response to the growing population and urbanisation in Türkiye. In this context, the roles and functions of institutions and entities that provide infrastructure services should be subjected to continuous review, necessitating restructuring in critical areas such as project inspection, management, financing, development, and assessment. Sustainable and stable plans have to be devised to improve the efficiency and effectiveness of infrastructure services, ensuring that investments are made prudently and effectively.

References

Aslan, M. (2014). Kentsel rantların vergilendirilmesi. *Ankara Barosu Dergisi, 3*, 117–134. https://dergipark.org.tr/en/download/article-file/398184. Accessed 27 September 2022

Bulutoğlu, K. (1976). *Türk Vergi Sistemi* (5th ed.). Fakülteler Matbaası.

Çelebi, T. (2003). *Avrupa Yerel Yönetimler Özerklik Şartı ve Türkiye'de İdari Vesayet Uygulamasının Değerlendirilmesi*. Master's thesis, Ankara University. Retrieved September 27, 2022, from https://dspace.ankara.edu.tr/xmlui/bitstream/handle/20.500.12575/27831/842.pdf?sequence=1&isAllowed=y

Collier, P., & Venables, A. J. (2016). Urban infrastructure for development. *Oxford Review of Economic Policy, 32*(3), 391–409. Retrieved April 7, 2025, from https://academic.oup.com/oxrep/article-abstract/32/3/391/1745327

Ferrer, A. L. C., Thomé, A. M. T., & Scavarda, A. J. (2018). Sustainable urban infrastructure: A review. *Resources, Conservation and Recycling, 128*, 360–372. Retrieved April 7, 2025, from https://www.sciencedirect.com/science/article/abs/pii/S0921344916301914

Global Infrastructure Outlook. (2020). *A G20 initiative*. https://outlook.gihub.org/
Harper, T., Hibbard, M., Costa, H., & Yeh, A. G. (2010). *Dialogues in urban and regional planning 4*. Routledge.
Hong, Y. H., & Brubaker, D. (2010). Integrating the proposed property tax with the public leasehold system. In J. Y. Man & Y. H. Hong (Eds.), *China's local public finance in transition* (pp. 165–187). Lincoln Institute of Land Policy.
Kalem, A. (2015). Türkiye'deki kamu yatırımlarının özel sektör yatırımlarına etkisinin incelenmesi. *Specialisation thesis, Republic of Türkiye Ministry of Development, Publication No: 2922.*
Keleş, R., Geray, C., Emre, C., & Mengi, A. (1999). *Kentsel toprak rantının kamuya kazandırılması*. Türkkent Publications.
Kılıçbay, A. (1991). *Türk Ekonomisinin Son 10 Yılı*. Milliyet Publications.
Kocabıyık, İ. (2016). Ankara–İstanbul arası yüksek hızlı tren projesinin ve işletmesinin açmazları, eksikleri ve sıkıntıları. *İnşaat Mühendisleri Odası*, 27–34. Retrieved September 27, 2022, from https://www.imo.org.tr/Eklenti/2044,174002301rtrtpdf.pdf?0&
Liu, L. X., Clegg, S., & Pollack, J. (2024). The effect of public–private partnerships on innovation in infrastructure delivery. *Project Management Journal, 55*(2), 123–145.
Meng, J., Ye, Z., & Wang, Y. (2024). Financing and investing in sustainable infrastructure: A review and research agenda. *Sustainable Futures*, 100312. Retrieved Aprilr 7, 2025, from https://www.sciencedirect.com/science/article/pii/S2666188824001618
Ministry of Environment, Urbanization and Climate Change (MEUCC). (2017). *Plan tadilatlarında ve kentsel dönüşüm uygulamalarında kentsel altyapı etki analizi modeli projesi araştırma geliştirme işi*. Directorate General for Infrastructure and Urban Transformation Services.
Presidency of Strategy and Budget (PSB). (2022). *KÖİ Proje Göstergeleri*. Retrieved September 27, 2022, from https://www.psb.gov.tr/koi-gostergeleri/
Public Administration Research. (1992). *Yerel Yönetimler Araştırma Grubu Raporu. TODAİE Publications, No: 247.*
Tanrıvermiş, H. (2022). *Gayrimenkul geliştirme ve değerlemede özel konular ders notu*. Ankara University Publications.
Tuna, M., & Bostancı, S. (2021). Mahalli idarelerde altyapı yatırımlarının finansman yöntemleri: Ankara Su ve Kanalizasyon İdaresi (ASKİ) Genel Müdürlüğü örneği. *Afyon Kocatepe Üniversitesi Sosyal Bilimler Dergisi, 23*(4), 1477–1499. Retrieved September 28, 2022, from https://dergipark.org.tr/tr/download/article-file/1678917
Turkish Statistical Institute. (2022). *Website: TSI*. Retrieved September 10, 2022, from https://www.tuik.gov.tr/
World Bank. (2015). *Rise of the Anatolian Tigers: Türkiye urbanization review*. The World Bank Publications.
World Bank. (2022). *Infrastructure finance, PPPs, and guarantees*. The World Bank Publications.
World Bank. (2025). *Urban development overview*. https://www.worldbank.org/en/topic/urbandevelopment/overview
Yılmaz, N. (2008). Bir otokontrol sistemi olarak belediyelerde harcamalara katılma payı. *Türk Hukuk Sisteminde Normlar Hiyerarşisi ve Sayıştay Denetimine Etkileri, 3*, 75.
Yılmaz, M. S. (2020). *Değer artış kazancı ile sağlanan kaynaklarla kamu projelerinin finansmanı uygulamalarının incelenmesi ve Türkiye'de uygulanabilirliğinin değerlendirilmesi*. Master's thesis, Ankara University. Retrieved September 30, 2022, from https://acikbilim.yok.gov.tr/bitstream/handle/20.500.12812/44214/yokAcikBilim_10320422.pdf?sequence=-1&isAllowed=y

Mustafa Tuna is a former mayor of Sican district in Ankara province, a former mayor of Ankara Municipality, and a full professor at the Department of Real Estate Development and Management, Faculty of Applied Sciences at Ankara University. He graduated from the Civil Engineering program at Istanbul Technical University in 1980, and then he completed his Ph.D. at the Department of Environmental Engineering at Istanbul Technical University in 1995. He was awarded an associate professorship in the field of environmental engineering in 1998 and appointed a full professor in 2023. His areas of expertise include hydraulics, water management in urban areas, wastewater treatment and treatment cost analysis, urban infrastructure and investment strategies, environmental impacts of investment projects and feasibility studies. He has both theoretical and practical knowledge and experience in urban infrastructure management, urban transformation, and life quality, serving as an academic, practitioner, and major in municipalities.

Sinan Güneş is lecturing in the Department of Real Estate Development and Management at Ankara University. He obtained his bachelor's degree in civil engineering from Erciyes University in 2013 and subsequently completed a master's degree in real estate development and management at Ankara University in 2019. His master's thesis focused on the decision-making processes pertaining to the repair or demolition of earthquake-affected reinforced concrete buildings. Mr. Güneş completed in doctoral studies at the same department at Ankara University in 2025. His research interests encompass financial economics, engineering management, numerical methods, and construction management, with a particular focus on energy efficiency and sustainability in the built environment. He has authored numerous academic publications addressing sustainable building practices, energy consumption forecasting, and near-zero energy building strategies. Through his teaching and research, he makes significant contributions to the advancement of knowledge in sustainable real estate development and energy-efficient building strategies.

Mustafa Tombul is a full professor in the Department of Real Estate Development and Management at Ankara University. He completed his PhD in Civil Engineering at Anadolu University in 1996, having previously obtained both his undergraduate and master's degrees from the same institution. His areas of expertise include hydraulics, structural engineering, and construction management, with a specific emphasis on water resources management, environmental engineering, and energy efficiency. Professor Tombul has authored numerous articles in esteemed SCI-indexed journals covering topics such as drought forecasting, environmental risk assessment, precipitation and streamflow modelling, and sustainable water management. His research contributions have been acknowledged with various awards, including a Silver Medal from the Turkish Patent and Trademark Office. He continues to spearhead significant research projects pertaining to energy efficiency in buildings and environmental sustainability, thereby making substantial contributions to both academic knowledge and practical applications within his discipline.

Sevilay Bostancı serves as a Department Manager at the EGO General Directorate. In 2017, she earned her master's degree in Real Estate Development from Ankara University with a thesis titled Feasibility of Rail System Investments in Local Governments: The Case of Ankara Metropolitan Municipality, Batıkent–Sincan–Törekent Subway Line. She subsequently completed her Ph.D. in Real Estate Development at the same university with a dissertation titled Investment Analysis and Management Models of Urban Rail Systems: The Case of Ankara Province.Her research interests include financial economics, local governments, rail systems, transportation, and accounting, with a particular focus on urban transportation. She has published numerous academic studies on topics such as urban transportation, rail systems, local governance, public transportation, financing methods of infrastructure investments, municipal borrowing practices, funding sources used in urban rail system investments, the necessity of asset management approaches in public infrastructure investments, financial statement analysis approaches in local governments, real estate management in municipalities, financial resources used in urban public transportation, urban transportation issues and proposed solutions, transit-oriented development, measurement of social impact and social benefit in urban rail system services, analysis of enterprise and property revenues of metropolitan municipalities, and the management and financing of public transportation. Her work, particularly on urban rail systems, local governments, and the financing and management of public transportation, has made significant contributions to both academic literature and practical applications in municipal governance.

Public–Private Partnership Practices in Infrastructure and Real Estate Projects and Policy Implications

Erol Demir and Sinan Terzioğlu

Abstract

The Public-Private Partnership (PPP) model represents a progressive approach to planning and management. PPP serves as a feasible alternative for governmental funding, facilitating shared governance with the private sector. This model not only guarantees that the proposed sub-projects address public requirements but also enables private partners to derive profit from substantial projects. Presently, this model is integral to numerous training instruments for PPP frameworks, with the potential to use private sector objectives more efficiently within investment strategies. As global PPP projects advance, Türkiye has seen parallel growth, implementing such initiatives across diverse sectors. Collaborative projects between the public and private sectors are particularly prominent in energy, transportation, communication, and health, both globally and within Türkiye. This chapter explores the characteristics of the PPP model, its historical development, the motivations for its adoption by various countries, the types of models employed in Türkiye, relevant examples, and the legal framework that underpins it.

Keywords

Public–Private Partnership · Infrastructure · Public–Private Partnership Model in Türkiye

E. Demir (✉) · S. Terzioğlu
Department of Real Estate Development and Management, Faculty of Applied Sciences, Ankara University, Ankara, Türkiye
e-mail: eroldemir@ankara.edu.tr; sinan.terzioglu@ankara.edu.tr

T. Just et al. (eds.), *Understanding Türkiye's Real Estate Markets*, Management for Professionals, https://doi.org/10.1007/978-3-032-13297-0_27

1 Introduction

A Public–Private Partnership (PPP) constitutes a collaborative arrangement between governmental entities and the private sector, focused on delivering essential public services. In contemporary contexts, the PPP service delivery model operates as a systemic partnership established to pursue a shared objective, characterised by a mutual division of labour and the allocation of shared risks among stakeholders (Güneş, 2009). This model has emerged from a novel comprehension that embraces the principle of shared risks, responsibilities, resources, capabilities, and collaborations, alongside the distribution of functions and authorities associated with public administration, in conjunction with the private sector, for the provision of services or the realisation of projects (Özer, 2016). It is not an approach favoured by governments to depend exclusively on public resources and place the burden of project risks upon the public to finance services intended for public provision. Presently, there is a marked increase in the willingness of private enterprises to engage in public service projects (Tanrıvermiş et al., 2022).

The PPP model plays a crucial role in delivering public services in both developing and developed countries. Due to limited public resources, private financing is often used for public investments (Mayburd, 2021). Presented as a viable option for governments to tackle financing, expertise, and risk sharing, PPPs have been used across various sectors and projects for many years (Zhang et al., 2016). "Public Private Partnership (PPP)" applications remain widespread globally, with their importance continuing to increase. The effective growth and popularity of PPP practices can be attributed to the rising investments, meeting public financing needs, improving service quality, and enabling the roles of investors and operators to adapt to the private sector's dynamism (Uysal and Presentation, 2008).

PPP is a broad concept with a rich scope that is applicable in many areas. As a result, the term COO lacks a unified definition in existing literature (Uygun, 2013). This conceptual ambiguity is also evident in international sources (Gökkaya, 2021). Traditionally, the PPP model is defined as a financing model designed to implement public goods and services, which the state partially funds while avoiding strain on the public budget (Sarikatipoğlu et al., 2016).

2 Public–Private Partnership Model

2.1 Historical Development of the PPP Model

Historically, the Roman Empire served as an exemplar of the successful collaboration between the public and private sectors in the realisation of projects following the advent of Christ. During this period, essential services deemed necessary by the state, including ports, marketplaces, and bathhouses, were made publicly accessible, with private enterprises engaging in investment through special agreements

(Atasoy, 2011). Following the Middle Ages, initial contracts involving the private sector in public services began to emerge, particularly in England and France, with a primary focus on transportation and infrastructure construction (Wettenhall, 2010).

In the seventeenth-century Europe, public investments began in England and France with road and canal construction projects that involved the private sector (Saiyed, 2015). It is noted that private companies participated in road construction investments in England during the 1660s. By the nineteenth century, canal and railway projects, along with PPP models, emerged. However, many investors faced bankruptcy as a result of the European economic crisis (Çekirge, 2006). The "Canal du Midi" project, initiated in France in 1681, was finalised through private financing organisations (Cartlidge, 2006). In the subsequent years, particularly during the nineteenth century, the industrial revolution and rapid urbanisation in Europe and America led to infrastructure developments, including public transportation, energy, and sewer systems. The private sector facilitated many of these initiatives through concession agreements (Babatunde, 2015). This trend has been observed in several countries since the mid-nineteenth century. The Suez Canal project, constructed in France in 1858, used the build-operate-transfer model as part of the PPP framework (Bergere, 2016).

By the twentieth century, the First and Second World Wars, coupled with the economic crisis of 1929, prompted nations to adopt more statist policies. Throughout this period, public investments were executed using the budgets allocated by the states. By the end of the twentieth century, a rapid transition towards privatisation emerged globally because of the neoliberal policies established under the Washington Consensus, which were championed by President Ronald Reagan of the United States of America and Prime Minister Margaret Thatcher of the United Kingdom during the 1980s. This novel financing stream has influenced governments across many countries and has endeavoured to implement neoliberal policies domestically. This phenomenon has been manifested in numerous states through the privatisation of public services, evolving towards a more market-oriented framework. As the neoliberal trend gained momentum worldwide, the PPP financing model has continued to grow, achieving greater applicability in numerous countries to this day (Mooney, 2014). Factors contributing to the preference for PPP models encompassed the financing needs that arose due to public sector inadequacies during the 1980s, the inefficiencies prevalent within public bureaucracy, and the technological progress that public entities struggled to keep pace with globally (Miles, 1995).

The inception of the contemporary PPP model took place in the United Kingdom, where it was designated as the "Private Sector Financing Initiative" (PFI) in 1992, under the administration of Prime Minister John Major. Following the successful implementation of the PPP model in the UK, this financing framework was subsequently adopted in Germany, Canada, the United States, and various other nations (Alfen, 2010). Throughout the 2000s, the majority of both developed and developing countries integrated applications of the PPP model into multiple projects, and they continue to use them (Grimsey & Lewis, 2007).

2.2 Attributes of PPP, Rationale for Preference, Advantages and Disadvantages

The PPP financing model presents distinct advantages by integrating characteristics from both the public and private sectors. This model facilitates the leveraging of each party's strengths (Li & Akintoye, 2003), thereby ensuring the delivery of public services in a manner that is most beneficial. The primary objective of the PPP model is to capitalise on the expertise and capabilities of the private sector through an equitable structuring of the relationship between the parties, thereby ensuring the project achieves enhanced value by permitting the partner best equipped to manage potential risks that may emerge (European Commission, 2003).

In projects realised using the PPP model, the state's priorities include the public interest, the quality of the services provided, the public's access to the most suitable pricing policy, and the achievement of intended social and political objectives. Simultaneously, the state assumes the responsibility of ensuring that the works carried out under the PPP project comply with these objectives (Commission of the European Communities, 2004). To complete projects on time and without exceeding the allocated budget, in partnership with the public and private sectors, to enhance project efficiency through proper risk planning, to deliver quality and comprehensive services to stakeholders, to reduce both project and operational costs, and to lower maintenance and repair costs during the operational period, the PPP model is favoured for various reasons such as providing capital, possessing advanced technology and current innovations, optimising limited resources, having the flexibility in project management that the private sector offers, and alleviating the pressures of legal regulations (Gökkaya, 2021). Furthermore, it is preferred in both developed and developing countries to meet the service expectations of a growing population in public services, to fulfil and enhance infrastructure needs, to provide public services promptly, to avert the depletion of public budget resources, to keep pace with current technology, and to develop new applications (Sekhri et al., 2011).

PPP models derive significant advantages from the experience, expertise, and technological innovations of the private sector, particularly in the provision of public services. Concurrently, within this financing model, the private sector fosters the timely execution of projects, adhering to the pre-established budget (Şahin & Uysal, 2012). It ensures the swift completion of certain public investments that may have been deferred due to budgetary limitations. As the private sector is compelled to expeditiously complete the investment for the project to commence generating revenue, it guarantees that the undertaking is finalised and delivered in a timely manner. In the PPP financing model, local or national private sector firms have collaborated with international companies to foster advancement. Moreover, progress has been noted through the provision of subcontracting and employment opportunities for local companies in various domains, including project management, engineering, construction works, facility management, security, cleaning, and maintenance services (Tharun Shastry, 2014).

The PPP model significantly enhances the quality of public facilities and services, resulting in increased citizen satisfaction due to improved public infrastructure development. Private sector financing is employed to meet the rising demand for services and to augment the limited capacity of public resources. This model enhances the country's competitiveness across various sectors by stimulating economic growth, expanding employment opportunities, and attracting new investments, which encourages foreign investors to establish operations within the country (Brzozowska, 2006; Chen et al., 2013; Zaharioaie, 2012). Additionally, it facilitates the successful implementation of large and complex public projects. Given that state budgets do not allocate resources for these investment initiatives, only minimal returns can activate certain projects (Yetgin, 2015). The PPP financing framework ensures that public funds may be redirected to other critical needs, supported by the infusion of private capital into public initiatives. Consequently, it re-evaluates the financial resources, incentives, and responsibilities of the public sector, leading to enhanced efficiency (Sapri et al., 2016).

PPP projects are inherently complex as they typically unfold in two distinct phases: construction and operation. Furthermore, these initiatives involve long-term investments. The different processes and diverse requirements emphasise the innovative complexity of each project. Generally, these undertakings demand intricate legal arrangements, with contracts laden with technical jargon. Within the PPP framework, long-term contracts typically last for approximately 30 years. Nevertheless, needs may evolve during the project lifecycle, potentially rendering these contracts inadequate to meet new demands. Additionally, if a contract fails to adapt to current requirements, it can create a less favourable legal position. Given the lengthy nature of these agreements, the services provided may need to be adjusted in response to changing public needs, necessitating updates to management practices, contract provisions, and pricing.

Generally, projects realised with PPP require substantial investments. The aim is to reduce the total project expenses through the public PPP model. However, both the development and operational costs of these projects are high. The presence of at least two contractual parties in the PPP financing model can lead to coordination issues (Boyer & Newcomer, 2015). Even when projects are infrequent, a lack of competition may result in lower productivity. Moreover, a cultural and structural gap might develop in the relationship between the public and private sectors, potentially eroding mutual trust. In this partnership model, the public seeks to meet citizens' service expectations in exchange for the services provided. Conversely, the primary objective of the private sector is profit generation, leading it to increase its earnings. This scenario can sometimes result in internal conflict (Brogaard, 2019). The private sector will also implement policies aimed at minimising costs while pursuing maximum profit. This could lead to reduced employment and pressure on wages and salaries for employees (Spraul & Thaler, 2020). Additionally, the risk of corruption is perceived to be lower in the PPP financing model, given the involvement of numerous stakeholders, individuals, and processes in the completion of the project (Tharun Shastry, 2014; Yalçın, 2014).

With the transfer of certain public services that the state can provide to the private sector under this model, its dependence on the private sector increases. A loss of public control, coordination, and management systems may lead to reduced operational capacity for the public. During the implementation of such projects, a management crisis may arise as a result of the bankruptcy of the private company involved (Amadi et al., 2014). Improper allocation of risks between the public and private sectors poses significant threats to the execution of the model. Furthermore, the private sector's inability to be accountable to the public sector, along with a contractor's liquidation of the project or alteration of the project's status, carries the risk of evading debts and responsibilities associated with the project. Additionally, the lack of competition that may arise due to a shortage of expert contractors or private companies during the execution of the public project can result in higher costs and lower service quality in the projects (Lee, 2005).

3 Development of PPP in Türkiye

The historical trajectory of the PPP model in Türkiye dates back to the era of the Ottoman Empire. The initial instances of concessions established for the execution of public services are documented in the legislation that came into effect on June 10, 1910, under the title "Law on Concessions Concerning Benefits". This legislation facilitated the establishment of the first public–private partnerships during the Ottoman era, permitting the allocation of specific public privileges to the private sector. In the latter half of the fourteenth century, the accumulation of private capital, especially in European countries, prompted the private sector to explore new investment opportunities beyond Europe. Consequently, the Ottoman Empire emerged as an appealing destination for foreign investments during this period. The profit rate, which fluctuated around 4% in European countries, could rise to approximately 9% in regions governed by the Ottoman Empire. The vast territory of the Ottoman Empire created a pressing need for investment in imperial lands, most notably in transportation infrastructure. In this context, France emerged as the primary investor in the railway sector within the Ottoman territories. During this period, France directed its investments towards both mining and railways, while Germany focused its efforts on the railway sector, and England primarily aimed its investments at the banking sector (Tan, 2014).

During the Republican Period, the concession method was rarely used, requiring services to be delivered through public means. Over time, increasing public demands have led to inadequate resources allocated by the government for investment. Coupled with inefficient resource utilisation and a lack of innovative service delivery, this situation has brought the implementation of PPP models back into focus. Consequently, the PPP method, serving as an alternative model for providing public services, has begun to be adopted. "In this context, various legislative arrangements have been made since the 1980s, establishing the legal framework for PPP models, allowing the private sector to deliver some public services". The use of the PPP model has expanded in Türkiye since the 1980s, particularly gaining momentum in the 2000s. Notably, in recent years, ministries including Transport and Infrastructure, Energy and Natural Resources, Environment, Urbanisation and Climate Change, and Health have employed the PPP model in various projects aimed at enhancing public service and infrastructure investments (Sarısu, 2009). Numerous projects and services across diverse sectors—such as electricity generation and distribution, highways, airports, city hospitals, and ports—have been realised through the PPP model. In Türkiye, various agreement models for PPP include (1) Build-Operate-Transfer (BOT), (2) Build-Lease-Transfer (BLT), (3) Build-Operate (BO), and (4) Transfer of Operating Rights (TOR), akin to concession models (Ministry of Development, 2022).

1. The BOT model allows the private sector to engage in construction activities related to public facilities. Project risks are shared between the private and public sectors. The private sector is responsible for managing the constructed facility for a predetermined duration, which includes performing maintenance and repairs. Upon the completion of the specified period, the facility is then transferred to the public sector without charge. This model encompasses a range of projects, including bridges, tunnels, and nature parks.
2. In the Build-Lease-Transfer (BLT) model, the private sector constructs the facility, furnishes the requisite physical equipment, and operates designated areas of the facility for the duration stipulated within the contract. Upon completion of this period, the facility is transferred to the public sector at no cost. Throughout the contract duration, the public sector remits annual rent to the contracting company. This model is notably employed in the construction of municipal hospitals within the healthcare sector.
3. The BO model is predominantly used in public electricity generation. Under its parameters, the private sector is authorised to establish and operate a power plant under its ownership. The government acquires the electricity produced at a predetermined price. At the conclusion of the contract period, the facility remains under private sector ownership.
4. In the Transfer of Operations and Responsibilities (TOR) model, the authority to manage the existing facility owned by the state is delegated to the private sector for a predetermined duration. This model does not incorporate the characteristics inherent to the customisation method. The existing facility is provisionally conveyed to the private sector; however, the property remains within the public domain.

In Türkiye, a PPP initiative encompasses 211 projects from 1986 to 2016, totalling USD 122 billion. Between 1986 and 2002, 67 projects were conducted using the PPP approach, involving an investment of USD 11.1 billion and a contract value of USD 11.6 billion. Consequently, about USD 500 million was disbursed. Between 2003 and 2016, an additional 144 projects were executed under the PPP model, with an overall investment of USD 42 billion and a contract value of USD 110 billion (Alagöz & Yokuş, 2017).

According to the eleventh Development Plan Report published by the Strategy and Budget Presidency of the Republic of Türkiye, the PPP model was implemented across various sectors, primarily in health and transportation, during the tenth Development Plan period from 2013 to 2018. As of 2013, 190 projects with contracts valued at USD 120 billion were executed under the PPP model. By 2018, the number of projects had risen to 242. The total investment made within the scope of the PPP model has reached USD 64 billion, while the total contract amount is USD 140 billion. According to the report, significant projects such as the Istanbul Airport Project, Yavuz Sultan Selim Bridge, Osmangazi Bridge, Eurasia Tunnel, and eight city hospitals were undertaken between 2014 and 2018 using this model. The report further emphasises the necessity for PPP projects to be managed within a holistic framework, aligned with macroeconomic policies, thereby enhancing the institutional capacity of the public sector. Numerous urban environmental infrastructure projects are planned to be implemented using the PPP financing model, alongside the Kanal Istanbul Project, Filyos Port Superstructure and Operation Project, the Great Istanbul Tunnel Project, and the Çandarlı Port Superstructure and Operation Project, which are intended to commence in the eleventh plan period. In addition, it is planned to complete eleven city hospital projects with a total capacity of 18,716 beds, various highway projects, the second phase of the Istanbul Airport project, Çeşme Airport, and several port projects currently under construction using the PPP model (Presidency of the Republic of Türkiye, 2019).

Considering the investments within the scope of the PPP model in Türkiye, it is evident that private sector entrepreneurs operate for profit and offer attractive interest rates for financiers. This model serves as a tool that develops and addresses the infrastructure needs of the managers. According to the 2015 World Bank report, three out of the 10 projects with the largest budgets in the world under the PPP model are taking place in Türkiye. These three projects represent approximately 75% of the total cost of the ten largest projects worldwide. Among these ten projects are the New Istanbul Airport project, which costs USD 35.58 billion; the Osmangazi Bridge and Highway project, which costs USD 6.35 billion; and the Dalaman Airport project, which is valued at USD 1.08 billion. In recent years, significant investment has been made in projects implemented using the PPP model in Türkiye, and this model is being extensively used in public investments (Alagöz & Yokuş, 2017).

3.1 PPP Models Used in Türkiye and Financing Structure

PPP was introduced in Türkiye in 1986. It features various approaches based on different sectors. The PPP models used in Türkiye can be categorised into four types: Build-Operate Transfer, Build-Operate, Build-Lease Transfer, and Transfer of Operating Rights (Ministry of Development, 2016).

3.1.1 Build Operate Transfer Model

The Build-Operate-Transfer (BOT) model is one of the investment models in which the private sector ensures that investments are made when public resources are inadequate to realise them. This model encourages the engagement of private sector capital. In return for the financing provided by private capital, the owner of that capital retains the project's profits or losses for a specified period until the end of the operational phase, after which the ownership transfers to the relevant public administration (Yerlikaya, 2002). In other words, the financial resources necessary for certain services that public administration must deliver are sometimes insufficient. The BOT model represents the financing approach used for investments requiring the technology and financial resources of the private sector (Emek, 1999).

The BOT model is regulated in Türkiye under Law No. 3996. This model, used to facilitate investments that require advanced technology and significant financing, indicates that the investment amount is paid to a capital firm or an international firm through the purchase of goods or services produced during the operational period by the public or those benefiting from the service. It involves the transfer of compulsory investments from the public to the private sector through a contract for a specified duration, with the stipulation that project and operational risks are transferred to the private sector contractor, drawing on the resources of the private sector. At the end of the contract period, the investment is returned to the public sector (Ministry of Development, 2018; Topdemir & Azaltun, 2019).

3.1.2 Build Operate Model

The Build-Operate Model (BO) refers to a system where certain public services are monopolised by the state and executed by the private sector under public oversight through a contract. The Council of Ministers Decision first established the GI model for Electric Power Generation Facilities, dated June 8, 1996, and numbered 96/8269. A communiqué based on this law was released. However, BKK chose to suspend the implementation of the regulations due to the legal foundations established by the rules created in accordance with this communiqué. Following this decision, the "Law on the Establishment and Operation of Electrical Energy Production Facilities with the Build-Operate Model and the Regulation of Energy Sales", dated July 16, 1997, and numbered 4283, was enacted (Tanrıvermiş et al., 2022). Under the BP model, the establishment and operation of thermal power plants, along with the sale of electricity produced by these plants, are governed by the BP model (Sarısu, 2009).

The primary characteristic that sets the BO model apart from the BOT model is that the private sector constructs the facilities under the contract without a time constraint, allowing for indefinite privatisation. In Türkiye, the GI model is prominently applied in electricity generation projects. Under the BO model, the private sector is permitted to build and operate power plants within these facilities indefinitely while retaining ownership. The state procures the electrical energy produced from these facilities. Once the contract related to this model is concluded, the facility continues to be the responsibility of the private entity indefinitely. Unlike the concession model, ownership of the facility does not have to revert to the relevant administration (Güngör, 2012). Essentially, in the BO model, the private sector investor retains the property rights of the facility and is not mandated to transfer it to the public after a designated period (Sarısu, 2009). The established facility is owned by a private investor company, which grants an operation permit to the public for a specified timeframe (Ersöz, 2010).

3.1.3 Build Lease Transfer Model

The Build Lease Transfer (BTL) model is a method for financing public infrastructure projects using private companies, which then lease these projects to the public for a designated time. This investment strategy is particularly useful in contexts where there may be concerns, as the investments made under the BTL model remain owned by the private company (Çınar et al., 2017). In the BTL model, the private firm contracts to provide the facility and necessary equipment, manages the operation of the facility for the agreed period, and then hands over the constructed facility to the public at no cost once this period concludes. According to the BTL contract, the public administration pays the private contractor an annual rent (Tanrıvermiş et al., 2022). Essentially, the BTL model entails the private sector taking charge of designing, financing, and building the investment project, which is subsequently leased to the government for the time frame indicated in the investment contract. Ownership of the facility is then transferred to the public administration when the contract period expires (Ersöz, 2010).

3.1.4 Transfer of Operating Rights Model

The Transfer of Operating Rights Model (TOR) can be defined as the operation of a publicly owned facility by private companies for a specified duration, ensuring that ownership rights remain with the public. Through the TOR model, the production of goods and services is facilitated by granting operating rights, leasing, or transferring ownership during the privatisation of physical assets. The BLT model is implemented within the framework of the "Law on Privatisation Practices" No. 4046 and Law No. 5335 (Ministry of Development, 2018).

3.2 Public–Private Partnership and Legal Framework in Türkiye

The PPP models implemented in Türkiye have been influenced by the models established by the European Union (EU). Public infrastructure investments in EU member states have used this model. Due to the funds allocated by EU member states for financing this model and the increasing efforts of private companies to form partnerships under it, member states have also initiated various programmes. The initial stage of investment in Türkiye has progressed while considering the legal frameworks established by the UK and EU member states (Pangal Çalışkan, 2019). To define the PPP model, it can be articulated as "it is a model that is realised by sharing the services and investments based on a certain contract, the risks and costs arising from the project, and the revenues to be obtained between the state and private institutions". Conversely, the PPP model is defined as "a method that unites the state and the private sector in the provision of public services, is based on the principles of equality and management, and in which the costs, risks and benefits that occur during the production of goods and services are mutually shared" (Altan et al., 2013). Notably, the medium-term plans prepared by the Ministry of Development in Türkiye in recent years aim to use the PPP model widely for public services. Consequently, the Department of Public-Private Cooperation was established within the Ministry of Development.

The initial regulation concerning the PPP model in Türkiye was implemented through amendments to the 1982 Constitution. Regulatory provisions pertaining to the model were incorporated into Law No. 4446 in 1999. With the introduction of two paragraphs to Article 47 of the Constitution, it is mandated that the procedures and principles governing the privatisation of public assets and enterprises shall be regulated by law (Sefa & Bilgiç, 2016). As a result, it has been enacted that the state may allocate and transfer specific services and investments to the private sector. Furthermore, the revised provision in the first paragraph of Article 125 of the Constitution states that disputes arising from public service conditions and contracts can be resolved through national and international arbitration. This provision provides enhanced flexibility in the organisation and financing of certain public services. Consequently, a foundation has been laid for the adoption of new models for the implementation of various public services (Kerman & Altan, 2012).

The PPP model, recognised as the first of its kind to be implemented globally in the United Kingdom, is particularly notable in projects related to City Hospital Campuses or Health Campuses in Türkiye. In England, the cost advantage of approximately 30% associated with the PPP model underscores its applicability (Tekin, 2007). A review of various PPP applications in Türkiye indicates that public investments have been executed using models such as Build-Operate-Transfer (BOT), Build-Own (BO), Build-Transfer-Lease (BTL), and Transfer of Rights (TOR) (Kasapoğlu Turhan, 2011). Furthermore, it is observed that instances of PPP models are especially conducted under the "Privatisation Practices Law", which was enacted in 1994 (Akıllı, 2013). As examples of PPP model applications carried out by the Privatisation Administration, one may include Ankara Natural Electricity Production, Atik Ali Paşa Mansion, İzmir Wholesale Fish Market Project, various Mining Licenses, TÜVTÜRK Vehicle Inspection Stations, and several marinas (Güler, 2016).

3.2.1 Legal Framework of PPP Contracts in Türkiye

The legal framework governing their contracts under the PPP model encompasses the establishment of the contract, its duration, the delineation of responsibilities between the participating parties, and the characteristics of those parties involved.

1. *The process of creating PPP contracts:* The public budget alone cannot sufficiently cover the construction, maintenance, and renewal of infrastructure and public service facilities necessary to address the demographic pressures arising from global economic crises; these pressures originate from migration and the growing needs of the population (Acartürk & Keskin, 2012). Consequently, states engage the private sector in providing public services through private law contracts to generate specific public goods and services. These operations are executed under specific guidelines, either within the framework of public administrative contracts or private law contracts. To facilitate particular investments employing PPP models, the administration is required to enter into an agreement

with a private entity in compliance with established regulations (Yıldırım & Çınarlı, 2020).
2. *Tender processes:* In the implementation of PPP models in Türkiye, the "PPP Law" should be applied instead of the "State Procurement Law" numbered 2886 and the "Public Procurement Law" numbered 4734. There are several reasons for using the provisions of the PPP Law for PPP contracts. Firstly, it is evident that the PPP contract differs from the tenders conducted under these two Laws and cannot be realised in the classical sense of purchasing or selling goods and services. Secondly, while PPP project tenders may be perceived as a form of public procurement practice, the only connection between the "Public Procurement Law" and the "PPP Law" lies in the term "tender". The methods, principles, and objectives of these tenders are, in fact, distinct. Article 11 of the Law governing the construction, renewal, and service procurement of health facilities under the Public-Private Cooperation Model, administered by the Ministry of Health, states: "It is not subject to the Law No. 4734" (Boz, 2013).

Although Laws No. 2886 and 4734 do not apply to PPP contracts, their fundamental characteristics are consistent with the tender features applicable to such contracts. Consequently, based on the fifth chapter on public procurement, it is apparent that Türkiye should ensure transparency in the tenders associated with the PPP model and implement uniform regulations regarding equality and free competition in Türkiye's endeavours to join the European Union. Nevertheless, similar to public procurement, projects conducted under the PPP model progress through several distinct phases, including tendering, project acceptance, consultant selection and preparation, as well as the evaluation and establishment of the tender commission (Acartürk & Keskin, 2012; Kerman & Altan, 2012).

3. *Signing the contract:* In contracts executed under the PPP model, the provisions of the contract and the articles governing the project's implementation are explicitly defined to guarantee that the project fulfils the administration's requirements and expectations. Consequently, the contracting parties are obligated to assess the anticipated risks and allocate them equitably to ensure mutual benefit for all parties involved. Moreover, the contract should delineate a mechanism that enables the contracting parties to evaluate the performance of each participant (Ersöz, 2010).

The financing, design, and construction of the facilities associated with the PPP contract involve the infrastructure being designed, constructed, operated, and maintained by the private sector. This scope further includes the stipulations regarding the transfer of services to the public by the private sector upon the termination of the PPP contract, the compensation allotted to the private sector for the construction or operation of the project, and the comprehensive expenditures related to the project. Moreover, it should encompass elements such as environmental and social requirements.

4. *The nature of the contracting parties:* In PPP contracts, the parties involved encompass private sector enterprises and the relevant public administration. By executing the contract, a private company or consortium has the potential to establish a cooperative relationship with the pertinent administration on behalf of the public. The most critical participant during the implementation of projects developed under the PPP model is the public administration. Local government bodies or state-funded organisations possessing legal personalities may represent the applicable state administration. In the context of a transportation project, the Ministry of Transport and Infrastructure, along with an associated public institution, may become a party to the PPP contract (Ersöz, 2010).

Currently, there is no comprehensive legislation applicable to all models of PPP in effect in Türkiye. In order to understand the private sector component of the contract, it is essential to examine the tariff provisions outlined within the relevant legal regulations that govern the various forms of PPP models. According to the initial article of the Law on the Construction, Renovation, and Service Procurement by the Ministry of Health under Law No. 6428, "one or more natural or legal persons can be a party to the PPP contract". This article further specifies the characteristics relevant to the involvement of the private sector. Law No. 6428 defines the tenderer selected by the administration following the tender process and the execution of the implementation contract as a "special purpose company". Conversely, it states that the operational scope of the entity entering into a contract with the public administration is limited to the subject matter of the contract. Furthermore, the article above specifies that the agreement established between natural or legal persons, identified as private law entities, to participate in the PPP tender invitation issued by the administration, is referred to as a "joint venture". A joint-stock company, whose operations are exclusively confined to the PPP contract, may enter a PPP contract with the administration for the provision of infrastructure and public services. Additionally, non-profit organisations recognised as private institutions under the law may also enter a PPP contract as a private entity (Boz, 2013).

5. *Contract duration:* Each entity engaged in the projects executed under the PPP model bears the responsibility of fulfilling the obligations delineated in the contract. In PPP initiatives, the private sector is tasked with the construction and commissioning of the facilities. For example, in the BOT model, the private sector participant does not receive any remuneration from the respective public administration for the services rendered. As a result, the private sector must be positioned to recoup its investments and generate a return on investment. The primary objective of private investors in this partnership is to achieve a profit. In alternative forms of PPP, such as the YKD model, the private sector investor leases the facility to the pertinent administration and, in exchange, acquires a rental fee for a designated period as specified in the investment contract (Pangal Çalışkan, 2019).

There exists no overarching legislation governing the PPP model in Türkiye. In accordance with the seventh article of Law No. 3359, a PPP contract, with a maximum duration of 49 years, may be entered into with legitimate individual or corporate entities for the leasing of healthcare facilities. Nevertheless, the first article of Law No. 6428 stipulates that the duration of any PPP contract cannot exceed 30 years, excluding the fixed investment period. Furthermore, Article 7 of Law No. 3996 specifies that the contract duration cannot exceed 49 years. Article 7 of Law No. 3096 articulates that the duration of contracts established within the electricity sector may be regulated for a term extending up to 90–9 years. The contractual period for investments executed under the PPP model in Türkiye is adequately prolonged to accommodate the recovery of investment costs incurred by the private sector.

3.2.2 Sharing Responsibilities Between the Relevant Public Administration and the Private Sector and Its Political Effects

In some projects, the state authorises public service delivery through private enterprises using the PPP method. However, the state does not fully disengage from the services rendered through this approach. The public's responsibility persists during the execution of the contract under the PPP framework. While the relevant administrative body delegates the provision of public services to the private sector, it continues to provide certain services within the project's scope. Although service delivery occurs within the project's parameters, the public concurrently bears responsibilities for areas not encompassed by the service obligations. Consequently, it remains the duty of the public to organise these services to protect the public interest. Upon the conclusion of the contract about PPP projects, the public assumes control of the facilities and continues to provide public services independently. Both parties share responsibilities during the implementation of PPP projects (Cebeci, 2011). In PPP projects, both parties must acknowledge the risks and domains in which they are proficient in managing. Each party assumes responsibility for activities that they can effectively control and manage. Thus, the likelihood of project success is enhanced.

In the implementation of PPP contracts, the state does not wholly delegate public services to the private sector; instead, it seeks assistance from the private sector in delivering services to citizens. In this context, it is asserted that the ultimate responsibility for public services resides with the state, a legal entity governed by public law. For instance, it is indicated that only the private sector is responsible for the construction, maintenance, and operation of hospital facilities within the health sector. In contrast, activities related to public health services will be conducted by the Ministry of Health (Acartürk & Keskin, 2012). Therefore, the PPP model signifies that the state has not entirely withdrawn from the sector, and it supports the private sector in enhancing and more effectively managing the quality of infrastructure and public services.

4 Conclusion

Due to the rapid population growth observed in the developing world, particularly since the 2000s, as well as the swift advancement of technology and the increasing human needs and expectations that arise from globalisation and neoliberal economic policies, it has become challenging for the public to depend solely on their resources to fulfil public service demands. Several customised models have been developed to address this situation; however, the anticipated benefits have not been fully realised. As a result, rather than transferring public projects to the private sector, public-private partnership models are presently favoured, thereby enabling the public to remain integrated within the system.

The preference for PPP in projects developed for public services arises from the model's focus on efficiency, productivity, and economic sustainability. However, the source of the projects to be implemented within this framework is provided by a consortium formed by multiple companies, which unite in direct proportion to the size of the project. The primary objective of this consortium is to uphold the efficiency and appropriateness of expenditures, ensure the fulfilment of requirements throughout the project's duration, and ultimately facilitate the transfer of assets to the public sector.

Particularly considering the public-private partnership practices in Türkiye, the financial models employed in the provision of public services reflect cooperation rather than a genuine partnership. Collaboration between the public and private sectors is used to meet the requirements of public service. This provision of public service is undertaken in alignment with free market principles, under state supervision, while taking into account the public interest. The objective is to deliver the service in a more effective, high quality, and efficient manner.

References

Acartürk, E., & Keskin, S. (2012). Türkiye'de sağlık sektöründe kamu özel ortaklığı modeli. *Süleyman Demirel Üniversitesi İktisadi ve İdari Bilimler Fakültesi Dergisi, 17*(3), 25–51.

Akıllı, H. (2013). Kamu hizmeti imtiyazından yap-işlet-devret yöntemine: Yasal serüven. *Sayıştay Dergisi, 89*, 91–114.

Alagöz, M., & Yokuş, T. (2017). Kamu özel işbirliği (KÖİ) yatırımları ve ekonomik illüzyon etkisi. *Sosyal ve Ekonomik Araştırmalar Dergisi, 19*(32), 115.

Alfen, H. (2010). Public-private partnership (PPP) as part of infrastructure management solutions—A structural approach of delimiting PPP from other private sector participation models. In *18th CIB world building congress*.

Altan, Y., Kerman, U., Aktel, M., Metin, Y., & Erdal, E. (2013). Yerel yönetimlerde kamu özel ortaklığı uygulaması: Büyükkabaca Belediyesi örneği. *Uluslararası Alanya İşletme Fakültesi Dergisi, 5*(3), 9–17.

Amadi, C., Carrillo, P., & Tuuli, M. (2014). Stakeholder management in public-private partnership projects in Nigeria: Towards a research agenda.

Atasoy, H. (2011). *Kamu özel işbirliği modeli ve Türkiye'de belediyelerin altyapı projelerinin finansmanında uygulanabilirliği*. Doctoral dissertation, Erciyes Üniversitesi, Sosyal Bilimler Enstitüsü.

Babatunde, S. O. (2015). *Developing a public-private partnership strategy for infrastructure delivery in Nigeria*. Doctoral dissertation, University of Northumbria at Newcastle.

Bergere, F. (2016). Ten years of PPP: An initial assessment. *OECD Journal on Budgeting, 15*(1), 31–123.
Boyer, E. J., & Newcomer, K. E. (2015). Developing government expertise in strategic contracting for public–private partnerships. *Journal of Strategic Contracting and Negotiation, 1*(2), 129–148.
Boz, S. S. (2013). Kamu özel işbirliği (PPP) modeli. *İnönü Üniversitesi Hukuk Fakültesi Dergisi, 4*(2), 277–332.
Brogaard, L. (2019). Business value in public-private partnerships: The positive impact of trust and task-relevant competencies on business outcomes in PPPs. *International Public Management Journal, 22*(4), 617–642.
Brzozowska, K. (2006). *Advantages and threats of public-private partnerships in large infrastructure projects*. CeDeWu.
Cartlidge, D. (2006). *Public-private partnerships in construction*. Routledge.
Cebeci, A. (2011). Kamu özel ortaklığı ve koordinasyonu sağlayan kurum olarak YOİKK. *Sağlık Alanında Kamu-Özel Ortaklığı Sempozyumu, 6*(7), 84–100.
Çekirge, H. L. (2006). *Dünyada ve Türkiye'de kamu özel sektör ortaklığı uygulamaları ve örnek bir projede modelin finansal ve genel avantajlarının incelenmesi*. Doctoral dissertation, İstanbul Teknik Üniversitesi.
Chen, C., Hubbard, M., & Liao, C. S. (2013). When public–private partnerships fail: Analysing citizen engagement in public–private partnerships—Cases from Taiwan and China. *Public Management Review, 15*(6), 839–857.
Çınar, N. F., Türkoğlu, Ç., & Tütünsatar, A. (2017). Kamu-özel ortaklığı/işbirliği modeli ve sağlık hizmetlerinin sunumunda hizmet memnuniyetinin ölçülmesi: Entegre sağlık kampüsleri için bir araştırma. *Journal of Suleyman Demirel University Institute of Social Sciences, 29*(4).
Commission of the European Communities. (2004). *Green paper on public-private partnerships and community law on public contracts and concessions*. Office for Official Publications of the European Communities.
Emek, U. (1999). *Yap-İşlet-Devret (YİD), Yap-İşlet (Yİ) ve Kamu Hizmeti İmtiyazı Mevzuatı*. Devlet Planlama Teşkilatı Yayınları.
Ersöz, M. (2010). *Avrupa Birliği ve Türk Hukuku Işığında Public Private Partnership Uygulamaları*. Master's thesis, Marmara Üniversitesi.
European Commission. (2003). *Guidelines for successful public-private partnerships*. Retrieved from https://ec.europa.eu/regional_policy/sources/docgener/guides/ppp_en.pdf
Gökkaya, D. (2021). Türkiye'de kamu özel ortaklığı bağlamında şehir hastanelerinin değerlendirilmesi: Nitel bir araştırma. *Uluslararası İktisadi ve İdari İncelemeler Dergisi, 31*, 73–96.
Grimsey, D., & Lewis, M. (2007). *Public-private partnerships: The worldwide revolution in infrastructure provision and project finance*. Edward Elgar Publishing.
Güler, E. (2016). *Sağlık hizmetlerinde kamu-özel ortaklığı modeli (Bursa ili örneği)*. Master's thesis, Atılım Üniversitesi.
Güneş, A. M. (2009). Kamu hizmetlerinin yürütülmesinde yeni bir yöntem: Kamu özel ortaklığı. *Güncel Hukuk Dergisi, 58*, 62.
Güngör, H. (2012). *Sağlık sektöründe kamu özel işbirliği uygulamaları ve Türkiye için bir değerlendirme*. Kalkınma Bakanlığı Uzmanlık Tezi.
Kalkınma Bakanlığı. (2016). *Dünyada ve Türkiye'de kamu-özel işbirliği uygulamalarına ilişkin gelişmeler raporu 2015*.
Kalkınma Bakanlığı. (2018). *Kamu-özel işbirliği raporu 2017*.
Kalkınma Bakanlığı. (2022). *Kamu özel işbirliği ile yürütülen projeler*. Retrieved August 25, 2022, from https://kamuozel.kalkinma.gov.tr
Kasapoğlu Turhan, M. (2011). Kamu özel ortaklığının hukuksal niteliği: Çeşitli ülkelerdeki kamu özel ortaklığı uygulamalarının hukuki açıdan değerlendirilmesi. In *Sağlık Alanında Kamu-Özel Ortaklığı Sempozyumu* (pp. 101–127). Türk Tabipleri Birliği Yayınları.
Kerman, U., & Altan, Y. (2012). Sağlık hizmetlerinde kamu özel ortaklığı uygulaması. *Süleyman Demirel Üniversitesi İktisadi ve İdari Bilimler Fakültesi Dergisi, 17*(3), 1–23.

Lee, V. (2005). *Public-private partnerships*. Legislative Council Secretariat.
Li, B., & Akintoye, A. (2003). An overview of public-private partnerships. In *Public-private partnerships: Managing risks and opportunities* (pp. 3–30).
Mayburd, A. (2021). A public-private partnership for the express development of antiviral leads: A perspective view. *Expert Opinion on Drug Discovery, 16*(1), 23–38.
Miles, D. (1995). *International project marketing* (Vol. No. 6). International Labour Organisation.
Mooney, G. (2014). *Ulusların sağlığı: Yeni bir ekonomi politiğe doğru* (Vol. 206). Yordam Kitap.
Özer, M. A. (2016). Sağlık sektöründe yeni bir hizmet sunum modeli: Kamu özel ortaklığı. *SGD-Sosyal Güvenlik Dergisi, 6*(1), 9–38.
Pangal Çalışkan, Z. (2019). *Türkiye'de sağlık sektöründe kamu özel ortaklığı modeli: Şehir hastanelerine yönelik ampirik bir araştırma*. Master's thesis, Trakya Üniversitesi.
Şahin, M., & Uysal, Ö. (2012). Kamu maliyesine etkileri açısından kamu özel sektör ortaklıkları üzerine bir değerlendirme. *Maliye Dergisi, 162*(1), 155–174.
Saiyed, A. A. (2015). Public-private partnership and legal education.
Sapri, M., Hariati, A. H., Ting, L. S., & Sipan, I. (2016). Public-private partnership benefits in delivering public facilities in Malaysia. *MATEC Web of Conferences, 66*, 00014.
Sarikatipoğlu, A., Yazıcı, C., Çapkın, T. A., & Yaka, P. (2016). Public-private partnership under Turkish law. *GSI Articletter, 14*, 195.
Sarısu, A. (2009). *Kamu-özel işbirlikleri*. Yaklaşım Yayınları.
Sefa, U. S. T. A., & Bilgiç, E. (2016). Yerel yönetimlerde hizmet sunumu: Kamu özel ortaklığı modeli. *Süleyman Demirel Üniversitesi Sosyal Bilimler Enstitüsü Dergisi, 23*, 249–268.
Sekhri, N., Feachem, R., & Ni, A. (2011). Public-private integrated partnerships demonstrate the potential to improve health care access, quality, and efficiency. *Health Affairs, 30*(8), 1498–1507.
Spraul, K., & Thaler, J. (2020). Partnering for good? An analysis of how to achieve sustainability-related outcomes in public–private partnerships. *Business Research, 13*(2), 485–511.
T.C. Cumhurbaşkanlığı Strateji ve Bütçe Başkanlığı. (2019). *On birinci kalkınma planı (2019–2023)*. Retrieved October 29, 2022, from https://www.sbb.gov.tr/kalkinma-planlari/
Tan, S. (2014). XIX. yüzyılda Osmanlı-Hindistan ticaretine bir örnek: At ihracatı. *Akdeniz İnsani Bilimler Dergisi, 4*(2), 239–247.
Tanrıvermiş, H., Tanrıvermiş, Y., & Demir, E. (2022). *Proje geliştirme ve finansmanı ders notları*. Retrieved September 22, 2022, from https://acikders.ankara.edu.tr/course/view.php?id=7293
Tekin, A. G. (2007). Kamu-özel sektör iş birlikleri—Kamu-özel ortaklıkları. *İdarecinin Sesi Dergisi, 21*(122).
Tharun Shastry, L. (2014). A study on public-private partnerships with reference to Indian infrastructural projects. *International Journal of Business and Management Invention, 3*(10), 56–62.
Topdemir, B., & Azaltun, M. (2019). Yap-işlet-devret ile yapılan havalimanı yatırımları üzerine bir değerlendirme. *Muhasebe ve Finansman Dergisi*, 33–54.
Uygun, B. (2013). Yeni bir ilişki türü: Kamu özel ortaklığı. *Hukuk Gündemi, 2*, 24–26.
Uysal, T., & UYDB Sunumu. (2008). *International PPP Platform Turkey Açılış Töreni Konuşma Metinleri*.
Wettenhall, R. (2010). Mixes and partnerships through time. In *The international handbook on public–private partnerships*.
Yalçın, F. C. (2014). *Kamu özel iş birlikleri*. Doctoral dissertation, Ankara Üniversitesi.
Yerlikaya, G. K. (2002). *Yap-işlet-devret modeli hukuki mahiyeti ve vergilendirme*. Seçkin Yayınları.
Yetgin, F. (2015). Kamu-özel sektör işbirliği modeli; konut üretiminde "arsa satışına yönelik gelir paylaşımı uygulamaları". *Marmara Üniversitesi Avrupa Araştırmaları Dergisi, 14*(1), 191–205.
Yıldırım, R., & Çınarlı, S. (2020). *Türk idare hukuku dersleri Cilt I*. Astana Yayınları.
Zaharioaie, M. (2012). The utility of using public-private partnerships for local governments. *Journal of Public Administration, Finance and Law, 02*, 17–24.
Zhang, S., Chan, A. P., Feng, Y., Duan, H., & Ke, Y. (2016). Critical review on PPP research—A search from the Chinese and international journals. *International Journal of Project Management, 34*(4), 597–612.

Erol Demir is a full professor at the Department of Real Estate Development and Management, Faculty of Applied Sciences, Ankara University, Türkiye. He holds a Ph.D. in Agricultural Economics from Ankara University and an M.Sc. in Business Administration from Gazi University. His research focuses on real estate taxation, accounting practices in the construction and property sectors, cooperative finance, and public sector economics. He has published extensively in peer-reviewed journals and authored several books. Prof. Demir has also served as Deputy Dean and contributed to multiple academic committees within Ankara University. He is currently an editorial board member of cited journals.

Sinan Terzioğlu graduated from Gazi University's Faculty of Engineering and Architecture with a degree in Civil Engineering in 2005. Following his graduation, he undertook various roles across a range of private firms. Since 2012, he has advanced in his career as a co-founding partner in a private enterprise. In 2023, he obtained his doctoral degree in "Facility Management/healthcare facility management" from Ankara University's Department of Real Estate Development and Management. In 2022, he had the honour of conducting research as a visiting scholar at Texas A&M University's Department of Construction Science in the United States. He is actively engaged with several non-governmental organisations and professional institutions. He has authored numerous papers, articles, and books, and has presented at various seminars and conferences focusing on facility management (FM), healthcare facility management (HFM), and construction engineering and management. Currently, Dr. Terzioğlu integrates both academic and commercial endeavours in the domains of facility management, healthcare facility management, quantitative methods in facility management, construction and civil engineering, as well as maintenance and performance.

Public Real Estate and Public Policies

Public Real Estate Management in Türkiye

İlhan Yıldırım, Ahmet Hilmi Erciyes, and İskender Duman

Abstract

In order to realise sustainable economic development, it is crucial to integrate all resources within the production process in line with the economy's needs. In countries like Türkiye, where the public owns and manages more than half of the nation's real estate assets, the public plays a significant role in the real estate and construction sectors, thereby necessitating a clearer understanding of the efficient and effective use and management of public real estate. Real estate varies in terms of ownership structures, characteristics, factors influencing its value, and the legal regulations applicable to it. Public real estate in Türkiye is generally classified as unclaimed properties, common properties, service properties, and real estate owned by the Treasury. While public administrations in Türkiye cannot exercise ownership rights over the real estate they own or manage in the same way as private ownership, public real estate is safeguarded under a complex and comprehensive legal framework.

Keywords

Public property · Management of public real estate · Treasury property · Special budget administrations and management of real estate

İ. Yıldırım (✉) · A. H. Erciyes
Department of Real Estate Development and Management, Faculty of Applied Sciences, Ankara University, Ankara, Türkiye
e-mail: ilhan.yildirim@msb.gov.tr; aherciyes@ankara.edu.tr

İ. Duman
Van Metropolitan Municipality, Deputy Secretary General, Ankara, Türkiye
e-mail: iskender.duman@van.bel.tr

T. Just et al. (eds.), *Understanding Türkiye's Real Estate Markets*, Management for Professionals, https://doi.org/10.1007/978-3-032-13297-0_28

1 Introduction

The effective management of public real estate assets by governmental entities significantly contributes to the enhancement of their overall performance, thereby facilitating more efficient operations and improving service delivery to communities (Van Den Beemt-Tjeerdsma & Veuger, 2016). To mitigate inefficiencies and prevent the misallocation of public assets, systematic management practices have become increasingly important as governmental real estate portfolios grow more diverse and complex (Rymarzak & Trojanowski, 2013). Moreover, the governance of public real estate is essential for economic development and stability. Public real estate management acts as a crucial driver of economic growth for both central and local governmental bodies, influencing employment and infrastructural progress. Beyond its role as a major investment area, real estate is an important factor in promoting economic resilience. (Liu & Chen, 2011; Yang, 2023). Particularly within the context of developing nations, the effective deployment of public real estate assets can enable the essential diversification of resources for governmental activities when confronted with declining financial resources (Manganelli et al., 2022).

Public institutions and organisations necessitate real estate classified as "service properties" to fulfil the services mandated by their governing legislation. Furthermore, they may own real estate with diverse legal statuses, which they administer under varying legal regulations. These properties, for which public institutions and organisations bear responsibility, are governed by either public or private law, contingent upon their classifications, property statuses, intended usages, public interest in their use, equitable access, and their function in sustaining the continuity of public services. Consequently, the public administration accountable for real estate management, alongside the processes regulating their protection statuses and management is undergoing evolution.

There is no legal definition of public property within the Turkish Legal System. Nevertheless, definitions of public property are provided by higher judicial bodies. The Constitutional Court characterises public property as "unclaimed properties that are open to the common use of everyone due to their natural characteristics, common properties allocated by public legal entities for the benefit of everyone or a part of the public, and properties that are the subject and tool of public service activities". Similarly, the eighth Chamber of the Council of State defines public property in alignment with the Constitutional Court's definition: "According to the principles of administrative law, the properties and properties belonging to or allocated for the use and benefit of the public and the properties that can be considered as an element and an integral part of a public service."

Although there is no definitive criterion within the framework of French law, which informs the theory of administrative law in the context of the Turkish legal system, an analysis of the decisions above by the high judicial authorities and the prevailing scholarly consensus shows that "the direct benefit of the public or a public service is allocated with a special arrangement made for that service". The definition of "properties" (Arslan, 2017; Gülan, 1999) is prominent among the interpretations of public properties. Properties that are publicly owned yet contribute indirectly to the public welfare through the revenues they generate are regarded as the private properties of the public. This distinction is not absolute. For instance, while coastal areas and forests are inherently not classified as private properties, services or common properties may be designated as private properties through a new allocation decision or by revoking an existing allocation decision (Şimşek, 2013).

In Türkiye, public administrations are mandated to manage the real estate allocated for their utilisation, whether directly or indirectly, in line with the principles of efficiency and frugality to fulfil the intended service objectives as articulated in the Public Financial Management and Control Law No. 5018, which is regarded as the foundational legislation of public finance. This chapter examines the concept of public real estate as delineated in various statutes in Türkiye and the stipulations concerning real estate qualifications. The management of public real estate is elucidated through data pertaining to real estate possession or administration within the framework of the administrative structure, predominantly outlined in Law No. 5018.

2 The Concept of Public Real Estate in Türkiye

It has been discerned that there is no universally accepted definition for the concept of public real estate in Türkiye. Furthermore, to regulate the structure, operation, and management of public financial administration, as well as the management procedures of real estate used by public administrations, Law No. 5018 has been enacted. Specifically, this includes the Regulation of the Allocation and Transfer of Real Estates Owned by Public Administrations (KIATTDHY) and the Registry of Real Estates Owned by Public Administrations established in 2006. Various legal frameworks, including the Regulation on the Related Regulation (KİATKİY) and the Regulation on the Administration of Treasury Real Estates (HTİHY), implemented in 2007, have also come into effect. The legislation above defines key concepts, such as the Treasury, Treasury real estate, and real estate, categorised as private property of the Treasury. Public administrations are classified based on their budgets, and detailed procedures regarding the registration of real estate used by these entities, their accounting records, and the protocols governing their use are expounded. Additionally, the concept of public resources was articulated in Law No. 5018, indicating that real estate falling under the ownership, management, and/or utilisation of these administrations constitutes public property.

Public administrations, as delineated in Law No. 5018, are classified into three categories under the overarching classification of general administration: (i) public administrations operating within the framework of central government, (ii) local administrations, and (iii) social security institutions. Furthermore, these administrations are listed under four distinct classifications in the tables appended to the Law. Moreover, by referencing the classification established in Law No. 5018 within KİATKİ, the procedures for recording the real estate owned, managed, or retained by these administrations for diverse purposes are outlined. With respect to the Regulation, the real estate used by these administrations is deemed public real estate.

Conversely, in KİATTDHY and HTİHY, the concepts pertaining to public real estate are elucidated in accordance with Law No. 5018 and its associated practices. In the regulations above, the Treasury is characterised as a broader concept denoting the name of the State's legal entity. "Real estate under the private ownership of the Treasury" is directly registered in the name of the Treasury in the title deed, while real estate explicitly designated as "under the rule and disposal of the State" in various statutes is classified as "Treasury real estate".

2.1 Public Properties

Public legal entities are obligated to fulfil their responsibilities in accordance with applicable legislation by employing a variety of legal methods and authorities. These methods may encompass expropriation under the Expropriation Law No. 2942, the transfer of real estate between two public administrations as delineated in Article 30, and purchases in compliance with the Public Procurement Law No. 4734 and the Reconstruction Law No. 3194. Such practices facilitate the acquisition of real estate through diverse legal powers, which include zoning applications in alignment with pertinent laws. Although various terms are used to describe the real estate necessitated by public administrations, the notion of "public property" has gained significant prominence in recent years (Gözübüyük, 1998; Onar, 1960).

Gözübüyük (1998) defines public properties as follows: "properties on which public services are carried out and reserved for the common use and benefit of society". Onar (1960) similarly defines it as: "The properties that can be considered as an element and complementary part of a public service, that is, the properties that have been connected to that service in such a way that the separation from it will interrupt the service or prevent it from being seen as it should, and the properties of the State that are substituted for the other in terms of national wealth and culture that "properties that cannot be substituted".

Public properties in Türkiye are delineated under three principal categories below.

2.1.1 Unclaimed Properties

Coasts, forests, natural wealth and resources, seas, mountains, and hills, as well as the air and areas within the atmosphere, which are inherently incapable of being subject to ownership, are classified as unclaimed property (Gözübüyük & Tan, 2021). The air and electromagnetic fields present in the atmosphere are similarly categorised as unclaimed property due to their inability to be privately owned (Onar, 1960; Söyler, 2005, 2011; Yayla, 1998). The principle that coasts and forests cannot be subject to private ownership is further reinforced by constitutional guarantees in Türkiye, as reiterated in Article 715 of the Turkish Civil Code No. 4721. Additionally, "ground waters", "mines", and "oil resources" are recognised as natural assets as defined in the Constitution and are categorised as unclaimed properties by applicable legislation. Consequently, authorised public administrations do not have to undertake any administrative actions for the benefit of public access to these properties.

Furthermore, Article 16/c of Cadastre Law No. 3402 categorises real estate governed by the State as unclaimed property. This classification indicates that such real estate is ineligible for registration and is exempt from restrictions, save for exceptional circumstances. In this regard, considering Türkiye's non-arable land, abundant water basins, coastal areas, and various other natural resources, a substantial portion of the land continues to remain under the jurisdiction of the State and is safeguarded from private ownership.

2.1.2 Common Properties

Properties used for very long time by the public for their designated purposes, or allocated for public use through administrative decisions, are classified as common properties (Kirbaş, 1988; Şimşek, 2014). According to this classification, Article 16/B of Law No. 3402 identifies pastures, winter pastures, threshing fields, and fairgrounds as common properties, specifying that these properties must be distinctly defined with parcel numbers and documented in a specialised registry. Conversely, it suffices to represent roads, squares, and bridges, which are likewise recognised as common properties, on maps without necessitating their registration in the private registry. Furthermore, the same article emphasises that the limitation of common properties does not result in their conversion to private property, except for the circumstances delineated in the relevant legislation.

2.1.3 Service Properties

Properties designated for public service through an administrative decision, or that have been used for public service since very long, are identified as service properties. Real estate may attain the classification of quality-of-service properties through acquisition, expropriation, or easement. Additionally, a property may qualify as a service property if it has been traditionally employed for public service or if there exists an administrative decision to allocate that real estate for public service (Kirbaş, 1988; Söyler, 2005). Furthermore, Law No. 3402 delineates real estate utilised and acquired for public services by providing examples such as administrative buildings, mosques, roads, and parks. The public administrations responsible for the ownership and management of this real estate are specified in accordance with the administrative framework established by Law No. 5018, thereby mitigating potential conflicts between ownership and authority.

2.2 Real Estate Privately Owned by the Treasury

Real estate within the private property of the Treasury refers to properties that are registered in the land registry under the name of the public administration. These properties do not directly contribute to public service performance, unlike public real estate, which contributes indirectly to funding sources such as public income. The Treasury owns these properties, excluding those assets designated and utilised for public service purposes. The owner of the public administration retains the authority to exercise powers conferred by Law No. 4721 (Kirbaş, 1988; Kapan,

1997) concerning these properties. Nonetheless, given that this property contributes indirectly to public services, its acquisition, disposal, and management are subject to specific limitations imposed by public law. Individuals can benefit indirectly from these properties by purchasing, renting, or employing various methods, such as establishing an easement right in their name. Thus, the real estate encompassed within this category is accessible for use or benefit by private individuals.

Article 45 of Law No. 5018 provides an indirect elucidation of the concept and registration of real estate under the private ownership of public administrations. As stipulated in this article, public administrations operating within the parameters of the general budget, as well as other entities, are permitted to register real estate acquired through purchase or financial leasing in the name of their respective legal entities (Gündoğan, 2011).

2.3 Characteristics of Public Real Estate

Public real estate possesses a privileged legal status attributable to its inherent qualities and the specific purposes for which it is designated. This distinctive status necessitates that public real estate undergo different regulatory processes. The attributes of public real estate can be examined under the following categories (Şimşek, 2013).

(i) Public properties shall not be subject to private ownership. According to Law No. 4721, as explicitly stated in Article 715, public properties cannot be converted into private property (Oğuzman et al., 2021). They may only become subject to private ownership if they relinquish this status (Gözler, 2009; Gözler & Kaplan, 2021; Gülan, 1999; Onar, 1960).

(ii) They cannot be registered in the land registry. Due to their classification as non-private property, they are exempt from registration in the land registry, except for extraordinary cases, such as the establishment of a real right on them (Ayanoğlu, 2016; Gözübüyük & Tan, 2021; Günday, 2013). Nevertheless, public commodities are documented in private registers, and roads and squares are solely represented on the map.

(iii) Real estate rights cannot be appropriated: Properties designated as private may be expropriated for reasons of public interest, while properties classified as public are protected from expropriation. Additionally, real estate that is privately owned by the public is likewise safeguarded against confiscation (Günday, 2013).

(iv) Public real estate is subject to privileged protection; public properties possess a special protection status as they are allocated for public use and public benefit, constituting an element of national wealth (Aydinli, 1991). Public real estate is regulated by statutes such as the Turkish Penal Code No. 5237, Coastal Law No. 3621, Village Law No. 442, National Parks Law No. 2873, and Bosphorus Law No. 2960, among others. Furthermore, there are specialised protective provisions in various laws, including Law No. 3091 on the Prevention of Infringement on the Possession of Real Estate Property.

(v) The utilisation of public real estate is generally without charge; in contrast to the private use of service-related real estate, all public real estate is accessible at no expense, and all individuals are permitted to make use of it.

(vi) Transfers and assignments are prohibited: Public properties are not subject to sale, nor can they be transformed into private properties via zoning or revival according to the ordinary and extraordinary statute of limitations (Gülan, 1999), as outlined in Articles 712 and 713 of Law No. 4721, or through zoning and restoration in accordance with Law No. 3402.

(vii) Exempt from seizure: The Treasury is prohibited from seizing public or private property. However, real estate that other public administrations own may be governed by distinct regulations in accordance with applicable laws (Gözler, 2009; Onar, 1960).

3 Management of Public Real Estate

Within the framework of public real estate, the properties acquired, managed, and utilised by the public administrations listed in Law No. 5018, in their capacity as representatives of a public legal entity, are governed by distinct regulations, principles, and procedures. The effective and prudent execution and utilisation of administrative functions, such as acquisition, leasing, allocation, and disposal of public real estate, must adhere to the guidelines established in the applicable legislation and reflect the intended uses for which these properties are designated. This adherence has become a legal obligation under Law No. 5018. Furthermore, administrative, judicial, and financial liabilities for public works exist that contravene these established principles.

Public administrations are permitted to receive real estate at no cost if it is used in the execution of their official duties. Furthermore, public administrations can allocate public real estate amongst themselves, either free of charge or under their management and responsibility, to deliver public services.

This part of the chapter subdivides public real estate management into five categories, each determined by its characteristics and the administrative structure responsible for its oversight.

3.1 Management of Real Estate Owned by the Treasury

The Ministry of Environment, Urbanisation and Climate Change (ÇŞB) is responsible for managing real estate owned by the Treasury in accordance with Law No. 5018. Pursuant to Article 46 of the Law above, the authority to conduct sales, allocate resources, and revoke allocations within the context of Article 47 is also granted to the same Ministry. The General Directorate of National Real Estate (MEGM) performs these responsibilities on behalf of the Ministry.

As of the conclusion of 2023, under the management of the Ministry of Environmental and Green Management (MEGM), there is a total of 4,859,732 properties encompassing an area of 424,109,849,286 m^2, which are registered under the authority and custody of the State Land and Property Agency (DHTA). Among these, 185,249 properties, accounting for an area of 61,671,169,615 m^2, fall under the jurisdiction of DHTA. In contrast, 101,325 properties, encompassing 5,822,727,216 m^2, are not owned by the Treasury for a variety of reasons. Nonetheless, these properties are categorised as "associated real estate" due to their status as defendants in legal proceedings or by virtue of established leasing or easement rights. Approximately 65.78% of the registered real estate is located within forested areas, 9.90% consists of land, 5.18% comprises agricultural fields, 16.56% consists of plots, and 0.26% pertains to buildings (MEGM, 2024). MEGM undertakes activities relating to the acquisition, management, and disposal of real estate:

Acquisition activities: The acquisition of real estate required for public services is executed by public institutions primarily through methods such as barter, purchases against tax debt, construction activities in exchange for land or floor space, or, in situations where these options are not feasible, through purchases conducted in accordance with Law No. 4734. Additionally, unregistered areas (DHTA-qualified real estate) that are classified as public real estate are registered in the name of the Treasury through an administrative registration process, thereby conferring upon them the status of privately owned real estate. An official document indicates that 3685 properties were registered in the name of the Treasury in 2018; this number rose to 7281 in 2019, 7978 in 2020, fell back to 6653 in 2021, and rose again to 8102 in 2022. However, it fell to 905 units in 2023 (MEGM, 2024) (Fig. 1).

Management activities: Real estate owned by the Treasury is leased for commercial activities, resulting in an accrual and establishing the associated easement rights. Additionally, the management of the real estate is delegated to various public administrations as part of an administrative function; public residences are allocated to public employees, and maintenance and repair operations for these properties are carried out (Kara, 2017; MEGM, 2024). Furthermore, procedures for establishing easement rights are executed to facilitate usage by private individuals for educational, industrial, social, agricultural, and tourism endeavours, and a real estate portfolio is developed for special investments in accordance with Additional Article 3 of Law No. 4706. As an aspect of incentive legislation, preliminary permits were issued for a total of 188 real estate projects from 2016 to 2023, resulting in an investment amounting to TL 4,202,567,405.50 aimed at generating employment for a total of 8443 individuals (MEGM, 2024).

Disposal activities: In order to divest real estate from public ownership there are mechanisms such as sale, transfer, and abandonment. In accordance with the general provisions, sale transactions are executed with public institutions, organisations, and associations dedicated to public interest, leading entities within the organised industrial zone at par value, and state-owned economic enterprises at both current and par values. Furthermore, lands that have lost their forest quality are allocated to beneficiaries and users of agricultural land. Consequently,, total income in 2023 amounted to TL 18,124,014,000, inclusive of TL 4,122,256,000 derived

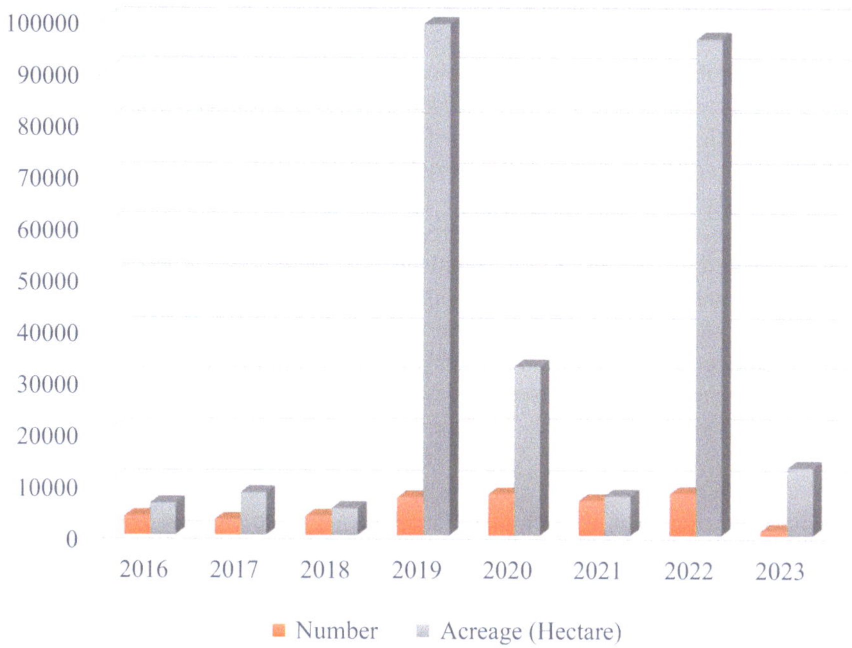

Fig. 1 Real estate acquisition with administrative registration (2016–2023). Source: MEGM (2024)

from rental income, TL 5,196,670,000 from the establishment of easement rights, and TL 8,737,544,000 generated from sales revenue.

3.2 Management of Real Estate of Public Administrations with Special Budgets

Public administrations endowed with special budgets are enumerated in Article 3 of Law No. 5018 and detailed in the Schedules appended to the Law. In contrast to other public administrations, they possess the authority to acquire real estate under the name of their legal entities, within the parameters outlined in the general budget as specified in Schedule I annexed to the Law, and to record such acquisitions in the title deed. Among these institutions, universities, local administrations, and the General Directorate of Forestry are prominent due to the volume of real estate properties they maintain and the breadth of their operational jurisdictions. These administrations function in accordance with Law No. 5018, the Regulations established for its execution, and the provisions delineated in their founding statutes and Presidential Decree No. 1.

3.3 Management of Forest Properties

The responsibilities of protection, development, operation, enhancement, maintenance, and the establishment of new forestry policies regarding forests, classified as public properties within the designation of unclaimed property, have been delegated to the Ministry of Agriculture and Forestry (TOB) in accordance with paragraph 1/ç of Article 410 of Presidential Decree No. 1. On behalf of the Ministry, these responsibilities are executed by the General Directorate of Forestry (OGM), a public institution endowed with a special budget and legal personality.

The fundamental provisions pertaining to forests are delineated in Forest Law No. 6831, particularly within the article entitled "Protection and development of forests" in Article 169 of the 1982 Turkish Constitution. Furthermore, additional regulations concerning the utilisation, leasing, servitude rights, and accessibility for forest villagers and public needs are stipulated in Article 7 of Law No. 6292, titled "Forest Cadaster", as well as in Articles 16, 17, 18, and the supplementary Article 8 (Coskun, 2009).

Within the scope of the activities undertaken by the General Directorate of Forestry (OGM), a total area of 23,363,000 hectares, which corresponds to 29.8% of the country as of the end of 2023, is classified as forest land. The ratio of forested areas globally in relation to the total surface area has decreased from 31.2% in the year 2000 to 30.7% in 2016 (World Bank, 2022). During the period from 1973 to 2023 the ratio of forested areas to the total surface area in Türkiye has been rising towards the global average (Fig. 2) (OGM, 2021; 2024a; ÇŞB, 2024a, b).

The "Ecosystem-Based Functional Forest Management Regulation dated 05.02.2008", which is predicated upon an ecosystem approach, participatory methods, and functional planning, has been enacted to govern the identification of forest areas and their functions for sustainable forest management. Pursuant to this regulation, and based on analyses conducted by the OGM, forest areas have been designated according to their principal economic, ecological, and socio-cultural functions. Consequently, as of the end of 2023, a total of 23,363,071 hectares of forest have been classified, which includes 9,346,665 hectares deemed to hold economic significance, 11,935,673 hectares recognised for ecological value, and 2,080,733 hectares acknowledged for socio-cultural importance (Fig. 3) (OGM, 2024b).

3.4 Management of Pasture-Qualified Real Estate

The management, determination, protection, and enhancement of Türkiye's rangelands, pastures, and highland regions are conducted in accordance with Pasture Law No. 4342 and the Pasture Regulation dated July 31, 1998, which was promulgated pursuant to this Law. According to Article 4 of Law No. 4342, pastures designated as common property may be owned by a single village or municipality or jointly by multiple villages or municipalities. Pastures, akin to coastal areas and forests, are exempt from private ownership. As a general principle, using these areas for purposes other than their designated use and diminishing their boundaries is strictly

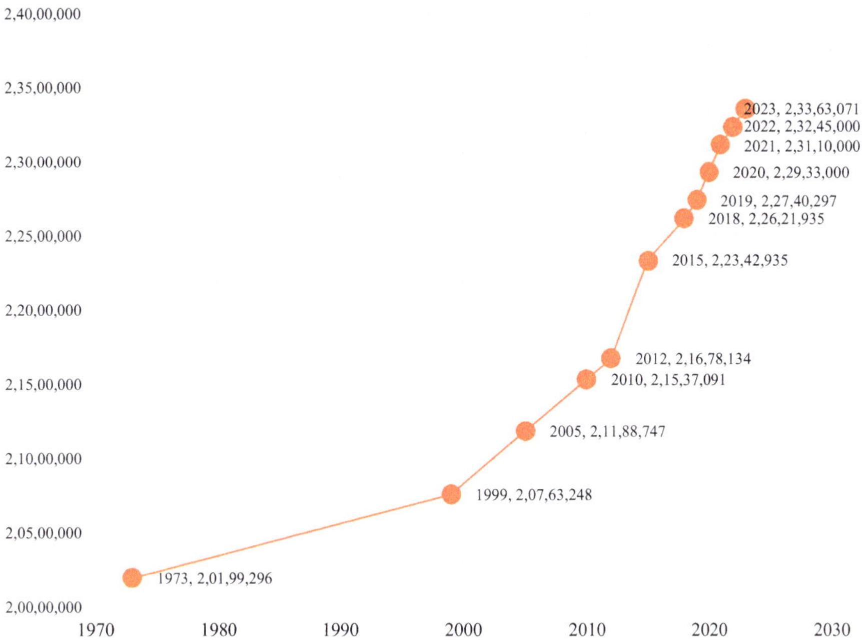

Fig. 2 Change of forest areas by years (1970–2023). Source: OGM (2024b) and ÇŞB (2024a)

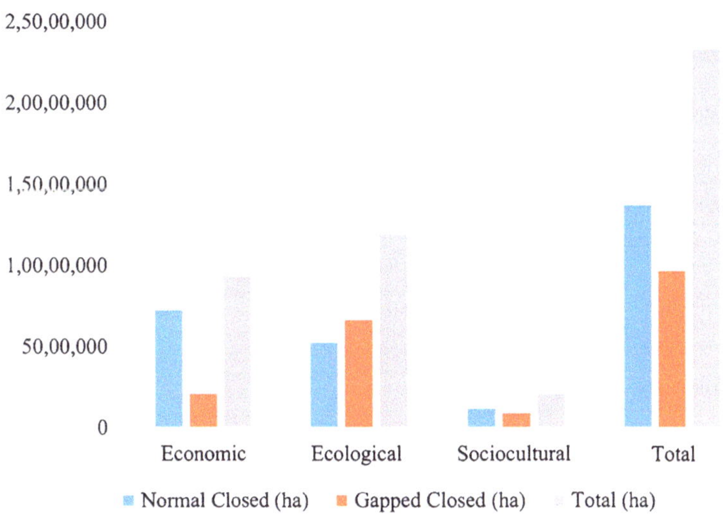

Fig. 3 Distribution of forest areas by main functions. Source: ÇSB (2024b)

prohibited, as they are subject to special protection. However, leasing of pasture areas is permissible under the circumstances specified in Law No. 4342. These areas are recorded in specialised registers at the land registry directorates, and the TOB provincial directorate maintains an inventory thereof. Based on data from 2020, there has been a 50% reduction in the rangeland area since 1970. Pasture areas, which amounted to 21,698,400 hectares according to the village services census in 1970, decreased to 14,616,687 hectares in the 2001 TUIK census and further to 13,616,687 hectares at the conclusion of 2022 (Fig. 4) (TOB, 2024).

The pasture commissions are responsible for identifying, restricting, and allocating real estate that meets rangeland qualifications on behalf of the TOB. These commissions designate rangelands, pastures, and winter quarters based upon the village or municipality in which they are situated and subsequently present this information to the governor of the respective province for approval. Pastures, plateaus, and winter quarters that exceed the requirements of the designated village or municipality may be leased to neighbouring villages or municipalities, as well as to individuals or legal entities engaged in animal husbandry. Although it is standard practice to use these areas for allocation purposes, modifications are permissible provided that the original allocation purpose remains intact. These areas may be registered under the name of the Treasury or a foundation, in accordance with the conditions specified in the twelfth and fourteenth articles of Law No. 4342. Moreover, the responsibility for the protection of the rangelands, pastures, and winter quarters is assigned to the headman or the mayor of the designated village, as stipulated in the nineteenth

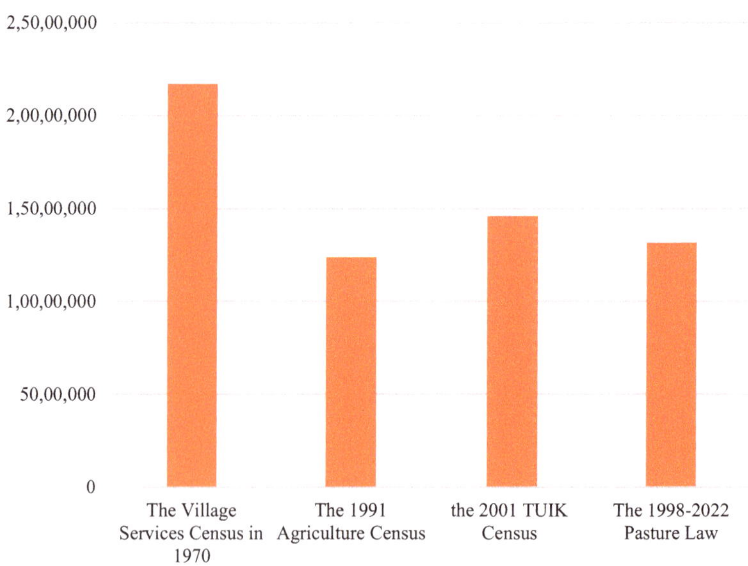

Fig. 4 Change in rangelands over the years. Source: TOB (2024)

Fig. 5 Rangeland determination, restriction, and allocation amounts (2000, 2005, 2010, 2015, 2020). Source: TOB (2022)

article of Law No. 4342. To support this initiative, the establishment of "Passage Management Unions" within the relevant local government units has been proposed. As of 2022, a total of 13,147,701 hectares of land have been identified, with 12,707,829 hectares restricted and 8,233,647 hectares allocated to local administration (Fig. 5) (TOB, 2024).

3.5 Management of Cultural and Natural Assets

Under Law No. 2863, enacted in 1983, concerning the Protection of Cultural and Natural Assets, cultural and natural assets are recognised as state property. In accordance with the provisions of this law, identification and registration procedures are conducted based on the characteristics of the properties and protected areas involved, the nature of their existence (including but not limited to mosques, masjids, tombs, and inns), as well as the administrative body responsible for their management and oversight, which may be either the Ministry of Culture and Tourism-KTB or the General Directorate of Foundations. The KTB carries out the determination procedures by consulting the pertinent public administrations regarding transactions initiated within this framework. The outcomes of these determinations are communicated to the land registry directorates, and corresponding annotations are made to the land registry records. Moreover, in these designated areas, conservation boards (namely the High Council for Conservation of Cultural Heritage and Regional Boards of Conservation) are vested with the authority to delineate protection boundaries and supervise construction activities.

Moreover, the KTB is entrusted with the responsibility of implementing essential measures to protect these assets, conducting thorough inspections, and collaborating with relevant public administrations. The sale or donation of such real estate is

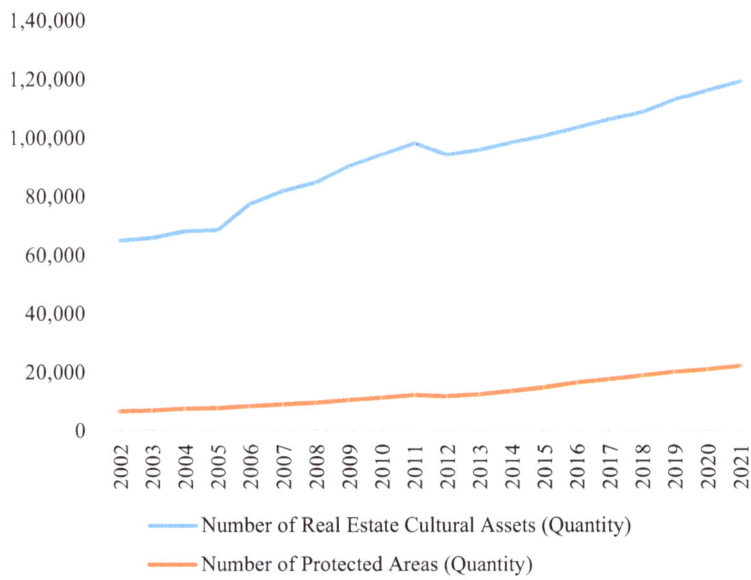

Fig. 6 Real estate, cultural assets, and protected areas throughout Türkiye. Source: KTB (2022)

strictly prohibited unless expressly authorised by the KTB. The KTB's consent is imperative for these assets to be maintained and utilised by public institutions and organisations, or for such properties to be transferred or subleased to these entities. Significant increases in real estate and protected areas were documented from 2002 to 2023. As of the end of 2023, a total of 124,671 real estate properties and 24,786 protected areas have been officially registered (Fig. 6) (KTB, 2024a; 2024b).

4 Conclusion

Within the Turkish legal framework, there is a clear demarcation among legislation, jurisprudence, doctrine, and both public and private real estate held by public institutions and organisations. Real estate transactions are governed by various legal regimes. Furthermore, the provisions outlined in Law No. 4721 regarding private property are inapplicable to public assets. The Turkish Constitution of 1982 has afforded special protection to coasts and forests, completely prohibiting the transfer of ownership in the case of forests. This restrictive regulation pertaining to forests does not extend to rangelands. In accordance with the conditions specified in the Pasture Law, the qualification of rangelands may be revoked by the pasture commission. Nevertheless, despite alterations in the status of these real properties, their sale to private entities and public legal bodies, as well as ownership transfer, including gratuitous transfer, has been prohibited. Conversely, there are no impediments to leasing, establishing easements, or allocating these properties for public services in alignment with the purpose of the classification change.

The immovables owned by the treasury may be sold under the conditions established for small industrial sites, public institutions and organisations, commodity exchanges, professional organisations, and technology development zones. In certain provinces, real estate located in Organised Industrial Zones may be transferred without charge, if there are no other impediments. Conversely, for investments associated with organised livestock breeding, projects operating under the build-operate-transfer model, technological and organic agriculture, geothermal greenhouse cultivation, and energy investments, an easement right may be established on the treasury-owned real estate for a fee, at no cost, or for 49 years.

The allocation of public real estate for investments, including private enterprises, has been recognised as a vital development tool in Türkiye in recent years. Considering the recent legislative changes, it is noteworthy that numerous regulations pertaining to the integration of public resources into the economy have been incorporated into Türkiye's legislative activities and other regulatory measures. Specifically, the rules established in the tourism sector have facilitated significant investments in this area. Promoting the allocation of real estate owned or managed by the public, which is not used for public services, to investments across various sectors represents a crucial initiative for economic development.

When the pasture and forest areas are incorporated into the Treasury real estate, approximately two-thirds of the total area of Türkiye consists of public real estate. In this regard, considering that most of the real estate within the country is overseen by public administrations and the significant influence they exert within the real estate market, it becomes imperative to determine effective management policies for this property and to develop policies and tools that contribute to the economy. Within this context, the registration of all real estate, the assessment of their value, the identification of their type and class, and the formulation of management policies that align with the development strategies of the nation, while also addressing food and energy security and sustainability—particularly during a period in which the socio-economic repercussions of the Covid-19 pandemic continue to be experienced—further emphasises the significance of achieving self-sufficiency.

Since a large proportion of land is owned by the public sector, this has a direct and significant impact on areas such as agriculture and housing policy. Türkiye effectively employed urban transformation projects in the 2000s, particularly in addressing the issue of informal settlements. By reducing the cost of land, recognised as a key expenditure in urban housing production, through the use of public lands, successful transformations were accomplished via public–private collaboration, thereby significantly alleviating the issue of informal settlements, particularly in metropolitan areas. It is imperative to ensure social equity, especially when the initiatives designed for vulnerable housing groups achieve success. Moreover, the projects developed by the Çevre ve Şehircilik Bakanlığı (ÇSB) to allocate treasury lands to farmers lacking adequate land for agricultural endeavours are anticipated to substantially augment the nation's agricultural production if successful and provide a meaningful resolution to income inequality.

It is essential that all public real estate, encompassing properties owned by public administrations with a designated budget that is not allocated for public service, is incorporated, either directly or indirectly, into economic activities and utilised strategically in investments by both the private and public sectors. Simultaneously, employing public transport as a financing source in both domestic and international markets through secondary markets (such as the issuance of rental and income certificates) emerges as a pivotal instrument that has been recently developed to enhance the nation's progress and foster increasing social welfare.

References

Arslan, K. O. (2017). Kamu malı niteliğinin tespiti ve kamu mallarından yararlanmanın esasları. *TBB Dergisi, 131*, 57–86.

Ayanoğlu, T. (2016). Kamu mallarından özel yararlanmaya ilişkin sözleşmelerin tabi olduğu hukuki rejim. *Legal Hukuk Dergisi, 14*(163), 3573–3600.

Aydinli, B. (1991). *Türk hukukunda kamu malları* (Controller thesis). Milli Emlak Genel Müdürlüğü, Ministry of Finance,

ÇŞB (2024a). *Forest area distribution in Turkey*, Ministry of Environment, Urbanisation and Climate Change. https://cevreselgostergeler.csb.gov.tr/ormanlik-alanlarin-dagilimi-i-85782. Accessed August 22, 2024,

ÇŞB (2024b). *Functional classification of forests in Turkey*, Ministry of Environment, Urbanisation and Climate Change. https://cevreselgostergeler.csb.gov.tr/ormanlarin-ana-fonksiyonlar-ina-gore-dagilimi-i-85786. Accessed August 22, 2024,

Gözler, K. (2009). *İdare hukuku (Administrative Law)*. Ekin Basım Yayın Dağıtım.

Gözler, K., & Kaplan, G. (2021). *İdare hukuku dersleri* (23rd ed.). Ekin Basım Yayın Dağıtım.

Gözübüyük, Ş. (1998). *Yönetim hukuku*. Turhan Kitabevi.

Gözübüyük, Ş., & Tan, T. (2021). *İdare hukuku* (Vol. 1). Turhan Kitabevi.

Gülan, A. (1999). *Kamu mallarından yararlanma usullerinin tâbi olduğu hukuki rejim*. Alfa Basım Yayım Dağıtım.

Günday, M. (2013). *İdare hukuku* (10th ed.). İmaj Yayınevi.

Gündoğan, S. (2011). *Türkiye'de kamu taşınmazlarının turizm yatırımlarına tahsisi ve sorunlarının analizi* (Master's thesis). Ankara University, , Real Estate Development Department

Kapan, G. (1997). Kamu toprakları ve belediyeler. *Çağdaş Yerel Yönetimler Dergisi, 6*(3), 22–24.

Kara, D. (2017). Türkiye'de hazine taşınmazlarının ekonomik kalkınma üzerindeki rolü. *Sosyal ve Beşeri Bilimler Dergisi, 9*(1), 93–107.

Kirbaş, S. (1988). *Devlet malları* (2nd ed.). Adım Yayınları.

KTB (2022). Statistics on immovable cultural assets in Turkey, Ministry of Culture and Tourism. https://kvmgm.ktb.gov.tr/TR-104412/turkiye-genelinde-yillara-gore-tasinmaz-kultur-varliklari-istatistigi.html. Accessed September 24, 2022

KTB (2024a). Turkey-wide real estate cultural assets in need of protection statistics, Ministry of Culture and Tourism. https://kvmgm.ktb.gov.tr/TR-44798/turkiye-geneli-korunmasi-gerekli-tasinmaz-kultur-varligi-istatistigi.html. Accessed August 22, 2024.

KTB (2024b). Turkey-wide protected areas statistics, Ministry of Culture and Tourism. https://kvmgm.ktb.gov.tr/TR-44798/turkiye-geneli-korunmasi-gerekli-tasinmaz-kultur-varligi-istatistigi.html. Accessed August 22, 2024.

Liu, Z., & Chen, L. (2011). Research on Chinese real estate development and the future trends. *Asian Social Science, 7*(9), 207.

Manganelli, B., Tataranna, S., Vona, M., & Del Giudice, F. P. (2022). An innovative approach for the enhancement of public real estate assets. *Sustainability, 14*(14), 8309.

MEGM (2024). 2023 annual report. Directorate General of National Property. https://webdosya.csb.gov.tr/db/milliemlak/icerikler/2024-m-ll-emlak-faal-yet-raporu-evren-01042024-web-20240401112236.pdf. Accessed August 22, 2024.

Oğuzman, K., Seliçi, Ö., & Özdemir, S. O. (2021). *Eşya hukuku*. Filiz Kitabevi.

OGM (2021). *2020 Forest Coverage in Türkiye*, Directorate General of Forestry. https://www.ogm.gov.tr/tr/ormanlarimiz-sitesi/TurkiyeOrmanVarligi/Yayinlar/2020%20T%C3%BCrkiye%20Orman%20Varl%C4%B1%C4%9F%C4%B1.pdf. Accessed September 24, 2022.
OGM (2024a). *Türkiye forest inventory*, Directorate General of Forestry. https://www.ogm.gov.tr/tr/ormanlarimiz/Turkiye-Orman-Varligi. Access ed August 22, 2024.
OGM (2024b). *Official forest statistics*, Directorate General of Forestry. https://www.ogm.gov.tr/tr/ekutuphane/resmi-istatistikler. Accessed August 22, 2024.
Onar, S. S. (1960). *İdare hukukunun umumi esasları*. Akgün Matbaası.
Rymarzak, M., & Trojanowski, D. (2013). Asset management of the public sector in Poland. *Real Estate Management and Valuation, 21*(1), 5–13.
Şimşek, S. (2013). Kamu malları teorisi açısından arazi ve arsa düzenlemesi işlemleri: Yargıtay ve Danıştay kararları ışığında bir değerlendirme. *Adalet Dergisi, 46*, 242–273.
Şimşek, S. (2014). Kamu mallarının özel mülkiyete konu olmaması ilkesinin mülkiyet hukukuna yansımaları. *Sayıştay Dergisi, 92*, 93–115.
Söyler, İ. (2005). *Devlet mallarının kamu finansmanı açısından değerlendirilmesi*. Ministry of Finance Research and Coordination Board.
Söyler, İ. (2011). Kamu malları teorisi açısından devletin hüküm ve tasarrufundaki yerler. *Sayıştay Dergisi, 83*, 57–68.
TOB (2022). *Pasture and forage crop statistics*, Ministry of Agriculture and Forestry. https://www.tarimorman.gov.tr/Konular/Bitkisel-Uretim/Cayir-Mera-ve-Yem-Bitkileri. Accessed September 24, 2022.
TOB (2024). *Updated statistics on meadows and pastures*, Ministry of Agriculture and Forestry. https://www.tarimorman.gov.tr/Konular/Bitkisel-Uretim/Cayir-Mera-ve-Yem-Bitkileri. Accessed: August 22, 2024.
Van Den Beemt-Tjeerdsma, A., & Veuger, J. (2016). Towards a more professionalised municipal real estate management. *Journal of Corporate Real Estate, 18*(2), 132–144.
World Bank. (2022). *GDP by sector data*. http://wdi.worldbank.org/table/3.1#. Accessed: September 24, 2022
Yang, Y. (2023). Factors affecting the continuity of public policies: China's real estate policy as an example. *Lecture Notes in Education, Psychology and Public Media, 24*, 249–255.
Yayla, Y. (1998). Kamu malının çağdaş tanımı. *Marmara Üniversitesi Hukuk Araştırmaları Dergisi, 7*(1–3), 7–17.

İlhan Yıldırım is a doctor and completed his master's and doctorate degrees at the Department of Real Estate Development and Management at Ankara University in 2024. He is currently employed as an expert at the Ministry of National Defence. Dr. Yildirim's areas of expertise encompass real estate finance, real estate law, real estate valuation, real estate projects, project valuation, and the management of public real estate.

Ahmet Hilmi Erciyes is a research assistant in the Department of Real Estate Development and Management at Ankara University. He graduated from the Department of Public Administration at Süleyman Demirel University in 2013. He completed his master's degree in real estate development and management at Ankara University in 2019 and is currently pursuing his doctoral studies in the same field. As a certified real estate appraiser, his academic work primarily focuses on local governments, urban land management, zoning plans, and urban economics.

İskender Duman was born in 1987 and completed his primary, secondary, and high school education in Van. He pursued his university studies at Yıldız Technical University, Faculty of Civil Engineering, Department of Geomatics Engineering, followed by his master's and doctoral studies at the Department of Real Estate Development and Management at Ankara University in 2011 and 2017, respectively. He held engineering and managerial roles at the Van Metropolitan Municipality. Between 2017 and 2023, Dr. Duman occupied managerial positions at various engineering and valuation firms, as well as the Eastern Anatolia Regional Directorate.

Policies and Practices for Reducing Emissions and Improving Energy Efficiency in Real Estate

Sinan Güneş and Mustafa Tombul

Abstract

Türkiye is dependent on energy imports, and this import dependency underscores Türkiye's goal to improve its energy efficiency, stimulate investment in renewable energy, and ensure the security of energy supply. The expansion of solar and wind energy capacities signifies the nation's commitment to these renewable energy sources. The prevailing dependence on fossil fuels contributes to rising CO_2 emissions, presenting challenges for achieving climate targets. The successful implementation of energy efficiency strategies will reduce energy intensity and promote sustainable development. Additionally, it is important to strengthen the capacity to utilise international climate finance. In summary, the augmented use of renewable energy and stronger energy efficiency policies will be crucial for helping Türkiye attain its sustainable energy goals.

Keywords

Carbon emissions · Energy efficiency · Renewable energy

1 Introduction

Sources of green energy production and the efficient management of energy demand are among the biggest challenges faced by production enterprises. Currently, a significant portion of the energy used in production is derived from fossil fuels.

S. Güneş (✉) · M. Tombul
Department of Real Estate Development and Management, Faculty of Applied Sciences, Ankara University, Ankara, Türkiye
e-mail: sngunes@ankara.edu.tr; mtombul@ankara.edu.tr

T. Just et al. (eds.), *Understanding Türkiye's Real Estate Markets*, Management for Professionals, https://doi.org/10.1007/978-3-032-13297-0_29

Therefore, optimising energy consumption is a good opportunity for reducing greenhouse gas emissions in the near future (Rahimifard et al., 2010).

Improving energy efficiency throughout energy production, transmission, and final consumption, while concurrently preventing waste, alleviating inefficient usage, and reducing energy intensity at both sectoral and macro levels, constitutes a crucial component of Türkiye's national energy policies (MENR 2016). This strategy is closely aligned with contemporary global initiatives for sustainable building development that emphasise the reduction of environmental impacts through the adoption of enhanced efficiency measures (Brotchie & Mathias, 2023; Vasilakopoulou & Santamouris, 2021).

This chapter analyses Türkiye's current state and potential strategies regarding energy consumption, efficiency, and sustainable energy policies. The following sections will explore the development of Türkiye's energy efficiency policies and the establishment of national strategies within this domain. Subsequently, the dynamics of energy consumption will be examined in relation to those of the European Union and OECD countries, with the objective of elucidating the reasons and methods by which Türkiye's energy policies diverge (Elsland et al., 2014).

Strategies to enhance the use of renewable energy sources and reduce emissions will also be examined. The initiatives implemented by Türkiye to fulfil its obligations under the Paris Agreement and to achieve its 2053 net-zero emissions target will be assessed (Guler & Kumar, 2022). Finally, sustainability practices within the energy and real estate sectors, including ongoing projects and policy recommendations, will be discussed.

The assessment of the initiatives undertaken in accordance with Türkiye's inaugural and subsequent National Energy Efficiency Action Plans (NEEAP) for the periods of 2012–2023 and 2024–2030 highlights the imperative of formulating a strategic and dynamic roadmap for energy efficiency (MENR, 2024). This roadmap has to incorporate the experiences and challenges encountered during execution and the prevailing global trends in the energy sector. A multitude of legal regulations have been enacted to promote collaboration between the public sector, the private sector, and non-governmental organisations. These endeavours are geared towards developing policies that are underpinned by tangible, results-oriented objectives, identifying the necessary actions required to achieve these objectives, and delineating the responsibilities that organisations will undertake throughout the process.

Data on Türkiye's primary energy consumption from 2011 to 2023 shows a significant increase. Primary energy consumption, which was recorded at 4.85 exajoules (EJ) in 2011, rose by 44% to 7.00 EJ in 2023. In 2020, a transitory decline occurred due to the global pandemic; the upward trajectory resumed in 2021.

Türkiye's primary energy consumption is correlated with economic output, industrialisation, and urbanisation. The observed reduction in energy consumption among EU member states can be attributed to stringent energy efficiency policies, low population growth rates, and an increased use of renewable energy sources. Türkiye's expanding industrial sector and young population are also important factors driving energy demand. While relatively stable energy consumption is noted among OECD countries, a distinct upward trend is evident in non-OECD countries.

Türkiye exhibits a lower rate of increase compared to non-OECD countries; Türkiye's trajectory is more closely aligned with that of OECD countries.

The unique dynamics of Türkiye's energy consumption, which differ from regional and global trends, underscore the necessity for customised approaches in the nation's energy policies and strategies. It is crucial to manage this growth potential in a sustainable manner (Fig. 1).

This upward trend highlights the need for strategic planning regarding energy supply security and the development of sustainable energy policies. To address the escalating energy demand, it is imperative to enhance the role of renewable energy sources and ensure the more effective implementation of energy efficiency policies (Toklu & Kaygusuz, 2012).

While Türkiye's total energy consumption experienced a modest decline from 7.10 exajoules (EJ) in 2022 to 7.00 EJ in 2023, substantial increases were observed in oil consumption, which rose by 5.5%, and renewable energy consumption, which increased by 2.9%. Conversely, natural gas and coal consumption declined by 5.4% and 6.3%, respectively. These transformations signify a positive shift in Türkiye's energy consumption patterns, indicating an increasing emphasis on renewable energy sources.

In contrast, energy consumption across EU member states and the broader European region exhibits a general downward trend, accompanied by notable reductions in natural gas and coal consumption, specifically a decline of 7.1% and 1.5%, respectively. At the same time, renewable energy consumption within EU member states has increased by 8.2%. Total energy consumption among OECD countries has decreased by 1.6%. In comparison, non-OECD countries have seen a 4.3% rise, primarily driven by increased consumption of oil and coal. Globally, energy consumption increased by 2.0% from 2022 to 2023, reaching a total of 619.63 EJ, driven by rises in oil and coal use. Stringent sustainable energy policies and climate change goals lead to higher growth in renewable energy within the EU. Türkiye has

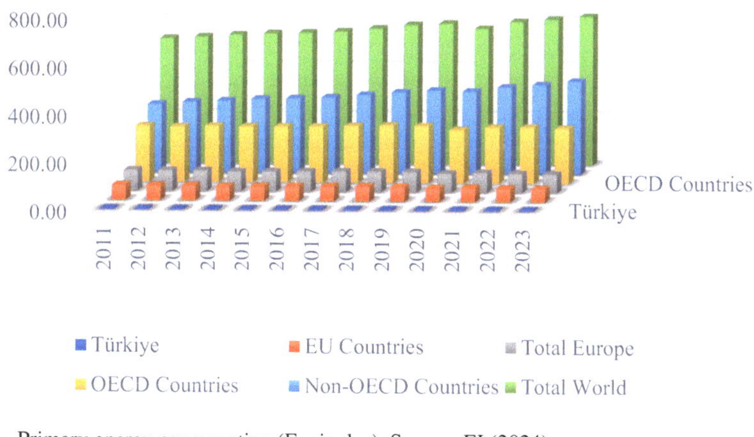

Fig. 1 Primary energy consumption (Exajoules). Source: EI (2024)

similarly increased its investments in renewable energy and expanded its capacity in this sector; however, the implementation and adaptation of its policies are relatively slow compared to those in EU countries. This difference stems from Türkiye's economic priorities and the need to ensure energy supply security.

Mitigating energy consumption among OECD member countries necessitates investments in energy efficiency technologies and a transition towards renewable energy sources. Türkiye's alignment with non-OECD countries regarding energy consumption trends suggests that there remains significant potential for improvements in energy efficiency. Given the country's growth and the close link between economic growth and energy consumption, a more effective execution of energy efficiency policies could aid Türkiye in lowering its energy intensity and achieving its goals.

The data indicate that the dynamics of energy consumption exhibit variability across different regions, reflecting the diverse energy policies and economic conditions prevalent in these regions. Türkiye prioritises economic growth and the security of energy supply within its energy policies, which results in fossil fuels maintaining a significant role in energy production. Nonetheless, strategies aimed at transitioning to renewable energy have been formulated, although complete implementation has required considerable time. This transition is poised to bolster economic growth while also aiding the attainment of environmental sustainability objectives. This scenario highlights the need for global energy policies to adopt a more balanced and diversified approach, ensuring both energy security and sustainability. This also holds for Türkiye's energy policies (Fig. 2).

The prominence of fossil fuels in Türkiye's energy consumption poses a significant challenge to the nation's energy supply and environmental sustainability objectives. The substantial reliance on fossil fuels, including natural gas and oil, exacerbates external dependency and contributes to elevated emission levels. Policymakers must expedite the transition towards renewable energy sources and, more critically, formulate robust policies aimed at reducing the dependency on fossil fuels (Kilickaplan et al., 2017).

Türkiye's per capita energy consumption has risen by 24% from 65.80 gigajoules per person (GJ/person) in 2011 to 81.60 GJ/person in 2023 (Fig. 3). The rise in per capita energy consumption has been particularly pronounced since 2016, reaching a peak in 2021 and 2022, before experiencing a slight decline to 81.60 in 2023. This growth is indicative of Türkiye's economic development. In contrast, per capita energy consumption among European Union member states exhibits a downward trajectory; it decreased from 145.80 GJ/person in 2011 to 125.60 in 2023, still 50% above the levels in Türkiye, though. Similar declining trends are evident across all European and OECD nations, where the effects of enhanced energy efficiency and the transition to renewable energy sources become apparent.

Conversely, per capita energy consumption in non-OECD countries has increased from 49.90 GJ/person in 2011 to 58.50 GJ/person in 2023, indicating an expansion in energy access and economic growth. On a global scale, per capita energy consumption increased by 4.1% from 74.00 GJ/person in 2011 to 77.00 GJ/person in 2023.

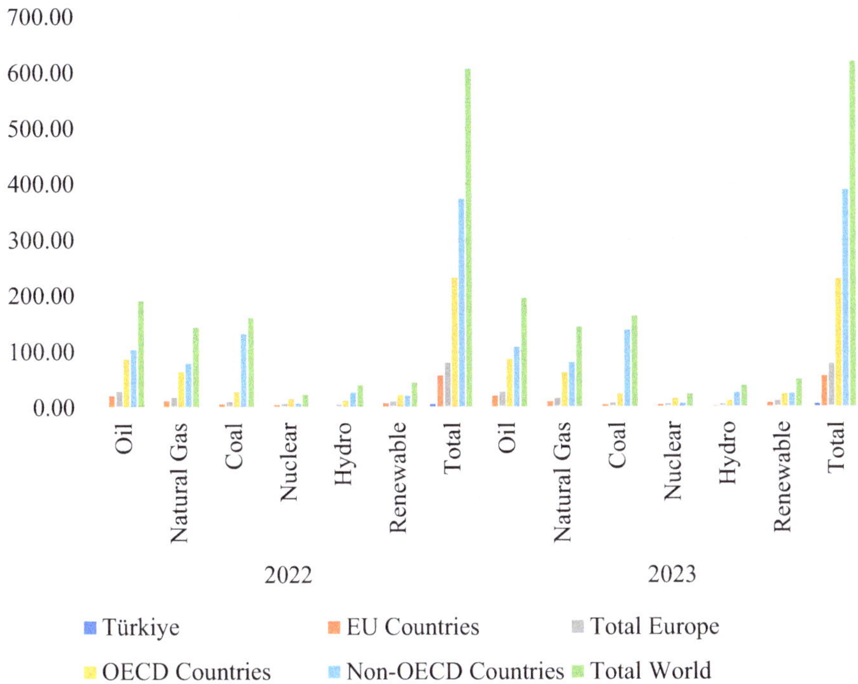

Fig. 2 Primary energy consumption by fuel type (Exajoules). Source: EI (2024)

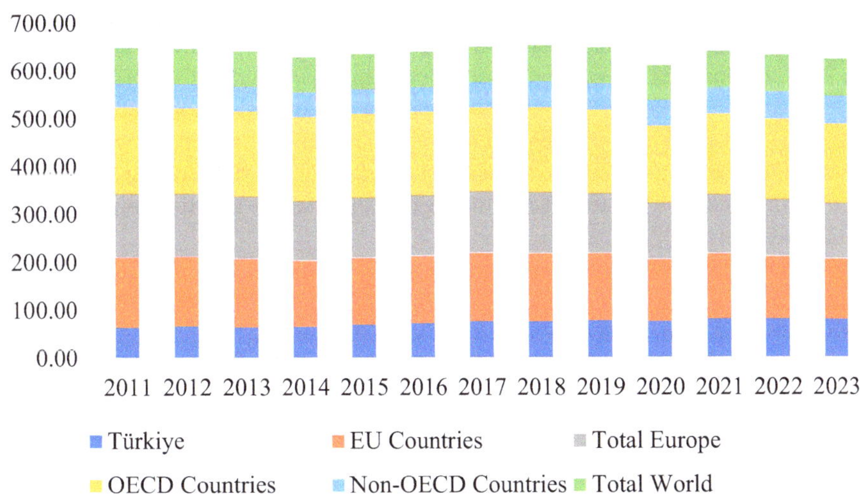

Fig. 3 Primary energy consumption per capita (Gigajoule/population). Source: EI (2024)

The increase in per capita energy consumption is associated with Türkiye's economic growth and the potential for further improvements in living standards. Policymakers should enact measures to enhance energy efficiency and reduce energy waste.

From 2011 to 2021, Türkiye's population increased by approximately 10 million persons, from 74.7 million to 84.7 million (Table 1). At the same time, Gross Domestic Product (GDP) fluctuated along an upward trend. Total energy supply (measured in petajoules) and electricity consumption (measured in terawatt-hours) rose during this period. The substantial increase in electricity consumption, particularly from 2017 onwards, reflects the impacts of industrialisation, urbanisation, and population growth. CO_2 emissions have risen in conjunction with increased energy consumption and economic activities. The rise in per capita energy supply and electricity consumption indicates improved living standards and enhanced access to energy. The energy efficiency ratio (TES/GDP) has improved since 2017, alongside a reduction in carbon intensity (CO_2/GDP), suggesting that Türkiye is transitioning towards cleaner or more carbon-efficient energy technologies. These trends provide critical insights into the balance between Türkiye's economic growth, energy consumption, and environmental impacts, offering guidance for shaping future energy policies.

2 Energy and Climate Change

Total greenhouse gas emissions categorised by sector offer a comprehensive overview of Türkiye's environmental footprint, as illustrated in Fig. 4. The 145% increase in total emissions, measured in million tons of CO_2 equivalent from 1990 to 2022, emphasises the ecological cost associated with Türkiye's rapid economic growth and urbanisation. The 180% increase in the energy sector exemplifies the nation's substantial ongoing dependence on fossil fuels to meet its growing energy demand. In contrast, the 208% rise in emissions from industrial processes and product use underscores the expansion of the industrial sector and the imperative for modernisation.

Although the 38% increase in the agricultural sector is lower than in other sectors, it reflects the impact of potent greenhouse gases such as methane and nitrous oxide resulting from farm activities. The 58% rise in the waste sector can be attributed to the growing population and evolving consumption patterns. Variations in emissions during exceptional periods, such as the global economic crisis of 2008–2009 and the COVID-19 pandemic of 2020, illustrate the close relationship between economic activity and greenhouse gas emissions.

Thus, Türkiye is poised to implement comprehensive and assertive sector-specific policies to fulfil its commitments under the Paris Agreement and achieve the 2053 net-zero emissions target (Guler & Kumar, 2022). Türkiye faces significant challenges in combating climate change, including the prevalence of high-carbon-emitting sectors, insufficient renewable energy infrastructure, and obstacles in accessing climate finance. To address these challenges, it is crucial to invest in

Table 1 Türkiye in numbers

Year	Population (M) (1)	GDP (billion USD) (2)	Growth (%)	GDP in PPP in billion USD) (3)	Net Import (TJ) (5)	Total Energy Supply (PJ) (6)	Electricity consumption (TWh) (7)	CO_2 emission (Mt CO_2) (8)	TES/Population (GJ/pop.) (6/1)	TES/GDP (GJ/000,$) (6/2)	TES/GDP (SAGP) (GJ/000, USD) (6/3)	Electricity consumption/pop. (kWh/pop.) (7/1)	CO_2/TES (tCO_2/TJ) (8/6)	CO_2/pop. (tCO_2/pop.) (8/1)	CO2/GDP (kg CO_2/USD) (8/2)	CO_2/GDP (SAGP) (kgCO_2/USD) (8/3)
2011	74.7	831.7	11.2	1450	3408	4707	186	298.8	63.0	5.61	3.25	2490	63.47	4.00	0.36	0.21
2012	75.6	871.1	4.8	1550	3774	4923	194.9	314.4	65.1	5.59	3.18	2577	63.87	4.16	0.36	0.20
2013	76.7	950.4	8.5	1700	3695	4794	198.1	303.3	62.5	5.01	2.82	2583	63.26	3.96	0.32	0.18
2014	77.7	934.9	4.9	1860	3926	4958	207.4	335.1	63.9	5.29	2.67	2669	67.46	4.31	0.36	0.18
2015	78.7	861.9	6.1	2020	4338	5379	217.3	341.1	68.3	6.22	2.66	2760	63.41	4.33	0.40	0.17
2016	79.8	862.8	3.3	2120	4424	5707	231.2	359.2	71.5	6.56	2.69	2897	62.95	4.50	0.42	0.17
2017	80.8	852.6	7.5	2260	4867	6149	249.0	404.2	76.1	7.16	2.72	3082	65.74	5.00	0.47	0.18
2018	82.0	789.0	5.0	2300	4578	6040	258.2	401.8	73.7	7.76	2.63	3149	66.53	4.90	0.51	0.17
2019	83.2	760.8	0.9	2240	4428	6136	257.3	394.0	73.8	8.06	2.74	3094	64.22	4.74	0.52	0.18
2020	83.6	717.1	1.8	2300	4414	6161	262.7	384.6	73.7	8.56	2.68	3142	62.42	4.60	0.54	0.17
2021	84.7	802.7	11.0	2590	4428	6134	286.7	420.7	72.4	7.64	2.37	3386	68.58	4.97	0.52	0.16

Note that all values were rounded for clarity

Sources: Own compilation using TurkStat, World Bank, EC and IEA data. (1) TurkStat (2011–2021); (2) World Bank (2025a); (3) World Bank (2025b); (4) World Bank (2025c) (5) IEA (2021b); (6) IEA (2011–2021); IEA (2021a); (7) IEA (2021c); (8) European Commission (2023)

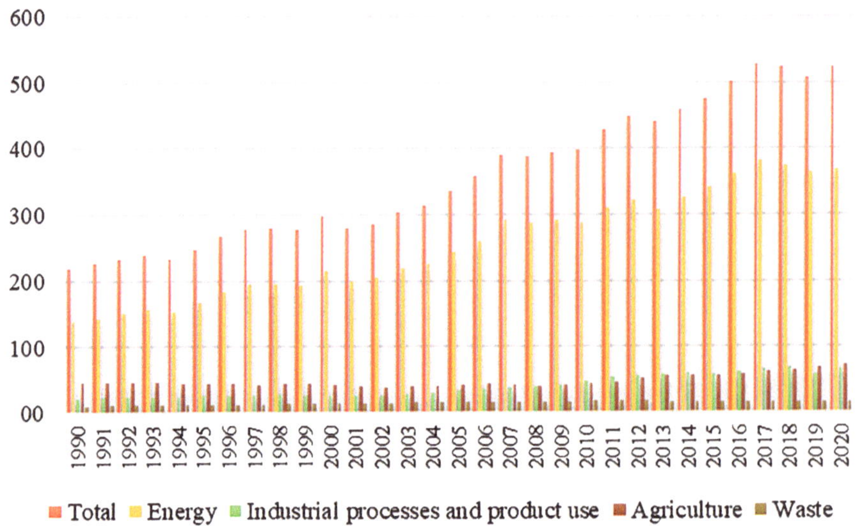

Fig. 4 Total greenhouse gas emissions by sectors. Source: TurkStat (2021)

low-carbon technologies, increase the number of renewable energy projects, and promote innovative solutions within the energy sector. Furthermore, diplomatic efforts should be intensified to facilitate access to international climate finance, and essential legal and institutional frameworks should be established to enable Türkiye to benefit from these funds.

Implementing carbon pricing mechanisms may be pivotal in attaining emission reduction targets. Enhancing energy efficiency, transitioning to renewable energy sources, modernising industrial processes through green technologies, adopting sustainable agricultural practices, and employing circular economy approaches in waste management are imperative (Zhao et al., 2023). Furthermore, the application of carbon pricing mechanisms and the augmentation of investments in low-carbon technologies will facilitate Türkiye's advancement toward sustainable development and contribute to the global endeavour against climate change.

The emissions of CO_2 resulting from fossil fuels are affected by a multitude of factors, including population growth, economic development, energy intensity (TES/GDP), and the carbon intensity of the energy supply (CO_2/TES) (IEA, 2021c). Türkiye's GDP has increased by 89% since 2000, while its population has grown by 29.7%. Simultaneously, energy intensity has decreased by 21.4%, and carbon intensity has fallen by 5.6%. In total, the total CO_2 emissions have risen by 82% during the same period (Fig. 5).

In Türkiye, the Ministry of Environment, Urbanisation, and Climate Change oversees high-level environmental policies, strategies addressing climate change, and corresponding action plans. Furthermore, the Ministry of Energy and Natural Resources (MENR) assists in coordinating climate and environmental policies relevant to the energy sector. Within MENR, the Directorate General for Energy

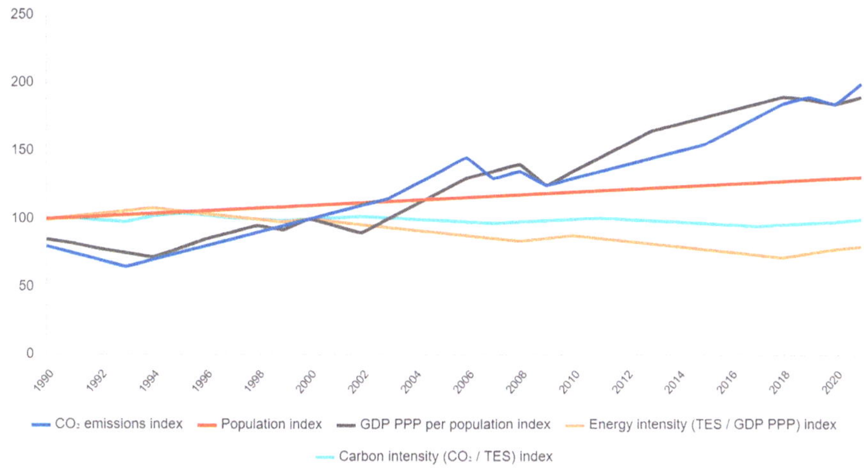

Fig. 5 CO_2 emissions drivers, republic of Türkiye, 1990–2021. Source: IEA (2021c)

Efficiency and Environment is tasked with the management of policies related to climate change and environmental stewardship. The primary activities categorised under climate change include participation in climate negotiations, implementation of mitigation actions, and management of greenhouse gas inventories. In terms of ecological management, the emphasis is placed on sustainability, including conducting environmental impact assessments, as well as managing the quality of water, air, and soil. The Ministry of Treasury and Finance spearheads efforts related to climate finance and ecological taxation. At the same time, the Ministry of Environment, Urbanisation, and Climate Change bears the responsibility for ensuring the maintenance of air quality.

To advance the National Climate Change Strategy (2010–2023), the Climate Change and Air Management Coordination Board was established in 2013. This strategic move was designed to temporarily unite public and private sector institutions, academia, civil society, and other stakeholders. It was chaired by the Minister of Environment, Urbanisation, and Climate Change. The board includes representatives from all ministries to facilitate coordination on climate change and air quality issues nationwide. Under this board, there are seven working groups composed of experts. MENR is also part of the Greenhouse Gas Mitigation Working Group.

Between 2013 and 2023, a discernible upward trend in fossil fuel consumption was observed in Türkiye (Table 2). Notably, oil consumption has increased at an annual rate of 6%, accounting for 1.1% of global oil consumption by 2023. Although the consumption of natural gas in Türkiye decreased by 5.5%, it still accounts for 1.2% of global natural gas consumption. Furthermore, coal consumption exhibited a decline of 6.3%; Türkiye's share of global coal consumption remains constant at 1%. In contrast, the European Union and OECD countries, in general, are reducing their fossil fuel consumption, reflecting their commitment to sustainable energy policies. The EU's coal consumption has declined by 20.4%, and significant

Table 2 Oil, natural gas and coal consumption in Türkiye

Oil consumption in thousands of barrels per day						
	Years			Annual growth (%)		Consumption (%)
Country/region	2013	2022	**2023**	2023	2013–2023	2023
Türkiye	734	1072	**1,136**	6.0	4.5	1.1
EU countries	10,961	10,687	**10,488**	−1.9	−0.4	10.5
Total europe	14,211	14,009	**13,904**	−0.8	−0.2	13.9
OECD countries	45,024	44,770	**44,731**	−0.1	−0.1	44.6
Non-OECD countries	445,077	52,913	**55,489**	4.9	2.1	55.4
Total world	90,101	97,683	**100,221**	2.6	1.1	100.0
Natural gas consumption (Billion m³)						
Country/region	**Years**			**Annual growth (%)**		**Consumption (%)**
	2013	2022	**2023**	2023	2013–2023	2023
Türkiye	44	51	**48**	−5.5	1.0	1.2
EU countries	375	344	**320**	−7.1	−1.6	8.0
Total europe	555	498	**463**	−6.9	−1.8	11.6
OECD countries	1617	1793	**1757**	−2.0	0.8	43.8
Non-OECD countries	1755	2215	**2253**	1.7	2.5	56.2
Total world	3372	4009	**4010**	0.0	1.7	100.0
Coal consumption (Exajoules)						
Country/region	**Years**			**Annual growth (%)**		**Consumption (%)**
	2013	2022	**2023**	2023	2013–2023	2023
Türkiye	1.3	1.8	**1.7**	−6.3	2.3	1.0
EU countries	10.5	6.9	**5.5**	−20.4	−6.3	3.3
Total europe	15.9	10.0	**8.4**	−16.2	−6.1	5.1
OECD countries	43.7	28.9	**25.2**	−12.9	−5.3	15.3
Non-OECD countries	117.3	132.7	**138.9**	4.7	1.7	84.7
Total world	161.0	161.5	**164.0**	1.6	0.2	100.0

Note that all figures are rounded to the neares whole number
Source: EI (2024)

reductions have also been achieved with regard to natural gas and oil. Conversely, non-OECD countries are increasing their fossil fuel consumption, which can be attributed to economic growth and rising energy demand.

The contemporary energy efficiency legislation in Türkiye, which encompasses the preparation of draft strategies and action plans, the execution of regulatory impact assessments, and the monitoring and evaluation of measures, is predominantly administered by the Ministry of Environment, Urbanisation, and Climate Change for the building sector. The Ministry of Transport and Infrastructure is responsible for implementing and regulating efficiency policies related to the transportation sector. The Ministry of Industry and Technology coordinates its efforts with the Directorate General for Energy Efficiency and Environment (DGEEE) within the industrial sector. Lastly, the Ministry of Agriculture and Forestry is responsible for energy efficiency policies and practices in the agricultural industry.

In addition to domestic energy efficiency and emission reduction initiatives, Türkiye is actively engaged in a range of project-based international collaborations. Noteworthy projects encompass the Energy Efficiency and Low Carbon Heating and Cooling Supply Project with Denmark, the Energy Efficiency Network Project with Germany, and the International Training Project on Energy Efficiency and Management in Industry and Buildings with Japan. Additionally, Türkiye participates in various technology collaboration programmes under the auspices of the International Energy Agency (IEA), focusing on energy efficiency and renewable energy, including Energy Storage, Hybrid and Electric Vehicles, Photovoltaic Power Systems, and Solar Heating and Cooling (IEA, 2021c). These collaborations with Denmark, Germany, and Japan have considerably advanced Türkiye's energy efficiency and low-carbon technology sectors, facilitating the transfer of essential technologies aimed at achieving energy savings and reducing greenhouse gas emissions. Looking ahead, it would be advantageous for Türkiye to broaden such collaborations into emerging fields such as renewable energy, energy storage, and carbon capture. By fostering enhanced international cooperation, Türkiye can effectively contribute to global initiatives aimed at combating climate change while simultaneously fulfilling its national objectives.

Analysing the distribution of energy-related carbon dioxide emissions over the years, it is apparent that emissions in Türkiye rose from 298.8 million tons in 2011 to 411.1 million tons in 2023. Türkiye reached its peak emission levels in 2017 and 2018, followed by a modest decline in 2020, likely attributable to the repercussions of the global pandemic. Nevertheless, emissions surged once more in 2023 (Fig. 6). This increase may be associated with Türkiye's economic expansion and increased energy consumption (IEA, 2025).

In contrast, CO_2 emissions associated with energy in European Union member states have fallen from 3,300.8 million metric tons in 2011 to 2,517.6 million metric tons in 2023. Countries within the OECD have exhibited a general trend of declining greenhouse gas emissions from 12,842.4 million tons in 2011 to 11,108.5 million tons in 2023. In contrast, emissions in non-OECD countries have continued to increase, rising from 19,062.2 million tons in 2011 to 24,021.3 million tons in 2023. Energy-related carbon dioxide emissions have fluctuated annually, but they have generally trended upward over time. Global emissions increased from 31,904.6 million tons in 2011 to 35,129.8 million tons in 2023.

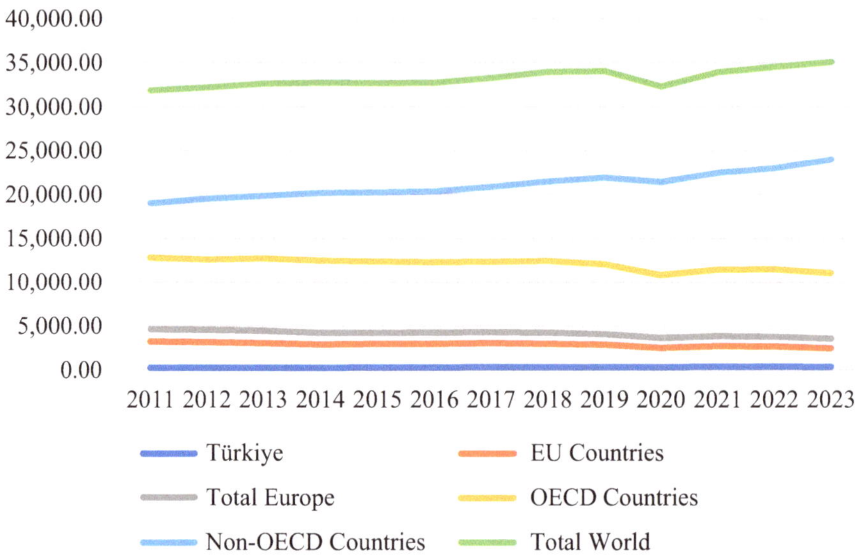

Fig. 6 CO_2 emissions from energy (million tons). Source: EI (2024)

3 Emission Reduction Targets and Policies

The substantial increase in energy consumption has influenced Türkiye's overarching energy policy, particularly in terms of energy imports, despite the ongoing efforts to reduce the nation's reliance on imported energy. In accordance with this, the energy sector has undergone a significant restructuring aimed at enhancing domestic production capacity, encompassing modernisation, liberalisation, and an increase in private and foreign investment. Within this framework, the Ministry of Energy and Natural Resources unveiled the National Energy and Mining Policy in 2017 (MENR, 2017). This policy underscores the imperative of reducing Türkiye's dependency on imported energy sources and is founded upon three main pillars:

- Enhancing energy supply security;
- Increasing the use of domestic energy resources to localise energy production;
- Improving predictability in energy markets.

3.1 The Twelfth Development Plan (2024 to 2028)

The Twelfth Development Plan (2024–2028) sets strategic objectives for Türkiye's energy sector, aiming to ensure a sustainable, secure, and economically viable energy supply (Presidency of Strategy and Budget, 2024). To realise this vision, the plan emphasises the importance of increasing domestic and renewable energy sources to bolster energy supply security and undertake essential measures toward achieving the net-zero emissions target by 2050. By advocating for the localisation of energy technologies and the integration of innovative technologies, the plan aspires to enhance Türkiye's strategic standing in the realm of international energy trade (Table 3). The primary objectives and policies, especially those pertinent to the real estate sector, are delineated as follows:

1. **Sustainable energy supply:** Ensuring a continuous, high-quality, and sustainable energy supply is central to Türkiye's energy policies. Diversifying energy sources to enhance energy security is a crucial objective. Increasing the use of renewable energy sources will help meet energy demands cleanly and sustainably (Atilgan & Azapagic, 2017).
2. **Increasing energy efficiency:** Energy efficiency plays a critical role in effectively managing energy consumption, minimising emissions, and preserving resources. The plan aims to optimise energy usage across all sectors by advancing energy efficiency initiatives and providing both economic and environmental benefits (Yilan & Çiftçioğlu, 2020).
3. **Nuclear energy and technological localisation:** Incorporating nuclear energy into Türkiye's energy mix will support objectives related to energy supply security and the production of low-carbon energy. Promoting the development and localisation of energy technologies will enhance Türkiye's autonomy within the energy sector.
4. **Flexibility of energy grids:** Enhancing the flexibility of electricity grids is essential for integrating renewable energy sources and mitigating the adverse impacts associated with intermittent energy supplies. This endeavour will strengthen energy supply security and promote the broader adoption of renewable energy.

Table 3 Targets for the energy sector in the twelfth development plan

Descriptions	2022	2023	2028
Primary energy demand (kTOE)	159,500	165,350	190,000
Primary energy consumption per capita (TOE/person)	1.87	1.9	2
Electrical energy demand (TWh)	331	325	430
Electrical energy consumption per capita (kWh/person)	3883	3780	4700
Installed power capacity (MW)	103,809	106,800	136,000
Installed wind power capacity (MW)	11,396	11,700	18,000
Installed wind solar capacity (MW)	9425	11,350	30,000
Amount of electricity generated from domestic sources (TWh)	190.4	176	270
Share of renewable resources in electricity generation (%)	42.4	40	50
Share of natural gas in electricity generation (%)	22.9	23	15
Underground natural gas storage capacity (billion m^3)	5.8	5.8	13
Amount of savings from energy efficiency (BTEP)	–	–	4500
Battery storage capacity (MW)	0	0	5000

Source: Own depiction based on the 12th development plan

5. **Development of human resources in the energy sector:** Training competent professionals for the energy sector is essential for its sustainable growth and development.

These objectives will facilitate Türkiye's transition to a sustainable, low-carbon energy future, thereby providing a robust foundation for reducing emissions and enhancing energy efficiency within the real estate sector. By augmenting energy efficiency and employing renewable energy sources, the plan aspires to optimise energy consumption in the real estate sector, thereby yielding both economic and environmental benefits.

Türkiye has achieved notable advances in its energy objectives, evidenced by the increase in the proportion of private ownership in electricity generation from 40% in 2002 to 85% in 2018. This expansion is further bolstered by a significant increase in renewable energy, particularly hydropower, which is supported by government incentive programmes. Looking forward, Türkiye intends to commission 10,000 MW of solar and wind capacity between 2017 and 2027, along with the establishment of 7500 MW of new domestic coal energy capacity, thereby indicating a more diverse and future-oriented energy supply. By 2023, it was projected that 84% of new energy capacity would be generated from domestic sources, with 76% of this capacity originating from renewable sources. By 2027, these numbers are anticipated to be 82% and 61%, respectively (IEA, 2021c).

Energy efficiency is central to the policies aimed at reducing energy consumption through the promotion of the effective and efficient use of energy resources. Energy efficiency regulations in Türkiye have been legally established by the Energy Efficiency Law No. 5627, which was published in the Official Gazette on April 18, 2007. While this law was enacted to advance energy efficiency, several challenges persist. These challenges encompass difficulties in financing energy efficiency projects, a lack of awareness, and insufficient technical expertise. To effectively address these challenges, it is imperative to expand financing options for energy efficiency projects, organise awareness campaigns, and enhance the availability of technical training in energy efficiency. Furthermore, local governments and the private sector should adopt a more active stance in enforcing energy efficiency laws, and monitoring mechanisms should be strengthened.

Subsequent to the enactment of the law, regulations and communiqués were disseminated widely to promote energy efficiency and ensure national coordination. These encompass the Regulation on Increasing Efficiency in the Use of Energy Resources and Energy, the Energy Performance Regulation for Buildings, the Energy Efficiency Audit Regulation, and the Regulation on Procedures and Principles for Enhancing Energy Efficiency in Transportation. These regulations have established a robust framework for energy efficiency initiatives, facilitating their effective implementation.

Through the implementation of the Energy Efficiency Strategy (2012–2023) and the inaugural National Energy Efficiency Action Plan (NEEAP) (2017–2023), Türkiye had established a target to reduce energy intensity by 20% by 2023, relative to 2011 levels. The 2022 energy balance sheet indicated a decline in energy supply by 1.0%, while energy intensity fell by 20.4%. This achievement, which surpasses the predetermined objectives, demonstrates the efficacy and dedication of Türkiye's energy efficiency policies, thereby offering reassurance regarding the country's future energy landscape.

Under the NEEAP, total energy savings of 23.9 million tons of oil equivalent (Mtoe) were projected for 2023, accompanied by an investment of USD 10.9 billion. Between 2017 and 2023, energy savings totalling 24.6 Mtoe were achieved, with assets valued at USD 8.5 billion. The reduction in technology costs facilitated the attainment of the targeted savings at more economical rates.

The accomplishment of the objectives outlined in the Energy Efficiency Strategy and the National Energy Efficiency Action Plan (NEEAP) exemplifies Türkiye's commitment to and progress in energy efficiency. Nevertheless, in light of factors such as variations in global energy prices, the ongoing battle against climate change, and the need for energy supply security, it is imperative to continue augmenting efforts toward energy efficiency.

Table 4 delineates the legal regulations and objectives pertaining to energy efficiency in Türkiye across a specified timeline, emphasising the advances and measures undertaken in this domain. Several crucial points merit emphasis:

1. **Development of the legal framework:** The initial legislative action taken by Türkiye concerning energy efficiency was the implementation of Energy Efficiency Law No. 5627 in 2007. Although this legislation established extensive regulations related to energy efficiency, it did not delineate explicit targets for energy efficiency. In subsequent years, further regulations were enacted, particularly addressing energy performance standards in buildings, strategies for combating climate change, energy identity certification, and an array of other legal provisions.
2. **Energy efficiency targets:** The articulation of clear energy efficiency targets commenced with the Energy Efficiency Strategy Document published in 2012, which aimed to reduce energy intensity by 20% by 2023, relative to 2011 levels. This target represented a significant advancement in establishing measurable and tangible objectives for energy efficiency in Türkiye. The National Energy Efficiency Action Plan (NEEAP), published in 2018, outlined a more specific goal of achieving cumulative energy savings of 23.9 million tons of oil equivalent (Mtoe) by 2023. This reflects a comprehensive approach to energy efficiency strategies, evaluated through specific metrics. The Twelfth Development Plan 2023 established a target to save 4500 thousand tons of oil equivalent (ttoe) and achieve at least 30% energy savings in public buildings. These ambitious targets signify a commitment to enhanced savings rates, particularly within the public sector.
3. **Continuously evolving and updating policies:** The table demonstrates that energy efficiency policies are subject to continuous modification and enhancement. The Energy Efficiency Strategy 2030, alongside the second National Energy Efficiency Action Plan, published in early 2024, seeks to further energy efficiency objectives and practices, drawing insights from historical experiences.

This consistent evolution of policies exemplifies Türkiye's adaptability and dedication to advancement, thereby aligning energy efficiency initiatives with global climate objectives (MENR, 2024).

4. **Targets for public buildings:** Presidential Circulars issued in 2019 and 2023 concentrate on augmenting energy savings in public buildings. These circulars outline specific objectives aimed at enhancing energy efficiency within public infrastructure, thereby underscoring substantial measures taken to promote energy efficiency in the public sector.

Table 4 clearly illustrates the evolution of energy efficiency legislation in Türkiye, a progress marked by significant advancements and the formulation of specific objectives. Starting in 2007, the legislative measures underscore the escalating importance of energy efficiency and its crucial role in energy policies. The establishment of precise, measurable objectives has enabled the monitoring and evaluation of progress in energy efficiency. As a result, Türkiye's energy efficiency policies are advancing in alignment with national objectives, with increasingly ambitious goals being set for the period following 2023.

Although the long-term objectives were delineated during the formulation of the National Energy Efficiency Strategy Document, the precise savings required to attain these objectives were not specified. To rectify this deficiency, the inaugural National Energy Efficiency Action Plan (NEEAP) incorporated calculations pertaining to the requisite investments, anticipated savings, and the financial implications of these savings. It was acknowledged that progress in energy efficiency is contingent upon various factors, including the nation's overall economic performance, growth in energy supply, and global energy pricing.

It is acknowledged that resources should be allocated towards priority areas, with energy efficiency regarded as a principal policy domain alongside disaster management and exceptional circumstances. Moreover, large-budget investment institutions and regional organisations have deemed energy efficiency a vital component for guaranteeing the effective use of existing resources. Strategies that rely exclusively on incentives and tax exemptions are considered inadequate, underscoring the need to connect private sector financing and international credit sources with investments in energy efficiency.

The private sector and non-governmental entities are not mere bystanders; rather, they are integral participants in the dissemination of energy efficiency measures. The significance of digital technological solutions in supporting energy efficiency has been recognised, and the integration of these solutions into energy efficiency policies has been proposed. This approach empowers these actors and reinforces their essentiality in the process.

Thus, the Energy Efficiency 2030 Strategy serves not only as a plan but also as a crucial instrument for achieving sustainable development goals and promoting progress in this realm. Reducing emissions and improving energy efficiency are regarded as indispensable objectives, with the real estate sector acknowledged as a focus area. This strategy underscores the importance of ongoing efforts and their potential impact on the future.

Table 4 Regulations on energy efficiency in Türkiye

Date	Yasal Düzenleme	Energy efficiency target
18.04.2007	Law No. 5627 Energy efficiency law	–
05.12.2008	Regulation on energy performance in buildings	–
03.05.2010	Republic of Türkiye climate change strategy 2010-2023	–
10.06.2010	Communiqué on training for energy identity certificate experts and training institutions	–
27.10.2011	Regulation on increasing efficiency in the use of energy resources and energy	–
25.02.2012	The energy efficiency strategy document for 2012–2023	The 2023 energy intensity is to be reduced by 20 per cent compared to 2011
2012	Republic of Türkiye climate change action plan 2011–2023	–
May 2016	Energy efficient building design strategies	–
01.11.2017	Communiqué on the national calculation method for energy performance in buildings	–
02.01.2018	National energy efficiency action plan 2017–2023	23.9 mtoe cumulative savings by 2023
06.07.2018	Regulation on energy efficiency audits	–
November 2018	Strategic plan of the ministry of energy and natural resources of the republic of Türkiye (2019–2023)	–
16.08.2019	Presidential circular on energy savings in public buildings (2019/18)	Minimum 15% energy saving in public buildings
07.12.2019	Presidential circular on the monitoring and steering committee of the national energy efficiency action plan (2019/27)	–
November 2022	Republic of Türkiye nationally determined contribution	–
19.01.2023	Türkiye national energy plan	51% improvement in energy intensity in the period 2000–2035
06.09.2023	Medium-term program (2024–2026)	–
01.11.2023	Twelfth development plan (2024–2028)	4500 ttoe savings
03.11.2023	Presidential circular on energy savings in public buildings (2023/15)	Minimum 30% energy saving in public buildings
08.01.2024	Energy efficiency 2030 strategy and second national energy efficiency action plan (2024–2030)	–

Source: Own depiction

To implement these regulations and objectives, the Ministry of Environment, Urbanisation, and Climate Change (MEUCC) published a comprehensive guide in 2020 regarding the energy-efficient renovation of public buildings. The main aim of this guide is to furnish guidance for energy-efficient renovations applicable to existing public buildings (MEUCC, 2020).

The Energy Efficiency and Environment Department (EEED) was established within the Ministry of Energy and Natural Resources to oversee energy efficiency policies and programmes by virtue of a Presidential Decree issued in January 2019. Subsequently, the National Energy Efficiency Action Plan Monitoring and Steering Committee was established under Decree No. 27 in December 2019, with the purpose of overseeing and directing the implementation of energy efficiency programmes and the NEEAP. The EEED, tasked with the execution of the NEEAP, administers a technical assistance programme designed to enhance institutional capacity and facilitate the implementation of efficiency strategies, particularly in alignment with European Union standards and directives.

3.2 Climate Transition Finance

Over the years, Türkiye has established successful partnerships with multilateral development banks on initiatives aimed at reducing greenhouse gas emissions. These initiatives are generally financed by grants and concessional loans from multilateral funds, including the Global Environment Facility (GEF) and the Climate Investment Funds. As of 2021, approximately USD 435 million has been expended from the Clean Technology Fund for climate transformation efforts. With the commencement of GEF utilisation, roughly USD 111 million in grants have been secured for 34 national projects. Furthermore, Türkiye has actively participated in 34 regional/global GEF projects, which amount to a total of USD 299 million and has attracted co-financing of approximately USD 1.3 billion (IEA, 2021c).

Türkiye possesses considerable potential for low-carbon technology and renewable energy projects. To secure international funding, enhance its project preparation capabilities, and foster collaborations with international financial institutions, Türkiye should align its national projects with the criteria prescribed for international funding. The development of innovative financing models and the promotion of public-private partnerships are vital for Türkiye to bolster its capacity to access international resources. Furthermore, Türkiye's strategic objectives in climate finance should be redefined to support sustainable development and facilitate the energy transition, necessitating the implementation of tangible measures in this direction.

These partnerships are considered significant opportunities to secure vital funding for innovative and sustainable initiatives, while fostering policy dialogues with international partners on climate change practices. Accordingly, Türkiye expresses its appreciation for the global community's technical assistance and climate finance support to assist in its efforts to combat climate change.

Türkiye is engaged in negotiations to modify its status under the United Nations Framework Convention on Climate Change (UNFCCC) in order to gain access to the Green Climate Fund. These negotiations involve a significant diplomatic endeavour to categorise Türkiye as a developing nation, thereby enabling equitable access to funding. The primary challenges encountered during these discussions stem from divergent interpretations of Türkiye's economic and developmental status. Gaining access to the Green Climate Fund is crucial for enhancing Türkiye's capacity to address climate change and achieve its low-carbon development objectives. The resources acquired from this fund would facilitate Türkiye's investment in renewable energy initiatives, enhance energy efficiency, and construct more resilient infrastructure to confront climate change.

3.3 Monitoring Emissions

Under the prevailing regulations, sectors delineated in the emissions data regulation are mandated to undergo annual monitoring, reporting, and verification processes. The prepared monitoring plans are submitted to the Ministry of Energy and Natural Resources through the Environmental Information System (MEUCC, 2022). Furthermore, according to a project conducted jointly by the Ministry of Environment, Urbanisation, and Climate Change and the German Federal Ministry for the Environment, Nature Conservation, and Nuclear Safety, the Capacity Building Project for the Implementation of the Monitoring, Reporting, and Verification System for Greenhouse Gas Emissions has been coordinated and implemented since 2014. The primary objective of the project is to assist in establishing a monitoring, reporting, and verification system that provides a robust and reliable data source for determining greenhouse gas emissions (ACSDC, 2022).

3.4 Climate Change Adaptation

Türkiye's adaptation policies are rooted in the National Climate Change Strategy and Action Plan (NCCSAP), which was adopted in 2011. This plan delineated short- and medium-term objectives and actions to be executed by 2023, covering water resource management, the agricultural sector, food security, ecosystem services, biodiversity and forestry, natural disaster risk management, and public health.

The analyses conducted within the scope of the plan indicate that Türkiye's geographic position in the Mediterranean Basin renders it more vulnerable to drought conditions and heat waves attributable to climate change. It is projected that the annual average temperature in Türkiye will rise by 2.5° to 4 °C in the forthcoming years, potentially reaching up to 4 °C in the Aegean and Eastern Anatolia regions and up to 5 °C in the interior regions (MEUCC, 2011). This scenario is anticipated to substantially amplify the demand for cooling technology in Türkiye in the future, in addition to its detrimental impacts on water and soil resources (Kılkış, 2021).

Fluctuations significantly influence the energy sector at sea level, as well as the effects of weather conditions on infrastructure. Notably, water scarcity is anticipated to have a direct impact on Türkiye's hydroelectric capacity, which currently constitutes approximately 30% of the nation's total electricity generation. Nevertheless, the potential of alternative energy sources, such as geothermal energy, provides optimism for the future. Consequently, the implications of climate change must be considered when selecting sites and planning hydroelectric projects

(MEUCC, 2011). Furthermore, enhancing the use of geothermal heat pumps and implementing district heating plans based on geothermal energy are critical strategies for adapting to climate change (MEUCC, 2011).

4 Energy Efficiency

Türkiye's strategic transition from an extensive dependence on oil and natural gas to a more diversified energy portfolio, encompassing renewable resources, nuclear energy, and lignite mining, signifies substantial progress in the global energy landscape (IEA, 2021c).

Recent increases in renewable energy production and capacity data indicate that the global energy transition is accelerating (Tables 5 and 6). In 2023, Türkiye generated 137.9 TWh of renewable energy, with 86% of this production originating from hydroelectric, solar, and wind sources. The production of solar energy has experienced substantial growth since 2013, achieving an average annual growth rate of 89.7%, thereby emphasising Türkiye's growing investments in solar energy. Türkiye's solar energy capacity attained 11,293 MW in 2023, while its wind energy capacity expanded to 11,697 MW, realising an average annual growth rate of 15.5% since 2013. This data underscores Türkiye's broadening investments in renewable energy and its swiftly increasing capacity within this sector.

Similarly, the production of renewable energy has increased across Europe. In 2023, the EU's renewable energy production reached an impressive 1,211.7 TWh, while the overall renewable energy production in Europe as a whole amounted to 1,769.3 TWh. The primary driving force behind this increase has been the growth of wind and solar energy. Europe's solar energy capacity has risen to 299,200 MW, reflecting an average annual growth rate of 13.5% since 2013. In contrast, wind energy capacity has expanded by 8.3% per year to 268,708 MW. On a global scale, renewable energy production reached 8,988.4 TWh in 2023, marking a 5.4% increase. This rise in global solar and wind energy production underscores the

Table 5 Renewable energy generation by sources (Terawatt-saat)

Country/region	Wind	Solar	Hy-dro	Other	2022	Wind	Solar	Hy-dro	Other	2023
Türkiye	34.9	16.9	66.8	19.2	138	34.1	20.5	63.9	19.5	**138**
EU countries	421	209	274	175	1080	481	247	326	158	**1212**
Total europe	555	249	564	239	1608	614	295	639	222	**1769**
OECD countries	1094	655	1395	400	3544	1149	755	1386	386	**3676**
Non-OECD countries	1014	667	2929	377	4986	1176	886	2855	396	**5312**
Total world	2108	1322	4323	777	8530	2325	1642	4240	782	**8988**

Note that larger values are rounded to the nearest whole number for clarity
Source: EI (2024)

Table 6 Solar and wind energy capacity (installed photovoltaic power, megawatt)

Renewable energy: solar capacity (installed photovoltaic power, megawatt)						
	Years			Annual growth rate (%)		Consumption (%)
Country/region	2013	2022	**2023**	2023	2013–2023	2023
Türkiye	19	9400	**11,300**	19.8	89.7	0.8
Total Europe	84,200	243,000	**299,200**	23.1	13.5	21.1
Total World	141,400	1,073,000	**1,419,000**	32.2	25.9	100.0
Renewable energy: wind power capacity (installed turbine capacity, megawatt)						
Country/region	**Years**			**Annual growth rate (%)**		**Consumption (%)**
	2013	2022	**2023**	2023	2013–2023	2023
Türkiye	2760	11,400	**11,700**	2.6	15.5	1.1
Total europe	120,900	251,600	**268,700**	6.8	8.3	26.4
Total world	299,900	901,200	**1,017,200**	12.9	13.0	100.0

All capacity values are rounded to the nearest hundred or thousand for readability. Growth rate and consumption shares are shown in percent, rounded to 1 decimal place

Source: EI (2024)

accelerated transition from fossil fuels to sustainable energy sources. Global solar energy capacity reached 1,418,969 MW, while wind energy capacity surged to 1,017,199 MW.

This strategy of increasing renewable energy aligns with the objectives outlined in the Twelfth Development Plan, which aims to enhance domestic electricity production, reduce reliance on external sources, and diversify supply, particularly in response to fossil fuel-producing nations (Figs. 7 and 8).

The electricity generation data for 2022 and 2023 reflect overarching global trends in energy production and the accelerated transition towards renewable energy sources (Figs. 7 and 8). Despite a marginal decline in Türkiye's total electricity generation from 328.4 TWh in 2022 to 328.0 TWh in 2023, the increase in renewable energy production to 74.1 TWh highlights the effectiveness of ongoing investments in this sector.

Electricity production within Europe is showing a downward trend attributed to a decline in the use of fossil fuels, primarily coal and natural gas. The total electricity generation within the EU fell from 2,812.4 TWh in 2022 to 2,737.2 TWh in 2023, while total production across Europe as a whole decreased from 3,899.4 TWh to 3,805.1 TWh. Increases in hydroelectric power and other renewable energy sources have partially mitigated this decline. A comparable trend is observed in OECD countries, where total electricity generation declined from 11,351.2 TWh in 2022 to 11,178.6 TWh in 2023. However, the increase in renewable energy production signifies the fortification of sustainable energy policies in these nations.

In non-OECD countries, electricity generation has experienced a significant increase, with production rising from 17,836.8 TWh in 2022 to 18,746.2 TWh in 2023. This growth can primarily be attributed to the increased output from both coal and renewable energy sources. On a global scale, total electricity generation

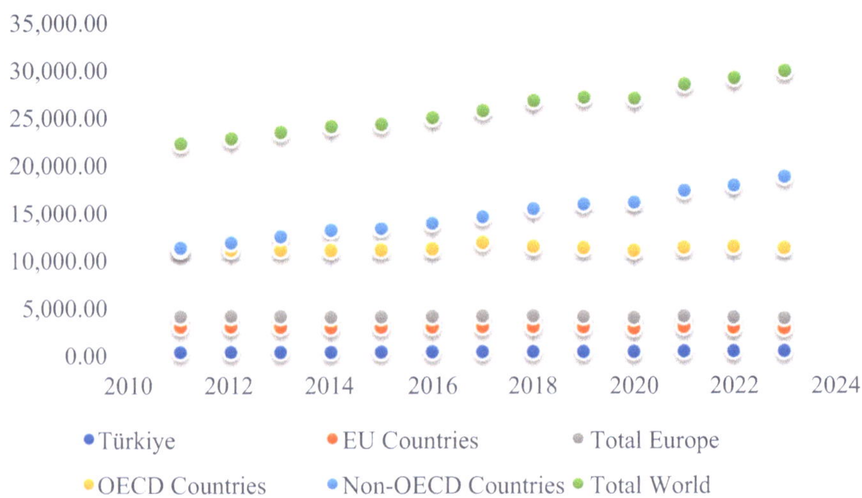

Fig. 7 Electricity generation (Terawatt-hour). Source: EI (2024)

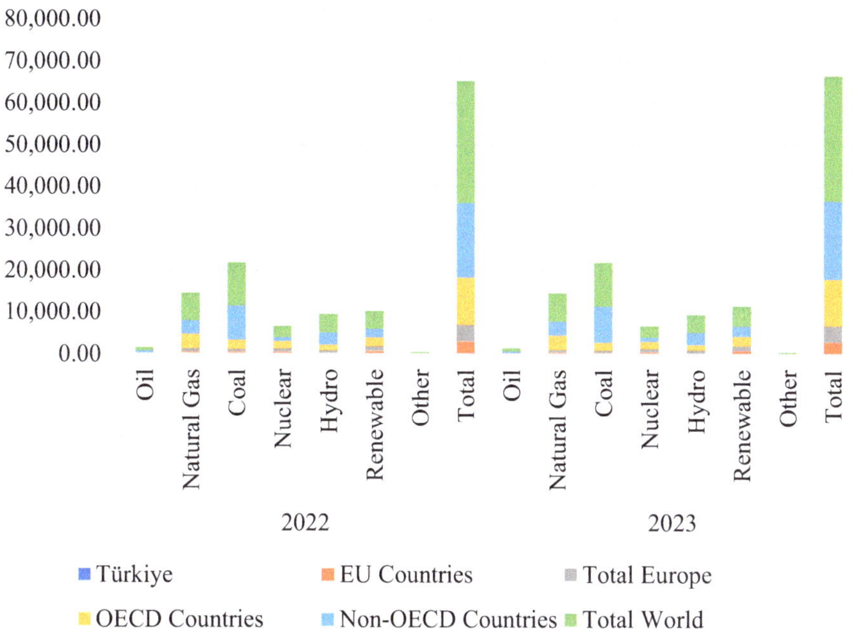

Fig. 8 Electricity generation by fuel types (Terawatt-hour). Source: EI (2024)

increased from 29,188.1 TWh in 2022 to 29,924.8 TWh in 2023. Renewable energy sources, such as solar and wind, are assuming an increasingly significant role.

Overall, these trends underscore the accelerating transition from fossil fuels to renewable energy sources and highlight the growing importance of sustainable energy policies. The increase in renewable energy production in Türkiye, the European Union, and worldwide plays a crucial role in combating climate change and ensuring energy supply security.

A comprehensive nuclear energy strategy has been instituted to reduce dependence on imported fuels for electricity generation. Initiatives are in progress to construct three nuclear power plants (NPPs) comprising 12 reactor units. The inaugural NPP, Akkuyu NPP, is currently under construction in Mersin, located on the southern coast of Türkiye. This facility will comprise four units, each with a total installed capacity of 800 megawatts (MW).

5 Conclusion

This chapter examines Türkiye's current condition and prospective strategies regarding energy consumption, energy efficiency, and sustainable energy policies. The findings provide insights into the alignment of Türkiye's energy policies with national and international dynamics, offering a critical assessment of their effectiveness. The increase in energy consumption necessitates the formulation of strategic planning and policy interventions to ensure sustainability and energy security.

The increase in Türkiye's primary energy consumption is intricately connected to economic growth, industrialisation, and urbanisation processes. In comparison to EU and OECD countries, Türkiye's elevated rate of increase in energy consumption indicates a need for intensified efforts to enhance the effectiveness of energy efficiency policies. The escalation in per capita energy consumption suggests that energy demand is likely to continue its upward trend, underscoring the importance of sustainably managing this demand.

Over the years, the increase in energy-related CO_2 emissions underscores Türkiye's considerable dependency on fossil fuel consumption, thereby presenting challenges in achieving emission reduction targets. The reduction in emissions noted in EU countries suggests that Türkiye should enhance energy efficiency and increase the utilisation of renewable energy sources.

Investments in renewable energy constitute a pivotal aspect of Türkiye's energy policy. The recent surge in renewable energy production has enabled Türkiye to make substantial advances in securing energy reliability and diminishing emissions. The augmentation of solar and wind energy capacity indicates that Türkiye is effectively leveraging its renewable energy potential. Nonetheless, additional investments and incentives remain essential to fully actualising this potential.

While advancements in energy efficiency present a promising avenue for effectively managing energy consumption and reducing waste, challenges such as difficulties in financing energy efficiency projects, a lack of awareness, and inadequate technical expertise must be addressed. By implementing energy efficiency strategies more effectively, Türkiye can substantially decrease energy intensity and ensure sustainable economic growth.

Türkiye's potential in climate finance enhances its capacity to invest in sustainable energy projects and low-carbon technologies. However, bureaucratic hurdles in accessing international funds and varying interpretations of Türkiye's economic status hinder the full realisation of this potential. The ongoing negotiations regarding access to the Green Climate Fund underscore the significance of international cooperation in Türkiye's efforts to combat climate change. Securing access to these funds is of strategic importance for increasing investments in renewable energy and achieving energy efficiency.

Enhancing investments in renewable energy is imperative for ensuring Türkiye's energy security and mitigating emissions. Policies that advocate for renewable sources, such as solar, wind, and geothermal energy, will be pivotal in securing the energy supply and minimising emissions. Fostering public-private partnerships can amplify the financing of energy efficiency projects, and the development of innovative financing models for these initiatives is essential. Expanding awareness campaigns and technical training will serve to elevate consciousness regarding energy efficiency. Türkiye is set to align its national projects with the criteria set forth by international funds and strengthen its diplomatic efforts to enhance access to global climate finance. The potential to benefit from sources such as the Green Climate Fund would substantially bolster Türkiye's efforts in combating climate change.

Reducing reliance on fossil fuels is crucial for Türkiye to meet its emission reduction targets and ensure energy security. Türkiye will likely continue investing in renewable energy initiatives and formulate policies that reduce fossil fuel consumption. Reinforcing emission reduction targets and policies will facilitate Türkiye in achieving its sustainable energy objectives. In this context, Türkiye should reassess its emission reduction targets and policies to ensure their alignment with the Paris Agreement and its commitment to achieving net-zero emissions by 2053. Comprehensive and robust policies have to be enacted across various sectors, enhancing investments in energy efficiency, renewable energy, and low-carbon technologies.

In summary, Türkiye has achieved notable advances in energy consumption, energy efficiency, and the formulation of sustainable energy policies. Nonetheless, the increasing demand for energy and the dependence on fossil fuels pose challenges to energy security and environmental sustainability. Hence, it is imperative to enhance the utilisation of renewable energy sources, ensure energy efficiency and optimise the utilisation of international climate finance to ensure the success of Türkiye's energy policies. Strategies oriented towards transformation and sustainability within the energy sector will bolster Türkiye's economic growth while making significant contributions to the fight against climate change.

References

Association of Civil Society Development Center. (2022). *Germany Federal Foreign Office - Almanya Federal Çevre Doğa Koruma Nükleer Güvenlik Bakanlığı*. https://www.stgm.org.tr/germany-federal-foreign-office-almanya-federal-cevre-doga-koruma-nukleer-guvenlik-bakanligi. Accessed 17 August 2024

Atilgan, B., & Azapagic, A. (2017). Energy challenges for Turkey: Identifying sustainable options for future electricity generation up to 2050. *Sustainable Energy Technologies and Assessments, 20*, 29–44. https://doi.org/10.1016/j.seta.2017.02.004

Brotchie, R., & Mathias, J. (2023). The value of energy efficiency in residential buildings – A matter of heterogeneity?! *Energy Economics, 116*, 106472. https://doi.org/10.1016/j.eneco.2022.106472

Elsland, R., Divrak, C., & Fleiter, T. (2014). Turkey's strategic energy efficiency plan – An Ex Ante impact assessment of the residential sector. *Energy Policy, 70*, 14–29. https://doi.org/10.1016/j.enpol.2014.03.010

Energy Institute. (2024). *Statistical Review of World Energy 2024*. https://www.energyinst.org/statistical-review. Accessed 29 August 2024

European Commission, Joint Research Centre. (2023). *Emission Database for Global Atmospheric Research (EDGAR), release EDGAR v8.0 GHG (1970-2022)*. European Commission, JRC (Dataset). https://edgar.jrc.ec.europa.eu/dataset_ghg80

Guler, Y., & Kumar, P. (2022). Climate change policy and performance of Turkiye in the EU harmonization process. Frontiers in Sustainable Cities, 4, 1070154.

International Energy Agency. (2011–2021). *Energy statistics data browser - Net energy imports*. IEA Publications. https://www.iea.org/data-and-statistics/data-tools/energy-statistics-data-browser

International Energy Agency. (2021a). *Key World Energy Statistics Statistics Report 2021*. https://www.iea.org/reports/key-world-energy-statistics-2021. Accessed 17 August 2024

International Energy Agency. (2021b). *Türkiye 2021 Energy Policy Review*. https://www.iea.org/reports/Türkiye-2021. Accessed 7 September 2024

International Energy Agency. (2021c). *Turkey 2021: Energy policy review. IEA Energy Policy Reviews*. IEA Publications. https://www.iea.org/reports/turkey-2021

International Energy Agency. (2025). *CO_2 emissions, Global Energy Review 2025. IEA Statistics*. IEA Publications. https://www.iea.org/reports/global-energy-review-2025/co2-emissions

Kilickaplan, A., Bogdanov, D., Peker, O., Caldera, U., Aghahosseini, A., & Breyer, C. (2017). An energy transition pathway for Turkey to achieve 100% renewable energy-powered electricity, desalination and non-energetic industrial gas demand sectors by 2050. *Solar Energy, 158*, 218–235. https://doi.org/10.1016/j.solener.2017.09.030

Kılkış, Ş. (2021). Impact of climate change on the existing residential building stock in Turkey: An analysis on energy use, greenhouse gas emissions and occupant comfort. *Renewable Energy, 153*, 1284–1276. https://doi.org/10.1016/j.renene.2019.11.100

Ministry of Energy and Natural Resources. (2016). *Türkiye National Energy Efficiency Action Plan 2012-23*. https://rise.esmap.org/data/files/library/Türkiye/EE%20Pillar/EE1.1.pdf. Accessed 17 September 2024

Ministry of Energy and Natural Resources. (2017). *National Energy Efficiency Action Plan*. https://enerji.gov.tr//Media/Dizin/EVCED/tr/EnerjiVerimlili%C4%9Fi/UlusalEnerjiVerimlili%C4%9FiEylemPlan%C4%B1/Belgeler/NEEAP.pdf. Accessed 17 September 2024

Ministry of Energy and Natural Resources. (2024). *Energy Efficiency 2030 Strategy and Second National Energy Efficiency Action Plan (2024-2030)*. Ministry of Energy and Natural Resources.

Ministry of Environment, Urbanization and Climate Change. (2011). *Türkiye National Climate Change Strategy and Action Plan*. https://webdosya.csb.gov.tr/db/destek/editordosya/Iklim_Degisikligi_Uyum_Stratejisi_ve_Eylem_Plani.pdf. Accessed 17 September 2024

Ministry of Environment, Urbanization and Climate Change. (2020). *Kamu binalarının enerji verimli yenilenmesine yönelik rehber*. Ministry of Environment, Urbanization and Climate Change.

Ministry of Environment, Urbanization and Climate Change. (2022). *Ministry of Environment, Urbanization and Climate Change Official Website*. https://www.cevre.gov.tr/. Accessed 17 September 2024

Ministry of Environment, Urbanization and Climate Change. (2024). *2024-2030 Climate Change Mitigation and Adaptation Strategy and Action Plan*. TC Çevre, Şehircilik ve İklim Değişikliği Bakanlığı İklim Değişikliği Başkanlığı.

Presidency of Strategy and Budget. (2024). *Twelfth Development Plan (2024-2028)*. Presidency of Türkiye.

Rahimifard, S., Seow, Y., & Childs, T. (2010). Minimising embodied product energy to support energy-efficient manufacturing. *CIRP Annals, 59*(1), 25–28. https://doi.org/10.1016/J.CIRP.2010.03.048

Toklu, E., & Kaygusuz, K. (2012). Renewable energy policies in Turkey. *Renewable Energy, 42*, 100–106. https://doi.org/10.1016/j.renene.2011.08.016

Turkish Statistical Institute. (2011–2021). *Address-Based Population Registration System results*. TurkStat. https://www.tuik.gov.tr/en/

Vasilakopoulou, K., & Santamouris, M. (2021). Present and future energy consumption of buildings: Challenges and opportunities towards decarbonization. *Energy and Climate Change, 2*(1), 100024. https://doi.org/10.1016/j.egycc.2021.100024

World Bank. (2025a). *GDP (current US$) - Turkey. World Development Indicators*. World Bank. https://data.worldbank.org/indicator/NY.GDP.MKTP.CD?locations=TR

World Bank. (2025b). *GDP, PPP (current international $) - Turkey. World Development Indicators*. World Bank. https://data.worldbank.org/indicator/NY.GDP.MKTP.PP.CD?locations=TR

World Bank. (2025c). *GDP growth (annual %) - Turkey. World Development Indicators*. World Bank. https://data.worldbank.org/indicator/NY.GDP.MKTP.KD.ZG?locations=TR

Yilan, G., & Çiftçioğlu, G. A. (2020). Profiling energy efficiency tendency: A case for Turkish households. *Energy Policy, 118*, 506–519. https://doi.org/10.1016/j.enpol.2018.03.078

Zhao, Q., Li, L., & Zhang, B. (2023). Building and carbon emissions: Evidence from real estate purchase restriction policy. *Sustainable Cities and Society, 91*, 104414. https://doi.org/10.1016/j.scs.2023.104414

Sinan Güneş is lecturing in the Department of Real Estate Development and Management at Ankara University. He obtained his bachelor's degree in civil engineering from Erciyes University in 2013 and subsequently completed a master's degree in real estate development and management at Ankara University in 2019. His master's thesis focused on the decision-making processes pertaining to the repair or demolition of earthquake-affected reinforced concrete buildings. Mr. Güneş completed in doctoral studies at the same department at Ankara University in 2025. His research interests encompass financial economics, engineering management, numerical methods, and construction management, with a particular focus on energy efficiency and sustainability in the built environment. He has authored numerous academic publications addressing sustainable building practices, energy consumption forecasting, and near-zero energy building strategies. Through his teaching and research, he makes significant contributions to the advancement of knowledge in sustainable real estate development and energy-efficient building strategies.

Mustafa Tombul is a full professor in the Department of Real Estate Development and Management at Ankara University. He completed his PhD in Civil Engineering at Anadolu University in 1996, having previously obtained both his undergraduate and master's degrees from the same institution. His areas of expertise include hydraulics, structural engineering, and construction management, with a specific emphasis on water resources management, environmental engineering, and energy efficiency. Professor Tombul has authored numerous articles in esteemed SCI-indexed journals covering topics such as drought forecasting, environmental risk assessment, precipitation and streamflow modelling, and sustainable water management. His research contributions have been acknowledged with various awards, including a Silver Medal from the Turkish Patent and Trademark Office. He continues to spearhead significant research projects pertaining to energy efficiency in buildings and environmental sustainability, thereby making substantial contributions to both academic knowledge and practical applications within his discipline.

Evaluation of Policies Regarding Productive Agricultural Land and Protected Natural Areas, Sustainability, and Their Impact on Real Estate Markets

Yeşim Tanrıvermiş, A. Filiz Zorlu Kaman, and Arda Özkan

Abstract

The natural values present in the world and within Türkiye possess strategic significance, particularly regarding human health, the continuation of species, and the sustainability of resources. Nonetheless, technological advancements, rapid population growth, and development policies contribute to the deterioration and depletion of these values. In Türkiye, it has been observed that the challenge of utilising agricultural lands for non-agricultural purposes, which is a primary concern among the existing issues related to agricultural land, poses a threat to both current and future agricultural production. Furthermore, this situation is known to have implications for the real estate sector, as the conversion of agricultural lands for non-agricultural uses increases real estate investments, especially in sectors such as housing and industry. To protect agricultural lands effectively, it appears essential to establish sustainable land management practices, promote policies that foster social awareness, and maintain an updated and reliable soil database. With the advent of the twentieth century, area-based protection approaches have emerged as critical considerations globally. In Türkiye, various categories of natural protected areas, including national parks, nature parks, and special environmental protection areas, have been designated. However, several factors may hinder the attainment of protection objectives, such as the delineation and registration of the boundaries of protected areas, the protracted duration

Y. Tanrıvermiş (✉) · A. Filiz Zorlu Kaman
Department of Real Estate Development and Management, Faculty of Applied Sciences, Ankara University, Ankara, Türkiye
e-mail: aliefendioglu@ankara.edu.tr; afzkaman@ankara.edu.tr

A. Özkan
Department of Basic Sciences, Faculty of Maritime, İstanbul Technical University, İstanbul, Türkiye
e-mail: ozkanar20@itu.edu.tr

T. Just et al. (eds.), *Understanding Türkiye's Real Estate Markets*, Management for Professionals, https://doi.org/10.1007/978-3-032-13297-0_30

of the protection zoning plan process, inadequate public participation, the inability to provide compensation for restrictions on property rights, and a lack of effective management models. In this context, consolidating the management of natural protected areas in Türkiye under a single organisation and establishing a legislative framework for these areas are among the primary recommendations. Furthermore, it is emphasised that achieving the protection objective will have a positive impact on the real estate sector.

Keywords

Fertile agricultural lands · Natural protected areas · Sustainability

1 Introduction

The protection of natural resources and values, along with ensuring their sustainability, remains one of the most pressing challenges facing humanity. In this regard, soil emerges as a vital and strategic natural resource, essential for life. Likewise, nationally declared and internationally recognised natural protected areas, with their varying quality and status, constitute the collective wealth of humanity. Nevertheless, factors such as rapid population growth, migration, illegal construction, investments, and the excessive and inappropriate use of natural resources are intensifying the pressure on both fertile agricultural lands and natural protected areas.

Under these circumstances, the development and implementation of projects aimed at the efficient utilisation of land resources is of growing importance in developing nations. This is particularly true for countries such as Türkiye, where the agricultural sector continues to play a crucial role in the national economy, due to factors including agricultural production, employment, and foreign trade (Tanrıvermiş & Tanrıvermiş, 2019).

In this chapter, sustainability policies and fundamental legal regulations concerning agricultural lands and naturally protected areas are analysed in the first instance. Subsequently, the methodology for classifying agricultural lands, the conditions under which classification may be altered, the risks associated with conversion to non-agricultural uses, and additional challenges are assessed. Ultimately, an examination is conducted on how the practices and experiences related to these areas influence the real estate sector, followed by several recommendations.

2 Fertile Agricultural Lands

The protection of fertile agricultural lands is of paramount importance for nations. This scarce, irreplaceable resource, which cannot be produced, must be used in accordance with its designated purpose. Otherwise, restoring productive agricultural lands for farming can often become unattainable. At this juncture, it is fitting to evaluate the efficacy of policies and regulations pertaining to the protection of agricultural lands and to scrutinise their effects on the real estate sector in light of ongoing challenges.

2.1 Policies and Legal Arrangements on the Protection of Agricultural Lands

The comprehensive framework of agricultural policies in Türkiye is outlined within the Constitution. Article 44 of the Constitution articulates that "The State shall take necessary measures to protect and develop the productive use of land." Additionally, Article 45 stipulates that "The State shall facilitate the provision of tools and equipment and other inputs to those engaged in agriculture and animal husbandry in order to prevent the improper use and destruction of agricultural lands, meadows and pastures."

In Türkiye, the policies and objectives regarding the protection of agricultural lands are integrated into all planning frameworks, commencing with the First Five-Year Development Plan (1963–1967) and extending through to the Eleventh Development Plan (2019–2023). In the Eleventh Development Plan, in alignment with preceding plans, pivotal policies comprise the safeguarding and efficient management of agricultural lands, the establishment of comprehensive agricultural information systems, and the enhancement of inspections through the finalisation of regulations aimed at alleviating the pressures stemming from the conversion of agricultural lands to non-agricultural uses.

Law No. 5403 on Soil Protection and Land Use, which took effect on 19 July 2005, aims to safeguard and enhance soil quality, categorise agricultural lands, establish minimum sizes for adequate income-generating agricultural lands, prevent fragmentation, and facilitate the planned utilisation of these lands in alignment with the principle of sustainable development, prioritising environmental considerations. A notable regulation introduced by this legislation is the formation of the Soil Protection Board. "The Regulation on the Implementation of the Law on Soil Protection and Land Use" and "the Regulation on the Protection and Use of Agricultural Lands and Land Consolidation", enacted pursuant to this law, delineate the conditions under which agricultural lands may be employed for purposes other than their designated use.

The comprehensive nature of these legal regulations, the adequacy of technical and institutional capacity, and the presence of non-governmental organisations are acknowledged as strengths of the system. However, there exists a deficiency in social awareness regarding the fact that agricultural lands, which serve as the principal production area for food, constitute a finite and irreplaceable resource. In addition to the shortcomings identified in the planning, management, and oversight of these areas, the exceptional regulations enshrined in legislation intended for protection, which lead to the improper use of agricultural lands, have become a prevalent practice due to administrative and political pressures (Ministry of Agriculture and Forestry, 2019). Furthermore, the absence of appropriate legal frameworks governing land ownership, land management, and the regulation of land markets until recent years has adversely affected the sustainable management of land resources, thereby contributing to challenges such as land fragmentation, improper utilisation, and soil degradation (Tanrıvermiş et al., 2024).

2.2 Use of Agricultural Lands and Current Problems

According to data from TUIK (Turkish Statistical Institute), Türkiye's agricultural land holdings were recorded at 38,757 thousand hectares in 2000, subsequently decreasing to 38,619 thousand hectares by 2024, following a trend characterised by fluctuations over time (Table 1). The proportional distribution of agricultural land usage information for the year 2024 is illustrated in Fig. 1 with further details.

To ensure the protection, development, and sustainable utilisation of agricultural lands, it is imperative to identify the lands suitable for agricultural production along with their associated qualities. The classification of land serves as the foundation for land use planning. The primary objective is to ensure that these areas are committed to agricultural production and to prevent their designation for non-agricultural purposes. Three classification methods are used in line with the applicable legislation:

- Land Capability Classification,
- Land Suitability Classification,
- Agricultural Land Classification (Topçu, 2012).

The "Land Capability Classification" is the most widely employed method for assessing land use. This method categorises lands into eight distinct classes, with

Table 1 Agricultural land utilisation from 2000 to 2024

Year	Total agricultural land	Processed agricultural land	Meadow and pasture land
2000	38,757	26,379	14,617
2005	41,223	26,606	14,617
2010	39,011	24,394	14,617
2015	38,551	23,934	14,617
2020	37,762	23,145	14,617
2024	38,619	24,002	14,617

Source: TURKSTAT (2024)

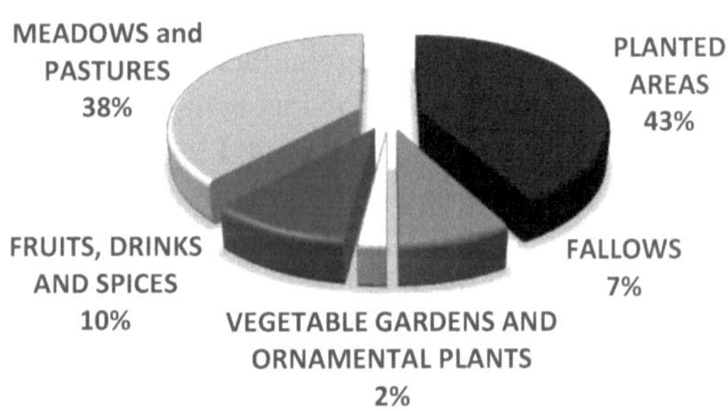

Fig. 1 Agricultural land utilisation in 2024. Source: TURKSTAT (2024)

the initial four classes recognised as agricultural lands that are suitable for cultivated agriculture and the cultivation of perennial plants. The "Land Suitability Classification" ascertains the soil, climate, and topographical requirements essential for various plants, in addition to evaluating the characteristics of land that could potentially be repurposed for non-agricultural uses (Ministry of Development, 2014). Furthermore, the "Agricultural Land Classification" introduced by Law No. 5403 serves as a means to determine the qualifications of agricultural lands based on their significance to the nation's agriculture through the analysis of soil and other land characteristics. These lands are classified as follows:

- Absolute agricultural lands
- Special crop lands
- Planted agricultural lands
- Marginal agricultural lands.

According to Law No. 5403, absolute agricultural lands are defined as those that do not hinder crop production due to a combination of the physical, chemical, and biological properties of the soil. Such lands demonstrate minimal or no topographical limitations and are recognised as significant at the national, regional, or local levels. Currently, these lands are used for agricultural production or are considered suitable for such use, thereby rendering them essential and highly productive for the country's agriculture. In the analysis of the distribution of land assets within the framework of agricultural land classification, the proportion of absolute agricultural land is 42.2 % (Table 2).

A new and more reliable database on agricultural land in Türkiye is urgently needed. The current data fails to illuminate the present conditions. In this regard, it is clear that transferring land to future generations, without compromising its productivity, can be achieved through careful and strategic use (Yüzal, 2019).

When examining the issues impacting agricultural lands in Türkiye, the primary concern is their conversion for non-agricultural purposes (Ministry of Development, 2018). Additionally, problems such as soil degradation due to careless farming practices, along with factors like erosion, insufficient drainage, slope, soil depth, salinity, alkalinity, and stoniness, are also related (Yüzal, 2019).

Table 2 Distribution of Agricultural Land in Türkiye

Land class	Area	Share (%)
Absolute agricultural land	11,613,090	42.2
Marginal agricultural land	12,135,961	44.1
Planted agricultural land	2,883,105	10.5
Special crop land	878,594	3.2
General total	27,510,750	100.0

Source: Ministry of Development (2014)

2.3 Misuse of Productive Agricultural Lands

The misuse of agricultural land in Türkiye poses a significant problem that endangers both current and future agricultural output. Rapid population growth, coupled with Türkiye's developing country status, accelerates the expansion of non-agricultural sectors, further intensifying the pressure on agricultural lands (Yüzal, 2019). This issue is critical due to the concentration of misuse on highly productive agricultural lands. Moreover, disorganisation and shortcomings in existing policies, along with inadequate legislation, contribute to problems. Additionally, the lack of independent and coordinated operations among implementing institutions is identified as a key factors that lead to the use of productive agricultural lands for non-agricultural purposes (Ministry of Development, 2018).

The rent generated from city development and expansion exceeds agricultural returns, leading to the rapid conversion of fertile agricultural land into urban use (Table 3). Studies in the Mediterranean region suggest that protecting prime agricultural land for production is becoming more difficult due to rapid population growth and existing industrial and tourism investments in the region (Tanrıvermiş, 2003). Consequently, these lands are viewed as opportunities for residential development, small-scale manufacturing, tourism investments, mining, and public projects that require extensive land use, often disregarding their agricultural productivity (Dağlı, 2019). In public investment projects, such as highways and airports, the land's efficiency is frequently overlooked, with cost factors prioritised. Similarly, in some organised industrial zones, the high investment costs push investors toward lower-cost agricultural lands. For instance, in Kocaeli, 1.13 hectares of land designated for organised industrial zones and small industrial sites comprises class I, II, III, and IV agricultural lands. Furthermore, industrial facilities along the Izmit-Yalova coast occupy fertile agricultural land (Topçu, 2012).

Several factors contribute to this issue, including unemployment in agriculture, low agricultural product prices, insufficient awareness of natural resource conservation, and fragmented agricultural land ownership. Furthermore, the absence of national land use strategies, poor adherence to existing regulations, and lack of oversight represent further aspects of the problem (Yüzal, 2019). Additionally, fluctuations in the demand for non-agricultural land usage are associated with economic growth and periods of economic downturn (Topçu, 2012).

Another major concern is the pressure on fertile agricultural areas caused by urban sprawl. However, proponents suggest that implementing a land value

Table 3 Sectoral distribution of areas excluded from agriculture (2011–2016)

Sector	Housing	In-dustry	Other	Energy	Tou-rism	Tran-sport	Edu-cation	Health	Total
Area	80,182	36,853	30,341	29,408	6190	4217	2399	1125	190,715
Share (%)	42	19.3	15.9	15.5	3.2	2.2	1.3	0.6	100.0

Source: Ministry of Agriculture and Forestry (2020)

increment tax could deter the prolonged ownership of undeveloped land, mitigate land speculation, and help curb the outward expansion of cities (Var et al., 2017).

Table 4 illustrates the area of agricultural land prepared by the abolished Ministry of Environment and Urbanisation as part of environmental indicators, along with the annual size of agricultural land designated for unintended use. In contrast, the area permitted for conversion from agriculture is fluctuating around a long-term upward trend. An analysis following Law No. 5403 regarding the land classes allowed for non-agricultural use from 2005 to 2018 shows that 63.9% were marginal agricultural lands, while 23.7% were absolute agricultural lands.

According to the Regulation on the Protection and Use of Agricultural Lands and Land Consolidation established under Law No. 5403, the conversion of agricultural land to non-agricultural uses may be allowed if the relevant opinion from the provincial Soil Protection Boards is obtained. The key responsibilities of the Soil Protection Board include: taking actions to resolve soil protection and associated issues, forming opinions to guarantee their enforcement, monitoring and overseeing the execution of local plans or projects, developing proposals, and reviewing applications related to the concerns outlined in the law.

According to the regulation mentioned above, the Ministry may permit the off-purpose use of these lands for strategic defence needs, temporary settlements due to natural disasters, oil and natural gas exploration, mining activities, and investments with public benefit decisions if there is no alternative area and the Soil Protection Board approves the decision. This rule also applies to road, infrastructure, and superstructure projects, as well as renewable energy and geothermal greenhouse investments. The Ministry can also delegate the authority to the governorships.

Each province has a Soil Protection Board chaired by the governor. This board includes the head of the provincial agriculture unit, three senior representatives from planning authorities, including institutions and universities, three members from the provincial Ministry of Finance, and three local representatives from professional and non-governmental organisations that operate as public institutions involved in planning and/or national soil protection issues. The Board meets during the first week of every month to discuss the agenda, and decisions require a majority vote of 3 out of 5 members.

Table 4 Area allocated for non-agricultural use of land (2001–2018)

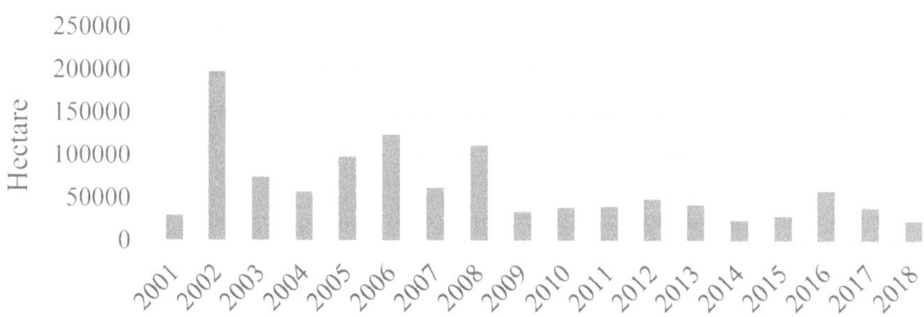

Source: Ministry of Environment, Urbanisation and Climate Change 2023

The Soil Protection Board's decisions face criticisms (Dağlı, 2019). These criticisms are inter alia (1) public institution representatives on the boards are too dominant, (2) the board chairman in overseeing most members during decision-making is not sufficiently effective, (3) there is a lack of detailed soil data necessary for informed decision-making, and (4) there is a potential lack of land specialists among the members.

In the US, in contrast, soil experts lead local soil protection boards. Furthermore, while the process for converting agricultural lands to non-agricultural uses differs between states, at least three public officials and six representatives from universities and NGOS should grant their approval (Topçu, 2012).

Taking all factors into account, we can conclude that Soil Protection Boards now serve as entities that assess and decide on applications to convert agricultural land for non-agricultural purposes based on any written request, and they gather primarily for this reason (Topçu, 2012).

In contrast, Law No. 5403 has designated areas with significant agricultural production potential that are experiencing rapid soil loss and land degradation as great plain protection areas, following a Decree from the Council of Ministers and a Presidential Decree. As a result, non-agricultural activities in these regions are largely restricted (Ministry of Agriculture and Forestry, 2020).

Amendments have been made to certain provisions of the Soil Conservation and Land Use Law to tackle the fragmentation of fertile agricultural land caused by inheritance and its conversion to non-agricultural uses. These revisions create regulations that enforce compulsory agricultural land ownership and aim to reduce land fragmentation from inheritance and sales (Tanrıvermiş & Uisso, 2021).

Proposals exist to designate productive agricultural lands as "agricultural protected areas" in order to prevent their loss and degradation (Ministry of Development, 2018). For lands that have been improperly converted to non-agricultural uses, a recommendation is made to allocate a percentage of the resulting economic value increase to a special account within the Ministry. This funding would be used to support the consolidation, drainage, irrigation, and reclamation of alternative lands, thereby tackling land degradation (Ministry of Agriculture and Forestry, 2019).

Consequently, policies aimed at achieving effective and sustainable land management, along with the creation of a current and dependable soil database, are deemed crucial for addressing the identified issues (Yüzal, 2019). Formulating land use and production plans based on this data is vital to prevent the unplanned and inappropriate conversion of agricultural land into non-agricultural uses (Ministry of Development, 2018).

2.4 Reflections and Recommendations for the Real Estate Sector

While the real estate sector is primarily linked to housing, industry, and commerce, agricultural land is also a significant component. Historically, the rapid increase in population has intensified the demand for agricultural production, resulting in a greater need for agricultural land. At the same time, urban expansion has started to jeopardise these lands. Consequently, the growing need for food has made agricultural lands increasingly important, leading to a stronger focus on sustainability policies and laws aimed at their protection.

A significant criticism of the legislation intended to safeguard productive agricultural lands is that it inadvertently promotes their conversion for non-agricultural purposes. This issue is exacerbated by the extensive investments in housing and industry occupying these lands. Although urban expansion is considered vital to meet growing demands, it is evident that unchecked development that compromises productive agricultural land results in increased social costs. Additionally, this trend affects the real estate market because transforming agricultural lands for other uses enhances investments in real estate, especially in the housing and industrial sectors.

Recent factors such as global epidemics, wars, and migration have highlighted the importance of soil and agriculture in our food supply chain. Furthermore, the efficient management of agricultural land has become increasingly relevant. Specifically, during epidemics, a safer lifestyle in rural areas is sought after. It is anticipated that these circumstances will prompt a reassessment of agricultural policies, particularly those related to sustainability, to prevent the conversion of agricultural land for non-agricultural purposes (Kayabaşı, 2020).

Several strategies can improve real estate investments in agricultural lands. Firstly, large-scale agricultural businesses that thrive in productivity and marketing have the potential to yield steady income. Therefore, if real estate investors invest in the stocks of these companies, it could result in notable progress in the agricultural sector. Additionally, agricultural lands are still largely overlooked by real estate investment trusts (REITs). Given the emphasis on food and agriculture, REITs could allocate funds toward agricultural enterprises on fertile land (Çıkılı, 2010).

3 Natural Protected Areas

Protected areas, due to their inherent qualities, serve multiple functions that support human life and maintain ecological balance across all living beings (WWF, 2021). Consequently, protection policies for natural assets have increasingly adopted a universal approach, resulting in the designation of various statuses for protected areas through national and international agreements. Nonetheless, uncontrolled expansion driven by rapid population growth and migration in Türkiye, along with the socio-economic challenges stemming from this trend, has led to significant losses in these natural protected areas. As a result, these lands are often viewed as potential sites for agriculture, housing, tourism, industry, and other sectors (Zorlu Kaman & Aliefendioğlu, 2017).

3.1 Policies, Legal Arrangements and Area Protection Statuses

Article 56 of the Constitution outlines the right to a healthy environment in Türkiye. The first two paragraphs state, "Everyone has the right to live in a healthy and balanced environment. The State and citizens must improve the environment, protect environmental health, and prevent environmental pollution".

To assess Türkiye's nature protection policies, development plans are important to look at. While the 8th Development Plan aspires to boost the number of protected natural areas, the 9th Development Plan highlights their shortage. The goals outlined in the 10th Development Plan, which incorporate both rural development and biodiversity protection, are significant. A key element for successful protection is enhancing the well-being of rural communities within and near protected areas. Conversely, the 11th Development Plan for 2019–2023 does not consider the interplay between rural development and protected areas; instead, it sets a goal to increase the number of protected areas by 2023. Again, in this plan, "*As the needs and diverse preferences of the growing population influence the development process, it becomes crucial to alleviate the pressure on the environment. In this framework, priority is given to the prevention of environmental pollution, the protection and sustainable use of biodiversity and natural resources*". The importance of protecting natural values is emphasised, and the goal of addressing nature protection and rural development together has transformed into the goal of protecting natural values (Koç & Soykan, 2020).

Türkiye establishes protected areas through the international conventions in which it participates. It joined the Convention for the Protection of the World Cultural and Natural Heritage on 14 April 1982. On 9 January 1984, Türkiye also became a party to the Convention on the Protection of European Wildlife and Habitats, which aims to safeguard wild plants and animals along with their habitats, resulting in the creation of lists for strictly protected species. Under the framework of the Barcelona Convention, Türkiye ratified the Protocol on Special Protection Areas in the Mediterranean Sea on 7 October 1988. This protocol seeks to protect marine areas and their surroundings as special protection sites, ensuring preservation of natural environments and cultural heritage in the Mediterranean region (Aliefendioğlu & Tanrıvermiş, 2011).

In Türkiye, two ministries are authorised in natural protected areas, and the main laws are outlined in Table 5:

In Türkiye, natural protected areas account for about 11% of the country's surface area (Fig. 2). Considering both the area size and the number of sites, it's clear that natural sites and special environmental protection areas represent roughly 62% of all natural protected areas (Table 6).

Designating a location as a natural protected area involves a process of identification, registration, and declaration. Although the current classifications of natural protected areas usually pursue the same objective, the criteria for designation and declaration vary and encompass key elements of qualification and categorisation. Additionally, it is important to note that different natural protected areas can partially or fully overlap, and may also intersect with historic sites and cultural resources (Zorlu Kaman & Aliefendioğlu, 2017). It is essential to provide an overview of national parks, nature parks, natural monuments, natural protected areas, natural sites, and special environmental protection areas, which are not exclusively forested, span extensive regions, and include provisions that limit ownership rights in Türkiye.

Table 5 Legal regulations on natural protected areas in Türkiye

Law no	Law name/year	Related organisation	Content related to Nature protection
6831	Forest Law/1956	Ministry of Agriculture and Forestry	Protection Forest, Urban Forest, Gene Protection Forest
2873	National Parks Law/1983		National Park, Natural Park, Natural Monument, Nature Reserve
4915	Land Hunting Law/2003		Wildlife Protection and Development Areas
2863	Law on the Protection of Cultural and Natural Heritage/1983	Ministry of Environment, Urbanisation and Climate Change	Natural Sites
2872	Environmental Law/1983		Wetlands, Ramsar Sites
383	Decree Law on the Establishment of the Special Environmental Protection Authority/1989		Special Environmental Protection Zones
644	Decree Law on the Organisation and Duties of the Ministry of Environment and Urbanisation (Decree Law)/2011		The Ministry of Environment and Urbanisation is authorised to register and declare Natural Sites, National Parks, Special Environmental Protection Areas, Environmental Protection Areas, Wetlands, etc.

Source: own depiction

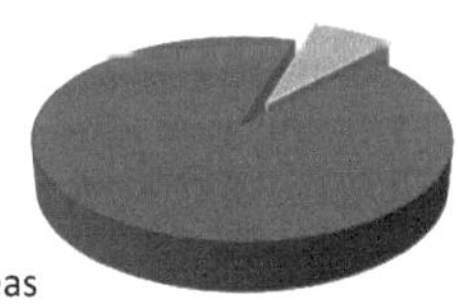

Fig. 2 Ratio of natural protected areas to Türkiye's surface area. Source: General Directorate for the Protection of Natural Assets and General Directorate of Nature Protection and National Parks (2021)

Law No. 2873 concerning National Parks:

- **National Park:** an area recognised for its unique national and international natural and cultural resources in terms of scientific and aesthetic significance, as well as areas for protection, recreation, and tourism.
- **Natural Park:** sections of nature characterised by distinct vegetation and wildlife, designated for public enjoyment and leisure while preserving the landscape's integrity.

Table 6 List of natural protected areas

Protected area	Number	Surface area (hectare)	Share (%)	Responsible institution
Natural site	4096	2,847,106	31.78	Ministry of Environment, Urbanisation and Climate Change
Special Environmental Protection Area	19	2,711,328[a]	30.27	
National Park	48	909,158	10.15	Ministry of Agriculture and Forestry
Wildlife Development Area	85	1,.165,448	13.01	
Wetland	106	976,718	10.90	
Ramsar Site	14	184,487	2.07	
Nature Park	266	108,036	1.21	
Nature Reserve	31	46,455	0.52	
Natural Monument	110	8356	0.09	
TOTAL	**4775**	**8,957,092**	**100**	

Source: General Directorate for the Protection of Natural Assets and General Directorate of Nature Protection and National Parks (2021)

[a]The Finike Submarine Mountains Special Environmental Protection Area is excluded because it encompasses only the marine region

- **Natural Monument:** segments of nature safeguarded under the principles governing national parks, possessing unique characteristics and scientific importance, shaped by natural processes.
- **Natural Protected Areas** are regions that harbour rare or endangered ecosystems and species, as well as exceptional natural phenomena, which are critical for scientific research and education. They necessitate strict protection and are reserved solely for scientific and educational use.

The Ministry of Agriculture and Forestry identifies these areas and submits them to the Ministry of Environment, Urbanisation and Climate Change. Once the proposal reaches the President for approval, the registration process is completed. Natural Parks, Natural Monuments, and Natural Protected Areas located within forest boundaries are registered by the Ministry of Agriculture and Forestry, while those outside fall under the jurisdiction of the Ministry of Environment, Urbanisation, and Climate Change.

The main management tool for national parks in Türkiye is the "Long Term Development Plan". This plan provides a broad framework for all practices to be carried out within a national park area. This plan determines the activities allowed in the area and land use. In areas subject to construction, in accordance with the zoning legislation, the zoning plans are approved by the authorised local administrations. From this point, various uses are permitted in national parks within the framework of certain criteria (Eroğlu, 2022).

Law No. 2863 regarding the Protection of Cultural and Natural Heritage defines natural sites as "protected areas above ground, underground, or underwater that originate from geological periods and which possess extraordinary characteristics due to their rarity". According to the Principal Decision of the High Council on the

Protection of Cultural and Natural Heritage, which addresses Natural Sites, their Protection, and Utilisation Conditions, these sites are classified into three categories: Grade I, II, and III Natural Sites.

- **Grade I Natural Site Areas** are intended to be preserved in their natural state, except for scientific studies focused on protection. Essential infrastructure, public amenities, and structures like piers and fishing harbours can be built to safeguard and improve the area's characteristics.
- **Grade II Natural Site Areas** are locations that can be opened for use, balancing public interest with the preservation and development of natural structures. In this framework, investments in tourism can be pursued.
- **Grade III Natural Site Areas** are identified as locations appropriate for residential development, taking into account the area's potential and usage traits. The goal is to conserve and improve natural conditions.

Decree Law No. 644 has transferred the authority for registering, approving, and declaring areas under the National Parks Law, along with the determination, registration, approval, amendment, and declaration of natural protected areas and special environmental protection zones, to the Ministry of Environment, Urbanisation, and Climate Change. The provisions set forth in the "Regulation on the Procedures and Principles Regarding the Determination, Registration and Approval of Protected Areas" have redefined the categories of natural protection areas. However, until the current statuses are assessed and new ones established, the existing grades of natural protected areas and associated principal decisions will remain valid. According to the regulation mentioned above:

- **Sensitive areas require strict protection:** These zones, designated by Presidential decree, limit all activities to safeguard the environment. Access is restricted when necessary, and special measures are implemented for scientific research.
- **Qualified natural protected areas** are those where the natural structure remains unchanged, having not been significantly affected by human activities. In these areas, traditional ways of life based on natural ecosystems are preserved. The Regional Commissions assess this for the Protection of Natural Assets (RCPNA).[1] These are areas where activities such as compulsory infrastructure, traditional agriculture and fishing activities, open sports areas, tented camping and caravanning, and daily activities can be carried out.

[1] It was created to guarantee that the responsibilities given to the Ministry of Environment, Urbanization, and Climate Change concerning immovable natural assets and areas requiring protection are fulfilled. It is composed of a minimum of five and a maximum of seven members. Its responsibilities encompass giving opinions on site designations, setting guidelines for protection during transitional periods, advising on zoning plans for protection, and reviewing requests for implementation.

- **Sustainable protection and controlled use areas** are defined as those allowing low-intensity activities, along with integrated facilities for agriculture, livestock breeding, hydroelectric, wind, and solar power plants, tourism investments, and settlements. This is based on the RCPNA's assessment of the region's natural structure, ecological values, silhouette, and landscape features. The Ministry of Environment, Urbanisation and Climate Change submits a report to the RCPNA to classify these areas as natural sites. If the Commission decides to register, the process concludes once the Minister approves the registration. However, if a building ban is included in the decision, the registration is finalised through the President's decision. Thus, "**sensitive areas to be strictly protected**" refer to regions that necessitate complete protection as specified by presidential decree.

Protection Zoning Plans for natural protected areas are submitted to the Ministry of Environment, Urbanisation, and Climate Change alongside the decision from the RCPNA. In cases where these areas intersect with other protection statuses, submissions to the Ministry include the RCPNA decision after obtaining feedback from the relevant ministries. Any necessary adjustments are made and subsequently approved by the Minister.

The Regulation of the Procedures and Principles for Determining, Registering, and Approving Protected Areas defines "**special environmental protection zones**" as "*land, water, and sea areas of ecological significance on both national and global scales, vulnerable to environmental pollution and degradation. These areas are essential for protecting and ensuring the sustainability of biological diversity, natural resources, and related cultural values, and are designated by Presidential Decree*." **Special environmental protection zones** are designated areas at risk of degradation or extinction due to agriculture, industry, tourism, and housing pressures. Their boundaries include settlements at provincial, district, town, and village levels to manage these threats (Zorlu Kaman, 2016). In this regard, the Ministry of Environment, Urbanisation and Climate Change prepares spatial plans of various types and scales for the region, which the Minister then approves. Local administrations are responsible solely for implementing these plans.

3.2 Problems Related to Natural Protected Areas

Discussing protection policies often emphasises that simply striving to maintain the ecological structure and integrity of an area is insufficient. Formulating policies without understanding the demographic and socio-economic conditions in these regions results in notable challenges. Literature highlights the necessity of creating management plans that cover essential aspects, from delineating the boundaries of natural protected areas to establishing sector-specific plans (Koç & Soykan, 2020). Nevertheless, Türkiye lacks binding legal requirements for the development and execution of these management plans. As a result, authorities responsible for protection operate solely based on their objectives, which hinders the completion of the tasks specified in these plans (Zorlu Kaman, 2016).

An evaluation of current policies and practices reveals that merely designating "protected areas" with specified borders is inadequate for effective protection. The identification of these areas often lacks a foundation in scientific research, and a deficiency in public involvement during this process is frequently mentioned as a significant issue (Zorlu Kaman & Aliefendioğlu, 2017). Additionally, it is suggested that protection efforts need to extend beyond the borders of these designated areas. Institutions often remain inactive, claiming that potentially destructive investments near protected areas fall outside their jurisdiction (Atmış & Artar, 2013). In contrast, the boundaries established for "**special environmental protection zones**" are crafted to accommodate activities from sectors such as settlement, industry, and tourism, which could threaten natural values; albeit to a certain degree, these risks can be mitigated.

In contrast, the primary goal is to safeguard natural values; a single area may simultaneously hold multiple natural protected area designations. It is feasible to register a national park, a nature reserve, and a special environmental protection area within the same region. An evaluation of current practices highlights that the management of areas with overlapping protection statuses, governed by various administrations and regulations, has resulted in several issues (Zorlu Kaman & Aliefendioğlu, 2017). Specifically, it is noted that the lengthy processes involved in designating new protected areas and approving spatial plans for existing ones hinder effective coordination and cohesive execution in the field, sometimes leading to duplicated efforts (WWF, 2021).

An important issue is the reduction or complete removal of protected area boundaries in order to accommodate specific investment needs or facilitate construction projects. One case is the reclassification of Yumurtalık Lagoon, İğneada Floodplain Forests, and Lake Gala national parks, recently designated as national parks, from their previous status as "natural protected areas", where development is not permitted. In a lawsuit concerning Yumurtalık Lagoon national park, the Council of State halted the procedure specifically based on "*the Council of Ministers' decision aimed at lowering the protection level of Yumurtalık Lagoon, and there was no compliance with the law in the transaction*", and the area was restored to its former status (Atmış & Artar, 2013).

In national parks and protected areas, 'absolute protection areas', 'natural protected areas of the first degree', and "sensitive areas to be strictly protected', along with 'sensitive zones' in special environmental protection areas, represent zones where property rights may be entirely restricted. In other classifications, these rights are limited to varying extents. Fundamental rights of individuals, as outlined in the Constitution, must be considered when making decisions about protection. Hence, finding a balance between public and individual interests is key to fulfilling the protection objectives. However, in Türkiye, the lack of compensation for restricted property rights complicates the enforcement of decisions regarding protected areas. This issue becomes evident in the degradation of protected areas and legal cases concerning actions that defy legislation and claims of property rights restrictions (Zorlu Kaman & Aliefendioğlu, 2017).

Although the inability to compensate for restrictions on the right to property is a problem, the interpretation of judicial decisions on the issue remains important. The Council of State decision[2] concerns a lawsuit instituted for the compensation of real estate confiscated without expropriation, consequent to the declaration of a Grade I Natural Protected Area in Doğanbey Village, located within the Söke District of Aydın Province. In conclusion, the ruling of the administrative court was reversed, indicating that the plaintiff cannot sell the immovable property because of the land's characteristics. It was classified not as agricultural land, situated in a tidal zone that is vulnerable to flooding. Furthermore, the plaintiff was required to prove the type of damage sustained, suggesting that no harm could arise from the property being unused. This ruling implies that claims of property rights violations cannot be made in regions where construction rights, though limited, exist or where agricultural uses are allowed. Moreover, for a violation of property rights to be recognised, the property's use must be completely non-existent (Zorlu Kaman & Aliefendioğlu, 2017).

An additional significant issue is that Mining Law No. 3213 and the Mining Activities Permit Regulation have enabled mining operations in all nature reserves across Türkiye (Atmış & Artar, 2013).

It can be asserted that the majority of the problems above arise from deficiencies in management and supervision rather than from the inadequacies of the pertinent legislation. Furthermore, the failure to implement the "Draft Law on the Protection of Nature and Biological Diversity", which serves as a framework law, constitutes one of the factors influencing this process.

In all instances, it is advised that the ownership and management systems of all public lands possessing characteristics of nature conservation, including pastures and forested areas, undergo a thorough review. Moreover, innovative approaches predicated on the notion of social ownership ought to be formulated, and models appropriate for maintaining a balance between protection and utilisation at the local level should be established (Sen et al., 2024).

3.3 Reflections and Recommendations for the Real Estate Sector

There is a necessity for strategic spatial plans that prioritise the efficient use of existing resources and underscore environmental quality, founded upon reliable cadastral systems, with the intention of promoting national and regional development (Tanrıvermiş & Tanrıvermiş, 2021). In this context, one of the critical instruments for crafting protection-use decisions is the implementation of protection zoning plans. However, the distribution of authorities and responsibilities related to planning within these areas, particularly in regions where protection statuses intersect,

[2] Republic of Türkiye, 6th Chamber of the Council of State, E: 2014/7813, K: 2015/4418, T: 19.06.2015.

results in further delays in the process and hinders the achievement of the protective objective. This scenario also engenders delays or deferrals in real estate investments.

Effective management of protected natural areas is regarded as a critical factor in safeguarding natural values and ensuring their preservation for future generations. In this context, the management model for such areas should be meticulously structured to establish and enact principles of both protection and sustainable use. It is imperative to assess the total surface area of the region, the number and dimensions of parcels, ownership classifications, usage patterns, population density in the event of inhabited settlements, the level of development in the vicinity, as well as spatial characteristics and construction demand (Aliefendioğlu & Tanrıvermiş, 2011).

While effective area management positively influences real estate values, investments, and use patterns both locally and in the surrounding regions, the challenge of addressing the decline in household income and property values, resulting from property rights restrictions in protected areas, through tools such as expropriation, barter, site certificates, and transfer of development rights, in accordance with legal frameworks, continues to represent a significant issue still.

Then, merging the protection sub-units of both ministries involved in nature conservation can reduce authority-related confusion and bureaucratic delays, ultimately saving labour, time, and financial resources. Additionally, a geographically focused organisation staffed with skilled personnel can improve the effectiveness of managing protected areas. A critical issue is the engagement of the public in the governance of these areas from a single source, which will help address existing challenges and raise awareness about conservation (WWF, 2021). Furthermore, for real estate markets to function effectively, it is essential to align a well-developed real estate market and financial system with sustainability principles throughout the planning, design, construction, and operational decision-making processes (Tanrıvermiş & Tanrıvermiş, 2021).

4 Conclusion

Natural resources and their associated values hold significant strategic importance for the protection and sustainability of ecosystems globally, specifically in Türkiye. In this context, the rational management of agricultural lands, which encompass both natural values and essential natural resources, will positively contribute to the enhancement of the living environment, agricultural productivity, and human health.

The process of rapid urbanisation continues in Türkiye. The pressure exerted by urban growth, particularly on fertile agricultural lands, gradually results in the loss of agricultural land, thereby threatening the future of agricultural production and food security (Yörür et al., 2018). Consequently, Türkiye has to manage its limited productive agricultural land and water resources most effectively. To achieve effective and sustainable land management, it is crucial to establish a current and reliable soil database.

Then, merely registering "protected areas" with defined boundaries is insufficient in achieving the protection objectives. One of the most fundamental and pressing issues is the encroachment upon or complete elimination of the boundaries of these protected areas, often to facilitate certain investment demands or construction activities. Furthermore, an additional challenge lies in the inability to adequately compensate for property rights affected by the restrictions imposed for protection purposes. Therefore, to fulfil the objective of protection, it is crucial to devise a comprehensive policy that integrates the protected area with its surrounding environment. Additionally, enhancing the management framework and developing sustainability strategies to foster social awareness regarding protection is imperative.

It is recommended that the management of natural protected areas in Türkiye should be consolidated under a single organisation, with protection decisions being implemented in collaboration with other pertinent institutions. Additionally, the continuous need for a comprehensive framework law that encompasses all aspects of nature protection is underscored. Consequently, the safeguarding of natural values and strategic natural resources such as agricultural lands is crucial for the sustainability of the ecosystem. The successful attainment of protection goals within these areas will also have a favourable impact on the real estate sector. Nevertheless, the value ascribed to real estate by various factors is connected to the preservation of the ecosystem, as well as the potential degradation of value in urban areas arising from issues such as desertification, drought, water scarcity, and food supply challenges, which result from over-exploitation, pollution, and the transformation of natural spaces into unproductive lands.

References

Aliefendioğlu, Y., & Tanrıvermiş, H. (2011). Land use and conservation decisions in environmental protection areas in Turkey: The case of Gökova special environmental protection zone. *The Third Sector Social Economy Review, 46*(1), 61–100.

Atmış, E., & Artar, M. (2013). Evaluation of Turkey's nature conservation policies shifting from protection to use. In *Towards 2023: 2nd Nature and Forestry Symposium* (pp. 403–422). Chamber of Forest Engineers. https://www.researchgate.net/publication/289526874

Çıkılı, G. (2010). *Real estate sector and real estate investment trusts in Turkey* (Master's thesis). Dokuz Eylül University, Institute of Social Sciences.

Dağlı, Z. (2019). Agricultural land protection policy and the case of Düzce (1999–2018). In *Rural Development and Cooperatives* (Publication No. 24). Ankara University, Ernst Reuter Settlement and Urbanism Research Center.

Eroğlu, S. (2022). Evaluation of national park management in Turkey in light of international practices: A comparative analysis. *Ankara University Journal of Environmental Sciences, 9*(1), 8–23. https://dergipark.org.tr/en/download/article-file/2283957

Kayabaşı, E. T. (2020). The impact of COVID-19 on agricultural production. *Eurasian Journal of Social and Economic Research, 7*(5), 38–45. https://dergipark.org.tr/tr/pub/asead/issue/54658/740039

Koç, Y., & Soykan, A. (2020). Theoretical foundations of nature conservation in the world and in Turkey. *IBAD Journal of Social Sciences, 7*, 86–99. https://dergipark.org.tr/tr/download/article-file/955969

Ministry of Agriculture and Forestry. (2019). *Global Soil Partnership and Turkey Soil Information System.*

Ministry of Agriculture and Forestry. (2020). *Agricultural Structure and Transformation Group Working Document.*

Ministry of Development. (2014). *10th Development Plan: Sustainable use of agricultural lands working group report.*

Ministry of Development. (2018). *11th Development Plan: Special commission report on sustainable use of land and water in agriculture.*

Sen, A., Tanrıvermiş, H., & Ahsan, M. M. (2024). Enforcement of forest regulations on selling forestlands that have lost their forest character in Türkiye: A study of Kızılcahamam District in Ankara Province. *Asia Pacific Journal of Environmental Law, 27*(2), 230–247.

Tanrıvermiş, H., & Tanrıvermiş, Y. (2019). Socio-economic impact assessment of land consolidation projects in Türkiye: A case study of Beyazaltın Village land consolidation project in Eskişehir Province. In *26th ERES Annual Conference*. European Real Estate Society.

Tanrıvermiş, Y., & Tanrıvermiş, H. (2021). Linkages between urbanisation, real estate investments and sustainability in Türkiye. In *Sustainable Real Estate in the Developing World* (pp. 13–37). Emerald Publishing.

Tanrıvermiş, Y., Tanrıvermiş, H., & Uisso, A. M. (2024). Assessment of farmland fragmentation and the role of the legal regulations for the prevention of farmland fragmentation in Türkiye. *Land Use Policy, 145.*

Tanrıvermiş, H. (2003). Agricultural land use change and sustainable use of land resources in the Mediterranean region of Türkiye. *Journal of Arid Environments, 54*(3).

Tanrıvermiş, H., & Uisso, A. (2021). The problems of farmland fragmentation and assessment of legal regulations for the prevention of farmland fragmentation in Türkiye. In *27th Annual European Real Estate Society Conference*, Germany.

Topçu, P. (2012). *Policies for the protection and efficient use of agricultural land* (Master's thesis). Ministry of Development.

Turkish Statistical Institute (TURSTAT). (2024). Agricultural Land Utilisation Statistics. https://data.tuik.gov.tr/

Var, G., Aliefendioğlu, Y., Canaz Sevgen, S., & Tanrıvermiş, H. (2017). Transformation of land to land lot, value gain, land speculation, and opportunities for sharing value increment: An evaluation of the Türkiye example. *Annual World Bank Conference on Land and Poverty.*

WWF. (2021). *We lose if we don't protect: Protected areas for a sustainable Turkey – 30% target by 2030.*

Yörür, N., Altınörs Çırak, A., Aydın, B. S., İncekőse, Ü., Erduran Nemutlu, F., Aydın, G., Atatanır, L., & Yorulmaz, A. (2018). Proposal of conservation-based planning approach for agricultural areas designated as Special Project Areas (ÖPA) in Türkiye: Example of Muğla Plain. *Journal of Planning, Supplement, 1*, 25–41. https://jag.journalagent.com/planlama/pdfs/PLAN_28_50_25_41.pdf

Yüzal, B. (2019). *Problems and policies regarding the protection and use of agricultural lands in Turkey* (Master's thesis). Çukurova University, Institute of Natural and Applied Sciences.

Zorlu Kaman, A. F. (2016). *Transfer of development rights in nature conservation areas and a case study on Gölbaşı Special Environmental Protection Area* (Master's thesis). Ankara University, Institute of Natural and Applied Sciences.

Zorlu Kaman, A. F., & Aliefendioğlu, Y. (2017). An evaluation on the practices of transferring development rights in nature conservation areas. *Ankara University SBF Journal, 72*(3), 715–743.

Yeşim Tanrıvermiş holds the position of full professor in the Department of Real Estate Development and Management at the Faculty of Applied Sciences, Ankara University, Türkiye. She attained her Master of Science (M.Sc.) degree in 2011 from the Department of Agricultural Economics at Ankara University. She received her Ph.D. in 2011 as the first Ph.D. program graduate of the Department of Real Estate Development and Management at Ankara University. Her research interests encompass the management and conservation of land resources, land resource economics, as well as real estate analysis and economics, in addition to studies in real estate and asset valuation. She has been delivering lectures for several years and has published academic papers since 2006. Her publications consist of 50 international and 40 national peer-reviewed articles. Additionally, she has made contributions to 110 international and 25 national full or abstract proceedings at various conferences and congresses and has authored 35 books and 30 book chapters. Presently, she serves as the Deputy Head of her department at Ankara University. Moreover, she is an active participant in various academic and professional organisations. Her experience encompasses working as a researcher and consultant across diverse public and private sectors, with a focus on real estate asset analysis, real estate finance and valuation, land and building conservation practices, as well as real estate economics and management. Furthermore, she actively engages in enhancing cooperation with both domestic and international institutions, mobilising financial resources for research projects.

A. Filiz Zorlu Kaman is a part-time lecturer at the Department of Real Estate Development and Management, Faculty of Applied Sciences, Ankara University, where she teaches undergraduate courses in housing economics and policies, real estate, and asset analysis. She obtained her M.Sc. and Ph.D. in Real Estate Development and Management from Ankara University, as well as a B.Sc. in City and Regional Planning from Gazi University. With over 30 years of experience in urban planning and real estate development, she has occupied influential roles within the public sector, notably in senior positions at the Ministry of Environment, Urbanisation, and Climate Change, as well as the former Special Environmental Protection Agency. Her professional expertise encompasses spatial planning, zoning regulations, environmental protection, and inter-institutional collaboration. She has led planning teams in the formulation, evaluation, and implementation of spatial plans for environmentally sensitive and protected areas. Dr. Kaman has contributed to the establishment of sustainable and compliant urban policies. Throughout her academic and professional endeavours, she has consistently emphasised the promotion of sustainable urban development, the optimisation of land use, and the enhancement of institutional collaboration.

A. Filiz Zorlu Kaman Arda Özkan graduated from the Department of International Relations at Karadeniz Technical University in 2007. He completed his master's degree in the same department in 2009 and obtained his doctoral degree from the Department of Political Science and International Relations at Istanbul University in 2018. During 2014-2015, he studied for one year at the Washington College of Law at American University in the United States, conducting doctoral research funded by a scholarship from the Scientific and Technological Research Council of Türkiye (TÜBİTAK). In 2022, he spent six months at the American University Washington College of Law in the United States, engaging in postdoctoral research with support from a TÜBİTAK scholarship. From 2009 to 2019, he served as a Research Assistant in the Department of International Relations at Giresun University. Subsequently, from 2020 to 2025, he served as an Assistant Professor in the Department of International Trade and Logistics at Ankara University. Since September 2025, he has been serving as an Assistant Professor at Istanbul Technical University's Faculty of Maritime Studies. His research interests encompass maritime security and the law of the sea, environmental security, Turkish foreign policy, sustainable development policies, and maritime energy security.

Heritage Conservation Policies and Real Estate Markets Linkages

Yeşim Tanrıvermiş and Emine Baydan

Abstract

The establishment of a unified global understanding is crucial for formulating conservation policies and developing conservation statuses related to the preservation of cultural heritage assets. International agreements and organisations facilitate the advancement of conservation policies and practices from local to regional, national, and international levels. Despite the inherently local nature of real estate markets, it is essential to recognise the evolution of conservation policies into regional and even global frameworks. This chapter provides an overview of the legal regulations, conservation statuses, and practices associated with heritage assets in Türkiye. Furthermore, it assesses the impact of expropriation tools and principle decisions within conservation areas on property ownership and the real estate market.

Keywords

Cultural assets · Property restrictions · Expropriation · Principle decision

1 Introduction

The concept of heritage encompasses all elements transmitted across generations. Intangible assets, such as national values, history, legends, language, and traditions, are regarded as heritage, as are tangible components, including settlements, places of worship, landscape features, transportation systems, and agricultural lands,

Y. Tanrıvermiş (✉) · E. Baydan
Department of Real Estate Development and Management, Faculty of Applied Sciences, Ankara University, Ankara, Türkiye
e-mail: aliefendioglu@ankara.edu.tr; ebaydan@ankara.edu.tr

T. Just et al. (eds.), *Understanding Türkiye's Real Estate Markets*, Management for Professionals, https://doi.org/10.1007/978-3-032-13297-0_31

which have been inherited over time. It is essential to acknowledge that heritage elements, beyond their functional roles, hold significance on both national and global levels, depending on their nature. In other words, these heritage assets are considered valuable for their intrinsic moral virtues beyond mere material worth (ISMEP Guidebooks, 2014). Documents produced by institutions engaged in conservation efforts on international platforms, such as the United Nations Educational, Scientific and Cultural Organization (UNESCO), define "cultural heritage" to encompass a range of concepts. Cultural heritage is fundamentally categorised into tangible heritage, underwater heritage, and intangible heritage. Tangible cultural heritage is further subdivided into movable items (such as sculptures, archaeological artefacts, paintings, etc.) and immovable sites (including archaeological sites, historic urban structures, etc.) (Kuşçuoğlu & Murat, 2017; Yüce, 2021).

Within the framework of international conventions to which Türkiye is a signatory, the protection and sustainable utilisation of natural and cultural heritage sites through the formulation of unified conservation policies bear significant importance. While each nation independently develops its conservation strategies and determines the conservation status within its legislative jurisdiction, it is imperative to establish a common vocabulary for delineating conservation statuses, ensuring the recognition of heritage assets, and safeguarding them under an international oversight mechanism (ISMEP Guidebooks, 2014). Each heritage asset maintains substantial local significance within real estate markets. Furthermore, it is noteworthy that conservation policies are increasingly adopting regional and global dimensions, in accordance with initiatives undertaken by various organisations and international agreements. By acceding to these international instruments, Türkiye has implemented specific legal regulations within its national legal framework and has established institutional arrangements domestically (Özdemir, 2005). Nonetheless, these institutional and legal provisions may be insufficient to ensure the comprehensive protection of cultural heritage.

The effectiveness of conservation policies hinges upon the organisational framework, statutory regulations, societal cultural contexts, and available financial resources. Conservation councils have formally established principles to protect cultural heritage assets, delineating protocols for their preservation and utilisation. While conservation practices are rooted in legal statutes, the expropriation of properties owned by private individuals or legal entities, or their exchange with treasury properties, has been codified as a necessary measure for conservation objectives. Furthermore, incentives are provided to promote the maintenance and repair of properties owned by private individuals or legal entities (Özdemir, 2005).

Cultural heritage in Türkiye is explicitly defined within the Code of Conservation of Cultural and Natural Properties (Law No. 2863), encompassing both movable and immovable assets as subjects of cultural heritage. This chapter focuses on cultural heritage properties, which are also relevant to the real estate market, by evaluating the policies and conservation processes related to these assets in Türkiye. In the initial section of this chapter, elements of cultural heritage classified within the legal framework are delineated, and the conservation and utilisation decisions mandated by legal regulations, along with the distribution of administrative authority in these areas, are scrutinised. The conservation process commences with identification, and the accurate and standardised identification of cultural heritage elements is of critical importance. Accordingly, the criteria for assessing cultural heritage assets requiring protection in Türkiye are discussed in the second section. The criteria employed in identifying cultural assets, as stipulated in conservation legislation, directly influence conservation and utilisation decisions. The conservation process, which begins with the identification and registration of cultural heritage elements, results in restrictions on property rights. Expropriation, considered a direct intervention in property rights, is one of the most frequently employed tools in Türkiye for protecting cultural heritage areas and assets. The expropriation procedures utilised in cultural heritage zones and for the safeguarding of cultural assets are analysed in the third section of this chapter, where the challenges encountered in Türkiye are identified and the property valuation processes are examined.

2 Cultural Heritage Elements and Conservation-Utilisation Decisions

The responsibility for conserving cultural and natural assets in Türkiye is entrusted to the state, as mandated by Article 63 of the Constitution. In accordance with this obligation, restrictions are imposed on privately owned heritage assets, and consequently, aid and exemptions for heritage asset owners are regulated through legislation. Beyond legal regulations, the formulation of principle decisions that restrict the uses of properties and establish guidelines for the preservation of cultural heritage elements falls under the jurisdiction of the High Council for the Conservation of Cultural and Natural Assets (HCCCN).

In addition to UNESCO member countries, Türkiye became a signatory to the "Convention Concerning the Protection of the World Cultural and Natural Heritage" in 1983. Under this convention, Türkiye has committed to protecting cultural and natural assets within its national borders (Ürün, 2016). The framework for safeguarding natural and cultural heritage, including operational procedures and the allocation of authority, has been established under Law No. 2863 on the Conservation of Cultural and Natural Properties since 1983. Despite subsequent amendments to the law, Law No. 2863 remains the primary legal framework for conservation practices.

According to conservation legislation, cultural heritage properties are safeguarded at both the individual and site levels. When cultural heritage properties constitute a coherent entity, a site-scale conservation approach is implemented by designating the area as a "protected site" (Öngören & Karali, 2020; Çolak, 2015, p. 494). At this juncture, the designation of a "protected site" alters the legal status of the area and directly influences the utilisation of properties under private ownership within the site, in accordance with the conservation status. Furthermore, the site designation specified in the decision also outlines the principles of conservation and utilisation that must be observed during the implementation of conservation practices within the protected areas. In addition to statutory regulations guiding conservation activities, principal decisions issued by HCCCN further establish the conservation and utilisation conditions to be adhered to in the implementation of conservation measures within site regions.

2.1 Cultural Heritage Areas

It has become necessary to categorise cultural assets that require site-wide preservation according to their specific characteristics under the designation "protected site". Although the attributes of heritage zones may vary, uniformly applying the same conservation and utilisation conditions across all these zones contradicts the fundamental objectives of conservation. Within this framework, legislation categorises cultural heritage zones into various types, including urban, historical, archaeological, and urban-archaeological protected sites. A review of the distribution of registered site areas in Türkiye reveals that, as of the conclusion of 2023, approximately 93% of these protected zones are categorised as archaeological sites, while 4% are classified as natural sites (Fig. 1).

In addition to evaluating the status of the site within the framework of site designation decisions, efforts are also directed towards delineating site categories. During the categorisation process, emphasis is placed on addressing issues related to permissible and impermissible practices within the conservation area, in accordance with the specific site categories, rather than on scientific attributes (Kortanoğlu, 2013). Except for natural protected areas, the processes of identification, registration, and inventory creation fall under the jurisdiction of the Ministry of Culture and Tourism (MCT) (Table 1). Consequently, the management of cultural heritage elements and natural heritage elements in Türkiye is allocated to two distinct ministries.

Archaeological sites are among the most frequently registered cultural heritage sites in Türkiye. Consequently, the usage and preservation restrictions established by principle decisions for privately-owned immovable properties within archaeological sites are of considerable importance in conservation practices. Furthermore,

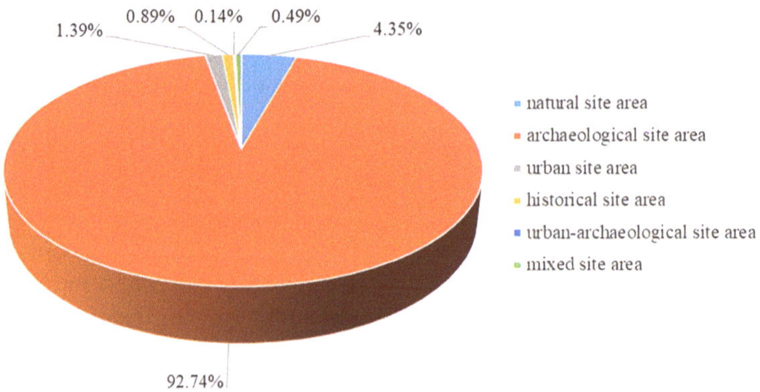

Fig. 1 Distribution of existing protected site status in Türkiye as of the end of 2023. Sources: Own depiction, based on Ministry of Culture and Tourism (MCT), 2024; and the Ministry of Environment, Urbanisation, and Climate Change (EUCC), 2024

Table 1 Authorised institutions and units for the identification and registration of conservation statuses

Conservation status	Authority		
	Identification	Registration	
Natural site area	EUCC: GDPNA[a]	In the case of a construction ban	In the absence of a construction ban;
		Presidential decision	EUCC Minister approval
Urban Site Area	MCT	Regional Council for the Conservation of Cultural Property	
Archaeological Site Area			
Urban–Archaeological Site Area			
Historical Site Area			

Source: Baydan (2021)
[a]GDPNA: General Directorate for Protection of Natural Assets

Table 2 Scope of Principle Decision No. 658 applied to archaeological sites

Principle Decision No 658: Principles for the Conservation and Utilisation of Archaeological Site Areas			
Decision date	5.11.1999		
Authorized institution	MCT		
Conservation grade	I. Grade	II. Grade	III. Grade
Construction permission	X	X (In unregistered structures, simple repair permits are allowed.)	Subject to COZP and the Transitional period conservation principles
Mining	X	X	X
Excavation work	X (Exception: scientific research)		With the conservation council's permission
Agriculture and livestock	X (Greenhouse cultivation and restricted seasonal agricultural activities can only be carried out with Conservation Council permission.)		–
Industry	X	X	–

Source: Baydan (2021)

the conservation and utilisation limitations outlined by principle decisions for privately owned properties within archaeological protected areas are also of significant importance. In regions designated as archaeological protected zones, the principles of conservation and utilisation are governed under Principle Decision No. 658 (Table 2), with construction permissions subject to variation according to the protection levels assigned to the sites.

For areas designated as urban site areas, the principles of conservation and utilisation are governed by Principle Decision No. 681. Permissions for new constructions are constrained by the existence of approved conservation-oriented zoning plans (COZP) for the respective area (Table 3). Repairs, whether minor or

Table 3 Scope of Principle Decision No. 681 applied to urban sites

Principle Decision No 681: Principles for the Conservation and Utilisation of Urban Site Areas			
Decision date	25.01.2017		
Authorized institution	MCT		
Conservation grade	If the transitional period conservation and utilisation conditions are not specified;	If the transitional period conservation and utilisation conditions are specified;	If a COZP exists;
Construction permission	(For new construction and unregistered structures: substantial repairs are not permitted; For registered structures: substantial and simple repairs are subject to Conservation Council permission.)	(Only the substantial and simple repairs of registered structures are subject to Conservation Council permission.)	
Mining	–	–	–
Excavation work	–	–	–
Agriculture and livestock	–	–	–
Industry	–	–	–

Source: Baydan (2021)

significant, require authorisation from the Cultural Heritage Preservation Department (KUDEB) or the Protection Board. These regulations concerning construction and repairs are implemented to prevent the distortion of the urban skyline within designated urban site areas.

In areas designated as historical sites, Long-Term Development Plans (LTDP) or conservation-oriented zoning plans (COZP) are formulated. Until such plans are enacted, construction activities within these zones are prohibited (Table 4). Conservation-oriented zoning plans govern decisions about agricultural operations in historical site regions.

In urban archaeological sites, regulations regarding land use are addressed under Principle Decision No. 702. In these areas, construction permits are not granted until conservation-oriented zoning plans are approved. However, restorations of individual cultural assets within the site can be conducted with the approval of the Conservation Council (Table 5). This decision aims to prevent irregular and unplanned construction while also ensuring that cultural real assets are not left neglected within the urban fabric.

2.2 Cultural Heritage Elements at the Building Scale

Within the scope of legal regulations, conservation efforts at the individual level are mainly carried out under the auspices of the ICOMOS Türkiye National Committee

Table 4 Scope of Principle Decision No. 1700 applied to historical sites

Principle Decision No 1700: Principles for the Conservation and Utilisation of Historical Site Areas	
Decision date	11.03.2021
Authorized institution	MCT
Conservation grade	Historical site
Construction permission	X (Construction is prohibited until the LTDP or COZP is approved.)
Mining	–
Excavation work	–
Agriculture and livestock	Ongoing agricultural activities that existed prior to this are permitted to continue.
Industry	–

Source: Baydan (2021)

Table 5 Scope of Principle Decision No. 702 applied to urban–archaeological sites

Principle Decision No: 702: Principles for the Conservation and Utilisation of Urban-Archaeological Site Areas	
Decision date	15.04.2005
Authorized institution	MCT
Conservation grade	Urban-Archaeological Site
Construction permission	X (Until the COZP is approved, restoration and survey projects (at the individual building scale) can be carried out with the approval of the Conservation Regional Council)
Mining	–
Excavation work	–
Agriculture and livestock	–
Industry	–

Source: Baydan (2021)

and the DOCOMOMO Türkiye National Working Group. Under the auspices of these two prominent organisations, preservation initiatives for both historic buildings and modern heritage examples have begun in Türkiye (Balamir, 2014). The Anatolian region, where Türkiye is located, has hosted various civilisations throughout different historical eras due to its geopolitical and geographical location. As a result of Anatolia's historical background, numerous archaeological, cultural, and architectural heritage assets are present. By the end of 2023, approximately 62% of the cultural heritage properties registered by the Ministry of Culture and Tourism in Türkiye were identified as "civil architecture" (Fig. 2). Consequently, conservation policies and decisions regarding privately owned cultural heritage assets also directly affect property rights. Furthermore, it is worth noting that beyond property interventions, these conservation decisions also have a direct impact on the real estate market.

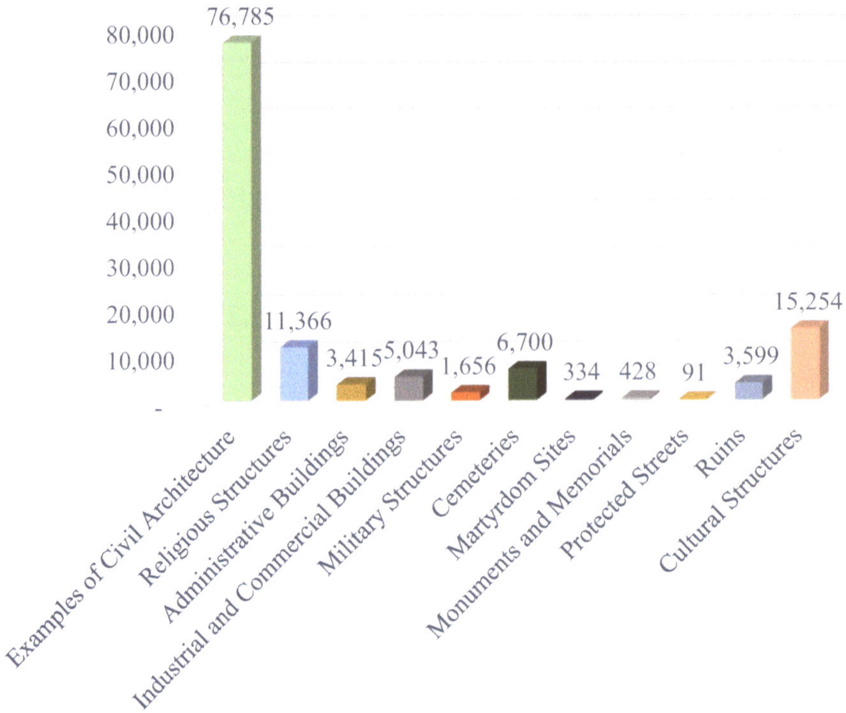

Fig. 2 Distribution of registered cultural heritage property types in Türkiye as of the end of 2023. Source: Own depiction based on Ministry of Culture and Tourism (MCT, 2024)

Considering the identification and registration procedures that have been carried out, it is evident that Türkiye possesses a significant wealth of cultural heritage elements. In terms of cultural heritage conservation, the Ministry of Culture and Tourism has both financial and administrative authority. While conserving cultural heritage is a universal responsibility for all nations, it is undertaken in accordance with national legislation.

3 Basic Criteria Used in the Evaluation of Cultural Heritage Properties

For a property to be covered by the provisions of Law No. 2863 and officially designated as a "cultural asset", it must meet specific criteria. Both international and national legal frameworks govern the key attributes that qualify properties. In the context of conservation legislation, precise criteria are established for a property to be registered as a "cultural property in need of protection".

Initially, the definition of "cultural asset" includes the historical dimension. According to this definition, the historical dimension is described as "belonging to prehistoric and historic periods". The qualitative dimension of the property is determined by criteria such as "related to science, religion, fine arts, and culture". Lastly, the spatial dimension is defined without specific restrictions to include all properties as "underground, overground, and underwater" (Arslan, 1990). Based on the criteria outlined within the definition of cultural assets, there is a barrier from a historical perspective in registering modern architectural structures as "cultural assets". Indeed, in the absence of historical restrictions, properties deemed necessary for protection by the relevant Ministry, based on their significance and characteristics, can be registered as cultural assets (Madran, 2006).

Under the law, the designation of a cultural heritage site as a "protected site" is evaluated based on historical, qualitative, and spatial factors, according to specific criteria. Primarily, the registration of cultural heritage sites depends on the criterion of "surviving from prehistoric times to the present". The qualitative aspect at the site level is defined by criteria such as "reflecting the social, architectural, and economic characteristics of the period in which it was inhabited" and "witnessing historical events". However, while these criteria mentioned by law serve as general assessment guidelines, detailed criteria are not specified. At the level of individual structures, the qualitative aspect includes criteria such as the property's "historical, regional, artistic, and other characteristics" (Law No. 2863 / Article 7) (Arslan, 1990).

Alongside the provisions outlined in Article 7 of the Conservation Law, specific criteria for assessing heritage elements are detailed by key decisions. The 1999 Principle Decision No. 660, issued by the HCCCN, categorises cultural heritage properties beyond the scope established by legal regulations. According to this Principle Decision, cultural heritage properties are classified as "Group I" if they naturally possess aesthetic and historical importance, and as "Group II" if they contribute to the historical identity of cities. The types of interventions—such as maintenance, repair, and restoration—applicable to these properties are determined based on their classification. These intervention definitions broadly apply to cultural heritage properties (Genim, 1990, p.49). Structures classified as "Group I" under this Principle Decision are also referred to as "monumental structures", including religious edifices, baths, palaces, rock tombs, and similar constructions. Conversely, "Group II" structures reflect local life and consist of traditional residential buildings (Yeşilbaş, 2022).

Identifying properties or cultural assets that require conservation, as well as establishing the criteria for this process, presents significant challenges. Although conservation approaches differ across countries, they can also evolve within a single nation over time, resulting in variations in the criteria used to identify cultural assets. While international documents address evaluation standards for elements of cultural heritage, specific guidelines are detailed within Türkiye's conservation legislation. The Conservation Law (Law No. 2863) employs criteria to define cultural heritage elements; however, these criteria are not explicitly specified within the law. The legislation considers factors such as temporal aspects, quality, authenticity, and spatial dimensions to identify cultural assets that require preservation. It also highlights the artistic, architectural, historical, aesthetic, local, and archaeological importance of cultural assets. Nevertheless, no precise definitions or clarifications are provided by these criteria. The scope of evaluation standards for the identification and registration of cultural assets at the individual structural level has been expanded through regulatory measures, emphasising values such as architectural, symbolic, documentary, historical, functional, aesthetic, decorative, perceptual, uniqueness, authenticity, memory, material, rarity, restorability, and homogeneity.

Within conservation legislation, the criteria for identifying and assessing cultural heritage elements, whether at the individual structure level or the site scale, have not been clearly established or defined. The identification of cultural heritage elements, the determination of intervention methods, the development of conservation policies, and the definition of common evaluation criteria are essential for interventions related to the use and protection of properties (Arslan, 1990, p. 28).

4 Expropriation Procedures and Issues in Cultural Properties and Heritage Sites

In Türkiye, the key decisions made by the Conservation Council are crucial for the preservation of cultural properties. These properties are categorised into different building groups according to the decisions, primarily as Group I and Group II. No repair or intervention can be undertaken on cultural properties without identifying their respective building groups. Properties or cultural assets within heritage sites may be privately owned. The restrictions imposed on protected properties directly impact private ownership. Consequently, one of the main challenges in conserving cultural assets in Türkiye is addressing ownership restrictions and securing funding for conservation efforts.

In the context of reflecting conservation policies onto spatial planning, conservation-oriented planning efforts involve subjecting certain uses of properties to the approval of the conservation council, in addition to utilising tools such as expropriation and land swaps to compensate for the loss of rights resulting from private ownership restrictions and to ensure conservation. Conservation practices are primarily carried out through planning decisions, principle decisions, use restrictions, and identification and registration processes (Aliefendioğlu, 2011, p. 496). However, the economic impacts of conservation decisions should not be overlooked. At this point, compensating for the loss of rights due to use restrictions is attempted through expropriation and land swap procedures.

Article 15 of Law No. 2863 governs the principles regarding the expropriation of cultural heritage elements. According to the relevant article, expropriation processes within conservation areas are conducted within the framework of expropriation programmes prepared by the Ministry of Culture and Tourism (Zorlu Kaman & Aliefendioğlu, 2017, p. 721). Municipalities and local administrations can also undertake expropriation processes for cultural properties, provided that the use function specified by the conservation council is not exceeded. However, Law No. 2863 states that the age, rarity, and artistic value of cultural properties should be disregarded when determining compensation for expropriation. The valuation of cultural properties should be based solely on the net costs of the structures.

Therefore, factors such as the rarity of the property or its artistic features are not considered as value-enhancing elements (Tanrıvermiş & Aliefendioğlu, 2008). At this point, debates emerge regarding the methods for determining the value of properties in expropriation practices. Considering that Türkiye is rich in cultural heritage, there is a considerable need for funding to support the preservation of cultural properties. The budget allocated to public institutions and organisations authorised to carry out expropriations is often insufficient to meet the demand (Yeşilbaş, 2022). Despite this, expropriation remains a tool that contributes to the preservation of historic structures and textures, enhancing the appreciation of architectural heritage elements.

In the case of Türkiye, numerous issues related to cultural heritage elements and property rights have been brought before the European Court of Human Rights (ECHR). An examination of the outcomes of cases submitted to the ECHR reveals that the court has primarily focused on the justification for expropriation and the compensation amounts awarded following the deprivation of property rights (Aliefendioğlu, 2011, p. 111). Indeed, even if expropriation for cultural heritage protection is deemed legitimate, it has been emphasised that the cultural characteristics of the property should be taken into account when determining appropriate compensation. The fundamental principle is that a balance must be maintained between the public interest and intervention in property rights to assess the true value of the property accurately (Özel, 2022).

5 General Assessment

The conservation of heritage elements has become a global issue that transcends national borders in the era of globalisation. In Türkiye, the conservation process primarily commences with the registration of these elements. The identification of cultural heritage elements and the subsequent registration by the conservation council initiate the conservation process. In addition to legal and regulatory frameworks, the principles established by these councils for the conservation and utilisation of heritage form the foundation of the national conservation approach. The usage restrictions imposed by these principles directly impact property rights. Therefore, adhering to the principle of proportionality in interventions related to property rights—within constitutional and legal frameworks—is essential to ensure that conservation decisions are effectively reflected in both spatial and economic dimensions.

Türkiye's rich cultural heritage necessitates certain international obligations concerning conservation policies. While it is essential to examine the legal, administrative, social, and environmental foundations of conservation practices, it is equally important to strengthen their financial aspects. Indeed, one of the most critical elements of conservation policies in Türkiye is the allocation of resources. The insufficient budget for conservation efforts significantly hampers the success of these policies. As a result, there is a continuous search for alternative management tools to fund conservation initiatives. However, the discussed or tested alternative tools often fail to be effectively utilised due to the neglect of national identity, culture, and legal framework.

The obligation to provide specific compensation for property rights that are forfeited as a consequence of safeguarding heritage elements under private ownership constitutes a fundamental tenet within expropriation procedures. Given that property rights are protected by both constitutional law and internationally recognised instruments, it is imperative to meticulously evaluate the value of properties subject to restrictions and designated for protection. In Türkiye, the principles and procedures governing expropriation in preservation zones are defined by Law No. 2863, which is the Expropriation Law. The Preservation Law does not delineate particular expropriation principles. It explicitly states that the "age value", "artistic value" and "rarity value" of expropriated properties are to be disregarded during the valuation process. Consequently, factors such as the rarity of similar structures within the area, construction techniques, architectural features, historical significance, and the quality of materials employed are not taken into account during valuation.

The fundamental issue encountered in the conservation of cultural heritage is the allocation of budget and the provision of financing for conservation expenses. However, the effective implementation of conservation policies is also directly related to national awareness of conservation. The insufficient recognition of heritage elements within the country, the lack of public engagement with conserved values, and the absence of discussion on methods and approaches during the conservation process constitute the social and cultural shortcomings of the system. It is essential to adopt the "conservation" approach as a cultural issue, ensuring that the public is informed alongside the registration decisions that initiate the conservation process and that local stakeholders are included. The success of conservation policies can only be achieved through a participatory approach that considers not only central administrative decisions but also social factors.

When determining and developing conservation policies, it is essential to establish national standards for the identification and registration of heritage elements, taking into account national needs and the cultural, social, economic, and legal infrastructure. Additionally, ethical guidelines for the use of cultural assets and, most importantly, legal frameworks specifically tailored for conservation areas must be established. However, the success of preservation policies is not solely dependent on legal regulations; it is crucial to emphasise that conservation should be regarded as a national cultural issue, and that conservation practices must be widely embraced and properly understood by the public. Therefore, legal regulations concerning conservation policies should not conflict with national culture and should be perceived as a social responsibility. In this regard, education emerges as another critical aspect of conservation policies. The acceptance of conservation culture as a social responsibility largely depends on educational programs, starting with family education.

References

Aliefendioğlu, Y. (2011). *Türkiyede koruma alanlarındaki taşınmazların kullanımı ve koruma statülerinin taşınmaz piyasaları ve değerlerine etkileri: Muğla ili örneği*. Ankara Üniversitesi, Fen Bilimleri Enstitüsü, Taşınmaz Geliştirme Anabilim Dalı.

Arslan, G (1990). 'Koruma planlamasında ilk aşama: tespit ve tescil' Kültür Bakanlığı, Kültür ve Tabiat Varlıklarını Koruma Genel Müdürlüğü (ed.) *Kültür Ve Tabiat Varlıklarını Koruma Kurultayı* (pp. 27–34). Ankara.

Balamir, A. (2014). Modern mirasın korunması, korumada sivil mimarlık çalıştay notları. In *Vehbi Koç Ankara Araştırmaları Uygulama ve Araştırma Merkezi (VEKAM)* (pp. 37–55). Ankara.

Baydan, E (2021). *Koruma alanlarında planlama ve mülkiyet ilişkileri: Nevşehir Kapadokya bölgesi örneği*. Yüksek Lisans Tezi. Ankara Üniversitesi, Fen Blimleri Enstitüsü, Gayrimenkul Geliştirme ve Yönetimi Anabilim Dalı.

Çolak, İ. (2015). *Kültür ve Tabiat Varlıklarını Koruma Hukuku* (p. 164). Onikilevha Yayıncılık.

Genim, S (1990). 'Koruma olgusunda onama ve denetleme mekanizmaları: koruma kurulları - kurul - yerel yönetim ilişkileri. In Kültür Bakanlığı, Kültür ve Tabiat Varlıklarını Koruma Genel Müdürlüğü (ed) *Kültür Ve Tabiat Varlıklarını Koruma Kurultayı* (pp. 49–54). Ankara.

İsmep Guidebooks. (2014). *Kültürel mirasın korunması*. İstanbul Valiliği, İstanbul Proje Koordinasyon Birimi (İPKB). Ünal, Z.G. (ed). İstanbul. Retrieved from https://www.guvenli-yasam.org/wp-content/uploads/2016/02/KULTUREL.pdf on 12 September 2024.

Kaman, A. F. Z., & Aliefendioğlu, Y. (2017). Doğa koruma alanlarında İmar Hakkı aktarımı uygulamaları üzerine bir değerlendirme. *Ankara Üniversitesi SBF Dergisi, 72*(3), 715–743.

Kortanoğlu, M. S. (2013). Arkeolojik sitler ve derecelendirme sorunu. *Colloquium Anatolicum, 12*, 271–290.

Kuşçuoğlu, G. Ö., & Murat, T. A. Ş. (2017). Sürdürülebilir kültürel miras yönetimi. *Yalvaç Akademi Dergisi, 2*(1), 58–67.

Madran, E. (2006). Modern mimarlık ürünlerinin belgelenmesi ve korunması süreci için bazı notlar. *Mimarlık Dergisi*, 332(1) [çevrimiçi]. Retrieved from http://www.mimarlikdergisi.com/index.cfm?sayfa=mimarlik&DergiSayi=50&RecID=1207 on 05 September 2024.

Öngören, G & Karali, E. (2020). *Sit Alanı İlanı Kararı, Hukuki Niteliği ve Sonuçları*. Retrieved from https://ongoren.av.tr/sit-alani-ilani-karari-hukuki-niteligi-ve-sonuclari/ on September 5, 2024.

Özdemir, M. Z. D. (2005). Türkiye'de kültürel mirasın korunmasına kısa bir bakış. *Planlama, 31*, 20–25.

Özel, K. C. (2022). Kültür varlıklarına ilişkin düzenlemelerin anayasalardaki ve uluslararası sözleşmelerdeki görünümü. In E. Yeşilbaş & C. Altıparmak (Eds.), *Uygulamaya yönelik, disiplinlerarası bir yaklaşımla kültürel miras (kültür varlıkları) hukuku*. Seçkin Hukuk.

Tanrıvermiş, H., & Aliefendioğlu, Y. (2008). Yapı değerlemesinin teorik esasları ve uygulamaları: Türkiye'de kamulaştırma, emlak vergisi ve imar düzenlemeleri yönünden bir inceleme. *Üçüncü Sektör Kooperatifçilik, 43*(4), 30–60.

Ürün, Ş (2016). *Dünya Kültürel ve Doğal Mirasın Korunmasına Dair Sözleşme: Doğal Miras Alanları Başvuru, Adaylık ve Değerlendirme Süreçleri*. Uzmanlık Tezi. Unesco Türkiye Millî Komisyonu, Ankara. Retrieved from: https://www.unesco.org.tr/Content_Files/Content/tez/sutez.pdf on 05 August 2024.

Yeşilbaş, E. (2022). Kültür varlıkları açısından sanat tarihinin önemi ve temel meseleleri. In E. Yeşilbaş & C. Altıparmak (Eds.), *Uygulamaya yönelik, disiplinlerarası bir yaklaşımla kültürel miras (kültür varlıkları) hukuku*. Seçkin Hukuk.

Yüce, İ (2021). Kültürel miras hukuku. *Sanat Hukuku Enstitüsü*. Retrieved from https://www.sanathukukuenstitusu.com/post/k%C3%BClt%C3%BCrel-miras-hukuku on 18 August 2024.

Yeşim Tanrıvermiş holds the position of full professor in the Department of Real Estate Development and Management at the Faculty of Applied Sciences, Ankara University, Türkiye. She attained her Master of Science (M.Sc.) degree in 2011 from the Department of Agricultural Economics at Ankara University. She received her Ph.D. in 2011 as the first Ph.D. program graduate of the Department of Real Estate Development and Management at Ankara University. Her research interests encompass the management and conservation of land resources, land resource economics, as well as real estate analysis and economics, in addition to studies in real estate and asset valuation. She has been delivering lectures for several years and has published academic papers since 2006. Her publications consist of 50 international and 40 national peer-reviewed articles. Additionally, she has made contributions to 110 international and 25 national full or abstract proceedings at various conferences and congresses and has authored 35 books and 30 book chapters. Presently, she serves as the Deputy Head of her department at Ankara University. Moreover, she is an active participant in various academic and professional organisations. Her experience encompasses working as a researcher and consultant across diverse public and private sectors, with a focus on real estate asset analysis, real estate finance and valuation, land and building conservation practices, as well as real estate economics and management. Furthermore, she actively engages in enhancing cooperation with both domestic and international institutions, mobilising financial resources for research projects.

Emine Baydan graduated from the Department of City and Regional Planning at Middle East Technical University in 2012. In 2021, she earned her master's degree from the Department of Real Estate Development and Management at the Graduate School of Natural and Applied Sciences at Ankara University. Her master's thesis examined planning and property relations in conservation areas, featuring a case study of the Cappadocia region in middle Anatolia. She is currently a Ph.D. candidate in the same department, concentrating on the interplay between transportation planning, land use, and real estate markets. Mrs Baydan commenced her academic career in 2018 as a research assistant in the Department of Real Estate Development at Ankara University. Her research interests encompass urban planning, real estate development, transportation, spatial transformation, and the application of digital tools, including sentiment analysis and artificial intelligence, in analysing real estate and urban policies.

Real Estate Education, Research Systems, and Professionalisation Trends in Türkiye

Harun Tanrıvermiş, Muhammed Said Yılmaz, and Amani Micheal Uisso

Abstract

This chapter analyses real estate education, training, research systems, and professionalisation processes in Türkiye from both global and local perspectives. With the expansion of globalisation and the deepening of the financial sector, the real estate industry has moved beyond providing for basic shelter needs, gaining greater significance as an economic and financial sector. This development requires examining real estate not only within the context of engineering and architecture, but also by a multidisciplinary approach that encompasses law, urban planning, finance, and valuation. In this chapter, the real estate educational models in the USA, the United Kingdom, and Continental Europe are analysed and compared with those in Türkiye. Within this context, the development of real estate education in Türkiye is evaluated, and areas for improvement are identified. Türkiye's real estate education systems should be advanced following an interdisciplinary approach, aligning with global trends. Furthermore, the importance of restructuring real estate education to meet contemporary needs such as

The authors of the chapter consider it a debt of gratitude to Prof. Dr. Mehmet Bülbül, who was staff and international coordinator of the Department of Real Estate Development and Management, Ankara University, Türkiye, and passed away on November 4, 2022, and whose efforts made great contributions to the initiation of real estate development education and research in Türkiye.

H. Tanrıvermiş (✉) · M. S. Yılmaz
Department of Real Estate Development and Management, Faculty of Applied Sciences, Ankara University, Ankara, Türkiye
e-mail: tanrivermis@ankara.edu.tr; mhsyilmaz@ankara.edu.tr

A. M. Uisso
President Office Ethics Secretariat, Dodoma, Tanzania
e-mail: amani.uisso@maadili.go.tz

T. Just et al. (eds.), *Understanding Türkiye's Real Estate Markets*, Management for Professionals, https://doi.org/10.1007/978-3-032-13297-0_32

technological progress, sustainability, and international economic integration is discussed. In conclusion, real estate education in Türkiye has developed in response to increasing demands, particularly since the market economy's rise in the 1980s. It is currently delivered through undergraduate and postgraduate programmes aimed at fostering professionalisation. The further integration of technological innovations, data analytics, and sustainability considerations into curricula can enhance the global competitiveness of Türkiye's real estate sector.

Keywords

Real estate · Professionalisation · Real estate education · Research strategies · Market trends and Turkish higher education system

1 Introduction

The real estate sector has experienced expanded income and population growth due to globalisation and advancements in the financial industry. Going beyond merely offering shelter, real estate now functions as an important economic and financial asset. This change has made it necessary to view real estate not only through engineering and architecture but from a broader perspective. Traditionally, academic departments related to real estate have developed in response to societal and sectoral demands.

While subjects such as land surveying, cadastre, and land registry systems have been core areas within the surveying profession, real estate ownership and law have been central topics in the legal field. The professions of civil engineering and architecture have evolved in tandem with construction activities for a long time; an interdisciplinary approach has emerged through the integration of methods from agriculture, forestry, and economics, which consider land as a factor of production. Expertise in real estate has evolved in tandem with technological progress, innovations in building materials, and shifting societal needs. The demand for real estate professionals has increased due to processes like the valuation and taxation of urban and rural properties for various purposes, differing land management and administrative approaches between countries, and methods of land acquisition and expropriation for investment purposes.

The process of specialisation within the real estate sector commenced in the twentieth century, generating demand for well-trained experts in this domain. During the ninetieth century, technical disciplines related to real estate were incorporated into curricula at engineering and architecture institutions, as well as at agriculture and forestry faculties. Legal and statutory procedures pertinent to the real estate industry were also included in law school programmes. Nonetheless, rapid urbanisation, the proliferation of private property development initiatives, and the increasing necessity for specialisation in areas such as land management, facilities management, and property management prompted faculties of business administration, law, engineering-architecture, agriculture, and forestry to dedicate attention to this field. The earliest recognised formal educational institution specialising in real estate was founded in 1923 at the University of Wisconsin-Madison. Initially, this education was integrated within the economics department, emphasising the interrelation between real estate and economic development. The post-World War II expansion of the real estate market significantly intensified the demand for qualified professionals. Consequently, real estate education in the United States evolved primarily within business schools; it adopted a finance-oriented approach, resulting in the creation of an integrated curriculum encompassing courses in finance, economics, law, and urban planning. From the 1960s onward, master's degree programmes were similarly introduced within economics faculties, alongside the establishment of new departments aimed at enhancing the expertise of undergraduates and graduates in the field of real estate.

In the final decade of the twentieth century, real estate education, which originated in Europe amidst the expansion of globalisation and real estate markets, began to gain prominence in Asian nations as well. During this period, the need for specialisation within real estate education became clear; consequently, sub-disciplines such as real estate finance, project development, land management and administration, facility and property management, and real estate valuation emerged as distinct fields. In the twenty-first century, the adoption of technological innovations within the real estate sector has accelerated. Technologies such as (big) data analytics, remote sensing, geographic information systems (GIS), building information systems, building information modelling (BIM), and software solutions for facility, property, and asset management are now widely used. Modern real estate education programmes adopt an interdisciplinary framework that integrates finance, law, urban planning, sustainability, and technological developments. Professionals are expected to tackle a diverse range of challenges, including zoning laws and environmental regulations, while managing the complexities inherent in real estate development and facility management. Within this context, the evolution of real estate education and training on a global scale is examined by a comparative perspective with the situation in Türkiye. The development of real estate education in Türkiye is analysed in terms of the knowledge, skills, and competencies expected of professionals, along with sectoral demands. Notably, discussions with selected experts from various countries have enabled an analysis of the current state of real estate education, training, and research strategies using a participatory approach, thereby identifying areas for improvement. The key issues to be addressed in this chapter include:

- What knowledge, skills, and competencies are essential for real estate professionals to provide high-quality services and effectively respond to the sector's changing demands?
- To what extent do the knowledge, skills, and competencies of real estate graduates meet the expectations of real estate consultancy and professional practice?
- In what ways should real estate education and its associated knowledge base be adapted to better address the evolving needs of the market and industry stakeholders?

2 Global Development of Real Estate Education and Training

As a result of urban growth and growing populations, managing land has become increasingly important. Since demand for land resources is constantly evolving and land itself is immovable, using these resources efficiently and establishing control are crucial. To achieve sustainable management, a professional approach to the "spatial control of real estate" is essential, covering aspects such as land conveyance (purchase and sale), land cadastre (survey), decision-making, valuation, registration, and resource distribution. The rise of land and real estate development, combined with the growing demand for diverse land uses, has heightened the need for knowledgeable and skilled professionals in the real estate sector. In line with globalisation, technological progress, and urban development, there is an increasing demand for expertise in areas such as construction, valuation methods, real estate finance and investment, capital market instruments related to real estate, and property and facility management. In this context, education and training in real estate have become strategic priorities to support sectoral sustainability and address the needs of the professional workforce.

The diverse approaches adopted by countries regarding the real estate sector have significantly contributed to the development of knowledge, content, and structural frameworks within international real estate education. This heterogeneity in educational and training methods is mainly rooted in the United States and the United Kingdom, which are widely recognised as pioneers in the global development of the real estate discipline (Kim & Pior, 2018; Schulte et al., 2005; Shi-Ming, 2001; Weeks & Finch, 2003). In line with the historical progress of nations, their social, economic, legal, and environmental systems have directly influenced the real estate industry, thereby shaping the evolution of related educational programmes. The ongoing changes and dynamics driven by globalisation have extended beyond rural and agricultural contexts, creating new demands in areas such as manufacturing, city development, housing needs, and spatial planning, which have significantly influenced the trajectory of real estate education (Kim & Pior, 2018; Shi-Ming, 2001). Within this context, the real estate paradigm needs to remain flexible, capable of evolving to meet the needs of contemporary society as well as technological and environmental challenges.

The evolution of globalisation, driven by technological change, shifts in political and economic power, clean energy policies, and capital flows, is shaping the direction of international markets. As a result, values and returns in the real estate sector are gaining strategic value. Capital moves opportunistically and flexibly across borders, while investor focus shifts from a national to a global perspective on real estate investment. Accordingly, urban development challenges such as the globalisation of real estate investment and finance markets, international mergers between real estate firms, and the future of major cities are increasingly highlighting the need for internationally proficient real estate experts. These developments have a direct impact on the structure and content of real estate education (Schulte et al., 2005). In the era of rapid technological change, a comprehensive and systematically structured real estate education becomes more important to meet the demands of this new epoch. Then, well-trained real estate professionals, who have been carefully designed curriculum, emerge as the agents guiding the sector's ongoing development (Kim & Pior, 2018).

Rapid technological progress has created a world that functions as a global ecosystem where information and capital cross borders instantly. In this evolving environment—during the shift to a knowledge-based economy—universities are vital. Their role has become important in developing individuals capable of thriving in a rapidly changing and highly competitive global landscape (Shi-Ming, 2001). According to Kim and Pior (2018), today's real estate education is mainly shaped by the core qualities shared by programmes accredited by the Royal Institution of Chartered Surveyors (RICS) and The Association to Advance Collegiate Schools of Business (AACSB-International).

A significant portion of real estate education in the United States takes place within business faculties specialising in land economics. Many of these programmes have gained accreditation from the international organisation now called The Association to Advance Collegiate Schools of Business International (AACSB), formerly known as the Association of Collegiate Business Schools (ACSB). Real estate education in the United States has been shaped by the concept of private property, which has evolved since the country's independence, and by a market structure based on the free transfer of property among parties. As a result, the educational focus is mainly on finance and investment (Kim & Pior, 2018). Bossard and Dewhurst (1931) noted that 24 of 42 AACSB member business schools included real estate courses in their curricula. By 1981, this number had risen considerably, with 35 of the 42 schools affiliated with the organisation offering real estate courses within their programmes (Garrigan & Wardrop, 1981). Meanwhile, much of the real estate education in the United Kingdom was influenced by the Royal Institution of Chartered Surveyors (RICS), formerly known as the "Institution of Surveyors". Traditional perspectives significantly shaped it within surveying and real estate practice (Kim & Pior, 2018). Since its establishment, the RICS has played a vital role in maintaining professional standards, developing professional practices, and setting ethical principles in the real estate sector. Particularly in recent years, the RICS has become an authority for many institutions, professionals, and graduates across Europe and Asia, aiding their registration and accreditation processes (Poon et al., 2011). Additionally, there has been a rise in the number of institutions offering real estate education, especially at the postgraduate level (D'Arcy & Taltavull, 2009).

Regional dynamics have significantly shaped the real estate sector and its related education over many years. Consequently, real estate education exhibits notable structural and content variations worldwide (Schulte et al., 2005). Although it is founded on certain professional principles and core tenets, similar to fields such as law, medicine, and engineering, it still enjoys less recognition as an academic discipline compared to established fields like law, economics, business, engineering, and architecture. This is widely acknowledged (Shi-Ming, 2001). The two main reasons for this status are the multidisciplinary nature of the field and its relatively brief history. Unlike disciplines such as law and engineering, which focus on a singular area, real estate education necessitates an interdisciplinary framework that integrates various fields, and the framework has to incorporate a holistic approach covering all facets of the real estate profession (Shi-Ming, 2001). The real estate education models employed by many universities are categorised into three main approaches (Schulte, 2012):

- The "interdisciplinary approach" adopted in continental Europe.
- The "surveying (real estate) approach" used in the United Kingdom and Commonwealth countries.
- The "investment and finance approach" prevalent in the United States.

University-level real estate education programmes have been a topic of global discussion, especially since 2000. Schulte (2012) classified real estate education programmes in 39 countries into three main models: the "real estate approach" used in the United Kingdom, the "investment and finance approach" common in the United States, and the "interdisciplinary approach" adopted by other European countries (excluding the United Kingdom). Conversely, Shi-Ming (2001), expanding the discussion at the National University of Singapore to a global scale, addressed real estate education under three categories: "the United Kingdom model, the U.S. model, and the "eclectic (mixed) approach" covering Asian and African nations. In this context, Schulte's (2012) "interdisciplinary approach" and Shi-Ming's (2001) "eclectic approach" reflect adaptations of the United Kingdom and U.S. models, blending them according to the specific needs of local real estate sectors (Kim & Pior, 2018). The mixed approach is characterised by universities offering both the U.K.'s practice-based professional education model and the U.S. finance-focused approach simultaneously. This has become a model for undergraduate real estate programmes across many universities today, providing a flexible and comprehensive structure capable of responding to the evolving global financial landscape.

In shaping modern real estate education, different schools of thought have developed based on each country's real estate markets and legal systems. However, these schools are not strictly separated by clear boundaries. For example, the "real estate approach" used in the United Kingdom and the "interdisciplinary approach" common in Continental Europe share many similarities. Nonetheless, these two approaches differ in their historical and institutional development processes (McGrath et al., 2020). Within this framework, the "interdisciplinary approach", the "real estate approach", and the "investment and finance approach" have evolved within the specific social, economic, and legal contexts of their respective countries; therefore, the development and application of these models should be analysed and evaluated on a country-by-country basis.

2.1 The Investment and Finance Approach

The approach to investment and finance is mainly linked to the United States, where real estate education has mostly developed within business faculties. Since the country's founding, a market framework has existed that allows land to be bought and sold freely. The fact that the government did not own land or have a royal family, combined with the ability for private property to be transferred without restrictions, sped up the growth of the real estate market. This situation, in turn, created demand for education among market participants and led to the institutionalisation of real estate education. The first real estate courses in the U.S. explicitly focused on the concept of property. In this context, the initial course, titled "Landed Property", was offered in 1886 at the University of Kansas by James H. Canfield. Similarly, in 1892, Fred M. Taylor gave lectures at the University of Michigan titled "The History and Theory of Land Tenure" and "The Agrarian Movement". However, these lectures were removed from the curriculum two years later. Although some universities started offering courses featuring "land economics" content during this period, these efforts were short-lived because academic administrators and industry stakeholders did not fully understand the scope of the subject. A significant development was the launch of a seminar called "Property and Rent of Land" by R. T. Ely at the University of Wisconsin in 1892. By 1915, this seminar had become a regular university course named "Land Economics", securing its place in the curriculum (K'Akumu, 2024).

The recognition of real estate brokerage as a professional field and the necessity for specialisation in this area originated from initiatives by the National Association of Real Estate Boards (NAREB). Within the capitalist production system, the formalisation of business education at universities made it essential for real estate brokers to possess basic business knowledge to conduct their commercial activities effectively. In this context, real estate education was first introduced at higher education institutions in 1905, at the Wharton School of Finance and Commerce in Philadelphia and the New York University School of Commerce, followed by the University of Pittsburgh School of Economics in 1908, in the form of evening classes. The primary aim of these courses was to raise the ethical standards of real estate brokers, enhance their understanding of economic and social issues, and develop professional skills, especially in real estate economics and valuation. The view that real estate brokerage should be regarded as a business-oriented profession, akin to accounting, fostered collaboration between the National Association of Real Estate Boards (NAREB) and the AACSB. These joint efforts played a substantial role in promoting academic education for the real estate brokerage profession.

In 1931, real estate education was integrated as a standard component of Master of Business Administration (MBA) programmes in the USA. From the 1920s to the mid-1950s, real estate education was predominantly organised as land economics and practice-oriented vocational training, with the objective of increasing the number of graduates. The expansion of MBA programmes in the 1950s established the groundwork for recognising real estate as an independent discipline. Nevertheless, this development was subject to criticism from prominent academic institutions.

Notably, the report titled "Higher Education for Business", published by the Ford Foundation, and the study "The Education of American Businessmen", conducted by the Carnegie Foundation, expressed sceptical views regarding these advancements. These reports argued that real estate education lacked sufficient content, was primarily aimed at increasing the number of certified graduates, and was deficient in academic rigour.

In the post-World War II era of the 1960s, economic growth and the move towards peaceful living increased the demand for more skilled professionals in the real estate sector (Black et al., 1996). In this context, university real estate programmes expanded their curricula; educational initiatives became more analytical, focusing on topics such as problem-solving and investment analysis. The American Real Estate and Urban Economics Association (AREUEA), founded in 1964, aimed to enhance the academic quality of research in real estate and deepen its analytical approach, making notable contributions to scholarly work in this field. From the 1970s onwards, problem-solving methods evolved into two main branches: one adopting an interdisciplinary framework, and the other a finance-management-oriented educational philosophy. During this period, investment and finance became the most popular specialisation in real estate education. With increasing globalisation in the 1990s, organisations like the American Real Estate Society (ARES) and the International Real Estate Society (IRES) actively supported the development of international real estate education. At the same time, the AACSB accredited its first school outside North America in 1997, aiming to expand its certification programmes internationally (Schulte et al., 2005). In light of these historical developments, it is clear that market logic shaped real estate education in the U.S., centred on the free transfer (purchase and sale) of land, dating back to the pre-independence era. In conclusion, the core of real estate education in the USA tends to focus on finance and investment within a business-oriented framework.

2.2 The Surveying (Real Estate) Approach

The development of the approach to real estate surveying originated in England and among the member nations of the Commonwealth of Nations. Its roots can be traced back to land surveying and valuation practices associated with real estate, dating to the Middle Ages within the historical evolution of the country. Formal training for land surveying as a profession commenced in the United Kingdom during the Middle Ages, employing a systematic methodology whereby apprentices succeeded family businesses and received instruction through guilds. Urbanisation advanced rapidly with the first and second enclosure movements, initiated in the sixteenth century, involving the fencing of large tracts of land to promote agricultural productivity. These developments, particularly with the onset of the Industrial Revolution in the eighteenth century, facilitated the emergence of new roles and expertise within land surveying and valuation, rendering these disciplines increasingly specialised. The increase in production capacity, trade volume, and urban population density following the Industrial Revolution created new economic opportunities for the business sector. It also made the real estate industry more complex both technically and financially (Kim & Pior, 2018). The Royal Institution of Chartered Surveyors (RICS) defines 22 distinct specialisations related to land, property, infrastructure, and construction management. These are: building control, building surveying, commercial real estate, corporate real estate, environmental surveying, facilities management, geomatics, infrastructure, land and natural resources, management consultancy, minerals and waste management, personal property (including arts and antiques), project management, project finance and investment, quantity surveying and construction management, research, residential property, rural property, taxation allowances, valuation, and business and intangible asset valuation. Among these, 12 specialisations are offered as secondary fields of expertise to RICS members, while the remaining 10 serve as primary pathways directly incorporated into the professional qualification process. RICS members are particularly authorised in the following areas within these specialisations: due diligence, building inspection, valuation, consultancy, and dispute resolution.

The foundations of modern real estate education in the United Kingdom were laid with the creation of the Institution of Surveyors in 1868 by William Sturge. This organisation was reorganised in 1947, adopting its current name, the Royal Institution of Chartered Surveyors (RICS), and establishing membership standards. To develop professional skills, RICS introduced a mandatory qualifying examination for its members, first held in 1881. These advancements introduced governance, quality assurance, and ethical principles into the real estate profession, while also forming the basis for higher education courses. The nineteenth century was a crucial period for modern education, particularly in real estate studies. During this era, topics shifted from rural land valuation towards urban property management and appraisal, driven by increasing urbanisation. Society's awareness of universal education grew, with the modern UK education system being formalised by the Education Act of 1870 and subsequent reforms in 1902 and 1918. In this context, estate management began to be recognised as an academic discipline at the university level. In 1918 and 1919, the University of London and the University of Cambridge introduced undergraduate degree programmes in estate management. Simultaneously, the College of Estate Management, part of the Chartered Auctioneers' and Estate Agents' Institute, founded in 1919, started offering sector-specific knowledge through evening classes and distance learning. This college joined the University of London in 1938 and later gained the authority to confer bachelor's degrees in estate management. In the 1960s, estate management diversified into new specialised fields. For example, in 1962, the University of Cambridge launched the "BSc in Land Economy" under the leadership of William Dampier. Its origins date back to estate management classes traditionally offered within the university's agricultural faculties. Finally, the School of Real Estate and Planning, established at the University of Reading in 1968, began delivering real estate programmes at both undergraduate and postgraduate levels. This milestone is regarded as a significant step in the development of contemporary, institutionally focused, and research-driven real estate education in the United Kingdom (Kim & Pior, 2018).

In the post-1994 period, undergraduate and postgraduate programmes at universities in England underwent rapid restructuring to cover all specialisation areas outlined by RICS and other international organisations. During this period, RICS evolved into a global entity and introduced quality control measures for chartered surveyors outside the United Kingdom through initiatives such as programme accreditation, the development of professional standards and ethical guidelines, the formation of collaborative partnerships with academic institutions, and the Bologna Process, which promotes globalisation within European higher education (Kim & Pior, 2018). Throughout these developments, real estate departments in the United Kingdom have predominantly based their educational structures on estate management principles and have been significantly influenced by the traditional "real estate approach" endorsed by RICS. The main paradigm of real estate education in the country has particularly developed within the context of the built environment and has become even more research-oriented. In the United Kingdom, real estate education has been established as a distinct academic discipline separate from business management; this field has expanded to include dimensions such as public benefit, environmental sustainability, spatial planning, and professional competencies. As a result, bachelor's, master's, and doctoral programmes in real estate have rapidly grown across universities. The number of undergraduate programmes exceeds that of other countries (Schulte, 2003), also thanks to the UK being a global financial hub and due to the integration of real estate investments with monetary and capital markets. However, in more recent years, a notable shift towards the American business school model has gained increased attention within the United Kingdom.

2.3 The Interdisciplinary Approach

The interdisciplinary approach in real estate education is mainly present across Continental Europe and Asia. Following the Second World War, urban reconstruction generated new demand that required expertise in the real estate sector. During this period, real estate education and practices largely developed from existing professional fields. In Germany or the Netherlands, where rapid post-war urbanisation took place, urban planning, land management, construction, property management, and real estate investment became prominent, increasing the need for specialisation in these domains. With globalisation, real estate transitioned from being purely a physical asset to an economic investment vehicle. This shift resulted in more international real estate investments and a heightened demand for specialised personnel in various countries. This educational requirement was often addressed through programmes developed within law, engineering, economics or urban planning. However, new real estate departments were significantly shaped by the curriculum models of the United States' finance-focused approach and the United Kingdom's vocational and applied approach, which incorporated relevant content from both (Black et al., 1996). Consequently, courses on real estate, previously outside the scope of civil engineering, architecture, planning, or business departments, began to be offered in these countries. Later, with the establishment of dedicated real estate departments, core subjects like economics, law, spatial planning, architecture, and engineering were integrated into the curricula within an interdisciplinary framework.

In the Netherlands, the initiation of real estate education occurred subsequent to the 1960s, marked by the introduction of specialised courses within business and civil engineering faculties. These courses were first established at Delft University of Technology. Presently, as part of programmes within the broader scope of Built Environment Management at numerous universities, a Department of Real Estate Management is also operational (Amsterdam School of Real Estate, 2024). Similarly, in Germany, the demand for real estate expertise arose in conjunction with globalisation and internationalisation; however, formal educational initiatives commenced only in 1990 with the establishment of the private European Business School (EBS) Real Estate Academy. Prior to this, real estate courses were predominantly offered at technical universities (Schulte, 2003). In Japan, the formal institutionalisation of real estate education was first realised in 1992 with the establishment of the Department of Real Estate at Meikai University (Kim & Pior, 2018).

It can be argued that the interdisciplinary approach has evolved in response to the expansion of the real estate sector, aiming to meet the real estate skills demanded by globalisation and internationalisation. The comprehensive curriculum framework for real estate education was established as foreign investors started investing in other nations and as the real estate market achieved a global status, thereby strengthening relationships between organisations within the field, such as IRES (International Real Estate Society) and RICS. Within the interdisciplinary approach, the content of the real estate education curriculum is tailored to the specific needs of each country. Since real estate encompasses various disciplines, the boundaries of these disciplines and the required level of knowledge differ depending on the specific country in which the real estate department is located. Particularly in Africa, where property ownership, systems of tenure, and land registry systems are insufficiently developed and institutionalised, there is a greater focus on property and registration issues within real estate education (Kariuki et al., 2022).

The interdisciplinary approach views real estate as both an investment tool and a field of study that encompasses various areas within its scope. As a result, it conducts analyses by synthesising economic theories, property rights, urban planning, and financial models. Since real estate is evaluated beyond its role as an investment or economic asset, understanding its spatial dynamics and the legal framework is crucial.

3 The Development of Real Estate Education and Training in Türkiye

3.1 Assessment of the Current Situation and Fundamental Problems

Real estate education is a complex system built on existing resources and knowledge, aligned with changing needs documented throughout its history. Over time, it has been delivered through the integration of various disciplines based on core subjects. Today, many specialised fields—such as agricultural, forestry, surveying, civil and geological engineering, architecture, urban and regional planning, law, economics, business administration, finance, public finance, and public administration—are interconnected with real estate topics. Each discipline approaches real estate from its own perspective. This highlights the need for experts who understand the connections between these disciplines and can synthesise relevant information in a balanced way. Therefore, in addition to its ongoing evolution, real estate education must be organised to meet the demand of the contemporary real estate industry.

Schulte (2003) states that achieving consistent results from a business perspective requires an integrated approach to real estate, involving disciplines such as economics, law, spatial planning, architecture, and engineering. Economic factors heavily influence every decision within the real estate sector. The links between the economy and real estate cycles, as well as the effects of specific economic policy instruments on the industry, need to be considered. The interaction between law and real estate includes the impact of property rights, real estate law, cadastre and land registry legislation, commercial law, urbanisation and zoning regulations, and tax legislation on the sector. Spatial planning, in turn, reflects the physical outcomes of strategic decisions made at national, regional, and local levels. Moreover, a balance must be maintained between decisions made in the public interest and those made by real estate investors seeking profit. The relationship between real estate and design can be established by analysing the elements that influence individuals' spatial preferences based on architectural knowledge and human-space-function relationships. Not only the physical design of the structure but also facility management—which addresses user needs and the operational and usage processes of the building—has become an important component. Facility management requires the integration of numerous disciplines into the real estate sector, including engineering, economics, business administration, finance, law, and behavioural sciences. This integration also requires that real estate professionals possess a broad range of knowledge and skills. With regards to business management, real estate is managed on three levels:

- **At the strategic level:** Real estate portfolio management, corporate real estate management, and general real estate strategies;
- **At the functional level:** Real estate analysis, valuation, finance, investment, and marketing;
- **At the process-oriented level:** Processes involved in project development, construction management, and facility management.

Within this scope, the active involvement of real estate experts at all these stages is crucial for sectoral success and sustainability (Schulte, 2003).

Real estate education in Türkiye has reflected the development of the country. Following the proclamation of the Republic, policies of statism and protectionism led to public sector investments in development projects. The central government launched urban planning initiatives. Solutions to housing problems in major cities were sought through cooperatives guided by the government (Keleş, 2015; Keskinok, 2010). Türkiye's neutrality during the Second World War helped avoid destruction in its cities. However, the absence of a strong real estate market, combined with a growing population at that time, resulted in increased unauthorised squatter settlements (Keleş, 2015). After 1980, with the adoption of neoliberal policies and a market economy, urbanisation was driven by commerce and capital flows, which also influenced the real estate sector. For many years, Türkiye's real estate market faced significant limitations due to inadequate housing finance options. The institution, established in 1984 and now functioning as the Housing Development Administration of Türkiye (TOKİ), was created to support housing finance and address this issue. Nonetheless, during this period, housing and real estate were mainly regarded as social needs for shelter; their recognition as economic, investment, or financial assets was limited. As a result, the institutional and financial development of the real estate market progressed slowly, hindering growth in demand for specialisation and a skilled workforce.

In Türkiye, real estate education started with courses related to the field, as well as conducting research and practical work across various professional disciplines. The foundations of real estate education were established in 1933 within the Faculty of Agriculture at the Ankara Higher Institute of Agriculture. Courses covering topics such as real estate valuation, land surveys, mapping, expropriation, and settlement were introduced at that time. Later, curricula at the Faculty of Political Sciences of Ankara University included subjects like development, urbanism, and local governments. In contrast, fields such as property law, zoning law, and real estate tax law were incorporated into the Faculty of Law. These initiatives, which began at Ankara University in the 1920s, only started to spread to other universities from the 1970s onwards. In this context, the Department of Geodesy and Photogrammetry (Surveying) Engineering at Yıldız Technical University became one of the first to include a "real estate valuation" course in its curriculum. Currently, some engineering faculties and faculties of economics and administrative sciences offer valuation courses either as electives or compulsory subjects. However, these courses often lack depth and tend to be superficial, failing to provide students with expert-level knowledge. While systematic education programmes in real estate began developing at universities worldwide after 1850, it is notable that academic specialisation in this area in Türkiye started relatively late.

The names and contents of associate, bachelor's, and graduate degree programmes in real estate professions in Türkiye differ considerably, both between each other and compared to international models. A general review reveals that most of these programmes use varied terms instead of a single, comprehensive term for real estate. The most common alternatives are the strictly legalistic term for "immovable property" ["taşınmaz"] or the more commercially-oriented term "emlak". The expression "immovable property" ["taşınmaz"] appears in the Turkish Civil Code No. 4721, where it legally encompasses assets such as land, rights recorded on land registers, and units registered in the condominium register. Conversely, "emlak" is more frequently used for properties involved in buying and selling, carrying a commercial connotation related to the property market rather than a technical or theoretical context. On the other hand, "gayrimenkul" ("real estate") refers to a multi-faceted domain that includes not only physical immovable assets but also natural and built environments, along with their associated social, economic, and spatial relationships. This broader interpretation aligns with the international understanding of "real estate", covering land, buildings, infrastructure, and the sectoral activities related to property rights, utilisation, and processes involved in acquisition, operation, and disposal. Therefore, the varied terminology used in Türkiye reflects not just lexical differences but also introduces conceptual ambiguity, which can lead to deviations from global standards. This situation complicates efforts to ensure consistency in educational content and to foster integration with international academic and professional communities (Ling & Archer, 2016).

The primary aim of the "Real Estate Management" ("Emlak Yönetimi") programmes offered at an associate degree level in Türkiye is to train real estate consultants and brokers. This indicates that the programmes are conceptually related to the real estate sector but are limited. In this context, the term "immovable property" ("taşınmaz") often encountered in programme names represents the legal aspect of ownership as defined in the Turkish Civil Code No. 4721. However, this expression does not fully capture the complex relationship that immovable assets establish with people through their social, spatial, economic, and technical dimensions. Therefore, it would be more appropriate to use the term "gayrimenkul" to denote this multifaceted structure. Within the scope of this research, institutions and programmes whose educational content includes the words "emlak","taşınmaz" or "gayrimenkul" have been considered. The Real Estate Management programmes at the associate degree level generally aim to develop foundational knowledge for real estate brokerage activities. These programmes are designed to train intermediate-level staff in fields such as economics, finance, law, legislation, valuation, accounting, management, and business administration. The first associate degree programme in Real Estate Management in Türkiye was established in 2000 within the Vocational School of Social Sciences at Istanbul University-Cerrahpasa. This development marks the first example of the institutionalisation of the need for intermediate staff for the sector within the higher education system ("Real Estate Management Program", 2024). The course content in Real Estate Management programmes comprises subjects focused on brokerage services within the framework of real estate economics and business education ("Real Estate Management Program Course Contents", 2024).

In Türkiye, a total of 21 universities have established Real Estate Management programmes at the diploma level. While 18 of these programmes offer face-to-face education, two provide only open and distance learning, and one university operates with both face-to-face and open/distance education models. As of 2025, a total of 2629 students were enrolled in these 21 programmes. Additionally, the quota for the Real Estate Management programmes conducted within open and distance learning faculties has been identified as 1665 students (ÖSYM, 2024). Considering that 37% of the diploma programme quotas are allocated to face-to-face learning and 63% to open and distance learning programmes, and taking into account that the number of vocational high schools providing education in the real estate field and their student numbers are very limited, allocating a high quota to the open and distance learning model seems impractical. Despite the limited number of academic staff specialising in real estate at some universities, the quotas for diploma programmes are high, raising concerns about the quality of education and training. Furthermore, assigning a very high quota for distance learning in an applied field such as real estate has significant challenges (Table 1).

Associate degree programmes typically span two years (comprising four semesters) and are designed to train intermediate-level personnel. In real estate management programmes, students usually focus on courses related to real estate consultancy. At the associate degree level, the curriculum of Real Estate Management programmes mainly highlights marketing topics. Additionally, these programmes include courses on law, cadastre, land registry, zoning legislation, accounting, economics, business administration, real estate valuation, and finance (Real Estate Management Programme, 2024). However, the course content remains limited, and the expected learning outcomes or programme competencies warrant further consideration. Although the term "management" appears in the programme titles, many Real Estate Management associate degree programmes primarily consist of a single "building management" course, based on national legislation. This reveals a gap in areas related to facility and property management within the curricula. Furthermore, topics associated with the operational principles of enterprises involved in real estate brokerage and consultancy, office management practices, and professional standards are completely absent. Additionally, many vocational institutions show limited sectoral engagement, which significantly restricts students' opportunities for practical or academic interactions with industry professionals. This situation clearly highlights the disparities between global trends in real estate education and their application within Türkiye.

For undergraduate programmes in real estate, the departments of real estate development and management were considered. By 2025, eight undergraduate departments will include the word "gayrimenkul" ("real estate") in their name or programme title (Table 2). According to the Council of Higher Education (YÖK) Information Management System, only three of these active departments admit students (YÖK, 2024; ÖSYM, 2024). The main aim of undergraduate real estate programmes is to train students as specialists in their field. An analysis of the curricula for the Departments of Real Estate Development and Management reveals that courses in economics, business administration, law, civil engineering, architecture, agricultural engineering, surveying engineering, city and regional planning, spatial economics, finance, project development and management, facility and property management, and real estate and asset valuation are covered more extensively (Ankara University Bologna Information System, 2024a; Sinop University Student Information System, 2024). Besides the departments of real estate development and management and land registry and cadastre, a limited number of real estate-related courses are offered in disciplines such as surveying engineering, law, civil engineering, architecture, political science and public administration, city and regional planning, agricultural engineering, and forestry engineering.

Two distinct structures exist in graduate education related to real estate development: it is either managed under related disciplines or as an independent department and programme. In fields connected to real estate development and management, 13

Table 1 Associate degree programmes in real estate in türkiye and their educational methods (ÖSYM, 2024)

University	Faculty /Vocational school	Educational format	Quota
Alanya Alaaddin Keykubat University	Alanya Chamber of Commerce and Industry Vocational School	Face-to-face	74
Anadolu University	Eskişehir Vocational School	Face-to-face	69
Aydın Adnan Menderes University	Yeni Pazar Vocational School	Face-to-face	42
Balıkesir University	Savaştepe Vocational School	Face-to-face	42
Bursa Uludağ University	Vocational School of Social Sciences	Face-to-face	57
Çukurova University	Adana Vocational School	Face-to-face	71
Giresun University	Keşap Vocational School	Face-to-face	32
Hatay Mustafa Kemal University	Antakya Vocational School	Face-to-face	40
Istanbul University-Cerrahpaşa	Vocational School of Social Sciences	Face-to-face	67
Karamanoğlu Mehmetbey University	Vocational School of Social Sciences	Face-to-face	49
Kırıkale University	Fatma Şenses Vocational School of Social Sciences	Face-to-face	69
Kocaeli University	Ali Rıza Veziroğlu Vocational School	Face-to-face	69
Kütahya Dumlupınar University	Kütahya Vocational School of Social Sciences	Face-to-face	59
Manisa Celal Bayar University	Salihli Vocational School	Face-to-face	59
Ondokuz Mayıs University	Havza Vocational School	Face-to-face	42
Pamukkale University	Çivril Atasay Kamer Vocational School	Face-to-face	27
Sakarya University of Applied Sciences	Geyve Vocational School	Face-to-face	42
Selçuk University	Vocational School of Social Sciences	Face-to-face	54
Subtotal			**964**
Anadolu University	Open Education Faculty	Online	1050
Atatürk University	Faculty of Open and Distance Education	Online	410
Istanbul University-Cerrahpaşa	Vocational School of Social Sciences	Online	205
Subtotal			**1665**
Grand Total			**2629**

Source: own compilation

thesis and non-thesis master's programmes and three doctoral programmes were established (Study in Türkiye, 2024). However, in practice, only two institutions offer doctoral-level education (Table 3). An examination of departments offering master's education in real estate reveals that they primarily focus on sub-disciplines such as development, valuation, finance, and management. In some programmes, a

Table 2 Undergraduate real estate programmes in türkiye (YÖK, 2024; ÖSYM, 2024)

University	Faculty	Department name	Quota
Akdeniz University	Serik Faculty of Business	Real Estate Development and Management	No student intake
Bolu Abant Izzet Baysal University	Gerede Faculty of Applied Sciences	Real Estate Development and Management	No student intake
Burdur Mehmet Akif Ersoy University	Gölhisar School of Applied Sciences	Real Estate Development and Management	No student intake
Giresun University	Bulancak Kadir Karabaş School of Applied Sciences	Real Estate Development and Management	No student intake
Özyeğin University	Faculty of Applied Sciences	Real Estate Development and Management	No student intake
Tokat Gaziosmanpaşa University	Faculty of Applied Sciences	Real Estate Valuation Management	No student intake
Ankara University	Faculty of Applied Sciences	Real Estate Development and Management	77
Sinop University	Boyabat Faculty of Economics and Administrative Sciences	Real Estate Development and Management	32
Ankara HACI Bayram Veli University	School of Land Registry and Cadastre	Real Estate and Real Estate Management	60

Source: own compilation

graduate programme in development and valuation has been set up under a specific profession rather than as part of an interdisciplinary structure. The terms "develop ment and valuation" are used together in programme names, despite "the science of valuation" being a fundamental component of real estate development. Although real estate development topics are closely associated with branches like surveying, agriculture, construction, as well as business and finance on a global scale, the established programmes do not serve as sub-branches of these sciences. Real estate development is too broad to be contained within these disciplines. Conversely, some universities have established doctoral programmes in real estate development without corresponding bachelor's or master's programmes, or have introduced master's programmes without offering a bachelor's degree, which creates significant gaps between expected programme outcomes or success and actual results. The creation of non-thesis distance learning master's programmes in real estate development and related areas, in a country where undergraduate education has not yet reached the desired standard, tends to emphasise financial considerations over academic aims, and this is not compatible with higher education quality standards.

Graduate education is primarily organised within departments called Anabilim Dalı (literally, "main branches of science"). However, active teaching and research

Table 3 Departments providing graduate education in real estate in türkiye and their programmes (Study in Türkiye, 2024)

University	Institute	Department	Graduate programs		
			Master's (with Thesis)	Master's (Non-Thesis)	Doctorate
Ankara University	Graduate School of Natural and Applied Sciences	Real Estate Development and Management	+	+	+
Ankara University	Graduate School of Natural and Applied Sciences	Real Estate Development and Management - Land Administration and Management	+	+	–
Çanakkale Onsekiz Mart University	Graduate School	Real Estate Development	+	–	–
Ankara HACI Bayram Veli University	Graduate School	Immovable Property Valuation and Management	+	+	–
Ankara HACI Bayram Veli University	Graduate School	Immovable Property Rights and Management	+	–	–
Istanbul University	Institute of Social Sciences	Real Estate Economics	+	+	–
Istanbul University	Institute of Social Sciences	Real Estate and Construction Law	–	+	–
Istanbul Kültür University	Graduate School	Real Estate Development	–	+	–
Istanbul Technical University	Graduate School of Natural and Applied Sciences	Real Estate Development	+	–	–
Istanbul Esenyurt University	Graduate School	Real Estate Finance and Valuation	+	+	–
Istanbul Okan University	Graduate School	Real Estate Finance and Valuation	+	+	–
Istanbul Okan University	Graduate School	Land Management and Utilisation	–	–	+

(continued)

Table 3 (continued)

University	Institute	Department	Graduate programs		
			Master's (with Thesis)	Master's (Non-Thesis)	Doctorate
Istanbul Ticaret University	Natural and Applied Sciences	Real Estate Development and Management	+	–	+
Konya Technical University	Graduate School	Land Management, Urban Transformation, and Immovable Property Valuation	–	+	–
Marmara University	Institute of Social Sciences	Department of Business Administration - Real Estate Finance and Valuation Program	+	+	–
Mersin University	Natural and Applied Sciences	Land Management, Immovable Property Valuation, and Development	+	–	–
Ondokuz Mayıs University	Graduate School	Immovable Property Valuation and Development	–	+	–
Sivas Cumhuriyet University	Natural and Applied Sciences	Immovable Property Valuation and Development	+	–	–
Tekirdağ Namık Kemal University	Natural and Applied Sciences	Immovable Property Valuation and Development	–	+	–
Yıldız Technical University	Natural and Applied Sciences	Immovable Property Valuation and Development	–	+	–

Note: (+) indicates that the programme is open, and (–) indicates that the programme is not open at the university
Source: own compilation

are not carried out in all programmes. Graduate programmes established at universities in major cities, such as Ankara and Istanbul, where economic activity is concentrated, are accepting students. Although programmes in other cities have admitted students in the past, many are currently unable to do so due to a lack of demand. Among these, Ankara University's Department of Real Estate Development and Management stands out for its undergraduate and postgraduate offerings, which are accredited by international bodies such as RICS, IFMA (International Facility Management Association), and CEPI (European Association for Real Estate Professions). Furthermore, the department is an academic member of the IVSC (International Valuation Standards Council), FIG (The International Federation of Surveyors), EuroFM (European Facility Management Network), and AACSB (Department of Real Estate Development and Management, 2024). Additionally, the department has begun establishing graduate programmes for sub-specialisations. In this context, the Land Management and Policy Master's Programmes (with thesis and non-thesis options), conducted in Turkish and English, have begun accepting students.

With the exception of a few universities and departments, it is noteworthy that many programmes have failed to establish collaboration with organisations that influence the profession, education, and sector at an international level. Additionally, internationalisation and cooperation are insufficient (Tanrivermiş; 2019, YÖK, 2024). With regards to the structure and operation of Ankara University Graduate Programmes, these programmes differ from other domestic examples in aspects such as course diversity, the number of experts with specialisations and professional qualifications in the real estate field, and the quantity of theoretical and applied research projects alongside the accumulated knowledge within the department. Emphasis is placed on integrating theory and practice, offering students opportunities to synthesise knowledge across sub-disciplines such as real estate development, land, facility, and property management (Ankara University Bologna Information System, 2024b). However, an analysis of programme titles reveals narrower specialisations within the real estate sector, including real estate valuation, immovable property valuation and management, and immovable property rights and management. It is essential to note that the operations of some programmes have a limited connection to the scope and functions of real estate development and management disciplines. Notably, "real estate development" should encompass the entire building life cycle, spanning from land acquisition and development through all stages of physical environment creation to ongoing management (Geltner, 2006; Healey, 1991; Miles et al., 2000). This includes areas such as property rights, valuation, finance, and economics. For instance, in the immovable property valuation and management programme, although the objective mentions "specialisation in the fields of real estate development and construction management", the scope appears narrower based on its name (Ankara HACI Bayram Veli University, 2024).

In Türkiye, real estate education is available at associate, bachelor's, and postgraduate levels. These programmes must align with the workforce needs of public and private sector organisations. The shift to a market economy and the growth of free enterprise have increased demand for expertise in the real estate sector, leading to the establishment of specialised departments within educational institutions. Beginning in the 2000s with associate degree programmes in real estate management and master's courses, development also facilitated the introduction of bachelor's degrees. However, it is important to recognise that the names, curricula, and operational structures of these programmes vary considerably across institutions compared to those in the USA, the United Kingdom, and Continental Europe, with professional competencies remaining a key challenge. For professional development and standardisation, it is necessary to review and harmonise programme titles and contents, giving priority to training faculty members in specialised areas such as real estate development, facilities, and property management. In addition to permanent faculty, it is essential to involve industry professionals from both public and private sectors as part-time instructors for practical courses and where feasible, to establish departments and programmes in major cities where the real estate industry is big enough.

To develop expertise in sub-disciplines such as real estate development, valuation, investment and finance, and facility and property management, it would be beneficial to establish professional standards and complete the process of professional organisation. It will be necessary to define the sub-specialisations within the real estate field in relevant institutions and to continuously enhance the programme structure, considering job and employment opportunities. According to the Ankara University model, the job placement rate for bachelor's graduates within the first six months is approximately 90%. It would be advantageous to focus on improving graduates' qualifications to increase this rate above 95%.

Contemporary requirements and ongoing technological progress must be integrated into real estate education. The geographical location of real estate, its function as a hedge against inflation, its immobility, permanence, indivisibility, scarcity, locational fixity, durability (indestructibility), and other spatial characteristics have been extensively discussed regarding their potential to be influenced by technology (Veuger, 2018). Nevertheless, significant technological innovations have emerged that directly impact real estate development. In the context of residential and commercial properties, technologies such as blockchain, big data analytics, property technology (Proptech), automated valuation and management tools, artificial intelligence (AI), the Internet of Things (IoT), virtual reality, real estate development software, inspection drones, and similar innovations exemplify these advancements. Currently, the influence of technological progress is clearly reflected in education and research related to real estate development and management; emerging technologies are rapidly incorporated into academic curricula and scholarly analyses (Pryke, 2019; Scheurwater, 2017). Furthermore, education in urban land development and real estate construction should address the requirements for sustainable utilisation of existing resources, clean energy technologies, zero-waste design principles, and the certification of building schemes, in response to global climate change.

3.2 Opportunities for Developing Education and Research Strategies with a Participatory Approach

The Delphi technique was used to reassess real estate development and management education and training programmes by considering developments both globally and across countries. Applying the Delphi technique involves several stages aimed at identifying, examining, and reaching consensus on the approaches and perspectives of experts within the relevant field or representatives of the target audience on a specific problem (Şahin, 2001). For the Fourth International Conference on Real Estate Development and Management (ICREDM, 2025), a roundtable on "real estate education, institutionalisation, and research systems" was attended by 50 experts holding doctoral or higher academic positions from 21 countries outside of Türkiye, including the United Kingdom, South Africa, Sweden, Norway, Germany, Italy, France, Serbia, Morocco, Qatar, the UAE, Malaysia, Nigeria, Bangladesh, Canada, Singapore, the Russian Federation, Brazil, Japan, and the USA. During the meeting, the views of each expert were gathered regarding the current state and prospects of real estate education and training; changes in real estate expertise and the need for sub-specialisations in the coming years; the scope and functioning of educational activities; the internationalisation of academic programmes and the impact of accreditation; research and application strategies; and trends towards professionalisation within related sectors. The experts' views and recommendations were recorded, and the insights and suggestions are presented anonymously (ICREDM, 2025 Real Estate Education, Institutionalisation and Research System Round Table Discussion 2025).[1]

In the presentation delivered by the meeting moderator, it was stated that universities worldwide have faculties or departments named, for example, real estate development, facility and property management, land management and administration, real estate economics, and real estate investment and finance. These units offer bachelor's, master's, and doctoral programmes. It was also noted that these departments operate under different names and are affiliated with various faculties. With the establishment of the Department of Real Estate Development and Management at Ankara University, a hybrid model was developed, inspired by examples from other countries and universities, to launch its undergraduate and postgraduate programmes. This model is currently under review.

Moreover, it was stressed that undergraduate and postgraduate programmes in advanced technology institutes, faculties of architecture and the built environment, and business faculties—particularly in developed countries—are becoming more widespread. It was noted that there is a need to review all educational programmes related to real estate, establish a standardised curriculum, and hold forums to share views and build consensus on topics such as student and academic exchanges, as well as the development of joint programmes. In this regard, the moderator invited all participants to share their thoughts on the meeting's topics.

During the meeting, numerous participants highlighted the importance of institutionalising real estate to facilitate a transparent comprehension of the actual situation on the ground. It was suggested that universities establish centres of real estate research and that government authorities support activities, including participation in real estate conferences and contributions to academically supported journal publications, as integral components of real estate education. Furthermore, in order to understand the global standing and prospects of real estate, advanced technologies such as artificial intelligence, digitalisation, and blockchain must be swiftly incorporated into standard educational programmes. The participants underscored the necessity for education to possess an interconnected structure, whereby policymakers and industry leaders actively contribute to both the content and the implementation of the educational model. A professor provided the following assessment on this matter:

> Artificial intelligence, deep learning, and big data analysis are included in real estate courses. The hybrid models that surfaced after the pandemic have transformed not only our

[1] The authors would like to express their gratitude to all participants of the roundtable meeting at the ICREDM2025.

> working environments but also our perspective on education. Changes in physical working conditions have directly impacted the real estate sector. As the COVID-19 experience highlighted the need for collaboration with the industry, it is evident that responding to this transformation by training students who meet the sector's requirements is vital. Disciplines such as data science, economics, and urban design should also be integrated into real estate education. Through big data analysis, we can gain a better understanding of how the education sector will adapt to the new era (Participant No. 1)

It was emphasised that establishing strong relationships between academic institutions and all stakeholders in the real estate sector, as well as creating direct links between students and industry representatives, is essential for incorporating the real estate skills required by employers into educational programmes at every level. Such relationships help students to understand the needs of the business world better and motivate them. It was highlighted that the traditional learning approach is rapidly losing relevance; therefore, real estate education should be adapted to meet future, not just current, requirements. It was stated that the department curriculum should be able to answer key questions, such as what qualifications are expected of students and what skills a student should possess by the end of a four-year undergraduate course. Discussions highlighted industry expectations of graduates, their alignment with current curricula, and the importance of fostering entrepreneurship among students to start their own businesses rather than seeking employment after graduation. However, it was also notably acknowledged that adapting to global trends is costly and that building the necessary educational capacity involves challenges.

The extent to which undergraduate and postgraduate course content can be altered is regarded as a significant problem. The curriculum must be sustainable, promote diversity, and consider gender distribution. However, aligning these criteria with international standards remains challenging. At this stage, the principle of "Think globally, act locally" becomes increasingly relevant. For example, legal education provided locally in Sweden is accessible only to students who can overcome the language barrier. Additionally, it was observed that personnel and students with sufficient knowledge of Geographic Information Systems (GIS) can make substantial contributions to the real estate sector.

Many participants in the roundtable emphasised that the characteristics of the era or generation to which students belong should be taken into account when designing undergraduate and postgraduate curricula. Additionally, technological advances such as artificial intelligence (AI) and big data have a direct impact on educational programmes, and therefore, the "connected curriculum" approach should be adopted. It was also highlighted that education must remain open to ongoing reforms, and the importance of developing curricula within a flexible and innovative framework was emphasised. A participant offered the following assessment on the subject:

> Real estate education should be combined with fields closely related to technology. Incorporating data science is especially significant. However, it remains difficult to access the necessary data for research projects in a publicly available manner (Participant No. 2).

It was considered beneficial for the structures and operations of both undergraduate and postgraduate real estate programmes at universities to be adaptable, encouraging students to specialise by enrolling in courses from different programmes. A participant commented on this issue:

> Regardless of the discipline, students should be able to select the courses they wish to take. Students from diverse fields, such as civil engineering, sociology, and architecture, learn together through real estate-related courses that involve both individual and group assignments. Students from different disciplines adapt to the process by working collaboratively in teams. Topics such as sustainability, digitalisation, and innovation should be discussed collectively, and each student should contribute in relation to their area of expertise (Participant No. 3).

Another researcher also emphasised that the digitalisation process will significantly transform real estate education programmes, leading to the following assessment:

> Digitalisation is advancing rapidly in many areas and is swiftly transforming education and training systems. The integration of artificial intelligence (AI) with real estate technologies and its potential to offer procedural advantages must be thoroughly analysed. Simultaneously, this must also be compatible with local needs (Participant No. 4).

Research related to real estate is conducted not only in departments specialising in real estate at universities but also in other related fields. For example, Canada has a very large amount of land assets and real estate capital. However, housing accessibility for the local population is limited in cities like Vancouver and Toronto, which emphasises the importance of real estate development expertise. A new practice called house flipping has been introduced in Canada, involving the purchase of old properties and selling them after renovation. Additionally, topics such as green technology and green construction are increasingly popular in residential and commercial real estate. Nevertheless, a key issue is whether academic curricula align with sector requirements. Moreover, the clear boundaries between different professional disciplines further complicate academic collaboration.

In many countries, the residential and commercial real estate sector faces significant challenges, and there is no universally accepted standard approach within the realm of social housing. For instance, the United Kingdom employs a system centred on "public benefit", while the models used in other countries differ. Furthermore, the contributions of both real estate departments and professional organisations are of utmost importance in developing cohesive policies and effective implementation tools to address housing and shelter concerns.

In the general evaluation section, almost all participants emphasised that the three key elements—the real estate sector, academia, and research—must collaborate, and progress is necessary on issues related to education and training, professional principles and standards, and professionalisation. Expanding internship programmes or industry-based training, which lasts for two or three years at some universities and only covers the final semester at others, is important for linking theory with practice in education. Furthermore, it was conveyed that directing research projects according to sector needs and providing lifelong learning and updated training for sector employees are significant. It was stressed that the education and training policies of countries and regions in the field of real estate and settlement sciences should be developed through a participatory approach, with applications tailored accordingly. It is important to recognise that the outcomes of the search conference held within this framework are significant not only for Ankara University and Türkiye but also for other countries where real estate education is advancing.

4 Concluding Remarks

The establishment of associate, bachelor's, and graduate programmes in fields such as land, real estate, infrastructure, and construction management within higher education institutions has been achieved after a long-standing effort and a challenging journey. In developed countries, these programmes and educational models have been based on statutory requirements and market needs. In universities in developing countries like Türkiye, real estate education and research systems are also designed and implemented within an interdisciplinary framework, aligning with global trends and national needs. However, in many countries, there are issues in recognising and prioritising the importance of university-level programmes related to real estate, and these programmes are sometimes established to pursue international accreditation to enhance their credibility and attract more international students.

Over time, notable structural changes were documented in academic programmes related to real estate. Throughout this progression, many programmes were established, affiliated with faculties such as architecture and the built environment, economics, and business administration. While some of these programmes feature highly technical content, similar to engineering and architecture disciplines, others adopt a more qualitative, verbal approach rooted in economics and finance. Post-1980s, the growing demand within the real estate sector—driven by neoliberal policies and market economy—necessitated both the professionalisation of the educational system and the development of new professional roles. Initially, university programmes for real estate development, land, facility, and property management were formed through the integration of various disciplines—including agricultural engineering, forestry engineering, surveying engineering, city and regional planning, architecture, economics, business administration, public administration, and law—and were structured as a multidisciplinary amalgamation. These programmes, which were mainly multidisciplinary at inception, gradually evolved into an interdisciplinary framework, with sub-specialisations quickly emerging. However, the current dynamic real estate market, technological advancements, and ongoing global economic integration have increased the demand for more comprehensive and in-depth educational programmes. Since the real estate sector is regarded as a complex field—serving as both an economic investment vehicle and an area involving spatial dynamics—it requires an approach based on a thorough and balanced curriculum suited to its diverse nature. Nevertheless, educational programmes related to real estate development established within Turkish higher education institutions have experienced rapid growth in recent years. However, a shortage of qualified faculty remains within sub-disciplines that demand specialised expertise, and the outcomes and competencies of these programmes require further review and discussion.

The education and training programmes at various levels within academic real estate departments require continual updates; indeed, the curricula and outcomes of these programmes are seen to be undergoing rapid transformation over time. The future focus of associate, bachelor's, and postgraduate programmes is expected to be on technological innovations and sustainability. Technologies such as data analytics, artificial intelligence, geographic information systems, computer-aided design (CAD), and building information modelling are increasingly incorporated into the real estate sector, thereby boosting the demand for a skilled workforce within the industry. Furthermore, global challenges such as climate change and environmental sustainability must be given greater emphasis in urban development projects and appropriately reflected within educational curricula. Integrating real estate education in Türkiye with international practices and preparing professionals to meet global standards will help to enhance the sector's competitiveness and encourage the development of new business opportunities. Attention is required to address systems for illegal settlements, land ownership, tenure and security frameworks, urban infrastructure investments and their financing, land consolidation in rural areas, efficient land use, cadastre, land registry, valuation, and taxation—issues faced by many of the world's cities—that are crucial for improving citizens' quality of life. In line with these needs, it is expected that the demand for experts in real estate development and management will grow; consequently, interest in undergraduate and postgraduate programmes in this field at universities is projected to increase. However, for sustainable success in the medium and long term, it is essential to incorporate international professional standards and ethical frameworks in a manner consistent with national conditions, alongside developing an infrastructure for professionalisation.

References

Amsterdam School of Real Estate. (2024). *Our history* [Online]. Available: https://asre.nl/opleiding/master-of-real-estate/?gad_source=1&gclid=CjwKCAjwreW2BhBhEiwAavLwfHEsPOqyPUd_GYtErpxo43puCQ5ERR9s1O1P6m2fh7Nr6bjYvGA2NhoCOt0QAvD_BwE. Accessed 05 September 2024

Ankara HACI Bayram Veli Üniversitesi. (2024). *Taşınmaz Değerleme ve Yönetimi Yüksek Lisans Programı Bilgileri* [Online]. Available: https://obs.hacibayram.edu.tr/oibs/bologna/index.aspx?lang=tr&curOp=showPac&curUnit=95&curSunit=9281#. Accessed 06 October 2024

Ankara Üniversitesi Bologna Bilgi Sistemi. (2024a). *Gayrimenkul Geliştirme ve Yönetimi Bölümü Ders Listesi ve Kredilendirme* [Online]. Available: http://bbs.ankara.edu.tr/Ders_Plani.aspx?bno=3990&bot=1581. Accessed 07 October 2024

Ankara Üniversitesi Bologna Bilgi Sistemi. (2024b). *Gayrimenkul Geliştirme Ve Yönetimi Yüksek Lisans Programı Ders Listesi ve Kredilendirme* [Online]. Available: http://bbs.ankara.edu.tr/Ders_Plani.aspx?bno=3954&bot=1544. Accessed 01 October 2024

Black, R. T., Carn, N. G., Diaz, J., & Rabianski, J. S. (1996). The role of the American Real Estate Society in defining and promulgating the study of real estate. *Journal of Real Estate Research, 12*, 183–194.

Bossard, J., & Dewhurst, J. (1931). A study of existing needs and practices. Philadelphia: University of Pennsylvania Press.

D'Arcy, É., & Taltavull, P. (2009). Real estate education in Europe: Some perspectives on a decade of rapid change. *Journal of European Real Estate Research, 2*, 69–78.

Garrigan, R. T. & Wardrop, R. T. (1981). *Real Estate Programs at Business Schools Accredited by the American Assembly of Collegiate Schools of Business* and the National Association of Realtors.

Geltner, D. (2006). Commercial real estate. *A Companion to Urban Economics*, 211–227.

Healey, P. (1991). Urban regeneration and the development industry. *Regional Studies, 25*, 97–110.

ICREDM. (2025). Real Estate Education, Institutionalisation, and Research System Roundtable Discussion. 2025. In 4th International Conference on Real Estate Development and Management, 3-5 February 2025. Ankara, Türkiye [Online]. Available: https://2025.icredm.org/. Accessed 26 July 2025

K'Akumu, O. A. (2024). Centennium of collegiate real estate education: a prospectus on "the search for a discipline" in the American School of Business. *Journal of European Real Estate Research,* ahead-of-print.

Kariuki, C., Michell, K., & Mirembe, R. D. (2022). Real Estate Education in Africa South of the Sahara. In A. Karam, F. Viruly, C. Kariuki, & V. A. Akujuru (Eds.), *Understanding African Real Estate Markets*. Routledge.

Keleş, R. (2015). Kentleşme Politikası (14. Baskı). *Ankara, Türkiye: İmge Kitabevi*, 422–485.

Keskinok, Ç. (2010). Urban planning experience of Turkey in the 1930s. *Metu Journal of The Faculty of Architecture, 27*, 173–188.

Kim, D.-H., & Pior, M.-Y. (2018). A study on the mainstream of real estate education with core term analysis. *Education Sciences, 8*, 182.

Ling, D. C., & Archer, W. R. (2016). *Real estate principles: A value approach*. McGraw-Hill Education.

McGrath, K., Wang, B., Jackson, B., Kämpf-Dern, A., Malone, K., Funk, D., & Geurts, T. G. (2020). The future of real estate education: A multi-faceted perspective. *Journal of Real Estate Practice and Education, 22*, 40–55.

Miles, M. E., Berens, G., & Weiss, M. A. (2000). *Real estate development: Principles and process*. Urban Land Institute.

ÖSYM. (2024). *2024 Yüksek Öğretim Kurumları Sınavı Yerleştirme Sonuçlarına İlişkin Sayısal Bilgiler* [Online]. Available: https://www.osym.gov.tr/TR,29511/2024-yks-yerlestirme-sonuclarina-iliskin-sayisal-bilgiler.html. Accessed 07 September 2024

Poon, J., Hoxley, M., & Fuchs, W. (2011). Real estate education: An investigation of multiple stakeholders. *Property Management, 29*, 468–487.

Pryke, A. (2019). What can VR do for you? *Journal Property, 2019*, 8–9.

Real Estate Management Program. (2024). *İstanbul Üniversitesi Cerrahpaşa Sosyal Bilimler Meslek Yüksek Okulu Toptan ve Perakende Satış Bölümü Emlak Yönetimi Programı* [Online]. Available: https://sosyalbilimlermyo.iuc.edu.tr/tr/content/bolumler/toptan-ve-perakende-satis-bolumu. Accessed 07 September 2024

Real Estate Management Program Course Contents. (2024). *Anadolu Üniversitesi Eskişehir Meslek Yüksekokulu Emlak Yönetimi Programı Ders İçerikleri* [Online]. Available: https://abp.anadolu.edu.tr/tr/program/dersler/467/13. Accessed 07 September 2024

Şahin, A. E. (2001). Eğitim Araştırmalarında Delphi Tekniği ve Kullanımı. *Hacettepe Üniversitesi Eğitim Fakültesi Dergisi, 20*, 215–220.

Scheurwater, S. (2017). The future of valuations. *Report for Royal Institution of Chartered Surveyors*, 23–25.

Schulte, K. W. (2012). *Real estate education throughout the world: Past, present and future*. Springer US.

Schulte, K.-W. (2003). The role of investment and finance in real estate education and research throughout the world. *Property Management, 21*, 97–113.
Schulte, K.-W., Schulte-Daxbök, G., Holzmann, C. & Wiffler, M. (2005). *Internationalisation of real estate education*. ERES Conference: Dublin, Ireland, 2005.
Shi-Ming, Y. (2001). New paradigms in real estate education. *Pacific Rim Property Research Journal, 7*, 79–88.
Sinop Üniversitesi Öğrenci Bilgi Sistemi. (2024). *Gayrimenkul Geliştirme ve Yönetimi Bölümü Programı Bilgileri* [Online]. Available: https://obs.sinop.edu.tr/oibs/bologna/index.aspx?lang=tr&curOp=showPac&curUnit=9&curSunit=8091#. Accessed 01 October 2024
Study in Türkiye. (2024). *Gayrimenkul Alanında Lisansüstü Eğitim Programları* [Online]. Available: https://www.studyinturkiye.gov.tr/StudySearch/List?Length=11. Accessed 07 September 2024
Tanrivermiş, H. (2019). Türkiye Ekonomisinde İnşaat ve Gayrimenkul Sektörlerinin Rolleri ve Gelişme Eğilimlerinin Değerlendirilmesi (Assesment of The Roles of Construction and Real Estate Sectors and Their Development Trends in Turkey), In: *Kent, İnşaat ve Ekonomi Kongresi* (pp. 36–57). TMMOB Mimarlar Odası Gaziantep Şubesi, 2-3-4 Mayıs 2019, Gaziantep.
Veuger, J. (2018). Trust in a viable real estate economy with disruption and blockchain. *Facilities, 36*, 103–120.
Weeks, H. S., & Finch, J. H. (2003). An analysis of real estate curriculum requirements at AACSB International-Accredited Institutions. *Journal of Real Estate Practice and Education, 6*, 257–268.
YÖK. (2024). *Yükseköğretim Bilgi Yönetimi Sistemi Bölümler Hakkında Bilgiler* [Online]. Available: https://istatistik.yok.gov.tr/. Accessed 07 September 2024

Harun Tanrıvermiş is a distinguished professor who occupies the esteemed position at the Ankara University top management level as founder and head of the Department of Real Estate Development and Management, and founder and current dean of the Faculty of Applied Sciences at Ankara University. Professor Tanrıvermiş also currently works as the vice rector at Ankara University. He attained his B.Sc., M.Sc., and Ph.D. degrees from the Department of Agricultural Economics at Ankara University, specialising in land and real estate economics, land and real estate valuation, as well as natural resources and environmental economics. Furthermore, he earned an M.Sc. in environmental management through the MED-CAMPUS Programme in 1996. Professor Tanrıvermiş has published approximately 400 papers, including 43 international and 55 national peer-reviewed articles, which have been published in various high-impact journals. Additionally, he has presented 48 international and 74 national proceedings, either in full or as abstracts, at numerous conferences. He is also credited with writing 39 books and 17 book chapters. Moreover, his works concentrate on the land and real estate valuation, land and real estate economics, real estate development and project appraisal, urban transformation and sustainability, sustainable real estate development, facility and real estate management, land management, administration and polices, measuring and reporting of real estate sustainability and ESG, digital transformation in real estate and real estate technologies.

Muhammed Said Yılmaz is a lecturer at the Department of Real Estate Development and Management, Faculty of Applied Sciences, Ankara University, Türkiye. He graduated from the Department of City and Regional Planning at Middle East Technical University (METU) in 2014. He completed his master's degree in the Department of Real Estate Development and Management in 2020. He is currently pursuing his Ph.D. and working as a lecturer in the Department of Real Estate Development and Management at the Faculty of Applied Sciences, Ankara University. There, he conducts research in the fields of urban transformation, project development, and project financing.

Amani Michael Uisso is an expert in the fields of real estate development, urban transformation, and land management, boasting an extensive academic and professional career that spans both Tanzania and Türkiye. He holds a doctorate and a master's degree in real estate development and management from Ankara University, Türkiye, along with a bachelor's degree in land management and valuation from Ardhi University, Tanzania. Dr. Uisso's research centres on urban development, land management, and administration, providing valuable insights to the discipline through numerous publications. His work effectively bridges academic rigour with practical applications, addressing significant challenges in urban transformation and sustainable land use. Currently, Dr. Uisso holds a position within the President's Office, where he applies his expertise to inform policy and strategic initiatives. In addition to his contributions to public service, he is a certified real estate appraiser and a highly sought-after consultant in real estate development, offering specialised guidance to projects that shape urban environments. With a steadfast commitment to advancing knowledge and practice in the fields of real estate and urban development, Dr. Uisso consistently and significantly contributes to both academia and industry.

The Effect of Coastal Areas Management on Real Estate

Mehmet Ülger, Yeşim Tanrıvermiş, and F. Nihan Özdemir Sönmez

Abstract

In Türkiye, the 1982 Constitution and the Coastal Law of 1990 have established various restrictions regarding real estate along the coast and coastlines. These restrictions have led to legal challenges concerning the status of previously registered coastal real estate. The diverse practices among institutions have complicated the resolution of this issue. To address these challenges and other coastal concerns, the concept of integrated coastal zone management (ICZM) planning has been introduced in Türkiye. ICZM planning studies have commenced in numerous coastal cities. Nevertheless, the ownership status of the real estate encompassed within the ICZM plans is of paramount importance; issues related to coastline determination, deficiencies in modelling studies for estimating shoreline change, the scarcity of real estate appraisers in ICZM planning studies, and the observation that ICZM plans are not fully integrated into the planning stages but rather serve primarily as guiding documents for other planning studies have undermined the efficacy of ICZM plans. This chapter explores the status of coastal real estate while considering national and international legislation from historical and contemporary perspectives. It discusses the legal status of coastal real estate, the restrictive provisions of current legislation, and the implications of coastal management on real estate.

Keywords

Coastal zone management · Real estate value

M. Ülger (✉) · Y. Tanrıvermiş · F. Nihan Özdemir Sönmez
Department of Real Estate Development and Management, Faculty of Applied Sciences, Ankara University, Ankara, Türkiye
e-mail: mehmet.ulger@ankara.edu.tr; aliefendioglu@ankara.edu.tr; sonmezo@ankara.edu.tr

T. Just et al. (eds.), *Understanding Türkiye's Real Estate Markets*, Management for Professionals, https://doi.org/10.1007/978-3-032-13297-0_33

1 Introduction

Coastal regions serve as critical junctures where human activities and natural resources intersect, facilitating a variety of endeavours, such as tourism, industry, commerce, and transportation. This set of interests has led to a rise in population, settlement patterns, and urbanisation along the coast (Özelçi Eceral & Özdemir Sönmez, 2011). According to the 2012 population data for Türkiye, 60.6% of the total population resides within 100 kilometres of the coastal area (Karaburun & Karakuyu, 2015).

The prevalence of second homes acquired or leased for vacation purposes in coastal regions, combined with the disproportionate utilisation of Türkiye's coastlines, results in a decline in visual quality, inefficient investments, and an adverse effect on tourism (Emekli, 2014). In addition to the increase in second homes, there is also a notable rise in the number of constructions, including tourism facilities, ports, fishermen's shelters, coastal protection structures, and roadways. This level of human activity and construction underscores the imperative for a comprehensive planning process and the equitable distribution of responsibilities among institutions managing Türkiye's coastal areas, thereby elevating the concept of spatial planning as a critical consideration during the planning phase.

Spatial planning in Türkiye is delineated into three distinct stages: spatial strategy, environmental plans, and zoning plans, which are organised hierarchically from top to bottom. The decisions and regulations established by the upper-level plans shall not contradict those articulated within the lower-level plans. In accordance with the Spatial Plans Production Regulation, the Integrated Coastal Zone Plan (ICZP) has been emphasised prominently. Although the ICZP is not encompassed within the spatial planning stages, it is characterised as a strategic plan, serving as a guiding framework for sub-scale plans.

The Ministry of Environment, Urbanisation, and Climate Change oversees ICZM and ICZP studies that were initiated in Türkiye in 2007. However, the Directorate General of Spatial Planning, the BKAY, collaborates with numerous organisations and institutions (Gülbitti & Özüduru, 2020). In conjunction with the coastal legislation in Türkiye, ICZM and ICZP have a substantial impact on real estate in coastal or near-coastal areas. This chapter provides an examination of the current state of coastal real estate by analysing both national and international legislation from historical and contemporary perspectives. The discussion encompasses the legal status of coastal real estate, the restrictive provisions inherent in the existing legislation, and the influence of coastal management on real estate.

2 Historical Development of Coastal Legislation in Türkiye

The initial legal regulation in Türkiye about the coastal areas is encapsulated in the 1926 Constitution, which serves as the fundamental and most significant statute asserting that the coastlines are accessible to all, yet remain under the sovereignty and control of the State. Subsequent to the 1926 Constitution, the first legal provision addressing coastal matters was instituted through the Municipal Law of 1930. This Law specifies that maritime areas developed by the Municipality will be assigned to the Municipality. This regulation established, for the first time, a legal framework specifically addressing coastal matters related to marine reclamation. The "Municipal Building and Roads Law" of 1933 underscored the necessity for a designated area that is available for public use at a specified distance from the shoreline. This Law explicitly states that an area extending 10 meters from the shoreline shall be designated for communal use, accompanied by a prohibition of construction within this 10-meter zone. The 1961 Constitution introduced the principle of public interest concerning coastal areas. Furthermore, it was articulated that expropriation might occur with regard to public interest in order to safeguard coastal regions (Ülger, 2022).

To facilitate planned construction along the coastlines, the inaugural comprehensive legal regulation regarding construction and usage conditions was instituted in 1972 through an amendment to the Zoning Law of that period (Serdaroğlu Sağ & Yıldırım, 2011). In this context, the implementing regulation was promulgated in 1975. According to this regulation, no structures may be erected within the 30-meter coastal zone (Gezim & Kiper, 1991). However, the provisions outlined in the Constitution and subsequent laws were inadequate for the establishment of comprehensive coastal legislation. The constitutional provisions necessary for formulating the legislation concerning the legal status and utilisation of coastal areas could be enacted under the 1982 Constitution. The 1982 Constitution stipulates that the coastlines are under the sovereignty and authority of the state, prioritising public interest in benefiting from coastal areas and delineating the processes for coastline usage and the compensation for expropriation costs (Kurt, 2015). Upon examining the historical evolution of coastal legislation in Türkiye in relation to national law, it is imperative to assess the contemporary coastal legislation alongside the international conventions that influence the development of coastal zone management.

3 International Conventions

The United Nations Environment Programme (UN Environment) established the Regional Seas Programme in 1974 to coordinate activities directed at protecting the marine environment. The Mediterranean Action Plan (MAP) was adopted in 1975 as the inaugural UN environmental initiative. The "Convention on the Protection of the Mediterranean Sea against Pollution" (Barcelona Convention) was adopted in Barcelona on 16 February 1976 to establish the legal framework and subsequently entered into force in 1978 (UN, 2017).

In 1980, Türkiye ratified the Convention on the Protection of the Mediterranean Sea against Pollution, the "Protocol on the Protection of the Mediterranean Sea from Pollution as a Result of Unloading from Ships and Aircraft", and "the Protocol on Combating and Cooperating against the Pollution of the Mediterranean Sea with Oil and other Harmful Substances in Emergencies". The phrase "the development and protection of the Mediterranean Region within a broad set of interrelated measures", as stated in the Convention on the Protection of the Mediterranean Sea against Pollution, emphasises the necessity of considering and managing the required measures for the sea and coasts in Türkiye comprehensively (GNAT, 1980).

In accordance with the resolutions established at the UN Environment and Development Summit convened in Rio de Janeiro in 1992, the Barcelona Convention was formulated in 1995 to manage the marine environment and coastal regions. It encompasses various topics, including public participation, sustainable development, and environmental impact assessment. Furthermore, the title of the "Convention on the Protection of the Mediterranean Sea Against Pollution" was amended to "Convention on the Protection of the Marine Environment and Coastal Zone of the Mediterranean." Türkiye ratified this convention in 2002 (LG, 2002). Among the seven protocols associated with the Barcelona Convention is the "Protocol for Integrated Coastal Zone Management in the Mediterranean Sea". However, Türkiye has yet to accede to the "Mediterranean Integrated Coastal Zone Management Protocol".

The Athens Declaration was ratified during COP 19, which took place in Athens from February 9 to 12, 2016. At the culmination of this event, the UNEP (United Nations Environment Programme)/MAP 2016–2021 Mediterranean Strategy for Sustainable Development and the 2016–2021 Medium Term Strategy were both adopted. In addition, a Memorandum of Understanding was executed between the secretariats of the Convention on the Protection of the Black Sea against Pollution and the Convention on the Protection of the Marine Environment and Coastal Zone of the Mediterranean. Türkiye is the sole nation that is a party to both conventions (MFART, 2022). Furthermore, the 22nd meeting of the parties to the convention (COP22) of the Barcelona Convention and its Protocols occurred in Türkiye from December 7 to 10, 2021.

Although Türkiye has not signed the Protocol on Integrated Coastal Zone Management in the Mediterranean, one of the protocols of the Barcelona Convention, Türkiye actively participates in international meetings convened by the United Nations Environment Programme (UNEP). Türkiye formulates its national legislation in accordance with the decisions made during these meetings.

4 Current Coastal Legislation

The inaugural comprehensive constitutional regulation of the coasts was instituted in the 1982 Constitution. It delineated that the coasts are subject to the sovereignty and control of the State, emphasising the public interest in the utilisation of these coastal areas. The stipulations governing the usage and benefits derived from the coasts shall be regulated by law. Furthermore, the Constitution articulates that in instances where the public interest is involved, privately owned real estate may be appropriated, with compensation established in accordance with the law. The 1982 Constitution established a broad framework for the coasts, signifying that pertinent laws and regulations are to be enacted.

4.1 Coastal Law

The first and only specific legislation pertaining to the coastlines in Türkiye is the Coastal Law of 1990, which was formulated in accordance with the 1982 Constitution. This legislation was enacted to safeguard the coastal areas and shorelines, ensure public accessibility to these regions, and establish principles for their utilisation while taking into account public interest.

When this legislation is examined with respect to coastal regions, crucial definitions such as "coast," "coastline," "shore edge line," "shoreline," and "recreational areas" are elucidated, thereby averting any ambiguity that may arise from varying definitions in other statutes. In broader terms, the law.

- Shoreline: The virtual demarcation established by connecting the points at which the sea intersects with the land.
- Shoreline boundary: The demarcation that delineates regions such as coastal beaches, where marine influence is evident from the shoreline extending landward.
- Coast: The region situated between the shoreline and the edge of the shoreline.
- Coastline: A region extending a minimum of 100 metres from the shoreline to the land.
- Recreational Areas: Areas designated for relaxation and entertainment include outdoor seating arrangements, culinary and dining spaces, a swimming pool, a fountain, zones for recreational and athletic activities, and landscaped vegetation areas.

In accordance with the Coastal Law, it is imperative to delineate the shore edge line for any proposal or application regarding coastal areas. A committee establishes the shore edge line, the qualifications of which are outlined in the Law. The decisions rendered by this committee become effective only following approval by the Ministry of Environment, Urbanisation and Climate Change (MEUCC). The law explicitly forbids the construction of structures or the undertaking of excavations in coastal regions, as well as the creation of any obstructions. Proposed plans for coastal and shoreline areas must adhere strictly to the Coastal Law and the Regulation on the Implementation of the Coastal Law (RICL). The plans submitted attain finality upon approval within the framework of the Tourism Incentive Law (TIL). The municipality oversees applications in neighbouring areas, whereas governorships are responsible for managing other locations, with inspections being executed by the pertinent Ministries. The law notably emphasises the principle of public interest as well as the TIL.

The RICL has been enacted in accordance with the coastal law. This regulation delineates the coastline into two segments of 50 metres each, specifying the types of construction permitted within both segments. Accurately determining coastal boundaries is imperative for effective coastal planning and the identification of permissible construction zones. To define these areas, it is essential to establish the shoreline accurately (Fig. 1).

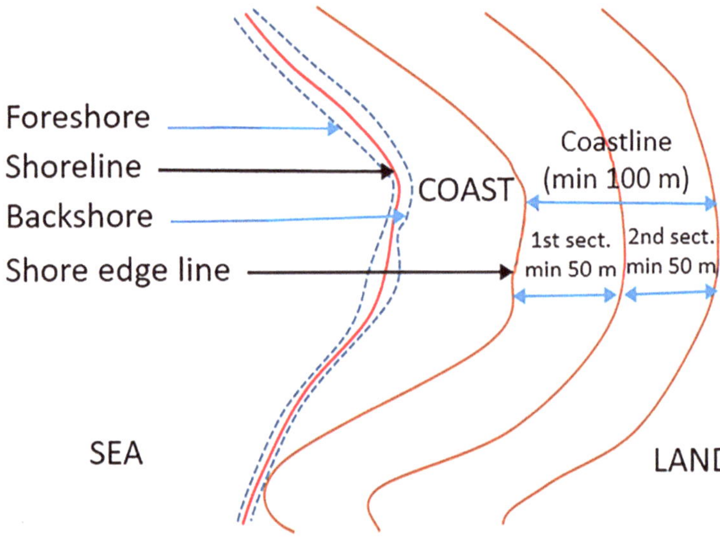

Fig. 1 Definitions in the Coastal Law. Source: own depiction

Prior to the enactment of the coastal law, the status of real estate registered with title deeds along the coasts was delineated by the RICL. In accordance with the regulation, the coastal sections of real estate will be identified, and the title deeds of privately owned real estate situated on the coast will be annulled. Nevertheless, the regulation established in 1994 introduced the notion of partial construction. In accordance with zoning plans sanctioned before July 11, 1992, a stipulation was formulated to delineate the coastline's boundaries, taking into account the zoning areas and constructions along the coast. The rights of proprietors whose buildings along the coastline were completed to at least the plinth level and who secured a construction permit under the prevailing plan or legislation prior to July 11, 1992, are safeguarded. These stipulations governing partial construction have instituted regulations for coastal development and do not extend to constructions situated along the coasts.

4.2 Tourism Incentive Law (TIL)

The Tourism Infrastructure Law (TIL) was enacted in 1982 to regulate and enhance the tourism sector. The law delineates the Culture and Tourism Protection and Development Zones (CTPDZ). To facilitate organised and sector-specific development, regions exhibiting significant tourism potential are to be used. A presidential decree establishes the boundaries of these regions. Furthermore, the concept of "Tourism Centres" is explicitly defined within the legal framework. These centres are recognised as locations that are primarily designated for development, with their respective locations and boundaries determined and publicly announced by presidential decree. The primary objective is to safeguard and use the coastlines within the specified regions and centres while taking public interest into account. Accordingly, it is stipulated that constructions and facilities may be established along the coastlines without the necessity of title deed registration in accordance with the zoning plans. These facilities are authorised for operation, and the characteristics of the coastlines may be leveraged without causing degradation.

According to the TIL, the Ministry of Culture and Tourism (MCT) is authorised to formulate, amend, and endorse all varieties of coastal planning plans within the confines of the designated regions and centres. The documents and viewpoints requested from other institutions and organisations for the planning and infrastructural activities undertaken by the Ministry in these areas must be submitted within three months. Failure to comply will result in the Ministry undertaking the necessary actions. Prior to the execution of projects such as leasing, allocation, sales, and projections pertaining to infrastructure and superstructure that may precipitate environmental impacts, an appropriate opinion should be procured from the Ministry by other institutions and organisations operating in these regions and centres.

The Ministry may allocate sub-regions, parcels, or the entirety of the CTPDZ to investors in alignment with the objectives of the plan. The Ministry grants the right of construction and easement on these properties in favour of the principal investor, subject to the conditions stipulated by the Ministry of Treasury and Finance. A zoning plan is formulated and sanctioned by the Ministry for these designated regions or sub-regions. The parcels delineated through the zoning plans may be operated and leased, and the construction rights conferred to the investors can be transferred. Pursuant to the Expropriation Law, urgent expropriation may be executed to facilitate the utilisation of privately owned real estate within the designated regions for tourism-related investments. Expropriated properties are registered under the ownership of the Treasury.

Within the framework of the law, the Regulation on Planning and Implementation in CTPDZ and Tourism Centres has been enacted. The regulation stipulates that the initial 50 meters of the coastline shall be designated as open space for communal usage. In the primary section, there may be recreational facilities, including a promenade and resting areas, pedestrian pathways, dining and seating spaces, swimming pools, cooking zones, exhibition areas, green spaces, fountains, playgrounds, sports facilities, landing ramps, and bicycle paths. It specifies that daily tourism structures may be constructed on the subsequent 50-meter section of the coastline.

4.3 Environmental Law

In legal terminology, water and soil regions possessing ecological significance and exhibiting sensitivity to environmental degradation and pollution may be designated as a "Special Environmental Protection Area (SEPA)" to facilitate essential amendments concerning natural resources and biological life. It has been indicated that the pertinent provisions of the Coastal Law are inapplicable to the plans and projects associated with the SEPA.

In the SEPA, multiple units have been established within the framework of the MEUCC to safeguard environmental values, address challenges, implement necessary precautions, identify protection and utilisation strategies, and formulate and ratify plans and revisions across various scales. In line with protection and construction principles, authorities have been delegated to the respective units. All constructions within the SEPA require permission and are subject to inspection in accordance with the guidelines set forth by the institution. All plans and projects will undergo re-evaluation, and density and floor limitations may be imposed on ongoing plans to prevent disruption to the natural environment and to ensure alignment with ecological principles while adhering to coastal legislative provisions. It is indicated that, contingent upon fulfilling the requisite facilities in the region, operating and construction permits may be granted. Structures that do not conform to the implementation and master development plans, as well as relevant legislation, are subject to demolition, and constructions that contravene the Zoning Law may be suspended.

4.4 Zoning Law

The Development Law of 1985 stipulates that the Privatisation Administration (PA) is empowered to formulate zoning plans and implement revisions of all varieties and scales, which encompasses areas governed by the Coastal Law and the TCC, pertaining to real estate incorporated within the privatisation program. It has been stipulated that privatised companies may not alter the plans approved in accordance with this provision for a period of five years from the date of transfer of the land and plots. During these 5 years, any amendments to the zoning plan will be executed by the PA in accordance with the judicial ruling concerning the zoning plans.

4.5 Environmental Impact Assessment Regulation

The Environmental Impact Assessment (EIA) Regulation was promulgated to govern all procedures and methodologies to be adhered to during the EIA process. It encompasses provisions concerning the categories of projects for which an EIA will be mandated and guidelines to be observed throughout the EIA process. Projects encompassed by the EIA, as stated in the regulation, are categorically divided into two segments: (a) projects subject to environmental impact assessment, and (b) projects contingent upon selection and elimination criteria.

Concerning the coasts, it is articulated that coastal structures (including breakwaters, spurs, etc.) capable of inducing alterations in coastal dynamics are integral to the selection and elimination criteria. The concept of "Sensitive Regions" is also addressed within the regulation. Sensitive Regions are delineated as locations that exhibit vulnerability to environmental impacts due to their qualitative and quantitative characteristics, wherein pollution levels have escalated to a degree that jeopardises public and environmental health. These areas necessitate protection owing to their alignment with local legislation or international conventions.

4.6 Spatial Plans Production Regulations

Spatial Plans Construction Regulation: This regulation aims to develop spatial plans that safeguard historical, cultural, natural, and physical values. It seeks to establish a balance between preservation and utilisation, promote sustainable development at national, urban, and regional levels, and create healthy and safe environments that ensure a high quality of life. Furthermore, it serves to inform decisions regarding construction and land use. In the realm of spatial planning, the various levels are categorised hierarchically from top to bottom as spatial strategy plans, environmental plans, master zoning plans, and implementation zoning plans.

The regulation elucidates the concept of integrated coastal zones for the first time. This concept encompasses spatial actions, strategies, target proposals, and management plans designed to equilibrate the use and preservation of coastal areas. It adheres to the schematic and graphic planning system at a scale of 1:25,000 or 1:50,000, situated within the broader framework of the strategic planning methodology consistent with the plan and report. It is defined as a plan formulated in collaboration with organisations.

Including the concept of an environmental plan within the regulation safeguarding and enhancing the natural characteristics of coastal regions, like numerous other areas, was considered fundamental during the preparation of the environmental plan. It is asserted that it is mandatory to depict the approved coastal edge line, as established in the zoning plans, on the layouts designated for coastal regions.

In formulating plans to identify settlement areas, data and studies pertaining to the geographical attributes collected from various institutions and organisations are meticulously evaluated. The current maps at the designated scales are superimposed, followed by the execution of a threshold analysis. This analysis systematically examines agricultural lands, forested regions, protected zones, sensitive areas, coastal locales, and other physical and environmental information, in addition to disaster scenarios.

4.7 Strategic Environmental Assessment Regulation

The Strategic Environmental Assessment (SEA) Regulation was promulgated to govern all procedures, principles, and methodologies to be adhered to during the SEA stages. This regulation is designed to incorporate environmental considerations into the process of formulating and sanctioning plans or programs that may substantially impact the environment, all within the parameters of a sustainable development approach to environmental protection. It has been developed in accordance with European Union legislation, considering the "European Parliament and Council Directive on the Evaluation of the Effects of Certain Plans and Programs on the Environment".

The regulation also incorporates coastal management. It encompasses all methodologies for preparing or completing SEA for the plans and programs pertaining to these areas. It offers the requisite training in accordance with the established processes. Furthermore, it stipulates that the provisions of the regulation shall not apply to the zoning plans.

The SEA plays a pivotal role in formulating the integrated management strategy in coastal regions. It incorporates research undertaken through a participatory methodology, which is compiled into a comprehensive report before public institutions endorse plans and programs.

4.8 Presidential Decree

The Presidential Decree No. 1, dated 2018, delineated the MEUCC's responsibilities and authorities. In this context, the Ministry is charged with establishing the principles and procedures to be adhered to by the respective administrations in the renewal, transformation, and enhancement practices to be executed in coastal regions and coastal environment facilities.

Through the issuance of the decree, the concept of integrated coastal area management and planning has been placed on the agenda within the array of responsibilities and authorities of the General Directorate of Spatial Planning (GDSP). The procedures to be carried out in accordance with the Coastal Areas Regulation include the approval of reports and projects resulting from geotechnical and geological investigations, the determination and confirmation of the coastline, the registration of these results, and the carrying out of investigations, research, and planning at all scales for coastal and reclamation areas and their adjacent regions. Furthermore, the GDSP will be responsible for creating, endorsing, and executing the requisite maps.

4.9 Integrated Coastal Zone Management Principles in Türkiye

The boundaries of integrated coastal areas in Türkiye have been approved by the MEUCC, taking into consideration the use, natural environment, and activities linked to the coasts in relation to historical, social, economic, and transportation aspects. When necessary, input from relevant institutions and organisations is incorporated. The plans are founded on a participatory management system and a holistic approach. To date, studies concerning ICZM planning have been completed or are approaching completion for the majority of Türkiye's coastlines (Fig. 2).

The ICZM Plan process in Türkiye comprises four principal stages: the preparatory phase, which encompasses the preparation of the research report, the development of alternative draft plans, and the formulation of the final plan.

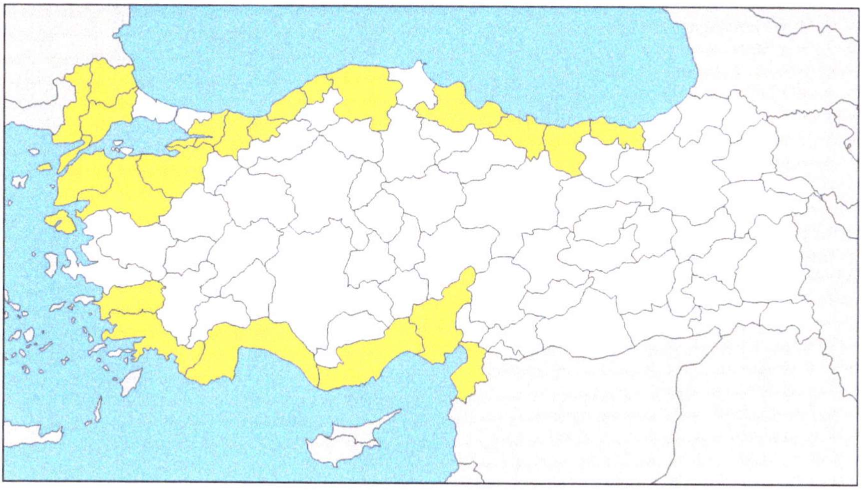

Fig. 2 Places where the ICZM plan has been completed or the plan studies are in progress in Türkiye. Source: own depiction

5 An Overview of ICZM Plans in Terms of Real Estate

ICZM plans in Türkiye are the result of thorough examination and research conducted within the framework of applicable legislation. Nevertheless, the provision within the legislation that designates ICZM plans merely as a guiding framework for additional planning studies undermines their effectiveness. During the formulation of integrated coastal zone plans, data is acquired from pertinent institutions and organisations, followed by comprehensive research and analysis based on this data. This research encompasses investigations into disaster hazards, including but not limited to tsunamis and floods, wind and wave climate, marine currents, sea level rise, storm surges, and applications about the coastline and shore edge line. Moreover, it has a direct impact on the evolving values and ownership statuses of real estate.

5.1 Factors Affecting Real Estate in ICZM Plans

In ICZM plans, it is essential to predict the changes, including erosion and agglomeration, that will occur along the shorelines of the proposed coastal infrastructure (such as harbours, piers, etc.). This necessitates a comprehensive verification of the wind and wave climate analysis pertaining to the coastal region, as well as the determination of the direction and magnitude of coastal sediment transport. Currently, numerical model analyses for estimating shoreline changes are not yet conducted within ICZM plans. Consequently, the coastal structures (e.g., harbours, piers) significantly alter the wave flow patterns, leading to notable movements of erosion and agglomeration along the coasts (see Fig. 3).

Fig. 3 Coastal erosion Karasu/Sakarya/Türkiye. Source: Ülger (2022)

Fig. 4 Underwater shore edge line (yellow line) and real estate Karasu/Sakarya/Türkiye. Source: Ülger and Tanrıvermiş (2022)

This erosion and agglomeration significantly impact the coastline and the shoreline. The necessity to redefine the shoreline, which is inundated due to erosion, becomes increasingly prominent. Furthermore, the redefined shoreline also modifies the property status and values of real estate in this coastal region (Fig. 4) (Ülger & Tanrıvermiş, 2022).

Table 1 Compensation amounts appraised by the ECHR

No	Amount requested by the real estate owner (Euro)	Compensation amounts appraised by the ECHR (Euro)
1	37,390.00	29,000.00
2	29,000.00	26,000.00
3	50,300.00	50,300.00
4	56,300.00	50,000.00
5	100,000.00	10,000.00
6	144,651.00	15,500.00
7	78,300.00	15,000.00
8	291,000.00	150,000.00

Source: Şimşek (2010)

Table 2 Compensation amounts appraised by Turkish Courts

No	City/ District	Zone	Parcel Area (m^2)	Payment Year	Compensation amounts appraised by Turkish Courts (Turkish Lira)
1	Sakarya/ Karasu	Aşağı incili	675	2020	25,343.60
2	Sakarya/ Karasu	Aşağı İncili	675	2020	207,042.43
3	Sakarya/ Karasu	Aşağı incili	675	2020	61,322.29

Source: Ülger (2022)

5.2 Ownership Status of Real Estate on the Coasts

In accordance with the prevailing legislation in Türkiye, the coasts are subject to the sovereignty and control of the State. Consequently, they cannot be subjected to private ownership. Prior to 1972, however, the legislation allowed for the acquisition of private property along the coasts. Given that the laws enacted subsequent to 1972 prohibit private ownership of coastal areas, the public has initiated legal proceedings to annul the title deeds of properties established before that year. The European Court of Human Rights (ECHR), to which Türkiye is a party, has ruled that the cancellation of title deed registrations without compensatory measures constitutes a violation of property rights. The ECHR has asserted that such cancellations disrupt the fair balance between individual rights and public interests. In acknowledgement of the ECHR's ruling, the Turkish judiciary has resolved to provide compensation to owners of real estate whose title deeds have been annulled due to the coastal location of their properties (Şimşek, 2010).

The primary issue at hand is that the judicial body possesses the discretion to ascertain the compensation amount to be allocated as a result of expropriation. The inconsistency observed in the compensation valuations provided by the ECHR (Table 1) and the Turkish Courts (Table 2), even when evaluated internally, impedes the resolution of the matter between the property owners and the public.

6 Conclusion

In Türkiye, where 60.6% of the total population resides within 100 km of the coast, the most effective legal regulations for the protection and utilisation of coastal areas were established with the enactment of the 1982 Constitution. Subsequently, the Coastal Law and its implementing regulations were introduced to address matters related to coastal real estate and coastlines. However, it has been observed that institutions undertook various applications regarding the real estate recorded in the title deed along the coasts and coastlines prior to the implementation of the Coastal Law, resulting in a jurisdictional conflict among institutions in the planning of these areas.

Following the issuance of the Presidential Decree aimed at resolving the conflict of authority among the various institutions, the roles and powers of the MEUCC have been articulated. The MEUCC is entrusted with delineating the principles and procedures that the pertinent administrations must adhere to during the processes of renewal, transformation, and improvement within the coastal regions and facilities that fall under its jurisdiction. The decree has introduced the concepts of ICZM and ICZP within the framework of the powers and responsibilities of the GDSP. The GDSP has commenced ICZM studies encompassing a substantial stretch of the Turkish coastlines, and a number of planning studies have been successfully concluded.

The exclusion of ICZM plans in Türkiye from the various stages of spatial planning, where they are used solely as guiding frameworks for other studies, diminishes their efficacy. The ICZM plans are hindered by insufficiently qualified studies necessary to delineate the shoreline, assess the impacts of coastal structures (including harbours, fishing shelters, piers, etc.) on the coastline, and conduct comprehensive evaluations of the real estate potentially affected by shoreline alterations. Moreover, persistent issues regarding property and the valuation of coastal real estate remain prevalent. The lack of detailed analyses for real estate presents a considerable challenge. In addition, the absence of an effective monitoring and inspection framework for ICZM plans, combined with inadequate institutional and local infrastructure as well as insufficient expert personnel, significantly undermines the overall effectiveness of these plans.

To address the adverse effects of ICZM plans on real estate,

- Define ICZM plans as an integral component of the spatial planning process in order to enhance their effectiveness.
- Incorporate reports regarding the effects of shoreline alterations on real estate in ICZM plans, along with analyses of compensation and fluctuations in value that may occur.
- In ICZM plans, reliable data essential for estimating shoreline changes is collected and maintained by a central authority through systematic measurements, including wind speed, wave heights, and sea level assessments.
- Establish a monitoring unit dedicated to supervising and overseeing ICZM plans in coastal cities is essential.
- Include experts in real estate valuation as participants in the commissions established to assess the relationship between the shoreline and property boundaries in ICZM plans.

References

UN. (2017). United Nations Environment Program. *Regional Seas programmes covering areas beyond national jurisdictions*. Retrived from https://www.un.org/Depts/los/biodiversity-workinggroup/Regional_seas_programmes_ABNJ.pdf. Accessed October 14, 2022

Emekli, G. (2014). The importance of tourism geography in terms of the second home concept and the development of second homes in Turkey. *Aegean Journal of Geography, 23*(1), 25–42.

Gezim, F., & Kiper, P. (1991). Coastal area planning problems and an evaluation of the last 30 years in Turkish urbanism. In *15th World Urbanism Day in Türkiye, 3rd Turkish Urbanism Congress* (pp. 363–369), İzmir.

Grand National Assembly of Türkiye (GNAT). (1980). *Law on the approval of the Convention for the Protection of the Mediterranean Sea Against Pollution signed in Barcelona on 16 February 1976 and its two protocols and annexes*. https://www5.tbmm.gov.tr/tutanaklar/KANUNLAR_KARARLAR/kanuntbmmc064/kanunmgkc064/kanunmgkc06402328.pdf. Accessed October 14, 2022

Gülbitti, M., & Özüduru, B. (2020). Evaluation of integrated coastal zone management processes in Turkey in relation to strategic spatial planning. *Planning, Union of Chambers of Turkish Engineers and Architects, 30*(1), 36–53.

Karaburun, A., & Karakuyu, M. (2015). Analysis of Turkish districts and their 2012 populations by elevation and proximity to the coast. *International Journal of Geography and Geography Education, 32*, 74–87.

Kurt, S. (2015). Historical development of coastal use laws and regulations in Turkey. *Eastern Geographical Review, 20*(33), 91–110. https://doi.org/10.17295/dcd.64190

Legal Gazette (LG). (2002). *International treaty*. https://www.resmigazete.gov.tr/eskiler/2002/08/20020822.htm#1. Accessed October 16, 2022

Ministry of Foreign Affairs of the Republic of Türkiye (MFART). (2022). *Barcelona Convention*. https://www.mfa.gov.tr/barselona-sozlesmesi.tr.mfa. Accessed October 5, 2022

Özelçi Eceral, T., & Özdemir Sönmez, N. (2011). Integrated coastal zone management and Turkey's coastal planning legislation and institutional structure. In *Legal and administrative dimensions of planning* (pp. 118–135). Technical Research and Application General Directorate Publications, Ministry of Public Works and Settlement. ISBN: 978-975-490-010-1

Serdaroğlu Sağ, N., & Yıldırım, H. H. (2011). Evaluation of the concept of public interest in coastal legislation. *Selcuk University Journal of Engineering, Science and Technology, 26*(2), 38–54.

Şimşek, S. (2010). The issue of ownership in coastal areas: A proposal for a solution in light of the annulment decisions of the European Court of Human Rights. *Journal of the Turkish Court of Accounts, 77*, 87–118.

Ülger, M. (2022). *Numerical modelling of the impact of coastal line change on real estate value* (Doctoral dissertation). Ankara University, Graduate School of Natural and Applied Sciences.

Ülger, M., & Tanrıvermiş, Y. (2022). Analysis of the impact of coastal erosion on real estate value. *Eurasian Academy of Sciences, Eurasian Business & Economics Journal, 29*, 41–59.

Mehmet Ülger earned his B.Sc. with a Civil Engineering degree from Erciyes University and holds an M.Sc. in Coastal Engineering from Gazi University. He completed his PhD in Real Estate Development and Management at Ankara University, specialising in modelling shoreline changes and their effect on real estate values. He has published numerous papers in top journals, including Q1 publications, addressing topics such as coastal erosion, real estate valuation, and coastal area planning. He is responsible for teaching graduate and doctoral courses in coastal area management and planning, building information modelling (BIM) in the real estate sector, and real estate and asset analysis at the department. His professional expertise encompasses numerical modelling of coastal sediment transport, assessing the impacts of climate change on coastal properties, and investigating Building Information Modelling (BIM) applications in infrastructure projects. Dr. Ülger's research focuses on the nexus of coastal engineering, real estate economics, and advanced modelling techniques for sustainable coastal and property development.

Yeşim Tanrıvermiş holds the position of full professor in the Department of Real Estate Development and Management at the Faculty of Applied Sciences, Ankara University, Türkiye. She attained her Master of Science (M.Sc.) degree in 2011 from the Department of Agricultural Economics at Ankara University. She received her Ph.D. in 2011 as the first Ph.D. program graduate of the Department of Real Estate Development and Management at Ankara University. Her research interests encompass the management and conservation of land resources, land resource economics, as well as real estate analysis and economics, in addition to studies in real estate and asset valuation. She has been delivering lectures for several years and has published academic papers since 2006. Her publications consist of 50 international and 40 national peer-reviewed articles. Additionally, she has made contributions to 110 international and 25 national full or abstract proceedings at various conferences and congresses and has authored 35 books and 30 book chapters. Presently, she serves as the Deputy Head of her department at Ankara University. Moreover, she is an active participant in various academic and professional organisations. Her experience encompasses working as a researcher and consultant across diverse public and private sectors, with a focus on real estate asset analysis, real estate finance and valuation, land and building conservation practices, as well as real estate economics and management. Furthermore, she actively engages in enhancing cooperation with both domestic and international institutions, mobilising financial resources for research projects.

F. Nihan Özdemir Sönmez is a professor at the Department of Real Estate Development and Management, Faculty of Applied Sciences, Ankara University, Türkiye. She graduated from Middle East Technical University in 1987 with a degree in City and Regional Planning. She subsequently obtained her master's degree in the same field from the University's City Planning Master's Programme in 1990. In 1998, she earned her Ph.D. in Urban Studies from the University of Kent, United Kingdom, with a dissertation entitled "The Transformation of Squatter Settlements into Authorised Apartment Blocks: A Case Study of Ankara, Türkiye". She commenced her academic career as a research assistant in the Department of City and Regional Planning at Gazi University in 1988. In 2005, she advanced to the position of assistant professor and was subsequently promoted to associate professor in 2012. Since March 2016, she has been a faculty member of Ankara University's Department of Real Estate Development and Management, achieving the rank of full professor in 2018. She specialises in research areas including urban planning, urban policies, and urban transformation.

Land Resources and Rural Land Management and Policies

Harun Tanrıvermiş and Yeşim Tanrıvermiş

Abstract

Land is the most essential resource for countries and a crucial part of their heritage. In every country, land management—covering the economics, administration, and policy of rural and urban land—is a vital element and an indispensable resource for local and regional development. However, in many developing countries, including Türkiye, land management is characterised by a fragmented institutional landscape where numerous organisations adopt different approaches, and a lack of cooperation between agencies prevents uniform implementation. In Türkiye, the involvement of multiple institutions in land management and administration, combined with poor coordination and overlapping jurisdictions, results in resource waste and an inefficient land management system. Therefore, aligning the legal mandates of various institutions is crucial to establishing an effective, accessible, and transparent land management system that guarantees property rights, ensures reliable property valuation for investments and transfers, and implements land use planning and sustainable land development. Rural land use has seen significant changes over the past century. Today, fragmented land holdings that do not generate sufficient income, combined with the declining viability of farming, have led to land abandonment and a continuous migration from rural to urban areas. Meanwhile, urban sprawl into rural zones is causing land degradation and an ongoing expansion of urban land. In the coming years, restructuring land management, administration, and policy will be necessary to meet the food and fibre demands of a growing population amid climate change.

H. Tanrıvermiş (✉) · Y. Tanrıvermiş
Department of Real Estate Development and Management, Faculty of Applied Sciences, Ankara University, Ankara, Türkiye
e-mail: tanrivermis@ankara.edu.tr; aliefendioglu@ankara.edu.tr

T. Just et al. (eds.), *Understanding Türkiye's Real Estate Markets*, Management for Professionals, https://doi.org/10.1007/978-3-032-13297-0_34

Keywords

Land · Rural and urban land · Land management · Land administration and policy

1 Introduction

The strength of nations is fundamentally connected to their land assets, natural resource potential, and the effective utilisation of these resources. Although the relationship between economic development and land and natural resources has been extensively examined in the post-1950 era (De Soto, 2003; Tanrıvermiş, 1999; Tanrıvermiş, 2011), challenges remain in clarifying core concepts within this field. Terms such as nature, natural resources, soil, land, and real estate (immovable property) are frequently used interchangeably; however, their meanings are distinct. It is, therefore, crucial to establish clear definitions and delineate their respective scopes. While soil constitutes a fundamental component supporting life on Earth, land is a three-dimensional natural resource encompassing the Earth's surface, its subsurface (to a certain depth), and the space above it (the atmosphere). In ecosystems, numerous biochemical processes are facilitated by organisms residing in the soil, a condition that significantly enhances the sustainability of life. The soil layer covering the Earth's surface, in conjunction with flora and fauna, climatic conditions, and natural phenomena, directly impacts land utilisation (Tanrıvermiş & Tanrıvermiş, 2023).

Soil is an essential component for sustaining life, existing not only within agricultural regions but also as a delicate layer beneath even the most challenging natural conditions. The development of ecosystems relies on air, water, and soil; at the confluence of these three elements is the soil itself. Land and natural resources are indispensable for the survival of societies. Sustainable growth and development should be grounded on a robust foundation of natural resources. The connection between land, agriculture, and food security is critical for human survival. Societies that have effectively secured food security have formulated agricultural and rural policies that reflect the productive capacity of their land in response to burgeoning populations. Over the past two centuries, humanity has expanded agricultural land to support population increases, thereby intensifying pressure on land resources. Notably, the population theory proposed by Thomas R. Malthus in his 1797 work, "An Essay on the Principle of Population", has contributed to the widespread and often indiscriminate utilisation of these resources.

The ownership, use rights, and tenure forms of land resources possess multifaceted implications across economic, environmental, and social domains. The delineation and assurance of land ownership are intrinsically linked to economic development (De Soto, 2003; Tanrıvermiş et al., 2024; Terzioğlu et al., 2022). While land ownership confers economic, social, and political authority on individuals, it also imposes significant obligations. These obligations concern the safeguarding of the land's productivity and its capacity to sustain economic functions. Historically, numerous civilisations have failed to uphold this responsibility, resulting in migrations driven by factors such as land degradation, drought, and desertification. The manner in which societies engage with their land constitutes a fundamental determinant of their long-term viability. Unfortunately, many societies have struggled to achieve a sustainable balance between land conservation and utilisation, thereby contributing to the depletion of fertile soils and desertification. As emphasised by neoclassical economics, unrestrained use of land resources is unsustainable without the implementation of necessary measures. Consequently, the delicate nature of fertile soils warrants protection and careful management. The integration of land and soil considerations into many of the United Nations' Sustainable Development Goals (SDGs) underscores the significance of these resources for all societies. This chapter provides an evaluation of the legal and institutional frameworks governing land management in Türkiye, identifies core issues, and proposes multiple potential solutions.

2 Soil and Land Resources and Their Fundamental Characteristics

Soil constitutes a dynamic living system that undergoes continuous change and development. The organic and inorganic substances, water, and air essential for plant growth—along with soil structure and climatic conditions—dictate the living conditions and developmental stages of the organisms inhabiting it. Soil is not merely a passive environment but also a complex product created by these organisms. It embodies the attributes of a living resource, serving as both a hub of life and a product of life.

Although the concepts of soil and land are frequently used interchangeably, their meanings are distinct. Soil, recognised as one of the natural resources, constitutes a vital asset for humanity, as it cannot be artificially produced. Despite the common use of the terms soil and land within the Turkish Legal System, regulations such as the Turkish Civil Code No. 4721, the Real Estate Tax Law No. 1319, the Law on Land Regulation in Irrigation Areas and Agricultural Reform No. 3083, the Cadastre Law No. 3402, the Land Registry Law No. 2644, and the Land Registry Regulation have failed to sufficiently define the concepts of real estate, land, and soil. According to the Law on Soil Protection and Land Use No. 5403, these concepts and the various types of land and soil are properly delineated. According to this law, land is defined as a portion of the Earth's surface that is influenced by various factors, including climate, soil, topography, hydrology, parent material, and living organisms. Conversely, soil is characterised as a living, natural resource covering the Earth's surface in a thin layer, formed through the decomposition of mineral and organic matter. The definition of land in Law No. 5403, which states it as "a part of the Earth's surface", reflects a unidimensional perspective. In contrast, land is a multidimensional entity encompassing the surface, depth, and height of the Earth.

The definition of land, as outlined in the glossary compiled by the former Ministry of Forestry and Water Affairs, is as follows: "*(i) a bio-productive terrestrial system that includes soil, vegetation, and other living organisms, along with the ecological and hydrological processes operating within this system, and (ii) a portion of the Earth's surface influenced by various factors such as soil, climate, topography, parent material, hydrology, and living organisms*" (Ministry of Forestry and Water Affairs, 2015). Consistent with this definition, land may be characterised as a segment of the Earth's surface accompanied by its natural resources. Land is a three-dimensional entity with defined boundaries and geographical coordinates, encompassing the Earth's surface, its elevation, and its subsurface. As corroborated by the definition provided by the Ministry, as mentioned earlier, it also encompasses soil, subterranean resources, existing vegetation, land-based water resources, the atmospheric layer surrounding the Earth, and geographical features such as proximity to the sea (Tanrıvermiş, 2017).

Land represents a naturally occurring or original (unproduced) resource. It offers the fundamental space necessary for the survival of living organisms and encompasses all elements that constitute terrestrial ecosystems. The growth in population and related activities increases the demand for land, which subsequently leads to deterioration in land quality, a reduction in agricultural productivity, and heightened competition for land resources (Tutorialspoint, 2022).

The concept of land is interpreted and understood differently across academic disciplines. For geographers, land is regarded as a landscape shaped by geological and geomorphological processes. Economists define land as a factor of production that, in conjunction with labour and capital, is developed and maintained to foster economic output and growth. According to legal scholars, land is described as a volume extending from the Earth's core to the atmosphere, encompassing the rights associated with use within this volume. In domains such as real estate development, land management, and administration, land is considered a living space and a spatial entity that encompasses the Earth's surface, including areas adjacent to bodies of water.

Land demonstrates both similarities and differences when compared to other factors of production, such as labour, capital, and entrepreneurship. For instance, unlike other factors, land cannot be transferred from one location to another due to its immobility. The immobility of land and the rigid nature of its supply accentuate its significance relative to other factors of production. In addition to fulfilling the population's needs for food and fibre, issues related to land use and sustainability for settlement and various other objectives become particularly important. In summary, the characteristics that distinguish land from other factors of production are as follows:

- Non-reproducibility and non-multiplicability (being an original factor).
- Indestructibility or, with precautions, non-depreciation (having no amortisation).
- Immobility or non-transportability (being real property).
- The applicability of the law of diminishing returns in its use (the inability to increase production to the desired level).
- Acquisition and use are subject to legal regulations (in every country, land ownership, acquisition, and use are regulated by law).

- Serving as the habitat for living beings and the locus of human activities (as societies cannot reside in a vacuum or on the water's surface, and states must have geographical space).

Conceptual differences in defining land also occur based on its location and intended use. The use of "land" (arazi) as a legal term in rural areas and "plot" (arsa) in urban areas clearly illustrates this distinction. In zoning districts, the area on which a building is situated is referred to as a parcel or zoning parcel. The use and development rights of plots and parcels are established through "zoning plans" within the scope set by zoning legislation. A plot refers to inhabited areas within or surrounding a settlement where development exists. However, for an area to be considered a plot, planning alone is not enough; it must also have a residential character and access to municipal services. The land remaining in cities outside parcels designated for building development should be regarded as rural land and classified based on its use, such as agricultural land, forest, pasture, and meadow. Each cadastral parcel not subject to a zoning application is defined as "land" (arazi). It is necessary to identify, register, and inventory this land according to its type, including agricultural lands (irrigated and dry land, orchard, vineyard, and meadow), pasture, forest, and vacant land.

The scope of land ownership pertains to the elements within the horizontal and vertical boundaries of the land owned by an individual. The owner generally holds rights over all components within these boundaries. Nonetheless, certain elements situated within these confines do not fall within the material scope of land ownership, as discussed by Eren (2016). According to the Turkish Civil Code No. 4721, the scope of ownership encompasses integral parts, natural products, and appurtenances. Significantly, Article 718 of Law No. 4721 explicitly delineates the three dimensions of land ownership, stating: "*ownership of land, to the extent that it is useful for its use, includes the air above and the layers of the earth below. Subject to legal restrictions, the scope of this ownership also includes structures, plants, and resources*".

Article 4 of Law No. 5403 stipulates: "When exercising the right of ownership over lands under the rule and disposal of the State and in the private ownership of the Treasury, as well as lands belonging to public institutions and real and legal persons, land users are obliged to take the measures stipulated by this Law to ensure that the soil's vegetative production function, and its industrial, socio-economic, and ecological functions are not completely, partially, or temporarily hindered". This provision underscores the obligation of owners of both public and private lands to implement all necessary protective measures in land use and to utilise land resources in a manner that aligns with the public interest. The rights of landowners are constrained by the public interest and, more broadly, by usage that benefits society. These rights and constraints result in the formation of varying rents or prices depending on the type of land, which occur independently of the owner's will. In other words, the use and value of land can be directly influenced and altered by legal and institutional regulations. The rights and restrictions associated with the use of capital and labour as factors of production are comparatively more limited than those pertaining to land resources. This is due to the extensive and diverse utilisation of land and its higher degree of scarcity (Tanrıvermiş, 2017).

3 Classification of Land Assets and Land Use Planning

Soil classification depends on its natural features and suitability for different technical uses. To determine land use categories for agriculture, pasture-meadow, forestry, wildlife, settlement, mining, community services, sports, and recreation, detailed soil maps are created using data from field studies and laboratory analyses. These maps are used in various technical fields, including soil engineering, transportation routes, infrastructure, water systems, land consolidation, and taxation. Soil survey and mapping studies can be used for various objectives, and their results indicate how suitable the land is for specific uses. The classification of land use capability relies on factors such as irrigability, drainage, crop suitability, erosion risk, and soil conservation qualities. These studies examine the physical, chemical, and biological properties of soils in relation to their formation. Surface features, vegetation, and colour are also evaluated through aerial photographs or remote sensing data. By linking the characteristics of different soil types with crop development potential from local agricultural trials, soils are categorised into different land-use capability classes (Tanrıvermiş & Tanrıvermiş, 2023).

For the sustainable use of land, it is crucial to conduct land use planning that considers soil characteristics. Land management also requires land use planning and involves the rational integration of agricultural and non-agricultural activities. However, this necessitates a thorough understanding of soils and the inclusion of essential details and information for their application in engineering operations. Soil maps created for this purpose are known as detailed soil maps. Land use planning conducted without this information usually fails to yield sound and rational outcomes. In many countries, soils were examined through thorough research, sampled, and analysed in the twentieth century, with mapping studies carried out based on their characteristics and distribution. In many European countries, soil maps are utilised in land use planning for agricultural purposes and within land management to develop recommendations on drainage, irrigation requirements, erosion hazards, and soil properties that limit crop yields. In Türkiye, the lack of completed, detailed soil survey studies and the unavailability of detailed soil maps at the national level have hindered the progress of land use planning efforts.

Eight different capability classes have been established based on an assessment of the soil's physical properties, susceptibility to erosion, organic matter content, plant nutrient availability, water saturation, groundwater level, salinity levels, and issues such as rock and gully formations, as well as climatic data including temperature and precipitation distribution. Additionally, factors such as effective soil depth, slope classes, drainage and erosion values, as well as salt and alkalinity characteristics, are taken into account. The first four classes are deemed suitable for cultivation as agricultural land. It is essential to avoid using lands classified in the first three capability classes for non-agricultural activities unless necessary. In practice, however, the opposite trend is often observed. The employment of land according to its capability class is essential for conserving land resources and ensuring sustainable use. First and second-class agricultural lands are valuable assets that should be reserved exclusively for agricultural production, with careful planning and sensitivity. Lands outside these first four classes are classified as susceptible to erosion due to factors such as stoniness, wetness, or steep slopes; having shallow profiles due to severe erosion; or being suitable for wildlife habitats, such as salt marshy areas.

The Land Use Capability Classification serves as a fundamental prerequisite for sustainable land use. It is a systematic classification that examines land and soil characteristics influencing land use, including soil properties, slope, location, vegetation, groundwater, salinity, alkalinity, drainage, and stoniness. This classification is executed across three tiers: capability class, capability subclass, and capability unit (Dengiz, 2011). The capability classes comprise eight distinct categories; notably, the first four classes are deemed suitable for cultivated agriculture, whereas the remaining four are not. A summary of this classification is provided below (Şimşek, 2018; Tanrıvermiş & Tanrıvermiş, 2023).

***Class I Lands*:** These lands are areas characterised by a gentle slope or flat terrain, possessing deep soil, minimal soil and water erosion, and exhibiting an absence of stoniness, salinity, or alkalinity. There is no risk of flooding, and the drainage is effective. These highly fertile lands with a high capacity for water retention can be cultivated using established agricultural practices. Additionally, they can be utilised as meadows, forests, and pastures.

***Class II Lands*:** These lands show moderate erosion, salinity, and alkalinity, and may occasionally experience flooding and wetness that can be managed through drainage. They are classified as lands that can be farmed if certain measures are implemented.

***Class III Lands*:** These lands are characterised by numerous factors that impose restrictions on land utilisation, thereby providing limited opportunities for various uses. They are suitable for cultivating crops, as well as for meadow, forestland, and pasture. The implementation of conservation measures is essential for crop cultivation, although conditions such as slope, inadequate soil depth, and the accumulation of salt and sodium influence their usability.

***Class IV Lands*:** These types of lands, characterised by severe water and wind erosion, salinity, alkalinity, and shallow soil structure, may be utilised provided that meticulous management practices are applied. On these terrains, where reclamation often entails significant costs, certain horticultural and field crops can be cultivated.

Class V, VI, and VII Lands: These lands are predominantly designated for use as meadow, forestland, pasture, or settlement areas and are deemed unsuitable for the cultivation of most crops, with the exception of specialised crops such as tea and hazelnuts.

***Class VIII Lands*:** These lands are unsuitable for agricultural purposes, such as mining quarries, coastal dunes, mountainous terrains, and stone and sand quarries that lack soil.

Class I lands, as delineated within the land use classification, are considered agricultural lands that are free from usage issues. However, from Class II through Class IV, there is a progressively increasing incidence of problems associated with agricultural production. Moreover, undertaking agricultural activities on these soils and lands without implementing appropriate conservation measures entails significant risks. It is essential to note that from second-class lands onwards, mismanagement of land use can lead to erosion problems (Dengiz, 2023; Şimşek, 2018).

In the case of lands designated under the VI and VII categories within the land capability classification system, the destruction of natural vegetation for the purpose of establishing agricultural land or constructing buildings and other settlement facilities is considered unfeasible. This is attributable to the inevitable soil erosion and environmental degradation that would result. Many of these areas comprise steep hillside terrains, making agricultural activities technically impractical (Dengiz, 2023). Consequently, conventional agricultural practices should not be undertaken on lands classified as Class VI and VII to prevent erosion and soil depletion. Certain portions of these lands may be appropriate for use as controlled hunting zones, camping centres, or recreational areas. Lands categorised as Class VIII refer to areas from which neither ecological nor economic vegetative products can be obtained. These lands are suitable for designation as settlement zones, including villages, towns, and cities; for the development of sectors such as industry and tourism; and for the conservation and development of wildlife.

In Türkiye, 47.31% of land assets are classified as Class VII, 13.35% as Class VI, 9.88% as Class III, 9.39% as Class IV, 8.81% as Class II, 6.54% as Class I, and 4.50% as Class VIII. Overall, 34.62% of the country's land assets fall within capability classes I to IV, with 81.32% of this land dedicated to agricultural production. Conversely, 13.09% of land within capability classes V to VII is utilised for agriculture, despite these lands not being used in accordance with their designated capability classes (Table 1). The presence of meadow-pasture, forest, and settlement areas—expected to be in classes V to VII—located in the first four classes, and the practice of irrigated farming in classes V to VII, suggests that land use is inconsistent with capability classifications, resulting in significant management and conservation issues.

4 The Institutional Structure of Land Management

4.1 Approaches to Land Management and Administration

Considering that soil functions as a sensitive system influenced by intricate environmental factors, soil management is recognised as a process that influences both ecological and economic conditions essential for sustainable agriculture. Human interventions within the soil ecosystem can induce alterations in soil structure and the activities of environmental groups. The most notable impact involves the utilisation of fertile and preservable lands for agricultural purposes. Agricultural systems markedly differ from natural ecosystems, which have evolved based on species diversity. Since agricultural practices predominantly target specific crops over extensive areas, they often lead to changes in biodiversity, as well as nutrient and water conservation measures. Additionally, mechanisation, organic matter depletion, and chemical inputs further complicate these systems. The residual organic matter in the soil is significantly reduced, and indiscriminate practices such as

Table 1 Land asset and use according to land use capability classification (1000 ha)

Land use types	Land use capability classification								
	I	II	III	IV	V	VI	VII	VIII	TOTAL
Cultivated land	4778	5987	6229	4593	18	3848	2246	–	27,699
Dry farming	3156	4876	5439	4063	14	3377	1684	–	22,609
Irrigated farming	1413	836	476	223	4	34	4	–	2990
Vineyards and orchards	176	188	206	172	–	202	115	–	1059
Specialty crops	33	87	109	135	–	235	443	–	1042
Meadow-pasture	178	547	826	1731	103	4104	14,257	–	21,746
Forest and shrubland	17	172	477	840	31	2237	19,694	–	23,468
Settlement areas	40	53	42	37	–	49	57	292	570
Other lands	–	–	–	–	13	–	35	3164	3212
Water surfaces	–	–	–	–	–	–	–	–	1102
Total land	5013	6759	7574	7201	165	10,238	36,289	3456	76,694
Share of total area (%)	**6.54**	**8.81**	**9.88**	**9.39**	**0.22**	**13.35**	**47.31**	**4.50**	**100.00**

Source: Dengiz (2023)

stubble burning severely disrupt organic matter management. It is essential to develop specialised land management systems to counteract these negative human-induced effects. Consequently, within the frameworks of agricultural production planning and environmental land management, strategies aimed at ensuring the sustainability of land productivity and ecological integrity have gained importance. These strategies include the dissemination of practices originating from the Green Revolution, such as sustainable agriculture, low external input agriculture, organic (ecological) agriculture, conservation agriculture, and good agricultural practices, as well as approaches like micro-farming, which involve localised fertilisation techniques tailored to soil structure, crop rotation, and no-till farming (Tanrıvermiş, 1999). The implementation of controlled techniques, such as drip irrigation in irrigated regions, and an awareness of the importance of preventing soil salinisation and enhancing organic matter content, constitute fundamental elements of soil and land management.

Challenges arise in defining and differentiating concepts such as land management, land administration, and land governance. According to the cadastre report of the International Federation of Surveyors (FIG), land management is described as the process of overseeing the use and development of land resources (Demirel & Gür, 2008). Another definition that views land management as a process states: "*the decision-making processes through which land resources are allocated in a manner that aligns with human needs and desires, within the framework of political and social institutions and legal and administrative regulations*" (O'Riordan, 1971). In this context, land management is regarded as the process through which land policies—aimed at enabling society to use land and land resources in accordance with sustainable development principles—are implemented.

The interconnected concepts of land management and land administration possess distinct meanings. Land administration is defined as "the process of creating, recording, and disseminating information about ownership, value, and use of land when implementing land management policies" (UNECE, 2004). Moreover, land administration can be characterised as the operations involved in obtaining data on ownership, value, and land use necessary for this process. For effective land administration, it is imperative to concentrate on the methods of: "(i) monitoring developments on land and immovable properties, (ii) regulating the use and conservation of land, (iii) generating income from land through sale, lease, and taxation, and (iv) resolving disputes related to the ownership and use of land" (Dale & McLaunghlin, 1999).

Land governance refers to the rules, processes, and structures that govern decisions regarding access to and utilisation of land, as well as the implementation of these decisions and the management of conflicts of interest. Consequently, land governance encompasses a range of institutions, including legal, traditional, religious, and informal ones. The concept of land governance encompasses traditional customs that regulate land transactions, inheritance, and dispute resolution, as well as the legal and political frameworks governing land use. In essence, land governance is primarily concerned with the distribution of power and the political economy related to land (FAO, 2022).

4.2 Institutions Conducting Activities Related to Soil and Land

Land regulations are delineated within the Constitution of the Republic of Türkiye, as well as in numerous laws, statutes, regulations, directives, and circulars. More than 50 public institutions are engaged in land-related activities (Çete & Yomralıoğlu, 2009), and several institutions undertake overlapping functions.

The former General Directorate of Soil and Water was specifically established to measure, map, and assess the potential of soil and water resources. It undertook a significant task by conducting reconnaissance-style soil surveys and mapping studies across the country between 1965 and 1971. However, these maps lack sufficient detail for land use planning. In 1984, the General Directorates of Roads, Water, and Electricity, along with Soil and Settlement, merged to form the General Directorate of Rural Services. This consolidation enabled the integration of soil survey and mapping activities, as well as the updating of existing maps. During this period, however, survey and mapping work slowed down, and there was no significant progress in detailed soil surveys. Following the closure of the General Directorate of Rural Services in 2005, an institutional gap emerged in creating the soil database necessary for implementing Law No. 5403 on Soil Protection and Land Use, dated 19 July 2005. Although Law No. 5403 and its regulations assign responsibility to the Ministry of Agriculture and Forestry for preparing soil maps, it is widely recognised that there are substantial deficiencies in producing national, regional, and local soil maps of the required accuracy and quality, as well as in making them accessible to all stakeholders.

The organisational structure pertaining to cadastre, land registration, surveying and mapping, land use, planning, and land management has progressively developed in accordance with international conventions, global transformations, and national mandates. The organisational framework related to soil and land resources can be categorised as central administrations, local administrations, and scholarly and civil society organisations. At the central level, activities concerning land resources are predominantly managed by the Ministry of Agriculture and Forestry and the Ministry of Environment, Urbanisation, and Climate Change, along with their affiliated and related institutions.

The general directorates affiliated with the Ministry of Agriculture and Forestry—including divisions such as Plant Production, Nature Conservation and National Parks, Agricultural Research and Policies, Agricultural Reform, and Water Management—alongside related entities such as the Atatürk Forest Farm, the State Hydraulic Works, the General Directorate of Forestry, and the Turkish Water Institute, undertake a broad spectrum of activities. These activities encompass land surveys, mapping, the development of soil and water resources, soil conservation, land use planning, environmental and watershed protection, expropriation, public land management, valuation, and infrastructure services. Regarding the Ministry's operational sectors, 49 research institutes—including 10 central, 13 regional, and 26 subject-specific institutions—conduct applied research projects at both local and regional levels. Their research areas include land conservation and utilisation, land economics, water resource management, soil surveying and mapping, and geographic information systems. The State Hydraulic Works, a public authority under the Ministry, actively participates in various activities, including hydroelectric power generation, provision of drinking and utility water to major cities, flood prevention, irrigation, land consolidation and field development, land acquisition and expropriation, as well as survey and mapping operations. The General Directorate of Forestry oversees forest resources, undertaking functions such as resource identification and surveying, management planning, mapping, watershed and soil conservation, forestry ownership and cadastre, and operational initiatives (Table 2).

The Ministry of Environment, Urbanisation and Climate Change engages in activities such as spatial planning, infrastructure development, geographic information systems, environmental impact assessments, environmental management, desertification and erosion control, treasury land management, land registry, cadastre operations, and housing production. All tasks related to land management fall under its responsibilities. The General Directorate of Land Registry and Cadastre, affiliated with the Ministry, manages cadastre, mapping, land registry, valuation, and various land management duties. The Bank of Provinces (İlbank) focuses on planning, financing infrastructure and superstructure projects, and resource mobilisation. Meanwhile, the Housing Development Administration (TOKİ) handles planning, expropriation, land development, project execution, squatter prevention, and social housing projects. It also constructs public buildings on treasury lands, other acquired lands, and designated zones for squatter prevention.

In addition to the responsibilities mentioned above, the General Directorate of Cultural Assets and Museums within the Ministry of Culture and Tourism is responsible for expropriation, planning, and the preservation of sites and monuments situated within historical, archaeological, and urban heritage zones. The General Directorate of Industrial Zones, under the Ministry of Industry and Technology, manages site selection, land surveys, expropriation, and the expansion of zone boundaries for organised industrial zones, industrial regions, and small industrial sites. Key authorities involved in land market activities include the Disaster and Emergency Management Presidency (AFAD), the General Directorate of Highways (KGM), the General Directorate of Mining and Petroleum Affairs (MAPEG), and the General Directorate of Mineral Research and Exploration (MTA). Additionally, corporations such as the Petroleum Pipeline Corporation (BOTAŞ), the Turkish Electricity Generation Corporation (EÜAŞ), the Turkish Electricity Transmission Corporation (TEİAŞ), the Turkish Electricity Distribution Corporation (TEDAŞ), and the Turkish Coal Enterprises (TKİ) participate in activities including land acquisition, expropriation, mapping, infrastructure development, valuation, and land reclamation (Table 2).

Among local authorities, municipalities and provincial special administrations hold substantial authority in the realm of soil and land management. In accordance with Law No. 6360 and the Metropolitan Municipality Law No. 5216, environmental plans for extensive urban areas are devised by metropolitan municipalities. Furthermore, the fundamental frameworks for land management and utilisation decisions are established across 30 provinces. Additionally, master and

Table 2 Institutions responsible and authorised for land management in Türkiye and their activities

Institutions \ Activities		Land Surveys and Map Production	Expropriation	Environmental and Land Conservation	Real Property Valuation	Planning	Infrastructure Services	Settlement and Resettlement	Administration of Treasury Lands Cadastre	Administration of Mines	Land (Plot) and Housing Production	Cadastre	Administration of Forests	Administration of Historical Assets	(Land) Consolidation	Squatter Prevention	Land Registry	Administration of Foundation Properties	Coastal Management	Policy Development
Local Governmen	Metropolitan Municipality	■	■	■	■	■	■	■	■		■			■		■				
	Other Municipalities	■	■	■	■	■	■	■	■		■			■		■				
	Special Provincial Administration	■	■	■	■	■	■	■						■	■					
Central Administration	GD of Agricultural Reform	■	■	■	■	■		■	■		■				■					
	GD of Plant Production		■	■											■					
	GD of State Hydraulic Works	■	■	■	■		■	■				■			■					
	GD of Water Management	■	■	■																■
	GD of Nature Conservation and National Parks			■									■							
	GD of Forestry	■	■	■	■				■	■			■							
	GD of Spatial Planning			■		■														■
	GD for the Protection of Natural Assets			■		■			■											
	GD of National Real Estate								■											
	GD of Land Registry and Cadastre	■			■				■			■					■			
	Housing Development Administration	■	■		■	■	■	■			■					■				
	GD of EIA, Permit and Inspection			■		■														
	GD of Environmental Management			■															■	
	GD of Construction Works	■				■														
	GD of the Bank of Provinces	■	■	■		■	■													
	GD of Infrastructure Investments					■	■													
	GD of Highways	■	■	■	■		■					■								
	TCDD (Turkish State Railways)	■	■		■		■													
	GD of Cultural Assets and Museums		■	■		■								■						
	GD of Foundations		■		■									■				■		
	GD of Investments and Enterprises		■	■		■														
	GD of Mining and Petroleum Affairs	■	■	■						■										
	GD Mineral Research and Exploration (MTA)	■		■						■										
	GD of Energy Affairs						■													
	TEDAŞ/TEİAŞ/EUAŞ[a]		■		■							■								
	GD of BOTAŞ (Petroleum Pipeline Corporation)	■	■	■	■	■	■	■												
	Turkish Coal Enterprises	■	■	■	■					■										
	TPAO (Turkish Petroleum Corporation)	■		■						■										
	Energy Market Regulatory Authority (EMRA)		■																	
	GD of Mapping	■																		
	GD of Logistics	■	■		■	■			■											■
	GD of Industrial Zones	■	■		■	■	■													■
	GD of Development Agencies	■		■		■														■
	Privatization Administration Presidency	■			■	■														
	GD of Free Zones		■			■	■													
	BRSA (Banking Regulation and Supervision Agency)				■															
	Capital Markets Board (CMB)				■															
	Regional Development Administrations	■				■	■													■
	Disaster and Emergency Management Presidency (AFAD)	■	■			■	■	■			■				■					
Other	Professional and Civil Society Organizations																			■
	Universities		■																	■
	R&D Institutions																			■
	International Organizations																			■

[a]TEDAŞ: Turkish Electricity Distribution Corporation / TEİAŞ: Turkish Electricity Transmission Corporation / EÜAŞ: Electricity Generation Corporation

Source: Prepared by updating from Demirci et al. (2007), Çete and Yomralıoğlu (2009), and Tanrıvermiş and Tanrıvermiş (2023)

implementation zoning plans are developed by individual municipalities, which also determine land use, development, as well as urban growth and sprawl within their jurisdictions. Provincial, district, and town municipalities engage in various activities related to land management, including conducting land surveys, zoning planning, environmental protection, and expropriation. Provincial special administrations operate in regions beyond the boundaries of municipal and adjacent areas—predominantly rural regions—focusing on site selection for settlements, resettlement, planning, rural physical infrastructure, rural development, and mining activities. Although village legal entities are also entrusted with responsibilities in land management, these duties are performed only to a limited extent.

Recent modifications in the administration of metropolitan municipalities have delegated responsibilities in agriculture and rural development to these entities. When both central and local governments duplicate efforts within the same jurisdiction, questions may arise concerning the efficient and effective use of public resources. Nonetheless, the shared regional needs of district centres and villages within metropolitan boundaries differ substantially from those of residents in the metropolitan area itself. The regional needs of populations are influenced by their modes of production; for instance, the requirements of urban dwellers working in offices differ from those of villagers engaged in agriculture or animal husbandry (Görmez, 2013). Recognising that the needs of residents in district centres and villages within metropolitan boundaries diverge from those of urban inhabitants, Law No. 6360 on the Establishment of Metropolitan Municipalities in Fourteen Provinces and Twenty-Seven Districts, along with amendments to various laws and decree-laws, authorises metropolitan municipalities "to engage in all kinds of activities and services to support agriculture and animal husbandry" (Art. 7). Typically, the most urbanised region in a country is designated as a "metropolis", where industrial and service sectors are expected to predominate over rural and agricultural pursuits. However, the delegation of agricultural and service responsibilities to metropolitan municipalities—roles also managed by provincial and district directorates and research institutes of the Ministry of Agriculture and Forestry—results in task overlaps among local and central authorities. Such overlaps may hinder the balanced and rational allocation of resources among local settlements (Tanrıvermiş & Tanrıvermiş, 2023).

Professional and scientific associations, chambers, academic institutions, and international organisations also undertake significant activities beyond the scope of central and local administrations. Among scientific and professional organisations, the research, congress, and consultancy initiatives of the Union of Chambers of Turkish Engineers and Architects (TMMOB), the Soil Science Society of Türkiye, and other associations are widely recognised. Concerning academic institutions, the activities of the Faculties of Agriculture and Forestry, the Faculties of Engineering and Architecture, and the Departments of Real Estate Development and Management within the Faculties of Applied Sciences are important. Prof. Dr. Ömer Kerim Çağlar laid the foundation of soil science in Türkiye and established the Soil Science Department at Ankara University's Faculty of Agriculture. Currently, the work conducted by the Soil Science and Plant Nutrition Departments in the Faculties of

Agriculture, the Soil Science and Ecology Departments in the Forest Engineering programmes of the Faculties of Forestry, and the disciplines of Facility and Real Estate Management within the Departments of Real Estate Development and Management are prominent. Recognising the growing importance of land management and the need for developing interdisciplinary studies in this domain, the "*Land Management and Policy Master's Programmes*" have been established within the Department of Real Estate Development and Management at Ankara University. These programmes are designed to promote scientific research at both national and international levels in areas such as land management, land administration and policy, land governance and sustainability, climate change and environmental land management, urban land development, rural settlement planning and rural infrastructure investments, cadastre, taxation, valuation, information systems, as well as climate, environment, and land investments.

On a global level, the efforts of organisations such as the Food and Agriculture Organisation (FAO), the United Nations Human Settlements Programme (UN-HABITAT), the United Nations Environment Programme (UNEP), the United Nations Development Programme (UNDP), the World Bank, and the Organisation for Economic Co-operation and Development (OECD) are significant. The successes of agreements and projects established at international and regional levels, as well as the initiatives created to fund them, remain somewhat limited. Nevertheless, significant efforts were made in areas such as climate agreements, tackling desertification, forest fires, erosion control, climate change mitigation, climate-related investments and financing, and sustainable urban development. It is vital to promote cooperation among organisations operating at national, regional, and international levels and to undertake joint research, particularly on land management, sustainability, environmental land use, desertification, and climate change policies, as well as the development of preventive strategies, institutional capacity building, and financial mechanisms.

Activities pertaining to soil, water, and land resources are undertaken by various public institutions, each possessing distinct objectives, scopes, and characteristics. Moreover, inter-agency coordination remains insufficient, and there is an imperative to develop new standards and methodologies for data generation and sharing to avoid redundant procedures (Tanrıvermiş, 2003). In this context, it is of public interest to ensure that the production of maps and orthophotos by a single institution satisfies the requirements of other organisations. Furthermore, completing soil survey and mapping initiatives at the local, regional, and national levels is vital for finalising the Soil Map of Türkiye and Land Use Plans, thus making them accessible to all public and private stakeholders. Experts frequently assert that, owing to the strategically significant information contained within soil maps, their creation, utilisation, and dissemination should be overseen by a public institution.

Public institutions and organisations engaged in land-related activities operate within a complex legislative framework that encompasses e.g. zoning laws, infrastructure services, squatter prevention, coastal zone management, land registry, property valuation, environmental protection, land consolidation, expropriation, and the creation of plots and housing. However, due to the highly diverse and fragmented nature of land legislation, numerous institutions possess similar authorities and responsibilities. This frequently results in jurisdictional conflicts between local and central governments. The current institutional framework lacks a cohesive system; instead, it comprises a fragmented structure formed through an additive process driven by evolving needs. Consequently, the same activities may be duplicated across several institutions, or gaps may emerge. Furthermore, increasing demands and evolving processes, particularly those prompted by technological progress, necessitate the reorganisation of obsolete institutional structures.

For effective restructuring, it is imperative to initially identify current land activities and subsequently reform legal and institutional regulations accordingly. It is crucial to eliminate institutional fragmentation within the land management and administration sectors by consolidating these entities under a unified framework. Furthermore, issues such as gaps in institutional responsibilities concerning map production, land valuation, agricultural land information systems, models for joint cultivation and land banking to utilise idle lands, reclamation of problematic lands, regulation of land tenure systems, and rural settlement and physical infrastructure investments must be addressed during the restructuring process. The necessity to establish leading institutions within land-related sectors is frequently highlighted by stakeholders (Çete & Yomralıoğlu, 2009; Yomralıoğlu, 2011). This strategy minimises confusion caused by multiple institutions executing similar functions, as a specialised institution will manage each activity. Consequently, clarity regarding responsible entities improves, coordination and efficiency are enhanced, inconsistencies in application are reduced, and standardisation is achieved. Additionally, service quality is expected to improve, and the requisite institutional infrastructure for land information systems can be developed. To formulate effective land policies and manage land proficiently, it is essential to restructure the existing land administration framework first and establish a sustainable national land management and administration system next.

5 Legal Aspects of Land Management and Administration

5.1 Global Land Assets and Relevant International Agreements

The total surface area of the Earth is estimated at 510 million km^2 (51 trillion hectares), with a terrestrial surface of roughly 14.86 trillion hectares. The land area of the 193 nations recognised by the United Nations is approximately 13.5 trillion hectares. When water bodies are excluded, the total land asset of the globe amounts to about 13.0 trillion hectares. Cultivated lands account for around 10 to 12% of the total land, while total agricultural lands make up 34 to 37%. At the national level, the proportion of cultivated land within the total land area varies from 30% to 33%, and the share of irrigated land within the total cultivated area ranges from 28% to 30%. Globally, the ratio of agricultural land assets to total land assets is between 34% and 38%. Notably, there was a significant reduction in total agricultural land between 2000 and 2024. During this period, there was a decrease of approximately 787.05 million hectares in total agricultural land, representing about 2% of the peak agricultural land asset of 4.878 trillion hectares in 2000 (Table 3). A similar decline was observed in meadow, pasture, and forest lands, while settlement areas and other land uses increased. The utilisation and transformation of land at both global and national levels serve as key indicators for environmental protection and sustainable management of natural resources. In particular, monitoring changes in land use related to agriculture, forestry, pasture, and natural land is essential for ecosystem monitoring, biodiversity conservation, and assessing the impacts of climate change.

The Principles of the Soil Charter No. 720, adopted by the Council of Europe's Committee of Ministers, demonstrate that perspectives on land resources in Europe shifted rapidly, especially after the Second World War. These principles emphasise that soil is a vital natural resource for human survival, and that even in Europe, soil remains insufficiently protected against degradation, which can cause irreversible effects. Consequently, the Council of Europe's Committee of Ministers approved the European Soil Charter No. 720 on May 19, 1972. This charter, comprising 12 principles and recommendations, prioritises the risk of soil degradation and the threat it poses to the future of industrial societies.

During the period after 1970, the management of global land resources became an important topic in scholarly and policy discussions. In this context, the United Nations Food and Agriculture Organisation (FAO) formalised the World Soil Charter in 1982; at the same time, the United Nations Environment Programme (UNEP) released the World Soils Policy document (FAO, 1982; UNEP, 1980). Initial international efforts began with the "United Nations Conference on Environment and Development" (UNCED, 1992) (Table 4). Afterwards, international agreements such as the United Nations Convention to Combat Desertification (UNCCD), the Framework Convention on Climate Change (UNFCCC), and the Convention on Biological Diversity (CBD) came into effect. These conventions led to broader global initiatives aimed at increasing awareness within the international community. Although soil conservation, sustainable land management, and land-use change were not the main focus of these agreements, they are nonetheless considered from both human and ecological viewpoints (Hurni et al., 2006).

The UN Food and Agriculture Organisation describes soil resource management as "*one of the essential pillars of sustainable agriculture and offers significant leverage for climate regulation as well as a pathway for the preservation of ecosystem services and biodiversity*". In 2015, it issued the World Soil Charter, which outlines nine guiding principles (FAO, 2015a). These principles are designed to sustainably manage soil resources and enhance the resource inventory through the rehabilitation of degraded soils.:

- **First Principle:** "*Soils are a vital resource, essential for producing a range of goods and services that are key components of ecosystems and human well-being. Protecting or enhancing the global soil resource is crucial for humanity to meet its needs for inclusive food, water, and energy security, respecting each State's sovereign rights over its natural resources. In particular, the anticipated*

Table 3 Global land asset and its distribution by use type

Years	Total country surface area (million hectares)	Total land asset (million hectares)	Total cultivated area (million hectares)	Meadow and pasture land (million hectares)	Forest area (million hectares)	Other lands (million hectares)	Irrigated agricultural land (million hectares)	Agricultural land (million hectares)
1960	13,444.9	13,040.6	1350.0	3,090.6	–	–	401.6	4440.6
1980	13,444.9	13,040.4	1420.0	3217.3	–	–	401.8	4637.3
2000	13,437.5	13,004.8	1492.4	3385.6	4158.0	3968.7	429.9	4878.0
2005	13,441.2	13,020.1	1510.2	3310.2	4132.2	4067.5	418.4	4820.4
2010	13,461.0	13,018.4	1521.3	3272.8	4106.3	4117.9	439.9	4794.1
2015	13,499.2	13,030.9	1550.3	3181.3	4083.9	4215.5	428.0	4731.6
2020	13,500.3	13,031.2	1561.7	3182.8	4058.9	4227.8	427.4	4744.5
2024	14,094.5	13,016.8	1571.5	3229.5	4043.9	4148.7	355.0	4799.3

Note: All figures are rounded to million hectares for clarity
Source: FAO (2025)

Table 4 International regulations concerning land governance and sustainable development

Years	International regulations
1982	FAO world soil charter
1988	Intergovernmental panel on climate change (IPCC)
1992	UN conference on environment and development
	Rio declaration
	Agenda 21
	Global environment facility
	UN convention to combat desertification (UNCCD)
	UN framework convention on climate change (UNFCCC)
	Convention on biological diversity (CBD)
1997	Kyoto protocol
2000	United nations millennium development goals
2005	Millennium ecosystem assessment
2008	Zero net lnd degradation approach (UNCCD)
2011	Global soil partnership (FAO/EU)
2012	Rio+20 conference
	Foundation of the sustainable development goals (SDGs) and the post-2015 development agenda
2013	GSP's intergovernmental technical panel on soils (ITPS)
	Updated FAO world soil charter
	Land and soils integrated into the open working group on sustainable development goals (SDGs)
	GSP's regional land partnerships
2015	International year of soils declared by the UN general assembly
2017	FAO global soil map

Source: own compilation

growth in food, fibre, and fuel production needed to secure food and energy supplies will increasingly exert pressure on land".

- **Second Principle:** *"Soils result from complex actions and interactions of processes across different times and spaces, leading to a diverse range of forms, properties, and levels of ecosystem services they provide. Effective soil governance requires a comprehensive understanding of these diverse soil capabilities and the promotion of land use practices that recognise and respect these varying capacities, thereby supporting poverty alleviation and food security".*
- **Third Principle:** *"Soil management is regarded as sustainable when the supporting, provisioning, regulating, and cultural services supplied by soil are maintained or improved without inflicting substantial damage on either the soil functions that support these services or on biodiversity. An important concern pertains to balancing supporting and provisioning services vital for plant production with the regulating services that soil provides in relation to water quality, availability, and atmospheric greenhouse gas levels".*
- **Fourth Principle:** *"The execution of soil management decisions is predominantly conducted at the local level and occurs within varied socio-economic contexts. Formulating appropriate specific measures for the adoption by local*

decision-makers often requires multi-level, interdisciplinary efforts involving multiple stakeholders. A strong commitment to integrating local and indigenous knowledge is essential".

- **Fifth Principle:** *"The specific functions a soil provides are largely determined by its chemical, biological, and physical properties. Understanding the current condition of these properties, their roles in soil functions, and how natural and human-induced changes influence them is vital for sustainable soil management".*
- **Sixth Principle:** *"Soils form a vital reservoir of global biodiversity, including microorganisms, flora, and fauna. This biodiversity is essential for supporting soil functions and the ecosystem goods and services linked to soils. Therefore, conserving soil biodiversity is crucial to maintain these vital functions".*
- **Seventh Principle:** *"All soils, whether actively managed or not, provide ecosystem services related to global climate regulation and water management at various scales. Land use changes can reduce these vital global services performed by soils. The impacts of local or regional land-use modifications can be accurately evaluated within the framework of assessments of global effects, as well".*
- **Eighth Principle:** *"Soil degradation inherently diminishes or eliminates the capacity of soils to sustain their functions and ecosystem services, which are essential for human well-being. It is imperative to reduce or prevent soil degradation to preserve the services provided by soils, as such prevention is considerably more cost-effective than rehabilitating soils subsequent to damage".*
- **Ninth Principle:** *"Degraded soils can, in some instances, be restored to their fundamental functions and their contribution to ecosystem services through the use of suitable rehabilitation techniques. This process augments the available area for delivering services without necessitating land-use changes or conversion".* (FAO, 2015b).

While international conventions have concentrated on the effective and efficient use of resources, the importance of resources for future generations and their long-term availability became apparent in the 1970s, leading to a focus on sustainability. During that decade, the regulation of resource use and the equitable distribution of natural resources gained prominence. In the context of climate change and global warming, alongside the management of natural resources, various forms of intervention gained significance. By the 2000s, debates expanded to include the sustainable management of land, rural and urban development, and the relationships between land use, development, and spatial and environmental justice (Terzioğlu et al., 2022).

5.2 Land Assets and Relevant Legal Regulations in Türkiye

Türkiye's total surface area is estimated at 78.54 million km^2, with a land area of 76.96 million km^2. The cultivated agricultural land, which was 10 million hectares in 1934, expanded to 25.17 million hectares in 1960 and further increased to 28.48

million hectares in 1980. However, this area declined to 23.15 million hectares in 2020 before rising again to 24.00 million hectares in 2024. The decrease in agricultural land within the total land asset shows that lands suitable for agriculture are either remaining vacant for various reasons or being repurposed for non-agricultural uses. As of 2024, the share of total agricultural lands (including cultivated, meadow, and pasture lands) in the country's total land assets was recorded at 50.18%, while the proportion of cultivated lands was 31.19% (Table 5). A downward trend has been observed for both ratios recently. Similarly, although there has been no significant increase in the share of lands important for biodiversity, such as forests and meadow-pastures, the category of other lands—including settlement areas—continues to show an upward trend.

The "procedures and principles" for activities related to land management and administration are defined by legislation concerning land resources. These include the Agriculture Law No. 5488 of 18/04/2006; the Soil Protection and Land Use Law No. 5403 of 03/07/2005; and the Law on Land Regulation in Irrigation Areas and Agricultural Reform No. 3083 of 22/11/1984. The purpose of Agriculture Law No. 5488 is to "determine the necessary policies and make regulations for the development and support of the agricultural sector and rural areas in line with development plans and strategies". The purpose of Law No. 5403 is to "determine the procedures and principles to ensure the protection and development of soil, the classification of agricultural lands, the determination of minimum agricultural land and agricultural land of sufficient income sizes and the prevention of their division, and the planned use of agricultural land and agricultural land of sufficient income in accordance with the principle of environment-focused sustainable development". The scope of the Law includes "the classification of land and soil resources following scientific principles, the setting of minimum sizes for agricultural land and land of sufficient income, and the prevention of their division; the creation of land use plans; the assessment of social, economic and environmental factors in protection and development through participatory methods; the prevention of non-designated and incorrect uses; and the establishment of methods to ensure protection, along with procedures and principles related to duties, powers, and responsibilities" It is important to note that the duties and powers of central and local administrations designated or authorised by legal regulations concerning land resources often conflict, leading to significant implementation challenges.

Within the Turkish legal system, the concept of "land" (arazi) is regarded as the fundamental component of real estate. While certain legal provisions incorporate explanations regarding the concepts of soil and land, along with their classifications, explicit and precise definitions are often absent from many statutes. The Soil Protection and Land Conservation Law No. 5403 encompasses both concepts, providing definitions aligned with various land types. Under Law No. 5403, "land" is characterised as a portion of the Earth's surface affected by diverse factors such as climate, soil, parent material, topography, hydrology, and living organisms. Conversely, "soil" is described as a living, natural resource forming a thin layer covering the Earth's surface, resulting from the decomposition of mineral and organic matter. The law further delineates "agricultural land" as territories where

Table 5 Land assets in Türkiye by year and use type

Years	Total country surface area (Thousand hectares)	Total land asset area (Thousand hectares)	Total cultivated area (Thousand hectares)	Meadow and pasture (Thousand hectares)	Forest area (Thousand hectares)	Other lands (Thousand hectares)	Irrigated agricultural land (Thousand hectares)	Agricultural land (Thousand hectares)
1960	78,535	76,963	25,167	11,350	–	–	1572	36,517
1980	78,535	76,963	28,479	10,100	–	–	1572	38,579
2000	78,535	76,963	26,379	14,100	20,148	16,336	1572	40,479
2005	78,535	76,963	26,606	14,617	20,616	15,124	1572	41,223
2010	78,535	76,963	24,395	14,617	21,083	16,868	1572	39,012
2015	78,535	76,963	23,934	14,617	21,630	16,782	1572	38,551
2020	78,535	76,963	23,145	14,617	22,220	16,981	1572	37,762
2024	78,535	76,963	24,002	14,617	23,363	14,981	1572	38,619

Source: FAO (2025), TURKSTAT (2025)

soil, topography, and climatic conditions are conducive to agricultural activities, whether currently utilised for such purposes or suitable for agricultural production, or capable of being rendered suitable through development, reclamation, and improvement. In contrast, "non-agricultural areas" are defined as zones designated for tourism, industrial, recreational, infrastructure, settlement, and similar functions, as well as bare rocks lacking sufficient soil, riverbeds, expanses of snow-covered terrain, military zones, coastal dunes, reeds, and swamps. Significantly, non-agricultural areas are considered in conjunction with settlement zones or urban land, as well as lands not yet opened for utilisation, most of which are vacant or under the jurisdiction of the State for disposal and management.

The concepts and scopes of "land" and "soil" are not defined in accordance with scientific principles within the legislation. Primarily, the acceptance of land merely as a "part of the Earth's surface" and soil as a "living and natural resource", as delineated in Law No. 5403, is scientifically inappropriate. Essentially, the concept of soil pertains to the depth from the Earth's surface and is regarded as a resource that encases the Earth in a thin layer, which is of greater significance from an agricultural perspective. Conversely, land is considered a three-dimensional entity that includes the surface (comprising plant and animal communities, water resources), its height (the atmospheric layer), and its depth (such as underground resources). In summary, land is a factor of production that encompasses both the soil and all subterranean, surface, and supraterranean resources, thereby constituting a more comprehensive concept than soil.[1]

Law No. 3083 seeks to promote the efficient cultivation of soil, protect its utilisation, optimise economic productivity per unit area, and continuously improve and evaluate agricultural output. Moreover, it aims to augment employment opportunities within these sectors. The legislation applies to irrigation districts and other regions designated as necessary by the President. Additionally, it establishes regulations concerning the ownership and tenure of real properties and settlement zones for national security reasons in other regions, as deemed necessary by the President. Notably, Law No. 3083 and Law No. 5403 define the legal framework governing principles of soil and land protection and utilisation, emphasising land management within the context of human–environment interaction and sustainability.

Regulations related to land are found in many laws, decree-laws (KHK), statutes, regulations, directives, and circulars, with the Constitution and the Turkish Civil Code being the most prominent. Specifically, laws, KHKs, and ordinances are considered "rule-making", while regulations, directives, and circulars serve as "guideline" regulations for implementing the relevant legislation (Çete & Yomralıoğlu, 2009). There are approximately 90 laws, decree-laws, and statutes directly related to land management and administration. However, this number does not include

[1] In numerous economics textbooks, the term 'soil' is often employed as a substitute for 'land' within the section on factors of production, which is entirely incorrect. It would be more appropriate for Turkish textbooks to utilise the terms 'arazi' (land) or 'doğal kaynaklar' (natural resources) to correspond with the concepts of' land" or 'natural resources' as used as factors of production in English textbooks.

regulations that indirectly relate to land or the establishment laws defining the authorities and responsibilities of institutions involved in land activities. When these are included, the total number of regulations rises to about 300. Land laws are characterised by uncertainties and fragmentation, lacking a cohesive structure, with short-term regulations added over time to address emerging needs or solve problems. This process has created a fragmented legal framework with disconnected parts, repetitions, and contradictions. In light of this, there is a need to review, simplify, eliminate redundancies, and restructure the current legal regulations comprehensively. It would be advisable to consider all laws related to land collectively and unify them under a single "land law". Such an approach could eliminate fragmentation, repetitions, and contradictions within the legal framework; develop effective, clear, and holistic regulations aligned with long-term policies; establish a standard structure for land-related activities conducted by various institutions; address gaps in legal regulation areas such as real property valuation; ease the burden on courts by reviewing provisions that create legal disputes; and ultimately, transform existing laws that have been rendered ineffective through amendments over time into a dedicated land law.

6 The Use of Land Resources and Associated Problems in Türkiye

Over the past 70 years, driven by increased use of non-agricultural inputs and particularly rapid mechanisation, the agricultural land asset has expanded. It has become unavoidable to plough and convert pasture and forest lands for agriculture in addition to the existing fertile land assets. Consequently, the agricultural land asset, which was 11.68 million hectares in 1934, grew to 28 million hectares in 1980 (Tanrıvermiş, 2003). Due to factors like declining productivity and insufficient income, the agricultural land asset decreased to 24.00 million hectares in 2024 (Table 5), leaving 4.5 million hectares of land out of production and vulnerable to erosion. Despite this increase, industrialisation did not progress as desired, leading to a rise in the number of landless households in rural areas and an expansion of the operational areas of relatively large landowners (Tanrıvermiş & Tanrıvermiş, 2023). Although pasture and forest lands are sensitive areas with steep slopes and very shallow soils that should remain under permanent cover, their partial conversion to agriculture has been a significant human cause of increased erosion (Tanrıvermiş, 2003). The limited nature of the land asset, coupled with current cultivation practices that do not employ conservation farming techniques, widespread erosion, and soil pollution and degradation caused by incorrect irrigation, fertilisation, and pesticide use—alongside environmental pollution from industry and other sectors and the destruction of fertile agricultural lands for industrial, urban settlement, and infrastructure projects—all under the pressure of a growing population, pose serious potential problems for future food production and raw material supply for agro-based industries. In this context, key issues related to land resources can be categorised as erosion, soil pollution, the non-designated use of fertile lands, and desertification. These fundamental problems are briefly explained below (Haktanır, 2016).

6.1 Erosion

Although the area unaffected by erosion in Türkiye constitutes only 6.7% of the land, an erosion problem affects 73% of the total cultivated land. In extensive agricultural regions, the topsoil has been substantially depleted, and soil depths have diminished. This depletion not only reduces soil fertility but also impairs the water retention capacity of the soil. While erosion impacts a total of 25 million hectares across all European Union countries, approximately 68 million hectares are affected in Türkiye. The total affected agricultural area encompasses 23.2 million hectares, and based on sediment measurements in rivers, the annual soil loss is estimated at approximately 500 million tonnes. Furthermore, this soil loss includes the most fertile component of the soil in terms of humus, nutrients, and biological activity, which are vital to soil vitality. The adverse effects of losing the Earth's fertile soil layer extend beyond soil erosion alone, as erosion-related damages present various characteristics (Haktanır, 1999; Haktanır, 2016).

Along with transported soil, a significant portion of the chemical fertilisers and pesticides applied to the land is also lost, leading to yield reductions and considerable resource wastage. Furthermore, agricultural chemicals carried from farmlands degrade the quality of rivers, causing pollution. In Türkiye, 1000 tonnes of soil are lost annually from every square kilometre of land, 6 times more than the world average. Türkiye accounts for more than one third of the global land loss, and national efforts to combat erosion are deemed inadequate (Haktanır, 2016). Although most measures focus on forested areas, a large part of erosion occurs on tilled agricultural lands. At the current rate of mitigation, it will take very long to achieve erosion control across the country.

The concepts of erosion, desertification, and land degradation are often confused. The FAO defines land degradation as a decline in the capacity of the ecosystem to produce goods and services due to changes in soil health. Degraded lands, because of their poor structure, cannot maintain the typical soil characteristics of the ecosystem. Although this is often mistaken for the term "soil erosion", erosion specifically refers to the loss of topsoil and nutrients. While erosion is a clear sign of land degradation, it does not cover all aspects of it. In mountainous and high-altitude settlements, erosion is a natural process that is often worsened by poor management techniques, negatively impacting both production and living conditions in rural areas (FAO, 2022).

6.2 Non-Designated Use, Fragmentation, and Degradation of Fertile Agricultural Land

The increasing levels of industrialisation, infrastructure development, urbanisation, and tourism investments have accentuated the failure to adequately formulate and effectively implement national policies concerning the use and preservation of fertile lands, thereby becoming a significant issue. Adverse developments, including inadequate land use planning, frequent legislative amendments, and a gradual relaxation of protective regulations, have contributed to an increase in the unauthorised utilisation of agricultural lands, warranting safeguarding. Evidently, existing measures to prevent such processes are insufficient. The use of agricultural lands designated for farming—such as speciality and permanent crop areas—for non-agricultural purposes engenders complex problems. Such practices diminish the farm's potential and lead to the loss and degradation of fertile lands. Consequently, agricultural activities face restrictions, and the sector's contribution to the national economy continues to decline. Land degradation and the unauthorised use of land result in the irreversible loss of agricultural areas. If this trajectory remains unmitigated, the country will inevitably depend on imports to satisfy food demands or resort to developing marginal lands unsuitable for agriculture.

Half of the 4.5-million-hectare land portion has been taken out of production (left vacant), and a significant part has been allocated for non-designated uses such as sites for urban development, industry, tourism, and infrastructure investments. In regions where agricultural activities have lost their economic significance, especially in the arid farming conditions of the Central and Eastern Anatolia Regions, the abandonment of lands and the desertion of villages have become widespread. This is largely seen as a result of low agricultural income and insufficient welfare (Tanrıvermiş et al., 2024).

The fundamental challenges encountered in agricultural activities can be summarised as the insufficiency of land assets, the fragmented structure of lands, shared ownership, irrigation deficiencies, and the imbalance between input and product prices. A comprehensive evaluation of agricultural census results and Farmer Registration System (FRS) data indicates that agricultural enterprises are confronted with significant structural issues pertaining to fragmentation and tenure arrangements. There are regions where the quantity of agricultural land per household exceeds the national average. Conversely, the land owned by an average enterprise comprises approximately 6 parcels. Land consolidation projects implemented in certain neighbourhoods [villages] over the past 20 years have yielded positive outcomes in reducing the number of parcels.

In rural areas, most households or agricultural enterprises have small, highly fragmented, and scattered lands. This indicates that efforts to consolidate land and enlarge agricultural enterprises have not been sufficiently effective. Indeed, data from 2016 shows that the proportion of enterprises with 10 hectares or less of land is 78.2% of the total. This structure hampers capital accumulation in agriculture, which in turn limits technology use and productivity growth. The average size of enterprise land increased, especially after 1990, due to a rapid decline in the rural population and the number of agricultural enterprises. The cultivated land asset per agricultural enterprise was on average 7.7 hectares in 1950, 6.2 hectares in 1980, 6.1 hectares in 2000, and 11.3 hectares in 2016. The number of farmers registered in the Ministry of Agriculture and Forestry's Farmer Registration System was 2,132,491 in 2017, with an average land asset per farmer of 7 hectares. This database records only titled lands of farmers seeking state support and lands cultivated under notarised lease agreements. However, a substantial portion of rural households also cultivates land through verbal leases or de facto occupation. Consequently, the total number of enterprises (3.02 million) and the average land asset per household are likely lower than the figures derived from administrative records (Tanrıvermiş et al., 2024).

Efforts to address agricultural land fragmentation include land consolidation initiatives and new legal regulations aimed at preventing land division and inheritance problems. Since 1960, these efforts have covered 7.59 million hectares by the end of 2024 (Ministry of Agriculture and Forestry, 2025). However, regulations and support systems to prevent re-fragmentation after consolidation are still insufficient, and their impacts are rarely evaluated (Dönmez et al., 2022). To effectively combat fragmentation, Law No. 5403, amended by Law No. 6537 on April 14, 2014, prohibits dividing fertile agricultural lands into parcels smaller than two hectares. It also sets conditions for transferring inherited lands, requiring beneficiaries to demonstrate sufficient income. In Türkiye, minimum land sizes that ensure adequate income are determined at the provincial and district levels based on land type (e.g. dry, irrigated, permanent crops and greenhouse cultivation), established in 2014. Inherited lands must meet these size criteria for division and transfer. Inheritance must be declared within a year, and the land either transferred to eligible heirs or sold with a sales permit from the Ministry of Agriculture and Forestry, with proceeds shared among beneficiaries. Nevertheless, landowners, users, and both public and private organisations show insufficient concern for protecting and efficiently using fertile agricultural land. Despite rising risks from climate change and food crises, land degradation continues extensively.

6.3 Soil Pollution

Unlike soil problems such as erosion or more visible effects like water and air pollution, soil pollution does not have an immediately apparent nature. Polluting agents contaminate soils either indirectly or through direct application. Soils are considered the most vital natural decomposition centres on Earth, where organic residues of various types are broken down into their main components by the action of diverse microorganisms and soil organisms. In this way, soil and its microorganisms are crucial elements of the ecosystem, preventing the Earth from becoming a giant dumpsite. However, current practices have reached a point where they can harm this characteristic of the soil system. Among the pollutants that reach soils, heavy metals and residues of chemical fertilisers and pesticides are particularly significant. Heavy metal deposits in soils occur through atmospheric deposition,[2] the effects of chemical fertilisers and pesticides, irrigation waters with high pollution loads and wastewater treatment sludge (Haktanır, 2016; Haktanır & Arcak, 1997). It will be necessary to give special importance and priority to reclamation efforts for contaminated lands to restore them to productive use and back to nature, as well as to rehabilitation works for former industrial and commercial areas, mining sites, and other infrastructure investment zones after they fall out of use, steering them towards uses such as agriculture, meadows, and forestry where possible.

6.4 Desertification

According to the United Nations Convention to Combat Desertification, desertification is defined as the "degradation of the natural structure of land" resulting from various factors, including climate variations and human activities, in arid, semi-arid, and dry sub-humid areas. This degradation impairs the sustainability of its original natural ecological role or its appropriate economic function due to natural events or human activities. To address desertification, it is essential to prevent and/or mitigate land degradation, reclaim partially degraded lands, and rehabilitate desertified regions. Currently, under the "2019-2030 National Action Plan for Combating Desertification", the Ministry of Agriculture and Forestry is conducting studies such as monitoring systems, greening initiatives, and the promotion of drought-tolerant crop production within the framework of the "Türkiye Desertification Model and Risk Map Project".

In Türkiye, natural, technical, socio-economic, administrative, and legal factors all contribute to desertification trends. Climate fluctuations that cause the lengthening or shortening of the growing seasons (vegetation periods) of crops, which in turn reduce crop production efficiency, are natural drivers of desertification. Land management and administrative issues such as land fragmentation, intensive land use, the promotion of capital-intensive production models, salinisation, alkalinisation, desertification of lands, and the destruction or improper use of agricultural, meadow, and forest areas are among the main technical causes. Specifically, the uncertainty in land tenure systems, insecurity of use rights beyond ownership, the dominance of small family farms, the persistent reliance on traditional land

[2] Pollutants from industrial emissions, mining operations, and combustion, after being present at a certain level in the troposphere, return to the earth's surface in the form of dry and wet deposition. Research shows that the concentrations of heavy metals such as lead, cadmium, copper, and nickel, which have negative effects on the ecosystem, mostly accumulate in the top 5 cm of the soil layer. However, depending on precipitation and soil acidity, they can reach deep soil layers and groundwater or be taken up by plants and soil organisms. Surveys from an environmental ecology perspective show that soils worldwide, especially in developed countries, are being enriched with heavy metals. The increased use of coal with the industrial revolution, followed by the global proliferation of leaded gasoline consumption, and then the introduction of developing metal activities and agricultural pesticides containing heavy metals, have increased the dimensions of pollution (Haktanır, 2016, pp. 160–165).

cultivation practices on small parcels, and inadequate technical training are managerial and legal factors that exacerbate poor land use and accelerate desertification.

6.5 Evaluation of Agro-Environmental and Land Protection Measures and Their Effectiveness

Agro-environmental and land management tools are generally classified into two categories: traditional (remedial) tools and economic-financial (preventive) tools. Traditional tools include measures such as prohibitions, standards, monetary fines, and direct inspections. In contrast, economic and financial tools involve measures like taxes, fees, deposit-refund systems, tradable pollutant permits (emission allowances), subsidies, loans, market mechanisms, and liability insurance (Aliefendioğlu & Tanrıvermiş, 2011). To improve environmental and land quality in agriculture and promote sustainable land management, it is essential to utilise tools such as land use planning, banning the allocation of land for purposes other than those specified in the plan, regulating the use of agrochemicals, and encouraging sustainable and organic farming and agroforestry practices. In other words, success requires using both economic and traditional tools in a comprehensive and integrated manner. This approach is justified by the limited management capacity of environmental and agricultural organisations, the ineffective enforcement of traditional tools, the high costs of implementing traditional measures, and the fact that these tools alone often do not suffice to raise environmental quality to the desired level (Gökçe & Kaya, 1997; Tanrıvermiş, 1997; Turner et al., 1994).

Traditional instruments are generally employed to address environmental pollution stemming from crop and livestock activities. For example, discharge standards and tolerance limits have been established under the Water Pollution Control Regulation; regulations concerning agricultural pesticides, such as the minimum interval between application and harvest and residue limits for foodstuffs, have also been implemented. Furthermore, measures such as the prohibition of stubble burning, restrictions on fishing for aquatic products and hunting wild animals during specific periods, and bans on the production, importation, and sale of certain agricultural and veterinary pharmaceuticals are commonplace. Nevertheless, these conventional tools frequently prove inadequate in achieving the desired environmental management outcomes in agriculture. Consequently, it becomes necessary to integrate economic instruments alongside traditional approaches. Such examples include the collection of agricultural pesticide and fertiliser packaging via a deposit system, the promotion of environmentally friendly agricultural inputs, support for sustainable production methods such as organic farming, and, notably, in the 2000s, the taxation of polluting agricultural inputs. In addition, the implementation of awareness campaigns, projects, and training programmes aimed at fostering environmental consciousness remains essential.

For the sustainability of land management, it is imperative to regulate usage conditions and conduct comprehensive studies on land, species, and variety conservation. Primarily, the Soil Protection and Land Use Law No. 5403 explicitly prohibits the utilisation of prime agricultural lands, marginal lands, speciality crop zones, and irrigated lands for non-agricultural purposes. As part of efforts to protect agricultural land under Law No. 5403, geographic designation studies of' great plains' are undertaken, and these plains are subsequently safeguarded through Presidential Decisions. By the end of 2024, a total of 440 large agricultural plains have been designated as "Great Plain Conservation Areas" and are under protection; as a result, the protected fertile agricultural land encompasses 9.38 million hectares. This initiative has significantly contributed to the preservation of fertile lands and the promotion of sustainability in food production. Nevertheless, partial expropriation of fertile land assets for infrastructure projects such as highways, railways, ports, and pipelines, along with the subdivision of land into smaller plots for raw material supply for brick and tile manufacturing, impairs the capacity to conduct agricultural activities effectively. These restrictions on operations such as cultivation, maintenance, and harvesting reduce productivity. Consequently, infrastructure routes should be planned with consideration for fertile agricultural lands, great plains, and consolidated areas; preventing land fragmentation must be regarded as a fundamental environmental and social obligation of the pertinent institutions.

The area of fertile agricultural land (Class I–IV) designated for urbanisation, industrialisation, or tourism is approximately 1.27 million hectares, representing 4.6% of the total agricultural land (Dengiz, 2023; MEUCC, 2025). In 1980, 27.8 million hectares of land were allocated to agriculture, and by 2020, the farmland remained at 27.8 million hectares (Tanrıvermiş et al., 2024). About half of the 4.5-million-hectare share of the total agricultural land has been taken out of production and left vacant. At the same time, the remaining area has been converted to non-agricultural uses such as urban development, industry, tourism, and infrastructure projects. The decline in the economic importance of agricultural activities has led to land abandonment and village depopulation, especially in the Central and Eastern Anatolia Regions, where production occurs under arid conditions. This trend is largely related to low agricultural income levels and insufficient rural welfare. To ensure sustainable agricultural production, it is important to increase the scale of production, restructure the system, and develop cooperative land cultivation models such as "group farming". These approaches are crucial for the sustainable production of food and fibre materials.

At the national level, protected areas such as national parks, nature conservation areas, nature parks, and wildlife conservation zones have been established to safeguard specific natural resources. As a result, 2.43 million hectares of land have been designated for protection. Additionally, 2.58 million hectares of land in 18 environmentally sensitive special protection areas have also been protected (Aliefendioğlu & Tanrıvermiş, 2011; MEUCC, 2025; Ministry of Agriculture and Forestry, 2025). Although around 18% of the country's total land and 60% of its agricultural land are under protection through various legal regulations, the ongoing use of high-energy agricultural practices within conservation areas and special environmental protection zones, coupled with the inadequacy of legal rules to incentivise the development of low-input or sustainable agriculture, diminishes the effectiveness of site protection policies.

Furthermore, in land use planning, it is important to identify intensive production areas—those capable of supporting high population and consumption levels—as well as conservation and restoration zones, or to classify the national land asset accordingly. From the perspective of sustainable land management, organic farming and low external input farming practices are also deemed significant. Based on 2024 data, there were 36,412 producers engaged in organic agriculture, and the land converted for organic farming amounted to 241,490 hectares. The land where good agricultural practices are implemented has reached 393,146 hectares across 71 provinces (Ministry of Agriculture and Forestry, 2025). The proportion of land used for both production techniques relative to total cultivated land is 2.64%, and considering the presence of sensitive ecosystems and natural values within soil and water basins, it is evident that greater emphasis should be placed on sustainable land use applications. Particularly with the provisions of the climate law enacted in 2025, legislation on desertification, agriculture, and the environment, along with support systems, should be integrated to prioritise land conservation and utilisation, ensuring that principles of spatial and environmental justice are upheld.

One of the initiatives aimed at developing agro-environmental policies suitable for Türkiye's conditions is the "Programme for the Conservation of Agricultural Lands for Environmental Purposes (ÇATAK)", which was launched in 2016. The programme aims to protect areas to conserve water and soil quality, prevent erosion, ensure the sustainability of natural resources, and reduce the negative impacts of agricultural activities. ÇATAK, which began implementation under the Agricultural Reform Implementation Project, has gradually evolved from being a project solely funded externally to becoming a key part of agricultural incentives and has started to be implemented in designated areas across 58 provinces (Hasdemir & Hasdemir, 2012; Ministry of Agriculture and Forestry, 2025).

7 Evaluation and Conclusion

In Türkiye's land management practices, prohibitions and standard-setting—such as restrictions on land activities, stubble burning, and the use of fertilisers and pesticides—are frequently employed, along with direct monitoring and administrative and monetary penalties. However, economic and financial instruments have not been sufficiently developed. As a result, these instruments have not been integrated (Aliefendioğlu & Tanrıvermiş, 2011). Conversely, numerous central and local institutions hold responsibility and authority in the field of land management, leading to conflicts of authority and duties. The fundamental principle for the effective protection of land resources should be the implementation of rational land use planning at national, regional, and local levels, with data obtained from this planning forming the basis for zoning plans and land use decisions. It is essential to define a comprehensive "National Land Use and Protection Policy" and to implement this policy effectively to ensure that land is used in accordance with its capabilities. Within this framework, not only physical characteristics but also socioeconomic, legal, and institutional factors must be evaluated in a coordinated manner. It is necessary to reclaim lands that have lost productivity due to erosion and improper practices, establish a balance among agricultural, meadow-pasture, and forest assets, comply with legislative provisions when selecting areas for non-designated uses, and utilise natural resources within a "conservation-use balance". In agricultural production, quality should be given equal priority with quantity; accordingly, timely protective measures must be ensured through regular monitoring and evaluation of pollutant loads on agricultural lands.

Türkiye has ratified several international conventions and agreements concerning land resources and has embraced the responsibilities derived from this framework. In environmental planning for industrial investments, highways, railways, ports, organised industrial zones, individual industrial and commercial enterprises, and urban development and transformation projects, the principle of safeguarding fertile agricultural lands must be upheld. Accordingly, the rational selection of alternative sites should be considered within a coherent national policy framework. Decision-makers must base their judgments on analyses of the highest and best use of these areas. Furthermore, coordination among institutions and organisations responsible for land management and administration must be enhanced, and their operational effectiveness in implementation must be elevated. The main policy objectives in the process of conserving and using land assets should include the following:

- Prioritising the public interest over individual interests,
- Making population mobility directable and controllable through land policies,
- Restructuring land ownership and tenure systems,
- Continuously monitoring and evaluating the land market and prices.

Land and other natural resources should be prioritised in the country's development and conservation policies. Agricultural lands threatened by desertification are being degraded due to physical issues such as salinisation, pollution, and compaction caused by natural factors or human activities, as well as erosion and conversion to non-agricultural uses. Fertile lands are continually lost to unplanned urbanisation, industrialisation, tourism, and infrastructure projects, threatening the sustainability of agricultural production. It is essential to establish a "National Soil and Land Policy" focused on protecting and developing land resources through planned land use. This policy should be grounded in sustainable development goals and supported by long-term strategies.

The concept of the highest and best use of land resources is a core principle in the fields of real estate development and management, especially in land management and administration. This concept considers not only current uses but also the land's potential value for alternative uses. When making decisions about the highest and best use of land, four key criteria are taken into account:

Physical Possibility and Suitability of the Land: The highest and best use analysis aims to assess the land's usability for a particular purpose. The initial stage in this analysis, excluding legal restrictions such as ownership and zoning rights, is to determine whether the proposed use is physically feasible. In this regard, a land development study should be carried out considering the land's topography, type, parcel size and shape, surface and groundwater conditions, and climate. If ground conditions are unsuitable, a land use decision should not be made without undertaking necessary ground improvement works. For instance, constructing a marina in desert conditions, enabling heavy or marble structures on areas with soft clay soil, or building a structure with a 250,000 m^2 footprint on a 200,000 m^2 parcel, is not feasible. Therefore, in land management and especially in valuation applications, it is essential to analyse not only the current use but also the use that would generate the highest income and value potential for the land. In this process, the suitability of physical and environmental conditions should be evaluated as the primary criterion.

Legal Use Rights: The second fundamental element to evaluate is the legal use rights and any existing legal restrictions. For example, it is generally not possible to conduct crop production on pasture and forest lands or to obtain permits for non-agricultural uses on absolute agricultural, speciality crop, permanent crop, and olive grove lands—even if alternative areas are available. Therefore, the proposed land use must comply with existing legal rights. In cases such as wanting to build a structure in an area with restrictive zoning laws, the feasibility of the proposed development plans will be limited. To assess whether the proposed use is legally possible, the relevant legal regulations and restrictions from both public and private law must be considered together.

Financial Feasibility Analysis: To assess the financial feasibility of the proposed use, a thorough market analysis must be carried out, and potential cash flows should be estimated. If the land is intended for areas such as agricultural production or forestry, it should be directed towards the use that will generate the highest income or yield. In urban settings, for land development, data must be gathered and analysed for factors like construction and development costs, operating expenses, rental rates, vacancy and absorption rates, the discount rate, and the residual value. Accordingly, the use option that offers the highest net present value should be identified.

Maximisation of Land Use Productivity and Value: After identifying physically, environmentally, legally, and financially suitable land use options, the choice that offers the greatest productivity and value is selected. At this stage, different use options are compared based on their productivity, net present value, and risk levels. For example, a proposed use might show a higher net present value and internal rate of return than all other options. However, this higher return could also be associated with a greater level of risk. Therefore, to appropriately manage the risk linked with the proposed use, a discount rate that reflects the risk must be applied in the net present value analysis. As a result, the option with the highest internal rate of return and net present value is deemed the most productive and economically optimal use for the land.

The effective management and utilisation of land assets engender long-term spatial, economic, social, and environmental impacts, while also influencing the relationship between land use and economic development. In this regard, it is imperative to inventory land assets, conduct soil surveys and mapping studies, and establish land information systems both nationally and regionally within countries. It must be ensured that land use plans developed from these studies serve as the foundation for spatial strategy plans, environmental layout plans, and zoning schemes. By implementing land management and administration in accordance with these plan decisions, the efficient and effective utilisation of land resources can be achieved, thereby enabling the sustainable use of limited national natural resources in alignment with conservation and utilisation objectives. Such a balance will further support regional development initiatives aimed at mitigating disparities in economic development among regions. Land use plans and policies, which are aligned with the strategic objectives articulated in national and regional development plans, will provide a fundamental basis for land development, sustainable utilisation, conservation, and the formulation of suitable management models.

References

Aliefendioğlu, Y., & Tanrıvermiş, H. (2011). Türkiye'de Çevre Koruma Alanlarında Arazi Kullanımı ve Koruma Kararlarının Arazi Piyasalarına Etkileri: Gökova Özel Çevre Koruma Bölgesi Örneği. *Üçüncü Sektör Kooperatifçilik (Yeni ismiyle Üçüncü Sektör Sosyal Ekonomi Dergisi), 46*(1), 64–102.

Çete, M., & Yomralıoğlu, T. (2009). Türkiye İçin Bir Arazi İdare Sistemi Yaklaşımı. *Harita ve Kadastro Mühendisleri Odası Dergisi, 100*, 1–43.

Dale, P. F., & McLaunghlin, J. D. (1999). *Land administration*. Oxford University Press.

De Soto, H. (2003). *The mystery of capital: Why capitalism triumphs in the west and fails everywhere else* (Reprint ed.). Basic Books.

Demirci, R., Tanrıvermiş, H., & Aliefendioğlu, Y. (2007). Türkiye'de Arazi Yönetimi ve Piyasası: Temel Özellikleri, Yasal ve Kurumsal Düzenlemeler, Sorunlar ve Değerleme Çalışmaları Üzerine Etkileri. *Üçüncü Sektör Kooperatifçilik (Yeni ismiyle Üçüncü Sektör Sosyal Ekonomi Dergisi), 42*(4), 38–63.

Demirel, Z., & Gür, M. (2008). Arazi Yönetimi ve Mesleğimizdeki Değişime Etkileri. *Jeodezi ve Jeoinformasyon Dergisi, 98*, 5–11.

Dengiz, O. (2011). Samsun İlinin Potansiyel Tarım Alanlarının Genel Dağılımları ve Toprak Etüd ve Haritalama Çalışmalarının Önemi. *Anadolu Tarım Bilimleri Dergisi, 26*(3), 241–250.

Dengiz, O. (2023). *Arazi Yetenek Sınıflaması ve Türkiye'deki Dağılımı*. https://avys.omu.edu.tr/storage/app/public/odengiz/118332/4.pdf, Accessed Date: 07.03.2023.

Dönmez, İ. F., Tanrıvermiş, H., & Tanrıvermiş, Y. (2022). An evaluation of land consolidation in the context of social, spatial and environmental justice in terms of rural land management in Türkiye: The case of Çubuk District of Ankara Province. In *11th Interdisciplinary Symposium of the European Academy of Land Use and Development (EALD)*, 1-2 September 2022, UAS Frankfurt, Germany.

Eren, F. (2016). *Mülkiyet Hukuku, Gözden Geçirilmiş 4*. Baskı.

FAO. (1982). *World Soil Charter*. https://www.fao.org/3/t0389e/T0389E0b.htm, Accessed Date: 05.11.2022.

FAO. (2015a). *Status of the World's Soil Resources Main Report*. İtalya, https://www.fao.org/documents/card/en/c/c6814873-efc3-41db-b7d3-2081a10ede50/, Accessed Date: 07.03.2023.

FAO. (2015b). *Revised World Soil Charter*. İtalya, https://www.fao.org/documents/card/fr/c/e60df30b-0269-4247-a15f-db564161fee0/, Accessed Date: 07.03.2023.

FAO. (2022). *Land and Water*. https://www.fao.org/land-water/land/en/, Accessed Date: 08.11.2022.

FAO. (2025). *Land Use*. https://www.fao.org/faostat/en/#data/RL, Accessed Date: 10.07.2025.

Gökçe, O., & Kaya, F. (1997). Tarımsal Üretimde Çevresel Girdilerin Maliyete Yansıtılması, 3. Verimlilik Kongresi-Bildirileri 14-16 Mayıs 1997, MPM Yayınları:599, Ankara, ss.342-359.

Görmez, K. (2013). 6360 Sayılı Kanun Hakkında Eleştiriler. *Legal Hukuk Dergisi, 11*(122): 37–82 (www.idare.gen.tr/6360-elestiriler.pdf), Accessed Date: 05.03.2023.

Haktanır, K. (1999). Toprak Sorunları, İçinde Türkiye'nin Çevre Sorunları, Türkiye Çevre Vakfı Yayını, Ankara.

Haktanır, K. (2016). Yeryüzünün Gizemli Örtüsü Toprak, İçinde İnsan Çevre Toplum, Yayına Hazırlayan Ruşen Keleş, İMGE Kitabevi, 3. Baskı, Ankara, ss.129–172.

Haktanır, K., & Arcak, S. (1997). Toprak Biyolojisi (Toprak Ekosistemine Giriş), Yayınevi: Ankara Üniversitesi Ziraat Fakültesi Yayınlan Yayın No: 1486.

Hasdemir, M., & Hasdemir, M. (2012). *Çevre Amaçlı Tarım Arazilerini Koruma Programı ve Bu Programı Uygulamada Görevli Personellerin Çevre Duyarlılıkları*. Türkiye 10. Ulusal Tarım Ekonomisi Kongresi, Konya, ss. 1276–1283.

Hurni, H., Giger, M., & Meyer, K. (Eds.). (2006). *Soils on the global agenda. Developing international mechanisms for sustainable land management. Prepared with the support of an international group of specialists of the IASUS Working Group of the International Union of Soil Sciences (IUSS), Centre for Development and Environment* (pp. 1–64). University of Bern.

Ministry of Agriculture and Forestry (MAF). (2025). Tarım ve Orman Bakanlığı Kayıtları, Republic of Türkiye, www.tarim.gov.tr, Accessed Date: 12.05.2025.

Ministry of Environment, Urbanization and Climate Change (MEUCC). (2025). *Çevre, Şehircilik ve İklim Değişikliği Bakanlığı Kayıtları*. Republic of Türkiye, www.csb.gov.tr, Accessed Date: 12.04.2025.

Ministry of Forestry and Water Affairs (Orman ve Su İşleri Bakanlığı), (2015). Çölleşme/Arazi Bozulumu ve Kuraklıkla Mücadele Terimler Sözlüğü, Çölleşme ve Erozyonla Mücadele Genel Müdürlüğü, https://www.tarimorman.gov.tr/CEM/Belgeler/collesme%20belgeleri%20arsiv/Sayfa02/CollesmeSozluk.pdf, Accesed Date: 07.02.2025.

O'Riordan, T. (1971). *Perspectives on Research Management*. Pion Ltd.

Şimşek, O. (2018). *Alüvyal Ovalarda Farklı Fizyografyalarda Gelişen Toprakların Arazi Kullanım Planlaması ve Coğrafi Bilgi Sistemleri ile Haritalanması: Aksu Ovası Örneği*. Yayımlanmış Yüksek Lisans Tezi, Akdeniz Üniversitesi, Fen Bilimleri Enstitüsü, Antalya.

Tanrıvermiş, H. (1997). Çevre Kirliliğinin Vergilendirilmesi: İlkeler, Uygulamaları ve Türkiye Açısından Genel Değerlendirme. Gazi Üniversitesi İ.İ.B.F. İktisat Bölümü, Ekonomik Yaklaşım, Levent Sanin Özel Sayısı:27:303–328.

Tanrıvermiş, H. (1999). Çevre Koruma ve Sürdürülebilir Kalkınma Yönünden Karadeniz Bölgesi Tarımının Değerlendirilmesi. *Üçüncü Sektör Kooperatifçilik (Yeni ismiyle Üçüncü Sektör Sosyal Ekonomi Dergisi), 126*, 49–70.

Tanrıvermiş, H. (2003). Agricultural land use change and sustainable use of land resources in the Mediterranean Region of Türkiye. *Journal of Arid Environments., 54*, 553–564.

Tanrıvermiş, H. (2011). Doğal Kaynaklar Ekonomisi. İçinde: Tarım Ekonomisi, Editör: A.Özçelik, TC Anadolu Üniversitesi Yayını No:2226, Açıköğretim Fakültesi Yayını No:1125, Eskişehir, ss.126-169.

Tanrıvermiş, H. (2017). *Gayrimenkul Değerleme Esasları*. SPL Lisanslama Sınavları Çalışma Kitabı.

Tanrıvermiş, H., & Tanrıvermiş, Y. (2023). Toprak ve Arazi Kaynakları, İçinde: Türkiye'de Kent ve Çevre Yönetimi, Editörler: R.Keleş ve H.Kuran, Nika Yayınevi, Ankara, ss.209–243.

Tanrıvermiş, H., Terzioğlu, A. G., & Aliefendioğlu, Y. (2024). Kentsel ve Çevresel Adalet Bağlamında Mülkiyet ve İmar Hakkı Analizi: İstanbul İli Sultanbeyli İlçesi Örneği. *İDEALKENT, 16*(43), 69–108. https://doi.org/10.31198/idealkent.1400451

Tanrıvermiş, Y., Tanrıvermiş, H., & Uisso, A. M. (2024). Assessment of farmland fragmentation and the role of the legal regulations for the prevention of farmland fragmentation in Türkiye. *Land Use Policy, 145*, 107289.

Terzioğlu, A. G., Tanrıvermiş, H., & Tanrıvermiş, Y. (2022). An evaluation of the rights of property and zoning in Urban land management in terms of Urban and environmental justice: The case of Sultanbeyli District of Istanbul (Türkiye). In 11th Interdisciplinary Symposium of the European Academy of Land Use and Development (EALD), 1-2 September 2022, UAS Frankfurt, Germany.

TURKSTAT (TÜİK) (2025). *Tarım ve Orman Alanları 1988-2024.* https://data.tuik.gov.tr/Kategori/GetKategori?p=tarim-111, Accessed Date: 08.03.2025.

Turner, R. K., Pearce, D. W., & Bateman, I. (1994). *Environmental economics: An elementary introduction.* J Press Ltd.

Tutorialspoint. (2022). *Environmental Studies Land Resources.* https://www.tutorialspoint.com/environmental_studies/environmental_studies_land_resources.htm, Accessed Date: 08.11.2023.

UNCED. (1992). United Nations Conference on Environment and Development, Rio de Janeiro, Brazil, 3-14 June 1992, https://www.un.org/en/conferences/environment/rio1992, Accessed Date: 05.03.2023.

UNECE. (2004). *Guidelines on real property units and identifiers.* United Nations Economic Commission for Europe. https://unece.org/DAM/hlm/documents/Publications/guidelines.real.property.e.pdf, Accessed Date: 09.03.2023.

UNEP. (1980). *World Soils Policy.* Nairobi, United Nations Environmental Programme, https://digitallibrary.un.org/record/56456, Accessed Date: 05.03.2023.

Yomralıoğlu, T. (2011). Dünya'da arazi yönetimi. Türkiye'de Sürdürülebilir Arazi Yönetimi Çalıştayı, İstanbul, ss. 26–27.

Harun Tanrıvermiş is a distinguished professor who occupies the esteemed position at the Ankara University top management level as founder and head of the Department of Real Estate Development and Management, and founder and current dean of the Faculty of Applied Sciences at Ankara University. Professor Tanrıvermiş also currently works as the vice rector at Ankara University. He attained his B.Sc., M.Sc., and Ph.D. degrees from the Department of Agricultural Economics at Ankara University, specialising in land and real estate economics, land and real estate valuation, as well as natural resources and environmental economics. Furthermore, he earned an M.Sc. in environmental management through the MED-CAMPUS Programme in 1996. Professor Tanrıvermiş has published approximately 400 papers, including 43 international and 55 national peer-reviewed articles, which have been published in various high-impact journals. Additionally, he has presented 48 international and 74 national proceedings, either in full or as abstracts, at numerous conferences. He is also credited with writing 39 books and 17 book chapters. Moreover, his works concentrate on the land and real estate valuation, land and real estate economics, real estate development and project appraisal, urban transformation and sustainability, sustainable real estate development, facility and real estate management, land management, administration and polices, measuring and reporting of real estate sustainability and ESG, digital transformation in real estate and real estate technologies.

Yeşim Tanrıvermiş holds the position of full professor in the Department of Real Estate Development and Management at the Faculty of Applied Sciences, Ankara University, Türkiye. She attained her Master of Science (M.Sc.) degree in 2011 from the Department of Agricultural Economics at Ankara University. She received her Ph.D. in 2011 as the first Ph.D. program graduate of the Department of Real Estate Development and Management at Ankara University. Her research interests encompass the management and conservation of land resources, land resource economics, as well as real estate analysis and economics, in addition to studies in real estate and asset valuation. She has been delivering lectures for several years and has published academic papers since 2006. Her publications consist of 50 international and 40 national peer-reviewed articles. Additionally, she has made contributions to 110 international and 25 national full or abstract proceedings at various conferences and congresses and has authored 35 books and 30 book chapters. Presently, she serves as the Deputy Head of her department at Ankara University. Moreover, she is an active participant in various academic and professional organisations. Her experience encompasses working as a researcher and consultant across diverse public and private sectors, with a focus on real estate asset analysis, real estate finance and valuation, land and building conservation practices, as well as real estate economics and management. Furthermore, she actively engages in enhancing cooperation with both domestic and international institutions, mobilising financial resources for research projects.

Perspectives

Prospects for Improvement in the Real Estate Sector in Türkiye

Harun Tanrıvermiş, Yeşim Tanrıvermiş, and Tobias Just

Abstract

Türkiye is a transcontinental country that bridges Asia and Europe. Its geographical location between these continents enables a rapid increase in demand for real estate and infrastructure. Over the past two decades, Türkiye's real estate industry has experienced substantial growth, propelled by demand from locals and international stakeholders. Additionally, enhancements in governance structures have played a crucial role in supporting these achievements. Simultaneously, both the public and private sectors have increased housing supply, but not enough to meet the existing demand. This chapter explains the drivers of real estate demand in Türkiye and summarises the key messages of the preceding chapters in seven categories: macro environment, institutional and legal framework, real estate financing and investment, real estate market characteristics, urban planning and restructuring, public real estate and public policies, and prospects. In that sense, this chapter applies the analytical PESTEL framework: political, economic, social, technological, legal, and environmental drivers for real estate in Türkiye are presented, and provide a short SWOT (Strengths, Weaknesses, Opportunities, and Threats) analysis. The chapter concludes with an outlook and recommendations for improving the real estate sector in Türkiye.

H. Tanrıvermiş · Y. Tanrıvermiş
Department of Real Estate Development and Management, Faculty of Applied Sciences, Ankara University, Ankara, Türkiye
e-mail: tanrivermis@ankara.edu.tr; aliefendioglu@ankara.edu.tr

T. Just (✉)
International Real Estate Business School (IREBS), Regensburg University, Regensburg, Germany
e-mail: tobias.just@irebs.academy

T. Just et al. (eds.), *Understanding Türkiye's Real Estate Markets*, Management for Professionals, https://doi.org/10.1007/978-3-032-13297-0_35

1 Macro Environment

Both the construction and the real estate industry play significant roles in the economy, employing approximately two million people. At the same time, socioeconomic factors, including demographic change, income and employment growth, have influenced the development of Türkiye's real estate market. Türkiye has shown an improvement in economic indicators; still, progress remains slow. Between 2010 and 2022, Türkiye's economy grew at an average annual rate of about 5%, whereas the EU27 average was approximately 2%. Despite this growth difference, Türkiye is still lagging countries like Poland or Romania.

The urban growth driven by population growth and infrastructure projects raises costs for local authorities, however, unevenly. Furthermore, Türkiye's urbanisation challenges in post-World War II, with rapid growth causing significant issues such as unaddressed disparities and ineffective slum policies. Similarly, the dissolution of the State Planning Organisation and the sale of public lands have hindered urban development. Despite being a signatory to the European Charter of Local Self-Government, Türkiye has yet to establish a successful national urbanisation policy. Coalition governments and related issues have historically hindered progress, and even in recent stable years, effective urban and housing policies that ensure human dignity have remained elusive (see Keleş et al. in Chap. 4).

Data shows disparities among provinces, affecting housing sales and financing. A 2017 study found strong links between development scores and housing sales, especially mortgage sales. Since 2018, economic challenges have lowered initial housing sales, with interest rates and consumer confidence playing key roles. For understanding future real estate market development, it is important to understand these drivers, and yet, market research in Türkiye is still often insufficient. This also includes understanding the positive connection between education, population growth and house price growth, as well as the close relationship between the economic development of a region and its financial institutions (see Tanrıvermiş et al. in Chap. 5).

To analyse the market better, better data on the real estate market is crucial. And this applies similarly to better analysis methods and the technical data infrastructure. Today, most reliable data comes from public institutions, while the private sector provides reports on property markets and price indices and valuations on different real estate asset classes. However, there are still several data-related challenges like legal and actual property status, unreliable transaction information, limited building data in land registers, and generally poor data quality. These flaws complicate property taxation. This partly stems from a lack of standardisation and coverage gaps, which cause misleading information on housing stock and vacancies. Better collaboration between institutions and integrated data could improve quality (see Güneş et al. in Chap. 6).

International real estate investors reflect this macroeconomic dynamic and lack of available data with a split between hopeful optimism and cautious pessimism while investing in Türkiye. Favourable demographic trends bolster the positive outlook, with significant catch-up potential across key real estate asset classes in both quality and quantity, alongside the economic momentum. Türkiye's unique geographical and political position lends support to this optimism (Yıldız, 2021). The framework of beta convergence suggests that catch-up could lead to long-term growth, provided institutions are elevated to Western standards, allowing per capita economic output to align with that of the West. The institutional backlog is still keeping international investors careful, as this backlog is reflected not only in limited transparency and inadequate financial, capital, and regulatory institutions, but also in increased volatility of key economic indicators, elevated inflation rates, and consequently higher interest rates. Such conditions create significant obstacles for risk-averse investors entering the market. Overall, Türkiye has developed in many senses, but at the same time several economic institutional aspects resemble the situation of 15 years ago (Kudatgobilik et al., 2008). While substantial long-term opportunities exist, institutional barriers continue to impede progress in the short and medium term (see Just and Dietl in Chap. 3).

And these institutional settings demonstrate their importance, particularly during times of crisis when a region and consequently its property market are sensitive. Türkiye experienced a series of crises with the COVID-19 pandemic, the Russia–Ukraine invasion, and the 2023 earthquake, and all three events have significantly impacted the volatility of Türkiye's real estate market (Salami et al., 2024). These shocks revealed the market's sensitivity to macroeconomic, political, and natural disruptions. Findings suggest government intervention is crucial during crises (see Tanrıvermiş et al. in Chap. 7).

2 Institutional and Legal Framework

Türkiye's real estate market stakeholders include developers, financiers, and regulatory bodies that play crucial roles in the market activities through land exchanges, service rendering, tax collection, investments, and transactions. T-REITs have governance structures based on real estate activities and workforce, reflecting diversification and risk levels. Larger T-REITs invest in multiple indices, are less risky, and are often led by directors with sufficient experience in the sector. Just and Tanrıvermiş suggest in Chap. 2 that future research could explore seasonal variations in risk to assess resilience.

The best instrument to protect against risk, however, is a stable and reliable judicial and tax system: Türkiye's real estate rights outline fundamental entitlements that enable real estate owners to use and dispose of properties, as governed by Türkiye's law in Articles 2, 13, and 35 of the Constitution. Still, public interest, personal rights, and democratic order limit these rights. Owners cannot exercise these rights against public interests (Eren, 2016). The law also clarifies that real estate is a right, not a duty, and such rights cannot be limited contrary to the democratic order. The 1976 Constitutional Court ruling declared partial expropriation without full compensation unconstitutional. Viewing the State as a social institution requires recognising private land ownership, which is protected by public, international, and private law (see Öcal and Keskin in Chap. 8).

Spatial use, renewal efforts, and effective space management are important. Especially when considering future projections in cities that grow and change without strategic planning, zoning plans. Within this context, fair value distribution, fostering a sense of belonging, and justly integrating increased value into the urban fabric are priorities. In this regard, consistent practices in Türkiye are vital at both local and national levels. Each zoning decision impacts the balance of urban growth and development, ensuring that value distribution does not disrupt this balance over time helps to guide public investments and urban development through careful location planning. Following spatial use decisions, parcel-level distribution supports spatial management by strategically positioning infrastructure and social facilities. Decisions at the parcel scale influence not only local administrations but also strategies at the city level. Settlement patterns in urban centres and their outskirts develop based on comparative land use decisions across different regions. Achieving a rural–urban settlement balance depends on effective spatial organisation, while land and parcel readjustment practices seek to promote healthy regional development. In line with the principle of value equality, urban land readjustment often employs area-based distribution models rather than evaluating each parcel individually, as seen in land consolidation projects. This approach reduces the likelihood of achieving fair outcomes. Implementing a value-based distribution model for zoning and parcelling in urban areas fosters a more equitable system. Additionally, collaboration between real estate professionals and technical experts involved in these processes is recommended to ensure sound decision-making. When the Dedication for Public Facilities (DOP) mechanism, recognised by legislation as the land acquisition method for common use areas, falls short, expropriation is often applied. Then, land consolidation or zoning boundary modifications can be beneficial for zoning implementation. Zoning practices, which are highly significant within Türkiye's legal framework, are seen as tools for urban and spatial management. Land and parcel readjustment is a widely used and effective strategy—both in Türkiye and internationally—for promoting planned development in urban peripheries and blending rural and urban areas. Still, it is important to recognise the significant challenges involved in its implementation. Therefore, efforts to review and improve these processes will be of great importance (see Tanrıvermiş et al. in Chap. 9).

Real estate's strategic role in Türkiye is vital for economic and social growth. The construction sector is linked to approximately 100 other sectors; this means any disruption in the construction sector heavily impacts the overall economy. Despite classification challenges, real estate value is mainly derived from land and buildings. Land management depends on economics, policies, cadastre, zoning, and land consolidation, all of which require effective valuation. Progress has been made in market valuation, but tax, expropriation, and land sharing activities are inadequate, with reports often below standards. A comprehensive evaluation system, including mass appraisal and value maps, is crucial. Creating detailed value maps will aid risk analysis, urban planning, and audits. Efforts to achieve this have remained incomplete. The system needs reform, strengthening valuation authority and aligning with international standards like IVSC, RICS, IASB, and IPMSC. Establishing institutions like a value information system and real estate exchange, possibly under Borsa

Istanbul, is vital for transparency, investor protection, and data use. Adopting international standards, professionalising valuation, and improving reporting are essential for competitiveness and growth.

Since 2010, protocols involving various institutions have served as models for training experts, especially RICS graduates, enhancing quality and foreign investment. Disciplines like development, management, and valuation are key for integration. Türkiye's past reliance on untrained individuals caused quality issues. Recently, programmes and regulations stressing qualified experts linked to GIS and the Land Registry are emerging. Aligning property tax values with market prices could raise revenues, but regulations must be reviewed comprehensively for a system reform (see Tanrıvermiş and Tanrıvermiş in Chap. 10).

Taxation for construction and real estate involves specialised sector issues, with challenges from sector traits and existing laws being outlined. The sector's vital role in Türkiye's economy stems from strong housing demand, while its production process boosts connected industries, production and employment. Tax obligations arise at various stages and encompass taxes on profits, transactions, and ownership, necessitating an approach that considers the overall burden and avoids double taxation. The sector displays a fragmented, complex structure with policies that lack integration, highlighting the need for a comprehensive taxation system to ensure fairness. Property values are often uncertain; adopting international valuation standards by professionals could improve revenue. Challenges include legislation, tax obligations, weak accounting, and oversight, which hinder efficiency. Public authorities should implement regulations to address these issues. A simplified, balanced tax structure, stakeholder involvement, and measures to reduce double taxation are crucial for curbing informality, boosting direct tax revenues, and reducing income inequality (see Töremen and Demir in Chap. 11).

3 Real Estate Financing and Investment

A well-functioning real estate financing system can boost demand and enable supply by securing terms, relying on good relations between government, financial institutions, developers, and households. New financial instruments, aligned with international standards, are needed to meet the financing demand for real estate. Real estate-based capital market instruments facilitate access to financing, aiming to enable homeownership and provide alternative development financing.

In Türkiye, the number of real estate-related financial instruments is growing, along with product diversity, user base, and transaction volume. However, most housing finance is still provided by commercial banks, which use deposit accounts as funding sources, thereby risking a maturity mismatch. To address this, new products are needed to ensure sustainable financing, depending on secondary markets and expanding mortgage banking, supported by Law No. 5582. Regulation of secondary markets and the introduction of real estate derivatives are crucial for increasing investor participation (see Güneş et al. in Chap. 12).

Since their inception, T-REITs have become a popular investment, primarily due to the psychological trust associated with real estate. These trusts offer opportunities through securities funds, enhancing the competitive landscape and increasing mobility in secondary markets. REITs pool investors' capital, allowing individuals to benefit from real estate without funding, acquiring, or managing properties directly. Publicly listed REITs are common and more liquid than direct real estate investments. However, the Turkish REIT market is underdeveloped due to restrictions including borrowing capacity, property eligibility, expertise, and subsidiaries. Corporate taxpayers holding shares in real estate investment funds are exempt from certain taxes, unlike REIT investors. Improving the legal framework and growth prospects for REITS could help expand Türkiye's real estate market and support larger projects (see Hepşen et al. in Chap. 13).

Türkiye's foreign real estate laws underwent significant changes between 1984 and 2012, during its outward growth strategy. The legislation set limits per person and district, but Law No. 6302 of 2012 removed reciprocity and some of the restrictions. Despite reforms, foreign investment remains below expectations:

While desirable for residence, citizenship through purchasing real estate by international buyers faces criticism; many suggest residence permits instead. Foreign demand, driven by conflicts and exchange rates, has pushed up rental and sale prices (Salami et al., 2023). As policy persists, targeted measures are needed to improve Turkish citizens' housing access. Current policies focus mainly on economics, neglecting social, cultural, and environmental effects. Agency systems are inadequate for managing foreign ownership, and regions with high foreign property activity require better support and integration measures (see Tanrıvermiş et al. in Chap. 14).

The primary motive for real estate investments in Türkiye is to achieve a higher target as quickly as possible. The decisions and strategies of real estate market investors in Türkiye have been adversely affected by various sector-specific factors, such as increases in construction and labour costs, depreciation of the Turkish Lira, and rising energy prices. Policies related to housing and land development—such as urban transformation initiatives and housing acquisition support schemes introduced through reduced mortgage interest rates as well as tax incentives, can significantly influence investment decisions and investor preferences. Furthermore, fluctuations in regional supply and demand within the real estate sector have affected investment options and their associated returns. Indirect investment options, comprising financial assets backed by real estate, have lagged direct investments in Türkiye and are still less prevalent compared to developed countries. The main reason for this is Turkish economic and political instability. Additionally, increasing and incentivising options aimed at qualified investors, such as real estate investment funds, will strengthen the market (see Ulusoy et al. in Chap. 15).

Furthermore, Real Estate Investment Funds (REIFs), investment options, and the prerequisites for Islamic real estate investment funds in Türkiye were investigated. It was found that multiple categorisations exist based on the development stage of REIFs within specific markets. In addition, the success of REIFs largely hinges on the participation of qualified investors. Quarterly net asset value (NAV) data for each T-REIF were collected and analysed, along with asset allocation percentages, to estimate the distribution of investments across sectors. The results indicate that T-REIFs are guided not only by Western regulations but also by Islamic law, as indicated by the non-convergence of prices, which constrains the scope of permissible investments (see Güneş et al. in Chap. 16).

Besides capital market instruments, technology will have to play a bigger role: Technologies like AI, IoT, digital twins, and bio-based materials are transforming buildings into proactive, adaptable systems, supporting regenerative design and reducing environmental impact. But PropTech applications can also foster a more effective utilisation of *Sukuk* investments. As the world shifts from traditional methods to virtual approaches, so will investment strategies. Applying PropTech in capital allocation for real estate through—for example—*Sukuk*, aimed at affordable and social housing, warrants proper attention. The adoption of *Sukuk* in financing Türkiye's housing market has established a long-term relationship. Additionally, investors can make consistent decisions on where and what kinds of projects to invest in through PropTech applications. The transparency embedded in PropTech could provide investors with more and better information. Since *Sukuk* is an Islamic finance project, ethical investment and societal contribution should take precedence over profit maximisation for investors (see Salami et al. in Chap. 17).

Next to the social affordability question is the broader challenge of sustainable real estate development. Sustainable practices have moved from niche to mainstream, creating value across economic, environmental, social, and technological spheres. Research has shown that projects within the "Quadruple Net Value Analysis" framework generate economic, environmental, social, and sensory benefits, saving up to 30% on operating costs, increasing asset values by 15 to 20%, and enhancing user health. Green buildings offer 82% cleaner indoor air, 215 to 309% more natural light, and 25 dB less noise. Türkiye's potential to lead this change relies on its youth, its infrastructure, and technological growth. ESG criteria are now vital for investments, with research confirming a positive link between environmental performance and returns. Türkiye could be a regional leader, aligned with its 2053 Net Zero goals and the EU's Green Deal. Success depends on promoting innovations such as regenerative design, enhancing governance, and developing green finance tools (see Tanrıvermiş et al. in Chap. 18).

4 Real Estate Market Characteristics

Türkiye has the potential to rise as a real estate hub, driven by internal factors such as its large and young population, as well as increasing purchasing power, and external influences, including migration and geopolitical events. The country's natural beauty, history, infrastructure, and socioeconomic improvements attract investors, fuelling sector growth. COVID-19 has spurred technological changes affecting shopping, transportation, communication, and home design, alongside shifts in energy use and regulations. Energy's role in real estate highlights the importance of using renewable sources, incorporating green buildings, leveraging smart technology, and implementing automation to enhance sustainability. Establishing clear regulations and legal reforms is essential for sustainable urbanisation and sector growth, impacting both domestic and international investors, as well as the national economy. Future adaptations will focus on technology, development, marketing, and management practices (see Parsa et al. in Chap. 19).

Given the size and social and economic relevance of the housing sector, the emergence of a housing bubble would pose a serious threat. A housing bubble would imply that housing prices are escalating beyond their intrinsic and justified levels. Given current market conditions, significant declines are not evident. The price increases are primarily attributable to fundamental factors within Türkiye's housing market, a speculative bubble is currently unlikely. However, that does not make the affordability issue less challenging (see Ahsan et al. in Chap. 20).

With reference to European standards, the facility, property, and asset management market in Türkiye is an early stage of development. Sectors like facility management are gaining recognition, institutionalisation, standard-setting, certification, legislation, and best practices are developing. The industry needs to professionalise, especially in commercial and infrastructure projects. Improving asset, portfolio, corporate, and investment management is urgently needed for large organisations and investors. Türkiye lacks specific regulation and an administrative structure for the sector. Regulation and increased outsourcing will likely boost sector growth, improving regulatory oversight and service quality through standardised metrics and restructuring companies, including ancillary support firms. Establishing a legal framework and creating sector associations are essential, though current structures are fragmented. Collaboration with European and US institutions will enhance training and research, fostering skilled personnel and academic ties. The growing demand and international cooperation will facilitate experience sharing, developing occupational standards and a qualified workforce (see Tanrıvermiş et al. in Chap. 21).

Technologies such as big data, IoT, virtual reality, and digital twins facilitate industry transformation. This is supported by policies such as the Eleventh and Twelfth Development Plans and the National Smart Cities Strategy, government initiatives such as the Web Tapu system and pilot projects with 3D city models promote a digital real estate ecosystem. Solutions like online platforms, virtual tours, and intelligent facilities improve efficiency and transparency. Challenges include data system integration, legal alignment, workforce readiness, and scaling pilots. Collaboration across sectors is crucial for maximising digitalisation benefits. (see Sunguroğlu et al. in Chap. 22).

The inherent risks associated with real estate investment and project development are escalating due to evolving environmental conditions. Maintaining a comprehensive, sector-specific database is indispensable for effective analysis of market and corporate risks. Monitoring country-specific and systematic risks holds equal importance. Project scheduling should be determined through methodologies such as real options, scenario analyses, and simulations.

The deployment of skilled human capital is essential for analysing risks and devising management techniques, particularly in rapidly changing nations. Topics such as land acquisition, development, design, contractual agreements, construction, and risk assessment are crucial areas of research, along with regional studies. Both public and private entities are mandated to conduct risk analyses, develop Decision Support Systems (DSS), and recognise these as central to their operational framework (see Öztürk and Tanrıvermiş in Chap. 23).

5 Urban Planning and Restructuring

Urban welfare planning aims at anticipating and meeting future needs. Limited participatory mechanisms lead to lawsuits over perceived interests. While oversight based on "public interest" exists, legislative gaps cause challenges. Sharing urban development benefits among property owners, the municipality, and residents, as well as clarifying regulations regarding illegal construction, are key elements of addressing challenges of urban planning. Deterrents and reducing reliance on amnesties are crucial. A comprehensive urban policy and a strong legal framework are essential to address legislative shortcomings and prioritise public interest (see Keskin and Öcal in Chap. 24).

The growth of informal housing in Türkiye has been a big challenge in the last few decades and triggered several policies towards better urban transformation projects. Post-1980s, converting low-income areas into upscale developments, backed by private investment, has become the norm. The focus lies on the causes behind the demand for such transformations. While Gecekondu owners initially led the implementation of amnesty laws for redevelopment, they now oppose ongoing efforts. Improving social and economic conditions is important alongside physical renewal. Achieving holistic, participatory urban change remains crucial, despite challenges. Often, project eligibility excludes the urban poor and benefits middle- and upper-income groups. Measures include recognising the demand's origins, avoiding forced transformations, and using social impact assessments to ensure projects to improve life quality. Inclusive, well-planned and economically viable approaches should be adopted (see Özdemir et al. in Chap. 25).

Furthermore, there have been serious issues with urban infrastructure improvements in Türkiye with regard to legislation and implementation since the 2000s, mainly due to historical urbanisation challenges. Establishing a secure, accessible, and sustainable urban transport system is crucial, emphasising efficiency in time and cost. Strategies for water resource management must be aligned, with wastewater and potable water services meeting standards. Investment and institutional performance should improve, with opportunities identified to enhance solid waste management. PPC models should promote environmental responsibility, while local facilities need financial support. Coordination in urban transit and zoning is vital, with master plans being updated regularly. Policies should favour mass transit over private vehicles and promote sustainable, eco-friendly modes, including non-motorised transport. Similarly, a national strategy is needed for demand management and safety. Urban infrastructure services face financing challenges, requiring diverse approaches, supportive legal frameworks, and more adoption of PPP. As urbanisation expands, institutional roles must be reviewed and restructured (see Tuna et al. in Chap. 26).

While public–private partnerships (PPP) aim to boost efficiency, productivity, and sustainability, projects often involve consortia, ensuring cost efficiency and asset transfer back to the public, leading to complications. In Türkiye, these collaborations primarily reflect cooperation within a regulated market, rather than true partnerships.

The use of public land for investments has become vital for the Türkiye's economy, especially in the tourism and technology sectors. Incorporating pasture and forest lands into the treasury's portfolio means about two-thirds of Türkiye's land is public real estate. Effective management, valuation, and classification of these assets are crucial for supporting economic growth, sustainability, and security. Extensive public land impacts agriculture and housing, with urban transformation projects in the 2000s reducing land costs and alleviating informal settlements through public-private collaborations. Projects to allocate treasury lands to farmers aim to boost agriculture and reduce income inequality. All public real estate should be integrated into economic activities to support investments (see Demir and Terzioğlu in Chap. 27).

6 Public Real Estate and Public Polices

Different legal regimes regulate real estate transactions. The 1982 Constitution protects coastline and forest areas, prohibiting full forest ownership transfer, but not rangelands. The pasture commission can revoke rangeland classification; however, sale or transfer to private or public entities is not permitted. Treasury-owned properties can be sold under specific conditions, and in some provinces, properties in Organised Industrial Zones can be transferred free of charge if no restrictions exist.

Public real estate allocation has become a vital development tool, with recent laws integrating public resources into the economy, especially in tourism. Allocating unused public real estate for investment promotes economic growth. Türkiye's public real estate necessitates effective management and strategic policies to support development, food security, and energy security. The public land assets influence agricultural and housing policies; urban transformation projects in the 2000s used public lands to reduce informal settlements, especially in metros, improving social equity. Projects by the Ministry aim to allocate treasury lands to farmers, boosting agriculture and addressing income inequality. All public real estate should be integrated into economic activities and used strategically for investment, with public transport revenues also serving as financing sources to advance national progress and social welfare (see Yıldırım et al. in Chap. 28).

Türkiye's energy policies reflect economic growth, industrialisation, and urbanisation. Compared to EU and OECD countries, faster energy growth in Türkiye indicates a need for better efficiency and renewable energy use. Dependence on fossil fuels raises emission concerns, while investments in renewables, especially solar and wind, are enhancing energy security. Challenges like funding, awareness, and technical skills must be addressed to boost energy efficiency. Access to climate finance, such as the Green Climate Fund, is crucial but hindered by bureaucratic hurdles for achieving the net-zero goal by 2053. (see Güneş and Tombul in Chap. 29).

Furthermore, natural resources and their related values are critically important for protecting and maintaining ecosystems worldwide, especially within Türkiye. Sensible management of agricultural lands, including natural assets and vital resources, greatly supports improving the environment, agricultural yields, and human health. Urbanisation puts pressure on fertile agricultural lands, leading to their gradual loss and threatening future food security and agricultural productivity. Therefore, Türkiye must efficiently manage its limited agricultural land and water resources. Developing an accurate and reliable soil database is essential for effective and sustainable land management. Together with an assessment of current policies and practices, it shows that simply registering protected areas with defined boundaries is not enough to meet protection goals. One urgent issue is the encroachment upon or the complete removal of boundaries of protected areas, often to enable specific investments or construction projects. Additionally, a major challenge is the insufficient compensation for property rights affected by restrictions for conservation purposes. Recommendations also include centralising the management of natural protected areas in Türkiye under a single organisation, with protection decisions made collaboratively with relevant institutions. Furthermore, there is a need for a comprehensive legal framework covering all facets of nature conservation. Ultimately, safeguarding natural assets and strategic resources like agricultural lands is fundamental to ecosystem sustainability. (see Tanrıvermiş et al. in Chap. 30).

Similarly, heritage preservation has become an international issue due to globalisation. In Türkiye, conservation primarily begins with the registration of heritage elements, driven by conservation councils that establish principles that impact property rights. Interventions must follow proportionality within legal boundaries to ensure effective spatial and economic conservation. Türkiye's rich heritage requires reviewing legal, administrative, social, and environmental practices and improving funding, which remains a challenge. Alternative management tools are explored but underused due to neglect of cultural and legal factors. Compensation for expropriated private property rights is essential. Budget constraints and public awareness are key challenges; social and cultural engagement is crucial. Success depends on legal, cultural, and educational initiatives, starting from family education (see Tanrıvermiş and Baydan in Chap. 31).

The education and research system in real estate highlights progress in establishing associate, bachelor's, and graduate programmes in land, real estate, infrastructure, and construction management, achieved through professionalisation in the field. In developed countries, these programmes mainly adhere to statutory requirements and market demands. Developing countries such as Türkiye are also progressing in real estate education within an interdisciplinary framework, aligning with global trends. Nonetheless, many countries face challenges in recognising and prioritising university real estate programmes, often establishing them for international accreditation and to attract international students. The complexity of real estate calls for comprehensive curricula covering economic, spatial, and technological aspects. Türkiye's higher education has experienced rapid growth in real estate programmes, though shortages of qualified faculty and the need to review outcomes persist. Aligning Türkiye's real estate education with international standards will enhance sector competitiveness. To attain sustainable success, it is essential to integrate international standards, ethical frameworks, and professionalisation infrastructure (see Tanrıvermiş et al. in Chap. 32).

In Türkiye, approximately 60.6% of the population resides within 100 km of the coast, and the 1982 Constitution established the legal framework for coastal protection and use. The Coastal Law and regulations followed, but different institutions applied them divergently, creating jurisdictional conflicts. A Presidential Decree clarified the roles of different public administrative bodies in order to reduce uncertainties that result from different regulations (see Ülger et al. in Chap. 33).

Türkiye's land management instruments include bans, standards, and penalties for land activities, while acknowledging that economic tools are underdeveloped and lack proper integration (Aliefendioğlu & Tanrıvermiş 2011). Many institutions share responsibilities for land management, which often leads to conflict. Effective land protection depends on rational land-use planning, supported by precise zoning data. The enactment of a comprehensive "National Land Use and Protection Policy" is essential to ensure that land use aligns with its potential. Eroded land requires reclamation, and a harmonious balance between agricultural, pasture, and forested lands must be maintained. Legislation should govern non-designated land uses, emphasising sustainable resource management. In agriculture, the quality of produce should correspond with quantity, accompanied by pollution monitoring. Türkiye remains dedicated to comply with international land agreements. Urban planning must prioritise the protection of fertile land through informed site selection within a unified national policy framework. Institutional coordination should be strengthened to facilitate optimal land use, with a focus on public interests, management of population mobility, restructuring of land systems, and monitoring land markets.

Prioritisation of land and natural resources within development and conservation policies is imperative. Agricultural lands threatened by desertification are degrading and their conversion to non-agricultural uses—driven by both natural processes and human activities. Fertile lands are lost to urbanisation, industrialisation, tourism, and infrastructure development, endangering agricultural sustainability. The establishment of a "National Soil and Land Policy" focused on land protection and sustainable utilisation is urgent. Such a policy should align with the Sustainable Development Goals and long-term strategic plans.

If ground conditions are unfavourable, land use decisions should not proceed without the necessary ground improvement measures. Therefore, in land management and valuation, it is crucial to analyse not only current uses but also potential uses, with an emphasis on physical and environmental suitability.

The second critical component involves evaluating legal rights and restrictions pertaining to land use. For example, crop production may be unviable on pasturelands, forests, or designated agricultural zones such as absolute agricultural, speciality crop, permanent crop, or olive grove areas, even if alternative lands are available. Developing structures within zones subject to restrictive zoning laws will limit developmental potential.

Effective management of land assets contributes to sustainable spatial, economic, social, and environmental development, shaping the nexus between land use and economic progress. It is vital to inventory land assets, conduct soil surveys and mapping studies, and develop comprehensive land information systems at both national and regional levels. Land use plans founded on these studies should serve as the basis for spatial strategy plans, environmental schemes, and zoning regulations. Proper land resource management and administration, in accordance with these plans, enable sustainable utilisation, support conservation efforts, and promote the responsible use of limited natural resources. This balanced approach fosters regional development initiatives aimed at reducing disparities in economic progress across different areas and regions. Land use plans and policies aligned with the strategic objectives of national and regional development plans will serve as a fundamental basis for land development, sustainable utilisation, conservation, and the establishment of suitable management models (see Tanrıvermiş and Tanrıvermiş in Chap. 34).

7 Development Trends of Real Estate in Türkiye

Due to the country's economic and financial system, the emerging real estate issue in major cities has persisted as a significant challenge since the 1950s. Following the 1999 Marmara Earthquake, Türkiye's urban transformation agenda prioritised urban settlements at risk of disasters, accompanied by relevant legislative amendments. The implementation of this transformation agenda has facilitated substantial progress in management within the real estate sector. After the 2001 recession, under the "Transition to a Strong Economy" programme, Türkiye achieved economic growth and stability in the construction and real estate industries. The legal framework for these rapid developments was established with the enactment of the "Sales of Real Estate to Foreigners" law in 2003 and the "Long-term Mortgage System" law in February 2007. Post-2005, the real estate sector experienced its highest growth rates until 2007, leading to a notable reduction in the country's housing problems. Despite the global recession of 2007/2008, Türkiye lagged developed nations, particularly in green infrastructure and shopping centres. Nonetheless, it has been viewed as a market with growth potential for foreign investors, notwithstanding the decline and stagnation of such investments. Furthermore, the role of the government regarding structural reforms prior to the crisis renders Türkiye's economy relatively underdeveloped in this context, which was affected (Tanrıvermiş, 2020). Over the past few decades, Türkiye has experienced significant urban renewal and development initiatives within the real estate sector, particularly in housing. The government intends to construct 500,000 social housing units over five years; however, this will likely not meet the entire demand in this segment.

8 Opportunities and Challenges of the Real Estate Sector

Summarising the opportunities and challenges for Türkiye's real estate sector with a PESTEL analysis:

8.1 Political

Türkiye's liberal policies have fostered political stability, encouraging investors to participate in the real estate market. It has become a target market for Western and Arab investors, as well as individuals escaping unstable conditions in their home countries, seeking to acquire residence in Türkiye. The country advocates for liberal trade and investment policies, facilitating open commerce among various countries within the European Union. Its objective is to attract a broader spectrum of real estate investors. Nevertheless, one of the prevailing political challenges in Türkiye is the occurrence of recurrent violent terrorist attacks, which have taken place and continue to pose a threat.

8.2 Economical

The influx of foreign investment from abroad used to be one of Türkiye's economic drivers. On the back of stable real economic growth, the unemployment rate in Türkiye came down in the last few years—though it remains elevated.

Between 2005 and 2020, a total of 72,053 properties, covering 309 million square metres, were sold.[1] However, the overall inflow of Foreign Direct Investment was volatile over the last few years (Table 1). To enhance foreign direct investments, particularly in real estate, the processes for establishing businesses should be streamlined, and market transparency should be improved.

One of the principal economic challenges confronting Türkiye is the current account deficit, and inflation remains too high with regard to both consumer and producer prices, and consequently, interest rates are also high.

The housing transaction market is stagnating due to loan restrictions and diminished purchasing power. However, housing prices and rents have stabilised since 2024 indicating a more balanced housing market. Given that the proportion of second-hand homes in total housing transactions remains high shows that affordability and access to new homes are still a problem. Under these circumstances, it is imperative to expedite the transformation of risky buildings, promote new projects—especially in large cities and coastal regions where demand is high—and adopt targeted measures to enhance housing affordability for middle- and low-income households. These actions are essential to reorient policies related to the real estate sector's supply and demand dynamics, as well as monetary and fiscal policies.

[1] https://www.duvarenglish.com/president-erdogan-the-worlds-biggest-real-estate-agent-news-57329.

Table 1 Main economic indicators of Türkiye during 2018–2024

Economic Indicators	2018	2020	2022	2023	2024
GDP (Current Billion US $)	797.73	717.14	905.81	1153.24	1358.26
GDP per Capita (Current US $)	9799	8600	10,659	13,008	15,325
Growth (%)	3.6	1.6	5.2	5.0	3.5
Inflation (CPI (2003 = 100), Annual Average, %)	16.33	12.28	72.31	53.86	58.51
Foreign Direct Investment (Billion USD)	12.5	7.5	13.8	10.7	11.3
Current Account Deficit (Billion US$)	12.5	7.7	13.7	10.7	11.3
Current Account Balance /GDP (%)	−14.6	−31.1	−46.3	−39.9	−10.2
USD/TL (USD Sales Average)	4.82025	7.01823	16.58555	24.05339	32.83261
Unemployment Rate (%)	11.0	13.2	10.4	9.4	8.7

Source: Republic of Türkiye Ministry of Trade (2025)

8.3 Social

One of the strengths of the social system in Türkiye is the high share of the young population, with more than half of the population being under 30 years of age (Ahsan and Duman, 2022). This is a strategic advantage for Türkiye, as it signifies a robust supply of a young, motivated workforce.

Türkiye's unemployment rate declined to 8.7% in 2024 from 13.2% in 2020, but is still significantly above a "natural" rate of unemployment. Thus, one of the challenges within Türkiye's social framework is the elevated level of unemployment. Of a total workforce of 35.7 million, the number of unemployed individuals has reached 3.0 million, and unemployment rates are negatively correlated with education level and also related to gender, with women registering more often for unemployment (11.4%) than men (6.9%). Additionally, open and hidden unemployment rates differ between rural and urban regions. Meanwhile, the labour force participation rate remained steady at 54.1%. Notably, the youth unemployment rate for individuals aged 15 to 24 years was 15.6%. The fact that youth unemployment is nearly twice as high as the national unemployment rate and that unemployed young graduates from higher education institutions underscores the necessity to address the content of academic education curricula, talent mismatch, and employment policies conjointly.

8.4 Technological

Türkiye is advancing technologically quickly in the ICT sector. Since 2021, Türkiye has continued the technological progress through several projects in ICT, defence, and aviation—including domestically designed automobiles, new communication satellites, and advanced defence products. Over the past decade, Türkiye's ICT sector has expanded at double-digit growth rates: in 2020, the ICT industry experienced a 36% growth, surpassing the initial forecast of 10%. The information technology sector grew by an average of 29% during the same period, while growth in communication technologies reached 19%. In the previous year, the value of information technologies was TL 114.5 billion, constituting 29% of the total industry, while communication technologies accounted for TL 120.1 billion. The privatisation of the ICT sector has attracted increased foreign investment and has contributed to the creation of additional employment opportunities within Türkiye.

8.5 Legal

One of Türkiye's strengths is the comprehensive legal framework. The judicial system consists of general courts, which handle domestic cases, and specialised penal courts for more serious offences. Military courts oversee military-related cases, while the Constitutional Court, the highest tribunal, deals with key cases involving the Türkiye's government, including war crimes. Türkiye's government is strict about enforcing the law. This ensures fair trials in case of legal issues for all parties, including trade union issues.

Another advantage in Türkiye is the strong legal framework for business entities. Companies looking to invest in Türkiye have the freedom to start, operate, and close a business within Türkiye's regulatory framework. For example, in Türkiye, it takes on average 6 days to start a business, compared to 43 days in other countries.

One of the current challenges in Türkiye is judicial inefficiency and partly ineffectiveness, as there are delays in Türkiye's judicial system. This is a disadvantage for bringing the plant into Türkiye, as a decision against the company in a legal battle may be influenced by biases.

8.6 Environmental

Türkiye possesses a rich natural resource base and ranks ninth in biodiversity among European countries. One of the current environmental issues in Türkiye are the high pollution levels and the resulting global warming. The water treatment facilities, wastewater treatment equipment, and solid waste management systems in Türkiye need urgent improvement, as there is significant pollution, with an increase in chemical and detergent pollutants that are released into the air and can cause health problems, especially in urban areas.

Additionally, another disadvantage of high pollution levels is that emitted greenhouse gases contribute to global warming. Türkiye needs to reduce pollution levels to meet EU standards for future cooperation prospects.

References

Ahsan, M. M., & Duman, D. (2022). Kırsal Yerleşimlerde Gençlerin Göç Etme Eğilimleri ve Etkileri: Bitlis İli Adilcevaz İlçesi Örneği. *Journal of Academic Value Studies, 8*(3), 231–243. https://doi.org/10.29228/javs.63782

Aliefendioğlu, Y., & Tanrıvermiş, H. (2011). Türkiye'de Çevre Koruma Alanlarında Arazi Kullanımı ve Koruma Kararlarının Arazi Piyasalarına Etkileri: Gökova Özel Çevre Koruma Bölgesi Örneği. *Üçüncü Sektör Kooperatifçilik (Yeni ismiyle Üçüncü Sektör Sosyal Ekonomi Dergisi), 46*(1), 64–102.

Eren, F. (2016). Mülkiyet hukuku. Yetkin Publications See, for example, Ankara, Türkiye.

Kudatgobilik, Z., Ruppert, E., Topintzi, E. & Just, T. (2008). *Real estate investment in Turkey: Look beyond Istanbul*. Deutsche Bank Current Issues, August 26, 2008.

Republic of Türkiye Ministry of Trade. (2025, August). *Economic Outlook 2025: August*. https://www.trade.gov.tr/data/602cd44013b876f918da9c8c/Economic%20Outlook%202025%20August.pdf

Salami, M. A., Tanrıvermiş, H., & Tanrıvermiş, Y. (2023). Interdependence between foreigner housing acquisitions and housing price increase in Turkey during the COVID-19 pandemic era. *International Journal of Housing Markets and Analysis, 16*(3), 575–597. https://doi.org/10.1108/IJHMA-08-2022-0109

Salami, M. A., Tanrıvermiş, H., & Tanrıvermiş, Y. (2024). The impact of the Russian invasion of Ukraine on Turkish Markets. *The Journal of Economic Asymmetries, 29*, 1–17. https://doi.org/10.1016/j.jeca.2023.e00348

Tanrıvermiş, H. (2020). Possible impacts of the COVID-19 outbreak on the real estate sector and possible changes to adopt: A situation analysis and general assessment from a Turkish perspective. *Journal of Urban Management, 9*(3), 263–269.

Yildiz, K. M. (2021). *President Erdoğan: The world's biggest real estate agent*. Duvar English. https://www.duvarenglish.com/president-erdogan-the-worlds-biggest-real-estate-agent-news-57329

Harun Tanrıvermiş is a distinguished professor who occupies the esteemed position at the Ankara University top management level as founder and head of the Department of Real Estate Development and Management, and founder and current dean of the Faculty of Applied Sciences at Ankara University. Professor Tanrıvermiş also currently works as the vice rector at Ankara University. He attained his B.Sc., M.Sc., and Ph.D. degrees from the Department of Agricultural Economics at Ankara University, specialising in land and real estate economics, land and real estate valuation, as well as natural resources and environmental economics. Furthermore, he earned an M.Sc. in environmental management through the MED-CAMPUS Programme in 1996. Professor Tanrıvermiş has published approximately 400 papers, including 43 international and 55 national peer-reviewed articles, which have been published in various high-impact journals. Additionally, he has presented 48 international and 74 national proceedings, either in full or as abstracts, at numerous conferences. He is also credited with writing 39 books and 17 book chapters. Moreover, his works concentrate on the land and real estate valuation, land and real estate economics, real estate development and project appraisal, urban transformation and sustainability, sustainable real estate development, facility and real estate management, land management, administration and polices, measuring and reporting of real estate sustainability and ESG, digital transformation in real estate and real estate technologies.

Yeşim Tanrıvermiş holds the position of full professor in the Department of Real Estate Development and Management at the Faculty of Applied Sciences, Ankara University, Türkiye. She attained her Master of Science (M.Sc.) degree in 2011 from the Department of Agricultural Economics at Ankara University. She received her Ph.D. in 2011 as the first Ph.D. program graduate of the Department of Real Estate Development and Management at Ankara University. Her research interests encompass the management and conservation of land resources, land resource economics, as well as real estate analysis and economics, in addition to studies in real estate and asset valuation. She has been delivering lectures for several years and has published academic papers since 2006. Her publications consist of 50 international and 40 national peer-reviewed articles. Additionally, she has made contributions to 110 international and 25 national full or abstract proceedings at various conferences and congresses and has authored 35 books and 30 book chapters. Presently, she serves as the Deputy Head of her department at Ankara University. Moreover, she is an active participant in various academic and professional organisations. Her experience encompasses working as a researcher and consultant across diverse public and private sectors, with a focus on real estate asset analysis, real estate finance and valuation, land and building conservation practices, as well as real estate economics and management. Furthermore, she actively engages in enhancing cooperation with both domestic and international institutions, mobilising financial resources for research projects.

Tobias Just is Managing Director at the IRE|BS Immobilienakademie and professor for Real Estate at the Regensburg University. Tobias studied economics in Hamburg and Uppsala (Sweden). In 1997, he graduated and started to work at the University of the Federal Armed Forces Hamburg. His Ph.D. dissertation was awarded the university science prize in 2001. For more than ten years, Tobias worked at Deutsche Bank Research, the economics research unit of Deutsche Bank. He headed the units' sector and real estate research team and was a member of Deutsche Bank's group-wide Environmental Steering Committee. In summer 2006, Tobias was a Research Fellow at the American Institute of Contemporary German Studies at Johns Hopkins University in Washington, DC. Tobias published 17 books and more than 250 papers in professional and academic journals and books. Since November 2011, Tobias has been Managing Director at the IRE|BS Immobilienakademie and holds a Chair for Real Estate at the University of Regensburg. He was President of the German Society of Property Researchers (GIF) from 2014-2021 and is editor of the ZIÖ—the German Journal of Real Estate Research. From 2016 to 2023, Tobias was a member of the Supervisory Board of Helaba Invest Kapitalanlagegesellschaft mbH. In 2017, Tobias became a Fellow of the RICS by nomination.

Correction to: Understanding Türkiye's Real Estate Markets

Tobias Just, Harun Tanrıvermiş,
and Yeşim Tanrıvermiş

Correction to:
T. Just et al. (eds.), *Understanding Türkiye's Real Estate Markets*, Management for Professionals, https://doi.org/10.1007/978-3-032-13297-0

The original version of the book was inadvertently published with the following corrections:

Errors	Page No.	Corrections
Harun vermis	viii, 267	Harun Tanrıvermiş
Hacı Bayram Mahallesi, Altındağ, Ankara Türkiye	xi, 565	EGO General Directorate, Ankara Metropolitan Municipality, Ankara, Türkiye
F. Nihan Özdemir Sönmez	xii	Name repitition
For Şebnem Akipek Öcal	xii, 141, 533	The institution is **TED University** not **Ankara University**
For Ardan Özkan	page xii	Institution is '**Department of Basic Sciences, Faculty of Maritime, İstanbul Technical University, İstanbul, Türkiye**'
Professor Tanrivermis	11, 40, 96, 137, 204, 269, 354, 393, 530, 710, 764, 783	Professor Tanrıvermiş
Tanrıvermis	39, 93, 95, 120, 226, 330, 331, 783	Tanrıvermiş

The updated version of this book can be found at
https://doi.org/10.1007/978-3-032-13297-0

T. Just et al. (eds.), *Understanding Türkiye's Real Estate Markets*, Management for Professionals, https://doi.org/10.1007/978-3-032-13297-0_36

Errors	Page No.	Corrections
Muhammed Said Yilmaz	72, 710	Muhammed Said Yılmaz
Ilhan Yildirim	249, 619	İlhan Yıldırım
Hepsen	252, 255, 256, 258, 260, 261, 262, 264, 306, 310	Hepşen
Coskum et al., 2021	262	Coşkun et al., 2021
dots (.) before H_1, H_2 and H_3	320	Should be removed
Kiyilar & Hepsen	327, 330	Kıyılar & Hepşen
Salih Demirkaye	428	Salih Demirkaya
Şebnem Akipek Öca	546	Şebnem Akipek Öcal
Sevilay Dinçer	582	Sevilay Bostancı
Iskender Duman	619	İskender Duman
A. Filiz Zorlu Kaman	668	Arda Özkan
Yildiz	769	Yıldız
Güneş et al	774	Parsa et al.
Keskin et al.	775	Keskin and Öcal
Terzioglu	776	Terzioğlu
Yildirim	776	Yıldırım

These changes have now been corrected.

MIX
Papier aus verantwortungsvollen Quellen
Paper from responsible sources
FSC® C105338

If you have any concerns about our products,
you can contact us on
ProductSafety@springernature.com

In case Publisher is established outside the EU,
the EU authorized representative is:
Springer Nature Customer Service Center GmbH
Europaplatz 3, 69115 Heidelberg, Germany

Printed by Libri Plureos GmbH
in Hamburg, Germany